My Dear Students,

When I decided to use a custom edition for this course, it meant that t.. .... text would be reduced. In addition, I was able to choose the design of the cover. I am walking my two beloved dogs. Riley is the big golden retriever and Olive is the border collie mix. They are both rescues. Olive had been neglected and abused. When she came to me at the age of three and a half years old, she was emaciated and anxious. She had spent most of her life in a small cage with little food or water and had been left alone for days at a time. Riley's human could no longer care for her. She was twelve years old when I adopted her in April of 2015.

Today, they are given lots of love, attention, daily walks (at least two a day) and are essentially my children with fur. I love them dearly and they are loyal and loving in return.

Every dog deserves a loving home. The decision to get a dog should never be made on impulse. Pets require a lot of care and time. If you feel you can make a commitment to a pet, I would urge you to rescue, rather than buy, a dog. Millions of dogs languish in shelters and are ultimately killed.

Lastly, if you become aware of an animal that is being abused or neglected, please be his or her voice. Call the police. Call an animal control officer. You can do it anonymously. Thank you for reading this and, if you have a dog, give him or her lots of attention and daily walks.

Here's to a great semester,

Sherry Corneal

Laura E. Berk

Exploring Lifespan Development

Second Custom Edition for HDFS 129 at Penn State University

Taken from:
Exploring Lifespan Development, Third Edition
by Laura E. Berk

Cover Art: Courtesy of Sherry Corneal.

Taken from:

Exploring Lifespan Development, Third Edition
by Laura E. Berk
Copyright © 2014, 2011, 2008 by Pearson Education, Inc.
New York, New York, 10013

Pearson Learning Solutions, 330 Hudson Street, New York, New York 10013
A Pearson Education Company
www.pearsoned.com

Printed in the United States

3   16

000200010271987217

JK

ISBN 10: 1-323-23874-3
ISBN 13: 978-1-323-23874-5

About the Author

Laura E. Berk is a distinguished professor of psychology at Illinois State University, where she has taught human development to both undergraduate and graduate students for more than three decades. She received her bachelor's degree in psychology from the University of California, Berkeley, and her master's and doctoral degrees in child development and educational psychology from the University of Chicago. She has been a visiting scholar at Cornell University, UCLA, Stanford University, and the University of South Australia.

Berk has published widely on the effects of school environments on children's development, the development of private speech, and the role of make-believe play in development. Her research has been funded by the U.S. Office of Education and the National Institute of Child Health and Human Development. It has appeared in many prominent journals, including *Child Development, Developmental Psychology, Merrill-Palmer Quarterly, Journal of Abnormal Child Psychology, Development and Psychopathology,* and *Early Childhood Research Quarterly.* Her empirical studies have attracted the attention of the general public, leading to contributions to *Psychology Today* and *Scientific American.* She has also been featured on National Public Radio's *Morning Edition* and in *Parents Magazine, Wondertime,* and *Reader's Digest.*

Berk has served as a research editor of *Young Children* and as a consulting editor for *Early Childhood Research Quarterly.* Currently, she is associate editor of the *Journal of Cognitive Education and Psychology.* She is a frequent contributor to edited volumes on early childhood development, having recently authored chapters on the importance of parenting, on make-believe play, and on the kindergarten child. She has also written the article on social development for *The Child: An Encyclopedic Companion;* the article on Vygotsky for the *Encyclopedia of Cognitive Science;* and the chapter on storytelling as a teaching strategy for *Voices of Experience: Memorable Talks from the National Institute on the Teaching of Psychology* (Association for Psychological Science). She is coauthor of the forthcoming chapter on make-believe play and self-regulation in the *Sage Handbook of Play and Learning in Early Childhood.*

Berk's books include *Private Speech: From Social Interaction to Self-Regulation; Scaffolding Children's Learning: Vygotsky and Early Childhood Education; Landscapes of Development: An Anthology of Readings;* and *A Mandate for Playful Learning in Preschool: Presenting the Evidence.* In addition to *Development Through the Lifespan* and *Exploring Lifespan Development,* she is author of the best-selling texts *Child Development* and *Infants, Children, and Adolescents,* published by Pearson. Her book for parents and teachers is *Awakening Children's Minds: How Parents and Teachers Can Make a Difference.*

Berk is active in work for children's causes. In addition to service in her home community, she is a member of the national board of directors and chair of the Chicago advisory board of Jumpstart, a nonprofit organization that provides intensive literacy intervention to thousands of low-income preschoolers across the United States, using college and university students as interveners. Berk is a fellow of the American Psychological Association, Division 7: Developmental Psychology.

Features at a Glance

Contents

A Personal Note to Students

My more than 30 years of teaching human development have brought me in contact with thousands of students like you—students with diverse college majors, future goals, interests, and needs. Some are affiliated with my own field, psychology, but many come from other related fields—education, sociology, anthropology, family studies, social service, nursing, and biology, to name just a few. Each semester, my students' aspirations have proved to be as varied as their fields of study. Many look toward careers in applied work—counseling, caregiving, nursing, social work, school psychology, and program administration. Some plan to teach, and a few want to do research. Most hope someday to become parents, whereas others are already parents who come with a desire to better understand and rear their children. And almost all arrive with a deep curiosity about how they themselves developed from tiny infants into the complex human beings they are today.

My goal in preparing this third edition of *Exploring Lifespan Development* is to provide a textbook that meets the instructional goals of your course as well as your personal interests and needs. To achieve these objectives, I have grounded this book in a carefully selected body of classic and current theory and research. In addition, the text highlights the lifespan perspective on development and the interacting contributions of biology and environment to the developing person. It also illustrates commonalities and differences among ethnic groups and cultures and discusses the broader social contexts in which we develop. I have provided a unique pedagogical program that will assist you in mastering information, integrating various aspects of development, critically examining controversial issues, applying what you have learned, and relating the information to your own life.

I hope that learning about human development will be as rewarding for you as I have found it over the years. I would like to know what you think about both the field of human development and this book. I welcome your comments; please feel free to send them to me at Department of Psychology, Box 4620, Illinois State University, Normal, IL 61790.

Laura E. Berk

Preface for Instructors

I wrote *Exploring Lifespan Development* with the goal of retaining all the vital features of *Development Through the Lifespan* while providing students with a clear, efficient read of the most important concepts and empirical findings in the field of lifespan development. The text has been refashioned with an exceptionally strong emphasis on applications. Classical, contemporary, and cutting-edge theories and research are made accessible to students in a manageable and relevant way. This third edition represents rapidly transforming aspects of the field, with a wealth of new content and teaching tools:

■ *Diverse pathways of change are highlighted.* Investigators have reached broad consensus that variations in biological makeup and everyday tasks lead to wide individual differences in paths of change and resulting competencies. This edition pays more attention to variability in development and to recent theories—including ecological, sociocultural, and dynamic systems—that attempt to explain it. Multicultural and cross-cultural findings, including international comparisons, are enhanced throughout the text. Biology and Environment and Cultural Influences boxes also accentuate the theme of diversity in development.

■ *The lifespan perspective is emphasized.* As in previous editions, the lifespan perspective—development as lifelong, multidimensional, multidirectional, plastic, and embedded in multiple contexts—continues to serve as a unifying approach to understanding human change and is woven thoroughly into the text.

■ *The complex bidirectional relationship between biology and environment is given greater attention.* Accumulating evidence on development of the brain, motor skills, cognitive and language competencies, temperament and personality, emotional and social understanding, and developmental problems underscores the way biological factors emerge in, are modified by, and share power with experience. Interconnections between biology and environment are integral to the lifespan perspective and are revisited throughout the text narrative and in the Biology and Environment boxes with new and updated topics.

■ *Inclusion of interdisciplinary research is expanded.* The move toward viewing thoughts, feelings, and behavior as an integrated whole, affected by a wide array of influences in biology, social context, and culture, has motivated developmental researchers to strengthen their ties with other fields of psychology and with other disciplines. Topics and findings included in this edition increasingly reflect the contributions of educational psychology, social psychology, health psychology, clinical psychology, neurobiology, pediatrics, geriatrics, sociology, anthropology, social service, and other fields.

■ *The links among theory, research, and applications are strengthened.* As researchers intensify their efforts to generate findings relevant to real-life situations, I have placed even greater weight on social policy issues and sound theory- and research-based applications. Further applications are provided in the Applying What We Know tables, which give students concrete ways of building bridges between their learning and the real world.

■ *The role of active student learning is made more explicit.* TAKE A MOMENT..., a feature built into the chapter narrative, asks students to think deeply and critically or to engage in an exercise or application as they read. Ask Yourself questions at the end of each major section have been thoroughly revised and expanded to promote four approaches to engaging actively with the subject matter— *Review, Connect, Apply,* and *Reflect.* This feature assists students in thinking about what they have learned from multiple vantage points. A new LOOK AND LISTEN feature asks students to observe what real children, adolescents, and adults say and do; speak with them or with professionals invested in their well-being; and inquire into community programs and practices that influence lifespan development. In addition, highlighting of key terms within the text narrative reinforces student learning in context.

Text Philosophy

The basic approach of this book has been shaped by my own professional and personal history as a teacher, researcher, and parent. It consists of seven philosophical ingredients that I regard as essential for students to emerge from a course with a thorough understanding of lifespan development. Each theme is woven into every chapter:

1. **An understanding of the diverse array of theories in the field and the strengths and shortcomings of each.** The first chapter begins by emphasizing that only knowledge of multiple theories can do justice to the richness of human development. As I take up each age period and domain of development, I present a variety of theoretical perspectives, indicate how each highlights previously overlooked aspects of development, and discuss research that evaluates it. Consideration of contrasting theories also serves as the context for an evenhanded analysis of many controversial issues.

2. **A grasp of the lifespan perspective as an integrative approach to development.** I introduce the lifespan perspective as an organizing framework in the first chapter and refer to and illustrate its assumptions throughout the text, in an effort to help students construct an overall vision of development from conception to death.

3. **Knowledge of both the sequence of human development and the processes that underlie it.** Students are provided with a discussion of the organized sequence of development

along with processes of change. An understanding of process—how complex combinations of biological and environmental events produce development—has been the focus of most recent research. Accordingly, the text reflects this emphasis. But new information about the timetable of change has also emerged. In many ways, the very young and the old have proved to be far more competent than they were believed to be in the past. In addition, many milestones of adult development, such as finishing formal education, entering a career, getting married, having children, and retiring, have become less predictable. Current evidence on the sequence and timing of development, along with its implications for process, is presented for all periods of the lifespan.

4. **An appreciation of the impact of context and culture on human development.** A wealth of research indicates that people live in rich physical and social contexts that affect all domains of development. Throughout the book, students travel to distant parts of the world as I review a growing body of cross-cultural evidence. The text narrative also discusses many findings on socioeconomically and ethnically diverse people within the United States. Furthermore, the impact of historical time period and cohort membership receives continuous attention. In this vein, gender issues—the distinctive but continually evolving experiences, roles, and life paths of males and females—are granted substantial emphasis. Besides highlighting the effects of immediate settings, such as family, neighborhood, and school, I make a concerted effort to underscore the influence of larger social structures—societal values, laws, and government policies and programs—on lifelong well-being.

5. **An understanding of the joint contributions of biology and environment to development.** The field recognizes more powerfully than ever before the joint roles of hereditary/constitutional and environmental factors—that these contributions to development combine in complex ways and cannot be separated in a simple manner. Numerous examples of how biological dispositions can be maintained as well as transformed by social contexts are presented throughout the book.

6. **A sense of the interdependency of all domains of development—physical, cognitive, emotional, and social.** Every chapter emphasizes an integrated approach to human development. I show how physical, cognitive, emotional, and social development are interwoven. Within the text narrative, and in a special series of Ask Yourself questions at the end of major sections, students are referred to other sections of the book to deepen their grasp of relationships among various aspects of change.

7. **An appreciation of the interrelatedness of theory, research, and applications.** Throughout this book, I emphasize that theories of human development and the research stimulated by them provide the foundation for sound, effective practices with children, adolescents, and adults. The link among theory, research, and applications is reinforced by an organizational format in which theory and research are presented first, followed by practical implications. In addition, a current focus in the field—harnessing knowledge of human development to shape social policies that support human needs throughout the lifespan—is reflected in every chapter. The text addresses the current condition of children, adolescents, and adults in the United States and elsewhere in the world and shows how theory and research have combined with public interest to spark successful interventions. Many important applied topics are considered, such as family planning, infant mortality, maternal employment and child care, teenage pregnancy and parenthood, domestic violence, exercise and adult health, religiosity and well-being, lifelong learning, grandparents rearing grandchildren, caring for aging adults with dementia, adjustment to retirement, optimal aging, and palliative care for the dying.

Text Organization

I have chosen a chronological organization for *Exploring Lifespan Development*. The book begins with an introductory chapter that describes the scientific history of the field, influential theories, and research strategies. It is followed by two chapters on the foundations of development. Chapter 2 combines an overview of genetic and environmental contexts into a single integrated discussion of these multifaceted influences on development. Chapter 3 is devoted to prenatal development, birth, and the newborn baby. With this foundation, students are ready to look closely at seven major age periods: infancy and toddlerhood (Chapters 4, 5, and 6), early childhood (Chapters 7 and 8), middle childhood (Chapters 9 and 10), adolescence (Chapters 11 and 12), early adulthood (Chapters 13 and 14), middle adulthood (Chapters 15 and 16), and late adulthood (Chapters 17 and 18). Topical chapters within each chronological division cover physical development, cognitive development, and emotional and social development. The book concludes with a chapter on death, dying, and bereavement (Chapter 19).

The chronological approach assists students in thoroughly understanding each age period. It also eases the task of integrating the various domains of development because each is discussed in close proximity. At the same time, a chronologically organized book requires that theories covering several age periods be presented piecemeal. This creates a challenge for students, who must link the various parts together. To assist with this task, I frequently remind students of important earlier achievements before discussing new developments, referring back to related sections with page references. Also, chapters or sections devoted to the same topic (for example, cognitive development) are similarly organized, making it easier for students to draw connections across age periods and construct an overall view of developmental change.

New Coverage in the Third Edition

Lifespan development is a fascinating and ever-changing field of study, with constantly emerging new discoveries and refinements in existing knowledge. The sixth edition represents this burgeoning contemporary literature, with over 1,500 new citations. Cutting-edge topics throughout the text underscore the book's major themes. Here is a sampling:

CHAPTER 1: Updated Biology and Environment box on resilience • Updated section on developmental cognitive neuroscience • Increased coverage of evolutionary developmental psychology, with special attention to the adaptiveness of human longevity • Updated Cultural Influences box on immigrant youths • Clarified explanation of sequential designs

CHAPTER 2: Updated Social Issues: Health box on the pros and cons of reproductive technologies • Updated section on development of adopted children • Enhanced attention to the impact of poverty on development • Expanded introduction to family influences on development, including the importance of coparenting • Updated research on neighborhood influences on children's physical and mental health • Current statistics on the condition of children, families, and the aged in the United States compared with other Western nations • Introduction to the concept of gene–environment interaction, with illustrative research findings • Expanded section on epigenesis, including new examples of environmental influences on gene expression • New Biology and Environment box highlighting a case of epigenesis—prenatal smoking modifies gene expression

CHAPTER 3: Enhanced attention to fetal brain development, sensory capacities, and behavior • Expanded and updated consideration of a wide range of teratogens • New evidence on the long-term consequences of emotional stress during pregnancy • Updated evidence on the contributions of doula support to the birth process and to newborn adjustment • New research on parenting and development of preterm and low-birth-weight infants • Expanded and updated Social Issues: Health box on health care and other policies for parents and newborn babies • New Social Issues: Health box on the Nurse–Family Partnership—reducing maternal stress and enhancing child development through social support • Updated findings on the roles of impaired brain functioning, maternal smoking, and maternal drug abuse in sudden infant death syndrome (SIDS) • New evidence on the role of sleep in infant learning • Updated research on touch sensitivity in newborns, including techniques for reducing infant stress to painful medical procedures

CHAPTER 4: Updated introduction to major methods of assessing brain functioning, including the EEG geodesic sensor net (GSN) and near-infrared spectroscopy (NIRS) • Updated discussion of advances in brain development, with special attention to the prefrontal cortex • New research on children adopted from Romanian orphanages, including neurobiological evidence bearing on the question of whether infancy is a sensitive period of development • Updated Cultural Influences box on cultural variation in infant sleeping arrangements • Updated section on breastfeeding • New dynamic systems research on development of walking and reaching • Enhanced attention to cultural influences—including infant sleep and motor development • New evidence on the perceptual narrowing effect in speech, music, and species-related face perception, and in gender- and race-related face perception

CHAPTER 5: Revised and updated section on infant and toddler imitation, revealing toddlers' ability to infer others' intentions • New section on symbolic understanding, including toddlers' developing grasp of words and pictures as symbolic tools • New Social Issues: Education box on baby learning from TV and video, including discussion of the video deficit effect • Revised section introducing information-processing concepts, including working memory, automatic processes, speed of processing, and executive function • Revised and updated section on infant and toddler categorization skills • New research on babies' joint attention and preverbal gestures, revealing their developing capacity to participate in cooperative processes necessary for effective communication • Updated findings on toddlers' earliest spoken words, including cultural variations • New findings on adult–child conversation and early vocabulary development, with special attention to SES differences

CHAPTER 6: New research on consequences of effortful control—the self-regulatory dimension of temperament—for cognitive, emotional, and social development • Special attention to the role of child genotype in parenting effects on temperament • Revised and updated section on consequences of early availability of a consistent caregiver for attachment security, emotion processing, and adjustment, highlighting studies of children adopted from Eastern European orphanages • Updated findings on employed fathers' increased involvement in caregiving • Revised and updated Social Issues: Health box on child care, attachment, and later development • New evidence on toddlers' scale errors, with implications for body self-awareness

CHAPTER 7: Increased attention to brain development in early childhood, with special attention to the prefrontal cortex and executive function • Updated statistics and research on the health status of U.S. young children, including tooth decay, immunizations, unintentional injury, and overall health status • New research on development of handedness, including cultural variations • New evidence on preschoolers' magical beliefs • Revised and updated section on preschoolers' understanding of symbol–real-world relations • New research on cultural variations in effective scaffolding • New Social Issues: Education box on children's questions as a catalyst for cognitive development • Updated discussion of gains in executive function in early childhood, including attention, inhibition, and planning • Recent findings on toddlers' early, implicit false-belief understanding and its relationship to preschoolers explicit grasp of false belief • New evidence on cognitive attainments and social experiences that contribute to mastery of false belief • Enhanced discussion of SES differences in emergent literacy and math knowledge • Updated discussion of the effects of television and computers on academic learning

CHAPTER 8: Updated consideration of emotional self-regulation in early childhood, including the influence of temperament and parenting • Enhanced Cultural Influences box on ethnic differences in the consequences of physical punishment • New section on the role of positive peer relations in school readiness • New longitudinal evidence on the relationship of early corporal punishment to later behavior problems • Enhanced attention to aggressive children's distorted view of the social world • Updated discussion of parent training programs to reduce child conduct problems, with special attention to Incredible Years • New findings on the harmful impact of parental psychological control on children's adjustment • Updated consideration of consequences of child maltreatment, including new evidence on central nervous system damage

CHAPTER 9: Revised and updated section on overweight and obesity, including current U.S. prevalence rates, international comparisons, and coverage of contributing factors and consequences • Updated statistics on physical activity and fitness among U.S. school-age children • New sections on working-memory capacity and executive function in middle childhood, with implications for academic learning • Revised and updated Biology and Environment box on children with attention-deficit hyperactivity disorder • New research on development of planning in middle childhood • Updated evidence on the school-age child's theory of mind • Discussion of secular trends in IQ, including implications for understanding ethnic variations in IQ • Attention to the impact of the U.S. No Child Left Behind Act on quality of U.S. education • New research on educational consequences of widespread SES and ethnic segregation in American schools • New Social Issues: Education box on magnet schools as a means of attaining equal access to high-quality education • Revised and updated section on U.S. academic achievement in international perspective, including comparisons with high-performing nations

CHAPTER 10: Enhanced attention to cultural variations in self-concept, with special attention to Asian versus U.S. comparisons • Updated research on parenting practices and children's achievement-related attributions, including the influence of cultural values on likelihood of developing learned helplessness • New section on children's understanding of diversity and inequality, development of racial and ethnic prejudice, and strategies for reducing prejudice • Updated evi-

dence on implications of peer-acceptance categories for bullying and victimization • Updated Biology and Environment box on bullies and their victims • New evidence on sex differences in development of gender identity in middle childhood • Enhanced attention to the role of effective coparenting in children's adjustment to parental divorce and remarriage • New research on the implications of self-care and after-school programs for school-age children's adjustment • Revised and updated Cultural Influences box on impact of ethnic and political violence on children • Updated findings on the consequences of child sexual abuse

CHAPTER 11: New section on adolescent brain development, focusing on the imbalance between the cognitive control network and the emotional/social network, with implications for teenage reward-seeking, emotional reactivity, and risk-taking • Updated evidence on teenage pregnancy and parenthood prevention and intervention strategies • Expanded and updated research on adolescent decision making • New research on the impact of school transitions on adolescent adjustment • New Social Issues: Education box on the impact of "media multitasking" on learning

CHAPTER 12: New research on personal and social factors contributing to identity development in adolescence • Updated Social Issues: Health box on adolescent suicide • Updated evidence on adolescents' capacity to integrate moral, social-conventional, and personal concerns • Enhanced consideration of factors that promote moral identity, along with its relationship to moral behavior • New evidence on gender intensification in adolescence • Updated section on parenting and adolescent autonomy, including research on immigrant families • Expanded and updated section on Internet friendships, with special attention to teenagers' use of social networking sites • New findings on long-term outcomes of multisystemic therapy for violent juvenile offenders

CHAPTER 13: Updated Biology and Environment box on telomere length as a marker of the impact of life circumstances on biological aging • New controversial evidence on the role of free radicals in aging • New research on SES variations in adult health • Updated statistics on the continued rise in adult overweight and obesity • New findings on negative stereotyping and discrimination experienced by overweight adults • Updated discussion of treatment of adult obesity • New evidence on the Internet as a contemporary way to initiate dating relationships • Updated research on psychological stress and unfavorable health outcomes • Enhanced discussion of the psychological impact of attending college, including benefits of opportunities to interact with racially and ethnically diverse peers • New findings on the role of gender stereotypes in women's likelihood of choosing STEM careers • Updated Social Issues: Education box on men who choose nontraditional careers

CHAPTER 14: Revised and updated section on emerging adulthood, including new findings on emerging adults' religiosity, spirituality, and commitment to community service • Enhanced discussion of the controversy over whether emerging adulthood really is a distinct period of development • Special attention to parenting of emerging adults, including "helicopter parenting" • Updated consideration of increasingly flexible age-graded expectations for early adulthood life events • Updated consideration of factors that contribute to enduring romantic relationships • New findings on social networking sites as contexts for early adulthood friendship • Expanded discussion of the rise in average age of leaving the parental home • Increased attention to parent–young-adult child relationships • New findings on sharing of household tasks in dual-earner marriages, including cross-national evidence • Updated research on relationship qualities and communication skills contributing to marital satisfaction • Updated consideration of the dramatic increase in never-married single parents, including SES and ethnic variations • New findings on career development in early adulthood, with special attention to obstacles to success faced by women and ethnic minorities • Enhanced discussion of combining work and family

CHAPTER 15: Updated Biology and Environment box on anti-aging effects of dietary calorie restriction • Updated evidence on the risks of hormone therapy to reduce physical discomforts of menopause • New survey findings on sexual activity of U.S. middle-aged adults • Updated sections on risk of cancer and heart disease in midlife • New findings on midlife changes in attention and memory • New Social Issues: Education box on how lessons in the art of acting improve memory in older adults

CHAPTER 16: Enhanced consideration of the contribution of parenting to generativity in midlife • Updated Social Issues: Health box on grandparents rearing grandchildren in skipped-generation families • Updated evidence on relationships between middle-aged adults and their aging parents, including ethnic variations • New findings on midlife intergenerational assistance to both children and aging parents • Enhanced discussion of care of aging parents in poor health, with emphasis on gender disparities, ethnic variations, and emotional, physical, and financial consequences • New research on middle-aged adults' use of social networking sites • Updated discussion of the glass ceiling in career advancement faced by women and ethnic minorities • Discussion of the impact of the late-2000s recession on delayed retirement

CHAPTER 17: Updated statistics on life expectancy in late adulthood, including gender and SES variations • Updated international comparisons in healthy life expectancy • New research on brain development, including neurological changes that enable older adults to compensate for declines in cen-

tral nervous system functioning • Updated findings on risk and protective factors associated with various aspects of physical aging • Updated section on assistive technologies • Expanded and updated discussion of stereotypes of aging, including stereotype threat, with implications for physical and cognitive performance • Updated consideration of SES and ethnic variations in health in late adulthood • Expanded consideration of progress in compression of morbidity • Updated survey findings on sexual activity in late adulthood • New findings on neurological changes associated with Alzheimer's disease, including efforts to understand how abnormal amyloid and tau damage neurons • New evidence on genetic and environmental risks for Alzheimer's, and on protective factors, with special emphasis on diet, education, and physical activity • Updated Social Issues: Health box on interventions for caregivers of older adults with dementia, with increased attention to respite and caregiving skills • Expanded discussion of episodic memory and prospective memory in late adulthood • Enhanced consideration of the impact of cognitive training on older adults' mental functioning, including broadening programs to target self-efficacy • New evidence on the rapid rise in use of computers and the Internet among older people

CHAPTER 18: Updated research on reminiscence in late adulthood • New findings on personality development in late adulthood, with special attention to openness to experience • Enhanced consideration of the benefits of spirituality and religiosity in late life • Consideration of sustaining an effective person–environment fit in older adults' social contexts, including caregiving and housing arrangements • New research on divorce, remarriage, and cohabitation in late adulthood, including aging baby boomers' use of online dating services • Updated findings on late-life friendships • New evidence on retirement as a dynamic process with multiple transitions and wide individual variation

CHAPTER 19: Updated research on diverse factors influencing people's adaptation to dying • Updated discussion of dying at home, in hospitals, and in nursing homes • New findings on hospice, including reducing patient suffering, improving family functioning, and increasing ability to sustain patient care at home • Updated statistics on public attitudes toward passive euthanasia, voluntary active euthanasia, and assisted suicide • New research on the role of expressions of happiness and humor in bereavement adjustment • New evidence on bereavement interventions, with special attention to support groups based on the dual-process model of coping with loss

Pedagogical Features

Maintaining a highly accessible writing style—one that is lucid and engaging without being simplistic—continues to be one of my major goals. I frequently converse with students, encouraging them to relate what they read to their own lives. In doing so, I hope to make the study of human development involving and pleasurable.

CHAPTER INTRODUCTIONS AND VIGNETTES ABOUT REAL PEOPLE. To provide a helpful preview, I include an outline and overview of chapter content in each chapter introduction. To help students construct a clear image of development and to enliven the text narrative, each chronological age division is unified by case examples woven throughout that set of chapters. For example, the middle childhood section highlights the experiences and concerns of 10-year-old Joey; 8-year-old Lizzie; their divorced parents, Rena and Drake; and their classmates. In the chapters on late adulthood, students get to know Walt and Ruth, a vibrant retired couple, along with Walt's older brother Dick, Dick's wife Goldie, and Ruth's sister Ida, a victim of Alzheimer's disease. Besides a set of main characters who bring unity to each age period, many additional vignettes offer vivid examples of development and diversity among children, adolescents, and adults.

END-OF-CHAPTER SUMMARIES. Chapter summaries are organized by learning objectives, encouraging active study. They also include bolded key terms, which help students acquire and master the vocabulary of the field.

TAKE A MOMENT... Built into the text narrative, this feature asks students to "take a moment" to think about an important point, integrate information on human development, or engage in an exercise or an application to clarify a challenging concept. *TAKE A MOMENT...* highlights and reinforces the text's strength in conversing with and actively engaging the student in learning and in inspiring critical thinking.

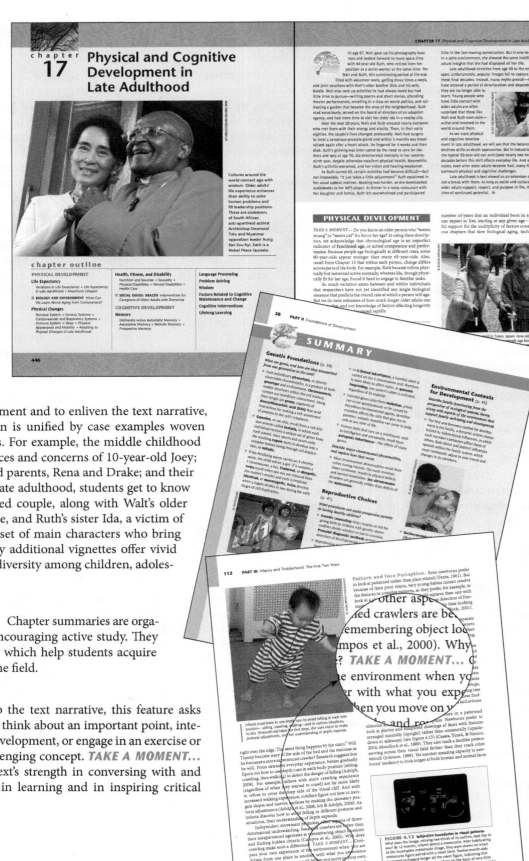

LOOK AND LISTEN. This new active-learning feature asks students to observe what real individuals say and do; speak with or observe parents, teachers, or other professionals; and inquire into community programs and practices that influence children, adolescents, and adults.

ASK YOURSELF QUESTIONS. Active engagement with the subject matter is also supported by study questions at the end of each major section. Three types of questions prompt students to think about human development in diverse ways: *Review* questions help students recall and comprehend information they have just read; *Apply* questions encourage the application of knowledge to controversial issues and problems faced by children, adolescents, adults, and professionals who work with them; and *Reflect* questions help make the study of human development personally meaningful by asking students to reflect on their own development and life experiences. Each question is answered on the text's MyDevelopmentLab website.

FEATURE BOXES. Thematic boxes accentuate the philosophical themes of this book. *(See page iv for a complete listing.)*

***Biology and Environment* boxes** highlight the growing attention to the complex, bidirectional relationship between biology and environment during development. Examples include *A Case of Epigenesis: Smoking During Pregnancy Alters Gene Expression; Children with Attention-Deficit Hyperactivity Disorder; Anti-Aging Effects of Dietary Calorie Restriction;* and *Music as Palliative Care for Dying Patients.*

***Cultural Influences* boxes** deepen the attention to culture threaded throughout the text and accentuate both cross-cultural and multicultural variations in human development—for example, *Immigrant Youths: Adapting to a New Land; Impact of Ethnic and Political Violence on Children; Is Emerging Adulthood Really a Distinct Period of Development?;* and *The New Old Age.*

Social Issues boxes discuss the impact of social conditions on children, adolescents, and adults and emphasize the need for sensitive social policies to ensure their well-being:

New *Social Issues: Education* boxes focus on home, school, and community influences on learning. Examples include *Baby Learning from TV and Video: The Video Deficit Effect; Media Multitasking Disrupts Attention and Learning; Magnet Schools: Equal Access to High-Quality Education;* and *The Art of Acting Improves Memory in Older Adults.*

New *Social Issues: Health* boxes address values and practices relevant to physical and mental health. Examples include *The Nurse–Family Partnership: Reducing Maternal Stress and Enhancing Child Development Through Social Support; A Cross-National Perspective on Health Care and Other Policies for Parents and Newborn Babies;* and *Interventions for Caregivers of Older Adults with Dementia.*

APPLYING WHAT WE KNOW TABLES. To accentuate the link between theory and research and applications, Applying What We Know tables provide easily accessible practical advice on the importance of caring for oneself and others throughout the lifespan. The tables also speak directly to students as parents or future parents and to those pursuing child- and family-related careers or areas of study, such as teaching, health care, counseling, or social work. They include: *Do's and Don'ts of a Healthy Pregnancy, Signs of Developmentally Appropriate Infant and Toddler Child Care, Positive Parenting, Helping Children Adjust to Their Parents' Divorce, Resources That Foster Resilience in Emerging Adulthood, Relieving the Stress of Caring for an Aging Parent,* and *Fostering Adaptation to Widowhood in Late Adulthood. (See page iv for a complete listing.)*

MILESTONES TABLES. A Milestones table appears at the end of each age division of the text. These tables summarize major physical, cognitive, language, emotional, and social attainments, providing a convenient aid for reviewing the chronology of lifespan development.

ENHANCED ART AND PHOTO PROGRAM. A revised art style presents concepts and research findings with clarity and attractiveness, thereby aiding student understanding and retention. Each photo has been carefully selected to complement the text discussion and to represent the diversity of people in the United States and around the world.

IN-TEXT KEY TERMS WITH DEFINITIONS, END-OF-CHAPTER TERM LIST, AND END-OF-BOOK GLOSSARY. Mastery of terms that make up the central vocabulary of the field is promoted through in-text highlighting of key terms and concept definitions, which encourages students to review the terminology of the field in greater depth by rereading related information. Key terms also appear in an end-of-chapter page-referenced list of important terms and concepts and an end-of-book page-referenced glossary.

Acknowledgments

The dedicated contributions of many individuals helped make this book a reality and contributed to refinements and improvements in this third edition. An impressive cast of reviewers provided many helpful suggestions, constructive criticisms, and enthusiasm for the organization and content of the text. I am grateful to each one of them.

Reviewers for the Third Edition

Cheryl Anagnopoulos, Black Hills State University
Carolyn M. Barry, Loyola University
Lori Bica, University of Wisconsin, Eau Claire
Linda Curry, Texas Christian University
Manfred Diehl, Colorado State University
Mary Anne Erickson, Ithaca College
Karen Fingerman, University of Texas, Austin
Linda Halgunseth, Pennsylvania State University
Melinda Heinz, Iowa State University
Joseph Kishton, University of North Carolina, Wilmington
Dale Lund, California State University, San Bernardino
Debra McGinnis, Oakland University
Celinda Reese-Melancon, Oklahoma State University
Mathew Shake, Western Kentucky University
Kim Shifren, Towson University
Gregory Smith, Kent State University
Stephanie Stein, Central Washington University
JoNell Strough, West Virginia University
Bruce Thompson, University of Southern Maine
Laura Thompson, New Mexico State University

Reviewers for Previous Editions

Gerald Adams, University of Guelph
Jackie Adamson, South Dakota School of Mines and Technology
Paul C. Amrhein, University of New Mexico
Cheryl Anagnopoulos, Black Hills State University
Doreen Arcus, University of Massachusetts, Lowell
René L. Babcock, Central Michigan University
Sherry Beaumont, University of Northern British Columbia
W. Keith Berg, University of Florida
James A. Bird, Weber State University
Toni Bisconti, University of Akron
Joyce Bishop, Golden West College
Kimberly Blair, University of Pittsburgh
Tracie L. Blumentritt, University of Wisconsin, La Crosse
Ed Brady, Belleville Area College
Michele Y. Breault, Truman State University
Dilek Buchholz, Weber State University
Lanthan Camblin, University of Cincinnati
Judith W. Cameron, Ohio State University
Joan B. Cannon, University of Massachusetts, Lowell
Michael Caruso, University of Toledo
Susan L. Churchill, University of Nebraska—Lincoln

Gary Creasey, Illinois State University
Rhoda Cummings, University of Nevada—Reno
Rita M. Curl, Minot State University
Carol Lynn Davis, University of Maine
Lou de la Cruz, Sheridan Institute
Byron Egeland, University of Minnesota
Beth Fauth, Utah State University
Karen Fingerman, Purdue University
Maria P. Fracasso, Towson University
Elizabeth E. Garner, University of North Florida
Laurie Gottlieb, McGill University
Dan Grangaard, Austin Community College
Clifford Gray, Pueblo Community College
Marlene Groomes, Miami Dade College
Laura Gruntmeir, Redlands Community College
Laura Hanish, Arizona State University
Traci Haynes, Columbus State Community College
Vernon Haynes, Youngstown State University
Bert Hayslip, University of North Texas
Bob Heller, Athabasca University
Karl Hennig, St. Francis Xavier University
Paula Hillman, University of Wisconsin—Whitewater
Deb Hollister, Valencia Community College
Hui-Chin Hsu, University of Georgia
Lera Joyce Johnson, Centenary College of Louisiana
Janet Kalinowski, Ithaca College
Kevin Keating, Broward Community College
Wendy Kliewer, Virginia Commonwealth University
Marita Kloseck, University of Western Ontario
Karen Kopera-Frye, University of Nevada, Reno
Valerie Kuhlmeier, Queens University
Deanna Kuhn, Teachers College, Columbia University
Rebecca A. López, California State University—Long Beach
Dale Lund, California State University, San Bernardino
Pamela Manners, Troy State University
Ashley Maynard, University of Hawaii
Robert B. McLaren, California State University, Fullerton
Kate McLean, University of Toronto at Mississauga
Randy Mergler, California State University
Karla K. Miley, Black Hawk College
Carol Miller, Anne Arundel Community College
Teri Miller, Milwaukee Area Technical College
David Mitchell, Kennesaw State University
Steve Mitchell, Somerset Community College
Gary T. Montgomery, University of Texas, Pan American
Feleccia Moore-Davis, Houston Community College
Ulrich Mueller, University of Victoria
Karen Nelson, Austin College
Bob Newby, Tarleton State University
Jill Norvilitis, Buffalo State College
Patricia O'Brien, University of Illinois at Chicago
Nancy Ogden, Mount Royal College
Peter Oliver, University of Hartford
Verna C. Pangman, University of Manitoba

Robert Pasnak, George Mason University
Ellen Pastorino, Gainesville College
Julie Patrick, West Virginia University
Marion Perlmutter, University of Michigan
Warren H. Phillips, Iowa State University
Leslee K. Polina, Southeast Missouri State University
Dana Plude, University of Maryland
Dolores Pushkar, Concordia University
Leon Rappaport, Kansas State University
Pamela Roberts, California State University, Long Beach
Stephanie J. Rowley, University of North Carolina
Elmer Ruhnke, Manatee Community College
Randall Russac, University of North Florida
Marie Saracino, Stephen F. Austin State University
Edythe H. Schwartz, California State University—Sacramento
Bonnie Seegmiller, City University of New York, Hunter College
Richard Selby, Southeast Missouri State University
Aurora Sherman, Oregon State University
Carey Sherman, University of Michigan
David Shwalb, Southeastern Louisiana University
Paul S. Silverman, University of Montana
Judi Smetana, University of Rochester
Glenda Smith, North Harris College
Jacqui Smith, University of Michigan
Jeanne Spaulding, Houston Community College
Thomas Spencer, San Francisco State University
Bruce Stam, Chemeketa Community College
JoNell Strough, West Virginia University
Vince Sullivan, Pensacola Junior College
Bruce Thompson, University of Southern Maine
Laura Thompson, New Mexico State University
Mojisola Tiamiyu, University of Toledo
Ruth Tincoff, Harvard University
Joe Tinnin, Richland College
Catya von Károlyi, University of Wisconsin, Eau Claire
L. Monique Ward, University of Michigan
Rob Weisskirch, California State University, Fullerton
Nancy White, Youngstown State University
Ursula M. White, El Paso Community College
Carol L. Wilkinson, Whatcom Community College
Lois J. Willoughby, Miami-Dade Community College
Paul Wink, Wellesley College
Deborah R. Winters, New Mexico State University

I cannot begin to express what a great pleasure it has been, once again, to work with Tom Pauken, Managing Editor. His careful review of manuscript, keen organizational skills, responsive day-to-day communication, insightful suggestions, astute problem solving, interest in the subject matter, and thoughtfulness greatly enhanced the quality of the text and eased the immense challenges that arose during its preparation. Judy Ashkenaz, Development Editor, commented on each chapter, helping to ensure that every thought and concept would be clearly expressed and well-developed. She also assisted with

preparation of photo specifications, drafting of photo captions, and, as needs arose, graciously took on extra tasks, including updating of diverse aspects of the Instructor's Resource Manual. Rachel Trapp, editorial assistant, has been extraordinary. In addition to spending countless hours searching, gathering, and organizing scholarly literature, she assisted with an array of editorial and production tasks. In a pinch, she diligently took over the responsibility of preparing and editing many of the assessments in MyDevelopmentLab (MDL).

The supplements package benefited from the talents and dedication of several other individuals. Leah Shriro revised the IRM brief summaries and lecture outlines. Kimberly Michaud prepared a superb Test Bank and many of the MDL assessments. Judy Ashkenaz and Rachel Trapp assisted me in designing and writing a highly attractive PowerPoint presentation. Maria Henneberry and Phil Vandiver of Contemporary Visuals in Bloomington, IL, prepared an artistic and inspiring set of new video segments addressing diverse topics in lifespan development.

Donna Simons, Senior Production Project Manager, coordinated the complex production tasks that resulted in an exquisitely beautiful third edition. I am grateful for her keen aesthetic sense, attention to detail, flexibility, efficiency, and thoughtfulness. I thank Sarah Evertson and Tom Pauken for photo research that contributed to the exceptional photographs that illustrate the text narrative. Margaret Pinette provided outstanding copy-editing and careful compilation of the references list, and Julie Hotchkiss offered meticulous proofreading.

Wendy Albert, Executive Marketing Manager, prepared the beautiful print ads and informative e-mails to the field about *Exploring Lifespan Development,* Third Edition. She has also ensured that accurate and clear information reached Pearson Education's sales force and that the needs of prospective and current adopters were met.

A final word of gratitude goes to my family, whose love, patience, and understanding have enabled me to be wife, mother, teacher, researcher, and text author at the same time. My sons, David and Peter, grew up with my texts, passing from childhood to adolescence and then to adulthood as successive editions were written. David has a special connection with the books' subject matter as an elementary school teacher. Peter is now an experienced attorney, and his vivacious and talented wife Melissa joins a new generation of university faculty dedicated to creative teaching and research. All three continue to enrich my understanding through reflections on events and progress in their own lives. Last, but certainly not least, I thank my husband, Ken, for joining me on a wonderfully fulfilling lifespan journey. Over the past two decades, he willingly made room in our lives for the immensely demanding endeavor of authoring three editions of *Exploring Lifespan Development* and six editions of its parent text, *Development Through the Lifespan.* His reflections, support, and astute counsel made all the difference during the project's final months.

Laura E. Berk

Teaching Resources

A variety of teaching tools are available to assist instructors in organizing lectures, planning demonstrations and examinations, and ensuring student comprehension.

- **MyDevelopmentLab for *Exploring Lifespan Development.*** Authored by Laura Berk, MyDevelopmentLab includes a variety of assessments that enable continuous evaluation of students' learning. Extensive video footage, multimedia simulations, "Careers in Human Development," and interactive activities—all unique to *Exploring Lifespan Development*—are also included.

- **Instructor's Resource Manual (IRM).** This thoroughly revised IRM can be used by first-time or experienced instructors to enrich classroom experiences. Each chapter includes a Chapter-at-a-Glance grid, Brief Chapter Summary, Learning Objectives, detailed Lecture Outline, Learning Activities, "Ask Yourself" questions with answers, Suggested Readings, and Media Materials list.

- **Test Bank.** The Test Bank contains over 2,000 multiple-choice and essay questions, all of which are page-referenced to the chapter content and also classified by type.

- **Pearson MyTest.** This secure online environment allows instructors to easily create exams, study guide questions, and quizzes from any computer with an Internet connection.

- **PowerPoint Presentation.** The PowerPoint presentation provides outlines and illustrations of key topics for each chapter of the text.

- ***Explorations in Lifespan Development* DVD and Guide.** This new DVD is over four hours in length and contains over 70 four- to ten-minute narrated segments, designed for classroom use, that illustrate the many theories, concepts, and milestones of human development. New additions include *Preterm Birth; Autism; First-Grade Science Education; Civic Engagement in Adolescence; Changing Parent–Adolescent Relationships; Adult Obesity;* and *Expertise, Practical Problem Solving, and Leadership in Middle Adulthood.* The DVD and Guide are available to instructors who adopt the text and to students as a supplement when packaged with the text. The DVD Guide helps students use the DVD in conjunction with the textbook, deepening their understanding and applying what they have learned to everyday life.

MyDevelopmentLab

Authored by Laura Berk, MyDevelopmentLab for *Exploring Lifespan Development* engages students through personalized learning and helps instructors with course preparation, content delivery, and assessment. It helps students better prepare for class, quizzes, and exams. It provides educators with a dynamic set of tools for tracking individual and class performance.

- A **Personalized Study Plan** analyzes students' study needs into three levels: Remember, Understand, and Apply.

- The **Gradebook** helps students track progress and get immediate feedback. Automatically graded assessments flow into the Gradebook, which can be viewed in MyDevelopmentLab or exported.

- The **eText** allows students to highlight relevant passages and add notes. Access the eText through a laptop, iPad®, or tablet—or download the free app to use on tablets.

- **Extensive video footage** includes NEW video segments such as *Preterm Birth; Autism; First-Grade Science Education; Civic Engagement in Adolescence; Changing Parent–Adolescent Relationships; Adult Obesity;* and *Expertise, Practical Problem Solving, and Leadership in Middle Adulthood.*

- **Multimedia simulations** include NEW *Reducing Gender Stereotyping, Create an Older Adult,* and *Working Memory.*

- **Careers in Human Development** explains how studying lifespan development is essential for a wide range of career paths. This tool features over 25 career overviews, which contain interviews with actual practitioners, educational requirements, typical day-to-day activities, and links to websites for additional information.

- **Biographies** of major figures in the field. Examples include Erik Erikson, Jean Piaget, Lev Vygotsky, and Lawrence Kohlberg.

- NEW **MyVirtualLife** includes two simulations. In the first, students observe the effects of their parenting decisions on a child's development. In the second, they simulate their own progress through adulthood, making personal choices and reflecting on their lives.

MyDevelopmentLab can be used by itself or linked to any learning management system. To learn more about how the new MyDevelopmentLab combines learning applications with powerful assessment, visit *www.mydevelopmentlab.com.*

Legend for Photos Accompanying Sofie's Story

Sofie's story is told in Chapters 1 and 19, from her birth to her death. The photos that appear at the beginning of Chapter 1 follow her through her lifespan and include family members of two succeeding generations.

Page 1

1. Sofie, age 18, high school graduation in 1926.
2. Sofie as a baby, with her mother in 1908.
3. Sofie, age 6, with her brother, age 8, in 1914.
4. Sofie's German passport.
5. Sofie, age 60, and daughter Laura on Laura's wedding day in 1968.
6. Sofie and Phil in 1968, less than two years before Sofie died.
7. Sofie's grandsons, David and Peter, ages 5 and 2, children of Laura and Ken.
8. Laura, Ken, and sons Peter and David, ages 10 and 13, on the occasion of David's Bar Mitzvah in 1985.
9. Peter and Melissa on their wedding day in 2007.
10. Laura, Ken, sons David and Peter, and Peter's wife Melissa, with acclaimed pianist Awadagin Pratt, at the naming of a Pratt Foundation piano scholarship in Sofie's memory.

Page 2 top

Sofie, age 61, and her first grandchild, Ellen, October 1969, less than three months before Sofie died.

Page 2 bottom

Sofie and Phil in their mid-thirties, during World War II, when they became engaged.

chapter
1

History, Theory, and Research Strategies

This photo essay chronicles the life course and family legacy of Sofie Lentschner. It begins in 1908 with Sofie's infancy and concludes in 2012, four decades after Sofie's death, at an event celebrating the naming of a piano scholarship in her memory. For a description of each photo, see the legend on page xxvii.

chapter outline

A Scientific, Applied, and Interdisciplinary Field

Basic Issues

Continuous or Discontinuous Development? • One Course of Development or Many? • Relative Influence of Nature and Nurture?

The Lifespan Perspective: A Balanced Point of View

Development Is Lifelong • Development Is Multidimensional and Multidirectional • Development Is Plastic • Development Is Influenced by Multiple, Interacting Forces

■ **BIOLOGY AND ENVIRONMENT** Resilience

■ **CULTURAL INFLUENCES** The Baby Boomers Reshape the Life Course

Scientific Beginnings

Darwin: Forefather of Scientific Child Study • The Normative Period • The Mental Testing Movement

Mid-Twentieth-Century Theories

The Psychoanalytic Perspective • Behaviorism and Social Learning Theory • Piaget's Cognitive-Developmental Theory

Recent Theoretical Perspectives

Information Processing • Developmental Cognitive Neuroscience • Ethology and

Evolutionary Developmental Psychology • Vygotsky's Sociocultural Theory • Ecological Systems Theory

Comparing Theories

Studying Development

Common Research Methods • General Research Designs • Designs for Studying Development

■ **CULTURAL INFLUENCES** Immigrant Youths: Adapting to a New Land

Ethics in Lifespan Research

Sofie Lentschner was born in 1908, the second child of Jewish parents who made their home in Leipzig, Germany. Her father was a successful businessman and community leader, her mother a socialite well-known for her charm, beauty, and hospitality. As a baby, Sofie displayed the determination and persistence that would be sustained throughout her life. She sat for long periods inspecting small objects with her eyes and hands. As soon as Sofie could crawl, she steadfastly pulled herself up to the keys of the piano in the parlor and marveled at the tinkling sounds.

By the time Sofie entered elementary school, she was an introspective child, often ill at ease at the festive parties that girls of her family's social standing were expected to attend. She immersed herself in schoolwork, especially in mastering foreign languages. Twice a week, she took piano lessons from the finest teacher in Leipzig. By the time Sofie graduated from high school, she spoke English and French fluently and had become an accomplished pianist. Whereas most German girls of her time married by age 20, Sofie postponed serious courtship in favor of entering the university.

Sofie wanted marriage as well as education, but her plans were thwarted by the political turbulence of her times. When Hitler rose to power in the early 1930s, Sofie's father, fearing for the safety of his wife and children, moved the family to Belgium. Conditions for

Jews in Europe quickly worsened. The Nazis plundered Sofie's family home and confiscated her father's business. By the end of the 1930s, Sofie had lost contact with all but a handful of her aunts, uncles, cousins, and childhood friends, many of whom (she later learned) were herded into cattle cars and transported to Nazi death camps. In 1939, as anti-Jewish laws and atrocities intensified, Sofie's family fled to the United States.

As Sofie turned 30, her parents, convinced that she would never marry and would need a career for financial security, agreed to support her return to school. Sofie earned two master's degrees, one in music and the other in librarianship.

Then, on a blind date, she met Philip, a U.S. army officer. Philip's calm, gentle nature complemented Sofie's intensity and worldliness. Within six months they married. During the next four years, two daughters and a son were born.

When World War II ended, Philip left the army and opened a small men's clothing store. Sofie divided her time between caring for the children and helping Philip in the store. Now in her forties, she was a devoted mother, but few women her age were still rearing young children. As Philip struggled with the business, he spent longer hours at work, and Sofie often felt lonely. She rarely touched the piano, which brought back painful memories of youthful life plans shattered by war. Sofie's sense of isolation and lack of fulfillment frequently left her short-tempered. Late at night, she and Philip could be heard arguing.

As Sofie's children grew older, she returned to school again, this time to earn a teaching credential. Finally, at age 50, she launched a career. For the next decade, she taught German and French to high school students and English to newly arrived immigrants. Besides easing her family's financial difficulties, she felt a gratifying sense of accomplishment and creativity. These years were among the most energetic and satisfying of Sofie's life. She had an unending enthusiasm for teaching—for transmitting her facility with language and her practical understanding of how to adapt to life in a new land. She watched her children adopt many of her values and commitments and begin their marital and vocational lives at the expected time.

Sofie approached age 60 with an optimistic outlook. Released from the financial burden of paying for their children's college education, she and Philip looked forward to greater leisure. Their affection and respect for each other deepened. Once again, Sofie began to play the piano. But this period of contentment was short-lived.

One morning, Sofie felt a hard lump under her arm. Several days later, her doctor diagnosed cancer. Sofie's spirited disposition and capacity to adapt to radical life changes helped her meet the illness head on, defining it as an enemy to be fought and overcome. As a result, she lived five more years. Despite the exhaustion of chemotherapy, Sofie maintained a full schedule of teaching duties and continued to visit and run errands for her elderly mother. But as she weakened physically, she no longer had the stamina to meet her classes. Bedridden for the last few weeks, she slipped quietly into death with Philip at her side. The funeral chapel overflowed with hundreds of Sofie's students. She had granted each a memorable image of a woman of courage and caring.

One of Sofie's three children, Laura, is the author of this book. Married a year before Sofie died, Laura and her husband, Ken, often think of Sofie's message, spoken privately to them on the eve of their wedding day: "I learned from my own life and marriage that you must build a life together but also a life apart. You must grant each other the time, space, and support to forge your own identities, your own ways of expressing yourselves and giving to others. The most important ingredient of your relationship must be respect."

Laura and Ken settled in a small Midwestern city, near Illinois State University, where they have served on the faculty for many years—Laura in the Department of Psychology, Ken in the

Department of Mathematics. They have two sons, David and Peter, who carry Sofie's legacy forward. David shares his grandmother's penchant for teaching; he is a second-grade teacher. Peter, a lawyer, shares his grandmother's love of music, and his wife Melissa—much like Sofie—is both a talented linguist and a musician.

Sofie's story raises a wealth of fascinating issues about human life histories:

- What determines the features that Sofie shares with others and those that make her unique—in physical characteristics, mental capacities, interests, and behaviors?
- What led Sofie to retain the same persistent, determined disposition throughout her life but to change in other essential ways?
- How do historical and cultural conditions—for Sofie, the persecution that destroyed her childhood home, caused

the death of family members and friends, and led her family to flee to the United States—affect well-being throughout life?

- How does the timing of events—for example, Sofie's early exposure to foreign languages and her delayed entry into marriage, parenthood, and career—affect development?
- What factors—both personal and environmental—led Sofie to die sooner than expected?

These are central questions addressed by **developmental science,** a field of study devoted to understanding constancy and change throughout the lifespan (Lerner, 2006; Lerner et al., 2011). Great diversity characterizes the interests and concerns of investigators who study development. But all share a single goal: to identify those factors that influence consistencies and transformations in people from conception to death. ●

A Scientific, Applied, and Interdisciplinary Field

The questions just listed are not merely of scientific interest. Each has *applied,* or practical, importance as well. Research about development has also been stimulated by social pressures to improve people's lives. For example, the beginning of public education in the early twentieth century led to a demand for knowledge about what and how to teach children of different ages. The interest of the medical profession in improving people's health required an understanding of physical development, nutrition, and disease. The social service profession's desire to treat emotional problems and to help people adjust to major life events required information about personality and social development. And parents have continually sought expert advice about child-rearing practices and experiences that would promote their children's well-being.

Our large storehouse of information about development is *interdisciplinary.* It has grown through the combined efforts of people from many fields of study. Because of the need for solutions to everyday problems at all ages, researchers from psychology, sociology, anthropology, biology, and neuroscience have joined forces in research with professionals from education, family studies, medicine, public health, and social service, to name just a few. Together, they have created the field as it exists today—a body of knowledge that is not just scientifically important but also relevant and useful.

Basic Issues

Speculations about how people grow and change have existed for centuries. As they combined with research, they inspired the construction of *theories* of development. A **theory** is an

orderly, integrated set of statements that describes, explains, and predicts behavior. For example, a good theory of infant–caregiver attachment would (1) *describe* the behaviors of babies of 6 to 8 months of age as they seek the affection and comfort of a familiar adult, (2) *explain* how and why infants develop this strong desire to bond with a caregiver, and (3) *predict* the consequences of this emotional bond for future relationships.

Theories are vital tools for two reasons. First, they provide organizing frameworks for our observations of people, *guiding and giving meaning* to what we see. Second, theories that are verified by research provide a sound basis for practical action. Once a theory helps us *understand* development, we are in a much better position to know *how to improve* the welfare and treatment of children and adults.

As we will see, theories are influenced by the cultural values and belief systems of their times. But theories differ from mere opinion or belief: A theory's continued existence depends on *scientific verification.* Every theory must be tested using a fair set of research procedures agreed on by the scientific community, and findings must endure, or be replicated over time.

The field of developmental science contains many theories about what people are like and how they change. Humans are complex beings; they change physically, mentally, emotionally, and socially. And investigators do not always agree on the meaning of what they see. But the existence of many theories helps advance knowledge as researchers try to support, contradict, and integrate these different points of view.

This chapter introduces you to major theories of human development and research strategies used to test them. Although there are many theories, we can easily organize them by looking at the stand they take on three basic issues: (1) Is the course of development continuous or discontinuous? (2) Does one course of development characterize all people, or are there many possible courses? (3) Are genetic or environmental factors more important in influencing development?

Continuous or Discontinuous Development?

How can we best describe the differences in capacities among infants, children, adolescents, and adults? As Figure 1.1 illustrates, major theories recognize two possibilities.

One view holds that infants and preschoolers respond to the world in much the same way as adults do. The difference between the immature and mature being is simply one of *amount or complexity*. For example, when Sofie was a baby, her perception of a piano melody, memory for past events, and ability to categorize objects may have been much like our own. Perhaps her only limitation was that she could not perform these skills with as much information and precision as we can. If this is so, then changes in her thinking must be **continuous**—a process of gradually augmenting the same types of skills that were there to begin with.

According to a second view, infants and children have *unique ways of thinking, feeling, and behaving,* ones quite different from adults. If so, then development is **discontinuous**—a process in which new ways of understanding and responding to the world emerge at specific times. From this perspective, Sofie could not yet perceive, remember, and categorize experiences as a mature person can. Rather, she moved through a series of developmental steps, each of which has unique features, until she reached the highest level of functioning.

Theories that accept the discontinuous perspective regard development as taking place in **stages**—*qualitative* changes in thinking, feeling, and behaving that characterize specific periods of development. In stage theories, development is like climbing a staircase, with each step corresponding to a more mature, reorganized way of functioning. The stage concept also assumes that people undergo periods of rapid transformation as they step up from one stage to the next. In other words, change is fairly sudden rather than gradual and ongoing.

One Course of Development or Many?

Stage theorists assume that people everywhere follow the same sequence of development. Yet children and adults live in distinct **contexts**—unique combinations of personal and environmental circumstances that can result in different paths of change. For example, a shy individual who fears social encounters develops in very different contexts from those of an outgoing agemate who readily seeks out other people (Kagan, 2008a). Children and adults in non-Western village societies have experiences that differ sharply from those of people in large Western cities, which result in markedly different intellectual capacities, social skills, and feelings about the self and others (Shweder et al., 2006).

As you will see, contemporary theorists regard the contexts that shape development as many-layered and complex. On the personal side, they include heredity and biological makeup. On the environmental side, they include home, school, and neighborhood as well as circumstances more remote from everyday life: community resources, societal values, and historical time period. Finally, researchers have become increasingly conscious of cultural diversity in development.

Relative Influence of Nature and Nurture?

In addition to describing the course of human development, each theory takes a stand on a major question about its underly-

FIGURE 1.1 Is development continuous or discontinuous? (a) Some theorists believe that development is a smooth, continuous process. Individuals gradually add more of the same types of skills. (b) Other theorists think that development takes place in discontinuous stages. People change rapidly as they step up to a new level and then change very little for a while. With each new step, the person interprets and responds to the world in a reorganized, qualitatively different way. As we will see later, still other theorists believe that development is characterized by both continuous and discontinuous change.

Infancy   **Adulthood**

(a) Continuous Development

Infancy   **Adulthood**

(b) Discontinuous Development

ing causes: Are genetic or environmental factors more important? This is the age-old **nature–nurture controversy.** By *nature,* we mean the hereditary information we receive from our parents at the moment of conception. By *nurture,* we mean the complex forces of the physical and social world that influence our biological makeup and psychological experiences before and after birth.

Although all theories grant roles to both nature and nurture, they vary in emphasis. A theory's position affects how it explains individual differences. Theorists who emphasize *stability*—that individuals who are high or low in a characteristic (such as verbal ability, anxiety, or sociability) will remain so at later ages—typically stress the importance of *heredity.* If they regard environment as important, they usually point to *early experiences* as establishing a lifelong pattern of behavior. Powerful negative events in the first few years, they argue, cannot be fully overcome by later, more positive ones (Bowlby, 1980; Sroufe, Coffino, & Carlson, 2010). Other theorists, taking a more optimistic view, see development as having substantial **plasticity** throughout life—as open to change in response to influential experiences (Baltes, Lindenberger, & Staudinger, 2006; Overton, 2010).

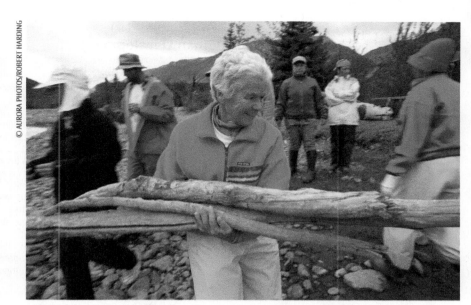

Since the 1960s, researchers have moved from focusing only on child development to investigating development over the entire life course. This woman and her companions on a river rafting trip illustrate the health, vitality, and life satisfaction of many contemporary older adults.

The Lifespan Perspective: A Balanced Point of View

So far, we have discussed basic issues of human development in terms of extremes—solutions favoring one side or the other. But as we trace the unfolding of the field, you will see that positions have softened. Today, some theorists believe that both continuous and discontinuous changes occur. Many acknowledge that development has both universal features and features unique to each individual and his or her contexts. And a growing number regard heredity and environment as inseparably interwoven, each affecting the potential of the other to modify the child's traits and capacities (Gottlieb, 2007; Overton, 2010).

These balanced visions owe much to the expansion of research from a nearly exclusive focus on the first two decades to include adulthood. In the first half of the twentieth century, it was widely assumed that development stopped at adolescence. Adulthood was viewed as a plateau and aging as a period of decline. The changing character of the North American population awakened researchers to the idea that gains in functioning are lifelong.

Because of improvements in nutrition, sanitation, and medical knowledge, *average life expectancy* (the number of years an individual born in a particular year can expect to live) gained more in the twentieth century than in the preceding 5,000 years. In 1900, life expectancy was just under age 50; today, it is 78.5 years in the United States and even higher in most other industrialized nations. Life expectancy continues to increase; in the United States, it is predicted to reach 84 years in 2050 (U.S. Census Bureau, 2013).

Older adults are not only more numerous but also healthier and more active. Challenging the earlier stereotype of the withering person, they have contributed to a profound shift in our view of human change. Increasingly, researchers are envisioning *development as a dynamic system*—a perpetually ongoing process, extending from conception to death, that is molded by a complex network of biological, psychological, and social influences (Lerner et al., 2011). A leading dynamic systems approach is the **lifespan perspective.** Four assumptions make up this broader view: that development is (1) lifelong, (2) multidimensional and multidirectional, (3) highly plastic, and (4) affected by multiple, interacting forces (Baltes, Lindenberger, & Staudinger, 2006; Staudinger & Lindenberger, 2003).

Development Is Lifelong

According to the lifespan perspective, no single age period is supreme in its impact on the life course. Rather, events occurring during each major period, summarized in Table 1.1 on page 6, can have equally powerful effects on future change.

TABLE 1.1   Major Periods of Human Development

PERIOD	APPROXIMATE AGE RANGE	BRIEF DESCRIPTION
Prenatal	Conception to birth	The one-celled organism transforms into a human baby with remarkable capacities to adjust to life outside the womb.
Infancy and toddlerhood	Birth–2 years	Dramatic changes in the body and brain support the emergence of a wide array of motor, perceptual, and intellectual capacities and first intimate ties to others.
Early childhood	2–6 years	During the "play years," motor skills are refined, thought and language expand at an astounding pace, a sense of morality is evident, and children establish ties with peers.
Middle childhood	6–11 years	The school years are marked by improved athletic abilities; more logical thought processes; mastery of basic literacy skills; advances in self-understanding, morality, and friendship; and the beginnings of peer-group membership.
Adolescence	11–18 years	Puberty leads to an adult-sized body and sexual maturity. Thought becomes abstract and idealistic and school achievement more serious. Adolescents focus on defining personal values and goals and establishing autonomy from the family.
Early adulthood	18–40 years	Most young people leave home, complete their education, and begin full-time work. Major concerns are developing a career, forming an intimate partnership, and marrying, rearing children, or establishing other lifestyles.
Middle adulthood	40–65 years	Many people are at the height of their careers and attain leadership positions. They must also help their children begin independent lives and their parents adapt to aging. They become more aware of their own mortality.
Late adulthood	65 years–death	People adjust to retirement, to decreased physical strength and health, and often to the death of a spouse. They reflect on the meaning of their lives.

Within each period, change occurs in three broad domains: *physical, cognitive,* and *emotional/social,* which we separate for convenience of discussion (see Figure 1.2 for a description of each). Yet, as you already know from the first part of this chapter, these domains overlap and interact.

Development Is Multidimensional and Multidirectional

Think back to Sofie's life and how she continually faced new demands and opportunities. From a lifespan perspective, the challenges and adjustments of development are *multidimensional*—affected by an intricate blend of biological, psychological, and social forces.

Lifespan development is also *multidirectional.* At every period, development is a joint expression of growth and decline. When Sofie mastered languages and music as a school-age child, she gave up refining other skills. Later, when she chose to become a teacher, she let go of other career options. Although gains are especially evident early in life, and losses during the final years, people of all ages can improve current skills and develop new ones (Lang, Rohr, & Williger, 2010; Scheibe, Freund, & Baltes, 2007). Most older adults, for example, devise compensatory techniques for dealing with their increasing memory failures, such as relying more on external aids like calendars and lists.

Besides being multidirectional over time, change is multidirectional within each domain of development. Although some qualities of Sofie's cognitive functioning (such as memory) likely declined in her mature years, her knowledge of both English and French grew throughout her life. And she also developed new forms of thinking—for example, expertise in practical matters, a quality of reasoning called *wisdom.* Recall Sofie's wise advice to Laura and Ken on the eve of their wedding day. Notice how the lifespan perspective includes both continuous and discontinuous change.

Development Is Plastic

Lifespan researchers emphasize that development is plastic at all ages. Consider Sofie's social reserve in childhood and her decision to study rather than marry as a young adult. As new opportunities arose, Sofie moved easily into marriage and childbearing in her thirties. And although parenthood and financial difficulties posed challenges to Sofie's and Philip's happiness, their relationship gradually became richer and more fulfilling. In Chapter 17, we will see that intellectual performance also remains flexible with advancing age. Older people respond to special training with substantial (but not unlimited) gains in a wide variety of mental abilities (Stine-Morrow & Basak, 2011).

Evidence on plasticity reveals that aging is not an eventual "shipwreck," as has often been assumed. Instead, the metaphor

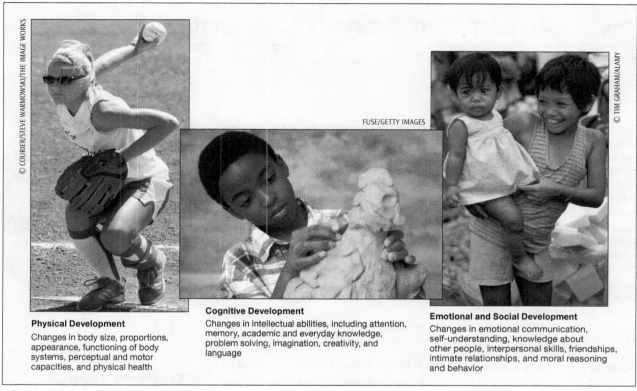

Physical Development

Changes in body size, proportions, appearance, functioning of body systems, perceptual and motor capacities, and physical health

Cognitive Development

Changes in intellectual abilities, including attention, memory, academic and everyday knowledge, problem solving, imagination, creativity, and language

Emotional and Social Development

Changes in emotional communication, self-understanding, knowledge about other people, interpersonal skills, friendships, intimate relationships, and moral reasoning and behavior

| **FIGURE 1.2** **Major domains of development.** The three domains are not really distinct. Rather, they overlap and interact.

of a "butterfly"—of metamorphosis and continued potential—provides a more accurate picture of lifespan change. Still, development gradually becomes less plastic, as both capacity and opportunity for change are reduced. And plasticity varies across individuals. Some children and adults experience more diverse life circumstances. Also, as the Biology and Environment box on page 8 indicates, some adapt more easily than others to changing conditions.

Development Is Influenced by Multiple, Interacting Forces

According to the lifespan perspective, *development is influenced by multiple forces:* biological, historical, social, and cultural. Although these wide-ranging influences can be organized into three categories, they work together, combining in unique ways to fashion each life course.

Age-Graded Influences. Events that are strongly related to age and therefore fairly predictable in when they occur and how long they last are called **age-graded influences.** For example, most individuals walk shortly after their first birthday, acquire their native language during the preschool years, reach puberty around age 12 to 14, and (for women) experience menopause in their

late forties or early fifties. These milestones are influenced by biology, but social customs—such as starting school around age 6, getting a driver's license at age 16, and entering college around age 18—can create age-graded influences as well.

For these 18-year-olds, moving into their college dorm is a major life transition, offering new freedoms and responsibilities. Entering college is an age-graded influence, occurring at about the same age for most young people.

Biology and Environment

Resilience

John and his best friend, Gary, grew up in a rundown, crime-ridden, inner-city neighborhood. By age 10, each had experienced years of family conflict followed by parental divorce. Reared from then on in mother-headed households, John and Gary rarely saw their fathers. Both dropped out of high school and were in and out of trouble with the police.

Then their paths diverged. By age 30, John had fathered two children with women he never married, had spent time in prison, was unemployed, and drank alcohol heavily. In contrast, Gary had returned to finish high school, had studied auto mechanics at a community college, and had become manager of a gas station and repair shop. Married with two children, he had saved his earnings and bought a home. He was happy, healthy, and well-adapted to life.

A wealth of evidence shows that environmental risks—poverty, negative family interactions and parental divorce, job loss, mental illness, and drug abuse—predispose children to future problems (Masten & Gewirtz, 2006; Sameroff, 2006; Wadsworth & Santiago, 2008). Why did Gary "beat the odds" and come through unscathed?

Research on **resilience**—the ability to adapt effectively in the face of threats to development—is receiving increased attention as investigators look for ways to protect young people from the damaging effects of stressful life conditions (Masten & Powell, 2003). This interest has been inspired by long-term studies on the relationship of life stressors in childhood to competence and adjustment in adolescence and adulthood (Werner, 2013). In each study, some individuals were shielded from negative outcomes, whereas others had lasting problems. Four broad factors offered protection from the damaging effects of stressful life events.

Personal Characteristics

A child's genetically influenced characteristics can reduce exposure to risk or lead to experiences that compensate for early stressful events. High intelligence and socially valued talents (in music or athletics, for example) increase the chances that a child will have rewarding experiences in school and in the

community that offset the impact of a stressful home life. Temperament is particularly powerful. Children who have easygoing, sociable dispositions and who can readily inhibit negative emotions and impulses tend to have an optimistic outlook on life and a special capacity to adapt to change—qualities that elicit positive responses from others. In contrast, emotionally reactive and irritable children often tax the patience of people around them (Vanderbilt-Adriance & Shaw, 2008; Wang & Deater-Deckard, 2013). For example, both John and Gary moved several times during their childhoods. Each time, John became anxious and angry, whereas Gary looked forward to making new friends.

A Warm Parental Relationship

A close relationship with at least one parent who provides warmth, appropriately high expectations, monitoring of the child's activities, and an organized home environment fosters resilience (Taylor, 2010). But this factor (as well as the next one) is not independent of children's personal characteristics. Children who are relaxed, socially responsive, and able to deal with change are easier to rear and more likely to enjoy positive relationships with parents and other people. At the same time, some children develop more attractive dispositions as a result of parental warmth and attention (Gulotta, 2008).

Social Support Outside the Immediate Family

The most consistent asset of resilient children is a strong bond with a competent, caring adult. For children who do not have a close bond with either parent, a grandparent, aunt, uncle, or teacher who forms a special relationship with the child can promote resilience (Masten & Reed, 2002). Gary received support in adolescence from his grandfather, who listened to Gary's concerns and helped him solve problems.

Associations with rule-abiding peers who value school achievement are also linked to resilience (Tiet, Huizinga, & Byrnes, 2010). But children who have positive relationships with adults are far more likely to establish these supportive peer ties.

© ROBERT BRENNER/PHOTOEDIT

This child's close relationship with his father helps shield him from the damaging effects of stressful life conditions.

Community Resources and Opportunities

Community supports—good schools, convenient and affordable health care and social services, libraries, and recreation centers—foster both parents' and children's well-being. In addition, engaging in extracurricular activities at school and in religious youth groups, scouting, and other organizations teaches important social skills, such as cooperation, leadership, and contributing to others' welfare. As participants acquire these competencies, they gain in self-reliance, self-esteem, and community commitment (Benson et al., 2006). As a student, Gary volunteered for Habitat for Humanity, joining a team building affordable housing in low-income neighborhoods. Community involvement offered Gary opportunities to form meaningful relationships, which further strengthened his resilience.

Research on resilience highlights the complex connections between heredity and environment. Armed with positive characteristics, which stem from native endowment, favorable rearing experiences, or both, children and adolescents can act to reduce stressful situations.

But when many risks pile up, they are increasingly difficult to overcome (Obradović et al., 2009). To inoculate children against the negative effects of risk, interventions must not only reduce risks but also enhance children's protective relationships at home, in school, and in the community.

History-Graded Influences. Development is also profoundly affected by forces unique to a historical era. Examples include epidemics, wars, and periods of economic prosperity or depression; technological advances, such as the introduction of television, computers, and the Internet; and changes in cultural values, such as attitudes toward women and ethnic minorities. These **history-graded influences** explain why people born around the same time—called a *cohort*—tend to be alike in ways that set them apart from people born at other times.

Consider the *baby boomers*, a term used to describe people born between 1946 and 1964, the post–World War II period during which birth rates soared in most Western nations, with an especially sharp increase in the United States. The sheer size of the baby-boom generation made it a powerful social force from the time its members became young adults; today, the baby boomers are redefining our view of middle and late adulthood (see the Cultural Influences box on page 10).

LOOK AND LISTEN

Identify a history-graded influence in your life, and speculate about its impact on people your age. Then ask someone a generation older than you to identify a history-graded influence in his or her life and to reflect on its impact. ●

Nonnormative Influences. Age-graded and history-graded influences are *normative*—meaning typical, or average—

Lessons from an inspiring music teacher is a nonnormative influence that may powerfully affect the direction of this child's life.

because each affects large numbers of people. **Nonnormative influences** are events that are irregular: They happen to just one person or a few people and do not follow a predictable timetable. Nonnormative influences that had a major impact on the direction of Sofie's life included piano lessons in childhood with an inspiring teacher; delayed marriage, parenthood, and career entry; and a battle with cancer.

Nonnormative influences have become more powerful and age-graded influences less so in contemporary adult development. Compared with Sofie's era, much greater diversity exists today in the ages at which people finish their education, enter careers, get married, have children, and retire. Indeed, Sofie's "off-time" accomplishments would have been less unusual had she been born two generations later!

Notice that instead of a single line of development, the lifespan perspective emphasizes many potential pathways and outcomes—an image more like tree branches extending in diverse directions (see Figure 1.3). Now let's turn to scientific foundations of the field as a prelude to major theories that address various aspects of change.

ASK YOURSELF

REVIEW Distinguish age-graded, history-graded, and nonnormative influences on lifespan development. Cite an example of each in Sofie's story.

APPLY Anna, a high school counselor, has devised a program that integrates classroom learning with vocational training to help adolescents at risk for school dropout stay in school. What is Anna's position on *stability versus plasticity* in development? Explain.

REFLECT Describe an aspect of your development that differs from a parent's or a grandparent's when he or she was your age. Using influences highlighted by the lifespan perspective, explain this difference in development.

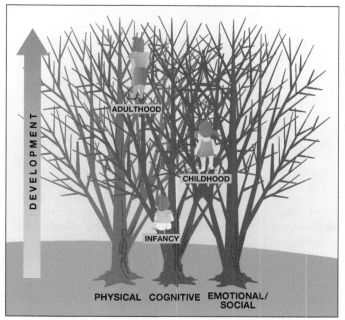

FIGURE 1.3 The lifespan view of development. Rather than envisioning a single line of stagewise or continuous change (see Figure 1.1 on page 4), lifespan theorists conceive of development as more like tree branches extending in diverse directions. Many potential pathways are possible, depending on the contexts that influence the individual's life course. Each branch in this treelike image represents a possible skill within one of the major domains of development. The crossing of the branches signifies that the domains—physical, cognitive, emotional, and social—are interrelated.

Cultural Influences

The Baby Boomers Reshape the Life Course

From 1946 to 1964, 92 percent of all American women of childbearing age gave birth, averaging almost four children each (Croker, 2007). This splurge of births, which extended for nearly two decades, yielded a unique generation often credited with changing the world. Today, the baby boomers comprise more than 80 million adults—nearly 30 percent of the U.S. population (U.S. Census Bureau, 2013). Most are middle-aged, with the oldest having recently entered late adulthood.

Several interrelated factors sparked the post–World War II baby boom. Many people who had postponed marriage and parenthood throughout the Great Depression of the 1930s started families in the 1940s, once the economy had improved. With the end of World War II, returning GIs also began to have children. And as economic prosperity accelerated in the 1950s, making larger families affordable, more people married at younger ages and had several children closely spaced (Stewart & Malley, 2004). Finally, after a war, the desire to make babies generally strengthens. Besides replacing massive loss of life, new births signify hope that "human life will continue" (Croker, 2007, p. 9).

Compared with the previous generation, many more young baby boomers were economically privileged. They were also the recipients of deep emotional investment from their parents, who—having undergone the deprivations of depression and war—often ranked children as the most enduring benefit of their adult lives. These factors may have engendered optimism, confidence, even a sense of entitlement (Elder, Nguyen, & Caspi, 1985). At the same time, their huge numbers—evident in overflowing school classrooms—may have sparked an intense struggle for individual recognition. By the time the boomers reached early adulthood, this set of traits led critics to label them a narcissistic, indulged, "me" generation.

From the mid-1960s to the early 1970s, the "leading-edge" baby boomers (born in the late 1940s and early 1950s) entered colleges and universities in record numbers, becoming better educated than any previous generation. This cohort—self-focused, socially aware, and in search of distinction—broke away from their parents' family- and marriage-centered lifestyles. Starting in the mid-sixties, marriage rates declined, age of first marriage rose, and divorce rates increased. And the baby boomers responded to the turbulence of those times—the assassination of President Kennedy in 1963, the Vietnam War, and growing racial tensions—by mobilizing around the antiwar, civil rights, and women's movements, yielding a generation of student activists.

By the time the "trailing-edge" boomers (born in the late 1950s and early 1960s) came of age, these movements had left an enduring mark. Even as they turned toward family life and career development, the boomers continued to search for personal meaning, self-expression, and social responsibility. By midlife, the generation had produced an unusually large number of socially concerned writers, teachers, filmmakers, and labor and community organizers, as well as innovative musicians and artists (Cole & Stewart, 1996; Dickstein, 1992). And a multitude of ordinary citizens worked to advance social causes.

In addition, as baby-boom women entered the labor market and struggled for career advancement and equal pay, their self-confidence grew, and they paved the way for the next generation: On average, younger women attained this same level of self-confidence at a much earlier age (Twenge, 1997, 2001). And as baby-boom activists pressed for gender and racial equality, they influenced national policy. The 1960s saw laws passed that banned discrimination in employment practices, in racial access to public accommodations, and in sale or rental of housing. By the 1970s, progress in civil rights served as the springboard for the gay and lesbian rights movement.

Today, the baby boomers are healthier, better educated, and financially better off than

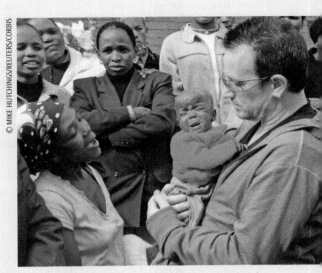

Rock star Bono, born in 1960, shares his cohort's sense of social responsibility. Shown here at a health clinic in Lesotho, he is a leader in the fight against AIDS and poverty in Africa.

any previous midlife cohort (Whitbourne & Willis, 2006). Their sense of self-empowerment and innovativeness is bringing new vitality to this period of the lifespan, including efforts to increase the personal meaningfulness of their careers and to deepen their lifelong engagement with social causes.

Nevertheless, though advantaged as a generation, the baby boomers are diverse in health status and sense of control over their lives. Those higher in education and income considerably better off. And because retirement savings were heavily hit by the economic recession of 2007 to 2009, many are working longer than they otherwise had planned.

What lies ahead as this gigantic population bulge moves into late adulthood? Most analysts focus on societal burdens, such as rising social security and health-care costs. At the same time, as the boomers could become "our only increasing natural resource" (Freedman, 1999). After retirement, they will have more time to care about others—and more relevant experience and years left to do so—than any previous generation. Policies and programs aimed at recruiting older adults into volunteer and service roles may be one of the best ways to "channel good will into good deeds," combat social ills, and enhance development during all periods of life.

© MIKE HUTCHINGS/REUTERS/CORBIS

Scientific Beginnings

Scientific study of human development dates back to the late nineteenth and early twentieth centuries. Early observations of human change were soon followed by improved methods and theories, contributing to the firm foundation on which the field rests today.

Darwin: Forefather of Scientific Child Study

British naturalist Charles Darwin (1809–1882) observed the infinite variation among plant and animal species. He saw that within a species, no two individuals are exactly alike. From these observations, he constructed his famous *theory of evolution.*

The theory emphasized two related principles: *natural selection* and *survival of the fittest.* Darwin explained that certain species survive in particular environments because they have characteristics that fit with, or are adapted to, their surroundings. Individuals within a species who best meet the environment's survival requirements live long enough to reproduce and pass their more beneficial characteristics to future generations. Darwin's (1859/1936) emphasis on the adaptive value of physical characteristics and behavior found its way into important developmental theories.

Darwin's theory of evolution emphasizes the adaptive value of physical characteristics and behavior. Affection and care in families promote survival and psychological well-being throughout the lifespan. Here, a son helps his father adjust to using a walker.

During his explorations, Darwin discovered that early prenatal growth is strikingly similar in many species. Other scientists concluded from Darwin's observations that the development of the human child follows the same general plan as the evolution of the human species. Although this belief eventually proved inaccurate, efforts to chart parallels between child growth and human evolution prompted researchers to make careful observations of all aspects of children's behavior. As a result, scientific child study was born.

The Normative Period

G. Stanley Hall (1844–1924), one of the most influential American psychologists of the early twentieth century, is regarded as the founder of the child study movement (Cairns & Cairns, 2006). He also wrote one of the few books of his time on aging, foreshadowing lifespan research. Inspired by Darwin's work, Hall and his well-known student Arnold Gesell (1880–1961) devised theories based on evolutionary ideas. They regarded development as a *maturational process*—a genetically determined series of events that unfold automatically, much like a flower (Gesell, 1933; Hall, 1904).

Hall and Gesell are remembered less for their one-sided theories than for their intensive efforts to describe all aspects of development. This launched the **normative approach,** in which measures of behavior are taken on large numbers of individuals, and age-related averages are computed to represent typical development. Using this procedure, Hall constructed elaborate questionnaires asking children of different ages almost everything they could tell about themselves—interests, fears, imaginary playmates, dreams, friendships, everyday knowledge, and more. Through careful observations and parent interviews, Gesell collected detailed normative information on infants' and children's motor achievements, social behaviors, and personality characteristics.

Gesell was also among the first to make knowledge about child development meaningful to parents. His books, along with Benjamin Spock's *Baby and Child Care,* became central to a rapidly expanding child-rearing literature for parents.

The Mental Testing Movement

While Hall and Gesell were developing their theories and methods in the United States, French psychologist Alfred Binet (1857–1911) was also taking a normative approach, but for a different reason. In the early 1900s, Binet and his colleague Theodore Simon were asked by Paris school officials to find a way to identify children with learning problems for placement in special classes. To address this practical educational concern, they constructed the first successful intelligence test.

In 1916, at Stanford University, Binet's test was adapted for use with English-speaking children. Since then, the English version has been known as the *Stanford-Binet Intelligence Scale.* Besides providing a score that successfully predicted school achievement, the Binet test sparked tremendous interest in individual differences in development.

Mid-Twentieth-Century Theories

In the mid-twentieth century, the study of human development expanded into a legitimate discipline. A variety of theories emerged, each of which still has followers today.

The Psychoanalytic Perspective

In the 1930s and 1940s, as more people sought help from professionals to deal with emotional difficulties, a new question had to be addressed: How and why do people become the way they are? To treat psychological problems, psychiatrists and social workers turned to an approach to personality development that emphasizes each individual's unique life history.

According to the **psychoanalytic perspective,** people move through a series of stages in which they confront conflicts between biological drives and social expectations. How these conflicts are resolved determines the person's ability to learn, to get along with others, and to cope with anxiety. Among the many contributors to the psychoanalytic perspective, two were especially influential: Sigmund Freud, founder of the psychoanalytic movement, and Erik Erikson.

Freud's Theory. Freud (1856–1939), a Viennese physician, treated emotionally troubled adults by having them talk freely about painful childhood events. Working with these recollections, he examined the unconscious motivations of his patients and constructed his **psychosexual theory,** which emphasizes that how parents manage their child's sexual and aggressive drives in the first few years is crucial for healthy personality development.

In Freud's theory, three parts of the personality—id, ego, and superego—become integrated during five stages, summarized in Table 1.2. The *id,* the largest portion of the mind, is the source of basic biological needs and desires. The *ego,* the conscious, rational part of personality, emerges in early infancy to redirect the id's impulses into acceptable behaviors.

Between 3 and 6 years of age, the *superego,* or conscience, develops as parents insist that children conform to the values of society. Now the ego faces the increasingly complex task of reconciling the demands of the id, the external world, and conscience (Freud, 1923/1974). According to Freud, relations established among the id, ego, and superego during the preschool years determine the individual's basic personality.

Freud (1938/1973) believed that during childhood, sexual impulses shift their focus from the oral to the anal to the genital regions of the body. In each stage, parents walk a fine line between permitting too much or too little gratification of their child's basic needs. If parents strike an appropriate balance, then children grow into well-adjusted adults with the capacity for mature sexual behavior and investment in family life.

Freud's theory was the first to stress the influence of the early parent–child relationship on development. But his perspective was eventually criticized. First, it overemphasized the influence of sexual feelings in development. Second, because it was based on the problems of sexually repressed, well-to-do adults in nineteenth-century Viennese society, it did not apply in other cultures. Finally, Freud had not studied children directly.

Erikson's Theory. Several of Freud's followers improved on his vision, the most important of whom was Erik Erikson (1902–1994). In his **psychosocial theory,** Erikson emphasized that in addition to mediating between id impulses and superego demands, the ego makes a positive contribution to development, acquiring attitudes and skills that make the individual an active, contributing member of society. A basic psychosocial conflict, which is resolved along a continuum from positive to negative, determines healthy or maladaptive outcomes at each stage. As Table 1.2 shows, Erikson's first five stages parallel Freud's stages, but Erikson added three adult stages.

Unlike Freud, Erikson pointed out that normal development must be understood in relation to each culture's life situation. For example, in the 1940s, he observed that Yurok Indians of the northwest coast of the United States deprived babies of breastfeeding for the first 10 days after birth and instead fed them a thin soup. At age 6 months, infants were abruptly weaned—an experience that, from our cultural vantage point, might seem cruel. But Erikson explained that the Yurok lived in a world in which salmon filled the river just once a year, a circumstance requiring considerable self-restraint for survival.

Contributions and Limitations of the Psychoanalytic Perspective. A special strength of the psychoanalytic perspective is its emphasis on understanding the individual's unique life history. Consistent with this view, psychoanalytic theorists accept the *clinical,* or *case study, method,* yields a detailed picture of the personality of a single person.

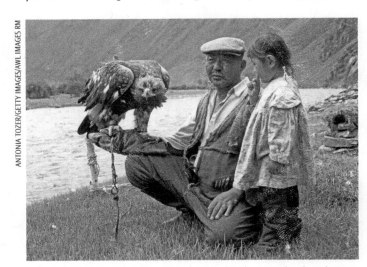

A child of the Kazakh people of Mongolia observes closely as her grandfather demonstrates how to train an eagle to hunt small animals, essential for the heavily meat-based Kazakh diet. As Erikson recognized, this parenting practice is best understood in relation to the competencies valued and needed in Kazakh culture.

ANTONIA TOZER/GETTY IMAGES/AWL IMAGES RM

TABLE 1.2
Freud's Psychosexual Stages and Erikson's Psychosocial Stages Compared

APPROXIMATE AGE	FREUD'S PSYCHOSEXUAL STAGE	ERIKSON'S PSYCHOSOCIAL STAGE
Birth–1 year	*Oral:* The new ego directs the baby's sucking activities toward breast or bottle. If oral needs are not met, the individual may develop such habits as thumb sucking, fingernail biting, overeating, or smoking.	*Basic trust versus mistrust:* From warm, responsive care, infants gain a sense of trust, or confidence, that the world is good. Mistrust occurs if infants are neglected or handled harshly.
1–3 years	*Anal:* Toddlers and preschoolers enjoy holding and releasing urine and feces. If parents toilet train before children are ready or make too few demands, conflicts about anal control may appear in the form of extreme orderliness or disorder.	*Autonomy versus shame and doubt:* Using new mental and motor skills, children want to decide for themselves. Parents can foster autonomy by permitting reasonable free choice and not forcing or shaming the child.
3–6 years	*Phallic:* As preschoolers take pleasure in genital stimulation, Freud's Oedipus conflict for boys and Electra conflict for girls arise: Children feel a sexual desire for the other-sex parent. To avoid punishment, they give up this desire and adopt the same-sex parent's characteristics and values. As a result, the superego is formed, and children feel guilty when they violate its standards.	*Initiative versus guilt:* Through make-believe play, children gain insight into the person they can become. Initiative—a sense of ambition and responsibility—develops when parents support their child's sense of purpose. But if parents demand too much self-control, children experience excessive guilt.
6–11 years	*Latency:* Sexual instincts die down, and the superego strengthens as the child acquires new social values from adults and same-sex peers.	*Industry versus inferiority:* At school, children learn to work and cooperate with others. Inferiority develops when negative experiences at home, at school, or with peers lead to feelings of incompetence.
Adolescence	*Genital:* With puberty, sexual impulses reappear. Successful development during earlier stages leads to marriage, mature sexuality, and child rearing.	*Identity versus role confusion:* By exploring values and vocational goals, the young person forms a personal identity. The negative outcome is confusion about future adult roles.
Early adulthood		*Intimacy versus isolation:* Young adults establish intimate relationships. Because of earlier disappointments, some individuals cannot form close bonds and remain isolated.
Middle adulthood		*Generativity versus stagnation:* Generativity means giving to the next generation through child rearing, caring for others, or productive work. The person who fails in these ways feels an absence of meaningful accomplishment.
Old age		*Integrity versus despair:* Integrity results from feeling that life was worth living as it happened. Older people who are dissatisfied with their lives fear death.

© OLIVE PIERCE/BLACK STAR

Erik Erikson

The psychoanalytic approach has also inspired a wealth of research on many aspects of emotional and social development, including infant–caregiver attachment, aggression, sibling relationships, child-rearing practices, morality, gender roles, and adolescent identity.

Despite its contributions, the psychoanalytic perspective is no longer in the mainstream of human development research. Psychoanalytic theorists were so strongly committed to in-depth study of individuals that they failed to consider other methods. In addition, many psychoanalytic ideas, such as psychosexual stages and ego functioning, are so vague that they are difficult or impossible to test empirically (Crain, 2005; Thomas, 2005). Nevertheless, Erikson's broad outline of lifespan change

captures the essence of personality development during each major period, so we will return to it in later chapters.

Behaviorism and Social Learning Theory

As the psychoanalytic perspective gained in prominence, the study of development was also influenced by a very different perspective. According to **behaviorism,** directly observable events—stimuli and responses—are the appropriate focus of study. North American behaviorism began in the early twentieth century with the work of John Watson (1878–1958), who wanted to create an objective science of psychology.

Traditional Behaviorism. Watson was inspired by Russian physiologist Ivan Pavlov's studies of animal learning. Pavlov knew that dogs release saliva as an innate reflex when they are given food. But he noticed that his dogs were salivating before they tasted any food—when they saw the trainer who usually fed them. The dogs, Pavlov reasoned, must have learned to associate a neutral stimulus (the trainer) with another stimulus (food) that produces a reflexive response (salivation). Because of this association, the neutral stimulus alone could bring about a response resembling the reflex. Eager to test this idea, Pavlov successfully taught dogs to salivate at the sound of a bell by pairing it with the presentation of food. He had discovered *classical conditioning.*

In a historic experiment that applied classical conditioning to children's behavior, Watson taught an 11-month-old infant, Albert, to fear a neutral stimulus—a soft white rat—by presenting it several times with a sharp, loud sound, which naturally scared the baby. Little Albert, who at first had reached out eagerly to touch the furry rat, began to cry and turn his head away at the sight of it (Watson & Raynor, 1920). Watson concluded that environment is the supreme force in development and that adults can mold children's behavior by carefully controlling stimulus–response associations. He viewed development as a continuous process—a gradual increase with age in the number and strength of these associations.

Another form of behaviorism was B. F. Skinner's (1904–1990) *operant conditioning theory.* According to Skinner, the frequency of a behavior can be increased by following it with a wide variety of *reinforcers,* such as food, praise, or a friendly smile. It can also be decreased through *punishment,* such as disapproval or withdrawal of privileges. We will consider these conditioning techniques further in Chapter 4.

Social Learning Theory. Psychologists wondered whether behaviorism might offer a more direct and effective explanation of the development of social behavior than the less precise concepts of psychoanalytic theory. This sparked approaches that built on the principles of conditioning, offering expanded views of how children and adults acquire new responses.

Several kinds of **social learning theory** emerged. The most influential, devised by Albert Bandura (1925–), emphasizes *modeling,* also known as *imitation* or *observational learning,* as a powerful source of development. The baby who claps her hands after her mother does so and the child who angrily hits a playmate in the same way that he has been punished at home are displaying observational learning. In his early work, Bandura found that diverse factors affect children's motivation to imitate: their own history of reinforcement or punishment for the behavior, the promise of future reinforcement or punishment, and even observing the model being reinforced or punished.

Bandura's work continues to influence much research on social development. But today, his theory stresses the importance of *cognition,* or thinking. In fact, the most recent revision of Bandura's (1992, 2001) theory places such strong emphasis

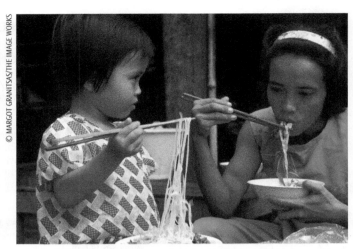

Social learning theory recognizes that children acquire many skills through modeling. By observing and imitating her mother, this Vietnamese preschooler learns to use chopsticks.

on how we think about ourselves and other people that he calls it a *social-cognitive* rather than a social learning approach.

In Bandura's revised view, children gradually become more selective in what they imitate. From watching others engage in self-praise and self-blame and through feedback about the worth of their own actions, children develop *personal standards* for behavior and *a sense of self-efficacy*—the belief that their own abilities and characteristics will help them succeed. These cognitions guide responses in particular situations (Bandura, 1999, 2001). For example, imagine a parent who often remarks, "I'm glad I kept working on that task, even though it was hard," and who encourages persistence by saying, "I know you can do a good job on that homework!" Soon the child starts to view herself as hard-working and high-achieving and selects people with these characteristics as models. In this way, as individuals acquire attitudes, values, and convictions about themselves, they control their own learning and behavior.

Contributions and Limitations of Behaviorism and Social Learning Theory. Behaviorism and social learning theory have been helpful in treating adjustment problems. **Behavior modification** consists of procedures that combine conditioning and modeling to eliminate undesirable behaviors and increase desirable responses. It has been used to relieve difficulties in children and adults, ranging from poor time management and unwanted habits to serious problems, such as language delays and persistent aggression (Martin & Pear, 2011).

Nevertheless, many theorists believe that behaviorism and social learning theory offer too narrow a view of important environmental influences, which extend beyond immediate reinforcement, punishment, and modeled behaviors to people's rich physical and social worlds. Behaviorism and social learning theory have also been criticized for underestimating people's contributions to their own development. Bandura, in emphasiz-

TABLE 1.3 **Piaget's Stages of Cognitive Development**

STAGE	PERIOD OF DEVELOPMENT	DESCRIPTION
Sensorimotor	Birth–2 years	Infants "think" by acting on the world with their eyes, ears, hands, and mouth. As a result, they invent ways of solving sensorimotor problems, such as pulling a lever to hear the sound of a music box, finding hidden toys, and putting objects into and taking them out of containers.
Preoperational	2–7 years	Preschool children use symbols to represent their earlier sensori-motor discoveries. Development of language and make-believe play takes place. However, thinking lacks the logic of the two remaining stages.
Concrete operational	7–11 years	Children's reasoning becomes logical. School-age children understand that a certain amount of lemonade or play dough remains the same even after its appearance changes. They also organize objects into hierarchies of classes and subclasses. However, children think in a logical, organized fashion only when dealing with concrete information they can perceive directly.
Formal operational	11 years on	The capacity for abstract, systematic thinking enables adolescents, when faced with a problem, to start with a hypothesis, deduce testable inferences, and isolate and combine variables to see which inferences are confirmed. Adolescents can also evaluate the logic of verbal statements without referring to real-world circumstances.

© BETTMANN/CORBIS

Jean Piaget

ing cognition, is unique among theorists whose work grew out of the behaviorist tradition in granting children and adults an active role in their own learning.

Piaget's Cognitive-Developmental Theory

If one individual has influenced research on child development more than any other, it is Swiss cognitive theorist Jean Piaget (1896–1980). North American investigators did not grant Piaget's work much attention until the 1960s, mainly because Piaget's ideas were at odds with behaviorism, which dominated North American psychology in the mid-twentieth century (Cairns & Cairns, 2006). Piaget did not believe that children's learning depends on reinforcers, such as rewards from adults. According to his **cognitive-developmental theory,** children actively construct knowledge as they manipulate and explore their world.

Piaget's Stages. Piaget's view of development was greatly influenced by his early training in biology. Central to his theory is the biological concept of *adaptation* (Piaget, 1971). Just as structures of the body are adapted to fit with the environment, so structures of the mind develop to better fit with, or represent, the external world. In infancy and early childhood, Piaget claimed, children's understanding is different from adults'. For example, he believed that young babies do not realize that an object hidden from view continues to exist. He also concluded that preschoolers' thinking is full of faulty logic. For example,

children younger than age 7 commonly say that the amount of a liquid changes when it is poured into a different-shaped container. According to Piaget, children eventually revise these incorrect ideas in their ongoing efforts to achieve an *equilibrium,* or balance, between internal structures and information they encounter in their everyday worlds.

In Piaget's theory, as the brain develops and children's experiences expand, they move through four broad stages, each characterized by qualitatively distinct ways of thinking. Table 1.3 provides a brief description of Piaget's stages.

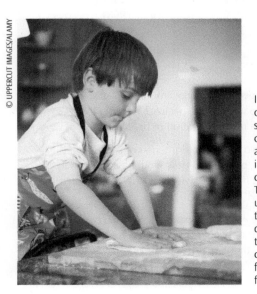
© UPPERCUT IMAGES/ALAMY

In Piaget's concrete operational stage, school-age children think in an organized, logical fashion about concrete objects. This 7-year-old understands that the quantity of pie dough remains the same after he changes its shape from a ball to a flattened circle.

Piaget devised special methods for investigating how children think. Early in his career, he carefully observed his three infant children and presented them with everyday problems, such as an attractive object that could be grasped, mouthed, kicked, or searched for. From their responses, Piaget derived his ideas about cognitive changes during the first two years. To study childhood and adolescent thought, Piaget adapted the clinical method of psychoanalysis, conducting open-ended *clinical interviews* in which a child's initial response to a task served as the basis for Piaget's next question.

Contributions and Limitations of Piaget's Theory. Piaget convinced the field that children are active learners whose minds consist of rich structures of knowledge. Besides investigating children's understanding of the physical world, Piaget explored their reasoning about the social world. His stages have sparked a wealth of research on children's conceptions of themselves, other people, and human relationships. In practical terms, Piaget's theory encouraged the development of educational philosophies and programs that emphasize discovery learning and direct contact with the environment.

Despite Piaget's overwhelming contributions, his theory has been challenged. Research indicates that Piaget underestimated the competencies of infants and preschoolers. When young children are given tasks scaled down in difficulty and relevant to their everyday experiences, their understanding appears closer to that of the older child and adult than Piaget assumed. Furthermore, many studies show that children's performance on Piagetian problems can be improved with training—findings that call into question Piaget's assumption that discovery learning rather than adult teaching is the best way to foster development (Siegler & Svetina, 2006). Critics also point out that Piaget's stagewise account pays insufficient attention to social and cultural influences on development. Finally, some lifespan theorists disagree with Piaget's conclusion that no major cognitive changes occur after adolescence. Several have proposed important transformations in adulthood (Labouvie-Vief, 2006; Moshman, 2011; Perry, 1970/1998).

ASK YOURSELF

REVIEW What aspect of behaviorism made it attractive to critics of the psychoanalytic perspective? How did Piaget's theory respond to a major limitation of behaviorism?

APPLY A 4-year-old becomes frightened of the dark and refuses to go to sleep at night. How would a psychoanalyst and a behaviorist differ in their views of how this problem developed?

REFLECT Describe a personal experience in which you received feedback from another person that strengthened your sense of self-efficacy—belief that your abilities and characteristics will help you succeed.

 # Recent Theoretical Perspectives

New ways of understanding development are constantly emerging—questioning, building on, and enhancing of earlier theories. Today, a burst of fresh approaches is broadening our insights into lifespan development.

Information Processing

In the 1970s and 1980s, researchers turned to the field of cognitive psychology for ways to understand the development of thinking. The design of digital computers that use mathematically specified steps to solve problems suggested to psychologists that the human mind might also be viewed as a symbol-manipulating system through which information flows—a perspective called **information processing** (Munakata, 2006). From the time information is presented to the senses at *input* until it emerges as a behavioral response at *output,* information is actively coded, transformed, and organized.

Information-processing researchers often design flowcharts to map the precise steps individuals use to solve problems and complete tasks. They seek to clarify how both task characteristics and cognitive limitations—for example, memory capacity or available knowledge—influence performance (Birney & Sternberg, 2011). To see the usefulness of this approach, let's look at an example.

In a study of problem solving, a researcher asked school-age children to build a bridge across a "river" too wide for any single block to span (Thornton, 1999). Whereas older children easily built successful bridges, only one 5-year-old did. Careful tracking of her efforts revealed that she repeatedly tried unsuccessful strategies, such as pushing two planks together and pressing down on their ends to hold them in place. But eventually, her experimentation triggered the idea of using the blocks as counterweights, as shown in Figure 1.4. Her mistaken procedures helped her understand why the counterweight approach worked.

Some information-processing models, like the one just considered, track children's mastery of one or a few tasks. Others describe the human cognitive system as a whole (Gopnik & Tenenbaum, 2007; Johnson & Mareschal, 2001; Westermann et al., 2006). These general models are used as guides for asking questions about broad changes in thinking: Does a child's ability to solve problems become more organized and "planful" with age? Are declines in memory during old age evident on all types of tasks or only some?

Like Piaget's theory, the information-processing approach regards people as active, sense-making beings (Munakata, 2006). But unlike Piaget's theory, it does not divide development into stages. Rather, most information-processing researchers regard the thought processes studied—perception, attention, memory, planning, categorization of information, and comprehension of written and spoken prose—as similar at all ages but

FIGURE 1.4 **Information-processing flowchart showing the steps that a 5-year-old used to solve a bridge-building problem.** Her task was to use blocks varying in size, shape, and weight, some of which were planklike, to construct a bridge across a "river" (painted on a floor mat) too wide for any single block to span. The child discovered how to counterweight and balance the bridge. The arrows reveal that, even after building a successful counterweight, she returned to earlier, unsuccessful strategies, which seemed to help her understand why the counterweight approach worked. (Adapted from Thornton, 1999.)

present to a lesser or greater extent. Their view of development is one of continuous change.

A great strength of the information-processing approach is its commitment to rigorous research methods. Because it has provided precise accounts of how children and adults tackle many cognitive tasks, its findings have important implications for education (Blumenfeld, Marx, & Harris, 2006; Siegler, 2009). But information processing has been better at analyzing thinking into its components than at putting them back together into a comprehensive theory. And it has little to say about aspects of cognition that are not linear and logical, such as imagination and creativity.

Developmental Cognitive Neuroscience

Over the past three decades, as information-processing research has expanded, a new area of investigation arose, called **developmental cognitive neuroscience.** It brings together researchers from psychology, biology, neuroscience, and medicine to study the relationship between changes in the brain and the developing person's cognitive processing and behavior patterns.

Improved methods for analyzing brain activity while children and adults perform various tasks have greatly enhanced knowledge of relationships between brain functioning, cognitive capacities, and behavior (Pennington, Snyder, & Roberts, 2007; Westermann et al., 2007). Armed with these brain-imaging techniques (which we will consider in Chapter 4), neuroscientists are tackling questions like these: How does genetic makeup combine with specific experiences to influence the growth and organization of the child's brain? What neurological changes are related to declines in various aspects of cognitive processing in old age?

During the first five years, the brain is highly plastic—especially open to growth as a result of experience. But it retains

considerable plasticity throughout life. Neuroscientists are identifying the types of experiences that support or undermine brain development at various ages. They are also clarifying the brain bases of many learning and behavior disorders and contributing to the design of effective interventions (Durston & Conrad, 2007; Luciana, 2007; Schlaggar & McCandliss, 2007).

An advantage of having many theories is that they encourage researchers to attend to previously neglected dimensions of people's lives. The final three perspectives we will discuss focus on *contexts* for development. The first of these views emphasizes that the development of many capacities is influenced by our long evolutionary history.

Ethology and Evolutionary Developmental Psychology

Ethology is concerned with the adaptive, or survival, value of behavior and its evolutionary history. Its roots can be traced to the work of Darwin. Two European zoologists, Konrad Lorenz and Niko Tinbergen, laid its modern foundations. Watching diverse animal species in their natural habitats, Lorenz and Tinbergen observed behavior patterns that promote survival. The best known of these is *imprinting,* the early following behavior of certain baby birds, such as geese, that ensures that the young will stay close to the mother and be fed and protected from danger. Imprinting takes place during an early, restricted period of development (Lorenz, 1952). If the mother goose is absent during this time but an object resembling her in important features is present, young goslings may imprint on it instead.

Observations of imprinting led to a major concept in human development: the *critical period.* It refers to a limited time span during which the individual is biologically prepared to acquire certain adaptive behaviors but needs the support of a stimulating environment. Many researchers have investigated whether

Ethology focuses on the adaptive, or survival, value of behavior and on similarities between human behavior and that of other species, especially our primate relatives. Observing this chimpanzee mother cuddling her infant helps us understand the human caregiver–infant relationship.

complex cognitive and social behaviors must be learned during certain time periods. For example, if children are deprived of adequate physical and social stimulation during their early years, will their intelligence be impaired? If language learning is impeded in childhood due to limited parent–child communication, is the capacity to acquire language later reduced?

In later chapters, we will see that the term *sensitive period* applies better to human development than the strict notion of a critical period (Bornstein, 1989). A **sensitive period** is a time that is optimal for certain capacities to emerge and in which the individual is especially responsive to environmental influences. However, its boundaries are less well-defined than those of a critical period. Development can occur later, but it is harder to induce.

Inspired by observations of imprinting, British psychoanalyst John Bowlby (1969) applied ethological theory to the understanding of the human infant–caregiver relationship. He argued that infant smiling, babbling, grasping, and crying are built-in social signals that encourage the caregiver to approach, care for, and interact with the baby. By keeping the parent near, these behaviors help ensure that the infant will be fed, protected from danger, and provided with stimulation and affection necessary for healthy growth. The development of attachment in humans is a lengthy process that leads the baby to form a deep affectionate tie with the caregiver (Thompson, 2006). Bowlby believed that this bond has lifelong consequences for human relationships. In later chapters, we will consider research that evaluates this assumption.

Recently, researchers have extended this effort in a new area of research called **evolutionary developmental psychology.** It seeks to understand the adaptive value of specieswide cognitive, emotional, and social competencies as those competencies change with age (Geary, 2006b; King & Bjorklund, 2010).

Evolutionary developmental psychologists ask questions like these: What role does the newborn's visual preference for facelike stimuli play in survival? Does it support older infants' capacity to distinguish familiar caregivers from unfamiliar people? Why do children play in gender-segregated groups? What do they learn from such play that might lead to adult gender-typed behaviors, such as male dominance and female investment in caregiving?

As these examples suggest, evolutionary psychologists are not just concerned with the genetic and biological roots of development. They recognize that humans' large brain and extended childhood resulted from the need to master an increasingly complex environment, so they are also interested in learning (Bjorklund, Causey, & Periss, 2009).

Recently, evolutionary psychologists have addressed the adaptiveness of human longevity—why adults live as much as one-fourth to one-third of their years after their children are grown (Greve & Bjorklund, 2009). The most common explanation involves the support that grandparents (especially grandmothers) offer in rearing young grandchildren. Another view emphasizes the adaptive value of aging adults' vast knowledge, experience, and sage advice—a rich resource for younger people as they tackle life's many challenges.

Vygotsky's Sociocultural Theory

The field of human development has recently seen a dramatic increase in studies addressing the cultural context of people's lives. Investigations that make comparisons across cultures, and between ethnic groups within cultures, provide insight into whether developmental pathways apply to all people or are limited to particular environmental conditions (Goodnow, 2010).

Today, much research is examining the relationship of *culturally specific beliefs and practices* to development. The contributions of Russian psychologist Lev Vygotsky (1896–1934) have played a major role in this trend. Vygotsky's (1934/1987) perspective, called **sociocultural theory**, focuses on how *culture*—the values, beliefs, customs, and skills of a social group—is transmitted to the next generation. According to Vygotsky, *social interaction*—in particular, cooperative dialogues with more knowledgeable members of society—is necessary for children to acquire the ways of thinking and behaving that make up a community's culture. Vygotsky believed that as adults and more expert peers help children master culturally meaningful activities, the communication between them becomes part of children's thinking. As children internalize the features of these dialogues, they can use the language within them to guide their own thought and actions and to acquire new skills (Winsler, Fernyhough, & Montero, 2009).

In Vygotsky's theory, children undergo certain stagewise changes. For example, when they acquire language, they gain

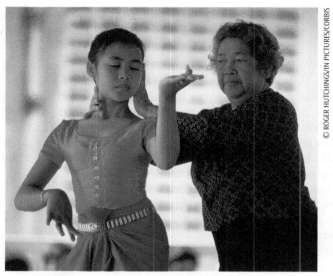

A Cambodian girl learns traditional dance forms from her grandmother. She acquires a culturally valued skill by interacting with an older, more experienced member of her culture.

in ability to participate in dialogues with others, and mastery of culturally valued competencies surges forward. When children enter school, they spend much time discussing language, literacy, and other academic concepts—experiences that encourage them to reflect on their own thinking (Bodrova & Leong, 2007). As a result, they advance dramatically in reasoning and problem solving.

At the same time, Vygotsky stressed that dialogues with experts lead to continuous changes in cognition that vary greatly from culture to culture. Consistent with this view, a major finding of cross-cultural research is that cultures select tasks for their members, and social interaction surrounding those tasks leads to competencies essential for success in a particular culture. For example, in industrialized nations, teachers help people learn to read, drive a car, or

use a computer. Among the Zinacanteco Indians of southern Mexico, adult experts guide young girls as they master complicated weaving techniques (Greenfield, 2004).

Research stimulated by Vygotsky's theory reveals that people in every culture develop unique strengths. But Vygotsky's emphasis on social experiences led him to neglect the biological side of development. Although he recognized the importance of heredity and brain growth, he said little about their role in cognitive change.

Ecological Systems Theory

Urie Bronfenbrenner (1917–2005) is responsible for an approach that has moved to the forefront of the field because it offers the most differentiated and complete account of contextual influences on development. **Ecological systems theory** views the person as developing within a complex *system* of relationships affected by multiple levels of the surrounding environment. Because the child's biologically influenced dispositions join with environmental forces to mold development, Bronfenbrenner characterized his perspective as a *bioecological model* (Bronfenbrenner & Morris, 2006).

Bronfenbrenner envisioned the environment as a series of nested structures, including but also extending beyond the home, school, neighborhood, and workplace settings in which people spend their everyday lives (see Figure 1.5). Each layer of the environment joins with the others to powerfully affect development.

FIGURE 1.5 Structure of the environment in ecological systems theory. The *microsystem* concerns relations between the developing person and the immediate environment; the *mesosystem,* connections among immediate settings; the *exosystem,* social settings that affect but do not contain the developing person; and the *macrosystem,* the values, laws, customs, and resources of the culture that affect activities and interactions at all inner layers. The *chronosystem* (not pictured) is not a specific context. Instead, it refers to the dynamic, ever-changing nature of the person's environment.

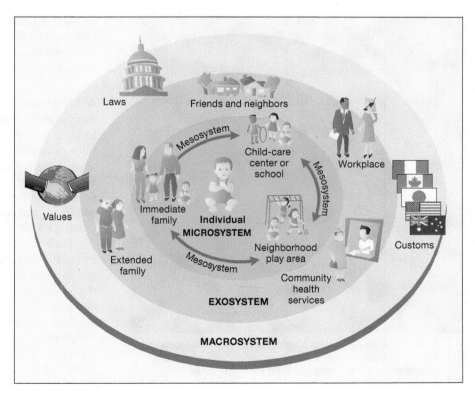

The Microsystem. The innermost level of the environment, the **microsystem,** consists of activities and interaction patterns in the person's immediate surroundings. Bronfenbrenner emphasized that to understand development at this level, we must keep in mind that all relationships are *bidirectional.* For example, adults affect children's behavior, but children's biologically and socially influenced characteristics—their physical attributes, personalities, and capacities—also affect adults' behavior. A friendly, attentive child is likely to evoke positive, patient reactions from parents, whereas an irritable or distractible child is more likely to receive impatience, restriction, and punishment (Crockenberg & Leerkes, 2003).

Third parties—other individuals in the microsystem—also affect the quality of any two-person relationship. If they are supportive, interaction is enhanced. For example, when parents encourage each other in their child-rearing roles, each engages in more effective parenting. In contrast, marital conflict is associated with inconsistent discipline and hostile reactions toward children, who often react with fear and anxiety or with anger and aggression (Caldera & Lindsey, 2006; Low & Stocker, 2012).

The Mesosystem. The second level of Bronfenbrenner's model, the **mesosystem,** encompasses connections between microsystems. For example, a child's academic progress depends not just on activities that take place in classrooms but also on parent involvement in school life and on the extent to which academic learning is carried over into the home (Jeynes, 2012). Among adults, how well a person functions as spouse and parent at home is affected by relationships in the workplace, and vice versa (Gottfried, Gottfried, & Bathurst, 2002).

The Exosystem. The **exosystem** consists of social settings that do not contain the developing person but nevertheless affect experiences in immediate settings. These can be formal organizations, such as the board of directors in the individual's workplace, religious institution, or community health and welfare services. Flexible work schedules, paid maternity and paternity leave, and sick leave for parents whose children are ill are examples of ways that work settings can help parents rear children and, indirectly, enhance the development of both adult and child. Exosystem supports can also be informal. Children are affected by their parents' social networks—friends and extended-family members who provide advice, companionship, and even financial assistance.

LOOK AND LISTEN

Ask a parent to explain his or her most worrisome child-rearing challenge. Cite one source of support at each level of Bronfenbrenner's model that could ease parental stress and promote child development. ●

The Macrosystem. The outermost level of Bronfenbrenner's model, the **macrosystem,** consists of cultural values, laws, customs, and resources. The priority that the macrosystem gives to the needs of children and adults affects the support they receive at inner levels of the environment. For example, in countries that set high standards for the quality of child care and workplace benefits for employed parents, children are more likely to have favorable experiences in their immediate settings. And governments that provide a generous pension plan for retirees support the well-being of older people.

A Dynamic, Ever-Changing System. The environment is not a static force that affects people in a uniform way. Instead, it is ever-changing. Whenever individuals alter the roles or settings in their lives, the breadth of their microsystems changes. These shifts in contexts—or *ecological transitions,* as Bronfenbrenner called them—are often important turning points in development. Starting school, entering the workforce, marrying, becoming a parent, getting divorced, moving, and retiring are examples.

Bronfenbrenner called the temporal dimension of his model the **chronosystem** (the prefix *chrono* means "time"). Life changes can be imposed externally or can arise from within the person, since individuals shape many of their own settings and experiences. How they do so depends on their age; their physical, intellectual, and personality characteristics; and their environmental opportunities. Therefore, in ecological systems theory, people are both products and producers of their environments: The person and the environment form a network of interdependent effects.

© ELLEN B. SENISI PHOTOGRAPHY

A father says good-bye to his daughter at the start of the school day. The child's experiences at school (microsystem) and the father's experiences at work (exosystem) affect the father–daughter relationship.

ASK YOURSELF

REVIEW Explain how each recent theoretical perspective regards children and adults as active contributors to their own development.

APPLY Mario wants to find out precisely how children of different ages recall stories. Anna is interested in how adult–child communication in different cultures influences children's storytelling. Which theoretical perspective has Mario probably chosen? How about Anna? Explain.

REFLECT To illustrate the chronosystem in ecological systems theory, select an important event from your childhood, such as a class with an inspiring teacher, or parental divorce. How did the event affect you? How might its impact have differed had you been five years younger? How about five years older?

Comparing Theories

In the preceding sections, we reviewed major theoretical perspectives in human development research. They differ in many respects. First, they focus on different domains of development. Some, such as the psychoanalytic perspective and ethology, emphasize emotional and social development. Others, such as Piaget's cognitive-developmental theory, information processing, and Vygotsky's sociocultural theory, stress changes in thinking. The remaining approaches—behaviorism, social learning theory, evolutionary developmental psychology, ecological systems theory, and the lifespan perspective—discuss many aspects of human functioning. Second, every theory contains a point of view about development. *TAKE A MOMENT...* As we conclude our review of theoretical perspectives, identify the stand each theory takes on the controversial issues presented at the beginning of this chapter. Then check your analysis against Table 1.4 on page 22.

Studying Development

In every science, research is usually based on a *hypothesis*—a prediction about behavior drawn from a theory. Theories and hypotheses, however, merely initiate the many activities that result in sound evidence on human development. Conducting research according to scientifically accepted procedures involves many steps and choices. Investigators must decide which participants, and how many, to include. Then they must figure out what the participants will be asked to do and when, where, and how many times each will be seen. Finally, they must examine and draw conclusions from their data.

In the following sections, we look at research strategies commonly used to study human development. We begin with common *research methods*—the specific activities of participants, such as taking tests, answering questionnaires, responding to interviews, or being observed. Then we turn to *research designs*—overall plans for research studies that permit the best possible test of the investigator's hypothesis. Finally, we discuss ethical issues involved in doing research with human participants.

Why learn about research strategies? Why not leave these matters to research specialists and concentrate, instead, on what is known about the developing person and how this knowledge can be applied? There are two reasons. First, each of us must be a wise and critical consumer of knowledge. Knowing the strengths and limitations of various research strategies is important in separating dependable information from misleading results. Second, individuals who work directly with children or adults may be in a unique position to build bridges between research and practice by conducting studies, either on their own or in partnership with experienced investigators. Community agencies such as schools, mental health facilities, and parks and recreation programs are increasingly collaborating with researchers in designing, implementing, and evaluating interventions aimed at enhancing development (Guerra, Graham, & Tolan, 2011). To broaden these efforts, a basic understanding of the research process is essential.

LOOK AND LISTEN

Ask a teacher, counselor, social worker, or nurse to describe a question about development he or she would like researchers to address. After reading the rest of this chapter, recommend research strategies best suited to answering that question, citing their strengths and limitations. ●

This preschool teacher is in a unique position to conduct research with important practical implications for young children's learning. To do so, she must be well versed in basic research strategies.

TABLE 1.4

Stances of Major Theories on Basic Issues in Human Development

THEORY	CONTINUOUS OR DISCONTINUOUS DEVELOPMENT?	ONE COURSE OF DEVELOPMENT OR MANY?	RELATIVE INFLUENCE OF NATURE AND NURTURE?
Psychoanalytic perspective	*Discontinuous:* Psychosexual and psychosocial development takes place in stages.	*One course:* Stages are assumed to be universal.	*Both nature and nurture:* Innate impulses are channeled and controlled through child-rearing experiences. *Early experiences* set the course of later development.
Behaviorism and social learning theory	*Continuous:* Development involves an increase in learned behaviors.	*Many possible courses:* Behaviors reinforced and modeled may vary from person to person.	*Emphasis on nurture:* Development is the result of conditioning and modeling. *Both early and later experiences* are important.
Piaget's cognitive-developmental theory	*Discontinuous:* Cognitive development takes place in stages.	*One course:* Stages are assumed to be universal.	*Both nature and nurture:* Development occurs as the brain grows and children exercise their innate drive to discover reality in a generally stimulating environment. *Both early and later experiences* are important.
Information processing	*Continuous:* Children and adults change gradually in perception, attention, memory, and problem-solving skills.	*One course:* Changes studied characterize most or all children and adults.	*Both nature and nurture:* Children and adults are active, sense-making beings who modify their thinking as the brain grows and they confront new environmental demands. *Both early and later experiences* are important.
Ethology and evolutionary developmental psychology	*Both continuous and discontinuous:* Children and adults gradually develop a wider range of adaptive behaviors. Sensitive periods occur in which qualitatively distinct capacities emerge fairly suddenly.	*One course:* Adaptive behaviors and sensitive periods apply to all members of a species.	*Both nature and nurture:* Evolution and heredity influence behavior, and learning lends greater flexibility and adaptiveness to it. In sensitive periods, *early experiences* set the course of later development.
Vygotsky's sociocultural theory	*Both continuous and discontinuous:* Language development and schooling lead to stagewise changes. Dialogues with more expert members of society also lead to continuous changes that vary from culture to culture.	*Many possible courses:* Socially mediated changes in thought and behavior vary from culture to culture.	*Both nature and nurture:* Heredity, brain growth, and dialogues with more expert members of society jointly contribute to development. *Both early and later experiences* are important.
Ecological systems theory	*Not specified.*	*Many possible courses:* Biologically influenced dispositions join with environmental forces at multiple levels to mold development in unique ways.	*Both nature and nurture:* The individual's characteristics and the reactions of others affect each other in a bidirectional fashion. *Both early and later experiences* are important.
Lifespan perspective	**Both continuous and discontinuous: Continuous gains and declines and discontinuous, stagewise emergence of new skills occur.**	**Many possible courses: Development is influenced by multiple, interacting biological, psychological, and social forces, many of which vary from person to person, leading to diverse pathways of change.**	**Both nature and nurture: Development is multidimensional, affected by an intricate blend of hereditary and environmental factors. Emphasizes plasticity at all ages. Both early and later experiences are important.**

Common Research Methods

How does a researcher choose a basic approach to gathering information? Common methods include systematic observation, self-reports (such as questionnaires and interviews), clinical or case studies of a single individual, and ethnographies of the life circumstances of a specific group of people. Table 1.5 summarizes the strengths and limitations of each of these methods.

Systematic Observation. Observations of behavior can be made in different ways. One approach is to go into the field, or natural environment, and record the behavior of interest—a method called **naturalistic observation.**

A study of preschoolers' responses to their peers' distress provides a good example (Farver & Branstetter, 1994). Observing 3- and 4-year-olds in child-care centers, the researchers recorded each instance of crying and the reactions of nearby

TABLE 1.5

Strengths and Limitations of Common Research Methods

METHOD	DESCRIPTION	STRENGTHS	LIMITATIONS
SYSTEMATIC OBSERVATION			
Naturalistic observation	Observation of behavior in natural contexts	Reflects participants' everyday lives.	Cannot control conditions under which participants are observed.
Structured observation	Observation of behavior in a laboratory, where conditions are the same for all participants	Grants each participant an equal opportunity to display the behavior of interest.	May not yield observations typical of participants' behavior in everyday life.
SELF-REPORTS			
Clinical interview	Flexible interviewing procedure in which the investigator obtains a complete account of the participant's thoughts	Comes as close as possible to the way participants think in everyday life. Great breadth and depth of information can be obtained in a short time.	May not result in accurate reporting of information. Flexible procedure makes comparing individuals' responses difficult.
Structured interview, questionnaires, and tests	Self-report instruments in which each participant is asked the same questions in the same way	Permits comparisons of participants' responses and efficient data collection. Researchers can specify answer alternatives that participants might not think of in an open-ended interview.	Does not yield the same depth of information as a clinical interview. Responses are still subject to inaccurate reporting.
CLINICAL, OR CASE STUDY, METHOD			
	A full picture of one individual's psychological functioning, obtained by combining interviews, observations, and test scores	Provides rich, descriptive insights into factors that affect development.	May be biased by researchers' theoretical preferences. Findings cannot be applied to individuals other than the participant.
ETHNOGRAPHY			
	Participant observation of a culture or distinct social group. By making extensive field notes, the researcher tries to capture the culture's unique values and social processes	Provides a more complete description than can be derived from a single observational visit, interview, or questionnaire.	May be biased by researchers' values and theoretical preferences. Findings cannot be applied to individuals and settings other than the ones studied.

children—whether they ignored, watched, commented on the child's unhappiness, scolded or teased, or shared, helped, or expressed sympathy. Caregiver behaviors—explaining why a child was crying, mediating conflict, or offering comfort—were noted to see if adult sensitivity was related to children's caring responses. A strong relationship emerged. The great strength of naturalistic observation is that investigators can see directly the everyday behaviors they hope to explain.

Naturalistic observation also has a major limitation: Not all individuals have the same opportunity to display a particular behavior in everyday life. In the study just described, some children might have witnessed a child crying more often than others or been exposed to more cues for positive social responses from caregivers. For these reasons, they might have displayed more compassion.

Researchers commonly deal with this difficulty by making **structured observations,** in which the investigator sets up a laboratory situation that evokes the behavior of interest so that every participant has equal opportunity to display the response. In one such study, 2-year-olds' emotional reactions to harm that

they thought they had caused were observed by asking each of them to take care of a rag doll that had been modified so its leg would fall off when the child picked it up. Researchers recorded children's facial expressions of sadness, efforts to help the doll, and body tension—responses indicating worry, remorse, and a desire to make amends for the mishap. In addition, mothers were asked to engage in brief conversations about emotions with their children (Garner, 2003). Toddlers whose mothers more often explained the causes and consequences of emotion were more likely to express concern for the injured doll.

Systematic observation provides invaluable information on how children and adults actually behave, but it tells us little about the reasoning behind their responses. For that information, researchers must turn to self-report techniques.

Self-Reports. Self-reports ask research participants to provide information on their perceptions, thoughts, abilities, feelings, attitudes, beliefs, and past experiences. They range from relatively unstructured interviews to highly structured interviews, questionnaires, and tests.

In a **clinical interview**, researchers use a flexible, conversational style to probe for the participant's point of view. In the following example, Piaget questioned a 5-year-old child about his understanding of dreams:

> *Where does the dream come from?*—I think you sleep so well that you dream.—*Does it come from us or from outside?*—From outside.—*When you are in bed and you dream, where is the dream?*—In my bed, under the blanket. I don't really know. If it was in my stomach, the bones would be in the way and I shouldn't see it.—*Is the dream there when you sleep?*—Yes, it is in the bed beside me. (Piaget, 1926/1930, pp. 97–98)

Although a researcher conducting clinical interviews with more than one participant would typically ask the same first question to establish a common task, individualized prompts are used to provide a fuller picture of each person's reasoning.

The clinical interview has two major strengths. First, it permits people to display their thoughts in terms that are as close as possible to the way they think in everyday life. Second, the clinical interview can provide a large amount of information in a fairly brief period. For example, in an hour-long session, we can obtain a wide range of information on child rearing from a parent or on life circumstances from an older adult—much more than we could capture by observing for the same amount of time.

A major limitation of the clinical interview has to do with accuracy. Some participants, wishing to please the interviewer, may make up answers that do not represent their actual thinking. When asked about past events, some may have trouble recalling exactly what happened. And because the clinical interview depends on verbal ability and expressiveness, it may underestimate the capacities of individuals who have difficulty putting their thoughts into words.

The clinical interview has also been criticized because of its flexibility. When questions are phrased differently for each participant, responses may reflect the manner of interviewing rather than real differences in the way people think about a topic. **Structured interviews** (including tests and questionnaires), in which each participant is asked the same set of questions in the same way, eliminate this problem. But structured interviews do not yield the same depth of information as clinical interviews. And they can still be affected by the problem of inaccurate reporting. Currently, more researchers are combining the two approaches to see if they yield consistent findings (Yoshikawa et al., 2008). And blending the two methods is likely to offer a clearer picture than either method can alone.

The Clinical, or Case Study, Method. An outgrowth of psychoanalytic theory, the **clinical, or case study, method** brings together a wide range of information on one person, including interviews, observations, and test scores. The aim is to obtain as complete a picture as possible of that individual's psychological functioning and the experiences that led up to it.

The clinical method is well-suited to studying the development of certain types of individuals who are few in number but

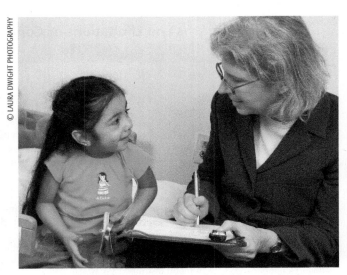

Using the clinical, or case study, method, this researcher interacts with a 3-year-old during a home visit. Interviews and observations will contribute to an in-depth picture of this child's psychological functioning.

vary widely in characteristics. For example, the method has been used to find out what contributes to the accomplishments of *prodigies*—extremely gifted children who attain adult competence in a field before age 10. Consider Adam, a boy who read, wrote, and composed musical pieces before he was out of diapers. Clinical research indicates that such children rarely realize their extraordinary potential without nurturing, committed parents, and exceptional teachers who guide and encourage the child's special gift (Goldsmith, 2000; Moran & Gardner, 2006).

The clinical method yields richly detailed case narratives that offer valuable insights into the many factors influencing development. Nevertheless, because information often is collected unsystematically and subjectively, researchers' theoretical preferences may bias their observations and interpretations. In addition, investigators cannot assume that their conclusions apply, or generalize, to anyone other than the person studied (Stanovich, 2013). Even when patterns emerge across several cases, it is wise to confirm these with other research strategies.

Methods for Studying Culture. To study the impact of culture, researchers adjust the methods just considered or tap procedures specially devised for cross-cultural and multicultural research (Triandis, 2007). Which approach investigators choose depends on their research goals.

Sometimes researchers are interested in characteristics that are believed to be universal but that vary in degree from one society to the next: Are parents warmer or more directive in some cultures than others? How strong are gender stereotypes in different nations? In each instance, several cultural groups will be compared, and all participants must be questioned or observed in the same way. Therefore, researchers draw on the observational and self-report procedures we have already considered, adapting them through translation so they can be understood in each cultural context. Still, investigators must be mindful of cultural differences in familiarity with being observed and responding to self-report instruments, which may bias their findings (Van de Vijver, Hofer, & Chasiotis, 2010).

At other times, researchers want to uncover the *cultural meanings* of children's and adults' behaviors by becoming as familiar as possible with their way of life. To achieve this goal, investigators rely on a method borrowed from the field of anthropology—**ethnography**. Like the clinical method, ethnographic research is a descriptive, qualitative technique. But instead of aiming to understand a single individual, it is directed toward understanding a culture or a distinct social group through *participant observation*. Typically, the researcher spends months, and sometimes years, in the cultural community, participating in its daily life. Extensive field notes are gathered, consisting of a mix of observations, self-reports from members of the culture, and careful interpretations by the investigator (Miller, Hengst, & Wang, 2003; Shweder et al., 2006). Later, these notes are put together into a description of the community that tries to capture its unique values and social processes.

In some ethnographies, investigators look at many aspects of experience, as one team of researchers did in describing what it is like to grow up in a small American town. Others focus on one or a few settings and issues—for example, barriers to effective parent–school communication in a Mexican-American community or African-Caribbean adults' reactions to a diagnosis of high blood pressure, signaling elevated risk for heart disease (Higginbottom, 2006; Peshkin, 1997; Valdés, 1998). Researchers may supplement traditional self-report and obser-

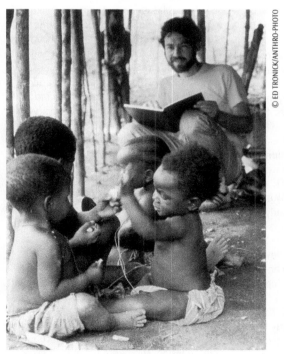

This Western researcher spent months living among the Efe people of the Republic of Congo in an effort to understand their way of life. Here he observes young children sharing food.

vational methods with ethnography if they suspect that unique meanings underlie cultural differences, as the Cultural Influences box on page 26 reveals.

Ethnographers strive to minimize their own influence on the culture they are studying by becoming part of it. Nevertheless, as with clinical studies, investigators' cultural values and theoretical commitments sometimes lead them to observe selectively or misinterpret what they see. In addition, the findings of ethnographic studies cannot be assumed to generalize beyond the people and settings in which the research was conducted.

ASK YOURSELF

REVIEW Why might a researcher choose structured observation over naturalistic observation? How about the reverse?

APPLY A researcher wants to study the thoughts and feelings of parents on active duty in the military and those of their school-age and adolescent children. Which method should she use? Why?

REFLECT Reread the description of nonnormative influences on page 9, and cite an example from your own life. Which method would be best-suited to studying the impact of such an event on development?

General Research Designs

In deciding on a research design, investigators choose a way of setting up a study that permits them to test their hypotheses with the greatest certainty possible. Two main types of designs are used in all research on human behavior: *correlational* and *experimental*.

Correlational Design. In a **correlational design**, researchers gather information on individuals, generally in natural life circumstances, without altering their experiences. Then they look at relationships between participants' characteristics and their behavior or development. Suppose we want to answer the following question: Do parents' styles of interacting with their children have any bearing on children's intelligence? In this and many other instances, the conditions of interest are difficult or impossible to arrange and control and must be studied as they currently exist.

Correlational studies have one major limitation: We cannot infer cause and effect. For example, if we were to find that parental interaction is related to children's intelligence, we would not know whether parents' behavior actually *causes* intellectual differences among children. In fact, the opposite is possible: The behaviors of highly intelligent children may be so attractive that they cause parents to interact more favorably. Or a third variable that we did not even consider, such as the amount of noise and distraction in the home, may cause changes in both parental interaction and children's intelligence.

Cultural Influences

Immigrant Youths: Adapting to a New Land

Over the past several decades, a rising tide of immigrants has come to North America, fleeing war and persecution in their homelands or seeking better life chances. Today, nearly one-fourth of U.S. children and adolescents have foreign-born parents, making them the fastest growing sector of the U.S. youth population. About 20 percent of these young people are foreign-born themselves, mostly from Latin America, the Caribbean, and Asia (Hernandez, Denton, & Macartney, 2008; Suárez-Orozco, Todorova, & Qin, 2006).

How well are immigrant youths adapting to their new country? To find out, researchers use multiple research methods—academic testing, questionnaires assessing psychological adjustment, and in-depth ethnographies.

Academic Achievement and Adjustment

Although educators and laypeople often assume that the transition to a new country has a negative impact on psychological well-being, evidence reveals that children of immigrant parents adapt well. Students who are first-generation (foreign-born) and second-generation (American-born, with immigrant parents) often achieve in school as well as or better than students of native-born parents (Fuligni, 2004; Hao & Woo, 2012; Hernandez, Denton, & Macartney, 2008). Findings on psychological adjustment are similar. Compared with their agemates, adolescents from immigrant families are less likely to commit delinquent and violent acts, to use drugs and alcohol, or to have early sex. They are also less likely to be obese or to have missed school because of illness. And they tend to report just as high, and at times higher, self-esteem as young people with native-born parents (Fuligni, 1998; Saucier et al., 2002; Supple & Small, 2006).

These outcomes are strongest for Chinese, Filipino, Japanese, Korean, and East Indian youths (Fuligni, 2004; Louie, 2001; Portes & Rumbaut, 2005). Variation in adjustment is greater among Mexican, Central American, and Southeast Asian (Hmong, Cambodian, Laotian, Thai, and Vietnamese) young people, who show elevated rates of school dropout, delinquency, teenage parenthood, and drug use. Disparities in parental economic resources, education, English-language proficiency, and support of children contribute to these trends (García Coll & Marks, 2009; Pong & Landale, 2012).

Still, even youths whose parents face considerable financial hardship and who speak little English are successful (Hao & Woo, 2012; Hernandez, Denton, & Macartney, 2008). Factors other than income are responsible.

Family and Community Influences

Ethnographies reveal that immigrant parents view education as the surest way to improve life chances (García Coll & Marks, 2009; Goldenberg et al., 2001). They remind their children that, because educational opportunities were not available in their native countries, they themselves are often limited to menial jobs. And while preserving their culture's values, these parents also make certain adaptations—for example, supporting education for daughters even though their culture of origin endorses it only for sons.

Adolescents from these families internalize their parents' valuing of education, endorsing it more strongly than agemates with native-born parents (Fuligni, 2004; Su & Costigan, 2008). Because minority ethnicities usually stress allegiance to family and community over individual goals, first- and second-generation young people feel a strong sense of obligation to their parents. They view school success as both their own and their parents' success and as a way of repaying their parents for the hardships they have endured (Bacallao & Smokowski, 2007; Fuligni, Yip, & Tseng, 2002). Both family relationships and school achievement protect these youths from delinquency, early pregnancy and drug use, and other risky behav-

These Hmong boys perform in an ethnic festival in St. Paul, Minnesota, where many Hmong immigrants have settled. Cultural values that foster allegiance to family and community promote high achievement and protect many immigrant youths from involvement in risky behaviors.

iors (see the Biology and Environment box on resilience on page 8).

Immigrant parents of successful youths typically develop close ties to an ethnic community, which exerts additional control through a high consensus on values and constant monitoring of young people's activities. As one 16-year-old straight-A student remarked, "My parents know pretty much all the kids in the neighborhood. . . . Everybody here knows everybody else. It's hard to get away with much" (Zhou & Bankston, 1998, pp. 93, 130).

The experiences of well-adjusted immigrant youths are not problem-free. Chinese adolescents who had arrived in the United States within the previous year described their adjustment as very difficult because they were not proficient in English and, as a result, found many everyday tasks challenging and felt socially isolated (Yeh et al., 2008). Young immigrants also encounter racial and ethnic prejudices and experience tensions between family values and the new culture—challenges we will take up in Chapter 12. In the long term, however, family and community cohesion, supervision, and high expectations promote favorable outcomes.

Will the death of her husband affect this elderly widow's physical health and psychological well-being? A correlational design can be used to answer this question, but it does not permit researchers to determine the precise cause of their findings.

In correlational studies and in other types of research designs, investigators often examine relationships by using a **correlation coefficient**—a number that describes how two measures, or variables, are associated with each other. We will encounter the correlation coefficient in discussing research findings throughout this book, so let's look at what it is and how it is interpreted. A correlation coefficient can range in value from +1.00 to −1.00. The *magnitude*, or *size, of the number* shows the *strength of the relationship*. A zero correlation indicates no relationship; the closer the value is to +1.00 or −1.00, the stronger the relationship. For instance, a correlation of −.78 is high, −.52 is moderate, and −.18 is low. Note, however, that correlations of +.52 and −.52 are equally strong. The *sign of the number* (+ or −) refers to the *direction of the relationship*. A positive sign (+) means that as one variable *increases,* the other also *increases.* A negative sign (−) indicates that as one variable *increases,* the other *decreases.*

Let's look at some examples of how a correlation coefficient works. One researcher reported a +.55 correlation between a measure of maternal language stimulation and the size of children's vocabularies at 2 years of age (Hoff, 2003). This is a moderate correlation, which indicates that mothers who spoke more to their toddlers had children who were more advanced in language development. In two other studies, maternal sensitivity was modestly associated with children's cooperativeness in consistent ways. First, maternal warmth during play correlated positively with 2-year-olds' willingness to comply with their mother's directive to clean up toys, at +.34 (Feldman & Klein, 2003). Second, the extent to which mothers spoke harshly, interrupted, and controlled their 4-year-olds' play correlated negatively with children's compliance, at −.31 for boys and −.42 for girls (Smith et al., 2004).

TAKE A MOMENT… Are you tempted to conclude from these correlations that the maternal behaviors influenced children's responses? Although the researchers suspected this was so, they could not be sure of cause and effect. Can you think of other possible explanations? Finding a relationship in a corre-

lational study does suggest that tracking down its cause—using a more powerful experimental strategy, if possible—would be worthwhile.

Experimental Design. An **experimental design** permits inferences about cause and effect because researchers use an evenhanded procedure to assign people to two or more treatment conditions. In an experiment, the events and behaviors of interest are divided into two types: independent and dependent variables. The **independent variable** is the one the investigator expects to cause changes in another variable. The **dependent variable** is the one the investigator expects to be influenced by the independent variable. Cause-and-effect relationships can be detected because the researcher directly *controls* or *manipulates* changes in the independent variable by exposing participants to the treatment conditions. Then the researcher compares their performance on measures of the dependent variable.

In one *laboratory experiment,* investigators explored the impact of adults' angry interactions on children's adjustment (El-Sheikh, Cummings, & Reiter, 1996). They hypothesized that the way angry encounters end (independent variable) affects children's emotional reactions (dependent variable). Four- and 5-year-olds were brought to a laboratory one at a time, accompanied by their mothers. One group was exposed to an *unresolved-anger treatment,* in which two adult actors entered the room and argued but did not work out their disagreements. The other group witnessed a *resolved-anger treatment,* in which the adults ended their disputes by apologizing and compromising. When witnessing a follow-up adult conflict, children in the resolved-anger treatment showed fewer behavioral signs of distress, such as anxious facial expressions. The experiment revealed that anger resolution can reduce the stressful impact of adult conflict on children.

In experimental studies, investigators must control for participants' characteristics that could reduce the accuracy of their findings. In the study just described, if a greater number of children from homes high in parental conflict ended up in the unresolved-anger treatment, we could not tell what produced the results—the independent variable or the children's backgrounds. To protect against this problem, researchers engage in **random assignment** of participants to treatment conditions. By using an unbiased procedure, such as drawing numbers out of a hat or flipping a coin, investigators increase the chances that participants' characteristics will be equally distributed across treatment groups.

Modified Experimental Designs: Field and Natural Experiments. Most experiments are conducted in laboratories, where researchers can achieve the maximum possible control over treatment conditions. But, as we have already indicated, findings obtained in laboratories may not always apply to everyday situations. In *field experiments,* investigators assign participants randomly to treatment conditions in natural settings. In the experiment just described, we can conclude that the emotional climate established by adults affects

TABLE 1.6 **Strengths and Limitations of Research Designs**

DESIGN	DESCRIPTION	STRENGTHS	LIMITATIONS
GENERAL			
Correlational	The investigator obtains information on participants without altering their experiences.	Permits study of relationships between variables.	Does not permit inferences about cause-and-effect relationships.
Experimental	Through random assignment of participants to treatment conditions, the investigator manipulates an independent variable and examines its effect on a dependent variable. Can be conducted in the laboratory or the natural environment.	Permits inferences about cause-and-effect relationships.	When conducted in the laboratory, findings may not generalize to the real world. In *field experiments,* control over the treatment is usually weaker than in the laboratory. In *natural,* or *quasi-, experiments,* lack of random assignment substantially reduces the precision of research.
DEVELOPMENTAL			
Longitudinal	The investigator studies the same group of participants repeatedly at different ages.	Permits study of common patterns and individual differences in development and relationships between early and later events and behaviors.	Age-related changes may be distorted because of participant dropout, practice effects, and cohort effects.
Cross-sectional	The investigator studies groups of participants differing in age at the same point in time.	More efficient than the longitudinal design. Not plagued by such problems as participant dropout and practice effects.	Does not permit study of individual developmental trends. Age differences may be distorted because of cohort effects.
Sequential	The investigator conducts several similar cross-sectional or longitudinal studies (called sequences). These might study participants over the same ages but in different years, or they might study participants over different ages but during the same years.	When the design includes longitudinal sequences, permits both longitudinal and cross-sectional comparisons. Also reveals cohort effects. Permits tracking of age-related changes more efficiently than the longitudinal design.	May have the same problems as longitudinal and cross-sectional strategies, but the design itself helps identify difficulties.

children's behavior in the laboratory. But does it also do so in daily life?

Another study helps answer this question. Ethnically diverse, poverty-stricken families with a 2-year-old child were randomly assigned to either a brief intervention condition, called the Family Check-Up, or a no-intervention control group. The intervention consisted of three home-based sessions in which a consultant gave parents feedback about their child-rearing practices and their child's adjustment, explored parents' willingness to improve, and identified community services appropriate to each family's needs (Dishion et al., 2008). Findings showed that families assigned to the Family Check-Up (but not controls) gained in positive parenting, which predicted a reduction in child problem behaviors—sometimes still evident a year later.

When researchers cannot randomly assign participants and manipulate conditions in the real world, they can sometimes compromise by conducting *natural, or quasi-, experiments,* comparing treatments that already exist, such as different family environments, schools, workplaces, or retirement villages. These studies differ from correlational research only in that groups of participants are carefully chosen to ensure that their

characteristics are as much alike as possible. In this way, investigators do their best to rule out alternative explanations for their treatment effects, though they cannot achieve the precision and rigor of true experimental research.

Table 1.6 summarizes the strengths and limitations of correlational and experimental designs. It also includes an overview of designs for studying development, to which we turn next.

Designs for Studying Development

Scientists interested in human development require information about the way research participants change over time. To answer questions about development, they must extend correlational and experimental approaches to include measurements at different ages using longitudinal and cross-sectional designs.

The Longitudinal Design. In a **longitudinal design,** participants are studied repeatedly, and changes are noted as they get older. The time spanned may be relatively short (a few months to several years) or very long (a decade or even a lifetime). The longitudinal approach has two major strengths. First, because it tracks the performance of each person over time, researchers can identify common patterns as well as individual differences in development. Second, longitudinal studies permit investigators to examine relationships between early and later events and behaviors. Let's illustrate these ideas.

A group of researchers wondered whether children who display extreme personality styles—either angry and explosive or shy and withdrawn—retain the same dispositions when they become adults and, if so, the consequences for long-term adjustment. To answer these questions, the researchers delved into the archives of the Guidance Study, a well-known longitudinal investigation initiated in 1928 at the University of California, Berkeley, and continued for several decades (Caspi, Elder, & Bem, 1987, 1988).

Results revealed that the two personality styles were moderately stable. Between ages 8 and 30, a good number of individuals remained the same, whereas others changed substantially. When stability did occur, it appeared to be due to a "snowballing effect," in which children evoked responses from adults and peers that acted to maintain their dispositions. Explosive youngsters were likely to be treated with anger, whereas shy children were apt to be ignored. As a result, explosive children came to view others as hostile, while shy children regarded them as unfriendly (Caspi & Roberts, 2001). Together, these factors led explosive children to sustain or increase their unruliness and shy children to continue to withdraw—patterns that tended to persist into adulthood and to negatively affect adjustment to marriage, parenting, and work life. Shy women, however, were an exception. Because a withdrawn, unassertive style was socially acceptable for females at that time, they showed no special adjustment problems.

Problems in Conducting Longitudinal Research.
Despite their strengths, longitudinal investigations pose a number of problems. For example, participants may move away or drop out of the research for other reasons. This biases the sample so that it no longer represents the population to whom researchers would like to generalize their findings. Also, from repeated study, people may become more aware of their own thoughts, feelings, and actions and revise them in ways that have little to do with age-related change. In addition, they may become "test-wise." Their performance may improve as a result of *practice effects*—better test-taking skills and increased familiarity with the test—not because of factors commonly associated with development.

The most widely discussed threat to longitudinal findings is **cohort effects** (see page 9): Individuals born in the same time period are influenced by a particular set of historical and cultural conditions. Results based on one cohort may not apply to people developing at other times. For example, unlike the findings on female shyness described in the preceding section, which were gathered in the 1950s, today's shy adolescent girls and young women tend to be poorly adjusted—a difference that may be due to changes in gender roles in Western societies. Shy young people, whether male or female, feel more anxious, depressed, and lonely and may do less well in educational and

Cohort effects are particular historical and cultural conditions that affect individuals born in the same time period. Young people who witnessed Barack Obama and his family celebrating his election victory in 2008 and again in 2012 came away with a new sense of what is possible for members of America's ethnic minorities.

career attainment than their agemates (Karevold et al., 2012; Mounts et al., 2006). Similarly, a longitudinal study of lifespan development would probably result in quite different findings if it were carried out around the time of World War II versus in the second decade of the twenty-first century.

Cohort effects don't just operate broadly on an entire generation. They also occur when specific experiences influence some groups of individuals but not others in the same generation—for example, some children and adults more profoundly affected than others by an economic recession, a natural disaster, or a terrorist attack.

The Cross-Sectional Design. The length of time it takes for many behaviors to change, even in limited longitudinal studies, has led researchers to turn toward a more efficient strategy for studying development. In the **cross-sectional design,** groups of people differing in age are studied at the same point in time. Because participants are measured only once, researchers need not be concerned about such difficulties as participant dropout or practice effects.

A study in which students in grades 3, 6, 9, and 12 filled out a questionnaire about their sibling relationships provides a good illustration (Buhrmester & Furman, 1990). Findings revealed that feelings of sibling companionship declined during adolescence. The researchers speculated that as adolescents move from psychological dependence on the family to greater involvement with peers, they may have less time and emotional need to invest in siblings. As we will see in Chapter 12, subsequent research has confirmed this age-related trend.

Problems in Conducting Cross-Sectional Research.
Despite its convenience, cross-sectional research does not provide evidence about development at the level at which it actually occurs: the individual. For example, in the cross-sectional study of sibling relationships just discussed, comparisons are limited to age-group averages. We cannot tell if important individual differences exist. Indeed, longitudinal findings reveal that adolescents vary considerably in the changing quality of their sibling relationships. Although many become more distant, others become more supportive and intimate, still others more rivalrous and antagonistic (Kim et al., 2006; Whiteman & Loken, 2006).

Cross-sectional studies—especially those that cover a wide age span—have another problem. Like longitudinal research, they can be threatened by cohort effects. For example, comparisons of 10-year-old cohorts, 20-year-old cohorts, and 30-year-old cohorts—groups born and reared in different years—may not really represent age-related changes. Instead, they may reflect unique experiences associated with the historical period in which the age groups were growing up.

Improving Developmental Designs. Researchers have devised ways of building on the strengths and minimizing the weaknesses of longitudinal and cross-sectional approaches. Several modified developmental designs have resulted.

Sequential Designs. To overcome some of the limitations of traditional developmental designs, investigators sometimes use **sequential designs,** in which they conduct several similar cross-sectional or longitudinal studies (called *sequences*). The sequences might study participants over the same ages but in different years, or they might study participants over different ages but during the same years. Figure 1.6 illustrates the first of these options. As it also reveals, some sequential designs combine longitudinal and cross-sectional strategies, an approach that has two advantages:

- We can find out whether cohort effects are operating by comparing participants of the same age who were born in different years. In the example in Figure 1.6, we can compare the three longitudinal samples at ages 20, 30, and 40. If they do not differ, we can rule out cohort effects.

- We can make longitudinal and cross-sectional comparisons. If outcomes are similar in both, then we can be especially confident about our findings.

In a study that used the design in Figure 1.6, researchers wanted to find out whether adult personality development progresses as Erikson's psychosocial theory predicts (Whitbourne et al., 1992). Questionnaires measuring Erikson's stages were given to three cohorts of 20-year-olds, each born a decade apart. The cohorts were reassessed at ten-year intervals. Consistent with Erikson's theory, longitudinal and cross-sectional gains in identity and intimacy occurred between ages 20 and 30—a trend unaffected by historical time period. But a powerful cohort effect emerged for the sense of industry: At age 20, Cohort 1 scored substantially below Cohorts 2 and 3. Notice that members of Cohort 1 reached age 20 in the mid-1960s. As college students, they were part of an era of political protest that reflected disenchantment with the work ethic. Once out of college, they caught up with the other cohorts in industry. Followed up in 2001 at age 54, Cohort 1 showed a decline in focus on identity issues and a gain in ego integrity—trends expected to continue through late adulthood (Sneed, Whitbourne, & Culang, 2006). Future tracking of Cohorts 2 and 3 will reveal whether they, too, follow this Erikson-predicted psychosocial path.

By uncovering cohort effects, sequential designs help explain diversity in development. Yet to date only a small number of sequential studies have been conducted.

Combining Experimental and Developmental Designs. Perhaps you noticed that all the examples of longitudinal and cross-sectional research we have considered permit only correlational, not causal, inferences. Sometimes researchers can explore the causal link between experiences and development by experimentally manipulating the experiences. If, as a result, development improves, then we have strong evidence for a

FIGURE 1.6 Example of a sequential design.
Three cohorts, born in 1945 (blue), 1955 (pink), and 1965 (green), are followed longitudinally from 20 to 40 years of age. The design permits the researcher to check for cohort effects by comparing people of the same age who were born in different years. In a study that used this design, the 20-year-olds in Cohort 1 differed substantially from the 20-year-olds in Cohorts 2 and 3, indicating powerful cohort effects. This design also permits longitudinal and cross-sectional comparisons. Similar findings lend additional confidence in the results.

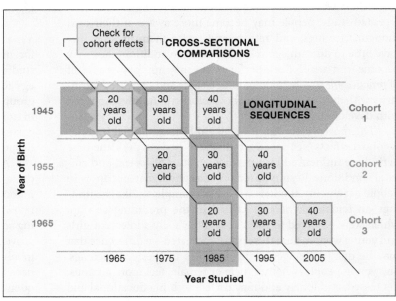

causal association. Today, research that combines an experimental strategy with either a longitudinal or a cross-sectional approach is becoming increasingly common.

ASK YOURSELF

REVIEW Explain how cohort effects can affect the findings of both longitudinal and cross-sectional studies. How do sequential designs reveal cohort effects?

APPLY A researcher compares older adults with chronic heart disease to those with no major health problems and finds that the first group scores lower on mental tests. Can the researcher conclude that heart disease causes a decline in intellectual functioning in late adulthood? Explain.

REFLECT Suppose a researcher asks you to enroll your baby in a 10-year longitudinal study. What factors would lead you to agree and stay involved? Do your answers shed light on why longitudinal studies often have biased samples?

Ethics in Lifespan Research

Research into human behavior creates ethical issues because, unfortunately, the quest for scientific knowledge can sometimes exploit people. For this reason, special guidelines for research have been developed by the federal government, by funding agencies, and by research-oriented associations, such as the American Psychological Association (2002) and the Society for Research in Child Development (2007). Table 1.7 presents a summary of basic research rights drawn from these guidelines. **TAKE A MOMENT...** After examining them, read about the following research situations, each of which poses a serious ethical dilemma. What precautions do you think should be taken in each instance?

- In a study of moral development, an investigator wants to assess children's ability to resist temptation by videotaping their behavior without their knowledge. She promises 7-year-olds a prize for solving difficult puzzles but tells them not to look at a classmate's correct solutions, which are deliberately placed at the back of the room. Informing children ahead of time that cheating is being studied or that their behavior is being monitored will destroy the purpose of the study.

- A researcher wants to study the impact of mild daily exercise on the physical and mental health of elderly patients in nursing homes. He consults each resident's doctor to make sure that the exercise routine will not be harmful. But when he seeks the residents' consent, he finds that many do not comprehend the purpose of the research. And some appear to agree simply to relieve feelings of loneliness.

As these examples indicate, when children or the aged take part in research, the ethical concerns are especially complex. Immaturity makes it difficult or impossible for children to evaluate for themselves what participation in research will mean. And because mental impairment rises with very advanced age, some older adults cannot make voluntary and informed choices (Dubois et al., 2011; Society for Research in Child Development, 2007). The life circumstances of others make them unusually vulnerable to pressure for participation.

TABLE 1.7

Rights of Research Participants

RESEARCH RIGHT	DESCRIPTION
Protection from harm	Participants have the right to be protected from physical or psychological harm in research. If in doubt about the harmful effects of research, investigators should seek the opinion of others. When harm seems possible, investigators should find other means for obtaining the desired information or abandon the research.
Informed consent	All participants, including children and aging adults, have the right to have explained to them, in language appropriate to their level of understanding, all aspects of the research that may affect their willingness to participate. When children are participants, informed consent of parents as well as of others who act on the child's behalf (such as school officials) should be obtained, preferably in writing. Older adults who are cognitively impaired should be asked to appoint a surrogate decision maker. If they cannot do so, then someone should be named by an institutional review board (IRB) after careful consultation with relatives and professionals who know the person well. All participants have the right to discontinue participation in the research at any time.
Privacy	Participants have the right to concealment of their identity on all information collected in the course of research. They also have this right with respect to written reports and any informal discussions about the research.
Knowledge of results	Participants have the right to be informed of the results of research in language that is appropriate to their level of understanding.
Beneficial treatments	If experimental treatments believed to be beneficial are under investigation, participants in control groups have the right to alternative beneficial treatments if they are available.

Sources: American Psychological Association, 2002; Society for Research in Child Development, 2007.

This older adult requires only typical informed-consent procedures to participate in research. But some elders with cognitive impairments or chronic illnesses may need the assistance of a surrogate decision maker.

them to better understand basic scientific principles and the needs of others. Researchers should respect and enhance these new capacities by giving school-age children a full explanation of research activities in language they can understand (Fisher, 1993). Extra care must be taken when telling children that the information they provide will be kept confidential and that they can end their participation at any time. Even adolescents may not understand, and sometimes do not believe, these promises (Bruzzese & Fisher, 2003; Ondrusek et al., 1998).

Most older adults require no more than the usual informed-consent procedures. Yet many investigators set upper age limits in studies relevant to the elderly, thereby excluding the oldest adults (Bayer & Tadd, 2000). Older adults should not be stereotyped as incompetent to decide about their own participation or to engage in research activities. Nevertheless, extra measures, such as the appointment of a surrogate decision maker to safeguard the older person's welfare, must be taken to protect those who are cognitively impaired or chronically ill.

The ultimate responsibility for the ethical integrity of research lies with the investigator. But researchers are advised—and often required—to seek advice from others. Committees for this purpose, called *institutional review boards (IRBs),* exist in colleges, universities, and other institutions. If there are any risks to participants' safety and welfare that the research does not justify, then the IRB always favors the participants' interests.

The ethical principle of *informed consent* requires special interpretation when participants cannot fully appreciate the research goals and activities. Parental consent is meant to protect the safety of children, whose ability to decide is not yet mature. But as soon as children are old enough to appreciate the purpose of the research, and certainly by age 7, their own informed consent should be obtained in addition to parental consent. Around this age, changes in children's thinking permit

Finally, all ethical guidelines advise that special precautions be taken in the use of deception and concealment, as occurs when researchers observe people from behind one-way mirrors, give them false feedback about their performance, or do not tell them the truth about the real purpose of the research. When these kinds of procedures are used, *debriefing,* in which the investigator provides a full account and justification of the activities, occurs after the research session is over. But young children often lack the cognitive skills to understand the reasons for deceptive procedures, and despite explanations, even older children may leave the research situation with their trust in adults undermined. Ethical standards permit deception if investigators satisfy IRBs that a study's potential benefits to society are great enough to justify infringing on participants' right to informed consent and risking other harm (Fisher, 2005). Nevertheless, because deception may have serious emotional consequences for some youngsters, many experts in research ethics believe that investigators should use it only if the risk of harm is minimal.

SUMMARY

A Scientific, Applied, and Interdisciplinary Field

(p. 3)

What is developmental science, and what factors stimulated expansion of the field?

- **Developmental science** is an interdisciplinary field devoted to understanding human constancy and change throughout the lifespan. Research on human development has been stimulated by both scientific curiosity and social pressures to improve people's lives.

Basic Issues (p. 3)

Identify three basic issues on which theories of human development take a stand.

- Each **theory** of human development takes a stand on three basic issues: (1) development as a **continuous** process or a series of **discontinuous stages;** (2) one course of development characterizing all individuals, or many possible courses, depending on **contexts;** (3) development determined primarily by genetic or environmental factors and either stable or characterized by substantial **plasticity.**

The Lifespan Perspective: A Balanced Point of View

(p. 5)

Describe the lifespan perspective on development.

- The **lifespan perspective** envisions development as a dynamic system and as lifelong, multidimensional (affected by biological, psychological, and social forces), multidirectional (a joint expression of growth and decline), and plastic (open to change through new experiences).

- Furthermore, in the lifespan perspective, three categories of influences shape the life course: (1) **age-graded influences,** which are predictable in timing and duration; (2) **history-graded influences,** unique to a particular historical era; and (3) **nonnormative influences,** unique to one or a few individuals.

Scientific Beginnings (p. 11)

Describe the major early influences on the scientific study of development.

- Darwin's theory of evolution influenced important developmental theories and inspired scientific child study. In the early twentieth century, Hall and Gesell introduced the **normative approach,** which produced a large body of descriptive facts about development.

- Binet and Simon constructed the first successful intelligence test, which sparked interest in individual differences in development and led to a heated **nature–nurture controversy.**

Mid-Twentieth-Century Theories (p. 12)

What theories influenced human development research in the mid-twentieth century?

- In the 1930s and 1940s, psychiatrists and social workers turned to the **psychoanalytic perspective** for help in treating people's emotional problems. In Freud's **psychosexual theory,** the individual moves through five stages, during which three portions of the personality—id, ego, and superego—become integrated. Erikson's **psychosocial theory** expands Freud's theory by emphasizing the development of culturally relevant attitudes and skills and the lifespan nature of development.

- As the psychoanalytic perspective gained in prominence, **behaviorism** and **social learning theory** emerged, emphasizing principles of conditioning and modeling and practical procedures of **behavior modification.**

- In contrast to behaviorism, Piaget's **cognitive-developmental theory** emphasizes children's active role in constructing knowledge as they manipulate and explore their world. According to Piaget, children move through four stages, from the baby's sensorimotor action patterns to the adolescent's capacity for abstract, systematic thinking.

Recent Theoretical Perspectives (p. 16)

Describe recent theoretical perspectives on human development.

- **Information processing** views the mind as a complex symbol-manipulating system and development as undergoing continuous change. This approach provides precise accounts of how children and adults tackle cognitive tasks.

- Researchers in **developmental cognitive neuroscience** study the relationship between changes in the brain and the development of cognitive processing and behavior patterns. They are identifying the types of experiences to which the brain is sensitive at various ages and the brain bases of learning and behavior disorders.

- Three contemporary perspectives emphasize contexts of development. **Ethology** stresses the adaptive value of behavior and inspired the **sensitive period** concept. In **evolutionary developmental psychology,** which extends this emphasis, researchers seek to understand the adaptiveness of specieswide competencies as they change with age.

- Vygotsky's **sociocultural theory** focuses on how culture is transmitted from one generation to the next through social interaction. Through cooperative dialogues with more expert members of society, children acquire culturally relevant knowledge and skills.

- **Ecological systems theory** views the individual as developing within a complex system of relationships affected by multiple, nested layers of the surrounding environment— **microsystem, mesosystem, exosystem,** and **macrosystem.** The **chronosystem** represents the dynamic, ever-changing nature of individuals and their experiences.

Comparing Theories (p. 21)

Identify the stand taken by each major theory on the three basic issues of human development.

- Theories vary widely in their focus on different domains of development and in their view of how development occurs. (For a full summary, see Table 1.4 on page 22.)

Studying Development (p. 21)

Describe methods commonly used in research on human development.

- **Naturalistic observations,** gathered in everyday environments, permit researchers to see directly the everyday behaviors they hope to explain. In contrast, **structured observations,** which take place in laboratories, give every participant an equal opportunity to display the behaviors of interest.

- Self-report methods can be flexible and open-ended like the **clinical interview.** Alternatively, in **structured interviews** (including tests and questionnaires), each participant is asked the same questions in the same way. Investigators use the **clinical,** or **case study, method** to gain an in-depth understanding of a single individual.

- To understand the unique values and social processes of a culture or distinct social group, researchers rely on **ethnography,** engaging in participant observation.

Distinguish between correlational and experimental research designs, noting the strengths and limitations of each.

- The **correlational design** examines relationships between variables without altering people's experiences. The **correlation coefficient** is often used to measure the association between variables.

- An **experimental design** permits cause-and-effect inferences. Researchers manipulate an **independent variable** by exposing participants to two or more treatment conditions. Then they determine what effect this variable has on a **dependent variable. Random assignment** to treatment conditions reduces the chances that participant characteristics will affect the accuracy of experimental findings.

- Field and natural, or quasi-, experiments compare treatments in natural environments. However, these approaches are less rigorous than laboratory experiments.

Describe designs for studying development, noting the strengths and limitations of each.

- The **longitudinal design** permits researchers to identify common patterns and individual differences in development and to examine relationships between early and later events and behaviors. Longitudinal research poses several problems, including biased sampling, practice effects, and **cohort effects.**

AP IMAGES/CHRIS CARLSON

- The **cross-sectional design** is an efficient way to study age-related trends, but it is limited to comparisons of age-group averages. Cross-sectional studies, especially those that cover a wide age span, are also vulnerable to cohort effects.

- By comparing participants of the same age who were born in different years, investigators use **sequential designs** to discover whether cohort effects are operating. When researchers combine experimental and developmental designs, they can examine causal influences on development.

Ethics in Lifespan Research
(p. 31)

What special ethical concerns arise in research on human development?

- Because the quest for scientific knowledge has the potential to exploit people, the ethical principle of informed consent requires special safeguards for children and for elderly people who are cognitively impaired or chronically ill. The use of deception in research with children is especially risky because it may undermine their basic faith in the honesty of adults.

Important Terms and Concepts

age-graded influences (p. 7)
behavior modification (p. 14)
behaviorism (p. 13)
chronosystem (p. 20)
clinical interview (p. 24)
clinical, or case study, method (p. 24)
cognitive-developmental theory (p. 15)
cohort effects (p. 29)
contexts (p. 4)
continuous development (p. 4)
correlational design (p. 25)
correlation coefficient (p. 27)
cross-sectional design (p. 29)
dependent variable (p. 27)
developmental cognitive neuroscience (p. 17)
developmental science (p. 3)
discontinuous development (p. 4)

ecological systems theory (p. 19)
ethnography (p. 25)
ethology (p. 17)
evolutionary developmental psychology (p. 18)
exosystem (p. 20)
experimental design (p. 27)
history-graded influences (p. 9)
independent variable (p. 27)
information processing (p. 16)
lifespan perspective (p. 5)
longitudinal design (p. 28)
macrosystem (p. 20)
mesosystem (p. 20)
microsystem (p. 20)
naturalistic observation (p. 22)
nature–nurture controversy (p. 5)
nonnormative influences (p. 9)

normative approach (p. 11)
plasticity (p. 5)
psychoanalytic perspective (p. 12)
psychosexual theory (p. 12)
psychosocial theory (p. 12)
random assignment (p. 27)
resilience (p. 8)
sensitive period (p. 18)
sequential designs (p. 30)
social learning theory (p. 14)
sociocultural theory (p. 18)
stage (p. 4)
structured interview (p. 24)
structured observation (p. 23)
theory (p. 3)

chapter
6

Emotional and Social Development in Infancy and Toddlerhood

© LAURA DWIGHT PHOTOGRAPHY

This father takes time to build a strong, affectionate bond with his infant daughter. His warmth and sensitivity engender a sense of security in the baby—a vital foundation for all aspects of early development.

chapter outline

Erikson's Theory of Infant and Toddler Personality

Basic Trust versus Mistrust • Autonomy versus Shame and Doubt

Emotional Development

Development of Basic Emotions • Understanding and Responding to the Emotions of Others • Emergence of Self-Conscious Emotions • Beginnings of Emotional Self-Regulation

■ **BIOLOGY AND ENVIRONMENT** Parental Depression and Child Development

Temperament and Development

The Structure of Temperament • Measuring Temperament • Stability of Temperament • Genetic and Environmental Influences • Temperament and Child Rearing: The Goodness-of-Fit Model

■ **BIOLOGY AND ENVIRONMENT** Development of Shyness and Sociability

Development of Attachment

Ethological Theory of Attachment • Measuring the Security of Attachment • Stability of Attachment • Cultural Variations • Factors That Affect Attachment Security • Multiple Attachments • Attachment and Later Development

■ **SOCIAL ISSUES: HEALTH** Does Child Care in Infancy Threaten Attachment Security and Later Adjustment?

Self-Development

Self-Awareness • Categorizing the Self • Self-Control

As Caitlin reached 8 months of age, her parents noticed that she had become more fearful. One evening, when Carolyn and David left her with a babysitter, she wailed as they headed for the door—an experience she had accepted easily a few weeks earlier. Caitlin and Timmy's caregiver Ginette also observed an increasing wariness of strangers. At the mail carrier's knock at the door, they clung to Ginette's legs, reaching out to be picked up.

At the same time, each baby seemed more willful. Removing an object from the hand produced little response at 5 months. But at 8 months, when Timmy's mother, Vanessa, took away a table knife he had managed to reach, Timmy burst into angry screams and could not be consoled or distracted.

All Monica and Kevin knew about Grace's first year was that she had been deeply loved by her destitute, homeless mother. Separation from her had left Grace in shock. At first she was extremely sad, turning away when Monica or Kevin picked her up. But as Grace's new parents held her close, spoke gently, and satisfied her craving for food, Grace returned their affection. Two weeks after her arrival, her despondency gave way to a sunny, easy-going disposition. As her second birthday approached, she pointed to herself, exclaiming "Gwace!" and laid claim to treasured possessions. "Gwace's teddy bear!"

Taken together, the children's reactions reflect two related aspects of personality development during the first two years: close ties to others and a sense of self. We begin with Erikson's psychosocial theory, which provides an overview of infant and toddler personality development. Then, as we chart the course of emotional development, we will discover why fear and anger became more apparent in Caitlin's and Timmy's range of emotions by the end of the first year. Our attention then turns to the origins and developmental consequences of individual differences in temperament.

Next, we take up attachment to the caregiver, the child's first affectionate tie. We will see how the feelings of security that grow out of this important bond support the child's sense of independence and expanding social relationships. Finally, we consider how cognitive advances combine with social experiences to foster early self-development and the beginnings of self-control in the second year. ●

Erikson's Theory of Infant and Toddler Personality

Our discussion in Chapter 1 revealed that the psychoanalytic perspective is no longer in the mainstream of human development research. But one of its lasting contributions is its ability to capture the essence of personality during each period of development. Recall that Sigmund Freud believed that psychological health and maladjustment could be traced to the quality of the child's relationships with parents during the early years. Although Freud came to be heavily criticized, the basic outlines of his theory were elaborated in several subsequent theories. The most influential is Erik Erikson's *psychosocial theory,* also introduced in Chapter 1.

Basic Trust versus Mistrust

Erikson accepted Freud's emphasis on the importance of the parent–infant relationship during feeding, but he expanded and enriched Freud's view. A healthy outcome during infancy, Erikson believed, depends on the *quality* of caregiving: relieving discomfort promptly and sensitively, waiting patiently until the baby has had enough milk, and weaning when the infant shows less interest in breast or bottle.

Erikson recognized that many factors affect parental responsiveness—personal happiness, current life conditions (for example, additional young children in the family), and culturally valued child-rearing practices. But when the *balance of care* is

sympathetic and loving, the psychological conflict of the first year—**basic trust versus mistrust**—is resolved on the positive side. The trusting infant expects the world to be good and gratifying, so he feels confident about venturing out and exploring it. The mistrustful baby cannot count on the kindness and compassion of others, so she protects herself by withdrawing from people and things around her.

Autonomy versus Shame and Doubt

With the transition to toddlerhood, Freud viewed the parents' manner of toilet training as decisive for psychological health. In Erikson' view, toilet training is only one of many influential experiences. The familiar refrains of newly walking, talking toddlers—"No!" "Do it myself!"—reveal a period of budding selfhood. The conflict of **autonomy versus shame and doubt** is resolved favorably when parents provide young children with suitable guidance and reasonable choices. A self-confident, secure 2-year-old has parents who do not criticize or attack him when he fails at new skills—using the toilet, eating with a spoon, or putting away toys. And they meet his assertions of independence with tolerance and understanding—for example, by giving him an extra five minutes to finish his play before leaving for the grocery store. In contrast, when parents are over- or undercontrolling, the outcome is a child who feels forced and shamed or who doubts his ability to control his impulses and act competently on his own.

In sum, basic trust and autonomy grow out of warm, sensitive parenting and reasonable expectations for impulse control

On a visit to a science museum, a 2-year-old insists on exploring a flight simulator. As the mother supports her toddler's desire to "do it myself," she fosters a healthy sense of autonomy.

starting in the second year. If children emerge from the first few years without sufficient trust in caregivers and without a healthy sense of individuality, the seeds are sown for adjustment problems.

Emotional Development

Researchers have conducted careful observations to find out how babies convey their emotions and interpret those of others. They have discovered that emotions play powerful roles in organizing the attainments that Erikson regarded as so important: social relationships, exploration of the environment, and discovery of the self (Halle, 2003; Saarni et al., 2006).

Development of Basic Emotions

Basic emotions—happiness, interest, surprise, fear, anger, sadness, and disgust—are universal in humans and other primates and have a long evolutionary history of promoting survival. Do newborns express basic emotions? Although signs of some emotions are present, babies' earliest emotional life consists of little more than two global arousal states: attraction to pleasant stimulation and withdrawal from unpleasant stimulation (Camras et al., 2003; Fox, 1991). Only gradually do emotions become clear, well-organized signals.

According to one view, sensitive, contingent caregiver communication, in which parents selectively mirror aspects of the baby's diffuse emotional behavior, helps infants construct emotional expressions that more closely resemble those of adults (Gergely & Watson, 1999). With age, face, voice, and posture form organized patterns that vary meaningfully with environmental events. For example, Caitlin typically responded to her parents' playful interaction with a joyful face, pleasant babbling, and a relaxed posture, as if to say, "This is fun!" In contrast, an

unresponsive parent often evokes a sad face, fussy sounds, and a drooping body (sending the message, "I'm despondent") or an angry face, crying, and "pick-me-up" gestures (as if to say, "Change this unpleasant event!") (Weinberg & Tronick, 1994; Yale et al., 1999).

Four basic emotions—happiness, anger, sadness, and fear—have received the most research attention. Let's see how they develop.

Happiness. Happiness—expressed first in blissful smiles and later through exuberant laughter—contributes to many aspects of development. When infants achieve new skills, they smile and laugh, displaying delight in motor and cognitive mastery. As the smile encourages caregivers to be affectionate and stimulating, the baby smiles even more (Aksan & Kochanska, 2004). Happiness binds parent and baby into a warm, supportive relationship that fosters the infant's developing competencies.

During the early weeks, newborn babies smile when full, during REM sleep, and in response to gentle stroking of the skin, rocking, and the mother's soft, high-pitched voice. By the end of the first month, infants smile at dynamic, eye-catching sights, such as a bright object jumping suddenly across their field of vision. Between 6 and 10 weeks, the parent's communication evokes a broad grin called the **social smile** (Lavelli & Fogel, 2005; Sroufe & Waters, 1976). These changes parallel the development of infant perceptual capacities—in particular, sensitivity to visual patterns, including the human face (see Chapter 4).

Laughter, which appears around 3 to 4 months, reflects faster processing of information than smiling. As with smiling, the first laughs occur in response to very active stimuli, such as the parent saying playfully, "I'm gonna get you!" and kissing the baby's tummy. As infants understand more about their world, they laugh at events with subtler elements of surprise, such as a silent game of peekaboo (Sroufe & Wunsch, 1972).

Around the middle of the first year, infants smile and laugh more when interacting with familiar people, a preference that strengthens the parent–child bond. Between 8 and 10 months, the smile becomes a deliberate social signal: Infants interrupt their play with an interesting toy to relay their delight to an attentive adult (Venezia et al., 2004).

Anger and Sadness. Newborn babies respond with generalized distress to a variety of unpleasant experiences, including hunger, changes in body temperature, and too much or too little stimulation. From 4 to 6 months into the second year, angry expressions increase in frequency and intensity (Braungart-Rieker, Hill-Soderlund, & Karrass, 2010). Older infants also react with anger in a wider range of situations—when an object is taken away, an expected pleasant event does not occur, the caregiver leaves for a brief time, or they are put down for a nap (Camras et al., 1992; Stenberg & Campos, 1990; Sullivan & Lewis, 2003).

Why do angry reactions increase with age? As infants become capable of intentional behavior (see Chapter 5), they

Biology and Environment

Parental Depression and Child Development

About 8 to 10 percent of women experience chronic depression—mild to severe feelings of sadness, distress, and withdrawal that continue for months or years. Sometimes, depression emerges or strengthens after childbirth and fails to subside. Julia experienced this type—called *postpartum depression.*

Although less recognized and studied, fathers, too, experience chronic depression. About 3 to 5 percent of fathers report symptoms after the birth of a child (Madsen & Juhl, 2007; Thombs, Roseman, & Arthurs, 2010). Parental depression can interfere with effective parenting and seriously impair children's development. Genetic makeup increases the risk of depressive illness, but social and cultural factors are also involved.

Maternal Depression

During Julia's pregnancy, her husband, Kyle, showed so little interest in the baby that Julia worried that having a child might be a mistake. Shortly after Lucy was born, Julia's mood plunged. She felt anxious and weepy, overwhelmed by Lucy's needs, and angry at loss of control over her own schedule. When Julia approached Kyle about her own fatigue and his unwillingness to help with the baby, he snapped that she was overreacting.

Julia's depressed mood quickly affected her baby. The more extreme the depression and the greater the number of stressors in a mother's life (such as marital discord, little or no social support, and poverty), the more the parent–child relationship suffers (Simpson et al., 2003). Julia rarely smiled at, comforted, or talked to Lucy, who responded to her mother's sad, vacant gaze by turning away, crying, and often looking sad or angry herself (Feldman et al., 2009; Field, 2011). By age 6 months, Lucy showed symptoms common

in babies of depressed mothers—delays in motor and mental development, an irritable mood, and attachment difficulties (Cornish et al., 2005; McMahon et al., 2006).

Depressed mothers use inconsistent discipline—sometimes lax, at other times too forceful. As we will see in later chapters, children who experience these maladaptive parenting practices often have serious adjustment problems. Some withdraw into a depressed mood themselves; others become impulsive and aggressive. In one study, infants born to mothers who had been depressed during pregnancy were four times more likely than babies of nondepressed mothers to engage in violent antisocial behavior by age 16, after other maternal stressors that could contribute to youth antisocial conduct had been controlled (Hay et al., 2010).

Paternal Depression

Paternal depression is also linked to dissatisfaction with marriage and family life after childbirth and to other life stressors, including job loss and divorce (Bielawska-Batorowicz & Kossakowska-Petrycka, 2006). Persistent paternal depression strongly predicts child behavior problems—especially overactivity, defiance, and aggression in boys (Ramchandani et al., 2008).

Paternal depression is linked to frequent father–child conflict as children grow older (Kane & Garber, 2004). Over time, children subjected to parental negativity develop a pessimistic world view—one in which they lack self-confidence and perceive their parents and other people as threatening. Children who constantly feel endangered are especially likely to become overly aroused in stressful situations, easily losing control in the face of cognitive and social challenges (Sturge-Apple et al., 2008).

This father appears completely disengaged from his wife and toddler. If his depression continues, disruptions in the parent–child relationship will likely lead to serious child behavior problems.

Interventions

Early treatment is vital to prevent parental depression from interfering with the parent–child relationship. Julia's doctor referred her to a therapist, who helped Julia and Kyle with their marital problems. At times, antidepressant medication is prescribed.

In addition to alleviating parental depression, therapy that encourages depressed mothers to engage in emotionally positive, responsive caregiving is vital for reducing young children's attachment and other developmental problems (Forman et al., 2007). When a depressed parent does not respond easily to treatment, a warm relationship with the other parent or another caregiver can safeguard children's development (Mezulis, Hyde, & Clark, 2004).

---

want to control their own actions. They are also more persistent about obtaining desired objects (Mascolo & Fischer, 2007). Furthermore, older infants are better at identifying who caused them pain or removed a toy. The rise in anger is also adaptive. New motor capacities enable an angry infant to defend herself or overcome an obstacle (Izard & Ackerman, 2000).

Although expressions of sadness also occur in response to pain, removal of an object, and brief separations, they are less frequent than anger (Alessandri, Sullivan, & Lewis, 1990). But when caregiver–infant communication is seriously disrupted, infant sadness is common—a condition that impairs all aspects of development (see the Biology and Environment box above).

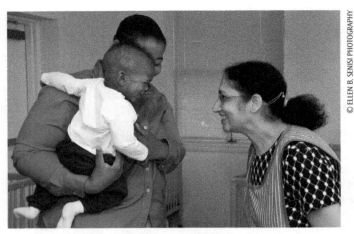

Stranger anxiety appears in many infants after 6 months of age. But this baby, safe in his mother's arms, also expresses curiosity, reaching out warily toward an unfamiliar adult who eases his fear by smiling and approaching slowly.

Fear. Like anger, fear rises from the second half of the first year into the second year (Braungart-Rieker, Hill-Soderland, & Karrass, 2010). Older infants hesitate before playing with a new toy, and newly crawling infants soon back away from heights (see Chapter 4). But the most frequent expression of fear is to unfamiliar adults, a response called **stranger anxiety.** Many infants and toddlers are quite wary of strangers, although the reaction varies with temperament (some babies are generally more fearful), past experiences with strangers, and the current situation. When an unfamiliar adult picks up the infant, stranger anxiety is likely. But if the adult sits still or acts warmly and playfully and a parent is nearby, infants often show positive and curious behavior (Horner, 1980).

Cross-cultural research reveals that infant-rearing practices can modify stranger anxiety. Among the Efe hunters and gatherers of the Republic of Congo, where the maternal death rate is high, infant survival is safeguarded by a collective caregiving system in which, starting at birth, Efe babies are passed from one adult to another. Consequently, Efe infants show little stranger anxiety (Tronick, Morelli, & Ivey, 1992).

LOOK AND LISTEN

While observing an 8- to 18-month-old with his or her parent, gently approach the baby, offering a toy. Does the baby respond with stranger anxiety? To better understand the baby's behavior, ask the parent to describe his or her temperament and past experiences with strangers. ●

The rise in fear after age 6 months keeps newly mobile babies' enthusiasm for exploration in check. Once wariness develops, babies use the familiar caregiver as a **secure base,** or point from which to explore, venturing into the environment and then returning for emotional support. As part of this adaptive system, encounters with strangers lead to two conflicting tendencies: approach (indicated by interest and friendliness) and avoidance (indicated by fear). The infant's behavior is a balance between the two.

As toddlers learn to discriminate more effectively between threatening and nonthreatening people and situations, stranger anxiety and other fears of the first two years decline. Fear also wanes as toddlers acquire more strategies for coping with it, as you will see when we discuss emotional self-regulation.

Understanding and Responding to the Emotions of Others

Infants' emotional expressions are closely tied to their ability to interpret the emotional cues of others. We have seen that in the first few months, babies match the feeling tone of the caregiver in face-to-face communication. Perhaps infants respond in kind to others' emotions through a built-in, automatic process of *emotional contagion* (Stern, 1985). Alternatively, they may acquire these emotional contingencies through operant conditioning—for example, learning that a smile generally triggers pleasurable feedback and that distress prompts a comforting response (Saarni et al., 2006).

Around 3 to 4 months, infants become sensitive to the structure and timing of face-to-face interactions. When they gaze, smile, or vocalize, they now expect their social partner to respond in kind (Markova & Legerstee, 2006; Rochat, Striano, & Blatt, 2002). Recall from Chapter 4 (see page 105) that out of this early imitative communication, infants start to view others as "like me"—an awareness believed to lay the foundation for understanding others' thoughts and feelings (Meltzoff, 2007).

From 5 months on, infants perceive facial expressions as organized patterns (see Chapter 4). As skill at establishing joint attention improves, infants realize that an emotional expression not only has meaning but is also a meaningful reaction to a specific object or event (Moses et al., 2001; Tomasello, 1999).

Once these understandings are in place, beginning at 8 to 10 months, infants engage in **social referencing**—actively seeking emotional information from a trusted person in an uncertain situation (Mumme et al., 2007). Many studies show that the caregiver's emotional expression (happy, angry, or fearful) influences whether a 1-year-old will be wary of strangers, play with an unfamiliar toy, or cross the deep side of the visual cliff (see Chapter 4, page 111) (de Rosnay et al., 2006; Stenberg, 2003; Striano & Rochat, 2000).

Parents can take advantage of social referencing to teach their baby how to react to many everyday events. And around the middle of the second year, as toddlers begin to appreciate that others' emotional reactions may differ from their own, social referencing allows them to compare their own and others' assessments of events. In one study, an adult showed 14- and 18-month-olds broccoli and crackers and acted delighted with one food but disgusted with the other (Repacholi & Gopnik, 1997). When asked to share the food, 18-month-olds gave the adult whichever food she appeared to like, regardless of their own preferences.

In sum, in social referencing, toddlers move beyond simply reacting to others' emotional messages. They use those signals to evaluate the safety of their surroundings, to guide their own actions, and to gather information about others' intentions and preferences.

Emergence of Self-Conscious Emotions

Besides basic emotions, humans are capable of a second, higher-order set of feelings, including guilt, shame, embarrassment, envy, and pride. These are called **self-conscious emotions** because each involves injury to or enhancement of our sense of self. We feel guilt when we have harmed someone and want to correct the wrongdoing. When we are ashamed or embarrassed, we have negative feelings about our behavior, and we want to retreat so others will no longer notice our failings. In contrast, pride reflects delight in the self's achievements, and we are inclined to tell others what we have accomplished and to take on further challenges (Saarni et al., 2006).

Self-conscious emotions appear in the middle of the second year, as 18- to 24-month-olds become firmly aware of the self as a separate, unique individual. Toddlers show shame and embarrassment by lowering their eyes, hanging their heads, and hiding their faces with their hands. They show guiltlike reactions, too: One 22-month-old returned a toy she had grabbed and patted her upset playmate. Pride also emerges around this time, and envy by age 3 (Barrett, 2005; Garner, 2003; Lewis et al., 1989).

Besides self-awareness, self-conscious emotions require an additional ingredient: adult instruction in *when* to feel proud,

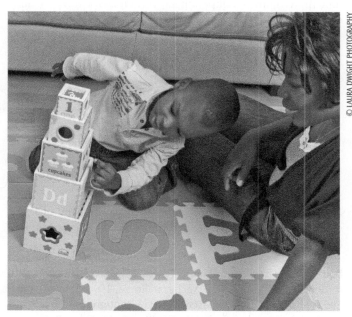

A mother praises her 2-year-old's success at tower-building. To experience self-conscious emotions, such as pride, young children need self-awareness as well as adult instruction.

© LAURA DWIGHT PHOTOGRAPHY

ashamed, or guilty. Situations in which adults encourage these feelings vary from culture to culture. In Western individualistic nations, most children are taught to feel pride in personal achievement. But in collectivist cultures such as China and Japan, calling attention to individual success evokes embarrassment and self-effacement. And violating cultural standards by failing to show concern for others—a parent, a teacher, or an employer—sparks intense shame (Akimoto & Sanbonmatsu, 1999; Lewis, 1992).

Beginnings of Emotional Self-Regulation

Besides expressing a wider range of emotions, infants and toddlers begin to manage their emotional experiences. **Emotional self-regulation** refers to the strategies we use to adjust our emotional state to a comfortable level of intensity so we can accomplish our goals (Thompson & Goodvin, 2007). When you remind yourself that an anxiety-provoking event will be over soon, suppress your anger at a friend's behavior, or decide not to see a scary horror film, you are engaging in emotional self-regulation.

Emotional self-regulation requires voluntary, effortful management of emotions, a capacity that improves gradually, as a result of development of the prefrontal cortex and the assistance of caregivers (Fox & Calkins, 2003; Rothbart, Posner, & Kieras, 2006). A good start in regulating emotion during the first two years contributes greatly to autonomy and mastery of cognitive and social skills (Eisenberg et al., 2004; Lawson & Ruff, 2004).

In the early months, infants are easily overwhelmed by intense emotions. They depend on the soothing interventions of caregivers—being lifted to the shoulder, rocked, gently stroked, and talked to softly—for distraction and reorienting of attention. More effective functioning of the prefrontal cortex increases the baby's tolerance for stimulation. Between 2 and 4 months, caregivers build on this capacity by initiating face-to-face play and attention to objects. In these interactions, parents arouse pleasure in the baby while adjusting the pace of their behavior so the infant does not become distressed. As a result, the baby's tolerance for stimulation increases further (Kopp & Neufeld, 2003).

By 4 to 6 months, the ability to shift attention away from unpleasant events helps infants control emotion (Crockenberg & Leerkes, 2003). At the end of the first year, crawling and walking enable infants to regulate emotion more effectively by approaching or retreating from various situations.

Infants whose parents "read" and respond contingently and sympathetically to their emotional cues tend to be less fussy and fearful, to express more pleasurable emotion, to be more interested in exploration, and to be easier to soothe (Braungart-Rieker, Hill-Soderlund, & Karrass, 2010; Crockenberg & Leerkes, 2004; Volling et al., 2002). In contrast, parents who respond impatiently or angrily or who wait to intervene until the infant has become extremely agitated reinforce the baby's rapid rise to intense distress. Consequently, brain structures that buffer stress may not develop properly, resulting in an anxious, reactive child who has a reduced capacity for managing emotional problems (Blair & Raver, 2012; Feldman, 2007).

Caregivers also provide lessons in socially approved ways of expressing feelings. As early as the first few months, parents encourage infants to suppress negative emotion by imitating their expressions of interest, happiness, and surprise more often than their expressions of anger and sadness. Boys get more of this training than girls, in part because boys have a harder time regulating negative emotion (Else-Quest et al., 2006; Malatesta et al., 1986). As a result, the well-known sex difference—females as emotionally expressive and males as emotionally controlled—is promoted at a tender age. Collectivist cultures place particular emphasis on socially appropriate emotional behavior. Compared with Americans, Japanese and Chinese adults discourage the expression of strong emotion in babies (Fogel, 1993; Kuchner, 1989). By the end of the first year, Chinese and Japanese infants smile and cry less than American infants (Camras et al., 1998; Gartstein et al., 2010).

Toward the end of the second year, a vocabulary for talking about feelings—"happy," "scary," "yucky"—develops rapidly, but toddlers are not yet good at using language to manage their emotions. Temper tantrums tend to occur when an adult rejects their demands, particularly when toddlers are fatigued or hungry (Mascolo & Fischer, 2007). Toddlers whose parents are emotionally sympathetic but set limits (by not giving in to tantrums), who distract the child by offering acceptable alternatives, and who later suggest better ways to handle adult refusals display more effective anger-regulation strategies and social skills during the preschool years (Lecuyer & Houck, 2006).

Patient, sensitive parents also encourage toddlers to describe their internal states. Then, when 2-year-olds feel distressed, they can guide caregivers in helping them (Cole, Armstrong, & Pemberton, 2010). For example, while listening to a story about monsters, Grace whimpered, "Mommy, scary." Monica put the book down and gave Grace a comforting hug.

ASK YOURSELF

REVIEW Why do many infants show stranger anxiety in the second half of the first year? What factors can increase or decrease wariness of strangers?

APPLY At age 14 months, Reggie built a block tower and gleefully knocked it down. But at age 2, he called to his mother and pointed proudly to his tall block tower. What explains this change in Reggie's emotional behavior?

REFLECT How do you typically manage negative emotion? How might your early experiences, gender, and cultural background have influenced your style of emotional self-regulation?

Temperament and Development

When we describe one person as cheerful and "upbeat," another as active and energetic, and still others as calm, cautious, persistent, or prone to angry outbursts, we are referring to **temperament**—early-appearing, stable individual differences in reactivity and self-regulation. *Reactivity* refers to quickness and intensity of emotional arousal, attention, and motor activity. *Self-regulation,* as we have seen, refers to strategies that modify that reactivity (Rothbart & Bates, 2006). The psychological traits that make up temperament are believed to form the cornerstone of the adult personality.

In 1956, Alexander Thomas and Stella Chess initiated the New York Longitudinal Study, a groundbreaking investigation of the development of temperament that followed 141 children from early infancy well into adulthood. Results showed that temperament can increase a child's chances of experiencing psychological problems or, alternatively, protect a child from the negative effects of a highly stressful home life. At the same time, Thomas and Chess (1977) discovered that parenting practices can modify children's temperaments considerably.

These findings stimulated a growing body of research on temperament. Let's begin with the structure, or makeup, of temperament and how it is measured.

The Structure of Temperament

Thomas and Chess's model of temperament inspired all others that followed. When detailed descriptions of infants' and children's behavior obtained from parent interviews were rated on nine dimensions of temperament, certain characteristics clustered together, yielding three types of children:

- The **easy child** (40 percent of the sample) quickly establishes regular routines in infancy, is generally cheerful, and adapts easily to new experiences.

- The **difficult child** (10 percent of the sample) is irregular in daily routines, is slow to accept new experiences, and tends to react negatively and intensely.

- The **slow-to-warm-up child** (15 percent of the sample) is inactive, shows mild, low-key reactions to environmental stimuli, is negative in mood, and adjusts slowly to new experiences.

Note that 35 percent of the children did not fit any of these categories. Instead, they showed unique blends of temperamental characteristics.

Difficult children are at high risk for adjustment problems—both anxious withdrawal and aggressive behavior in early and middle childhood (Bates, Wachs, & Emde, 1994; Ramos et al., 2005; Thomas, Chess, & Birch, 1968). Although slow-to-warm-up children present fewer problems, they tend to show excessive fearfulness and slow, constricted behavior in the late preschool and school years, when they are expected to respond actively

TABLE 6.1 Rothbart's Model of Temperament

DIMENSION	DESCRIPTION
REACTIVITY	
Activity level	Level of gross-motor activity
Attention span/persistence	Duration of orienting or interest
Fearful distress	Wariness and distress in response to intense or novel stimuli, including time to adjust to new situations
Irritable distress	Extent of fussing, crying, and distress when desires are frustrated
Positive affect	Frequency of expression of happiness and pleasure
SELF-REGULATION	
Effortful control	Capacity to voluntarily suppress a dominant, reactive response in order to plan and execute a more adaptive response

and quickly in classrooms and peer groups (Chess & Thomas, 1984; Schmitz et al., 1999).

Today, the most influential model of temperament is Mary Rothbart's, described in Table 6.1. It combines related traits proposed by Thomas and Chess and other researchers, yielding a concise list of six dimensions that represent the three underlying components included in the definition of temperament: (1) *emotion* ("fearful distress," "irritable distress," "positive affect," and "soothability"), (2) *attention* ("attention span/persistence"), and (3) *action* ("activity level"). According to Rothbart, individuals differ not only in their reactivity on each dimension but also in the self-regulatory dimension of temperament, **effortful control**—the capacity to voluntarily suppress a dominant response in order to plan and execute a more adaptive response (Rothbart, 2003; Rothbart & Bates, 2006). Variations in effortful control are evident in how effectively a child can focus and shift attention, inhibit impulses, and manage negative emotion.

Beginning in early childhood, effortful control predicts favorable development and adjustment in cultures as diverse as China and the United States (Zhou, Lengua, & Wang, 2009). Positive outcomes include persistence, task mastery, academic achievement, cooperation, moral maturity (such as concern about wrongdoing and willingness to apologize), and positive social behaviors of sharing and helpfulness (Eisenberg, 2010; Harris et al., 2007; Kochanska & Aksan, 2006; Posner & Rothbart, 2007; Valiente et al., 2010). *TAKE A MOMENT...* Turn back to page 127 in Chapter 5 to review the concept of executive function, and note its resemblance to effortful control. These converging concepts, which are associated with similar positive outcomes, reveal that the same mental activities lead to effective regulation in both the cognitive and emotional/social domains.

Measuring Temperament

Temperament is often assessed through interviews or questionnaires given to parents. Behavior ratings by pediatricians, teachers, and others familiar with the child and laboratory observations by researchers have also been used. Parental reports are convenient and take advantage of parents' depth of knowledge about their child across many situations (Gartstein & Rothbart, 2003). Although information from parents has been criticized as biased, parental reports are moderately related to researchers' observations of children's behavior (Majdandžić & van den Boom, 2007; Mangelsdorf, Schoppe, & Buur, 2000).

Observations by researchers avoid the subjectivity of parental reports but can lead to other inaccuracies. In homes, observers find it hard to capture rare but important events, such as infants' response to frustration. And in the unfamiliar lab setting, fearful children may become too upset to complete the session (Wachs & Bates, 2001). Still, researchers can better control children's experiences in the lab. And they can conveniently combine observations of behavior with neurobiological measures to gain insight into the biological bases of temperament.

Most neurobiological research has focused on children who fall at opposite extremes of the positive-affect and fearful-distress dimensions of temperament: **inhibited,** or **shy, children,** who react negatively to and withdraw from novel stimuli, and **uninhibited,** or **sociable, children,** who display positive emotion to and approach novel stimuli. As the Biology and Environment box on page 150 reveals, biologically based reactivity differentiates children with inhibited and uninhibited temperaments.

Stability of Temperament

Young children who score low or high on attention span, irritability, sociability, shyness, or effortful control tend to respond similarly when assessed again several months to a few years later and, occasionally, even into the adult years (Caspi et al., 2003; Kochanska & Knaack, 2003; Majdandžić & van den Boom, 2007; Rothbart, Ahadi, & Evans, 2000; van den Akker et al., 2010). However, the overall stability of temperament is low in infancy and toddlerhood and only moderate from the preschool years on (Putnam, Samson, & Rothbart, 2000).

A major reason is that temperament itself develops with age. To illustrate, let's look at irritability. Recall from Chapter 3 that most babies fuss and cry in the early months. As infants better regulate their attention and emotions with the help of patient, supportive parenting, many who initially seemed irritable become calm and content.

These discrepancies help us understand why long-term prediction from early temperament is best achieved after age 3, when styles of responding are better established (Roberts & DelVecchio, 2000). In line with this idea, between age 2½ and 3, children improve substantially on tasks requiring effortful control, such as waiting for a reward and selectively attending to one stimulus while ignoring competing stimuli (Kochanska,

Biology and Environment

Development of Shyness and Sociability

Two 4-month-old babies, Larry and Mitch, visited the laboratory of Jerome Kagan, who observed their reactions to various unfamiliar experiences. When exposed to new sights and sounds, such as a moving mobile decorated with colorful toys, Larry moved his arms and legs with agitation and cried. In contrast, Mitch remained relaxed and quiet, smiling and cooing.

As toddlers, Larry and Mitch returned to the lab, where they experienced several procedures designed to induce uncertainty. Electrodes were placed on their bodies and blood pressure cuffs on their arms to measure heart rate; toy robots, animals, and puppets moved before their eyes; and unfamiliar people behaved in unexpected ways. While Larry whimpered and quickly withdrew, Mitch watched with interest, laughed, and approached the toys and strangers.

On a third visit, at age 4½, Larry barely talked or smiled during an interview with an unfamiliar adult. In contrast, Mitch expressed pleasure at each new activity. In a playroom with two unfamiliar peers, Larry pulled back and watched, while Mitch quickly made friends.

In longitudinal research on several hundred children, Kagan found that about 20 percent of 4-month-old babies were, like Larry, easily upset by novelty; 40 percent, like Mitch, were comfortable, even delighted, with new experiences. About 20 to 30 percent of these groups retained their temperamental styles as they grew older (Kagan, 2003; Kagan & Saudino, 2001; Kagan et al., 2007). But most children's dispositions became less extreme over time. Biological makeup and child-rearing experiences jointly influenced stability and change in temperament.

Neurobiological Correlates of Shyness and Sociability

Individual differences in arousal of the *amygdala,* an inner brain structure devoted to processing emotional information, contrib-

ute to these contrasting temperaments. fMRI research reveals that in shy, inhibited children, novel stimuli easily excite the amygdala and its connections to the prefrontal cortex and the sympathetic nervous system, which prepares the body to act in the face of threat. In sociable, uninhibited children, the same level of stimulation evokes minimal neural excitation (Kagan & Fox, 2006). And the two emotional styles are distinguished by additional neurobiological responses known to be mediated by the amygdala:

- *Heart rate.* From the first few weeks of life, the heart rates of shy children are consistently higher than those of sociable children, and they speed up further in response to unfamiliar events (Schmidt et al., 2007; Snidman et al., 1995).

- *Cortisol.* Saliva concentrations of the stress hormone cortisol tend to be higher, and to rise more in response to a stressful event, in shy than in sociable children (Schmidt et al., 1997, 1999; Zimmermann & Stansbury, 2004).

- *Pupil dilation, blood pressure, and skin surface temperature.* Compared with sociable children, shy children show greater pupil dilation, rise in blood pressure, and cooling of the fingertips when faced with novelty (Kagan et al., 1999, 2007).

Furthermore, shy children show greater EEG activity in the right than in the left frontal lobe of the cerebral cortex, which is associated with negative emotional reactivity; sociable children show the opposite pattern (Fox et al., 2008; Kagan et al., 2007). Neural activity in the amygdala, which is transmitted to the frontal lobes, probably contributes to these differences.

Child-Rearing Practices

According to Kagan, extremely shy or sociable children inherit a physiology that biases them toward a particular temperamental style. Yet experience, too, has a powerful

A strong physiological response to uncertain situations prompts this toddler to cling to her father. With patient but insistent encouragement, her parents can help her overcome the urge to retreat.

impact. Warm, supportive parenting reduces shy infants' and preschoolers' intense reaction to novelty, whereas cold, intrusive parenting heightens anxiety (Coplan, Arbeau, & Armer, 2008; Hane et al., 2008). And if parents overprotect infants and young children who dislike novelty, they make it harder for their child to overcome an urge to retreat. Parents who make appropriate demands for their child to approach new experiences help shy youngsters overcome fear (Rubin & Burgess, 2002).

When inhibition persists, it leads to excessive cautiousness, low self-esteem, and loneliness and, in adolescence, increases the risk of severe anxiety, especially social phobia— intense fear of being humiliated in social situations (Kagan & Fox, 2006). To acquire effective social skills, inhibited children need parenting tailored to their temperaments— a theme we will encounter again in this and later chapters.

Murray, & Harlan, 2000; Li-Grining, 2007). Researchers believe that around this time, areas in the prefrontal cortex involved in suppressing impulses develop rapidly (Rothbart & Bates, 2006).

Nevertheless, the ease with which children manage their reactivity depends on the type and strength of the reactive emotion. Preschoolers who were highly fearful as toddlers score slightly better than their agemates in effortful control. In contrast, angry, irritable toddlers tend to be less effective at effortful control at later ages (Bridgett et al., 2009; Kochanska & Knaack, 2003).

In sum, many factors affect the extent to which a child's temperament remains stable, including development of the biological systems on which temperament is based, the child's capacity for effortful control, the success of her efforts (which depend on the quality and intensity of her emotional reactivity), and rearing experiences. With these ideas in mind, let's turn to genetic and environmental contributions to temperament and personality.

Genetic and Environmental Influences

Research indicates that identical twins are more similar than fraternal twins across a wide range of temperamental and personality traits (Bouchard, 2004; Bouchard & Loehlin, 2001; Caspi & Shiner, 2006; Goldsmith, Pollak, & Davidson, 2008). In Chapter 2, we noted that heritability estimates suggest a moderate role for heredity in personality: About half of individual differences have been attributed to differences in genetic makeup.

Although genetic influences are clear, environment is also powerful. For example, we have seen in early chapters that persistent nutritional and emotional deprivation profoundly alters temperament, resulting in maladaptive emotional reactivity. Other evidence shows that heredity and environment often jointly contribute to temperament, since a child's approach to the world affects the experiences to which she is exposed—an instance of gene–environment correlation (see page 55 in Chapter 2). To see how this works, let's look at ethnic and gender differences.

Ethnic and Gender Differences.
Compared with American Caucasian infants, Chinese and Japanese babies tend to be less active, irritable, and vocal, more easily soothed when upset, and better at quieting themselves (Kagan et al., 1994; Lewis, Ramsay, & Kawakami, 1993). Chinese and Japanese babies are also more fearful and inhibited, remaining closer to their mothers in an unfamiliar playroom and displaying more anxiety when interacting with a stranger (Chen, Wang, & DeSouza, 2006).

These variations may have genetic roots, but they are supported by cultural beliefs and practices. Japanese mothers usually say that babies come into the world as independent beings who must learn to rely on their mothers through close physical contact. American mothers typically believe just the opposite—that they must wean babies away from dependency toward autonomy. And while Asian cultures tend to view calmness as an ideal emotional state, Americans highly value the arousal and excitement generated by new places and activities (Kagan, 2010). Consistent with these beliefs, Asian mothers interact gently, soothingly, and gesturally with their babies, whereas Caucasian mothers use a more active, stimulating, verbal approach (Rothbaum et al., 2000a). Also, recall from our discussion of emotional self-regulation that Chinese and Japanese adults discourage babies from expressing strong emotion, which contributes further to their infants' tranquility.

Similarly, gender differences in temperament are evident as early as the first year, suggesting a genetic foundation. Boys are more active and daring, more irritable when frustrated, and slightly more impulsive—factors that contribute to their higher injury rates throughout childhood and adolescence. And girls' large advantage in effortful control undoubtedly contributes to their greater compliance, better school performance, and lower incidence of behavior problems (Eisenberg et al., 2004; Else-Quest et al., 2006). At the same time, parents more often encourage their young sons to be physically active and their daughters to seek help and physical closeness—through the toys they provide (trucks and footballs for boys, dolls and tea sets for girls) and through more positive reactions when the child exhibits temperamental traits consistent with gender stereotypes (Bryan & Dix, 2009; Ruble, Martin, & Berenbaum, 2006).

Children's Unique Experiences.
In families with several children, an additional influence on temperament is at work. *TAKE A MOMENT...* Ask several parents to describe each of their children's personalities. You will see that they often look for differences between siblings: "She's a lot more active," "He's more sociable," "She's far more persistent." As a result, parents often regard siblings as more distinct than other observers do (Saudino, 2003). Parents' tendency to emphasize each child's unique qualities affects their child-rearing practices. In an investigation of identical-twin toddlers, mothers' differential treatment predicted differences in psychological adjustment. The twin who received more warmth and less harshness was more positive in mood and social behavior (Deater-Deckard et al., 2001).

Besides different experiences within the family, siblings have distinct experiences with teachers, peers, and others in their community that affect personality development. And in middle childhood and adolescence, they often seek ways to differ from one another. For all these reasons, both identical and fraternal twins tend to become increasingly dissimilar in personality with age (Loehlin & Martin, 2001; McCartney, Harris, & Bernieri, 1990). In sum, temperament and personality can be understood only in terms of complex interdependencies between genetic and environmental factors.

Temperament and Child Rearing: The Goodness-of-Fit Model

If a child's disposition interferes with learning or getting along with others, adults must gently but consistently counteract the child's maladaptive style. Thomas and Chess (1977) proposed a **goodness-of-fit model** to describe how temperament and environment together can produce favorable outcomes. Goodness of fit involves creating child-rearing environments that recognize each child's temperament while encouraging more adaptive functioning.

Difficult children frequently experience parenting that fits poorly with their dispositions. By the second year, their parents tend to resort to angry, punitive discipline, which undermines the development of effortful control. As the child reacts with

A parent's firm but affectionate approach to discipline can help temperamentally difficult children gain in effortful control, managing negative emotion.

defiance and disobedience, parents become increasingly stressed (Bridgett et al., 2009; Paulussen-Hoogeboom et al., 2007). As a result, they continue their coercive tactics and also discipline inconsistently, at times rewarding the child's noncompliance by giving in to it—practices that sustain the child's conflict-ridden style (van Aken et al., 2007; Pesonen et al., 2008). In contrast, when parents are positive and sensitive, difficultness declines by age 2 or 3 (Feldman, Greenbaum, & Yirmiya, 1999). In toddlerhood and childhood, parental sensitivity, support, clear expectations, and limits foster effortful control, also reducing the likelihood that difficultness will persist (Cipriano & Stifter, 2010).

Recent evidence indicates that temperamentally difficult children function much worse than other children when exposed to inept parenting, yet benefit most from good parenting (Pluess & Belsky, 2011). Using molecular genetic analyses, researchers are investigating gene–environment interactions (see page 54 in Chapter 2) that explain this finding. In one study, 2-year-olds with a chromosome 17 gene that interferes with functioning of the neurotransmitter serotonin (involved in regulating negative mood) became increasingly irritable as their mothers' anxiety about parenting increased (Ivorra et al., 2010). Maternal anxiety had little impact on toddlers without this genetic marker. In another investigation, preschoolers with this gene benefited, especially, from positive parenting, displaying unusually large gains in effortful control (Kochanska, Philibert, & Barry, 2009).

The goodness-of-fit model reminds us that children have unique dispositions that adults must accept. Parents can neither take full credit for their children's virtues nor be blamed for all their faults. But parents can turn an environment that exaggerates a child's problems into one that builds on the child's strengths. As we will see, goodness of fit is also at the heart of infant–caregiver attachment. This first intimate relationship grows out of interaction between parent and baby, to which the emotional styles of both partners contribute.

ASK YOURSELF

REVIEW How do genetic and environmental factors work together to influence temperament? Cite several examples from research.

APPLY Mandy and Jeff are parents of 2-year-old inhibited Sam and 3-year-old difficult Maria. Explain the importance of effortful control to Mandy and Jeff, and suggest ways they can strengthen it in each of their children.

REFLECT How would you describe your temperament as a young child? Do you think your temperament has remained stable, or has it changed? What factors might be involved?

Development of Attachment

Attachment is the strong affectionate tie we have with special people in our lives that leads us to feel pleasure when we interact with them and to be comforted by their nearness in times of stress. By the second half of the first year, infants have become attached to familiar people who have responded to their needs. *TAKE A MOMENT...* Watch how babies of this age single out their parents for special attention. When the parent enters the room, the baby breaks into a broad, friendly smile. When she picks him up, he snuggles against her. When he feels anxious or afraid, he crawls into her lap and clings closely.

Attachment has also been the subject of intense theoretical debate. Recall that the *psychoanalytic perspective* regards feeding as the central context in which caregivers and babies build

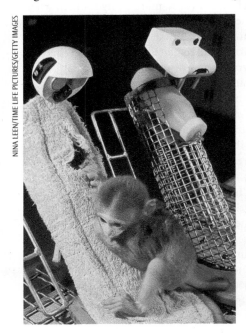

Baby monkeys reared with "surrogate mothers" preferred to cling to a soft terry-cloth "mother" over a wire-mesh "mother" holding a bottle—evidence that parent–infant attachment is based on more than satisfaction of hunger.

this close emotional bond. *Behaviorism,* too, emphasizes the importance of feeding, but for different reasons. According to a well-known behaviorist explanation, infants learn to prefer the mother's soft caresses, warm smiles, and tender words because these events are paired with tension relief as she satisfies the baby's hunger.

Although feeding is an important context for building a close relationship, attachment does not depend on hunger satisfaction. In the 1950s, a famous experiment showed that rhesus monkeys reared with terry-cloth and wire-mesh "surrogate mothers" clung to the soft terry-cloth substitute, even though the wire-mesh "mother" held the bottle and infants had to climb onto it to be fed (Harlow & Zimmerman, 1959). Human infants, too, become attached to family members who seldom feed them, including fathers, siblings, and grandparents. And toddlers in Western cultures who sleep alone and experience frequent daytime separations from their parents sometimes develop strong emotional ties to cuddly objects, such as blankets and teddy bears, that play no role in infant feeding!

Ethological Theory of Attachment

Today, **ethological theory of attachment,** which recognizes the infant's emotional tie to the caregiver as an evolved response that promotes survival, is the most widely accepted view. John Bowlby (1969), who first applied this idea to the infant–caregiver bond, was inspired by Konrad Lorenz's studies of imprinting (see Chapter 1). Bowlby believed that the human infant, like the young of other animal species, is endowed with a set of built-in behaviors that help keep the parent nearby to protect the infant from danger and to provide support for exploring and mastering the environment (Waters & Cummings, 2000).

The infant's relationship with the parent begins as a set of innate signals that call the adult to the baby's side. Over time, a true affectionate bond forms, supported by new cognitive and emotional capacities as well as by a history of warm, sensitive care. Attachment develops in four phases:

1. *Preattachment phase* (birth to 6 weeks). Built-in signals—grasping, smiling, crying, and gazing into the adult's eyes—help bring newborn babies into close contact with other humans, who comfort them.
2. *"Attachment-in-the-making" phase* (6 weeks to 6–8 months). During this phase, infants respond differently to a familiar caregiver than to a stranger. For example, at 4 months, Timmy smiled, laughed, and babbled more freely when interacting with his mother and quieted more quickly when she picked him up. As infants learn that their own actions affect the behavior of those around them, they begin to develop a *sense of trust*—the expectation that the caregiver will respond when signaled—but they still do not protest when separated from her.
3. *"Clear-cut" attachment phase* (6–8 months to 18 months– 2 years). Babies display **separation anxiety,** becoming upset when their trusted caregiver leaves. Like stranger anxiety (see page 146), separation anxiety does not always

occur; it depends on infant temperament and the current situation. But in many cultures, separation anxiety increases between 6 and 15 months. Besides protesting the parent's departure, older infants and toddlers approach, follow, and climb on her in preference to others. And they use the familiar caregiver as a secure base from which to explore.

LOOK AND LISTEN

Watch an 8- to 18-month-old at play for 20 to 30 minutes. Describe the baby's use of the parent or other familiar caregiver as a secure base from which to explore. ●

4. *Formation of a reciprocal relationship* (18 months to 2 years and on). Rapid growth in representation and language permits toddlers to understand some of the factors that influence the parent's coming and going and to predict her return. As a result, separation protest declines. Now children negotiate with the caregiver to alter her goals. At age 2, Caitlin asked Carolyn and David to read a story before leaving her with a babysitter. The extra time with her parents, along with a better understanding of when they would be back ("right after you go to sleep"), helped Caitlin withstand her parents' absence.

According to Bowlby (1980), out of their experiences during these four phases, children construct an enduring affectionate tie to the caregiver that they can use as a secure base in the parents' absence. This image serves as an **internal working model,** or set of expectations about the availability of attachment figures and their likelihood of providing support during times of stress. The internal working model becomes a vital part of personality, serving as a guide for all future close relationships (Bretherton & Munholland, 2008). With age, children continually revise and expand their internal working model as their cognitive, emotional, and social capacities increase and as they interact with parents and form other bonds with adults, siblings, and friends.

Because this 2-year-old has the language and representational skills to predict his mother's return, separation anxiety declines. He accepts his mother's departure.

Measuring the Security of Attachment

Although all family-reared babies become attached to a familiar caregiver, the quality of this relationship varies. A widely used laboratory procedure for assessing the quality of attachment between 1 and 2 years of age is the **Strange Situation.** Designed by Mary Ainsworth, it takes the baby through eight short episodes in which brief separations from and reunions with the parent occur in an unfamiliar playroom (see Table 6.2).

Observing infants' responses to these episodes, researchers identified a secure attachment pattern and three patterns of insecurity (Ainsworth et al., 1978; Barnett & Vondra, 1999; Main & Solomon, 1990; Thompson, 2006). *TAKE A MOMENT...* From the description at the beginning of this chapter, which pattern do you think Grace displayed after adjusting to her adoptive family?

- **Secure attachment.** These infants use the parent as a secure base. When separated, they may or may not cry, but if they do, it is because the parent is absent and they prefer her to the stranger. When the parent returns, they actively seek contact, and their crying is reduced immediately. About 60 percent of North American infants in middle-SES families show this pattern. (In low-SES families, a smaller proportion of babies are secure, with higher proportions falling into the insecure patterns.)

TABLE 6.2
Episodes in the Strange Situation

EPISODE	EVENTS	ATTACHMENT BEHAVIOR OBSERVED
1	Researcher introduces parent and baby to playroom and then leaves.	
2	Parent is seated while baby plays with toys.	Parent as a secure base
3	Stranger enters, is seated, and talks to parent.	Reaction to unfamiliar adult
4	Parent leaves room. Stranger responds to baby and offers comfort if baby is upset.	Separation anxiety
5	Parent returns, greets baby, and offers comfort if necessary. Stranger leaves room.	Reaction to reunion
6	Parent leaves room.	Separation anxiety
7	Stranger enters room and offers comfort.	Ability to be soothed by stranger
8	Parent returns, greets baby, offers comfort if necessary, and tries to reinterest baby in toys.	Reaction to reunion

Note: Episode 1 lasts about 30 seconds; each of the remaining episodes lasts about 3 minutes. Separation episodes are cut short if the baby becomes very upset. Reunion episodes are extended if the baby needs more time to calm down and return to play.
Source: Ainsworth et al., 1978.

- **Avoidant attachment.** These infants seem unresponsive to the parent when she is present. When she leaves, they usually are not distressed, and they react to the stranger in much the same way as to the parent. During reunion, they avoid or are slow to greet the parent, and when picked up, they often fail to cling. About 15 percent of North American infants in middle-SES families show this pattern.

- **Resistant attachment.** Before separation, these infants seek closeness to the parent and often fail to explore. When the parent leaves, they are usually distressed, and on her return they combine clinginess with angry, resistive behavior, sometimes hitting and pushing. Many continue to cry after being picked up and cannot be comforted easily. About 10 percent of North American infants in middle-SES families show this pattern.

- **Disorganized/disoriented attachment.** This pattern reflects the greatest insecurity. At reunion, these infants show confused, contradictory behaviors—for example, looking away while the parent is holding them or approaching the parent with flat, depressed emotion. About 15 percent of North American infants in middle-SES families show this pattern.

An alternative method, the **Attachment Q-Sort,** suitable for children between 1 and 4 years, depends on home observation (Waters et al., 1995). Either the parent or a highly trained observer sorts 90 behaviors ("Child greets mother with a big smile when she enters the room," "If mother moves very far, child follows along") into nine categories ranging from "highly descriptive" to "not at all descriptive" of the child. Then a score, ranging from high to low in security, is computed. The Q-Sort responses of expert observers correspond well with babies' secure-base behavior in the Strange Situation, but parents' Q-Sorts do not (van IJzendoorn et al., 2004). Parents of insecure children, especially, may have difficulty accurately reporting their child's attachment behaviors.

Stability of Attachment

Research on the stability of attachment patterns between 1 and 2 years of age yields a wide range of findings (Thompson, 2006). Quality of attachment is usually secure and stable for middle-SES babies experiencing favorable life conditions. And infants who move from insecurity to security typically have well-adjusted mothers with positive family and friendship ties. Perhaps many became parents before they were psychologically ready but, with social support, grew into the role. In contrast, in low-SES families with many daily stresses and little social support, attachment generally moves away from security or changes from one insecure pattern to another (Fish, 2004; Levendosky et al., 2011; Vondra et al., 2001).

These findings indicate that securely attached babies more often maintain their attachment status than insecure babies. The exception is disorganized/disoriented attachment, an insecure pattern that is either highly stable or that consistently predicts later insecurity of another type (Aikens, Howes, & Hamilton, 2009; Sroufe et al., 2005; Weinfield, Whaley, & Egeland, 2004).

As you will soon see, many disorganized/disoriented infants and children experience extremely negative caregiving, which may disrupt emotional self-regulation so severely that confused, ambivalent feelings toward parents often persist.

Cultural Variations

Cross-cultural evidence indicates that attachment patterns may have to be interpreted differently in certain cultures. For example, as Figure 6.1 reveals, German infants show considerably more avoidant attachment than American babies do. But German parents value independence and encourage their infants to be nonclingy (Grossmann et al., 1985). In contrast, a study of infants of the Dogon people of Mali, Africa, revealed that none showed avoidant attachment to their mothers (True, Pisani, & Oumar, 2001). Even when grandmothers are primary caregivers (as they are with firstborn sons), Dogon mothers remain available, holding their babies close and nursing promptly in response to hunger and distress.

Japanese infants, as well, rarely show avoidant attachment (refer again to Figure 6.1). Rather, many are resistantly attached, but this reaction may not represent true insecurity. Japanese mothers rarely leave their babies in others' care, so the Strange Situation probably induces greater stress in them than in infants who experience frequent maternal separations (Takahashi, 1990). Also, Japanese parents view the attention seeking that is part of resistant attachment as a normal indicator of infants' efforts to satisfy dependency and security needs (Rothbaum et al., 2007). Despite such cultural variations, the secure pattern is still the most common attachment quality in all societies studied (van IJzendoorn & Sagi-Schwartz, 2008).

Dogon mothers of Mali, West Africa, stay close to their babies and respond promptly and gently to infant hunger and distress. With their mothers consistently available, none of the Dogon babies show avoidant attachment.

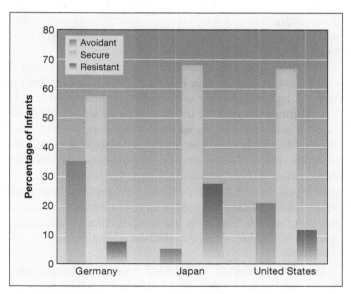

FIGURE 6.1 A cross-cultural comparison of infants' reactions in the Strange Situation. A high percentage of German babies seem avoidantly attached, whereas a substantial number of Japanese infants appear resistantly attached. Note that these responses may not reflect true insecurity. Instead, they are probably due to cultural differences in child-rearing practices. (Adapted from van IJzendoorn & Kroonenberg, 1988; van IJzendoorn & Sagi-Schwartz, 2008.)

Factors That Affect Attachment Security

What factors might influence attachment security? Researchers have looked closely at four important influences: (1) early availability of a consistent caregiver, (2) quality of caregiving, (3) the baby's characteristics, and (4) family context, including parents' internal working models.

Early Availability of a Consistent Caregiver. Although adopted children who spent their first year or more in deprived Eastern European orphanages where they had no opportunity to establish a close tie to a caregiver are able to bond with their adoptive parents, they nevertheless show elevated rates of attachment insecurity (van den Dries et al., 2009; Smyke et al., 2010). They are also at high risk for emotional and social difficulties. Many are overly friendly to unfamiliar adults; others are sad, anxious, and withdrawn. These symptoms are associated with wide-ranging mental health problems in middle childhood and adolescence, including cognitive impairments, inattention and hyperactivity, depression, and either social avoidance or aggressive behavior (Kreppner et al., 2007, 2010; Rutter et al., 2007, 2010; Zeanah, 2000).

Furthermore, as early as 7 months, institutionalized children show reduced ERP brain waves in response to facial expressions of emotion and have trouble discriminating such expressions—outcomes that suggest disrupted formation of neural structures involved in "reading" emotions (Parker et al., 2005). Consistent with these findings, in adopted children with longer institutional stays, the volume of the *amygdala* (see page 150) is atypically large (Tottenham et al., 2011). The larger the amygdala, the worse adopted children perform on tasks assessing understanding of emotion and the poorer their emotional self-regulation. Overall, the evidence indicates that fully normal emotional development depends on establishing a close tie with a caregiver early in life.

Quality of Caregiving. Dozens of studies report that **sensitive caregiving**—responding promptly, consistently, and appropriately to infants and holding them tenderly and carefully—is moderately related to attachment security in diverse cultures and SES groups (Belsky & Fearon, 2008; De Wolff & van IJzendoorn, 1997; van IJzendoorn et al., 2004). In contrast, insecurely attached infants tend to have mothers who engage in less physical contact, handle them awkwardly or "routinely," and are resentful and rejecting, particularly in response to infant distress (Ainsworth et al., 1978; Isabella, 1993; McElwain & Booth-LaForce, 2006; Pederson & Moran, 1996).

Cultures, however, vary in their view of sensitivity toward infants. Among the Gusii people of Kenya, for example, mothers rarely cuddle, hug, or interact playfully with their babies, although they are very responsive to their infants' needs. Yet most Gusii infants appear securely attached (LeVine et al., 1994). This suggests that security depends on attentive caregiving, not necessarily on frequent physical affection or face-to-face interaction. Puerto Rican mothers, who highly value obedience and socially appropriate behavior, often physically direct and limit their babies' actions—a caregiving style linked to attachment security in Puerto Rican culture (Carlson & Harwood, 2003). Yet in many Western cultures, such physical control and restriction of exploration predict insecurity (Belsky & Fearon, 2008; Whipple, Bernier, & Mageau, 2011).

Compared with securely attached infants, avoidant babies tend to receive overstimulating, intrusive care. By avoiding the mother, these infants appear to be escaping from overwhelming interaction. Resistant infants often experience inconsistent care. Their mothers are unresponsive to infant signals. Yet when the baby begins to explore, these mothers interfere, shifting the infant's attention back to themselves. As a result, the baby is overly dependent as well as angry at the mother's lack of involvement (Cassidy & Berlin, 1994; Isabella & Belsky, 1991).

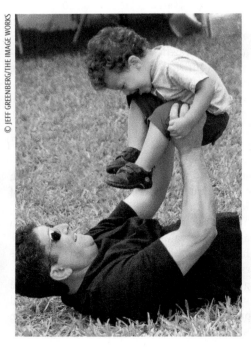

This father's sensitive, affectionate interaction contributes to his child's attachment security.

Highly inadequate caregiving is a powerful predictor of disruptions in attachment. Child abuse and neglect are associated with all three forms of attachment insecurity. Among maltreated infants, disorganized/disoriented attachment is especially high (van IJzendoorn, Schuengel, & Bakermans-Kranenburg, 1999). Persistently depressed mothers, mothers with very low marital satisfaction, and parents suffering from a traumatic event, such as loss of a loved one, also tend to promote the uncertain behaviors of this pattern (Campbell et al., 2004; Madigan et al., 2006; Moss et al., 2005). Some of these mothers display frightening, contradictory, and unpleasant behaviors—looking scared, teasing the baby, holding the baby stiffly at a distance, or seeking reassurance from the upset child (Abrams, Rifkin, & Hesse, 2006; Moran et al., 2008).

Infant Characteristics. Because attachment is the result of a *relationship* that builds between two partners, infant characteristics should affect how easily it is established. Babies whose temperament is emotionally reactive and difficult are more likely to develop later insecure attachments (van IJzendoorn et al., 2004; Vaughn, Bost, & van IJzendoorn, 2008). However, caregiving is also involved. In a study extending from birth to age 2, difficult infants more often had highly anxious mothers—a combination that, by the second year, often resulted in a "disharmonious relationship" characterized by both maternal insensitivity and attachment insecurity (Symons, 2001).

Other research on disorganized/disoriented attachment has uncovered gene–environment interactions (Gervai, 2009). In one investigation, mothers' experience of unresolved loss of a loved one or other trauma was associated with attachment disorganization only in infants with a chromosome-11 gene linked to deficient self-regulation (van IJzendoorn & Bakermans-Kranenburg, 2006). Babies with this genetic marker, who face special challenges in managing intense emotion, were more negatively affected by maternal adjustment problems.

Overall, infant characteristics are only weakly related to attachment quality because *many* child attributes can lead to secure attachment as long as the caregivers behave sensitively. Interventions that teach parents to interact with difficult-to-care-for infants are highly successful in enhancing both sensitive care and attachment security (Velderman et al., 2006). But when parents' capacity is strained—by their own personalities or by stressful living conditions—then infants with illnesses, disabilities, and difficult temperaments are at risk for attachment problems. Child care—as the Social Issues: Health box on the following page indicates—is yet another context with consequences for the infant–parent attachment relationship.

Parents' Internal Working Models. Parents bring to the family context their own history of attachment experiences, from which they construct internal working models that they apply to the bonds they establish with their children. Monica, who recalled her mother as tense and preoccupied, expressed regret that they had not had a closer relationship. Is her image of parenthood likely to affect Grace's attachment security?

Social Issues: Health

Does Child Care in Infancy Threaten Attachment Security and Later Adjustment?

Are infants who experience daily separation from their employed parents and early placement in child care at risk for attachment insecurity and development problems? Some researchers think so, but others disagree. Evidence from the National Institute of Child Health and Development (NICHD) Study of Early Child Care, the largest longitudinal investigation to date, including more than 1,300 infants and their families—reveals that nonparental care by itself does not affect attachment quality (NICHD Early Child Care Research Network, 1997, 2001). Rather, the relationship between child care and emotional well-being depends on both family and child-care experiences.

Family Circumstances

We have seen that family conditions affect children's attachment security and later adjustment. The NICHD Study confirmed that parenting quality, assessed using a combination of maternal sensitivity and HOME scores (see page 133 in Chapter 5), exerts a more powerful impact on children's adjustment than does exposure to child care (NICHD Early Childhood Research Network, 1998; Watamura et al., 2011).

For employed parents, balancing work and caregiving can be stressful. Mothers who feel overloaded by work and family pressures may respond less sensitively to their babies, thereby risking the infant's security. And as paternal involvement in caregiving has risen (see page 158), many more U.S. fathers in dual-earner families also report work–family life conflict (Galinsky, Aumann, & Bond, 2009).

Quality and Extent of Child Care

Nevertheless, poor-quality child care may contribute to a higher rate of insecure attachment. In the NICHD Study, when babies were exposed to combined home and child-care risk factors—insensitive caregiving at home

along with insensitive caregiving in child care, long hours in child care, or more than one child-care arrangement—the rate of attachment insecurity increased. Overall, mother–child interaction was more favorable when children attended higher-quality child care and also spent fewer hours in child care (NICHD Early Child Care Research Network, 1997, 1999).

Furthermore, when these children reached age 3, a history of higher-quality child care predicted better social skills (NICHD Early Child Care Research Network, 2002b). However, at age 4½ to 5, children averaging more than 30 child-care hours per week displayed more behavior problems, especially defiance, disobedience, and aggression (NICHD Early Child Care Research Network, 2003a, 2006).

This does not necessarily mean that child care causes behavior problems. Rather, heavy exposure to substandard care, which is widespread in the United States, may promote these difficulties, especially when combined with family risk factors. A closer look at the NICHD participants during the preschool years revealed that those in both poor-quality home and child-care environments fared worst in social skills and problem behaviors, whereas those in both high-quality home and child-child care environments fared best. In between were preschoolers in high-quality child care but poor-quality homes (Watamura et al., 2011). These children benefited from the *protective influence* of high-quality child care.

Evidence from other industrialized nations confirms that full-time child care need not harm children's development. In Australia, for example, infants who spend full days in government-funded, high-quality child-care centers have a higher rate of secure attachment than infants informally cared for by relatives, friends, or babysitters. And amount of time spent in child care is

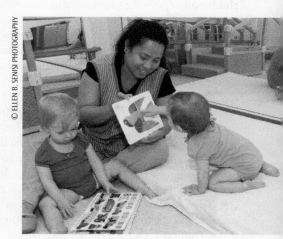

© ELLEN B. SENISI PHOTOGRAPHY

High-quality child care, with generous caregiver–child ratios, small group sizes, and knowledgeable caregivers, can be part of a system that promotes all aspects of development, including attachment security.

unrelated to Australian children's behavior problems (Love et al., 2003).

Conclusions

Taken together, research suggests that some infants may be at risk for attachment insecurity and later adjustment problems due to inadequate child care, long hours in such care, and parental pressures of full-time employment and child rearing. But it is inappropriate to use these findings to justify a reduction in child-care services. When family incomes are limited or mothers who want to work are forced to stay at home, children's emotional security is not promoted.

Instead, it makes sense to increase the availability of high-quality child care and to relieve work–family-life conflict by providing parents with paid employment leave (see page 81 in Chapter 3) and opportunities for part-time work. In the NICHD study, part-time (as opposed to full-time) employment during the baby's first year was associated with greater maternal sensitivity and a higher-quality home environment, which yielded more favorable development in early childhood (Brooks-Gunn, Han, & Waldfogel, 2010).

To assess parents' internal working models, researchers ask them to evaluate childhood memories of attachment experiences (Main & Goldwyn, 1998). Parents who discuss their childhoods with objectivity and balance, regardless of whether their experiences were positive or negative, tend to have

securely attached children. In contrast, parents who dismiss the importance of early relationships or describe them in angry, confused ways usually have insecurely attached children and are less warm, sensitive, and encouraging of learning and mastery (Behrens, Hesse, & Main, 2007; Coyl, Newland,

& Freeman, 2010; Steele, Steele, & Fonagy, 1996; van IJzendoorn, 1995).

But we must not assume any direct transfer of parents' childhood experiences to quality of attachment with their own children. Internal working models are *reconstructed memories* affected by many factors, including relationship experiences over the life course, personality, and current life satisfaction. Longitudinal research reveals that negative life events can weaken the link between an individual's own attachment security in infancy and a secure internal working model in adulthood. And insecurely attached babies who become adults with insecure internal working models often have lives that, based on self-reports in adulthood, are filled with family crises (Waters et al., 2000; Weinfield, Sroufe, & Egeland, 2000).

In sum, our early rearing experiences do not destine us to become either sensitive or insensitive parents. Rather, the way we *view* our childhoods—our ability to come to terms with negative events, to integrate new information into our working models, and to look back on our own parents in an understanding, forgiving way—is far more influential in how we rear our children than the actual history of care we received (Bretherton & Munholland, 2008).

Multiple Attachments

Babies develop attachments to a variety of familiar people—not just mothers but also fathers, grandparents, siblings, and professional caregivers. Although Bowlby (1969) believed that infants are predisposed to direct their attachment behaviors to a single special person, especially when they are distressed, his theory allows for these multiple attachments.

Fathers. Fathers' sensitive caregiving with infants, like mothers', predicts attachment security (Lundy, 2003; van IJzendoorn et al., 2004). But in many cultures—Australia, Canada, Germany, India, Israel, Italy, Japan, and the United States—mothers and fathers tend to interact differently with their babies. Mothers devote more time to physical care and expressing affection, fathers to playful interaction (Freeman & Newland, 2010; Roopnarine et al., 1990).

Mothers and fathers also play differently. Mothers more often provide toys, talk to infants, and gently play conventional games like pat-a-cake. In contrast, fathers—especially with their infant sons—tend to engage in highly stimulating physical play with bursts of excitement (Feldman, 2003). As long as fathers are also sensitive, this stimulating, startling play style helps babies regulate emotion in intensely arousing situations, including novel physical environments and play with peers (Hazen et al., 2010; Paquette, 2004).

FIGURE 6.2 Average amount of time per workday U.S. employed mothers and fathers reported spending with their children (age 12 and younger) in 1977 and 2008. In national surveys of several thousand employed parents, mothers' time with children remained fairly stable from 1977 to 2008; fathers' time increased substantially. (Adapted from Galinsky, Aumann, & Bond, 2009.)

In cultures such as Japan, where long work hours prevent most fathers from sharing in infant caregiving, play is a vital context in which fathers build secure attachments (Hewlett, 2004; Newland, Coyl, & Freeman, 2008). In many Western nations, however, a strict division of parental roles—mother as caregiver, father as playmate—has changed over the past several decades in response to women's workforce participation.

Recent surveys indicated that U.S. fathers under age 29 devote about 85 percent as much time to children as mothers do—on average, just over 4 hours per workday, nearly double the hours young fathers reported three decades ago. Although fathers age 29 to 42 spend somewhat less time with children, their involvement has also increased substantially (see Figure 6.2). Today, nearly one-third of U.S. employed women say that their spouse or partner shares equally in or takes most responsibility for child-care tasks (Galinsky, Aumann, & Bond, 2009). Paternal availability to children is fairly similar across SES and ethnic groups, with one exception: Hispanic fathers spend more time engaged, probably because of the particularly high value that Hispanic cultures place on family involvement (Cabrera & García Coll, 2004; Parke et al., 2004).

A warm marital bond promotes both parents' sensitivity and involvement and children's attachment security, but it is particularly important for fathers (Brown et al., 2010; Sevigny & Loutzenhiser, 2010). And in studies carried out in many societies and ethnic groups, fathers' affectionate care of young children predicted later cognitive, emotional, and social competence as strongly as did mothers' warmth—and occasionally more strongly (Rohner & Veneziano, 2001; Veneziano, 2003).

Siblings. Despite declines in family size, 80 percent of North American and European children grow up with at least one sibling (Dunn, 2004). The arrival of a new baby is a difficult expe-

The arrival of a baby brother or sister is a difficult experience for most preschoolers. Maternal warmth toward both children assures the older sibling of continuing parental love and is related to positive sibling interaction.

rience for most preschoolers, who often become demanding, clingy, and deliberately naughty for a time. Attachment security also declines, especially for children over age 2 (old enough to feel threatened and displaced) and for those with mothers under stress (Baydar, Greek, & Brooks-Gunn, 1997; Teti et al., 1996).

Yet resentment is only one feature of a rich emotional relationship that soon develops between siblings. Older children also show affection and concern when the infant cries. By the end of the first year, babies are comforted by the presence of a preschool-age brother or sister during short parental absences. Throughout childhood, children continue to treat older siblings as attachment figures, turning to them for comfort in stressful situations when parents are unavailable (Seibert & Kerns, 2009).

Nevertheless, individual differences in sibling relationships emerge early. Certain temperamental traits—high emotional reactivity or activity level—increase the chances of sibling conflict (Brody, Stoneman, & McCoy, 1994; Dunn, 1994). And maternal warmth toward both children is related to positive sibling interaction and to preschoolers' support of a distressed younger sibling (Volling, 2001; Volling & Belsky, 1992). In contrast, maternal harshness and lack of involvement are linked to antagonistic sibling relationships (Howe, Aquan-Assee, & Bukowski, 2001).

Finally, a good marriage and effective coparenting are linked to preschool siblings' capacity to cope adaptively with jealousy and conflict (Volling, McElwain, & Miller, 2002). Perhaps good communication between parents serves as a model of effective problem solving. It may also foster a generally happy family environment, giving children less reason to feel jealous.

Attachment and Later Development

According to psychoanalytic and ethological theories, the inner feelings of affection and security that result from a healthy attachment relationship support all aspects of psychological development. Yet contrary evidence exists. In longitudinal research, secure infants generally fared better than insecure infants, but not always (Fearon et al., 2010; McCartney et al., 2004; Schneider, Atkinson, & Tardif, 2001; Stams, Juffer, & van IJzendoorn, 2002).

What accounts for this inconsistency? Mounting evidence indicates that *continuity of caregiving* determines whether attachment security is linked to later development (Lamb et al., 1985; Thompson, 2006). When a large sample of children were tracked from ages 1 to 3 years, those experiencing secure attachment followed by sensitive parenting scored highest in cognitive, emotional, and social outcomes. Those experiencing insecure attachment followed by parental insensitivity scored lowest, while those with mixed histories of attachment and maternal sensitivity scored in between (Belsky & Fearon, 2002a).

In sum, secure attachment in infancy launches the parent–child relationship on a positive path. An early warm, positive parent–child tie, sustained over time, predicts a more confident and complex self-concept, more advanced emotional understanding and social skills, a stronger sense of moral responsibility, and higher motivation to achieve in school (Thompson, 2006, 2008). But the effects of early attachment security are *conditional*—dependent on the quality of the baby's future relationships.

ASK YOURSELF

REVIEW What factors explain stability in attachment pattern for some children and change for others? Are these factors also involved in the link between attachment in infancy and later development? Explain.

APPLY Explain how the caregiving experiences of securely attached infants promote development of emotional self-regulation, described on page 147.

REFLECT How would you characterize your internal working model? What factors, in addition to your relationship with your parents, might have influenced it?

 ## Self-Development

Infancy is a rich formative period for the development of both physical and social understanding. In Chapter 5, you learned that infants develop an appreciation of the permanence of objects. In this chapter, we have seen that over the first year, infants recognize and respond appropriately to others' emotions and distinguish familiar from unfamiliar people. That both objects and people achieve an independent, stable existence for the infant implies that knowledge of the self as a separate, permanent entity is also emerging.

Self-Awareness

When Carolyn held Caitlin in front of a mirror, as early as the first few months Caitlin smiled and returned friendly behaviors to her image. At what age did she realize that the charming baby gazing and smiling back was herself?

Beginnings of Self-Awareness. Infants' remarkable capacity for *intermodal perception* (see page 113 in Chapter 4) supports the beginnings of self-awareness (Rochat, 2003). As they feel their own touch, feel and watch their limbs move, and feel and hear themselves cry, babies experience intermodal matches that differentiate their own body from surrounding bodies and objects.

Over the first few months, infants distinguish their own visual image from other stimuli. When shown two side-by-side video images of their kicking legs, one from their own perspective (camera behind the baby) and one from an observer's perspective (camera in front of the baby), 3-month-olds looked longer at the observer's view (Rochat, 1998). By 4 months, infants look and smile more at video images of others than at video images of themselves, indicating that they treat another person (as opposed to the self) as a social partner (Rochat & Striano, 2002).

Self-Recognition. During the second year, toddlers become consciously aware of the self's physical features. In several studies, 9- to 28-month-olds were placed in front of a mirror. Then, under the pretext of wiping the baby's face, each mother rubbed red dye on her child's nose or forehead. Toddlers older than 20 months touched or rubbed their noses or foreheads, indicating awareness of their unique appearance (Bard et al., 2006; Lewis & Brooks-Gunn, 1979). Around age 2, **self-recognition**—identification of the self as a physically unique being—is well under way. Children point to themselves in photos

This 20-month-old's response to her mirror image indicates that she recognizes her unique physical features and is aware of herself as a separate being, distinct from other people and objects.

and refer to themselves by name or with a personal pronoun ("I" or "me") (Lewis & Ramsay, 2004). Nevertheless, toddlers make **scale errors,** attempting to do things that their body size makes impossible. For example, they will try to put on dolls' clothes or walk through a doorway too narrow for them to pass through (Brownell, Zerwas, & Ramani, 2007; DeLoache, Uttal, & Rosengren, 2004). Possibly, toddlers lack an accurate understanding of their own body dimensions. Alternatively, they may simply be exploring the consequences of squeezing into restricted spaces, as they are far less likely to try when the risk of harming themselves is high (the too-narrow doorway is next to a ledge where they could fall) (Franchak & Adolph, 2012). Scale errors decline around age 2, but many 2½-year-olds still make them.

According to many theorists, self-awareness and self-recognition develop as infants and toddlers increasingly realize that their own actions cause objects and people to react in predictable ways (Nadel, Prepin, & Okanda, 2005). For example, batting a mobile and seeing it swing in a pattern different from the infant's own actions informs the baby about the relation between self and physical world. Smiling and vocalizing at a caregiver who smiles and vocalizes back helps clarify the relation between self and social world. The contrast between these experiences helps infants sense that they are separate from external reality.

Cultural variations exist in early self-development (Keller et al., 2004, 2005). Mothers of the Nso people of Cameroon, a collectivist farming society, engage in less face-to-face communication and object stimulation and more body contact and physical stimulation of their babies than do urban German and Greek mothers. Nso "proximal" parenting, which emphasizes interdependence, is associated with later attainment of self-recognition but earlier emergence of toddlers' compliance with adult requests.

Self-Awareness and Early Emotional and Social Development. Recall that self-conscious emotions depend on a strengthening sense of self. Self-awareness also leads to first efforts to appreciate others' perspectives. Toddlers express first signs of **empathy**—the ability to understand another's emotional state and *feel with* that person, or respond emotionally in a similar way. For example, they communicate concern when others are distressed and may offer what they themselves find comforting—a hug, a reassuring comment, or a favorite doll or blanket (Hoffman, 2000; Moreno, Klute, & Robinson, 2008).

At the same time, toddlers demonstrate clearer awareness of how to upset others. One 18-month-old heard her mother talking to another adult about an older sibling: "Anny is really frightened of spiders" (Dunn, 1989, p. 107). The innocent-looking toddler ran to the bedroom, returned with the toy spider, and pushed it in front of Anny's face!

Categorizing the Self

By the end of the second year, language becomes a powerful tool in self-development. Between 18 and 30 months, children develop a **categorical self** as they classify themselves and others on the basis of age ("baby," "boy," or "man"), sex ("boy" or "girl"), physical characteristics ("big," "strong"), and even goodness versus badness ("I a good girl." "Tommy mean!") and competencies ("Did it!" "I can't") (Stipek, Gralinski, & Kopp, 1990).

Toddlers use their limited understanding of these social categories to organize their own behavior. As early as 17 months, they select and play in a more involved way with toys that are stereotyped for their own gender—dolls and tea sets for girls, trucks and cars for boys. Their ability to label their own gender predicts a sharp rise in these play preferences over the next few months (Zosuls et al., 2009). Then parents encourage gender-typed behavior by responding more positively when toddlers display it (Ruble, Martin, & Berenbaum, 2006). As we will see in Chapter 8, gender typing increases dramatically in early childhood.

Self-Control

Self-awareness also contributes to strengthening of effortful control (see page 149). To behave in a self-controlled fashion, children must think of themselves as separate, autonomous beings who can direct their own actions. And they must have the representational and memory capacities to recall a caregiver's directive ("Caitlin, don't touch that light socket!") and apply it to their own behavior.

As these capacities emerge between 12 and 18 months, toddlers first become capable of **compliance.** They show clear awareness of caregivers' wishes and expectations and can obey simple requests and commands. And as every parent knows, they can also decide to do just the opposite! But for most, assertiveness and opposition occur alongside compliance with an eager, willing spirit, which suggests that the child is beginning to adopt the adult's directives as his own (Dix et al., 2007; Kochanska, Murray, & Harlan, 2000). Compliance quickly leads to toddlers' first consciencelike verbalizations—for example, correcting the self by saying "No!" before touching a delicate object or jumping on the sofa.

Researchers often study self-control by giving children tasks that, like the situations just mentioned, require **delay of gratification**—waiting for an appropriate time and place to engage in a tempting act. Between ages 1½ and 3, children show an increasing capacity to wait before eating a treat, opening a present, or playing with a toy (Vaughn, Kopp, & Krakow, 1984). Children who are advanced in development of attention and language tend to be better at delaying gratification (Else-Quest et al., 2006). These findings help explain why girls are typically more self-controlled than boys.

Like effortful control in general, young children's capacity to delay gratification is influenced by both biologically based temperament and quality of caregiving (Kochanska & Aksan, 2006; Kochanska & Knaack, 2003). Inhibited children find it easier to wait than angry, irritable children do. But toddlers who experience parental warmth and simple (as opposed to lengthy, detailed) statements that patiently redirect their behavior are more likely to be cooperative and resist temptation (Blandon

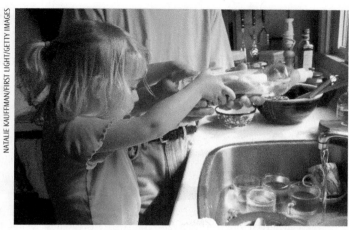

NATALIE KAUFFMAN/FIRST LIGHT/GETTY IMAGES

This toddler demonstrates compliance and the beginnings of self-control as she helps her father wash dishes. She eagerly joins in the task, suggesting that she is adopting the adult's directives as her own.

& Volling, 2008; Hakman & Sullivan, 2009). Recall that such parenting, which encourages and models patient, nonimpulsive behavior, is particularly important for emotionally reactive children (see page 152).

As self-control improves, parents gradually increase the range of rules they expect toddlers to follow, from safety and respect for property and people to family routines, manners, and simple chores (Gralinski & Kopp, 1993). Still, toddlers' control over their own actions depends on constant parental oversight and reminders. Several prompts ("Remember, we're going to go in just a minute") and gentle insistence were usually necessary to get Caitlin to stop playing so that she and her parents could go on an errand. Applying What We Know on page 162 summarizes ways to help toddlers develop compliance and self-control.

As the second year of life drew to a close, Carolyn, Monica, and Vanessa were delighted at their children's readiness to learn the rules of social life. As we will see in Chapter 8, advances in cognition and language, along with parental warmth and reasonable demands for maturity, lead preschoolers to make tremendous strides in this area.

ASK YOURSELF

REVIEW What type of early parenting fosters the development of emotional self-regulation, secure attachment, and self-control? Why, in each instance, is it effective?

APPLY Len, a caregiver of 1- and 2-year-olds, wonders whether toddlers recognize themselves. List signs of self-recognition in the second year that Len can observe.

REFLECT Do you think that "the terrible twos," a commonly used expression to characterize toddler behavior, is an apt description? Explain.

Applying What We Know

Helping Toddlers Develop Compliance and Self-Control

Suggestion	Rationale
Respond with sensitivity and encouragement.	Toddlers whose parents are sensitive and supportive actively resist at times, but they are also more compliant and self-controlled.
Provide advance notice when the toddler must stop an enjoyable activity.	Toddlers find it more difficult to stop a pleasant activity that is already under way than to wait before engaging in a desired action.
Offer many prompts and reminders.	Toddlers' ability to remember and comply with rules is limited; they need continuous adult oversight and patient assistance.
Respond to self-controlled behavior with verbal and physical approval.	Praise and hugs reinforce appropriate behavior, increasing the likelihood that it will occur again.
Encourage selective and sustained attention (see Chapter 5, page 127).	Development of attention is related to self-control. Children who can shift attention from a captivating stimulus and focus on a less attractive alternative are better at controlling their impulses.
Support language development (see Chapter 5, page 139).	In the second year, children begin to use language to remind themselves of adult expectations and to delay gratification.
Gradually increase rules in a manner consistent with the toddler's developing capacities.	As cognition and language improve, toddlers can follow more rules related to safety, respect for people and property, family routines, manners, and simple chores.

SUMMARY

Erikson's Theory of Infant and Toddler Personality (p. 143)

According to Erikson's psychosocial theory, how do infants and toddlers resolve the psychological conflicts of the first two years?

- Warm, responsive caregiving leads infants to resolve the psychological conflict of **basic trust versus mistrust** on the positive side. During toddlerhood, **autonomy versus shame and doubt** is resolved favorably when parents provide appropriate guidance and reasonable choices.

Emotional Development (p. 144)

Describe the development of basic emotions over the first year.

- During the first half-year, **basic emotions** gradually become clear, well-organized signals. The **social smile** appears between 6 and 10 weeks, laughter around 3 to 4 months. Happiness strengthens the parent–child bond and both reflects and supports physical and cognitive mastery.

- Anger and fear, especially in the form of **stranger anxiety,** increase in the second half-year as infants' cognitive and motor capacities improve. Newly mobile babies use the familiar caregiver as a **secure base** from which to explore.

Summarize changes during the first two years in understanding others' emotions, expression of self-conscious emotions, and emotional self-regulation.

- As infants' ability to detect the meaning of emotional expressions improves over the first year, **social referencing,** appears. By the middle of the second year, toddlers appreciate that others' emotional reactions may differ from their own.

- During toddlerhood, self-awareness and adult instruction provide the foundation for **self-conscious emotions. Emotional self-regulation** emerges as the prefrontal cortex functions more effectively and as caregivers build on the infants' increasing tolerance for stimulation. When caregivers are emotionally sympathetic but set limits, children develop more effective anger-regulation strategies in the preschool years.

Temperament and Development (p. 148)

What is temperament, and how is it measured?

- **Temperament** refers to early-appearing, stable individual differences in reactivity and self-regulation. The New York Longitudinal Study identified three patterns: the **easy child,** the **difficult child,** and the **slow-to-warm-up child.** Mary Rothbart's model of temperament includes **effortful control,** the ability to regulate one's reactivity.

- Temperament is assessed through parental reports, behavior ratings by others familiar with the child, and laboratory observations. Most neurobiological research has focused on distinguishing **inhibited,** or **shy, children** from **uninhibited,** or **sociable, children.**

What roles do heredity and environment play in the stability of temperament?

- Stability of temperament is generally low to moderate. Temperament has a genetic foundation, but child rearing and cultural beliefs and practices have much to do with maintaining or changing it.

- According to the **goodness-of-fit model,** parenting practices that fit well with the child's temperament help children achieve more adaptive functioning.

Development of Attachment
(p. 152)

Describe the development of attachment during the first two years.

- **Ethological theory,** the most widely accepted perspective on **attachment,** recognizes the infant's emotional tie to the caregiver as an evolved response that promotes survival. In early infancy, a set of built-in behaviors encourages the parent to remain close to the baby.

- Around 6 to 8 months, **separation anxiety** and use of the caregiver as a secure base indicate that a true attachment bond has formed. As representation and language develop, separation protest declines. From early caregiving experiences, children construct an **internal working model** that guides future close relationships.

How do researchers measure attachment security, what factors affect it, and what are its implications for later development?

- Using the **Strange Situation,** a laboratory technique for assessing the quality of attachment between 1 and 2 years, researchers have identified four attachment patterns: **secure, avoidant, resistant,** and **disorganized/ disoriented.** The **Attachment Q-Sort,** a home observation method suitable for 1- to 4-year-olds, yields a score ranging from high to low in security.

- Securely attached babies more often maintain their attachment pattern than insecure babies, although the disorganized/disoriented pattern is highly stable. Cultural conditions must be considered in interpreting attachment patterns.

- Attachment quality is influenced by early availability of a consistent caregiver, **sensitive caregiving,** the fit between the baby's temperament and parenting practices, and family circumstances, including parents' internal working models.

- Continuity of caregiving is the crucial factor determining whether attachment security is linked to later development. If caregiving improves, children can recover from an insecure attachment history.

Describe infants' capacity for multiple attachments.

- Infants develop strong affectionate ties to fathers, who tend to engage in more exciting, physical play with babies than mothers do. Infants begin to build rich emotional relationships with siblings that mix affection and caring with rivalry and resentment. Individual differences in the quality of sibling relationships are influenced by temperament and parenting.

Self-Development (p. 159)

Describe the development of self-awareness in infancy and toddlerhood, along with the emotional and social capacities it supports.

- Babies' capacity for intermodal perception supports early self-awareness. Around age 2, **self-recognition**—identification of the self as a physically unique being—is well under way. However, toddlers make **scale errors,** attempting to do things that their body size makes impossible.

- Self-awareness leads to first signs of **empathy.** As language strengthens, toddlers develop a **categorical self** based on age, sex, physical characteristics, goodness versus badness, and competencies.

- Self-awareness provides the foundation for the emergence of **compliance** between 12 and 18 months and gains in **delay of gratification** between 1½ and 3 years. Children who are advanced in development of attention and language and who have warm, encouraging parents tend to be more self-controlled.

Important Terms and Concepts

attachment (p. 152)
Attachment Q-Sort (p. 154)
autonomy versus shame and doubt (p. 143)
avoidant attachment (p. 154)
basic emotions (p. 144)
basic trust versus mistrust (p. 143)
categorical self (p. 160)
compliance (p. 161)
delay of gratification (p. 161)
difficult child (p. 148)
disorganized/disoriented attachment (p. 154)
easy child (p. 148)

effortful control (p. 149)
emotional self-regulation (p. 147)
empathy (p. 160)
ethological theory of attachment (p. 153)
goodness-of-fit model (p. 151)
inhibited, or shy, child (p. 149)
internal working model (p. 153)
resistant attachment (p. 154)
scale errors (p. 160)
secure attachment (p. 154)
secure base (p. 146)
self-conscious emotions (p. 147)

self-recognition (p. 160)
sensitive caregiving (p. 156)
separation anxiety (p. 153)
slow-to-warm-up child (p. 148)
social referencing (p. 146)
social smile (p. 144)
stranger anxiety (p. 146)
Strange Situation (p. 154)
temperament (p. 148)
uninhibited, or sociable, child (p. 149)

milestones

Development in Infancy and Toddlerhood

ARIEL SKELLY/BLEND IMAGES/GETTY IMAGES

Birth–6 months

PHYSICAL

- Height and weight increase rapidly. (93)
- Newborn reflexes decline. (83)
- Distinguishes basic tastes and odors; shows preference for sweet-tasting foods. (86–87)
- Responses can be classically and operantly conditioned. (103–104)
- Habituates to unchanging stimuli; recovers to novel stimuli. (104)
- Sleep is increasingly organized into a night–day schedule. (98)
- Holds head up, rolls over, and grasps objects. (106, 108)
- Perceives auditory and visual stimuli as organized patterns. (109, 111, 112)
- Shows sensitivity to motion, then binocular, and finally pictorial depth cues. (111)
- Recognizes and prefers human facial pattern; recognizes features of mother's face. (112–113)
- Masters a wide range of intermodal (visual, auditory, and tactile) relationships. (113–114)

COGNITIVE

- Engages in immediate and deferred imitation of adults' facial expressions. (105, 122)
- Repeats chance behaviors that lead to pleasurable and interesting results. (119–120)

- Has some awareness of many physical properties (including object permanence) and basic numerical knowledge. (121, 125)
- Recognition memory for visual events improves. (127–128)
- Attention becomes more efficient and flexible. (127)
- Categorizes objects on the basis of similar physical features. (128)

LANGUAGE

- Coos and, by end of this period, babbles. (137)
- Begins to establish joint attention with caregiver, who labels objects and events. (137)

EMOTIONAL/SOCIAL

- Social smile and laughter emerge. (144)
- Matches feeling tone of caregiver in face-to-face communication; later, expects matched responses. (146)

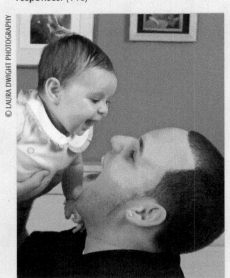

© LAURA DWIGHT PHOTOGRAPHY

- Emotional expressions become well-organized and meaningfully related to environmental events. (144)

- Regulates emotion by shifting attention and self-soothing. (147)
- Awareness of self as physically distinct from surroundings increases. (160)

7–12 months

PHYSICAL

- Approaches adultlike sleep–wake schedule. (98)
- Sits alone, crawls, and walks. (106)

JGI/BLEND IMAGES/GETTY IMAGES

- Reaching and grasping improve in flexibility and accuracy; shows refined pincer grasp. (108–109)
- Intermodal perception continues to improve. (113–114)

COGNITIVE

- Engages in intentional, or goal-directed, behavior. (120)
- Finds object hidden in an initial location. (120)
- Recall memory improves, as indicated by ability to find hidden objects and engage in deferred imitation. (122–123, 128)
- Solves simple problems by analogy to a previous problem. (123)
- Categorizes objects on the basis of subtle sets of features, even when the perceptual contrast between categories is minimal. (128)

Note: Numbers in parentheses indicate the page or pages on which each milestone is discussed.

LANGUAGE

- Babbling expands to include many sounds of spoken languages and patterns of the child's language community. (137)
- Joint attention with caregiver becomes more accurate. (137)
- Takes turns in games, such as pat-a-cake and peekaboo. (137)
- Comprehends some word meanings. (138)
- Uses preverbal gestures (showing, pointing) to influence others' behavior. (137)

- Around end of this period, understands displaced reference of words and says first words. (123, 138)

EMOTIONAL/SOCIAL

- Smiling and laughter increase in frequency and expressiveness. (144)
- Anger and fear increase in frequency and intensity. (144, 146)
- Stranger anxiety and separation anxiety appear. (146, 153)
- Uses caregiver as a secure base for exploration. (146)
- Shows "clear-cut" attachment to familiar caregivers. (153)
- Increasingly detects the meaning of others' emotional expressions and engages in social referencing. (146)
- Regulates emotion by approaching and retreating from stimulation. (147)

13–18 months

PHYSICAL

- Height and weight gain are rapid, but not as great as in first year. (93)
- Walking is better coordinated. (106, 107)
- Manipulates small objects with improved coordination. (108–109)

COGNITIVE

- Explores the properties of objects by acting on them in novel ways. (120)
- Searches in several locations for a hidden object. (120)
- Engages in deferred imitation of adults' actions with objects over longer delays and across a change in context—for example, from child care to home. (122–123)
- Sustained attention improves. (127)
- Recall memory improves further. (128)
- Sorts objects into categories. (128, 130)
- Realizes that pictures can symbolize real objects. (123)

LANGUAGE

- Steadily adds to vocabulary. (138)

EMOTIONAL/SOCIAL

- Joins in play with familiar adults and siblings. (158, 159)

- Realizes that others' emotional reactions may differ from one's own. (146)
- Complies with simple directives. (161)

19–24 months

PHYSICAL

- Jumps, walks on tiptoe, and runs. (106)
- Manipulates small objects with good coordination. (108–109)

COGNITIVE

- Solves simple problems using representation. (120)
- Finds a hidden object that has been moved while out of sight. (120)
- Engages in make-believe play, using simple actions experienced in everyday life. (121, 131)

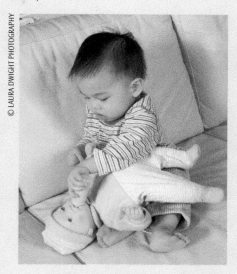

- Engages in deferred imitation of actions an adult tries to produce, even if not fully realized. (123)
- Categorizes objects conceptually, on the basis of common function or behavior. (130)

LANGUAGE

- Produces 200 to 250 words. (138)
- Combines two words. (138)

EMOTIONAL/SOCIAL

- Self-conscious emotions (shame, embarrassment, guilt, envy, and pride) emerge. (147)
- Acquires a vocabulary for talking about feelings. (148)
- Begins to use language to assist with emotional self-regulation. (148)
- Begins to tolerate caregiver's absences more easily; separation anxiety declines. (154)
- Recognizes image of self and, by end of this period, uses own name or personal pronoun to refer to self. (160)
- Less often makes scale errors. (160)
- Shows signs of empathy. (160)
- Categorizes self and others on the basis of age, sex, physical characteristics, and goodness and badness. (160–161)
- Shows gender-stereotyped toy preferences. (161)
- Self-control, as indicated by delay of gratification, emerges. (161)

chapter 8

Emotional and Social Development in Early Childhood

© ELLEN B. SENISI PHOTOGRAPHY

During the preschool years, children make great strides in understanding the thoughts and feelings of others, and they build on these skills as they form first friendships—special relationships marked by attachment and common interests.

chapter outline

As the children in Leslie's classroom moved through the preschool years, their personalities took on clearer definition. By age 3, they voiced firm likes and dislikes as well as new ideas about themselves. "See, I'm great at this game," Sammy announced with confidence, as he aimed a beanbag toward the mouth of a large clown face—an attitude that kept him trying, even though he missed most of the throws.

The children's conversations also revealed early notions about morality. Often they combined adults' statements about right and wrong with forceful attempts to defend their own desires. "You're 'posed to share," stated Mark, grabbing the beanbag out of Sammy's hand.

"I was here first! Gimme it back," demanded Sammy, pushing Mark. The two boys struggled until Leslie intervened, provided an extra set of beanbags, and showed them how they could both play.

As the interaction between Sammy and Mark reveals, preschoolers quickly become complex social beings. Young children argue, grab, and push, but cooperative exchanges are far more frequent. Between ages 2 and 6, first friendships form, in which children converse, act out complementary roles, and learn that their own desires for companionship and toys are best met when they consider others' needs and interests.

The children's developing understanding of their social world was especially apparent in their growing attention to gender roles. While Priti and Karen cared for a sick baby doll in the housekeeping area, Sammy, Vance, and Mark transformed the block corner into a busy intersection. "Green light, go!" shouted police officer Sammy as Vance and Mark pushed large wooden cars and trucks across the floor. Already, the children preferred peers of their own gender, and their play themes mirrored their culture's gender stereotypes.

This chapter is devoted to the many facets of early childhood emotional and social development. We begin with Erik Erikson's view of personality change in the preschool years. Then we consider children's concepts of themselves, their insights into their social and moral worlds, their gender typing, and their increasing ability to manage their emotional and social behaviors. Finally, we ask, What is effective child rearing? And we discuss the complex conditions that support good parenting or lead it to break down. ●

Erikson's Theory: Initiative versus Guilt

According to Erikson (1950), once children have a sense of autonomy, they become less contrary than they were as toddlers. Their energies are freed for tackling the psychological conflict of the preschool years: **initiative versus guilt**. As the word *initiative* suggests, young children have a new sense of purposefulness. They are eager to tackle new tasks, join in activities with peers, and discover what they can do with the help of adults. They also make strides in conscience development.

Erikson regarded play as a means through which young children learn about themselves and their social world. Play creates a small social organization of children who try out culturally meaningful roles and skills and who cooperate to achieve common goals. Around the world, children act out family scenes and highly visible occupations—police officer, doctor, and nurse in Western societies, hut builder and spear maker among the Baka of West Africa (Göncü, Patt, & Kouba, 2004).

Through patient, reasonable adult guidance and play experiences with peers, preschoolers also acquire both the moral and gender-role standards of their society. For Erikson, the negative outcome of early childhood is an overly strict conscience, or superego (see Chapter 1, page 12) that causes children to feel too much guilt because they have been threatened, criticized, and punished excessively by adults. When this happens, preschoolers' exuberant play and bold efforts to master new tasks break down.

As we will see, Erikson's image of initiative captures the diverse changes in young children's emotional and social lives. Early childhood is, indeed, a time when children develop a confident self-image, more effective control over their emotions, new social skills, the foundations of morality, and a sense of themselves as boy or girl.

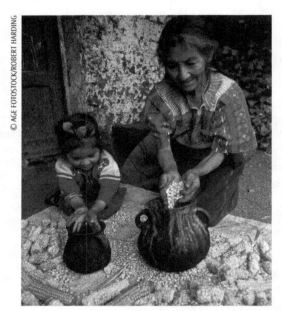

A Guatemalan 3-year-old pretends to shell corn. By acting out family scenes and highly visible occupations, young children around the world develop a sense of initiative, gaining insight into what they can do and become in their culture.

Self-Understanding

In Chapter 7, we noted that young children acquire a vocabulary for talking about their inner mental lives and gain in understanding of mental states. As self-awareness strengthens, preschoolers focus more intently on qualities that make the self unique. They begin to develop a **self-concept,** the set of attributes, abilities, attitudes, and values that an individual believes defines who he or she is.

Foundations of Self-Concept

Ask a 3- to 5-year-old to tell you about himself, and you are likely to hear something like this: "I'm Tommy. See, I got this new red T-shirt. I'm 4 years old. I have a new Tinkertoy set, and I made this big, big tower." Preschoolers' self-concepts consist largely of observable characteristics, such as their name, physical appearance, possessions, and everyday behaviors (Harter, 2006; Watson, 1990).

By age 3½, children also describe themselves in terms of typical emotions and attitudes—"I'm happy when I play with my friends"; "I don't like scary TV programs"; "I usually do what Mommy says"—suggesting a beginning understanding of their unique psychological characteristics (Eder & Mangelsdorf, 1997). And by age 5, children's degree of agreement with such statements coincides with maternal reports of their personality traits, indicating that older preschoolers have a sense of their own timidity, agreeableness, and positive or negative affect (Brown et al., 2008). But preschoolers do not yet say, "I'm helpful" or "I'm shy." Direct references to personality traits must wait for greater cognitive maturity.

A warm, sensitive parent–child relationship seems to foster a more positive, coherent early self-concept. In one study, 4-year-olds with a secure attachment to their mothers were more likely than their insecurely attached agemates to describe themselves in favorable terms at age 5—with statements that reflect agreeableness and positive affect (Goodvin et al., 2008). Also recall from Chapter 7 that securely attached preschoolers participate in more elaborative parent–child conversations about personally experienced events, which help them understand themselves (see page 186).

As early as age 2, parents use narratives of past events to impart rules, standards for behavior, and evaluative information about the child: "You added the milk when we made the mashed potatoes. That's a very important job!" (Nelson, 2003). These self-evaluative narratives are a major means through which caregivers imbue the young child's self-concept with cultural values. In observational research on Irish-American families in Chicago and Chinese families in Taiwan, Chinese parents frequently told their preschoolers long stories about the child's misdeeds. In a warm, caring tone, they stressed the impact of the child's misbehavior on others ("You made Mama lose face."). Irish-American parents, in contrast, rarely dwelt on children's transgressions and, when they did, interpreted these acts positively ("He's got a lot of spunk!") (Miller et al., 1997, 2002, 2012).

Consistent with these narrative differences, the Chinese child's self-image emphasizes obligations to others, whereas the American child's is more autonomous.

Emergence of Self-Esteem

Another aspect of self-concept emerges in early childhood: **self-esteem,** the judgments we make about our own worth and the feelings associated with those judgments. *TAKE A MOMENT...* Make a list of your own self-judgments. Notice that, besides a global appraisal of your worth as a person, you have a variety of separate self-evaluations concerning how well you perform at different activities. These evaluations are among the most important aspects of self-development because they affect our emotional experiences, future behavior, and long-term psychological adjustment.

By age 4, preschoolers have several self-judgments—for example, about learning things in school, making friends, getting along with parents, and treating others kindly (Marsh, Ellis, & Craven, 2002). But because they have difficulty distinguishing between their desired and their actual competence, they usually rate their own ability as extremely high and underestimate task difficulty, as when Sammy asserted, despite his many misses, that he was great at beanbag throwing (Harter, 2006).

High self-esteem contributes greatly to preschoolers' initiative. By age 3, children whose parents criticize their worth and performance give up easily when faced with a challenge and express shame and despondency after failing (Kelley, Brownell, & Campbell, 2000). Adults can avoid promoting these self-defeating reactions by adjusting their expectations to children's capacities, scaffolding children's attempts at difficult tasks (see Chapter 7, page 182), and pointing out effort and improvement in children's behavior.

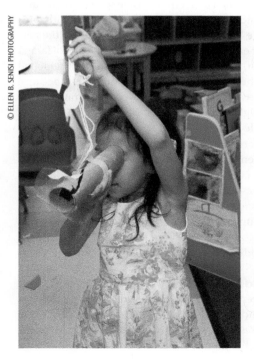

After creating a "camera" and "flash," this preschooler pretends to take pictures. Her high self-esteem contributes greatly to her initiative in mastering many new skills.

Emotional Development

Gains in representation, language, and self-concept support emotional development in early childhood. Between ages 2 and 6, children achieve a better understanding of their own and others' feelings, and *emotional self-regulation* improves. In addition, preschoolers more often experience *self-conscious emotions* and *empathy*, which contribute to their developing sense of morality.

Understanding Emotion

Early in the preschool years, children refer to causes, consequences, and behavioral signs of emotion, and over time their understanding becomes more accurate and complex (Stein & Levine, 1999). By age 4 to 5, children correctly judge the causes of many basic emotions ("He's happy because he's swinging very high"; "He's sad because he misses his mother"). Preschoolers' explanations tend to emphasize external factors over internal states, a balance that changes with age (Levine, 1995). After age 4, children appreciate that both desires and beliefs motivate behavior (Chapter 7). Then their grasp of how internal factors can trigger emotion expands.

Preschoolers can also predict what a playmate expressing a certain emotion might do next. Four-year-olds know that an angry child might hit someone and that a happy child is more likely to share (Russell, 1990). And they realize that thinking and feeling are interconnected—that a person reminded of a previous sad experience is likely to feel sad (Lagattuta, Wellman, & Flavell, 1997). Furthermore, they come up with effective ways to relieve others' negative feelings, such as hugging to reduce sadness (Fabes et al., 1988).

The more parents label emotions, explain them, and express warmth and enthusiasm when conversing with preschoolers, the more "emotion words" children use and the better developed their emotional understanding (Fivush & Haden, 2005). Furthermore, 3- to 5-year-olds who are securely attached to their mothers better understand emotion, likely because attachment security is related to parent–child narratives that more often highlight the emotional significance of events (Laible, 2004; Laible & Song, 2006; Raikes & Thompson, 2006).

As preschoolers learn about emotion from interacting with adults, they engage in more emotion talk with siblings and friends, especially during make-believe play (Hughes & Dunn, 1998). Make-believe, in turn, contributes to emotional understanding, especially when children play with siblings (Youngblade & Dunn, 1995). The intense nature of the sibling relationship, combined with frequent acting out of feelings, makes pretending an excellent context for learning about emotions.

As early as 3 to 5 years of age, knowledge about emotions is linked to children's friendly, considerate behavior, willingness to make amends after harming another, and constructive responses to disputes with agemates (Dunn, Brown, & Maguire,

1995; Garner & Estep, 2001; Hughes & Ensor, 2010). Also, the more preschoolers refer to feelings when interacting with playmates, the better liked they are by their peers (Fabes et al., 2001). Children seem to recognize that acknowledging others' emotions and explaining their own enhance the quality of relationships.

Emotional Self-Regulation

Language also contributes to preschoolers' improved *emotional self-regulation* (Cole, Armstrong, & Pemberton, 2010). By age 3 to 4, children verbalize a variety of strategies for adjusting their emotional arousal to a more comfortable level. For example, they know they can blunt emotions by restricting sensory input (covering their eyes or ears to block out an unpleasant sight or sound), talking to themselves ("Mommy said she'll be back soon"), or changing their goals (deciding that they don't want to play anyway after being excluded from a game) (Thompson & Goodvin, 2007). As children use these strategies, emotional outbursts decline. *Effortful control*—in particular, inhibiting impulses and shifting attention—also continues to be vital in managing emotion. Three-year-olds who can distract themselves when frustrated tend to become cooperative school-age children with few problem behaviors (Gilliom et al., 2002).

Warm, patient parents who explain strategies for controlling feelings strengthen children's capacity to handle stress (Colman et al., 2006; Morris et al., 2011). In contrast, when parents rarely express positive emotion, dismiss children's feelings as unimportant, and have difficulty controlling their own anger, children have continuing problems in managing emotion (Thompson & Goodman, 2010; Thompson & Meyer, 2007).

As with infants and toddlers, preschoolers who experience negative emotion intensely find it harder to shift attention away from disturbing events. They are more likely to be anxious and fearful, respond with irritation to others' distress, react angrily or aggressively when frustrated, and get along poorly with teachers and peers (Chang et al., 2003; Eisenberg et al., 2005a; Raikes et al., 2007).

Self-Conscious Emotions

One morning in Leslie's classroom, a group of children crowded around for a bread-baking activity. Leslie asked them to wait patiently while she got a baking pan. But Sammy reached over to feel the dough, and the bowl tumbled off the table. When Leslie returned, Sammy looked at her, then covered his eyes with his hands. He felt ashamed and guilty.

As their self-concepts develop, preschoolers become increasingly sensitive to praise and blame or to the possibility of such feedback. They more often experience *self-conscious emotions*—feelings that involve injury to or enhancement of their sense of self (see Chapter 6). By age 3, self-conscious emotions are clearly linked to self-evaluation (Lewis, 1995; Thompson, Meyer, & McGinley, 2006). But because preschoolers are still developing standards of excellence and conduct, they depend on the messages of parents, teachers, and others who matter to them to know *when* to feel proud, ashamed, or guilty (Thompson, Meyer, & McGinley, 2006).

When parents repeatedly comment on the worth of the child and her performance ("That's a bad job! I thought you were a good girl!"), children experience self-conscious emotions intensely—more shame after failure, more pride after success. In contrast, parents who focus on how to improve performance ("You did it this way; now try it that way") induce moderate, more adaptive levels of shame and pride and greater persistence on difficult tasks (Kelley, Brownell, & Campbell, 2000; Lewis, 1998).

Among Western children, intense shame is associated with feelings of personal inadequacy ("I'm stupid"; "I'm a terrible person") and with maladjustment—withdrawal and depression as well as intense anger and aggression toward those who shamed them (Lindsay-Hartz, de Rivera, & Mascolo, 1995; Mills, 2005). In contrast, guilt—when it occurs in appropriate circumstances and is not accompanied by shame—is related to good adjustment. Guilt helps children resist harmful impulses, and it motivates a misbehaving child to repair the damage and behave more considerately (Mascolo & Fischer, 2007; Tangney, Stuewig, & Mashek, 2007). But overwhelming guilt—involving such high emotional distress that the child cannot make amends—is linked to depressive symptoms as early as age 3 (Luby et al., 2009).

The consequences of shame for children's adjustment, however, may vary across cultures. As Chinese parents' narratives about their child's misdeeds illustrate (see page 201), adults in Asian collectivist societies more often induce shame in children, viewing it as an adaptive reminder of the importance of others' judgments (Bedford, 2004).

Empathy and Sympathy

Another emotional capacity, *empathy,* serves as an important motivator of **prosocial,** or **altruistic, behavior**—actions that benefit another person without any expected reward for the self (Spinrad & Eisenberg, 2009). Compared with toddlers, preschoolers rely more on words to communicate empathic feelings. And as the ability to take another's perspective improves, empathic responding increases.

Yet in some children, empathy—*feeling with* another person and responding emotionally in a similar way—does not yield acts of kindness and helpfulness but, instead, escalates into personal distress. In trying to reduce these feelings, the child focuses on his own anxiety rather than the person in need. As a result, empathy does not lead to **sympathy**—feelings of concern or sorrow for another's plight.

Temperament plays a role in whether empathy prompts sympathetic, prosocial behavior or self-focused personal distress. Children who are sociable, assertive, and good at regulating emotion are more likely to help, share, and comfort others in distress (Bengtsson, 2005; Eisenberg et al., 1998; Valiente et al., 2004). But poor emotion regulators, who are often over-

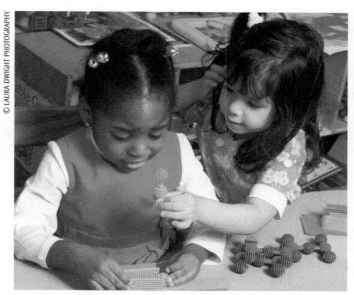

As children's language skills and capacity to take the perspective of others improve, empathy also increases, motivating prosocial, or altruistic, behavior.

whelmed by their feelings, less often display sympathetic concern and prosocial behavior.

As with other aspects of emotional development, parenting affects empathy and sympathy. When parents show sensitive, empathic concern for their preschoolers' feelings, children are likely to react in a concerned way to the distress of others—relationships that persist into adolescence and early adulthood (Koestner, Franz, & Weinberger, 1990; Michalik et al., 2007). Besides modeling sympathy, parents can teach children the importance of kindness and can intervene when they display inappropriate emotion—strategies that predict high levels of sympathetic responding (Eisenberg, 2003).

Peer Relations

As children become increasingly self-aware and better at communicating and understanding others' thoughts and feelings, their skill at interacting with peers improves rapidly. Peers provide young children with learning experiences they can get in no other way. Because peers interact on an equal footing, children must keep a conversation going, cooperate, and set goals in play. With peers, children form friendships—special relationships marked by attachment and common interests.

Advances in Peer Sociability

Mildred Parten (1932), one of the first to study peer sociability among 2- to 5-year-olds, noticed a dramatic rise with age in joint, interactive play. She concluded that social development proceeds in a three-step sequence. It begins with **nonsocial activity**—unoccupied, onlooker behavior and solitary play.

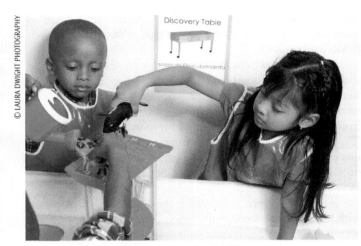

These 4-year-olds (left) engage in parallel play. Cooperative play (right) develops later than parallel play, but preschool children continue to move back and forth between the two types of sociability, using parallel play as a respite from the complex demands of cooperation.

Then it shifts to **parallel play,** in which a child plays near other children with similar materials but does not try to influence their behavior. At the highest level are two forms of true social interaction. In **associative play,** children engage in separate activities but exchange toys and comment on one another's behavior. Finally, in **cooperative play,** a more advanced type of interaction, children orient toward a common goal, such as acting out a make-believe theme.

Follow-Up Research on Peer Sociability. Longitudinal evidence indicates that these play forms emerge in the order suggested by Parten but that later-appearing ones do not replace earlier ones (Rubin, Bukowski, & Parker, 2006). Rather, all types coexist in early childhood.

TAKE A MOMENT... Watch children move from one type of play to another in a play group or preschool classroom, and you will see that they often transition from onlooker to parallel to cooperative play and back again (Robinson et al., 2003). Preschoolers seem to use parallel play as a way station—a respite from the demands of complex social interaction and a crossroad to new activities. Also, both solitary and parallel play remain fairly stable from 3 to 6 years, accounting for as much of the child's play as cooperative interaction (Rubin, Fein, & Vandenberg, 1983).

We now understand that the *type,* not the amount, of solitary and parallel play changes in early childhood. In studies of preschoolers' play in Taiwan and the United States, researchers rated the *cognitive maturity* of nonsocial, parallel, and cooperative play, using the categories shown in Table 8.1. Within each play type, older children displayed more cognitively mature behavior than younger children (Pan, 1994; Rubin, Watson, & Jambor, 1978).

Often parents wonder whether a preschooler who spends much time playing alone is developing normally. But only *certain types* of nonsocial activity—aimless wandering, hovering near peers, and functional play involving repetitive motor action—are cause for concern. Children who watch peers without playing are usually temperamentally inhibited—high in social fearfulness (Coplan et al., 2004). And preschoolers who engage in solitary, repetitive behavior (banging blocks, making a doll jump up and down) tend to be immature, impulsive children who find it difficult to regulate anger and aggression (Coplan et al., 2001). In the classroom, both reticent and impulsive children tend to experience peer ostracism (Coplan & Arbeau, 2008). But most preschoolers with low rates of peer interaction simply like to play alone, and their solitary activities are positive and constructive. When they do play with peers, they show socially skilled behavior (Coplan & Armer, 2007).

TABLE 8.1

Developmental Sequence of Cognitive Play Categories

PLAY CATEGORY	DESCRIPTION	EXAMPLES
Functional play	Simple, repetitive motor movements with or without objects, especially common during the first two years	Running around a room, rolling a car back and forth, kneading clay with no intent to make something
Constructive play	Creating or constructing something, especially common between 3 and 6 years	Making a house out of toy blocks, drawing a picture, putting together a puzzle
Make-believe play	Acting out everyday and imaginary roles, especially common between 2 and 6 years	Playing house, school, or police officer; acting out storybook or television characters

Source: Rubin, Fein, & Vandenberg, 1983.

Agta village children in the Philippines play a tug-of-war game. Large-group, highly cooperative play is typical of peer sociability in collectivist societies.

Cultural Variations.   Peer sociability in collectivist societies, which stress group harmony, takes different forms than in individualistic cultures (Chen & French, 2008). For example, children in India generally play in large groups, which require high levels of cooperation. Much of their behavior is imitative, occurs in unison, and involves close physical contact. In a game called Bhatto Bhatto, children act out a script about a trip to the market, touching one another's elbows and hands as they pretend to cut and share a tasty vegetable (Roopnarine et al., 1994).

Cultural beliefs about the importance of play also affect early peer associations. Caregivers who view play as mere entertainment are less likely to provide props or to encourage pretend than those who value its cognitive and social benefits (Gaskins, 2000). Preschoolers of Korean-American parents, who emphasize task persistence as vital for learning, spend less time than Caucasian-American children in joint make-believe and more time unoccupied and in parallel play (Farver, Kim, & Lee, 1995).

First Friendships

As preschoolers interact, first friendships form that serve as important contexts for emotional and social development. Preschoolers understand that a friend is someone "who likes you," with whom you spend a lot of time playing, and with whom you share toys. But friendship does not yet have a long-term, enduring quality based on mutual trust (Damon, 1988a; Hartup, 2006). "Mark's my best friend," Sammy would declare on days when the boys got along well. But when a dispute arose, he would reverse himself: "Mark, you're not my friend!"

Nevertheless, interactions between young friends are unique. Preschool friends are more cooperative and emotionally expressive—talking, laughing, and looking at each other more often than nonfriends do (Hartup, 2006). Furthermore, children who begin kindergarten with friends in their class or readily make new friends adjust to school more favorably (Ladd, Birch, & Buhs, 1999; Ladd & Price, 1987). The company of friends seems to serve as a secure base from which to develop new relationships, enhancing children's feelings of comfort in the new classroom.

Peer Relations and School Readiness

The ease with which kindergartners are accepted by their classmates predicts cooperative participation in classroom activities and self-directed completion of learning tasks—behaviors linked to gains in achievement (Ladd, Birch, & Buhs, 1999; Ladd, Buhs, & Seid, 2000). Positive peer relationships enable kindergartners to integrate themselves into classroom environments in ways that foster both academic and social competence. In one study, 4-year-olds of average intelligence but with above-average social skills fared better in academic achievement in first grade than children of equal mental ability who were socially below average (Konold & Pianta, 2005).

Because social maturity in early childhood contributes to later academic performance, a growing number of experts propose that kindergarten readiness be assessed in terms of not just academic skills but also social skills (Ladd, Herald, & Kochel, 2006; Thompson & Raikes, 2007). Preschool programs, too, should attend to these vital social prerequisites. Warm, responsive teacher–child interaction is vital. In studies involving several thousand 4-year-olds in public preschools in six states, teacher sensitivity and emotional support were strong predictors of children's social competence, both during preschool and after kindergarten entry (Curby et al., 2009; Mashburn et al., 2008).

Parental Influences on Early Peer Relations

Children first acquire skills for interacting with peers within the family. Parents influence children's peer sociability both *directly,* through attempts to influence children's peer relations, and *indirectly,* through their child-rearing practices and play behaviors (Ladd & Pettit, 2002; Rubin et al., 2005).

Direct Parental Influences.   Preschoolers whose parents frequently arrange informal peer play activities tend to have larger peer networks and to be more socially skilled (Ladd, LeSieur, & Profilet, 1993). In providing play opportunities, parents show children how to initiate peer contacts. And parents' skillful suggestions for managing conflict, discouraging teasing, and entering a play group are associated with preschoolers' social competence and peer acceptance (Mize & Pettit, 2010; Parke et al., 2004).

Indirect Parental Influences.   Many parenting behaviors not directly aimed at promoting peer sociability nevertheless influence it. For example, secure attachments to parents are linked to more responsive, harmonious peer interaction, larger peer networks, and warmer, more supportive friendships during the preschool and school years (Laible, 2007; Lucas-Thompson

Through involved, emotionally positive play, this father promotes his child's capacity to engage in harmonious, supportive peer interaction.

& Clarke-Stewart, 2007; Wood, Emmerson, & Cowan, 2004). The sensitive, emotionally expressive communication that contributes to attachment security may be responsible. In several studies, involved, emotionally positive parent–child conversations and play predicted preschoolers' prosocial behavior and positive peer relations (Clark & Ladd, 2000; Lindsey & Mize, 2000).

As we have seen, some preschoolers already have great difficulty with peer relations. In Leslie's classroom, Robbie was one of them. Wherever he happened to be, comments like "Robbie ruined our block tower" and "Robbie hit me for no reason" could be heard. As we take up moral development in the next section, you will learn more about how parenting contributed to Robbie's peer problems.

ASK YOURSELF

REVIEW Among children who spend much time playing alone, what factors distinguish those who are likely to have adjustment difficulties from those who are well-adjusted and socially skilled?

APPLY Three-year-old Ben lives in the country, with no other preschoolers nearby. His parents wonder whether it is worth driving Ben into town once a week to participate in a peer play group. What advice would you give Ben's parents, and why?

REFLECT What did your parents do, directly and indirectly, that might have influenced your earliest peer relationships?

Foundations of Morality

Children's conversations and behavior provide many examples of their developing moral sense. By age 2, they use words to evaluate behavior as "good" or "bad" and react with distress to aggressive or otherwise harmful acts (Kochanska, Casey, & Fukumoto, 1995).

Adults everywhere take note of this budding capacity to distinguish right from wrong. Some cultures have special terms for it. The Utku Indians of Hudson Bay say the child develops *ihuma* (reason). The Fijians believe that *vakayalo* (sense) appears. In response, parents hold children more responsible for their behavior (Dunn, 2005). By the end of early childhood, children can state many moral rules: "Don't take someone's things without asking!" "Tell the truth!" In addition, they argue over matters of justice: "It's not fair. He got more!"

All theories of moral development recognize that conscience begins to take shape in early childhood. And most agree that at first, the child's morality is *externally controlled* by adults. Gradually, it becomes regulated by *inner standards*. Truly moral individuals do not do the right thing just to conform to others' expectations. Rather, they have developed compassionate concerns and principles of good conduct, which they follow in many situations.

Each major theory emphasizes a different aspect of morality. Psychoanalytic theory stresses the *emotional side* of conscience development—in particular, identification and guilt as motivators of good conduct. Social learning theory focuses on how *moral behavior* is learned through reinforcement and modeling. Finally, the cognitive-developmental perspective emphasizes *thinking*—children's ability to reason about justice and fairness.

The Psychoanalytic Perspective

Recall from Chapter 1 that according to Freud, young children form a *superego*, or conscience, by adopting the same-sex parent's moral standards. Children obey the superego to avoid *guilt*, a painful emotion that arises each time they are tempted to misbehave. Moral development, Freud believed, is largely complete by 5 to 6 years of age.

Today, most researchers disagree with Freud's view of conscience development. In his theory, fear of punishment and loss of parental love motivate conscience formation and moral behavior. Yet children whose parents frequently use threats, commands, or physical force tend to violate standards often and feel little guilt, whereas parental warmth and responsiveness predict greater guilt following transgressions (Kochanska et al., 2005, 2008). And if a parent withdraws love after misbehavior—for example, refuses to speak to or states a dislike for the child—children often respond with high levels of self-blame, thinking "I'm no good." Eventually, to protect themselves from overwhelming guilt, these children may deny the emotion and, as a result, also develop a weak conscience (Kochanska, 1991).

A teacher uses inductive discipline to explain to a child the impact of her transgression on others, pointing out classmates' feelings. Induction encourages empathy, sympathy, and commitment to moral standards.

Inductive Discipline. In contrast, conscience formation is promoted by a type of discipline called **induction,** in which an adult helps the child notice feelings by pointing out the effects of the child's misbehavior on others. For example, a parent might say, "She's crying because you won't give back her doll" (Hoffman, 2000). Preschoolers with warm parents who use induction are more likely to refrain from wrongdoing, confess and repair damage after misdeeds, and display prosocial behavior (Kerr et al., 2004; Volling, Mahoney, & Rauer, 2009; Zahn-Waxler, Radke-Yarrow, & King, 1979).

The success of induction may lie in its power to motivate children's active commitment to moral standards. By emphasizing the impact of the child's actions on others, it encourages empathy and sympathy (Krevans & Gibbs, 1996). And giving children reasons for changing their behavior encourages them to adopt moral standards because they make sense.

The Child's Contribution. Although good discipline is crucial, children's characteristics also affect the success of parenting techniques. Twin studies suggest a modest genetic contribution to empathy (Knafo et al., 2009). A highly empathic child is more responsive to induction.

Temperament is also influential. Mild, patient tactics—requests, suggestions, and explanations—are sufficient to prompt guilt reactions in anxious, fearful preschoolers (Kochanska et al., 2002). But with fearless, impulsive children, gentle discipline has little impact. Power assertion also works poorly. It undermines the child's capacity for effortful control, which strongly predicts good conduct, empathy, sympathy, and prosocial behavior (Kochanska & Aksan, 2006; Kochanska & Knaack, 2003). Parents of impulsive children can foster conscience development by ensuring a secure attachment relationship and combining firm correction with induction (Kochanska, Aksan, & Joy, 2007). When children are so low in anxiety that parental disapproval causes them little discomfort, a close parent–child bond motivates them to listen to parents as a means of preserving an affectionate, supportive relationship.

The Role of Guilt. Although little support exists for Freudian ideas about conscience development, Freud was correct that guilt is an important motivator of moral action. Inducing *empathy-based guilt* (expressions of personal responsibility and regret, such as "I'm sorry I hurt him") by explaining that the child is harming someone and has disappointed the parent is a means of influencing children without using coercion. Empathy-based guilt reactions are associated with stopping harmful actions, repairing damage caused by misdeeds, and engaging in future prosocial behavior (Baumeister, 1998; Eisenberg, Eggum, & Edwards, 2010).

But contrary to what Freud believed, guilt is not the only force that compels us to act morally. Nor is moral development complete by the end of early childhood. Rather, it is a gradual process, extending into adulthood.

Social Learning Theory

According to social learning theory, moral behavior is acquired just like any other set of responses: through reinforcement and modeling.

Importance of Modeling. *Operant conditioning*—reinforcement for good behavior with approval, affection, and other rewards—is not enough for children to acquire moral responses. For a behavior to be reinforced, it must first occur spontaneously. Yet many prosocial acts, such as sharing, helping, or comforting an unhappy playmate, occur so rarely at first that reinforcement cannot explain their rapid development in early childhood. Rather, social learning theorists believe that children learn to behave morally largely through *modeling*—observing and imitating people who demonstrate appropriate behavior (Bandura, 1977; Grusec, 1988). Once children acquire a moral response, reinforcement in the form of praise increases its frequency (Mills & Grusec, 1989).

Many studies show that having helpful or generous models increases young children's prosocial responses. Models are most

As this preschooler imitates his father's laundry folding, he internalizes a family prosocial rule: everyone helps with household chores.

influential in the early years. In one study, toddlers' eager, willing imitation of their mothers' behavior predicted moral conduct (not cheating in a game) and guilt following transgressions at age 3 (Forman, Aksan, & Kochanska, 2004). At the end of early childhood, children who have had consistent exposure to caring adults have internalized prosocial rules and follow them whether or not a model is present (Mussen & Eisenberg-Berg, 1977).

Effects of Punishment.

A sharp reprimand or physical force to restrain or move a child is justified when immediate obedience is necessary—for example, when a 3-year-old is about to run into the street. In fact, parents are most likely to use forceful methods under these conditions. But to foster long-term goals, such as acting kindly toward others, they tend to rely on warmth and reasoning (Kuczynski, 1984). And in response to very serious transgressions, such as lying and stealing, they often combine power assertion with reasoning (Grusec, 2006).

Frequent punishment, however, promotes only momentary compliance. For example, Robbie's parents often punished by hitting, criticizing, and shouting at him. But as soon as they were out of sight, Robbie usually engaged in the unacceptable behavior again. The more harsh threats, angry physical control, and physical punishment children experience, the more likely they are to develop serious, lasting mental health problems. These include weak internalization of moral rules; depression, aggression, antisocial behavior, and poor academic performance in childhood and adolescence; and depression, alcohol abuse, criminality, and partner and child abuse in adulthood (Afifi et al., 2006; Bender et al., 2007; Gershoff, 2002a; Kochanska, Aksan, & Nichols, 2003; Lynch et al., 2006).

Repeated harsh punishment has wide-ranging, undesirable side effects:

- It models aggression.

- It induces a chronic sense of being personally threatened, which prompts children to focus on their own distress rather than respond sympathetically to others.

- It causes children to avoid the punishing adult, who, as a result, has little opportunity to teach desirable behaviors.

- By stopping children's misbehavior temporarily, it offers immediate relief to adults, who may then punish more often—a course of action that can spiral into serious abuse.

- Adults whose parents used corporal punishment—the use of physical force to inflict pain but not injury—are more accepting of it (Deater-Deckard et al., 2003; Vitrup & Holden, 2010). In this way, use of physical punishment may transfer to the next generation.

Although corporal punishment spans the SES spectrum, its frequency and harshness are elevated among less educated, economically disadvantaged parents (Lansford et al., 2004, 2009). And consistently, parents with conflict-ridden marriages and with mental health problems are more likely to be punitive and also to have hard-to-manage children (Berlin et al., 2009; Erath et al., 2006; Taylor et al., 2010). These parent–child similarities

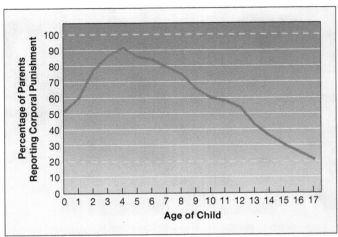

FIGURE 8.1 **Prevalence of corporal punishment by children's age.** Estimates are based on the percentage of parents in a nationally representative U.S. sample of nearly 1,000 reporting one or more instances of spanking, slapping, pinching, shaking, or hitting with a hard object in the past year. Physical punishment increases sharply during early childhood and then declines, but it is high at all ages. (From M. A. Straus & J. H. Stewart, 1999, "Corporal Punishment by American Parents: National Data on Prevalence, Chronicity, Severity, and Duration, in Relation to Child and Family Characteristics," *Clinical Child and Family Psychology Review, 2,* p. 59. Adapted with kind permission from Springer Science+Business Media and Murray A. Straus.)

suggest that heredity contributes to the link between punitive discipline and children's adjustment difficulties.

But heredity is not a complete explanation. Return to page 56 in Chapter 2 to review findings indicating that good parenting can shield children who are genetically at risk for aggression and antisocial activity from developing those behaviors. Furthermore, longitudinal studies reveal that parental harshness and corporal punishment predict child and adolescent emotional and behavior problems, even after child, parenting, and family characteristics that might otherwise account for the relationship were controlled (Berlin et al., 2009; Lansford et al., 2009, 2011; Taylor et al., 2010).

Surveys of nationally representative samples of U.S. families reveal that although corporal punishment increases from infancy to age 5 and then declines, it is high at all ages (see Figure 8.1) (Gershoff et al., 2012; Straus & Stewart, 1999). And more than one-fourth of physically punishing parents report having used a hard object, such as a brush or a belt (Gershoff, 2002b).

A prevailing American belief is that corporal punishment, if implemented by caring parents, is harmless, perhaps even beneficial. But as the Cultural Influences box on the following page reveals, this assumption is valid only under conditions of limited use in certain social contexts.

Alternatives to Harsh Punishment.

Alternatives to criticism, slaps, and spankings can reduce the side effects of punishment. A technique called **time out** involves removing children from the immediate setting—for example, by sending them to their rooms—until they are ready to act appropriately. When a child is out of control, a few minutes in time out can

Cultural Influences

Ethnic Differences in the Consequences of Physical Punishment

In an African-American community, six elders, who had volunteered to serve as mentors for parents facing child-rearing challenges, met to discuss parenting issues at a social service agency. Their attitudes toward discipline were strikingly different from those of the white social workers who had brought them together. Each elder argued that successful child rearing required appropriate physical tactics. At the same time, they voiced strong disapproval of screaming or cursing at children, calling such out-of-control parental behavior "abusive." Ruth, the oldest and most respected member of the group, characterized good parenting as a complex combination of warmth, teaching, talking nicely, and disciplining physically. She related how an older neighbor advised her to handle her own children when she was a young parent:

> She said to me says, don't scream . . . you talk to them real nice and sweet and when they do something ugly . . . she say you get a nice little switch and you won't have any trouble with them and from that day that's the way I raised 'em. (Mosby et al., 1999, pp. 511–512)

In several studies, corporal punishment predicted externalizing problems similarly among white, black, Hispanic, and Asian children (Gershoff et al., 2012; Pardini, Fite, & Burke, 2008). But other investigations point to ethnic variations.

In one, researchers followed several hundred families for 12 years, collecting information on disciplinary strategies and problem behaviors (Lansford et al., 2004). Even after many child and family characteristics were controlled, the findings were striking: In Caucasian-American families, physical punishment was positively associated with adolescent aggression and anti-social behavior. In African-American families, by contrast, the more mothers had disciplined physically in childhood, the less their teenagers displayed angry, acting-out behavior and got in trouble at school and with the police.

African-American and Caucasian-American parents seem to mete out physical punishment differently. In black families, such discipline is typically culturally approved and often mild, delivered in a context of parental warmth, and aimed at helping children become responsible adults. White parents, in contrast, consider physical punishment to be wrong, so when they resort to it, they are usually highly agitated and rejecting of the child (Dodge, McLoyd, & Lansford, 2006). As a result, many black children may view spanking as a practice carried out with their best interests in mind, whereas white children may regard it as an "act of personal aggression" (Gunnoe & Mariner, 1997, p. 768).

In support of this view, when several thousand ethnically diverse children were followed from the preschool through the early

In African-American families, discipline often includes mild physical punishment. Because the practice is culturally approved and delivered in a context of parental warmth, children may view it as an effort to encourage maturity, not as an act of aggression.

school years, spanking was associated with a rise in behavior problems if parents were cold and rejecting, but not if they were warm and supportive (McLoyd & Smith, 2002). And in another study, spanking predicted depressive symptoms only among African-American children whose mothers disapproved of the practice and, as a result, tended to use it when they were highly angry and frustrated (McLoyd et al., 2007).

These findings are not an endorsement of physical punishment. Other forms of discipline, including the positive strategies listed on page 210, are far more effective. But it is noteworthy that the meaning and impact of physical discipline vary sharply with its intensity level, context of warmth and support, and cultural approval.

---

be enough to change behavior while also giving angry parents a cooling-off period (Morawska & Sanders, 2011). Another approach is *withdrawal of privileges,* such as watching a favorite TV program. When parents do decide to use these forms of punishment, they can increase their effectiveness in three ways:

- *Consistency.* Permitting children to act inappropriately on some occasions confuses them, and the unacceptable act persists (Acker & O'Leary, 1996).

- *A warm parent–child relationship.* Children of involved, caring parents find the interruption in parental affection that accompanies punishment especially unpleasant. They want to regain parental warmth and approval as quickly as possible.

- *Explanations.* Providing reasons for mild punishment helps children relate the misdeed to expectations for future behavior, resulting in far greater reduction in misbehavior than using punishment alone (Larzelere et al., 1996).

Positive Relationships, Positive Parenting. The most effective forms of discipline encourage good conduct—by building a mutually respectful bond with the child, letting the child know ahead of time how to act, and praising mature behavior. When sensitivity, cooperation, and shared positive emotion are evident in joint activities between parents and preschoolers, children show firmer conscience development—expressing empathy after transgressions, playing fairly in games, and considering others' welfare (Kochanska et al., 2005, 2008).

Applying What We Know

Positive Parenting

Strategy	Explanation
Use transgressions as opportunities to teach.	When a child engages in harmful or unsafe behavior, intervene firmly, and then use induction, which motivates children to make amends and behave prosocially.
Reduce opportunities for misbehavior.	On a long car trip, bring back-seat activities that relieve children's restlessness. At the supermarket, converse with children and let them help with shopping. As a result, children learn to occupy themselves constructively when options are limited.
Provide reasons for rules.	When children appreciate that rules are rational, not arbitrary, they are more likely to strive to follow the rules.
Arrange for children to participate in family routines and duties.	By joining with adults in preparing a meal, washing dishes, or raking leaves, children develop a sense of responsible participation in family and community life and acquire many practical skills.
When children are obstinate, try compromising and problem solving.	When a child refuses to obey, express understanding of the child's feelings, suggest a compromise, and help the child think of ways to avoid the problem in the future. Responding firmly but kindly and respectfully increases the likelihood of willing cooperation.
Encourage mature behavior.	Express confidence in children's capacity to learn and appreciation for effort and cooperation: "You gave that your best!" Adult encouragement fosters pride and satisfaction in succeeding, thereby inspiring children to improve further.

Sources: Berk, 2001; Grusec, 2006.

Consult Applying What We Know above for ways to parent positively. Parents who use these strategies focus on long-term social and life skills—cooperation, problem solving, and consideration for others. This greatly reduces the need for punishment.

The Cognitive-Developmental Perspective

The psychoanalytic and behaviorist approaches to morality focus on how children acquire ready-made standards of good conduct from adults. In contrast, the cognitive-developmental perspective regards children as *active thinkers* about social rules. As early as the preschool years, children make moral judgments, deciding what is right or wrong on the basis of concepts they construct about justice and fairness (Gibbs, 2010a; Turiel, 2006).

Young children have some well-developed ideas about morality. As long as researchers emphasize people's intentions, 3-year-olds say that a person with bad intentions—someone who deliberately frightens, embarrasses, or otherwise hurts another—is more deserving of punishment than a well-intentioned person (Helwig, Zelazo, & Wilson, 2001). Around age 4, children know that a person who expresses an insincere intention—saying, "I'll come over and help you rake leaves," while not intending to do so—is lying (Maas, 2008). And 4-year-olds approve of telling the truth and disapprove of lying, even when a lie remains undetected (Bussey, 1992).

Furthermore, preschoolers distinguish **moral imperatives,** which protect people's rights and welfare, from two other types

of rules and expectations: **social conventions,** customs determined solely by consensus, such as table manners and politeness rituals (saying "hello," "please," "thank you"); and **matters of personal choice,** such as friends, hairstyle, and leisure activities, which do not violate rights and are up to the individual (Killen, Margie, & Sinno, 2006; Nucci, 1996; Smetana, 2006). Interviews with 3- and 4-year-olds reveal that they judge moral violations (stealing an apple) as more wrong than violations of social conventions (eating ice cream with your fingers). And preschoolers' concern with personal choice, conveyed through statements like "I'm gonna wear *this* shirt," serves as the springboard for moral concepts of individual rights (Nucci, 2005).

Within the moral domain, however, preschool and young school-age children tend to reason *rigidly,* making judgments based on salient features and consequences while neglecting other important information. For example, they are more likely than older children to claim that stealing and lying are always wrong, even when a person has a morally sound reason for engaging in these acts (Lourenco, 2003). Their explanations for why hitting others is wrong, even in the absence of rules against hitting, are simplistic and centered on physical harm: "When you get hit, it hurts, and you start to cry" (Nucci, 2008). And their focus on outcomes means that they fail to realize that a promise is still a promise, even if it is unfulfilled (Maas, 2008; Maas & Abbeduto, 2001).

Cognition and language support preschoolers' moral understanding, but social experiences are vital. Disputes with siblings and peers over rights, possessions, and property allow preschoolers to negotiate, compromise, and work out their first ideas about justice and fairness. Children also learn from warm, sensitive parental communication and from observing the way adults handle rule violations to protect the welfare of others (Turiel & Killen, 2010). Children who are advanced in moral thinking tend to have parents who adapt their communications about fighting, honesty, and ownership to what their children can understand, tell stories with moral implications, encourage prosocial behavior, and gently stimulate the child to think further, without being hostile or critical (Janssens & Deković, 1997; Walker & Taylor, 1991a).

Preschoolers who verbally and physically assault others, often without provocation, are already delayed in moral reasoning (Helwig & Turiel, 2004; Sanderson & Siegal, 1988). Without special help, such children show long-term disruptions in moral development.

The Other Side of Morality: Development of Aggression

Beginning in late infancy, all children display aggression at times. As interactions with siblings and peers increase, so do aggressive outbursts. By the second year, aggressive acts with two distinct purposes emerge. Initially, the most common is **proactive** (or *instrumental*) **aggression**, in which children act to fulfill a need or desire—obtain an object, privilege, space, or social reward, such as adult or peer attention—and unemotionally attack a person to achieve their goal. The other type, **reactive** (or *hostile*) **aggression**, is an angry, defensive response to provocation or a blocked goal and is meant to hurt another person (Dodge, Coie, & Lynam, 2006; Little et al., 2003).

Proactive and reactive aggression come in three forms:

- **Physical aggression** harms others through physical injury—pushing, hitting, kicking, or punching others or destroying another's property.
- **Verbal aggression** harms others through threats of physical aggression, name-calling, or hostile teasing.
- **Relational aggression** damages another's peer relationships through social exclusion, malicious gossip, or friendship manipulation.

In early childhood, verbal aggression gradually replaces physical aggression (Alink et al., 2006; Tremblay et al., 1999). And proactive aggression declines as preschoolers' improved capacity to delay gratification enables them to avoid grabbing others' possessions. But reactive aggression in verbal and relational forms tends to rise over early and middle childhood (Côté et al., 2007; Tremblay, 2000). Older children are better able to recognize malicious intentions and, as a result, more often respond in hostile ways.

By age 17 months, boys are more physically aggressive than girls—a difference found throughout childhood in many cultures (Baillargeon et al., 2007; Card et al., 2008). The sex difference is due in part to biology—in particular, to male sex hormones

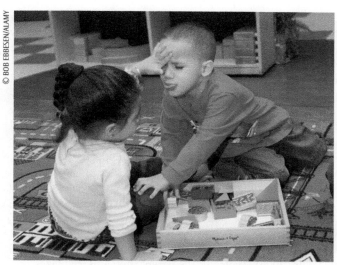

These preschoolers display proactive aggression, pushing and grabbing as they argue over a game. As children learn to compromise and share, and as their capacity to delay gratification improves, proactive aggression declines.

(androgens) and temperamental traits (activity level, irritability, impulsivity) on which boys exceed girls. Gender-role conformity is also important. As soon as preschoolers are aware of gender stereotypes—that males and females are expected to behave differently—physical aggression drops off more sharply for girls than for boys (Fagot & Leinbach, 1989).

Although girls have a reputation for being both more verbally and relationally aggressive than boys, the sex difference is small (Crick et al., 2004, 2006; Crick, Ostrov, & Werner, 2006). Beginning in the preschool years, girls concentrate most of their aggressive acts in the relational category. Boys inflict harm in more variable ways and, therefore, display overall rates of aggression that are much higher than girls'.

At the same time, girls more often use indirect relational tactics that—in disrupting intimate bonds especially important to girls—can be particularly mean. Whereas physical attacks are usually brief, acts of indirect relational aggression may extend for hours, weeks, or even months (Nelson, Robinson, & Hart, 2005; Underwood, 2003). In one instance, a 6-year-old girl formed a "pretty-girls club" and—for nearly an entire school year—convinced its members to exclude several classmates by saying they were "ugly and smelly."

An occasional aggressive exchange between preschoolers is normal. But children who are emotionally negative, impulsive, and disobedient are prone to early, high rates of physical or relational aggression (or both) that often persist, placing them at risk for internalizing and externalizing difficulties, social skills deficits, and antisocial activity in middle childhood and adolescence (Campbell et al., 2006; Côté et al., 2007). These negative outcomes, however, depend on child-rearing conditions.

The Family as Training Ground for Aggressive Behavior. "I can't control him, he's impossible," Robbie's mother, Nadine, complained to Leslie one day. When Leslie asked if Robbie might be troubled by something happening at home, she discovered that his parents fought constantly and resorted to harsh, inconsistent discipline. The same child-rearing practices that undermine moral internalization—love withdrawal, power assertion, critical remarks, physical punishment, and inconsistent discipline—are linked to aggression from early childhood through adolescence in diverse cultures, with most of these practices predicting both physical and relational forms (Bradford et al., 2003; Casas et al., 2006; Côté et al., 2007; Gershoff et al., 2010; Kuppens et al., 2009; Nelson et al., 2006a).

In families like Robbie's, anger and punitiveness quickly create a conflict-ridden family atmosphere and an "out-of-control" child. The pattern begins with forceful discipline, which occurs more often with stressful life experiences, a parent with an unstable personality, or a difficult child (Dodge, Coie, & Lynam, 2006). Typically, the parent threatens, criticizes, and punishes, and the child angrily resists until the parent "gives in." As these cycles become more frequent, they generate anxiety and irritability among other family members, including siblings, who soon join in the hostile interactions. Destructive sibling conflict, in turn, quickly spreads to peer relationships, contributing to poor impulse control and antisocial behavior (Garcia et al., 2000; Ostrov, Crick, & Stauffacher, 2006).

Boys are more likely than girls to be targets of harsh, inconsistent discipline because they are more active and impulsive and therefore harder to control. When children who are extreme in these characteristics are exposed to emotionally negative, inept parenting, their capacity for emotional self-regulation, empathic responding, and guilt after transgressions is disrupted (Eisenberg, Eggum, & Edwards, 2010). Consequently, they lash out when disappointed, frustrated, or faced with a sad or fearful victim.

Children subjected to these family processes acquire a distorted view of the social world, often seeing hostile intent where it does not exist and, as a result, making many unprovoked attacks (Lochman & Dodge, 1998; Orbio de Castro et al., 2002). And some, who conclude that aggression "works" to access rewards and control others, callously use it to advance their own goals and are unconcerned about causing suffering in others—an aggressive style associated with later more severe conduct problems, violent behavior, and delinquency (Marsee & Frick, 2010).

Violent Media and Aggression. In the United States, 57 percent of TV programs between 6 A.M. and 11 P.M. contain violent scenes, often portraying repeated aggressive acts that go unpunished. Victims of TV violence are rarely shown experiencing serious harm, and few programs condemn violence or depict other ways of solving problems (Center for Communication and Social Policy, 1998). Verbally and relationally aggressive acts are particularly frequent in reality TV shows (Coyne, Robinson, & Nelson, 2010). And violent content is 9 percent above average in children's programming, with cartoons being the most violent.

Reviewers of thousands of studies have concluded that TV violence increases the likelihood of hostile thoughts and emotions and of verbally, physically, and relationally aggressive behavior (Ostrov, Gentile, & Crick, 2006; Scharrer, 2013). And a growing number of studies confirm that playing violent video games has similar effects (Anderson et al., 2008; Hofferth, 2010).

LOOK AND LISTEN

Watch a half-hour of Saturday morning cartoons and a prime-time movie on TV, and tally the number of violent acts, including those that go unpunished. How often did violence occur in each type of program? What do young viewers learn about the consequences of violence? ●

Violent programming not only creates short-term difficulties in parent and peer relations but also has lasting negative consequences. In longitudinal research, time spent watching TV in childhood and adolescence predicted aggressive behavior in adulthood, after other factors linked to TV viewing (such as prior child and parent aggression, IQ, parent education, family income, and neighborhood crime) were controlled (Graber et al., 2006; Huesmann, 1986; Huesmann et al., 2003; Johnson et al., 2002). Aggressive children and adolescents have a greater appetite for violent TV and computer games. And boys devote more time to violent media than girls, in part because of male-oriented themes of conquest and adventure. But even in nonaggressive children, violent TV sparks hostile thoughts and behavior; its impact is simply less intense (Bushman & Huesmann, 2001).

The ease with which television and video games can manipulate children's attitudes and behavior has led to strong public pressure to improve media content. In the United States, the First Amendment right to free speech has hampered efforts to regulate TV broadcasting. Instead, all programs must be rated for violent and sexual content, and all new TV sets are required to contain the V-chip, which allows parents to block undesired material. In general, parents bear most responsibility for regulating their children's exposure to media violence and other inappropriate content. As with the V-chip for TV, parents can control children's Internet access by using filters or programs that monitor website visits. Yet surveys of U.S. parents indicate that 20 to 30 percent of preschoolers and about half of school-age children experience no limits on TV or computer use at home (Rideout, Foehr, & Roberts, 2010; Rideout & Hamel, 2006; Varnhagen, 2007). Besides regulating media exposure, parents are best off participating in children's TV and computer use—expressing disapproval of onscreen violent acts and encouraging discussion, with the aim of helping children understand and critique media content.

Helping Children and Parents Control Aggression. Treatment for aggressive children is best begun early, before their antisocial behavior becomes well-practiced and difficult to change. Breaking the cycle of hostilities between family members and promoting effective ways of relating to others are crucial.

Leslie suggested that Robbie's parents enroll in a parent training program aimed at improving the parenting of children with conduct problems. In one approach, called *Incredible Years,* parents complete 18 weekly group sessions facilitated by two professionals, who teach positive parenting techniques for promoting preschool and school-age children's academic, emotional, and social skills and for managing disruptive behaviors (Webster-Stratton & Reid, 2010b). A complementary six-day training program for teachers, aimed at improving classroom management strategies and strengthening children's social skills, is also available. And a 22-week program intervenes directly with children, teaching appropriate classroom behavior, self-control, and social skills.

Evaluations in which families with aggressive children were randomly assigned to either Incredible Years or control groups reveal that the program improves parenting and reduces child behavior problems. Combining parent training with teacher and/or child intervention strengthens child outcomes (Webster-Stratton & Herman, 2010). And effects of parent training endure. In one long-term follow-up, 75 percent of young children with serious conduct problems whose parents participated in Incredible Years were well-adjusted as teenagers (Webster-Stratton & Reid, 2010a; Webster-Stratton, Rinaldi, & Reid, 2011).

Other interventions focus on modifying aggressive children's distorted social perspectives, by encouraging them to attend to nonhostile social cues, seek additional information before acting, and take the perspective of others, which promotes empathy and sympathetic concern for others. Another approach is to teach effective conflict-resolution skills. At preschool, Robbie participated in a social problem-solving intervention. Over several months, he met with Leslie and a small group of classmates to act out common conflicts using puppets, discuss alternatives for settling disputes, and practice successful strategies. Children who receive such training show gains in social competence still present several months later (Bierman & Powers, 2009; Shure & Aberson, 2005).

Finally, Robbie's parents sought counseling for their marital problems. When parents receive help in coping with stressors in their own lives, interventions aimed at reducing children's aggression are even more effective (Kazdin & Whitley, 2003).

ASK YOURSELF

REVIEW What must parents do to foster conscience development in fearless, impulsive children? How does this illustrate the concept of goodness of fit (see page 151 in Chapter 6)?

APPLY Alice and Wayne want their two children to become morally mature, caring individuals. List some parenting practices they should use and some they should avoid.

REFLECT Which types of punishment for a misbehaving preschooler do you endorse, and which types do you reject? Why?

As these preschoolers' imaginative play reveals, they have already acquired the gender-stereotyped belief that cooking is a "feminine" activity.

Gender Typing

Gender typing refers to any association of objects, activities, roles, or traits with one sex or the other in ways that conform to cultural stereotypes (Liben & Bigler, 2002). Already, the children in Leslie's classroom had acquired many gender-linked beliefs and preferences and tended to play with peers of their own sex.

Social learning theory, with its emphasis on modeling and reinforcement, and *cognitive-developmental theory,* with its focus on children as active thinkers about their social world, offer contemporary explanations of children's gender typing. As we will see, neither is adequate by itself. *Gender schema theory,* a third perspective that combines elements of both, has gained favor. In the following sections, we consider the early development of gender typing.

Gender-Stereotyped Beliefs and Behavior

Recall from Chapter 6 that around age 2, children use such words as *boy, girl, lady,* and *man* appropriately. As soon as gender categories are established, children sort out what they mean in terms of activities and behavior. Preschoolers associate toys, articles of clothing, tools, household items, games, occupations, colors (blue and pink), and behaviors (physical and relational aggression) with one sex or the other (Banse et al., 2010; Giles & Heyman, 2005; Poulin-Dubois et al., 2002). And their actions reflect their beliefs, not only in play preferences but in personality traits as well. As we have seen, boys tend to be more active, impulsive, assertive, and physically aggressive. Girls tend to be more fearful, dependent, emotionally sensitive, compliant, advanced in effortful control, and skilled at understanding self-conscious emotions and at inflicting indirect relational aggression (Bosacki & Moore, 2004; Else-Quest et al., 2006; Underwood, 2003).

During early childhood, gender-stereotyped beliefs strengthen—so much so that many children apply them as blanket rules rather than as flexible guidelines. When children were asked whether gender stereotypes could be violated, half or more of 3- and 4-year-olds answered "no" to clothing, hairstyle, and play with certain toys (Barbie dolls and G.I. Joes) (Blakemore, 2003). Furthermore, most 3- to 6-year-olds are firm about not wanting to be friends with a child who violates a gender stereotype (a boy who wears nail polish, a girl who plays with trucks) or to attend a school where such violations are allowed (Ruble et al., 2007). These one-sided judgments are a joint product of gender stereotyping in the environment and young children's cognitive limitations (Trautner et al., 2005). Most preschoolers do not yet realize that characteristics *associated with* being male or female—activities, toys, occupations, hairstyle, and clothing—do not *determine* a person's sex.

Biological Influences on Gender Typing

The sex differences just described appear in many cultures around the world (Munroe & Romney, 2006). Certain ones—male activity level and physical aggression, female emotional sensitivity, and preference for same-sex playmates—are widespread among mammalian species (de Waal, 1993, 2001). According to an evolutionary perspective, the adult life of our male ancestors was largely oriented toward competing for mates, that of our female ancestors toward rearing children. Therefore, males became genetically primed for dominance and females for intimacy, responsiveness, and cooperativeness (Konner, 2010; Maccoby, 2002).

Experiments with animals reveal that prenatally administered androgens increase active play and aggression and suppress maternal caregiving in both male and female mammals (Sato et al., 2004). Eleanor Maccoby (1998) argues that sex hormones also affect human play styles, leading to rough, noisy movements among boys and calm, gentle actions among girls. Then, as children interact with peers, they choose partners whose interests and behaviors are compatible with their own. Preschool girls increasingly seek out other girls and like to play in pairs because they share a preference for quieter activities involving cooperative roles. Boys come to prefer larger-group play with other boys, who share a desire to run, climb, play-fight, and compete (Fabes, Martin, & Hanish, 2003). By age 6, children spend 11 times as much time with same-sex as with other-sex playmates (Martin & Fabes, 2001).

Even stronger support for the role of biology in human gender typing comes from research on girls exposed prenatally to high levels of androgens. These girls showed more "masculine" behavior—a preference for trucks and blocks over dolls, for active over quiet play, and for boys as playmates—even when

parents encouraged them to engage in gender-typical play (Cohen-Bendahan, van de Beek, & Berenbaum, 2005; Pasterski et al., 2005).

Research on boys with low early androgen exposure, either because production by the testes is reduced or because body cells are androgen-insensitive, also yields consistent findings (Jürgensen et al., 2007). The greater the degree of impairment, the more these boys display "feminine" behaviors, including toy choices and preference for girl playmates.

Environmental Influences on Gender Typing

A wealth of evidence reveals that environmental forces—at home, at school, and in the community—build on genetic influences to promote vigorous gender typing in early childhood.

Parents. Beginning at birth, parents have different expectations of sons than of daughters. Many describe achievement, competition, and control of emotion as important for sons and warmth, "ladylike" behavior, and closely supervised activities as important for daughters (Brody, 1999; Turner & Gervai, 1995).

Parenting practices reflect these beliefs. Parents typically give their sons toys that stress action and competition (cars, tools, footballs) and their daughters toys that emphasize nurturance, cooperation, and physical attractiveness (dolls, tea sets, jewelry) (Leaper, 1994; Leaper & Friedman, 2007). Parents also actively reinforce independence in boys and closeness and dependency in girls. For example, parents react more positively when a son plays with cars and trucks, demands attention, runs and climbs, or tries to take toys from others. When interacting with daughters, parents more often direct play activities, provide help, encourage participation in household tasks, refer to emo-

CAVAN IMAGES/GETTY IMAGES

Of the two sexes, boys are more gender-typed. Fathers, especially, promote "masculine" behavior in their preschool sons through activities that stress action and competition.

tions, and express approval and agreement (Clearfield & Nelson, 2006; Fagot & Hagan, 1991; Kuebli, Butler, & Fivush, 1995).

Language is a powerful indirect means for teaching children about gender stereotypes. Even parents who believe strongly in gender equality unconsciously use language that highlights gender distinctions and informs children about traditional gender roles (see the Social Issues: Education box on page 216).

LOOK AND LISTEN

Observe a parent discussing a picture book with a 3- to 6-year-old. How many times did the parent make generic statements about gender? How about the child? Did the parent accept or correct the child's generic utterances? ●

Of the two sexes, boys are more gender-typed, and fathers, especially, insist that boys conform to gender roles. They place more pressure to achieve on sons than on daughters and are less tolerant of "cross-gender" behavior in sons—more concerned when a boy acts like a "sissy" than when a girl acts like a "tomboy" (Wood, Desmarais, & Gugula, 2002). But parents who hold nonstereotyped values and consciously avoid behaving in these ways have children who are less gender-typed (Tenenbaum & Leaper, 2002).

Teachers. Like parents, preschool teachers give girls more encouragement to participate in adult-structured activities. Girls frequently cluster around the teacher, following directions, whereas boys are attracted to play areas where teachers are minimally involved (Campbell, Shirley, & Candy, 2004; Powlishta, Serbin, & Moller, 1993). As a result, boys and girls practice different social behaviors. Compliance and bids for help occur more often in adult-structured contexts; assertiveness, leadership, and creative use of materials in unstructured pursuits.

Furthermore, as early as kindergarten, teachers give more overall attention (both positive and negative) to boys than to girls—a difference evident in diverse countries, including China, England, and the United States. They tend to praise boys more for their academic knowledge, perhaps as a means of motivating them because boys' school performance is behind that of girls. Teachers also use more disapproval and controlling discipline with boys (Chen & Rao, 2011; Davies, 2008; Swinson & Harrop, 2009). They seem to expect boys to misbehave more often—a belief based partly on boys' actual behavior and partly on gender stereotypes.

Peers. Children's same-sex peer association make the peer context a potent source of gender-role learning (Martin & Fabes, 2001). By age 3, same-sex peers positively reinforce one another for gender-typed play by praising, imitating, or joining in. In contrast, when preschoolers engage in "cross-gender" activities—for example, when boys play with dolls or girls with cars and trucks—peers criticize them. Boys are especially intolerant of cross-gender play in other boys (Thorne, 1993).

Children also develop different styles of social influence in gender-segregated peer groups. To get their way in large-group play, boys often rely on commands, threats, and physical force. Girls' preference for playing in pairs leads to greater concern with a partner's needs, evident in polite requests, persuasion, and acceptance. Girls soon find that these tactics succeed with other girls but not with boys, who ignore their courteous overtures (Leaper, 1994; Leaper, Tenenbaum, & Shaffer, 1999). Boys' unresponsiveness gives girls another reason to stop interacting with them.

As boys and girls separate, *in-group favoritism*—more positive evaluations of members of one's own gender—becomes another factor that sustains the separate social worlds of boys and girls. As a result, "two distinct subcultures" of knowledge, beliefs, interests, and behaviors form (Maccoby, 2002).

Gender Identity

As adults, each of us has a **gender identity**—an image of oneself as relatively masculine or feminine in characteristics. By middle childhood, researchers can measure gender identity by asking children to rate themselves on personality traits. A child or adult with a "masculine" identity scores high on traditionally masculine items (such as *ambitious, competitive,* and *self-sufficient*) and low on traditionally feminine items (such as *affectionate, cheerful,* and *soft-spoken*). Someone with a "feminine" identity does the reverse. And a substantial minority (especially females) have a gender identity called **androgyny,** scoring high on both masculine and feminine personality characteristics.

"Masculine" and androgynous children and adults have higher self-esteem than "feminine" individuals (Boldizar, 1991; DiDonato & Berenbaum, 2011; Harter, 2006). Also, androgynous individuals are more adaptable—able to show masculine independence or feminine sensitivity, depending on the situation (Huyck, 1996; Taylor & Hall, 1982). The existence of an androgynous identity demonstrates that children can acquire a mixture of positive qualities traditionally associated with each gender—an orientation that may best help them realize their potential.

Emergence of Gender Identity. How do children develop a gender identity? According to *social learning theory,* behavior comes before self-perceptions. Preschoolers first acquire gender-typed responses through modeling and reinforcement and only later organize these behaviors into gender-linked ideas about themselves. In contrast, *cognitive-developmental theory* maintains that self-perceptions come before behavior. Over the preschool years, children acquire a cognitive appreciation of the permanence of their sex. They develop **gender constancy**—a full understanding of the biologically based permanence of their gender, including the realization that sex remains the same even if clothing, hairstyle, and play activities change. Then children use this knowledge to guide their behavior.

Children younger than age 6 who watch an adult dress a doll in "other-gender" clothing typically insist that the doll's

Social Issues: Education

Young Children Learn About Gender Through Mother–Child Conversations

In an investigation of the power of language to shape preschoolers' beliefs about gender, mothers were asked to converse with their 2- to 6-year-olds about picture books containing images both consistent and inconsistent with gender stereotypes (Gelman, Taylor, & Nguyen, 2004). Each picture was accompanied by the question, "Who can X?" where X was the activity on the page.

Analyses of picture-book conversations revealed that mothers' directly expressed gender attitudes were neutral, largely because they mostly posed questions to their children, such as, "Who's driving that boat?" "Who can be a sailor? Boys and girls?" But by age 4, children often voiced stereotypes ("No, only boys can do that!"), and nearly one-third of the time, mothers affirmed them ("OK, only boys"). Rarely—just 2 percent of the time—did they explicitly counter a child's stereotype, and usually only when the book itself included stereotype-inconsistent pictures.

Although the mothers were not asked to discuss gender, they called attention to it even when they did not need to do so. In English, many nouns referring to people convey age-related information (*kid, baby, 2-year-old, preschooler, teenager, grownup, senior*), whereas only a few encode gender (*male, female, sister, brother, aunt, uncle*). Yet when referring to persons, mothers

called attention to gender more than half the time, even though the people shown in the books varied as much in age as in gender. Referring often to gender encourages young children to sort the social world into gender categories.

Furthermore, both mothers and children frequently expressed *generic utterances*—ones that were broad in scope, referring to many, or nearly all, males and females: "Boys can be sailors." "Most girls don't like trucks." Even generics that were gender-neutral ("Lots of girls in this book") or that denied a stereotype ("Boys can be ballet dancers") prompted children to view individuals of the same gender as alike and to ignore exceptions.

Mothers' and children's use of generics increased with age. At age 2, mothers introduced these generalizations nearly three times as often as children. But by age 6 children were producing generics more often than mothers. Generics were especially common in speech to and from boys, likely contributing to boys' stronger gender typing.

Even though these mothers overwhelmingly believed in gender equality, in conversing with their children, they provided a wealth of implicit cues that foster gender-stereotyping. Adults can combat children's gender stereotyped beliefs by refraining from

While reading, this mother may unconsciously teach her child to see the world in gender-linked terms—by referring to gender unnecessarily or by making generic gender statements ("Most girls prefer X"; "Boys usually don't like X").

labeling gender unnecessarily (substituting *friend* for *boy* or *girl*), using references to individuals ("That person wants to be firefighter") or qualifiers ("Some boys and some girls want to be firefighters"), countering children's stereotypical claims, and asking children to avoid using gender labels and generics.

---

sex has also changed (Chauhan, Shastri, & Mohite, 2005; Fagot, 1985). Attainment of gender constancy is strongly related to ability to pass verbal appearance–reality tasks (see page 177 in Chapter 7) (Trautner, Gervai, & Nemeth, 2003). Indeed, gender constancy tasks can be considered a type of appearance–reality problem, in that children must distinguish what a person looks like from who he or she really is.

Is cognitive-developmental theory correct that gender constancy is responsible for children's gender-typed behavior? Evidence for this assumption is weak. "Gender-appropriate" behavior appears so early in the preschool years that its initial appearance must result from modeling and reinforcement, as social learning theory suggests. Although outcomes are not entirely consistent, some evidence suggests that gender con-

stancy actually contributes to more flexible gender-role attitudes during the school years (Ruble et al., 2007). But overall, the impact of gender constancy on gender typing is not great. As research in the following section reveals, gender-role adoption is more powerfully affected by children's beliefs about how close the connection must be between their own gender and their behavior.

Gender Schema Theory. Gender schema theory is an information-processing approach that combines social learning and cognitive-developmental features. It explains how environmental pressures and children's cognitions work together to shape gender-role development (Martin & Halverson, 1987; Martin, Ruble, & Szkrybalo, 2002). At an early age, children pick up gender-typed preferences and behaviors from others. At the same time, they organize their experiences into *gender schemas,* or masculine and feminine categories, that they use to interpret their world. As soon as preschoolers can label their own gender, they select gender schemas consistent with it ("Only boys can be doctors" or "Cooking is a girl's job") and apply those categories to themselves. Their self-perceptions then become gender-typed and serve as additional schemas that children use to process information and guide their own behavior.

We have seen that individual differences exist in the extent to which children endorse gender-typed views. Children who acquire rigid gender schemas use them to filter their experiences (Liben & Bigler, 2002). When such children see others behaving in "gender-inconsistent" ways, they often cannot remember the information or distort it to make it "gender-consistent." For example, when shown a picture of a male nurse, they may remember him as a doctor (Martin & Ruble, 2004). And because gender-schematic preschoolers typically conclude, "What I like, children of my own sex will also like," they often use their own preferences to add to their gender biases. For example, a girl who dislikes oysters may conclude that only boys like oysters even though she has never actually been given information promoting such a stereotype. At least partly for this reason, young children's gender schemas contain both culturally standard and nonstandard ideas (Tenenbaum et al., 2010). Not until well into the school years do children's gender schemas fully resemble those of adults.

Reducing Gender Stereotyping in Young Children

How can we help young children avoid developing gender schemas? No easy recipe exists. Biology clearly affects children's gender typing, channeling boys toward active, competitive play and girls toward quieter, more intimate interaction. But most aspects of gender typing are not built into human nature (Ruble, Martin, & Berenbaum, 2006).

Because young children's cognitive limitations lead them to assume that cultural practices determine gender, adults are wise to try to delay preschoolers' exposure to gender-stereotyped messages. Parents and teachers can begin by limiting traditional gender roles in their own behavior and by providing children with nontraditional alternatives—for example, giving boys and girls both trucks and dolls, avoiding use of language that conveys gender stereotypes, and shielding children from media presentations that do the same.

Once children notice the vast array of gender stereotypes in their society, parents and teachers can point out exceptions. For example, they can arrange for children to see men and women pursuing nontraditional careers and can explain that interests and skills, not sex, should determine a person's occupation. Research shows that such reasoning is highly effective in reducing children's tendency to view the world in a gender-biased fashion. By middle childhood, children who hold flexible

beliefs about what boys and girls can do are more likely to notice instances of gender discrimination (Brown & Bigler, 2004). And as we will see next, a rational approach to child rearing promotes healthy, adaptable functioning in many other areas as well.

ASK YOURSELF

REVIEW Explain how the social environment and young children's cognitive limitations jointly contribute to rigid gender stereotyping in early childhood.

APPLY List findings indicating that language and communication—between parents and children, between teachers and children, and between peers—powerfully affect children's gender typing. What recommendations would you make to counteract these influences?

REFLECT Would you describe your own gender identity as "masculine," "feminine," or androgynous? What biological and social factors might have influenced your gender identity?

Child Rearing and Emotional and Social Development

In this and previous chapters, we have seen how parents can foster children's competence—by building a parent–child relationship based on affection and cooperation, by serving as models and reinforcers of mature behavior, by using reasoning and inductive discipline, and by guiding and encouraging children's mastery of new skills. Now let's put these practices together into an overall view of effective parenting.

Styles of Child Rearing

Child-rearing styles are combinations of parenting behaviors that occur over a wide range of situations, creating an enduring child-rearing climate. In a landmark series of studies, Diana Baumrind (1971) gathered information on child rearing by watching parents interact with their preschoolers. Her findings, and those of others who have extended her work, reveal three features that consistently differentiate an effective style from less effective ones: (1) acceptance and involvement, (2) control, and (3) autonomy granting (Gray & Steinberg, 1999; Hart, Newell, & Olsen, 2003). Table 8.2 on page 218 shows how child-rearing styles differ in these features.

Authoritative Child Rearing. The **authoritative child-rearing style**—the most successful approach—involves high acceptance and involvement, adaptive control techniques, and

TABLE 8.2 **Features of Child-Rearing Styles**

CHILD-REARING STYLE	ACCEPTANCE AND INVOLVEMENT	CONTROL	AUTONOMY GRANTING
Authoritative	Is warm, responsive, attentive, patient, and sensitive to the child's needs	Makes reasonable demands for maturity and consistently enforces and explains them	Permits the child to make decisions in accord with readiness Encourages the child to express thoughts, feelings, and desires When parent and child disagree, engages in joint decision making when possible
Authoritarian	Is cold and rejecting and frequently degrades the child	Makes many demands coercively, using force and punishment Often uses psychological control, withdrawing love and intruding on the child's individuality	Makes decisions for the child Rarely listens to the child's point of view
Permissive	Is warm but overindulgent or inattentive	Makes few or no demands for maturity	Permits the child to make many decisions before the child is ready
Uninvolved	Is emotionally detached and withdrawn	Makes few or no demands for maturity	Is indifferent to the child's decision making and point of view

appropriate autonomy granting. Authoritative parents are warm, attentive, and sensitive, establishing an enjoyable, emotionally fulfilling parent–child relationship that draws the child into close connection. At the same time, authoritative parents exercise firm, reasonable control. They insist on appropriate maturity and give reasons for their expectations. Finally, authoritative parents engage in gradual, appropriate autonomy granting, allowing the child to make decisions in areas where he is ready to do so (Kuczynski & Lollis, 2002; Russell, Mize, & Bissaker, 2004).

Throughout childhood and adolescence, authoritative parenting is linked to many aspects of competence—an upbeat mood, self-control, task persistence, cooperativeness, high self-esteem, social and moral maturity, and favorable school performance (Amato & Fowler, 2002; Aunola, Stattin, & Nurmi, 2000; Gonzalez & Wolters, 2006; Mackey, Arnold, & Pratt, 2001; Milevsky et al., 2007; Steinberg, Darling, & Fletcher, 1995).

Authoritarian Child Rearing. The **authoritarian child-rearing style** is low in acceptance and involvement, high in coercive control, and low in autonomy granting. Authoritarian parents appear cold and rejecting. To exert control, they yell, command, criticize, and threaten, demanding unquestioning obedience. If the child resists, authoritarian parents resort to force and punishment.

Children of authoritarian parents are likely to be anxious, unhappy, and low in self-esteem and self-reliance. When frustrated, they tend to react with hostility and, like their parents, resort to force when they do not get their way. Boys, especially, show high rates of anger and defiance. Although girls also engage in acting-out behavior, they are more likely to be dependent and overwhelmed by challenging tasks (Hart, Newell, & Olsen, 2003; Kakihara et al., 2010; Thompson, Hollis, & Richards, 2003). Children and adolescents exposed to the authoritarian style typically do poorly in school, but because of their parents' concern with control, they tend to achieve better than peers with undemanding parents—that is, whose parents use one of the styles we will consider next (Steinberg, Blatt-Eisengart, & Cauffman, 2006).

In addition to unwarranted direct control, authoritarian parents engage in a more subtle type called **psychological control**—behaviors that intrude on and manipulate children's verbal expression, individuality, and attachments to parents. In an attempt to decide virtually everything for the child, these parents frequently interrupt or put down the child's ideas, decisions, and choice of friends. When they are dissatisfied, they withdraw love, making their affection or attention contingent on the child's compliance. They also hold excessively high expectations that do not fit the child's developing capacities. Children subjected to psychological control exhibit adjustment problems involving both anxious, withdrawn behavior and defiance and aggression—especially the relational form, which (like parental psychological control) damages relationships through manipulation and exclusion (Barber et al., 2005; Kuppens et al., 2009; Nelson et al., 2006b; Silk et al., 2003).

Permissive Child Rearing. The **permissive child-rearing style** is warm and accepting but uninvolved. Permissive parents are either overindulgent or inattentive and, thus, engage in little control. Instead of gradually granting autonomy, they allow children to make many of their own decisions at an age when they are not yet capable of doing so. Their children can eat meals and go to bed whenever they wish and can watch as much television as they want. They do not have to learn good manners or do any household chores. Although some permissive parents truly believe in this approach, many others simply lack confidence in their ability to influence their child's behavior (Oyserman et al., 2005).

Children of permissive parents tend to be impulsive, disobedient, and rebellious. Compared with children whose parents exert more control, they are also overly demanding and dependent on adults, and they show less persistence on tasks, poorer school achievement, and more antisocial behavior (Barber & Olsen, 1997; Baumrind, 1971; Steinberg, Blatt-Eisengart, & Cauffman, 2006).

Uninvolved Child Rearing. The **uninvolved child-rearing style** combines low acceptance and involvement with little control and general indifference to issues of autonomy. Often these parents are emotionally detached and depressed and so overwhelmed by life stress that they have little time and energy for children. At its extreme, uninvolved parenting is a form of child maltreatment called *neglect*. Especially when it begins early, it disrupts virtually all aspects of development (see Chapter 6, page 145). Even with less extreme parental disengagement, children and adolescents display many problems—poor emotional self-regulation, school achievement difficulties, depression, anger, and antisocial behavior (Aunola, Stattin, & Nurmi, 2000; Kurdek & Fine, 1994; Schroeder et al., 2010).

What Makes Authoritative Child Rearing Effective?

Like all correlational findings, the relationship between the authoritative style and children's competence is open to interpretation. Perhaps parents of well-adjusted children are authoritative because their youngsters have especially cooperative dispositions. But although temperamentally fearless, impulsive children and emotionally negative, difficult children are more likely to evoke coercive, inconsistent discipline, extra warmth and firm control succeed in modifying these children's maladaptive styles (Cipriano & Stifter, 2010; Kochanska, Philibert, & Barry, 2009; Pettit et al., 2007). Furthermore, a variant of authoritativeness in which parents exert strong control—becoming directive but not coercive—yields just as favorable long-term outcomes as a more democratic approach (Baumrind, Larzelere, & Owens, 2010). Indeed, some children, because of their dispositions, require "heavier doses" of certain authoritative features.

In sum, authoritative child rearing seems to create a positive emotional context for parental influence in the following ways:

- Warm, involved parents who are secure in the standards they hold for their children provide models of caring concern as well as confident, self-controlled behavior.

- Children are far more likely to comply with and internalize control that appears fair and reasonable, not arbitrary.

- Authoritative parents appropriately make demands and grant autonomy. By conveying a sense of competence to their children, parents foster favorable self-esteem and cognitive and social maturity.

- Supportive aspects of the authoritative style are a powerful source of *resilience*, protecting children from the negative effects of family stress and poverty (Beyers et al., 2003).

LOOK AND LISTEN

Ask several parents to explain their style of child rearing, inquiring about acceptance and involvement, control, and autonomy granting. Look, especially, for variations in authoritativeness—more or less control over the child's behavior—along with parents' rationales. ●

Cultural Variations

Although authoritative parenting is broadly advantageous, parents of different ethnicities often have distinct child-rearing beliefs and practices that reflect cultural values. Let's take some examples.

Compared with Western parents, Chinese parents describe their parenting as more controlling. They are more directive in teaching and scheduling their children's time, as a way of fostering self-control and high achievement. Chinese parents may appear less warm than Western parents because they withhold praise, which they believe results in self-satisfied, poorly motivated children (Chao, 1994; Chen et al., 2001). Chinese parents report expressing affection and using induction and other reasoning-oriented discipline as much as American parents do (Cheah et al., 2009; Shwalb et al., 2004; Wu et al., 2002). When Chinese parents engage in psychological or coercive control, Chinese children display the same negative outcomes as Western children: poor academic achievement, anxiety, depression, and aggressive behavior (Chan, 2010; Nelson et al., 2006b; Pong, Johnston, & Chen, 2010).

In Hispanic families, Asian Pacific Island families, and Caribbean families of African and East Indian origins, firm insistence on respect for parental authority is paired with high parental warmth—a combination suited to promoting cognitive and social competence and family loyalty (Halgunseth, Ispa, & Rudy, 2006; Roopnarine & Evans, 2007). Hispanic fathers often spend much time with their children and are warm and sensitive (Cabrera & Bradley, 2012). In Caribbean families that have immigrated to the United States, fathers' authoritativeness—but not mothers'—predicted preschoolers' literacy and math skills, probably because Caribbean fathers take a larger role in guiding their children's academic progress (Roopnarine et al., 2006).

In low-SES African-American families, parents tend to expect immediate obedience, regarding strictness as fostering self-control and a watchful attitude in risky surroundings. Consistent with these beliefs, African-American parents who use more controlling strategies tend to have more cognitively and socially competent children (Brody & Flor, 1998). Recall, also, that a history of physical punishment is associated with a reduction in antisocial behavior among African-American youths but with an increase among Caucasian Americans (see page 209). Most African-American parents who use strict, "no-nonsense"

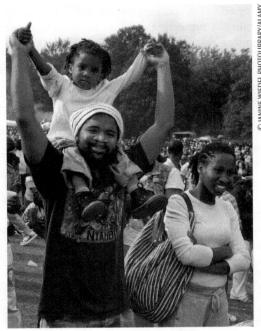

© JANINE WIEDEL PHOTOLIBRARY/ALAMY

In Caribbean families of African origin, respect for parental authority is paired with high parental warmth—a combination that promotes competence and family loyalty.

discipline use physical punishment sparingly and combine it with warmth and reasoning.

These cultural variations remind us that child-rearing styles must be viewed in their larger context. As we have seen, many factors contribute to good parenting: personal characteristics of child and parent, SES, access to extended family and community supports, cultural values and practices, and public policies. As we turn to the topic of child maltreatment, our discussion will underscore, once again, that effective child rearing is sustained not just by the desire of mothers and fathers to be good parents. Almost all want to be. Unfortunately, when vital supports for parenting break down, children—as well as parents—can suffer terribly.

Child Maltreatment

Child maltreatment is as old as human history, but only recently has the problem been widely acknowledged and research aimed at understanding it. Perhaps public concern has increased because child maltreatment is especially common in large industrialized nations. In the most recently reported year, about 700,000 U.S. children (9 out of every 1,000) were identified as victims (U.S. Department of Health and Human Services, 2011b). Most cases go unreported, so the true figures are much higher.

Child maltreatment takes the following forms:

- *Physical abuse:* Assaults, such as kicking, biting, shaking, punching, or stabbing, that inflict physical injury

- *Sexual abuse:* Fondling, intercourse, exhibitionism, commercial exploitation through prostitution or production of pornography, and other forms of exploitation
- *Neglect:* Failure to meet a child's basic needs for food, clothing, medical attention, education, or supervision
- *Emotional abuse:* Acts that could cause serious mental or behavioral disorders, including social isolation, repeated unreasonable demands, ridicule, humiliation, intimidation, or terrorizing

Parents commit more than 80 percent of abusive incidents. Other relatives account for about 7 percent. The remainder are perpetrated by parents' unmarried partners, school officials, camp counselors, and other adults. Maternal and paternal rates of physical and emotional abuse are fairly similar. Infants and young preschoolers are at greatest risk for neglect; preschool and school-age children for physical, emotional, and sexual abuse (Trocmé & Wolfe, 2002; U.S. Department of Health and Human Services, 2011b). Because most sexual abuse victims are identified in middle childhood, we will pay special attention to this form of maltreatment in Chapter 10.

Origins of Child Maltreatment. For help in understanding child maltreatment, researchers turned to *ecological systems theory* (see Chapters 1 and 2). They discovered that many interacting variables—at the family, community, and cultural levels—contribute.

The Family. Within the family, children whose characteristics make them more challenging to rear are more likely to become targets of abuse. These include premature or very sick babies and children who are temperamentally difficult, are inattentive and overactive, or have other developmental problems. Child factors, however, only slightly increase the risk (Jaudes & Mackey-Bilaver, 2008; Sidebotham et al., 2003). Whether such children are maltreated largely depends on parents' characteristics.

Maltreating parents are less skillful than other parents in handling discipline confrontations. They also suffer from biased thinking about their child. For example, they often attribute their baby's crying or their child's misdeeds to a stubborn or bad disposition, evaluate child transgressions as worse than they are, and feel powerless in parenting—perspectives that lead them to move quickly toward physical force (Bugental & Happaney, 2004; Crouch et al., 2008).

Most parents have enough self-control not to respond with abuse to their child's misbehavior or developmental problems. Other factors combine with these conditions to prompt an extreme response. Abusive parents react to stressful situations with high emotional arousal. And low income, low education (less than a high school diploma), unemployment, alcohol and drug use, marital conflict, overcrowded living conditions, frequent moves, and extreme household disorganization are common in abusive homes (Wekerle et al., 2007; Wulczyn, 2009).

Each year, fourth to sixth graders across Los Angeles County enter a poster contest to celebrate National Child Abuse Prevention Month. This 2012 winner expresses a heartfelt appeal: "Don't Let Our Children Live in Fear." (Gillian Lih Bautista, 6th Grade, St. Genevieve Elementary, Panorama City, CA. Courtesy ICAN Associates, Los Angeles County Inter-Agency Council on Child Abuse and Neglect, ican4kids.org.)

These conditions increase the chances that parents will be too overwhelmed to meet basic child-rearing responsibilities or will vent their frustrations by lashing out at their children.

The Community. The majority of abusive and neglectful parents are isolated from both formal and informal social supports. Because of their life histories, many have learned to mistrust and avoid others and are poorly skilled at establishing and maintaining positive relationships. Also, maltreating parents are more likely to live in unstable, rundown neighborhoods that provide few links between family and community, such as preschool programs, recreation centers, and religious institutions (Coulton et al., 2007; Guterman et al., 2009). They lack "lifelines" to others and have no one to turn to for help during stressful times.

The Larger Culture. Cultural values, laws, and customs profoundly affect the chances that child maltreatment will occur when parents feel overburdened. Although the United States has laws to protect children from maltreatment, widespread support exists for use of physical force with children (refer back to page 208). Many countries—including Austria, Croatia, Cyprus, Denmark, Finland, Germany, Israel, Italy, Latvia, Norway, Sweden, and Uruguay—have outlawed corporal punishment, a measure that dampens both physical discipline and abuse (Zolotor & Puzia, 2010). Furthermore, all industrialized nations except the United States and France now prohibit corporal punishment in schools. The U.S. Supreme Court has twice upheld the right of school officials to use corporal punishment. Fortunately, 31 U.S. states and the District of Columbia have passed laws that ban it.

Consequences of Child Maltreatment. The family circumstances of maltreated children impair the development of emotional self-regulation, empathy and sympathy, self-concept, social skills, and academic motivation. Over time, these youngsters show serious adjustment problems—cognitive deficits (including impaired working memory and executive function), severe depression, aggressive behavior, peer difficulties, substance abuse, and violent crime—that persist into adulthood (Gould et al., 2010; Kaplow & Widom, 2007; Sanchez & Pollak, 2009).

How do these damaging consequences occur? Think back to our earlier discussion of hostile cycles of parent–child interaction. For abused children, these are especially severe. Also, a family characteristic strongly associated with child abuse is partner abuse (Graham-Bermann & Howell, 2011). Clearly, the home lives of abused children overflow with experiences that evoke profound distress and with opportunities to learn to use aggression to solve problems.

Furthermore, the trauma of repeated abuse is associated with central nervous system damage, including abnormal EEG brain-wave activity; fMRI-detected reduced size and impaired functioning of the cerebral cortex, corpus callosum, and cerebellum; and atypical production of the stress hormone cortisol—initially too high but, after months of abuse, often too low. Over time, the massive trauma of persistent abuse seems to blunt children's normal physiological response to stress (Cicchetti, 2007; Hart & Rubia, 2012). These effects increase the chances that cognitive and emotional problems will endure.

Preventing Child Maltreatment. Because child maltreatment is embedded in families, communities, and society as a whole, efforts to prevent it must be directed at each of these levels. Many approaches have been suggested, from teaching high-risk parents effective child-rearing strategies to developing broad social programs aimed at improving community services and economic conditions.

Providing social supports to families eases parental stress, sharply reducing child maltreatment. Parents Anonymous, a U.S. organization with affiliate programs around the world, helps child-abusing parents learn constructive parenting practices, largely through social supports. Its local chapters offer self-help group meetings, daily phone calls, and regular home visits to relieve social isolation and teach child-rearing skills.

Early intervention aimed at strengthening both child and parent competencies can reduce child maltreatment. Healthy Families America, a program that began in Hawaii and has spread to 440 sites across the United States and Canada, identifies at-risk families during pregnancy or at birth. Each receives three years of home visitation, in which a trained worker helps parents manage crises, encourages effective child rearing, and puts parents in touch with community services (Healthy Families America, 2011). In an evaluation of its effectiveness, Healthy Families home visitation alone reduced only neglect, not abuse (Duggan et al., 2004). But adding a *cognitive component* dramatically increased its impact. When home visitors helped parents change negative appraisals of their children, physical punishment and abuse dropped sharply after one year of intervention (Bugental et al., 2002).

Child maltreatment is a sad note on which to end our discussion of a period of childhood that is so full of excitement, awakening, and discovery. But there is reason to be optimistic. Great strides have been made over the past several decades in understanding and preventing child maltreatment.

ASK YOURSELF

REVIEW Is the concept of authoritative parenting useful for understanding effective parenting across cultures? Explain.

APPLY Chandra heard a news report about 10 severely neglected children, living in squalor in an inner-city tenement. She wondered, "Why would parents so mistreat their children?" How would you answer Chandra?

REFLECT How would you classify your parents' child-rearing styles? What factors might have influenced their approach to parenting?

SUMMARY

Erikson's Theory: Initiative versus Guilt (p. 200)

What personality changes take place during Erikson's stage of initiative versus guilt?

- Preschoolers develop a new sense of purposefulness as they grapple with Erikson's psychological conflict of **initiative versus guilt.** A healthy sense of initiative depends on exploring the social world through play, forming a conscience, and experiencing supportive parenting.

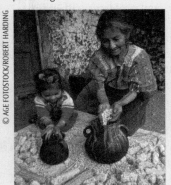

Self-Understanding (p. 201)

Describe preschoolers' self-concepts and the development of self-esteem.

- As preschoolers think more intently about themselves, they construct a **self-concept** consisting largely of observable characteristics and typical emotions and attitudes. A warm, sensitive parent–child relationship seems to foster a more positive, coherent early self-concept.

- During early childhood, high **self-esteem** contributes to a mastery-oriented approach to the environment. But even a little adult disapproval can undermine a young child's self-esteem and enthusiasm for learning.

Emotional Development (p. 202)

Identify changes in understanding and expressing emotion during early childhood, citing factors that influence those changes.

- Preschoolers' impressive understanding of the causes, consequences, and behavioral signs of basic emotions is supported by cognitive and language development, secure attachment, and conversations about feelings. By age 3 to 4, children are aware of various strategies for emotional self-regulation. Temperament and parental communication about coping strategies influence preschoolers' capacity to handle stress and negative emotion.

- As their self-concepts develop, preschoolers more often experience self-conscious emotions. They depend on feedback from parents and other adults to know when to feel each of these emotions.

- Empathy also becomes more common. Temperament and parenting influence the extent to which empathy leads to **sympathy** and results in **prosocial, or altruistic, behavior.**

Peer Relations (p. 203)

Describe peer sociability and friendship in early childhood, along with parental influences on early peer relations.

- During early childhood, peer interaction increases as children move from **nonsocial activity** to **parallel play,** then to **associative** and **cooperative play.** Nevertheless, both solitary and parallel play remain common.

- Preschoolers understand something about the uniqueness of friendship, but their friendships do not yet have an enduring quality. Children's social maturity contributes to later academic performance. Parents affect peer sociability both directly, through attempts to influence their child's peer relations, and indirectly, through their child-rearing practices.

Foundations of Morality (p. 206)

What are the central features of psychoanalytic, social learning, and cognitive-developmental approaches to moral development?

- Psychoanalytic theory emphasizes the emotional side of moral development, especially identification and guilt as motivators of good conduct. Contrary to Freud's theory, conscience formation is promoted not by fear of punishment and loss of parental love but by **induction,** in which an adult points out the effects of the child's misbehavior on others.

- Social learning theory focuses on how moral behavior is learned through reinforcement and modeling. Effective adult models of pro-social responses are warm and powerful, and they practice what they preach.

- Alternatives to harsh punishment such as **time out** and withdrawal of privileges can help parents avoid undesirable side effects of punishment. Parents can increase the effectiveness of punishment by being consistent, maintaining a warm parent–child relationship, and offering explanations.

- The cognitive-developmental perspective views children as active thinkers about social rules. By age 4, children consider intentions in making moral judgments. Preschoolers also distinguish **moral imperatives** from **social conventions** and **matters of personal choice.** However, they tend to reason rigidly about morality, focusing on outcomes and on physical harm.

Describe the development of aggression in early childhood, including family and media influences and effective approaches to reducing aggressive behavior.

- During early childhood, **proactive aggression** declines while **reactive aggression** increases. Proactive and reactive aggression come in three forms: **physical aggression** (more common in boys), **verbal aggression,** and **relational aggression.**

- Ineffective discipline and a conflict-ridden family atmosphere promote children's aggression, as does media violence. Effective approaches to reducing aggressive behavior include training parents in effective child-rearing practices, teaching children conflict-resolution skills, helping parents cope with stressors in their own lives, and shielding children from violent media.

Gender Typing (p. 213)

Discuss genetic and environmental influences on preschoolers' gender-stereotyped beliefs and behavior.

- **Gender typing** is well under way in the preschool years. Preschoolers acquire a wide range of gender-stereotyped beliefs, often applying them rigidly.

- Prenatal sex hormones contribute to boys' higher activity level and rougher play and to children's preference for same-sex playmates. But parents, teachers, peers, and the broader social environment also encourage many gender-typed responses.

CAVAN IMAGES/GETTY IMAGES

Describe and evaluate theories that explain the emergence of gender identity.

- Although most people have a traditional **gender identity,** some are **androgynous,** combining both masculine and feminine characteristics. Masculine and androgynous identities are linked to better psychological adjustment.

- According to social learning theory, preschoolers first acquire gender-typed responses through modeling and reinforcement and then organize these behaviors into gender-linked ideas about themselves. Cognitive-developmental theory maintains that children must master **gender constancy** before they develop gender-typed behavior.

- **Gender schema theory** combines features of social learning and cognitive-developmental perspectives. As children acquire gender-typed preferences and behaviors, they form masculine and feminine categories, or gender schemas, that they apply to themselves and their world.

Child Rearing and Emotional and Social Development (p. 217)

Describe the impact of child-rearing styles on children's development, and note cultural variations in child rearing.

- Three features distinguish **child-rearing styles:** (1) acceptance and involvement, (2) control, and (3) autonomy granting. In contrast to the **authoritarian, permissive,** and **uninvolved** styles, the **authoritative style** promotes cognitive, emotional, and social competence. Warmth, explanations, and reasonable demands for mature behavior account for the effectiveness of this style. **Psychological control,** associated with authoritarian parenting, contributes to adjustment problems.

- Certain ethnic groups, including Chinese, Hispanic, Asian Pacific Island, and African-American, combine parental warmth with high levels of control. But when control becomes harsh and excessive, it impairs academic and social competence.

Discuss the multiple origins of child maltreatment, its consequences for development, and effective prevention.

- Maltreating parents use ineffective discipline, hold a negatively biased view of their child, and feel powerless in parenting. Unmanageable parental stress and social isolation greatly increase the likelihood of abuse and neglect. Societal approval of physical force as a means of solving problems promotes child abuse.

- Maltreated children are impaired in emotional self-regulation, empathy and sympathy, self-concept, social skills, and academic motivation. The trauma of repeated abuse is associated with central nervous system damage and serious, lasting adjustment problems. Successful prevention requires efforts at the family, community, and societal levels.

Important Terms and Concepts

androgyny (p. 215)
associative play (p. 204)
authoritarian child-rearing style (p. 218)
authoritative child-rearing style (p. 217)
child-rearing styles (p. 217)
cooperative play (p. 204)
gender constancy (p. 215)
gender identity (p. 215)
gender schema theory (p. 216)
gender typing (p. 213)

induction (p. 207)
initiative versus guilt (p. 200)
matters of personal choice (p. 210)
moral imperatives (p. 210)
nonsocial activity (p. 203)
parallel play (p. 204)
permissive child-rearing style (p. 218)
physical aggression (p. 211)
proactive aggression (p. 211)
prosocial, or altruistic, behavior (p. 203)

psychological control (p. 218)
reactive aggression (p. 211)
relational aggression (p. 211)
self-concept (p. 201)
self-esteem (p. 201)
social conventions (p. 210)
sympathy (p. 203)
time out (p. 208)
uninvolved child-rearing style (p. 219)
verbal aggression (p. 211)

milestones

Development in Early Childhood

PHYSICAL

- Running, jumping, hopping, throwing, and catching become better coordinated. (173)
- Pedals and steers tricycle. (173)

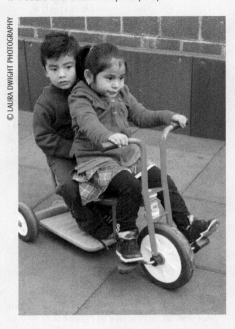

- Galloping and one-foot skipping appear. (173)
- Fastens and unfastens large buttons. (173)
- Uses scissors. (173)
- Uses fork effectively. (173)
- Draws first picture of a person, using tadpole image. (174)

COGNITIVE

- Understands the symbolic function of drawings and of models of real-world spaces. (174, 176–177)
- Distinguishes appearance from reality. (177)
- Grasps conservation, reasons about transformations, reverses thinking, and understands cause–effect sequences in familiar contexts. (178)
- Sorts familiar objects into hierarchically organized categories. (178)
- Uses private speech to guide behavior during challenging tasks. (182)
- Improves in sustained attention. (185)
- Uses scripts to recall familiar events. (185)
- Understands that both beliefs and desires determine behavior. (186)
- Knows the meaning of numbers up to 10, counts correctly, and grasps cardinality. (189)

2 years

PHYSICAL

- Throughout early childhood, height and weight increase more slowly than in toddlerhood. (167)
- Balance improves; walks more rhythmically; hurried walk changes to run. (173)
- Jumps, hops, throws, and catches with rigid upper body. (173)
- Puts on and removes simple items of clothing. (173)
- Uses spoon effectively. (173)
- First drawings are gestural scribbles. (174)

COGNITIVE

- Make-believe becomes less dependent on realistic objects, less self-centered, and more complex; sociodramatic play increases. (175–176)
- Understands the symbolic function of photos and realistic-looking pictures. (176–177)

- Takes the perspective of others in simplified, familiar situations and in face-to-face communication. (179)
- Recognition memory is well-developed. (185)
- Shows awareness of the distinction between inner mental and outer physical events. (186)
- Begins to count. (189)

LANGUAGE

- Vocabulary increases rapidly. (193)
- Uses a coalition of cues—perceptual and, increasingly, social and linguistic—to figure out word meanings. (194)
- Speaks in simple sentences that follow basic word order of native language, gradually adding grammatical markers. (194–195)
- Displays effective conversational skills. (195)

EMOTIONAL/SOCIAL

- Understands causes, consequences, and behavioral signs of basic emotions. (202)
- Begins to develop self-concept and self-esteem. (201)
- Shows early signs of developing moral sense—verbal evaluations of own and others' actions and distress at harmful behaviors. (206)
- May display proactive (instrumental) aggression. (211)
- Gender-stereotyped beliefs and behavior increase. (213)

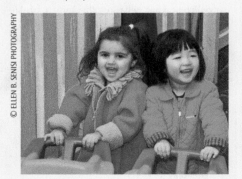

Note: Numbers in parentheses indicate the page or pages on which each milestone is discussed.

LANGUAGE

- Aware of some meaningful features of written language. (187–188)
- Coins new words based on known words; extends language meanings through metaphor. (194)
- Masters increasingly complex grammatical structures, occasionally overextending grammatical rules to exceptions. (195)
- Adjusts speech to fit the age, sex, and social status of listeners. (195)

EMOTIONAL/SOCIAL

- Describes self in terms of observable characteristics and typical emotions and attitudes. (201)
- Has several self-esteems, such as learning things in school, making friends, getting along with parents, and treating others kindly. (201)
- Emotional self-regulation improves. (202)
- Experiences self-conscious emotions more often. (202)
- Relies more on language to express empathy. (203)

- Engages in associative and cooperative play with peers, in addition to parallel play. (204)
- Forms first friendships, based on pleasurable play and sharing of toys. (205)
- Distinguishes truthfulness from lying. (210)
- Distinguishes moral imperatives from social conventions and matters of personal choice. (210)
- Proactive aggression declines, while reactive aggression (verbal and relational) increases. (211)
- Preference for same-sex playmates strengthens. (214)

5–6 years

PHYSICAL

- Starts to lose primary teeth. (167)
- Increases running speed, gallops more smoothly, and engages in true skipping. (173)
- Displays mature, flexible throwing and catching patterns. (173)
- Uses knife to cut soft foods. (173)
- Ties shoes. (173–174)

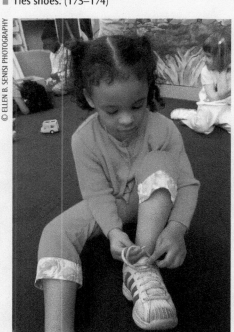

- Draws more complex pictures. (174)
- Copies some numbers and simple words; prints name. (174)

COGNITIVE

- Magical beliefs decline. (179)
- Improves in ability to distinguish appearance from reality. (177)

- Improves in sustained attention and planning. (185)
- Recognition, recall, scripted memory, and autobiographical memory improve. (185–186)

- Understanding of false belief strengthens. (186)

LANGUAGE

- Understands that letters and sounds are linked in systematic ways. (188)
- Uses invented spellings. (188)
- By age 6, vocabulary reaches about 10,000 words. (193)
- Uses most grammatical constructions competently. (195)

EMOTIONAL/SOCIAL

- Improves in emotional understanding (ability to interpret, predict, and influence others' emotional reactions). (202)

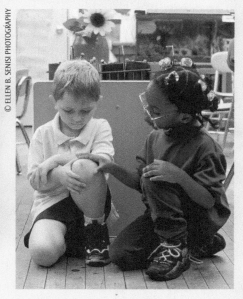

- Has acquired many morally relevant rules and behaviors. (207)
- Gender-stereotyped beliefs and behavior and preference for same-sex playmates continue to strengthen. (214)
- Understands gender constancy. (215–216)

chapter
10

Emotional and Social Development in Middle Childhood

© ELLEN B. SENISI PHOTOGRAPHY

Social understanding expands greatly in middle childhood. Like others their age around the world, these third graders choose friends based on personal qualities, and they count on those friends for understanding and emotional support.

chapter outline

Late one afternoon, Rena heard her son Joey burst through the front door, run upstairs, and phone his best friend. "Terry, gotta talk to you," Joey pleaded breathlessly. "Everything was going great until I got that word—*porcupine,*" Joey went on, referring to the fifth-grade spelling bee at school that day. "Just my luck! *P-o-r-k,* that's how I spelled it! I can't believe it. Maybe I'm not so good at social studies," Joey confided, "but I *know* I'm better at spelling than that stuck-up Belinda Brown. I knocked myself out studying those spelling lists. Then *she* got all the easy words. If I *had* to lose, why couldn't it be to a nice person?"

Joey's conversation reflects new emotional and social capacities. By entering the spelling bee, he shows *industriousness,* the energetic pursuit of meaningful achievement in his culture. Joey's social understanding has also expanded: He can size up strengths, weaknesses, and personality characteristics. Furthermore, friendship means something different than it did earlier—Joey counts on his best friend, Terry, for understanding and emotional support.

For an overview of the personality changes of middle childhood, we return to Erikson's theory. Then we look at children's views of themselves and of others, their moral understanding, and their peer relationships. Each increases in complexity as children reason more effectively and spend more time in school and with agemates.

ELISA CICINELLI/BRAND X PICTURES/GETTY IMAGES

Despite changing parent–child relationships, the family remains powerfully influential in middle childhood. Today, family lifestyles are more diverse than ever before. Through Joey and his younger sister Lizzie's experiences with parental divorce, we will see that family functioning is far more important than family structure in ensuring children's well-being. Finally, we look at some common emotional problems of middle childhood. ●

Erikson's Theory: Industry versus Inferiority

According to Erikson (1950), children whose previous experiences have been positive enter middle childhood prepared to redirect their energies toward realistic accomplishment. Erikson believed that the combination of adult expectations and children's drive toward mastery sets the stage for the psychological conflict of middle childhood, **industry versus inferiority,** which is resolved positively when children develop a sense of competence at useful skills and tasks.

In industrialized nations and increasingly in developing regions of the world, the beginning of formal schooling marks the transition to middle childhood. In school, children discover their own and others' unique capacities, learn the value of division of labor, and develop a sense of moral commitment and responsibility. The danger at this stage is *inferiority,* reflected in the pessimism of children who lack confidence in their ability to do things well. This sense of inadequacy can develop when family life has not prepared children for school life or when teachers and peers destroy children's self-confidence with negative responses.

Erikson's sense of industry combines several developments of middle childhood: a positive but realistic self-concept, pride in accomplishment, moral responsibility, and cooperative participation with agemates. How do these aspects of self and social relationships change over the school years?

Self-Understanding

In middle childhood, children begin to describe themselves in terms of psychological traits, compare their own characteristics with those of their peers, and speculate about the causes of their strengths and weaknesses. These transformations in self-understanding have a major impact on self-esteem.

Self-Concept

During the school years, children refine their self-concept, organizing their observations of behaviors and internal states into general dispositions. A major change takes place between ages 8 and 11, as the following self-description by an 11-year-old illustrates:

> My name is A. I'm a human being. I'm a girl. I'm a truthful person. I'm not pretty. I do so-so in my studies. I'm a very good cellist. . . . I try to be helpful. I'm always ready to be friends with anybody. Mostly I'm good, but I lose my temper. (Montemayor & Eisen, 1977, pp. 317–318)

Instead of specific behaviors, this child emphasizes competencies: "I'm a very good cellist" (Damon & Hart, 1988). She also describes her personality, mentioning both positive and negative traits: "truthful" but short-tempered. Older school-age children are far less likely than younger children to describe themselves in extreme, all-or-none ways. These qualified, trait-based self-descriptions result from cognitive advances—specifically, the ability to combine typical experiences and behaviors into psychological dispositions. Children also become better at *perspective taking*—inferring others' attitudes toward the child—and incorporating those attitudes into their self-definitions. These cognitive capacities, combined with more experiences in which children are evaluated against agemates, prompt **social comparisons**—judgments of one's own appearance, abilities, and behavior in relation to those of others. For example, Joey observed that he was better than his peers at spelling but not so good at social studies (Harter, 2006). As children internalize others' expectations and make social comparisons, they form an *ideal self* that they use to evaluate their *real self*. As we will see, a large discrepancy between the two can undermine self-esteem, leading to sadness, hopelessness, and depression.

In middle childhood, children look to more people beyond the family for information about themselves as they enter a wider range of settings in school and community. And self-descriptions now include frequent reference to social groups: "I'm a Boy Scout, a paper boy, and a Prairie City soccer player," said Joey. As children move into adolescence, although parents and other adults remain influential, self-concept is increasingly vested in feedback from close friends (Oosterwegel & Oppenheimer, 1993).

But recall that the makeup of self-concept varies from culture to culture. In earlier chapters, we noted that Asian parents stress harmonious interdependence, whereas Western parents stress independence and self-assertion. When asked to recall personally significant past experiences (their last birthday, a time their parent scolded them), U.S. school-age children gave longer accounts including more personal preferences, interests, skills, and opinions. Chinese children, in contrast, more often referred to social interactions and to others. Similarly, in their self-descriptions, U.S. children listed more personal attributes ("I'm smart," "I like hockey"), Chinese children more attributes involving group membership and relationships ("I'm in second grade," "My friends are crazy about me") (Wang, 2006; Wang, Shao, & Li, 2010).

Finally, although school-age children from diverse cultures view themselves as more knowledgeable about their own inner attributes than significant adults, Japanese children credit their parents and teachers with considerably more knowledge than Western children do (Mitchell et al., 2010, p. 249). Perhaps because of their more interdependent self, Japanese children assume that their inner states are more transparent to others.

Self-Esteem

Recall that most preschoolers have extremely high self-esteem. But as children enter school and receive more feedback about how well they perform compared with their peers, self-esteem differentiates and also adjusts to a more realistic level.

Researchers have asked children to indicate the extent to which statements such as "I am good at reading" or "I'm usually the one chosen for games" are true of themselves. By age 6 to 7, children have formed at least four broad self-evaluations: academic competence, social competence, physical/athletic competence, and physical appearance. Within these are more refined categories that become increasingly distinct with age (Marsh, 1990; Marsh & Ayotte, 2003; Van den Bergh & De Rycke, 2003). Furthermore, the capacity to view the self in terms of stable dispositions permits school-age children to combine their separate self-evaluations into a general psychological image of themselves—an overall sense of self-esteem (Harter, 2003, 2006). As a result, self-esteem takes on the hierarchical structure shown in Figure 10.1 on page 262.

Children attach greater importance to certain self-evaluations than to others. Although individual differences exist, during childhood and adolescence, perceived physical appearance correlates more strongly with overall self-worth than any other self-esteem factor (Klomsten, Skaalvik, & Espnes, 2004; Shapka & Keating, 2005). Emphasis on appearance—in the media, by parents and peers, and in society—has major implications for young people's overall satisfaction with themselves.

Over the first few years of elementary school, level of self-esteem declines as children evaluate themselves in various areas (Marsh, Craven, & Debus, 1998; Wigfield et al., 1997). Typically, the drop is not great enough to be harmful. Most (but not all) children appraise their characteristics and competencies realistically while maintaining an attitude of self-respect. Then, from fourth grade on, self-esteem rises for the majority of young people, who feel especially good about their peer relationships and athletic capabilities (Impett et al., 2008; Twenge & Campbell, 2001).

Influences on Self-Esteem

From middle childhood on, individual differences in self-esteem become increasingly stable (Trzesniewski, Donnellan, & Robins, 2003). And positive relationships among self-esteem, valuing of various activities, and success at those activities emerge and strengthen (Denissen, Zarrett, & Eccles, 2007; Valentine, DuBois, & Cooper, 2004; Whitesell et al., 2009). What social influences might lead self-esteem to be high for some children and low for others?

Culture. An especially strong emphasis on social comparison in school may explain why Chinese and Japanese children, despite their higher academic achievement, score lower than U.S. children in self-esteem (Harter, 2006; Hawkins, 1994; Twenge & Crocker, 2002). And because their culture values

In response to feedback from classmates and teachers, the self-esteem of these schoolchildren in India gradually adjusts to a more realistic level.

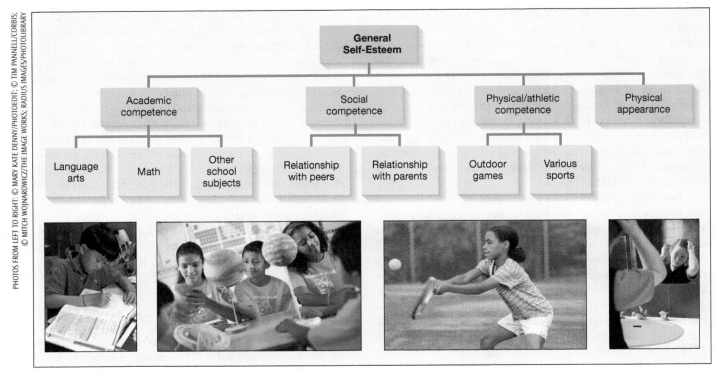

FIGURE 10.1 **Hierarchical structure of self-esteem in the mid-elementary school years.** From their experiences in different settings, children form at least four separate self-esteems: academic competence, social competence, physical/athletic competence, and physical appearance. These differentiate into additional self-evaluations and combine to form a general sense of self-esteem.

social harmony, Asian children tend to be reserved about judging themselves positively but generous in their praise of others (Falbo et al., 1997).

Gender-stereotyped expectations also affect self-esteem. In one study, the more 5- to 8-year-old girls talked with friends about the way people look, watched TV shows focusing on physical appearance, and perceived their friends as valuing thinness, the greater their dissatisfaction with their physical

An 11-year-old performs a traditional African dance at a community Kwanzaa celebration. A stronger sense of ethnic pride may be partly responsible for African-American children's higher self-esteem relative to their Caucasian agemates.

self and the lower their overall self-esteem a year later (Dohnt & Tiggemann, 2006). In academic self-judgments, girls score higher in language arts self-esteem, whereas boys have higher math, science, and physical/athletic self-esteem—even when children of equal skill levels are compared (Fredricks & Eccles, 2002; Jacobs et al., 2002; Kurtz-Costes et al., 2008). At the same time, girls exceed boys in self-esteem dimensions of close friendship and social acceptance. And despite a widely held assumption that boys' overall self-worth is much higher than girls', the difference is slight (Marsh & Ayotte, 2003; Young & Mroczek, 2003). Girls may think less well of themselves because they internalize this negative cultural message.

Compared with their Caucasian agemates, African-American children tend to have slightly higher self-esteem, possibly because of warm extended families and a stronger sense of ethnic pride (Gray-Little & Hafdahl, 2000). Finally, children and adolescents who attend schools or live in neighborhoods where their SES and ethnic groups are well-represented feel a stronger sense of belonging and have fewer self-esteem problems (Gray-Little & Carels, 1997).

Child-Rearing Practices. Children whose parents use an *authoritative* child-rearing style (see Chapter 8) feel especially good about themselves (Lindsey et al., 2008; Wilkinson, 2004). Warm, positive parenting lets children know that they are accepted as competent and worthwhile. And firm but appropriate expectations, backed up with explanations, help them evaluate their own behavior against reasonable standards.

Controlling parents—those who too often help or make decisions for their child—communicate a sense of inadequacy to children. Having parents who are repeatedly disapproving is also linked to low self-esteem (Kernis, 2002; Pomerantz & Eaton, 2000). Children subjected to such parenting need constant reassurance, and many rely heavily on peers to affirm their self-worth—a risk factor for adjustment difficulties, including aggression and antisocial behavior (Donnellan et al., 2005). In contrast, indulgent parenting is correlated with unrealistically high self-esteem. These children tend to lash out at challenges to their overblown self-images and, thus, are also likely to be hostile and aggressive (Hughes, Cavell, & Grossman, 1997; Thomaes et al., 2008).

The best way to foster a positive, secure self-image is to encourage children to strive for worthwhile goals. Over time, achievement fosters self-esteem, which contributes to further effort and gains in performance (Gest, Domitrovich, & Welsh, 2005; Marsh et al., 2005). What can adults do to promote, and to avoid undermining, this mutually supportive relationship between motivation and self-esteem? Some answers come from research on the precise content of adults' messages to children in achievement situations.

Achievement-Related Attributions.

Attributions are our common, everyday explanations for the causes of behavior—our answers to the question, "Why did I or another person do that?" Notice how Joey, in talking about the spelling bee at the beginning of this chapter, attributes his disappointing performance to *luck* (Belinda got all the easy words) and his usual success to *ability* (he *knows* he's a better speller than Belinda). Joey also appreciates that *effort* matters: "I knocked myself out studying those spelling lists."

Cognitive development permits school-age children to separate all these variables in explaining performance (Dweck, 2002). Those who are high in academic self-esteem and motivation make **mastery-oriented attributions,** crediting their successes to ability—a characteristic they can improve through trying hard and can count on when facing new challenges. And they attribute failure to factors that can be changed or controlled, such as insufficient effort or a very difficult task (Heyman & Dweck, 1998). Whether these children succeed or fail, they take an industrious, persistent approach to learning.

In contrast, children who develop **learned helplessness** attribute their failures, not their successes, to ability. When they succeed, they conclude that external factors, such as luck, are responsible. Unlike their mastery-oriented counterparts, they believe that ability is fixed and cannot be improved by trying hard (Cain & Dweck, 1995). When a task is difficult, these children experience an anxious loss of control—in Erikson's terms, a pervasive sense of inferiority. They give up without really trying.

Children's attributions affect their goals. Mastery-oriented children seek information on how best to increase their ability through effort. Hence, their performance improves over time (Blackwell, Trzesniewski, & Dweck, 2007). In contrast, learned-

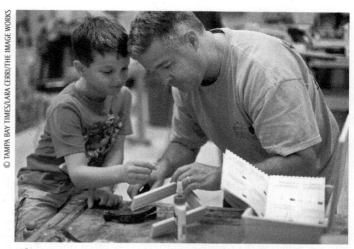

A 7-year-old in a woodworking class seeks additional information on how to assemble a jewelry box. Using this mastery-oriented, effortful approach to overcoming obstacles, his performance will improve over time.

helpless children focus on obtaining positive and avoiding negative evaluations of their fragile sense of ability. Over time, their ability no longer predicts how well they do (Pomerantz & Saxon, 2001). Because they fail to connect effort with success, learned-helpless children do not develop the metacognitive and self-regulatory skills necessary for high achievement (see Chapter 9). Lack of effective learning strategies, reduced persistence, and a sense of loss of control sustain one another in a vicious cycle (Chan & Moore, 2006).

Influences on Achievement-Related Attributions.

Adult communication plays a key role in the different attributions of mastery-oriented and learned-helplessness children (Pomerantz & Dong, 2006). Children with a learned-helpless style often have parents who believe that their child is not very capable. When the child fails, the parent might say, "You can't do that, can you? It's OK if you quit." When the child succeeds, the parent might offer feedback that evaluates the child's traits ("You're so smart"). Such trait statements—even when positive—encourage children to adopt a fixed view of ability (Mueller & Dweck, 1998). This leads them to question their competence in the face of challenges.

LOOK AND LISTEN

Observe a school-age child working on a challenging homework assignment under the guidance of a parent or other adult. What features of the adult's communication likely foster mastery-oriented attributions? How about learned helplessness? Explain. ●

Despite their higher achievement, girls more often than boys blame poor performance on lack of ability. When girls do not do well, they tend to receive messages from teachers and parents that their ability is at fault, and negative stereotypes (for example, that girls are weak at math) undermine their interest and effort (Bleeker & Jacobs, 2004; Cole et al., 1999). And as

Chapter 9 revealed, low-SES ethnic minority students often receive less favorable feedback from teachers—conditions that result in a drop in academic self-esteem and achievement (Harris & Graham, 2007).

Finally, cultural values affect the likelihood that children will develop learned helplessness. Asian parents and teachers are more likely than their American counterparts to view effort as key to success and as a moral responsibility—messages they transmit to children (Mok, Kennedy, & Moore, 2011; Pomerantz, Ng, & Wang, 2008). Asians also attend more to failure than to success because failure indicates where corrective action is needed. Americans, in contrast, focus more on success because it enhances self-esteem. Observations of U.S. and Chinese mothers' responses to their fourth and fifth graders' puzzle solutions revealed that the U.S. mothers offered more praise after success, whereas the Chinese mothers more often pointed out the child's inadequate performance. And Chinese mothers made more task-relevant statements aimed at ensuring that children exerted sufficient effort ("You concentrated on it": "You got only 6 out of 12") (Ng, Pomerantz, & Lam, 2007). When children continued with the task after mothers left the room, the Chinese children showed greater gains in performance.

Fostering a Mastery-Oriented Approach. Attribution research suggests that well-intended messages from adults sometimes undermine children's competence. An intervention called *attribution retraining* encourages learned-helpless children to believe that they can overcome failure by exerting more effort. Children are given tasks difficult enough that they will experience some failure, followed by repeated feedback that helps them revise their attributions: "You can do it if you try harder." After they succeed, children receive additional feedback—"You're really good at this" or "You really tried hard on that one"—so that they attribute their success to both ability and effort, not chance. Another approach is to encourage low-effort students to focus less on grades and more on mastering a task for individual improvement (Hilt, 2004; Yeh, 2010). Instruction in effective strategies and self-regulation is also vital, to compensate for development lost in this area and to ensure that renewed effort pays off (Wigfield et al., 2006).

ASK YOURSELF

REVIEW How does level of self-esteem change in middle childhood, and what accounts for these changes?

APPLY Should parents promote children's self-esteem by telling them they're "smart" or "wonderful"? Are children harmed if they do not feel good about everything they do? Why or why not?

REFLECT Recall your own attributions for academic successes and failures when you were in elementary school. What are those attributions like now? What messages from others may have contributed to your attributions?

 # Emotional Development

Greater self-awareness and social sensitivity support gains in emotional competence in middle childhood. Changes take place in experience of self-conscious emotions, emotional understanding, and emotional self-regulation.

Self-Conscious Emotions

In middle childhood, the self-conscious emotions of pride and guilt become clearly governed by personal responsibility. Children experience pride in a new accomplishment and guilt over a transgression, even when no adult is present (Harter & Whitesell, 1989).

Pride motivates children to take on further challenges, whereas guilt prompts them to make amends and to strive for self-improvement. But in Chapter 8 we noted that excessive guilt is linked to depressive symptoms. And harsh, insensitive reprimands from adults ("Everyone else can do it! Why can't you?") can lead to intense shame, which is particularly destructive, yielding both internalizing and externalizing problems (see page 203).

Emotional Understanding

School-age children's understanding of mental activity means that, unlike preschoolers, they are likely to explain emotion by referring to internal states, such as happy or sad thoughts (Flavell, Flavell, & Green, 2001). Also, between ages 6 and 12, children become more aware of circumstances likely to spark mixed emotions, each of which may be positive or negative and may differ in intensity (Larsen, To, & Fireman, 2007; Pons et al., 2003). For example, Joey reflected, "I was very happy that I got a birthday present from my grandma but a little sad that I didn't get just what I wanted."

Appreciating mixed emotions helps children realize that people's expressions may not reflect their true feelings (Misailidi, 2006). It also fosters awareness of self-conscious emotions. For example, between ages 6 and 7, children improve sharply in ability to distinguish pride from happiness and surprise (Tracy, Robins, & Lagattuta, 2005). And 8- and 9-year-olds understand that pride combines two sources of happiness—joy in accomplishment and joy that a significant person recognized that accomplishment (Harter, 1999).

As with self-understanding, gains in emotional understanding are supported by cognitive development and social experiences, especially adults' sensitivity to children's feelings and willingness to discuss emotions. Together, these factors lead to a rise in empathy as well. As children move closer to adolescence, advances in perspective taking permit an empathic response not just to people's immediate distress but also to their general life condition (Hoffman, 2000). As Joey and Lizzie imagined how people who are chronically ill or hungry feel and evoked those emotions in themselves, they gave part of their allowance to charity and joined in school and scouting fundraising projects.

Detroit-area schoolchildren prepare meal packages for families in need. Gains in emotional understanding and perspective taking enable children to expand their empathic responding to include people's general life condition.

Emotional Self-Regulation

Rapid gains in emotional self-regulation occur in middle childhood. As children engage in social comparison and care more about peer approval, they must learn to manage negative emotion that threatens their self-esteem.

By age 10, most children shift adaptively between two general strategies for managing emotion. In **problem-centered coping,** they appraise the situation as changeable, identify the difficulty, and decide what to do about it. If problem solving does not work, they engage in **emotion-centered coping,** which is internal, private, and aimed at controlling distress when little can be done about an outcome (Kliewer, Fearnow, & Miller, 1996; Lazarus & Lazarus, 1994). For example, when faced with an anxiety-provoking test or an angry friend, older school-age children view problem solving and seeking social support as the best strategies. But when outcomes are beyond their control—for example, after receiving a bad grade—they opt for distraction or try to redefine the situation: "Things could be worse. There'll be another test." School-age children's improved ability to appraise situations and reflect on thoughts and feelings means that, compared with preschoolers, they more often use these internal strategies to manage emotion (Brenner & Salovey, 1997).

When emotional self-regulation has developed well, school-age children acquire a sense of *emotional self-efficacy*—a feeling of being in control of their emotional experience (Saarni, 2000; Thompson & Goodman, 2010). This fosters a favorable self-image and an optimistic outlook, which further help children face emotional challenges. As at younger ages, school-age children whose parents respond sensitively and helpfully when the child is distressed are emotionally well-regulated—generally upbeat in mood and also empathic and prosocial. In contrast, poorly regulated children often experience hostile, dismissive parental reactions to distress (Davidov & Grusec, 2006; Zeman, Shipman, & Suveg, 2002). These children are overwhelmed by negative emotion, a response that interferes with empathy and prosocial behavior.

 ## Moral Development

Recall from Chapter 8 that preschoolers pick up many morally relevant behaviors through modeling and reinforcement. By middle childhood, they have had time to internalize rules for good conduct: "It's good to help others in trouble" or "It's wrong to take something that doesn't belong to you." This change leads children to become considerably more independent and trustworthy.

In Chapter 8, we also saw that children do not just copy their morality from others but actively think about right and wrong. An expanding social world, the capacity to consider more information when reasoning, and perspective taking lead moral understanding to advance greatly in middle childhood.

Moral and Social-Conventional Understanding

During the school years, children construct a flexible appreciation of moral rules. By age 7 to 8, they no longer say truth telling is always good and lying is always bad but also consider prosocial and antisocial intentions. They evaluate certain types of truthfulness very negatively—for example, blunt statements, particularly when made in public contexts where they are especially likely to have negative social consequences (telling a classmate that you don't like her drawing) (Bussey, 1999; Ma et al., 2011).

As children's ideas about justice take into account an increasing number of variables, they clarify and link moral imperatives and social conventions. School-age children, for example, distinguish social conventions with a clear *purpose* (not running in school hallways to prevent injuries) from ones with no obvious justification (crossing a "forbidden" line on the playground). They regard violations of purposeful social conventions as closer to moral transgressions (Buchanan-Barrow & Barrett, 1998). With age, they also realize that people's *intentions* and the *contexts* of their actions affect the moral implications of violating a social convention. In one study, 8- to 10-year-olds

This 10-year-old understands the moral implications of observing social conventions, such as expressing respect for his country's flag. He also grasps that flag burning is sometimes justifiable as a form of freedom of expression.

stated that because of a flag's symbolic value, burning it to express disapproval of a country or to start a cooking fire is worse than burning it accidentally. But they recognized that flag burning is a form of freedom of expression, and most agreed that it would be acceptable in a country that treated its citizens unfairly (Helwig & Prencipe, 1999).

Children in Western and non-Western cultures reason similarly about moral and social-conventional concerns (Neff & Helwig, 2002; Nucci, 2005, 2008). When a directive is fair and caring, such as telling children to stop fighting or to share candy, school-age children view it as right, regardless of who states it—a principal, a teacher, or a child with no authority. In contrast, even in Korean culture, which places a high value on deference to authority, 7- to 11-year-olds evaluate negatively a teacher's or principal's order to engage in immoral acts, such as stealing or refusing to share (Kim, 1998; Kim & Turiel, 1996). In sum, children everywhere seem to realize that higher principles, independent of rule and authority, must prevail when people's personal rights and welfare are at stake.

Understanding Individual Rights

When children challenge adult authority, they typically do so within the personal domain. As their grasp of moral imperatives and social conventions strengthens, so does their conviction that certain choices, such as hairstyle, friends, and leisure activities, are up to the individual.

Notions of personal choice, in turn, enhance children's moral understanding. As early as age 6, children view freedom of speech and religion as individual rights, even if laws exist that deny those rights (Helwig, 2006). And they regard laws that discriminate against individuals—for example, denying certain people access to medical care or education—as wrong and worthy of violating (Helwig & Jasiobedzka, 2001). In justifying their responses, children appeal to personal privileges and, by the end of middle childhood, to the importance of individual rights for maintaining a fair society.

At the same time, older school-age children place limits on individual choice, depending on circumstances. Fourth graders faced with conflicting moral and personal concerns—such as whether or not to befriend a classmate of a different race or gender—typically decide in favor of kindness and fairness (Killen et al., 2002). Partly for this reason, as we will see next, prejudice usually declines during middle childhood.

Understanding Diversity and Inequality

By the early school years, children associate power and privilege with white people and poverty and inferior status with people of color. They do not necessarily acquire these views directly from parents or friends, whose attitudes often differ from their own (Aboud & Doyle, 1996). Rather, children seem to pick up prevailing societal attitudes from social contexts that present a world sorted into groups, such as racial and ethnic segregation in schools and communities.

In-Group and Out-Group Biases: Development of Prejudice. Studies in diverse Western nations confirm that by age 5 to 6, white children generally evaluate their own racial group favorably and other racial groups less favorably or negatively. *In-group favoritism* emerges first; children simply prefer their own group, generalizing from self to similar others (Bennett et al., 2004; Nesdale et al., 2004). And the ease with which a trivial group label supplied by an adult can induce in-group favoritism is striking. In one study, Caucasian-American 5-year-olds were told that they were members of a group based on T-shirt color. Although no information was provided about group status and the children never met any group members, they still displayed vigorous in-group favoritism (Dunham, Baron, & Carey, 2011). When shown photos of unfamiliar agemates wearing either an in-group or an out-group shirt, the children claimed to like members of their own group better, gave them more resources, and engaged in positively biased recall of group members' behavior.

Out-group prejudice requires a more challenging social comparison between in-group and out-group. But it does not take long for white children to acquire negative attitudes toward ethnic minority out-groups when such attitudes are encouraged by their environments. When white Canadian 4- to 7-year-olds living in a white community and attending nearly all-white schools sorted positive and negative adjectives into boxes labeled as belonging to a white child and a black child, out-group prejudice emerged at age 5. Unfortunately, many minority children show a reverse pattern: *out-group favoritism,* in which they assign positive characteristics to the privileged white majority and negative characteristics to their own group (Averhart & Bigler, 1997; Corenblum, 2003).

But recall that with age, children pay more attention to inner traits. The capacity to classify the social world in multiple ways enables school-age children to understand that people who look different need not think, feel, or act differently (Aboud, 2008). Consequently, voicing of negative attitudes toward minorities declines. After age 7 to 8, both majority and minority children express in-group favoritism, and white children's openly expressed prejudice against out-group members often weakens (Nesdale et al., 2005; Ruble et al., 2004). Yet even in children aware of the injustice of discrimination, prejudice can operate automatically without awareness—through subtle negative emotional reactions toward the out-group—as it does in many white adults (Degner & Wentura, 2010; Dunham, Baron, & Banaji, 2006). At least to some degree, then, older school-age children's desire to present themselves in a socially acceptable light may contribute to reduced overt expressions of prejudice with age.

The extent to which children hold racial and ethnic biases varies, depending on the following personal and situational factors:

- *A fixed view of personality traits.* Children who believe that people's personality traits are fixed rather than changeable readily form prejudices on the basis of limited information.

For example, they might infer that "a new child at school who tells a lie to get other kids to like her" is simply a bad kid (Levy & Dweck, 1999).

● *Overly high self-esteem.* Children (and adults) with very high self-esteem are more likely to hold racial and ethnic prejudices (Baumeister et al., 2003; Bigler, Brown, & Markell, 2001). These individuals seem to belittle disadvantaged people or groups to justify their own extremely favorable, yet insecure, self-evaluations.

● *A social world in which people are sorted into groups.* The more adults highlight group distinctions and the less interracial contact children experience, the more likely white children will express out-group prejudice (Killen et al., 2010).

Reducing Prejudice. Research confirms that an effective way to reduce prejudice is through intergroup contact, in which racially and ethnically different children have equal status, work toward common goals, and become personally acquainted. Children assigned to cooperative learning groups with peers of diverse backgrounds show low levels of prejudice in their expressions of likability and in their behavior. For example, they form more cross-race friendships (Pettigrew & Tropp, 2006). Sharing thoughts and feelings with close, cross-race friends, in turn, reduces even subtle, unintentional prejudices (Turner, Hewstone, & Voci, 2007). But these positive effects seem not to generalize to out-group members who are not part of these learning teams.

Long-term contact and collaboration among neighborhood, school, and community groups may be the best way to reduce prejudice (Rutland, Killen, & Abrams, 2010). Classrooms that expose children to ethnic diversity, teach them to value those differences, directly address the damage caused by preju-

dice, and encourage perspective taking and empathy both prevent children from forming negative biases and reduce already acquired biases (Dweck, 2009).

Finally, inducing children to view others' traits as changeable, by discussing with them the many possible influences on those traits, is helpful. The more children believe that people can change their personalities, the more they report liking and perceiving themselves as similar to members of disadvantaged out-groups. Furthermore, children who believe in the changeability of human attributes spend more time volunteering to help the needy (Karafantis & Levy, 2004). Volunteering may, in turn, promote a changeable view of others by helping children appreciate the social conditions that lead to disadvantage.

ASK YOURSELF

REVIEW How does emotional self-regulation improve in middle childhood? What implications do these changes have for children's self-esteem?

APPLY Seven-year-old Tracy heard her parents discussing an older cousin's fiancé. "Molly can marry whomever she wants," Tracy chimed in. "That's *her* choice." How is Tracy's reasoning contributing to her moral understanding?

REFLECT Did you attend an integrated elementary school? Why is school integration vital for reducing racial and ethnic prejudice?

Peer Relations

In middle childhood, the society of peers becomes an increasingly important context for development. Peer contact, as we have seen, contributes to perspective taking and understanding of self and others. These developments, in turn, enhance peer interaction. Compared with preschoolers, school-age children resolve conflicts more effectively, using persuasion and compromise (Mayeux & Cillessen, 2003). Sharing, helping, and other prosocial acts also increase. In line with these changes, aggression declines. But the drop is greatest for physical attacks (Côte et al., 2007). As we will see, verbal and relational aggression continue as children form peer groups.

Peer Groups

TAKE A MOMENT... Watch children in the schoolyard or neighborhood, and notice how often they gather in groups of three to a dozen or more. In what ways are members of the same group noticeably alike? By the end of middle childhood, children display a strong desire for group belonging. They form **peer groups,** collectives that generate unique values and standards for behavior and a social structure of leaders and

THE STAR-LEDGER/STEVE HOCKSTEIN/THE IMAGE WORKS

Third graders perform a traditional Chinese dance at their culturally diverse school. Long-term contact and collaboration with members of other ethnic groups reduces prejudice.

followers. Peer groups organize on the basis of proximity (being in the same classroom) and similarity in sex, ethnicity, academic achievement, popularity, and aggression (Rubin, Bukowski, & Parker, 2006).

The practices of these informal groups lead to a "peer culture" that typically involves a specialized vocabulary, dress code, and place to "hang out." These customs bind peers together, creating a sense of group identity. Within the group, children acquire many social skills—cooperation, leadership, follower-ship, and loyalty to collective goals.

Most school-age children believe a group is wrong to exclude a peer (Killen, Crystal, & Watanabe, 2002). Neverthe-less, children do exclude, often using relationally aggressive tactics. Peer groups—at the instigation of their leaders, who can be skillfully aggressive—frequently oust no longer "respected" children. Some of these castouts, whose own previous behavior toward outsiders reduces their chances of being included else-where, turn to other low-status peers with poor social skills (Farmer et al., 2010; Werner & Crick, 2004). Socially anxious children, when ousted, often become increasingly peer-avoidant and thus more isolated (Buhs, Ladd, & Herald-Brown, 2010). In either case, opportunities to acquire socially competent behav-ior diminish.

School-age children's desire for group membership can also be satisfied through formal group ties such as scouting, 4-H, and religious youth groups. Adult involvement holds in check the negative behaviors associated with children's informal peer groups.

DAVID ROTH/TAXI/GETTY IMAGES

These boys have probably established a peer-group structure of leaders and followers as they gather for joint activities. Their relaxed body language and similar way of dressing suggest a strong sense of group belonging.

Friendships

Whereas peer groups provide children with insight into larger social structures, friendships contribute to the development of trust and sensitivity. During the school years, friendship becomes more complex and psychologically based. Consider the follow-ing 8-year-old's ideas:

How come you like Shelly better than anyone else? She's done the most for me. She never disagrees, she never eats in front of me, she never walks away when I'm crying, and she helps me with my homework. . . . *How do you get someone to like you?* . . . If you're nice to [your friends], they'll be nice to you. (Damon, 1988b, pp. 80–81)

As these responses show, friendship has become a mutually agreed-on relationship in which children like each other's per-sonal qualities and respond to one another's needs and desires. And once a friendship forms, *trust* becomes its defining feature. Consequently, older children regard violations of trust, such as not helping when others need help, breaking promises, and gos-siping behind the other's back, as serious breaches of friendship (Hartup & Abecassis, 2004).

LOOK AND LISTEN

Ask an 8- to 11-year-old to tell you what he or she looks for in a best friend. Is *trust* centrally important? Does the child mention personality traits, just as school-age children do in describing themselves? ●

Because of these features, school-age children's friendships are more selective. Whereas preschoolers say they have lots of friends, by age 8 or 9, children name only a handful of good friends, and their friendships last longer—sometimes for sev-eral years. Girls, who demand greater closeness than boys, are more exclusive in their friendships (Markovits, Benenson, & Dolensky, 2001).

In addition, children tend to select friends similar to them-selves in age, sex, ethnicity, and SES. Friends also resemble one another in personality (sociability, inattention/hyperactiv-ity, aggression, depression), popularity, academic achievement, prosocial behavior, and judgments (including biased percep-tions) of other people (Hartup, 2006; Mariano & Harton, 2005). But friendship opportunities offered by children's environments also affect their choices. As noted earlier, in integrated class-rooms with mixed-race collaborative learning groups, students form more cross-race friendships.

Through friendship, children come to realize that close relationships can survive disagreements if friends are secure in their liking for each other (Hartup, 2006). In this way, friendship provides an important context in which children learn to toler-ate criticism and resolve disputes.

Yet the impact of friendships on development depends on the nature of those friends. Children who bring kindness and compassion to their friendships strengthen each other's pro-social tendencies and form more lasting ties. When aggressive children make friends, the relationship is often riddled with

Cross-race friendships are common in integrated classrooms with rich opportunities for collaborative learning.

hostile interaction and is at risk for breakup, especially when just one member of the pair is aggressive (Ellis & Zarbatany, 2007). Aggressive girls' friendships are full of jealousy, conflict, and betrayal. Aggressive boys' friendships involve frequent expressions of anger, coercive statements, physical attacks, and enticements to rule-breaking behavior (Bagwell & Coie, 2004; Crick & Nelson, 2002; Werner & Crick, 2004). These findings indicate that the social problems of aggressive children operate within their closest peer ties.

Peer Acceptance

Peer acceptance refers to likability—the extent to which a child is viewed by a group of agemates, such as classmates, as a worthy social partner. Unlike friendship, likability is not a mutual relationship but a one-sided perspective, involving the group's view of an individual. Nevertheless, certain social skills that contribute to friendship also enhance peer acceptance. Better-accepted children tend to have more friends and more positive relationships with them (Lansford et al., 2006).

To assess peer acceptance, researchers usually use self-reports that measure *social preferences*—for example, asking children to identify classmates whom they "like very much" or "like very little" (Hymel et al., 2004). Another approach assesses *social prominence*—children's judgments of the peers most of their classmates admire. Only moderate correspondence exists between the classmates children identify as prominent (looked up to by many others) and those they say they personally prefer (Prinstein & Cillessen, 2003).

Children's self-reports yield four general categories of peer acceptance:

- **Popular children,** who get many positive votes (are well-liked)
- **Rejected children,** who get many negative votes (are disliked)

- **Controversial children,** who get a large number of positive and negative votes (are both liked and disliked)
- **Neglected children,** who are seldom mentioned, either positively or negatively

About two-thirds of students in a typical elementary school classroom fit one of these categories (Coie, Dodge, & Coppotelli, 1982). The remaining one-third, who do not receive extreme scores, are *average* in peer acceptance.

Peer acceptance is a powerful predictor of psychological adjustment. Rejected children, especially, are anxious, unhappy, disruptive, and low in self-esteem. Both teachers and parents rate them as having a wide range of emotional and social problems. Peer rejection in middle childhood is also strongly associated with poor school performance, absenteeism, dropping out, substance use, depression, antisocial behavior, and delinquency in adolescence and with criminality in early adulthood (Ladd, 2005; Laird et al., 2001; Rubin, Bukowski, & Parker, 2006).

However, earlier influences—children's characteristics combined with parenting practices—may largely explain the link between peer acceptance and adjustment. School-age children with peer-relationship problems are more likely to have weak emotion regulation skills and to have experienced family stress due to low income, insensitive child rearing, and coercive discipline (Cowan & Cowan, 2004; Trentacosta & Shaw, 2009). Nevertheless, peer rejection adds to the risk of maladjustment, beyond rejected children's maladaptive behavioral styles (Sturaro et al., 2011).

Determinants of Peer Acceptance. Why is one child liked while another is rejected? A wealth of research reveals that social behavior plays a powerful role.

Popular Children. Two subtypes of popular children exist. The majority are **popular-prosocial children,** who combine academic and social competence, performing well in school and communicating with peers in sensitive, friendly, and cooperative ways (Cillessen & Bellmore, 2004). A smaller number are admired for their socially adept yet belligerent behavior. These **popular-antisocial children** include "tough" boys—athletically skilled but poor students who cause trouble and defy adult authority—and relationally aggressive boys and girls who enhance their own status by ignoring, excluding, and spreading rumors about other children (Rodkin et al., 2000; Rose, Swenson, & Waller, 2004; Vaillancourt & Hymel, 2006). With age, peers like these high-status, aggressive youths less and less and may eventually reject them.

Rejected Children. Rejected children display a wide range of negative social behaviors. The largest subtype, **rejected-aggressive children,** show high rates of conflict, physical and relational aggression, and hyperactive, inattentive, and impulsive behavior. They are even more belligerent than popular-aggressive children and are also deficient in perspective taking and emotion regulation (Dodge, Coie, & Lynam, 2006; Hoza et al., 2005). In contrast, **rejected-withdrawn children** are passive

Biology and Environment

Bullies and Their Victims

Follow the activities of aggressive children over a school day, and you will see that they reserve their hostilities for certain peers. A particularly destructive form of interaction is **peer victimization**, in which certain children become targets of verbal and physical attacks or other forms of abuse. What sustains these repeated assault–retreat cycles?

About 20 percent of children are bullies, while 25 percent are repeatedly victimized. Most bullies are boys who use both physically, verbally, and relationally aggressive tactics, but a considerable number of girls bombard vulnerable classmates with verbal and relational hostility (Cook et al., 2010). As bullies move into adolescence, gender harassment increases—powerful youths (more often boys) delivering insults of a sexual nature against weaker agemates, and heterosexual youths targeting sexual minority peers (Pepler et al., 2006). Furthermore, many youths amplify their attacks through electronic means. About 20 to 40 percent of youths have experienced "cyberbullying" through text messages, e-mail, chat rooms, or other electronic tools (Tokunaga, 2010). They often do not report it to parents or adults at school.

Many bullies are disliked because of their cruelty. But a substantial number are socially prominent youngsters, who are broadly admired for their physical attractiveness, leadership, or athletic abilities (Vaillancourt et al., 2010c). To preserve their high social status, bullies often target already peer-rejected children, whom classmates are unlikely to defend (Veenstra et al., 2010). This helps explain why peers rarely intervene to help victims, and why 20 to 30 per-

cent of onlookers actually encourage bullies, even joining in (Salmivalli & Voeten, 2004).

Chronic victims tend to be passive when active behavior is expected. On the playground, they hang around chatting or wander on their own. When bullied, they give in, cry, and assume defensive postures (Boulton, 1999). Biologically based traits—an inhibited temperament and a frail physical appearance—contribute to victimization. But victims also have histories of resistant attachment, overly controlling child rearing, and maternal overprotection—parenting that prompts anxiety, low self-esteem, and dependency, resulting in a fearful demeanor that marks these children as vulnerable (Snyder et al., 2003). Victims' adjustment problems include depression, loneliness, poor school performance, unruly behavior, and school avoidance (Paul & Cillessen, 2003). And like persistent child abuse, victimization is linked to impaired production of cortisol, suggesting a disrupted physiological response to stress (Vaillancourt et al., 2010b).

Interventions that change victimized children's negative opinions of themselves and that teach them to respond in nonreinforcing ways to their attackers are helpful. Another way to assist victimized children is to help them form and maintain a gratifying friendship (Fox & Boulton, 2006). When children have a close friend to whom they can turn for help, bullying episodes usually end quickly.

Although modifying victimized children's behavior can help, this does not mean they

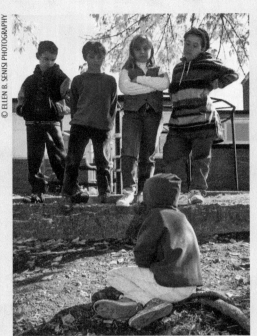

Some bullies are high-status youngsters, but many are disliked, or become so, because of their cruelty. And chronic victims are often easy targets—physically weak, passive, and inhibited.

are to blame. The best way to reduce bullying is to promote prosocial attitudes and behaviors. Effective approaches include developing school and community codes against bullying; teaching child bystanders to intervene; strengthening adult supervision of high-bullying areas in schools, such as hallways and schoolyard; enlisting parents' assistance in changing bullies' behaviors; and (if necessary) moving socially prominent bullies to another class or school (Kiriakidis & Kavoura, 2010; Vaillancourt et al., 2010a).

and socially awkward. These timid children are overwhelmed by social anxiety, hold negative expectations for treatment by peers, and worry about being scorned and attacked (see the Biology and Environment box above) (Hart et al., 2000; Rubin, Bowker, & Gazelle, 2010; Troop-Gordon & Asher, 2005). As rejected children are excluded, their classroom participation declines, their feelings of loneliness rise, their academic achievement falters, and they want to avoid school (Buhs, Ladd, & Herald-Brown, 2010; Gooren et al., 2011). Most have few friends, and some have none—a circumstance that predicts severe adjustment difficulties (Ladd et al., 2011).

LOOK AND LISTEN

Contact a nearby elementary school or a school district to find out what practices are in place to prevent bullying. Inquire about a written antibullying policy, and request a copy. ●

Controversial and Neglected Children. Consistent with the mixed peer opinion they engender, controversial children display a blend of positive and negative social behaviors. They are hostile and disruptive, but they also engage in positive, prosocial acts (de Bruyn & Cillessen, 2006; Newcomb, Bukowski, & Pattee, 1993). But like their popular-antisocial and rejected-aggressive counterparts, they often bully others and engage in calculated relational aggression to sustain their dominance (DeRosier & Thomas, 2003; Putallaz et al., 2007).

Perhaps the most surprising finding is that neglected children, once thought to be in need of treatment, are usually well-adjusted. Although they engage in low rates of interaction, most are just as socially skilled as average children. They do not report feeling lonely or unhappy, and when they want to, they can break away from their usual pattern of playing alone, cooperating well with peers and forming positive, stable friendships (Ladd & Burgess, 1999; Ladd et al., 2011). Neglected, socially competent children remind us that an outgoing, gregarious personality style is not the only path to emotional well-being.

Helping Rejected Children. A variety of interventions exist to improve the peer relations and psychological adjustment of rejected children. Most involve coaching, modeling, and reinforcing positive social skills, such as how to initiate interaction with a peer, cooperate in play, and respond to another child with friendly emotion and approval. Several of these programs have produced lasting gains in social competence and peer acceptance (Asher & Rose, 1997; DeRosier, 2007).

Still another approach focuses on training in perspective taking and in solving social problems. But many rejected-aggressive children are unaware of their poor social skills and do not take responsibility for their social failures (Mrug, Hoza, & Gerdes, 2001). Rejected-withdrawn children, in contrast, are likely to develop a *learned-helpless* approach to peer difficulties—concluding, after repeated rebuffs, that they will never be liked (Wichmann, Coplan, & Daniels, 2004). Both types of children need help attributing their peer difficulties to internal, changeable causes.

As rejected children gain in social skills, teachers must encourage peers to alter their negative opinions. Accepted children often selectively recall rejected classmates' negative acts while overlooking their positive ones (Mikami, Lerner, & Lun, 2010; Peets et al., 2007). Consequently, even in the face of contrary evidence, rejected children's negative reputations tend to persist. Teachers' praise and expressions of liking can modify peer judgments.

Finally, because rejected children's social incompetence often originates in harsh, authoritarian parenting, interventions focusing on the child alone may not be sufficient (Bierman & Powers, 2009). If the parent–child interaction does not change, children may soon return to their old behavior patterns.

Gender Typing

Children's understanding of gender roles broadens in middle childhood, and their gender identities (views of themselves as relatively masculine or feminine) change as well. We will see that development differs for boys and girls.

Gender-Stereotyped Beliefs

Research in many countries reveals that stereotyping of personality traits increases steadily in middle childhood, becoming adultlike around age 11 (Best, 2001; Heyman & Legare, 2004). For example, children regard "tough," "aggressive," "rational," and "dominant" as masculine and "gentle," "sympathetic," and "dependent" as feminine (Serbin, Powlishta, & Gulko, 1993).

Children derive these distinctions from observing sex differences in behavior as well as from adult treatment. When helping a child with a task, for example, parents (especially fathers) behave in a more mastery-oriented fashion with sons, setting higher standards, explaining concepts, and pointing out important features of tasks—particularly during gender-typed pursuits, such as science activities (Tenenbaum & Leaper, 2003; Tenenbaum et al., 2005). Furthermore, parents less often encourage girls to make their own decisions. And both parents and teachers more often praise boys for knowledge and accomplishment, girls for obedience (Good & Brophy, 2003; Leaper, Anderson, & Sanders, 1998; Pomerantz & Ruble, 1998).

Also in line with adult stereotypes, school-age children quickly figure out which academic subjects and skill areas are "masculine" and which are "feminine." They often regard reading, spelling, art, and music as more for girls and mathematics, athletics, and mechanical skills as more for boys (Cvencek, Meltzoff, & Greenwald, 2011; Eccles, Jacobs, & Harold, 1990). These attitudes influence children's preferences and sense of competence. As we saw earlier (page 262), boys tend to feel more competent at math, science, and athletics, whereas girls feel more competent at language arts—gender differences still evident after controlling for actual performance.

An encouraging sign is that in several recent investigations carried out in Canada, France, and the United States, a majority of elementary and secondary students disagreed with the idea that math is a "masculine" subject (Martinot & Désert, 2007; Plante, Théoret, & Favreau, 2009; Rowley et al. 2007). And although school-age children are aware of many stereotypes, they also develop a more open-minded view of what males and females *can do* (Trautner et al., 2005). The ability to classify flexibly contributes to this change. School-age children realize that a person's sex is not a certain predictor of his or her personality traits, activities, and behavior. Similarly, by the end of middle childhood, most children regard gender typing as socially rather than biologically influenced (Taylor, Rholdes, & Gelman, 2009).

Nevertheless, acknowledging that people *can* cross gender lines does not mean that children always *approve* of doing so. In one longitudinal study, between ages 7 and 13, children of both genders became more open-minded about girls being offered the same opportunities as boys. This increasing flexibility, however, was less pronounced among boys (Crouter et al., 2007). Furthermore, many children take a harsh view of certain violations—boys playing with dolls and wearing girls' clothing, girls acting noisily and roughly. They are especially intolerant when boys engage in these "cross-gender" acts (Blakemore, 2003).

Gender Identity and Behavior

From third to sixth grade, boys tend to strengthen their identification with "masculine" personality traits, whereas girls' identification with "feminine" traits declines. Girls are more *androgynous,* often describing themselves as having some "other-gender" characteristics (Serbin, Powlishta, & Gulko, 1993). And whereas boys usually stick to "masculine" activities, many girls experiment with a wider range of options—from cooking and sewing to sports and science fairs—and consider traditionally male future work roles (Liben & Bigler, 2002).

These changes are due to a mixture of cognitive and social forces. School-age children of both sexes are aware that society attaches greater prestige to "masculine" characteristics. For example, they rate "masculine" occupations as having higher status than "feminine" occupations (Liben, Bigler, & Krogh, 2001; Weisgram, Bigler, & Liben, 2010). Messages from adults and peers are also influential. In Chapter 8, we saw that parents (especially fathers) are far less tolerant when sons, as opposed to daughters, cross gender lines. Similarly, a tomboyish girl can make her way into boys' activities without losing the approval of her female peers, but a boy who engages in "feminine" pursuits is likely to be ridiculed and rejected.

As school-age children make social comparisons and characterize themselves in terms of stable dispositions, their gender identity expands to include the following self-evaluations, which greatly affect their adjustment:

● *Gender typicality*—the degree to which the child feels he or she "fits in" with others of the same gender (Egan & Perry, 2001).

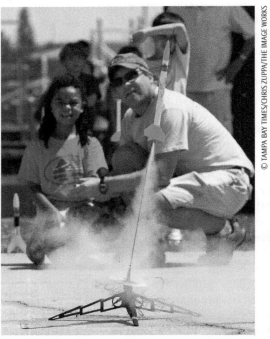

An 8-year-old launches the rocket she made in her school's Young Astronaut Club. Whereas school-age boys usually stick to "masculine" pursuits, girls experiment with a wider range of options.

● *Gender contentedness*—the degree to which the child feels comfortable with his or her gender assignment.

● *Felt pressure to conform to gender roles*—the degree to which the child feels parents and peers disapprove of his or her gender-related traits.

In a longitudinal study of third through seventh graders, *gender-typical* and *gender-contented* children gained in self-esteem over the following year. In contrast, children who were *gender-atypical* and *gender-discontented* declined in self-worth. Furthermore, gender-atypical children who reported *intense pressure to conform to gender roles* experienced serious difficulties—withdrawal, sadness, disappointment, and anxiety (Yunger, Carver, & Perry, 2004). Intervening with parents and peers to help them become more accepting of children's gender-atypical interests and behaviors can protect gender-atypical children's well-being (Bigler, 2007; Conway, 2007; Crawford, 2003).

ASK YOURSELF

REVIEW Why are girls more androgynous than boys in middle childhood?

APPLY What changes in parent–child relationships are probably necessary to help rejected children?

REFLECT As a school-age child, did you have classmates you would classify as popular-aggressive? What were they like, and why do you think peers admired them?

 Family Influences

As children move into school, peer, and community contexts, the parent–child relationship changes. At the same time, children's well-being continues to depend on the quality of family interaction. In the following sections, we will see that contemporary diversity in family life—divorce, remarriage, maternal employment, and dual-earner families—can have positive as well as negative effects on children. In later chapters, we take up other family structures, including gay and lesbian families, never-married single-parent families, and the increasing numbers of grandparents rearing grandchildren.

Parent–Child Relationships

In middle childhood, the amount of time children spend with parents declines dramatically. Children's growing independence means that parents must deal with new issues. "I've struggled with how many chores to assign, how much allowance to give, whether their friends are good influences, and what to do about problems at school," Rena remarked. "And then there's the challenge of keeping track of them when they're out—or even when they're home and I'm not there to see what's going on."

Despite these new concerns, child rearing becomes easier for those parents who established an authoritative style during the early years. Reasoning is more effective with school-age children because of their greater capacity for logical thinking and their increased respect for parents' expert knowledge (Collins, Madsen, & Susman-Stillman, 2002).

As children demonstrate that they can manage daily activities and responsibilities, effective parents engage in **coregulation,** a form of supervision in which parents exercise general oversight while letting children take charge of moment-by-moment decision making. Coregulation grows out of a warm, cooperative relationship between parent and child based on give-and-take. Parents must guide and monitor from a distance and effectively communicate expectations when they are with their children. And children must inform parents of their whereabouts, activities, and problems so parents can intervene when necessary (Maccoby, 1984).

As at younger ages, mothers tend to spend more time than fathers with school-age children. Still, many fathers are highly involved (Galinsky, Aumann, & Bond, 2009). Each parent, however, tends to devote more time to children of his or her own sex (Lamb & Lewis, 2004; Tucker, McHale, & Crouter, 2003). And parents are more vigilant about monitoring the activities of same-sex children while their children are away from home.

Siblings

Sibling rivalry tends to increase in middle childhood. As children participate in a wider range of activities, parents often compare siblings' traits and accomplishments (Dunn, 2004; Tamrouti-Makkink et al., 2004). The child who gets less parental affection, more disapproval, or fewer material resources is likely to be resentful and show poorer adjustment.

For same-sex siblings who are close in age, parental comparisons are more frequent, resulting in more antagonism. This effect is particularly strong when parents are under stress as a result of financial worries, marital conflict, single parenthood, or child negativity (Jenkins, Rasbash, & O'Connor, 2003). Parents whose energies are drained become less careful about being fair.

To reduce this rivalry, siblings often strive to be different from one another. For example, two brothers I know deliberately selected different athletic pursuits and musical instruments. Parents can limit the effects of rivalry by making an effort not to compare children, but some feedback about their competencies is inevitable. As siblings strive to win recognition for their own uniqueness, they shape important aspects of each other's development.

Although conflict rises, school-age siblings continue to rely on each other for companionship and support (Seibert & Kerns, 2009; Tucker, McHale, & Crouter, 2001). But for siblings to reap these benefits, parental encouragement of warm, considerate sibling ties is vital. The more positive their relationship, the

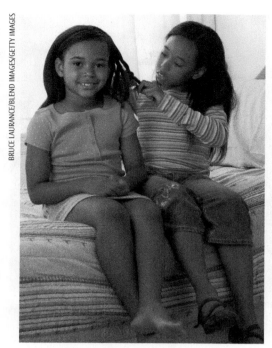

Although sibling rivalry tends to increase in middle childhood, siblings also provide each other with emotional support and help with difficult tasks.

more siblings resolve disagreements constructively, provide each other with various forms of assistance, and contribute to resilience in the face of major stressors, such as parental divorce (Conger, Stocker, & McGuire, 2009; Soli, McHale, & Feinberg, 2009).

When siblings get along well, the older sibling's academic and social competence tends to "rub off on" the younger sibling, fostering more favorable achievement and peer relations (Brody & Murry, 2001; Lamarche et al., 2006). But destructive sibling conflict in middle childhood is associated with negative outcomes, including conflict-ridden peer relationships, anxiety, depressed mood, and later substance use and delinquency, even after other family relationship factors are controlled (Criss & Shaw, 2005; Kim et al., 2007; Stocker, Burwell, & Briggs, 2002).

Only Children

Although sibling relationships bring many benefits, they are not essential for healthy development. Contrary to popular belief, only children are not spoiled, and in some respects, they are advantaged. U.S. children growing up in one-child and multichild families do not differ in self-rated personality traits (Mottus, Indus, & Allik, 2008). And compared to children with siblings, only children are higher in self-esteem, do better in school, and attain higher levels of education. One reason may be that only children have somewhat closer relationships with parents, who may exert more pressure for mastery and accomplishment (Falbo, 1992). However, only children tend to be less well-accepted in the peer group, perhaps because they have not

BRUCE LAURANCE/BLEND IMAGES/GETTY IMAGES

WANG ZHAO/AFP/GETTY IMAGES

Limiting family size has been a national policy in China for more than three decades. In urban areas, the majority of couples have no more than one child.

had opportunities to learn effective conflict-resolution strategies through sibling interactions (Kitzmann, Cohen, & Lockwood, 2002).

Favorable development also characterizes only children in China, where a one-child family policy has been enforced in urban areas for more than three decades to control population growth (Yang, 2008). Compared with agemates who have siblings, Chinese only children are advanced in cognitive development and academic achievement. They also feel more emotionally secure, perhaps because government disapproval promotes tension in families with more than one child (Falbo & Poston, 1993; Jiao, Ji, & Jing, 1996; Yang et al., 1995).

China's birth rate, at 1.5 overall and 0.7 in its largest cities, is now lower than that of many developed nations. As a result, its elderly population is rapidly increasing while its working-age population has leveled off—an imbalance that threatens the country's economic progress. And because sons are more highly valued than daughters, the policy has resulted in an epidemic of abortions of female fetuses and abandonment of girl babies, yielding a vastly skewed population sex ratio (130 male births for every 100 female births) that jeopardizes social stability (Zhu & Hesketh, 2009). Consequently, China is considering relaxing the one-child policy, but it is now so culturally ingrained that couples typically say they would not have a second child, even if offered the opportunity (LaFraniere, 2011).

Divorce

Children's interactions with parents and siblings are affected by other aspects of family life. Joey and Lizzie's relationship, Rena told me, had been particularly negative only a few years before. Joey pushed, hit, and taunted Lizzie and called her names—fighting that coincided with Rena and her husband's growing

marital unhappiness. When Joey was 8 and Lizzie 5, their father, Drake, moved out.

Between 1960 and 1985, divorce rates in Western nations rose dramatically before stabilizing in most countries. The United States has experienced a decline in divorces over the past decade, largely due to a rise in age at first marriage (Amato & Dorius, 2010). Nevertheless, the United States continues to have the highest divorce rate in the world (see Figure 10.2). Of the 45 percent of American marriages that end in divorce, half involve children. At any given time, one-fourth of U.S. children live in single-parent households. Although most reside with their mothers, the percentage in father-headed households has increased steadily, to about 12 percent (Federal Interagency Forum on Child and Family Statistics, 2011).

Children of divorce spend an average of five years in a single-parent home. About two-thirds of divorced parents marry again. Half of their children eventually experience a third major change—the end of a parent's second marriage (Hetherington & Kelly, 2002).

These figures reveal that divorce is a transition that leads to a variety of new living arrangements, accompanied by changes in housing, income, and family roles and responsibilities. Since the 1960s, many studies have reported that marital breakup is stressful for children. But how well children fare depends on

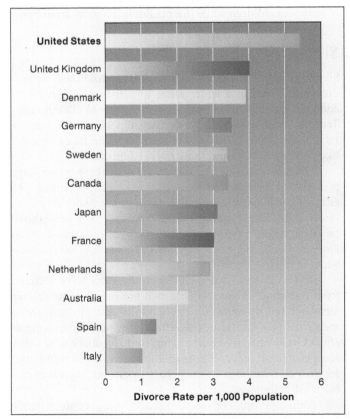

FIGURE 10.2 Divorce rates in 12 industrialized nations. The U.S. divorce rate is the highest in the industrialized world, far exceeding divorce rates in other countries. (Adapted from U.S. Census Bureau, 2013.)

many factors: the custodial parent's psychological health, the child's characteristics, and social supports within the family and surrounding community (Fine, Ganong, & Demo, 2010).

Immediate Consequences.

"Things were worst during the period Drake and I decided to separate," Rena reflected. "We fought over division of our belongings and custody of the children, and the kids suffered. Sobbing, Lizzie told me she was 'sorry she made Daddy go away.' Joey kicked and threw things at home and didn't do his work at school. In the midst of everything, I could hardly deal with their problems. We had to sell the house, and I needed a better-paying job."

Family conflict often rises around the time of divorce as parents try to settle disputes over children and possessions. Once one parent moves out, additional events threaten supportive interactions between parents and children. Many mother-headed households experience a sharp drop in income. In the United States, 27 percent of divorced mothers with young children live in poverty, and more are low-income, getting less than the full amount of child support from the absent father or none at all (Grall, 2011).

The transition from marriage to divorce typically leads to high maternal stress, depression, and anxiety and to a disorganized family situation. Declines in well-being are greatest for mothers of young children (Williams & Dunne-Bryant, 2006). "Meals and bedtimes were at all hours, and I stopped taking Joey and Lizzie on weekend outings," said Rena. As children react with distress and anger to their less secure home lives, discipline may become harsh and inconsistent. Contact with noncustodial fathers often decreases over time (Hetherington & Kelly, 2002). Fathers who see their children only occasionally are inclined to be permissive and indulgent, making the mother's task of managing the child even more difficult.

The more parents argue and fail to provide children with warmth, involvement, and consistent guidance, the poorer children's adjustment. About 20 to 25 percent of children in divorced families display severe problems, compared with about 10 percent in nondivorced families (Lansford, 2009; Noller et al., 2008). At the same time, reactions vary with children's age, temperament, and sex.

Children's Age.

Preschool and young school-age children often blame themselves for a marital breakup (as Lizzie did) and fear that both parents may abandon them. And although older children have the cognitive maturity to understand that they are not responsible for their parents' divorce, many react strongly, declining in school performance, becoming unruly, and escaping into undesirable peer activities, especially when family conflict is high (D'Onofrio et al., 2006; Lansford et al., 2006). Some older children—especially the oldest child in the family—display more mature behavior, willingly taking on extra household tasks as well as emotional support of a depressed, anxious mother. But if these demands are too great, these children may eventually become resentful and engage in angry, acting-out behavior (Hetherington, 1999).

Children's Temperament and Sex.

Exposure to stressful life events and inadequate parenting magnifies the problems of temperamentally difficult children (Lengua et al., 2000). In contrast, easy children are less often targets of parental anger and also cope more effectively with adversity.

These findings help explain sex differences in response to divorce. Girls sometimes respond as Lizzie did, with internalizing reactions such as crying, self-criticism, and withdrawal. More often, children of both sexes show demanding, attention-getting behavior. But in mother-custody families, boys are at slightly greater risk for serious adjustment problems (Amato, 2010). Recall from Chapter 8 that boys are more active and noncompliant—behaviors that increase with exposure to parental conflict and inconsistent discipline.

Long-Term Consequences.

Rena eventually found better-paying work and gained control over the daily operation of the household. And after several meetings with a counselor, Rena and Drake realized the harmful impact of their quarreling on Joey and Lizzie. Drake visited regularly and handled Joey's unruliness with firmness and consistency. Soon Joey's school performance improved, his behavior problems subsided, and both children seemed calmer and happier.

Most children show improved adjustment by two years after divorce. Yet overall, children and adolescents of divorced parents continue to score slightly lower than children of continuously married parents in academic achievement, self-esteem, social competence, and emotional and behavior problems (Lansford, 2009). And divorce is linked to problems with adolescent sexuality and development of intimate ties. Young people who experienced parental divorce—especially more than once—display higher rates of early sexual activity and adolescent parenthood. Some experience other lasting difficulties—reduced educational attainment, troubled romantic relationships and marriages, and divorce in adulthood (Amato, 2006, 2010).

The overriding factor in positive adjustment following divorce is effective parenting—shielding the child from family conflict and using authoritative child rearing (Leon, 2003; Wolchik et al., 2000). Where the custodial parent is the mother, contact with fathers is important. In the United States, paternal contact has risen over the past three decades, with about one-third of children today experiencing at least weekly visits (Amato & Dorius, 2010).

The more paternal contact and the warmer the father–child relationship, the less children react with defiance and aggression (Dunn et al., 2004). For girls, a good father–child relationship protects against early sexual activity and unhappy romantic involvements. For boys, it seems to affect overall psychological well-being. In fact, several studies indicate that outcomes for sons are better when the father is the custodial parent (Clarke-Stewart & Hayward, 1996; McLanahan, 1999). Fathers' greater economic security and image of authority seem to help them engage in effective parenting with sons.

Although divorce is painful for children, remaining in an intact but high-conflict family is much worse than making the

Applying What We Know

Helping Children Adjust to Their Parents' Divorce

Suggestion	Explanation
Shield children from conflict.	Witnessing intense parental conflict is very damaging to children. If one parent insists on expressing hostility, children fare better if the other parent does not respond in kind.
Provide children with as much continuity, familiarity, and predictability as possible.	Children adjust better during the period surrounding divorce when their lives have some stability—for example, the same school, bedroom, babysitter, playmates, and daily schedule.
Explain the divorce, and tell children what to expect.	Children are more likely to develop fears of abandonment if they are not prepared for their parents' separation. They should be told that their parents will not be living together anymore, which parent will be moving out, and when they will be able to see that parent. Parents should provide a reason that each child can understand and assuring children that they are not to blame.
Emphasize the permanence of the divorce.	Fantasies of parents getting back together can prevent children from accepting the reality of their current life. Children should be told that the divorce is final and that they cannot change this fact.
Respond sympathetically to children's feelings.	For children to adjust well, their painful emotions must be acknowledged, not denied or avoided.
Engage in authoritative parenting.	Parents who engage in authoritative parenting—providing affection and acceptance, reasonable demands for mature behavior, and consistent, rational discipline—greatly reduce their children's risk of maladjustment.
Promote a continuing relationship with both parents.	When parents disentangle their lingering hostility toward the former spouse from the child's need for a continuing relationship with the other parent, children adjust well. Grandparents and other extended-family members can help by not taking sides.

Source: Teyber, 2001.

transition to a low-conflict, single-parent household (Greene et al., 2003; Strohschein, 2005). However, more parents today are divorcing because they are moderately (rather than extremely) dissatisfied with their relationship. Research suggests that children in these low-discord homes are especially puzzled and upset. Perhaps these youngsters' inability to understand the marital breakup and grief over the loss of a seemingly happy home life explain why the adjustment problems of children of divorce have intensified over time (Amato, 2001; Lansford, 2009). Regardless of the extent of their friction, divorcing parents who manage to engage in *coparenting* (see page 46 in Chapter 2), supporting each other in their child-rearing roles, greatly improve the chances of favorable child outcomes.

Divorce Mediation, Joint Custody, and Child Support. Community-based services aimed at helping divorcing families include *divorce mediation,* a series of meetings between divorcing adults and a trained professional aimed at reducing family conflict, including legal battles over property division and child custody. Research reveals that mediation increases out-of-court settlements, cooperation and involvement of both parents in child rearing, and parents' and children's feelings of well-being (Emery, Sbarra, & Grover, 2005).

Joint custody, which grants parents equal say in important decisions about the child's upbringing, is becoming increasingly common. Children usually reside with one parent and see the other on a fixed schedule, similar to the typical sole-custody

situation. In other cases, parents share physical custody, and children move between homes—transitions that can be especially hard on some children. Joint-custody parents report little conflict—fortunately so, since the success of the arrangement depends on effective coparenting. And their children tend to be better-adjusted than children in sole-maternal-custody homes (Bauserman, 2002).

Finally, many single-parent families depend on child support from the noncustodial parent to relieve financial strain. All U.S. states have procedures for withholding wages from parents who fail to make these payments. Noncustodial fathers who have generous visitation schedules and who often see their children are more likely to pay child support regularly (Amato & Sobolewski, 2004). Applying What We Know above summarizes ways to help children adjust to their parents' divorce.

Blended Families

"If you get married to Wendell, and Daddy gets married to Carol," Lizzie wondered aloud to Rena, "then I'll have two sisters and one more brother. And let's see, how many grandmothers and grandfathers? A lot!" exclaimed Lizzie.

About 60 percent of divorced parents remarry within a few years. Others *cohabit,* or share a sexual relationship and a residence with a partner outside of marriage. Parent, stepparent, and children form a new family structure called the **blended,** or **reconstituted, family.** For some children, this expanded family network is positive, bringing greater adult attention. But children in blended families usually have more adjustment problems than children in stable, first-marriage families (Jeynes, 2007; Nicholson et al., 2008). Switching to stepparents' new rules and expectations can be stressful, and children often view steprelatives as intruders. How well they adapt is, again, related to the quality of family functioning (Hetherington & Kelly, 2002). This depends on which parent forms a new relationship, the child's age and sex, and the complexity of blended-family relationships. As we will see, older children and girls seem to have the hardest time.

Mother–Stepfather Families. Because mothers generally retain custody of children, the most common form of blended family is a mother–stepfather arrangement. Boys tend to adjust quickly, welcoming a stepfather who is warm and who refrains from exerting his authority too quickly. Mothers' friction with sons also declines as a result of greater economic security, another adult to share household tasks, and an end to loneliness (Visher, Visher, & Pasley, 2003). Girls, however, often react with sulky, resistant behavior when a new stepfather disrupts the close ties they have established with their mothers (Bray, 1999; Ganong, Coleman, & Jamison, 2011).

But age affects these findings. Older school-age children and adolescents of both sexes display more irresponsible, acting-out behavior than their peers not in stepfamilies (Hetherington & Stanley-Hagan, 2000; Robertson, 2008). If parents are warmer and more involved with their biological children than with their stepchildren, older children are more likely to notice and challenge unfair treatment. And adolescents often view the new stepparent as a threat to their freedom. But when teenagers have affectionate, cooperative relationships with their mothers, many eventually develop good relations with their stepfathers—a circumstance linked to better adjustment (King, 2009; Yuan & Hamilton, 2006).

To help these teenagers adapt to life in a complex blended family, both father and stepmother must avoid favoring their much younger children, born after remarriage.

Father–Stepmother Families. Remarriage of non-custodial fathers often leads to reduced contact with their biological children, especially when fathers remarry quickly, before they have established postdivorce parent–child routines (Dunn, 2002; Juby et al., 2007). When fathers have custody, children typically react negatively to remarriage. One reason is that children living with fathers often start out with more problems. Perhaps the biological mother could no longer handle the difficult child (usually a boy), so the father and his new partner are faced with a youngster who has behavior problems. In other instances, the father has custody because of a very close relationship with the child, and his remarriage disrupts this bond (Buchanan, Maccoby, & Dornbusch, 1996).

Girls, especially, have a hard time getting along with their stepmothers, either because the remarriage threatens the girl's bond with her father or because she becomes entangled in loyalty conflicts between the two mother figures. But the longer girls live in father–stepmother households, the more positive their interaction with stepmothers becomes (King, 2007). Eventually, most girls benefit from the support of a second mother figure.

Support for Blended Families. Parenting education and couples counseling can help parents and children adapt to the complexities of blended families. Effective approaches encourage stepparents to move into their new roles gradually by first building a warm relationship with the child (Nicholson et al., 2008). Counselors can offer couples guidance in coparenting to limit loyalty conflicts and provide consistency in child rearing.

Unfortunately, the divorce rate for second marriages is even higher than for first marriages. Parents with antisocial tendencies and poor child-rearing skills are particularly likely to have several divorces and remarriages, and their children have greater adjustment difficulties (Amato, 2010). These families usually require prolonged, intensive therapy.

Maternal Employment and Dual-Earner Families

Today, more than three-fourths of mothers, whether single or married, with school-age children are employed (U.S. Census Bureau, 2013). In previous chapters, we saw that the impact of maternal employment on early development depends on the quality of child care and the continuing parent–child relationship. The same is true in middle childhood.

Maternal Employment and Child Development. When mothers enjoy their work and remain committed to parenting, children show favorable adjustment—higher self-esteem, more positive family and peer relations, less gender-stereotyped beliefs, and better grades in school. Girls, especially, profit from the image of female competence. Regardless of SES, daughters of employed mothers are more achievement- and career-oriented (Hoffman, 2000).

Parenting practices contribute to these benefits. Employed mothers who value their parenting role are more likely to use authoritative child rearing and coregulation. And maternal employment leads fathers—especially those who believe in the importance of the paternal role and who feel successful at parenting—to take on greater child-care responsibilities (Gottfried, Gottfried, & Bathurst, 2002; Jacobs & Kelley, 2006). Paternal involvement is associated in childhood and adolescence with higher intelligence and achievement, more mature social behavior, and a flexible view of gender roles (Pleck & Masciadrelli, 2004).

But when employment places heavy demands on a mother's or a father's schedule or is stressful for other reasons, children are at risk for ineffective parenting—reduced parental sensitivity, fewer joint parent–child activities, and poorer cognitive development throughout childhood and adolescence (Brooks-Gunn, Han, & Waldfogel, 2002; Bumpus, Crouter, & McHale, 2006; Strazdins et al., 2006). In contrast, part-time employment and flexible work schedules, which help parents meet children's needs, are associated with sensitive, involved parenting and good child adjustment (Buehler & O'Brien, 2011).

Child Care for School-Age Children. High-quality child care is vital for children's well-being, even in middle childhood. An estimated 5 million 5- to 14-year-olds in the United States are **self-care children** who regularly look after themselves for some period of time after school (Afterschool Alliance, 2009). Self-care increases with age and also with SES, perhaps because of the greater safety of higher-income neighborhoods. But when lower-SES parents lack alternatives, their children spend more hours on their own (Casper & Smith, 2002).

Younger school-age children who spend many hours alone have emotional and social difficulties (Vandell & Posner, 1999). As children become old enough to look after themselves, those who have a history of authoritative child rearing, are monitored by parental telephone calls, and have regular after-school chores appear responsible and well-adjusted. In contrast, children left to their own devices are more likely to bend to peer pressures and engage in antisocial behavior (Coley, Morris, & Hernandez, 2004; Vandell et al., 2006).

Before age 8 or 9, most children need supervision because they are not yet competent to handle emergencies (Galambos & Maggs, 1991). Also, throughout middle childhood, attending high-quality after-school programs with stimulating activities is linked to good school performance and emotional and social adjustment (Durlak & Weissberg, 2007; Granger, 2008). Low-SES children who participate in "after-care" programs offering academic assistance and enrichment activities (scouting, music and art lessons, clubs) show special benefits. They exceed their self-care counterparts in classroom work habits, academic achievement, and prosocial behavior and display fewer behavior problems (Lauer et al., 2006; Vandell et al., 2006).

Unfortunately, good after care is in especially short supply in low-income neighborhoods (Afterschool Alliance, 2009;

High-quality after-school programs with enrichment activities yield academic and social benefits for low-SES children.

Dearing et al., 2009). A special need exists for well-planned programs in these areas—ones that provide safe environments, warm relationships with adults, and enjoyable, goal-oriented activities.

ASK YOURSELF

REVIEW Describe and explain changes in sibling relationships during middle childhood.

APPLY Steve and Marissa are in the midst of an acrimonious divorce. Their 9-year-old son Dennis has become hostile and defiant. How can Steve and Marissa help Dennis adjust?

REFLECT What after-school child-care arrangements did you experience in elementary school? How do you think they influenced your development?

Some Common Problems of Development

We have considered a variety of stressful experiences that place children at risk for future problems. Next, we address two more areas of concern: school-age children's fears and anxieties and the consequences of child sexual abuse. Finally, we sum up factors that help children cope effectively with stress.

Fears and Anxieties

Although fears of the dark, thunder and lightning, and supernatural beings persist into middle childhood, older children's anxieties are also directed toward new concerns. Common fears of the school years include poor academic performance, peer rejection, the possibility of personal harm (being robbed or shot), threats to parents' health, and media events (Gullone, 2000; Weems & Costa, 2005).

Children's fears are shaped in part by their culture. Children in Western nations mention exposure to negative information in the media as the most frequent source of their fears, followed by direct exposure to frightening events (Muris et al., 2001). Nevertheless, as we saw in Chapter 8, many parents have no rules about their children's TV viewing or computer use, including Internet access.

Most children handle fears constructively, and they decline with age (Gullone, 2000). But about 5 percent of school-age children develop an intense, unmanageable fear called a **phobia.** Children with inhibited temperaments are at high risk (Ollendick, King, & Muris, 2002).

For example, in *school phobia,* children feel severe apprehension about attending school, often accompanied by physical complaints (dizziness, nausea, and stomachaches). About one-third of children with school phobia are 5- to 7-year-olds for whom the real fear is maternal separation. Family therapy helps these children, whose difficulty can often be traced to parental overprotection (Elliott, 1999).

Most cases of school phobia appear around age 11 to 13, in children who usually find a particular aspect of school frightening—an overcritical teacher, a school bully, or too much parental pressure to achieve. A change in school environment or parenting practices may be needed (Silverman & Pina, 2008). Firm insistence that the child return to school, along with training in how to cope with difficult situations, is also helpful.

Severe childhood anxieties may arise from harsh living conditions. In inner-city ghettos and in war-torn areas of the world, children live in the midst of constant danger and deprivation. As the Cultural Influences box on page 280 reveals, these youngsters are at risk for long-term difficulties. Finally, as we saw in our discussion of child abuse in Chapter 8, too often violence and other destructive acts become part of adult–child relationships. During middle childhood, child sexual abuse increases.

Child Sexual Abuse

Until recently, child sexual abuse was considered rare, and adults often dismissed children's claims of abuse. In the 1970s, efforts by professionals and media attention led to recognition of child sexual abuse as a serious and widespread problem. About 65,000 cases in the United States were confirmed in the most recently reported year (U.S. Department of Health and Human Services, 2011b).

Characteristics of Abusers and Victims. Sexual abuse is committed against children of both sexes, but more often against girls. Most cases are reported in middle childhood, but for some victims, abuse begins early in life and continues for many years (Hoch-Espada, Ryan, & Deblinger, 2006; Goodyear-Brown, Fath, & Myers, 2012).

Typically, the abuser is male, either a parent or someone the parent knows well—a father, stepfather, or live-in boyfriend, somewhat less often an uncle or older brother. But in about 25 percent of cases, mothers are the offenders, more often with sons (Boroughs, 2004). If the abuser is a nonrelative, the person is usually someone the child has come to know and trust. However, the Internet and mobile phones have become avenues through which other adults commit sexual abuse—for example, by exposing children and adolescents to pornography and online sexual advances as a way of "grooming" them for sexual acts offline (Wolak et al., 2008).

Many offenders blame the abuse on the willing participation of a seductive youngster. Yet children are not capable of making a deliberate, informed decision to enter into a sexual relationship! Even adolescents are not free to say yes or no. Rather, the responsibility lies with abusers, who tend to have characteristics that predispose them toward sexual exploitation of children. They have great difficulty controlling their impulses and may suffer from psychological disorders, including alcohol and drug abuse. Often they pick out children who are unlikely to defend themselves or to be believed—those who are physically weak, emotionally deprived, socially isolated, or affected by disabilities (Bolen, 2001).

Reported cases of child sexual abuse are linked to poverty and marital instability. Children who live in homes with a constantly changing cast of characters—repeated marriages, separations, and new partners—are especially vulnerable (Goodyear-Brown, Fath, & Myers, 2012). But children in economically advantaged, stable families are also victims, although their abuse is more likely to escape detection.

Consequences. The adjustment problems of child sexual abuse victims—including anxiety, depression, low self-esteem,

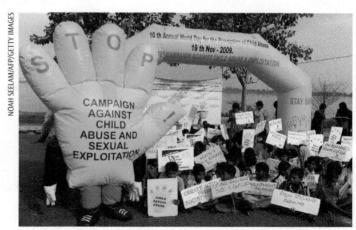

NOAH SEELAM/AFP/GETTY IMAGES

Children in Hyderabad, India, participate in a "Stay Safe" campaign against child abuse and sexual exploitation—part of a global effort to prevent all forms of abuse.

Cultural Influences

Impact of Ethnic and Political Violence on Children

At a refugee camp in Jordan, Syrian children wearing face-masks to protect against blowing sand play games with a caring adult. Most have witnessed violent atrocities and lost family members in Syria's civil war. Sensitive adult support can help them regain a sense of safety.

Around the world, many children live with armed conflict, terrorism, and other acts of violence stemming from ethnic and political tensions. Some children may participate in fighting, either because they are forced or because they want to please adults. Others are kidnapped, assaulted, and tortured. Those who are bystanders often come under direct fire and may be killed or physically maimed. And many watch in horror as family members, friends, and neighbors flee, are wounded, or die. In the past decade, wars have left 6 million children physically disabled, 20 million homeless, and more than 1 million separated from their parents (UNICEF, 2011).

When war and social crises are temporary, most children do not show long-term emotional difficulties. But chronic danger can seriously impair their psychological functioning. Many children of war lose their sense of safety, become desensitized to violence, are haunted by terrifying intrusive memories, display immature moral reasoning, and build a pessimistic view of the future. Anxiety and depression increase, as do aggression and antisocial behavior (Eisenberg & Silver, 2011; Klingman, 2006). These outcomes appear to be culturally universal, observed among children in every war zone studied—from Bosnia, Angola, Rwanda, and the Sudan to the West Bank, Gaza, Afghanistan, and Iraq (Barenbaum, Ruchkin, & Schwab-Stone, 2004).

Parental affection and reassurance are the best protection against lasting problems. When parents offer security, discuss traumatic experiences sympathetically, and serve as role models of calm emotional strength, most children can withstand even extreme war-related violence (Gewirtz, Forgatch, & Wieling, 2008). Children who are separated from parents must rely on help from their communities. Orphans in Eritrea who were placed in residential settings where they could form a close emotional tie with an adult showed less emotional stress five years later than orphans placed in impersonal settings (Wolff & Fesseha, 1999). Education and recreation programs are powerful safeguards, too, providing children with consistency in their lives along with teacher and peer supports.

With the September 11, 2001, terrorist attacks on the World Trade Center, some U.S. children experienced extreme wartime violence firsthand. Most children, however, learned about the attacks indirectly—from the media or from caregivers or peers. Although both direct and indirect exposure triggered child and adolescent distress, extended exposure—having a family member affected or repeatedly witnessing the attacks on TV—resulted in more severe symptoms (Agronick et al., 2007; Otto et al., 2007; Rosen & Cohen, 2010). During the following months, distress reactions declined, though more slowly for children with conflict-ridden parent–child relationships or preexisting adjustment problems.

Unlike many war-traumatized children in the developing world, students in New York's Public School 31, who watched from their classroom windows as the towers collapsed, received immediate intervention—a "trauma curriculum" in which they expressed their emotions through writing, drawing, and discussion and participated in experiences aimed at restoring trust and tolerance (Lagnado, 2001). Older children learned about the feelings of their Muslim classmates, the dire condition of children in Afghanistan, and ways to help victims as a means of overcoming a sense of helplessness.

When wartime drains families and communities of resources, international organizations must step in and help children. Efforts to preserve children's physical, psychological, and educational well-being may be the best way to stop transmission of violence to the next generation.

mistrust of adults, and anger and hostility—are often severe and can persist for years after the abusive episodes. Younger children frequently react with sleep difficulties, loss of appetite, and generalized fearfulness. Adolescents may run away and show suicidal reactions, eating disorders, substance abuse, and delinquency (Hornor, 2010; Wolfe, 2006). And repeated sexual abuse, like physical abuse, is associated with central nervous system damage (Gaskill & Perry, 2012).

Sexually abused children frequently display precocious sexual knowledge and behavior. In adolescence, abused young people often become promiscuous, and as adults, they show increased arrest rates for sex crimes (mostly against children) and prostitution (Salter et al., 2003; Whipple, 2006). Furthermore, women who were sexually abused are likely to choose partners who abuse them and their children, and they often engage in child abuse and neglect themselves (Pianta, Egeland, & Erickson, 1989). In all these ways, the harmful impact of sexual abuse is transmitted to the next generation.

Prevention and Treatment. Because sexual abuse typically appears in the midst of other serious family problems, long-term therapy with both children and parents is often needed

(Saunders, 2012). The best way to reduce the suffering of victims is to prevent sexual abuse from continuing. Today, courts are prosecuting abusers more vigorously and taking children's testimony more seriously.

Educational programs that teach children to recognize inappropriate sexual advances and identify sources of help reduce the risk of abuse (Finkelhor, 2009). Yet because of controversies over educating children about sexual abuse, few schools offer these interventions. New Zealand is the only country with a national, school-based prevention program targeting sexual abuse. In Keeping Ourselves Safe, children and adolescents learn that abusers are rarely strangers. Parent involvement ensures that home and school collaborate in teaching children self-protection skills. Evaluations reveal that virtually all New Zealand parents and children support the program and that it has helped many children avoid or report abuse (Sanders, 2006).

Fostering Resilience in Middle Childhood

Throughout middle childhood—and other periods of development—children encounter challenging and sometimes threatening situations that require them to cope with psychological stress. In this and the previous chapter, we have considered such topics as chronic illness, learning disabilities, achievement expectations, divorce, harsh living conditions and wartime trauma, and sexual abuse. Each taxes children's coping resources, creating serious risks for development.

Nevertheless, only a modest relationship exists between stressful life experiences and psychological disturbance in childhood (Masten & Reed, 2002). Recall from Chapter 1 that four broad factors protect against maladjustment: (1) the child's personal characteristics, including an easy temperament and a mastery-oriented approach to new situations; (2) a warm parental relationship; (3) an adult outside the immediate family who offers a support system; and (4) community resources, such as good schools, social services, and youth organizations and recreation centers (Commission on Children at Risk, 2008; Wright & Masten, 2005).

Often just one or a few of these ingredients account for why one child is "stress-resilient" and another is not. Usually, however, personal and environmental factors are interconnected: Each resource favoring resilience strengthens others. For example, safe, stable neighborhoods with family-friendly community services reduce parents' daily hassles and stress, thereby promoting good parenting (Chen, Howard, & Brooks-Gunn, 2011). In contrast, unfavorable home and neighborhood experiences increase the chances that children will act in ways that expose them to further hardship.

Rather than a preexisting attribute, *resilience* is a capacity that develops, enabling children to use internal and external resources to cope with adversity (Dessel, 2010; Riley & Masten, 2004). As the next two chapters will reveal, young people whose childhood experiences helped them learn to control impulses, overcome obstacles, strive for self-direction, and respond considerately and sympathetically to others meet the challenges of the next period—adolescence—quite well.

ASK YOURSELF

REVIEW Describe adjustment problems of victims of child sexual abuse. How can the harmful consequences of sexual abuse carry over to the next generation?

APPLY Claire told her 6-year-old daughter never to talk to or take candy from strangers. Why will Claire's warning not protect her daughter from sexual abuse?

REFLECT Describe a challenging time during your childhood. What aspects of the experience increased stress? What resources helped you cope with adversity?

SUMMARY

Erikson's Theory: Industry versus Inferiority (p. 260)

What personality changes take place during Erikson's stage of industry versus inferiority?

- According to Erikson, children who successfully resolve the psychological conflict of **industry versus inferiority** develop a sense of competence at useful skills and tasks, learn the value of division of labor, and develop a sense of moral commitment and responsibility.

Self-Understanding (p. 260)

Describe school-age children's self-concept and self-esteem, and discuss factors that affect their achievement-related attributions.

- During middle childhood, children's self-concepts include personality traits, competencies, and **social comparisons.**
- Self-esteem differentiates further, becoming hierarchically organized and more realistic. Authoritative parenting is linked to favorable self-esteem.

- Children who hold **mastery-oriented attributions** believe ability can be improved by trying hard and attribute failure to controllable factors, such as insufficient effort. In contrast, children who receive negative feedback about their ability are likely to develop **learned helplessness,** attributing success to external factors, such as luck, and failure to low ability.

Emotional Development

(p. 264)

Cite changes in self-conscious emotions, emotional understanding, and management of emotion in middle childhood.

- Self-conscious emotions of pride and guilt become clearly governed by personal responsibility. Intense shame is particularly destructive, yielding both internalizing and externalizing problems.

- School-age children develop an appreciation of mixed emotions. Empathy increases and includes sensitivity to both people's immediate distress and their general life condition.

© JIM WEST/THE IMAGE WORKS

- By age 10, most children shift adaptively between **problem-centered** and **emotion-centered coping** to regulate emotion. Children who acquire a sense of emotional self-efficacy are upbeat, empathic, and prosocial.

Moral Development (p. 265)

Describe changes in moral understanding during middle childhood, including children's understanding of diversity and inequality.

- By middle childhood, children have internalized rules for good conduct. They clarify and link moral imperatives and social conventions and develop a better understanding of personal choice and individual rights.

- Children of all races pick up prevailing societal attitudes about race and ethnicity. With age, voicing of prejudice typically declines though automatic prejudice may persist. Children most likely to hold biases are those who believe that personality traits are fixed, who have inflated self-esteem, and who live in a social world that highlights group differences. Long-term intergroup contact is most effective at reducing prejudice.

Peer Relations (p. 267)

How do peer sociability and friendship change in middle childhood?

- Peer interaction becomes more prosocial, and physical aggression declines. By the end of middle childhood, children organize themselves into **peer groups.**

- Friendships develop into mutual relationships based on trust. Children tend to select friends similar to themselves in many ways.

Describe categories of peer acceptance and ways to help rejected children.

- On measures of **peer acceptance, popular children** are well-liked by many agemates; **rejected children** are actively disliked; **controversial children** are both liked and disliked; and **neglected children** arouse little response, either positive or negative.

- **Popular-prosocial children** combine academic and social competence, while **popular-antisocial children** are aggressive but admired. **Rejected-aggressive children** are especially high in conflict and hostility; in contrast, **rejected-withdrawn children** are passive, socially awkward, and frequent targets of **peer victimization.**

- Coaching in social skills, academic tutoring, and training in perspective taking and in solving social problems have been used to help rejected children gain in social competence and peer acceptance. Intervening to improve the quality of parent–child interaction is often necessary.

Gender Typing (p. 271)

What changes in gender-stereotyped beliefs and gender identity occur during middle childhood?

- School-age children extend their awareness of gender stereotypes to personality traits and academic subjects. But they also develop a more open-minded view of what males and females can do.

- Boys strengthen their identification with masculine traits, whereas girls more often experiment with "other-gender" activities. Gender identity includes self-evaluations of gender typicality, contentedness, and felt pressure to conform to gender roles—each of which affects adjustment.

Family Influences (p. 272)

How do parent–child communication and sibling relationships change in middle childhood?

- Despite declines in time spent with parents, **coregulation** allows parents to exercise general oversight over children, who increasingly make their own decisions.

- Sibling rivalry tends to increase with participation in a wider range of activities and more frequent parental comparisons. Compared to children with siblings, only children are higher in self-esteem, school performance, and educational attainment.

BRUCE LAURANCE/BLEND IMAGES/GETTY IMAGES

What factors influence children's adjustment to divorce and blended family arrangements?

- Marital breakup is often quite stressful for children. Individual differences are affected by parental psychological health, child characteristics (age, temperament, and sex), and social supports. Children with difficult temperaments are at greater risk for adjustment problems. Divorce is linked to early sexual activity, adolescent parenthood, and long-term relationship difficulties.

- The overriding factor in positive adjustment following divorce is effective parenting. Positive father–child relationships are protective, as are supports from extended-family members, teachers, siblings, and friends. Divorce mediation can reduce parental conflict in the period surrounding divorce. The success of joint custody depends on effective coparenting.

- When divorced parents enter new relationships and form **blended,** or **reconstituted, families,** girls, older children, and children in father–stepmother families tend to have more adjustment problems. Stepparents who move into their roles gradually help children adjust.

How do maternal employment and life in dual-earner families affect school-age children?

● When employed mothers enjoy their work and remain committed to parenting, their children benefit from higher self-esteem, more positive family and peer relations, less gender-stereotyped beliefs, and better school grades. In dual-earner families, the father's willingness to share responsibilities is a crucial factor. Workplace supports help parents in their child-rearing roles.

● Authoritative child rearing, parental monitoring, and regular after-school chores lead **self-care children** to be responsible and well-adjusted. Good "after-care" programs also aid school performance and emotional and social adjustment, especially for low-SES children.

Some Common Problems of Development (p. 278)

Cite common fears and anxieties in middle childhood.

● School-age children's fears are directed toward new concerns, including poor academic performance, peer rejection, physical harm, parents' health, and medial events. Children with inhibited temperaments are at higher risk of developing **phobias.** Harsh living conditions can also cause severe anxiety.

Discuss factors related to child sexual abuse and its consequences for children's development.

● Child sexual abuse is typically committed by male family members, more often against girls than boys. Abusers have characteristics that predispose them toward sexual exploitation of children. Reported cases are strongly associated with poverty and marital instability. Abused children often have severe adjustment problems.

Cite factors that foster resilience in middle childhood.

● Only a modest relationship exists between stressful life experiences and psychological disturbance in childhood. Children's personal characteristics, a warm family life, authoritative parenting, and school, community, and societal resources predict resilience.

Important Terms and Concepts

blended, or reconstituted, families (p. 276)
controversial children (p. 269)
coregulation (p. 273)
emotion-centered coping (p. 265)
industry versus inferiority (p. 260)
learned helplessness (p. 263)
mastery-oriented attributions (p. 263)

neglected children (p. 269)
peer acceptance (p. 269)
peer group (p. 267)
peer victimization (p. 270)
phobia (p. 279)
popular-antisocial children (p. 269)
popular children (p. 269)

popular-prosocial children (p. 269)
problem-centered coping (p. 265)
rejected-aggressive children (p. 269)
rejected children (p. 269)
rejected-withdrawn children (p. 269)
self-care children (p. 278)
social comparisons (p. 260)

milestones

Development in Middle Childhood

- Self-concept begins to include personality traits, competencies, and social comparisons. (260)
- Self-esteem differentiates, becomes hierarchically organized, and declines to a more realistic level. (261)
- Self-conscious emotions of pride and guilt are governed by personal responsibility. (264)
- Recognizes that individuals can experience more than one emotion at a time and that people's expressions may not reflect their true feelings. (264)

- Awareness of memory strategies and the impact of psychological factors, such as mental inferences, on performance improves. (240)
- Appreciates second-order false beliefs. (240)
- Uses informal knowledge of number concepts and counting to master increasingly complex mathematical skills. (241–242)

- Empathy increases. (264)
- Becomes more independent and trustworthy. (265)
- Constructs a flexible appreciation of moral rules, taking prosocial and antisocial intentions into account. (265)
- Physical aggression declines; verbal and relational aggression continue. (267)
- Resolves conflicts more effectively. (267)

6–8 years

PHYSICAL

- Slow gains in height and weight continue until adolescent growth spurt. (227)
- Permanent teeth gradually replace primary teeth. (227)
- Legibility of writing increases, preparing children to master cursive writing. (231)
- Drawings become more organized and detailed and include some depth cues. (231)
- Games with rules and rough-and-tumble play become common. (232)

COGNITIVE

- Thought becomes more logical, as shown by the ability to pass Piagetian conservation, class inclusion, and seriation problems. (234)
- Attention becomes more selective, adaptable, and planful. (238)
- Uses memory strategies of rehearsal and then organization. (238)
- Views the mind as an active, constructive agent, capable of transforming information. (240)

LANGUAGE

- Vocabulary increases rapidly throughout middle childhood, eventually exceeding comprehension of 40,000 words. (248)
- Word definitions are concrete, referring to functions and appearance. (248)
- Narratives increase in organization, detail, and expressiveness. (248)
- Transitions from emergent literacy to conventional reading. (241)
- Language awareness improves. (248)
- Conversational strategies become more refined. (248)

9–11 years

PHYSICAL

- Adolescent growth spurt begins two years earlier in girls than in boys. (227)

Note: Numbers in parentheses indicate the page or pages on which each milestone is discussed.

- Executes gross-motor skills of running, jumping, throwing, catching, kicking, batting, and dribbling more quickly and with better coordination. (230)
- Steady gains in attention and reaction time contribute to improved motor performance. (231)
- Representation of depth in drawings expands. (231)

COGNITIVE

- Continues to master Piagetian tasks in a step-by-step fashion. (235)
- Spatial reasoning improves; readily draws and reads maps of large-scale spaces, and grasps the notion of scale. (235)

- Selective attention and planning improve further. (238)
- Uses memory strategies of rehearsal and organization more effectively. (238)
- Applies several memory strategies simultaneously; begins to use elaboration. (238)
- Long-term knowledge base grows larger and becomes better organized. (238)
- Theory of mind becomes more elaborate and refined. (240)
- Cognitive self-regulation improves. (240–241)

LANGUAGE

- Thinks about and uses words more precisely; word definitions emphasize synonyms and categorical relations. (248)

- Grasps double meanings of words, as reflected in comprehension of metaphors and humor. (248)
- Continues to master complex grammatical constructions. (248)
- Continues to refine conversational strategies. (248)
- Narratives lengthen, become more coherent, and include more evaluative comments. (248)

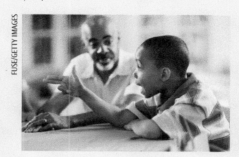

EMOTIONAL/SOCIAL

- Self-esteem tends to rise. (261)
- Distinguishes ability, effort, and external factors (such as luck) in attributions for success and failure. (263)
- Empathic responding extends to general life conditions. (264)

- Shifts adaptively between problem-centered and emotion-centered strategies in regulating emotion. (265)

- Clarifies and links moral rules and social conventions. (265)
- Convictions about matters of personal choice strengthen, and understanding of individual rights expands. (266)
- Overt expressions of outgroup prejudice decline. (266)
- Friendships become more selective and are based on mutual trust. (268)
- Peer groups emerge. (267–268)

- Becomes aware of more gender stereotypes, including personality traits and achievement, but has a flexible appreciation of what males and females can do. (271)
- Gender identity expands to include self-evaluations of typicality, contentedness, and felt pressure to conform. (272)
- Sibling rivalry tends to increase. (273)

chapter
12
Emotional and Social Development in Adolescence

JOHN GIUSTINA/ICONICA/GETTY IMAGES

As adolescents spend less time with family members, peer groups become more tightly knit into cliques. Mixed-sex cliques prepare teenagers for dating by providing models of how to interact and opportunities to do so without having to be intimate.

chapter outline

Erikson's Theory: Identity versus Role Confusion

Self-Understanding

Changes in Self-Concept • Changes in Self-Esteem • Paths to Identity • Identity Status and Psychological Well-Being • Factors Affecting Identity Development

■ **CULTURAL INFLUENCES** Identity Development Among Ethnic Minority Adolescents

Moral Development

Kohlberg's Theory of Moral Development • Are There Sex Differences in Moral Reasoning? • Coordinating Moral, Social-Conventional, and Personal Concerns • Influences on Moral Reasoning • Moral Reasoning and Behavior • Religious Involvement and Moral Development • Further Challenges to Kohlberg's Theory

Gender Typing

The Family

Parent–Child Relationships • Family Circumstances • Siblings

Peer Relations

Friendships • Cliques and Crowds • Dating

Problems of Development

Depression • Suicide • Delinquency

■ **BIOLOGY AND ENVIRONMENT** Two Routes to Adolescent Delinquency

Louis sat on the grassy hillside overlooking the high school, waiting for his best friend, Darryl, to arrive from his fourth-period class. Watching as hundreds of students poured onto the school grounds, Louis reflected on what he had learned in government class that day. "Suppose I *had* been born in the People's Republic of China. I'd be sitting here, speaking a different language, being called by a different name, and thinking about the world in different ways. Wow," Louis pondered. "I am who I am through some quirk of fate."

Louis awoke from his thoughts with a start to see Darryl standing in front of him. "Hey, dreamer! I've been shouting and waving from the bottom of the hill for five minutes. How come you're so spaced out lately, Louis?"

"Oh, just wondering about stuff—what I want, what I believe in. You ever feel that way?"

"Yeah, a lot," Darryl admitted, looking at Louis seriously. "I wonder, what am I really like? Who will I become?"

Louis and Darryl's introspective remarks are signs of a major reorganization of the self at adolescence: the development of identity. Both young people are attempting to formulate who they are—their personal values and the directions they will pursue in life.

We begin this chapter with Erikson's account of identity development and the research it has stimulated on teenagers' thoughts and feelings about themselves. The quest for identity extends to many aspects of development. We will see how a sense of cultural belonging, moral understanding, and masculine and feminine self-images are refined during adolescence. And as parent–child relationships are revised and young people become increasingly independent of the family, friendships and peer networks become crucial contexts for bridging the gap between childhood and adulthood. Our chapter concludes with a discussion of several serious adjustment problems of adolescence: depression, suicide, and delinquency. ●

© MARY KATE DENNY/ALAMY

Erikson's Theory: Identity versus Role Confusion

Erikson (1950, 1968) was the first to recognize **identity** as the major personality achievement of adolescence and as a crucial step toward becoming a productive, content adult. Constructing an identity involves defining who you are, what you value, and the directions you choose to pursue in life. One expert described it as an explicit theory of oneself as a rational agent—one who acts on the basis of reason, takes responsibility for those actions, and can explain them (Moshman, 2005). This search for what is true and real about the self drives many choices—vocation, interpersonal relationships, community involvement, ethnic-group membership, and expression of one's sexual orientation, as well as moral, political, and religious ideals.

Although the seeds of identity formation are planted early, not until late adolescence and early adulthood do young people become absorbed in this task. According to Erikson, in complex societies, teenagers experience an *identity crisis*—a temporary period of distress as they experiment with alternatives before settling on values and goals. They go through a process of inner soul-searching, sifting through characteristics that defined the self in childhood and combining them with emerging traits, capacities, and commitments. Then they mold these into a solid inner core that provides a mature identity—a sense of self-continuity as they move through various roles in daily life. Once formed, identity continues to be refined in adulthood as people reevaluate earlier commitments and choices.

Erikson called the psychological conflict of adolescence **identity versus role confusion.** If young people's earlier conflicts were resolved negatively or if society limits their choices to ones that do not match their abilities and desires, they may appear shallow, directionless, and unprepared for the challenges of adulthood.

Current theorists agree with Erikson that questioning of values, plans, and priorities is necessary for a mature identity, but they no longer describe this process as a "crisis" (Côté, 2009; Kroger, 2007). For most young people, identity development is not traumatic and disturbing but, rather, a process of *exploration* followed by *commitment*. As young people try out life possibilities, they gather important information about themselves and their environment and move toward making enduring decisions. In doing so, they forge an organized self-structure (Arnett, 2000, 2006; Moshman, 2005). In the following sections, we will see that adolescents go about the task of defining the self in ways that closely match Erikson's description.

Self-Understanding

During adolescence, the young person's vision of the self becomes more complex, well-organized, and consistent. Compared with younger children, adolescents evaluate an increasing variety of aspects of the self. Over time, they construct a balanced, integrated representation of their strengths and limitations.

Changes in Self-Concept

In describing themselves, adolescents unify separate traits ("smart" and "curious") into more abstract descriptors ("intelligent"). But at first, their generalizations are not interconnected and are often contradictory. For example, 12- to 14-year-olds might mention opposing traits—"intelligent" and "dork," "extrovert" and "introvert." These disparities result from the expansion of adolescents' social world, which creates pressure to display different selves in different relationships. As adolescents' awareness of these inconsistencies grows, they frequently agonize over "which is the real me" (Harter, 2003, 2006).

Gradually, cognitive changes enable teenagers to combine their traits into an organized system. Their use of qualifiers ("I have a *fairly* quick temper," "I'm not *thoroughly* honest") reveals an increasing awareness that psychological qualities can vary from one situation to the next. Older adolescents also add integrating principles that make sense of formerly troublesome contradictions. "I'm very adaptable," said one young person. "When I'm around my friends, who think what I say is important, I'm talkative; but around my family I'm quiet because they're never interested enough to really listen to me" (Damon, 1990, p. 88).

Compared with school-age children, teenagers place more emphasis on social virtues, such as being friendly, considerate, kind, and cooperative. Among older adolescents, personal and moral values also appear as key themes as young people revise their views of themselves to include enduring beliefs and plans.

Changes in Self-Esteem

Self-esteem, the evaluative side of self-concept, continues to differentiate in adolescence. Teenagers add several new dimensions of self-evaluation—close friendship, romantic appeal, and job competence—to those of middle childhood (see Chapter 10, pages 261–262) (Harter, 2003, 2006).

Level of self-esteem also changes. Though some adolescents experience temporary or persisting declines after school transitions (see Chapter 11, pages 309–310), self-esteem rises for most young people (Impett et al., 2008; Twenge & Campbell, 2001). Teenagers often assert that they have become more mature, capable, personable, and attractive. In longitudinal research on a nationally representative sample of U.S. youths, an increasing sense of mastery—feeling competent and in control of one's life—strongly predicted this age-related rise in self-esteem (Erol & Orth, 2011).

In adolescence, authoritative parenting continues to predict high self-esteem, as does encouragement from teachers (Lindsey et al., 2008; McKinney, Donnelly, & Renk, 2008; Wilkinson, 2004). In contrast, feedback that is negative, inconsistent, or not contingent on performance triggers, at best, uncertainty about the self's capacities and, at worst, a sense of being incompetent and unloved. Teenagers who experience such parenting tend to rely only on peers, not on adults, to affirm their self-esteem—a risk factor for adjustment difficulties (DuBois et al., 1999, 2002).

Paths to Identity

Adolescents' well-organized self-descriptions and differentiated sense of self-esteem provide the cognitive foundation for forming an identity. Through interviews or questionnaires,

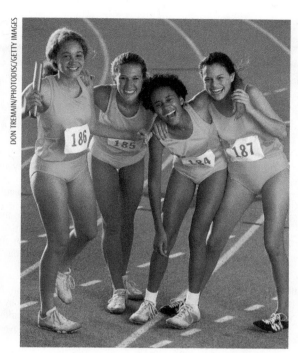

During adolescence, self-esteem rises for most young people, who feel especially good about their peer relationships and athletic capabilities.

researchers commonly evaluate progress in identity development on two key criteria derived from Erikson's theory: *exploration* and *commitment*. Their various combinations yield four *identity statuses,* summarized in Table 12.1 on page 320: **identity achievement,** commitment to values, beliefs, and goals following a period of exploration; **identity moratorium,** exploration without having reached commitment; **identity foreclosure,** commitment in the absence of exploration; and **identity diffusion,** an apathetic state characterized by lack of both exploration and commitment.

Identity development follows many paths. Some young people remain in one status, whereas others experience many status transitions. And the pattern often varies across *identity domains,* such as sexual orientation, vocation, and religious and political values. Most young people change from "lower" statuses (foreclosure or diffusion) to higher ones (moratorium or achievement) between their mid-teens and mid-twenties, but as many remain stable, and some move in the reverse direction (Kroger, 2007; Kroger, Martinussen, & Marcia, 2010; Meeus et al., 2012).

Because attending college provides opportunities to explore values, career options, and lifestyles, college students make more identity progress than they did in high school (Klimstra et al., 2010; Montgomery & Côté, 2003). After college, they often sample a broad range of life experiences before choosing a life course. Those who go to work immediately after high school graduation often settle on a self-definition earlier. But if they encounter obstacles to realizing their occupational goals because of lack of training or vocational choices, they are at risk for identity foreclosure or diffusion (Cohen et al., 2003; Eccles et al., 2003).

TABLE 12.1 **The Four Identity Statuses**

IDENTITY STATUS	DESCRIPTION	EXAMPLE
Identity achievement	Having already explored alternatives, identity-achieved individuals are committed to a clearly formulated set of self-chosen values and goals. They feel a sense of psychological well-being, of sameness through time, and of knowing where they are going.	When asked how willing she would be to give up going into her chosen occupation if something better came along, Lauren responded, "Well, I might, but I doubt it. I've thought long and hard about law as a career. I'm pretty certain it's for me."
Identity moratorium	*Moratorium* means "delay or holding pattern." These individuals have not yet made definite commitments. They are in the process of exploring—gathering information and trying out activities, with the desire to find values and goals to guide their lives.	When asked whether he had ever had doubts about his religious beliefs, Ramón said, "Yes, I guess I'm going through that right now. I just don't see how there can be a God and yet so much evil in the world."
Identity foreclosure	Identity-foreclosed individuals have committed themselves to values and goals without exploring alternatives. They accept a ready-made identity chosen for them by authority figures—usually parents but sometimes teachers, religious leaders, or romantic partners.	When asked if she had ever reconsidered her political beliefs, Emily answered, "No, not really, our family is pretty much in agreement on these things."
Identity diffusion	Identity-diffused individuals lack clear direction. They are not committed to values and goals, nor are they actively trying to reach them. They may never have explored alternatives or may have found the task too threatening and overwhelming.	When asked about his attitude toward nontraditional gender roles, Justin responded, "Oh, I don't know. It doesn't make much difference to me. I can take it or leave it."

Identity Status and Psychological Well-Being

A wealth of research verifies that both identity achievement and moratorium are psychologically healthy routes to a mature self-definition. Long-term foreclosure and diffusion, in contrast, are maladaptive.

Adolescents in moratorium resemble identity-achieved individuals in using an active, *information-gathering cognitive style* to make personal decisions and solve problems: They seek out relevant information, evaluate it carefully, and critically reflect on and revise their views (Berzonsky, 2003, 2011). Young people who are identity-achieved or exploring have higher self-esteem, feel more in control of their lives, are more likely to view school and work as feasible avenues for realizing their aspirations, and are more advanced in moral reasoning (Berzonsky et al., 2011; Kroger, 2007; Serafini & Adams, 2002).

Adolescents stuck in either foreclosure or diffusion are passive in the face of identity concerns and have adjustment difficulties. Foreclosed individuals display a *dogmatic, inflexible cognitive style,* internalizing the values and beliefs of parents and others without deliberate evaluation and resisting information that threatens their position (Berzonsky & Kuk, 2000; Berzonsky et al., 2011). Most fear rejection by people on whom they depend for affection and self-esteem.

Long-term diffused individuals are the least mature in identity development. They typically use a *diffuse-avoidant cognitive style* in which they avoid dealing with personal decisions and problems and, instead, allow current situational pressures to dictate their reactions (Berzonsky & Kuk, 2000; Krettenauer, 2005). Taking an "I don't care" attitude, they entrust themselves to luck or fate, tend to go along with the crowd, and are focused on short-term personal pleasures. As a result, they experience time management and academic difficulties and, of all young people, are most likely to commit antisocial acts and to use and abuse drugs (Berzonsky et al., 2011; Schwartz et al., 2005). Often at the heart of their apathy is a sense of hopelessness about the future.

Factors Affecting Identity Development

Adolescent identity formation begins a lifelong, dynamic process in which a change in either the individual or the context opens up the possibility of reformulating identity (Kunnen & Bosma, 2003). A wide variety of factors influence identity development.

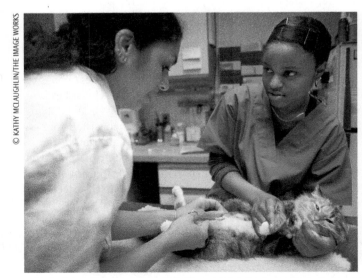

An internship in a veterinary office enables this teenager to explore a real-world career related to her love of animals, thereby fostering identity development.

Applying What We Know

Supporting Healthy Identity Development

Strategy	Explanation
Engage in warm, open communication.	Provides both emotional support and freedom to explore values and goals.
Initiate discussions that promote high-level thinking at home and at school.	Encourages rational and deliberate selection among beliefs and values.
Provide opportunities to participate in extracurricular activities and vocational training programs.	Permits young people to explore the real world of adult work.
Provide opportunities to talk with adults and peers who have worked through identity questions.	Offers models of identity achievement and advice on how to resolve identity concerns.
Provide opportunities to explore ethnic heritage and learn about other cultures in an atmosphere of respect.	Fosters identity achievement in all areas and ethnic tolerance, which supports the identity explorations of others.

Identity status, as we have just seen, is both cause and consequence of personality characteristics. Adolescents who assume that absolute truth is always attainable tend to be foreclosed, while those who doubt that they will ever feel certain about anything are more often identity-diffused. Young people who appreciate that they can use rational criteria to choose among alternatives are likely to be exploring or identity achieved (Berzonsky & Kuk, 2000; Berzonsky et al., 2011).

Parenting practices are associated with identity statuses. Adolescents who feel attached to their parents but also free to voice their own opinions tend to be in a state of moratorium or identity achievement (Berzonsky, 2004; Luyckx, Goossens, & Soenens, 2006; Schwartz et al., 2005). Foreclosed teenagers usually have close bonds with parents but lack opportunities for healthy separation. And diffused young people report the lowest levels of parental support and of warm, open communication (Reis & Youniss, 2004; Zimmerman & Becker-Stoll, 2002).

Interaction with diverse peers through school and community activities encourages adolescents to explore values and role possibilities (Barber et al., 2005). In one study, 15-year-olds with warm, trusting peer ties were more involved in exploring relationship issues—for example, thinking about what they valued in close friends and in a life partner (Meeus, Oosterwegel, & Vollebergh, 2002). In another study, young people's attachment to friends predicted progress in choosing a career (Felsman & Blustein, 1999).

Schools and communities can help by offering rich and varied opportunities for exploration. Supportive experiences include classrooms that promote high-level thinking, teachers and counselors who encourage low-SES students to go to college, extracurricular activities that offer teenagers responsible roles consistent with their interests and talents, and vocational training that immerses adolescents in the real world of adult work (Coatsworth et al., 2005; Hardy et al., 2011; McIntosh, Metz, & Youniss, 2005).

Finally, societal forces also are responsible for the special challenges faced by gay, lesbian, and bisexual youths (see Chapter 11) and by ethnic minority adolescents in forming a secure identity (see the Cultural Influences box on page 322). Applying What We Know above summarizes ways that adults can support adolescents in their quest for identity.

ASK YOURSELF

REVIEW List personal and contextual factors that promote identity development.

APPLY Return to the conversation between Louis and Darryl in the opening of this chapter. Which identity status best characterizes each of the two boys, and why?

REFLECT Does your identity status vary across the domains of sexuality, close relationships, vocation, religious beliefs, and political values? Describe factors that may have influenced your identity development in an important domain.

Moral Development

Eleven-year-old Sabrina sat at the kitchen table reading the Sunday newspaper, her eyes wide with interest. "Look at this!" she said to 16-year-old Louis, who was munching cereal. Sabrina held up a page of large photos showing a 70-year-old woman standing in her home. The floor and furniture were piled with stacks of newspapers, cardboard boxes, tin cans, glass containers, food, and clothing. The accompanying article described crumbling plaster on the walls, frozen pipes, and nonfunctioning sinks, toilet, and furnace. The headline read: "Loretta Perry: My Life Is None of Their Business."

"Look what they're trying to do to this poor lady," exclaimed Sabrina. "They wanna throw her out of her house and tear it down! Those city inspectors must not care about anyone. Here it says, 'Mrs. Perry has devoted much of her life to doing favors for people.' Why doesn't someone help *her*?"

Cultural Influences

Identity Development Among Ethnic Minority Adolescents

Most adolescents are aware of their cultural ancestry but relatively unconcerned about it. However, for teenagers who are members of minority groups, **ethnic identity**—a sense of ethnic group membership and attitudes and feelings associated with that membership—is central to the quest for identity. As they develop cognitively and become more sensitive to feedback from the social environment, minority youths become painfully aware that they are targets of prejudice and discrimination. This discovery complicates their efforts to develop a sense of cultural belonging and a set of personally meaningful goals.

In many immigrant families from collectivist cultures, adolescents' commitment to obeying their parents and fulfilling family obligations lessens the longer the family has been in the immigrant-receiving country—a circumstance that induces **acculturative stress,** psychological distress resulting from conflict between the minority and the host culture (Phinney, Ong, & Madden, 2000). When immigrant parents tightly restrict their teenagers through fear that assimilation into the larger society will undermine their cultural traditions, their youngsters often rebel, rejecting aspects of their ethnic background.

At the same time, discrimination can interfere with the formation of a positive ethnic identity. In one study, Mexican-American youths who had experienced more discrimination were less likely to explore their ethnicity and to report feeling good about it (Romero & Roberts, 2003). Those with low ethnic pride showed a sharp drop in self-esteem in the face of discrimination.

With age, many minority young people strengthen their ethnic identity. But because the process of forging an ethnic identity can be painful and confusing, others show no change, and still others regress (Huang & Stormshak, 2011). Young people with parents of different ethnicities face extra challenges. In a large survey of high school students, part-black biracial teenagers reported as much discrimination as their monoracial black counterparts, yet they felt less positively about their ethnicity. And compared with monoracial minorities, many biracial young people—including black–white, black–Asian, white–Asian, black–Hispanic, and white–Hispanic—regarded ethnicity as less central to their identities (Herman, 2004). Perhaps these adolescents encountered fewer opportunities in their homes and communities to forge a strong sense of belonging to either culture.

Adolescents whose family members encourage them to disprove ethnic stereotypes of low achievement or antisocial behavior typically surmount the threat that discrimination poses to a favorable ethnic identity. These young people manage experiences of unfair treatment effectively, by seeking social support and engaging in direct problem solving (Phinney & Chavira, 1995; Scott, 2003). Also, adolescents whose families taught them the history, traditions, values, and language of their ethnic group and who frequently interact with same-ethnicity peers are more likely to forge a favorable ethnic identity (Hughes et al., 2006; McHale et al., 2006).

How can society help minority adolescents resolve identity conflicts constructively? Here are some relevant approaches:

- Promote effective parenting, in which children and adolescents benefit from family ethnic pride yet are encouraged to explore the meaning of ethnicity in their own lives.

- Ensure that schools respect minority youths' native languages, unique learning styles, and right to high-quality education.

- Foster contact with peers of the same ethnicity, along with respect between ethnic groups (García Coll & Magnuson, 1997).

Stilt walkers celebrate their heritage at a Caribbean youth festival. Minority youths whose culture is respected in their community are more likely to incorporate ethnic values and customs into their identity.

A strong, secure ethnic identity is associated with higher self-esteem, optimism, and sense of mastery over the environment (St. Louis & Liem, 2005; Umaña-Taylor & Updegraff, 2007; Worrell & Gardner-Kitt, 2006). For these reasons, adolescents with a positive connection to their ethnic group cope more effectively with stress, show higher achievement in school, and have fewer emotional and behavior problems than agemates who identify only weakly with their ethnicity (Ghavami et al., 2011; Greene, Way, & Pahl, 2006; Seaton, Scottham, & Sellers, 2006; Umaña-Taylor & Alfaro, 2006).

Forming a **bicultural identity**—by exploring and adopting values from both the adolescent's subculture and the dominant culture—offers added benefits. Biculturally identified adolescents tend to be achieved in other areas of identity as well and to have especially favorable relations with members of other ethnic groups (Phinney, 2007; Phinney et al., 2001). In sum, achievement of ethnic identity enhances many aspects of emotional and social development.

"Sabrina, you're missing the point," Louis responded. "Mrs. Perry is violating the law—30 building code standards! And she's not just a threat to herself—she's a danger to her neighbors, too. Suppose her house caught on fire. You can't live around other people and say your life is nobody's business."

"You don't just knock someone's home down," Sabrina replied angrily. "Why aren't her friends and neighbors over there fixing up that house? You're just like those building inspectors, Louis. You've got no feelings!"

As Louis and Sabrina's disagreement over Loretta Perry's plight illustrates, cognitive development and expanding social experiences permit adolescents to better understand larger social structures—societal institutions and law-making systems—that govern moral responsibilities. As their grasp of social arrangements expands, adolescents construct new ideas about what should be done when the needs and desires of people conflict. As a result, they move toward increasingly just, fair, and balanced solutions to moral problems.

Kohlberg's Theory of Moral Development

Early work by Piaget on the moral judgment of the child inspired Lawrence Kohlberg's more comprehensive cognitive-developmental theory of moral understanding. Kohlberg used a clinical interviewing procedure in which he presented a sample of 10- to 16-year-old boys with hypothetical *moral dilemmas*—stories involving a conflict between two moral values—and asked them what the main actor should do and why. Then he followed the participants longitudinally, reinterviewing them at 3- to 4-year intervals over the next 20 years. The best known of Kohlberg's dilemmas, the "Heinz dilemma," pits the value of obeying the law (not stealing) against the value of human life (saving a dying person):

> In Europe a woman was near death from cancer. There was one drug the doctors thought might save her. A druggist in the same town had discovered it, but he was charging ten times what the drug cost him to make. The sick woman's husband, Heinz, went to everyone he knew to borrow the money, but he could only get together half of what it cost. The druggist refused to sell the drug for less or let Heinz pay later. So Heinz became desperate and broke into the man's store to steal the drug for his wife. Should Heinz have done that? Why or why not? (paraphrased from Colby et al., 1983, p. 77)

Kohlberg emphasized that it is *the way an individual reasons about the dilemma,* not *the content of the response* (whether or not to steal), that determines moral maturity. Individuals who believe Heinz should take the drug and those who think he should not can be found at each of Kohlberg's first four stages. Only at the two highest stages do moral reasoning and content come together in a coherent ethical system (Kohlberg, Levine, & Hewer, 1983). Given a choice between obeying the law and preserving individual rights, the most advanced moral thinkers support individual rights (in the Heinz dilemma, stealing the drug to save a life).

Kohlberg's Stages. Kohlberg organized moral development into three levels, each with two stages, yielding six stages in all. He believed that moral understanding is promoted by the same factors Piaget thought were important for cognitive development: (1) actively grappling with moral issues and noticing weaknesses in one's current reasoning and (2) gains in perspective taking, which permit individuals to resolve moral conflicts in more effective ways. *TAKE A MOMENT...* As we examine Kohlberg's developmental sequence and illustrate it with responses to the Heinz dilemma, look for changes in perspective taking that each stage assumes.

The Preconventional Level. At the **preconventional level,** morality is externally controlled. Children accept the rules of authority figures and judge actions by their consequences. Behaviors that result in punishment are viewed as bad, those that lead to rewards as good.

- *Stage 1: The punishment and obedience orientation.* Children at this stage find it difficult to consider two points of view in a moral dilemma. As a result, they overlook people's intentions. Instead, they focus on fear of authority and avoidance of punishment as reasons for behaving morally.

  Prostealing: "If you let your wife die, you will . . . be blamed for not spending the money to help her and there'll be an investigation of you and the druggist for your wife's death." (Kohlberg, 1969, p. 381)

  Antistealing: "You shouldn't steal the drug because you'll be caught and sent to jail if you do. If you do get away, [you'd be scared that] the police would catch up with you any minute." (Kohlberg, 1969, p. 381)

- *Stage 2: The instrumental purpose orientation.* Children become aware that people can have different perspectives in a moral dilemma, but at first this understanding is

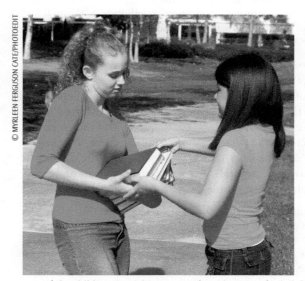

If the child on the right expects a favor in return for helping her friend, she is at Kohlberg's preconventional level. If she is motivated by ideal reciprocity, as in the Golden Rule, she has advanced to the conventional level.

concrete. They view right action as flowing from self-interest and understand reciprocity as equal exchange of favors: "You do this for me and I'll do that for you."

Prostealing: "[I]f Heinz decides to risk jail to save his wife, it's his life he's risking; he can do what he wants with it. And the same goes for the druggist; it's up to him to decide what he wants to do." (Rest, 1979, p. 26)

Antistealing: "[Heinz] is running more risk than it's worth [to save a wife who is near death]." (Rest, 1979, p. 27)

The Conventional Level. At the **conventional level,** individuals continue to regard conformity to social rules as important, but not for reasons of self-interest. Rather, they believe that actively maintaining the current social system ensures positive relationships and societal order.

- *Stage 3: The "good boy–good girl" orientation, or the morality of interpersonal cooperation.* The desire to obey rules because they promote social harmony first appears in the context of close personal ties. Stage 3 individuals want to maintain the affection and approval of friends and relatives by being a "good person"—trustworthy, loyal, respectful, helpful, and nice. The capacity to view a two-person relationship from the vantage point of an impartial, outside observer supports this new approach to morality. At this stage, individuals understand *ideal reciprocity:* They express the same concern for the welfare of another as they do for themselves—a standard of fairness summed up by the Golden Rule: "Do unto others as you would have them do unto you."

  Prostealing: "No one will think you're bad if you steal the drug, but your family will think you're an inhuman husband if you don't. If you let your wife die, you'll never be able to look anyone in the face again." (Kohlberg, 1969, p. 381)

  Antistealing: "It isn't just the druggist who will think you're a criminal, everyone else will too. . . . [Y]ou'll feel bad thinking how you've brought dishonor on your family and yourself." (Kohlberg, 1969, p. 381)

- *Stage 4: The social-order-maintaining orientation.* At this stage, the individual takes into account a larger perspective—that of societal laws. Moral choices no longer depend on close ties to others. Instead, rules must be enforced in the same evenhanded fashion for everyone, and each member of society has a personal duty to uphold them. The Stage 4 individual believes that laws should never be disobeyed because they are vital for ensuring societal order and cooperation between people.

  Prostealing: "Heinz has a duty to protect his wife's life; it's a vow he took in marriage. But it's wrong to steal, so he would have to take the drug with the idea of paying the druggist for it and accepting the penalty for breaking the law later."

  Antistealing: "Even if his wife is dying, it's still [Heinz's] duty as a citizen to obey the law. . . . If everyone starts breaking the law in a jam, there'd be no civilization, just crime and violence." (Rest, 1979, p. 30)

The Postconventional or Principled Level. Individuals at the **postconventional level** move beyond unquestioning support for their own society's rules and laws. They define morality in terms of abstract principles and values that apply to all situations and societies.

- *Stage 5: The social contract orientation.* At Stage 5, individuals regard laws and rules as flexible instruments for furthering human purposes. They can imagine alternatives to their own social order, and they emphasize fair procedures for interpreting and changing the law. When laws are consistent with individual rights and the interests of the majority, each person follows them because of a *social contract orientation*—free and willing participation in the system because it brings about more good for people than if it did not exist.

  Prostealing: "Although there is a law against stealing, the law wasn't meant to violate a person's right to life. . . . If Heinz is prosecuted for stealing, the law needs to be reinterpreted to take into account situations in which it goes against people's natural right to keep on living."

  Antistealing: At this stage, there are no antistealing responses.

- *Stage 6: The universal ethical principle orientation.* At this highest stage, right action is defined by self-chosen ethical principles of conscience that are valid for all people, regardless of law and social agreement. Stage 6 individuals typically mention such abstract principles as respect for the worth and dignity of each person.

  Prostealing: "It doesn't make sense to put respect for property above respect for life itself. [People] could live together without private property at all. Respect for human life and personality is absolute and accordingly [people] have a mutual duty to save one another from dying." (Rest, 1979, p. 37)

  Antistealing: At this stage, there are no antistealing responses.

Research on Kohlberg's Stage Sequence. Kohlberg's original research and other longitudinal studies provide the most convincing evidence for his stage sequence. With few exceptions, individuals move through the first four stages in the predicted order (Boom, Wouters, & Keller, 2007; Dawson, 2002; Walker & Taylor, 1991b). Moral development is slow and gradual: Reasoning at Stages 1 and 2 decreases in early adolescence, while Stage 3 increases through midadolescence and then declines. Stage 4 reasoning rises over the teenage years until, among college-educated young adults, it is the typical response.

Few people move beyond Stage 4. In fact, postconventional morality is so rare that no clear evidence exists that Kohlberg's Stage 6 actually follows Stage 5. This poses a key challenge to Kohlberg's theory: If people must reach Stages 5 and 6 to be considered truly morally mature, few individuals anywhere would measure up! According to one reexamination of Kohlberg's stages, moral maturity can be found in a revised understanding of Stages 3 and 4 (Gibbs, 2014). These stages are not "conventional"—based on social conformity—as Kohlberg assumed. Rather, they require profound moral constructions—an understanding of ideal reciprocity as the basis for relationships (Stage 3) and for widely accepted moral standards, set forth in rules and laws (Stage 4). In this view, "postconventional" morality is a highly reflective endeavor limited to a handful of people who have attained advanced education, usually in philosophy.

TAKE A MOMENT... Think of an actual moral dilemma you faced recently. How did you solve it? Did your reasoning fall at the same stage as your thinking about Heinz? Real-life conflicts often elicit moral reasoning below a person's actual capacity because they involve practical considerations and mix cognition with intense emotion (Walker, 2004).

The influence of situational factors on moral judgments indicates that like Piaget's cognitive stages, Kohlberg's moral stages are loosely organized and overlapping. Rather than developing in a neat, stepwise fashion, people draw on a range of moral responses that vary with context. With age, this range shifts upward as less mature moral reasoning is gradually replaced by more advanced moral thought.

Are There Sex Differences in Moral Reasoning?

In the discussion at the beginning of this section, notice how Sabrina's moral argument focuses on caring and commitment to others. Carol Gilligan (1982) is the best-known of those who have argued that Kohlberg's theory does not adequately represent the morality of girls and women. Gilligan believes that feminine morality emphasizes an "ethic of care" that Kohlberg's system devalues. Sabrina's reasoning falls at Stage 3 because it is based on mutual trust and affection, whereas Louis's is at Stage 4 because he emphasizes following the law. According to Gilligan, a concern for others is a *different* but no less valid basis for moral judgment than a focus on impersonal rights.

Most studies, however, do not support the claim that Kohlberg's approach underestimates the moral maturity of females (Turiel, 2006; Walker, 2006). On hypothetical dilemmas as well as everyday moral problems, adolescent and adult females display reasoning at the same stage as their male agemates and often at a higher stage. And themes of justice and caring appear in the responses of both sexes (Jadack et al., 1995; Walker, 1995).

Nevertheless, some evidence indicates that although the morality of males and females taps both orientations, females tend to emphasize care, whereas males either stress justice or focus equally on justice and care (Jaffee & Hyde, 2000; Wark & Krebs, 1996; Weisz & Black, 2002). This difference in emphasis, which appears more often in real-life dilemmas than in hypothetical ones, may reflect women's greater involvement in daily activities involving care and concern for others.

Coordinating Moral, Social-Conventional, and Personal Concerns

Adolescents' moral advances are also evident in their reasoning about situations that raise competing moral, social-conventional, and personal issues. In diverse Western and non-Western cul-

tures, concern with matters of personal choice strengthens during the teenage years—a reflection of adolescents' quest for identity and increasing independence (Neff & Helwig, 2002; Nucci, 2002). As young people firmly insist that parents not encroach on the personal arena (dress, hairstyle, diary records, friendships), disputes over these issues increase (Hasebe, Nucci, & Nucci, 2004).

As they enlarge the range of issues they regard as personal, adolescents think more intently about conflicts between personal choice and community obligations—for example, whether, and under what conditions, it is permissible to restrict speech, religion, marriage, childbearing, group membership, and other individual rights (Wainryb, 1997). When asked if it is OK to exclude a child from a peer group on the basis of race or gender, fourth graders usually say exclusion is always unfair. But by tenth grade, young people, though increasingly mindful of fairness, indicate that under certain conditions—in intimate relationships (friendship) and private contexts (at home or in a small club), and on the basis of gender more often than race—exclusion is OK (Killen et al., 2002, 2007; Rutland, Killen, & Abrams, 2010). In explaining, they mention the right to personal choice as well as concerns about effective group functioning.

As adolescents integrate personal rights with ideal reciprocity, they demand that the protections they want for themselves extend to others. For example, with age, they are more likely to defend the government's right to limit the individual freedom to engage in risky health behaviors such as smoking and drinking, in the interest of the larger public good (Flanagan, Stout, & Gallay, 2008). Similarly, they eventually realize that violating strongly held conventions in favor of asserting personal choices—showing up at a wedding in a T-shirt, talking out of turn at a student council meeting—can harm others, either by inducing distress or by undermining fair treatment (Nucci, 2001). As their grasp of fairness deepens, young people realize that many social conventions have moral implications: They are

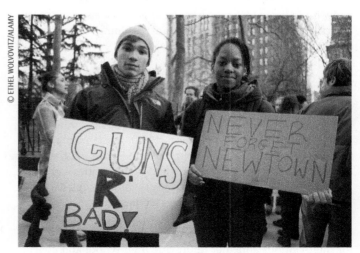

These teenagers participate in a demonstration in favor of gun control. Adolescent moral development involves thinking intently about conflicts between personal choice and community obligation—for example, whether, and under what conditions, individuals' right to bear arms should be restricted.

vital for maintaining a just and peaceful society. Notice how this understanding is central to Kohlberg's Stage 4, which is typically attained as adolescence draws to a close.

Influences on Moral Reasoning

Many factors influence moral understanding, including child-rearing practices, schooling, peer interaction, and culture. Growing evidence suggests that, as Kohlberg believed, these experiences work by presenting young people with cognitive challenges, which stimulate them to think about moral problems in more complex ways.

Child-Rearing Practices. Adolescents who gain most in moral understanding have parents who engage in moral discussions, encourage prosocial behavior, and create a supportive atmosphere by listening sensitively, asking clarifying questions, and presenting higher-level reasoning (Carlo et al., 2011; Pratt, Skoe, & Arnold, 2004; Wyatt & Carlo, 2002). In one study, 11-year-olds were asked what they thought an adult would say to justify a moral rule, such as not lying, stealing, or breaking a promise. Those with warm, demanding, communicative parents were far more likely than their agemates to point to the importance of ideal reciprocity: "You wouldn't like it if I did it to you" (Leman, 2005). In contrast, when parents lecture, use threats, or make sarcastic remarks, adolescents show little or no change in moral reasoning over time (Walker & Taylor, 1991a).

Schooling. Years of schooling is a powerful predictor of movement to Kohlberg's Stage 4 or higher (Dawson et al., 2003; Gibbs et al., 2007). Higher education introduces young people to social issues that extend beyond personal relationships to entire political or cultural groups. Consistent with this idea, college students who report more perspective-taking opportunities (for example, classes that emphasize open discussion of opinions, friendships with others of different cultural backgrounds) and who indicate that they have become more aware of social diversity tend to be advanced in moral reasoning (Comunian & Gielen, 2006; Mason & Gibbs, 1993a, 1993b).

Peer Interaction. Interaction among peers who present differing viewpoints promotes moral understanding. When young people negotiate and compromise, they realize that social life can be based on cooperation between equals rather than authority relations (Killen & Nucci, 1995). Furthermore, recall from Chapter 10 that intergroup contact—cross-race friendships and interactions in schools and communities—reduces racial and ethnic prejudice. It also affects young people morally, strengthening their conviction that race-based and other forms of peer exclusion are wrong (Crystal, Killen, & Ruck, 2008).

Peer discussions of moral problems have provided the basis for interventions aimed at improving high school and college students' moral understanding. But for these to be effective, young people must be highly engaged—confronting and critiquing one another's viewpoints, as Sabrina and Louis did when they argued over Mrs. Perry's plight (Berkowitz & Gibbs, 1983;

Comunian & Gielen, 2006). And because moral development occurs gradually, many peer interaction sessions over weeks or months are needed to produce moral change.

Culture. Individuals in industrialized nations move through Kohlberg's stages more quickly and advance to a higher level than individuals in village societies, who rarely move beyond Stage 3. One explanation is that in village societies, moral cooperation is based on direct relations between people and does not allow for the development of advanced moral understanding (Stages 4 to 6), which depends on appreciating the role of larger social structures, such as laws and government institutions (Gibbs et al., 2007).

A second possible reason for cultural variation is that responses to moral dilemmas in collectivist cultures (including village societies) are often more other-directed than in Western Europe and North America (Miller, 2006). In both village and industrialized cultures that highly value interdependency, statements portraying the individual as vitally connected to the social group are common. In one study, Japanese adolescents, who almost always integrated care- and justice-based reasoning, placed greater weight on care, which they regarded as a communal responsibility (Shimizu, 2001). Similarly, in research conducted in India, even highly educated people (expected to have attained Kohlberg's Stages 4 and 5) viewed solutions to moral dilemmas as the responsibility of the entire society, not of a single person (Miller & Bersoff, 1995).

These findings raise the question of whether Kohlberg's highest level represents a culturally specific way of thinking—one limited to Western societies that emphasize individualism and an appeal to an inner, private conscience. At the same time, a review of over 100 studies confirmed an age-related trend consistent with Kohlberg's Stages 1 to 4 across diverse societies (Gibbs et al., 2007). A common justice morality is clearly evident in the dilemma responses of people from vastly different cultures.

Members of this small village community in Mozambique experience moral cooperation as based on direct relations between people. Consequently, their moral reasoning is unlikely to advance beyond Kohlberg's Stage 3.

Moral Reasoning and Behavior

A central assumption of the cognitive-developmental perspective is that moral understanding should affect moral action. According to Kohlberg, mature moral thinkers realize that behaving in line with their beliefs is vital for creating and maintaining a just social world (Gibbs, 2014). Consistent with this idea, higher-stage adolescents more often act prosocially by helping, sharing, and defending victims of injustice and by volunteering in their communities (Carlo et al., 1996, 2011; Comunian & Gielen, 2000, 2006). Also, they less often engage in cheating, aggression, and other antisocial behaviors (Gregg, Gibbs, & Fuller, 1994; Raaijmakers, Engels, & van Hoof, 2005; Stams et al., 2006).

Yet the connection between mature moral reasoning and action is only modest. As we have seen, moral behavior is influenced by many factors besides cognition, including the emotions of empathy, sympathy, and guilt; individual differences in temperament; and a long history of cultural experiences and intuitive beliefs that affect moral decision making (Haidt & Kesebir, 2010). **Moral identity**—the degree to which morality is central to self-concept—also affects moral behavior (Hardy & Carlo, 2011). In a study of low-SES African-American and Hispanic teenagers, those who emphasized moral traits and goals in their self-descriptions displayed exceptional levels of community service (Hart & Fegley, 1995). But they did not differ from their agemates in moral reasoning.

Researchers have begun to identify factors that strengthen moral identity. Certain parenting practices—inductive discipline (see page 207 in Chapter 8) and clearly conveyed moral expectations—augment adolescents' moral identity (Patrick & Gibbs, 2011). And *just educational environments*—in which teachers guide students in democratic decision making and rule setting, resolving disputes civilly, and taking responsibility for others' welfare—are influential (Atkins, Hart, & Donnelly, 2004). In one study, tenth graders who reported fair teacher treatment were more likely than those who had experienced unjust treatment (an unfair detention or a lower grade than they deserved) to regard excluding a peer on the basis of race as a moral transgression (Crystal, Killen, & Ruck, 2010).

LOOK AND LISTEN

Would you characterize your high school as a *just educational environment?* Cite specific features and experiences that may have contributed to students' moral development and civic engagement. ●

Religious Involvement and Moral Development

Religion is especially important in U.S. family life. In recent national polls, nearly two-thirds of Americans reported actively practicing religion, compared with one-half of those in Canada, one-third of those in Great Britain and Italy, and even fewer elsewhere in Europe (CIA, 2012; Gallup News Service, 2006;

Playing in a brass quartet at church gives these adolescents a sense of connection to their faith. Religious involvement promotes teenagers' moral development, encouraging responsible academic work and community service.

Jones, 2003). As adolescents search for a personally meaningful identity, formal religious involvement tends to decline (Kerestes & Youniss, 2003; Pew Research Center, 2010b). Nevertheless, teenagers who remain part of a religious community are advantaged in moral values and behavior. Compared with nonaffiliated youths, they are more involved in community service activities aimed at helping the less fortunate (Kerestes, Youniss, & Metz, 2004). And religious involvement promotes responsible academic and social behavior and discourages misconduct (Dowling et al., 2004).

A variety of factors probably contribute to these favorable outcomes. In a study of inner-city high school students, religiously involved young people were more likely to report trusting relationships with parents, adults, and friends who hold similar worldviews. The more activities they shared with this network, the higher they scored in empathy and prosocial behavior (King & Furrow, 2004). Furthermore, religious education and youth activities directly teach concern for others and provide opportunities for moral discussions and civic engagement. And adolescents who feel connected to a higher being may develop certain inner strengths, including prosocial values and a strong moral identity, that help them translate their thinking into action (Hardy & Carlo, 2005; Sherrod & Spiewak, 2008). An exception is evident in religious cults, where rigid indoctrination into the group's beliefs, suppression of individuality, and estrangement from society all work against moral maturity (Scarlett & Warren, 2010).

Further Challenges to Kohlberg's Theory

Although much evidence is consistent with the cognitive-developmental approach to morality, Kohlberg's has faced major challenges. The most radical opposition comes from researchers who—referring to wide variability in moral reasoning across situations—claim that Kohlberg's stage sequence inadequately accounts for morality in everyday life (Krebs and Denton, 2005). These investigators favor abandoning Kohlberg's stages for a *pragmatic approach to morality.* They assert that everyday moral judgments—rather than being efforts to arrive at just solutions—are practical tools that people use to achieve their goals. To benefit personally, they often must advocate cooperation with others. But people often act first and then invoke moral judgments to rationalize their actions, regardless of whether their behavior is self-centered or prosocial (Haidt, 2001; Haidt & Kesebir, 2010).

Is the pragmatic approach correct that people strive to resolve moral conflicts fairly only when they themselves have nothing to lose? Supporters of the cognitive-developmental perspective point out that people frequently rise above self-interest to defend others' rights. For example, moral leaders in business—rather than resorting to Stage 2 reasoning—endorse trust, integrity, good faith, and just laws and codes of conduct (Damon, 2004; Gibbs, 2006). Also, adolescents and adults are well aware of the greater adequacy of higher-stage moral reasoning, which some people act on despite highly corrupt environments. And individuals who engage in sudden altruistic action may have previously considered relevant moral issues so thoroughly that their moral judgment activates automatically, triggering an immediate response (Gibbs et al., 2009; Pizarro & Bloom, 2003). In these instances, people who appear to be engaging in after-the-fact moral justification are actually behaving with great forethought.

In sum, the cognitive-developmental approach to morality has done much to clarify our profound moral potential. And despite opposition, Kohlberg's central assumption—that with age, humans everywhere construct a deeper understanding of fairness and justice that guides moral action—remains powerfully influential.

Gender Typing

As Sabrina entered adolescence, she began to worry about walking, talking, eating, dressing, laughing, and competing in ways consistent with a feminine gender role. According to one hypothesis, the arrival of adolescence is typically accompanied by **gender intensification**—increased gender stereotyping of attitudes and behavior, and movement toward a more traditional gender identity. Research on gender intensification, however, is mixed, with some studies finding evidence for it and others reporting few instances (Basow & Rubin, 1999; Galambos, Almeida, & Petersen, 1990; Huston & Alvarez, 1990; Priess, Lindberg, & Hyde, 2009). When gender intensification is evident, it seems to be stronger for adolescent girls. Although girls continue to be less gender-typed than boys, some may feel less free to experiment with "other-gender" activities and behaviors than they did in middle childhood.

In young people who do exhibit gender intensification, biological, social, and cognitive factors likely are involved. As puberty magnifies sex differences in appearance, teenagers may

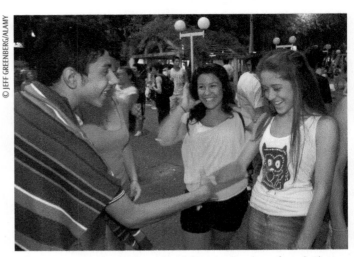

For some young people, early adolescence is a time of gender intensification. Pubertal changes in appearance, traditional gender-role expectations of parents, and increased concern with what others think can prompt a move toward a more traditional gender identity.

spend more time thinking about themselves in gender-linked ways. Pubertal changes might also prompt gender-typed pressures from others. Parents with traditional gender-role beliefs may encourage "gender-appropriate" activities and behavior more than they did earlier (Shanahan et al., 2007). And when adolescents start to date, they may become more gender-typed as a way of increasing their attractiveness. Finally, cognitive changes—in particular, greater concern with what others think—might make young teenagers more responsive to gender-role expectations.

Gender intensification declines by late adolescence, but not all affected young people move beyond it to the same degree. Teenagers who are encouraged to explore non-gender-typed options and to question the value of gender stereotypes for themselves and society are more likely to build an androgynous gender identity (see Chapter 8, page 215). Overall, androgynous adolescents, especially girls, tend to be psychologically healthier—more self-confident, more willing to speak their own mind, better-liked by peers, and identity-achieved (Bronstein, 2006; Dusek, 1987; Harter, 2006).

ASK YOURSELF

REVIEW How does an understanding of ideal reciprocity contribute to moral development? Why are Kohlberg's Stages 3 and 4 morally mature?

APPLY Tam grew up in a small village culture, Lydia in a large industrial city. At age 15, Tam reasons at Kohlberg's Stage 3, Lydia at Stage 4. What factors might account for the difference?

REFLECT Do you favor a cognitive-developmental or a pragmatic approach to morality, or both? Explain, drawing on research evidence and personal experiences.

The Family

Franca and Antonio remember their son Louis's freshman year of high school as a difficult time. Because of a demanding project at work, Franca was away from home many evenings and weekends. In her absence, Antonio took over, but when business declined and he had to cut costs at his hardware store, he, too, had less time for the family. That year, Louis and two friends used their computer know-how to gain entry to their classmates' systems to pirate video game software. Louis's grades fell, and he often left the house without saying where he was going. When Franca and Antonio noticed the video-game icons covering Louis's computer desktop, they knew they had cause for concern.

During adolescence, striving for **autonomy**—a sense of oneself as a separate, self-governing individual—becomes a salient task. Teenagers strive to rely more on themselves and less on parents for decision making (Collins & Laursen, 2004; Steinberg & Silk, 2002). Nevertheless, parent–child relationships remain vital for helping adolescents become autonomous, responsible individuals.

Parent–Child Relationships

A variety of changes within the adolescent support autonomy. In Chapter 11, we saw that puberty triggers psychological distancing from parents. In addition, as young people look more mature, parents give them more independence and responsibility (McElhaney et al., 2009). Gradually, adolescents solve problems and make decisions more effectively. And an improved ability to reason about social relationships leads teenagers to *deidealize* their parents, viewing them as "just people." Consequently, they no longer bend as easily to parental authority as they did when younger.

Parent–child relationships are vital for helping adolescents attain autonomy. Though teenagers benefit from freedom to explore ideas and make their own decisions, they need guidance and protection from dangerous situations.

Yet as Franca and Antonio's episode with Louis illustrates, teenagers still need guidance and protection from dangerous situations. In diverse ethnic groups and cultures, warm, supportive parenting that grants young people freedom to explore while making appropriate demands for maturity fosters autonomy, predicting high self-reliance, effortful control, academic achievement, positive work orientation, favorable self-esteem, and ease of separation in the transition to college (Bean, Barber, & Crane, 2007; Eisenberg et al., 2005b; Supple et al., 2009; Wang, Pomerantz, & Chen, 2007).

Conversely, parents who are coercive or psychologically controlling interfere with the development of autonomy. These tactics are linked to low self-esteem, depression, drug and alcohol use, and antisocial behavior—outcomes that often persist into early adulthood (Barber, Stolz, & Olsen, 2005; Bronte-Tinkew, Moore, & Carrano, 2006; Wissink, Deković, & Meijer, 2006).

In Chapter 2, we described the family as a *system* that must adapt to changes in its members. The rapid physical and psychological changes of adolescence trigger conflicting expectations in parent–child relationships. Parents and teenagers—especially young teenagers—differ sharply on the appropriate age for granting certain privileges, such as control over clothing, school courses, going out with friends, and dating (Smetana, 2002). Consistent parental monitoring of the young person's daily activities, through a cooperative relationship in which the adolescent willingly discloses information, is linked to a variety of positive outcomes—prevention of delinquency, reduction in sexual activity, improved school performance, and positive psychological well-being (Crouter & Head, 2002; Jacobson & Crockett, 2000).

LOOK AND LISTEN

Ask an early adolescent and his or her parent for their views on when the young person is mature enough to begin dating, own a cell phone, create a Facebook page, and be given other privileges. Do adolescent and parent perspectives differ? ●

Immigrant parents from cultures that highly value family closeness and obedience to authority have greater difficulty adapting to their teenagers' push for autonomy, often reacting more strongly to adolescent disagreement. And as adolescents acquire the host culture's language and are increasingly exposed to its individualistic values, immigrant parents may become even more critical, causing teenagers to rely less on the family network for social support (Yau, Tasopoulos-Chan, & Smetana, 2009). The resulting *acculturative stress* is associated with a decline in self-esteem and a rise in anxiety, depressive symptoms, and deviant behavior, including alcohol use and delinquency (Park, 2009; Suarez-Morales & Lopez, 2009; Warner et al., 2006).

Throughout adolescence, the quality of the parent–child relationship is the single most consistent predictor of mental health. In well-functioning families, teenagers remain attached to parents and seek their advice, but they do so in a context of greater freedom (Collins & Steinberg, 2006). The mild conflict that typically arises facilitates adolescent identity and autonomy by helping family members express and tolerate disagreement. Conflicts also inform parents of teenagers' changing needs and expectations, signaling a need for adjustments in the parent–child relationship. By middle to late adolescence, most parents and children achieve this mature, mutual relationship, and harmonious interaction is on the rise.

Family Circumstances

As Franca and Antonio's experience with Louis reminds us, adult life stress can interfere with warm, involved parenting and, in turn, with children's adjustment at any period of development. But parents who are financially secure, not overloaded with job pressures, and content with their marriages usually find it easier to grant teenagers appropriate autonomy and experience less conflict with them (Cowan & Cowan, 2002; Crouter & Bumpus, 2001). When Franca and Antonio's work stress eased and they recognized Louis's need for more involvement and guidance, his problems subsided.

Among the minority of families with seriously troubled parent–adolescent relationships, most difficulties began in childhood (Collins & Laursen, 2004). Teenagers who develop well despite family stress continue to benefit from factors that fostered resilience in earlier years: an appealing, easy-going disposition; a parent who combines warmth with high expectations; and (especially if parental supports are lacking) bonds with prosocial adults outside the family who care deeply about the adolescent's well-being (Masten, 2001; Masten & Shaffer, 2006).

Siblings

Like parent–child relationships, sibling interactions adapt to development at adolescence. As younger siblings become more self-sufficient, they accept less direction from their older brothers and sisters, and sibling influence declines. Also, as teenagers become more involved in friendships and romantic relationships, they invest less time and energy in siblings, who are part of the family from which they are trying to establish autonomy (Hetherington, Henderson, & Reiss, 1999; Kim et al., 2006). As a result, sibling relationships often become less intense, in both positive and negative feelings.

Nevertheless, attachment between siblings remains strong for most young people. Overall, siblings who established a positive bond in early childhood continue to display greater affection and caring, which contribute to more favorable adolescent adjustment (Kim et al., 2007; Samek & Rueter, 2011). Culture also influences quality of sibling relationships. In one study, Mexican-American adolescents who expressed a strong Mexican cultural orientation resolved sibling conflicts more cooperatively than did those more oriented toward U.S. individualistic values (Killoren, Thayer, & Updegraff, 2008).

Finally, mild sibling differences in perceived parental affection no longer trigger jealousy but, instead, predict greater sibling warmth (Feinberg et al., 2003). Perhaps adolescents interpret a unique relationship with parents, as long as it is generally accepting, as a gratifying sign of their own individuality.

Peer Relations

As adolescents spend less time with family members, peers become increasingly important. In industrialized nations, young people spend most of each weekday with agemates in school. Teenagers also spend much out-of-class time together, more in some cultures than others. For example, U.S. young people have about 50 hours of free time per week, Europeans about 45 hours, and East Asians about 33 hours (Larson, 2001). A shorter school year and less demanding academic standards, which lead American youths to devote much less time to schoolwork, account for this difference.

In the following sections, we will see that adolescent peer relations can be both positive and negative. At their best, peers serve as critical bridges between the family and adult social roles.

Friendships

Number of best friends declines from about four to six in early adolescence to one or two in adulthood (Hartup & Stevens, 1999). At the same time, the nature of the relationship changes.

Characteristics of Adolescent Friendships.
When asked about the meaning of friendship, teenagers stress three characteristics. The most important is *intimacy,* or psychological closeness, which is supported by *mutual understanding* of each other's values, beliefs, and feelings. In addition, more than younger children, teenagers want their friends to be *loyal*—to stick up for them and not leave them for somebody else (Collins & Madsen, 2006).

As frankness and faithfulness increase, *self-disclosure* (sharing of private thoughts and feelings) between friends rises over the adolescent years (see Figure 12.1). As a result, teenage friends get to know each other better as personalities. In addition to the many characteristics that school-age friends share (see page 268 in Chapter 10), adolescent friends tend to be alike in identity status, educational aspirations, political beliefs, and willingness to try drugs and engage in lawbreaking acts (Berndt & Murphy, 2002; Selfhout, Branje, & Meeus, 2008). Occasionally, however, teenagers choose friends with differing attitudes and values, which permits them to explore new perspectives within the security of a compatible relationship.

During adolescence, cooperation and mutual affirmation between friends increase—changes that reflect greater skill at preserving the relationship and sensitivity to a friend's needs and desires (De Goede, Branje, & Meeus, 2009). Adolescents also are less possessive of their friends than they were in childhood (Parker et al., 2005). Desiring a certain degree of autonomy for themselves, they recognize that friends need this, too.

Sex Differences in Friendships. TAKE A MOMENT...
Ask several adolescents to describe their close friendships. You are likely to find a consistent sex difference: Emotional closeness is more common between girls than between boys (Markovits, Benenson, & Dolensky, 2001). Girls frequently get together to

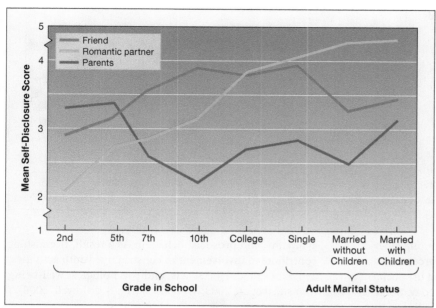

FIGURE 12.1 **Age changes in reported self-disclosure to parents and peers, based on findings of several studies.** Self-disclosure to friends increases steadily during adolescence, reflecting intimacy as a major basis of friendship. Self-disclosure to romantic partners also rises, but it does not surpass intimacy with friends until the college years. Self-disclosure to parents declines in early adolescence, a time of mild parent–child conflict. As family relationships readjust to the young person's increasing autonomy, self-disclosure to parents rises. (From D. Buhrmester, 1996, "Need Fulfillment, Interpersonal Competence, and the Developmental Contexts of Early Adolescent Friendship," in W. M. Bukowski, A. F. Newcomb, & W. W. Hartup [Eds.], *The Company They Keep: Friendship in Childhood and Adolescence,* New York: Cambridge University Press, p. 168. Reprinted with permission of Cambridge University Press.)

"just talk," and their interactions contain more self-disclosure and supportive statements. In contrast, boys more often gather for an activity—usually sports and competitive games. Boys' discussions usually focus on accomplishments and involve more competition and conflict (Brendgen et al., 2001; Rubin, Bukowski, & Parker, 2006).

Friendship closeness has costs as well as benefits. When friends focus on deeper thoughts and feelings, they tend to *coruminate,* or repeatedly mull over problems and negative

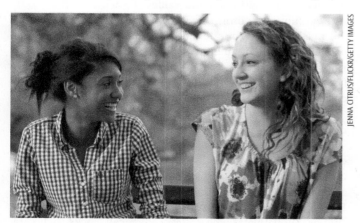

Compared to boys, adolescent girls place a higher value on emotional closeness, engaging in more self-disclosure and supportive statements with friends.

emotions—an activity that, while contributing to high friendship quality, also triggers anxiety and depression, symptoms more common among girls (Hankin, Stone, & Wright, 2010; Rose, Carlson, & Waller, 2007). And when conflict arises between intimate friends, more potential exists for one party to harm the other through relational aggression—for example, by divulging sensitive personal information to outsiders. Partly for this reason, girls' closest same-sex friendships tend to be of shorter duration than boys' (Benenson & Christakos, 2003).

Friendships on the Internet. Teenagers frequently use cell phones and the Internet to communicate with friends. About 75 percent of U.S. 12- to 17-year-olds own a cell phone, a rate that has nearly doubled during the past decade. Cell-phone texting has become the preferred means of electronic interaction between teenage friends, with cell calling second, followed by social networking sites and instant messaging (see Figure 12.2 on page 332). Girls use cell phones to text and call their friends considerably more often than boys (Lenhart et al., 2010). These forms of online interaction seem to support friendship closeness. In several studies, as amount of online messaging between preexisting friends increased, so did young people's perceptions of intimacy in the relationship and feelings of well-being (Reich, Subrahmanyam, & Espinoza, 2012; Valkenburg & Peter, 2007a, 2007b, 2009). The effect is largely due to friends' online disclosure of personal information, such as worries, secrets, and romantic feelings.

Although mostly communicating with friends they know, teenagers are also drawn to meeting new people over the Internet. Social networking sites such as Facebook and MySpace (used by nearly three-fourths of U.S. teenagers) along with blogs, message boards, and chat rooms open up vast alternatives beyond their families, schools, and communities (Lenhart et al., 2010). Through these online ties, young people explore central adolescent issues—sexuality, challenges in parent and peer relationships, and identity issues, including attitudes and values—in contexts that may feel less threatening than similar everyday conversations (Subrahmanyam, Smahel, & Greenfield, 2006; Valkenburg & Peter, 2011). Online interactions with strangers also offer some teenagers vital social support. Young people suffering from depression, eating disorders, and other problems can access message boards where participants provide mutual assistance (Whitlock, Powers, & Eckenrode, 2006).

But online communication also poses dangers. In unmonitored chat rooms, teenagers are likely to encounter degrading racial and ethnic slurs and sexually obscene and harassing remarks (Subrahmanyam & Greenfield, 2008). Furthermore, in a survey of a nationally representative sample of U.S. 10- to 17-year-olds, 14 percent reported having formed online close

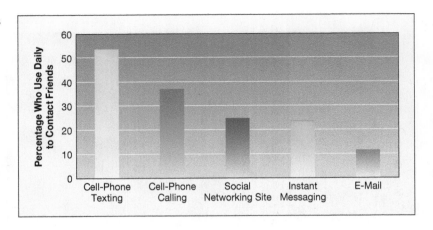

FIGURE 12.2 **Percentage of U.S. 12- to 17-year-olds who use various communication channels daily to contact friends.** A nationally representative sample of 800 U.S. 12- to 17-year-olds responded to a survey about their communication strategies with friends. Cell-phone texting emerged as the preferred channel, with over half of teenagers reporting that they used it daily. (Adapted from Lenhart et al., 2010.)

friendships or romances. Although some of these youths were well-adjusted, many reported high levels of conflict with parents, peer victimization, depression, and delinquency (Wolak, Mitchell, & Finkelhor, 2003). They also more often had been asked by online friends for face-to-face meetings and had attended those meetings—without telling their parents.

Finally, time devoted to social media is rising among older children and adolescents. For example, nearly 45 percent send more than 50 texts per day, and more than 70 percent use social networking sites for an average of 37 minutes per day. Some evidence suggests that very high social media use is linked to unsatisfying face-to-face social experiences, boredom, unhappiness, and Internet addiction (obsessive Internet use) (Pea et al., 2012; Rideout, Foehr, & Roberts, 2010; Smahel, Brown, & Blinka, 2012). Furthermore, high Internet consumers often engage in "face-to-face multitasking," such as texting at the dinner table or web surfing while chatting with friends (Abelson, Ledeen, & Lewis, 2008). These behaviors detract from high-quality face-to-face communication.

In sum, the Internet's value for enabling convenient and satisfying interaction among teenage friends must be weighed against its potential for facilitating harmful social consequences. Parents are wise to point out the risks of Internet communication, including excessive use, harassment, and exploitation, and to insist that teenagers follow Internet safety rules (see *www.safeteens.com*).

Friendship and Adjustment. As long as adolescent friendships are high in trust, intimate sharing, and support and not characterized by relational aggression or attraction to antisocial behavior, they contribute to many aspects of psychological health and competence into early adulthood (Bukowski, 2001; Waldrip, 2008), for several reasons:

● *Close friendships provide opportunities to explore the self and develop a deep understanding of another.* Through open, honest communication, friends become sensitive to each other's strengths and weaknesses, needs and desires—a process that supports the development of self-concept, perspective taking, and identity.

● *Close friendships provide a foundation for future intimate relationships.* Conversations with teenage friends about sexuality and romance, along with the intimacy of friendship itself, may help adolescents establish and work out problems in romantic partnerships (Connolly & Goldberg, 1999).

● *Close friendships help young people deal with the stresses of adolescence.* Supportive friendships promote empathy,

sympathy, and prosocial behavior. As a result, friendships contribute to involvement in constructive youth activities, avoidance of antisocial acts, and psychological well-being (Lansford et al., 2003; Wentzel, Barry, & Caldwell, 2004).

● *Close friendships can improve attitudes toward and involvement in school.* Close friendships promote good school adjustment, academically and socially (Wentzel, Barry, & Caldwell, 2004). When teenagers enjoy interacting with friends at school, they may begin to view all aspects of school life more positively.

LOOK AND LISTEN

Interview several adolescents about qualities they value most in their best friends. Ask how friendships have helped them cope with stress and resulted in other personal benefits. ●

Cliques and Crowds

In early adolescence, *peer groups* (see Chapter 10) become increasingly common and tightly knit. They are organized into **cliques**, groups of about five to seven members who are friends and, therefore, usually resemble one another in family background, attitudes, and values (Brown & Dietz, 2009). At first, cliques are limited to same-sex members. Among girls but not boys, being in a clique predicts academic and social competence. Clique membership is more important to girls, who use it as a context for expressing emotional closeness (Henrich et al., 2000). By midadolescence, mixed-sex cliques are common.

Among Western adolescents attending high schools with complex social structures, often several cliques with similar values form a larger, more loosely organized group called a **crowd.** Unlike the more intimate clique, membership in a crowd is based on reputation and stereotype, granting the adolescent an identity within the larger social structure of the school. Prominent crowds in a typical high school might include "brains" (nonathletes who enjoy academics), "jocks" (who are very involved in sports), "populars" (class leaders who are highly social and involved in activities), "partyers" (who value social-

These high school drama club members form a crowd, establishing relationships on the basis of shared abilities and interests. Crowd membership grants them an identity within the larger social structure of the school.

izing but care little about schoolwork), "nonconformists" (who like unconventional clothing and music), "druggies" (who frequently use substances, engage in sexual risk-taking, and otherwise get into trouble), and "normals" (average to good students who get along with most other peers) (Kinney, 1999; Stone & Brown, 1999).

What influences the sorting of teenagers into cliques and crowds? Crowd affiliations are linked to strengths in adolescents' self-concepts, which reflect their abilities and interests (Prinstein & La Greca, 2002). Ethnicity also plays a role. Minority teenagers who associate with an ethnically defined crowd, as opposed to a crowd reflecting their abilities and interests, may be motivated by discrimination in their school or neighborhood. Alternatively, they may be expressing a strong ethnic identity (Brown et al., 2008). Family factors are important, too. In a study of 8,000 ninth to twelfth graders, adolescents who described their parents as authoritative were members of "brain," "jock," and "popular" groups that accepted both adult and peer reward systems. In contrast, boys with permissive parents aligned themselves with the "partyers" and "druggies," suggesting lack of identification with adult reward systems (Durbin et al., 1993).

As interest in dating increases, boys' and girls' cliques come together. Mixed-sex cliques provide boys and girls with models of how to interact and a chance to do so without having to be intimate (Connolly et al., 2004). By late adolescence, when boys and girls feel comfortable enough about approaching each other directly, the mixed-sex cliques disappear (Connolly & Goldberg, 1999).

Crowds also decline in importance. As adolescents settle on personal values and goals, they no longer feel a need to broadcast, through dress, language, and activities, who they are. From tenth to twelfth grade, about half of young people switch crowds, mostly in favorable directions (Strouse, 1999). "Brains" and "normal" crowds grow and deviant crowds lose members as teenagers focus more on their future.

Dating

The hormonal changes of puberty increase sexual interest, but cultural expectations determine when and how dating begins. Asian youths start dating later and have fewer dating partners than young people in Western societies, which tolerate and even encourage romantic involvements from middle school on. At age 12 to 14, these relationships are usually casual, lasting only briefly. But by age 16, they continue, on average, for nearly two years (Carver, Joyner, & Udry, 2003). Early adolescents tend to mention recreation and achieving peer status as reasons for dating. By late adolescence, as young people are ready for greater psychological intimacy, they seek dating partners who offer personal compatibility, companionship, affection, and social support (Collins & van Dulmen, 2006b; Meier & Allen, 2009).

The achievement of intimacy between dating partners typically lags behind that between friends. And recall from Chapter 6 that according to ethological theory, early attachment bonds lead to an *internal working model,* or set of expectations about attachment figures, that guides later close relationships. Consistent with this idea, secure attachment to parents in infancy and childhood—together with recollections of that security in adolescence—predicts quality of teenagers' friendship and romantic ties (Collins & van Dulmen, 2006a; Collins, Welsh, & Furman, 2009).

Perhaps because early adolescent dating relationships are shallow and stereotyped, early dating is related to drug use, delinquency, and poor academic achievement (Eaton et al., 2007; Miller et al., 2009). These factors, along with a history of uninvolved parenting and aggression in family and peer relationships, increase the likelihood of dating violence. About 10 to 20 percent of adolescents are physically or sexually abused by dating partners, with boys and girls equally likely to report being victims, and violence by one partner often returned by the other (Cyr, McDuff, & Wright, 2006; Williams et al., 2008). Mental health consequences are severe, including increased

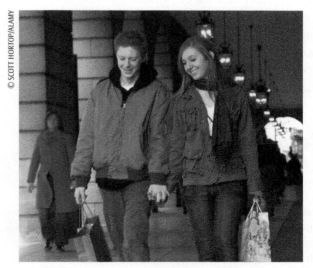

For this young couple out shopping together, dating extends the benefits of adolescent friendships, promoting sensitivity, empathy, self-esteem, and identity development.

anxiety, depression, suicide attempts, and risky sexual behavior (Wekerle & Avgoustis, 2003). Young teenagers are better off sticking with group activities, such as parties and dances, before becoming involved with a steady boyfriend or girlfriend.

Gay and lesbian youths face special challenges in initiating and maintaining visible romances. Their first dating relationships seem to be short-lived and to involve little emotional commitment, but for reasons different from those of heterosexuals: They fear peer harassment and rejection (Diamond & Lucas, 2004). In addition, many have difficulty finding a same-sex partner because their gay and lesbian peers have not yet come out. Often their first contacts with other sexual-minority youths occur in support groups, where they are free to date publicly (Diamond, 2003).

As long as it does not begin too soon, dating promotes sensitivity, empathy, self-esteem, social support, compromise, and identity development, thereby enhancing the quality of other peer relationships (Collins, Welsh, & Furman, 2009). Still, about half of first romances do not survive high school graduation, and those that do usually become less satisfying (Shaver, Furman, & Buhrmester, 1985). Because young people are still forming their identities, high school couples often find that they have little in common after graduation. Nevertheless, warm, caring romantic ties in adolescence can have long-term implications. They are positively related to gratifying, committed relationships in early adulthood (Meier & Allen, 2009).

ASK YOURSELF

REVIEW Describe the distinct positive functions of friendships, cliques, and crowds in adolescence. What factors lead some friendships and peer-group ties to be harmful?

APPLY Thirteen-year-old Mattie's parents are warm, firm in their expectations, and consistent in monitoring her activities. At school, Mattie met some girls who want her to tell her parents she's going to a friend's house but, instead, join them at the beach for a party. Is Mattie likely to comply? Explain.

REFLECT How did family experiences influence your crowd membership in high school? How did your crowd membership influence your behavior?

 ## Problems of Development

Most young people move through adolescence with little disturbance. But as we have seen, some encounter major disruptions in development, such as early parenthood, substance abuse, and school failure. In each instance, biological and psychological changes, families, schools, peers, communities, and culture combine to yield particular outcomes. Serious difficulties rarely occur in isolation but are usually interrelated—as is apparent in three additional problems of the teenage years: depression, suicide, and delinquency.

Depression

Depression—feeling sad, frustrated, and hopeless about life, accompanied by loss of pleasure in most activities and disturbances in sleep, appetite, concentration, and energy—is the most common psychological problem of adolescence. About 15 to 20 percent of teenagers have had one or more major depressive episodes, a rate comparable to that of adults. From 2 to 8 percent are chronically depressed—gloomy and self-critical for many months and sometimes years (Graber & Sontag, 2009; Rushton, Forcier, & Schectman, 2002).

Serious depression affects only 1 to 2 percent of children, many of whom (especially girls) remain depressed in adolescence. In addition, depression increases sharply from ages 12 to 16 in industrialized nations, with many more girls than boys displaying adolescent onset. Teenage girls are twice as likely as boys to report persistent depressed mood—a difference sustained throughout the lifespan (Dekker et al., 2007; Hankin & Abela, 2005; Nolen-Hoeksema, 2006).

Factors Related to Depression. Kinship studies reveal that heredity plays an important role in depression (Glowinski et al., 2003). Genes can induce depression by affecting the balance of neurotransmitters in the brain, the development of brain regions involved in inhibiting negative emotion, or the body's hormonal response to stress.

But experience can also promote these biological changes. In earlier chapters we saw that depressed or otherwise stressed parents often engage in maladaptive parenting. As a result, their child's emotional self-regulation, attachment, and self-esteem may be impaired, with serious consequences for many cognitive and social skills (Abela et al., 2005; Yap, Allen, & Ladouceur, 2008). In a vulnerable young person, numerous events can spark depression—for example, failing at something important, parental divorce, or the end of a close friendship or romantic partnership.

Sex Differences. Why are girls more prone to depression than boys? Biological changes associated with puberty cannot be responsible because in many developing countries, rates of depression are similar for males and females and occasionally higher in males (Culbertson, 1997). And in industrialized nations, the extent to which females exceed males in depression varies widely.

Instead, gender-typed coping styles seem to be responsible. Early-maturing girls are especially prone to depression (see Chapter 11). Adolescent gender intensification may strengthen girls' passivity, dependency, and tendency to ruminate on their anxieties and problems—maladaptive approaches to tasks expected of teenagers in complex cultures. Consistent with this explanation, adolescents who identify strongly with "feminine" traits ruminate more and are more depressed, regardless of their sex (Lopez, Driscoll, & Kistner, 2009; Papadakis et al., 2006). And having friends with depressive symptoms is linked to a rise in teenagers' own depressive symptoms, perhaps because corumination is high in such relationships (Conway et al., 2011).

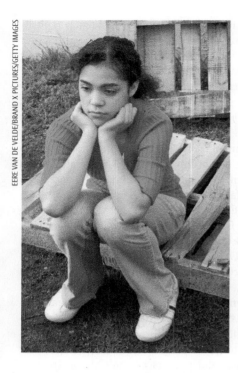

In industrialized nations, stressful life events and gender-typed coping styles—passivity, dependency, and rumination—make adolescent girls more prone to depression than boys.

Girls who repeatedly feel troubled and insecure develop an overly reactive physiological stress response and cope more poorly with future challenges (Hyde, Mezulis, & Abramson, 2008; Nolen-Hoeksema, 2006). In this way, stressful experiences and stress reactivity feed on one another, sustaining depression. Profound depression can lead to suicidal thoughts, which all too often are translated into action.

Suicide

The suicide rate increases from childhood to old age, but it jumps sharply at adolescence. Currently, suicide is the third-leading cause of death among American youths, after motor vehicle collisions and homicides. At the same time, rates of adolescent suicide vary widely among industrialized nations—low in Greece, Italy, the Netherlands, and Spain; intermediate in Australia, Canada, Japan, and the United States; and high in Finland, New Zealand, and Singapore (Bridge, Goldstein, & Brent, 2006). These international differences remain unexplained.

Factors Related to Adolescent Suicide. Despite girls' higher rates of depression, the number of boys who kill themselves exceeds the number of girls by a ratio of 3 or 4 to 1. Girls make more unsuccessful suicide attempts and use methods from which they are more likely to be revived, such as a sleeping pill overdose. In contrast, boys tend to choose techniques that lead to instant death, such as firearms (Langhinrichsen-Rohling, Friend, & Powell, 2009). Gender-role expectations may contribute; less tolerance exists for feelings of helplessness and failed efforts in males.

Possibly due to greater extended-family support, African Americans and Hispanics have lower suicide rates than Caucasian Americans. Recently, however, suicide has risen among African-American adolescent males; the current rate approaches that of Caucasian-American males. And Native-American youths commit suicide at rates two to six times national averages (Balis & Postolache, 2008; U.S. Census Bureau, 2013). High rates of profound family poverty, school failure, alcohol and drug use, and depression probably underlie these trends. Gay, lesbian, and bisexual youths are also at high risk, attempting suicide three times as often as other adolescents. Those who have tried to kill themselves report more family conflict over their gender-atypical behavior, inner turmoil about their sexuality, and peer victimization (D'Augelli et al., 2005).

Suicide tends to occur in two types of young people. The first group includes adolescents who are highly intelligent but solitary, withdrawn, and unable to meet their own standards or those of important people in their lives. Members of the second, larger group show antisocial tendencies (Evans, Hawton, & Rodham, 2004). Besides being hostile and destructive, they turn their anger and disappointment inward.

Suicidal adolescents often have a family history of emotional and antisocial disorders. In addition, they are likely to have experienced multiple stressful life events, including economic disadvantage, parental divorce, frequent parent–child conflict, and abuse and neglect (Beautrais, 2003; Kaminski et al., 2010). Triggering events include parental blaming of the teenager for family problems, the breakup of an important peer relationship, or the humiliation of having been caught engaging in antisocial acts.

Why does suicide increase in adolescence? One factor seems to be teenagers' improved ability to plan ahead. Although some act impulsively, many young people take purposeful steps toward killing themselves. Other cognitive changes also contribute. Belief in the personal fable (see Chapter 11) leads many depressed young people to conclude that no one could possibly understand their intense pain.

Prevention and Treatment. To prevent suicides, parents and teachers must be trained to pick up on the signals that a troubled teenager sends (see Table 12.2 on page 336). Schools and community settings, such as recreational and religious organizations, can help by providing counseling and support (Goldston et al., 2008; Miller, 2011). Once a teenager takes steps toward suicide, staying with the young person, listening, and expressing compassion and concern until professional help can be obtained are essential.

Treatments for depressed and suicidal adolescents range from antidepressant medication to individual, family, and group therapy. On a broader scale, gun-control legislation that limits adolescents' access to the most frequent and deadly suicide method in the United States would greatly reduce both the number of suicides and the high teenage homicide rate (Commission on Adolescent Suicide Prevention, 2005).

Teenage suicides often occur in clusters, with one death increasing the likelihood of others among depressed peers who knew the young person (Bearman & Moody, 2004; Feigelman & Gorman, 2008). In view of this trend, an especially watchful eye must be kept on vulnerable adolescents after a suicide happens.

TABLE 12.2
Warning Signs of Suicide

Efforts to put personal affairs in order—smoothing over troubled relationships, giving away treasured possessions
Verbal cues—saying goodbye to family members and friends, making direct or indirect references to suicide ("I won't have to worry about these problems much longer"; "I wish I were dead")
Feelings of sadness, despondency, "not caring" anymore
Extreme fatigue, lack of energy, boredom
No desire to socialize; withdrawal from friends
Easily frustrated
Emotional outbursts—spells of crying or laughing, bursts of energy
Inability to concentrate, distractible
Decline in grades, absence from school, discipline problems
Neglect of personal appearance
Sleep change—loss of sleep or excessive sleepiness
Appetite change—eating more or less than usual
Physical complaints—stomachaches, backaches, headaches

Delinquency

Juvenile delinquents are children or adolescents who engage in illegal acts. Although youth crime has declined in the United States since the mid-1990s, 12- to 17-year-olds account for about 14 percent of police arrests, although they constitute only 8 percent of the population (U.S. Department of Justice, 2010). When asked directly and confidentially about lawbreaking, almost all teenagers admit to having committed some sort of offense—usually a minor crime, such as petty stealing or disorderly conduct (Flannery et al., 2003).

Both police arrests and self-reports show that delinquency rises over early and middle adolescence and then declines (Farrington, 2009; U.S. Department of Justice, 2010). Antisocial behavior increases among teenagers as a result of heightened reward seeking and desire for peer approval. Over time, peers become less influential; decision making, emotional self-regulation, and moral reasoning improve; and young people enter social contexts (such as higher education, work, marriage, and career) that are less conducive to lawbreaking.

For most adolescents, a brush with the law does not forecast long-term antisocial behavior. But repeated arrests are cause for concern. Teenagers are responsible for 15 percent of violent offenses in the United States (U.S. Department of Justice, 2010). A small percentage become recurrent offenders, who commit most of these crimes, and some enter a life of crime.

Factors Related to Delinquency. In adolescence, the gender gap in physical aggression widens. Although girls account for about one in five adolescent arrests for violence,

their offenses are largely limited to simple assault (such as pushing or spitting). Serious violent crime is mostly the domain of boys (Dahlberg & Simon, 2006). SES and ethnicity are strong predictors of arrests but only mildly related to teenagers' self-reports of antisocial acts. The difference is due to the tendency to arrest, charge, and punish low-SES ethnic minority youths more often than their higher-SES white and Asian counterparts (Farrington, 2009; U.S. Department of Justice, 2010).

Difficult temperament, low intelligence, poor school performance, peer rejection in childhood, and association with antisocial peers are linked to chronic delinquency (Laird et al., 2005). How do these factors fit together? One of the most consistent findings about delinquent youths is that their families are low in warmth, high in conflict, and characterized by harsh, inconsistent discipline and low monitoring (Barnes et al., 2006; Capaldi et al., 2002). Our discussion on page 212 in Chapter 8 explained how ineffective parenting can promote and sustain children's aggression, with boys—who are more active and impulsive—more often targets of parental anger, physical punishment, and inconsistency. When these child temperamental traits combine with emotionally negative, inept parenting, aggression rises sharply during childhood, leads to violent offenses in adolescence, and persists into adulthood (see the Biology and Environment box on the following page).

Teenagers commit more crimes in poverty-stricken neighborhoods with limited recreational and employment opportunities and high adult criminality (Leventhal, Duprere, & Brooks-Gunn, 2009). In such neighborhoods, adolescents have easy access to deviant peers, drugs, and firearms and are likely to be recruited into antisocial gangs, whose members commit the vast majority of violent delinquent acts. Furthermore, schools in these locales typically fail to meet students' developmental needs (Chung, Mulvey, & Steinberg, 2011; Flannery et al., 2003). Large classes, weak instruction, rigid rules, and reduced academic

© CHROMORANGE/PICTURE-ALLIANCE/NEWSCOM

Delinquency—usually petty stealing and disorderly conduct—rises over early and middle adolescence and then declines. But a small percentage of young people engage in repeated, serious offenses and are at risk for a life of crime.

Biology and Environment

Two Routes to Adolescent Delinquency

Persistent adolescent delinquency follows two paths, one involving a small number of youths with an onset of conduct problems in childhood, the second a larger number with an onset in adolescence. The early-onset type is far more likely to lead to a life-course pattern of aggression and criminality (Moffitt, 2007). The late-onset type usually does not persist beyond the transition to early adulthood.

Why does antisocial activity more often continue and escalate into violence in the first group? Longitudinal studies yield similar answers to this question. Most research has focused on boys, but several investigations report that girls who were physically aggressive in childhood are also at risk for later problems—occasionally violent delinquency but more often other norm-violating behaviors and psychological disorders (Broidy et al., 2003; Chamberlain, 2003). Early relational aggression is linked to adolescent conduct problems as well.

Early-Onset Type

Early-onset youngsters seem to inherit traits that predispose them to aggressiveness. Violence-prone boys are emotionally negative, restless, willful, and physically aggressive as early as age 2. They also show subtle deficits in cognitive functioning that seem to contribute to disruptions in the development of language, memory, and cognitive and

emotional self-regulation (Moffitt, 2007; Shaw et al., 2003). Some have attention-deficit hyperactivity disorder (ADHD), which compounds their learning and self-control problems (see Chapter 9, page 239).

Yet these biological risks are not sufficient to sustain antisocial behavior: Most early-onset boys decline in aggression over time. Among those who follow the life-course path, inept parenting transforms their undercontrolled style into defiance and persistent aggression (Brame, Nagin, & Tremblay, 2001; Broidy et al., 2003). As they fail academically and are rejected by peers, they befriend other deviant youths, who facilitate one another's violent behavior (see Figure 12.3) (Hughes, 2010; Lacourse et al., 2003). Limited cognitive and social skills result in high rates of school dropout and unemployment, contributing further to antisocial involvements (Patterson & Yoerger, 2002).

Preschoolers high in relational aggression also tend to be hyperactive and frequently in conflict with peers and adults. As these behaviors trigger peer rejection, relationally aggressive girls befriend other girls high in relational hostility, and their relational aggression rises (Werner & Crick, 2004). Adolescents high in relational aggression are often angry, vengeful, and defiant of adult rules. Among teenagers who combine physical and relational hostility, these oppositional reactions intensify, increasing

the likelihood of serious antisocial activity (Harachi et al., 2006; Prinstein, Boergers, & Vernberg, 2001).

Late-Onset Type

Other youths first display antisocial behavior around the time of puberty, gradually increasing their involvement. Their conduct problems arise from the peer context, not from biological deficits and a history of unfavorable development. For some, quality of parenting may decline for a time, perhaps due to family stresses or the challenges of disciplining an unruly teenager (Moffitt, 2007). When age brings gratifying adult privileges, these youths draw on prosocial skills mastered before adolescence and abandon their antisocial ways.

A few late-onset youths do continue to engage in antisocial acts. The seriousness of their adolescent offenses seems to trap them in situations that close off opportunities for responsible behavior. Being employed or in school and forming positive, close relationships predict an end to criminal offending by age 20 to 25 (Clingempeel & Henggeler, 2003; Stouthamer-Loeber et al., 2004). In contrast, the longer antisocial young people spend in prison, the more likely they are to sustain a life of crime.

These findings suggest a need for a fresh look at policies aimed at stopping youth crime. Keeping youth offenders locked up for many years disrupts their vocational lives and access to social support during a crucial period of development, condemning them to a bleak future.

FIGURE 12.3 Path to chronic delinquency for adolescents with childhood-onset antisocial behavior. Difficult temperament and cognitive deficits characterize many of these youths in early childhood; some have attention-deficit hyperactivity disorder. Inept parenting transforms biologically based self-control difficulties into hostility and defiance.

expectations and opportunities are associated with higher rates of lawbreaking, even after other influences are controlled.

Prevention and Treatment. Because delinquency has roots in childhood and results from events in several contexts, prevention must start early and take place at multiple levels (Frey et al., 2009). Positive family relationships, authoritative parenting, high-quality teaching in schools, and communities with healthy economic and social conditions go a long way toward reducing adolescent antisocial acts.

Lacking resources for effective prevention, many U.S. schools have implemented *zero tolerance policies,* which punish all disruptive and threatening behavior, usually with suspension or expulsion. Yet often these policies are implemented inconsistently: Low-SES minority students are two to three times as likely to be punished, especially for minor misbehaviors (Goode & Goode, 2007; Reppucci, Meyer, & Kostelnik, 2011). No evidence exists that zero tolerance reduces youth misconduct (Stinchcomb, Bazemore, & Riestenberg, 2006). To the contrary, some studies find that these policies heighten high school dropout and antisocial behavior.

Treating serious offenders requires an intensive, often lengthy approach, also directed at the multiple determinants of delinquency. In a program called *multisystemic therapy,* counselors combined family intervention with integrating violent youths into positive school, work, and leisure activities and disengaging them from deviant peers. Compared with conventional services or individual therapy, the intervention led to greater improvement in parent–adolescent relationships and school performance and a dramatic drop in number of arrests. Multisystemic therapy also helped limit family instability once youth offenders reached adulthood, as measured by involvement in civil suits over divorce, paternity, or child support (Borduin, 2007; Henggeler et al., 2009; Sawyer & Borduin, 2011). Efforts to create nonaggressive environments—at the family, community, and cultural levels—are needed to help delinquent youths and to foster healthy development of all young people.

ASK YOURSELF

REVIEW Why are adolescent girls at greater risk for depression and adolescent boys at greater risk for suicide?

APPLY Zeke had been well-behaved in elementary school, but at age 13 he started spending time with the "wrong crowd." At 16, he was arrested for property damage. Is Zeke likely to become a long-term offender? Why or why not?

SUMMARY

Erikson's Theory: Identity versus Role Confusion (p. 318)

According to Erikson, what is the major personality achievement of adolescence?

- Erikson viewed **identity** as the major personality achievement of adolescence. Young people who successfully resolve the psychological conflict of **identity versus role confusion** construct a unified self-definition based on self-chosen values and goals.

Self-Understanding (p. 318)

Describe changes in self-concept and self-esteem during adolescence.

- Cognitive changes enable adolescents to develop more organized, consistent self-descriptions, with social, personal, and moral values as key themes.

- Self-esteem further differentiates and, for most adolescents, rises. Authoritative parenting and encouragement from teachers support positive self-esteem.

Describe the four identity statuses, along with factors that promote identity development.

- Researchers evaluate progress in identity development on two key criteria: exploration and commitment. **Identity achievement** (exploration followed by commitment to values, beliefs, and goals) and **identity moratorium** (exploration without having reached commitment) are psychologically healthy identity statuses. Long-term **identity foreclosure** (commitment without exploration) and **identity diffusion** (lack of both exploration and commitment) are related to adjustment difficulties.

© KATHY McLAUGHLIN/THE IMAGE WORKS

- An information-gathering cognitive style, healthy parental attachment, interaction with diverse peers, and schools and communities offering rich and varied opportunities promote healthy identity development. To forge a strong, secure **ethnic identity,** minority adolescents often must overcome **acculturative stress.** A **bicultural identity** offers additional emotional and social benefits.

Moral Development (p. 321)

Describe Kohlberg's theory of moral development, and evaluate its accuracy.

- Kohlberg organized moral development into three levels, each with two stages. At the **preconventional level,** morality is externally controlled and actions are judged by their consequences; at the **conventional level,** conformity to laws and rules is regarded as necessary for positive human relationships and societal order; and at the **postconventional level,** morality is defined by abstract, universal principles.

- A reexamination of Kohlberg's stages suggests that moral maturity can be found at Stages 3 and 4; few people attain the postconventional level. Because situational factors influence moral judgments, Kohlberg's stages are best viewed as loosely organized and overlapping.

- Contrary to Gilligan's claim, Kohlberg's theory does not underestimate the moral maturity of females but instead taps both justice and caring orientations.

- Compared with children, teenagers display more subtle reasoning about conflicts between personal choice and community obligation and are increasingly aware of the moral implications of following social conventions.

Describe influences on moral reasoning and its relationship to moral behavior.

- Factors contributing to moral maturity include warm, rational child-rearing practices, education level, and peer discussions of moral issues. In village societies, moral reasoning rarely moves beyond Kohlberg's Stage 3. In collectivist cultures, moral dilemma responses are more other-directed than in Western societies.

- Maturity of moral reasoning is only modestly related to moral behavior. Moral action is also influenced by empathy and guilt, temperament, history of morally relevant experiences, and **moral identity.** Although formal religious involvement declines in adolescence, most religiously affiliated teenagers are advantaged in moral values and behavior.

- Researchers favoring a pragmatic approach to morality assert that moral maturity varies depending on context and motivations.

Gender Typing (p. 328)

How does gender typing change in adolescence?

- Some research suggests that adolescence is a time of **gender intensification,** in which gender stereotyping of attitudes and behavior increases, though evidence is mixed.

The Family (p. 329)

Discuss changes in parent–child and sibling relationships during adolescence.

- In their quest for **autonomy,** adolescents rely more on themselves and less on parents for decision making. Teenagers deidealize their parents, often questioning parental authority. Warm, supportive parenting, appropriate demands for maturity, and consistent monitoring predict favorable outcomes.

- Sibling influence declines as adolescents separate from the family and turn toward peers. Still, attachment to siblings remains strong for most young people.

Peer Relations (p. 330)

Describe adolescent friendships, peer groups, and dating relationships and their consequences for development.

- Adolescent friendships are based on intimacy, mutual understanding, and loyalty and contain more self-disclosure. Girls place greater emphasis on emotional closeness, boys on shared activities and accomplishments.

- Online communication supports closeness with existing friends. Though online communication with strangers provides some teenagers with vital social support, it also poses risks. High social media use is linked to unsatisfying face-to-face social experiences.

- Adolescent friendships—when not characterized by relational aggression or attraction to antisocial behavior—promote self-concept, perspective taking, identity, and the capacity for intimate relationships. They also help young people deal with stress and can foster improved attitudes toward and involvement in school.

- Adolescent peer groups are organized into **cliques,** particularly important to girls, and **crowds,** which grant teenagers an identity within the larger social structure of the school. With interest in dating, mixed-sex cliques increase in importance. Both cliques and crowds diminish as teenagers settle on personal values and goals.

- Intimacy in dating relationships lags behind that between friends. Positive relationships with parents and friends contribute to secure romantic ties.

© SCOTT HORTOP/ALAMY

Problems of Development (p. 334)

Describe factors related to adolescent depression and suicide.

- Depression is the most common psychological problem of adolescence, with girls at greater risk in industrialized nations. Combinations of biological and environmental factors are implicated, including heredity, maladaptive parenting, and negative life events.

- The suicide rate increases sharply at adolescence. Although teenage girls make more unsuccessful suicide attempts, boys account for more deaths. Teenagers at risk for suicide may be withdrawn but more often are antisocial. Family turmoil is common in the backgrounds of suicidal adolescents.

Discuss factors related to delinquency.

- Delinquency rises over early and middle adolescence and then declines. But only a few teenagers are serious repeat offenders— usually boys with a childhood history of conduct problems.

- A family environment low in warmth, high in conflict, and characterized by inconsistent discipline and low monitoring is consistently related to delinquency, as are poverty-stricken neighborhoods with high crime rates and ineffective schools.

Important Terms and Concepts

milestones

Development in Adolescence

© RUDY VON BRIEL/PHOTOEDIT

© BOB DAEMMRICH/PHOTOEDIT

■ Becomes more self-conscious and self-focused. (308)

■ Becomes more idealistic and critical. (308)

■ Metacognition and self-regulation continue to improve. (291, 306)

EMOTIONAL/SOCIAL

■ Self-concept includes abstract descriptors unifying separate personality traits, but these are not interconnected and often contradictory. (318–319)

■ In striving for autonomy, spends less time with parents and siblings, more time with peers. (330)

■ Friendships decline in number and are based on intimacy, mutual understanding, and loyalty. (330)

■ Peer groups become organized around same-sex cliques. (332)

■ In high schools with complex social structures, cliques with similar values form crowds. (332)

© CINDY CHARLES/PHOTOEDIT

Middle Adolescence: 14–16

PHYSICAL

■ If a girl, completes growth spurt. (288)

■ If a boy, reaches peak of growth spurt. (288)

■ If a boy, voice deepens. (290)

■ If a boy, adds muscle while body fat declines. (289)

■ If a boy, motor performance improves dramatically. (289)

■ May have had sexual intercourse. (298)

COGNITIVE

■ Continues to improve in hypothetico-deductive reasoning and propositional thought. (304–305)

■ Continues to improve in scientific reasoning. (307)

© BOB DAEMMRICH/PHOTOEDIT

Early Adolescence: 11–14

PHYSICAL

■ If a girl, reaches peak of growth spurt. (288)

■ If a girl, adds more body fat than muscle. (289)

■ If a girl, starts to menstruate. (290)

■ If a boy, begins growth spurt. (288)

■ If a boy, starts to ejaculate seminal fluid. (290)

■ Is likely to be aware of sexual orientation. (299)

■ If a girl, motor performance increases gradually, leveling off by age 14. (289)

■ Reacts more strongly to stressful events; shows heightened sensation-seeking and risk-taking behavior. (292)

COGNITIVE

■ Gains in hypothetico-deductive reasoning and propositional thought. (304–305)

■ Gains in scientific reasoning—coordinating theory with evidence—on complex, multivariable tasks. (307)

Note: Numbers in parentheses indicate the page or pages on which each milestone is discussed.

- Becomes less self-conscious and self-focused. (308)
- Improves in decision making. (308–309)

EMOTIONAL/SOCIAL

- Combines features of the self into an organized self-concept. (319)
- Self-esteem differentiates further and tends to rise. (319)
- In most cases, begins to move from "lower" to "higher" identity statuses. (319)
- Increasingly emphasizes ideal reciprocity and societal laws as the basis for resolving moral dilemmas. (324)
- Engages in more subtle reasoning about conflicts between moral, social-conventional, and personal-choice issues. (325)

- Mixed-sex cliques become common. (332)
- Has probably started dating. (333)

Late Adolescence: 16–18

PHYSICAL

- If a boy, completes growth spurt. (288)
- If a boy, gains in motor performance continue. (289)

COGNITIVE

- Continues to improve in metacognition, scientific reasoning, and decision making. (306–309)

EMOTIONAL/SOCIAL

- Self-concept emphasizes personal and moral values. (319)
- Continues to construct an identity, typically moving to higher identity statuses. (319)
- Continues to advance in maturity of moral reasoning. (324)
- Cliques and crowds decline in importance. (333)
- Seeks psychological intimacy in romantic ties, which last longer. (333–334)

chapter
14

Emotional and Social Development in Early Adulthood

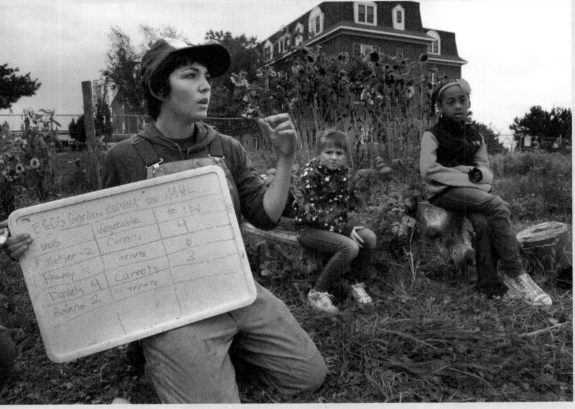

THE WASHINGTON POST/ GETTY IMAGES

This college student, a volunteer for a nonprofit organization called FoodCorps, helps children in economically disadvantaged communities plant a school garden, teaching them about healthy foods and how they grow. For many young people in industrialized nations, the transition to early adulthood is a time of prolonged exploration of attitudes, values, and life possibilities.

chapter outline

A Gradual Transition: Emerging Adulthood

Unprecedented Exploration • Cultural Change, Cultural Variation, and Emerging Adulthood • Risk and Resilience in Emerging Adulthood

■ **CULTURAL INFLUENCES** Is Emerging Adulthood Really a Distinct Period of Development?

Erikson's Theory: Intimacy versus Isolation

Other Theories of Adult Psychosocial Development

Levinson's Seasons of Life • Vaillant's Adaptation to Life • The Social Clock

Close Relationships

Romantic Love • Friendships

■ **SOCIAL ISSUES: HEALTH** Childhood Attachment Patterns and Adult Romantic Relationships

The Family Life Cycle

Leaving Home • Joining of Families in Marriage • Parenthood

■ **SOCIAL ISSUES: HEALTH** Partner Abuse

The Diversity of Adult Lifestyles

Singlehood • Cohabitation • Childlessness • Divorce and Remarriage • Varied Styles of Parenthood

Career Development

Establishing a Career • Women and Ethnic Minorities • Combining Work and Family

After completing her master's degree at age 26, Sharese returned to her hometown, where she and Ernie would soon be married. During their year-long engagement, Sharese had vacillated about whether to follow through. At times, she looked with envy at Heather, still unattached and free to choose from an array of options before her. After graduating from college, Heather accepted a Peace Corps assignment in a remote region of Ghana, forged a romance with another Peace Corps volunteer that she ended at the conclusion of her tour of duty, and then traveled for eight months before returning to the United States to contemplate next steps.

Sharese also pondered the life circumstances of Christy and her husband, Gary—married and first-time parents by their mid-twenties. Despite his good teaching performance, Gary's relationship with the high school principal deteriorated, and he quit his job at the end of his first year. A tight job market impeded Gary's efforts to find another teaching position, and financial pressures and parenthood put Christy's education and career plans on hold. Sharese wondered whether it was really possible to combine family and career.

As her wedding approached, Sharese's ambivalence intensified, and she admitted to Ernie that she didn't feel ready to marry. But Ernie reassured her of his love. His career had been under way for two years, and at age 28, he looked forward to marriage and starting a family. Uncertain and conflicted, Sharese felt swept toward the altar as relatives and friends arrived. On the appointed day, she walked down the aisle.

In this chapter, we take up the emotional and social sides of early adulthood. Notice that Sharese, Ernie, and Heather moved toward adult roles slowly, at times vacillating along the way. Not until their mid- to late twenties did they make lasting career and romantic choices and attain full economic independence—markers of adulthood that young people of previous generations reached considerably earlier. Each received financial and other forms of support from parents and other family members, which enabled them to postpone taking on adult roles. We consider whether prolonged exploration of life options has become so widespread that it merits a new developmental period—*emerging adulthood*—to describe and understand it.

Recall from Chapter 12 that identity development continues to be a central focus from the late teens into the mid-twenties (see page 319). As they achieve a secure identity and independence from parents, young adults seek close, affectionate ties. Yet the decade of the twenties is accompanied by a rise in feelings of personal control over events in their lives—in fact, a stronger sense of control than they will ever experience again (Grob, Krings, & Bangerter, 2001). Perhaps for this reason, like Sharese, young people often fear losing their freedom. Once this struggle is resolved, early adulthood leads to new family units and parenthood, accomplished in the context of diverse lifestyles. At the same time, young adults must master the tasks of their chosen career.

Our discussion will reveal that identity, love, and work are intertwined. In negotiating these arenas, young adults do more choosing, planning, and changing course than any other age group. When their decisions are in tune with themselves and their social and cultural worlds, they acquire many new competencies, and life is full and rewarding. ●

A Gradual Transition: Emerging Adulthood

TAKE A MOMENT... Think about your own development. Do you consider yourself to have reached adulthood? When a large sample of American 18- to 25-year-olds was asked this question, the majority gave an ambiguous answer: "yes and no." Only after reaching their late twenties and early thirties did most feel that they were truly adult—findings evident in a wide range of industrialized nations (Arnett, 2001, 2003, 2007a; Buhl & Lanz, 2007; Macek, Bejček, & Vaníčková, 2007; Nelson, 2009; Sirsch et al., 2009). The life pursuits and subjective judgments of many contemporary young people indicate that the transition to adult roles has become so delayed and prolonged that it has spawned a new transitional period extending from the late teens to the mid- to late-twenties, called **emerging adulthood**.

Unprecedented Exploration

Psychologist Jeffrey Arnett is the leader of a movement that regards emerging adulthood as a distinct period of life. As Arnett explains, emerging adults have left adolescence but are still a considerable distance from taking on adult responsibilities. Their parents agree: In a survey of parents of a large sample of ethnically and religiously diverse U.S. undergraduate and graduate students, most viewed their children as not yet fully adult (Nelson et al., 2007). Rather, young people who have the economic resources to do so explore alternatives in education, work, and personal values and behavior more intensely than they did as teenagers.

Not yet immersed in adult roles, many emerging adults can engage in activities of the widest possible scope. Because so little is normative, or socially expected, routes to adult responsibilities are highly diverse in timing and order across individuals (Côté, 2006). For example, more college students than in past generations pursue their education in a drawn-out, nonlinear way—changing majors as they explore career options, taking courses while working part-time, or interrupting school to work, travel, or participate in national or international service programs. About one-third of U.S. college graduates enter graduate school, taking still more years to settle into their desired career track (U.S. Department of Education, 2012b).

As a result of these experiences, young people's interests, attitudes, and values broaden (see page 361 in Chapter 13). Exposure to multiple viewpoints also encourages development of a more complex self-concept that includes awareness of their own changing traits and values over time, along with enhanced self-esteem rises (Labouvie-Vief, 2006; Orth, Robins, & Widaman, 2012). Together, these changes contribute to advances in identity.

Identity Development. During the college years, young people refine their approach to constructing an identity. Besides exploring in *breadth* (weighing multiple possibilities), they also explore in *depth*—evaluating existing commitments (Luyckx et al., 2006). For example, if you have yet selected your major, you may be taking classes in a broad array of disciplines. Once you choose a major, you are likely to embark on an in-depth evaluation of your choice—reflecting on your interest, motivation, and performance and on your career prospects as you take additional classes in that field. Depending on the outcome of your evaluation, either your commitment to your major strengthens, or you return to a broad exploration of options.

In a longitudinal study extending over the first two years of college, most students cycled between making commitments and evaluating commitments in various identity domains. Fluctuations in students' certainty about their commitments sparked movement between these two states (Luyckx, Goossens, & Soenens, 2006). *TAKE A MOMENT...* Consider your own identity progress. Does it fit this *dual-cycle model,* in which identity formation is a lengthy process of feedback loops? Notice how

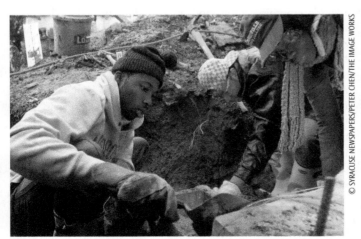

Volunteers with Habitat for Humanity help low-income home owners with major repairs. Despite a widespread view of today's young adults as self-centered, many emerging adults are committed to improving their communities, nation, and world.

© SYRACUSE NEWSPAPERS/PETER CHEN/THE IMAGE WORKS

the model helps explain the movement between identity statuses displayed by many young people, described in Chapter 12. College students who move toward exploration in depth and certainty of commitment are higher in self-esteem, psychological well-being, and academic, emotional, and social adjustment. Those who spend much time exploring in breadth without making commitments, or who are identity diffused (engaging in no exploration), tend to be poorly adjusted—anxious, depressed, and higher in alcohol and drug use, casual and unprotected sex, and other health-compromising behaviors (Kunnen et al., 2008; Schwartz et al., 2011).

Many aspects of the life course that were once socially structured—marriage, parenthood, religious beliefs, and career paths—are increasingly left to individual decision. As a result, emerging adults are required to "individualize" their identities—a process that requires a sense of self-efficacy, purpose, determination to overcome obstacles, and responsibility for outcomes. Among young people of diverse ethnicities and SES levels, this set of qualities, termed *personal agency,* is positively related to an information-gathering cognitive style and identity exploration followed by commitment (Schwartz, Côté, & Arnett, 2005; Stringer & Kerpelman, 2010).

Religion and Worldview. Most emerging adults say that constructing a worldview, or a set of beliefs and values to live by, is essential for attaining adult status—even more important than finishing their education and settling into a career and marriage (Arnett, 2006, 2007b). During the late teens and twenties, attendance at religious services drops to its lowest level throughout the lifespan as young people continue to question the beliefs they acquired in their families (Kunnen et al., 2008; Schwartz et al., 2011). About one-fourth of U.S. 18- to 29-year-olds are unaffiliated with a particular faith—considerably more than in their parents' generation at the same age (see Figure 14.1).

Nevertheless, religion is more important in the lives of U.S. young people than it is for their agemates in other developed countries. More than one-third of those who are religiously affiliated say they are "strong" members of their faith—equivalent to same-age individuals who said so a decade earlier (Pew Forum on Religion and Public Life, 2010). Women are more religious than men, a difference evident in other Western nations and throughout the lifespan. Also among the more religious are immigrants and certain ethnic minorities, including African Americans and Hispanics (Barry et al., 2010). And whether or not they are involved in organized religion, many young people begin to construct their own individualized faith and, if attending college, frequently discuss religious beliefs and experiences with friends (Montgomery-Goodnough & Gallagher, 2007; Stoppa & Lefkowitz, 2010). Often they weave together beliefs and practices from diverse sources, including Eastern and Western religious traditions, science, and popular culture.

As with adolescents, U.S. emerging adults who are religious or spiritual tend to be better-adjusted. They are higher in self-esteem, less likely to commit antisocial acts, and more likely to engage in community service (Barry & Nelson, 2008; Knox, Langehough, & Walters, 1998; White et al., 2006).

FIGURE 14.1 U.S. 18- to 29-year-olds' religiosity across generations. The percentage of unaffiliated young people rose substantially from the 1970s to 2000s. At the same time, among those in the 2000s cohort who are religiously affiliated, about one-third say they are strong members of their faith—similar to the 1990s cohort. (Adapted from Pew Forum on Religion and Public Life, 2010.)

Perhaps because emerging adults are so focused on exploring and "finding themselves," a widespread opinion is that that they forge self-centered worldviews, as the descriptor "generation me" suggests (Arnett, 2010). This issue has generated heated controversy. Analyses of large, nationally representative samples of U.S. young people, collected repeatedly over several decades, suggest that compared to past generations, the Millennial generation reports greater narcissism (egotistical self-admiration) and materialism—valuing of money and leisure and reduced empathy for the less fortunate (Gentile, Twenge, & Campbell, 2010; O'Brien, Hsing, & Konrath, 2010; Twenge, Campbell, & Freeman, 2012).

But other researchers claim that generational changes in egotism and other traits are too small to be meaningful (Trzesniewski & Donnellan, 2009, 2010). And gradual, age-related gains in self-esteem extending from adolescence through emerging adulthood and into mid-life are similar across generations, with average self-esteem of today's young people no higher than that of past cohorts (Orth, Robins, & Widaman, 2012; Orth, Trzesniewski, & Robins, 2010). Over these years, adults derive a greater sense of competence from making identity commitments, entering and succeeding at their careers, and becoming involved in their communities.

Additional evidence supports the view that many emerging adults are committed to improving their communities, nation, and world. In a survey of several hundred thousand first-year students enrolled in nearly 300 U.S. colleges and universities, a record number—nearly 30 percent—said that there is "a very

good chance" they will participate in community service—nearly double the number two decades earlier (Pryor et al., 2009). An additional 41 percent expressed "some chance" of participating, and only 6 percent said they would not volunteer. Among college students who expect to volunteer, the overwhelming majority actually do so within their first year (DeAngelo, Hurtado, & Pryor, 2010).

LOOK AND LISTEN

Ask 10 to 15 of your college classmates to answer the following question: What would you do if you had a million dollars? How often do respondents mention prosocial as opposed to self-centered acts? ●

Finally, compared to previous generations, contemporary 18- to 29-year-olds have been labeled "apathetic no shows" when it comes to voting. But in the 2012 U.S. presidential election, they made up more of the total electorate (19 percent) than did citizens over age 65 (16 percent), who traditionally have been the highest participants. In this respect, emerging adults' civic involvement appears to have strengthened.

Cultural Change, Cultural Variation, and Emerging Adulthood

Rapid cultural change explains the recent appearance of emerging adulthood. First, entry-level positions in many fields require more education than in the past, prompting young adults to seek higher education in record numbers and thus delaying financial independence and career commitment. Second, wealthy nations with longer-lived populations have no pressing need for young people's labor, freeing those who are financially able for extended exploration.

Indeed, emerging adulthood is limited to cultures that postpone entry into adult roles until the twenties. In developing nations such as Brazil, China, India, and Mexico, only a privileged few—usually those from wealthier families who are admitted to universities—experience it, often for a shorter time than their Western counterparts (Arnett, 2011; Nelson & Chen, 2007). Furthermore, the overwhelming majority of young people in traditional non-Western countries—those who have few economic resources or who remain in the rural regions where they grew up—have no emerging adulthood (UNICEF, 2010b). With limited education, they typically enter marriage, parenthood, and lifelong work early.

In industrialized countries, many young people experience these transitional years. Typically, their families are sufficiently well-off to provide them with financial support, without which few could advance their education, explore career possibilities, and travel to—as one emerging adult put it—"experience as much as possible." And although most emerging adults are pursuing higher education or have earned an advanced degree, some non-college-bound young people also benefit from this extended transition (Tanner, Arnett, & Leis, 2009). But they may do so by trying out different types of work rather than college majors or travel.

Cultural Influences

Is Emerging Adulthood Really a Distinct Period of Development?

Although broad consensus exists that cultural change has prolonged the transition to adult roles for many young people, disagreement persists over whether these years of "emergence" merit the creation of a new developmental period (Hendry & Kloep, 2007, 2010). Critics of the concept of emerging adulthood offer the following arguments.

First, burgeoning higher education enrollment, delayed career entry, and later marriage and parenthood are cultural trends that began as early as the 1970s in industrialized nations, only gradually becoming more conspicuous. At no time has adulthood in complex societies been attained at a distinct moment (Côté & Bynner, 2008). Rather, young people in the past reached adult status earlier in some domains and later in others, just as they do today. They also may reverse direction—for example, move back to the parental home to get their bearings after finishing college or being laid off from a job. In accord with the lifespan perspective, development is multidimensional and multidirectional, for 18- to 29-year-olds as it is for adults of all ages. Transitions occur during all periods of adult life, with societal conditions heavily influencing their timing, length, and complexity.

Second, the term *emerging adulthood* fails to describe the experiences of the majority of the world's youths (Galambos & Martinez, 2007). In most developing countries, young people—particularly women—are limited in education and marry and have children early. According to one estimate, over 1 billion individuals—nearly 70 percent of young people—follow this traditional route to adulthood (World Health Organization, 2011).

Third, research on emerging adulthood largely emphasizes its personal and societal benefits. But the extended exploration that defines this period can be risky for those who have not developed the personal agency to make good choices and acquire adult skills. These young people may remain uncommitted for too long— an outcome that impedes the focused learning required for a successful work life. A favorable emerging adulthood, then, depends on whether it is used to acquire competencies essential for contemporary living.

Finally, the financial upheaval of the late 2000s has left large numbers of bachelor's degree holders under age 25 with restricted options. In 2011, over 9 percent were unemployed and 20 percent underemployed—in low-paid jobs not requiring a college degree and, thus, without experiences necessary for advancing their skills (Shierholz, Sabadish, & Wething, 2012). Rather than a period of unparalleled opportunities, these graduates' delayed leap into adult roles is filled with anxiety and frustration. One young person, who might have been high in personal agency in a stable economy, remarked, "It has been tough finding a job that keeps me wanting to stick with something" (Kotkin, 2012).

Proponents of emerging adulthood as a distinct developmental period respond that, though not universal, it applies to most young people in industrialized societies and is spreading in developing nations that play major roles in our global economy (Tanner & Arnett, 2011). But skeptics counter that

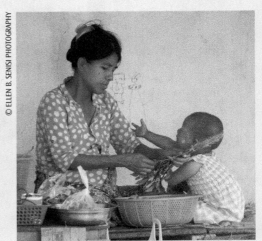

This young woman in Burma cares for her baby while working as a food vendor. Like most young people in developing countries, she has no emerging adulthood.

emerging adulthood is unlikely to become a prominent period of life in developing countries with high concentrations of poverty or, in industrialized countries, among low-income youths or those not involved in higher education (Côté & Bynner, 2008; Kloep & Hendry, 2011). And for college graduates, societal conditions can readily restrict the prospects and rewards of this period.

Critics also emphasize that in developed nations, age-graded influences have declined in favor of nonnormative influences throughout contemporary adulthood (see page 9 in Chapter 1 to review) (Hendry & Kloep, 2010). In their view, rather than being unique, emerging adults are part of a general trend toward blurring of age-related expectations, yielding multiple transitions and increased diversity in development across the adult years.

Nevertheless, for the large numbers of U.S. low-SES young people who are burdened by early parenthood, do not finish high school, are otherwise academically unprepared for college, or do not have access to vocational training, emerging adulthood is limited or nonexistent (see Chapters 11 and 13). Because of its strong association with SES and higher education, some researchers reject the notion of emerging adulthood as a distinct period of development (see the Cultural Influences box above). Others disagree, predicting that emerging adulthood will become increasingly common as *globaliza-*

tion—the exchange of ideas, information, trade, and immigration among nations—accelerates. As globalization proceeds, gains in higher education and the formation of a common "global identity" among young people may lead to the spread of emerging adulthood (Arnett, 2007a; Nelson & Chen, 2007). But, as the Cultural Influences box above points out, the recession's weak labor market has also left many college graduates with limited options. In sum, societal conditions enabling an emerging adulthood abundant in opportunity have recently contracted.

Applying What We Know

Resources That Foster Resilience in Emerging Adulthood

Type of Resource	Description
Cognitive attributes	Effective planning and decision making
	Information-gathering cognitive style and mature epistemic cognition
	Good school performance
	Knowledge of vocational options and necessary skills
Emotional and social attributes	Positive self-esteem
	Good emotional self-regulation and flexible coping strategies
	Good conflict-resolution skills
	Confidence in one's ability to reach one's goals
	Sense of personal responsibility for outcomes
	Persistence and effective use of time
	Healthy identity development—movement toward exploration in depth and commitment certainty
	Strong moral character
	Sense of meaning and purpose in life, engendered by religion, spirituality, or other sources
	Desire to contribute meaningfully to one's community
Social supports	Positive relationships with parents, peers, teachers, and mentors
	Financial assistance from parents or others
	Sense of connection to social institutions, such as school, church, workplace, and community center

Sources: Benson et al., 2006; Eccles and Gootman, 2002.

Risk and Resilience in Emerging Adulthood

In grappling with momentous choices and acquiring the skills to succeed in demanding life roles, emerging adults often encounter disappointments in love and work that require them to adjust, and sometimes radically change, their life path. Their vigorous explorations also extend earlier risks, including unprotected sexual activity, substance use, and hazardous driving behavior (see Chapter 13). And feelings of loneliness are higher at this time than at any other time of life (Rokach, 2003). As emerging adults move through school and employment settings, they must constantly separate from friends and forge new relationships.

Longitudinal research shows that the personal attributes and social supports listed in Applying What We Know above foster successful passage through these years, as indicated by completing a college education, forging a warm, stable intimate relationship, finding and keeping a well-paying job, and volunteering in one's community (Benson et al., 2006; Eccles & Gootman, 2002). Notice how the resources in the table overlap with ones discussed in previous chapters that promote development through *resilience,* the capacity to overcome challenge and adversity.

Relationships with parents have an especially wide-ranging influence. A secure, affectionate parent–emerging adult bond that extends the balance of connection and separation estab-lished in adolescence—an empathic approach in which parents recognize the weighty challenges the young person faces and encourage personally valued choices—predicts many aspects of adaptive functioning: favorable self-esteem, identity progress, successful transition to college life, higher academic achievement, more rewarding friendships and romantic ties, and positive psychological well-being (Aquilino, 2006, p. 201).

In contrast, excessive parental rule-setting and regulation of the young person's daily life (including taking over when the young person encounters challenges) and psychological control (invalidating the young person's thoughts and feelings) are linked to poor adjustment, including low self-esteem, inability to make commitments in identity formation, and increased anxiety, depression, and alcohol use (Luyckz et al., 2007; Nelson et al., 2011; Patock-Peckam & Morgan-Lopez, 2009). In another form of parenting—called *helicopter parenting* in popular culture—warm, well-intentioned parents "hover" over the emerging adult out of excessive concern for his or her well-being. They might, for example, take the child to college but refuse to leave and contact professors to discuss the child's grades. Perhaps because helicopter parenting is motivated by strong parental affection and involvement, it is not associated with the negative outcomes just noted. But it is related to reduced school engagement (going to class, completing assignments) (Padilla-Walker & Nelson, 2012). And it likely interferes with emerging adults' ability to acquire the skills they need to act on their own.

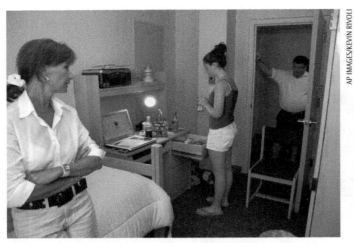

Although well-intentioned, these hovering "helicopter" parents make it harder for their daughter to acquire the skills she needs to manage the challenges of college life on her own.

Finally, exposure to multiple negative life events—family conflict, abusive intimate relationships, repeated romantic breakups, academic or employment difficulties, and financial strain—undermines development, even in emerging adults whose childhood and adolescence prepared them well for this transition (Masten et al., 2004). In sum, supportive family, school, and community environments are crucial, just as they were at earlier ages. The overwhelming majority of young people with access to these resources are optimistic about their future and likely to transition successfully to adult roles (Arnett, 2006). Now let's turn to theories of psychosocial development in early adulthood.

ASK YOURSELF

REVIEW What cultural changes have led to the appearance of emerging adulthood?

APPLY List supports that your college environment offers emerging adults in its health and counseling services, academic advising, residential living, and extracurricular activities. How does each help young people transition to adult roles?

REFLECT Should emerging adulthood be considered a distinct developmental period? Why or why not?

 ## Erikson's Theory: Intimacy versus Isolation

Erikson's vision has influenced all contemporary theories of adult personality development. His psychological conflict of early adulthood is **intimacy versus isolation,** reflected in the young person's thoughts and feelings about making a permanent commitment to an intimate partner.

As Sharese discovered, establishing a mutually gratifying close relationship is challenging. Intimacy requires that young people redefine their identity to include both partners' values and interests. Those in their late teens and early twenties frequently say they don't feel ready for a lasting tie (Carroll et al., 2009). During their first year of marriage, Sharese separated from Ernie twice as she tried to reconcile her desire for self-determination with her desire for intimacy. Maturity involves balancing these forces. Without intimacy, young adults face the negative outcome of Erikson's early adulthood stage: loneliness and self-absorption. Ernie's patience and stability helped Sharese realize that committed love requires generosity and compromise but not total surrender of the self.

Research confirms that—as Erikson emphasized—a secure identity fosters attainment of intimacy. Commitment to personally meaningful values and goals prepares young adults for interpersonal commitments, which increase as early adulthood progresses. Among large samples of college students, identity achievement was positively correlated with fidelity (loyalty in relationships) and love, for both men and women. In contrast, identity moratorium—a state of searching prior to commitment—was negatively associated with fidelity and love (Markstrom et al., 1997; Markstrom & Kalmanir, 2001). Other studies show that advanced identity development strongly predicts involvement in a deep, committed love partnership or readiness to establish such a partnership (Beyers & Seiffge-Krenke, 2010; Montgomery, 2005). Still, the coordination of identity and intimacy is more complex for women, who are more likely than men to consider the impact of their personal goals on important relationships (Archer, 2002).

Erikson believed that successful resolution of intimacy versus isolation prepares the individual for the middle adulthood stage, which focuses on *generativity*—caring for the next generation and helping to improve society. But childbearing and child rearing, as well as contributions to society through work and community service, are under way in the twenties and thirties. Still, in line with Erikson's ideas, high friendship or romantic intimacy in early adulthood does predict a stronger generative orientation (Mackinnon et al., 2011).

In sum, identity, intimacy, and generativity are concerns of early adulthood, with shifts in emphasis that differ among individuals. Recognizing that Erikson's theory provides only a broad sketch of adult personality development, other theorists have expanded his stage approach, adding detail.

 ## Other Theories of Adult Psychosocial Development

In the 1970s, growing interest in adult development led to several widely read books on the topic. Daniel Levinson's *The Seasons of a Man's Life* (1978) and *The Seasons of a Woman's Life* (1996), and George Vaillant's *Adaptation to Life* (1977) and *Aging Well* (2002), present psychosocial theories in the tradition of Erikson.

Levinson's Seasons of Life

On the basis of in-depth biographical interviews with 35- to 45-year-old men—and, later, similar interviews with women in the same age range—Levinson (1978, 1996) depicted adult development as a sequence of qualitatively distinct eras (or "seasons") coinciding with Erikson's stages and separated by *transitions*. The *life structure*, a key concept in Levinson's theory, is the underlying design of a person's life, consisting of relationships with significant others—individuals, groups, and institutions. Of its many components, usually only a few, relating to family, close friendships, and occupation, are central. But wide individual differences exist in the weights of central and peripheral components.

Levinson found that during the transition to early adulthood, most young people constructed a *dream*—an image of themselves in the adult world that guides their decision making. For men, the dream usually emphasized achievement in a career, whereas most career-oriented women had "split dreams" involving both marriage and career. Young adults also formed a relationship with a *mentor* who facilitated realization of their dream—often a senior colleague at work but occasionally a more experienced friend, neighbor, or relative.

Around age 30, a second transition occurred: Young people who had been preoccupied with career and were single usually focused on finding a life partner, while women who had emphasized marriage and family often developed more individualistic goals. For example, Christy, who had dreamed of becoming a professor, finally earned her doctoral degree in her mid-thirties and secured a college teaching position. For young people without a satisfying intimate tie or a vocational direction, this can be a time of crisis.

To create an early adulthood culminating life structure, men usually "settled down" by focusing on certain relation-

ships and aspirations, in an effort to establish a niche in society consistent with their values, whether those be wealth, prestige, artistic or scientific achievement, or forms of family or community participation. In his late thirties, Ernie became a partner in his firm, coached his son's soccer team, and was elected treasurer of his church. He paid less attention to golf, travel, and playing the guitar than previously.

Many women, however, remained unsettled in their thirties, often because they added an occupational or relationship commitment. When her two children were born, Sharese felt torn between her research position in the state health department and her family. She took three months off after the arrival of each baby. When she returned to work, she did not pursue attractive administrative openings that required travel and time away from home. And shortly after Christy began teaching, she and Gary divorced. Becoming a single parent while starting her professional life introduced new strains. Not until middle age did many women reach career maturity and take on more authority in the community.

Vaillant's Adaptation to Life

Vaillant (1977) followed the development of nearly 250 men born in the 1920s, selected for study while they were students at a competitive liberal arts college. Participants were interviewed extensively while in college and answered lengthy questionnaires during each succeeding decade. Then Vaillant (2002) interviewed them at ages 47, 60, and 70 about work, family, and physical and mental health.

Looking at how the men altered themselves and their social world to adapt to life, Vaillant—like Levinson—confirmed Erikson's stages but filled gaps between them. After focusing on intimacy concerns in their twenties, the men turned to career consolidation in their thirties. During their forties, they became more generative. In their fifties and sixties, they extended that generativity; they became "keepers of meaning," or guardians of their culture, expressing a deep need to preserve and pass on cultural traditions by teaching others what they had learned from life experience (Vaillant & Koury, 1994). Finally, in their seventies, the men became more spiritual and reflective. In a later lifelong study of a sample of well-educated women, Vaillant (2002) identified a similar series of changes.

Nevertheless, the developmental patterns Vaillant and Levinson described are based largely on interviews with people born in the first few decades of the twentieth century. As our discussion of emerging adulthood illustrates, development is far more variable today—so much so that some researchers doubt that adult psychosocial changes can be organized into distinct stages (Newton & Stewart, 2010). Rather, people may assemble the themes and dilemmas identified by these theorists into individualized arrangements, in a *dynamic system* of interacting biological, psychological, and social forces. Studies of new generations—both men and women of diverse backgrounds—are needed to shed light on the extent of commonality and variation among young people in psychosocial development.

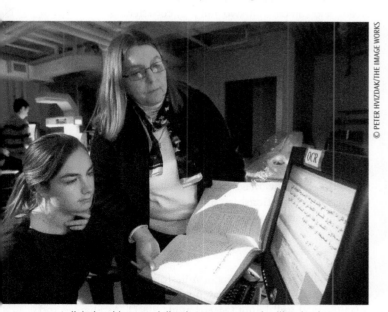

A digital archives specialist shows an apprentice librarian how to scan text. For young people starting out in a career, an effective mentor can serve as a role model and guide in overcoming challenges.

© PETER HVIZDAK/THE IMAGE WORKS

The Social Clock

As we have seen, changes in society from one generation to the next can affect the life course. Bernice Neugarten (1968a, 1979) identified an important cultural and generational influence on adult development: the **social clock**—age-graded expectations for major life events, such as beginning a first job, getting married, birth of the first child, buying a home, and retiring. All societies have such timetables. Research of two to three decades ago revealed that conformity to or departure from the social clock can be a major source of adult personality change, affecting self-esteem, independence, responsibility, and other attributes because adults (like children and adolescents) make social comparisons, measuring their progress against that of agemates (Helson, 1992; Vandewater & Stewart, 1997).

Among economically better-off young people, finishing one's education, marrying, and having children occur much later in the lifespan than they did a generation or two ago. Furthermore, departures from social-clock life events have become increasingly common. As we will see later, a growing number of women, mostly of lower income, are not marrying and, instead, rearing children as single mothers, turning not to a spouse but rather to their extended families for assistance (Furstenberg, 2010).

LOOK AND LISTEN

Describe your social clock, listing major life events along with the age you expect to attain each. Then ask a parent and/or grandparent to recall his or her own early adulthood social clock. Analyze generational differences. ●

These conditions can create intergenerational tensions when parents expect their young-adult children to attain adult milestones on an outdated schedule, at odds with their children's current opportunities and desires. Young adults may also feel distressed because their own timing of major milestones is not widely shared by their contemporaries or supported by current public policies, thereby weakening both informal and formal social supports (Settersten, 2007). And while rendering greater flexibility and freedom to young people's lives, an ill-defined social clock likely causes them to feel inadequately grounded—unsure of what others expect and of what to expect of themselves.

In sum, following a social clock of some kind seems to foster confidence and social stability because it guarantees that young people will develop skills, engage in productive work, and gain in understanding of self and others (Hendry & Kloep, 2007). In contrast, "crafting a life of one's own," whether self-chosen or the result of circumstances, is risky—more prone to breakdown (Settersten, 2007, p. 244). With this in mind, let's take a closer look at how men and women traverse major tasks of young adulthood.

ASK YOURSELF

REVIEW Return to page 319 in Chapter 12, and review the contributions of exploration and commitment to a mature identity. Using the two criteria, explain why identity achievement is positively related to attainment of intimacy (fidelity and love), whereas identity moratorium is negatively predictive.

APPLY In view of contemporary changes in the social clock, explain Sharese's conflicted feelings about marrying Ernie.

REFLECT Describe your early adulthood dream. Then ask a friend or classmate of the other gender to describe his or her dream, and compare the two. Are they consistent with Levinson's findings?

VSTOCK LLC/TANYA CONSTANTINE/GETTY IMAGES

Because the social clock has become increasingly flexible, this 30-year-old attorney, committed to her challenging, demanding career, may not feel pressure to conform to a strict timetable for major life events such as marriage and parenthood.

 ## Close Relationships

To establish an intimate tie to another person, people must find a partner and build an emotional bond that they sustain over time. Although young adults are especially concerned with romantic love, the need for intimacy can also be satisfied through other relationships involving mutual commitment—with friends, siblings, and co-workers.

Romantic Love

Finding a life partner is a major milestone of early adult development, with profound consequences for self-concept and psychological well-being (Meeus et al., 2007). As Sharese and Ernie's relationship reveals, it is also a complex process that unfolds over time and is affected by a variety of events.

Selecting a Mate. Recall from Chapter 13 that intimate partners generally meet in places where they are likely to find people of their own age, ethnicity, SES, and religion, or they connect through dating websites. People usually select partners who resemble themselves in other ways—attitudes, personality, educational plans, intelligence, physical attractiveness, and even height (Keith & Schafer, 1991; Simpson & Harris, 1994). Romantic partners sometimes have complementary personality traits—one self-assured and dominant, the other hesitant and submissive. Because this difference permits each to sustain their preferred style of behavior, it contributes to compatibility (Sadler, Ethier, & Woody, 2011). But overall, little support exists for the idea that "opposites attract." Rather, partners who are similar in personality and other attributes tend to be more satisfied with their relationship and more likely to stay together (Furnham, 2009; Markey & Markey, 2007).

Nevertheless, men and women differ in the importance they place on certain characteristics. In diverse industrialized and developing countries, women assign greater weight to intelligence, ambition, financial status, and moral character, whereas men place more emphasis on physical attractiveness and domestic skills. In addition, women prefer a same-age or slightly older partner, men a younger partner (Buunk, 2002; Cramer, Schaefer, & Reid, 2003; Stewart, Stinnett, & Rosenfeld, 2000).

According to an evolutionary perspective, because their capacity to reproduce is limited, women seek a mate with traits, such as earning power and emotional commitment, that help ensure children's survival and well-being. In contrast, men look for a mate with traits that signal youth, health, sexual pleasure, and ability to give birth to and care for offspring. As further evidence for this difference, men often want a relationship to move quickly toward physical intimacy, whereas women typically prefer to take the time to achieve psychological intimacy first (Buss, 2012).

In an alternative, social learning view, gender roles profoundly influence criteria for mate selection. Beginning in childhood, men learn to be assertive and independent—behaviors needed for success in the work world. Women acquire nurturant behaviors, which facilitate caregiving. Then each sex learns to value traits in the other that fit with this traditional division of labor (Eagly & Wood, 2012). In support of this theory, in cultures and in younger generations experiencing greater gender equity, men and women are more alike in their mate preferences. For example, compared with men in China and Japan, American men place more emphasis on their mate's financial prospects, less on her domestic skills. And both sexes care somewhat less about their mate's age relative to their own. Rather, they place a high value on relationship satisfaction (Buss et al., 2001; Toro-Morn & Sprecher, 2003).

As the Social Issues: Health box on page 378 reveals, young people's choice of an intimate partner and the quality of their relationship also are affected by memories of their early parent–child bond. Finally, for romance to lead to a lasting partnership, it must happen at the right time. If one or both do not feel ready to marry, the relationship is likely to dissolve.

© ALEX FARNSWORTH/THE IMAGE WORKS

The warmth and intimacy of this couple's communication form the basis for mutual affection, caring, acceptance, and respect, which are vital for a satisfying, enduring bond.

The Components of Love. How do we know that we are in love? Robert Sternberg's (1988, 2000, 2006) **triangular theory of love** identifies three components—intimacy, passion, and commitment—that shift in emphasis as romantic relationships develop. *Intimacy,* the emotional component, involves warm, tender communication, expressions of concern about the other's well-being, and a desire for the partner to reciprocate. *Passion,* the desire for sexual activity and romance, is the physical- and psychological-arousal component. *Commitment* is the cognitive component, leading partners to decide that they are in love and to maintain that love.

At the beginning of a relationship, **passionate love**—intense sexual attraction—is strong. Gradually, passion declines in favor of intimacy and commitment, which form the basis for **companionate love**—warm, trusting affection and caregiving (Acker & Davis, 1992; Fehr, 1994). Each aspect of love, however, helps sustain the relationship. Early passionate love is a strong predictor of whether partners keep dating. But without the quiet intimacy, predictability, and shared attitudes and values of companionate love, most romances eventually break up (Hendrick & Hendrick, 2002).

Couples whose relationships endure generally report that they love each other more than they did earlier (Sprecher, 1999). In the transformation of romantic involvements from passionate to companionate, *commitment* may be the aspect of love that determines whether a relationship survives. Communicating that commitment in ways that strengthen *intimacy*—through warmth, attentiveness, empathy, caring, acceptance, and respect—strongly predicts relationship maintenance and satisfaction (Neff & Karney, 2008; Lavner & Bradbury, 2012). For example, Sharese's doubts about getting married subsided largely because of Ernie's warm expressions of commitment.

Partners who consistently express their commitment report higher-quality and longer-lasting relationships (Fitzpatrick &

Social Issues: Health

Childhood Attachment Patterns and Adult Romantic Relationships

In Bowlby's ethological theory of attachment, the early attachment bond leads to construction of an *internal working model,* or set of expectations about attachment figures, that serves as a guide for close relationships throughout life. Adults' evaluations of their early attachment experiences are related to their parenting behaviors—specifically, to the quality of attachments they build with their children (see pages 156–158 in Chapter 6). Additional evidence indicates that recollections of childhood attachment patterns predict romantic relationships in adulthood.

In studies carried out in Australia, Israel, and the United States, researchers asked people about their early parental bonds (attachment history), their attitudes toward intimate relationships (internal working model), and their actual experiences with romantic partners. In a few studies, investigators also observed couples' behaviors. Consistent with Bowlby's theory, adults' memories and interpretations of childhood attachment patterns were good indicators of internal working models and relationship experiences. (To review patterns of attachment, see Chapter 6, page 154.)

Secure Attachment

Adults who described their attachment history as secure (warm, loving, and supportive parents) had internal working models that reflected this security. They viewed themselves as likable, were comfortable with intimacy, and rarely worried about abandonment. They characterized their most important love relationship in terms of trust, happiness, and friendship (Cassidy, 2001). Their behaviors toward their partner were empathic and supportive and their conflict resolution strategies constructive. They were also at ease in turning to their partner for comfort and assistance (Collins et al., 2006; Creasey & Jarvis, 2009; Roisman et al., 2002).

Avoidant Attachment

Adults who reported an avoidant attachment history (demanding, disrespectful, and critical parents) displayed internal working models that stressed independence, mistrust of love partners, and anxiety about people getting too close. They were convinced that others disliked them and that romantic love is hard to find and rarely lasts. Jealousy, emotional distance, lack of support in response to their partner's distress, and little enjoyment of physical contact pervaded their most important love relationship (Collins et al., 2006). They endorsed many unrealistic beliefs about relationships—for example, that partners cannot change, that males' and females' needs differ, and that "mind reading" is expected (Stackert & Bursik, 2003).

Resistant Attachment

Adults recalling a resistant attachment history (parents who responded unpredictably and unfairly) presented internal working models in which they sought to merge completely with another person and fall in love quickly (Cassidy, 2001). At the same time, they worried that their intense feelings would overwhelm others, who really did not love them and would not want to stay with them. Their most important love relationship was riddled with jealousy, emotional highs and lows, and desperation about whether the partner would return their affection (Feeney, 1999). Resistant adults, though offering support, do so in ways that fit poorly with their partner's needs (Collins et al., 2006).

Are adults' descriptions of their childhood attachment experiences accurate? In several longitudinal studies, quality of parent–child interactions, observed or assessed through family interviews 5 to 23 years earlier, were good predictors of internal working models and romantic-relationship quality in early adulthood (Donnellan, Larsen-Rife, & Conger, 2005; Ogawa et al., 1997; Roisman et al., 2001). However, attributes of the current

Did the internal working model constructed by this baby influence the relationship he later forged with his wife? Research indicates that early attachment is associated with the quality of later intimate ties.

partner also influence internal working models and intimate ties. When generally insecure individuals manage to form a secure representation of their partner, they report stronger feelings of affection and concern and reduced relationship conflict and anxiety (Sibley & Overall, 2010; Sprecher & Fehr, 2011).

In sum, negative parent–child experiences can be carried forward into adult close relationships. At the same time, internal working models are continuously "updated." When adults with a history of unhappy love lives have a chance to form a satisfying intimate tie, they may revise their internal working model.

Sollie, 1999; Madey & Rodgers, 2009). An important feature of their communication is constructive conflict resolution—directly expressing wishes and needs, listening patiently, asking for clarification, compromising, accepting responsibility,

forgiving their partner, and avoiding the escalation of negative interaction sparked by criticism, contempt, defensiveness, and stonewalling (Johnson et al., 2005; Schneewind & Gerhard, 2002). In a longitudinal study, newlyweds' negativity during problem solving predicted marital dissatisfaction and divorce over the following decade (Sullivan et al., 2010). Those who displayed little warmth and caring often resorted to anger and contempt when dealing with problems. These findings reveal that deficits in intimacy foreshadow poor conflict-resolution skills and eventual weakening of the marital tie.

Compared with women, men are less skilled at communicating in ways that foster intimacy, offering less comfort and helpful support in their close relationships. Men also tend to be less effective at negotiating conflict, frequently avoiding discussion (Burleson & Kunkel, 2006; Wood, 2009).

Finally, for gay and lesbian couples, widespread social stigma complicates the process of forging a satisfying, committed bond. Those who worry most about being stigmatized, who try to conceal their romance, or who harbor negative attitudes toward their own sexual orientation report lower-quality and less enduring love relationships (Mohr & Daly, 2008; Mohr & Fassinger, 2006).

Culture and the Experience of Love. Passion and intimacy, which form the basis for romantic love, became the dominant basis for marriage in twentieth-century Western nations as the value of individualism strengthened. From this vantage point, mature love is based on autonomy, appreciation of the partner's unique qualities, and intense emotion (Hatfield, Rapson, & Martel, 2007). Trying to satisfy dependency needs through an intimate bond is regarded as immature.

This Western view contrasts sharply with the perspectives of Eastern cultures, such as China and Japan, where lifelong dependency is accepted and viewed positively and the self is defined through role relationships—son or daughter, brother or sister, husband or wife. Furthermore, in choosing a mate, Chinese and Japanese young people are expected to consider obligations to others, especially parents. College students of Asian

Although arranged marriages are still common in parts of Southeast Asia, young couples increasingly expect love to be a prerequisite for marriage, and their parents are likely to acquiesce.

heritage are less likely than those of American or European descent to endorse a view of love based solely on physical attraction and deep emotion (Hatfield, Rapson, & Martel, 2007; Hatfield & Sprecher, 1995). Instead, compared to Westerners, they place greater weight on companionship and practical matters—similarity of background, career promise, and likelihood of being a good parent.

Still, even in countries where arranged marriages are still fairly common (including China, India, and Japan), parents and prospective brides and grooms consult one another before moving forward (Goodwin & Pillay, 2006). If parents try to force their children into an unappealing marriage, sympathetic extended family members may come to children's defense. And in developing countries, women who attain higher education—and who therefore have acquired more of an autonomous identity—are more likely to insist on actively participating in an arranged marriage (Bhopal, 2011). In sum, today young people in many countries consider love to be a prerequisite for marriage, though Westerners assign greater importance to love—especially, its passionate component.

Friendships

Like romantic partners and childhood friends, adult friends are usually similar in age, sex, and SES. As in earlier years, friends in adulthood enhance self-esteem and psychological well-being through affirmation, acceptance, autonomy support (permitting disagreement and choice), and support in times of stress (Collins & Madsen, 2006; Deci et al., 2006). Friends also make life more interesting by expanding social opportunities and access to knowledge and points of view.

Trust, intimacy, and loyalty, along with shared interests and values and enjoyment of each other's company, continue to be important in adult friendships, as they were in adolescence (Blieszner & Roberto, 2012). Sharing thoughts and feelings is sometimes greater in friendship than in marriage, although commitment is less strong as friends come and go over the life course. Even so, some adult friendships continue for many years, at times throughout life. Female friends get together more than male friends do, which contributes to greater friendship continuity for women (Sherman, de Vries, & Lansford, 2000).

But because of the dramatic rise in social media use, today's friendships are no longer as constrained by physical proximity. Nearly three-fourths of 18- to 29-year-olds who access the Internet use social networking sites; Facebook reports more than 500 million active users worldwide. Consequently, networks of "friends" have expanded. Do social networking sites lead young adults to form a large number of acquaintances at the expense of intimate friendships? Research reveals that people with 500 or more Facebook friends actually interact individually—by "liking" posts, leaving comments on walls, or engaging in Facebook chats—with far fewer. Among these large-network Facebook users, men engaged in one-on-one communication with an average of just 10 friends, women with just 16 (Henig & Henig, 2012). Facebook led passive tracking of casual relationships to rise while core friendships remained limited.

LOOK AND LISTEN

Ask your Facebook friends to indicate the size of their Facebook network along with the number of friends they interacted with individually during the past month. Do large-network users have only a limited number of core friendships? ●

Same-Sex Friendships. Extending a pattern evident in childhood and adolescence, women have more intimate same-sex friendships than men (see Chapter 12, pages 330–331). Barriers to intimacy between male friends include competitiveness, which may make men unwilling to disclose weaknesses, and concern that if they tell about themselves, their friends will not reciprocate (Reid & Fine, 1992). Because of greater intimacy and give-and-take, women generally evaluate their same-sex friendships more positively than men do. But they also have higher expectations of friends (Blieszner & Roberto, 2012). Thus, they are more disapproving if friends do not meet their expectations.

Of course, individual differences in friendship quality exist. The longer-lasting men's friendships are, the closer they become and the more they include disclosure of personal information (Sherman, de Vries, & Lansford, 2000). And gay and lesbian romantic relationships often develop out of close same-sex friendships, with lesbians, especially, forging compatible friendships before becoming involved romantically (Diamond, 2006).

As they develop romantic ties and marry, young adults—especially men—direct more of their disclosures toward their partners (Kito, 2005). Still, friendships continue to be vital contexts for personal sharing throughout adulthood. A best friendship can augment well-being when a marriage is not fully satisfying (but not when the marriage is low in quality) (Birditt & Antonucci, 2007). Turn back to Figure 12.1 on page 331 to view developmental trends in self-disclosure to romantic partners and friends.

Men often experience barriers to friendship intimacy due to competitiveness. But the longer-lasting men's friendships are, the more intimate they become, increasingly including disclosure of personal information.

Other-Sex Friendships. From the college years through career exploration and settling into work roles, other-sex friendships increase. After marriage, they decline for men but continue to rise for women, who more often form them in the workplace. Highly educated, employed women have the largest number of other-sex friends. Through these relationships, young adults often gain in companionship and self-esteem and learn about masculine and feminine styles of intimacy (Bleske & Buss, 2000). Because men confide especially easily in their female friends, such friendships offer them a unique opportunity to broaden their expressive capacity. And women sometimes say male friends offer objective points of view on problems and situations—perspectives not available from female friends (Monsour, 2002).

Many people try to keep other-sex friendships platonic to safeguard their integrity (Messman, Canary, & Hause, 2000). But sometimes the relationship changes into a romantic bond. When a solid other-sex friendship does evolve into a romance, it may be more stable and enduring than a romantic relationship formed without a foundation in friendship. And emerging adults, especially, are flexible about people they include in their friendship networks (Barry & Madsen, 2010). After a breakup, they may even keep a former romantic partner on as a friend.

Siblings as Friends. As young people marry and invest less time in developing a romantic partnership, siblings—especially sisters whose earlier bond was positive—become more frequent companions (Birditt & Antonucci, 2007). A childhood history of intense parental favoritism and sibling rivalry can disrupt sibling bonds in adulthood (Panish & Stricker, 2002). But when family experiences have been positive, relationships between adult siblings can be especially close and are important sources of psychological well-being (Sherman, Lansford, & Volling, 2006).

In families with five to ten siblings, common in industrialized nations in the past and still widespread in some cultures, close sibling bonds may replace friendships (Fuller-Iglesias, 2010). One 35-year-old with five siblings, who all—with their partners and children—resided in the same small city, remarked, "With a family like this, who needs friends?"

ASK YOURSELF

REVIEW Describe gender differences in traits usually desired in a long-term partner. What findings indicate that both biological and social forces contribute to those differences?

APPLY After dating for two years, Mindy and Graham reported greater love and relationship satisfaction than during their first few months of dating. What features of communication probably deepened their bond, and why is it likely to endure?

REFLECT Do you have a nonromantic, close other-sex friendship? If so, how has it enhanced your emotional and social development?

The Family Life Cycle

For most young people, the life course takes shape within the **family life cycle**—a series of phases characterizing the development of most families around the world. In early adulthood, people typically live on their own, marry, and bear and rear children. In middle age, as their children leave home, their parenting responsibilities diminish. Late adulthood brings retirement, growing old, and (more often for women) death of one's spouse (McGoldrick & Shibusawa, 2012). Stress tends to be greatest during transitions between phases, as family members redefine and reorganize their relationships.

But today, wide variations exist in the sequence and timing of family life-cycle phases—high rates of out-of-wedlock births, delayed marriage and childbearing, divorce, and remarriage, among others. And some people, voluntarily or involuntarily, do not experience all phases. Still, the family life-cycle model offers an organized way of thinking about how the family system changes over time and the impact of each phase on the family unit and its members.

Leaving Home

Departure from the parental home is a major step toward assuming adult responsibilities. The average age of leaving has risen since the 1960s; today, it resembles the departure age at the beginning of the twentieth century. But reasons for coresidence have changed: Early twentieth-century young adults resided with parents so they could contribute to the family economy. Twenty-first-century young adults living at home are typically financially dependent on their parents. This trend toward later home-leaving is evident in most industrialized nations, though substantial variation in timing exists. Because government support is available, young adults in the Scandinavian countries move out relatively early (Furstenberg, 2010). In contrast, cultural traditions in Mediterranean countries promote lengthy coresidence, extending for men into the mid-thirties.

Departures for education tend to occur at earlier ages, those for full-time work and marriage later. Because the majority of U.S. young adults enroll in higher education, many leave home around age 18. Those from divorced, single-parent homes tend to be early leavers, perhaps because of family stress (Cooney & Mortimer, 1999). Compared with the previous generation, fewer North American and Western European young people leave home to marry; more do so just to be "independent"—to express their adult status.

Slightly over half of U.S. 18- to 25-year-olds return to their parents' home for brief periods after first leaving (U.S. Census Bureau, 2013). Usually, role transitions, such as the end of college or military service, bring young people back. But tight job markets, high housing costs, or failures in work or love can also prompt a temporary return home.

The extent to which young people live on their own before marriage varies with SES and ethnicity. Those who are economically well-off are more likely to establish their own residence. Among African-American, Hispanic, and Native-American groups, poverty and a cultural tradition of extended-family living lead to lower rates of leaving home, even among young people in college or working (De Marco & Berzin, 2008; Fussell & Furstenberg, 2005). Unmarried Asian young adults also tend to live with their parents. But the longer Asian families have lived in the United States, where they are exposed to individualistic values, the more likely young people are to move out before marriage (Lou, Lalonde, & Giguère, 2012).

Parents of young adults living at home are usually highly committed to helping their children move into adult roles. Many provide wide-ranging assistance—not just financial support, but material resources, advice, companionship, and emotional support as well (Fingerman et al., 2009, 2012b). Still, in homes where parents and young adults live together, conflict over personal and moral values related to the young person's future tends to rise (Rodríguez & López, 2011). But when young adults feel securely attached to parents and well-prepared for independence, departure from the home is linked to more satisfying parent–child interaction and successful transition to adult roles, even among ethnic minorities that strongly emphasize family loyalty and obligations (Smetana, Metzger, & Campione-Barr, 2004; Whiteman, McHale, & Crouter, 2010). And regardless of living arrangements, young people doing well typically have close, enjoyable relationships with their parents, who offer help because they see it as key to their child's future success (Fingerman et al., 2012c).

In contrast, leaving home very early because of a lack of parental financial and emotional support is associated with less successful educational, marriage, and work lives. U.S. poverty-stricken young people are more likely than their nonpoor counterparts to leave home by age 18 (Berzin & De Marco, 2010). But if still at home beyond that age, they often remain

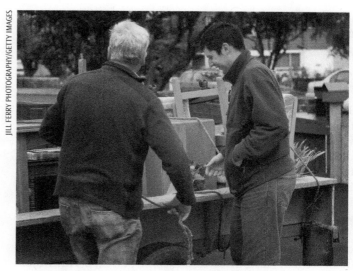

A father helps his son move belongings back into the parental home after graduation. Parents usually respond to their children's return with generous support, doing everything possible to help them move into adult roles.

there well into their thirties—a trend that may reflect the steep challenges they face in attaining self-sufficiency and exiting poverty.

Joining of Families in Marriage

The average age of first marriage in the United States has risen from about 20 for women and 23 for men in 1960 to 26½ for women and 29 for men today. Consequently, just 20 percent of contemporary U.S. 18- to 29-year-olds are married, compared to 60 percent a half-century ago (U.S. Census Bureau, 2012b). Postponement of marriage is even more marked in Western Europe—to the early thirties for men and the late twenties for women.

The number of first and second marriages has declined over the last few decades as more people stay single, cohabit, or do not remarry after divorce. In 1960, 85 percent of Americans had been married at least once; today, the figure is 70 percent. At present, 51 percent of U.S. adults, only a slight majority, live together as married couples (U.S. Census Bureau, 2012b). In one recent survey, 4 out of 10 American adults agreed that "marriage is becoming obsolete." Nevertheless, marriage remains a central life goal for young people (Pew Forum on Religion and Public Life, 2010; Smith & Snell, 2009). Irrespective of SES and ethnicity, most U.S. 18- to 23-year-olds say they want to marry and have children.

Same-sex marriages are recognized nationwide in Argentina, Belgium, Brazil, Canada, Denmark, France, Iceland, the Netherlands, New Zealand, Norway, Portugal, South Africa, Spain, Sweden, and Uruguay. In the United States, 14 states—California, Connecticut, Delaware, Iowa, Maine, Maryland, Massachusetts, Minnesota, New Hampshire, New Jersey, New York, Rhode Island, Vermont, and Washington—and the District of Columbia have legalized same-sex marriage. Several other states either grant people in same-sex unions the same legal status as married couples or extend nearly all spousal rights to same-sex partnerships. Because legalization is so recent, research on same-sex couples in the context of marriage is scant. But evidence on cohabiting same-sex couples suggests that the same factors that contribute to happiness in other-sex marriages do so in same-sex unions (Diamond, 2006).

Marriage is more than the joining of two individuals. It also requires that two systems—the spouses' families—adapt and overlap to create a new subsystem. Consequently, marriage presents complex challenges.

Marital Roles. Their honeymoon over, Sharese and Ernie turned to a multitude of issues they had previously decided individually or their families of origin had prescribed—from everyday matters (when and how to eat, sleep, talk, work, relax, have sex, and spend money) to family traditions and rituals (which to retain, which to work out for themselves). And as they related to their social world as a couple, they modified relationships with parents, siblings, extended family, friends, and co-workers.

Contemporary alterations in the context of marriage, including changing gender roles and living farther from family members, mean that couples must work harder than in the past to define their relationships. Although partners are usually similar in religious and ethnic background, "mixed" marriages are increasingly common today. Among new marriages in the United States, 15 percent are between partners of a different race or ethnicity, more than double the rate in 1980 (Taylor et al., 2012). Because of increased opportunities for interracial contact in colleges, workplaces, and neighborhoods and more positive attitudes toward intermarriage, highly educated young adults are more likely than their less educated counterparts to marry partners of another race or ethnicity (Qian & Lichter, 2011). Nevertheless, couples whose backgrounds differ face extra challenges in transitioning to married life.

Age of marriage is the most consistent predictor of marital stability. Young people who marry in their teens to mid-twenties are more likely to divorce than those who marry later (Lehrer & Chen, 2011). Both early marriage followed by childbirth and childbirth before marriage are more common among low-SES adults (U.S. Census Bureau, 2012b). This acceleration of family formation complicates adjustment to life as a couple.

Despite progress in the area of women's rights, **traditional marriages,** involving a clear division of roles—husband as head of household responsible for family economic well-being, wife as caregiver and homemaker—still exist in Western nations. In recent decades, however, these marriages have changed, with many women who focused on motherhood while their children were young returning to the work force later.

In **egalitarian marriages,** partners relate as equals, sharing power and authority. Both try to balance the time and energy they devote to their occupations, their children, and their relationship. Most well-educated, career-oriented women expect this form of marriage. And college-student couples who eventually intend to marry often plan in advance how they will coor-

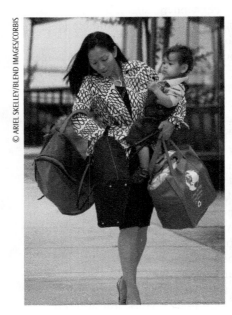

Arms laden with her toddler, a briefcase, and a bag of groceries, an employed mother heads home to prepare dinner. In industrialized nations, women in dual-earner marriages continue to shoulder most housework responsibilities.

dinate work and family roles, especially if the woman intends to enter a male-dominated career (Peake & Harris, 2002).

In Western nations, men in dual-earner marriages participate much more in child care than in the past. U.S. fathers in such marriages put in 85 percent as much time as mothers do. But housework—cleaning, cooking, laundry, and picking up clutter—reveals a different story. Recent surveys indicate that women in the United States and most Western European nations spend nearly twice as much time as men on housework, and women in Australia spend four times as much (Sayer, 2010). In Sweden, which places a high value on gender equality, men do more than in other nations. In contrast, men typically do little housework or child care in Japan, where corporate jobs demand long work hours and traditional marriages are common (Geist, 2010; Shwalb et al., 2004).

Women's housework hours do decline as their employment hours increase. But a close look at gender differences in most industrialized countries reveals that men fail to compensate (Cooke, 2010; Lippe, 2010). As Figure 14.2 shows for Australia, the United Kingdom, and the United States, men spend the same amount of time at housework, irrespective of their partners' employment schedules. Therefore, employed women's reduced housework hours are made possible by either purchase of time-saving services (cleaning help, prepackaged meals) or greater tolerance for unkempt homes, or both (Lachance-Grzela & Bouchard, 2010). In sum, true equality in marriage is still rare, and couples who strive for it usually attain a form of marriage in between traditional and egalitarian.

Marital Satisfaction. Despite its rocky beginnings, Sharese and Ernie's marriage grew to be especially happy. In contrast, Christy and Gary became increasingly discontented. Differences between these two couples mirror the findings of a large body of research on personal and contextual factors, summarized in Table 14.1.

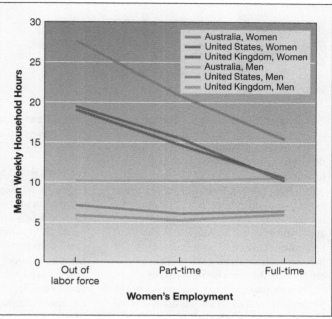

FIGURE 14.2 Women's and men's housework hours by women's employment for couples in Australia, the United Kingdom, and the United States. In each nation, as women's employment hours increase, they devote less time to housework. Men's contribution to housework is substantially less than women's. And women's level of employment has no influence on men's housework hours. (From L. P. Cooke, 2010, "The Politics of Housework," in J. Treas & S. Drobnic, [Eds.], *Dividing the Domestic: Men, Women, and Household Work in Cross-National Perspective*, p. 70. Copyright © 2010 by the Board of Trustees of the Leland Stanford Jr. University. Adapted with the permission of Stanford University Press, www.sup.org.)

Christy and Gary had children early and struggled financially. Gary's negative, critical personality led him to get along poorly with Christy's parents and to feel threatened when he and Christy disagreed. Christy tried to offer Gary encouragement

TABLE 14.1
Factors Related to Marital Satisfaction

FACTOR	HAPPY MARRIAGE	UNHAPPY MARRIAGE
Family backgrounds	Partners similar in SES, education, religion, and age	Partners very different in SES, education, religion, and age
Age at marriage	After mid-20s	Before mid-20s
Timing of first pregnancy	After first year of marriage	Before or within first year of marriage
Relationship to extended family	Warm and positive	Negative; wish to maintain distance
Marital patterns in extended family	Stable	Unstable; frequent separations and divorces
Financial and employment status	Secure	Insecure
Family responsibilities	Shared; perception of fairness	Largely the woman's responsibility; perception of unfairness
Personality characteristics and behavior	Emotionally positive; common interests; good conflict-resolution skills	Emotionally negative and impulsive; lack of common interests; poor conflict-resolution skills

Note: The more factors present, the greater the likelihood of marital happiness or unhappiness.

Sources: Diamond, Fagundes, & Butterworth, 2010; Gere et al., 2011; Johnson et al., 2005.

Social Issues: Health

Partner Abuse

Violence in families is a widespread health and human rights issue, occurring in all cultures and SES groups. Often one form of domestic violence is linked to others. Recall the story of Karen in Chapter 13. Her husband, Mike, not only assaulted her sexually and physically but also abused her psychologically—isolating, humiliating, and demeaning her. Violent adults also break their partner's favorite possessions, punch holes in walls, or throw objects. If children are present, they may become victims.

Partner abuse in which husbands are perpetrators and wives are physically injured is most likely to be reported to authorities. But many acts of family violence are not reported. When researchers ask American couples about fights that led to acts of hostility, men and women report similar rates of assault (Dutton, 2007). Women victims are more often physically injured, but sex differences in severity of abuse are small (Dutton, 2012; Ehrensaft, Moffitt, & Caspi, 2004). Partner abuse occurs at about the same rate in same-sex relationships as in heterosexual relationships (Schwartz & Waldo, 2004). "Getting my partner's attention," "gaining

control," and "expressing anger" are reasons that partners typically give for abusing each other.

Factors Related to Partner Abuse

In abusive relationships, dominance–submission sometimes proceeds from husband to wife, sometimes from wife to husband. In about one-third to one-half of cases, both partners are violent (Dutton, Nicholls, & Spidel, 2005). Marvin and Pat's relationship helps us understand how partner abuse escalates. Shortly after their wedding, Pat began complaining about the demands of Marvin's work and insisted that he come home early to spend time with her. When he resisted, she hurled epithets, threw objects, and slapped him. One evening, Marvin became so angry at Pat's hostilities that he smashed a dish against the wall, threw his wedding ring at her, and left the house. The next morning, Pat apologized and promised not to attack again. But her outbursts became more frequent and desperate.

These violence–remorse cycles, in which aggression escalates, characterize many abusive relationships. Personality and devel-

opmental history, family circumstances, and cultural factors combine to make partner abuse more likely (Diamond, Fagundes, & Butterworth, 2010).

Many abusers are overly dependent emotionally on their spouses as well as jealous, possessive, and controlling. For example, the thought of Karen ever leaving induced such high anxiety in Mike that he monitored all her activities. And because they have great difficulty managing anger, trivial events—such as an unwashed shirt or a late meal—can trigger abusive episodes. When asked to explain their offenses, they attribute greater blame to their partner than to themselves (Henning, Jones, & Holdford, 2005).

A high proportion of spouse abusers grew up in homes where parents engaged in hostile interactions, used coercive discipline, and were abusive toward their children (Ehrensaft, 2009). Perhaps this explains why conduct problems in childhood and violent delinquency in adolescence also predict partner abuse (Dutton, 2007). Stressful life events, such as job loss or financial difficulties, increase the likelihood of partner abuse. Because of widespread poverty, African Americans and Native Americans report high rates of partner violence (Hoff, 2001). Alcohol abuse is another related factor.

and support, but her own needs for nurturance and individuality were not being met. Gary was uncomfortable with Christy's career aspirations. As she came closer to attaining them, the couple grew further apart. In contrast, Sharese and Ernie married later, after their educations were complete. They postponed having children until their careers were under way and they had built a sense of togetherness that allowed each to thrive as an individual. Patience, caring, common values and interests, humor, affection, sharing of personal experiences through conversation, cooperating in household responsibilities, and good conflict-resolution skills contributed to their compatibility.

Although quality of the marital relationship predicts mental health similarly for both genders, men tend to report feeling slightly happier with their marriages than women do (Howard, Galambos, & Krahn, 2010; Kurdek, 2005). Women feel particularly dissatisfied when the demands of husband, children, housework, and career are overwhelming (Forry, Leslie, & Letiecq, 2007; Saginak & Saginak, 2005). Equal power in the relationship and sharing of family responsibilities usually enhance both partners' satisfaction, largely

by strengthening marital harmony (Amato & Booth, 1995; Xu & Lai, 2004).

Of course, from time to time, individuals are bound to say or do something upsetting to their partner. When this happens, the partner's attributions, or explanations for the behavior, make a difference. For example, a wife who interprets her husband's critical remark about her weight as unintentional ("He just isn't aware I'm sensitive about that") is far more likely to express both current and long-term marital satisfaction than a wife who views such comments as malicious ("He's trying to hurt my feelings") (Barelds & Dijkstra, 2011; Fincham & Bradbury, 2004). In fact, partners who hold overly positive (but still realistic) biases concerning each other's attributes are happier with their relationships (Claxton et al., 2011). As they turn to each other for feedback about themselves, these "positive illusions" enhance self-esteem and psychological well-being.

In contrast, people who feel devalued by their partner tend to react with anxiety and insecurity—more so when they are low in self-esteem, which heightens fear of rejection. To protect themselves, they often mete out criticism and contempt in kind,

At a societal level, cultural norms that endorse male dominance and female submissiveness promote partner abuse (Kaya & Cook, 2010). As Figure 14.3 shows, in economically distressed countries that also sanction gender inequality, partner violence against women is especially high, affecting nearly half or more of the female population.

Victims are chronically anxious and depressed and experience frequent panic attacks (Warshaw, Brashler, & Gil, 2009). Yet a variety of situational factors discourage them from leaving these destructive relationships. A victimized wife may depend on her husband's earning power or fear even worse harm to herself or her children. Extreme assaults, including homicide, tend to occur after partner separation (Campbell & Glass, 2009). And victims of both sexes, but especially men, are deterred by the embarrassment of going to the police.

Intervention and Treatment

Community services available to battered women include crisis telephone lines that provide anonymous counseling and social support and shelters that offer safety and treatment (see page 356). Because many women return to their abusive partners several times before making their final move, community agencies usually offer therapy to male batterers (Whitaker, Baker, & Arias, 2007). Most rely on several months to a year of group sessions that confront rigid gender stereotyping; teach communication, problem solving, and anger control; and use social support to motivate behavior change.

Although existing treatments are better than none, most are not effective at dealing with relationship difficulties or alcohol abuse. Consequently, many treated perpetrators repeat their violent behavior with the same or a new partner (Hamberger et al., 2009). At present, few interventions acknowledge that men also are victims. Yet ignoring their needs perpetuates domestic violence. When victims do not want to separate from a violent partner, a whole-family treatment approach that focuses on changing partner interaction and reducing high life stress is crucial.

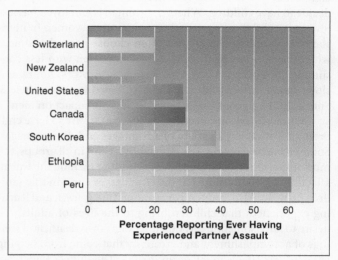

FIGURE 14.3 **Assaults by intimate partners against women in seven nations.** In each country, samples of women were asked to indicate whether they had ever experienced partner physical abuse. The incidence, always underreported, is high in all nations. It is especially high in countries that endorse traditional gender roles and suffer from widespread poverty. (From Kaya & Cook, 2010; World Health Organization, 2000, 2005.)

setting in motion hostile, defensive exchanges that create the very rejection they fear (Murray, 2008). Alternatively, individuals may disengage emotionally, suppressing negative feelings so as not to poison the relationship (Driver et al., 2012). In the process, shared positive emotion also declines, and intimacy erodes.

At their worst, marital relationships can become contexts for intense opposition, dominance–submission, and emotional and physical violence. As the Social Issues: Health box above explains, although women are more often targets of severe partner abuse, both men and women play both roles: perpetrator and victim.

High school and college courses in family life education can promote better mate selection and teach communication skills that contribute to gratifying romantic partnerships and marriages. And counseling aimed at helping couples listen to each other with understanding and empathy, focus on positive traits and memories, and use effective conflict-resolution strategies can cultivate the self-esteem, affection, and respect needed for the relationship to be resilient and enduring (Gottman, 2011).

Parenthood

In the past, the issue of whether to have children was, for many adults, a biological given or a compelling social expectation. Today, in Western industrialized nations, it is a matter of true individual choice. Effective birth control techniques enable adults to avoid having children in most instances. And changing cultural values allow people to remain childless with far less fear of social criticism.

In 1950, 78 percent of American married couples were parents. Today, 70 percent bear children, and they tend to be older when they have their first child. Consistent with this pattern of delayed childbearing and with the decision of most women to divide their energies between family and work, family size in industrialized nations has declined. In 1950, the average number of children per woman was 3.1. Currently, it is 2.1 in the United States, 1.9 in the United Kingdom, 1.7 in Sweden, 1.6 in Canada, 1.4 in Germany, and 1.3 in Italy and Japan (U.S. Census Bureau, 2012a, 2013). Nevertheless, the vast majority of married people continue to embrace parenthood as one of life's most meaningful experiences.

The Decision to Have Children. The choice of parenthood is affected by a complex array of factors, including financial circumstances, personal and religious values, and health conditions. Women with traditional gender identities usually decide to have children. Whether a woman is employed has less impact on childbearing than her occupation. Women in high-status, demanding careers less often choose parenthood and, when they do, more often delay it than women with less consuming jobs. Parenthood typically reduces work hours and slows career progress among career-oriented women (Abele & Spurk, 2011). In contrast, it generally has no impact on men.

When Americans are asked about their desire to have children, they mention a variety of advantages and disadvantages. Some ethnic and regional differences exist, but in all groups, the most important reasons for having children include the warm, affectionate relationship and the stimulation and fun that children provide. Also frequently mentioned are growth and learning experiences that children bring to the lives of adults, the desire to have someone carry on after one's own death, and feelings of accomplishment and creativity that come from helping children grow (Cowan & Cowan, 2000; O'Laughlin & Anderson, 2001).

Among disadvantages of parenthood, Americans cite loss of freedom most often, followed by concerns about role overload (not enough time for both family and work responsibilities) and about the financial strains. According to a conservative estimate, today's new parents in the United States will spend about $280,000 to rear a child from birth to age 18, and many will incur substantial additional expense for higher education and financial dependency during emerging adulthood (U.S. Department of Agriculture, 2012).

Transition to Parenthood. The early weeks after a baby enters the family are full of profound changes: constant caregiving, added financial responsibilities, and less time for the couple's relationship. In response, gender roles of husband and wife usually become more traditional—even for couples like Sharese and Ernie who are strongly committed to gender equality (Katz-Wise, Priess, & Hyde, 2010; Lawrence et al., 2010).

For most new parents, however, the arrival of a baby—though often associated with mild declines in relationship satisfaction and communication quality—does not cause significant marital strain. Marriages that are gratifying and supportive tend to remain so (Doss et al., 2009; Feeney et al., 2001). But troubled marriages usually become even more distressed after childbirth (Houts et al., 2008; Kluwer & Johnson, 2007). And when expectant mothers anticipate lack of partner support in parenting, their prediction generally becomes reality, yielding an especially difficult postbirth adjustment (Driver et al., 2012; McHale & Rotman, 2007).

Violated expectations about division of labor in the home powerfully affect new parents' well-being. In dual-earner marriages, the larger the difference in men's and women's caregiving responsibilities, the greater the decline in marital satisfaction after childbirth, especially for women—with negative consequences for parent–infant interaction. In contrast, sharing

Compared to a first birth, a second birth typically requires that fathers become more actively involved in parenting, sharing in the high demands of tending to both a baby and a young child.

caregiving predicts greater parental happiness and sensitivity to the baby (McHale et al., 2004; Moller, Hwang, & Wickberg, 2008).

Postponing childbearing until the late twenties or thirties, as more couples do today, eases the transition to parenthood. Waiting permits couples to pursue occupational goals, gain life experience, and strengthen their relationship. Under these circumstances, men are more enthusiastic about becoming fathers and therefore more willing to participate. And women whose careers are well under way and whose marriages are happy are more likely to encourage their husbands to share housework and child care, which fosters fathers' involvement (Lee & Doherty, 2007; Schoppe-Sullivan et al., 2008).

A second birth typically requires that fathers take an even more active role in parenting—by caring for the firstborn while the mother is recuperating and by sharing in the high demands of tending to both a baby and a young child. Consequently, well-functioning families with a newborn second child typically pull back from the traditional division of responsibilities that occurred after the first birth. Fathers' willingness to place greater emphasis on the parenting role is strongly linked to mothers' adjustment after the arrival of a second baby (Stewart, 1990).

Generous, paid employment leave—widely available in industrialized nations but not in the United States—is crucial for parents of newborns (see Chapter 3, page 81). But financial pressures mean that many new mothers who are eligible for unpaid work leave take far less than they are guaranteed by U.S. federal law, while new fathers take little or none. When favorable workplace policies exist and parents take advantage of them, couples are more likely to support each other and experience family life as gratifying (Feldman, Sussman, & Zigler, 2004). As a result, the stress caused by the birth of a baby stays at manageable levels.

Families with Young Children. In today's complex world, men and women are less certain about how to rear children than in previous generations. Clarifying child-rearing values and implementing them in warm, involved, and appropriately demanding ways are crucial for the welfare of the next generation and society. Yet cultures do not always place a high priority on parenting, as indicated by lack of many societal supports for children and families (see Chapter 2, pages 50–51). Furthermore, changing family forms mean that the lives of today's parents differ substantially from those of past generations.

In previous chapters, we discussed a wide variety of influences on child-rearing styles, including personal characteristics of children and parents, SES, and ethnicity. The couple's relationship is also vital. Parents who engage in effective coparenting, collaborating and showing solidarity and respect for each other in parenting roles, are more likely to gain in warm marital interaction, feel competent as parents, use effective child-rearing practices, and have children who are developing well (McHale et al., 2002a; Schoppe-Sullivan et al., 2004).

For employed parents, a major struggle is finding good child care and, when their child is ill or otherwise in need of emergency care, taking time off from work or making other urgent arrangements. The younger the child, the greater parents' sense of risk and difficulty—especially low-income parents, who must work longer hours to pay bills; who often, in the United States, have no workplace benefits (health insurance or paid sick leave); who typically cannot afford the cost of child care; and who experience more immediate concerns about their children's safety (Halpern, 2005b; Nomaguchi & Brown, 2011). When competent, convenient child care is not available, the woman usually faces added pressures. She must either curtail or give up her work, with profound financial consequences in low-income families, or endure unhappy children, missed workdays, and constant searches for new arrangements.

Despite its challenges, rearing young children is a powerful source of adult development. Parents report that it expands their emotional capacities, enriches their lives, and enhances psychological well-being (Nomaguchi & Milkie, 2003; Schindler, 2010). For example, involved parents say that parenthood helped them tune in to others' feelings and needs, required that they become more tolerant, self-confident, and responsible, and broadened their extended family, friendship, and community ties. In a survey of a large, nationally representative sample of U.S. fathers, engagement with children predicted greater community service and assistance of extended family members in middle adulthood (Eggebeen, Dew, & Knoester, 2010).

Families with Adolescents. Adolescence brings sharp changes in parental roles. In Chapters 11 and 12, we noted that parents must establish a revised relationship with their adolescent children—blending guidance with freedom and gradually loosening control. As adolescents gain in autonomy and explore values and goals in their search for identity, parents often complain that their teenager is too focused on peers and no longer cares about being with the family. Heightened parent–child bick-

ering over everyday issues takes a toll, especially on mothers, who do most of the negotiating with teenagers.

Overall, children seem to navigate the challenges of adolescence more easily than parents, many of whom report a dip in marital and life satisfaction. More people seek family therapy during this period of the family life cycle than during any other (Steinberg & Silk, 2002).

Parent Education. In the past, family life changed little from one generation to the next, and adults learned what they needed to know about parenting through modeling and direct experience. Today's world confronts adults with a host of factors that impinge on their ability to succeed as parents.

Contemporary parents eagerly seek information on child rearing. In addition to popular parenting books, magazines, and websites, new mothers access knowledge about parenting through social media, including chat rooms and blogs. They also reach out to networks of other women for knowledge and assistance. Fathers, by contrast, rarely have social networks through which they can learn about child care and child rearing. Consequently, they frequently turn to mothers to figure out how to relate to their child, especially if they have a close, confiding marriage (Lamb & Lewis, 2004; McHale, Kuersten-Hogan, & Rao, 2004). Recall from Chapter 6 that marital harmony fosters both parents' positive engagement with babies, but it is especially important for fathers.

Parent education courses exist to help parents clarify child-rearing values, improve family communication, understand how children develop, and apply more effective parenting strategies. A variety of programs yield positive outcomes, including enhanced knowledge of effective parenting practices, improved parent–child interaction, and heightened awareness by parents of their role as educators of their children (Bert, Farris, & Borkowski, 2008; Smith, Perou, & Lesesne, 2002). Another benefit is social support—opportunities to discuss concerns with experts and other dedicated parents.

© JENNIFER HULSHIZER/STAR LEDGER/CORBIS

Men are less likely than women to learn about child rearing through informal social networks. Fathers especially may benefit from parent education programs that help them clarify child-rearing values, learn about child development, and parent effectively.

REVIEW What strategies can couples use to ease the transition to parenthood?

APPLY After her wedding, Sharese was convinced she had made a mistake. Cite factors that sustained her marriage and led it to become especially happy.

REFLECT Do you live with your parents or on your own? Describe factors that contributed to your current living arrangements. How would you characterize the quality of your relationship with your parents? Do your responses match the findings of research?

The Diversity of Adult Lifestyles

The current array of adult lifestyles dates back to the 1960s, when young people began to question the conventional wisdom of previous generations and to ask, "What kinds of commitments should I make to live a full and rewarding life?" As the public became more accepting of diverse lifestyles, choices such as staying single, cohabiting, remaining childless, and divorcing seemed more available.

Today, nontraditional family options have penetrated the American mainstream. As we will see, some adults make a deliberate decision to adopt a lifestyle, whereas others drift into it. The lifestyle may be imposed by society, as is the case for cohabiting same-sex couples in the United States, who cannot marry legally in most states. Or people may choose a certain lifestyle because they feel pushed away from another, such as a marriage gone sour. In sum, the adoption of a lifestyle can be within or beyond the person's control.

Singlehood

On finishing her education, Heather joined the Peace Corps and spent four years in Ghana. Though open to a long-term relationship, she had only fleeting romances. After she returned to the United States, she went from one temporary job to another until, at age 30, she finally found steady employment in a large international travel company as a tour director. A few years later, she advanced into a management position. At age 35, over lunch with Sharese, she reflected on her life: "I was open to marriage, but after I got my career going, it would have interfered. Now I'm so used to independence that I question whether I could adjust to living with another person. I like being able to pick up and go where I want, when I want. But there's a tradeoff: I sleep alone, eat most of my meals alone, and spend a lot of my leisure time alone."

Singlehood—not living with an intimate partner—has increased in recent years, especially among young adults. For example, the rate of never-married Americans in their twenties has nearly tripled since 1960, to 75 percent of young people. As they move into their thirties, more people marry: By 30 to 34 years of age, about 32 percent remain single. More people marry later or not at all, and divorce has added to the numbers of single adults—slightly more than half when adults of all ages are considered. In view of these trends, it is likely that most Americans will spend a substantial part of their adult lives single, and a growing minority—about 8 to 10 percent—will stay that way (Pew Research Center, 2010a; U.S. Census Bureau, 2013).

Because they marry later, more young-adult men than women are single. But women are far more likely than men to remain single for many years or their entire life. With age, fewer men are available with characteristics that most women seek in a mate—the same age or older, equally or better educated, and professionally successful. In contrast, men can choose partners from a large pool of younger unmarried women. Because of the tendency for women to "marry up" and men to "marry down," men with a high school diploma or less and highly educated women in prestigious careers are overrepresented among singles after age 30.

Ethnic differences also exist. For example, the percentage of never-married African Americans is nearly twice as great as that of Caucasian Americans in early adulthood (U.S. Census Bureau, 2013). As we will see later, high unemployment among black men interferes with marriage. Many African Americans eventually marry in their late thirties and forties, a period in which black and white marriage rates come closer together.

The most commonly mentioned advantages of singlehood are freedom and mobility. But singles also recognize drawbacks—loneliness, the dating grind, limited sexual and social life, reduced sense of security, and feelings of exclusion from the

Compared with single men, single women more easily come to terms with their lifestyle, in part because of the greater social support available to women through intimate same-sex friendships.

world of married couples. Single men have more physical and mental health problems than single women, who more easily come to terms with their lifestyle, in part because of the greater social support available to women through intimate same-sex friendships (Pinquart, 2003). But overall, people over age 35 who have always been single are content with their lives (DePaulo & Morris, 2005; Lucas et al., 2003). Though not quite as happy as married people, they report feeling considerably happier than people recently widowed or divorced.

Nevertheless, many single people go through a stressful period in their late twenties or early thirties, when most of their friends have married. Widespread veneration of marriage, along with negative stereotyping of singles as socially immature and self-centered, contributes (Morris et al., 2008). The mid-thirties is another trying time for women, as the biological deadline for pregnancy approaches (Sharp & Ganong, 2011). A few decide to become parents through artificial insemination or a love affair. And an increasing number are adopting, often from overseas countries.

Among U.S. couples, making a long-term commitment by becoming engaged before cohabiting predicts an enduring marriage. U.S. young people who cohabit prior to engagement are at increased risk for divorce.

Cohabitation

Cohabitation refers to the lifestyle of unmarried couples who have a sexually intimate relationship and who share a residence. Until the 1960s, cohabitation in Western nations was largely limited to low-SES adults. Since then, it has increased in all groups, with an especially dramatic rise among well-educated, economically advantaged young people. Today's young adults are much more likely than those of a generation ago to form their first conjugal union through cohabitation. Among American young people, cohabitation is now the preferred mode of entry into a committed intimate partnership, chosen by over 60 percent of couples (U.S. Census Bureau, 2013). Cohabitation rates are even higher among adults with failed marriages.

Although Americans are more open to cohabitation than in the past, their attitudes are not as positive as those of Western Europeans. In the Netherlands, Norway, and Sweden, cohabitation is thoroughly integrated into society, with cohabiters having many of the same legal rights and responsibilities as married couples. Consequently, they are nearly as committed to each other as married people (Fussell & Gauthier, 2005; Perelli-Harris & Gassen, 2012). Compared with those in Western Europe, U.S. cohabiting unions are far more likely to dissolve within two years. Furthermore, U.S. couples who cohabit before they are engaged to be married are more prone to divorce than couples who wait to live together until after they have made a commitment to each other. But this association is less strong or absent in Western European nations (Jose, O'Leary, & Moyer, 2010; Rhoades, Stanley, & Markman, 2006). U.S. young people who cohabit prior to engagement tend to have less conventional values. They have had more sexual partners and are more politically liberal, less religious, and more androgynous. In addition, a larger number have parents who divorced (Kurdek, 2006).

These personal characteristics may contribute to the negative outcomes associated with U.S. cohabitation. But the cohabitation experience itself also plays a role. U.S. cohabiters have poorer-quality relationships (Kline et al., 2004). Perhaps the open-ended nature of the cohabiting relationship reduces motivation to develop effective conflict-resolution skills. When cohabiters carry negative communication into marriage, it undermines marital satisfaction.

Certain couples, however, are exceptions to the trends just described. People who cohabit after separation or divorce often test a new relationship carefully to prevent another failure, especially when children are involved. As a result, they cohabit longer and are less likely to move toward marriage. Similarly, cohabitation is often an alternative to marriage among low-SES couples (Pew Research Center, 2010a). Many regard their earning power as too uncertain for marriage and continue living together, sometimes giving birth to children and marrying when their financial status improves.

Finally, U.S. cohabiting gay and lesbian couples report strong relationship commitment (Kurdek, 2006). When their relationships become difficult, they end more often than those of heterosexual cohabiters and married couples because of fewer barriers to separating. For example, in 36 U.S. states, same-sex cohabiters cannot legalize their relationship because of laws or constitutional provisions that limit marriage to a man and a woman. Furthermore, same-sex cohabiters are less likely to have children in common and more likely to have extended family members who are unsupportive (Lau, 2012; Rothblum, Balsam, & Solomon, 2011). In a study in which same-sex couples in Vermont were followed over three years, cohabiters were more likely than couples in civil unions to have ended their relationships (Balsam et al., 2008). Civil unions were as stable as heterosexual marriages.

Childlessness

At work, Sharese got to know Beatrice and Daniel. Married for seven years and in their mid-thirties, they did not have children and were not planning any. To Sharese, their relationship seemed especially caring and affectionate. "At first, we were open to becoming parents," Beatrice explained, "but eventually we decided to focus on our marriage."

Childlessness in the United States has increased steadily, from 9 percent of women between ages 20 and 44 in 1975 to about 20 percent today, with similar trends occurring in other Western nations (Livingston & Cohn, 2010). Some people are *involuntarily childless* because they did not find a partner with whom to share parenthood or their efforts at fertility treatments did not succeed. Beatrice and Daniel are in another category—men and women who are *voluntarily childless*. But voluntary childlessness is not always a permanent condition. A few people decide early that they do not want to be parents and stick to their plans. But most, like Beatrice and Daniel, make their decision after they are married and have developed a lifestyle they do not want to give up. Later, some change their minds.

Besides marital satisfaction and freedom from child-care responsibilities, common reasons for not having children include the woman's career and economic security (Amba & Martinez, 2006; Kemkes-Grottenhaler, 2003). Consistent with these motives, the voluntarily childless are usually college-educated, have prestigious occupations, and are highly committed to their work.

Voluntarily childless adults are just as content with their lives as parents who have warm relationships with their children. But adults who cannot overcome infertility are likely to be dissatisfied—some profoundly disappointed, others more ambivalent, depending on compensations in other areas of their lives (Letherby, 2002; Nichols & Pace-Nichols, 2000). Childlessness seems to interfere with adjustment and life satisfaction only when it is beyond a person's control.

Divorce and Remarriage

Divorce rates have stabilized since the mid-1980s, partly because of rising age of marriage, which is linked to greater financial stability and marital satisfaction. In addition, the increase in cohabitation has curtailed divorce: Many relationships that once would have been marriages now break up before marriage. Still, 45 percent of U.S. marriages dissolve (U.S. Census Bureau, 2013). Because most divorces occur within seven years of marriage, many involve young children. Divorces are also common during the transition to midlife, when people have adolescent children—a period (as noted earlier) of reduced marital satisfaction.

Factors Related to Divorce. Why do so many marriages fail? As Christy and Gary's divorce illustrates, the most obvious reason is a disrupted husband–wife relationship. Christy and Gary did not argue more than Sharese and Ernie.

But their problem-solving style was ineffective. When Christy raised concerns, Gary reacted with contempt, resentment, defensiveness, and retreat. This demand–withdraw pattern is found in many partners who split up, with women more often insisting on change and men more often retreating (Birditt et al., 2010; Haltzman, Holstein, & Moss, 2007). Another typical style involves little conflict, but partners increasingly lead separate lives because they have different expectations of family life and few shared interests, activities, or friends (Gottman & Levenson, 2000).

What problems underlie these maladaptive communication patterns? In a nine-year longitudinal study, researchers asked a U.S. national sample of 2,000 married people about marital problems and followed up three, six, and nine years later to find out who had separated or divorced (Amato & Rogers, 1997). Wives reported more problems than husbands, with the gender difference largely involving the wife's emotions, such as anger and hurt feelings. Husbands seemed to have difficulty sensing their wife's distress, which contributed to her view of the marriage as unhappy. Regardless of which spouse reported the problem or was judged responsible for it, the strongest predictors of divorce during the following decade were infidelity, spending money foolishly, drinking or using drugs, expressing jealousy, engaging in irritating habits, and moodiness.

Background factors that increase the chances of divorce are younger age at marriage, not attending religious services, being previously divorced, and having parents who had divorced. Low religious involvement subtracts an influential context for instilling positive marital attitudes and behaviors. And research following families over two decades reveals that parental divorce elevates risk of divorce in at least two succeeding generations, in part because it promotes child adjustment problems and reduces commitment to the norm of lifelong marriage (Amato & Cheadle, 2005; Wolfinger, 2005).

FREDERICK BASS/GETTY IMAGES

An ineffective problem-solving style can lead to divorce. Partners who split up often follow a pattern in which one partner raises concerns, and the other reacts with resentment, anger, and retreat.

Poorly educated, economically disadvantaged couples who suffer multiple life stresses are especially likely to split up (Clarke-Stewart & Brentano, 2006). But Christy's case represents another trend—rising marital breakup among well-educated, career-oriented, economically independent women. When a woman's workplace status and income exceed her husband's, the risk of divorce increases—an association explained by differing gender-role beliefs between the spouses. A husband's lack of support for his wife's career can greatly heighten her unhappiness and, therefore, the chances that she will end the marriage. Overall, women are twice as likely as men to initiate divorce proceedings.

In addition to the relationship factors just described, American individualism—which includes the belief that each person has the right to pursue self-expression and personal happiness—contributes to the unusually high U.S. divorce rate (see page 276 in Chapter 10) (Cherlin, 2009). Whether cohabiting or married, Americans partner, split up, and repartner more often than anywhere else in the industrialized world.

Consequences of Divorce. Divorce involves the loss of a way of life and therefore a part of the self sustained by that way of life. As a result, it provides opportunities for both positive and negative change. Immediately after separation, both men and women experience disrupted social networks, a decline in social support, and increased anxiety, depression, and impulsivity (Amato, 2000). For most, these reactions subside within two years. Nonworking women who organized their identities around their husbands have an especially hard time (Coleman, Ganong, & Leon, 2006). And some noncustodial fathers feel disoriented and rootless as a result of decreased contact with their children.

Finding a new partner contributes most to the life satisfaction of divorced adults (Forste & Heaton, 2004; Wang & Amato, 2000). But it is more crucial for men, who adjust less well than women to living on their own. Despite loneliness and a drop in income (see Chapter 10), women tend to bounce back more easily from divorce. However, a few women—especially those who are anxious and fearful, who remain strongly attached to their ex-spouses, or who lack education and job skills—experience a drop in self-esteem and persistent depression (Amato, 2000; Coleman, Ganong, & Leon, 2006). Job training, continued education, career advancement, and social support from family and friends play vital roles in the economic and psychological well-being of many divorced women.

Remarriage. On average, people remarry within four years of divorce, men somewhat faster than women. Remarriages are especially vulnerable to breakup for several reasons. First, practical matters—financial security, help in rearing children, relief from loneliness, and social acceptance—figure more heavily into a second marriage. Second, some people transfer the negative patterns of interaction learned in their first marriage to the second. Third, people with a failed marriage behind them are more likely to view divorce as an acceptable solution when marital difficulties resurface. Finally, remarried couples experience more stress from stepfamily situations (Coleman, Ganong, & Leon, 2006). As we will see, stepparent–stepchild ties are powerful predictors of marital happiness.

Blended families generally take three to five years to develop the connectedness and comfort of intact biological families. Family life education, couples counseling, and group therapy can help divorced and remarried adults adapt to the complexities of their new circumstances.

Varied Styles of Parenthood

Diverse family forms result in varied styles of parenthood. Each type of family—blended, never-married, gay or lesbian, among others—presents unique challenges to parenting competence and adult psychological well-being.

Stepparents. Whether stepchildren live in the household or visit only occasionally, stepparents are in a difficult position. Stepparents enter the family as outsiders and, too often, move into their new parental role too quickly. Lacking a warm attachment bond to build on, their discipline is usually ineffective (Ganong & Coleman, 2004). Compared with first-marriage parents, remarried parents typically report higher levels of tension and disagreement, most centering on child-rearing issues. When both adults have children from prior marriages, rather than only one, more opportunities for conflict exist.

Stepmothers are especially likely to experience conflict. Those who have not previously been married and had children may have an idealized image of family life, which is quickly shattered. Expected to be in charge of family relationships, stepmothers quickly find that stepparent–stepchild ties do not develop instantly. After divorce, biological mothers are frequently jealous, uncooperative, and possessive of their children. Even when their husbands do not have custody, stepmothers feel stressed (Church, 2004; MacDonald & DeMaris, 1996). As stepchildren go in and out of the home, stepmothers find life easier without resistant children and then may feel guilty about their "unmaternal" feelings.

Stepfathers with children of their own tend to establish positive bonds with stepchildren relatively quickly, perhaps because they are experienced in building warm parent–child ties and feel less pressure than stepmothers to plunge into parenting (Ganong et al., 1999). But stepfathers without biological children (like their stepmother counterparts) can have unrealistic expectations. Or their wives may push them into the father role, sparking negativity from children.

In interviews in which young-adult stepchildren provided retrospective accounts of their stepparent relationships, the quality of these ties varied widely. A caring husband–wife bond, sensitive relationship-building behaviors by the stepparent, cooperation from the biological parent, and supportive extended family members all affected stepparent–stepchild ties. Over time, many couples built a coparenting partnership that improved interactions with stepchildren (Ganong, Coleman, & Jamison, 2011). But because stepparent–stepchild bonds are hard to establish, the divorce rate is higher for remarried couples with stepchildren than for those without them.

Never-Married Single Parents.

Today, about 40 percent of U.S. births are to single mothers, more than double the percentage in 1980. Whereas teenage parenthood has declined (see page 300 in Chapter 11), unwed parenthood among mothers in their twenties and older has risen. About 11 percent of U.S. children live with a single mother who has never married (U.S.Census Bureau, 2013).

In the United States, African-American young women make up the largest group of never-married parents. About 64 percent of births to black mothers in their twenties are to women without a partner, compared with 28 percent of births to white women (U.S. Census Bureau, 2013). African-American women postpone marriage more and childbirth less than women in other U.S. ethnic groups. Job loss, persisting unemployment, and consequent inability of many black men to support a family have contributed to the number of African-American never-married, single-mother families.

Never-married African-American mothers tap the extended family, especially their own mothers and sometimes male relatives, for help in rearing their children (Gasden, 1999; Jayakody & Kalil, 2002). For about one-third, marriage—not necessarily to the child's biological father—occurs within a decade after birth of the first child (Wu, Bumpass, & Musick, 2001). These couples function much like other first-marriage parents. Their children are often unaware that the father is a stepfather, and parents do not report the child-rearing difficulties typical of blended families (Ganong & Coleman, 1994).

Still, for low-SES women, never-married parenthood generally increases financial hardship; about half live in poverty (Mather, 2010). Nearly 50 percent of white mothers and 60 percent of black mothers have a second child while unmarried. And children of never-married mothers who lack father involvement achieve less well in school and display more antisocial behavior than children in low-SES, first-marriage families—problems that make life more difficult for mothers (Waldfogel, Craigie, & Brooks-Gunn, 2010). But marriage to the child's biological father benefits children only when the father is a reliable source of economic and emotional support. For example, adolescents who feel close to their nonresident father fare better in school performance and emotional and social adjustment than do those in two-parent homes where a close father tie is lacking (Booth, Scott, & King, 2010). Unfortunately, most unwed fathers—who usually are doing poorly financially—gradually spend less and less time with their children (Lerman,

2010). Strengthening parenting skills, social support, education, and employment opportunities for low-SES parents would greatly enhance the well-being of unmarried mothers and their children.

Gay and Lesbian Parents.

About 20 to 35 percent of lesbian couples and 5 to 15 percent of gay couples are parents, most through previous heterosexual marriages, some through adoption, and a growing number through reproductive technologies (Gates et al., 2007; Goldberg, 2010; Patterson & Riskind, 2010). In the past, because of laws assuming that homosexuals could not be adequate parents, those who divorced a heterosexual partner lost custody of their children. Today, some U.S. states hold that sexual orientation by itself is irrelevant to custody. A few U.S. states, however, ban gay and lesbian couples from adopting children. Among other countries, gay and lesbian adoptions are legal in Argentina, Belgium, Brazil, Canada, Iceland, Mexico, the Netherlands, Norway, South Africa, Spain, Sweden, the United Kingdom, and Uruguay.

Most research on homosexual parents and children is limited to volunteer samples. Findings indicate that gay and lesbian parents are as committed to and effective at child rearing as heterosexual parents and sometimes more so (Bos, van Balen, & van den Boom, 2007; Tasker, 2005). Also, whether born to or adopted by their parents or conceived through donor insemination, children in gay and lesbian families did not differ from the children of heterosexuals in mental health, peer relations, gender-role behavior, or sexual orientation (Allen & Burrell, 1996; Bos & Sandfort, 2010; Farr, Forssell, & Patterson, 2010; Goldberg, 2010). Three additional studies, which surmounted the potential bias associated with volunteer participants by including representative samples of lesbian-mother

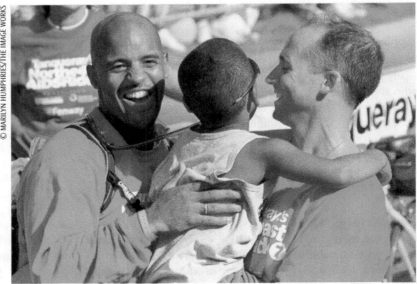

© MARILYN HUMPHRIES/THE IMAGE WORKS

Gay and lesbian parents are as committed to and effective at child rearing as heterosexual parents. Overall, families headed by same-sex partners are distinguishable only by issues related to a nonsupportive society.

families, also reported that children were developing favorably (Brewaeys et al., 1997; Chan, Raboy, & Patterson, 1998; Golombok et al., 2003).

When extended-family members withhold acceptance, homosexual mothers and fathers often build "families of choice" through friends, who assume the roles of relatives. Usually, however, parents of gays and lesbians cannot endure a permanent rift (Fisher, Easterly, & Lazear, 2008). With time, interactions between homosexual parents and their families of origin become more positive and supportive.

A major concern of gay and lesbian parents is that their children will be stigmatized by their parents' sexual orientation. Most studies indicate that incidents of teasing or bullying are rare because parents and children carefully manage the information they reveal to others (Tasker, 2005). Overall, families headed by homosexuals can be distinguished from other families only by issues related to living in a nonsupportive society.

ASK YOURSELF

REVIEW Return to Chapter 10, pages 275–276, and review the impact of divorce and remarriage on children and adolescents. How do those findings resemble outcomes for adults? What might account for the similarities?

APPLY After dating for three months, Wanda and Scott decided to live together. Their parents worried that cohabitation would reduce the couple's chances for a successful marriage. Is this fear justified? Why or why not?

REFLECT Do your own experiences or those of your friends match research findings on cohabitation, singlehood, never-married parents, or gay and lesbian parents? Select one instance and discuss.

 ## Career Development

Besides family life, vocational life is a vital domain of social development in early adulthood. Young people must learn how to perform work tasks well, get along with co-workers, respond to authority, and protect their own interests. When work experiences go well, adults develop new competencies, feel a sense of personal accomplishment, make new friends, and become financially independent and secure. And as we have seen, aspirations and accomplishments in the workplace and the family are interwoven.

Establishing a Career

Our discussion earlier in this chapter highlighted diverse paths and timetables for career development. *TAKE A MOMENT...*

Consider, once again, the wide variations among Sharese, Ernie, Christy, and Gary. Notice that Sharese and Christy, like many women, had *discontinuous* career paths—ones that were interrupted or deferred by child rearing and other family needs (Huang & Sverke, 2007; Moen & Roehling, 2005). Furthermore, not all people embark on the vocation of their dreams. As noted in our consideration of emerging adulthood, the late-2000s recession greatly increased the number of young people in jobs that do not match their educational preparation.

Even for those who enter their chosen field, initial experiences can be discouraging. At the health department, Sharese discovered that paperwork consumed much of her day. Because each project had a deadline, the pressure of productivity weighed heavily on her. Adjusting to unanticipated disappointments in salary, supervisors, and co-workers is difficult. As workers in their twenties become aware of the gap between their expectations and reality, they change jobs often.

Recall from our discussion of Levinson's theory that career progress often depends on the quality of a mentoring relationship. Access to an effective mentor is jointly affected by the availability of willing people and the individual's capacity to select an appropriate individual (Ramaswami & Dreher, 2007). The best mentors are seldom top executives, who tend to be preoccupied and therefore less helpful and sympathetic. Usually, young adults fare better with mentors who are just above them in experience and advancement or who are members of their professional associations (Allen & Finkelstein, 2003). Furthermore, mentoring early in a worker's career increases the likelihood of mentoring later on (Bozionelos et al., 2011). The professional and personal benefits of mentoring induce employees to provide it to others and to seek it again for themselves.

Women and Ethnic Minorities

Women and ethnic minorities have penetrated nearly all professions, but their talents often are not developed to the fullest. Women, especially those who are members of economically disadvantaged minorities, remain concentrated in occupations that offer little opportunity for advancement, and they are underrepresented in executive and managerial roles (see Chapter 13, pages 363–364). And although the overall difference between men's and women's earnings is smaller today than 30 years ago, it remains considerable in all industrialized countries (Rampell, 2010). U.S. government surveys following 9,000 U.S. college-educated workers for a decade revealed that a year after receiving their bachelor's degrees, women working full time earned just 80 percent as much as men. The difference was largely (but not entirely) due to gender differences in college majors: Women more often chose education and service fields, men higher-paying scientific and technical fields. Ten years after graduation, the gender pay gap had widened: Women's pay was only 69 percent of men's, and in no profession did women's earnings equal men's (Dey & Hill, 2007). Gender disparities in career development accounted for about 90 percent of the gap, with the remaining 10 percent attributed to on-the-job discrimination.

Especially for women in traditionally feminine occupations, career planning is often short-term and subject to change. Many women enter and exit the labor market several times, or reduce their work hours from full-time to part-time as they give birth to and rear children (Furchtgott-Roth, 2009; Lips, 2013). Time away from a career greatly hinders advancement—a major reason that women in prestigious, male-dominated careers tend to delay or avoid childbearing (Blair-Loy & DeHart, 2003).

In addition, low self-efficacy with respect to male-dominated fields limits women's career progress. Women who pursue nontraditional careers usually have "masculine" traits—high achievement orientation, self-reliance, and belief that their efforts will result in success. But even those with high self-efficacy are less certain than their male counterparts that they can overcome barriers to career success. In a study of women scientists on university faculties, those reporting a sexist work climate (sexual harassment or discrimination in salary, promotion, or resources) were less satisfied with their jobs and less productive (Settles et al., 2006).

Gender-stereotyped images of women as followers rather than leaders slow advancement into top-level management positions. And because men dominate high-status fields, they must be willing to mentor women into leadership positions and take time from their work responsibilities to do so. Mentoring by a senior-male executive predicts progress into management roles and pay gains more strongly for women in male-dominated industries than for men (Ramaswami et al., 2010). When a powerful male leader *sponsors* the advancement of a talented woman, designating her as having the qualities to succeed, senior-level decision makers are far more likely to take notice.

Despite laws guaranteeing equality of opportunity, racial and ethnic bias in career opportunities remains strong (Smith, Brief, & Colella, 2010). In one study, researchers recruited two three-member teams consisting of a white, a black, and a Hispanic male job applicant, each 22 to 26 years old and matched on verbal and interpersonal skills and physical attractiveness. The applicants were assigned identical fictitious résumés (with the exception that the résumé of the white member of the second team disclosed a criminal record) and sent out to apply for 170 entry-level jobs in New York City (Pager, Western, & Bonikowski, 2009). The white applicant received callbacks or job offers from employers slightly more often than the Hispanic applicant, with the black applicant trailing far behind. When the experiment was repeated with the second team, the white felon remained slightly preferred over both minority applicants, despite their clean records. In line with these findings, African Americans spend more time searching for work, experience less stable employment, and acquire less work experience than Caucasian Americans with equivalent job qualifications (Pager & Shepherd, 2008).

Ethnic minority women often must surmount combined gender and racial discrimination to realize their career poten-

Women in male-dominated fields, such as this scientist, usually have "masculine" traits, such as high achievement orientation and self-reliance. Nevertheless, many encounter workplace barriers to career success.

tial. Those who succeed frequently display an unusually high sense of self-efficacy, attacking problems head-on despite repeated obstacles to achievement. In interviews with African-American women who had become leaders in diverse fields, all reported intense persistence, fueled by supportive relationships with other women, including teachers and peers. Many described their mothers as inspiring role models who had set high standards for them (Richie et al., 1997). Others felt empowered by a deep sense of connection to their African-American communities.

Combining Work and Family

The majority of women with children are in the work force (see page 277 in Chapter 10), most in dual-earner marriages or cohabiting relationships. More women than men report moderate to high levels of stress in trying to meet both work and family responsibilities (Higgins, Duxbury, & Lyons, 2010; Zhao, Settles, & Sheng, 2011).

TAKE A MOMENT... Think about a dual-earner family you know well. What are the main sources of strain? When Sharese returned to her job after her children were born, she felt a sense of *role overload,* or conflict between the demands of work and family responsibilities. In addition to a challenging career, she also (like most employed women) shouldered more household and child-care tasks. And both Sharese and Ernie felt torn between the desire to excel at their jobs and the desire to spend more time with each other, their children, and their friends and relatives. Role overload is linked to increased psychological stress, physical health problems, poorer marital relations, less effective parenting, child behavior problems, and poorer job performance (Perry-Jenkins, Repetti, & Crouter, 2000; Saginak & Saginak, 2005; ten Brummelhuis et al., 2012).

Applying What We Know

Strategies That Help Dual-Earner Couples Combine Work and Family Roles

Strategy	Description
Devise a plan for sharing household tasks.	As soon as possible in the relationship, discuss relative commitment to work and family and division of household responsibilities. Decide who does a particular chore on the basis of who has the needed skill and time, not on the basis of gender. Schedule regular times to rediscuss your plan.
Begin sharing child care right after the baby's arrival.	For fathers, strive to spend equal time with the baby early. For mothers, refrain from imposing your standards on your partner. Instead, share the role of "child-rearing expert" by discussing parenting values and concerns often. Attend a parent education course together.
Talk over conflicts about decision making and responsibilities.	Face conflict through communication. Clarify your feelings and needs and express them to your partner. Listen and try to understand your partner's point of view. Then be willing to negotiate and compromise.
Establish a balance between work and family.	Critically evaluate the time you devote to work in view of your family values and priorities. If it is too much, cut back.
Press for workplace and public policies that assist dual-earner-family roles.	Encourage your employer to provide benefits that help combine work and family, such as flexible work hours, parental leave with pay, and on-site high-quality, affordable child care. Communicate with lawmakers and other citizens about improving public policies for children and families.

Workplace supports can greatly reduce role overload, yielding substantial payoffs for employers. Among a large, nationally representative sample of U.S. working adults, the greater the number of time-flexible policies available in their work settings (for example, time off to care for a sick child, choice in start and stop times, and opportunities to work from home), the better their work performance (Halpern, 2005a). Employees with several time-flexible options missed fewer days of work, less often arrived at work late or left early, felt more committed to their employer, and worked harder. They also reported fewer stress-related health symptoms.

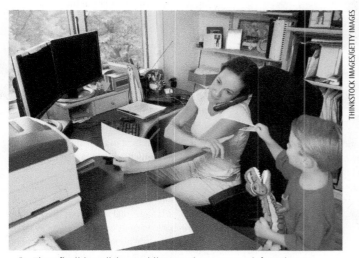

THINKSTOCK IMAGES/GETTY IMAGES

Time-flexible policies enabling employees to work from home help parents adjust work roles to meet family needs. As a result, employees work harder, take less time off, and feel more committed to their jobs.

LOOK AND LISTEN

Talk with one or more dual-earner couples about workplace supports for good parenting. Which policies are available? Which additional ones would they find especially helpful? ●

Effectively balancing work and family brings many benefits—a better standard of living, improved work productivity, enhanced psychological well-being, greater self-fulfillment, and happier marriages. Ernie took great pride in Sharese's dedication to both family life and career. And the skills, maturity, and self-esteem each derived from coping successfully with challenges at home strengthened their capacity to surmount difficulties at work (Graves, Ohlott, & Ruderman, 2007). Applying What We Know above lists strategies that help dual-earner couples attain mastery and pleasure in both spheres of life.

ASK YOURSELF

REVIEW Why do professionally accomplished women, especially those who are members of economically disadvantaged minorities, typically display high self-efficacy?

APPLY Write an essay aimed at convincing a company executive that family-friendly policies are "win-win" situations for both workers and employers.

REFLECT Ask someone who has succeeded in a career of interest to you to describe mentoring relationships that aided his or her progress.

SUMMARY

A Gradual Transition: Emerging Adulthood (p. 369)

What is emerging adulthood, and how has cultural change contributed to it?

- In **emerging adulthood,** young people from the late teens to the mid- to late-twenties have not yet taken on adult responsibilities. Instead, those with economic resources engage in extended exploration of alternatives in education, work, and personal values. Identity development extends into the college years, with young people exploring possibilities in breadth and depth.

- During the late teens and early twenties, religious attendance drops to its lowest level. Regardless of whether they participate in organized religion, many emerging adults begin to construct an individualized faith. They are also committed to improving their world, often engaging in community service.

- Increased education required for entry-level positions in many fields, gains in economic prosperity, and reduced need for young people's labor in industrialized nations have prompted the appearance of emerging adulthood. But because of its strong association with SES and higher education, some researchers do not view emerging adulthood as a distinct period of development.

- In exploring possibilities, emerging adults must adjust to disappointments in love and work, and their explorations may extend risky behaviors of adolescence. A wide array of personal attributes and social supports foster resilience. Relationships with parents are especially influential.

Erikson's Theory: Intimacy versus Isolation (p. 374)

According to Erikson, what personality changes take place during early adulthood?

- In Erikson's theory, young adults must resolve the conflict of **intimacy versus isolation** as they form a close relationship with a partner. The negative outcome is loneliness and self-absorption.

- Young people also focus on aspects of generativity, including parenting and contributions to society through work and community service.

Other Theories of Adult Psychosocial Development (p. 374)

Describe and evaluate Levinson's and Vaillant's psychosocial theories of adult personality development.

- Expanding Erikson's stage approach, Levinson described a series of eras in which people revise their life structure. Young adults usually construct a dream, typically involving career for men and both marriage and career for women, and form a relationship with a mentor. In their thirties, men tend to settle down, whereas many women remain unsettled into middle adulthood.

- Also in the tradition of Erikson, Vaillant portrayed the twenties as devoted to intimacy, the thirties to career consolidation, the forties to generativity, and the fifties and sixties to passing on cultural values.

- Young adults' development is far more variable today than Levinson's and Vaillant's theories depict.

What is the social clock, and how does it affect personality in adulthood?

- Following a **social clock**—age-graded expectations for major life events—grants confidence to young adults. Deviating from it can bring psychological distress.

- As age-graded expectations for appropriate behavior have become increasingly flexible, departures from social-clock life events are common and can create intergenerational tensions.

Close Relationships (p. 376)

Describe factors affecting mate selection and the role of romantic love in the young adult's quest for intimacy.

- Romantic partners tend to resemble each other in age, education level, ethnicity, religion, and various personal and physical attributes.

- According to an evolutionary perspective, women seek a mate with traits that help ensure children's survival, while men look for characteristics signaling sexual pleasure and ability to bear offspring. From a social learning perspective, gender roles profoundly influence criteria for mate selection. Research suggests that both biological and social forces are involved.

- According to Sternberg's **triangular theory of love,** the balance among intimacy, passion, and commitment changes as romantic relationships move from **passionate love** toward **companionate love.** The Western emphasis on romantic love in mate selection does not characterize all cultures.

Describe adult friendships and sibling relationships.

- Adult friendships, like earlier friendships, are based on trust, intimacy, and loyalty. Women's same-sex friendships tend to be more intimate than men's. After marriage, other-sex friendships decline with age for men but increase for women, who tend to form them in the workplace. When family experiences have been positive, adult sibling relationships often resemble friendships

The Family Life Cycle (p. 381)

Trace phases of the family life cycle that are prominent in early adulthood, and cite factors that influence these phases today.

- Wide variations exist in the sequence and timing of the **family life cycle.** A trend toward later home-leaving has occurred in most industrialized nations. Departures generally occur earlier for education than for full-time work or marriage; role transitions may prompt a move back. Parents of young adults living at home are usually highly committed to helping their children move into adult roles.

- The average age of first marriage in the United States and Western Europe has risen. Many countries and a growing number of U.S. states recognize same-sex marriages.

VSTOCK LLC/TANYA CONSTANTINE/GETTY IMAGES

- Both **traditional marriages** and **egalitarian marriages** are affected by women's participation in the work force. Women in Western nations spend nearly twice as much time as men on housework, although men participate much more in child care than in the past. Women feel particularly dissatisfied when the combined demands of work and family roles are overwhelming. Partners who hold overly positive (but still realistic) biases concerning each other's attributes express greater relationship satisfaction.

© ARIEL SKELLEY/BLEND IMAGES/CORBIS

- Although most couples in industrialized nations become parents, they do so later and have fewer children than in the past. The arrival of a child brings increased responsibilities, often prompting a shift to more traditional roles. After the birth of a second child, this may reverse. Shared caregiving predicts greater parental happiness and positive parent–infant interaction.

- Couples with young children face challenges of clarifying and implementing child-rearing values. Those who engage in effective coparenting are more likely to gain in warm marital interaction, use effective child-rearing practices, and have children who are developing well.

- Parents of adolescents must establish revised relationships with their increasingly autonomous teenagers, blending guidance with freedom and gradually loosening control. Marital satisfaction often declines in this phase.

The Diversity of Adult Lifestyles (p. 388)

Discuss the diversity of adult lifestyles, focusing on singlehood, cohabitation, and childlessness.

- Postponement of marriage and a high divorce rate have contributed to a rise in singlehood. Despite an array of drawbacks, singles typically appreciate their freedom and mobility.

- **Cohabitation** among U.S. couples has increased, becoming the preferred mode of entry into a committed intimate partnership. Compared with their Western European counterparts, Americans who cohabit before marriage tend to be less conventional in values and less committed to their partner, and their subsequent marriages are more likely to fail. But gay and lesbian couples who cohabit because they cannot legally marry report commitment equal to that of married couples.

- Voluntarily childless adults tend to be college-educated, career-oriented, and content with their lives. But involuntary childlessness interferes with adjustment and life satisfaction.

Cite factors that contribute to today's high rates of divorce and remarriage.

- Almost half of U.S. marriages dissolve. Although nearly two-thirds of divorced people remarry, many divorce again. Maladaptive communication patterns, younger ages at marriage, a family history of divorce, poverty, the changing status of women, and American individualism all contribute to divorce.

- Remarriages are especially vulnerable to breakup. Reasons include the prominence of practical concerns in the decision to remarry, the persistence of negative styles of communication, the acceptance of divorce as a solution to marital difficulties, and problems adjusting to a stepfamily.

Discuss challenges associated with varied styles of parenthood, including stepparents, never-married parents, and gay and lesbian parents.

- Establishing stepparent–stepchild ties is difficult, especially for stepmothers and for stepfathers without children of their own. A caring husband–wife bond that includes a coparenting partnership, cooperation from the biological parent, and extended-family support promote positive stepparent–stepchild ties.

- Never-married single parenthood is especially high among African-American women in their twenties. Even with help from extended family members, these mothers find it difficult to overcome poverty.

- Gay and lesbian parents are as effective at child rearing as heterosexual parents, and their children are as well-adjusted as those reared by heterosexual parents.

Career Development (p. 393)

Discuss patterns of career development, and cite difficulties faced by women, ethnic minorities, and couples seeking to combine work and family.

- Men's career paths are usually continuous, whereas women's are often interrupted by family needs. Once young adults settle into an occupation, their progress is affected by opportunities and access to an effective mentor.

- Women and ethnic minorities have penetrated most professions, but their career advancement has been hampered by time away from the labor market, low self-efficacy, lack of mentoring, and gender stereotypes. Racial and ethnic bias remains strong. Ethnic minority women who succeed display an unusually high sense of self-efficacy.

© NOEL HENDRICKSON/DIGITAL VISION/GETTY IMAGES

- Couples in dual-earner marriages often experience role overload. Effectively balancing work and family enhances standard of living, work productivity, psychological well-being, and marital happiness.

Important Terms and Concepts

cohabitation (p. 389)
companionate love (p. 377)
egalitarian marriage (p. 382)
emerging adulthood (p. 369)

family life cycle (p. 381)
intimacy versus isolation (p. 374)
passionate love (p. 377)
social clock (p. 376)

traditional marriage (p. 382)
triangular theory of love (p. 377)

milestones

Development in Early Adulthood

- Gains in cognitive–affective complexity. (359)
- Develops expertise in a field of endeavor, which enhances problem solving. (360)
- May increase in creativity. (360–361)

- As basal metabolic rate declines, gradual weight gain begins in the middle of this decade and continues through middle adulthood. (350)
- Sexual activity increases. (353–354)

COGNITIVE

- If college educated, dualistic thinking declines in favor of relativistic thinking. (358)
- Moves from hypothetical to pragmatic thought. (359)
- Narrows vocational options and settles on a specific career. (362)

EMOTIONAL/SOCIAL

- In the first half of this decade, if life circumstances permit, may engage in the extended exploration that characterizes emerging adulthood. (369–370)
- Forms a more complex self-concept that includes awareness of own changing traits and values. (370)
- Is likely to achieve a personally meaningful identity. (370)
- Leaves the parental home permanently. (381)
- Strives to make a permanent commitment to an intimate partner. (374, 376–377)

18–30 years

PHYSICAL

- Athletic skills that require speed of limb movement, explosive strength, and gross motor coordination peak early in this decade, then decline. (347–348)
- Athletic skills that depend on endurance, arm–hand steadiness, and aiming peak at the end of this decade, then decline. (347–348)
- Declines in touch sensitivity, cardiovascular and respiratory capacity, immune system functioning, and skin elasticity begin and continue throughout adulthood. (346–347)

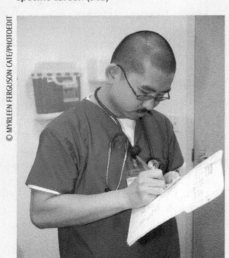

- Usually constructs a dream—an image of the self in the adult world that guides decision making. (375)

Note: Numbers in parentheses indicate the page or pages on which each milestone is discussed.

- Typically forms a relationship with a mentor. (375)
- If in a high-status career, acquires professional skills, values, and credentials. (375)
- Develops mutually gratifying adult friendships and work ties. (379–380)
- May cohabit, marry, and bear children. (382, 385–386, 389)
- Sibling relationships become more companionate. (380)

30–40 years

PHYSICAL

- Declines in vision, hearing, and the skeletal system begin and continue throughout adulthood. (347)
- In women, reproductive capacity declines, and fertility problems increase sharply after the middle of this decade. (348)

- In men, semen volume, sperm motility, and percentage of normal sperm decrease gradually in the second half of this decade. (348)
- Hair begins to gray and thin in the middle of this decade. (347)
- Sexual activity declines, probably as a result of the demands of daily life. (353–354)

COGNITIVE

- May develop commitment within relativistic thinking. (358)
- Creative accomplishment often peaks in the second half of this decade, although this varies across disciplines. (360)

EMOTIONAL/SOCIAL

- May cohabit, marry, and bear children. (382, 385–386, 389)

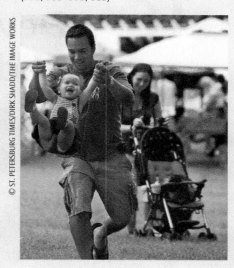

- Increasingly establishes a stable niche in society through family, occupation, and community activities. (375)

chapter 16

Emotional and Social Development in Middle Adulthood

HAGEN HOPKINS/GETTY IMAGES FOR NZOC

Midlife is a time of increased generativity—giving to and guiding younger generations. Charles Callis, director of New Zealand's Olympic Museum, shows visiting schoolchildren how to throw a discus. His enthusiastic demonstration conveys the deep sense of satisfaction he derives from generative activities.

chapter outline

Erikson's Theory: Generativity versus Stagnation

Other Theories of Psychosocial Development in Midlife

Levinson's Seasons of Life • Vaillant's Adaptation to Life • Is There a Midlife Crisis?

Stability and Change in Self-Concept and Personality

Possible Selves • Self-Acceptance, Autonomy, and Environmental Mastery • Coping with Daily Stressors • Gender Identity • Individual Differences in Personality Traits

■ **BIOLOGY AND ENVIRONMENT** What Factors Promote Psychological Well-Being in Midlife?

Relationships at Midlife

Marriage and Divorce • Changing Parent–Child Relationships • Grandparenthood • Middle-Aged Children and Their Aging Parents • Siblings • Friendships

■ **SOCIAL ISSUES: HEALTH** Grandparents Rearing Grandchildren: The Skipped-Generation Family

Vocational Life

Job Satisfaction • Career Development • Planning for Retirement

One weekend when Devin, Trisha, and their 24-year-old son, Mark, were vacationing together, the two middle-aged parents knocked on Mark's hotel room door. "Your dad and I are going off to see a crafts exhibit," Trisha explained.

"Feel free to stay behind," she offered, recalling Mark's antipathy toward attending such events as an adolescent.

"That exhibit sounds great!" Mark replied. "I'll meet you in the lobby."

"Sometimes I forget he's an adult!" exclaimed Trisha as she and Devin returned to their room to grab their coats. "It's been great to have Mark with us—like spending time with a good friend."

In their forties and fifties, Trisha and Devin built on earlier strengths and intensified their commitment to leaving a legacy for those who would come after them. When Mark faced a difficult job market after graduating from college, he returned home to live with Trisha and Devin and remained there for several years. With their support, he took graduate courses while working part-time, found steady employment in his late twenties, and married in his mid-thirties. With each milestone, Trisha and Devin felt a sense of pride at having escorted a member of the next generation into responsible adult roles. Family activities, which had declined during Mark's adolescent and college years, increased as Trisha and Devin related to their son as an enjoyable adult companion. Challenging careers and more time for community involvement, leisure pursuits, and each other contributed to a richly diverse and gratifying time of life.

The midlife years were not as smooth for two of Trisha and Devin's friends. Fearing that she might grow old alone, Jewel frantically pursued her quest for an intimate partner. She attended singles events, registered with dating services, and traveled in hopes of meeting a like-minded companion. "I can't stand the thought of turning 50," she lamented in a letter to Trisha. Jewel also had compensating satisfactions—friendships that had grown more meaningful, a warm relationship with a nephew and niece, and a successful consulting business.

Tim, Devin's best friend from graduate school, had been divorced for over five years. Recently, he had met Elena and had come to love her deeply. But in addition to her own divorce, Elena was dealing with a troubled daughter, a new career, and other life changes. Whereas Tim had reached the peak of his career and was ready to enjoy life, Elena wanted to recapture much of what she had missed in earlier decades, including opportunities to realize her talents. "I don't know where I fit into Elena's plans," Tim wondered aloud on the phone with Trisha.

Increasing awareness of limited time ahead prompts adults to reevaluate the meaning of their lives, refine and strengthen their identities, and reach out to future generations. Most make modest adjustments in their outlook, goals, and daily lives. But a few experience profound inner turbulence and initiate major changes, often in an effort to make up for lost time. Together with advancing years, family and work transitions contribute greatly to emotional and social development.

More midlifers are addressing these tasks than ever before, now that the baby boomers have reached their forties, fifties, and sixties (see page 10 in Chapter 1 to review how baby boomers have reshaped the life course). As our discussion will reveal, they have brought increased self-confidence, social consciousness, and vitality—along with great developmental diversity—to this period of the lifespan.

A monumental survey called *Midlife Development in the United States (MIDUS)*, conducted in the mid-1990s, has contributed enormously to our understanding of midlife emotional and social development. Its nationally representative sample included over 7,000 U.S. 25- to 75-year-olds, enabling those in the middle years to be compared with

PHOTOALTO/ODILON DIMIER/GETTY IMAGES

younger and older individuals. Through telephone interviews and self-administered questionnaires, participants responded to over 1,100 items addressing wide-ranging psychological, health, and background factors, yielding unprecedented breadth of information in a single study (Brim, Ryff, & Kessler, 2005). The research endeavor also included "satellite" studies, in which subsamples of respondents were questioned in greater depth on key topics. And it has been extended longitudinally, with 75 percent of the sample recontacted at first follow-up, in the mid-2000s (Radler & Ryff, 2010).

MIDUS has greatly expanded our knowledge of the *multidimensional* and *multidirectional* nature of midlife change. Hence, our discussion repeatedly draws on MIDUS, at times delving into its findings, at other times citing them alongside those of other investigations. Let's turn now to Erikson's theory and related research, to which MIDUS has contributed. ●

Erikson's Theory: Generativity versus Stagnation

Erikson's psychological conflict of midlife is called **generativity versus stagnation.** Generativity involves reaching out to others in ways that give to and guide the next generation. It is under way in early adulthood through work, community service, and childbearing and child rearing. Generativity expands greatly in midlife, when adults focus more intently on extending commitments beyond oneself and one's life partner to a larger group—family, community, or society (McAdams & Logan, 2004). The generative adult combines the need for self-expression with the need for communion, integrating personal goals with the welfare of the larger social world.

Erikson (1950) selected the term *generativity* to encompass everything generated that can outlive the self and ensure society's continuity and improvement: children, ideas, products,

Through his work with severely malnourished children in Niger, this nurse, affiliated with the Nobel Prize–winning organization Doctors Without Borders, integrates personal goals with a broader concern for society.

works of art. Although parenting is a major means of realizing generativity, it is not the only means: Adults can be generative in other family relationships (as Jewel was with her nephew and niece), as mentors in the workplace, in volunteer endeavors, and through many forms of productivity and creativity.

Notice, from what we have said so far, that generativity brings together personal desires and cultural demands. On the personal side, middle-aged adults feel a need to be needed—to attain symbolic immortality by making a contribution that will survive their death (Kotre, 1999; McAdams, Hart, & Maruna, 1998). This desire may stem from a deep-seated evolutionary urge to protect and advance the next generation. On the cultural side, society imposes a social clock for generativity in midlife, requiring adults to take responsibility for the next generation through their roles as parents, teachers, mentors, leaders, and coordinators (McAdams & Logan, 2004). And according to Erikson, a culture's "belief in the species"—the conviction that life is good and worthwhile, even in the face of human destructiveness and deprivation—is a major motivator of generative action, which has improving humanity as its goal.

The negative outcome of this stage is stagnation: Once people attain certain life goals, such as marriage, children, and career success, they may become self-centered and self-indulgent. Adults may express a sense of stagnation in many ways—through lack of interest in young people (including their own children), through a focus on what they can get from others rather than what they can give, and through taking little interest in being productive at work, developing their talents, or bettering the world in other ways.

Much research indicates that generativity tends to increase in midlife. For example, in longitudinal and cross-sectional studies of college-educated women, and in an investigation of middle-aged adults diverse in SES, self-rated generativity rose throughout middle adulthood (see Figure 16.1). At the same time, participants expressed greater concern about aging, increased security with their identities, and a stronger sense of competence (Miner-Rubino, Winter, & Stewart, 2004; Newton & Stewart, 2010; Stewart, Ostrove, & Helson, 2001; Zucker, Ostrove, & Stewart, 2002).

Just as Erikson's theory suggests, highly generative people appear especially well-adjusted—low in anxiety and depression; high in autonomy, self-acceptance, and life satisfaction; and more likely to have successful marriages and close friends (Ackerman, Zuroff, & Moskowitz, 2000; An & Cooney, 2006; Grossbaum & Bates, 2002; Westermeyer, 2004). They are also more open to differing viewpoints, possess leadership qualities, desire more from work than financial rewards, and care greatly about the welfare of their children, their partner, their aging parents, and the wider society (Peterson, 2002; Peterson, Smirles, & Wentworth, 1997). Furthermore, generativity is associated with more effective child rearing—higher valuing of trust, open communication, transmission of generative values to children, and an authoritative style (Peterson, 2006; Peterson & Duncan, 2007; Pratt et al., 2008).

Although these findings characterize adults of all backgrounds, individual differences in contexts for generativity exist. Having children seems to foster generative development in both men and women. In several studies, including the MIDUS survey, fathers scored higher in generativity than childless men (Marks, Bumpass, & Jun, 2004; McAdams & de St. Aubin, 1992; Snarey et al., 1987). Similarly, in an investigation of well-educated women from ages 43 to 63, those with family commit-

FIGURE 16.1 Age-related changes in self-rated generativity, concern about aging, identity security, and sense of competence. In a longitudinal study of over 300 college-educated women, self-rated generativity increased from the thirties to the fifties, as did concern about aging. The rise in generativity was accompanied by other indicators of psychological health—greater security with one's identity and sense of competence. (Adapted from Stewart, Ostrove, & Helson, 2001.)

ments (with or without a career) expressed greater generative concerns than childless women who were solely focused on their careers (Newton & Stewart, 2010). Parenting seems to spur especially tender, caring attitudes toward succeeding generations.

For low-SES men with troubled pasts, fatherhood can provide a context for highly generative, positive life change (Roy & Lucas, 2006). As one former gang member, who earned an associate's degree and struggled to keep his teenage sons off the streets, explained, "I came through the depths of hell to try to be a father. I let my sons know, 'You're never without a daddy, don't you let anybody tell you that.' I tell them that if me and your mother separate, I make sure that wherever I go, I build something for you to come to" (p. 153).

Finally, compared with Caucasians, African Americans more often engage in certain types of generativity. They are more involved in religious groups and activities, offer more social support to members of their community, and are more likely to view themselves as role models and sources of wisdom for their children (Hart et al., 2001). A life history of strong support from church and extended family may strengthen these generative values and actions. Among Caucasian Americans, religiosity and spirituality are also linked to greater generative activity (Dillon & Wink, 2004; Son & Wilson, 2011; Wink & Dillon, 2008). Highly generative middle-aged adults often indicate that as children and adolescents, they internalized moral values rooted in a religious tradition and sustained their commitment to those values, which provided lifelong encouragement for generative action (McAdams, 2006). Especially in individualistic societies, belonging to a religious community or believing in a higher being may help preserve generative commitments.

Other Theories of Psychosocial Development in Midlife

Erikson's broad sketch of psychosocial change in midlife has been extended by Levinson and Vaillant. Let's revisit their theories, which were introduced in Chapter 14.

Levinson's Seasons of Life

Return to page 375 to review Levinson's eras (seasons of life). His interviews with adults revealed that middle adulthood begins with a transition, during which people evaluate their success in meeting early adulthood goals. Realizing that from now on, more time will lie behind than ahead, they regard the remaining years as increasingly precious. Consequently, some make drastic revisions in their life structure: divorcing, remarrying, changing careers, or displaying enhanced creativity. Others make smaller changes in the context of marital and occupational stability.

Whether these years bring a gust of wind or a storm, most people turn inward for a time, focusing on personally meaning-

ful living (Neugarten, 1968b). According to Levinson, to reassess and rebuild their life structure, middle-aged adults must confront four developmental tasks. Each requires the individual to reconcile two opposing tendencies within the self, attaining greater internal harmony.

- *Young–old:* The middle-age person must seek new ways of being both young and old. This means giving up certain youthful qualities, transforming others, and finding positive meaning in being older. Perhaps because of the double standard of aging (see page 412 in Chapter 15), most middle-aged women express concern about appearing less attractive as they grow older (Rossi, 2005). But middle-aged men—particularly non-college-educated men, who often hold blue-collar jobs requiring physical strength and stamina—are also highly sensitive to physical aging (Miner-Rubino, Winter, & Stewart, 2004).

  Compared with previous midlife cohorts, U.S. baby boomers are especially interested in controlling physical changes—a desire that has helped energize a huge industry of anti-aging cosmetic products and medical procedures (Jones, Whitbourne, & Skultety, 2006; Lachman, 2004). And sustaining a youthful *subjective age* (feeling younger than one's actual age) is more strongly related to self-esteem and psychological well-being among American than Western-European middle-aged and older adults (Westerhof & Barrett, 2005; Westerhof, Whitbourne, & Freeman, 2012). In the more individualistic U.S. context, a youthful self-image seems more important for viewing oneself as self-reliant and capable of planning for an active, fulfilling late adulthood.

- *Destruction–creation:* With greater awareness of mortality, the middle-aged person focuses on ways he or she has acted destructively. Past hurtful acts toward parents, intimate partners, children, friends, and co-workers are countered by a strong desire to participate in activities that advance human welfare and leave a legacy for future generations. The image of a legacy can be satisfied in many ways—through charitable gifts, creative products, volunteer service, or mentoring young people.

- *Masculinity–femininity:* The middle-aged person must create a better balance between "masculine" and "feminine" parts of the self. For men, this means greater acceptance of traits of nurturance and caring, which enhance close relationships and compassionate exercise of authority in the workplace. For women, it generally means being more open to characteristics of autonomy and assertiveness. Recall from Chapter 8 that people who combine masculine and feminine traits have an androgynous gender identity. Later we will see that androgyny is associated with favorable adjustment.

- *Engagement–separateness:* The middle-aged person must forge a better balance between engagement with the external world and separateness. For many men, and for women who have had successful careers, this may mean reducing concern with ambition and achievement and attending more fully to oneself. But women who have been devoted to child rearing or an unfulfilling job often feel compelled to move in the other direction (Levinson, 1996). At age 48, Elena left her position as a reporter for a small-town newspaper, pursued an advanced degree in creative writing, accepted a college teaching position, and began writing a novel. Tim, in contrast, recognized his overwhelming desire for a gratifying romantic partnership. By scaling back his own career, he realized he could grant Elena the time and space she needed to build a rewarding work life.

People who flexibly modify their identities in response to age-related changes yet maintain a sense of self-continuity are more aware of their own thoughts and feelings and are higher in self-esteem and life satisfaction (Jones, Whitbourne, & Skultety, 2006; Sneed et al., 2012). But when poverty, unemployment, and lack of a respected place in society dominate the life course, energies are directed toward survival rather than realistically approaching age-related changes. And even adults whose jobs are secure and who live in pleasant neighborhoods may find that employment conditions restrict possibilities for growth by placing too much emphasis on productivity and profit and too little on the meaning of work. In her early forties, Trisha left a large law firm, where she felt constant pressure to bring in high-fee clients and received little acknowledgment of her efforts, for a small practice.

Opportunities for advancement ease the transition to middle adulthood. Yet these are far less available to women than to men. Individuals of both sexes in blue-collar jobs also have few possibilities for promotion (Christensen & Larsen, 2008). Many men find compensating rewards in moving to the senior generation of their families.

Vaillant's Adaptation to Life

Whereas Levinson interviewed 35- to 45-year-olds, Vaillant (1977, 2002)—in his longitudinal research on well-educated men and women—followed participants past the half-century mark. Recall from Chapter 14 how adults in their late fifties and sixties extend their generativity, becoming "keepers of meaning," or guardians of their culture (see page 375). "Passing the torch"—concern that the positive aspects of their culture survive—became a major preoccupation.

In societies around the world, older people are guardians of traditions, laws, and cultural values. This stabilizing force holds in check too-rapid change sparked by the questioning and challenging of adolescents and young adults. As people approach the end of middle age, they focus on longer-term, less-personal goals, such as the state of human relations in their society. And they become more philosophical, accepting the fact that not all problems can be solved in their lifetime.

Is There a Midlife Crisis?

Levinson (1978, 1996) reported that most men and women in his samples experienced substantial inner turmoil during the transition to middle adulthood. Yet Vaillant (1977, 2002) saw few examples of crisis but, rather, slow and steady change. These contrasting findings raise the question of how much personal upheaval actually accompanies entry to midlife. Are self-doubt and stress especially great during the forties, and do they prompt major restructuring of the personality, as the term **midlife crisis** implies?

Consider the reactions of Trisha, Devin, Jewel, Tim, and Elena to middle adulthood. Trisha and Devin moved easily into this period, whereas Jewel, Tim, and Elena sought alternative life paths. Clearly, wide individual differences exist in response to midlife. *TAKE A MOMENT...* Now ask several individuals in their twenties and thirties whether they expect to encounter a midlife crisis between ages 40 and 50. You are likely to find that Americans often anticipate it, perhaps because of culturally induced apprehension of aging (Wethington, Kessler, & Pixley, 2004). Yet little evidence supports this view of middle age as a turbulent time.

When MIDUS participants were asked to describe "turning points" (major changes in the way they felt about an important aspect of their lives) that had occurred during the past five years, most of the ones reported concerned work. Women's work-related turning points peaked in early adulthood, when many adjusted their work lives to accommodate marriage and childrearing (see Chapter 14). The peak for men, in contrast, came at midlife, a time of increased career responsibility and advancement. Other common turning points in early and middle adulthood were positive: They involved fulfilling a dream and learning something good about oneself (Wethington, Kessler, & Pixley, 2004). Overall, turning points rarely resembled midlife crises. Even negative work-related turning points generally led to personal growth—for example, a layoff that

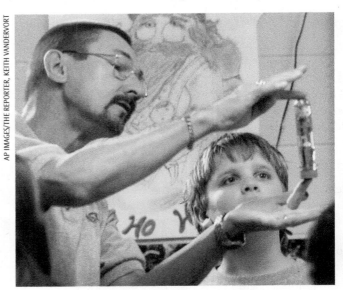

Like many midlifers, elementary school teacher Jaime Malwitz modified his career in ways that resemble a turning point, not a crisis. He designed a scientist-in-residence program for elementary schools. Here he serves as a resident physicist, discussing a density experiment with a fifth grader.

sparked a positive career change or a shift in energy from career to personal life.

Asked directly if they had ever experienced something they would consider a midlife crisis, only one-fourth of the MIDUS respondents said yes. And they defined such events much more loosely than researchers do. Some reported a crisis well before age 40, others well after age 50. And most attributed it not to age but rather to challenging life events (Wethington, 2000).

Another way of exploring midlife questioning is to ask adults about life regrets—attractive opportunities for career or other life-changing activities they did not pursue or lifestyle changes they did not make. In two investigations of women in their early forties, those who acknowledged regret without making life changes, compared to those who modified their lives, reported less favorable psychological well-being and poorer physical health over time (Landman et al., 1995; Stewart & Vandewater, 1999).

By late midlife, with less time ahead to make life changes, people's interpretation of regrets plays a major role in their well-being. Mature, contented adults acknowledge a past characterized by some losses but are able to disengage from them, investing in current, personally rewarding goals (King & Hicks, 2007). Among a sample of several hundred 60- to 65-year-olds diverse in SES, about half expressed at least one regret. Compared to those who had not resolved their disappointments, those who had come to terms with them (accepted and identified some eventual benefits) or had "put the best face on things" (identified benefits but still had some lingering regret) reported better physical health and greater life satisfaction (Torges, Stewart, & Miner-Rubino, 2005).

In sum, life evaluation is common during middle age. Most people make changes that are best described as turning points rather than drastic alterations of their lives. Those who cannot modify their life paths often look for the "silver lining" in life's difficulties (King & Hicks, 2007; Wethington, Kessler, & Pixley, 2004). The few midlifers who are in crisis typically have had early adulthoods in which gender roles, family pressures, or low income and poverty severely limited their ability to fulfill personal needs and goals, at home or in the wider world.

ASK YOURSELF

REVIEW What personal and cultural forces motivate generativity? Why does it increase and contribute vitally to favorable adjustment in midlife?

APPLY After years of experiencing little personal growth at work, 42-year-old Mel looked for a new job and received an attractive offer in another city. Although he was distressed at moving away from extended family and close friends, after several weeks of soul searching, he took the new job. Was Mel's dilemma a midlife crisis? Why or why not?

REFLECT Think of a middle-aged adult whom you admire. Describe the various ways that individual expresses generativity.

Stability and Change in Self-Concept and Personality

Midlife changes in self-concept and personality reflect growing awareness of a finite lifespan, longer life experience, and generative concerns. Yet certain aspects of personality remain stable, revealing the persistence of individual differences established during earlier periods.

Possible Selves

On a business trip, Jewel found a spare afternoon to visit Trisha. Sitting in a coffee shop, the two women reminisced about the past and thought aloud about the future. "It's been tough living on my own and building the business," Jewel said. "What I hope for is to become better at my work, to be more community-oriented, and to stay healthy and available to my friends. Of course, I would rather not grow old alone, but if I don't find that special person, I suppose I can take comfort in the fact that I'll never have to face divorce or widowhood."

Jewel is discussing **possible selves,** future-oriented representations of what one hopes to become and what one is afraid of becoming. Possible selves are the temporal dimension of self-concept—what the individual is striving for and attempting to avoid. To lifespan researchers, these hopes and fears are just as vital in explaining behavior as people's views of their current characteristics. Indeed, possible selves may be an especially strong motivator of action in midlife, as adults attach increased meaning to time (Frazier & Hooker, 2006). As we age, we may rely less on social comparisons in judging our self-worth and more on temporal comparisons—how well we are doing in relation to what we had planned.

Throughout adulthood, the personality traits people assign to their current selves show considerable stability. A 30-year-old who says he is cooperative, competent, outgoing, or successful is likely to report a similar picture at a later age. But reports of possible selves change greatly. Adults in their early twenties mention many possible selves, and their visions are lofty and idealistic—being "perfectly happy," "rich and famous," "healthy throughout life," and not being "a person who does nothing important." With age, possible selves become fewer in number and more modest and concrete. They are largely concerned with performance of roles and responsibilities already begun—"being competent at work," "being a good husband and father," "putting my children through college," "staying healthy," and not being "a burden to my family" (Bybee & Wells, 2003; Cross & Markus, 1991; Ryff, 1991).

What explains these shifts in possible selves? Because the future no longer holds limitless opportunities, adults preserve mental health by adjusting their hopes and fears. To stay motivated, they must maintain a sense of unachieved possibility, yet they must still manage to feel good about themselves and their lives despite disappointments (Bolkan & Hooker, 2012). For example, although Jewel feared loneliness in old age, she reminded herself that marriage can lead to equally negative outcomes, such as divorce and widowhood—possibilities that made not having attained an important interpersonal goal easier to bear.

Self-Acceptance, Autonomy, and Environmental Mastery

An evolving mix of competencies and experiences leads to changes in certain aspects of personality during middle adulthood. In Chapter 15, we noted that midlife brings gains in expertise and practical problem solving. Middle-aged adults also offer more complex, integrated descriptions of themselves than do younger and older individuals (Labouvie-Vief, 2003). Furthermore, midlife is typically a period in which the number of social roles peaks—spouse, parent, worker, and engaged community member. And status at work and in the community typically rises, as adults take advantage of opportunities for leadership and other complex responsibilities (Helson, Soto, & Cate, 2006).

These changes in cognition and breadth of roles undoubtedly contribute to other gains in personal functioning. In research on adults ranging in age from the late teens into the seventies, and in cultures as distinct as the United States and Japan, three qualities increased from early to middle adulthood:

- *Self-acceptance:* More than young adults, middle-aged people acknowledged and accepted both their good and bad qualities and felt positively about themselves and life.
- *Autonomy:* Middle-aged adults saw themselves as less concerned about others' expectations and evaluations and more concerned with following self-chosen standards.
- *Environmental mastery:* Middle-aged people saw themselves as capable of managing a complex array of tasks easily and effectively (Karasawa et al., 2011; Ryff & Keyes, 1995).

As these findings indicate, midlife is generally a time of increased comfort with the self, independence, assertiveness, commitment to personal values, and life satisfaction (Helson, Jones, & Kwan, 2002; Keyes, Shmotkin, & Ryff, 2002; Stone et al., 2010). Perhaps because of this rise in overall psychological well-being, middle age is sometimes referred to as "the prime of life."

At the same time, factors contributing to psychological well-being differ substantially among cohorts, as self-reports gathered from 25- to 65-year-old MIDUS survey respondents reveal (Carr, 2004). Among women who were born during the baby-boom years or later, and who thus benefited from the women's movement, balancing career with family predicted greater self-acceptance and environmental mastery. But also consider that women born before or during World War II who sacrificed career to focus on child rearing—expected of young mothers in the 1950s and 1960s—were similarly advantaged in

self-acceptance. Likewise, men who were in step with prevailing social expectations scored higher in well-being. Baby-boom and younger men who modified their work schedules to make room for family responsibilities—who fit their cohort's image of the "good father"—were more self-accepting. But older men who made this accommodation scored much lower in self-acceptance than those who focused on work and thus conformed to the "good provider" ideal of their times. (See the Biology and Environment box on the following page for additional influences on midlife psychological well-being.)

Coping with Daily Stressors

In a MIDUS satellite study in which more than 1,000 participants were interviewed on eight consecutive evenings, researchers found an early- to mid-adulthood plateau in frequency of daily stressors, followed by a decline as work and family responsibilities ease and leisure time increases (Almeida & Horn, 2004). Compared with older people, young and midlife adults also perceived their stressors as more disruptive and unpleasant, perhaps because they often experienced several at once, and many involved financial risks and children.

But recall from Chapter 15 that midlife brings an increase in effective coping strategies. Middle-aged individuals are more likely to identify the positive side of difficult situations, postpone action to permit evaluation of alternatives, anticipate and plan ways to handle future discomforts, and use humor to express ideas and feelings without offending others (Diehl, Coyle, & Labouvie-Vief, 1996). Notice how these efforts flexibly draw on both problem-centered and emotion-centered strategies.

Why might effective coping increase in middle adulthood? Other personality changes seem to support it. Complex, integrated self-descriptions—which increase in midlife, indicating an improved ability to blend strengths and weaknesses into an organized picture—predict a stronger sense of personal control over outcomes and good coping strategies (Hay & Diehl, 2010; Labouvie-Vief & Diehl, 2000). Midlife gains in emotional stability and confidence in handling life's problems may also contribute (Roberts et al., 2007; Roberts & Mroczek, 2008). These attributes predict work and relationship effectiveness—outcomes that reflect the sophisticated, flexible coping of middle age.

Gender Identity

In her forties and early fifties, Trisha appeared more assertive at work, taking on leadership roles and speaking out freely. She was also more dominant in family relationships, expressing her opinions to her husband and son more readily than she had 10 or 15 years earlier. In contrast, Devin's sense of empathy and caring became more apparent, and he was less assertive and more accommodating to Trisha's wishes.

Many studies report an increase in "masculine" traits in women and "feminine" traits in men across middle age (Huyck, 1990; James et al., 1995). Women become more confident, self-sufficient, and forceful, men more emotionally sensitive, caring,

Biology and Environment

What Factors Promote Psychological Well-Being in Midlife?

These yoga students express a sense of purpose and accomplishment. Maintaining an exercise regimen contributes greatly to midlife psychological well-being.

What factors contribute to individual differences in psychological well-being at midlife? Consistent with the lifespan perspective, biological, psychological, and social forces are involved, and their effects are interwoven.

Good Health and Exercise

Good health affects energy and zest for life at any age. But during middle and late adulthood, taking steps to improve health and prevent disability becomes a better predictor of psychological well-being. Many studies confirm that engaging in regular exercise—walking, dancing, jogging, or swimming—is more strongly associated with self-rated health and a positive outlook in older than in younger adults (Bherer, 2012). Middle-aged people who maintain an exercise regimen are likely to perceive themselves as particularly active for their age and, therefore, to feel a special sense of accomplishment (Netz et al., 2005). In addition, physical activity enhances self-efficacy and effective stress management (see page 411 in Chapter 15).

Sense of Control and Personal Life Investment

Middle-aged adults who report a high sense of control over events in various aspects of their lives—health, family, and work—also report more favorable psychological well-being. Sense of control contributes further to self-efficacy. It also predicts use of more effective coping strategies, including seeking of social support, and thereby helps sustain a positive outlook in the face of health, family, and work difficulties (Lachman, Neupert, & Agrigoroaei, 2011).

Personal life investment—firm commitment to goals and involvement in pursuit of those goals—also adds to mental health and life satisfaction (Staudinger & Bowen, 2010). According to Mihaly Csikszentmihalyi, a vital wellspring of happiness is *flow*—the psychological state of being so engrossed in a demanding, meaningful activity that one loses all sense of time and self-awareness.

People describe flow as the height of enjoyment, even as an ecstatic state. The more people experience flow, the more they judge their lives to be gratifying (Nakamura & Csikszentmihalyi, 2009). Flow depends on perseverance and skill at complex endeavors that offer potential for growth. These qualities are well-developed in middle adulthood.

Close Friendships and a Good Marriage

Supportive friendships improve mental health by promoting positive emotions and protecting against stress (Fiori, Antonucci, & Cortina, 2006; Powdthavee, 2008). In a survey of college alumni, those who preferred occupational prestige and high income to close friends were twice as likely as other respondents to describe themselves as "fairly" or "very" unhappy (Perkins, 1991, as cited by Myers, 2000).

A good marriage boosts psychological well-being even more. When interviews with over 13,000 U.S. adults were repeated five years later, people who remained married reported greater happiness than those who remained single. Those who separated or divorced became less happy, reporting considerable depression (Marks & Lambert, 1998). The role of marriage in mental health increases with age, becoming a powerful predictor by late midlife (Marks, Bumpass, & Jun, 2004; Marks & Greenfield, 2009).

Although not everyone is better off married, the link between marriage and well-being is similar in many nations, suggesting that marriage changes people's behavior in ways that make them better off (Diener et al., 2000; Lansford et al., 2005). Married partners monitor each other's health and offer care in times of illness. They also earn and save more money than single people,

and higher income is modestly linked to psychological well-being (Myers, 2000). Furthermore, sexual satisfaction predicts mental health, and married couples have more satisfying sex lives than singles (see Chapter 13).

Mastery of Multiple Roles

Success in handling multiple roles—spouse, parent, worker, community volunteer—is linked to psychological well-being. In the MIDUS survey, as role involvement increased, both men and women reported greater environmental mastery, more rewarding social relationships, heightened sense of purpose in life, and more positive emotion. Furthermore, adults who occupied multiple roles and who also reported high control (suggesting effective role management) scored especially high in well-being—an outcome that was stronger for less-educated adults (Ahrens & Ryff, 2006). Control over roles may be vital for individuals with lower educational attainment, whose role combinations may be particularly stressful and who have fewer economic resources.

Finally, among nonfamily roles, community volunteering in the latter part of midlife contributes uniquely to psychological well-being (Choi & Kim, 2011; Ryff et al., 2012). It may do so by strengthening self-efficacy, generativity, and altruism.

In middle age, gender identity becomes more androgynous for both sexes. Men tend to show an increase in "feminine" traits, becoming more emotionally sensitive, caring, considerate, and dependent.

considerate, and dependent. These trends appear in not just Western industrialized nations but also village societies such as the Maya of Guatemala, the Navajo of the United States, and the Druze of the Middle East (Fry, 1985; Gutmann, 1977; Turner, 1982). Consistent with Levinson's theory, gender identity in midlife becomes more androgynous—a mixture of "masculine" and "feminine" characteristics.

Although the existence of these changes is well-accepted, explanations for them are controversial. A well-known evolutionary view, **parental imperative theory**, holds that identification with traditional gender roles is maintained during the active parenting years to help ensure the survival of children. Men become more goal-oriented, while women emphasize nurturance (Gutmann & Huyck, 1994). After children reach adulthood, parents are free to express the "other-gender" side of their personalities.

But this biological account has been criticized. As discussed in earlier chapters, parents need both warmth and assertiveness (in the form of firmness and consistency) to rear children effectively. And although children's departure from the home is related to men's openness to the "feminine" side of their personalities, the link to a rise in "masculine" traits among women is less apparent (Huyck, 1996, 1998). In longitudinal research, college-educated women in the labor force became more independent by their early forties, regardless of whether they had children (Helson & Picano, 1990; Wink & Helson, 1993). Furthermore, cohort effects can contribute to this trend: In one study, middle-aged women of the baby-boom generation—who experienced new career opportunities as a result of the women's movement—more often described themselves as having masculine and androgynous traits than did older women (Strough et al., 2007).

Additional demands of midlife may prompt a more androgynous orientation. For example, among men, a need to enrich a marital relationship after children have departed, along with reduced chances for career advancement, may be involved in the awakening of emotionally sensitive traits. Women are far more likely than men to face economic and social disadvantages. A greater number remain divorced, are widowed, and encounter discrimination in the workplace. Self-reliance and assertiveness are vital for coping with these circumstances.

In adulthood, androgyny is associated with cognitive flexibility, creativity, advanced moral reasoning, and psychosocial maturity (Prager & Bailey, 1985; Runco, Cramond, & Pagnani, 2010; Waterman & Whitbourne, 1982). People who integrate the masculine and feminine sides of their personalities tend to be psychologically healthier, perhaps because they are able to adapt more easily to the challenges of aging.

Individual Differences in Personality Traits

Although Trisha and Jewel both became more self-assured and assertive in midlife, in other respects they differed. Trisha had always been more organized and hard-working, Jewel more gregarious and fun-loving. Once, the two women traveled together. At the end of each day, Trisha was disappointed if she had not kept to a schedule and visited every tourist attraction. Jewel liked to "play it by ear"—wandering through streets and stopping to talk with shopkeepers and residents.

In previous sections, we considered personality changes common to many middle-aged adults, but stable individual differences also exist. The hundreds of personality traits on which people differ have been reduced to five basic factors, often referred to as the **"big five" personality traits**: neuroticism, extroversion, openness to experience, agreeableness, and conscientiousness. Table 16.1 provides a description of each. Notice that Trisha is high in conscientiousness, whereas Jewel is high in extroversion.

Longitudinal and cross-sectional studies of U.S. men and women in many countries reveal that agreeableness and conscientiousness increase from the teenage years through middle age, whereas neuroticism declines, and extroversion and openness to experience do not change or decrease slightly—changes that reflect "settling down" and greater maturity (McCrae & Costa, 2006; Roberts, Walton, & Viechtbauer, 2006; Schmitt et al., 2007; Soto et al., 2011; Srivastava et al., 2003). The consistency of these cross-cultural findings has led some researchers to conclude that adult personality change is genetically influenced. They note that individual differences in the "big five" traits are large and highly stable: A person who scores high or low at one age is likely to do the same at another, over intervals ranging from 3 to 30 years (McCrae & Costa, 2006).

How can there be high stability in personality traits, yet significant changes in aspects of personality discussed earlier? Theorists concerned with change due to experience focus on how personal needs and life events induce new strategies and goals; their interest is in "the human being as a complex adaptive system" (Block, 2011, p. 19). In contrast, those who emphasize stability due to heredity measure personality traits on which individuals can easily be compared and that are present at any time of life.

TABLE 16.1

The "Big Five" Personality Traits

TRAIT	DESCRIPTION
Neuroticism	Individuals who are high on this trait are worrying, temperamental, self-pitying, self-conscious, emotional, and vulnerable. Individuals who are low are calm, even-tempered, self-content, comfortable, unemotional, and hardy.
Extroversion	Individuals who are high on this trait are affectionate, talkative, active, fun-loving, and passionate. Individuals who are low are reserved, quiet, passive, sober, and emotionally unreactive.
Openness to experience	Individuals who are high on this trait are imaginative, creative, original, curious, and liberal. Individuals who are low are down-to-earth, uncreative, conventional, uncurious, and conservative.
Agreeableness	Individuals who are high on this trait are soft-hearted, trusting, generous, acquiescent, lenient, and good-natured. Individuals who are low are ruthless, suspicious, stingy, antagonistic, critical, and irritable.
Conscientiousness	Individuals who are high on this trait are conscientious, hard-working, well-organized, punctual, ambitious, and persevering. Individuals who are low are negligent, lazy, disorganized, late, aimless, and nonpersistent.

Source: McCrae, 2011; McCrae & Costa, 2006.

To resolve this apparent contradiction, we can think of adults as changing in overall organization and integration of personality but doing so on a foundation of basic, enduring dispositions that support a coherent sense of self as people adapt to changing life circumstances. When more than 2,000 individuals in their forties were asked to reflect on their personalities during the previous six years, 52 percent said they had "stayed the same," 39 percent said they had "changed a little," and 9 percent said they had "changed a lot" (Herbst et al., 2000). Again, these findings contradict a view of middle adulthood as a period of great turmoil and change. But they also underscore that personality remains an "open system," responsive to the pressures of life experiences. Indeed, certain midlife personality changes may strengthen trait consistency! Improved self-understanding, self-acceptance, and skill at handling challenging situations can result in less need to modify basic personality dispositions over time.

ASK YOURSELF

REVIEW Summarize personality changes at midlife. How can these changes be reconciled with increasing stability of the "big five" personality traits?

APPLY Jeff, age 46, suggested to his wife, Julia, that they set aside time once a year to discuss their relationship—both positive aspects and ways to improve. Julia was surprised because Jeff had never before expressed interest in working on their marriage. What midlife developments probably fostered this new concern?

REFLECT List your hoped-for and feared possible selves. Then ask family members in early and middle adulthood to do the same. Are their reports consistent with age-related research findings? Explain.

 ## Relationships at Midlife

The emotional and social changes of midlife take place within a complex web of family relationships and friendships. Although some middle-aged people live alone, the vast majority—87 percent in the United States—live in families, most with a spouse (U.S. Census Bureau, 2013). Partly because they have ties to older and younger generations in their families and partly because their friendships are well-established, people tend to have a larger number of close relationships during midlife than at any other period (Antonucci, Akiyama, & Takahashi, 2004).

The middle adulthood phase of the family life cycle is often referred to as "launching children and moving on." In the past, it was called the "empty nest," but this phrase implies a negative transition, especially for women who have devoted themselves entirely to their children and for whom the end of active parenting can trigger feelings of emptiness and regret. But for most people, middle adulthood is a liberating time, offering a sense of completion and opportunities to strengthen social ties and rekindle interests.

As our discussion in Chapter 14 revealed, increasing numbers of young adults are living at home because of tight job markets and financial challenges, yielding launch–return–relaunch patterns for many middle-aged parents. As adult children depart and marry, middle-aged parents must adapt to new roles of parent-in-law and grandparent. At the same time, they must establish a different type of relationship with their aging parents, who may become ill or infirm and die.

Middle adulthood is marked by the greatest number of exits and entries of family members. Let's see how ties within and beyond the family change during this period of life.

Marriage and Divorce

Although not all couples are financially comfortable, middle-aged households are well-off compared with other age groups.

LORI ADAMSKI PEEK/WORKBOOK STOCK/GETTY IMAGES

For many middle-aged couples, having forged a relationship that permits satisfaction of both family and individual needs results in deep feelings of love.

Americans between 45 and 54 have the highest average annual income. And the baby boomers—more of whom have earned college and postgraduate degrees and live in dual-earner families—are financially better off than previous midlife generations (Eggebeen & Sturgeon, 2006; U.S. Census Bureau, 2013). Partly because of increased education and financial security, the contemporary social view of marriage in midlife is one of expansion and new horizons.

These forces strengthen the need to review and adjust the marital relationship. For Devin and Trisha, this shift was gradual. By middle age, their marriage had permitted satisfaction of family and individual needs, endured many changes, and culminated in deeper feelings of love. Elena's marriage, in contrast, became more conflict-ridden as her teenage daughter's problems introduced added strains and as departure of children made marital difficulties more obvious. Tim's failed marriage revealed yet another pattern. With passing years, the number of problems declined, but so did the love expressed (Rokach, Cohen, & Dreman, 2004). As less happened in the relationship, good or bad, the couple had little to keep them together.

As the Biology and Environment box on page 429 revealed, marital satisfaction is a strong predictor of midlife psychological well-being. As in early adulthood, divorce is one way of resolving an unsatisfactory marriage. The divorce rate of U.S. 50- to 65-year-olds has doubled over the past two decades (Brown & Lin, 2012). Divorce at any age takes a heavy psychological toll, but midlifers seem to adapt more easily than younger people (Marks & Lambert, 1998). Midlife gains in practical problem solving and effective coping strategies may reduce the stressful impact of divorce.

Nevertheless, for many women, marital breakup—especially when it is repeated—severely reduces standard of living (see page 275 in Chapter 10). For this reason, in midlife and earlier, it is a strong contributor to the **feminization of poverty**—a trend in which women who support themselves or their families have become the majority of the adult population living in poverty, regardless of age and ethnic group. Because of weak public policies safeguarding families (see Chapter 2), the gender gap in poverty is higher in the United States than in other Western industrialized nations (U.S. Census Bureau, 2013).

Longitudinal evidence reveals that middle-aged women who weather divorce successfully tend to become more tolerant, comfortable with uncertainty, nonconforming, and self-reliant in personality—factors believed to be fostered by divorce-forced independence. And both men and women reevaluate what they consider important in a healthy relationship, placing greater weight on equal friendship and less on passionate love than they had the first time (Baum, Rahav, & Sharon, 2005; Schneller & Arditti, 2004). Little is known about long-term adjustment following divorce among middle-aged men, perhaps because most enter new relationships and remarry within a short time.

Changing Parent–Child Relationships

Parents' positive relationships with their grown children are the result of a gradual process of "letting go," starting in childhood, gaining momentum in adolescence, and culminating in children's independent living. As mentioned earlier, most middle-aged parents adjust well to the launching phase of the family life cycle (Mitchell & Lovegreen, 2009). Investment in nonparental relationships and roles, children's characteristics, parents' marital and economic circumstances, and cultural forces affect the extent to which this transition is expansive and rewarding or sad and distressing.

After their son Mark secured a career-entry job and moved out of the family home permanently, Devin and Trisha felt a twinge of nostalgia. Beyond this, they returned to rewarding careers and community participation and delighted in having more time for each other.

Wide cultural variations exist in the social clock for children's departure. Recall from Chapter 13 that many young people from low-SES homes and with cultural traditions of extended-family living do not leave home early. In the southern European countries of Greece, Italy, and Spain, parents often actively delay their children's leaving. In Italy, for example, parents believe that moving out without a "justified" reason signifies that something is wrong in the family. Hence, many more Italian young adults reside with their parents until marriage than in other Western nations. At the same time, Italian parent–adult-child relationships are usually positive, making shared living attractive (Rusconi, 2004).

With the end of parent–child coresidence, parental authority declines sharply. But continued positive communication is important to middle-aged adults. Departure of children is a relatively minor event as long as parent–child contact and affection are sustained (Mitchell & Lovegreen, 2009). When it results in little or no communication or persistent conflict, parents' psychological well-being declines.

Whether or not they reside with parents, adolescent and young-adult children who are "off-time" in development— who deviate from parental expectations about how the path to adult responsibilities should unfold—can prompt parental strain (Fingerman et al., 2012a; Settersten, 2003). Consider Elena, whose daughter was doing poorly in her college courses and in danger of not graduating. The need for extensive parental guidance, at a time when she expected her daughter to be more responsible and independent, caused anxiety and unhappiness for Elena.

Throughout middle adulthood, parents continue to give more assistance to children than they receive, especially while children are unmarried or when they face difficulties, such as marital breakup or unemployment. Support in Western countries typically flows "downstream": Although ethnic variations exist, most middle-aged parents provide more financial, practical, emotional, and social support to their offspring than to their aging parents, unless a parent has an urgent need (declining health or other crises) (Fingerman & Birditt, 2011; Fingerman et al., 2011a). In explaining their generous support of adult children, parents usually mention the importance of the relationship. And providing adult children with assistance enhances midlife psychological well-being (Marks & Greenfield, 2009). Clearly, middle-aged adults remain invested in their adult children's development and continue to reap deep personal rewards from the parental role.

When children marry, parents must adjust to an enlarged family network that includes in-laws. Difficulties occur when parents do not approve of their child's partner or when the young couple adopts a way of life inconsistent with parents' values. Parents who take steps to forge a positive tie with a future daughter- or son-in-law generally experience a closer relationship after the couple marries (Fingerman et al., 2012b). And when warm, supportive relationships endure, intimacy between parents and children increases over the adult years, with great benefits for parents' life satisfaction (Ryff, Singer, & Seltzer, 2002). Members of the middle generation, especially mothers, usually take on the role of **kinkeeper,** gathering the family for celebrations and making sure everyone stays in touch.

Grandparenthood

Two years after Mark married, Devin and Trisha were thrilled to learn that a granddaughter was on the way. Although the stereotypical image of grandparents as elderly persists, today the average age of becoming a grandparent is 50 years for American women, 52 for American men (Legacy Project, 2012). A longer life expectancy means that many adults will spend one-third or more of their lifespan in the grandparent role.

Meanings of Grandparenthood. Middle-aged adults typically rate grandparenthood as highly important, following closely behind the roles of parent and spouse but ahead of worker, son or daughter, and sibling (Reitzes & Mutran, 2002).

Why did Trisha and Devin, like many others their age, greet the announcement of a grandchild with such enthusiasm? Most people experience grandparenthood as a significant milestone, mentioning one or more of the following gratifications:

- *Valued elder*—being perceived as a wise, helpful person
- *Immortality through descendants*—leaving behind not just one but two generations after death
- *Reinvolvement with personal past*—being able to pass family history and values to a new generation
- *Indulgence*—having fun with children without major child-rearing responsibilities (AARP, 2002; Hebblethwaite & Norris, 2011)

Grandparent–Grandchild Relationships. Grandparents' styles of relating to grandchildren vary as widely as the meanings they derive from their new role. The grandparent's and grandchild's age and sex make a difference. When their granddaughter was young, Trisha and Devin enjoyed an affectionate, playful relationship with her. As she got older, she looked to them for information and advice in addition to warmth and caring. By the time their granddaughter reached adolescence, Trisha and Devin had become role models, family historians, and conveyers of social, vocational, and religious values.

Living nearby is the strongest predictor of frequent, face-to-face interaction with young grandchildren. Most grandparents in Western nations live close enough to at least one grandchild to enable regular visits, but because time and resources are limited, number of "grandchild sets" (households with grandchildren) reduces contact (Uhlenberg & Hammill, 1998). As grandchildren get older, distance becomes less influential and relationship quality more so: The extent to which adolescent or young-adult grandchildren believe their grandparent values contact is a good predictor of a close bond (Brussoni & Boon, 1998).

© BLUE JEAN IMAGES/ALAMY

Many grandparents derive great joy from an affectionate, playful relationship with young grandchildren. As this grandchild gets older, he may look to his grandfather for advice, as a role model, and for family history in addition to warmth and caring.

Maternal grandmothers report more frequent visits with grandchildren than do paternal grandmothers, who are slightly advantaged over both maternal and paternal grandfathers (Uhlenberg & Hammill, 1998). Typically, relationships are closer between grandparents and grandchildren of the same sex and, especially, between maternal grandmothers and granddaughters—a pattern found in many countries (Brown & Rodin, 2004). Grandmothers also report higher satisfaction with the grandparent role than grandfathers, perhaps because grandmothers are more likely to participate in recreational, religious, and family activities with grandchildren (Reitzes & Mutran, 2004; Silverstein & Marenco, 2001). The grandparent role may be a vital means through which women satisfy their kinkeeping function.

SES and ethnicity also influence grandparent–grandchild ties. In low-income families, grandparents are more likely to perform essential activities. For example, many single parents live with their families of origin and depend on grandparents' financial and caregiving assistance to reduce the impact of poverty. Compared with grandchildren in intact families, grandchildren in single-parent and stepparent families report engaging in more diverse, higher-quality activities with their grandparents (Kennedy & Kennedy, 1993).

In some cultures, grandparents are absorbed into an extended-family household and become actively involved in child rearing. When a Chinese, Korean, or Mexican-American maternal grandmother is a homemaker, she is the preferred caregiver while parents of young children are at work (Kamo, 1998; Williams & Torrez, 1998). Similarly, involvement in child care is high among Native-American grandparents. In the absence of a biological grandparent, an unrelated aging adult may be integrated into the family to serve as a mentor and disciplinarian for children (Werner, 1991).

Increasingly, grandparents have stepped in as primary caregivers in the face of serious family problems. As the Social Issues: Health box on the following page reveals, a rising number of American children live apart from their parents in grandparent-headed households. Despite their willingness to help and their competence at child rearing, grandparents who take full responsibility for young children experience considerable emotional and financial strain. They need more assistance from community and government agencies than is currently available.

Because parents usually serve as gatekeepers of grandparents' contact with grandchildren, relationships between grandparents and their daughter-in-law or son-in-law strongly affect the closeness of grandparent–grandchild ties. A positive bond with a daughter-in-law seems particularly important in the relationship between grandparents and their son's children (Fingerman, 2004). And after a marital breakup, grandparents who are related to the custodial parent (typically the mother) have more frequent contact with grandchildren.

When family relationships are positive, grandparenthood provides an important means of fulfilling personal and societal needs in midlife and beyond. Grandparents are a frequent source of pleasure, support, and knowledge for grandchildren, while providing them with firsthand experience in how older people think and function. In return, grandchildren become deeply attached to grandparents and keep them abreast of social change.

Middle-Aged Children and Their Aging Parents

The percentage of middle-aged Americans with living parents has risen dramatically—from 10 percent in 1900 to over 50 percent in the first decade of the twenty-first century (U.S. Census Bureau, 2013). A longer life expectancy means that adult children and their parents are increasingly likely to grow old together.

Frequency and Quality of Contact. Approximately two-thirds of older adults in the United States live close to at least one of their children, and frequency of contact is high through both visits and telephone calls (U.S. Census Bureau, 2013). Proximity increases with age: Aging adults who move usually do so in the direction of kin, and younger people tend to move in the direction of their aging parents.

Middle age is a time when adults reassess relationships with their parents, just as they rethink other close ties. Many adult children become more appreciative of their parents' strengths and generosity and mention positive changes in the quality of the relationship, even after parents show physical declines. A warm, enjoyable relationship contributes to both parent and adult-child well-being (Fingerman et al., 2007, 2008; Pudrovska,

In midlife, many adults develop warmer, more supportive relationships with their aging parents. At a birthday party for her mother, this daughter expresses love and appreciation for her mother's strengths and generosity.

Social Issues: Health

Grandparents Rearing Grandchildren: The Skipped-Generation Family

Nearly 2.4 million U.S. children—4 to 5 percent of the child population—live with grandparents but apart from parents, in **skipped-generation families** (U.S. Census Bureau, 2013). The number of grandparents rearing grandchildren has increased over the past two decades. The arrangement occurs in all ethnic groups, though more often in African-American, Hispanic, and Native-American families than in Caucasian families. Although grandparent caregivers are more likely to be women than men, many grandfathers participate (Fuller-Thomson & Minkler, 2005, 2007; Minkler & Fuller-Thomson, 2005). Grandparents generally step in when parents' troubled lives—as a result of substance abuse, child abuse and neglect, family violence, or physical or mental illness—threaten children's well-being (Langosch, 2012). Often these families take in two or more children.

As a result, grandparents usually assume the parenting role under highly stressful life circumstances. Unfavorable child-rearing experiences have left their mark on the children, who show high rates of learning difficulties, depression, and antisocial behavior. Absent parents' adjustment difficulties strain family relationships. These children also introduce financial burdens into households that often are already low-income (Mills, Gomez-Smith, & De Leon, 2005; Williamson, Softas-Nall, & Miller, 2003). All these factors heighten grandparents' emotional distress.

Grandparent caregivers, at a time when they anticipated having more time for spouses, friends, and leisure, instead have less. Many report feeling emotionally drained, depressed, and worried about what will happen to the children if their own health fails (Hayslip & Kaminski, 2005; Langosch, 2012). Some families are extremely burdened. Native-American caregiving grandparents are especially likely to be unemployed, to have a disability, to be caring for several grandchildren, and to be living in extreme poverty (Fuller-Thomson & Minkler, 2005).

Despite great hardship, these grandparents seem to realize their widespread image as "silent saviors," often forging close emotional bonds with their grandchildren and using effective child-rearing practices (Fuller-Thomson & Minkler, 2000; Gibson, 2005). Compared with children in divorced, single-parent families, blended families, or foster families, children reared by grandparents fare better in adjustment (Rubin et al., 2008; Solomon & Marx, 1995).

Skipped-generation families have a tremendous need for social and financial support and intervention services for troubled children. Custodial grandparents describe support groups—both for themselves and for their grandchildren—as especially helpful, yet few make use of such interventions (Smith, Rodriguez, & Palmieri, 2010). This suggests that grandparents need special help

A custodial grandmother helps her 8-year-old granddaughter with homework. Although grandparents usually assume the parenting role under highly stressful circumstances, most find compensating rewards in rearing grandchildren.

in finding out about and accessing support services.

Although their everyday lives are often stressful, caregiving grandparents—even those rearing children with serious problems—report as much fulfillment in the grandparent role as typical grandparents do. The warmer the grandparent–grandchild bond, the greater grandparents' long-term life satisfaction (Goodman, 2012). Many grandparents mention joy from sharing children's lives and feelings of pride at children's progress, which help compensate for difficult circumstances. And some grandparents view the rearing of grandchildren as a "second chance"—an opportunity to make up for earlier, unfavorable parenting experiences and "do it right" (Dolbin-MacNab, 2006).

2009). Trisha, for example, felt closer to her parents and often asked them to tell her more about their earlier lives.

Research indicates that middle-aged daughters forge closer, more supportive relationships with aging parents, especially mothers, than do middle-aged sons (Fingerman, 2003). But this gender difference may be declining. Sons report closer ties and greater assistance to aging parents in recent than in previous studies (Fingerman et al., 2007, 2008). Changing gender roles are likely responsible. Because the majority of contemporary middle-aged women are employed, they face many competing demands on their time and energy. Consequently, men are becoming more involved in family responsibilities, including with aging parents (Fingerman & Birditt, 2011). Despite this shift, women's investment continues to exceed men's.

In collectivist cultures, older adults most often live with their married children. For example, traditionally, Chinese, Japanese, and Korean seniors moved in with a son and his wife and children; today, many live with a daughter and her family, too. This tradition of coresidence, however, is declining in some parts of Asia and in the United States, as more Asian and Asian-American aging adults choose to live on their own (Davey & Takagi, 2013; Zhan & Montgomery, 2003; Zhang, 2004). In

African-American and Hispanic families as well, coresidence is common. Regardless of whether coresidence and daily contact are typical, relationship quality usually reflects patterns established earlier: Positive parent–child ties generally remain so, as do conflict-ridden interactions.

The more positive the history of the parent–child tie, the more help given and received. Also, aging parents give more help to unmarried adult children and to those with disabilities. Similarly, adult children give more to elderly parents who are widowed or in poor health—usually emotional support and practical help, less often financial assistance. At the same time, middle-aged adults do what they can to maximize the overall quantity of help offered, as needed: While continuing to provide generous assistance to their young-adult children, they augment the aid they give to elderly parents as parental health problems increase (Kunemund, Motel-Klingebiel, & Kohli, 2005; Stephens et al., 2009).

Even when parent–child relationships have been emotionally distant, adult children offer more support as parents age, out of a sense of altruism and family duty (Silverstein et al., 2002). And although the baby-boom generation is often described as self-absorbed, baby-boom midlifers actually express a stronger commitment to caring for their aging parents than the preceding middle-aged generation (Gans & Silverstein, 2006).

In sum, as long as multiple roles are manageable and the experiences within each are high in quality, midlife intergenerational assistance as family members (aging parents) have increased needs is best characterized as *resource expansion* rather than as merely conflicting demands that inevitably drain energy and detract from psychological well-being (Grundy & Henretta, 2006; Stephens et al., 2009). Recall from the Biology and Environment box on page 429 that midlifers derive great personal benefits from successfully managing multiple roles. Their enhanced self-esteem, mastery, and sense of meaning and purpose expand their motivation and energy to handle added family-role demands, from which they reap additional personal rewards.

Caring for Aging Parents. About 25 percent of U.S. adult children provide unpaid care to an aging adult (MetLife, 2011). The burden of caring for aging parents can be great. In Chapter 2, we noted that as birthrates have declined, the family structure has become increasingly "top-heavy," with more generations alive but fewer younger members. Consequently, more than one older family member is likely to need assistance, with fewer younger adults available to provide it.

The term **sandwich generation** is widely used to refer to the idea that middle-aged adults must care for multiple generations above and below them at the same time (Riley & Bowen, 2005). Although only a minority of contemporary middle-aged adults who care for aging parents have children younger than age 18 at home, many are providing assistance to young-adult children and to grandchildren—obligations that, when combined with work and community responsibilities, can lead middle-aged caregivers to feel "sandwiched," or squeezed, between the pressures of older and younger generations. As more baby

Caring for an aging parent with a chronic illness or disability is highly stressful. But social support reduces physical and emotional strain, enabling adult children to find satisfactions and rewards in tending to parents' needs.

boomers move into late adulthood, the number of sandwiched midlifers will increase.

Middle-aged adults living far from aging parents who are in poor health often substitute financial help for direct care, if they have the means. But when parents live nearby and have no spouse to meet their needs, adult children usually engage in direct care. Regardless of family income level, African-American, Asian-American, and Hispanic adults give aging parents more direct care and financial help than Caucasian-American adults do (Shuey & Hardy, 2003). Compared with their white counterparts, African Americans and Hispanics express a stronger sense of obligation, and find it more personally rewarding, to support their aging parents (Fingerman et al., 2011b; Swartz, 2009). And African Americans often draw on close, family-like relationships with friends and neighbors for caregiving assistance.

In all ethnic groups, responsibility for providing care to aging parents falls more on daughters than on sons. Families turn to the person who seems most available—living nearby and with fewer commitments that might interfere with the ability to assist. These unstated rules, in addition to parents' preference for same-sex caregivers (aging mothers live longer), lead more women to fill the role (see Figure 16.2). Daughters also feel more obligated than sons to care for aging parents (Gans & Silverstein, 2006; Stein, 2009).

As Figure 16.2 shows, nearly one-fourth of American working women are caregivers; others quit their jobs to provide care. And the time they devote to caring for a disabled aging parent

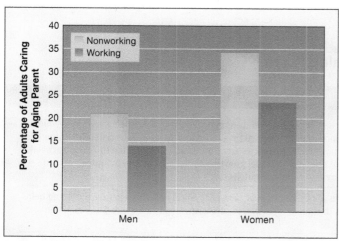

FIGURE 16.2 Baby boomers, by work status and gender, who provide basic personal care to an aging parent in poor health. A survey of a nationally representative sample of 1,100 U.S. men and women over age 50 with at least one parent living revealed that more nonworking than working adults engaged in basic personal care (assistance with such activities as dressing, feeding, and bathing). Regardless of work status, many more women than men were caregivers. (Adapted from *The MetLife Study of Caregiving Costs to Working Caregivers: Double Jeopardy for Baby Boomers Caring for Their Parents*, June 2011, Figure 3. Reprinted by permission of The MetLife Mature Market Institute, New York, NY.)

is substantial, averaging 10 to 20 hours per week (Metlife, 2011; Takamura & Williams, 2002). Nevertheless, men—although doing less than women—do contribute. In one investigation, employed men spent an average of 7½ hours per week caring for parents or parents-in-law (Neal & Hammer, 2007). Tim, for example, looked in on his father, a recent stroke victim, every evening, reading to him, running errands, making household repairs, and taking care of finances. His sister, however, provided more hands-on care—cooking, feeding, bathing, managing medication, and doing laundry. The care sons and daughters provide tends to be divided along gender-role lines (Pinquart & Sörensen, 2006).

As adults move from early to later middle age, the sex difference in parental caregiving declines. Perhaps as men reduce their vocational commitments and feel less need to conform to a "masculine" gender role, they grow more able and willing to provide basic care (Marks, 1996; MetLife, 2011). At the same time, parental caregiving may contribute to men's greater openness to the "feminine" side of their personalities. A man who cared for his mother, severely impaired by Alzheimer's disease, commented on how the experience altered his outlook: "It was so difficult to do these tasks; things a man, a son, is not supposed to do. I have definitely modified my views on conventional expectations" (Hirsch, 1996, p. 112).

Although most adult children help willingly, caring for a chronically ill or disabled parent is highly stressful. Over time, the parent usually gets worse, and the caregiving task escalates. As Tim explained to Devin and Trisha, "One of the hardest aspects is the emotional strain of seeing my father's physical and mental decline up close."

Caregivers who share a household with ill parents—about 23 percent of U.S. adult children—experience the most stress. When a parent and child who have lived separately for years must move in together, conflicts generally arise over routines and lifestyles. But the greatest source of stress is problem behavior, especially for caregivers of parents who have deteriorated mentally (Alzheimer's Association, 2012b). Tim's sister reported that their father would wake during the night, ask repetitive questions, follow her around the house, and become agitated and combative.

Parental caregiving often has emotional, physical, and financial consequences. It leads to role overload, high job absenteeism, exhaustion, inability to concentrate, feelings of hostility, anxiety about aging, and high rates of depression, with women more profoundly affected than men (Neal & Hammer, 2007; Pinquart & Sörensen, 2006). Despite having more time to care for an ill parent, women who quit work fare especially poorly in adjustment, probably because of social isolation and financial strain (Bookman & Kimbrel, 2011). Positive experiences at work can actually reduce the stress of parental care as caregivers bring a favorable self-evaluation and a positive mood home with them.

In cultures and subcultures where adult children feel an especially strong sense of obligation to care for aging parents, the emotional toll is also high (Knight & Sayegh, 2010). In research on Korean, Korean-American, and Caucasian-American caregivers of parents with mental disabilities, the Koreans and Korean Americans reported higher levels of family obligation and care burden—and also higher levels of anxiety and depression—than the Caucasian Americans (Lee & Farran, 2004; Youn et al., 1999). And among African-American caregivers, women who strongly endorsed cultural reasons for providing care ("It's what my people have always done") fared less well in mental health two years later than women who moderately endorsed cultural reasons (Dilworth-Anderson, Goodwin, & Williams, 2004).

LOOK AND LISTEN

Ask a middle-aged adult caring for an aging parent in declining health to describe both the stressful and rewarding aspects of caregiving. What strategies does he or she use to reduce stress? ●

Social support is highly effective in reducing caregiver stress. In Denmark, Sweden, and Japan, a government-sponsored home helper system eases the burden of parental care by making specially trained nonfamily caregivers available, based on seniors' needs (Saito, Auestad, & Waerness, 2010). In the United States, in-home care by a nonfamily caregiver is too costly for most families; only 10 to 20 percent arrange it (Family Caregiver Alliance, 2009). And unless they must, few people want to place their parents in formal care, such as nursing homes, which also are expensive. Applying What We Know on page 438 summarizes ways to relieve the stress of caring for an aging parent—at the individual, family, community, and societal levels. We will address additional care options, along with interventions for caregivers, in Chapter 17.

Applying What We Know

Relieving the Stress of Caring for an Aging Parent

Strategy	Description
Use effective coping strategies.	Use problem-centered coping to manage the parent's behavior and caregiving tasks. Delegate responsibilities to other family members, seek assistance from friends and neighbors, and recognize the parent's limits while calling on capacities the parent does have. Use emotion-centered coping to reinterpret the situation positively, such as emphasizing the opportunity it offers for personal growth. Avoid denial of anger, depression, and anxiety in response to the caregiving burden, which heightens stress.
Seek social support.	Confide in family members and friends about the stress of caregiving, seeking their encouragement and help. So far as possible, avoid quitting work to care for an ill parent; doing so is associated with social isolation and loss of financial resources.
Make use of community resources.	Contact community organizations to seek information and assistance, in the form of caregiver support groups, in-home respite help, home-delivered meals, transportation, and adult day care.
Press for workplace and public policies that relieve the emotional and financial burdens of caring for an aging parent.	Encourage your employer to provide care benefits, such as flexible work hours and employment leave for caregiving. Communicate with lawmakers and other citizens about the need for improved health insurance plans that reduce the financial strain of caring for an aging parent on middle- and low-income families.

Siblings

A survey of a large sample of ethnically diverse Americans revealed that sibling contact and support decline from early to middle adulthood, rebounding only after age 70 for siblings living near each other (White, 2001). Decreased midlife contact is probably due to the demands of middle-aged adults' diverse roles. However, most adult siblings report getting together or talking on the phone at least monthly (Antonucci, Akiyama, & Merline, 2002).

Despite reduced contact, many siblings feel closer in midlife, often in response to major life events (Stewart et al., 2001).

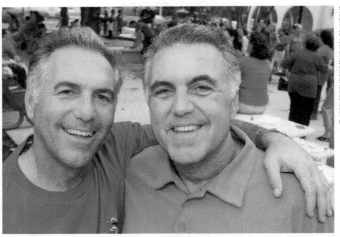

These brothers, both in their fifties, express their mutual affection at a family reunion. Even when they have only limited contact, siblings often feel closer in midlife.

© JEFF GREENBERG/THE IMAGE WORKS

Launching and marriage of children seem to prompt siblings to think more about each other. When a parent becomes seriously ill, brothers and sisters who previously had little to do with one another may find themselves in touch about parental care. And when parents die, adult children realize they have become the oldest generation and must look to each other to sustain family ties.

Not all sibling bonds improve, of course. Recall Trisha's negative encounters with her sister, Dottie (see page 409 in Chapter 15). Dottie's difficult temperament had made her hard to get along with since childhood, and her temper flared when their father died and problems arose over family finances. Large inequities in division of labor in parental caregiving can also unleash intense sibling conflict (Silverstein & Giarrusso, 2010). As siblings grow older, good relationships often get better and poor relationships get worse.

In industrialized nations, sibling relationships are voluntary. In village societies, they are generally involuntary and basic to family functioning. For example, among Asian Pacific Islanders, family social life is organized around strong brother–sister attachments. A brother–sister pair is often treated as a unit in exchange marriages with another family. After marriage, brothers are expected to protect sisters, and sisters serve as spiritual mentors to brothers (Cicirelli, 1995). Cultural norms reduce sibling conflict, thereby ensuring family cooperation.

Friendships

As family responsibilities declined in middle age, Devin found he had more time to spend with friends. On Friday afternoons, he met several male friends at a coffee house, and they chatted for a couple of hours. But most of Devin's friendships were couple-based—relationships he shared with Trisha. Compared with Devin, Trisha more often got together with friends on her own.

Middle-aged friendships reflect the same trends discussed in Chapter 14. At all ages, men's friendships are less intimate than women's. Men tend to talk about sports, politics, and business, whereas women focus on feelings and life problems. Women report a greater number of close friends and say they both receive and provide their friends with more emotional support (Antonucci, Akiyama, & Takahashi, 2004).

Over the past decade, the average number of friendships rose among U.S. midlifers, perhaps because of ease of keeping in touch through social media (Wang & Wellman, 2010). Though falling short of young adults' use, connecting regularly with friends through Facebook or other social networking sites has risen rapidly among middle-aged adults (see Figure 16.3) (Brenner, 2013; Hampton et al., 2011). As in early adulthood, women are more active users. And users have more offline close relationships, sometimes using Facebook to revive "dormant" friendships.

Still, for both sexes, number of friends declines from middle to late adulthood, probably because people become less willing to invest in nonfamily ties unless they are very rewarding. As selectivity of friendship increases, older adults try harder to get along with friends (Antonucci & Akiyama, 1995). Having chosen a friend, middle-aged people attach great value to the relationship and take extra steps to protect it.

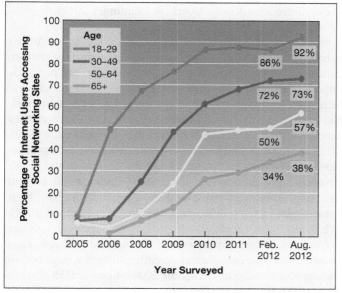

FIGURE 16.3 Gains in use of social networking sites by age group from 2005 to 2012. Repeated surveys of large representative samples of U.S. adults who use the Internet revealed that social networking site use increased substantially for all age groups. Though not as avid users as young adults, most middle-aged adults use social networking sites, primarily Facebook. (From J. Brenner, 2013, "Pew Internet: Social Networking." Pew Research Center's Internet & American Life Project, Washington, D.C. February 14, 2013, *www.pewinternet.org*. Adapted by permission.)

LOOK AND LISTEN

Ask a middle-aged couple you know well to describe the number and quality of their friendships today compared with their friendships in early adulthood. Does their report match research findings? Explain. ●

By midlife, family relationships and friendships support different aspects of psychological well-being. Family ties protect against serious threats and losses, offering security within a long-term timeframe. In contrast, friendships serve as current sources of pleasure and satisfaction (Levitt & Cici-Gokaltun, 2011). As middle-aged couples renew their sense of companionship, they may combine the best of family and friendship.

ASK YOURSELF

REVIEW How do age, sex, proximity, and culture affect grandparent–grandchild ties?

APPLY Raylene and her brother Walter live in the same city as their aging mother, Elsie. When Elsie could no longer live independently, Raylene took primary responsibility for her care. What factors probably contributed to Raylene's involvement in caregiving and Walter's lesser role?

REFLECT Ask one of your parents for his or her view of how the parent–child relationship changed as you transitioned to new adult roles, such as college student, career-entry worker, married partner, or parent. Do you agree?

 # Vocational Life

Work continues to be a salient aspect of identity and self-esteem in middle adulthood. More so than in earlier or later years, people attempt to increase the personal meaning and self-direction of their vocational lives. The large tide of baby boomers currently moving through midlife and (as we will see in Chapter 18) the desire of most to work longer than the previous generation means that the number of older workers will rise dramatically over the next few decades (Leonesio et al., 2012). Yet a favorable transition from adult worker to older worker is hindered by negative stereotypes of aging—incorrect assumptions of limited learning capacity, slower decision making, and resistance to change and supervision (Posthuma & Campion, 2009). Furthermore, gender discrimination continues to restrict the career attainments of many women. Let's take a close look at middle-aged work life.

Job Satisfaction

Job satisfaction increases in midlife in diverse nations and at all occupational levels, from executives to hourly workers. The trend is weaker for women than for men, probably because women's reduced chances for advancement result in a sense of unfairness. It is also weaker for blue-collar than for white-collar workers, perhaps because blue-collar workers have less control over their own work schedules and activities (Avolio & Sosik, 1999). When different aspects of jobs are considered, intrinsic satisfaction—happiness with the work itself—shows a strong age-related gain. Extrinsic satisfaction—contentment with supervision, pay, and promotions—changes very little (Barnes-Farrell & Matthews, 2007).

What explains the rise in job satisfaction during middle adulthood? An improved capacity to cope effectively with difficult situations and a broader time perspective probably contribute. "When I first started teaching, I complained a lot," remarked Devin. "Now, I can tell a big problem from a trivial one." Moving out of unrewarding work roles, as Trisha did, can also boost morale. And older people tend to have greater access to key job characteristics that predict well-being—involvement in decision making, reasonable workloads, and good physical working conditions. Furthermore, having fewer alternative positions into which they can move, older workers generally reduce their career aspirations (Barnes-Farrell & Matthews, 2007). As the perceived gap between actual and possible achievements narrows, job involvement—importance of one's work to self-esteem—increases (Warr, 2001).

Although emotional engagement with work is usually psychologically healthy, it can also result in **burnout**—a condition in which long-term job stress leads to mental exhaustion, a sense of loss of personal control, and feelings of reduced accomplishment. Burnout occurs more often in the helping professions, including health care, human services, and teaching, which place high emotional demands on employees. And it is especially likely to occur in unsupportive work environments, where work assignments exceed time available to complete them and encouragement and feedback from supervisors are scarce (Schmidt, Neubach, & Heuer, 2007). Burnout tends to occur more often in the United States than in Western Europe, perhaps because of Americans' greater achievement orientation (Maslach, Schaufeli, & Leiter, 2001).

To prevent burnout, employers can make sure workloads are reasonable, provide opportunities for workers to take time out from stressful situations, limit hours of stressful work, and offer social support. Interventions that enlist employees' participation in designing higher-quality work environments show promise for increasing work engagement and effectiveness and reducing burnout (Leiter, Gascón, & Martínez-Jarreta, 2010). And provisions for working at home may respond to the needs of some people for a calmer, quieter work atmosphere.

Career Development

After several years as a parish nurse, Anya felt a need for additional training to do her job better. Trisha appreciated her firm's generous support of workshop and course attendance, which helped her keep abreast of new legal developments. As these experiences reveal, career development is vital throughout work life.

Job Training. When Anya asked her supervisor, Roy, for time off to upgrade her skills, he replied, "You're in your fifties. What're you going to do with so much new information at this point in your life?" Roy's insensitive, narrow-minded response, though usually unspoken, is all too common among managers—even some who are older themselves! Training and on-the-job career counseling are less available to older workers. And when career development activities are offered, older employees may be less likely to volunteer for them (Barnes-Farrell & Matthews, 2007; Hedge, Borman, & Lammlein, 2006). What influences willingness to engage in job training and updating?

Personal characteristics are important: With age, growth needs give way somewhat to security needs. Perhaps for this reason, older employees depend more on co-worker and supervisor encouragement for vocational development. Yet as we have seen, they are less likely to have supportive supervisors. Furthermore, negative stereotypes of aging reduce older workers' self-efficacy, or confidence that they can get better at their jobs (Maurer, 2001; Maurer, Wrenn, & Weiss, 2003).

Workplace characteristics matter, too. An employee given work that requires new learning must pursue that learning to complete the assignment. Unfortunately, older workers sometimes receive more routine tasks than younger workers. In companies with a more favorable *age climate* (view of older workers), mature employees participate frequently in further education and report greater self-efficacy and commitment to the organization (Bowen, Noack, & Staudinger, 2011).

Gender and Ethnicity: The Glass Ceiling. In her thirties, Jewel became a company president by starting her own business. Having concluded that, as a woman, she had little chance of rising to a top executive position in a large corporation, she didn't even try. Although women and ethnic minorities have gradually gained in access to managerial careers, they remain a long distance from gender and ethnic equality (Huffman, 2012). From career entry on, inequalities in promotion between men and women and between whites and blacks become more pronounced over time—findings still evident after education, work skills, and work productivity have been controlled (Barreto, Ryan, & Schmitt, 2009; Maume, 2004). When the most prestigious high-level management jobs are considered, white men are overwhelmingly advantaged: They account for 70 percent of chief executive officers at large corporations and 93 percent at Fortune 500 companies (U.S. Census Bureau, 2013).

Women and ethnic minorities face a **glass ceiling**, or invisible barrier to advancement up the corporate ladder. Why is this so? Management is an art and skill that must be taught. Yet women and ethnic minorities have less access to mentors, role models, and informal networks that serve as training routes (Baumgartner & Schneider, 2010). And stereotyped doubts about women's career commitment and managerial ability

Facebook executive Sheryl Sandberg is among a handful of women who have attained top positions in major corporations. In her best-selling book, *Lean In*, she urges women to be more assertive in demonstrating qualities linked to leadership at work.

(especially women with children) also contribute, leading supervisors to underrate their competence and not to recommend them for formal management training programs (Hoobler, Lemmon, & Wayne, 2011).

Furthermore, women who demonstrate qualities linked to leadership and advancement—assertiveness, confidence, force-fulness, and ambition—encounter prejudice because they deviate from traditional gender roles, even though they more often combine these traits with a democratic, collaborative style of leading than do men (Cheung & Halpern, 2010; Eagly & Carli, 2007). To overcome this bias, women in line for top positions must demonstrate greater competence than their male counterparts. In an investigation of several hundred senior managers at a multinational financial services corporation, promoted female managers had earned higher performance ratings than promoted male managers (Lyness & Heilman, 2006). In contrast, no gender difference existed in performance of managers not selected for promotion.

Like Jewel, many women have dealt with the glass ceiling by going around it, leaving the corporate environment and going into business for themselves. Today, more than half of all startup businesses in the United States are owned and successfully operated by women (Ahuja, 2005; U.S. Census Bureau, 2013). But when women and ethnic minorities leave the corporate world, companies not only lose valuable talent but also fail to address the leadership needs of an increasingly diverse work force.

Planning for Retirement

One evening, Devin and Trisha met Anya and her husband, George, for dinner. Halfway through the meal, Devin inquired, "George, tell us what you and Anya are going to do

about retirement. Are you planning to work part-time or stop entirely? Do you think you'll stay here or move out of town?"

Three or four generations ago, the two couples would not have had this conversation. In 1900, about 70 percent of American men age 65 and over were in the labor force. By 1970, however, the figure had dropped to 27 percent, and in the early twenty-first century it declined to 16 percent (U.S. Census Bureau, 2013). Because of government-sponsored retirement benefits (begun in the United States in 1935), retirement is no longer a privilege reserved for the wealthy. The federal government pays Social Security to the majority of the aged, and others are covered by employer-based private pension plans.

As the trend just noted suggests, the average age of retirement has declined over the past several decades. Currently, it is age 63 in the United States and hovers between 60 and 63 in other Western nations (U.S. Census Bureau, 2013). The recent recession led to an increase in the number of Americans at risk for being unable to sustain their preretirement standard of living after leaving the workforce. Consequently, a survey of a large, nationally representative sample of baby boomers revealed that the majority expect to delay retirement (Jones, 2012). But current estimates indicate that most will need to work just a few extra years to be financially ready to retire (Munnell et al., 2012). For the healthy, active, long-lived baby-boom generation, up to one-fourth of their lives may lie ahead after they leave their jobs.

Retirement is a lengthy, complex process that begins as soon as the middle-aged person first thinks about it (Kim & Moen, 2002b). Planning is important because retirement leads to a loss of two important work-related rewards—income and status—and to a change in many other aspects of life. Yet nearly half of middle-aged people engage in no concrete retirement planning (Hershey et al., 2007).

Because income typically drops by 50 percent, more people engage in financial planning than in other forms of preparation. But even those who attend financial education programs often fail to look closely at their financial well-being and to make wise decisions (Keller & Lusardi, 2012). Many could benefit from an expert's financial analysis and counsel.

LOOK AND LISTEN

Contact the human resources division of a company or institution in your community, and inquire about the retirement planning services it offers. How comprehensive are those services, and what percentage of its recent retirees made use of them? ●

Retirement leads to ways of spending time that are largely guided by one's interests rather than one's obligations. Planning for an active life has an even greater impact on happiness after retirement than financial planning. Participation in activities promotes many factors essential for psychological well-being, including a structured time schedule, social contact, and self-esteem (Schlossberg, 2004). Carefully considering whether or not to relocate at retirement is related to an active life, since it affects access to health care, friends, family, recreation, entertainment, and part-time work.

Devin retired at age 62, George at age 66. Though several years younger, Trisha and Anya—like many married women—coordinated their retirements with those of their husbands. In contrast, Jewel—in good health but without an intimate partner to share her life—kept her consulting business going until age 75. Tim took early retirement and moved to be near Elena, where he devoted himself to public service—tutoring second graders in a public school and coaching after-school and weekend youth sports.

Unfortunately, less well-educated people with lower lifetime earnings are least likely to attend retirement preparation programs—yet they stand to benefit the most. And compared with men, women do less planning for retirement, instead relying on their husband's preparations. This gender gap seems to be narrowing, however, as women increasingly contribute to family income (Adams & Rau, 2011). Employers must take extra steps to encourage lower-paid workers and women to participate in planning activities. In addition, enhancing retirement adjustment among the economically disadvantaged depends on access to better vocational training, jobs, and health care at early ages. Clearly, a lifetime of opportunities and experiences affects the transition to retirement. In Chapter 18, we will consider the decision to retire and retirement adjustment in greater detail.

ASK YOURSELF

REVIEW What factors contribute to the rise in job satisfaction with age?

APPLY An executive wonders how his large corporation can foster advancement of women and ethnic minorities to upper management positions. What strategies would you recommend?

SUMMARY

Erikson's Theory: Generativity versus Stagnation (p. 423)

According to Erikson, how does personality change in middle age?

- Generativity expands as middle-aged adults face Erikson's psychological conflict of **generativity versus stagnation.** Personal desires and cultural demands jointly shape adults' generative activities.

JEAN-MARC GIBOUX/GETTY IMAGES

- Highly generative people, who contribute to society through parenthood, other family relationships, the workplace, and volunteer endeavors, appear especially well-adjusted. Stagnation occurs when people become self-centered and self-indulgent in midlife.

Other Theories of Psychosocial Development in Midlife (p. 425)

Describe Levinson's and Vaillant's views of psychosocial development in middle adulthood, and discuss similarities and differences between men and women.

- According to Levinson, middle-aged adults confront four developmental tasks, each requiring them to reconcile two opposing tendencies within the self: young–old, destruction–creation, masculinity–femininity, and engagement–separateness.

- Middle-aged men show greater acceptance of "feminine" traits of nurturance and caring, while women are more open to "masculine" characteristics of autonomy and assertiveness. Men and successful career-oriented women may reduce their concern with ambition and achievement. Women who have devoted themselves to child rearing or an unfulfilling job often seek rewarding work or community engagement.

- Vaillant found that adults in their late forties and fifties become guardians of their culture, seeking to "pass the torch" to later generations.

Does the term midlife crisis ***reflect most people's experience of middle adulthood, and is middle adulthood accurately characterized as a stage?***

- Most people respond to midlife with changes that are better described as "turning points" than as a crisis. Only a minority experience a **midlife crisis** characterized by intense self-doubt and stress that lead to drastic life alterations.

Stability and Change in Self-Concept and Personality (p. 427)

Describe changes in self-concept, personality, and gender identity in middle adulthood.

- Middle-aged individuals maintain self-esteem and stay motivated by revising their **possible selves,** which become fewer in number as well as more modest and concrete.

- Midlife typically brings enhanced psychological well-being, through greater self-acceptance, autonomy, and environmental mastery. Factors contributing to well-being, however, vary widely among cohorts and cultures.

- Daily stressors plateau in early to mid-adulthood, and then decline as work and family responsibilities ease. Midlife gains in emotional stability and confidence in handling life's problems lead to increased effectiveness in coping with stressors.

- Both men and women become more androgynous in middle adulthood. Biological explanations, such as **parental imperative theory,** are controversial. A combination of social roles and life conditions is more likely responsible.

Discuss stability and change in the "big five" personality traits in adulthood.

- Among the **"big five" personality traits,** agreeableness and conscientiousness increase into middle age, while neuroticism declines, and extroversion and openness to experience do not change or decrease slightly. Individual differences are large and highly stable: Although adults change in overall organization and integration of personality, they do so on a foundation of basic, enduring dispositions.

Relationships at Midlife

(p. 431)

Describe the middle adulthood phase of the family life cycle.

- "Launching children and moving on" is the midlife phase of the family life cycle. Adults must adapt to many entries and exits of family members as their children launch–return–relaunch, marry, and produce grandchildren, and as their own parents age and die.

- When divorce occurs, middle-aged adults seem to adapt more easily than younger people. For women, midlife marital breakup often severely reduces standard of living, contributing to the **feminization of poverty.**

- Most middle-aged parents adjust well to launching adult children, especially if positive parent–child relationships are sustained, but adult children who are "off-time" in development can prompt parental strain. As children marry, middle-aged parents, especially mothers, often become **kinkeepers.**

- Grandparents' contact and closeness with grandchildren depend on proximity, number of grandchild sets, sex of grandparent and grandchild, and in-law relationships. In low-income families and in some ethnic groups, grandparents provide essential financial and child-care assistance. When serious family problems exist, grandparents may become primary caregivers in **skipped-generation families.**

- Middle-aged adults reassess their relationships with aging parents, often becoming more appreciative. Mother–daughter relationships tend to be closer than other parent–child ties. The more positive the history of the parent–child tie and the greater the need for assistance, the more help exchanged.

- Middle-aged adults, often caught between caring for aging parents, assisting young-adult children and grandchildren, and meeting work and community responsibilities, are called the **sandwich generation.** The burden of caring for ill or frail parents falls most heavily on adult daughters, though the sex difference declines in later middle age.

- Parental caregiving has emotional and health consequences, especially in cultures and subcultures where adult children feel a particularly strong obligation to provide care. Social support is highly effective in reducing caregiver stress.

Describe midlife sibling relationships and friendships.

- Sibling contact and support decline from early to middle adulthood, probably because of the demands of diverse roles. But many middle-aged siblings feel closer, often in response to major life events. Sister–sister ties are typically closest in industrialized nations. In nonindustrialized societies, strong brother–sister attachments may be basic to family functioning.

- In midlife, friendships become fewer, more selective, and more deeply valued. Men continue to be less expressive with their friends than women, who have more close friendships. Viewing a spouse as a best friend can contribute greatly to marital happiness.

Vocational Life (p. 439)

Discuss job satisfaction and career development in middle adulthood, with special attention to sex differences and experiences of ethnic minorities.

- Vocational readjustments are common as middle-aged people seek to increase the personal meaning and self-direction of their work lives. Job satisfaction increases, more so for men than for women. **Burnout** is a serious occupational hazard, especially for those in helping professions and in unsupportive work environments.

- Both personal and workplace characteristics influence the extent to which older workers engage in career development. In companies with a more favorable age climate, mature employees report greater self-efficacy and commitment to the organization.

- Women and ethnic minorities face a **glass ceiling** because of limited access to management training and prejudice against women who demonstrate strong leadership qualities. Many women further their careers by leaving the corporate world, often to start their own businesses.

Discuss the importance of planning for retirement.

- Retirement brings major life changes, including loss of income and status and increase in free time. Besides financial planning, planning for an active life is vital, with a strong impact on happiness after retirement. Low-paid workers and women need extra encouragement to participate in retirement planning.

Important Terms and Concepts

"big five" personality traits (p. 430)
burnout (p. 440)
feminization of poverty (p. 432)
generativity versus stagnation (p. 423)

glass ceiling (p. 440)
kinkeeper (p. 433)
midlife crisis (p. 426)
parental imperative theory (p. 430)

possible selves (p. 427)
sandwich generation (p. 436)
skipped-generation family (p. 435)

milestones

Development in Middle Adulthood

40–50 years

PHYSICAL

■ Accommodative ability of the lens of the eye, ability to see in dim light, and color discrimination decline; sensitivity to glare increases. (402)

■ Hearing loss at high frequencies occurs. (402)

■ Hair grays and thins. (401)

■ Lines on the face become more pronounced; skin loses elasticity and begins to sag. (402–403)

■ Weight gain continues, accompanied by a rise in fatty deposits in the torso, while fat beneath the skin declines. (403)

■ Loss of lean body mass (muscle and bone) occurs. (403)

■ In women, production of estrogen drops, leading to shortening and irregularity of the menstrual cycle. (403)

■ In men, quantity of semen and sperm declines. (406)

■ Intensity of sexual response declines, but frequency of sexual activity drops only slightly. (407)

■ Rates of cancer and cardiovascular disease increase. (407–408)

COGNITIVE

■ Consciousness of aging increases. (401, 425)

■ Crystallized intelligence increases; fluid intelligence declines. (413–414)

■ Speed of processing declines, but adults can compensate through experience and practice. (415)

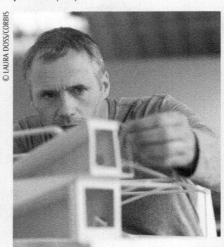

■ Ability to attend selectively and to adapt attention—switching from one task to another—declines, but adults can compensate through experience and practice. (415–416)

■ Amount of information retained in working memory declines, in part because of reduced use of memory strategies. (416)

■ Retrieving information from long-term memory becomes more difficult. (416)

■ General factual knowledge, knowledge related to one's occupation, and metacognitive knowledge remain unchanged or may increase. (416)

■ Practical problem solving and expertise increase. (417–418)

■ Creativity may become more deliberately thoughtful, emphasize integrating ideas, and shift from self-expression to more altruistic goals. (418)

Note: Numbers in parentheses indicate the page or pages on which each milestone is discussed.

EMOTIONAL/SOCIAL

- Generativity increases. (423–424)
- Focus shifts toward personally meaningful living. (425)

- Possible selves become fewer in number and more modest and concrete. (427)
- Self-acceptance, autonomy, and environmental mastery increase. (428)
- Strategies for coping with stressors become more effective. (428)
- Gender identity becomes more androgynous; "masculine" traits increase in women, "feminine" traits in men. (425, 428, 430)
- Agreeableness and conscientiousness increase, while neuroticism declines. (430)
- May launch children. (432)
- May become a kinkeeper, especially if a mother. (433)
- May become a parent-in-law and a grandparent. (433)
- Becomes more appreciative of parents' strengths and generosity; quality of relationships with parents increase. (434–436)
- May care for a parent with a disability or chronic illness. (436–438)
- Siblings may feel closer. (438)

- Number of friends generally declines. (439)
- Intrinsic job satisfaction—happiness with one's work—typically increases. (439–440)

50–65 years

PHYSICAL

- Lens of the eye loses its capacity to adjust to objects at varying distances entirely. (402)
- Hearing loss gradually extends to all frequencies but remains greatest for high frequencies. (402)
- Skin continues to wrinkle and sag, "age spots" increase, and blood vessels in the skin become more visible. (402–403)
- In women, menopause occurs; as estrogen declines further, genitals are less easily stimulated, and the vagina lubricates more slowly during arousal. (403)
- In men, inability to attain an erection when desired becomes more common. (406)
- Loss of bone mass continues; rates of osteoporosis rise. (403, 408–409)
- Collapse of disks in the spinal column causes height to drop by as much as 1 inch. (403)
- Rates of cancer and cardiovascular disease continue to increase. (407–408)

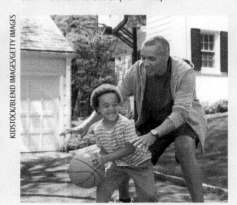

COGNITIVE

- Cognitive changes previously listed continue.

EMOTIONAL/SOCIAL

- Emotional and social changes previously listed continue.

- Parent-to-child help-giving declines, and child-to-parent support and practical assistance increase. (435–437)

- May retire. (441–442)

c h a p t e r
18

Emotional and Social Development in Late Adulthood

© DESIGN PICS/CORBIS

As family responsibilities and vocational pressures lessen, friendships—like the relaxed companionship of these Guatemalan seniors—take on increasing importance. Having friends is an especially strong predictor of mental health in late adulthood.

chapter outline

With Ruth at his side, Walt spoke to the guests at their sixtieth-anniversary party. "Even when things were hard," he reflected, "the time of life I liked best always seemed to be the current one. When I was a kid, I adored playing baseball. In my twenties, I loved learning the photography business. And of course," Walt continued, glancing affectionately at Ruth, "our wedding was the most memorable day of all."

He went on: "And then Sybil was born. Looking back at my parents and grandparents and forward at Sybil, Marci, and Marci's son Jamel, I feel a sense of unity with past and future generations."

Walt and Ruth greeted old age with calm acceptance, grateful for the gift of long life and loved ones. Yet not all older adults find such peace of mind. Walt's brother Dick was contentious, complaining about petty issues and major disappointments alike: "Goldie, why'd you serve cheesecake? No one eats cheesecake on birthdays!" "Know why we've got financial worries? Uncle Louie wouldn't lend me the money to keep the bakery going, so I *had* to retire."

A mix of gains and losses characterizes these twilight years, extending the multidirectionality of development. On one hand,

old age is a time of pleasure and tranquility, when children are grown, life's work is nearly done, and responsibilities are lightened. On the other hand, it brings concerns about declining physical functions, unwelcome loneliness, and the growing specter of imminent death.

In this chapter, we consider how older adults reconcile these opposing forces. Although some are weary and discontented, most attach deeper significance to life and reap great benefits from family and friendship bonds, leisure activities, and community involvement. We will see how personal attributes and life history combine with home, neighborhood, community, and societal conditions to mold emotional and social development in late life. ●

Erikson's Theory: Ego Integrity versus Despair

The final psychological conflict of Erikson's (1950) theory, **ego integrity versus despair,** involves coming to terms with one's life. Adults who arrive at a sense of integrity feel whole, complete, and satisfied with their achievements. They have adapted to inevitable triumphs and disappointments and realize that the paths they followed, abandoned, and never selected were necessary for fashioning a meaningful life course.

The capacity to view one's life in the larger context of all humanity—as the chance combination of one person and one segment in history—contributes to the serenity and contentment that accompany integrity. "These last few decades have been the happiest," Walt murmured, clasping Ruth's hand—only weeks before the heart attack that would end his life. At peace with himself, his wife, and his children, Walt had accepted his life course as something that had to be the way it was. In a study that followed a sample of women diverse in SES throughout adulthood, midlife generativity predicted ego integrity in late adulthood. Ego integrity, in turn, was associated with more favorable psychological well-being—a more upbeat mood, greater self-acceptance, higher marital satisfaction, closer relationships with adult children, greater community involvement, and increased ease in accepting help from others when it is needed (James & Zarrett, 2007).

Scanning the newspaper, Walt pondered, "I keep reading these percentages: One out of five people will get heart disease, one out of three will get cancer. But the truth is, one out of one will die. We are all mortal and must accept this fate." The

year before, Walt had given his granddaughter, Marci, his collection of prized photos, which had absorbed him for over half a century. With the realization that the integrity of one's own life is part of an extended chain of human existence, Erikson

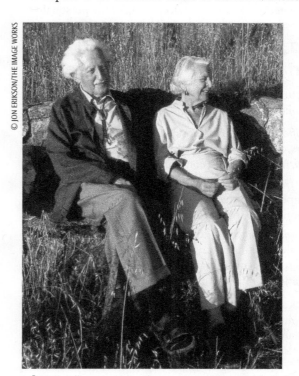

Erik Erikson and his wife Joan exemplified the ideal of Erikson's final stage. They aged gracefully, felt satisfied with their achievements, and were often seen together, contented and deeply in love.

suggested, death loses its sting. In support of this view, older adults who report having attained intrinsic (personally gratifying) life goals typically express acceptance of their own death (Van Hiel & Vansteenkiste, 2009). Those who emphasize attainment of extrinsic goals (such as money or prestige) more often fear life's end.

The negative outcome of this stage, despair, occurs when aging adults feel they have made many wrong decisions, yet time is too short to find an alternate route to integrity. Without another chance, the despairing person is overwhelmed with bitterness, defeat, and hopelessness. According to Erikson, these attitudes are often expressed as anger and contempt for others, which disguise contempt for oneself. Dick's argumentative, fault-finding behavior, tendency to blame others for his personal failures, and regretful view of his own life reflect this deep sense of despair.

Other Theories of Psychosocial Development in Late Adulthood

As with Erikson's stages of early and middle adulthood, other theorists have clarified and refined his vision of late adulthood, specifying the tasks and thought processes that contribute to a sense of ego integrity. All agree that optimal development involves greater integration and deepening of the personality.

Peck's Tasks of Ego Integrity and Joan Erikson's Gerotranscendence

According to Robert Peck (1968), attaining ego integrity involves three distinct tasks:

- *Ego differentiation:* For those who invested heavily in their careers, finding other ways to affirm self-worth—through family, friendship, and community life

- *Body transcendence:* Surmounting physical limitations by emphasizing the compensating rewards of cognitive, emotional, and social powers

- *Ego transcendence:* As contemporaries die, facing the reality of death constructively through efforts to make life more secure, meaningful, and gratifying for younger generations

In Peck's theory, ego integrity requires older adults to move beyond their life's work, their bodies, and their separate identities. Research suggests that as seniors grow older, both *body transcendence* (focusing on psychological strengths) and *ego transcendence* (orienting toward a larger, more distant future) increase. In a study of women, those in their eighties and nineties stated with greater certainty than those in their sixties that they "accept the changes brought about by aging," "have moved beyond fear of death," "have a clearer sense of the meaning of

life," and "have found new, positive spiritual gifts to explore" (Brown & Lowis, 2003).

Erikson's widow Joan Erikson suggested that these attainments actually represent development beyond ego integrity (which requires satisfaction with one's past life) to an additional psychosocial stage that she calls **gerotranscendence**—a cosmic and transcendent perspective directed forward and outward, beyond the self. Drawing on her own experience of aging, her observations of her husband's final years, and the work of others on the positive potential of the years shortly before death, Joan Erikson speculated that success in attaining gerotranscendence is apparent in heightened inner calm and contentment and additional time spent in quiet reflection (Erikson, 1998; Tornstam, 2000, 2011).

Although interviews with people in their ninth and tenth decades reveal that many (but not all) experience this peaceful, contemplative state, more research is needed to confirm the existence of a distinct, transcendent late-life stage. Besides focusing more intently on life's meaning, many of the very old continue to report investments in the real world—visiting friends, keeping up with current events, striving to be a good neighbor, and engaging in leisure and volunteer pursuits.

Labouvie-Vief's Emotional Expertise

In Chapter 13, we discussed Gisella Labouvie-Vief's research on development of adults' reasoning about emotion (see page 359). Recall that cognitive-affective complexity (awareness and coordination of positive and negative feelings into an organized self-description) increases from adolescence through middle adulthood and then declines as basic information-processing skills diminish in late adulthood.

But older people display a compensating emotional strength: They gain in **affect optimization,** the ability to maximize positive emotion and dampen negative emotion (Labouvie-Vief, 2005; Labouvie-Vief et al., 2007; Labouvie-Vief, Grühn, & Studer, 2010). Compared with younger people, older adults selectively attend to and better recall emotionally positive over negative information, which contributes to their remarkable resilience (Mather & Carstensen, 2005). Despite physical declines, increased health problems, a restricted future, and death of loved ones, most older people sustain a sense of optimism, emotional stability, and good psychological well-being—an upbeat attitude linked to longer survival (Boyle et al., 2009; Carstensen et al., 2011). Furthermore, about 30 to 40 percent not only are high in affect optimization but also retain considerable capacity for cognitive-affective complexity—a combination related to especially effective emotional self-regulation.

Furthermore, many aging individuals describe their emotional reactions to personal experiences more vividly than younger people—evidence of being more in touch with their feelings. Older adults' emotional perceptiveness helps them separate interpretations from objective aspects of situations. Consequently, their coping strategies often include making sure they fully understand their own feelings before deciding on a

Despite serious medical problems, this aging adult asserts, "Being an invalid does not invalidate your life." Her adopted rescue dog gives her great pleasure. The ability to maximize positive emotion and dampen negative emotion contributes to older people's remarkable resilience.

course of action. And they readily use emotion-centered coping strategies (controlling distress internally) in negatively charged situations (Blanchard-Fields, 2007). In sum, a significant late-life psychosocial attainment is becoming expert at reflecting on one's own feelings and regulating negative affect.

Reminiscence

We often think of older adults as engaged in **reminiscence**—telling stories about people and events from their past and reporting associated thoughts and feelings. Indeed, the widespread image of a reminiscing older person ranks among negative stereotypes of aging. In this common view, older people live in the past to escape the realities of a shortened future. Yet research consistently reveals no age differences exist in total quantity of reminiscing! Rather, younger and older adults often use reminiscence for different purposes (Westerhof, Bohlmeijer, & Webster, 2010). And certain types of reminiscence are positive and adaptive.

In his comments on major events in his life at the beginning of this chapter, Walt was engaging in a special form of reminiscence called *life review*—calling up past experiences with the goal of achieving greater self-understanding. According to Robert Butler (1968), most older adults engage in life review as part of attaining ego integrity. Older adults who participate in counselor-led life review report increased self-esteem, greater sense of purpose in life, and reduced depression (O'Rourke, Cappeliez, & Claxton, 2011; Westerhof, Bohlmeijer, & Webster, 2010).

But many older people who are high in self-acceptance and life satisfaction spend little time evaluating their past (Wink, 2007; Wink & Schiff, 2002). Indeed, in several studies in which older people were asked what they considered to be the best time of life, 10 to 30 percent identified one of the decades of late adulthood. Early and middle adulthood received especially high marks, whereas childhood and adolescence ranked as less satisfying (Field, 1997; Mehlson, Platz, & Fromholt, 2003). These findings challenge the widespread belief that older adults inevitably focus on the past and wish to be young again. To the contrary, today's seniors in industrialized nations are largely present- and future-oriented: They seek avenues for personal growth and fulfillment (see the Cultural Influences box on page 482).

Clearly, life review is not essential for adapting well to late adulthood. Indeed, reminiscence that is *self-focused*, engaged in to reduce boredom and revive bitter events, is linked to adjustment problems. Compared with younger people, older adults less often engage in this ruminative form of reminiscence (Bohlmeijer et al., 2007; O'Rourke, Cappeliez, & Claxton, 2011). Rather, extroverted seniors favor *other-focused* reminiscence directed at social goals, such as solidifying family and friendship ties and reliving relationships with lost loved ones. And at times, older adults—especially those who score high in openness to experience—engage in *knowledge-based* reminiscence, drawing on their past for effective problem-solving strategies and for teaching younger people (Cappeliez, Rivard, & Guindon, 2007). These socially engaged, mentally stimulating forms of reminiscence help make life rich and rewarding.

For young and old alike, reminiscence often occurs during times of life transition. Older adults who have recently retired, been widowed, or moved to a new residence may turn temporarily to the past to sustain a sense of personal continuity (Cappeliez & Robitaille, 2010). During these times, reminiscing about positive memories probably helps them recapture a sense of meaning.

Stability and Change in Self-Concept and Personality

Longitudinal research reveals continuing stability of the "big five" personality traits from mid- to late life (see Chapter 16, page 431). Yet the ingredients of ego integrity—wholeness, contentment, and image of the self as part of a larger world order—are reflected in several significant late-life changes in both self-concept and personality.

Secure and Multifaceted Self-Concept

Older adults have accumulated a lifetime of self-knowledge, leading to more secure and complex conceptions of themselves than at earlier ages (Diehl et al., 2011; Labouvie-Vief & Diehl, 1999). Ruth, for example, knew with certainty that she was good at growing a flower garden, budgeting money, counseling

Cultural Influences

The New Old Age

After retiring, pediatrician Jack McConnell tried a relaxing lifestyle near a lake and golf course, but it worked poorly for the energetic 64-year-old. As his desire for a more fulfilling retirement grew, he noticed that outside his comfortable, gated neighborhood were many people serving community needs as gardeners, laborers, fast-food workers, and the like, yet who lived in or near poverty. The contrast galvanized Jack to found Volunteers in Medicine, a free clinic for working-poor adults and their families who lack health insurance (Croker, 2007). Five years later, at age 69, Jack was overseeing a highly cost-effective operation involving 200 retired doctors, nurses, and lay volunteers, who treat 6,000 patients a year.

Increasingly, older adults are using their freedom from work and parenting responsibilities to pursue personally enriching interests and goals. In doing so, they are giving back to their communities in significant ways and serving as role models for younger generations.

Added years of longevity and health plus financial stability have granted this active, opportunistic time of life to so many contemporary seniors that some experts believe a new phase of late adulthood has evolved called the **Third Age**—a term originating over a decade ago in France that spread through Western Europe and recently has stretched to North America. According to this view, the First Age is childhood, the Second Age is the adult period of earning a living and rearing children, and the Third Age—extending from ages 65 to 79, and sometimes longer—is a time of personal fulfillment (James & Wink, 2007). The Fourth Age brings physical decline and need for care.

The baby boomers—healthier and financially better off than any preceding aging generation—are approaching late life with the conviction that their old age will not begin until 80 (Gergen & Gergen, 2003). This self-perception has helped define the Third Age as a time of self-realization and high life satisfaction. As we will see later in this chapter, retirement is no longer a one-way, age-graded event. In one survey of 300 older Americans, very few self-identified as retired (Trafford, 2004). Instead, they were building hybrid lives—leaving career jobs to work at different jobs that utilized their skills and devoting themselves to community service (Moen & Altobelli, 2007).

Although policy makers often express concern about the huge, impending baby-boomer burden on Social Security and Medicare, this large pool of vigorous, publicly minded future seniors has the potential to make enormous economic and social contri-

For many, late adulthood is a time of personal enrichment. Since retiring from her university faculty position, 82-year-old Freda Briggs continues as an advocate for abused children while also embracing new adventures, such as parasailing.

butions. Today's Third Agers donate billions to the global economy in volunteer work and continue to participate in the work force in large numbers.

But as midlife roles shrink and terminate, too few alternatives are available for the many aging adults eager to make a difference (Bass, 2011). Societies need to provide abundant volunteer, national service, and other public interest opportunities, thereby harnessing their rich elder resources to solve pressing problems. The U.S. Serve America Act, signed into law in 2009, offers expanded service incentives and options to American adults of all ages and, thus, is a major step in that direction.

---

others, giving dinner parties, and figuring out who could be trusted and who couldn't. Furthermore, when young and older adults were asked for several life-defining memories, 65- to 85-year-olds were more likely to mention events with a consistent theme—such as the importance of relationships or personal independence—and to explain how the events were interrelated (McLean, 2008). Their autobiographical selves emphasized coherence and consistency, despite physical, cognitive, and occupational changes.

Ruth's firm and multifaceted self-concept allowed for self-acceptance—a key feature of integrity. In a study of old (70 to 84 years) and very old (85 to 103 years) German seniors asked to respond to the question "Who am I?," participants mentioned more positive than negative self-evaluations. And positive, multifaceted self-definitions predicted psychological well-being (Freund & Smith, 1999).

As the future shortens, most older adults, into their eighties and nineties, continue to mention—and actively pursue—hoped-for selves in the areas of physical health, cognitive functioning, personal characteristics, relationships, social responsibility, and leisure (Frazier, 2002; Markus & Herzog, 1992). At the same time, possible selves reorganize well into old age. When the German 70- to 103-year-olds just mentioned were followed longitudinally for four years, the majority deleted some possible selves and replaced them with new ones (Smith & Freund, 2002). Older adults often characterize hoped-for selves in terms of "improving," "achieving," or "attaining," and those with hoped-for goals usually take concrete steps to attain them. Engaging in hope-related activities, in turn, is associated with gains in life satisfaction and with longer life (Hoppmann et al., 2007). Clearly, late adulthood is not a time of withdrawal from future planning!

Agreeableness, Acceptance of Change, and Openness to Experience

A flexible, optimistic approach to life, which fosters resilience in the face of adversity, is common in old age. Both open-ended interviews and personality tests reveal that older adults gain in *agreeableness*, becoming increasingly generous, acquiescent, and good-natured well into late life (Allemand, Zimprich, & Martin, 2008; Field & Millsap, 1991; Weiss et al., 2005). Agreeableness seems to characterize people who have come to terms with life despite its imperfections.

At the same time, older adults show modest age-related dips in *extroversion*, perhaps reflecting a narrowing of social contacts as people become more selective about relationships—a trend we will take up in a later section. Older people also tend to decline in *openness to experience*, likely due to their awareness of cognitive declines (Allemand, Zimprich, & Martin, 2008; Donnellan & Lucas, 2008). But engaging in cognitively challenging activities can promote openness to experience! In one study, 60- to 94-year-olds participated in a 16-week cognitive training program in reasoning, which included experience in solving challenging but enjoyable puzzles. During the program, the trained group showed steady gains in both reasoning and openness to experience not displayed by untrained controls. Sustained intellectual engagement seemed to induce seniors to view themselves as more open (Jackson et al., 2012). Openness, in turn, predicts pursuit of intellectual stimulation, thereby contributing to enhanced cognitive functioning.

Another late-life development is greater *acceptance of change* (Rossen, Knafl, & Flood, 2008). When asked about dissatisfactions in their lives, many seniors respond that they are not unhappy about anything! Acceptance of change is also evident in most older people' effective coping with the loss of loved ones, including death of a spouse, which they describe as the most stressful event they ever experienced (Lund, Caserta, & Dimond, 1993). The capacity to accept life's twists and turns, many of which are beyond one's control, is vital for adaptive functioning in late adulthood.

Most older adults are resilient, bouncing back in the face of adversity—especially if they did so earlier in their lives. And their heightened capacity for positive emotion contributes greatly to their resilience. Older adults' general cheerfulness strengthens their physiological resistance to stress, enabling them to conserve physical and mental resources needed for effective coping (Ong, Mroczek, & Riffin, 2011). The minority who are high in neuroticism—emotionally negative, short-tempered, and dissatisfied—tend to cope poorly with stressful events, experience mounting negative affect, and are at risk for health problems and earlier death (Mroczek & Spiro, 2007; Mroczek, Spiro, & Turiano, 2009).

Spirituality and Religiosity

How do older adults manage to accept declines and losses yet still feel whole and complete and anticipate death with calm composure? One possibility, consistent with Peck's and Erikson's emphasis on a transcendent perspective among seniors, is the development of a more mature sense of spirituality. Spirituality is not the same as religion: An inspirational sense of life's meaning can be found in art, nature, and social relationships. But for many people, religion provides beliefs, symbols, and rituals that guide this quest for meaning.

Older adults attach great value to religious beliefs and behaviors. In recent national surveys, over 70 percent of Americans age 65 and older said that religion is very important in their lives—the highest of any age group (Gallup News Service, 2006, 2012). Although health and transportation difficulties reduce organized religious participation in advanced old age, U.S. seniors generally become more religious or spiritual as they age.

The late-life increase in religiosity, however, is modest, and it is far from universal. Longitudinal research reveals that the majority of people show stability in religiosity throughout adulthood (Ai, Wink, & Ardelt, 2010; Dillon & Wink, 2007). Furthermore, in a British investigation following adults for two decades, one-fourth of seniors said they had become less religious, with some citing disappointment at the support they had received from their religious institution during stressful times (such as bereavement) as the reason (Coleman, Ivani-Chalian, & Robinson, 2004). Despite these differences, spirituality and faith may advance to a higher level in late adulthood—away from prescribed beliefs toward a more reflective approach that emphasizes links to others and is at ease with mystery and uncertainty and that accepts one's own belief system as one of many possible worldviews (Fowler & Dell, 2006).

Involvement in both organized and informal religious activities is especially high among low-SES ethnic minority older people, including African-American, Hispanic, and Native-American groups. African-American seniors look to religion as a powerful resource for social support beyond the family and for the inner strength to withstand daily stresses and physical impairments (Armstrong & Crowther, 2002). Compared with their Caucasian agemates, more African-American older adults report collaborating with God to overcome life problems (Lee & Sharpe, 2007).

Throughout adulthood, women are more likely than men to say that religion is very important to them, to participate in religious activities, and to engage in a personal quest for connectedness with a higher power (Gallup News Service, 2012; Wink & Dillon, 2002). Women's higher rates of poverty, widowhood, and participation in caregiving expose them to higher levels of stress and anxiety. As with ethnic minorities, they turn to religion for social support and for a larger vision of community that places life's challenges in perspective.

Religious involvement is associated with diverse benefits, including better physical and psychological well-being, more time devoted to exercising and leisure activities, greater sense of closeness to family and friends, and greater generativity (care for others) (Boswell, Kahana, & Dilworth-Anderson, 2006; Gillum et al., 2008; Krause, 2012; Wink, 2006, 2007). In longitudinal research, both organized and informal religious participation predicted longer survival, after many factors known to affect mortality were controlled (Helm et al., 2000; Strawbridge et al., 2001).

Contextual Influences on Psychological Well-Being

Personal and situational factors often combine to affect psychological well-being. Identifying these contextual influences is vital for designing interventions that foster positive adjustment.

Control versus Dependency

As Ruth's eyesight, hearing, and mobility declined in her eighties, Sybil visited daily to help with self-care and household tasks. During the hours mother and daughter were together, Sybil interacted most often with Ruth when she asked for help with activities of daily living. When Ruth handled tasks on her own, Sybil usually withdrew.

Observations of people interacting with older adults in both private homes and institutions reveal two highly predictable, complementary behavior patterns. In the first, called the **dependency–support script,** dependent behaviors are attended to immediately. In the second, the **independence–ignore script,** independent behaviors are mostly ignored. Notice how these sequences reinforce dependent behavior at the expense of independent behavior, regardless of the older person's competencies (Baltes, 1995, 1996). Even a self-reliant individual like Ruth did not always resist Sybil's unnecessary help because it brought about social contact.

Among older people who experience no difficulty with daily activities, opportunities to interact with others are related to high satisfaction with everyday life. In contrast, among older adults who have trouble performing daily activities, social contact is linked to a less positive everyday existence (Lang & Baltes, 1997). This suggests that social interaction while assisting seniors with physical care, household chores, and errands is often not meaningful and rewarding but, rather, demeaning and unpleasant. Consider these typical reactions of care recipients to a spouse's help with daily activities: "felt indebted," "felt like a weak, incapable person" (Newsom, 1999).

Longitudinal research shows that negative reactions to caregiving can result in persisting depression (Newsom &

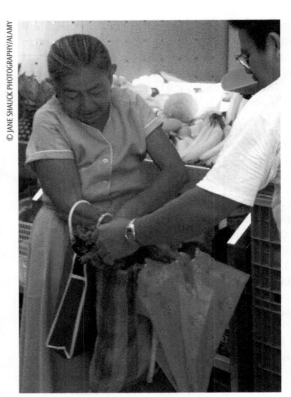

By letting her son help with grocery shopping, will this Mexican 80-year-old become too dependent? Not necessarily. When older adults assume personal control over areas of dependency, they can conserve their strength and invest it in highly valued activities.

Schulz, 1998). But whether assistance from others undermines well-being depends on many factors, including the quality of help, the caregiver–older adult relationship, and the social and cultural context in which helping occurs. In Western societies, which highly value independence, many older adults fear relinquishing control and becoming dependent on others (Curtiss, Hayslip, & Dolan, 2007; Frazier, 2002). As physical and cognitive limitations increase, granting older adults the freedom to choose those areas in which they desire help preserves their autonomy (Lachman, Neupert, & Agrigoroaei, 2011). Dependency can be adaptive if it permits older people to remain in control by choosing those areas in which they desire help. In this way, they can conserve their strength by investing it in self-chosen, highly valued activities, using a set of strategies considered in Chapter 17: *selective optimization with compensation.*

Assistance aimed at enabling older adults use their capacities fully in pursuit of their goals sustains an effective **person–environment fit**—a good match between their abilities and the demands of their living environments, which promotes adaptive behavior and psychological well-being. When people cannot maximize use of their capacities (have become excessively dependent), they react with boredom and passivity. When they encounter environmental demands that are too great (receive too little assistance), they experience overwhelming stress.

Physical Health

Physical declines and chronic disease can lead to a sense of loss of personal control—a powerful contributor to mental health problems. Physical illness resulting in disability is among the strongest risk factors for late-life depression (Morrison, 2008; Whitbourne & Meeks, 2011). Although fewer older than young and middle-aged adults are depressed (see Chapter 17), profound feelings of hopelessness rise with age as physical disability and consequent social isolation increase. But more than actual physical limitations, *perceived negative physical health* predicts depressive symptoms (Jang et al., 2007; Weinberger & Whitbourne, 2010). This helps explain the stronger physical impairment–depression relationship among higher-SES aging adults (Schieman & Plickert, 2007). Because of their lifetime of better physical health, they probably experience physical limitations as more unexpected and challenging.

Depression in old age is often lethal. People age 65 and older have the highest suicide rate of all age groups (see the Social Issues: Health box on page 486). What factors enable seniors like Ruth to surmount the physical impairment–depression relationship, remaining content? Personal characteristics discussed in this and earlier chapters—optimism, sense of self-efficacy, and effective coping—are vitally important (Morrison, 2008). But for frail aging adults to display these attributes, families and caregivers must avoid the dependency–support script and, instead, grant them autonomy.

Unfortunately, older adults generally do not get the mental health care they need—even in nursing homes, where depression and other mental health problems are widespread (Grabowski et al., 2010; Karel, Gatz, & Smyer, 2012). More than half of U.S. nursing home residents receive no regular mental health intervention.

Negative Life Changes

Ruth lost Walt to a heart attack, cared for her sister Ida as her Alzheimer's symptoms worsened, and faced health problems of her own—all within a span of a few years. Older adults are at risk for a variety of negative life changes—death of loved ones, illness and physical disabilities, declining income, and greater dependency. Negative life changes are difficult for everyone but may actually evoke less stress and depression in older than in younger adults (Charles, 2011). Many older people have learned to cope with hard times and to appraise negative changes as common and expected in late life.

Still, when negative changes pile up, they test the coping skills of older adults. In very old age, such changes are greater for women than for men. Women over age 75 are far less likely to be married, more often have lower incomes, and suffer from more illnesses—especially ones that restrict mobility. Furthermore, older women (as at younger ages) more often say that others depend on them for caregiving and emotional support. Thus, their social relations, even in very old age, are more often a source of stress (Antonucci, Ajrouch, & Birditt, 2008). And because of their own declining health, older women may not be able to meet others' needs for care—circumstances associated with chronic, high distress (Charles, 2010). Not surprisingly, women of advanced age tend to report lower psychological well-being than do men (Pinquart & Sörensen, 2001).

Social Support

In late adulthood, social support continues to reduce stress, thereby promoting physical health, psychological well-being, and longevity (Fry & Debats, 2006; Temkin-Greener et al., 2004). Usually, older adults receive informal assistance with tasks of daily living from family members—first from their spouse or, if none exists, from children and then from siblings.

Nevertheless, many older people place such high value on independence that they do not want extensive help from others close to them unless they can reciprocate. When assistance is excessive or cannot be returned, it often results in reduced self-efficacy and psychological stress (Liang, Krause, & Bennett, 2001; Warner et al., 2011). Perhaps for this reason, adult children express a deeper sense of obligation toward their aging parents than their parents expect from them. Formal support—a paid home helper or agency-provided services—as a complement to informal assistance not only helps relieve caregiving burden but also spares aging adults from feeling overly dependent in their close relationships.

Ethnic minority older adults are more willing to accept assistance when home helpers are connected to a familiar neighborhood organization, especially the church (Coke, 1992; Taylor, Lincoln, & Chatters, 2005). Support from religious congregants has psychological benefits for older people of all backgrounds, perhaps because recipients feel that it is motivated by genuine care and concern, not just obligation (Krause, 2001). Also, the warm atmosphere of religious organizations fosters a sense of social acceptance and belonging.

Overall, for social support to foster well-being, older adults must take personal control of it. As suggested earlier, this means consciously giving up primary control in some areas to remain in control of other, highly valued pursuits (Heckhausen, Wrosch, & Schultz, 2010). Help that is not wanted or needed or that exaggerates weaknesses results in poor person–environment fit, undermines mental health, and—if existing skills fall into disuse—accelerates physical disability. In contrast, help that increases autonomy—that frees up energy for endeavors that are personally satisfying and that lead to growth—enhances quality of life. These findings clarify why *perceived social support* (older adults' sense of being able to count on family or friends in times of need) is associated with a positive outlook in older adults with disabilities, whereas sheer *amount* of help family and friends provide has little impact (Uchino, 2009).

Finally, besides tangible assistance, older adults benefit from social support that offers affection, affirmation of their self-worth, and sense of belonging. As we will see in the next section, supportive social ties in old age have little to do with quantity of contact. Instead, high-quality relationships, involving expressions of kindness, encouragement, respect, and emotional closeness, have the greatest impact on mental health in late life.

Social Issues: Health

Elder Suicide

When 65-year-old Abe's wife died, he withdrew from life. Living far from his two daughters, he spent his nonworking days alone, watching television and reading mystery novels. As grandchildren were born, Abe visited his daughters' homes from time to time, carrying his despondent behavior with him.

After arthritis made walking difficult, Abe retired. With more empty days, his depression deepened. Gradually, he developed painful digestive difficulties, but he refused to see a doctor. "Don't need to," he said abruptly when one of his daughters begged him to get medical attention. Answering her invitation to a grandchild's tenth birthday party, Abe wrote, "Maybe—if I'm still around next month." Two weeks later, Abe died from an intestinal blockage. His body was found in the living room chair where he habitually spent his days. Although it may seem surprising, Abe's self-destructive acts are a form of suicide.

Factors Related to Elder Suicide

Recall from Chapter 12 that suicide increases over the lifespan. Although age differences in adulthood rates are shrinking, suicide continues to climb in late adulthood. Older adults are at increased risk in most countries throughout the world (World Health Organization, 2013b).

The higher suicide rate among males persists in late life. Five times as many U.S. aging men as women take their own lives. Suicide among white men age 70 and older rises steeply with age, whereas it actually declines after age 75 in women (U.S. Census Bureau, 2013). Compared with the white majority, most ethnic minority older adults have low suicide rates.

What explains these trends? Despite the lifelong pattern of higher rates of depression and more suicide attempts among females, older women's closer ties to family and friends, greater willingness to seek social support, and religiosity prevent many from taking their own lives. High levels of social support through extended families and church affiliations also may prevent suicide among ethnic minorities (Conwell, Van

Orden, & Caine, 2011). And within certain minority groups, such as Alaskan Natives, deep respect for older adults strengthens self-esteem and social integration (Kettl, 1998). This reduces elder suicide, making it nonexistent after age 80.

As in earlier years, the methods favored by older males (firearms, hanging) offer less chance of revival than those by older females (poisoning or drug overdose). Nevertheless, failed suicides are much rarer in old age than in adolescence (Conwell, Van Orden, & Caine, 2011). When seniors decide to die, they seem especially determined to succeed.

Underreporting of suicides probably occurs at all ages, but it is more common in old age. Medical examiners are less likely to pursue suicide as a cause of death when a person is old. And many older adults, like Abe, engage in indirect self-destructive acts rarely classified as suicide—refusing to eat or take prescribed medications. Among institutionalized seniors, these efforts to hasten death are widespread (Reiss & Tishler, 2008). Consequently, elder suicide is an even larger problem than official statistics indicate.

Two types of events prompt suicide in late life. Losses—retirement from a highly valued occupation, widowhood, or social isolation—place seniors who have difficulty coping with change at risk for persistent depression. Risks of another type arise when chronic and terminal illnesses severely reduce physical functioning or cause intense pain (Conwell et al., 2010). As comfort and quality of life diminish, feelings of hopelessness and helplessness deepen.

Prevention and Treatment

Warning signs of suicide in late adulthood, like those at earlier ages, include efforts to put personal affairs in order, statements about dying, despondency, and sleep and appetite changes. But family members, friends, and caregivers must also watch for indirect self-destructive acts that are unique to old age, such as refusing food or medical treatment. Too often, people in close touch with the elderly incorrectly assume that these symptoms are a "natural" consequence of aging.

Suicide reaches its highest rate among people age 75 and older. Warning signs include despondency, sleep and appetite changes, statements about dying, and efforts to put personal affairs in order.

When suicidal aging adults are depressed, the most effective treatment combines antidepressant medication with therapy, including help in coping with role transitions, such as retirement, widowhood, and dependency brought about by illness. Distorted ways of thinking ("I'm old—nothing can be done about my problems") must be countered and revised. Meeting with the family to find ways to reduce loneliness and desperation is also helpful.

Communities are beginning to recognize the importance of additional preventive steps, such as programs that help older adults cope with life transitions, telephone hot lines with trained volunteers who provide emotional support, and agencies that arrange for regular home visitors or "buddy system" phone calls (Lapierr et al., 2011). But so far, most of these efforts benefit women more than men because women are more likely to tell health professionals about high-risk symptoms and to use social resources.

Finally, elder suicide raises a controversial ethical issue: Do people with incurable illnesses have the right to take their own lives? We will take up this topic in Chapter 19.

ASK YOURSELF

REVIEW Many older people adapt effectively to negative life changes. List personal and situational factors that facilitate this generally positive outcome.

APPLY At age 85, Miriam took a long time to get dressed. Joan, her home helper, said, "From now on, don't get dressed until I get there. Then I can help, and it won't take so long." What impact is Joan's approach likely to have on Miriam's mental health? What alternative approach would you recommend?

REFLECT Among older people you know, do any fit the description of a Third Ager? Explain.

A Changing Social World

In late adulthood, extroverted individuals (like Walt and Ruth) continue to interact with a wider range of people than do introverts and people (like Dick) with poor social skills. Nevertheless, both cross-sectional and longitudinal research reveals that size of social networks and, therefore, amount of social interaction decline for virtually everyone (Antonucci, Akiyama, & Takahashi, 2004; Charles & Carstensen, 2009). This finding presents a curious paradox: If social interaction and social support are essential for mental health, how is it possible for older adults to interact less yet be generally satisfied with life and less depressed than younger adults?

Social Theories of Aging

Social theories of aging offer explanations for changes in aging adults' social activity. Two older perspectives—disengagement theory and activity theory—interpret declines in social interaction in opposite ways. More recent approaches—continuity theory and socioemotional selectivity theory—account for a wider range of findings.

Disengagement Theory. According to **disengagement theory**, mutual withdrawal between older adults and society takes place in anticipation of death (Cumming & Henry, 1961). Older people decrease their activity levels and interact less frequently, becoming more preoccupied with their inner lives. At the same time, society frees the old from employment and family responsibilities. The result is viewed as beneficial for both sides. Aging adults are granted a life of tranquility. And once they disengage, their deaths are less disruptive to society.

Clearly, however, most aging adults don't disengage! As we saw in Chapter 17 when we discussed wisdom, older people in many cultures move into new positions of prestige and power because of their long life experience. Even after retirement, many adults sustain aspects of their work; others develop new,

rewarding roles in their communities. Disengagement, then, may represent not older peoples' personal preference but, rather, a failure of the social world to provide opportunities for engagement. Indeed, an obvious application of disengagement theory—encouraging older people to withdraw from vital roles—can have profound negative consequences for their sense of self-worth and, at a societal level, waste valuable social resources!

As we will see shortly, older adults' retreat from interaction is more complex than disengagement theory implies. Instead of disengaging from all social ties, they let go of unsatisfying contacts and maintain satisfying ones.

Activity Theory. Attempting to overcome the flaws of disengagement theory, **activity theory** states that social barriers to engagement, not the desires of aging adults, cause declining rates of interaction. When older people lose certain roles (for example, through retirement or widowhood), they try to find others in an effort to stay about as active and busy as they were in middle age (Maddox, 1963). In this view, older adults' life satisfaction depends on conditions that permit them to remain engaged in roles and relationships.

Although people do seek alternative sources of meaning in response to social losses, activity theory fails to acknowledge any psychological change in old age. Many studies show that merely offering seniors opportunities for social contact does not lead to greater social activity. In nursing homes, for example, where social partners are abundant, social interaction is very low, even among the healthiest residents—a circumstance we will examine when we discuss housing arrangements for aging adults. Especially troubling for activity theory is the repeated finding that when health status is controlled, older people who have larger social networks and engage in more activities are not necessarily happier (Charles & Carstensen, 2009). Recall that quality, not quantity, of relationships predicts psychological well-being in old age.

Continuity Theory. According to **continuity theory**, rather than maintaining a certain activity level, most aging adults strive to maintain a personal system—an identity and a set of personality dispositions, interests, roles, and skills—that promotes life satisfaction by ensuring consistency between their past and anticipated future. This striving for continuity does not mean that older people's lives are static. To the contrary, aging produces inevitable change, but most older adults try to minimize stress and disruptiveness by integrating those changes into a coherent, consistent life path. As much as possible, they choose to use familiar skills and engage in familiar activities with familiar people—preferences that provide a secure sense of routine and direction in life.

Research confirms a high degree of continuity in older adults' everyday pursuits and relationships. Even after a change (such as retirement), people usually make choices that extend the previous direction of their lives, engaging in new activities but often within familiar domains. For example, a retired manager of a children's bookstore collaborated with friends to build a children's library and donate it to an overseas orphanage. A musician who, because of arthritis, could no longer play the violin arranged regular get-togethers with musically inclined friends to listen to and talk about music. Robert Atchley (1989), originator of continuity theory, noted, "Everyday life for most older people is like long-running improvisational theater in which . . . changes are mostly in the form of new episodes [rather] than entirely new plays" (p. 185).

Aging adults' reliance on continuity has many benefits. Participating in familiar activities with familiar people provides repeated practice that helps preserve physical and cognitive functioning, fosters self-esteem and mastery, and affirms identity (Finchum & Weber, 2000; Vacha-Haase, Hill, & Bermingham, 2012). Investing in long-standing, close relationships provides comfort, pleasure, and a network of social support. Finally, striving for continuity is essential for attaining Erikson's sense of ego integrity, which depends on preserving a sense of personal history (Atchley, 1999).

Socioemotional Selectivity Theory.

A final perspective addresses how people's social networks sustain continuity while also narrowing as they age. According to **socioemotional selectivity theory**, social interaction extends lifelong selection processes. In middle adulthood, marital relationships deepen, siblings feel closer, and number of friendships declines. In old

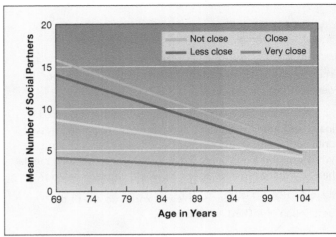

FIGURE 18.1 Age-related change in number of social partners varying in closeness. In interviews with over 500 older adults ranging in age from 69 to 104, the number of "not close" and "less close" partners fell off steeply with age, whereas the number of "close" and "very close" partners declined minimally. (From F. R. Lang, U. M. Staudinger, & L. L. Carstensen, 1998, "Perspectives on Socioemotional Selectivity in Late Life: How Personality and Social Context Do (and Do Not) Make a Difference," *Journal of Gerontology, 53B,* p. 24. Copyright © 1998 The Gerontological Society of America. Adapted by permission of Oxford University Press and F. R. Lang.)

age, contacts with family and long-term friends are sustained until the eighties, when they diminish gradually in favor of a few very close relationships. In contrast, as Figure 18.1 shows, contacts with acquaintances and willingness to form new social ties fall off steeply from middle through late adulthood (Carstensen, 2006; Carstensen, Fung, & Charles, 2003; Fung, Carstensen, & Lang, 2001).

What explains these changes? Socioemotional selectivity theory states that physical and psychological aspects of aging lead to changes in the functions of social interaction. *TAKE A MOMENT...* Consider the reasons you interact with members of your social network. At times, you approach them to get information. At other times, you seek affirmation of your worth as a person. You also choose social partners to regulate emotion, approaching those who evoke positive feelings and avoiding those who make you feel sad, angry, or uncomfortable. For older adults, who have gathered a lifetime of information, the information-gathering function becomes less significant. Also, they realize it is risky to approach people they do not know for self-affirmation: Negative stereotypes of aging increase the odds of receiving a condescending, hostile, or indifferent response.

Instead, as physical fragility makes it more important to avoid stress, older adults emphasize the emotion-regulating function of interaction. In one study, younger and older adults were asked to categorize their social partners. Younger people more often sorted them on the basis of information seeking and future contact, whereas older people emphasized anticipated feelings (Frederickson & Carstensen, 1990). They appeared highly motivated to approach pleasant relationships and avoid unpleasant

These sisters—ages 93 and 89—greet each other with enthusiasm. The one on the right traveled from Poland to New York City for this reunion. To preserve emotional equilibrium and reduce stress, older adults increasingly emphasize familiar, emotionally rewarding relationships.

ones. Interacting mostly with relatives and friends increases the chances that emotional equilibrium will be preserved. Within these close bonds, older adults actively apply their emotional expertise to promote harmony. They are less likely than younger people to respond to tensions with destructive tactics (yelling, arguing) and more likely to use constructive strategies, such as expressing affection or disengaging to calmly let the situation blow over (Birditt & Fingerman, 2005; Luong, Charles, & Fingerman, 2011). They also reinterpret conflict in less stressful ways—often by identifying something positive in the situation (Labouvie-Vief, 2003). Consequently, despite their smaller social networks, they are happier than younger people with their number of friends and report fewer problematic relationships (Blanchard-Fields & Coats, 2008; Fingerman & Birditt, 2003).

Research confirms that people's perception of time is strongly linked to their social goals. When remaining time is limited, adults *of all ages* shift from focusing on long-term goals to emphasizing emotionally fulfilling relationships in the here and now (Charles & Carstensen, 2010). Similarly, seniors—aware that time is "running out"—don't waste it on unlikely future payoffs but, instead, turn to close friends and family members. Furthermore, we generally take special steps to facilitate positive interaction with people dear to us whose time is limited—for example, treating older friends and relatives more kindly than younger ones, easily excusing or forgiving their social transgressions (Luong, Charles, & Fingerman, 2011). In this way, social partners contribute to older adults' gratifying relationship experiences. In sum, socioemotional selectivity theory views older adults' preference for high-quality, emotionally fulfilling relationships as resulting from changing life conditions.

Social Contexts of Aging: Communities, Neighborhoods, and Housing

The physical and social contexts in which aging adults live affect their social experiences and, consequently, their development and adjustment. Communities, neighborhoods, and housing arrangements vary in the extent to which they enable aging residents to satisfy their social needs.

Communities and Neighborhoods. About half of U.S. ethnic minority older adults live in cities, compared with just one-third of Caucasians. The majority of seniors reside in suburbs, where they moved earlier in their lives and usually remain after retirement. Suburban older adults have higher incomes and report better health than their inner-city counterparts do. But inner-city older people are better off in terms of public transportation. As declines in physical functioning compromise out-of-home mobility, convenient bus, tram, and rail lines become increasingly important to life satisfaction and psychological well-being (Mollenkopf, Hieber, & Wahl, 2011;

Oswald et al., 2010). Furthermore, city-dwelling seniors fare better in terms of health, income, and proximity of social services and cultural activities than do the one-fifth of U.S. older people who live in small towns and rural areas (U.S. Department of Health and Human Services, 2012e). In addition, small-town and rural seniors are less likely to live near their children, who often leave these communities in early adulthood.

Yet small-town and rural aging adults compensate for distance from children and social services by establishing closer relationships with nearby extended family and by interacting more with neighbors and friends (Hooyman & Kiyak, 2011; Shaw, 2005). Smaller communities have features that foster gratifying relationships—stability of residents, shared values and lifestyles, willingness to exchange social support, and frequent social visits as country people "drop in" on one another. And many suburban and rural communities have responded to aging residents' needs by developing transportation programs (such as special buses and vans) to take them to health and social services, senior centers, and shopping centers.

Both urban and rural older adults report greater life satisfaction when many senior citizens reside in their neighborhood and are available as like-minded companions. Presence of family is less crucial when neighbors and nearby friends provide social support (Gabriel & Bowling, 2004). This does not mean that neighbors replace family relationships. But older adults are content as long as their children and other relatives who live far away arrange occasional visits (Hooyman & Kiyak, 2011).

Housing Arrangements. Seniors' housing preferences reflect a strong desire for **aging in place**—remaining in a familiar setting where they have control over their everyday life. Overwhelmingly, older people in Western nations want to stay in the neighborhoods where they spent their adult lives; in fact, 90 percent remain in or near their old home. In the United States, fewer than 4 percent relocate to other communities (U.S.

Like many older adults, these dog lovers reap great satisfaction from residing in a neighborhood with like-minded senior residents. Presence of family is less crucial when neighbors and nearby friends provide social support.

Department of Health and Human Services, 2012e). These moves are usually motivated by a desire to live closer to children or, among the more economically advantaged and healthy, a desire for a more temperate climate and a place to pursue leisure interests.

Most aging adults' relocations occur within the same town or city and are prompted by declining health, widowhood, or disability (Sergeant, Ekerdt, & Chapin, 2008). As we look at housing arrangements for older adults, we will see that the more a setting deviates from home life, the harder it is for older people to adjust.

Ordinary Homes. For the majority of older adults, who are not physically impaired, staying in their own homes affords the greatest possible personal control. More seniors in Western countries live on their own today than ever before—a trend due to improved health and economic well-being (U.S. Department of Health and Human Services, 2012e). But when health and mobility problems appear, independent living poses risks to an effective person–environment fit. Most homes are not modified to suit the physical capacities of their aging residents. Living alone with a physical disability is linked to social isolation and loneliness (Adams, Sanders, & Auth, 2004).

When Ruth reached her mid-eighties, Sybil begged her to move into her home. Like many adult children of Southern, Central, and Eastern European descent (Greek, Italian, Polish, and others), Sybil felt an especially strong obligation to care for her frail mother. Older adults of these cultural backgrounds, as well as African Americans, Asians, Hispanics, and Native Americans, more often live in extended families (see page 434 in Chapter 16).

Yet increasing numbers of ethnic minority older adults want to live on their own. For example, two decades ago, most Asian-American older adults were living with their children, whereas today 65 percent live independently—a trend also evident in certain Asian nations, such as Japan (Federal Interagency Forum on Aging Related Statistics, 2012; Takagi, Silverstein, & Crimmins, 2007). With sufficient income to keep her home, Ruth refused to move in with Sybil. Continuity theory helps us understand why many older adults react this way, even after health problems accumulate. As the site of memorable life events, the home strengthens continuity with the past, sustaining a sense of identity in the face of physical declines and social losses. And it permits older adults to adapt to their surroundings in familiar, comfortable ways (Atchley, 1999). Older people also value their independence, privacy, and network of nearby friends and neighbors.

During the past half century, the number of unmarried, divorced, and widowed seniors living alone has risen dramatically. Approximately 30 percent of U.S. older adults live by themselves, a figure that rises to nearly 50 percent for those age 85 and older (U.S. Census Bureau, 2013). Over 40 percent of American seniors who live alone are poverty-stricken—rates many times greater than among older couples. More than 70 percent are widowed women. Because of lower earnings in

Residents of a retirement community join visiting Girl Scouts to bake dog treats for animal shelters. By sustaining an effective person–environment fit as capacities change, residential communities enable older adults to enjoy a more active lifestyle.

earlier years, some entered old age this way. Others became poor for the first time, often because they outlived a spouse who suffered a lengthy, costly illness. With age, their financial status worsens as their assets shrink and their own health-care costs rise (Biegel & Liebbrant, 2006; U.S. Census Bureau, 2013). Under these conditions, isolation, loneliness, and depression can pile up. Poverty among lone aging women is deeper in the United States than in other Western nations because of less generous government-sponsored income and health benefits.

Residential Communities. About 7 percent of U.S. adults age 65 and older live in residential communities, a proportion that rises with age as functional limitations increase. Among people age 85 and older, 22 percent live in these communities, which come in great variety (U.S. Department of Health and Human Services, 2012e). Housing developments for the aged, either single-dwelling or apartment complexes, differ from ordinary homes only in that they have been modified to suit older adults' capacities (featuring, for example, single-level living space and grab bars in bathrooms).

For older adults who need more help with everyday tasks, *assisted-living* arrangements are available (see Chapter 17, page 467). **Congregate housing**—an increasingly popular long-term care option—provides a variety of support services, including meals in a common dining room, along with watchful oversight of residents with physical and mental disabilities. **Life-care communities** offer a range of housing alternatives, from independent or congregate housing to full nursing home care. For a large initial payment and additional monthly fees, life care guarantees that seniors' changing needs will be met within the same facility as they age.

Dick and Goldie decided in their late sixties to move to nearby congregate housing. For Dick, the move was a positive turn of events that permitted him to set aside past failures and relate to peers on the basis of their current life together. Dick found gratifying leisure pursuits—leading an exercise class, organizing a charity drive with Goldie, and using his skills as a baker to make cakes for birthday and anniversary celebrations.

By sustaining an effective person–environment fit as older adults' capacities change, residential communities have positive effects on physical and mental health. A specially designed physical space and care on an as-needed basis help seniors overcome mobility limitations, enabling greater social participation and a more active lifestyle (Fonda, Clipp, & Maddox, 2002; Jenkins, Pienta, & Horgas, 2002). And in societies where old age leads to reduced status, age-segregated living can be gratifying, opening up useful roles and leadership opportunities. The more older adults perceive the environment as socially supportive, the more they collaborate with one another in coping with stressors of aging and in providing assistance to other residents (Lawrence & Schigelone, 2002).

Nevertheless, no U.S. federal regulations govern assisted-living facilities, which vary widely in quality. Low-income ethnic minority seniors are less likely to use assisted living, and, when they do, usually enter lower-quality settings—conditions associated with high stress (Ball et al., 2009). And in some states, assisted-living facilities are prohibited from providing any nursing care and monitoring, requiring seniors to leave when their health declines (Hernandez & Newcomer, 2007). Yet physical designs and support services that enable aging in place are vital for aging adults' well-being. These include homelike surroundings, division of large environments into smaller units to facilitate meaningful activities and social relationships, and the latest assistive technologies (Cutler, 2007; Oswald & Wahl, 2013).

Shared values and goals among residents with similar backgrounds also enhance life satisfaction. Older adults who feel socially integrated into the setting are more likely to consider it their home. But those who lack like-minded companions are at high risk for loneliness and depression (Adams, Sanders, & Auth, 2004; Cutchin, 2013).

LOOK AND LISTEN

Visit an assisted-living community, and explore its housing options, physical design, and social and leisure opportunities. How well does the living environment support aging in place and effective person–environment fit? ●

Nursing Homes. The 5 percent of Americans age 65 and older who live in nursing homes experience the most extreme restriction of autonomy and social integration. Although potential companions are abundant, interaction is low. To regulate emotion in social interaction (so important to aging adults), personal control over social experiences is vital. Yet nursing home residents have little opportunity to choose their social partners, and timing of contact is generally deter-

mined by staff. Social withdrawal is an adaptive response to these often overcrowded, hospital-like settings, which typically provide few ways for residents to use their competencies. Not surprisingly, nursing home residents with physical but not mental impairments are far more depressed, anxious, and lonely than their community-dwelling counterparts (Guildner et al., 2001).

Designing more homelike nursing homes could help increase residents' sense of security and control. U.S. nursing homes, usually operated for profit, are often packed with residents and institutional in their operation. In contrast, European facilities are liberally supported by public funds and resemble high-quality assisted living.

In a radically changed U.S. nursing home concept called THE GREEN HOUSE® model, a large, outdated nursing home in Mississippi was replaced by ten small houses, each with ten or fewer residents who live in private bedroom–bathroom suites surrounding a family-style communal space (Rabig et al., 2006). Besides providing personal care, a stable staff of nursing assistants fosters aging adults' control and independence. Residents determine their own daily schedules and are invited to join in both recreational and household activities. A professional support team—including licensed nurses, therapists, social workers, physicians, and pharmacists—visits regularly to serve residents' health needs.

In a comparison of Green House residents with traditional nursing home residents, Green House older adults reported

© 2009 LYNN JOHNSON

THE GREEN HOUSE® model blurs distinctions among nursing home, assisted living, and "independent" living. In this homelike setting, residents determine their own daily schedules and help with household tasks. Green House living environments now exist in more than 20 U.S. states.

substantially better quality of life, and they also showed less decline over time in ability to carry out activities of daily living (Kane et al., 2007). By making the home a central, organizing principle, the Green House approach includes all the aging-in-place and effective person–environment fit features that ensure late-life well-being.

ASK YOURSELF

REVIEW Cite features of neighborhoods and residential communities that enhance aging adults' life satisfaction.

APPLY Sam lives alone in the same home he has occupied for over 30 years. His adult children cannot understand why he won't move across town to a modern apartment. Using continuity theory, explain why Sam prefers to stay where he is.

REFLECT Imagine yourself as an aging resident in assisted living. List all the features you would want your living context to have, explaining how each helps ensure effective person–environment fit and favorable psychological well-being.

Relationships in Late Adulthood

The **social convoy** is an influential model of changes in our social networks as we move through life. *TAKE A MOMENT...* Picture yourself in the midst of a cluster of ships traveling together, granting one another safety and support. Ships in the inner circle represent people closest to you, such as a spouse, best friend, parent, or child. Those less close, but still important, travel on the outside. With age, ships exchange places in the convoy, and some drift off while others join the procession (Antonucci, Birditt, & Ajrouch, 2011; Antonucci, Birditt, & Akiyama, 2009). As long as the convoy continues to exist, you adapt positively.

In the following sections, we examine the ways older adults with diverse lifestyles sustain social networks of family members and friends. Although size of the convoy decreases as age-mates die, aging adults are rarely left without people in their inner circle who contribute to their well-being—a testament to their resilience in maintaining effective social networks (Fiori, Smith, & Antonucci, 2007). But for some, tragically, the social convoy breaks down. We will also explore the circumstances in which older people experience abuse and neglect at the hands of those close to them.

Marriage

Even with the high U.S. divorce rate, one in every four or five first marriages is expected to last at least 50 years. Walt's comment to Ruth that "the last few decades have been the happiest" characterizes the attitudes and behaviors of many aging couples

After retirement, couples have more time to devote to joint leisure activities, which contributes to the rise in marital satisfaction from middle to late adulthood.

who have spent their adult lives together. Marital satisfaction rises from middle to late adulthood, when it is at its peak (Ko et al., 2007). Several changes in life circumstance and couples' communication underlie this trend.

First, late-life marriages involve fewer stressful responsibilities that can negatively affect relationships, such as rearing children and balancing demands of career and family (Diamond, Fagundes, & Butterworth, 2010). Second, perceptions of fairness in the relationship increase as men participate more in household tasks after retirement (Kulik, 2001). Third, with extra time together, the majority of couples engage in more joint leisure activities, which—especially for women—enhances sense of marital closeness (Trudel et al., 2008).

Fourth, greater emotional understanding and emphasis on regulating emotion in relationships lead to more positive interactions between spouses. Compared to younger couples, aging couples rate their relationship as higher in quality, disagree less often, and resolve their differences in more constructive ways. Even in unhappy marriages, older adults are less likely to let their disagreements escalate into expressions of anger and resentment (Hatch & Bulcroft, 2004). As in other relationships, seniors protect themselves from stress by molding marital ties to make them as pleasant as possible.

Finally, compared to their single agemates, married seniors generally have larger social networks of both family members and friends, which provide for social engagement and support and are linked to higher psychological well-being (Birditt & Antonucci, 2007; Fiori, Smith, & Antonucci, 2007). When marital dissatisfaction exists, however, even having close, high-quality friendships cannot reduce its profoundly negative impact on adjustment. A poor marriage often takes a greater toll on women than on men (Birditt & Antonucci, 2007; Whisman et al., 2006). Recall from Chapter 14 that women more often try to work on a troubling relationship, yet in late life, expending energy in this way is especially taxing, both physically and mentally.

Gay and Lesbian Partnerships

Most older gays and lesbians in long-term partnerships report happy, highly fulfilling relationships, pointing to their partner as their most important source of social support. Compared with gay and lesbian seniors who live alone, couples rate their physical and mental health more favorably (Grossman, 2006).

A lifetime of effective coping with an oppressive social environment may have strengthened homosexuals' skill at dealing with late-life physical and social changes, thereby contributing to a satisfying partnership (Gabbay & Wahler, 2002). And changing social conditions, including the greater ease with which younger generations embrace their sexual minority identities and "come out," may have encouraged more older adults to do the same, with benefits for their well-being (Cohler & Hostetler, 2007). Also, greater gender-role flexibility enables gay and lesbian couples to adapt easily to sharing household tasks following retirement.

Nevertheless, because of continuing prejudice, aging gays and lesbians face unique challenges. Health-care systems are often unresponsive to their unique needs. And where gay and lesbian unions are not legally recognized (in most U.S. states), if one partner becomes frail or ill, the other may not be welcome in hospitals or nursing homes or be allowed to participate in health-care decisions—an issue we will return to in Chapter 19. These circumstances can make late-life declines and losses especially painful.

Divorce, Remarriage, and Cohabitation

When Walt's uncle Louie was 65, he divorced his wife Sandra after 32 years of marriage. Although she knew the marriage was far from perfect, Sandra had lived with Louie long enough that the divorce came as a shock. A year later, Louie married Rachella, a divorcée who shared his enthusiasm for sports and dance.

Couples who divorce in late adulthood constitute less than 5 percent of all U.S. divorces in any given year (Elliott & Simmons, 2011). But the divorce rate among people age 65 and older has increased over the past three decades as new generations of seniors—especially the baby boomers—have become accepting of marital breakup as a means of attaining self-fulfillment and as the divorce risk has risen for second and subsequent marriages.

Although one-fifth of older adults' dissolving marriages are of less than 10 years duration, about half are lengthy—30 years or more (Brown & Lin, 2012). Compared with younger adults, longtime married older people find it harder to separate their identity from that of their former spouse and, therefore, may experience a greater sense of personal failure. Relationships with family and friends shift at a time when close bonds are crucial for psychological well-being.

As in middle adulthood, aging women are more likely than men to initiate divorce. This is despite the fact that the financial consequences for women generally are severe—greater than for widowhood because many accumulated assets are lost in property settlements (McDonald & Robb, 2004; Wu & Schimmele, 2007). Still, older people of both genders seldom express regret over leaving an unhappy marriage (Bair, 2007). Usually, they experience a sense of relief.

Remarriage rates are low in late adulthood and decline with age, though remarriage is more likely after divorce than after widowhood. Aging baby boomers—accustomed to using the Internet for many purposes—are increasingly turning to contemporary ways of searching for new partners, including online dating services and personal ads, though they use dating sites far less often than younger people do. But older peoples' personal ads indicate that they are more selective with respect to the age, race, religion, and income of a potential dating partner (McIntosh et al., 2011). And as Figure 18.2 shows, they more often refer to their own health issues and loneliness and less often to romance, sex, desire for a soulmate, and adventure than middle-aged people do (Alterovitz & Mendelsohn, 2013). In their search for the right person, seniors seem to take a candid, no-nonsense approach!

Compared with younger people who remarry, seniors who do so enter more stable relationships, as their divorce rate is much lower. In Louie and Rachella's case, the second marriage lasted for 28 years! Perhaps late-life remarriages are more successful because they involve more maturity, patience, and a better balance of romantic with practical concerns. Remarried

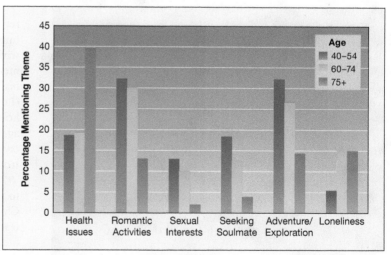

FIGURE 18.2 Themes in online personal ads of middle-aged and older adults seeking dating partners. An analysis of themes in 450 ads revealed that older adults more often mention health issues and loneliness, whereas middle-aged adults place greater emphasis on romance, sex, finding a soulmate, and adventure. Seniors appear to be practical and direct in their search for a partner. (From S. S. R. Alterovitz and G. A. Mendelsohn, 2013, "Relationship Goals of Middle-Aged, Young–Old, and Old–Old Internet Daters: An Analysis of Online Personal Ads." *Journal of Aging Studies, 27,* p. 163. Copyright © 2013, Elsevier. Reprinted by permission of Elsevier, Inc.)

older couples are generally very satisfied with their new relationships, although men tend to be more content than women (Clarke, 2005; Connidis, 2010). With fewer potential mates, perhaps women who remarry in late life settle for less desirable partners.

Rather than remarrying, seniors who enter a new relationship are increasingly choosing cohabitation. Like remarriage, cohabitation results in more stable relationships and higher relationship quality than it did at younger ages. And cohabiting seniors are as satisfied with their partnered lives as are their married counterparts (Brown & Kawamura, 2010). This suggests that cohabitation is distinctive in late adulthood, serving as a long-term alternative to marriage.

Widowhood

Walt died shortly after Ruth turned 80. Like over 70 percent of widowed seniors, Ruth described the loss of her spouse as the most stressful event of her life. As two researchers noted, being widowed means that the survivor has "lost the role and identity of being a spouse (being married and doing things as a couple), which is potentially one of the most pervasive, intense, intimate, and personal roles that they have ever had" (Lund & Caserta, 2004a, p. 29).

Widows make up about one-third of older adults in industrialized nations. Because women live longer than men and are less likely to remarry, more than 40 percent of U.S. women age 65 and older are widowed, compared with just 13 percent of men (U.S. Census Bureau, 2013). Ethnic minorities with high rates of poverty and chronic disease are more likely to be widowed.

The greatest problem for recently widowed older people is profound loneliness (Connidis, 2010). But adaptation varies widely, depending on age, social support, and personality. Aging adults have fewer lasting problems than younger individuals who are widowed, probably because death in later life is viewed as less unfair (Bennett & Soulsby, 2012). And most widowed seniors—especially those with outgoing personalities and high self-esteem—are resilient in the face of loneliness (Moore & Stratton, 2002; van Baarsen, 2002). To sustain continuity with their past, they try to preserve social relationships that were important before the spouse's death and report that relatives and friends respond in kind, contacting them at least as often as before (Utz et al., 2002). Also, the stronger aging adults' sense of self-efficacy in handling tasks of daily living, the more favorably they adjust (Fry, 2001).

Nevertheless, widowed individuals must reorganize their lives, reconstructing an identity that is separate from the deceased spouse. Overall, men show more physical and mental health problems and greater risk of mortality than women, for several reasons (Bennett, Smith, & Hughes, 2005; Shor et al., 2012). First, because most men relied on their wives for social connectedness, household tasks, promotion of healthy behaviors, and coping with stressors, they are less prepared than women for the challenges of widowhood. Second, because of gender-role expectations, men feel less free to express their emotions or to ask for help with meals, household tasks, and social relationships (Bennett, 2007; Lund & Caserta, 2004b). Finally, men tend to be less involved in religious activities—a vital source of social support and inner strength.

In two studies of older widowers, those in their seventies reported the most depression and showed the slowest rate of improvement over the following two years. The death of their wives occurred around the time they were adjusting to retirement, resulting in two major changes at once, with widowhood highly unexpected because most wives outlive their husbands (Lund & Caserta, 2001, 2004a). African-American widowers, however, show no elevated risk of mortality over their married agemates, and they report less depression than Caucasian widowers (Elwert & Christakis, 2006). Perhaps greater support from extended family and church is responsible.

Sex differences in the experience of widowhood contribute to men's higher remarriage rate. Women's kinkeeper role (see Chapter 16, page 433) and ability to form close friendships may lead them to feel less need to remarry. In addition, because many older women share the widowed state, they probably offer one another helpful advice and sympathy. In contrast, men often lack skills for maintaining family relationships, forming emotionally satisfying ties outside marriage, and handling the chores of their deceased wives.

Still, widowed seniors of both sexes who participated in several months of weekly classes providing information and support in acquiring daily living skills felt better prepared to

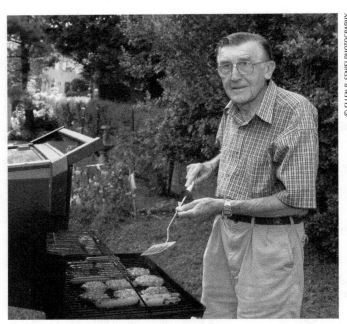

© ELLEN B. SENSI PHOTOGRAPHY

Because most men rely on their wives for social connectedness, they are less prepared than women to overcome the loneliness of widowhood. This widower, however, makes an effort to connect socially with neighbors by hosting a backyard barbecue.

Applying What We Know

Fostering Adaptation to Widowhood in Late Adulthood

Suggestion	Description
Self	
Mastery of new skills of daily living	Especially for men, learning how to perform household tasks such as shopping and cooking, to sustain existing family and friendship ties, and to build new relationships is vital for positive adaptation.
Family and Friends	
Social support and interaction	Social support and interaction must extend beyond the grieving period to ongoing assistance and caring relationships. Family members and friends can help most by making support available while encouraging the widowed older adult to use effective coping strategies.
Community	
Senior centers	Senior centers offer communal meals and other social activities, enabling widowed and other older adults to connect with people in similar circumstances and to gain access to other community resources, such as listings of part-time employment and available housing.
Support groups	Support groups can be found in senior centers, religious institutions, and other agencies. Besides new relationships, they offer an accepting atmosphere for coming to terms with loss, effective role models, and assistance with developing skills for daily living.
Religious activities	Involvement in a church, synagogue, or mosque can help relieve the loneliness associated with loss of a spouse and offer social support, new relationships, and meaningful roles.
Volunteer activities	One of the best ways for widowed older adults to find meaningful roles is through volunteer activities. Some are sponsored by formal service organizations, such as the Red Cross or the Retired and Senior Volunteer Program. Other volunteer programs exist in hospitals, senior centers, schools, and charitable organizations.

manage the challenges of widowed life (Caserta, Lund, & Obray, 2004). Those who emerge from this traumatic event with a sense of purpose in life and with confidence in their ability to meet everyday challenges often experience stress-related personal growth (Caserta et al., 2009). Many report a newfound sense of inner strength, greater appreciation of close relationships, and reevaluation of life priorities. Applying What We Know above suggests a variety of ways to foster adaptation to widowhood in late adulthood.

Never-Married, Childless Older Adults

Shortly after Ruth and Walt's marriage in their twenties, Ruth's father died. Her sister Ida continued to live with and care for their mother, who was in ill health until she died 16 years later. When, at age 25, Ida received a marriage proposal, she responded, "I can't marry anybody while my mother is still living. I'm expected to look after her." Ida's decision was not unusual for a daughter of her day. She never married or had children.

About 5 percent of older Americans have remained unmarried and childless throughout their lives. Almost all are conscious of being different from the norm, but most have developed alternative meaningful relationships. Ida, for example, formed a strong bond with a neighbor's son. In his childhood, she provided emotional support and financial assistance, which

helped him overcome a stressful home life. He included Ida in family events and visited her regularly until she died. Other nonmarried seniors speak of the centrality of extended family and of younger people in their social networks—often nieces

SUSAN WATTS/NY DAILY NEWS VIA GETTY IMAGES

For this never-married older adult, a warm relationship with his great-nephew provides a sense of family connection and an opportunity to influence a member of a younger generation.

and nephews—and of influencing them in enduring ways (Wenger, 2009; Wenger & Burholdt, 2001). In addition, same-sex friendships are key in never-married older women's lives (McDill, Hall, & Turell, 2006). These tend to be unusually close and often involve joint travel, periods of coresidence, and associations with each other's extended families.

Never-married, childless men are more likely than women to feel lonely and depressed. And without pressure from a partner to maintain a healthy lifestyle, they engage in more unhealthy behaviors. Hence, their physical and mental health is poor compared with their married counterparts (Kendig et al., 2007). Never-married older women report a level of well-being equivalent to that of married older adults and greater than that of divorcées and recently widowed seniors. Only when they cannot maintain social contacts because of declining health do they report feeling lonely (Dykstra, 2009).

Because friendships are not the same as blood ties when it comes to caregiving, being unmarried and childless in very old age reduces the likelihood of informal personal care (Chang, Wilber, & Silverstein, 2010; Wenger, 2009). Still, most say that some informal support is available.

Siblings

Nearly 80 percent of Americans age 65 and older have at least one living sibling. Most live within 100 miles of each other, communicate regularly, and visit at least several times a year. Both men and women describe closer bonds with sisters than with brothers. Perhaps because of women's greater emotional expressiveness and nurturance, the closer the tie to a sister, the higher older people's psychological well-being (Van Volkom, 2006).

Aging siblings in industrialized nations are more likely to socialize than to provide one another with direct assistance because most turn first to their spouse and children. Nevertheless, siblings seem to be an important "insurance policy" in late adulthood. After age 70, aid from siblings living near one another rises (White, 2001). Widowed and never-married seniors have more contacts with siblings, perhaps because they have fewer competing family relationships, and they also are more likely to receive sibling support when their health declines (Connidis, 2010). For example, when Ida's Alzheimer's symptoms worsened, Ruth came to her aid. Although Ida had many friends, Ruth was her only living relative.

Friendships

As family responsibilities and vocational pressures lessen, friendships take on increasing importance. Having friends is an especially strong predictor of mental health among seniors (Rawlins, 2004). Older adults report more favorable experiences with friends than with family members, in part because of the pleasurable leisure activities shared with friends (Larson, Mannell, & Zuzanek, 1986). Unique qualities of friendship interaction—openness, spontaneity, mutual caring, and common interests—are also influential.

Functions of Late-Life Friendships. The diverse functions of friendship in late adulthood clarify its profound significance:

- *Intimacy and companionship.* As Ida and her best friend, Rosie, took walks, went shopping, or visited each other, they disclosed their deepest sources of happiness and worry. Mutual interests, feelings of belongingness, and opportunities to confide in each other sustain these bonds over time (Field, 1999).

- *A shield against negative judgments stemming from stereotypes of aging.* "Where's your cane, Rosie?" Ida asked when the two women were about to leave for a restaurant. "Come on, don't be self-conscious. When y'get one of those 'you're finished' looks from someone, just remember: In the Greek village where my mother grew up, there was no separation between generations, so the young ones got used to wrinkled skin and weak knees and recognized older women as the wise ones [Deveson, 1994]. Why, we were midwives, matchmakers, experts in herbal medicine; we knew about everything!"

- *A link to the larger community.* For seniors who cannot go out as often, interactions with friends can keep them abreast of events in the wider world. "Rosie," Ida reported, "did you know the Thompson girl was named high school valedictorian?" Friends can also open up new experiences, such as travel or participation in community activities.

- *Protection from the psychological consequences of loss.* Older people in declining health who remain in contact with friends through phone calls and visits show improved psychological well-being (Fiori, Smith, & Antonucci, 2007). Similarly, when close relatives die, friends offer compensating social supports.

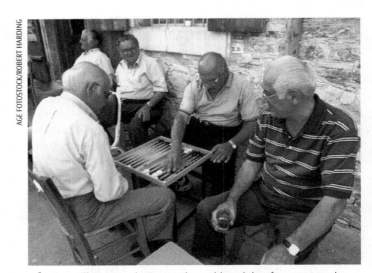

On a village street in Cyprus, these older adults often meet to play backgammon. Even after physical mobility declines, many seniors find ways to sustain ties with friends, who offer companionship, links to the larger community, and social support.

Characteristics of Late-Life Friendships. Although older adults prefer familiar, established relationships over new ones, friendship formation continues throughout life. Ties to old and dear friends who live far away are maintained, with growing numbers of seniors staying in touch with the aid of e-mail and social networking sites, such as Facebook (see page 475 in Chapter 17). Nevertheless, with age, seniors report that the friends they interact with most often and feel closest to live in the same community. As in earlier years, older people tend to choose friends whose age, sex, ethnicity, and values resemble their own. Compared with younger people, fewer report other-sex friendships. But some have them—usually long-standing ones dating back several decades (Monsour, 2002). As agemates die, the very old report more intergenerational friends—both same- and other-sex (Johnson & Troll, 1994). In her eighties, Ruth spent time with Margaret, a 55-year-old widow she met while serving on the board of directors of an adoption agency. Two or three times a month, Margaret came to Ruth's home for tea and lively conversation.

Sex differences in friendship, discussed in previous chapters, extend into late adulthood. Women are more likely to have intimate friends; men depend on their wives and, to a lesser extent, their sisters for warm, open communication (Waite & Das, 2013). Also, older women have more **secondary friends**—people who are not intimates but with whom they spend time occasionally, such as a group that meets for lunch, bridge, or museum tours. Through these associates, older adults meet new people, remain socially involved, and gain in psychological well-being (Blieszner & Roberto, 2012).

Relationships with Adult Children

About 80 percent of older adults in Western nations are parents of living children, most of whom are middle-aged. In Chapter 16, we noted that exchanges of help vary with the closeness of the parent–child bond and the needs of the parent and adult child. Recall, also, that over time, parent-to-child help declines, whereas child-to-parent assistance increases. Older adults and their adult children are often in touch, even when they live far from each other. But as with other ties, quality rather than quantity of interaction affects older adults' life satisfaction. In diverse ethnic groups and cultures, warm bonds with adult children reduce the negative impact of physical impairments and other losses (such as death of a spouse) on psychological well-being (Ajrouch, 2007; Milkie, Bierman, & Schieman, 2008). Alternatively, conflict or unhappiness with adult children contributes to poor physical and mental health.

Although aging parents and adult children in Western nations provide each other with various forms of help, level of assistance is typically modest. Older adults in their sixties and seventies—especially those who own their own home and who are married or widowed as opposed to divorced—are more likely to be providers than recipients of help, suggesting SES variations in the balance of support (Grundy, 2005). This balance shifts as older adults age, but well into late adulthood, seniors in Western nations give more than they receive, especially in financial support but also in practical assistance—a circumstance that contradicts stereotypes of older adults as "burdens" on younger generations (HSBC & Oxford Institute of Ageing, 2007).

Interviews with parents age 75 and older in five Western nations revealed that in all countries, aid received from adult children most often took the form of emotional support. Fewer than one-third said their children assisted with household chores and errands. Aging parents who provided more help of various kinds than they received scored highest in life satisfaction, those receiving more help than they gave scored lowest, while those in a balanced exchange fell in between (Lowenstein, Katz, & Gur-Yaish, 2007). To avoid dependency, older people usually do not seek children's practical assistance in the absence of a pressing need, and they express annoyance when children are overprotective or help unnecessarily (Spitze & Gallant, 2004). Moderate support, with many opportunities to reciprocate, is beneficial, fostering self-esteem and sense of family connection.

As social networks shrink in size, relationships with adult children become more important sources of family involvement. People 85 years and older with children have substantially more contacts with relatives than do those without children (Hooyman & Kiyak, 2011). Why is this so? Consider Ruth, whose daughter Sybil linked her to grandchildren, great-grandchildren, and relatives by marriage. When childless adults reach their eighties, siblings, other same-age relatives, and close friends may have become frail or died and hence may no longer be available as companions.

Elder Maltreatment

Although the majority of older adults enjoy positive relationships with family members, friends, and professional caregivers, some suffer maltreatment at the hands of these individuals. Through recent media attention, elder maltreatment has become a serious public concern.

Reports from many industrialized nations reveal widely varying rates of maltreatment, from 3 to 28 percent in general population studies. Overall, 7 to 10 percent of U.S. older adults say they were targets during the past month, amounting to 3 to 4 million victims (Acierno et al., 2010). Elder maltreatment crosses ethnic lines, although it is lower in Asian, Hispanic, and Native-American groups with strong traditions of respect for and obligation to the aged and highly disapproving attitudes toward harming them (Sherman, Rosenblatt, & Antonucci, 2008). Yet all figures underestimate the actual incidence because most abusive acts take place in private, and victims are often unable or unwilling to complain.

Elder maltreatment usually takes the following forms:

- *Physical abuse.* Intentional infliction of pain, discomfort, or injury, through hitting, cutting, burning, physical force, restraint, sexual assault, and other acts

- *Physical neglect.* Intentional or unintentional failure to fulfill caregiving obligations, resulting in lack of food, medication, or health services or in the older person being left alone or isolated

- *Emotional abuse.* Verbal assaults (such as name calling), humiliation (being treated as a child), and intimidation (threats of isolation or placement in a nursing home)

- *Sexual abuse.* Unwanted sexual contact of any kind

- *Financial abuse.* Illegal or improper exploitation of the aging person's property or financial resources, through theft or use without consent

Financial abuse, emotional abuse, and neglect are the most frequently reported types. Often several forms occur in combination (Anetzberger, 2005; National Academies Committee on National Statistics, 2010). The perpetrator is usually a person the older adult trusts and depends on for care and assistance.

Most abusers are family members—spouses (usually men), followed by children of both sexes and then by other relatives. Some are friends, neighbors, and in-home caregivers (National Center on Elder Abuse, 2013). Abuse in nursing homes is a major concern: From 6 to 40 percent of caregivers admit to having committed at least one act in the previous year (Schiamberg et al., 2011).

Over the past several decades, another form of neglect—referred to in the media as "granny dumping"—has risen: abandonment of older adults with severe disabilities by family caregivers, usually at hospital emergency rooms (Fulmer, 2008). Overwhelmed, their caregivers seem to have concluded that they have no other option but to take this drastic step. (See page 437 in Chapter 16 and page 465 in Chapter 17 for related research.)

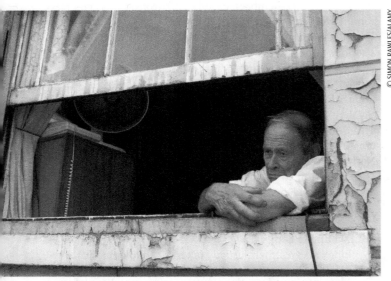

This older adult, who suffers from depression and physical disabilities, lives in a dilapidated rooming house. When conditions are ripe for elder maltreatment, those with severe impairments are least able to protect themselves.

Risk Factors. Characteristics of the victim, the abuser, their relationship, and its social context are related to the incidence and severity of elder maltreatment. The more of the following risk factors that are present, the greater the likelihood that abuse and neglect will occur.

Dependency of the Victim. When other conditions are ripe for maltreatment, older adults who are frail or severely disabled are at greater risk because they are least able to protect themselves (Reay & Browne, 2008; Selwood & Cooper, 2009). Those with physical or cognitive impairments may also have personality traits that make them vulnerable—a tendency to lash out when angry or frustrated, a passive or avoidant approach to handling problems, and a low sense of self-efficacy (Salari, 2011). The worse the caregiver–recipient relationship, the greater the risk of elder abuse of all kinds, particularly when that relationship has a long negative history.

Dependency of the Perpetrator. Many abusers are dependent, emotionally or financially, on their victims. Frequently the perpetrator–victim relationship is one of mutual dependency (Fryling, Summers, & Hoffman, 2006). The abuser needs the older person for money or housing, and the older person needs the abuser for assistance with everyday tasks or to relieve loneliness.

Psychological Disturbance and Stress of the Perpetrator. Abusers are more likely than other caregivers to have psychological problems and to be dependent on alcohol or other drugs (Nerenberg, 2010). Often they are socially isolated, have difficulties at work, or are unemployed. These factors increase the likelihood that they will lash out when caregiving is highly demanding or the behavior of an older adult with dementia is irritating or hard to manage.

History of Family Violence. Elder abuse is often part of a long history of family violence. Adults who were abused as children are at increased risk of harming older adults (Reay & Browne, 2008). In many instances, elder abuse is an extension of years of partner abuse (Walsh et al., 2007).

Institutional Conditions. Elder maltreatment is more likely to occur in nursing homes that are rundown and overcrowded and that have staff shortages, minimal staff supervision, high staff turnover, and few visitors (Schiamberg et al., 2011). Highly stressful work conditions combined with minimal oversight of caregiving quality set the stage for abuse and neglect.

Preventing Elder Maltreatment. Preventing elder maltreatment by family members is especially challenging. Victims may fear retribution; wish to protect abusers who are spouses, sons, or daughters; or feel embarrassed that they cannot control the situation. And they may be intimidated into silence or not know where to turn for help (Summers & Hoffman, 2006). Once abuse is discovered, intervention involves immediate protection and provision of unmet needs for the older adult and of mental health services and social support for the spouse or caregiver.

Prevention programs offer caregivers counseling, education, and respite services, such as adult day care and in-home help. Trained volunteer "buddies" who make visits to the home can combat social isolation of aging adults and assist them with problem solving to avoid further harm. Support groups help seniors identify abusive acts, practice appropriate responses, and form new relationships. And agencies that provide informal financial services to older people who are unable to manage on their own, such as writing and cashing checks and holding valuables in a safe, reduce financial abuse.

When elder abuse is extreme, legal action offers the best protection, yet many victims are reluctant to initiate court procedures or, because of mental impairments, cannot do so. In these instances, social service professionals must help caregivers rethink their role, even if it means that the aging person might be institutionalized. In nursing homes, improving staff selection, training, and working conditions can greatly reduce abuse and neglect.

LOOK AND LISTEN

Contact the your state's department of senior services. Find out about its policies and programs aimed at preventing elder abuse. ●

Combating elder maltreatment also requires efforts at the level of the larger society, including public education to encourage reporting of suspected cases and improved understanding of the needs of older people. As part of this effort, seniors benefit from information on where to go for help (National Center on Elder Abuse, 2013). Finally, countering negative stereotypes of aging reduces maltreatment because recognizing older adults' dignity, individuality, and autonomy is incompatible with acts of harm.

ASK YOURSELF

REVIEW Why is adjustment to late-life divorce usually more difficult for women and adjustment to widowhood more difficult for men?

APPLY At age 51, Mae lost her job, couldn't afford to pay rent, and moved in with her 78-year-old widowed mother, Beryl. Although Beryl welcomed Mae's companionship, Mae grew depressed, drank heavily, and stopped looking for work. When Beryl complained about Mae's behavior, Mae pushed and slapped her. Explain why this mother–daughter relationship led to elder abuse.

REFLECT Select one older member of your extended family whom you know well, and describe that person's social convoy, or cluster of close relationships providing safety and support. In what ways has the convoy changed over the past five to ten years?

Retirement

In Chapter 16, we noted that the period of retirement has lengthened because of increased life expectancy and a steady decline in average age of retirement—trends that have occurred in all Western industrialized nations. These changes have also led to a blurring of the distinction between work and retirement. Because mandatory retirement no longer exists for most workers in Western countries, older adults have more choices about when to retire and how they spend their time.

The late-2000s recession has had only a modest impact on raising the retirement age of the baby boomers (see page 441). Still, according to surveys of adults in many countries, the majority of baby boomers say they want to work longer, with one-third indicating that devoting some time to work is important for a happy retirement (HSBC & Oxford Institute of Ageing, 2007, 2011). Currently, nearly 40 percent of U.S. adults age 65 to 69, and nearly 20 percent of those in their seventies, are still working in some capacity.

As these figures suggest, the contemporary retirement process is highly variable: It may include a planning period, the decision itself, diverse acts of retiring, and continuous adjustment and readjustment of activities for the rest of the life course. The majority of U.S. older adults with career jobs retire gradually by cutting down their hours and responsibilities. Many take *bridge jobs* (new part-time jobs or full-time jobs of shorter duration) that serve as transitions between full-time career and retirement (Wang, 2011). Others leave their jobs but later return to paid work and even start new careers, desiring to introduce interest and challenge into their lives, to supplement limited financial resources, or both.

In the following sections, we examine factors that affect the decision to retire, happiness during the retirement years, and leisure and volunteer pursuits. We will see that the process of retirement and retired life reflect an increasingly diverse retired population.

The Decision to Retire

When Walt and Ruth retired, both had worked long enough to be eligible for comfortable income-replacement benefits— Walt's through the government-sponsored Social Security program, Ruth's through a private pension plan. In addition, they had planned for retirement (see Chapter 16, pages 441–442), with a projected date for leaving the work force. They wanted to retire early enough to pursue leisure activities while both were in good health. In contrast, Walt's brother Dick was forced to retire as the operating costs of his bakery rose while his clientele declined. He looked for temporary employment in sales while his wife, Goldie, kept her part-time job as a bookkeeper to help cover living expenses.

Affordability of retirement is usually the first consideration in the decision to retire. Yet despite economic concerns, many preretirees decide to let go of a steady work life in favor of alternative, personally meaningful work, leisure, or volunteer activities.

Retire

- Adequate retirement benefits
- Compelling leisure interests or family pursuits
- Low work commitment
- Declining health
- Spouse retiring
- Routine, boring job

A recent retiree enjoys an adult-education class in bookbinding.

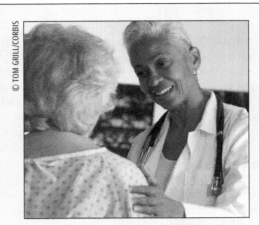

Continue Working

- Limited or no retirement benefits
- Few leisure interests or family pursuits
- High work commitment
- Good health
- Spouse working
- Flexible job demands and work schedule
- Pleasant, stimulating work environment

This doctor, in her 60s, continues to enjoy her fulfilling career.

FIGURE 18.3 **Personal and workplace factors that influence the decision to retire.**

"I had been working since I was 10 years old," said one retired auto worker. "I wanted a rest." Exceptions to this favorable outlook are people like Dick—forced into retirement or earning very low wages—who often take bridge jobs reluctantly to make ends meet (Cahill, Giandrea, & Quinn, 2006).

Figure 18.3 summarizes personal and workplace factors in addition to income that influence the decision to retire. People in good health, for whom vocational life is central to self-esteem, and whose work environments are pleasant and interesting are likely to keep on working. For these reasons, individuals in high-earning professional occupations usually retire later than those in blue-collar or clerical positions. And when they do retire, they more often shift to stimulating bridge jobs, with some retiring and returning to the work force multiple times (Feldman & Beehr, 2011; Wang et al., 2009). Self-employed older adults also work longer, probably because they can flexibly adapt their working hours to changing needs (Feldman & Vogel, 2009). In contrast, people in declining health, who are engaged in routine, boring work, or who have pleasurable leisure or family pursuits often opt for retirement.

In most Western nations, generous social security benefits make retirement feasible for the economically disadvantaged and sustain the standard of living of most workers after they retire. The United States is an exception: Many U.S. retirees, especially those who held low-income jobs without benefits, experience falling living standards. Denmark, France, Germany, Finland, and Sweden have gradual retirement programs in which older employees reduce their work hours, receive a partial pension to make up income loss, and continue to accrue pension benefits. Besides strengthening financial security, this approach introduces a transitional phase that fosters retirement planning and well-being (Peiró, Tordera, & Potocnik, 2012). And some countries' retirement policies are sensitive to women's more interrupted work lives. In Canada, France, and Germany, for example, time devoted to child rearing is given some credit when figuring retirement benefits (Service Canada, 2009).

In sum, individual preferences shape retirement decisions. At the same time, older adults' opportunities and limitations greatly affect their choices.

Adjustment to Retirement

Because retirement involves giving up roles that are a vital part of identity and self-esteem, it is often assumed to be a stressful process that contributes to declines in physical and mental health. Consider Dick, who reacted to the closing of his bakery with anxiety and depression. But recall that Dick had a cranky, disagreeable personality. In this respect, his psychological well-being after retirement was similar to what it had been before!

We must be careful not to assume a cause-and-effect relationship each time retirement is paired with an unfavorable reaction. For example, a wealth of evidence confirms that physical health problems lead older adults to retire, rather than the reverse (Shultz & Wang, 2007). The widely held belief that retirement inevitably leads to adjustment problems is contradicted by countless research findings. Contemporary seniors view retirement as a time of opportunity and personal growth and describe themselves as active and socially involved—major determinants of retirement satisfaction (Kloep & Hendry, 2007; Wang & Shultz, 2010). Still, about 10 to 30 percent mention some adjustment difficulties.

Workplace factors—especially financial worries and having to give up one's job—predict stress following retirement. And older adults who find it hard to give up the predictable schedule and social contacts of the work setting experience discomfort with their less structured way of life. But a sense of personal control over life events, including deciding to retire for internally motivated reasons (to do other things), is strongly linked to retirement satisfaction (Kubicek et al., 2011; Quine et al., 2007). Well-educated people with complex jobs typically adjust favorably (Kim & Moen, 2002a). Perhaps the satisfactions derived from challenging, meaningful work readily transfer to nonwork pursuits.

As with other major life events, social support reduces stress associated with retirement. Although social-network size typically shrinks as relationships with co-workers decline, quality of relationships remains fairly stable. And many seniors add to their social networks through leisure and volunteer pursuits (Kloep & Hendry, 2007). In Dick's case, entering congregate housing eased a difficult postretirement period, leading to new friends and rewarding leisure activities, some of which he shared with Goldie.

Finally, earlier in this chapter we noted that marital happiness tends to rise after retirement. When a couple's relationship is positive, it can buffer the uncertainty of retirement (van Solinge & Henkens, 2008). And retirement can enhance marital satisfaction by granting husband and wife more time for companionship. Consequently, a good marriage not only promotes adjustment to retirement but also benefits from the greater freedom of the retirement years. In line with continuity theory, people try to sustain lifestyle patterns, self-esteem, and values following retirement (Atchley, 2003). In favorable economic and social contexts, they usually succeed.

Leisure and Volunteer Activities

After a "honeymoon period" of trying out new options, many discover that interests and skills do not develop suddenly. Instead, meaningful leisure and community service pursuits are usually formed earlier and sustained or expanded during retirement (HSBC & Oxford Institute of Ageing, 2007; Pinquart & Schindler, 2009). For example, Walt's fondness for writing, theater, and gardening dated back to his youth. And Ruth's strong focus on her social work career led her to become an avid community volunteer.

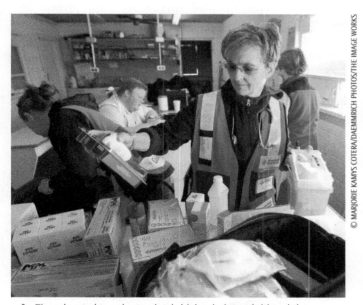

Time devoted to volunteering is higher in late adulthood than at any other time of life. As a Red Cross volunteer, this senior traveled to West, Texas, to provide services to those affected by the fertilizer plant explosion in April 2013.

Involvement in leisure activities and, especially, volunteer service is related to better physical and mental health and reduced mortality (Cutler, Hendricks, & O'Neill, 2011). But simply participating does not explain this relationship. Instead, older adults select these pursuits because they permit self-expression, new achievements, the rewards of helping others, or pleasurable social interaction. And those high in sense of self-efficacy are more engaged (Diehl & Berg, 2007). These factors account for gains in well-being.

Older people contribute enormously to society through volunteer work, a trend that is strengthening. About one-third of 60- and 70-year-olds in industrialized nations report volunteering. Of those who do, over half give 200 or more hours per year (HSBC & Oxford Institute of Ageing, 2007; Kloep & Hendry, 2007). Younger, better-educated, and financially secure seniors with social interests are more likely to volunteer, women more often than men. Although most extend an earlier pattern of civic engagement, nonvolunteers are especially receptive to volunteer activities in the first few years after retiring as they look for ways to compensate for work-role losses (Mutchler, Burr, & Caro, 2003). The retirement transition is a prime time to recruit seniors into these personally rewarding, socially useful pursuits.

LOOK AND LISTEN

Interview an older adult participating in a significant community service role about the personal meaning of the experience at this time of life. ●

In a survey of a large, nationally representative U.S. sample, time spent volunteering did not decline until the eighties (Hendricks & Cutler, 2004). Even then, it remained higher than at any other time of life! In accord with socioemotional selectivity theory, older adults eventually narrowed their volunteering to fewer roles, concentrating on one or two that meant the most to them (Windsor, Anstey, & Rodgers, 2008). They seemed to recognize that excessive volunteering reduces its emotional rewards and, thus, its benefits to life satisfaction.

Finally, older adults report greater awareness of and interest in public affairs and typically vote at a higher rate than any other age group. (The 2012 U.S. national election, in which 18- to 29-year-olds exceeded seniors in voter turnout, is an exception). After retiring, older people have more time to keep abreast of current events. Their political concerns are far broader than those that serve their own age group, and their voting behavior is not driven merely by self-interest (Campbell & Binstock, 2011). Rather, their political involvement may stem from a deep desire for a safer, more secure world for future generations.

 ## Optimal Aging

Walt, Ruth, Dick, Goldie, and Ida, and the research findings they illustrate, reveal great diversity in development during the final decades of life. Walt and Ruth fit contemporary experts' view of **optimal aging,** in which gains are maximized and losses

© MARJORIE KAMYS COTERA/DAEMMRICH PHOTOS/THE IMAGE WORKS

minimized. Both were actively engaged with their families and communities, coped well with negative life changes, enjoyed a happy intimate partnership and other close relationships, and led daily lives filled with gratifying activities. Ida, too, experienced optimal aging until the onset of Alzheimer's symptoms overwhelmed her ability to manage life's challenges. As a single adult, she built a rich social network that sustained her into old age, despite the hardship of having spent many years caring for her ailing mother.

People age optimally when their growth, vitality, and striving limit and, at times, overcome physical, cognitive, and social declines. Researchers want to know more about factors that contribute to optimal aging so they can help more seniors experience it. Yet theorists disagree on the precise ingredients of a satisfying old age. Some focus on easily measurable outcomes, such as excellent cardiovascular functioning, absence of disability, superior cognitive performance, and creative achievements. But this view has been heavily criticized (Aldwin, Spiro, & Park, 2006). Not everyone can become an outstanding athlete, an innovative scientist, or a talented artist. And many older adults do not want to keep on accomplishing and producing—the main markers of success in Western nations.

Recent views of a contented, fulfilling late adulthood have turned away from specific achievements toward processes people use to reach personally valued goals (Freund & Baltes, 1998; Kahana et al., 2005; Lund, 1998). In research on three samples of adults followed over the lifespan, George Vaillant found that factors people could control to some degree (such as health habits, coping strategies, marital stability, and years of education) far outweighed uncontrollable factors (parental SES, family warmth in childhood, early physical health, and longevity of family members) in predicting a happy, active old age (Vaillant & Mukamal, 2001). Consider the following description of one participant, who in childhood had experienced low SES, parental discord, a depressed mother, and seven siblings crowded into a tenement apartment. Despite these early perils, he became happily married and, through the GI bill, earned an accounting degree. At 70, he was aging well:

> Anthony Pirelli may have been *ill* considering his heart attack and open-heart surgery, but he did not feel *sick*. He was physically active as ever, and he continued to play tennis. Asked what he missed about his work, he exulted, "I'm so busy doing other things that I don't have time to miss work. . . . Life is not boring for me." He did not smoke or abuse alcohol; he loved his wife; he used mature [coping strategies]; he obtained 14 years of education; he watched his waistline; and he exercised regularly. (Adapted from Vaillant, 2002, pp. 12, 305.)

Vaillant concluded, "The past often predicts but never determines our old age" (p. 12). Optimal aging is an expression of remarkable resilience during this final phase of the lifespan.

In this and the previous chapter, we have considered the many ways that older adults realize their goals. *TAKE A MOMENT...* Look back and review the most important ones:

- Optimism and sense of self-efficacy in improving health and physical functioning (page 456)

- Selective optimization with compensation to make the most of limited physical energies and cognitive resources (pages 468 and 484)
- Strengthening of self-concept, which promotes self-acceptance and pursuit of hoped-for possible selves (pages 481–482)
- Enhanced emotional understanding and emotional self-regulation, which support meaningful, rewarding social ties (page 480)
- Acceptance of change, which fosters life satisfaction (page 483)
- A mature sense of spirituality and faith, permitting anticipation of death with calmness and composure (pages 483–484)
- Personal control over domains of dependency and independence (pages 484–485)
- High-quality relationships, which offer social support and pleasurable companionships (pages 488–489)

Optimal aging is facilitated by societal contexts that promote effective person–environment fit, enabling seniors to manage life changes effectively. Older adults need well-funded social security plans, good health care, safe housing, and diverse social services. Yet because of inadequate funding and difficulties reaching rural communities, many older adults' needs remain unmet. Isolated aging adults with little education may not know how to gain access to available assistance. Furthermore, the U.S. Medicare system of sharing health-care costs with seniors strains the financial resources of many. And housing that adjusts to changes in older people's capacities, permitting them to age in place without disruptive and disorienting moves, is available only to the economically well-off.

Besides improving policies that meet older adults' basic needs, new future-oriented approaches must prepare for increased aging of the population. More emphasis on lifelong learning for workers of all ages would help people maintain and expand their skills as they grow older. Also, reforms that prepare for expected growth in the number of frail aging adults are vital, including affordable help for family caregivers, adapted housing, and sensitive nursing home care.

All these changes involve recognizing, supporting, and enhancing the contributions that seniors make to society. A nation that takes care of its aging maximizes the chances that each of us, when our time comes to be old, will age optimally.

ASK YOURSELF

REVIEW What psychological and workplace factors predict favorable adjustment to retirement?

APPLY Nate, happily married to Gladys, adjusted well to retirement, and his marriage became even happier. How can a good marriage ease the transition to retirement? How can retirement enhance marital satisfaction?

REFLECT Think of someone you know who is aging optimally. What personal qualities led you to select that person?

SUMMARY

Erikson's Theory: Ego Integrity versus Despair (p. 479)

According to Erikson, how does personality change in late adulthood?

● The final psychological conflict of Erikson's theory, **ego integrity versus despair,** involves coming to terms with one's life. Adults who arrive at a sense of integrity feel whole and satisfied with their achievements. Despair occurs when older people feel time is too short to find an alternate route to integrity.

Other Theories of Psychosocial Development in Late Adulthood (p. 480)

Describe Peck's, Joan Erikson's, and Labouvie-Vief's views of psychosocial development in late adulthood, and discuss reminiscence in older adults' lives.

● According to Robert Peck, attaining ego integrity involves three distinct tasks: ego differentiation, body transcendence, and ego transcendence.

● Joan Erikson believes these attainments represent an additional psychosocial stage, **gerotranscendence,** evident in inner calm and quiet reflection.

● Gisella Labouvie-Vief points out that older adults improve in **affect optimization,** the ability to maximize positive emotion and dampen negative emotion. This bias toward the emotionally positive contributes an upbeat attitude that is linked to longer survival.

● **Reminiscence** can be positive and adaptive for older people. But many well-adjusted older adults spend little time seeking greater self-understanding through life review. Rather, as the term **Third Age** conveys, they are largely present- and future-oriented, seeking opportunities for personal fulfillment.

Stability and Change in Self-Concept and Personality (p. 481)

Cite stable and changing aspects of self-concept and personality, and discuss spirituality and religiosity in late adulthood.

● The "big five" personality traits remain stable from mid- to late life. Older adults' accumulation of a lifetime of self-knowledge leads to more secure and complex self-concepts. Those who continue to actively pursue hoped-for possible selves gain in life satisfaction.

● In late adulthood, resilience is fostered by gains in agreeableness and acceptance of change. Engaging in cognitively challenging activities promotes openness to experience.

● While U.S. seniors generally become more religious or spiritual as they age, this increase is modest and not universal. For the majority of people, religiosity is stable throughout adulthood. Religious involvement is especially high among low-SES ethnic minority older people and women and is linked to better physical and psychological well-being and longer survival.

Contextual Influences on Psychological Well-Being (p. 484)

Discuss the influence of control versus dependency, physical health, negative life changes, and social support on older adults' psychological well-being.

● In patterns of behavior called the **dependency–support script** and the **independence–ignore script,** older adults' dependency behaviors are attended to immediately while their independent behaviors are ignored. Dependency can be adaptive if older adults remain in control by selecting areas in which they desire help while conserving their strength for highly valued activities. Assistance that enables older adults to pursue their goals sustains an effective **person–environment fit,** which fosters psychological well-being.

● Physical declines and chronic disease can lead to a loss of personal control and high risk for late-life depression. Older adults have the highest suicide rate of all age groups.

● Although aging adults are at risk for a variety of negative life changes, these events evoke less stress and depression in older than in younger people. But when negative changes pile up, they test older adults' coping resources.

● By easing stress, social support promotes physical health and psychological well-being. But assistance that is excessive or cannot be returned often results in reduced self-efficacy and psychological stress. Consequently, perceived social support, rather than sheer amount of help, is associated with a positive outlook.

A Changing Social World (p. 487)

Describe social theories of aging, including disengagement theory, activity theory, continuity theory, and socioemotional selectivity theory.

● **Disengagement theory** holds that mutual withdrawal between older adults and society occurs in anticipation of death. Most aging adults, however, do not disengage but let go of unsatisfying contacts and maintain satisfying ones.

● **Activity theory** states that social barriers to engagement, not the desires of older adults, cause declining rates of interaction. Yet opportunities for social contact do not guarantee greater social activity.

- **Continuity theory** proposes that most aging adults strive to maintain consistency between their past and anticipated future. By using familiar skills and engaging in familiar activities with familiar people, older people integrate late-life changes into a coherent, consistent life path.

- **Socioemotional selectivity theory** states that social networks become more selective with age. Older adults emphasize the emotion-regulating function of interaction, preferring high-quality, emotionally fulfilling relationships.

How do communities, neighborhoods, and housing arrangements affect older adults' social lives and adjustment?

- Suburban older adults have higher incomes and report better health than their inner-city counterparts, but the latter are better off in terms of public transportation. Small-town and rural aging adults, who are less likely to live near their children, compensate by interacting more with nearby relatives, neighbors, and friends. Living in neighborhoods with many like-minded seniors promotes life satisfaction.

- Most older people prefer **aging in place,** remaining in a familiar setting where they have control over everyday life. But for those with health and mobility problems, independent living poses risks, and many older adults who live alone are poverty-stricken.

- Residential communities for older adults who need help with everyday tasks include assisted-living arrangements such as **congregate housing** and **life-care communities,** which guarantee that residents' changing needs will be met as they age.

- The small number of U.S. older adults who live in nursing homes experience extreme restriction of autonomy. Typically, social interaction among residents is low. Homelike nursing homes that achieve an effective person–environment fit foster late-life well-being.

Relationships in Late Adulthood (p. 492)

Describe changes in social relationships in late adulthood, including marriage, gay and lesbian partnerships, divorce, remarriage, and widowhood, and discuss never-married, childless older adults.

- As we move through life, a **social convoy,** or cluster of family members and friends, provides safety and support. As ties are lost, aging adults seek ways to maintain gratifying relationships.

- Marital satisfaction peaks in late adulthood as stressful responsibilities decline and gains in perceptions of relationship fairness, joint leisure activities, and positive communication increase. Most gay and lesbian older adults also report happy, highly fulfilling relationships.

- Divorce in late life brings greater stress than for younger people. Although older adults' remarriage rates are low, those who do remarry enter into more stable relationships. Seniors are increasingly choosing cohabitation as a long-term alternative to marriage.

- Adaptation to widowhood varies widely. Older adults fare better than younger individuals, and women better than men. Efforts to maintain social ties, an outgoing personality, high self-esteem, and a sense of self-efficacy in handling tasks of daily living promote resilience.

- Most older adults who remain unmarried and childless throughout their lives develop alternative meaningful relationships. Never-married childless women are better-adjusted than men, but—despite smaller social networks—both find social support.

How do sibling relationships, friendships, and relationships with adult children change in late life?

- In late adulthood, most siblings live nearby, communicate regularly, and visit several times a year. Perhaps because of fewer competing family relationships, widowed and never-married older people have more contact with siblings.

- Friendships in late adulthood serve diverse functions: intimacy and companionship, a shield against negative judgments, a link to the larger community, and protection from the psychological consequences of loss. Women, more than men, tend to have both intimate friends and **secondary friends,** with whom they spend time occasionally.

- Older adults are often in touch with their adult children, who more often provide emotional support than direct assistance. Many opportunities for aging parents to reciprocate is beneficial to well-being. Aging parents typically provide more help than they receive, especially financial support and practical assistance.

Discuss elder maltreatment, including risk factors and strategies for prevention.

- Some older adults suffer maltreatment at the hands of family members, friends, or professional caregivers. Risk factors include a dependent perpetrator–victim relationship, perpetrator psychological disturbance and stress, a history of family violence, and inadequate institutional conditions.

- Elder-abuse prevention programs provide counseling, education, and respite services for caregivers. Trained volunteers and support groups can help older persons avoid future harm. Societal efforts that encourage reporting of suspected cases and increase understanding of older people's needs are also vital.

Retirement (p. 499)

Discuss the decision to retire, adjustment to retirement, and involvement in leisure and volunteer activities.

- The decision to retire depends on affordability, health status, nature of the work environment, and opportunities to pursue meaningful activities.

- Seniors who view retirement as a time of personal growth and who remain active and socially involved adapt especially well. Factors affecting adjustment include health status, satisfactions previously derived from work, a sense of personal control over life events (including the retirement decision), social support, and marital happiness.

- Meaningful leisure and volunteer pursuits are typically formed earlier and sustained or expanded during retirement. Involvement is related to better physical and mental health and to reduced mortality.

Optimal Aging (p. 501)

Discuss the meaning of optimal aging.

- Older adults who experience **optimal aging** have developed many ways to minimize losses and maximize gains. Societal contexts that permit older adults to manage life changes effectively foster optimal aging. These include well-funded social security plans, good health care, safe housing, diverse social services, and opportunities for lifelong learning.

Important Terms and Concepts

activity theory (p. 487)
affect optimization (p. 480)
aging in place (p. 489)
congregate housing (p. 490)
continuity theory (p. 487)
dependency–support script (p. 484)

disengagement theory (p. 487)
ego integrity versus despair (p. 479)
gerotranscendence (p. 480)
independence–ignore script (p. 484)
life-care communities (p. 490)
optimal aging (p. 501)

person–environment fit (p. 484)
reminiscence (p. 481)
secondary friends (p. 497)
social convoy (p. 492)
socioemotional selectivity theory (p. 488)
Third Age (p. 482)

milestones

Development in Late Adulthood

65–80 years

PHYSICAL

- Performance of autonomic nervous system declines, impairing tolerance for extremes of heat and cold. (451)
- Declines in vision continue, with increased sensitivity to glare and impaired color discrimination, dark adaptation, depth perception, and visual acuity. (451)
- Declines in hearing continue throughout the frequency range. (452)
- Sensitivity to taste and odor may decline. (452)
- Touch sensitivity declines on the hands, especially the fingertips. (452)
- Declines in cardiovascular and respiratory functioning lead to greater physical stress during exercise. (453)

- Aging of the immune system increases risk for a variety of illnesses, including infectious diseases, cardiovascular disease, certain forms of cancer, and several autoimmune disorders. (453)

- Timing of sleep shifts to earlier bedtime and earlier morning wakening; sleep difficulties increase. (453)
- Graying and thinning of the hair continue; the skin wrinkles and sags further and becomes more transparent as it loses its fatty layer of support; "age spots" increase. (454)
- Height and weight decline because of loss of lean body mass. (454)

- Continued loss of bone mass leads to rising rates of osteoporosis. (454, 460)
- Frequency of sexual activity and intensity of sexual response decline, although most healthy married couples report regular sexual enjoyment. (458–459)

COGNITIVE

- Processing speed continues to decline, but crystallized intelligence is largely sustained. (467)

- Ability to attend selectively and to adapt attention, switching from one task to another, continues to decline. (468)
- Amount of information that can be held in working memory, use of memory strategies, and retrieval from long-term memory diminish further; problems are greatest on tasks requiring deliberate processing and associative memory. (468–469)
- Modest forgetting of remote memories occurs. (469–470)
- Use of external aids for prospective memory increases. (470)
- Retrieving words from long-term memory and planning what to say and how to say it become more difficult. (471)

- More often represents to-be-communicated information in terms of gist rather than details. (471)
- Hypothetical problem solving declines, but everyday problem solving remains adaptive. (471)
- May hold an important position of leadership in society, such as chief executive officer, religious leader, or court justice. (472)
- May develop wisdom. (471–472)
- Can improve a wide range of cognitive skills through training. (473)

Note: Numbers in parentheses indicate the page or pages on which each milestone is discussed.

EMOTIONAL/SOCIAL

- Comes to terms with life, developing ego integrity. (479–480)
- Cognitive-affective complexity declines as basic information-processing skills diminish. (480)
- Affect optimization—the ability to maximize positive emotion and dampen negative emotion—increases. (480)
- May engage in reminiscence and life review, but continues to seek avenues for personal growth and fulfillment. (481)

- Self-concept strengthens, becoming more secure and complex. (481–482)
- Agreeableness and acceptance of change increase, while extroversion and openness to experience tend to decline modestly. (483)
- Spirituality and faith may advance to a higher level, away from prescribed beliefs toward a more reflective approach. (483–484)

- Size of social network and amount of social interaction decline. (487)
- Selection of social partners is based on anticipated feelings, including pursuit of pleasant relationships and avoidance of unpleasant ones. (488)
- Marital satisfaction increases, peaking in late adulthood. (492)
- May be widowed. (494)
- Visits and support from siblings living nearby may increase. (496)
- Friendships take on increasing importance. (496–497)

- May retire. (499–500)
- Likely to increase involvement in leisure and volunteer activities (501)
- More likely to be knowledgeable about politics and to vote. (501)

80 years and older

PHYSICAL

- Physical changes previously listed continue.
- Mobility diminishes as muscle and bone strength and joint flexibility decline. (454)

COGNITIVE

- Cognitive changes previously listed continue.
- Fluid abilities decline further; crystallized abilities drop as well, though only modestly. (467)

EMOTIONAL/SOCIAL

- Emotional and social changes previously listed continue.
- May develop gerotranscendence, a cosmic perspective directed beyond the self. (480)

- Relationships with adult children become more important. (497)
- Frequency and variety of leisure and volunteer activities decline slightly. (501)

chapter
19 Death, Dying, and Bereavement

BRUNO MORANDI/ROBERT HARDING

Mourners on the island of Bali, Indonesia, perform a traditional Hindu ceremony marking the passage of the dead into the spirit realm. All cultures have rituals for celebrating the end of life and helping the bereaved cope with profound loss.

chapter outline

How We Die

Physical Changes • Defining Death • Death with Dignity

Attitudes Toward Death

Thinking and Emotions of Dying People

Do Stages of Dying Exist? • Contextual Influences on Adaptations to Dying

A Place to Die

Home • Hospital • Nursing Home • The Hospice Approach

■ **BIOLOGY AND ENVIRONMENT** Music as Palliative Care for Dying Patients

The Right to Die

Passive Euthanasia • Voluntary Active Euthanasia • Assisted Suicide

Bereavement: Coping with the Death of a Loved One

Grief Process • Personal and Situational Variations • Bereavement Interventions

■ **CULTURAL INFLUENCES** Cultural Variations in Mourning Behavior

Death Education

As every life is unique, so each death is unique. The final forces of the human spirit separate themselves from the body in manifold ways.

My mother Sofie's death was the culmination of a five-year battle against cancer. In her last months, the disease invaded organs throughout her body, attacking the lungs in its final fury. She withered slowly, with the mixed blessing of time to prepare against certain knowledge that death was just around the corner. My father, Philip, lived another 18 years. At age 80, he was outwardly healthy, active, and about to depart on a long-awaited vacation when a heart attack snuffed out his life suddenly, without time for last words or death-bed reconciliations.

As I set to work on this chapter, my 65-year-old neighbor Nicholas gambled for a higher quality of life. To be eligible for a kidney transplant, he elected bypass surgery to strengthen his heart. Doctors warned that his body might not withstand the operation. But Nicholas knew that without taking a chance, he would live only a few years, in debilitated condition. Shortly after the surgery, infection set in, traveling throughout his system and so weakening him that only extreme measures—a respirator to sustain breathing and powerful drugs to elevate his fading blood pressure—could keep him alive.

"Come on, Dad, you can do it," encouraged Nicholas's daughter Sasha, standing by his bedside and stroking his hand. But Nicholas could not. After two months in intensive care, he experienced brain seizures and slipped into a coma. Three doctors met with his wife, Giselle, to tell her there was no hope. She asked them to disconnect the respirator, and within half an hour Nicholas drifted away.

Death is essential for the survival of our species. We die so that our own children and the children of others may live. As hard as it is to accept the reality that we too will die, our greatest solace lies in knowing that death is part of ongoing life.

In this chapter, we address the culmination of lifespan development. Over the past century, technology has provided so many means to keep death at bay that many people regard it as a forbidden topic. But pressing social and economic dilemmas that are an outgrowth of the dramatic

increase in life expectancy are forcing us to attend to life's end—its quality, its timing, and ways to help people adjust to their own and others' final leave taking. The interdisciplinary field of **thanatology**, devoted to the study of death and dying, has expanded tremendously over the past 25 years.

Our discussion addresses the physical changes of dying; attitudes toward death, the thoughts and feelings of people as they stand face to face with death, where people die, hopelessly ill patients' right to die, and coping with the death of a loved one. The experiences of Sofie, Philip, Nicholas, their families, and others illustrate how each person's life history joins with social and cultural contexts to shape death and dying, lending great diversity to this universal experience. ●

How We Die

In industrialized countries, opportunities to witness the physical aspects of death are less available today than in previous generations. Most people in the developed world die in hospitals or nursing homes, where doctors and nurses, not loved ones, typically attend their last moments. Nevertheless, many want to know how we die, either to anticipate their own end or grasp what is happening to a dying loved one. As we look briefly at the physical dying, we must keep in mind that the dying person is more than a physical being requiring care of and attention to bodily functions. The dying are also mind and spirit—for whom the end of life is still life. They benefit profoundly in their last days and hours from social support responsive to their needs for emotional and spiritual closure.

Physical Changes

When asked how they would like to die, most people say they want "death with dignity"—either a quick, agony-free end during sleep or a clear-minded final few moments in which they can say farewell and review their lives. In reality, death is the culmination of a straightforward biological process. For about

20 percent of people, it is gentle—especially when narcotic drugs ease pain (Nuland, 1993). But most of the time it is not.

Of the one-quarter of deaths in industrialized nations that are sudden, 80 to 90 percent are due to heart attacks (American Heart Association, 2012; Winslow, Mehta, & Fuster, 2005). Though I longed for reassurance that my father's death had been painless, my wish was probably not fulfilled. Undoubtedly he felt the sharp, crushing sensation of a heart deprived of oxygen. As his heart twitched uncontrollably (called *fibrillation*) or stopped entirely, blood circulation slowed and ceased, and he was thrust into unconsciousness. A brain starved of oxygen for more than two to four minutes is irreversibly damaged. Other oxygen-deprived organs stop functioning as well.

Death is long and drawn out for three-fourths of people—many more than in times past, as a result of life-saving medical technology. Of those with heart disease, most have congestive heart failure, the cause of Nicholas's death (Gruenewald & White, 2006). His scarred heart could no longer contract with the force needed to deliver enough oxygen to his tissues. As it tried harder, its muscle weakened further. Without sufficient blood pressure, fluid backed up in Nicholas's lungs. This hampered his breathing and created ideal conditions for inhaled bacteria to multiply, enter the bloodstream, and run rampant in his system, leading many organs to fail.

Cancer also chooses diverse paths to inflict its damage. When it metastasizes, bits of tumor travel through the bloodstream and implant and grow in vital organs, disrupting their functioning. Medication made my mother's final days as comfortable as possible. But the preceding weeks involved physical suffering, including impaired breathing and digestion.

In the days or hours before death, activity declines; the person moves and communicates less and shows little interest in food, water, and surroundings. At the same time, body temperature, blood pressure, and circulation to the limbs fall, so the hands and feet feel cool and skin color changes to a duller, grayish hue (Hospice Foundation of America, 2005). When the transition from life to death is imminent, the person often moves through three phases:

1. The **agonal phase.** The Greek word *agon* means "struggle." Here agonal refers to gasps and muscle spasms during the first moments in which the regular heartbeat disintegrates (Manole & Hickey, 2006).
2. **Clinical death.** A short interval follows in which heartbeat, circulation, breathing, and brain functioning stop, but resuscitation is still possible.
3. **Mortality.** The individual passes into permanent death.

Defining Death

TAKE A MOMENT... Consider what we have said so far, and note the dilemma of identifying just when death occurs. Death is not an event that happens at a single point in time but, rather, a process in which organs stop functioning in a sequence that varies from person to person. Because the dividing line between life and death is fuzzy, societies need a definition of death to help doctors decide when life-saving measures should be terminated, to signal survivors that they must begin to grieve their loss and reorganize their lives, and to establish when donated organs can be removed.

A monk prays with mourners during a Shinto funeral in Japan. Shinto beliefs, emphasizing ancestor worship and time for the spirit to leave the corpse, may partly explain the Japanese discomfort with the brain death standard and organ donation.

Several decades ago, loss of heartbeat and respiration signified death. But these criteria are no longer adequate because resuscitation techniques frequently permit vital signs to be restored. Today, **brain death,** irreversible cessation of all activity in the brain and the brain stem (which controls reflexes), is used in most industrialized nations.

But not all countries accept this standard. In Japan, for example, doctors rely on traditional criteria—absence of heartbeat and respiration. This approach has hindered the development of a national organ transplant program because few organs can be salvaged from bodies without artificially maintaining vital signs. Buddhist, Confucian, and Shinto beliefs about death, which stress ancestor worship and time for the spirit to leave the corpse, may be partly responsible for the Japanese discomfort with brain death and organ donation. Today, Japanese law allows organ donation using the standard of brain death, even if the wishes of the deceased are not clear, as long as the family does not object (Ida, 2010). Otherwise, people are considered to be alive until the heart stops beating.

Often the brain death standard does not solve the problem of when to halt treatment. Consider Nicholas, who, though not brain dead, had entered a **persistent vegetative state,** in which the cerebral cortex no longer registered electrical activity but the brain stem remained active. Doctors were certain they could not restore consciousness or body movement. Because thousands of people in the United States and other nations are in a persistent vegetative state, with health-care costs totaling many millions of dollars annually, some experts believe that absence of activity in the cerebral cortex should be sufficient to declare a person dead. But others point to a few cases in which patients who had been vegetative for months regained cortical responsiveness and consciousness, though usually with very limited functioning (Laureys & Boly, 2007). In still other instances of illness, a fully conscious but suffering person refuses life-saving measures—an issue we will consider later when we take up the right to die.

Death with Dignity

We have seen that nature rarely delivers the idealized, easy end most people want, nor can medical science guarantee it. Therefore, the greatest dignity in death is in the integrity of the life that precedes it—an integrity we can foster by the way we communicate with and care for the dying person.

First, we can provide the majority of dying people, who succumb gradually, with the utmost in humane and compassionate care. This includes treating them through their physical and psychological distress. We can treat them with respect by taking interest in those aspects of their lives that they most value and by addressing their greatest concerns (Keegan & Drick, 2011).

Second, we can be candid about death's certainty. Unless people are aware that they are dying and understand (as far as possible) the likely circumstances of their death, they cannot plan for end-of-life care and decision making and share the

Dying patient Dick Warner's wife, Nancy, wears a nurse's hat she crafted from paper to symbolize her dual roles as medical and emotional caregiver. The evening of this photo, Nancy heard Dick's breaths shortening. She kissed him and whispered, "It's time to let go." Dick died as he wished, with his loving wife at his bedside.

AP IMAGES/COEUR D'ALENE PRESS, JEROME A. POLLOS

sentiments that bring closure to relationships they hold most dear. Because Sofie knew how and when her death would probably take place, she chose a time when she and Philip could express what their lives had meant to each other. Among those precious bedside exchanges was Sofie's last wish that Philip remarry after her death so he would not live out his final years alone. Openness about impending death granted Sofie a final generative act, helped her let go of the person closest to her, and offered comfort as she faced death.

Finally, doctors and nurses can help dying people learn enough about their condition to make reasoned choices about whether to fight on or say no to further treatment. An understanding of how the normal body works simplifies comprehension of how disease affects it—education that can begin as early as the childhood years.

In sum, we can ensure the most dignified exit possible by offering the dying person care, affection, companionship, and esteem; the truth about diagnosis; and the maximum personal control over this final phase of life (American Hospice Foundation, 2013). These are essential ingredients of a "good death," and we will revisit them throughout this chapter.

Attitudes Toward Death

A century ago, when most deaths occurred at home, people of all ages, including children, helped with care of the dying family member and were present at the moment of death. They saw their loved one buried on family property or in the local cemetery, where the grave could be visited regularly. Because infant and childhood mortality rates were high, all people were likely to know someone their own age, or even younger, who had died. And it was common for children to experience the death of a parent.

Compared with earlier generations, today more young people reach adulthood without having experienced the death of someone they know well (Morgan, Laungani, & Palmer, 2009). When a death does occur, professionals in hospitals and funeral homes take care of most tasks that involve confronting it directly.

This distance from death undoubtedly contributes to a sense of uneasiness about it. Despite frequent images of death in television shows, movies, and news reports of accidents, murders, wars, and natural disasters, we live in a death-denying culture. Adults are often reluctant to talk about death. And substitute expressions, such as "passing away," "going out," or "departing," permit us to avoid acknowledging it candidly. Not surprisingly, **death anxiety**—fear and apprehension of death—is widespread.

Even people who clearly accept the reality of death may fear it. What predicts whether thoughts of our own demise trigger intense distress, relative calm, or something in between? To answer this question, researchers measure both general death anxiety and specific factors—fear of no longer existing, loss of control, a painful death, decay of the body, separation from loved ones, and the unknown (Neimeyer, 1994). Findings reveal large individual and cultural variations in aspects of death that arouse fear. For example, in a study of devout Islamic Saudi Arabians, certain factors that appear repeatedly in the responses of Westerners, such as fear of the body decaying and of the unknown, were entirely absent (Long, 1985).

Among Westerners, spirituality—a sense of life's meaning—seems to be more important than religious commitment in limiting death anxiety (Ardelt, 2003; Routledge & Juhl, 2010). People with a well-developed personal philosophy of death are also less fearful. And in two studies, Christian older adults whose religious beliefs and behavior were contradictory—who believed in a rewarding afterlife but rarely prayed or attended services, or who regularly prayed and attended services but doubted the existence of an afterlife—reported higher death anxiety (Wink, 2006; Wink & Scott, 2005). Together, these findings indicate that both firmness of beliefs and consistency between beliefs and practices, rather than religiousness itself, reduce fear of death. Death anxiety is especially low among adults with deep faith in some form of higher force or being—faith that may or may not be influenced by religion (Cicirelli, 2002; Neimeyer et al., 2011).

TAKE A MOMENT... From what you have learned about adult psychosocial development, how do you think death anxiety might change with age? If you predicted it would decline, reaching its lowest level in late adulthood, you are correct (see Figure 19.1 on page 512) (Russac et al., 2007; Tomer, Eliason, & Smith, 2000). This age-related drop has been found in many cultures and ethnic groups. Recall from Chapter 18 that older adults are especially effective at regulating negative emotion. As a result, most cope with anxieties, including fear of death, effectively. Furthermore, attainment of ego integrity reduces death anxiety. Older people have had more time to develop symbolic immortality—the belief that one will continue to live

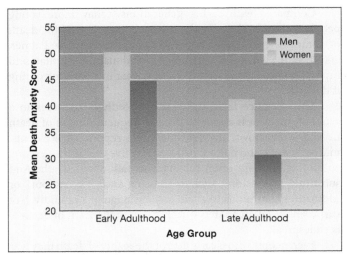

FIGURE 19.1 Relationship of age and gender to death anxiety. In this study comparing young and older adults, death anxiety declined with age. Women expressed greater fear of death than men. Many other studies show similar findings. (Adapted from Tomer, Eliason, & Smith, 2000.)

on through one's children or through one's work or personal influence (see Chapter 16, page 424).

As long as it is not overly intense, death anxiety can motivate people to live up to internalized cultural values—for example, to be kind to others and to work hard to reach one's goals. These efforts increase adults' sense of self-esteem, self-efficacy, and purpose in life—powerful antidotes against the terrifying thought that, in the overall scheme of things, they "are no more important or enduring than any individual potato, pineapple, or porcupine" (Fry, 2003; Pyszczynski et al., 2004,

Death anxiety declines in old age, and this 81-year-old from the Netherlands seems to have very little! She had this coffin made to serve as a bookshelf because, she said, "It's a waste to use a coffin just for burial." The pillow on the top will support her head after she dies.

p. 436). In a study of Israeli adults, symbolic immortality predicted reduced fear of death, especially among those with secure attachments (Florian & Mikulincer, 1998). Gratifying, close interpersonal ties seem to help people feel worthwhile and forge a sense of symbolic immortality. And people who view death as an opportunity to pass a legacy to future generations are less likely to fear it (Cicirelli, 2001; Mikulincer, Florian, & Hirschberger, 2003).

Regardless of age, in both Eastern and Western cultures, women appear more anxious about death than men do (refer again to Figure 19.1) (Madnawat & Kachhawa, 2007; Tomer, Eliason, & Smith, 2000). Women may be more likely to admit and men more likely to avoid troubled feelings about mortality—an explanation consistent with females' greater emotional expressiveness throughout the lifespan.

Experiencing some anxiety about death is normal and adaptive. But like other fears, very intense death anxiety can undermine effective adjustment. Although physical health in adulthood is not related to death anxiety, mental health clearly is. In cultures as different as China and the United States, people who are depressed or generally anxious are likely to have more severe death concerns (Neimeyer & Van Brunt, 1995; Wu, Tang, & Kwok, 2002). In contrast, people who are good at inhibition (keeping their minds from straying to irrelevant thoughts) and at emotional self-regulation report less death anxiety (Gailliot, Schmeichel, & Baumeister, 2006). They are better able to manage their concerns about death.

Death anxiety is largely limited to adolescence and adulthood. Children rarely display it unless they live in high-crime neighborhoods or war-torn areas where they are in constant danger (see the Cultural Influences box on the impact of ethnic and political violence on children on page 280 in Chapter 10). Terminally ill children are also at risk for high death anxiety. Compared with other same-age patients, children with cancer express more destructive thoughts and negative feelings about death (Malone, 1982). For those whose parents make the mistake of not telling them they are going to die, loneliness and death anxiety can be extreme (O'Halloran & Altmaier, 1996).

ASK YOURSELF

REVIEW Explain why death anxiety typically declines in late adulthood.

APPLY Considering factors that influence death anxiety, suggest several experiences that religious institutions or senior centers can offer that might reduce fear in highly death-anxious people.

REFLECT Ask members of earlier generations in your family about their childhood experiences with death. Compare these to your own experiences. What differences did you find, and how would you explain them?

Thinking and Emotions of Dying People

In the year before her death, Sofie did everything possible to surmount her illness. In between treatments to control the cancer, she tested her strength. She continued to teach high school, traveled to visit her children, cultivated a garden, and took weekend excursions with Philip. Hope pervaded Sofie's approach to her deadly condition, and she spoke often about the disease—so much so that her friends wondered how she could confront it so directly.

As Sofie deteriorated physically, she was frustrated, and at times angry and depressed, about her inability to keep on fighting. Once she asked when my husband and I, who were newly married, would have children. "If only I could live long enough to hold them in my arms!" she cried. In the last week, she appeared tired but free of struggle. Occasionally, she spoke of her love for us and commented on the beauty of the hills outside her window. But mostly, she looked and listened, rather than actively participating in conversation. One afternoon, she fell permanently unconscious.

Do Stages of Dying Exist?

As dying people move closer to death, are their reactions predictable? Do they go through a series of changes that are the same for everyone, or are their thoughts and feelings unique?

Kübler-Ross's Theory. Although her theory has been heavily criticized, Elisabeth Kübler-Ross (1969) is credited with awakening society's sensitivity to the psychological needs of dying patients. From interviews with over 200 terminally ill people, she devised a theory of five typical responses—initially proposed as stages—to the prospect of death and the ordeal of dying:

- *Denial.* On learning of the terminal illness, the person denies its seriousness. While the patient still feels reasonably well, denial is self-protective, allowing the individual to deal with the illness at his or her own pace. Kübler-Ross recommends that family members and health professionals not prolong denial by distorting the truth about the person's condition. In doing so, they prevent the dying person from adjusting to impending death and hinder necessary arrangements—for social support, for bringing closure to relationships, and for making decisions about medical interventions.

- *Anger.* Recognition that time is short promotes anger at having to die without having had a chance to do all one wants to do. Family members and health professionals may be targets of the patient's rage, resentment, and envy. Even so, they must tolerate rather than lash out at the patient's behavior, realizing that the underlying cause is the unfairness of death.

- *Bargaining.* Grasping the inevitability of death, the terminally ill person attempts to bargain for extra time—a deal he or she may try to strike with family members, friends, doctors, nurses, or God. The best response to these efforts to sustain hope is to listen sympathetically, as one doctor did to the pleas of a young AIDS-stricken father, whose wish was to live long enough to dance with his daughter—then 8 years old—at her wedding (Selwyn, 1996). Sometimes, bargains are altruistic acts. Tony, a 15-year-old leukemia patient, expressed to his mother:

  > I don't want to die yet. Gerry [youngest brother] is only 3 and not old enough to understand. If I could live just one more year, I could explain it to him myself and he will understand. Three is just too young. (Komp, 1996, pp. 69–70)

  Although many dying patients' bargains are unrealistic and impossible to fulfill, Tony lived for exactly one year—a gift to those who survived him.

- *Depression.* When denial, anger, and bargaining fail to postpone the illness, the person becomes depressed about the loss of his or her life. Unfortunately, many experiences associated with dying, including physical and mental deterioration, pain, lack of control, certain medications, and being hooked to machines, contribute to despondency. Compassionate medical and psychological treatment, aimed at clarifying and alleviating the patients concerns, can limit despair.

- *Acceptance.* Most people who reach acceptance, a state of peace and quiet about upcoming death, do so only in the last weeks or days. The weakened patient yields to death, disengaging from all but a few family members, friends, and caregivers. Some dying people, in an attempt to pull away from all they have loved, withdraw. "I'm getting my mental and emotional house in order," one patient explained (Samarel, 1995, p. 101).

Evaluation of Kübler-Ross's Theory. Kübler-Ross cautioned that her five stages should not be viewed as a fixed sequence and that not all people display each response. But her use of the term *stages* has made it easy for her theory to be interpreted simplistically, as the series of steps a "normal" dying person follows. Some health professionals, unaware of diversity in dying experiences, have insensitively tried to push patients through Kübler-Ross's sequence. And caregivers, through callousness or ignorance, can too easily dismiss a dying patient's legitimate complaints about treatment as "just what you would expect in Stage 2" (Corr & Corr, 2013; Kastenbaum, 2012).

Rather than stages, the five reactions Kübler-Ross observed are best viewed as coping strategies that anyone may call on in the face of threat. Furthermore, dying people react in many additional ways—for example, through efforts to conquer the disease, as Sofie displayed; through an overwhelming need to control what happens to their bodies during the dying process; through acts of generosity and caring, as seen in Tony's concern for his 3-year-old brother, Gerry; and through shifting their focus to living in a fulfilling way—"seizing the day" because so little time is left (Silverman, 2004; Wright, 2003).

As these examples suggest, the most serious drawback to Kübler-Ross's theory is that it looks at dying patients' thoughts and feelings outside the contexts that give them meaning. As we will see next, people's adaptations to impending death can be understood only in relation to the multidimensional influences that have contributed to their life course and that also shape this final phase.

Contextual Influences on Adaptations to Dying

From the moment of her diagnosis, Sofie spent little time in denial. Instead, she met the deadly disease head on, just as she had dealt with other challenges of life. Her impassioned plea to hold her grandchildren in her arms was less a bargain with fate than an expression of profound defeat that on the threshold of late adulthood, she would not live to enjoy its rewards. At the end, her quiet, withdrawn demeanor was probably resignation, not acceptance. All her life, she had been a person with a fighting spirit.

According to recent theorists, a single strategy, such as acceptance, is not best for every dying patient. Rather, an **appropriate death** is one that makes sense in terms of the individual's pattern of living and values and, at the same time, preserves or restores significant relationships and is as free of suffering as possible (Worden, 2000). When asked about a "good death," most patients mention the following goals:

- Maintaining a sense of identity, or inner continuity with one's past
- Clarifying the meaning of one's life and death

On September 18, 2007, Carnegie Mellon University computer science professor Randy Pausch, diagnosed with pancreatic cancer, gave his final lecture to a packed house. His message, which focused on achieving one's childhood dreams and enabling the dreams of others, can be viewed at *www.cmu.edu/homepage/multimedia/randy-pausch-lecture.shtml.* He died nine months later, at age 47, having approached his death in a way that suited his pattern of living and deepest values.

- Maintaining and enhancing relationships
- Achieving a sense of control over the time that remains
- Confronting and preparing for death (Goldsteen et al., 2006; Kleespies, 2004; Proulx & Jacelon, 2004)

Research reveals that biological, psychological, and social and cultural forces affect people's coping with dying and, therefore, the extent to which they attain these goals.

Nature of the Disease. The course of the illness and its symptoms affect the dying person's reactions. For example, the extended nature of Sofie's illness and her doctor's initial optimism about achieving a remission undoubtedly contributed to her attempts to try to conquer the disease. During the final month, when cancer had spread to Sofie's lungs and she could not catch her breath, she was agitated and fearful until oxygen and medication relieved her uncertainty about being able to breathe. In contrast, Nicholas's weakened heart and failing kidneys so depleted his strength that he responded only with passivity.

Because of the toll of the disease, about one-third of cancer patients experience severe depression—reactions distinct from the sadness, grief, and worry that typically accompany the dying process. Profound depression amplifies pain, impairs the immune response, interferes with the patient's capacity for pleasure, meaning, and connection, and is associated with poorer survival (Satin, Linden, & Phillips, 2009; Williams & Dale, 2006). It therefore requires immediate treatment. Among the most successful approaches are counselor-led life review (see page 481 in Chapter 18), medical control of pain, and advance care planning with the patient that ensures his or her end-of-life wishes are known and respected (Rosenstein, 2011).

Personality and Coping Style. Understanding the way individuals view stressful life events and have coped with them in the past helps us appreciate the way they manage the dying process. In a study in which terminally ill patients discussed their images of dying, responses varied greatly.

- Beth regarded *dying as imprisonment:* "I felt like the clock started ticking . . . like the future has suddenly been taken. . . . In a way, I feel like I'm already dead."
- To Faith, dying was *a mandate to live ever more fully:* "I have a saying: . . . 'You're not ready to live until you're ready to die.' . . . It never meant much to me until I . . . looked death in the eye, and now I'm living. . . . This life is a lot better than the one before."
- Dawn viewed dying as *part of life's journey:* "I learned all about my disease. . . . I would read, read, read. . . . I wanted to know as much as I can about it, and I don't think hiding . . . behind the door . . . could help me at all. And, I realized for the first time in my life—*really, really, really realized* that I could handle anything."

- Patty approached dying as *an experience to be transformed* so as to make it more bearable: "I am an avid, rabid fan of *Star Trek,* a trekkie like there never has been. . . . I watch it to the point that I've memorized it. . . . [In my mind, I play the various characters so] I'm not [always] thinking about cancer or dying. . . . I think that's how I get through it." (Wright, 2003, pp. 442–444, 447)

Each patient's view of dying helps explain her responses to worsening illness. Poorly adjusted individuals—those with conflict-ridden relationships and many disappointments in life—are usually more distressed (Kastenbaum, 2012).

Family Members' and Health Professionals' Behavior. Earlier we noted that a candid approach, in which everyone close to and caring for the dying person acknowledges the terminal illness, is best. Yet this also introduces the burden of participating in the work of dying with the patient—bringing relationships to closure, reflecting on life, and dealing with fears and regrets.

People who find it hard to engage in these tasks may pretend that the disease is not as bad as it is. In patients inclined toward denial, a "game" can be set in motion in which participants are aware that the patient is dying but act as though it were not so. Though this game softens psychological pain for the moment, it makes dying much more difficult. Besides impeding communication, it frequently leads to futile medical interventions, in which the patient has little understanding of what is happening and is subjected to great physical and emotional suffering. One attending physician provided this account of a cancer patient's death:

> The problem was that she had a young husband and parents who were pretty much in complete denial. We were trying to be aggressive up to the end. To the point that we actually hung a new form of chemotherapy about four hours before she died, even though everybody knew except her immediate family that she was going to die within the next four to eight hours. (Jackson et al., 2005, p. 653)

When doctors do want to inform patients of their prognosis, they may encounter resistance, especially within certain ethnic groups. Withholding information is common in Southern and Eastern Europe, Central and South America, much of Asia, and the Middle East. Japanese terminally ill cancer patients are seldom told the truth about their condition, partly because dying disrupts important interdependent relationships (Yamamoto, 2004). Many Mexican Americans and Korean Americans believe that informing patients is wrong and will hasten death (Blackhall et al., 1995, 2001). In these instances, providing information is complex. When a family insists that a patient not be told, the doctor can first offer information to the patient and then, if the patient refuses, ask who should receive information and make health-care decisions (Zane & Yeh, 2002). The patient's preference can be honored and reassessed at regular intervals.

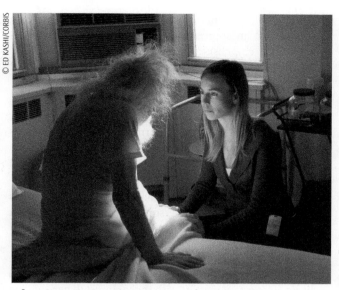

A doctor listens patiently to the concerns of a terminally ill 94-year-old. Through sensitive, open communication, health professionals help dying people prepare for death by bringing relationships to closure, reflecting on life, and dealing with fears and regrets.

Social support from family members also affects adaptation to dying. Dying patients who feel they have much unfinished business to attend to are more anxious about impending death. But family contact reduces their sense of urgency to prolong life (Mutran et al., 1997; Zimmerman, 2012). Perhaps it permits patients to work through at least some incomplete tasks.

Effective communication with the dying person is honest, fostering a trusting relationship, yet also oriented toward maintaining hope. Many dying patients move through a hope trajectory—at first, hope for a cure; later, hope for prolonging life; and finally, hope for a peaceful death with as few burdens as possible (Fanslow, 1981). Once patients near death stop expressing hope, those close to them must accept this. Family members who find letting go very difficult may benefit from expert guidance.

Spirituality, Religion, and Culture. Earlier we noted that a sense of spirituality reduces fear of death. Research indicates that this is as true for the dying as for people in general. Terminally ill patients who score higher in spiritual well-being (belief in life's meaning) experience less end-of-life despair (desire for a hastened death and suicidal thoughts) (McClain, Rosenfeld, & Breitbard, 2003; McClain-Jacobson et al., 2004). Vastly different cultural beliefs, guided by religious ideas, also shape people's dying experiences:

- Buddhism, widely practiced in China, India, and Southeast Asia, fosters acceptance of death. By reading sutras (teachings of Buddha) to the dying person to calm the mind and emphasizing that dying leads to rebirth in a heaven of peace and relaxation, Buddhists believe that it is possible to reach Nirvana, a state beyond the world of suffering (Kubotera, 2004; Yeung, 1996).

- In many Native-American groups, death is met with stoic self-control, an approach taught at an early age through stories that emphasize a circular, rather than linear, relationship between life and death and the importance of making way for others (Cox, 2002).

- For African Americans, a dying loved one signals a crisis that unites family members in caregiving (Crawley et al., 2000; Jenkins et al., 2005). The terminally ill person remains an active and vital force within the family until he or she can no longer carry out this role—an attitude of respect that undoubtedly eases the dying process.

- Among the Maori of New Zealand, relatives and friends gather around the dying person to give spiritual strength and comfort. Older adults, clergy, and other experts in tribal customs conduct a *karakia* ceremony, in which they recite prayers asking for peace, mercy, and guidance from the creator. After the ceremony, the patient is encouraged to discuss important matters with those closest to her—giving away of personal belongings, directions for interment, and completion of other unfinished tasks (Ngata, 2004).

In sum, dying prompts a multitude of thoughts, emotions, and coping strategies. Which ones are emphasized depends on a wide array of contextual influences. A vital assumption of the lifespan perspective—that development is multidimensional and multidirectional—is just as relevant to this final phase as to each earlier period.

 ## A Place to Die

Whereas in the past most deaths occurred at home, in the United States today about 40 percent take place in hospitals and another 20 percent in long-term care facilities, mostly nursing homes (Centers for Disease Control and Prevention, 2013). In the large, impersonal hospital environment, meeting the human needs of dying patients and their families is secondary, not because professionals lack concern, but because the work to be done focuses on saving lives. A dying patient represents a failure.

In the 1960s, a death awareness movement arose as a reaction to hospitals' death-avoiding practices—attachment of complicated machinery to patients with no chance of survival and avoidance of communication with dying patients. This movement soon led to medical care better suited to the needs of dying people and also to hospice programs, which have spread to many countries in the industrialized world. Let's visit each of these settings for dying.

Home

Had Sofie and Nicholas been asked where they wanted to die, undoubtedly each would have responded, "At home"—the preference of 80 to 90 percent of Americans (NHPCO, 2005; O'Connor, 2003). The reason is clear: The home offers an atmo-sphere of intimacy and loving care in which the terminally ill person is unlikely to feel abandoned.

However, only about one-fourth of Americans experience home death (Centers for Disease Control and Prevention, 2013). And it is important not to romanticize dying at home. Because of dramatic improvements in medicine, dying people tend to be sicker or much older than in the past. Consequently, their bodies may be extremely frail, making ordinary activities—eating, sleeping, taking a pill, toileting, and bathing—major ordeals for informal caregivers (Singer et al., 2005).

For many people, the chance to be with the dying person until the very end is a rewarding tradeoff for the high demands of caregiving. But to make dying at home feasible, adequate support for the caregiver is essential (Karlsson & Berggren, 2011; Newbury, 2011). A specially trained home health aide is usually necessary—a service (as we will see shortly) that hospice programs have made more accessible. Still, when family relationships are conflict-ridden, a dying patient introduces additional family strains and is subjected to increased distress, negating the benefits of home death. Furthermore, even with professional help, most homes are poorly equipped to handle the medical and comfort-care needs of the dying. Hospital-based equipment and technical support often must be transported to the home.

For all these reasons, older adults—although they view home as their ideal place to die—express concerns about quality of care, about burdening family and friends, and about the need for adult children to engage in unduly intimate caregiving tasks (Gott et al., 2004). And 10 months after a home death, family members continue to report more psychological stress than do family members whose loved one died elsewhere (Addington-Hall, 2000).

Hospital

Hospital dying takes many forms. Each is affected by the physical state of the dying person, the hospital unit in which it takes place, and the goal and quality of care.

Sudden deaths, due to injury or critical illness, typically occur in emergency rooms. Doctors and nurses must evaluate the problem and take action quickly. Little time is available for contact with family members. When staff break the news of death in a sympathetic manner and provide explanations, family members are grateful. Otherwise, feelings of anger, frustration, and confusion can add to their grief (Walsh & McGoldrick, 2004). Crisis intervention services are needed to help survivors cope with sudden death.

Nicholas died on an intensive care ward focused on preventing death in patients whose condition can worsen quickly. Privacy and communication with the family were secondary to monitoring his condition. To prevent disruption of nurses' activities, Giselle and Sasha could be at Nicholas's side only at scheduled times. Dying in intensive care—an experience unique to technologically sophisticated societies—is especially deper-

Dying in intensive care is a depersonalizing experience unique to technologically sophisticated societies. In such settings, medical responses supersede privacy and communication with patient and family.

sonalizing for patients like Nicholas, who linger between life and death while hooked to machines often for months.

Cancer patients, who account for most cases of prolonged dying, typically die in general or specialized cancer care hospital units. When hospitalized for a long time, they reach out for help with physical and emotional needs, too often with mixed success. In these settings, as in intensive care, a conflict of values is apparent (Costello, 2006). The tasks associated with dying must be performed efficiently so that all patients can be served and health professionals are not drained emotionally by repeated attachments and separations.

Although hospital comprehensive treatment programs aimed at easing physical, emotional, and spiritual suffering at the end of life have increased steadily over the past decade, one-third of hospitals still do not have them (Center to Advance Palliative Care, 2012). And because just 16 percent of U.S. and Canadian medical schools offer even a single pain-focused course (usually an elective), few doctors and nurses are specially trained in managing pain in chronically ill and dying people (Mezei & Murinson, 2011). At present, many people die in painful, frightening, and depersonalizing hospital conditions, without their wishes being met.

Nursing Home

Though deaths in U.S. nursing homes—mostly elderly patients—are common, care emphasizes rehabilitation rather than high-quality terminal care. The few studies that have addressed what it is like to die in nursing homes concur that many patients suffer from inattention to their emotional and spiritual needs and from high levels of untreated pain (Massachusetts Expert Panel on End of Life Care, 2010).

In one investigation, researchers conducted in-depth interviews with a nationally representative sample of nearly 600 family members whose loved one had spent at least 48 hours

of the final month of life in a nursing home. Respondents frequently mentioned unsatisfactory physical care of the dying patient, difficulty obtaining basic information from staff members on the patient's condition, staff members' lack of compassion and attentiveness to the patient's medical deterioration, and physicians who were "missing in action"—rarely seen in the nursing home (Shield et al., 2010; Wetle et al., 2005). Relatives often felt the need to advocate for their dying relative, though their efforts met with limited success—circumstances that greatly increased both patient and family distress.

The hospice approach—which we consider next—aims to reduce profound caregiving failures in hospitals and nursing homes. When combined with hospice, nursing home care of the dying improves greatly in pain management, emotional and spiritual support, and family satisfaction. But referrals of dying nursing home residents to hospice, though increasing, are often not made—or made too late to be useful (Zheng et al., 2012).

The Hospice Approach

In medieval times, a *hospice* was a place where travelers could find rest and shelter. In the nineteenth and twentieth centuries, the word referred to homes for dying patients. Today, **hospice** is not a place but a comprehensive program of support services for terminally ill people and their families. It aims to provide a caring community sensitive to the dying person's needs so patients and family members can prepare for death in ways that are satisfying to them. Quality of life is central to the hospice approach, which includes these main features:

● The patient and family as a unit of care

● Emphasis on meeting the patient's physical, emotional, social, and spiritual needs, including controlling pain, retaining dignity and self-worth, and feeling cared for and loved

A son and his dying mother share recollections as he shows her a photograph of her long-ago graduation. By creating opportunities for unpressured closeness and connection, hospice care enhances dying patients' quality of life rather than extending life.

Biology and Environment

Music as Palliative Care for Dying Patients

When Peter visits 82-year-old Stuart to play the harp, Stuart reports being transported to an idyllic place with water, children, and trees—far from the lung tumors that will soon take his life. "When Peter plays for me, . . . I am no longer frightened," Stuart says.

Peter is a specialist in *music thanatology,* an emerging specialty in music therapy that focuses on providing palliative care to the dying through music. He uses his harp, and sometimes his voice, to induce calm and give solace to the dying, their families, and their caregivers. Peter applies music systematically—matching it to each patient's breathing patterns and other responses, delivering different sounds to uplift or comfort, depending on his assessment of the patient's moment-by-moment needs.

Chaplains and counselors informally report that after music vigils, patients' conversations indicate that they more easily come to terms with their own death (Fyfe,

2006). And in a study of 65 dying patients in which pre- and post-intervention physiological measures were compared, music vigils averaging an hour in length resulted in decreased agitation and wakefulness and slower, deeper, less effortful breathing (Freeman et al., 2006). These physiological benefits extended to patients who, on the basis of their behavior, were clearly in pain.

Why is music effective in easing the distress of those who are dying? In patients close to death, hearing typically functions longer than other senses. Thus, responsiveness to music may persist until the individual's final moments. Besides reducing anxiety, music

Music thanatology focuses on providing palliative care for the dying through music. This practitioner uses her harp, and sometimes her voice, to induce calm and provide solace.

can, in some instances, enhance the effects of medication administered to control pain (Starr, 1999). For these reasons, music vigils may be an especially effective end-of-life therapy.

- Care provided by an interdisciplinary team: a doctor, a nurse or home health aide, a chaplain, a counselor or social worker, and a trained volunteer
- The patient kept at home or in an inpatient setting with a homelike atmosphere where coordination of care is possible
- Focus on protecting the quality of remaining life with **palliative,** or **comfort, care** that relieves pain and other symptoms (nausea, breathing difficulties, insomnia, and depression) rather than prolonging life
- In addition to regularly scheduled home care visits, on-call services available 24 hours a day, 7 days a week
- Follow-up bereavement services offered to families in the year after a death

Hospice programs everywhere encompass a continuum of care, from home to inpatient options, including hospitals and nursing homes. Central to the hospice approach is that the dying person and his or her family be offered choices that guarantee an appropriate death. Some programs offer hospice day care, which enables caregivers to continue working or be relieved of

the stresses of long-term care (Kernohan et al., 2006). Contact with others facing terminal illness is a supportive byproduct of many hospice arrangements. And to find out about a comforting musical intervention for patients near death, consult the Biology and Environment box above.

LOOK AND LISTEN

Contact a nearby hospice program, and find out about the varied ways it delivers comprehensive services to meet the needs of dying patients and their families. ●

Currently, the United States has over 5,300 hospice programs serving approximately 1.6 million terminally ill patients annually (NHPCO, 2012). Because hospice care is a cost-effective alternative to expensive life-saving treatments, U.S. government health-care benefits (Medicare and Medicaid) cover it, as do most private insurance plans. In addition, community and foundation contributions allow many hospices to provide free services to uninsured patients who cannot pay (Hospice Foundation of America, 2013). Consequently hospice is affordable for most dying patients and their families. Hospices also serve dying children—a tragedy so devastating that social support and bereavement intervention are vital.

Besides reducing patient physical suffering, hospice contributes to improved family functioning. The majority of patients and families report high satisfaction with quality of care and pain management, enhanced sense of social support, and (in the case of home hospice) increased ability to sustain patient care at home (Candy et al., 2011). In one study, family members experiencing hospice scored higher than nonhospice family members in psychological well-being one to two years after their loved one's death (Ragow-O'Brien, Hayslip, & Guarnaccia, 2000).

As a long-range goal, hospice organizations are striving for broader acceptance of their patient- and family-centered approach. Culturally sensitive approaches are needed to reach more ethnic minority patients, who are far less likely than white patients to participate in hospice (NHPCO, 2012). In developing countries, where millions die of cancer and other devastating illnesses each year, community-based teams working under a nurse's supervision sometimes deliver palliative care. But they face many obstacles, including lack of funding, pain-relieving drugs, and professional and public education about hospice (Ddungu, 2011).

ASK YOURSELF

REVIEW Why is the stage notion an inaccurate account of dying patients' mental and emotional reactions?

APPLY When 5-year-old Timmy's kidney failure was diagnosed as terminal, his parents could not accept the tragic news. Their hospital visits became shorter, and they evaded his anxious questions. Eventually, Timmy blamed himself. He died with little physical pain, but alone, and his parents suffered prolonged guilt. How could hospice care have helped Timmy and his family?

REFLECT If you were terminally ill, where would you want to die? Explain.

The Right to Die

In 1990, 26-year-old Terri Schiavo's heart stopped briefly, temporarily cutting off oxygen to her brain. Terri lay in a persistent vegetative state. Her husband and guardian, Michael, claimed that she had earlier told him she would not want to be kept alive artificially, but Terri's parents disagreed. In 1998, the Florida Circuit Court granted Michael's petition to have Terri's feeding tube removed. In 2001, after her parents had exhausted their appeals, the tube was taken out. But on the basis of contradic-

tory medical testimony, Terri's parents convinced a circuit court judge to order the feeding tube reinserted, and the legal wrangling continued. In 2002, Michael won a second judgment to remove the tube.

By that time, publicity over the case and its central question—who should make end-of-life decisions when the patient's wishes are unclear—had made Terri a political issue. In 2003, the Florida legislature passed a law allowing the governor to stay the circuit court's order to keep Terri alive, but on appeal, the law was declared unconstitutional. In 2005, the U.S. Congress entered the fray, passing a bill that transferred Terri's fate to the U.S. District Court. When the judge refused to intervene, the feeding tube was removed for a third time. In 2005—15 years after losing consciousness—Terri Schiavo died. The autopsy confirmed the original persistent vegetative state diagnosis: Her brain was half normal size.

The Schiavo case—and others like it—have brought right-to-die issues to the forefront of public attention. Today, all U.S. states have laws that honor patients' wishes concerning withdrawal of treatment in cases of terminal illness and, sometimes, in cases of a persistent vegetative state. But no uniform right-to-die policy exists, and heated controversy persists over how to handle the diverse circumstances in which patients and family members make requests.

Euthanasia is the practice of ending the life of a person suffering from an incurable condition. Its various forms are summarized in Table 19.1. As we will see, public acceptance of euthanasia is high, except when it involves ending the life of an anguished, terminally ill patient without his or her expressed permission.

TABLE 19.1

Forms of Euthanasia

FORM	DESCRIPTION
Passive euthanasia	At the patient's request, the doctor withholds or withdraws treatment, thereby permitting the patient to die naturally. For example, the doctor does not perform surgery or administer medication that could prolong life, or the doctor turns off the respirator of a patient who cannot breathe independently.
Voluntary active euthanasia	The doctor ends a suffering patient's life at the patient's request. For example, the doctor administers a lethal dose of drugs.
Assisted suicide	The doctor helps a suffering patient take his or her own life. For example, the doctor enables the patient to swallow or inject a lethal dose of drugs.
Involuntary active euthanasia	The doctor ends a suffering patient's life without the patient's permission. For example, without obtaining the patient's consent, the doctor administers a lethal dose of drugs.

Passive Euthanasia

In **passive euthanasia**, life-sustaining treatment is withheld or withdrawn, permitting a patient to die naturally. *TAKE A MOMENT...* Do you think Terri Schiavo should have been allowed to die sooner? Was it right for Nicholas's doctors to turn off his respirator at Giselle's request? When an Alzheimer's victim has lost all awareness and bodily functions, should life support be withheld?

In recent polls, more 70 percent of U.S. adults and 95 percent of physicians supported the right of patients or family members to end treatment when there is no hope of recovery (Curlin et al., 2008; Pew Research Center, 2006). In 1986, the American Medical Association endorsed withdrawing all forms of treatment from the terminally ill when death is imminent and from those in a permanent vegetative state. Consequently, passive euthanasia is widely practiced as part of ordinary medical procedure, in which doctors exercise professional judgment.

Still, a minority of citizens oppose passive euthanasia. Religious denomination has surprisingly little effect on people's opinions. For example, most Catholics hold favorable views, despite slow official church acceptance because of fears that passive euthanasia might be a first step toward government-approved mercy killing. However, ethnicity makes a difference: Nearly twice as many African Americans as Caucasian Americans desire all medical means possible, regardless of the patient's condition, and African Americans more often receive life-sustaining intervention, such as feeding tubes (Haley, 2013; Johnson et al., 2008). Their reluctance to forgo treatment reflects strong cultural and religious beliefs in overcoming adversity and in the power of God to promote healing (Johnson, Elbert-Avila, & Tulsky, 2005).

Because of controversial court cases like Terri Schiavo's, some doctors and health-care institutions are unwilling to end treatment without legal protection. In the absence of national consensus on passive euthanasia, people can best ensure that their wishes will be followed by preparing an **advance medical directive**—a written statement of desired medical treatment should they become incurably ill. U.S. states recognize two types of advance directives: a *living will* and a *durable power of attorney for health care* (U.S. Living Will Registry, 2005). Sometimes these are combined into one document.

In a **living will,** people specify the treatments they do or do not want in case of a terminal illness, coma, or other near-death situation. For example, a person might state that without reasonable expectation of recovery, he or she should not be kept alive through medical intervention of any kind. In addition, a living will sometimes specifies that pain-relieving medication be given, even though it might shorten life. In Sofie's case, her doctor administered a powerful narcotic to relieve labored breathing and quiet her fear of suffocation. The narcotic suppressed respiration, causing death to occur hours or days earlier than if the medication had not been prescribed, but without distress. Such palliative care is accepted as appropriate and ethical medical practice.

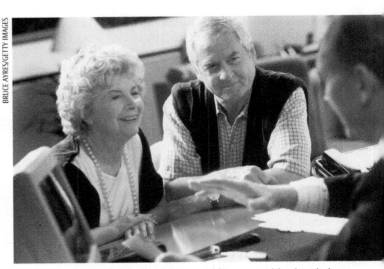

This couple discusses a durable power of attorney with a hospital chaplain. This advance directive authorizes a trusted spokesperson to make health-care decisions and helps ensure that one's desires will be granted.

Although living wills help ensure personal control, they do not guarantee it. Recognition of living wills is usually limited to patients who are terminally ill or are otherwise expected to die shortly. Only a few U.S. states cover people in a persistent vegetative state or aging adults who linger with many chronic problems, including Alzheimer's disease, because these conditions are not classified as terminal. Even when terminally ill patients have living wills, doctors sometimes do not follow them for a variety of reasons (van Asselt, 2006). These include fear of lawsuits, their own moral beliefs, failure to inquire about patients' directives, and inaccessibility of those directives—for example, located in the family safe or family members unaware of them.

Because living wills cannot anticipate all future medical conditions and can easily be ignored, a second form of advance directive has become common. The **durable power of attorney for health care** authorizes appointment of another person (usually, though not always, a family member) to make health-care decisions on one's behalf. It is more flexible than the living will because it permits a trusted spokesperson to confer with the doctor as medical circumstances arise. Because authority to speak for the patient is not limited to terminal illnesses, more latitude exists for dealing with unexpected situations. And in gay and lesbian and other close relationships not sanctioned by law, the durable power of attorney can ensure the partner's role in decision making and in advocating for the patient's health-care needs.

Whether or not a person supports passive euthanasia, it is important to have a living will, durable power of attorney, or both, because most deaths occur in hospitals or nursing homes. Yet only about 30 percent of Americans have executed such documents, perhaps because of widespread uneasiness about bringing up the topic of death, especially with relatives (Harris Interactive, 2011; Pew Research Center, 2006). The percentage with advance directives does increase with age; almost two-thirds of adults over age 65 have them. To encourage people to make decisions about potential treatment while they are able, U.S. federal law now requires that all medical facilities receiving federal funds provide information at admission about state laws and institutional policies on patients' rights and advance directives.

As happened with Terri Schiavo, health-care professionals—unclear about a patient's intent and fearing liability—will probably decide to continue treatment regardless of cost and a person's prior oral statements. Perhaps for this reason, some U.S. states permit appointment of a health-care proxy, or substitute decision maker, if a patient failed to provide an advance medical directive while competent. Proxies are an important means of covering children and adolescents, who cannot legally execute advance medical directives.

Voluntary Active Euthanasia

In recent years, the right-to-die debate has shifted from withdrawal of treatment for the hopelessly ill to more active alternatives. In **voluntary active euthanasia,** doctors or others act directly, at a patient's request, to end suffering before a natural end to life. The practice, a form of mercy killing, is a criminal offense in most countries, including almost all U.S. states. But support for voluntary active euthanasia has grown. As Figure 19.2 shows, about 70 to 90 percent of people in Western nations approve of it (World Federation of Right to Die Societies, 2006). When doctors engage in voluntary active euthanasia, judges are

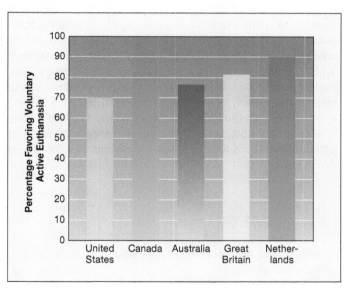

FIGURE 19.2 Public opinion favoring voluntary active euthanasia in five nations. A struggle exists between public opinion, which has increasingly favored voluntary active euthanasia over the past 30 years, and legal statutes, which prohibit it. The majority of people in Western nations believe that a hopelessly ill, suffering patient who asks for a lethal injection should be granted that request. Public support for voluntary active euthanasia is highest in the Netherlands—the only nation in the world where the practice is legal under certain conditions. (From Harris Interactive, 2011; Pew Research Center, 2006.)

usually lenient, granting suspended sentences or probation—a trend reflecting rising public interest in self-determination in death as in life.

Nevertheless, attempts to legalize voluntary active euthanasia have prompted heated controversy. Supporters believe it represents the most compassionate option for terminally ill people in severe pain. Opponents stress the moral difference between "letting die" and "killing" and point out that at times, even very sick patients recover. They also argue that involving doctors in taking the lives of suffering patients may impair people's trust in health professionals. Finally, a fear exists that legalizing this practice—even when strictly monitored to make sure it does not arise out of depression, loneliness, coercion, or a desire to diminish the burden of illness on others—could lead to a broadening of euthanasia. Initially limited to the terminally ill, it might be applied involuntarily to the frail, demented, or disabled—outcomes that most people find unacceptable and immoral. These concerns are warranted, as events in the Netherlands—where voluntary active euthanasia has been practiced for several decades and became legal in 2002—make clear. Dutch doctors are allowed to engage in it under the following conditions: when physical or mental suffering is severe, with no prospect of relief; when no doubt exists about the patient's desire to die; when the patient's decision is voluntary, well-informed, and stable over time; when all other options for care have been exhausted or refused; and when another doctor has been consulted. But despite these safeguards, some doctors admit to having actively caused a death when a patient did not ask for it (Rurup et al., 2005; von Tol, Rietjens, & van der Heide, 2010). They defend their actions by referring to the impossibility of treating pain, a low quality of life, or drawn-out dying in a patient near death. A small minority say they granted the euthanasia requests of physically healthy patients—usually older people who felt "weary of life."

Nevertheless, terminally ill individuals in severe pain continue to plead for legalization of voluntary active euthanasia. Probably all would agree that when doctors feel compelled to relieve suffering and honor self-determination by assisting a patient in dying, they should be subject to the most stringent monitoring possible.

Assisted Suicide

After checking Diane's blood count, Dr. Timothy Quill gently broke the news: leukemia. If she were to have any hope of survival, a strenuous course of treatment with only a 25 percent success rate would have to begin immediately. Convinced that she would suffer unspeakably from side effects and lack of control over her body, Diane chose not to undergo chemotherapy and a bone marrow transplant.

Dr. Quill made sure that Diane understood her options. As he adjusted to her decision, Diane raised another issue: She calmly insisted that when the time came, she desired to take her own life in the least painful way possible—a choice she had discussed with her husband and son, who respected it. Realizing that Diane could get the most out of the time she had left only

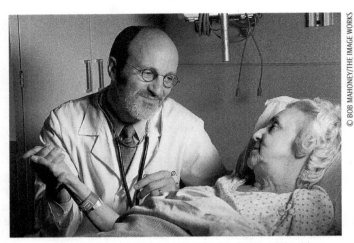

In a prestigious medical journal, Dr. Timothy Quill explained how and why he aided a terminally ill patient in taking her own life. Doctor-assisted suicide is legal in the states of Oregon, Washington, Montana, and Vermont and in several Western European countries.

if her fears of prolonged pain were allayed, Dr. Quill granted her request for sleeping pills, making sure she knew the amounts needed for both sleep and suicide.

Diane's next few months were busy and fulfilling. Her son took leave from college to be with her, and her husband worked at home as much as possible. Gradually, bone pain, fatigue, and fever set in. Saying goodbye to her family and friends, Diane asked to be alone for an hour, took a lethal dose of medication, and died at home (Quill, 1991).

Assisting a suicide is illegal in Canada and in most, but not all, U.S. states. In Western Europe, doctor-assisted suicide is legal in Belgium, the Netherlands, Luxembourg, and Switzerland and is tacitly accepted in many other countries. In the United States, Oregon's 1997 Death with Dignity Act explicitly allows physicians to prescribe drugs so terminally ill patients can end their lives. To get a prescription, patients must have two doctors agree that they have less than six months to live and must request the drugs at least twice, with an interval of at least 15 days. In January 2006, the U.S. Supreme Court rejected a challenge to the Oregon law, but the Court has also upheld the right of other states to ban assisted suicide. In 2008, the state of Washington passed legislation—similar to Oregon's—permitting assisted suicide. In 2013, the Montana and Vermont legislatures also legalized the practice.

Nearly 60 percent of Americans approve of assisted suicide for terminally ill patients in great pain (Harris Interactive, 2011). In a review of studies carried out in the United States, Canada, and Western Europe, level of support among terminally ill patients was about the same as for the general public, with about one-third of patients saying they would consider it for themselves in particular circumstances (Hendry et al., 2012). In Oregon, assisted suicide accounts for only one-fifth of 1 percent of deaths (Oregon Public Health Division, 2013). But thousands of Oregonians say they find comfort in knowing the option is available (Hedberg et al., 2009).

Public interest in assisted suicide was sparked in the 1990s by Dr. Jack Kevorkian, a vigorous proponent of euthanasia who devised "suicide machines" that permitted more than 100 terminally ill patients, after brief counseling, to self-administer lethal drugs and carbon monoxide. Less publicity surrounded Dr. Quill's decision to assist Diane—a patient he knew well after serving for years as her personal doctor. After he told her story in a prestigious medical journal, reactions were mixed, as they are toward assisted suicide in general. Some view doctors who help suffering people who want to die as compassionate and respectful of patients' personal choices. Others oppose assisted suicide on religious and moral grounds or believe that the role of doctors should be limited to saving, not taking, lives.

Like euthanasia, assisted suicide poses grave dilemmas. Juries have seldom returned guilty verdicts in cases involving doctor-assisted suicide. Yet in April 1999, Kevorkian—after giving a terminally ill man a lethal injection, videotaping the death, and permitting the event to be broadcast on the CBS television program *60 Minutes*—was convicted of second-degree murder and served 8 years of a 10- to 25-year sentence. The murder indictment prevented Kevorkian from introducing evidence indicating that the man wanted to kill himself—evidence that would have been permissible had the charge been assisted suicide or voluntary active euthanasia.

Public opinion consistently favors voluntary active euthanasia over assisted suicide. Yet in assisted suicide, the final act is solely the patient's, reducing the possibility of coercion. For this reason, some experts believe that legalizing assisted suicide is preferable to legalizing voluntary active euthanasia. However, in an atmosphere of high family caregiving burdens and intense pressure to contain health-care costs, legalizing either practice poses risks. The American Medical Association opposes both voluntary active euthanasia and assisted suicide. In a survey of 1,140 U.S. doctors, only 18 percent objected to sedating a dying patient to unconsciousness if pain can be controlled in no other way, whereas nearly 70 percent opposed assisted suicide—attitudes resembling those of physicians in other Western nations (Curlin et al., 2008; Seale, 2009). Helping incurable, suffering patients who yearn for death poses profound moral and legal problems.

ASK YOURSELF

REVIEW What benefits and risks does legalizing voluntary active euthanasia pose?

APPLY Ramón is certain that, if he ever became terminally ill, he would want doctors to halt life-saving treatment. To best ensure that his wish will be granted, what should Ramón do?

REFLECT Do you approve of passive euthanasia, voluntary active euthanasia, or assisted suicide? If you were terminally ill, would you consider any of these practices? Explain.

Bereavement: Coping with the Death of a Loved One

Loss is an inevitable part of existence throughout the lifespan. Even when change is for the better, we must let go of some aspects of experience so we can embrace others. In this way, our development prepares us for profound loss.

Bereavement is the experience of losing a loved one by death. The root of this word means "to be robbed," suggesting unjust and injurious theft of something valuable. Consistent with this image, we respond to loss with **grief**—intense physical and psychological distress. When we say someone is grief-stricken, we imply that his or her total way of being is affected.

Because grief can be overwhelming, cultures have devised ways of helping their members move beyond it to deal with the life changes demanded by death of a loved one. **Mourning** is the culturally specified expression of the bereaved person's thoughts and feelings. Customs—such as gathering with family and friends, dressing in black, attending the funeral, and observing a prescribed mourning period with special rituals—vary greatly among societies and ethnic groups. But all have in common the goal of helping people work through their grief and learn to live in a world that does not include the deceased.

Clearly, grief and mourning are closely linked—in everyday language, we often use the two words interchangeably. Let's look closely at how people respond to the death of a loved one.

Grief Process

Theorists formerly believed that bereaved individuals—both children and adults—moved through three phases of grieving, each characterized by a different set of responses (Bowlby, 1980; Rando, 1995). In reality, however, people vary greatly in behavior and timing and often move back and forth between these reactions. A more accurate account compares grief to a roller-coaster ride, with many ups and downs and, over time, gradual resolution (Lund, 1996). Rather than phases, the grieving process can be conceived as a set of *tasks*—actions the person must take to recover and return to a fulfilling life: (1) to accept the reality of the loss; (2) to work through the pain of grief; (3) to adjust to a world without the loved one; and (4) to develop an inner bond with the deceased and move on with life (Worden, 2009). According to this view, people can take active steps to overcome grief—a powerful remedy for the overwhelming feelings of vulnerability that the bereaved often experience.

Avoidance. On hearing the news, the survivor experiences shock followed by disbelief, which may last from hours to weeks. A numbed feeling serves as "emotional anesthesia" while the person begins the first task of grieving: becoming painfully aware of the loss.

Confrontation. As the mourner confronts the reality of the death, grief is most intense. The person often experiences a cascade of emotional reactions, including anxiety, sadness, protest, anger, helplessness, frustration, abandonment, and yearning for the loved one. Common responses include obsessively reviewing the circumstances of death, asking how it might have been prevented, and searching for meaning in it (Neimeyer, 2001). In addition, the grief-stricken person may be absent-minded, unable to concentrate, and preoccupied with thoughts of the deceased, and may experience loss of sleep and appetite. Self-destructive behaviors, such as taking drugs or driving too fast, may occur. Most of these responses are symptoms of depression—an invariable component of grieving.

Although confrontation is difficult, it enables the mourner to grapple with the second task: working through the pain of grief. Each surge of anguish brings the mourner closer to acceptance that the loved one is gone. As a result, the mourner makes progress on the third task: adjusting to a world in which the deceased is missing.

Restoration. Bereaved individuals must also deal with stressors that are secondary outcomes of the death—overcoming loneliness by reaching out to others; mastering skills (such as finances or cooking) that the deceased had performed; reorganizing daily life without the loved one; and revising one's identity from "spouse" to "widow" or from "parent" to "parent of a deceased child."

According to a recent perspective, called the **dual-process model of coping with loss**, effective coping requires people to oscillate between dealing with the emotional consequences of loss and attending to life changes, which—when handled successfully—have restorative, or healing, effects (Hansson & Stroebe, 2007; Stroebe & Schut, 1999, 2010). Much research indicates that confronting grief without relief has severe negative consequences for physical and mental health (Corr & Corr, 2007). Consistent with the dual-process model, in a study that assessed widowed older adults at 6, 18, and 48 months after the death of their spouses, both loss-oriented and restoration-oriented activities occurred throughout bereavement. As predicted, restoration-oriented activities—such as visiting friends, attending religious services, and volunteering—reduced the stress of grieving (Richardson, 2007). Using the dual-process approach, one 14-session intervention for older adults grieving the loss of a spouse addresses both emotional and life-change issues, alternating between them (Lund et al., 2004, 2010).

As grief subsides, emotional energies increasingly shift toward the fourth task—forging a symbolic bond with the deceased and moving on with life by meeting everyday responsibilities, investing in new activities and goals, strengthening old ties, and building new relationships. On certain days, such as family celebrations or the anniversary of death, grief reactions may resurface and require attention, but they do not interfere with a healthy, positive approach to life.

In fact, throughout the grieving process, individuals report experiencing positive as well as negative emotions, with expressions of happiness and humor aiding in coping with grief (Ong, Bergeman, & Bisconti, 2004). In an investigation of several hundred people age 50 and older whose spouse or partner had died within the previous six months, 90 percent agreed that "feeling happy" and "having humor" in daily life are important, and more than 75 percent said they had experienced humor, laughter, or happiness during the past week. The greater participants' valuing and experience of positive emotion, the better their bereavement adjustment, as indicated by reduced levels of grief and depression (Lund et al., 2008–2009). Expressions of happiness can be viewed as a restoration-oriented activity, offering distraction from grieving and strengthening bonds with others.

How long does grieving last? There is no single answer. Sometimes confrontation continues for a few months, at other times for several years. An occasional upsurge of grief may persist for a lifetime and is a common response to losing a much-loved spouse, partner, child, or friend.

Personal and Situational Variations

Like dying, grieving is affected by many factors, including personality, coping style, and religious and cultural background. Sex differences are also evident. Compared with women, men typically express distress and depression less directly and seek social support less readily—factors that may contribute to the much higher mortality rate among bereaved men than women (Doka & Martin, 2010; Lund & Caserta, 2004b; McGoldrick, 2004).

Furthermore, the quality of the mourner's relationship with the deceased is important. An end to a loving, fulfilling bond leads to more anguished grieving, but it is less likely to leave a long-term residue of anger, guilt, and regret than the dissolution of a conflict-ridden, ambivalent tie (Abakoumkin, Stroebe, & Stroebe, 2010; Mikulincer & Shaver, 2008). And end-of-life care makes a difference: Widowed older adults whose spouses experienced a painful death reported more anxiety, intrusive thoughts, and yearning for the loved one six months later (Carr, 2003).

Circumstances surrounding the death—whether it is sudden and unanticipated or follows a prolonged illness—also shape mourners' responses. The nature of the lost relationship and the timing of the death within the life course make a difference as well.

Sudden, Unanticipated Deaths versus Prolonged, Expected Deaths.
In instances of sudden, unexpected deaths—usually the result of murder, suicide, war, accident, or natural disaster—avoidance may be especially pronounced and confrontation highly traumatic because shock and disbelief are extreme. In contrast, during prolonged dying, the bereaved person has had time to engage in **anticipatory grieving**—acknowledging that the loss is inevitable and preparing emotionally for it. Survivors may feel less overwhelmed immediately following the death (Johansson & Grimby, 2013). But they may

display more persistent anxiety due to long-term stressors, such as highly demanding caregiving and having watched a loved one suffer from a debilitating illness (Carr et al., 2001).

Adjusting to a sudden death is easier when the survivor understands the reasons for it. This barrier to confronting loss is tragically apparent in cases of sudden infant death syndrome (SIDS), in which doctors cannot tell parents exactly why their apparently healthy baby died (see Chapter 3, page 84). That death seems "senseless" also complicates grieving after suicides, terrorist attacks, school and drive-by shootings, and natural disasters. In Western societies, people tend to believe that momentous events should be comprehensible and nonrandom (Lukas & Seiden, 2007). A death that is sudden and unexpected can threaten basic assumptions about a just, benevolent, and controllable world.

Suicide, particularly that of a young person, is especially hard to bear. Compared with survivors of other sudden deaths, people grieving a suicidal loss are more likely to conclude that they contributed to or could have prevented it—self-blame that can trigger profound guilt and shame. These reactions are likely to be especially intense and persisting when a mourner's culture or religion condemns suicide as immoral (Dunne & Dunne-Maxim, 2004). Typically, recovery from grief after a suicide is prolonged.

Parents Grieving the Loss of a Child.
The death of a child, whether unexpected or foreseen, is the most difficult loss an adult can face (Dent & Stewart, 2004). Children are extensions of parents' feelings about themselves—the focus of hopes and dreams, including parents' sense of immortality. Also, because children depend on, admire, and appreciate their parents in a deeply gratifying way, they are an unmatched source

A father weeps while holding the body of his son, killed during the Syrian armed conflict in 2012. The death of a child, whether unexpected or foreseen, is the most difficult loss an adult can face.

of love. Finally, the death of a child is unnatural: Children are not supposed to die before their parents. Parents who have lost a child often report considerable distress many years later, along with frequent thoughts of the deceased.

If parents can reestablish a sense of life's meaning through valuing the lost child's impact on their lives and investing in other children and activities, then the result can be firmer family commitments and personal growth. The process, which often takes years, is associated with improved physical and mental health and gains in marital satisfaction (Murphy, 2008; Price et al., 2011). Five years after her son's death, one parent reflected on her progress:

> I was afraid to let go [of my pain, which was] a way of loving him. . . . Finally I had to admit that his life meant more than pain, it also meant joy and happiness and fun—and living. . . . When we release pain we make room for happiness in our lives. My memories of S. became lighter and more spontaneous. Instead of hurtful, my memories brought comfort, even a chuckle. . . . realized S. was still teaching me things. (Klass, 2004, p. 87)

Children and Adolescents Grieving the Loss of a Parent or Sibling. The loss of an attachment figure has long-term consequences for children. When a parent dies, children's basic sense of security and being cared for is threatened. And the death of a sibling not only deprives children of a close emotional tie but also informs them, often for the first time, of their own vulnerability.

Children grieving a family loss describe frequent crying, trouble concentrating in school, sleep difficulties, headaches, and other physical symptoms several months to years after a death. And clinical studies reveal that persistent depression, anxiety, angry outbursts, social withdrawal, loneliness, and worries about dying themselves are common (Luecken, 2008; Marshall & Davies, 2011). At the same time, many children say they have actively maintained mental contact with their dead parent or sibling, dreaming about and speaking to them frequently (Silverman & Nickman, 1996). These images, reported by bereaved adults as well, seem to facilitate coping with loss.

Cognitive development contributes to the ability to grieve. Children with an immature understanding of death may believe the dead parent left voluntarily, perhaps in anger, and that the other parent may also disappear. For these reasons, young children need careful, repeated explanations assuring them that the parent did not want to die and was not angry at them (Christ, Siegel, & Christ, 2002). Keeping the truth from children isolates them and often leads to profound regrets. One 8-year-old who learned only a half-hour in advance that his sick brother was dying reflected, "If only I'd known, I could have said goodbye."

Regardless of children's level of understanding, honesty, affection, and reassurance help them tolerate painful feelings of loss. Grief-stricken school-age children are usually more willing than adolescents to confide in parents. To appear normal, teenagers tend to keep their grieving from both adults and peers. Consequently, they are more likely than children to

become depressed or to escape from grief through acting-out behavior (Granot, 2005). Overall, effective parenting—warmth combined with rational discipline—fosters adaptive coping and positive long-term adjustment in both children and adolescents (Luecken, 2008).

Adults Grieving the Loss of an Intimate Partner. Recall from Chapter 18 that after the death of a spouse, adaptation to widowhood varies greatly, with age, social support, and personality making a difference. After a period of intense grieving, most widowed older adults in Western nations fare well, while younger individuals display more negative outcomes (see page 494 to review). Older widows and widowers have many more contemporaries in similar circumstances. And most have already attained important life goals or adjusted to the fact that some goals will not be attained.

In contrast, loss of a spouse or partner in early or middle adulthood is a nonnormative event that profoundly disrupts life plans. Interviews with a large, U.S. nationally representative sample of adults who had been widowed from less than 1 to 64 years previously (typically in middle adulthood) revealed that thoughts about and conversations with the lost spouse occurred often in the first few years, then declined gradually (Carnelley et al., 2006). But they did not reach their lowest level for several decades, when the typical respondent still thought about the deceased partner once every week or two and conversed with him or her about once a month.

In addition to dealing with feelings of loss, young and middle-aged widows and widowers often must assume a greater role in comforting others, especially children. They also face the stresses of single parenthood and rapid shrinking of the social network established during their life as a couple. The death of an intimate partner in a gay or lesbian relationship presents unique challenges. When relatives limit or bar the partner from participating in funeral services, the survivor experiences *disenfranchised grief*—a sense of loss without the opportunity to mourn publicly and benefit from others' support—which can profoundly disrupt the grieving process (Doka, 2008). Fortunately, gay and lesbian communities provide helpful alternative support in the form of memorial services and other rituals.

Bereavement Overload. When a person experiences several deaths at once or in close succession, bereavement overload can occur. Multiple losses deplete the coping resources of even well-adjusted people, leaving them emotionally overwhelmed and unable to resolve their grief (Lattanzi-Licht & Doka, 2003).

Because old age often brings the death of spouse, siblings, and friends in close succession, aging adults are at risk for bereavement overload (Kastenbaum, 2008). But recall from Chapter 18 that compared with young people, older adults are often better equipped to handle these losses.

Public tragedies—terrorist attacks, natural disasters, random murders in schools, or widely publicized kidnappings—can

Applying What We Know

Suggestions for Resolving Grief After a Loved One Dies

Suggestion	Description
Give yourself permission to feel the loss.	Permit yourself to confront all thoughts and emotions associated with the death. Make a conscious decision to overcome your grief, recognizing that this will take time.
Accept social support.	In the early part of grieving, let others reach out to you by making meals, running errands, and keeping you company. Be assertive; ask for what you need so people who would like to help will know what to do.
Be realistic about the course of grieving.	Expect to have some negative and intense reactions, such as feeling anguished, sad, and angry, that last from weeks to months and may occasionally resurface years after the death. There is no one way to grieve, so find the best way for you.
Remember the deceased.	Review your relationship to and experiences with the deceased, permitting yourself to see that you can no longer be with him or her as before. Form a new bond based on memories, keeping it alive through photographs, commemorative donations, prayers, and other symbols and actions.
When ready, invest in new activities and relationships, and master new tasks of daily living.	Identify which roles you must give up and which ones you must assume as a consequence of the death, and take deliberate steps to modify daily life accordingly. Set small goals at first, such as a night at the movies, a dinner date with a friend, a cooking or household repair class, or a week's vacation.

spark bereavement overload (Rynearson & Salloum, 2011). Many survivors who lost loved ones, co-workers, or friends in the September 11, 2001, terrorist attacks (including an estimated 3,000 children who lost a parent) experienced repeated images of horror and destruction, which impeded coming to terms with loss. The greater the bereaved individual's exposure to the catastrophic death scene, the more severe these reactions.

Funerals and other bereavement rituals, illustrated in the Cultural Influences box on the following page, assist mourners of all ages in resolving grief with the help of family and friends.

Villagers in Sichuan Province, China, grieve for relatives who died in a massive earthquake in 2013 that left nearly 200 dead. Public tragedies can spark bereavement overload, leaving mourners at risk for prolonged, overwhelming grief.

AP IMAGES/ZHANG HAO/COLOR CHINA PHOTO

Bereaved individuals who remain preoccupied with loss and who have difficulty resuming interest in everyday activities benefit from special interventions designed to help them adjust.

Bereavement Interventions

Sympathy and understanding are sufficient to enable most people to undertake the tasks necessary to recover from grief (see Applying What We Know above). Yet effective support is often difficult to provide, and relatives and friends can benefit from training in how to respond. Sometimes they give advice aimed at hastening recovery or ask questions aimed at managing their own anxiety ("Were you expecting him to die?" Was she in a lot of pain?")—approaches that most bereaved people dislike (Kastenbaum, 2012). Listening patiently and assuring the bereaved of "being there" for them—"I'm here if you need to talk," "Let me know what I can do"—are among the best ways to help.

Bereavement interventions typically encourage people to draw on their existing social network, while providing additional social support through group or individual counseling. Controversy exists over whether grief counseling benefits most bereaved people, or whether it helps only those experiencing profound difficulties (CFAH, 2003; Jordan & Neimeyer, 2003). One analysis of research expressed optimism about broadly favorable effects (Larson & Hoyt, 2007). Furthermore, evidence is mounting that bereaved adults who struggle with and surmount challenges and losses often experience stress-related personal growth, including greater awareness of their own strengths, enhanced appreciation of close relationships, and new spiritual insights (Calhoun et al., 2010).

Cultural Influences

Cultural Variations in Mourning Behavior

The ceremonies that commemorated Sofie's and Nicholas's deaths—the first Jewish, the second Quaker—were strikingly different. Yet they served common goals: announcing that a death had occurred, ensuring social support, commemorating the deceased, and conveying a philosophy of life after death.

At the funeral home, Sofie's body was washed and shrouded, a Jewish ritual signifying return to a state of purity. Then it was placed in a plain wooden (not metal) coffin, so as not to impede the natural process of decomposition. To underscore the finality of death, Jewish tradition does not permit viewing of the body; it remains in a closed coffin. Traditionally, the coffin is not left alone until burial; in honor of the deceased, the community maintains a day-and-night vigil.

To return the body quickly to the life-giving earth from which it sprang, Sofie's funeral was scheduled as soon as relatives could gather—just three days after death. Sofie's husband and children symbolized their anguish by cutting a black ribbon and pinning it to their clothing. The rabbi recited psalms of comfort, followed by a eulogy. The service continued at the graveside. Once the coffin had been lowered into the ground, relatives and friends took turns shoveling earth onto it, each participating in the irrevocable act of burial. The service concluded with the *Kaddish* prayer, which affirms life while accepting death.

At home, the family lit a memorial candle, which burned throughout *shiva,* the seven-day mourning period. A meal of consolation prepared by others followed, creating a warm feeling of community. Jewish custom prescribes that after 30 days, life should gradually return to normal. When a parent dies,

the mourning period is extended to 12 months.

In the Quaker tradition of simplicity, Nicholas was cremated promptly. During the next week, relatives and close friends gathered with Giselle and Sasha at their home. Together, they planned a memorial service to celebrate Nicholas's life.

When people arrived on the appointed day, a clerk of the Friends (Quaker) Meeting welcomed them and explained to newcomers the Quaker custom of worshipping silently, with those who feel moved to speak rising at any time to share thoughts and feelings. Many mourners offered personal statements about Nicholas or read poems and selections from Scripture. After concluding comments from Giselle and Sasha, everyone joined hands to close the service. A reception for the family followed.

Variations in mourning behavior are vast, both within and across societies. At African-American funerals, for example, grief is expressed freely: Eulogies and music are usually designed to trigger release of deep emotion (McGoldrick et al., 2004). In contrast, the Balinese of Indonesia believe they must remain calm in the face of death so that the gods can hear their prayers. While acknowledging their underlying grief, Balinese mourners work hard to maintain their composure (Rosenblatt, 2008).

In recent years, a new ritual has arisen: "virtual cemeteries" on the Internet, which allow postings whenever bereaved individuals feel ready to convey their thoughts and

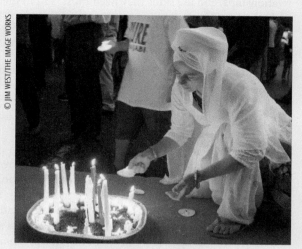

Mourners light candles at a memorial service for six Sikhs who died in a shooting rampage in Wisconsin in 2012. Sikh funeral customs include singing hymns, saying prayers, and offering remembrances of the deceased, followed by cremation and scattering of the ashes.

feelings, creation of tributes at little or no cost, and continuous, easy access to the memorial. Most creators of Web tributes choose to tell personal stories, highlighting a laugh, a favorite joke, or a touching moment. Some survivors use Web memorials to grieve openly, others to converse with the lost loved one. Cemetery guestbooks offer a place for visitors to connect with other mourners. Web cemeteries also provide a means for people excluded from traditional death rituals to engage in public mourning (Roberts, 2006; Stroebe, van der Houwen, & Schut, 2008). The following "gravesite" message captures the unique qualities of this highly flexible medium for mourning:

I wish I could maintain contact with you, to keep alive the vivid memories of your impact on my life. . . . Because I cannot visit your grave today, I use this means to tell you how much you are loved.

Support groups that bring together mourners who have experienced the same type of loss seem highly effective in promoting recovery. In a program for recently widowed older adults based on the dual-process model of coping with loss, a participant expressed the many lasting benefits:

We shared our anger at being left behind, . . . our fright of that aloneness. We shared our favorite pictures, so each of us could know the others' families and the fun we used to have. We shared

our feelings of guilt if we had fun . . . and found out that it was okay to keep on living! . . . We cheered when one of us accomplished a new task. We also tried to lend a helping hand and heart when we would have one of our bad days! . . . This group will always be there for me and I will always be there for them. I love you all! (Lund, 2005)

Follow-up research suggests that group sessions are best suited for fostering loss-oriented coping (confronting and resolving grief), whereas an individually tailored approach works best for restoration-oriented coping (reorganizing daily life) (Lund et al., 2010). Bereaved adults differ widely in the new roles, relationships, and life skills they need most, and in the formats and schedules best suited to acquiring them.

LOOK AND LISTEN

Arrange to sit in on a bereavement support group session sponsored by a local hospice program or hospital, noting both emotional and daily living challenges expressed by group members. Ask participants to explain how the group has helped them. ●

Interventions for children and adolescents following violent deaths must protect them from unnecessary reexposure and assist parents and teachers with their own distress so they can effectively offer comfort (Dowd, 2013). In the aftermath of horrific tragedies—such as the December 14, 2012, mass shooting at Sandy Hook Elementary School in Newtown, Connecticut, or the April 15, 2013, Boston Marathon bombings—nurturing and caring relationships with adults are the most powerful way to help children recover from trauma.

A sudden, violent, and unexplainable death; the loss of a child; a death that the mourner feels he or she could have prevented; or an ambivalent or dependent relationship with the deceased makes it harder for bereaved people to overcome their loss. In these instances, grief therapy, or individual counseling with a specially trained professional, can be helpful. Assisting bereaved adults in finding some value in the grieving experience—for example, gaining insight into the meaning of relationships, discovering their own capacity to cope with adversity, or crystallizing a sense of purpose in their lives—is particularly effective (Neimeyer et al., 2010).

Nevertheless, most bereaved individuals do not participate in bereavement interventions. In several studies, only 30 to 50 percent of family caregivers of dying patients made use of bereavement services—such as phone support, support groups, and referrals for counseling—even though these were readily available through hospice, hospitals, or other community organizations (Bergman, Haley, & Small, 2010, 2011; Cherlin et al., 2007). Many who refused bereavement services were severely distressed yet did not realize that intervention could be helpful.

Death Education

Preparatory steps can help people of all ages cope with death more effectively. The death awareness movement that sparked increased sensitivity to the needs of dying patients has also led to the rise of college and university courses in death, dying, and bereavement. Instruction has been integrated into the training

of doctors, nurses, psychologists, and social workers, although most professional offerings are limited to only a few lectures (Wass, 2004). Death education is also found in adult education programs in many communities and even in a few elementary and secondary schools.

Death education at all levels has the following goals:

- Increasing students' understanding of the physical and psychological changes that accompany dying
- Helping students learn how to cope with the death of a loved one
- Preparing students to be informed consumers of medical and funeral services
- Promoting understanding of social and ethical issues involving death

Educational format varies widely. Although using a lecture approach focused on conveying information leads to gains in knowledge, it often leaves students more uncomfortable about death than when they entered. In contrast, experiential programs that help people confront their own mortality—through discussions with the terminally ill, visits to mortuaries and cemeteries, and personal awareness exercises—are less likely to heighten death anxiety and may sometimes reduce it (Hurtig & Stewin, 2006; Maglio & Robinson, 1994).

Whether acquired in the classroom or in our daily lives, our thoughts and feelings about death are forged through interactions with others. Dying people have at times confided in those close to them that awareness of the limits of their lifespan permitted them to focus on what is truly important in their lives. As one terminally ill patient summed up, "[It's] kind of like life, just speeded up"—an accelerated process in which, over a period of weeks to months, one grapples with issues that normally would have taken years or decades to resolve (Selwyn, 1996, p. 36). Applying this lesson to ourselves, we learn that by being in touch with death and dying, we can live ever more fully.

ASK YOURSELF

REVIEW What circumstances are likely to induce bereavement overload? Cite examples.

APPLY List features of self-help groups likely to contribute to their effectiveness in helping people cope with loss.

REFLECT Visit a Web cemetery, such as Virtual Memorials (*virtualmemorials.com*). Select examples of Web tributes, guest book entries, and testimonials that illustrate the unique ways in which virtual cemeteries help people cope with death.

SUMMARY

How We Die (p. 509)

Describe the physical changes of dying, along with their implications for defining death and the meaning of death with dignity.

● Death is long and drawn-out for three-fourths of people, many more than in times past, as a result of life-saving medical technology. Of those who die suddenly, 80 to 90 percent are victims of heart attacks.

● In general, dying takes place in three phases: the **agonal phase,** in which regular heartbeat disintegrates; **clinical death,** a short interval in which resuscitation is still possible; and **mortality,** or permanent death.

● In most industrialized nations, **brain death** is accepted as the definition of death. But for incurable patients who remain in a **persistent vegetative state,** the brain death standard does not solve the problem of when to halt treatment.

● We can best ensure death with dignity by supporting dying patients through their physical and psychological distress, being candid about death's certainty, and helping them learn enough about their condition to make reasoned choices about treatment.

Attitudes Toward Death (p. 511)

Discuss factors that influence attitudes toward death, including death anxiety.

● Compared with earlier generations, more young people reach adulthood having had little contact with death, contributing to a sense of unease about it.

● Wide individual and cultural variations exist in **death anxiety.** People with a sense of spirituality or a well-developed personal philosophy of death are less fearful, as are those with deep faith in a higher force or being. Older adults' greater ability to regulate negative emotion and their sense of symbolic immortality reduce death anxiety. Women exhibit more death anxiety than men.

Thinking and Emotions of Dying People (p. 513)

Describe and evaluate Kübler-Ross's theory, citing factors that influence dying patients' responses.

● Elisabeth Kübler-Ross proposed that dying people typically express five responses, initially proposed as stages: denial, anger, bargaining, depression, and acceptance. These reactions do not occur in fixed sequence, and dying people often display other coping strategies.

● An **appropriate death** is one that makes sense in terms of the individual's pattern of living and values, preserves or restores significant relationships, and is as free of suffering as possible. The extent to which people attain these goals depends on many contextual variables—nature of the disease, personality and coping style, family members' and health professionals' behavior, and spirituality, religion, and cultural background.

A Place to Die (p. 516)

Evaluate the extent to which homes, hospitals, nursing homes, and the hospice approach meet the needs of dying people and their families.

● Although most people say they want to die at home, only about one-fourth of Americans do. Even with professional help and hospital-supplied equipment, caring for a dying patient is highly demanding.

● Sudden deaths typically occur in hospital emergency rooms, where sympathetic explanations from staff can reduce family members' anger, frustration, and confusion. Intensive care is especially depersonalizing for patients, lingering between life and death while hooked to machines. Many U.S. hospitals still lack comprehensive treatment programs aimed at easing end-of-life suffering.

● Though deaths in U.S. nursing homes are common, high-quality terminal care is lacking. Too many patients die in pain without having their needs met.

● The **hospice** approach is a comprehensive program of support services designed to meet the dying person's physical, emotional, social, and spiritual needs by providing **palliative,** or **comfort, care,** rather than prolonging life. Hospice care also contributes to improved family functioning and better psychological well-being among family survivors.

The Right to Die (p. 519)

Discuss controversies surrounding euthanasia and assisted suicide.

● **Euthanasia**—ending the life of a person suffering from an incurable condition—takes various forms.

● **Passive euthanasia,** withholding or withdrawing life-sustaining treatment from a hopelessly ill patient, is widely accepted and practiced. People can best ensure that their wishes will be followed by preparing an **advance medical directive.** A **living will** contains instructions for treatment, whereas the **durable power of attorney for health care** names another person to make health care decisions on one's behalf.

● Public support for **voluntary active euthanasia,** in which doctors or others act directly, at a patient's request, to end suffering before a natural end to life, is high. Nevertheless, the practice remains a criminal offense in most countries and has sparked heated controversy.

● Less public support exists for assisted suicide. But because the final act is solely the patient's, some experts believe that legalizing assisted suicide is preferable to legalizing voluntary active euthanasia.

Bereavement: Coping with the Death of a Loved One

(p. 523)

Describe the phases of grieving, factors that underlie individual variations, and bereavement interventions.

- **Bereavement** refers to the experience of losing a loved one by death, **grief** to the intense physical and psychological distress that accompanies loss. **Mourning** is the culturally prescribed expression of the bereaved person's thoughts and feelings.

- Although theorists previously believed that grieving occurred in orderly phases—avoidance, confrontation, and finally restoration—a more accurate image is a roller-coaster ride, with the mourner engaging in a set of tasks to overcome grief. According to the **dual-process model of coping with loss,** effective coping involves oscillating between dealing with the emotional consequences of loss and attending to life changes, which can have restorative effects. Bereaved individuals who experience positive as well as negative emotions cope more effectively.

- Like dying, grieving is affected by many personal and situational factors. Bereaved men express grief less directly than bereaved women. After a sudden, unanticipated death, avoidance may be especially pronounced and confrontation highly traumatic. In contrast, a prolonged, expected death grants the bereaved person time to engage in **anticipatory grieving.**

AP IMAGES/MANU BRABO

- When a parent loses a child or a child loses a parent or sibling, grieving is generally intense and prolonged. Because early loss of a life partner is a nonnormative event with a major impact on life plans, younger widowed individuals usually fare less well than widowed older people. Disenfranchised grief can profoundly disrupt the process of grieving.

- People who experience several deaths at once or in close succession may suffer from bereavement overload.

- Sympathy and understanding are sufficient for most people to recover from grief. Support groups are highly effective in aiding recovery, whereas individually tailored approaches help mourners reorganize their daily lives. Interventions for children and adolescents following violent deaths must protect them from unnecessary reexposure and assist parents and teachers in offering comfort.

Death Education (p. 528)

Explain how death education can help people cope with death more effectively.

- Today, instruction in death, dying, and bereavement is integrated into training programs for doctors, nurses, psychologists, and social workers. It is also found in adult education programs and in a few elementary and secondary schools. Courses with an experiential component may reduce death anxiety.

Important Terms and Concepts

advance medical directive (p. 520)
agonal phase (p. 510)
anticipatory grieving (p. 524)
appropriate death (p. 514)
bereavement (p. 523)
brain death (p. 510)
clinical death (p. 510)

death anxiety (p. 511)
dual-process model of coping with loss (p. 523)
durable power of attorney for health care (p. 520)
euthanasia (p. 519)
grief (p. 523)
hospice (p. 517)
living will (p. 520)

mortality (p. 510)
mourning (p. 523)
palliative, or comfort, care (p. 518)
passive euthanasia (p. 520)
persistent vegetative state (p. 510)
thanatology (p. 509)
voluntary active euthanasia (p. 521)

Glossary

A

academic programs Preschool and kindergarten programs in which teachers structure children's learning, teaching academic skills through formal lessons that often involve repetition and drill. Distinguished from *child-centered programs*. (p. 190)

accommodation In Piaget's theory, that part of adaptation in which new schemes are created and old ones adjusted to produce a better fit with the environment. Distinguished from *assimilation*. (p. 119)

acculturative stress Psychological distress resulting from conflict between an individual's minority culture and the host culture. (p. 322)

activities of daily living (ADLs) Basic self-care tasks required to live on one's own, such as bathing, dressing, getting in and out of bed or a chair, and eating. (p. 449)

activity theory A social theory of aging that states that declining rates of interaction in late adulthood reflect social barriers to engagement, not the desires of aging adults. Older people try to preserve life satisfaction by finding roles that allow them to remain about as active and busy as they were in middle age. Distinguished from *disengagement theory, continuity theory,* and *socioemotional selectivity theory*. (p. 487)

adaptation In Piaget's theory, the process of building schemes through direct interaction with the environment. Consists of two complementary activities: *assimilation* and *accommodation*. (p. 118)

adolescence The transition between childhood and adulthood that begins with puberty. It involves accepting one's full-grown body, acquiring adult ways of thinking, attaining greater independence from one's family, developing more mature ways of relating to peers of both sexes, and beginning to construct an identity. (p. 287)

advance medical directive A written statement of desired medical treatment should a person become incurably ill. (p. 520)

affect optimization The ability to maximize positive emotion and dampen negative emotion. An emotional strength of late adulthood. (p. 480)

age-graded influences Influences on lifespan development that are strongly related to age and therefore fairly predictable in when they occur and how long they last. (p. 7)

age of viability The age at which the fetus can first survive if born early. Occurs sometime between 22 and 26 weeks. (p. 65)

aging in place In late adulthood, remaining in a familiar setting where one has control over one's everyday life. (p. 489)

agonal phase The phase of dying in which gasps and muscle spasms occur during the first moments in which the regular heart beat disintegrates. Distinguished from *clinical death* and *mortality*. (p. 510)

alcohol-related neurodevelopmental disorder (ARND) The least severe form of fetal alcohol spectrum disorder, involving brain injury but with typical physical growth and absence of facial abnormalities. Distinguished from *fetal alcohol syndrome (FAS)* and *partial fetal alcohol syndrome (p-FAS)*. (p. 69)

allele Each of two or more forms of a gene located at the same place on corresponding pairs of chromosomes. (p. 38)

Alzheimer's disease The most common form of dementia, in which structural and chemical brain deterioration is associated with gradual loss of many aspects of thought and behavior, including memory, skilled and purposeful movements, and comprehension and production of speech. (p. 462)

amnion The inner membrane that that encloses the prenatal organism in amniotic fluid, which helps keep temperature constant and provides a cushion against jolts caused by the mother's movements. (p. 63)

amyloid plaques A structural change in the cerebral cortex associated with Alzheimer's disease, in which dense deposits of a deteriorated protein called *amyloid* develop, surrounded by clumps of dead nerve and glial cells. (p. 462)

androgyny The gender identity held by individuals who score high on both traditionally masculine and traditionally feminine personality characteristics. (p. 215)

anorexia nervosa An eating disorder in which young people, mainly females, starve themselves because of a compulsive fear of getting fat and an extremely distorted body image. (p. 296)

anoxia Inadequate oxygen supply. (p. 77)

anticipatory grieving Before a prolonged, expected death, acknowledging the inevitability of the loss and preparing emotionally for it. (p. 524)

Apgar Scale A rating system used to assess a newborn baby's physical condition immediately after birth on the basis of five characteristics: heart rate, respiratory effort, reflex irritability, muscle tone, and color. (p. 76)

appropriate death A death that makes sense in terms of the individual's pattern of living and values, preserves or restores significant relationships, and is as free of suffering as possible. (p. 514)

assimilation In Piaget's theory, that part of adaptation in which the external world is interpreted in terms of current schemes. Distinguished from *accommodation*. (p. 118)

assisted living A homelike housing arrangement for older adults who require more care than can be provided at home but less than is usually provided in nursing homes. (p. 467)

assistive technology An array of devices that permits people with disabilities, including older adults, to improve their functioning. (p. 455)

associative memory deficit Age-related difficulty creating and retrieving links between pieces of information—for example, two items or an item and its context. (p. 469)

associative play A form of social interaction in which children engage in separate activities but interact by exchanging toys and commenting on one another's behavior. Distinguished from *nonsocial activity, parallel play,* and *cooperative play*. (p. 204)

attachment The strong affectionate tie that humans have with special people in their lives, which leads them to feel pleasure when interacting with those people and to be comforted by their nearness in times of stress. (p. 152)

Attachment Q-Sort A method for assessing the quality of attachment in children between 1 and 4 years of age through home observations of a variety of attachment-related behaviors. (p. 154)

attention-deficit hyperactivity disorder (ADHD) A childhood disorder involving inattention, impulsivity, and excessive motor activity, resulting in academic and social problems. (p. 239)

authoritarian child-rearing style A child-rearing style that is low in acceptance and involvement, high in coercive control, and low in autonomy granting. Distinguished from *authoritative, permissive,* and *uninvolved child-rearing styles*. (p. 218)

authoritative child-rearing style A child-rearing style that is high in acceptance and involvement, emphasizes adaptive control techniques, and includes gradual, appropriate autonomy granting. Distinguished from *authoritarian, permissive,* and *uninvolved child-rearing styles*. (p. 217)

autobiographical memory Long-lasting recollections of personally meaningful one-time events from both the recent and the distant past. (p. 129)

autoimmune response A malfunction of the immune system in which it turns against normal body tissues. (p. 453)

automatic processes Cognitive activities that are so well-learned that they require no space in working memory and, therefore, permit an individual to focus on other information while performing them. (p. 126)

autonomy At adolescence, a sense of oneself as a separate, self-governing individual. Involves relying more on oneself and less on parents for support and guidance and engaging in careful, well-reasoned decision making. (p. 329)

autonomy versus shame and doubt In Erikson's theory, the psychological conflict of toddlerhood, which is resolved favorably when parents provide young children with suitable guidance and reasonable choices. (p. 143)

autosomes The 22 matching chromosome pairs in each human cell. (p. 37)

average healthy life expectancy The number of years that an individual born in a particular year can expect to live in full health, without disease or injury. Distinguished from *maximum lifespan* and *average life expectancy*. (p. 448)

average life expectancy The number of years that an individual born in a particular year can expect to live, starting at any given age. Distinguished from *maximum lifespan* and *average healthy life expectancy*. (p. 447)

avoidant attachment The attachment pattern characterizing infants who seem unresponsive to the parent when she is present, are usually not distressed by parental separation, react to the stranger in much the same way as to the parent, and avoid or are slow to greet the parent when she returns. Distinguished from *secure, resistant,* and *disorganized/disoriented attachment.* (p. 154)

B

babbling Repetition of consonant–vowel combinations in long strings, beginning around 6 months of age. (p. 137)

basal metabolic rate (BMR) The amount of energy the body uses at complete rest. (p. 350)

basic emotions Emotions such as happiness, interest, surprise, fear, anger, sadness, and disgust that are universal in humans and other primates and have a long evolutionary history of promoting survival. (p. 144)

basic trust versus mistrust In Erikson's theory, the psychological conflict of infancy, which is resolved positively when the balance of care is sympathetic and loving. (p. 143)

behavioral genetics A field devoted to uncovering the contributions of nature and nurture to the diversity of human traits and abilities. (p. 53)

behaviorism An approach that regards directly observable events—stimuli and responses—as the appropriate focus of study and views the development of behavior as taking place through classical and operant conditioning. (p. 13)

behavior modification Procedures that combine conditioning and modeling to eliminate undesirable behaviors and increase desirable responses. (p. 14)

bereavement The experience of losing a loved one by death. (p. 523)

bicultural identity The identity constructed by individuals who explore and adopt values from both their family's subculture and the dominant culture. (p. 322)

"big five" personality traits Five basic factors into which hundreds of personality traits have been organized: neuroticism, extroversion, openness to experience, agreeableness, and conscientiousness. (p. 430)

biological aging, or senescence Genetically influenced, age-related declines in the functioning of organs and systems that are universal in all members of our species. Sometimes called *primary aging.* (p. 343)

blended, or reconstituted, family A family structure resulting from remarriage or cohabitation that includes parent, child, and steprelatives. (p. 276)

body image Conception of and attitude toward one's physical appearance. (p. 294)

brain death Irreversible cessation of all activity in the brain and the brain stem. The definition of death accepted in most industrialized nations. (p. 510)

brain plasticity The capacity of various parts of the cerebral cortex to take over functions of damaged regions. Declines as hemispheres of the cerebral cortex lateralize. (p. 96)

breech position A position of the baby in the uterus that would cause the buttocks or feet to be delivered first. (p. 77)

bulimia nervosa An eating disorder in which individuals, mainly females, engage in strict dieting and excessive exercise accompanied by binge eating, often followed by deliberate vomiting and purging with laxatives. (p. 296)

burnout A condition in which long-term job stress leads to mental exhaustion, a sense of loss of personal control, and feelings of reduced accomplishment. (p. 440)

C

cardinality The mathematical principle specifying that the last number in a counting sequence indicates the quantity of items in the set. (p. 189)

carrier A heterozygous individual who can pass a recessive trait to his or her offspring. (p. 38)

cataracts Cloudy areas in the lens of the eye that increase from middle to old age, resulting in foggy vision and (without surgery) eventual blindness. (p. 451)

categorical self Classification of the self according to prominent ways in which people differ, such as age, sex, physical characteristics, and goodness and badness. Develops between 18 and 30 months. (p. 160)

central executive In information processing, the conscious, reflective part of our mental system that directs the flow of information, coordinating incoming information with information already in the system and selecting, applying, and monitoring strategies that facilitate memory storage, comprehension, reasoning, and problem solving. (p. 126)

centration In Piaget's theory, the tendency of preoperational children to focus on one aspect of a situation while neglecting other important features. (p. 178)

cephalocaudal trend An organized pattern of physical growth that proceeds from the upper to the lower part of the body ("head to tail"). Distinguished from *proximodistal trend.* (p. 93)

cerebellum A structure at the rear and base of the brain that aids in balance and control of body movements. (p. 169)

cerebral cortex The largest, most complex structure of the human brain, containing the greatest number of neurons and synapses and accounting for the highly developed intelligence of the human species. (p. 95)

cerebrovascular dementia A form of dementia that develops when a series of strokes leaves areas of dead brain cells, producing step-by-step degeneration of mental ability, with each step occurring abruptly after a stroke. (p. 464)

cesarean delivery A surgical delivery in which the doctor makes an incision in the mother's abdomen and lifts the baby out of the uterus. (p. 78)

child-centered programs Preschool and kindergarten programs in which teachers provide a variety of activities from which children select, and much learning takes place through play. Distinguished from *academic programs.* (p. 190)

child-rearing styles Combinations of parenting behaviors that occur over a wide range of situations, creating an enduring child-rearing climate. (p. 217)

chorion The outer membrane that forms a protective covering around the prenatal organism. It sends out tiny hairlike villi, from which the placenta begins to develop. (p. 63)

chromosomes Rodlike structures in the cell nucleus that store and transmit genetic information. (p. 36)

chronosystem In ecological systems theory, temporal changes in environments, either externally imposed or arising from within the person, that produce new conditions affecting development. Distinguished from *microsystem, mesosystem, exosystem,* and *macrosystem.* (p. 20)

circular reaction In Piaget's theory, a means of building schemes in which infants try to repeat a chance event caused by their own motor activity. (p. 119)

classical conditioning A form of learning that involves associating a neutral stimulus with a stimulus that leads to a reflexive response. Once the nervous system makes the connection between the two stimuli, the neutral stimulus alone produces the behavior. (p. 103)

climacteric The midlife transition in which fertility declines, bringing an end to reproductive capacity in women and diminished fertility in men. (p. 403)

clinical death The phase of dying in which heartbeat, circulation, breathing, and brain functioning stop, but resuscitation is still possible. Distinguished from *agonal phase* and *mortality.* (p. 510)

clinical interview An interview method in which the researcher uses a flexible, conversational style to probe for the participant's point of view. Distinguished from *structured interview.* (p. 24)

clinical, or case study, method A research method in which the aim is to obtain as complete a picture as possible of one individual's psychological functioning by bringing together interview data, observations, and sometimes test scores. (p. 24)

clique A group of about five to seven members who are good friends and, therefore, usually resemble one another in family background, attitudes, and values. (p. 332)

cognitive-affective complexity A form of thinking that increases from adolescence through middle adulthood, involving awareness of conflicting positive and negative feelings and coordination of them into a complex, organized structure that recognizes the uniqueness of individual experiences. (p. 359)

cognitive-developmental theory An approach introduced by Piaget that views children as actively constructing knowledge as they manipulate and explore their world and that regards cognitive development as taking place in stages. (p. 15)

cognitive maps Mental representations of familiar large-scale spaces, such as neighborhood or school. (p. 235)

cognitive self-regulation The process of continuously monitoring progress toward a goal, checking outcomes, and redirecting unsuccessful efforts. (p. 240)

cohabitation The lifestyle of unmarried couples who have a sexually intimate relationship and who share a residence. (p. 389)

cohort effects The effects of cultural–historical change on the accuracy of longitudinal and cross-sectional research findings. Results based on one cohort—individuals developing in the same time period, who are influenced by particular historical and cultural conditions—may not apply to other cohorts. (p. 29)

collectivist societies Societies in which people define themselves as part of a group and stress group goals over individual goals. Distinguished from *individualistic societies*. (p. 50)

commitment within relativistic thinking In Perry's theory, the mature individual's formulation of a perspective that synthesizes contradictions between opposing views, rather than choosing between them. (p. 358)

companionate love Love based on warm, trusting affection and caregiving. Distinguished from *passionate love*. (p. 377)

compliance Voluntary obedience to requests and commands. (p. 161)

compression of morbidity The public health goal of reducing the average period of diminished vigor before death as life expectancy extends. Medical advances, improved socioeconomic conditions, and good health habits all promote this goal. (p. 457)

concrete operational stage Piaget's third stage of cognitive development, extending from about 7 to 11 years of age, during which thought becomes logical, flexible, and organized in its application to concrete information, but the capacity for abstract thinking is not yet present. (p. 234)

conditioned response (CR) In classical conditioning, a new response produced by a conditioned stimulus (CS) that is similar to the unconditioned, or reflexive, response (UCR). (p. 103)

conditioned stimulus (CS) In classical conditioning, a neutral stimulus that, through pairing with an unconditioned stimulus (UCS), leads to a new, conditioned response. (CR). (p. 103)

congregate housing Housing for older adults that provides a variety of support services, including meals in a common dining room, along with watchful oversight of residents with physical and mental disabilities. (p. 490)

conservation The understanding that certain physical characteristics of objects remain the same, even when their outward appearance changes. (p. 178)

constructivist classroom A classroom grounded in Piaget's view of children as active agents who construct their own knowledge. Features include richly equipped learning centers, small groups and individuals solving self-chosen problems, a teacher who guides and supports in response to children's needs, and evaluation based on individual students' progress in relation to their own prior development. Distinguished from *traditional* and *social-constructivist classrooms*. (p. 250)

contexts Unique combinations of personal and environmental circumstances that can result in different paths of development. (p. 4)

continuity theory A social theory of aging that states that most aging adults, in their choice of everyday activities and social relationships, strive to maintain a personal system—an identity and a set of personality dispositions, interests, roles, and skills—that promotes life satisfaction by ensuring consistency between their past and anticipated future. Distinguished from *disengagement theory, activity theory*, and *socioemotional selectivity theory*. (p. 487)

continuous development The view that development is a process of gradually augmenting the same types of skills that were there to begin with. Distinguished from *discontinuous development*. (p. 4)

controversial children Children who receive many votes, both positive and negative, on self-report measures of peer acceptance, indicating that they are both liked and disliked. Distinguished from *popular, neglected*, and *rejected children*. (p. 269)

conventional level Kohlberg's second level of moral development, in which moral understanding is based on conforming to social rules to ensure positive human relationships and maintain societal order. (p. 324)

convergent thinking The type of cognition emphasized on intelligence tests, which involves arriving at a single correct answer to a problem. Distinguished from *divergent thinking*. (p. 254)

cooing Pleasant vowel-like noises made by infants beginning around 2 months of age. (p. 137)

cooperative learning Collaboration on a task by a small group of classmates who work toward common goals by resolving differences of opinion, sharing responsibilities, and providing one another with sufficient explanation to correct misunderstandings. (p. 251)

cooperative play A form of social interaction in which children orient toward a common goal, such as acting out a make-believe theme. Distinguished from *nonsocial activity, parallel play*, and *associative play*. (p. 204)

coparenting Parents' mutual support of each other's parenting behaviors. (p. 46)

coregulation A form of supervision in which parents exercise general oversight while letting children take charge of moment-by-moment decision making. (p. 273)

core knowledge perspective A perspective that states that infants are born with a set of innate knowledge systems, or core domains of thought, each of which permits a ready grasp of new, related information and therefore supports early, rapid development of certain aspects of cognition. (p. 125)

corpus callosum The large bundle of fibers connecting the two hemispheres of the cerebral cortex. (p. 170)

correlational design A research design in which the investigator gathers information on individuals without altering their experiences and then examines relationships between participants' characteristics and their behavior or development. Does not permit inferences about cause and effect. (p. 25)

correlation coefficient A number, ranging from +1.00 to −1.00, that describes the strength and direction of the relationship between two variables. (p. 27)

creativity The ability to produce work that is original yet appropriate—something others have not thought of that is useful in some way. (p. 254)

cross-linkage theory of aging A theory of biological aging asserting that the formation of bonds, or links, between normally separate protein fibers causes the body's connective tissue to become less elastic over time, leading to many negative physical outcomes. (p. 345)

cross-sectional design A research design in which groups of participants of different ages are studied at the same point in time. Distinguished from *longitudinal design*. (p. 29)

crowd A large, loosely organized social group consisting of several cliques with similar values. Membership is based on reputation and stereotype. (p. 332)

crystallized intelligence Intellectual skills that depend on accumulated knowledge and experience, good judgment, and mastery of social conventions—abilities acquired because they are valued by the individual's culture. Distinguished from *fluid intelligence*. (p. 413)

D

death anxiety Fear and apprehension of death. (p. 511)

deferred imitation The ability to remember and copy the behavior of models who are not present. (p. 121)

delay of gratification The ability to wait for an appropriate time and place to engage in a tempting act. (p. 161)

dementia A set of disorders occurring almost entirely in old age in which many aspects of thought and behavior are so impaired that everyday activities are disrupted. (p. 461)

deoxyribonucleic acid (DNA) Long, double-stranded molecules that make up chromosomes. (p. 36)

dependency–support script A typical pattern of interaction in which caregivers attend to older adults' dependent behaviors immediately, thereby reinforcing those behaviors. Distinguished from *independence-ignore script*. (p. 484)

dependent variable The variable the researcher expects to be influenced by the independent variable in an experiment. Distinguished from *independent variable*. (p. 27)

developmental cognitive neuroscience An area of investigation that brings together researchers from psychology, biology, neuroscience, and medicine to study the relationship between changes in the brain and the developing person's cognitive processing and behavior patterns. (p. 17)

developmentally appropriate practice A set of standards devised by the U.S. National Association for the Education of Young Children, specifying program characteristics that meet the developmental and individual needs of young children of varying ages, based on current research and consensus among experts. (p. 135)

developmental science An interdisciplinary field devoted to understanding constancy and change throughout the lifespan. (p. 3)

differentiation theory The view that perceptual development involves the detection of increasingly fine-grained, invariant features in the environment. (p. 114)

difficult child A child whose temperament is characterized by irregular daily routines, slow acceptance of new experiences, and a tendency to react negatively and intensely. Distinguished from *easy child* and *slow-to-warm-up child*. (p. 148)

discontinuous development The view that development is a process in which new ways of understanding and responding to the world emerge at specific times. Distinguished from *continuous development*. (p. 4)

disengagement theory A social theory of aging that states that declines in social interaction in late adulthood are due to mutual withdrawal between older adults and society in anticipation of death. Distinguished from *activity theory, continuity theory,* and *socioemotional selectivity theory*. (p. 487)

disorganized/disoriented attachment The attachment pattern reflecting the greatest insecurity, characterizing infants who show confused, contradictory responses when reunited with the parent after a separation. Distinguished from *secure, avoidant,* and *resistant attachment*. (p. 154)

displaced reference The realization that words can be used to cue mental images of things that are not physically present. (p. 123)

divergent thinking The type of thinking associated with creativity, which involves generating multiple and unusual possibilities when faced with a task or problem. Distinguished from *convergent thinking*. (p. 254)

dominant cerebral hemisphere The hemisphere of the cerebral cortex responsible for skilled motor action and other important abilities. In right-handed individuals, the left hemisphere is dominant; in left-handed individuals, motor and language skills are often shared between the hemispheres. (p. 169)

dominant–recessive inheritance A pattern of inheritance in which, under heterozygous conditions, the influence of only one allele is apparent. (p. 38)

dualistic thinking In Perry's theory, the cognitive approach typical of younger college students, who divide information, values, and authority into right and wrong, good and bad, we and they. Distinguished from *relativistic thinking*. (p. 358)

dual-process model of coping with loss A perspective that assumes that people cope most effectively with loss when they oscillate between dealing with the emotional consequences of loss and attending to life changes, which—when handled successfully—have restorative, or healing, effects. (p. 523)

dual representation The ability to view a symbolic object as both an object in its own right and a symbol. (p. 177)

durable power of attorney for health care A written statement authorizing appointment of another person (usually, though not always, a family member) to make health care decisions on one's behalf. (p. 520)

dynamic assessment An approach to testing consistent with Vygotsky's zone of proximal development, in which purposeful teaching is introduced into the testing situation to find out what the child can attain with social support. (p. 247)

dynamic systems theory of motor development A theory that views new motor skills as reorganizations of previously mastered skills, which lead to more effective ways of exploring and controlling the environment. Each new skill is a joint product of central nervous system development, the body's movement capacities, the child's goals, and environmental supports for the skill. (p. 107)

E

easy child A child whose temperament is characterized by quick establishment of regular routines in infancy, general cheerfulness, and easy adaptation to new experiences. Distinguished from *difficult child* and *slow-to-warm-up child*. (p. 148)

ecological systems theory Bronfenbrenner's approach, which views the person as developing within a complex system of relationships affected by multiple levels of the surrounding environment, from immediate settings of family and school to broad cultural values and programs. (p. 19)

educational self-fulfilling prophecies Teachers' positive or negative views of individual children, who tend to adopt and start to live up to those views. (p. 252)

effortful control The self-regulatory dimension of temperament, involving the capacity to voluntarily suppress a dominant response in order to plan and execute a more adaptive response. (p. 149)

egalitarian marriage A form of marriage in which partners relate as equals, sharing power and authority. Both try to balance the time and energy they devote to their occupations, their children, and their relationship. Distinguished from *traditional marriage*. (p. 382)

egocentrism Failure to distinguish others' symbolic viewpoints from one's own. (p. 177)

ego integrity versus despair In Erikson's theory, the psychological conflict of late adulthood, which is resolved positively when older adults come to terms with their lives and feel whole, complete, and satisfied with their achievements, recognizing that the paths they followed, abandoned, or never selected were necessary for fashioning a meaningful life course. (p. 479)

elaboration A memory strategy that involves creating a relationship, or shared meaning, between two or more pieces of information that do not belong to the same category in order to improve recall. (p. 238)

embryo The prenatal organism from 2 to 8 weeks after conception—the period when the groundwork for all body structures and internal organs is laid down. (p. 63)

emergent literacy Children's active efforts to construct literacy knowledge through informal experiences. (p. 187)

emerging adulthood A new transitional period of development, extending from the late teens to the mid- to late twenties, during which young people have left adolescence but have not yet assumed adult responsibilities. Rather, they continue to explore alternatives in education, work, personal beliefs and values, and love. (p. 369)

emotional self-regulation Strategies for adjusting our emotional state to a comfortable level of intensity so we can accomplish our goals. (p. 147)

emotion-centered coping A strategy for managing emotion that is internal, private, and aimed at controlling distress when little can be done to change an outcome. Distinguished from *problem-centered coping*. (p. 265)

empathy The ability to understand another's emotional state and to *feel with* that person, or respond emotionally in a similar way. (p. 160)

epigenesis Development resulting from ongoing, bidirectional exchanges between heredity and all levels of the environment. (p. 56)

episodic memory Memory for everyday experiences. (p. 185)

epistemic cognition Reflections on how one arrived at facts, beliefs, and ideas. (p. 358)

ethnic identity A sense of ethnic group membership and attitudes and feelings associated with that membership, as an enduring aspect of the self. (p. 322)

ethnography A method in which the researcher attempts to understand a culture or a distinct social group through participant observation—

living with its members and taking field notes for an extended time. (p. 25)

ethological theory of attachment Bowlby's theory, the most widely accepted view of attachment, which regards the infant's emotional tie to the caregiver as an evolved response that promotes survival. (p. 153)

ethology An approach concerned with the adaptive, or survival, value of behavior and its evolutionary history. (p. 17)

euthanasia The practice of ending the life of a person suffering from an incurable condition. (p. 519)

evolutionary developmental psychology An area of research that seeks to understand the adaptive value of specieswide cognitive, emotional, and social competencies as those competencies change with age. (p. 18)

executive function In information processing, the diverse cognitive operations and strategies that enable us to achieve our goals in cognitively challenging situations. Includes controlling attention, suppressing impulses, coordinating information in working memory, and flexibly directing and monitoring thought and behavior. (p. 127)

exosystem In ecological systems theory, social settings that do not contain the developing person but nevertheless affect experiences in immediate settings. Distinguished from *microsystem, mesosystem, macrosystem,* and *chronosystem.* (p. 20)

expansions Adult responses that elaborate on children's speech, increasing its complexity. (p. 196)

experience-dependent brain growth Growth and refinement of established brain structures as a result of specific learning experiences that vary widely across individuals and cultures. Distinguished from *experience-expectant brain growth.* (p. 98)

experience-expectant brain growth The young brain's rapidly developing organization, which depends on ordinary experiences—opportunities to explore the environment, interact with people, and hear language and other sounds. Distinguished from *experience-dependent brain growth.* (p. 98)

experimental design A research design in which the investigator randomly assigns participants to two or more treatment conditions and studies the effect that manipulating an independent variable has on a dependent variable. Permits inferences about cause and effect. (p. 27)

expertise Acquisition of extensive knowledge in a field or endeavor. (p. 360)

extended-family household A household in which three or more generations live together. (p. 50)

F

family life cycle A series of phases characterizing the development of most families around the world. In early adulthood, people typically live on their own, marry, and bear and rear children. In middle age, parenting responsibilities diminish. Late adulthood brings retirement, growing old, and (more often for women) death of one's spouse. (p. 381)

fantasy period Period of vocational development in which children gain insight into career options by fantasizing about them. Distinguished from *tentative period* and *realistic period.* (p. 362)

fast-mapping Children's ability to connect new words with their underlying concepts after only a brief encounter. (p. 193)

feminization of poverty A trend in which women who support themselves or their families have become the majority of the adult population living in poverty, regardless of age and ethnic group. (p. 432)

fetal alcohol spectrum disorder (FASD) A range of physical, mental, and behavioral outcomes caused by prenatal alcohol exposure, including *fetal alcohol syndrome (FAS), partial fetal alcohol syndrome (p-FAS),* and *alcohol-related neurodevelopmental disorder (ARND).* (p. 68)

fetal alcohol syndrome (FAS) The most severe form of fetal alcohol spectrum disorder, distinguished by slow physical growth, facial abnormalities, and brain injury. Usually affects children whose mothers drank heavily throughout pregnancy. Distinguished from *partial fetal alcohol syndrome (p-FAS)* and *alcohol-related neurodevelopmental disorder (ARND).* (p. 69)

fetal monitors Electronic instruments that track the baby's heart rate during labor. (p. 78)

fetus The prenatal organism from the ninth week to the end of pregnancy—the period during which body structures are completed and dramatic growth in size occurs. (p. 64)

fluid intelligence Intellectual skills that largely depend on basic information-processing skills—ability to detect relationships among visual stimuli, speed of analyzing information, and capacity of working memory. Influenced less by culture than by conditions in the brain and by learning unique to the individual. Distinguished from *crystallized intelligence.* (p. 413)

formal operational stage Piaget's highest stage, beginning around 11 years of age, in which adolescents develop the capacity for abstract, systematic, scientific thinking. (p. 304)

frailty Weakened functioning of diverse organs and body systems, which profoundly interferes with everyday competence and leaves older adults highly vulnerable in the face of infection, extremely hot or cold weather, or injury. (p. 459)

fraternal, or dizygotic, twins Twins resulting from the release and fertilization of two ova. They are genetically no more alike than ordinary siblings. Distinguished from *identical, or monozygotic, twins.* (p. 37)

free radicals Naturally occurring, highly reactive chemicals that form in the presence of oxygen and destroy nearby cellular material, including DNA, proteins, and fats essential for cell functioning. Believed to be involved in many disorders of aging. (p. 344)

functional age Actual competence and performance of an older adult, as distinguished from chronological age. (p. 447)

G

gametes Sex cells, or sperm and ova, which contain half as many chromosomes as regular body cells. (p. 37)

gender constancy A full understanding of the biologically based permanence of one's gender, including the realization that sex remains the same even if clothing, hairstyle, and play activities change. (p. 215)

gender identity An image of oneself as relatively masculine or feminine in characteristics. (p. 215)

gender intensification Increased gender stereotyping of attitudes and behavior and movement toward a more traditional gender identity, typical of early adolescence. (p. 328)

gender schema theory An information-processing approach to gender typing that explains how environmental pressures and children's cognitions work together to shape gender-role development. (p. 216)

gender typing Any association of objects, roles, or traits with one sex or the other in ways that conform to cultural stereotypes. (p. 213)

gene A segment of a DNA molecule that contains instructions for production of various proteins that contribute to growth and functioning of the body. (p. 36)

gene–environment correlation The idea that heredity influences the environments to which individuals are exposed. (p. 55)

gene–environment interaction The view that people have unique, genetically influenced reactions to particular experiences and qualities of the environment. (p. 54)

generativity versus stagnation In Erikson's theory, the psychological conflict of midlife, which is resolved positively if the adult can integrate personal goals with the welfare of the larger social world. The resulting strength is the capacity to give to and guide the next generation. (p. 423)

genetic counseling A communication process designed to help couples assess their chances of giving birth to a baby with a hereditary disorder and choose the best course of action in view of risks and family goals. (p. 42)

genomic imprinting A pattern of inheritance in which alleles are imprinted, or chemically marked, in such a way that one pair member is activated, regardless of its makeup. (p. 40)

genotype An individual's genetic makeup. Distinguished from *phenotype.* (p. 36)

gerotranscendence According to Joan Erikson, a psychosocial stage characterizing the very old and representing development beyond ego integrity. Involves a cosmic, transcendent perspective directed forward and outward, beyond the self. Apparent in heightened inner calm and contentment and in additional time spent in quiet reflection. (p. 480)

gifted Displaying exceptional intellectual strengths, such as high IQ, high potential for creativity, and specialized talent. (p. 254)

glass ceiling Invisible barrier to advancement up the corporate ladder, faced by women and ethnic minorities. (p. 440)

glaucoma A disease in which poor fluid drainage leads to a buildup of pressure within the eye, damaging the optic nerve. A leading cause of blindness among older adults. (p. 402)

glial cells Cells that are responsible for myelination of neural fibers, improving the efficiency of message transfer. (p. 94)

goodness-of-fit model A model that describes how favorable adjustment depends on an effective match, or good fit, between a child's temperament and the child-rearing environment. (p. 151)

grief Intense physical and psychological distress following the death of a loved one. (p. 523)

growth hormone (GH) A pituitary hormone that affects the development of all body tissues except the central nervous system and the genitals. (p. 170)

growth spurt Rapid gain in height and weight that is the first outward sign of puberty. (p. 288)

guided participation Shared endeavors between more expert and less expert participants, without specifying the precise features of communication in order to allow for variations across situations and cultures. A broader concept than *scaffolding*. (p. 183)

H

habituation A gradual reduction in the strength of a response due to repetitive stimulation. (p. 104)

hardiness A set of three personal qualities—control, commitment, and challenge—that, together, help people cope adaptively with stress brought on by inevitable life changes. (p. 411)

heritability estimate A statistic that measures the extent to which individual differences in complex traits, such as intelligence or personality, in a specific population are due to genetic factors. (p. 53)

heterozygous Having two different alleles at the same place on a pair of chromosomes. Distinguished from *homozygous*. (p. 38)

hierarchical classification The organization of objects into classes and subclasses on the basis of similarities and differences. (p. 178)

hippocampus An inner-brain structure that plays a vital role in memory and in images of space that help us find our way. (p. 169)

history-graded influences Influences on lifespan development that are unique to a particular historical era and explain why people born around the same time (called a *cohort*) tend to be alike in ways that set them apart from people born at other times. (p. 9)

Home Observation for Measurement of the Environment (HOME) A checklist for gathering information about the quality of children's home lives through observation and parental interview. (p. 133)

homozygous Having two identical alleles at the same place on a pair of chromosomes. Distinguished from *heterozygous*. (p. 38)

hormone therapy Low daily doses of estrogen, either alone or in combination with progesterone, aimed at reducing the physical discomforts of menopause. (p. 405)

hospice A comprehensive program of support services for terminally ill people and their families, which regards the patient and family as a unit of care and emphasizes meeting the patient's physical, emotional, social, and spiritual needs while also providing follow-up bereavement services to the family. (p. 517)

hypothetico-deductive reasoning A formal operational problem-solving strategy in which adolescents begin with a *hypothesis*, or prediction, about variables that might affect an outcome. From the hypothesis, they *deduce* logical, testable inferences. Then they systematically isolate and combine variables to see which of those inferences are confirmed in the real world. (p. 304)

I

identical, or monozygotic, twins Twins that result when a zygote, during early cell duplication, separates into two clusters of cells with the same genetic makeup, which develop into two individuals. Distinguished from *fraternal,* or *dizygotic, twins*. (p. 38)

identity A well-organized conception of the self, consisting of values, beliefs, and goals, to which the individual is solidly committed. (p. 318)

identity achievement The identity status of individuals who, after a period of exploration, have committed themselves to a clearly formulated set of self-chosen values and goals. Distinguished from *identity moratorium, identity foreclosure,* and *identity diffusion*. (p. 319)

identity diffusion The identity status of individuals who do not engage in exploration and are not committed to values and goals. Distinguished from *identity achievement, identity moratorium,* and *identity foreclosure*. (p. 319)

identity foreclosure The identity status of individuals who do not engage in exploration but, instead, are committed to ready-made values and goals chosen for them by authority figures. Distinguished from *identity achievement, identity moratorium,* and *identity diffusion*. (p. 319)

identity moratorium The identity status of individuals who are exploring but not yet committed to self-chosen values and goals. Distinguished from *identity achievement, identity foreclosure,* and *identity diffusion*. (p. 319)

identity versus role confusion In Erikson's theory, the psychological conflict of adolescence, which is resolved positively when adolescents achieve an identity through a process of exploration and inner soul-searching. (p. 318)

imaginary audience Adolescents' belief that they are the focus of everyone else's attention and concern. (p. 308)

imitation Learning by copying the behavior of another person. Also known as *modeling* or *observational learning*. (p. 104)

implantation Attachment of the blastocyst to the uterine lining, which occurs 7 to 9 days after fertilization. (p. 63)

implicit memory Memory without conscious awareness. (p. 469)

inclusive classrooms Classrooms in which students with learning difficulties learn alongside typical students in a regular educational setting for all or part of the school day—a practice designed to prepare them for participation in society and to combat prejudices against individuals with disabilities. (p. 252)

incomplete dominance A pattern of inheritance in which both alleles are expressed in the phenotype, resulting in a combined trait, or one that is intermediate between the two. (p. 39)

independence–ignore script A typical pattern of interaction in which older adults' independent behaviors are mostly ignored and, as a result, occur less often. Distinguished from *dependency–support script*. (p. 484)

independent variable In an experiment, the variable the investigator expects to cause changes in another variable and that the researcher manipulates by randomly assigning participants to treatment conditions. Distinguished from *dependent variable*. (p. 27)

individualistic societies Societies in which people think of themselves as separate entities and are largely concerned with their own personal needs. Distinguished from *collectivist societies*. (p. 50)

induction A type of discipline in which an adult helps the child notice feelings by pointing out the effects of the child's misbehavior on others. (p. 207)

industry versus inferiority In Erikson's theory, the psychological conflict of middle childhood, which is resolved positively when experiences lead children to develop a sense of competence at useful skills and tasks. (p. 260)

infant-directed speech (IDS) A form of communication used by adults to speak to infants and toddlers, consisting of short sentences with high-pitched, exaggerated expression, clear pronunciation, distinct pauses between speech segments, and repetition of new words in a variety of contexts. (p. 139)

infantile amnesia The inability of most older children and adults to retrieve events that happened before age 3. (p. 129)

infant mortality The number of deaths in the first year of life per 1,000 live births. (p. 81)

information-loss view A view that attributes age-related slowing of cognitive processing to greater loss of information as it moves through the system. As a result, the whole system must slow down to inspect and interpret the information. Distinguished from *neural network view*. (p. 415)

information processing A perspective that views the human mind as a symbol-manipulating system through which information flows and that regards cognitive development as a continuous process. (p. 16)

inhibited, or shy, child A child whose temperament is such that he or she reacts negatively to and withdraws from novel stimuli. Distinguished from *uninhibited, or sociable, child.* (p. 149)

initiative versus guilt In Erikson's theory, the psychological conflict of early childhood, which is resolved positively through play experiences that foster a healthy sense of initiative and through development of a superego, or conscience, that is not overly strict and guilt-ridden. (p. 200)

instrumental activities of daily living (IADLs) Tasks necessary to conduct the business of daily life and also requiring some cognitive competence, such as telephoning, shopping, food preparation, housekeeping, and paying bills. (p. 449)

intelligence quotient (IQ) A score that permits an individual's performance on an intelligence test to be compared to the performances of other individuals of the same age. (p. 132)

intentional, or goal-directed, behavior A sequence of actions in which schemes are deliberately coordinated to solve a problem. (p. 120)

intermodal perception The process of making sense of simultaneous input from more than one modality, or sensory system, perceiving them as an integrated whole. (p. 113)

internal working model A set of expectations about the availability of attachment figures and the likelihood that they will provide support in times of stress. It becomes a vital part of personality, serving as a guide for all future close relationships. (p. 153)

intimacy versus isolation In Erikson's theory, the psychological conflict of early adulthood, reflected in the young person's thoughts and feelings about making a permanent commitment to an intimate partner. (p. 374)

irreversibility The inability to mentally go through a series of steps in a problem and then reverse direction, returning to the starting point. Distinguished from *reversibility.* (p. 178)

J

joint attention A state in which the child attends to the same object or event as the caregiver, who often labels it. Supports language development. (p. 137)

K

kinkeeper Role assumed by members of the middle generation, especially mothers, who take responsibility for gathering the family for celebrations and making sure everyone stays in touch. (p. 433)

kinship studies Studies that compare the characteristics of family members to determine the importance of heredity in complex human characteristics. (p. 53)

kwashiorkor A disease caused by an unbalanced diet very low in protein that usually appears after weaning, between 1 and 3 years of age. Symptoms include an enlarged belly, swollen feet, hair loss, skin rash, and irritable, listless behavior. (p. 102)

L

language acquisition device (LAD) In Chomsky's theory, an innate system containing a universal grammar, or set of rules common to all languages, that enables children, no matter which language they hear, to understand and speak in a rule-oriented fashion as soon as they pick up enough words. (p. 136)

lanugo White, downy hair that covers the entire body of the fetus, helping the vernix stick to the skin. (p. 64)

lateralization Specialization of functions in the two hemispheres of the cerebral cortex. (p. 96)

learned helplessness Attribution of success to external factors, such as luck, and failure to low ability, which is fixed and cannot be improved through effort. Distinguished from *mastery-oriented attributions.* (p. 263)

learning disabilities Great difficulty with one or more aspects of learning, usually reading, resulting in achievement considerably behind what would be expected on the basis of a child's IQ. (p. 253)

life-care communities Housing for older adults that offers a range of alternatives, from independent or congregate housing to full nursing home care, guaranteeing that residents' changing needs will be met within the same facility as they age. (p. 490)

lifespan perspective A dynamic systems approach to development that assumes development is lifelong, multidimensional and multidirectional, highly plastic, and affected by multiple interacting forces. (p. 5)

living will A written statement specifying the treatments a person does or does not want in case of a terminal illness, coma, or other near-death situation. (p. 520)

longitudinal design A research design in which participants are studied repeatedly, and changes are noted as they get older. Distinguished from *cross-sectional design.* (p. 28)

long-term memory In information processing, the largest storage area in memory, containing our permanent knowledge base. (p. 126)

M

macrosystem In ecological systems theory, cultural values, laws, customs, and resources that influence experiences and interactions at inner levels of the environment. Distinguished from *microsystem, mesosystem, exosystem,* and *chronosystem.* (p. 20)

macular degeneration Blurring and eventual loss of central vision due to a breakdown of light-sensitive cells in the macula, or central region of the retina. (p. 451)

make-believe play A type of play in which children act out everyday and imaginary activities. (p. 121)

marasmus A wasted condition of the body caused by a diet low in all essential nutrients, which usually appears in the first year of life. (p. 101)

mastery-oriented attributions Attributions that credit success to ability, which can be improved through effort, and failure to insufficient effort. Distinguished from *learned helplessness.* (p. 263)

matters of personal choice Concerns that do not involve rights or others' welfare and, therefore, are up to the individual, such as choice of friends, hairstyle, and leisure activities. Distinguished from *moral imperatives* and *social conventions.* (p. 210)

maximum lifespan The species-specific biological limit to length of life (in years), corresponding to the age at which the oldest known individual died. Distinguished from *average life expectancy* and *average healthy life expectancy.* (p. 449)

meiosis The process of cell division through which gametes are formed and in which the number of chromosomes in each cell is halved. (p. 37)

memory strategies Deliberate mental activities that improve the likelihood of remembering. (p. 185)

menarche First menstruation. (p. 290)

menopause The end of menstruation and, therefore, of a woman's reproductive capacity. (p. 403)

mental representation An internal depiction of information that the mind can manipulate, including images and concepts. (p. 120)

mesosystem In ecological systems theory, connections between a person's microsystems, or immediate settings. Distinguished from *microsystem, exosystem, macrosystem,* and *chronosystem.* (p. 20)

metacognition Thinking about thought; a theory of mind, or coherent set of ideas about mental activities. (p. 186)

microsystem In ecological systems theory, the innermost level of the environment, consisting of activities and interaction patterns in the person's immediate surroundings. Distinguished from *mesosystem, exosystem, macrosystem,* and *chronosystem.* (p. 20)

midlife crisis Self-doubt and stress that prompt major restructuring of the personality during the transition to middle adulthood. Characterizes the experience of only a minority of adults. (p. 426)

mirror neurons Specialized cells in motor areas of the cerebral cortex in primates that underlie the ability to imitate by firing identically when a primate hears or sees an action and when it carries out the action on its own. (p. 105)

mitosis The process of cell duplication, in which each new cell receives an exact copy of the original chromosomes. (p. 37)

moral identity The degree to which morality is central to an individual's self-concept. (p. 327)

moral imperatives Rules and expectations that protect people's rights and welfare. Distinguished from *social conventions* and *matters of personal choice*. (p. 210)

mortality The phase of dying in which the individual passes into permanent death. Distinguished from *agonal phase* and *clinical death*. (p. 510)

mourning The culturally specified expression of the bereaved person's thoughts and feelings through funerals and other rituals. (p. 523)

mutation A sudden but permanent change in a segment of DNA. (p. 40)

myelination The coating of neural fibers with an insulating fatty sheath, called *myelin*, that improves the efficiency of message transfer. (p. 94)

N

naturalistic observation A research method in which the researcher goes into the field, or natural environment, and records the behavior of interest. Distinguished from *structured observation*. (p. 22)

natural, or prepared, childbirth A group of techniques designed to reduce pain and medical intervention and to make childbirth as rewarding an experience as possible. (p. 77)

nature–nurture controversy Disagreement among theorists about whether genetic or environmental factors are more important influences on development. (p. 5)

neglected children Children who are seldom mentioned, either positively or negatively, on self-report measures of peer acceptance. Distinguished from *popular, rejected,* and *controversial children*. (p. 269)

neural network view A view that attributes age-related slowing of cognitive processing to breaks in neural networks as neurons die. The brain adapts by forming bypasses—new synaptic connections that go around the breaks but are less efficient. Distinguished from *information-loss view*. (p. 415)

neural tube During the period of the embryo, the primitive spinal cord that develops from the ectoderm, the top of which swells to form the brain. (p. 63)

neurofibrillary tangles A structural change in the cerebral cortex associated with Alzheimer's disease, in which bundles of twisted threads appear that are the product of collapsed neural structures. (p. 462)

neurons Nerve cells that store and transmit information. (p. 93)

neurotransmitters Chemicals released by neurons that cross the synapse to send messages to other neurons. (p. 94)

niche-picking A type of gene–environment correlation in which individuals actively choose environments that complement their heredity. (p. 55)

nonnormative influences Influences on lifespan development that are irregular, in that they happen to just one or a few individuals and do not follow a predictable timetable. (p. 9)

non-rapid-eye-movement (NREM) sleep A "regular" sleep state during which the body is almost motionless and heart rate, breathing, and brain-wave activity are slow and even. Distinguished from *rapid-eye-movement (REM) sleep*. (p. 83)

nonsocial activity Unoccupied, onlooker behavior and solitary play. Distinguished from *parallel, associative,* and *cooperative play*. (p. 203)

normal distribution The bell-shaped distribution that results when individual differences are measured in large samples. Most scores cluster around the mean, or average, with progressively fewer falling toward the extremes. (p. 132)

normative approach An approach in which measures of behavior are taken on large numbers of individuals, and age-related averages are computed to represent typical development. (p. 11)

O

obesity A greater-than-20-percent increase over healthy body weight, based on body mass index, a ratio of weight to height associated with body fat. (p. 228)

object permanence The understanding that objects continue to exist when out of sight. (p. 120)

operant conditioning A form of learning in which a spontaneous behavior is followed by a stimulus that changes the probability that the behavior will occur again. (p. 104)

optimal aging Aging in which gains are maximized and losses minimized. (p. 501)

ordinality The mathematical principle specifying order relationships (more than and less than) between quantities. (p. 189)

organization In Piaget's theory, the internal rearrangement and linking together of schemes to create a strongly interconnected cognitive system. In information processing, a memory strategy that involves grouping related items together to improve recall. (p. 119, p. 238)

osteoarthritis A form of arthritis that involves deteriorating cartilage on the ends of bones of frequently used joints, which leads to swelling, stiffness, and loss of flexibility. Also known as "wear-and-tear" arthritis or "degenerative joint disease." Distinguished from *rheumatoid arthritis*. (p. 460)

osteoporosis Severe age-related bone loss, which greatly magnifies the risk of bone fractures. (p. 408)

overextension An early vocabulary error in which young children apply a word too broadly, to a wider collection of objects and events than is appropriate. Distinguished from *underextension*. (p. 138)

overregularization Overextension of regular grammatical rules to words that are exceptions. (p. 195)

P

palliative, or comfort, care Care for terminally ill, suffering patients that relieves pain and other symptoms (such as nausea, breathing difficulties, insomnia, and depression), with the goal of protecting the patient's quality of remaining life rather than prolonging life. (p. 518)

parallel play A form of limited social participation in which a child plays near other children with similar materials but does not try to influence their behavior. Distinguished from *nonsocial, associative,* and *cooperative play*. (p. 204)

parental imperative theory A theory that claims that identification with traditional gender roles is maintained during the active parenting years to help ensure the survival of children but that after children reach adulthood, parents are free to express the "other-gender" side of their personalities. (p. 430)

partial fetal alcohol syndrome (p-FAS) A form of fetal alcohol spectrum disorder characterized by facial abnormalities and brain injury, but less severe than fetal alcohol syndrome. Usually affects children whose mothers drank alcohol in smaller quantities during pregnancy. Distinguished from *fetal alcohol syndrome (FAS)* and *alcohol-related neurodevelopmental disorder (ARND)*. (p. 69)

passionate love Love based on intense sexual attraction. Distinguished from *companionate love*. (p. 377)

passive euthanasia The practice of withholding or withdrawing life-sustaining treatment, permitting a patient to die naturally. Distinguished from *voluntary active euthanasia*. (p. 520)

peer acceptance Likability, or the extent to which a child is viewed by a group of agemates as a worthy social partner. (p. 269)

peer group A collective of peers who generate unique values and standards for behavior and a social structure of leaders and followers. (p. 267)

peer victimization A destructive form of peer interaction in which certain children become frequent targets of verbal and physical attacks or other forms of abuse. (p. 270)

perceptual narrowing effect Perceptual sensitivity that becomes increasingly attuned with age to information most often encountered. (p. 110)

permissive child-rearing style A child-rearing style that is warm and accepting but uninvolved, low in control (either overindulgent or inattentive), and lenient rather than appropriate in autonomy granting. Distinguished from *authoritative, authoritarian,* and *uninvolved child-rearing styles*. (p. 218)

persistent vegetative state A state in which the cerebral cortex no longer registers electrical activity but the brain stem remains active. The person is unconscious and displays no voluntary movements. (p. 510)

personal fable Adolescents' inflated opinion of their own importance—a feeling that they are special and unique. (p. 308)

person–environment fit A good match between older adults' abilities and the demands of their living environments. Promotes adaptive behavior and psychological well-being. (p. 484)

phenotype An individual's directly observable physical and behavioral characteristics, which are determined by both genetic and environmental factors. Distinguished from *genotype.* (p. 36)

phobia An intense, unmanageable fear that leads to persistent avoidance of the feared situation. (p. 279)

phonics approach An approach to beginning reading instruction that emphasizes coaching children on phonics—the basic rules for translating written symbols into sounds—before exposing them to complex reading material. Distinguished from the *whole-language approach.* (p. 241)

phonological awareness The ability to reflect on and manipulate the sound structure of spoken language, as indicated by sensitivity to changes in sounds within words, to rhyming, and to incorrect pronunciation. A strong predictor of emergent literacy knowledge. (p. 188)

physical aggression A form of aggression that harms others through physical injury to themselves or their property. Distinguished from *verbal aggression* and *relational aggression.* (p. 211)

pituitary gland A gland located at the base of the brain that releases hormones that induce physical growth. (p. 170)

placenta The organ that permits exchange of nutrients and waste products between the bloodstreams of the mother and the embryo, while also preventing the mother's and embryo's blood from mixing directly. (p. 63)

plasticity Openness of development to change in response to influential experiences. (p. 5)

polygenic inheritance A pattern of inheritance in which many genes influence a characteristic. (p. 40)

popular-antisocial children A subgroup of popular children who are admired for their socially adept yet belligerent behavior. Includes "tough" boys who are athletically skilled, aggressive, and poor students, as well as relationally aggressive boys and girls. Distinguished from *popular-prosocial children.* (p. 269)

popular children Children who receive many positive votes on self-report measures of peer acceptance, indicating they are well-liked. Distinguished from *rejected, controversial,* and *neglected children.* (p. 269)

popular-prosocial children A subgroup of popular children who combine academic and social competence. Distinguished from *popular-antisocial children.* (p. 269)

possible selves Future-oriented representations of what one hopes to become and what one is afraid of becoming. The temporal dimension of self-concept. (p. 427)

postconventional level Kohlberg's highest level of moral development, in which individuals define morality in terms of abstract principles and values that apply to all situations and societies. (p. 324)

postformal thought Cognitive development beyond Piaget's formal operational stage. (p. 358)

practical problem solving Problem solving that requires people to size up real-world situations and analyze how best to achieve goals that have a high degree of uncertainty. (p. 418)

pragmatics The practical, social side of language, concerned with how to engage in effective and appropriate communication. (p. 195)

pragmatic thought In Labouvie-Vief 's theory, a structural advance in thinking in adulthood, in which logic becomes a tool for solving real-world problems and contradictions are accepted as part of existence. (p. 359)

preconventional level Kohlberg's first level of moral development, in which children accept the rules of authority figures and judge actions by their consequences, viewing behaviors that result in punishment as bad and those that lead to rewards as good. (p. 323)

prefrontal cortex The region of the cerebral cortex, lying in front of areas controlling body movement, that is responsible for thought—in particular, for consciousness, inhibition of impulses, integration of information, and use of memory, reasoning, planning, and problem-solving strategies. (p. 96)

prenatal diagnostic methods Medical procedures that permit detection of developmental problems before birth. (p. 43)

preoperational stage Piaget's second stage of cognitive development, extending from about 2 to 7 years of age, in which children undergo an extraordinary increase in representational, or symbolic, activity, although thought is not yet logical. (p. 175)

presbycusis Age-related hearing impairment, beginning around age 50 with a noticeable decline in sensitivity to high-frequency sounds, which gradually extends to all frequencies. (p. 402)

presbyopia A condition of aging in which, around age 60, the lens of the eye loses its capacity to adjust to objects at varying distances. (p. 402)

preterm infants Infants born several weeks or more before their due date. (p. 79)

primary aging Genetically influenced age-related declines in the functioning of organs and systems that affect all members of our species and occur even in the context of overall good health. Also called *biological aging.* Distinguished from *secondary aging.* (p. 459)

primary sexual characteristics Physical features that involve the reproductive organs (ovaries, uterus, and vagina in females; penis, scrotum, and testes in males). Distinguished from *secondary sexual characteristics.* (p. 290)

private speech Self-directed speech that children use to plan and guide their own behavior. (p. 182)

proactive aggression A type of aggression in which children act to fulfill a need or desire—obtain an object, privilege, space, or social reward, such as adult or peer attention—and unemotionally attack a person to achieve their goal. Also called *instrumental aggression.* Distinguished from *reactive aggression.* (p. 211)

problem-centered coping A strategy for managing emotion that involves appraising the situation as changeable, identifying the difficulty, and deciding what to do about it. Distinguished from *emotion-centered coping.* (p. 265)

programmed cell death An aspect of brain growth whereby, as synapses form, many surrounding neurons die, making space for these connective structures. (p. 94)

Project Head Start A U.S. federal early intervention program that provides children from low-income families with a year or two of preschool, along with nutritional and health services, and that encourages parent involvement in children's learning and development. (p. 191)

propositional thought A type of formal operational reasoning involving the ability to evaluate the logic of propositions, or verbal statements, without referring to real-world circumstances. (p. 305)

prosocial, or **altruistic**, **behavior** Actions that benefit another person without any expected reward for the self. (p. 203)

prospective memory Recall that involves remembering to engage in planned actions in the future. (p. 470)

proximodistal trend An organized pattern of physical growth that proceeds from the center of the body outward. Distinguished from *cephalocaudal trend.* (p. 93)

psychoanalytic perspective An approach to personality development introduced by Freud that assumes people move through a series of stages in which they confront conflicts between biological drives and social expectations. How these conflicts are resolved determines the person's ability to learn, to get along with others, and to cope with anxiety. (p. 12)

psychological control Parental behaviors that intrude on and manipulate children's verbal expressions, individuality, and attachments to parents. (p. 218)

psychosexual theory Freud's theory, which emphasizes that how parents manage children's sexual and aggressive drives in the first few years is crucial for healthy personality development. (p. 12)

psychosocial theory Erikson's theory, which emphasizes that in each Freudian stage, individuals not only develop a unique personality but also acquire attitudes and skills that make them active, contributing members of their society. Recognizes the lifespan nature of development and the impact of culture. (p. 12)

puberty Biological changes at adolescence that lead to an adult-sized body and sexual maturity. (p. 287)

public policies Laws and government programs designed to improve current conditions. (p. 50)

punishment In operant conditioning, removal of a desirable stimulus or presentation of an unpleasant one to decrease the occurrence of a response. (p. 104)

R

random assignment An unbiased procedure for assigning participants to treatment conditions in an experiment, such as drawing numbers out of a hat or flipping a coin. Increases the chances that participants' characteristics will be equally distributed across treatment groups. (p. 27)

rapid-eye-movement (REM) sleep An "irregular" sleep state in which brain-wave activity is similar to that of the waking state. Distinguished from *non-rapid-eye-movement (NREM) sleep*. (p. 83)

reactive aggression An angry, defensive response to provocation or a blocked goal that is meant to hurt another person. Also called *hostile aggression*. Distinguished from *proactive aggression*. (p. 211)

realistic period Period of vocational development in which older adolescents and young adults narrow their vocational options, engaging in further exploration before focusing on a general vocational category and, slightly later, settling on a single occupation. Distinguished from *fantasy period* and *tentative period*. (p. 362)

recall A type of memory that involves remembering something that is not present. Distinguished from *recognition*. (p. 128)

recasts Adult responses that restructure children's grammatically inaccurate speech into correct form. (p. 196)

recognition A type of memory that involves noticing whether a stimulus is identical or similar to one previously experienced. Distinguished from *recall*. (p. 128)

recovery Following habituation, an increase in responsiveness to a new stimulus. (p. 104)

reflex An inborn, automatic response to a particular form of stimulation. (p. 82)

rehearsal A memory strategy that involves repeating information to oneself to improve recall. (p. 238)

reinforcer In operant conditioning, a stimulus that increases the occurrence of a response. (p. 104)

rejected-aggressive children A subgroup of rejected children who show high rates of conflict, physical and relational aggression, and hyperactive, inattentive, and impulsive behavior. Distinguished from *rejected-withdrawn children*. (p. 269)

rejected children Children who receive many negative votes on self-report measures of peer acceptance, indicating they are actively disliked. Distinguished from *popular, controversial*, and *neglected children*. (p. 269)

rejected-withdrawn children A subgroup of rejected children who are passive and socially awkward. Distinguished from *rejected-aggressive children*. (p. 269)

relational aggression A form of aggression that damages another's peer relationships through social exclusion, malicious gossip, or friendship manipulation. Distinguished from *physical aggression* and *verbal aggression*. (p. 211)

relativistic thinking In Perry's theory, the cognitive approach typical of older college students, who view all knowledge as embedded in a framework of thought and, therefore, give up the possibility of absolute truth in favor of multiple truths, each relative to its context. Distinguished from *dualistic thinking*. (p. 358)

reminiscence The process of telling stories about people and events from the past and reporting associated thoughts and feelings. (p. 481)

reminiscence bump Older adults' heightened autobiographical memory for events that occurred between ages 10 and 30. (p. 470)

remote memory Very long-term recall. (p. 469)

resilience The ability to adapt effectively in the face of threats to development. (p. 8)

resistant attachment The attachment pattern characterizing infants who remain close to the parent and fail to explore before separation, are usually distressed when the parent leaves, and combine clinginess with angry, resistive behavior when the parent returns. Distinguished from *secure, avoidant*, and *disorganized/disoriented attachment*. (p. 154)

reticular formation A structure in the brain stem that maintains alertness and consciousness. (p. 169)

reversibility The ability to think through a series of steps in a problem and then mentally reverse direction, returning to the starting point. Distinguished from *irreversibility*. (p. 234)

rheumatoid arthritis A form of arthritis in which an autoimmune response leads to inflammation of connective tissue, particularly the membranes that line the joints, resulting in overall stiffness, inflammation, and aching. Leads to deformed joints and often serious loss of mobility. Distinguished from *osteoarthritis*. (p. 460)

Rh factor incompatibility A condition that arises when the Rh protein is present in the fetus's blood but not in the mother's, causing the mother to build up antibodies. If these enter the fetus's system, they destroy red blood cells, reducing the oxygen supply to organs and tissues. Mental retardation, miscarriage, heart damage, and infant death can occur. (p. 72)

rough-and-tumble play A form of peer interaction involving friendly chasing and play-fighting that emerges in the preschool years and peaks in middle childhood. In our evolutionary past, it may have been important for developing fighting skill. (p. 232)

S

sandwich generation A term used to describe middle-aged adults who must care for multiple generations above and below them at the same time. (p. 436)

scaffolding Adjusting the support offered during a teaching session to fit the learner's current level of performance. Direct instruction is offered when a task is new; less help is provided as competence increases, thereby keeping the task within the zone of proximal development. (p. 182)

scale errors Toddlers' attempts to do things that their body size makes impossible, possibly indicating lack of an accurate understanding of their own body dimensions. (p. 160)

scheme In Piaget's theory, a specific psychological structure, or organized way of making sense of experience, that changes with age. (p. 118)

scripts General descriptions of what occurs and when it occurs in a particular situation, used to organize and interpret everyday experiences. (p. 185)

secondary aging Age-related declines due to hereditary defects and environmental influences, such as poor diet, lack of exercise, disease, substance abuse, environmental pollution, and psychological stress. Distinguished from *primary aging*. (p. 459)

secondary friends People who are not intimates but with whom an individual spends time occasionally, such as a group that meets for lunch, bridge, or museum tours. (p. 497)

secondary sexual characteristics Physical features visible on the outside of the body that serve as signs of sexual maturity but do not involve the reproductive organs (for example, breast development in females, appearance of underarm and pubic hair in both sexes). Distinguished from *primary sexual characteristics*. (p. 290)

secular trend A change from one generation to the next in an aspect of development, such as body size or pubertal timing. (p. 291)

secure attachment The attachment pattern characterizing infants who use the parent as a secure base from which to explore, may be distressed by parental separation, but actively seek contact and are easily comforted by the parent when she returns. Distinguished from *avoidant, resistant*, and *disorganized/disoriented attachment*. (p. 154)

secure base The familiar caregiver as a point from which the baby explores, venturing into the environment and then returning for emotional support. (p. 146)

selective optimization with compensation A set of strategies used by older adults who sustain high levels of functioning. Narrowing their goals, they *select* personally valued activities to *optimize* returns from their diminishing energy and also find new ways to *compensate* for losses. (p. 468)

self-care children Children who are without adult supervision for some period of time after school. (p. 278)

self-concept The set of attributes, abilities, attitudes, and values that an individual believes defines who he or she is. (p. 201)

self-conscious emotions Emotions involving injury to or enhancement of the sense of self, including guilt, shame, embarrassment, envy, and pride. (p. 147)

self-esteem An aspect of self-concept that involves judgments about one's own worth and the feelings associated with those judgments. (p. 201)

self-recognition Identification of the self as a physically unique being. (p. 160)

sensitive caregiving Caregiving that involves responding promptly, consistently, and appropriately to infants and holding them tenderly and carefully. (p. 156)

sensitive period A time that is optimal for certain capacities to emerge and in which the individual is especially responsive to environmental influences. (p. 18)

sensorimotor stage Piaget's first stage, spanning the first two years of life, during which infants and toddlers "think" with their eyes, ears, hands, and other sensorimotor equipment. (p. 118)

sensory register The part of the information-processing system in which sights and sounds are represented directly and stored briefly. (p. 126)

separation anxiety An infant's distressed reaction to the departure of the familiar caregiver. (p. 153)

seriation The ability to order items along a quantitative dimension, such as length or weight. (p. 234)

sequential designs Developmental designs in which investigators conduct several similar cross-sectional or longitudinal studies (called *sequences*) at varying times, sometimes combining longitudinal and cross-sectional strategies. (p. 30)

sex chromosomes The twenty-third pair of chromosomes, which determines the sex of the individual. In females, it is called *XX*; in males, *XY*. (p. 37)

short-term memory store The part of the mind in which attended-to-information is retained briefly so that we can actively "work" on it to achieve our goals. (p. 126)

skipped-generation family A family structure in which children live with grandparents but apart from parents. (p. 435)

slow-to-warm-up child A child whose temperament is characterized by inactivity; mild, low-key reactions to environmental stimuli; negative mood; and slow adjustment to new experiences. Distinguished from *easy child* and *difficult child*. (p. 148)

small-for-date infants Infants whose birth weight is below their expected weight considering length of the pregnancy. Some are full-term; others are preterm infants who are especially underweight. (p. 79)

social clock Age-graded expectations for major life events, such as beginning a first job, getting married, birth of the first child, buying a home, and retiring. (p. 376)

social comparisons Judgments of one's own appearance, abilities, and behavior in relation to those of others. (p. 260)

social-constructivist classroom A classroom grounded in Vygotsky's sociocultural theory, in which children participate in a wide range of challenging activities with teachers and peers, with whom they jointly construct understandings. Distinguished from *traditional* and *constructivist classrooms*. (p. 251)

social conventions Customs determined solely by consensus within a society, such as table manners and politeness rituals. Distinguished from *moral imperatives* and *matters of personal choice*. (p. 210)

social convoy A model of age-related changes in social networks, which views the individual as moving through life within a cluster of relationships, with close ties in the inner circle and less close ties on the outside. With age, people change places in the convoy, new ties are added, and some are lost entirely. (p. 492)

social learning theory An approach that emphasizes the role of modeling, otherwise known as imitation or observational learning, in the development of behavior. (p. 14)

social referencing Actively seeking emotional information from a trusted person in an uncertain situation. (p. 146)

social smile The infant's broad grin, evoked by the parent's communication, that first appears between 6 and 10 weeks of age. (p. 144)

sociocultural theory Vygotsky's theory, in which children acquire the ways of thinking and behaving that make up their community's culture through social interaction—in particular, cooperative dialogues with more knowledgeable members of society. (p. 18)

sociodramatic play The make-believe with others that is under way by the end of the second year and increases rapidly in complexity during early childhood. (p. 176)

socioeconomic status (SES) A measure of an individual's or a family's social position and economic well-being that combines three related, but not completely overlapping, variables: years of education, the prestige of one's job and the skill it requires, and income. (p. 47)

socioemotional selectivity theory A social theory of aging that states that social interaction in late adulthood extends lifelong selection processes. Physical and psychological aspects of aging lead to an increased emphasis on the emotion-regulating function of social interaction, leading older adults to prefer familiar social partners with whom they have developed pleasurable relationships. Distinguished from *disengagement theory, activity theory,* and *continuity theory*. (p. 488)

spermarche First ejaculation of seminal fluid. (p. 290)

stage A qualitative change in thinking, feeling, and behaving that characterizes a specific period of development. (p. 4)

standardization The practice of giving a newly constructed test to a large, representative sample and using the results as the standard for interpreting individual scores. (p. 132)

states of arousal Different degrees of sleep and wakefulness. (p. 83)

statistical learning capacity The capacity to analyze the speech stream for regularly occurring sound sequences, through which infants acquire a stock of speech structures for which they will later learn meanings. (p. 109)

stereotype threat The fear of being judged on the basis of a negative stereotype, which can trigger anxiety that interferes with performance. (p. 246)

stranger anxiety The infant's expression of fear in response to unfamiliar adults, which appears in many babies in the second half of the first year. (p. 146)

Strange Situation A laboratory procedure used to assess the quality of attachment between 1 and 2 years of age by observing the baby's response to eight short episodes involving brief separations from and reunions with the caregiver in an unfamiliar playroom. (p. 154)

structured interview An interview method in which each participant is asked the same questions in the same way. Distinguished from *clinical interview*. (p. 24)

structured observation A research method in which the investigator sets up a laboratory situation that evokes the behavior of interest so that every participant has an equal opportunity to display the response. Distinguished from *naturalistic observation*. (p. 23)

subculture A group of people with beliefs and customs that differ from those of the larger culture. (p. 50)

sudden infant death syndrome (SIDS) The unexpected death, usually during the night, of an infant under 1 year of age that remains unexplained after thorough investigation. (p. 84)

sympathy Feelings of concern or sorrow for another's plight. (p. 203)

synapses The gaps between neurons, across which chemical messages are sent. (p. 94)

synaptic pruning Loss of synapses by seldom-stimulated neurons, a process that returns them to an uncommitted state so they can support future development. (p. 94)

T

talent Outstanding performance in a specific field. (p. 254)

telegraphic speech Toddlers' two-word utterances that, like a telegram, focus on high-content words while omitting smaller, less important words. (p. 138)

telomeres A special type of DNA located at the ends of chromosomes—serving as a "cap" to protect the ends from destruction—that shortens with each cell duplication. Eventually, so little remains that the cells no longer duplicate at all. (p. 344)

temperament Early-appearing, stable individual differences in reactivity (quickness and intensity of emotional arousal, attention, and motor activity) and self-regulation (strategies that modify that reactivity). (p. 148)

tentative period Period of vocational development in which adolescents begin to evaluate vocational options in terms of their interests, abilities, and values. Distinguished from *fantasy period* and *realistic period*. (p. 362)

teratogen Any environmental agent that causes damage during the prenatal period. (p. 66)

terminal decline Acceleration in deterioration of cognitive functioning prior to death. (p. 473)

thanatology An interdisciplinary field devoted to the study of death and dying. (p. 509)

theory An orderly, integrated set of statements that describes, explains, and predicts behavior. (p. 3)

theory of multiple intelligences Gardner's theory, which identifies eight independent intelligences, defined in terms of distinct sets of processing operations that permit individuals to engage in a wide range of culturally valued activities: linguistic, logico-mathematical, musical, spatial, bodily-kinesthetic, naturalist, interpersonal, and intrapersonal. (p. 244)

Third Age A new phase of late adulthood extending from ages 65 to 79 or longer, resulting from added years of longevity plus good health and financial stability, in which older adults pursue personally enriching interests and goals. (p. 482)

thyroid-stimulating hormone (TSH) A pituitary hormone that stimulates the thyroid gland to release thyroxine, which is necessary for brain development and for growth hormone to have its full impact on body size. (p. 170)

time out A form of mild punishment that involves removing children from the immediate setting until they are ready to act appropriately. (p. 208)

traditional classroom A classroom in which the teacher is the sole authority for knowledge, rules, and decision making and students are relatively passive learners whose progress is evaluated in relation to how well they keep pace with a uniform set of standards for their grade. Distinguished from *constructivist* and *social-constructivist classrooms*. (p. 250)

traditional marriage A form of marriage involving clear division of husband's and wife's roles, in which the man is the head of household and economic provider, and the woman devotes herself to caring for her husband and children and creating a nurturant, comfortable home. Distinguished from *egalitarian marriage*. (p. 382)

transitive inference The ability to seriate, or order items along a quantitative dimension, mentally. (p. 234)

triarchic theory of successful intelligence Sternberg's theory, in which intelligent behavior involves balancing three broad, interacting intelligences—analytical intelligence, creative intelligence, and practical intelligence—to achieve success in life according to one's personal goals and the requirements of one's cultural community. (p. 243)

triangular theory of love Sternberg's view of love as including three components—intimacy, passion, and commitment—that shift in emphasis as romantic relationships develop. (p. 377)

trimesters Three equal time periods, each lasting three months, into which prenatal development is sometimes divided. (p. 64)

Type A behavior pattern A behavior pattern characterized by extreme competitiveness, ambition, impatience, hostility, angry outbursts, and a sense of time pressure. (p. 409)

U

umbilical cord The long cord connecting the prenatal organism to the placenta that delivers nutrients and removes waste products. (p. 63)

unconditioned response (UCR) In classical conditioning, a reflexive response that is produced by an unconditioned stimulus (UCS). Distinguished from *conditioned response*. (p. 103)

unconditioned stimulus (UCS) In classical conditioning, a stimulus that leads to a reflexive response. Distinguished from *conditioned stimulus*. (p. 103)

underextension An early vocabulary error in which young children apply a word too narrowly, to a smaller number of objects and events than is appropriate. Distinguished from *overextension*. (p. 138)

uninhibited, or sociable, child A child whose temperament is such that he or she displays positive emotion to and approaches novel stimuli. Distinguished from *inhibited, or shy, child*. (p. 149)

uninvolved child-rearing style A child-rearing style that combines low acceptance and involvement with little control and general indifference to issues of autonomy. Distinguished from *authoritative, authoritarian,* and *permissive child-rearing styles*. (p. 219)

V

verbal aggression A type of aggression that harms others through threats of physical aggression, name-calling, or hostile teasing. Distinguished from *physical aggression* and *relational aggression*. (p. 211)

vernix A white, cheeselike substance that covers the fetus, preventing the skin from chapping due to constant exposure to amniotic fluid. (p. 64)

video deficit effect In toddlers, poorer performance on tasks after watching a video than after seeing a live demonstration. (p. 124)

violation-of-expectation method A method in which researchers show babies an expected event (one that follows physical laws) and an unexpected event (a variation of the first event that violates physical laws). Heightened attention to the unexpected event suggests that the infant is "surprised" by a deviation from physical reality and, therefore, is aware of that aspect of the physical world. (p. 121)

visual acuity Fineness of visual discrimination. (p. 87)

voluntary active euthanasia The practice of acting directly, at a patient's request, to end suffering before a natural end to life. Distinguished from *passive euthanasia*. (p. 521)

W

whole-language approach An approach to beginning reading instruction that exposes children to text in its complete form, using reading materials that are whole and meaningful, to promote appreciation of the communicative function of written language. Distinguished from *phonics approach*. (p. 241)

wisdom A capacity made up of multiple cognitive and personality traits, combining breadth and depth of practical knowledge; ability to reflect on and apply that knowledge in ways that make life more bearable and worthwhile; emotional maturity, including the ability to listen, evaluate, and give advice; and altruistic creativity, which involves contributing to humanity and enriching others' lives. (p. 471)

working memory The number of items that can be briefly held in mind while also engaging in some effort to monitor or manipulate those items—a "mental workspace" that we use to accomplish many activities in daily life. A contemporary view of the short-term memory store. (p. 126)

X

X-linked inheritance A pattern of inheritance in which a recessive gene is carried on the X chromosome, so that males are more likely than females to be affected. (p. 39)

Z

zone of proximal development In Vygotsky's theory, a range of tasks too difficult for a child to do alone but possible with the help of more-skilled partners. (p. 130)

zygote The newly fertilized cell formed by the union of sperm and ovum at conception. (p. 37)

References

A

Aalsma, M., Lapsley, D. K., & Flannery, D. J. (2006). Personal fables, narcissism, and adolescent adjustment. *Psychology in the Schools, 43,* 481–491.

Aarnoudse-Moens, C. S., Weisglas-Kuperus, N., & van Goudoever, J. B. (2009). Meta-analysis of neurobehavioral outcomes in very preterm and/or very low birth weight children. *Pediatrics, 124,* 717–728.

AARP. (2002). *The Grandparent Study 2002 report.* Washington, DC: Author.

Abakoumkin, G., Stroebe, W., & Stroebe, M. (2010). Does relationship quality moderate the impact of marital bereavement on depressive symptoms? *Journal of Social and Clinical Psychology, 29,* 510–526.

Abbey, A., & Jacques-Tiura, A. J. (2011). Sexual assault perpetrators' tactics: Associations with their personal characteristics and aspects of the incident. *Journal of Interpersonal Violence, 26,* 2866–2889.

Abbey, A., & McAuslan, P. (2004). A longitudinal examination of male college students' perpetration of sexual assault. *Journal of Consulting and Clinical Psychology, 72,* 747–756.

Abela, J. R. Z., Hankin, B. L., Haigh, E. A. P., Adams, P., Vinokuroff, T., & Trayhern, L. (2005). Interpersonal vulnerability to depression in high-risk children: The role of insecure attachment and reassurance seeking. *Journal of Clinical Child and Adolescent Psychology, 34,* 182–192.

Abele, A. E., & Spurk, D. (2011). The dual impact of gender and the influence of parenthood on men's and women's career development: Longitudinal findings. *International Journal of Behavioral Development, 35,* 225–232.

Abelson, H., Ledeen, K., & Lewis, H. (2008). *Blown to bits: Your life, liberty and happiness after the digital explosion.* New York: Addison-Wesley.

Aber, J. L., Jones, S. M., & Raver, C. C. (2007). Poverty and child development: New perspectives on a defining issue. In J. L. Aber, S. J. Bishop-Josef, S. M. Jones, K. T. McLearn, & D. Phillips (Eds.), *Child development and social policy: Knowledge for action* (pp. 149–166). Washington, DC: American Psychological Association.

Aboud, F. E. (2008). A social-cognitive developmental theory of prejudice. In S. M. Quintana & C. McKown (Eds.), *Handbook of race, racism, and the developing child* (pp. 55–71). Hoboken, NJ: Wiley.

Aboud, F. E., & Doyle, A. (1996). Parental and peer influences on children's racial attitudes. *International Journal of Intercultural Relations, 20,* 371–383.

Abrams, K. Y., Rifkin, A., & Hesse, E. (2006). Examining the role of parental frightened/ frightening subtypes in predicting disorganized attachment within a brief observational procedure. *Development and Psychopathology, 18,* 345–361.

Achenbach, T. M., Phares, V., Howell, C. T., Rauh, V. A., & Nurcombe, B. (1990). Seven-year outcome of the Vermont program for low-birthweight infants. *Child Development, 61,* 1672–1681.

Acierno R., Hernandez, M. A., Amstadter, A. B., Resnick, H. S., Steve, K., Muzzy, W., et al. (2010). Prevalence and correlates of emotional, physical, sexual, and financial abuse and potential neglect in the United States: The national elder mistreatment study. *American Journal of Public Health, 100,* 292–297.

Acker, M. M., & Davis, M. H. (1992). Intimacy, passion, and commitment in adult romantic relationships: A test of the triangular love theory. *Journal of Social and Personal Relationships, 9,* 21–50.

Acker, M. M., & O'Leary, S. G. (1996). Inconsistency of mothers' feedback and toddlers' misbehavior and negative affect. *Journal of Abnormal Child Psychology, 24,* 703–714.

Ackerman, S., Zuroff, D. C., & Moskowitz, D. S. (2000). Generativity in midlife and young adults: Links to agency, communion, and subjective wellbeing. *International Journal of Aging and Human Development, 50,* 17–41.

ACT. (2010). *2010 retention/completion summary tables.* Retrieved from www.act.org/research/policymakers/ pdf/10retain_trends.pdf

Adachi-Mejia, A. M., Longacre, M. R., Gibson, J. J., Beach, M. L., Titus-Ernstoff, L. T., & Dalton, M. A. (2007). Children with a TV in their bedroom at higher risk for being overweight. *International Journal of Obesity, 31,* 644–651.

Adams, G. A., Rau, B. L. (2011). Putting off tomorrow to do what you want today: Planning for retirement. *American Psychologist, 66,* 180–192.

Adams, K. B., Sanders, S., & Auth, E. A. (2004). Loneliness and depression in independent living retirement communities: Risk and resilience factors. *Aging and Mental Health, 8,* 475–485.

Adams, R. G., & Laursen, B. (2001). The organization and dynamics of adolescent conflict with parents and friends. *Journal of Marriage and the Family, 63,* 97–110.

Adamson, D. (2005). Regulation of assisted reproductive technologies in the United States. *Family Law Quarterly, 39,* 727–744.

Addington-Hall, J. (2000). Do home deaths increase distress in bereavement? *Palliative Medicine, 14,* 161–162.

Adhikari, B., Kahende, J., Malarcher, A., Pechacek, T., & Tong, V. (2009). Smoking-attributable mortality, years of potential life lost, and productivity losses. *Oncology Times, 31,* 40–43.

Adolph, K. E. (2008). Learning to move. *Current Directions in Psychological Science, 17,* 213–218.

Adolph, K. E., & Berger, S. E. (2006). Motor development. In D. Kuhn & R. Siegler (Eds.), *Handbook of child psychology: Vol. 2. Cognition, perception, and language* (6th ed., pp. 161–213). Hoboken, NJ: Wiley.

Adolph, K. E., & Eppler, M. A. (1998). Development of visually guided locomotion. *Ecological Psychology, 10,* 303–321.

Adolph, K. E., & Eppler, M. A. (1999). Obstacles to understanding: An ecological approach to infant problem solving. In E. Winograd, R. Fivush, & W. Hirst (Eds.), *Ecological approaches to cognition* (pp. 31–58). Mahwah, NJ: Erlbaum.

Adolph, K. E., Karasik, L. B., & Tamis-LeMonda, C. S. (2010). Motor skill. In M. H. Bornstein (Ed.), *Handbook of cultural developmental science* (pp. 61–88). New York: Psychology Press.

Adolph, K. E., Tamis-LeMonda, C. S., Ishak, S., Karasik, L. B., & Lobo, S. A. (2008). Locomotor experience and use of social information are posture specific. *Developmental Psychology, 44,* 1705–1714.

Adolph, K. E. A., Vereijken, B., & Shrout, P. E. (2003). What changes in infant walking and why. *Child Development, 74,* 475–497.

Afifi, T. O., Brownridge, D. A., Cox, B. J., & Sareen J. (2006). Physical punishment, childhood abuse and psychiatric disorders. *Child Abuse and Neglect, 30,* 1093–1103.

Afterschool Alliance. (2009). *America after 3 PM.* Retrieved from www.kidsdeservebetter.org/ AA3PM.cfm

Aggarwal, R., Sentz, J., & Miller, M. A. (2007). Role of zinc administration in prevention of childhood diarrhea and respiratory illnesses: A meta-analysis. *Pediatrics, 119,* 1120–1130.

Agronick, G., Stueve, A., Vargo, S., & O'Donnell, L. (2007). New York City young adults' psychological reactions to 9/11: Findings from the Reach for Health longitudinal study. *American Journal of Community Psychology, 39,* 79–90.

Agüero-Torres, H., von Strauss, E., Viitanen, M., Winblad, B., & Fratiglioni, L. (2001). Institutionalization in the elderly: The role of chronic diseases and dementia. Cross-sectional and longitudinal data from a population-based study. *Journal of Clinical Epidemiology, 54,* 795–801.

Aguiar, A., & Baillargeon, R. (2002). Developments in young infants' reasoning about occluded objects. *Cognitive Psychology, 45,* 267–336.

Ahlskog, J. E., Geda, Y. E., Graff-Radford, N. R., & Petersen, R. C. (2011). Physical exercise as a preventive or disease-modifying treatment of dementia and brain aging. *Mayo Clinics Proceedings, 86,* 876–884.

Ahrens, C. J. C., & Ryff, C. D. (2006). Multiple roles and well-being: Sociodemographic and psychological moderators. *Sex Roles, 55,* 801–815.

Ahuja, J. (2005). *Women's entrepreneurship in the United States.* Kansas City, MO: Kauffman Center for Entrepreneurial Leadership, Clearinghouse on Entrepreneurship Education. Retrieved from www.celcee.edu

Ai, A. L., Wink, P., & Ardelt, M. (2010). Spirituality and aging: A journey for meaning through deep interconnection in humanity. In J. C. Cavanaugh & C. K. Cavanaugh (Eds.), *Aging in America: Vol. 3. Societal issues* (pp. 222–246). Santa Barbara, CA: Praeger.

Aikens, J. W., Bierman, K. L., & Parker, J. G. (2005). Navigating the transition to junior high school: The influence of pre-transition friendship and self-system characteristics. *Social Development, 14,* 42–60.

Aikens, J. W., Howes, C., & Hamilton, C. (2009). Attachment stability and the emergence of unresolved representations in adolescence. *Attachment & Human Development, 11,* 491–512.

Ainsworth, M. D. S., Blehar, M. C., Waters, E., & Wall, S. (1978). *Patterns of attachment.* Hillsdale, NJ: Erlbaum.

Aisen, P. S., Schneider, L. S., Sano, M., Diaz-Arrastia, R., van Dyck, C. H., & Weiner, M. F. (2008). High-dose B vitamin supplementation and cognitive decline in Alzheimer disease: A randomized controlled trial. *Journal of the American Medical Association, 15,* 1774–1783.

Ajrouch, K. (2007). Health disparities and Arab-American elders: Does intergenerational support buffer the inequality–health link? *Journal of Social Issues, 63,* 745–758.

Akimoto, S. A., & Sanbonmatsu, D. M. (1999). Differences in self-effacing behavior between European and Japanese Americans: Effect on competence evaluations. *Journal of Cross-Cultural Psychology, 30,* 159–177.

Akinbami, L. J., Moorman, J. E., Garbe, P. L., & Sondik, E. J. (2009). Status of childhood asthma in the United States, 1980–2007. *Pediatrics, 123,* S123–S145.

Aksan, N., & Kochanska, G. (2004). Heterogeneity of joy in infancy. *Infancy, 6,* 79–94.

Akshoomoff, N. A., Feroleto, C. C., Doyle, R. E., & Stiles, J. (2002). The impact of early unilateral brain injury on perceptual organization and visual memory. *Neuropsychologia, 40,* 539–561.

Albers, C. A., & Grieve, A. J. (2007). Test review: Bayley, N. (2006). Bayley Scales of Infant and Toddler Development–Third Edition. San Antonio, TX: Harcourt Assessment. *Journal of Psychoeducational Assessment, 25,* 180–190.

Aldwin, C. M., Spiro, A., III, & Park, C. L. (2006). Health, behavior, and optimal aging: A life span developmental perspective. In J. E. Birren & K. W. Schaie (Eds.), *Handbook of the psychology of aging* (6th ed., pp. 85–104). Burlington, MA: Elsevier Academic Press.

Aldwin, C. M., & Yancura, L. (2011). Stress, coping, and adult development. In R. J. Contrada & A. Baum (Eds.), *Handbook of stress science: Biology, psychology, and health* (pp. 263–274). New York: Springer.

Aldwin, C. M., Yancura, L. A., & Boeninger, D. K. (2010). Coping across the life span. In M. E. Lamb, A. M. Freund, & R. M. Lerner (Eds.), *Handbook of life-span development. Vol. 2: Social and emotional development* (pp. 298–340). Hoboken, NJ: Wiley.

Alessandri, S. M., Sullivan, M. W., & Lewis, M. (1990). Violation of expectancy and frustration in early infancy. *Developmental Psychology, 26*, 738–744.

Alexander, J. M., Fabricius, W. V., Fleming, V. M., Zwahr, M., & Brown, S. A. (2003). The development of metacognitive causal explanations. *Learning and Individual Differences, 13*, 227–238.

Alink, L. R. A., Mesman, J., van Zeijl, J., Stolk, M. N., Juffer, F., & Koot, H. M. (2006). The early childhood aggression curve: Development of physical aggression in 10- to 50-month-old children. *Child Development, 77*, 954–966.

Alkema, G. E., Wilber, K. H., & Enguidanos, S. M. (2007). Community- and facility-based care. In J. A. Blackburn & C. N. Dulmus (Eds.), *Handbook of gerontology: Evidence-based approaches to theory, practice, and policy* (pp. 455–497). Hoboken, NJ: Wiley.

Allemand, M., Zimprich, D., & Martin, M. (2008). Long-term correlated change in personality traits in old age. *Psychology and Aging, 23*, 545–557.

Allen, J. P., Philliber, S., Herrling, S., & Kuperminc, G. P. (1997). Preventing teen pregnancy and academic failure: Experimental evaluation of a developmentally based approach. *Child Development, 64*, 729–742.

Allen, J. P., Seitz, V., & Apfel, N. H. (2007). The sexually mature teen as a whole person. In J. L. Aber, S. J. Bishop-Josef, S. M. Jones, K. T. McLearn, & D. A. Phillips (Eds.), *New directions in prevention and intervention for teen pregnancy and parenthood* (pp. 185–199). Washington, DC: American Psychological Association.

Allen, M., & Burrell, N. (1996). Comparing the impact of homosexual and heterosexual parents on children: Meta-analysis of existing research. *Journal of Homosexuality, 32*, 19–35.

Allen, P. A., Ruthruff, E., & Lien, M.-C. (2007). Attention. In J. E. Birren (Ed.), *Encyclopedia of gerontology* (2nd ed., pp. 120–129). San Diego: Academic Press.

Allen, S. E. M., & Crago, M. B. (1996). Early passive acquisition in Inuktitut. *Journal of Child Language, 23*, 129–156.

Allen, T. D., & Finkelstein, L. M. (2003). Beyond mentoring: Alternative sources and functions of developmental support. *Career Development Quarterly, 51*, 346–355.

Allison, B. N., & Schultz, J. B. (2004). Parent–adolescent conflict in early adolescence. *Adolescence, 39*, 101–119.

Alloway, T. P. (2009). Working memory, but not IQ, predicts subsequent learning in children with learning difficulties. *European Journal of Psychological Assessment, 25*, 92–98.

Almeida, D. M., & Horn, M. C. (2004). Is daily life more stressful during middle adulthood? In O. G. Brim, C. D. Ryff, & R. C. Kessler (Eds.), *How healthy are we? A national study of well-being at midlife* (pp. 425–451). Chicago: University of Chicago Press.

Almeida, D. M., Neupert, S. D., Banks, S. R., & Serido, J. (2005). Do daily stress processes account for socioeconomic health disparities? *Journal of Gerontology, 60B*, 34–39.

Almeida, J., Johnson, R. M., Corliss, H. L., Molnar, B. E., & Azrael, D. (2009). Emotional distress among LGBT youth: The influence of perceived discrimination based on sexual orientation. *Journal of Youth and Adolescence, 38*, 1001–1014.

Al-Namlah, A. S., Fernyhough, C., & Meins, E. (2006). Sociocultural influences on the development of verbal mediation: Private speech and phonological recoding in Saudi Arabian and British samples. *Developmental Psychology, 42*, 117–131.

Alonso-Fernández, P., & De la Fuente, M. (2011). Role of the immune system in aging and longevity. *Current Aging Science, 4*, 78–100.

Alsaker, F. D. (1995). Timing of puberty and reactions to pubertal changes. In M. Rutter (Ed.), *Psychosocial disturbances in young people* (pp. 37–82). New York: Cambridge University Press.

Alterovitz, S. S. R., & Mendelsohn, G. A. (2013). Relationship goals of middle-aged, young-old, and old-old Internet daters: An analysis of online personal ads. *Journal of Aging Studies, 27*, 159–165.

Althaus, J., & Wax, J. (2005). Analgesia and anesthesia in labor. *Obstetrics and Gynecology Clinics of North America, 32*, 231–244.

Alzheimer's Association. (2012a). *Communication: Best ways to interact with a person with dementia.* Chicago: Author.

Alzheimer's Association. (2012b). 2012 Alzheimer's disease facts and figures. *Alzeimer's and Dementia, 8* (Issue 2).

Amato, P. R. (2000). The consequences of divorce for adults and children. *Journal of Marriage and Family, 62*, 1269–1287.

Amato, P. R. (2001). Children of divorce in the 1990s: An update of the Amato and Keith (1991) meta-analysis. *Journal of Family Psychology, 15*, 355–370.

Amato, P. R. (2006). Marital discord, divorce, and children's well-being: Results from a 20-year longitudinal study of two generations. In A. Clarke-Stewart & J. Dunn (Eds.), *Families count: Effects on child and adolescent development* (pp. 179–202). New York: Cambridge University Press.

Amato, P. R. (2010). Research on divorce: Continuing trends and new developments. *Journal of Marriage and Family, 72*, 650–666.

Amato, P. R., & Booth, A. (1995). Change in gender role attitudes and perceived marital quality. *American Sociological Review, 60*, 58–66.

Amato, P. R., & Cheadle, J. (2005). The long reach of divorce: Divorce and child well-being across three generations. *Journal of Marriage and Family, 67*, 191–206.

Amato, P. R., & Dorius, C. (2010). Father, children, and divorce. In M. E. Lamb (Ed.), *The role of the father in child development* (5th ed., pp. 177–200). Hoboken, NJ: Wiley.

Amato, P. R., & Fowler, F. (2002). Parenting practices, child adjustment, and family diversity. *Journal of Marriage and the Family, 64*, 703–716.

Amato, P. R., & Rogers, S. J. (1997). A longitudinal study of marital problems and subsequent divorce. *Journal of Marriage and the Family, 59*, 612–624.

Amato, P. R., & Sobolewski, J. M. (2004). The effects of divorce on fathers and children: Nonresidential fathers and stepfathers. In M. E. Lamb (Ed.), *The role of the father in child development* (4th ed., pp. 341–367). Hoboken, NJ: Wiley.

Amba, J. C., & Martinez, G. M. (2006). Childlessness among older women in the United States: Trends and profiles. *Journal of Marriage and Family, 68*, 1045–1056.

American Academy of Orthopaedic Surgeons. (2009). *Position statement: Osteoporosis/bone health in adults as a national health priority.* Retrieved from www.aaos.org/about/papers/position/1113.asp

American Academy of Pediatrics. (2001). Committee on Public Education: Children, adolescents, and television. *Pediatrics, 104*, 341–343.

American Academy of Pediatrics. (2005). Breastfeeding and the use of human milk. *Pediatrics, 115*, 496–506.

American Academy of Pediatrics. (2006). Folic acid for the prevention of neural tube defects. *Pediatrics, 104*, 325–327.

American Academy of Pediatrics. (2012). SIDS and other sleep-related infant deaths: Expansion of recommendations for a safe sleep environment *Pediatrics, 128*, e1341.

American Cancer Society. (2012). *Stay healthy.* Retrieved from www.cancer.org/healthy/index

American College of Sports Medicine. (2011). Quantity and quality of exercise for developing and maintaining cardiorespiratory, musculoskeletal, and neuromotor fitness in apparently healthy adults: Guidance for prescribing exercise. *Medicine and Science in Sports and Exercise, 43*, 1334–1359.

American Heart Association. (2012). Heart disease and stroke statistics—2012 update. *Circulation, 125*, e2–e220.

American Hospice Foundation. (2013). *Talking about hospice: Tips for physicians.* Washington, DC: Author.

American Psychiatric Association. (2013). *Diagnostic and statistical manual of mental disorders* (5th ed.). Washington, DC: Author.

American Psychological Association. (2002). Ethical principles of psychologists and code of conduct. *American Psychologist, 57*, 1060–1073.

Amsel, E., & Brock, S. (1996). The development of evidence evaluation skills. *Cognitive Development, 11*, 523–550.

Amsterlaw, J., & Wellman, H. M. (2006). Theories of mind in transition: A micro-genetic study of the development of false belief understanding. *Journal of Cognition and Development, 7*, 139–172.

An, J. S., & Cooney, T. M. (2006). Psychological well-being in mid to late life: The role of generativity development and parent–child relationships across the lifespan. *International Journal of Behavioral Development, 30*, 410–421.

Anand, S. S., Yusuf, S., Jacobs, R., Davis, A. D., Yi, Q., & Gerstein, H. (2001). Risk factors, atherosclerosis, and cardiovascular disease among Aboriginal people in Canada: The study of health assessment and risk evaluation in Aboriginal peoples (SHARE-AP). *Lancet, 358*, 1147–1153.

Andel, R., Hyer, K., & Slack, A. (2007). Risk factors for nursing home placement in older adults with and without dementia. *Journal of Aging and Health, 19*, 213–228.

Anderson, C. A., Sakamoto, A., Gentile, D. A., Ihori, N., Shibuya, A., Yukawa, S., et al. (2008). Longitudinal effects of violent video games on aggression in Japan and the United States. *Pediatrics, 122*, e1067–e1072.

Anderson, D. M., Huston, A. C., Schmitt, K. L., Linebarger, D. L., & Wright, J. C. (2001). Early childhood television viewing and adolescent behavior. *Monographs of the Society for Research in Child Development, 66*(1, Serial No. 264).

Anderson, E. (2000). Exploring register knowledge: The value of "controlled improvisation." In L. Menn & N. B. Ratner (Eds.), *Methods for studying language production* (pp. 225–248). Mahwah, NJ: Erlbaum.

Anderson, J. L., Morgan, J. L., & White, K. S. (2003). A statistical basis for speech sound discrimination. *Language and Speech, 46*, 155–182.

Anderson, P. B., & Savage, J. S. (2005). Social, legal, and institutional context of heterosexual aggression by college women. *Trauma, Violence, and Abuse, 6*, 130–140.

Andreoletti, C., & Lachman, M. E. (2004). Susceptibility and resilience to memory aging stereotypes: Education matters more than age. *Experimental Aging Research, 30*, 129–148.

Andrews, G., & Halford, G. S. (1998). Children's ability to make transitive inferences: The importance of premise integration and structural complexity. *Cognitive Development, 13,* 479–513.

Andrews, G., & Halford, G. S. (2002). A cognitive complexity metric applied to cognitive development. *Cognitive Psychology, 45,* 475–506.

Aneshensel, C. S., Wight, R. G., Miller-Martinez, D., Botticello, A. L., Karlamangla, A. S., & Seeman, T. E. (2007). Urban neighborhoods and depressive symptoms among older adults. *Journal of Gerontology, 62B,* S52–S59.

Anetzberger, G. J. (2005). The reality of elder abuse. *Clinical Gerontologist, 28,* 2–25.

Anisfeld, M., Turkewitz, G., Rose, S. A., Rosenberg, F. R., Shelber, F. J., Couturier-Fagan, D. A., Ger, J. S., & Sommer, I. (2001). No compelling evidence that newborns imitate oral gestures. *Infancy, 2,* 111–122.

Annett, M. (2002). *Handedness and brain asymmetry: The right shift theory.* Hove, UK: Psychology Press.

Antonini, F. M., Magnolfi, S. U., Petruzzi, E., Pinzani, P., Malentacchi, F., Petruzzi, I., & Masotti, G. (2008). Physical performance and creative activities of centenarians. *Archives of Gerontology and Geriatrics, 46,* 253–261.

Antonucci, T. C., Ajrouch, K. J., & Birditt, K. (2008). Social relations in the Third Age: Assessing strengths and challenges using the convoy model. In J. B. James & P. Wink (Eds.), *Annual review of gerontology and geriatrics* (Vol. 26, pp. 193–209). New York: Springer.

Antonucci, T. C., & Akiyama, H. (1995). Convoys of social relations: Family and friendships within a life span context. In R. Blieszner & V. H. Bedford (Eds.), *Handbook of aging and the family* (pp. 355–371). Westport, CT: Greenwood Press.

Antonucci, T. C., Akiyama, H., & Merline, A. (2002). Dynamics of social relationships in midlife. In M. E. Lachman (Ed.), *Handbook of midlife development* (pp. 571–598). New York: Wiley.

Antonucci, T. C., Akiyama, H., & Takahashi, K. (2004). Attachment and close relationships across the lifespan. *Attachment and Human Development, 6,* 353–370.

Antonucci, T. C., Birditt, K. S., & Ajrouch, K. (2011). Convoys of social relations: Past, present, and future. In K. L. Fingerman, C. A. Berg, J. Smith, & T. C. Antonucci (Eds.), *Handbook of life-span development* (pp. 161–182). New York: Springer.

Antonucci, T. C., Birditt, K. S., & Akiyama, H. (2009). Convoys of social relations: An interdisciplinary approach. In V. Bengston, M. Silverstein, N. Putney, & D. Gans (Eds.), *Handbook of theories of aging* (pp. 247–260). New York: Springer.

Antonucci, T. C., Blieszner, R., & Denmark, F. L. (2010). Psychological perspectives on older women. In H. Landrine & N. F. Russo (Eds.), *Handbook of diversity in feminist psychology* (pp. 233–257). New York: Springer.

Anzuini, F., Battistella, A., & Izzotti, A. (2011). Physical activity and cancer prevention: A review of current evidence and biological mechanisms. *Journal of Preventive Medicine and Hygiene, 52,* 174–180.

Apgar, V. (1953). A proposal for a new method of evaluation in the newborn infant. *Current Research in Anesthesia and Analgesia, 32,* 260–267.

Aquilino, W. S. (2006). Family relationships and support systems in emerging adulthood. In J. J. Arnett & J. L. Tanner (Eds.), *Emerging adults in America: Coming of age in the 21st century* (pp. 193–218). Washington, DC: American Psychological Association.

Archer, J. (2002). Sex differences in aggression between heterosexual partners: A meta-analytic review. *Psychological Bulletin, 126,* 651–681.

Archibald, A. B., Graber, J. A., & Brooks-Gunn, J. (2006). Pubertal processes and physiological growth in adolescence. In G. R. Adams & M. D. Berzonsky (Eds.), *Blackwell handbook of adolescence* (pp. 24–48). Malden, MA: Blackwell.

Arcus, D., & Chambers, P. (2008). Childhood risks associated with adoption. In T. P. Gullotta & G. M Blau (Eds.), *Family influences on childhood behavior and development* (pp. 117–142). New York: Routledge.

Ardelt, M. (1998). Social crisis and individual growth: The long-term effects of the Great Depression. *Journal of Aging Studies, 12,* 291–314.

Ardelt, M. (2003). Effects of religion and purpose in life on elders' subjective well-being and attitudes toward death. *Journal of Religious Gerontology, 14,* 55–77.

Ardelt, M. (2011). Wisdom, age, and well-being. In K. W. Schaie & S. L. Willis (Eds.), *Handbook of the psychology of aging* (7th ed., pp. 279–291). San Diego, CA: Academic Press.

Arking, R. (2006). *Biology of aging: Observations and principles* (3rd ed.). New York: Oxford University Press.

Armstrong, T. D., & Crowther, M. R. (2002). Spirituality among older African Americans. *Journal of Adult Development, 9,* 3–12.

Arnett, J. J. (2000). Emerging adulthood: A theory of development from the late teens through the twenties. *American Psychologist, 55,* 469–480.

Arnett, J. J. (2001). Conceptions of the transition to adulthood: Perspectives from adolescence to midlife. *Journal of Adult Development, 8,* 133–143.

Arnett, J. J. (2003). Conceptions of the transition to adulthood among emerging adults in American ethnic groups. In J. J. Arnett & N. L. Galambos (Eds.), *New directions for child and adolescent development* (No. 100, pp. 63–75). San Francisco: Jossey-Bass.

Arnett, J. J. (2006). Emerging adulthood: Understanding the new way of coming of age. In J. J. Arnett & J. L. Tanner (Eds.), *Emerging adults in America: Coming of age in the 21st century* (pp. 3–19). Washington, DC: American Psychological Association.

Arnett, J. J. (2007a). Emerging adulthood, a 21st century theory: A rejoinder to Hendry and Kloep. *Child Development Perspectives, 1,* 80–82.

Arnett, J. J. (2007b). Emerging adulthood: What is it and what is it good for? *Child Development Perspectives, 1,* 68–73.

Arnett, J. J. (2010). Oh, grow up! Generational grumbling and the new life stage of emerging adulthood—commentary on Trzesniewski & Donnellan (2010). *Perspectives on Psychological Science, 5,* 89–92.

Arnett, J. J. (2011). Emerging adulthood(s): The cultural psychology of a new life stage. In L. A. Jensen (Ed.), *Bridging cultural and developmental psychology: New syntheses in theory, research, and policy* (pp. 255–275). New York: Oxford University Press.

Arnett, J. J. (2012). *New Clark Poll: 18- to 29-year-olds are traditional about roles in sex, marriage and raising children.* Retrieved from http://news .clarku.edu/news/2012/08/07/new-clark-poll-18-to-29-year-olds-are-traditional-about-roles-in-sex-marriage-and-raising-children

Arnon, S., Shapsa, A., Forman, L., Regev, R., Bauer, S., & Litmanovitz, I. (2006). Live music is beneficial to preterm infants in the neonatal intensive care unit. *Birth, 33,* 131–136.

Artman, L., & Cahan, S. (1993). Schooling and the development of transitive inference. *Developmental Psychology, 29,* 753–759.

Artman, L., Cahan, S., & Avni-Babad, D. (2006). Age, schooling, and conditional reasoning. *Cognitive Development, 21,* 131–145.

Asher, S. R., & Rose, A. J. (1997). Promoting children's social-emotional adjustment with peers. In P. Salovey & D. J. Sluyter (Eds.), *Emotional development and emotional intelligence* (pp. 193–195). New York: Basic Books.

Aslin, R. N., Jusczyk, P. W., & Pisoni, D. B. (1998). Speech and auditory processing during infancy: Constraints on and precursors to language. In D. Kuhn & R. S. Siegler (Eds.), *Handbook of child psychology: Vol. 2. Cognition, perception, and language* (5th ed., pp. 147–198). New York: Wiley.

Aslin, R. N., & Newport, E. L. (2009). What statistical learning can and can't tell us about language acquisition. In J. Colombo, P. McCardle, & L. Freund (Eds.), *Infant pathways to language: Methods, models, and research directions* (pp. 15–29). New York: Psychology Press.

Astington, J. W., Pelletier, J., & Homer, B. (2002). Theory of mind and epistemological development: The relation between children's second-order false belief understanding and their ability to reason about evidence. *New Ideas in Psychology, 20,* 131–144.

Atchley, R. C. (1989). A continuity theory of normal aging. *Gerontologist, 29,* 183–190.

Atchley, R. C. (1999). *Continuity and adaptation in aging: Creating positive experiences.* Baltimore, MD: Johns Hopkins University Press.

Atchley, R. C. (2003). Why people cope well with retirement. In J. L. Ronch & J. A. Goldfield (Eds.), *Mental wellness in aging: Strengths-based approaches* (pp. 123–138). Baltimore, MD: Health Professions Press.

Atkins, R., Hart, D., & Donnelly, T. M. (2004). Moral identity development and school attachment. In D. Lapsley & D. Narvaez (Eds.), *Moral development, self, and identity* (pp. 65–82). Mahwah, NJ: Erlbaum.

Au, T. K., Sidle, A. L., & Rollins, K. B. (1993). Developing an intuitive understanding of conservation and contamination: Invisible particles as a plausible mechanism. *Developmental Psychology, 29,* 286–299.

Aunola, K., Stattin, H., & Nurmi, J.-E. (2000). Parenting styles and adolescents' achievement strategies. *Journal of Adolescence, 23,* 205–222.

Averhart, C. J., & Bigler, R. S. (1997). Shades of meaning: Skin tone, racial attitudes, and constructive memory in African-American children. *Journal of Experimental Child Psychology, 67,* 368–388.

Aveyard, P., & Raw, M. (2012). Improving smoking cessation approaches at the individual level. *Tobacco Control, 21,* 252–257.

Avis, N. E., Crawford, S., & Johannes, C. B. (2002). Menopause. In G. M. Wingood & R. J. DiClemente (Eds.), *Handbook of women's sexual and reproductive health* (pp. 367–391). New York: Kluwer.

Avolio, B. J., & Sosik, J. J. (1999). A lifespan framework for assessing the impact of work on white-collar workers. In S. L. Willis & J. D. Reid (Eds.), *Life in the middle* (pp. 249–274). San Diego, CA: Academic Press.

Axelin, A., Salanterä, S., & Lehtonen, L. (2006). 'Facilitated tucking by parents' in pain management of preterm infants—a randomized crossover trial. *Early Human Development, 82,* 241–247.

Axia, G., & Baroni, R. (1985). Linguistic politeness at different age levels. *Child Development, 56,* 918–927.

Ayala, G. X., Rogers, M., Arredondo, E. M., Campbell, N. R., Baquero, B., Duerksen, S. C., & Elder, J. P. (2008). Away-from-home food intake and risk for obesity: Examining the influence of context. *Obesity, 16,* 1002–1008.

B

Bacallao, M. L., & Smokowski, P. R. (2007). The costs of getting ahead: Mexican family system changes after immigration. *Family Relations, 56,* 52–66.

Bagwell, C. L., & Coie, J. D. (2004). The best friendships of aggressive boys: Relationship quality, conflict management, and rule-breaking behavior. *Journal of Experimental Child Psychology, 88,* 5–24.

Bahrick, L. E. (2010). Intermodal perception and selective attention to intersensory redundancy: Implications for typical social development and autism. In G. Bremner & T. D. Wachs (Eds.), *Wiley-Blackwell handbook of infant development: Vol. 1. Basic research* (2nd ed., pp. 120–166). Malden, MA: Blackwell.

Bahrick, L. E., Gogate, L. J., & Ruiz, I. (2002). Attention and memory for faces and actions in infancy: The salience of actions over faces in dynamic events. *Child Development, 73,* 1629–1643.

Bahrick, L. E., Hernandez-Reif, M., & Flom, R. (2005). The development of infant learning about specific face–voice relations. *Developmental Psychology, 41,* 541–552.

Bahrick, L. E., Hernandez-Reif, M., & Pickens, J. N. (1997). The effect of retrieval cues on visual preferences and memory in infancy: Evidence for a four-phase attention function. *Journal of Experimental Child Psychology, 67,* 1–20.

Bahrick, L. E., Lickliter, R., & Flom, R. (2004). Intersensory redundancy guides the development of selective attention, perception, and cognition in infancy. *Current Directions in Psychological Science, 13,* 99–102.

Bahrick, L. E., Netto, D., & Hernandez-Reif, M. (1998). Intermodal perception of adult and child faces and voices by infants. *Child Development, 69,* 1263–1275.

Bailey, J. M., Bobrow, D., Wolfe, M., & Mikach, S. (1995). Sexual orientation of adult sons of gay fathers. *Developmental Psychology, 31,* 124–129.

Baillargeon, R. (2004). Infants' reasoning about hidden objects: Evidence for event-general and event-specific expectations. *Developmental Science, 7,* 391–424.

Baillargeon, R., & DeVos, J. (1991). Object permanence in young infants: Further evidence. *Child Development, 62,* 1227–1246.

Baillargeon, R., Scott, R. M., & He, Z. (2010). False-belief understanding in infants. *Trends in Cognitive Sciences, 14,* 110–118.

Baillargeon, R. H., Zoccolillo, M., Keenan, K., Côté, S., Pérusse, D., Wu, H.-X., & Boivin, M. (2007). Gender differences in physical aggression: A prospective population-based survey of children before and after 2 years of age. *Developmental Psychology, 43,* 13–26.

Bair, D. (2007). *Calling it quits: Late-life divorce and starting over.* New York: Random House.

Baird, B. M., & Bergeman, C. S. (2011). Life-span developmental behavior genetics. In K. L. Fingerman, C. A. Berg, J. Smith, & T. C. Antonucci (Eds.), *Handbook of life-span development* (pp. 701–744). New York: Springer.

Balasch, J. (2010). Ageing and infertility: An overview. *Gynecological Endocrinology, 26,* 855–860.

Bale, J. F. (2009). Fetal infections and brain development. *Clinical Perinatology, 36,* 639–653.

Balis, T., & Postolache, T. T. (2008). Ethnic differences in adolescent suicide in the United States. *International Journal of Child Health and Human Development, 1,* 282–296.

Ball, K., Berch, D. B., Helmers, K. F., Jobe, J. B., Leveck, M. D., & Marsiske, M. (2002). Effects of cognitive training interventions with older adults: A randomized controlled trial. *Journal of the American Medical Association, 288,* 2271–2281.

Ball, M. M., Perkins, M. M., Hollingsworth, C., Whittington, F. J., & King, S. V. (2004). Pathways to assisted living: The influence of race and class. *Journal of Applied Gerontology, 28,* 81–108.

Balsam, K. F., Beauchaine, T. P., Rothblum, E. D., & Solomon, S. E. (2008). Three-year follow-up of same-sex couples who had civil unions in Vermont, same-sex couples not in civil unions, and heterosexual married couples. *Developmental Psychology, 44,* 102–116.

Baltes, M. M. (1995, February). Dependency in old age: Gains and losses. *Psychological Science, 4*(1), 14–19.

Baltes, M. M. (1996). *The many faces of dependency in old age.* New York: Cambridge University Press.

Baltes, P. B., & Freund, A. M. (2003). Human strengths as the orchestration of wisdom and selective optimization with compensation (SOC). In L. G. Aspinwall & U. M. Staudinger (Eds.), *A psychology of human strengths: Fundamental questions and future directions for a positive psychology* (pp. 23–25). Washington, DC: American Psychological Association.

Baltes, P. B., Lindenberger, U., & Staudinger, U. M. (2006). Life span theory in developmental psychology. In R. M. Lerner (Ed.), *Handbook of child psychology: Vol. 1. Theoretical models of human development* (6th ed., pp. 569–664). Hoboken, NJ: Wiley.

Baltes, P. B., & Smith, J. (2003). New frontiers in the future of aging: From successful aging of the young old to the dilemmas of the fourth age. *Gerontology, 49,* 123–135.

Baltes, P. B., & Smith, J. (2008). The fascination of wisdom. *Perspectives on Psychological Science, 3,* 56–64.

Baltes, P. B., & Staudinger, U. M. (2000). Wisdom: A metaheuristic (pragmatic) to orchestrate mind and virtue toward excellence. *American Psychologist, 55,* 122–136.

Bancroft, J. (2002). The medicalization of female sexual dysfunction: The need for caution. *Archives of Sexual Behavior, 31,* 451–455.

Bandstra, E. S., Morrow, C. E., Accornero, V. H., Mansoor, E., Xue, L., & Anthony, J. C. (2011). Estimated effects of in utero cocaine exposure on language development through early adolescence. *Neurotoxicology and Teratology, 33,* 25–35.

Bandstra, E. S., Morrow, C. E., Mansoor, E., & Accornero, V. H. (2010). Prenatal drug exposure: Infant and toddler outcomes. *Journal of Addictive Diseases, 29,* 245–258.

Bandura, A. (1977). *Social learning theory.* Englewood Cliffs, NJ: Prentice-Hall.

Bandura, A. (1992). Perceived self-efficacy in cognitive development and functioning. *Educational Psychologist, 28,* 117–148.

Bandura, A. (1999). Social cognitive theory of personality. In L. A. Pervin (Ed.), *Handbook of personality: Theory and research* (2nd ed., pp. 154–196). New York: Guilford.

Bandura, A. (2001). Social cognitive theory: An agentic perspective. *Annual Review of Psychology, 52,* 1–26.

Banich, M. T., & Heller, W. (1998). Evolving perspectives on lateralization of function. *Current Directions in Psychological Science, 7,* 1–2.

Banks, M. S. (1980). The development of visual accommodation during early infancy. *Child Development, 51,* 646–666.

Banse, R., Gawronski, B., Rebetez, C., Gutt, H., & Morton, J. B. (2010). The development of spontaneous gender stereotyping in childhood: Relations to stereotype knowledge and stereotype flexibility. *Developmental Science, 13,* 298–306.

Barber, B. K., & Olsen, J. A. (1997). Socialization in context: Connection, regulation, and autonomy in the family, school, and neighborhood, and with peers. *Journal of Adolescent Research, 12,* 287–315.

Barber, B. K., & Olsen, J. A. (2004). Assessing the transitions to middle and high school. *Journal of Adolescent Research, 19,* 3–30.

Barber, B. K., Stolz, H. E., & Olsen, J. A. (2005). Parental support, psychological control, and behavioral control: Assessing relevance across time, culture, and method. *Monographs of the Society for Research in Child Development, 70*(4, Serial No. 282).

Barber, B. L., Stone, M. R., Hunt, J. E., & Eccles, J. S. (2005). Benefits of activity participation: The roles of identity affirmation and peer group norm sharing. In J. L. Mahoney, R. W. Larson, & J. S. Eccles (Eds.), *Organized activities as contexts of development: Extracurricular activities, after-school and community programs* (pp. 185–210). Mahwah, NJ: Erlbaum.

Bard, K. A., Todd, B. K., Bernier, C., Love, J., & Leavens, D. A. (2006). Self-awareness in human and chimpanzee infants: What is measured and what is meant by the mark and mirror test? *Infancy, 9,* 191–219.

Barelds, D. P. H., & Dijkstra, P. (2011). Positive illusions about a partner's personality and relationship quality. *Journal of Research in Personality, 45,* 37–43.

Barenbaum, J., Ruchkin, V., & Schwab-Stone, M. (2004). The psychosocial aspects of children exposed to war: Practice and policy initiatives. *Journal of Child Psychology and Psychiatry, 45,* 41–62.

Bar-Haim, Y., Ziv, T., Lamy, D., & Hodes, R. M. (2006). Nature and nurture in own-race face processing. *Psychological Science, 17,* 159–163.

Barker, D. J. (2008). Human growth and cardiovascular disease. *Nestlé Nutrition Workshop Series, 61,* 21–38.

Barkley, R. A. (2002). Psychosocial treatments of attention-deficit/hyperactivity disorder in children. *Journal of Clinical Psychology, 63*(Suppl. 12), 36–43.

Barkley, R. A. (2003a). Attention-deficit/hyperactivity disorder. In E. J. Mash & R. A. Barkley (Eds.), *Child psychopathology* (2nd ed., pp. 75–143). New York: Guilford Press.

Barkley, R. A. (2003b). Issues in the diagnosis of attention-deficit hyperactivity disorder in children. *Brain and Development, 25,* 77–83.

Barkley, R. A. (2006). Attention-deficit/hyperactivity disorder. In R. A. Barkley, D. A. Wolfe, & E. J. Mash (Eds.), *Behavioral and emotional disorders in adolescents: Nature, assessment, and treatment* (pp. 91–152). New York: Guilford.

Barnes, G. M., Hoffman, J. H., Welte, J. W., Farrell, M. P., & Dintcheff, B. A. (2006). Effects of parental monitoring and peer deviance on substance use and delinquency. *Journal of Marriage and Family, 68,* 1084–1104.

Barnes, J., Katz, I., Korbin, J. E., & O'Brien, M. (2007). *Children and families in communities: Theory, research, policy and practice.* Hoboken, NJ: Wiley.

Barnes-Farrell, J., & Matthews, R. A. (2007). Age and work attitudes. In K. S. Shultz & G. A. Adams (Eds.), *Aging and work in the 21st century* (pp. 139–162). Mahwah, NJ: Erlbaum.

Barnett, D., & Vondra, J. I. (1999). Atypical patterns of early attachment: Theory, research, and current directions. In J. I Vondra & D. Barnett (Eds.), *Atypical attachment in infancy and early childhood among children at developmental risk. Monographs of the Society for Research in Child Development, 64*(3, Serial No. 258), 1–24.

Barnett, W. S. (2011). Effectiveness of early educational intervention. *Science, 333,* 975–978.

Baron, I. S., & Rey-Casserly, C. (2010). Extremely preterm birth outcome: A review of four decades of cognitive research. *Neuropsychology Review, 20,* 430–452.

Baron-Cohen, S., & Belmonte, M. K. (2005). Autism: A window onto the development of the social and the analytic brain. *Annual Review of Neuroscience, 28,* 109–126.

Barr, H. M., Bookstein, F. L., O'Malley, K. D., Connor, P. D., Huggins, J. E., & Streissguth, A. P. (2006). Binge drinking during pregnancy as a predictor of psychiatric disorders on the structured clinical interview for DSM-IV in young adult offspring. *American Journal of Psychiatry, 163,* 1061–1065.

Barr, H. M., Streissguth, A. P., Darby, B. L., & Sampson, P. D. (1990). Prenatal exposure to alcohol, caffeine, tobacco, and aspirin: Effects on fine and gross motor performance in 4-year-old children. *Developmental Psychology, 26,* 339–348.

Barr, R., Marrott, H., & Rovee-Collier, C. (2003). The role of sensory preconditioning in memory retrieval by preverbal infants. *Learning and Behavior, 31,* 111–123.

Barr, R., Muentener, P., & Garcia, A. (2007). Age-related changes in deferred imitation from television by 6- to 18-month-olds. *Developmental Science, 10,* 910–921.

Barr, R. G. (2001). "Colic" is something infants do, rather than a condition they "have": A developmental approach to crying phenomena patterns, pacification and (patho)genesis. In R. G. Barr, I. St. James-Roberts, & M. R. Keefe (Eds.), *New evidence on unexplained infant crying* (pp. 87–104). St. Louis: Johnson & Johnson Pediatric Institute.

Barr, R. G., Paterson, J. A., MacMartin, L. M., & Lehtonen, L. (2005). Prolonged and unsoothable crying bouts in infants with and without colic. *Journal of Developmental and Behavioral Pediatrics, 26,* 14–23.

Barreto, M., Ryan, M. K., & Schmitt, M. T. (2009). *The glass ceiling in the 21st century: Understanding barriers to gender equality.* Washington, DC: American Psychological Association.

Barrett, K. C. (2005). The origins of social emotions and self-regulation in toddlerhood: New evidence. *Cognition and Emotion, 19,* 953–979.

Barrett, T. M., Traupman, E., & Needham, A. (2008). Infants' visual anticipation in grasp planning. *Infant Behavior and Development, 31,* 1–9.

Barros, R. M., Silver, E. J., & Stein, R. E. K. (2009). School recess and group classroom behavior. *Pediatrics, 123,* 431–436.

Barry, C. M., & Madsen, S. D. (2010). Friends and friendships in emerging adulthood. In T. Clydesdale (Ed.), *Who are emerging adults?* Washington, DC: Changing Spirituality of Emerging Adults Project. Retrieved from changingsea.org/barry.htm

Barry, C. M., & Nelson, L. J. (2008). The role of religious beliefs and practices in emerging adults' perceived competencies, perceived importance ratings, and global self-worth. *International Journal of Behavioral Development, 32,* 509–521.

Barry, C. M., Nelson, L., Davarya, S., & Urry, S. (2010). Religiosity and spirituality during the transition to adulthood. *International Journal of Behavioral Development, 34,* 311–324.

Bartlik, B., & Goldstein, M. Z. (2001). Men's sexual health after midlife. *Practical Geriatrics, 52,* 291–306.

Bartocci, M., Berggvist, L. L., Lagercrantz, H., & Anand, K. J. (2006). Pain activates cortical areas in the preterm newborn brain. *Pain, 122,* 109–117.

Bartrip, J., Morton, J., & de Schonen, S. (2001). Responses to mother's face in 3-week- to 5-monthold infants. *British Journal of Developmental Psychology, 19,* 219–232.

Bartsch, K., & Wellman, H. (1995). *Children talk about the mind.* New York: Oxford University Press.

Basak, C., & Verhaeghen, P. (2011). Aging and switching the focus of attention in working memory: Age differences in item availability but not in item accessibility. *Journal of Gerontology, 66B,* 519–526.

Basow, S. A., & Rubin, L. R. (1999). Gender influences on adolescent development. In N. G. Johnson & M. C. Roberts (Eds.), *Beyond appearance: A new look at adolescent girls* (pp. 25–52). Washington, DC: American Psychological Association.

Bass, S. (2011). From retirement to "productive aging" and back to work again. In D. C. Carr & K. Komp (Eds.), *Gerontology in the era of the Third Age: Implications and next steps* (pp. 169–188). New York: Springer.

Bassuk, S. S., & Manson, J. E. (2005). Epidemiological evidence for the role of physical activity in reducing risk of type 2 diabetes and cardiovascular disease. *Journal of Applied Physiology, 99,* 1193–1204.

Bates, E. (2004). Explaining and interpreting deficits in language development across clinical groups: Where do we go from here? *Brain and Language, 88,* 248–253.

Bates, J. E., Wachs, T. D., & Emde, R. N. (1994). Toward practical uses for biological concepts. In J. E. Bates & T. D. Wachs (Eds.), *Temperament: Individual differences at the interface of biology and behavior*

(pp. 275–306). Washington, DC: American Psychological Association.

Bauer, C. R., Langer, J. C., Shakaran, S., Bada, H. S., & Lester, B. (2005). Acute neonatal effects of cocaine exposure during pregnancy. *Archives of Pediatrics and Adolescent Medicine, 159,* 824–834.

Bauer, P. J. (2002). Early memory development. In U. Goswami (Ed.), *Blackwell handbook of child cognitive development* (pp. 127–150). Malden, MA: Blackwell.

Bauer, P. J. (2006). Event memory. In D. Kuhn & R. Siegler (Eds.), *Handbook of child psychology: Vol. 2. Cognition, perception, and language* (6th ed., pp. 373–425). Hoboken, NJ: Wiley.

Bauer, P. J. (2007). Recall in infancy: A neuro-developmental account. *Current Directions in Psychological Science, 16,* 142–146.

Baum, N., Rahav, G., & Sharon, D. (2005). Changes in the self-concepts of divorced women. *Journal of Divorce and Remarriage, 43,* 47–67.

Baumeister, R. F. (1998). Inducing guilt. In J. Bybee (Ed.), *Guilt and children* (pp. 185–213). San Diego: Academic Press.

Baumeister, R. F., Campbell, J. D., Krueger, J. I., & Vohs, K. D. (2003). Does high self-esteem cause better performance, interpersonal success, happiness, or healthier lifestyles? *Psychological Science in the Public Interest, 4*(1), 1–44.

Baumgartner, M. S., & Schneider, D. E. (2010). Perceptions of women in management: A thematic analysis of razing the glass ceiling. *Journal of Career Development, 37,* 559–576.

Baumrind, D. (1971). Current patterns of parental authority. *Developmental Psychology Monograph, 4*(No. 1, Pt. 2).

Baumrind, D., Lazelere, R. E., & Owens, E. B. (2010). Effects of preschool parents' power assertive patterns and practices on adolescent development. *Parenting, 10,* 157–201.

Bauserman, R. (2002). Child adjustment in joint-custody versus sole-custody arrangements: A meta-analytic review. *Journal of Family Psychology, 16,* 91–102.

Baydar, N., Greek, A., & Brooks-Gunn, J. (1997). A longitudinal study of the effects of the birth of a sibling during the first 6 years of life. *Journal of Marriage and the Family, 59,* 939–956.

Bayer, A., & Tadd, W. (2000). Unjustified exclusion of elderly people from studies submitted to research ethics committee for approval: Descriptive study. *British Medical Journal, 321,* 992–993.

Bayley, N. (1969). *Bayley Scales of Infant Development.* New York: Psychological Corporation.

Bayley, N. (1993). *Bayley Scales of Infant Development* (2nd ed.). San Antonio, TX: Psychological Corporation.

Bayley, N. (2005). *Bayley Scales of Infant and Toddler Development, Third Edition* (Bayley-III). San Antonio, TX: Harcourt Assessment.

Bean, R. A., Barber, B. K., & Crane, D. R. (2007). Parental support, behavioral control, and psychological control among African American youth: The relationships to academic grades, delinquency, and depression. *Journal of Family Issues, 27,* 1335–1355.

Bearman, P. S., & Moody, J. (2004). Suicide and friendships among American adolescents. *American Journal of Public Health, 94,* 89–95.

Beautrais, A. L. (2003). Life course factors associated with suicidal behaviors in young people. *American Behavioral Scientist, 46,* 1137–1156.

Becker, G., Beyene, Y., Newsome, E., & Mayen, N. (2003). Creating continuity through mutual assistance: Intergenerational reciprocity in four ethnic groups. *Journal of Gerontology, 38B,* S151–S159.

Becker, K., El-Faddagh, M., Schmidt, M. H., Esser, G., & Laucht, M. (2008). Interaction of dopamine transporter genotype with prenatal smoke exposure

on ADHD symptoms. *Journal of Pediatrics, 152,* 263–269.

Beckerman, M. B. (1990). Leos Janácek and "the late style" in music. *Gerontologist, 30,* 632–635.

Beckett, C., Maughan, B., Rutter, M., Castle, J., Colvert, E., & Groothues, C. (2006). Do the effects of early severe deprivation on cognition persist into early adolescence? Findings from the English and Romanian adoptees study. *Child Development, 77,* 696–711.

Bedford, O. A. (2004). The individual experience of guilt and shame in Chinese culture. *Culture and Psychology, 10,* 29–52.

Behnke, M., Smith, V., C., Committee on Substance Abuse, and Committee on Fetus and Newborn. (2013). Prenatal substance abuse: Short-and long-term effects on the exposed fetus. *American Academy of Pediatrics, 131,* e1009–e1024.

Behrens, K. Y., Hesse, E., & Main, M. (2007). Mothers' attachment status as determined by the Adult Attachment Interview predicts their 6-year-olds' reunion responses: A study conducted in Japan. *Developmental Psychology, 43*(6), 1553–1567.

Beier, M. E., & Ackerman, P. L. (2005). Age, ability, and the role of prior knowledge on the acquisition of new domain knowledge: Promising results in a real-world learning environment. *Psychology and Aging, 20,* 341–355.

Bekkouche, N. S., Holmes, S., Whittaker, K. S., & Krantz, D. S. (2011). Stress and the heart: Psychosocial stress and coronary heart disease. In R. J. Contrada & A. Baum (Eds.), *Handbook of stress science: Biology, psychology, and health* (pp. 385–398). New York: Springer.

Belcher, D., Lee, A., Solmon, M., & Harrison, L. (2003). The influence of gender-related beliefs and conceptions of ability on women learning the hockey wrist shot. *Research Quarterly for Exercise and Sport, 74,* 183–192.

Bell, J. H., & Bromnick, R. D. (2003). The social reality of the imaginary audience: A grounded theory approach. *Adolescence, 38,* 205–219.

Bell, M. L. (1995). Attitudes toward menopause among Mexican American women. *Health Care for Women International, 16,* 425–435.

Belle, S. H., Burgio, L., Burns, R., Coon, D., Czaja, S. J., Gallagher-Thompson, D., & Gitlin, L. N. (2006). Enhancing quality of life of dementia caregivers from different ethnic or racial groups: A randomized, controlled trial. *Annals of Internal Medicine, 145,* 727–738.

Bell-Scriber, M. J. (2008). Warming the nursing education climate for traditional-age nurses who are male. *Nursing Education Perspectives, 29,* 143–150.

Belsky, J. (2006). Early child care and early child development: Major findings of the NICHD Study of Early Child Care. *European Journal of Developmental Psychology, 3,* 95–110.

Belsky, J., & Fearon, R. M. P. (2002a). Early attachment security, subsequent maternal sensitivity, and later child development: Does continuity in development depend on caregiving? *Attachment and Human Development, 4,* 361–387.

Belsky, J., & Fearon, R. M. P. (2008). Precursors of attachment security. In J. Cassidy & P. R. Shaver (Eds.), *Handbook of attachment: Theory, research, and clinical applications* (2nd ed., pp. 295–316). New York: Guilford.

Belsky, J., Steinberg, L. D., Houts, R. M., Friedman, S. L., DeHart, G., Cauffman, E., Roisman, G. I., & Halpern-Felsher, B. (2007a). Family rearing antecedents of pubertal timing. *Child Development, 78,* 1302–1321.

Belsky, J., Steinberg, L., Houts, R. M., & Halpern-Felsher, B. L. (2010). The development of reproductive strategy in females: Early maternal harshness → earlier menarche → increased sexual risk taking. *Developmental Psychology, 46,* 120–128.

Belsky, J., Vandell, D. L., Burchinal, M., Clarke-Stewart, K. A., McCartney, K., & Owen, M. T. (2007b). Are there long-term effects of early child care? *Child Development, 78,* 681–701.

Bender, H. L., Allen, J. P., McElhaney, K. B., Antonishak, J., Moore, C. M., Kelly, H. L., & Davis, S. M. (2007). Use of harsh physical discipline and developmental outcomes in adolescence. *Development and Psychopathology, 19,* 227–242.

Benenson, J. F., & Christakos, A. (2003). The greater fragility of females' versus males' closest same-sex friendships. *Child Development, 74,* 1123–1129.

Bengtsson, H. (2005). Children's cognitive appraisal of others' distressful and positive experiences. *International Journal of Behavioral Development, 29,* 457–466.

Benner, A. D., & Graham, S. (2009). The transition to high school as a developmental process among multiethnic urban youth. *Child Development, 80,* 356–376.

Bennett, D. A., Schneider, J. A., Tang, Y., Arnold, S. E., & Wilson, R. S. (2006). The effect of social networks on the relation between Alzheimer's disease pathology and level of cognitive function in old people: A longitudinal cohort study. *Lancet Neurology, 5,* 406–412.

Bennett, K. M. (2007). "No sissy stuff": Toward a theory of masculinity and emotional expression in older widowed men. *Journal of Aging Studies, 21,* 347–356.

Bennett, K. M., Smith, P. T., & Hughes, G. M. (2005). Coping, depressive feelings and gender differences in late life widowhood. *Aging and Mental Health, 9,* 348–353.

Bennett, K. M., & Soulsby, L. K. (2012). Well-being in bereavement and widowhood. *Illness, Crisis & Loss, 20,* 321–337.

Bennett, M., Barrett, M., Karakozov, R., Kipiani, G., Lyons, E., Pavlenko, V., & Riazanova, T. (2004). Young children's evaluations of the ingroup and outgroups: A multi-national study. *Social Development, 13,* 124–141.

Benson, P. L., Scales, P. C., Hamilton, S. F., & Sesma, A., Jr. (2006). Positive youth development: Theory, research, and applications. In R. M. Lerner (Ed.), *Handbook of child psychology: Vol. 1. Theoretical models of human development* (6th ed., pp. 894–941). Hoboken, NJ: Wiley.

Berg, C. A., & Sternberg, R. J. (2003). Multiple perspectives on the development of adult intelligence. In J. Demick & C. Andreoletti (Eds.), *Handbook of adult development* (pp. 103–119). New York: Springer.

Berg, C. A., & Strough, J. (2011). Problem solving across the life span. In K. L. Fingerman, C. A. Berg, J. Smith, & T. C. Antonucci (Eds.), *Handbook of life-span development* (pp. 239–267). New York: Springer.

Berger, L. M., Paxson, C., & Waldfogel, J. (2009). Income and child development. *Children and Youth Services Review, 31,* 978–989.

Berger, S. E., Theuring, C., & Adolph, K. E. (2007). How and when infants learn to climb stairs. *Infant Behavior and Development, 30,* 36–49.

Bergman, E. J., Haley, W. E., & Small, B. J. (2010). The role of grief, anxiety, and depressive symptoms in the utilization of bereavement services. *Death Studies, 34,* 441–458.

Bergman, E. J., Haley, W. E., & Small, B. J. (2011). Who uses bereavement services? An examination of service use by bereaved dementia caregivers. *Aging and Mental Health, 15,* 531–540.

Bergman, H., Ferrucci, L., Guralnik, J., Hogan, D. B., Hummel, S., Karunananthan, S., & Wolfson. C. (2007). Frailty: An emerging research and clinical paradigm—issues and controversies. *Journal of Gerontology, 62A,* 731–737.

Bergman, I., Blomberg, M., & Almkvist, O. (2007). The importance of impaired physical health and age in

normal cognitive aging. *Scandinavian Journal of Psychology, 48,* 115–125.

Berk, L. E. (2001). *Awakening children's minds: How parents and teachers can make a difference.* New York: Oxford University Press.

Berk, L. E. (2006). Looking at kindergarten children. In D. Gullo (Ed.), *K today: Teaching and learning in the kindergarten year* (pp. 11–25). Washington, DC: National Association for the Education of Young Children.

Berk, L. E., & Harris, S. (2003). Vygotsky, Lev. In L. Nadel (Ed.), *Encyclopedia of cognitive science.* London: Macmillan.

Berk, L. E., Mann, T., & Ogan, A. (2006). Make-believe play: Wellspring for development of self-regulation. In D. Singer, K. Hirsh-Pasek, & R. Golinkoff (Eds.), *Play = learning.* New York: Oxford University Press.

Berk, L. E., & Spuhl, S. (1995). Maternal interaction, private speech, and task performance in preschool children. *Early Childhood Research Quarterly, 10,* 145–169.

Berkowitz, M. W., & Gibbs, J. C. (1983). Measuring the developmental features of moral discussion. *Merrill-Palmer Quarterly, 29,* 399–410.

Berlin, L. J., Ipsa, J. M., Fine, M. A., Malone, P. S., Brooks-Gunn, J., Brady-Smith, C., et al. (2009). Correlates and consequences of spanking and verbal punishment for low-income white, African-American, and Mexican-American toddlers. *Child Development, 80,* 1403–1420.

Berman, R. A. (2007). Developing linguistic knowledge and language use across adolescence. In K. Hirsh-Pasek & R. M. Golinkoff (Eds.), *Action meets word: How children learn verbs* (pp. 347–367). New York: Oxford University Press.

Berndt, T. J., & Murphy, L. M. (2002). Influences of friends and friendships: Myths, truths, and research recommendations. In R. V. Kail (Ed.), *Advances in child development and behavior* (Vol. 30, pp. 275–310). San Diego, CA: Academic Press.

Berner, M. M., Leiber, C., Kriston, L., Stodden, V., & Gunzler, C. (2008). Effects of written information material on help-seeking behavior in patients with erectile dysfunction: A longitudinal study. *Journal of Sexual Behavior, 5,* 436–447.

Bernier, J. C., & Siegel, D. H. (1994). Attention-deficit hyperactivity disorder: A family ecological systems perspective. *Families in Society, 75,* 142–150.

Bert, S. C., Farris, J. R., & Borkowski, J. G. (2008). Parent training: Implementation strategies for adventures in parenting. *Journal of Primary Prevention, 29,* 243–261.

Bertenthal, B. I. (1993). Infants' perception of biomechanical motions: Instrinsic image and knowledge-based constraints. In C. Granrud (Ed.), *Visual perception and cognition in infancy* (pp. 175–214). Hillsdale, NJ: Erlbaum.

Bertenthal, B. I., & Longo, M. R. (2007). Is there evidence of a mirror neuron system from birth? *Developmental Science, 10,* 513–523.

Bertenthal, B. I., Longo, M. R., & Kenny, S. (2007). Phenomenal permanence and the development of predictive tracking in infancy. *Child Development, 78,* 350–363.

Berzin, S. C., & De Marco, A. C. (2010). Understanding the impact of poverty on critical events in emerging adulthood. *Youth and Society, 42,* 278–300.

Berzlanovich, A. M., Keil, W. W., Sim, T., Fasching, P., & Fazeny-Dorner, B. (2005). Do centenarians die healthy? An autopsy study. *Journal of Gerontology, 60A,* 862–865.

Berzonsky, M. D. (2003). Identity style and well-being: Does commitment matter? *Identity: An International Journal of Theory and Research, 3,* 131–142.

Berzonsky, M. D. (2004). Identity style, parental authority, and identity commitment. *Journal of Youth and Adolescence, 33,* 213–220.

Berzonsky, M. D. (2011). A social-cognitive perspective on identity construction. In S. J. Schwartz, K. Luyckz, & V. L. Vignoles (Eds.), *Handbook of identity theory and research* (pp. 55–76). New York: Springer.

Berzonsky, M. D., Cieciuch, J., Duriez, B., & Soenens, B. (2011). The how and what of identity formation: Associations between identity styles and value orientations. *Personality and Individual Differences, 50,* 295–299.

Berzonsky, M. D., & Kuk, L. S. (2000). Identity status, identity processing style, and the transition to university. *Journal of Adolescent Research, 15,* 81–98.

Best, D. (2009). From the American Academy of Pediatrics: Technical report—Secondhand and prenatal tobacco smoke exposure. *Pediatrics, 124,* e1017–e1044.

Best, D. L. (2001). Gender concepts: Convergence in cross-cultural research and methodologies. *Cross-cultural Research: The Journal of Comparative Social Science, 35,* 23–43.

Beyers, J. M., Bates, J. E., Pettit, G. S., & Dodge, K. A. (2003). Neighborhood structure, parenting processes, and the development of youths' externalizing behaviors: A multilevel analysis. *American Journal of Community Psychology, 31,* 35–53.

Beyers, W., & Seiffge-Krenke, I. (2010). Does identity precede intimacy? Testing Erikson's theory of romantic development in emerging adults of the 21st century. *Journal of Adolescent Research, 25,* 387–415.

Bhanot, R., & Jovanovic, J. (2005). Parents' academic gender stereotypes influence whether they intrude on their children's work. *Sex Roles, 52,* 597–607.

Bhat, A., Heathcock, J., & Galloway, J. C. (2005). Toy-oriented changes in hand and joint kinematics during the emergence of purposeful reaching. *Infant Behavior and Development, 28,* 445–465.

Bhatt, R. S., Rovee-Collier, C., & Weiner, S. (1994). Developmental changes in the interface between perception and memory retrieval. *Developmental Psychology, 30,* 151–162.

Bhatt, R. S., Wilk, A., Hill, D., & Rovee-Collier, C. (2004). Correlated attributes and categorization in the first half-year of life. *Developmental Psychobiology, 44,* 103–115.

Bherer, L. (2012). Physical activity and exercise in older adults. In E. O. Acevedo (Ed.), *Oxford handbook of exercise psychology* (pp. 359–384). New York: Oxford University Press.

Bherer, L., Kramer, A. F., Peterson, M. S., Colcombe, S., Erickson, K., & Becic, E. (2006). Training effects on dual-task performance: Are there age-related differences in plasticity of attentional control? *Psychology and Aging, 20,* 695–709.

Bhopal, K. (2011). "Education makes you have more say in the way your life goes": Indian women and arranged marriages in the United Kingdom. *British Journal of Sociology of Education, 32,* 431–447.

Bialystok, E., Craik, F. I. M., Green, D. W., & Gollan, T. H. (2009). Bilingual minds. *Psychological Science in the Public Interest, 3,* 89–129.

Bialystok, E., & Martin, M. M. (2003). Notation to symbol: Development in children's understanding of print. *Journal of Experimental Child Psychology, 86,* 223–243.

Bianco, A., Stone, J., Lynch, L., Lapinski, R., Berkowitz, G., & Berkowitz, R. L. (1996). Pregnancy outcome at age 40 and older. *Obstetrics and Gynecology, 87,* 917–922.

Biederman, J., Kwon, A., Aleardi, M., Chouinard, V. A., Marino, T., & Cole, H. (2005). Absence of gender effects on attention-deficit hyperactivity disorder: Findings in nonreferred subjects. *American Journal of Psychiatry, 162,* 1083–1089.

Biegel, D., & Liebbrant, S. (2006). Elders living in poverty. In B. Berkman & S. D'Ambruoso (Eds.),

Handbook of social work in health and aging (pp. 161–180). New York: Oxford University Press.

Bielak, A. A. M., Anstey, K. J., Christensen, H., & Windsor, T. D. (2012). Activity engagement is related to level, but not change, in cognitive ability across adulthood. *Psychology and Aging, 27,* 219–228.

Bielak, A. A. M., Hultsch, D. F., Strauss, E., MacDonald, S. W. S., & Hunter, M. A. (2010). Intraindividual variability in reaction time predicts cognitive outcomes 5 years later. *Neuropsychology, 24,* 731–741.

Bielawska-Batorowicz, E., & Kossakowska-Petrycka, K. (2006). Depressive mood in men after the birth of their offspring in relation to a partner's depression, social support, fathers' personality and prenatal expectations. *Journal of Reproductive and Infant Psychology, 24,* 21–29.

Bierman, K. L., & Powers, L. M. (2009). Social skills training to improve peer relations. In K. H. Rubin, W. M. Bukowski, & B. Laursen (Eds.), *Handbook of peer interactions, relationships, and groups* (pp. 603–621). New York: Guilford Press.

Bifulco, R., Cobb, C. D., & Bell, C. (2009). Can interdistrict choice boost student achievement? The case of Connecticut's interdistrict magnet school program. *Educational Evaluation and Policy Analysis, 31,* 323–345.

Bigler, R. S. (2007, June). Personal communication.

Bigler, R. S., Brown, C. S., & Markell, M. (2001). When groups are not created equal: Effects of group status on the formation of intergroup attitudes in children. *Child Development, 72,* 1151–1162.

Bimmel, N., Juffer, F., van IJzendoorn, M. H., & Bakermans-Kranenburg, M. J. (2003). Problem behavior of internationally adopted adolescents: A review and meta-analysis. *Harvard Review of Psychiatry, 11,* 64–77.

Birch, L. L., & Fisher, J. A. (1995). Appetite and eating behavior in children. *Pediatric Clinics of North America, 42,* 931–953.

Birch, L. L., Fisher, J. O., & Davison, K. K. (2003). Learning to overeat: Maternal use of restrictive feeding practices promotes girls' eating in the absence of hunger. *American Journal of Clinical Nutrition, 78,* 215–220.

Bird, A., & Reese, E. (2006). Emotional reminiscing and the development of an autobiographical self. *Developmental Psychology, 42,* 613–626.

Birditt, K. S., & Antonucci, T. C. (2007). Relationship quality profiles and well-being among married adults. *Journal of Family Psychology, 21,* 595–604.

Birditt, K. S., Brown, E., Orbuch, T. L., & McIlvane, J. M. (2010). Marital conflict behaviors and implications for divorce over 16 years. *Journal of Marriage and Family, 72,* 1188–1204.

Birditt, K. S., & Fingerman, K. L. (2005). Do we get better at picking our battles? Age group differences in descriptions of behavioral reactions to interpersonal tensions. *Journal of Gerontology, 60B,* P121–P128.

Biringen, Z., Emde, R. N., Campos, J. J., & Appelbaum, M. I. (1995). Affective reorganization in the infant, the mother, and the dyad: The role of upright locomotion and its timing. *Child Development, 66,* 499–514.

Birkett, M., Espelage, D. L., & Koenig, B. (2009). LGB and questioning students in schools: The moderating effects of homophobic bullying and school climate on negative outcomes. *Journal of Youth and Adolescence, 38,* 989–1000.

Birney, D. P., & Sternberg, R. J. (2006). Intelligence and cognitive abilities as competencies in development. In E. Bialystok & F. I. M. Craik (Eds.), *Lifespan cognition: Mechanisms of change* (pp. 315–330). New York: Oxford University Press.

Birney, D. P., & Sternberg, R. J. (2011). The development of cognitive abilities. In M. H. Bornstein & M. E.

Lamb (Eds.), *Developmental science: An advanced textbook* (6th ed., pp. 353–388). New York: Psychology Press.

Birren, J. E. (2009). Gifts and talents of elderly people: The persimmon's promise. In F. D. Horowitz, R. F. Subotnik, & D. J. Matthews (Eds.), *The development of giftedness and talent across the life span* (pp. 171–185). Washington, DC: American Psychological Association.

Bjorklund, D. F. (2012). *Children's thinking* (5th ed.). Belmont, CA: Wadsworth Cengage Learning.

Bjorklund, D. F., Causey, K., & Periss, V. (2009). The evolution and development of human social cognition. In P. Kappeler & J. Silk (Eds.), *Mind the gap: Racing the origins of human universals* (pp. 351–371). Berlin: Springer Verlag.

Bjorklund, D. F., Schneider, W., Cassel, W. S., & Ashley, E. (1994). Training and extension of a memory strategy: Evidence for utilization deficiencies in high- and low-IQ children. *Child Development, 65,* 951–965.

Black, M. C., Basile, K. C., Breiding, M. J., Smith, S. G., Walters, M. L., et al. (2011). *National intimate partner and sexual violence survey: 2010 summary report.* Atlanta, GA: Centers for Disease Control and Prevention.

Black, R. E., Williams, S. M., Jones, I. E., & Goulding, A. (2002). Children who avoid drinking cow milk have low dietary calcium intakes and poor bone health. *American Journal of Clinical Nutrition, 76,* 675–680.

Blackhall, L. J., Frank, G., Murphy, S., & Michel, V. (2001). Bioethics in a different tongue: The case of truth-telling. *Journal of Urban Health, 78,* 59–71.

Blackhall, L. J., Murphy, S. T., Frank, G., Michel, V., & Azen, S. (1995). Ethnicity and attitudes toward patient autonomy. *Journal of the American Medical Association, 274,* 820–825.

Blackwell, L. S., Trzesniewski, K. H., & Dweck, C. S. (2007). Implicit theories of intelligence predict achievement across an adolescent transition: A longitudinal study and an intervention. *Child Development, 78,* 246–263.

Blair, C., & Raver, C. C. (2012). Child development in the context of adversity: Experiential canalization of brain and behavior. *American Psychologist, 67,* 309–318.

Blair, C., & Razza, R. P. (2007). Relating effortful control, executive function, and false belief understanding to emerging math and literacy ability in kindergarten. *Developmental Psychology, 78,* 647–663.

Blair-Loy, M., & DeHart, G. (2003). Family and career trajectories among African-American female attorneys. *Journal of Family Issues, 24,* 908–933.

Blakemore, J. E. O. (2003). Children's beliefs about violating gender norms: Boys shouldn't look like girls, and girls shouldn't act like boys. *Sex Roles, 48,* 411–419.

Blakemore, S.-J., & Choudhury, S. (2006). Development of the adolescent brain: Implications for executive function and social cognition. *Journal of Child Psychology and Psychiatry, 47,* 296–312.

Blanchard, R., & Bogaert, A. F. (2004). Proportion of homosexual men who owe their sexual orientation to fraternal birth order: An estimate based on two national probability samples. *American Journal of Human Biology, 16,* 151–157.

Blanchard-Fields, F. (2007). Everyday problem solving and emotion: An adult developmental perspective. *Current Directions in Psychological Science, 16,* 26–31.

Blanchard-Fields, F., & Coats, A. H. (2008). The experience of anger and sadness in everyday problems impacts age differences in emotion regulation. *Developmental Psychology, 44,* 1547–1556.

Blanchard-Fields, F., Mienaltowski, A., & Baldi, R. (2007). Age differences in everyday problem-solving effectiveness: Older adults select more

effective strategies for interpersonal problems. *Journal of Gerontology, 62B,* P61–P64.

Blandon, A. Y., & Volling, B. L. (2008). Parental gentle guidance and children's compliance within the family: A replication study. *Journal of Family Psychology, 22,* 355–366.

Blass, E. M., Ganchrow, J. R., & Steiner, J. E. (1984). Classical conditioning in newborn humans 2–48 hours of age. *Infant Behavior and Development, 7,* 223–235.

Blatteis, C. M. (2012). Age-dependent changes in temperature regulation—a mini review. *Gerontology, 58,* 289–295.

Bleeker, M. M., & Jacobs, J. E. (2004). Achievement in math and science: Do mothers' beliefs matter 12 years later? *Journal of Educational Psychology, 96,* 97–109.

Bleses, D., Vach, W., Slott, M., Wehberg, S., Thomsen, P., Madsen, T., et al. (2008). Early vocabulary development in Danish and other languages: A CDI-based comparison. *Journal of Child Language, 35,* 619–650.

Bleske, A. L., & Buss, D. M. (2000). Can men and women be just friends? *Personal Relationships, 7,* 131–151.

Blieszner, R., & Roberto, K. A. (2012). Partners and friends in adulthood. In S. K. Whitbourne & M. J. Sliwinski (Eds.), *The Wiley-Blackwell handbook of adulthood and aging* (pp. 381–398). Malden, MA: Wiley-Blackwell.

Block, J. (2011). The five-factor framing of personality and beyond: Some ruminations. *Psychological Inquiry, 21,* 2–25.

Blood-Siegfried, J. (2009). The role of infection and inflammation in sudden infant death syndrome. *Immunopharmacology and Immunotoxicology, 31,* 516–523.

Bloom, L. (1998). Language acquisition in its developmental context. In D. Kuhn & R. S. Siegler (Eds.), *Handbook of child psychology: Vol. 2. Cognition, perception, and language* (5th ed., pp. 309–370). New York: Wiley.

Blumenfeld, P. C., Marx, R. W., & Harris, C. J. (2006). Learning environments. In K. A. Renninger & I. E. Sigel (Eds.), *Handbook of child psychology: Vol. 4. Child psychology in practice* (6th ed., pp. 297–342). Hoboken, NJ: Wiley.

Blumenthal, H., Leen-Feldner, E. W., Babson, K. A., Gahr, J. L., Trainor, C. D., & Frala, J. L. (2011). Elevated social anxiety among early maturing girls. *Developmental Psychology, 47,* 1133–1140.

Boardman, J. D. (2004). Stress and physical health: The role of neighborhoods as mediating and moderating mechanisms. *Social Science and Medicine, 58,* 2473–2483.

Bobb, A. J., Castellanos, F. X., Addington, A. M., & Rapoport, J. L. (2006). Molecular genetic studies of ADHD: 1991 to 2004. *American Journal of Medical Genetics Part B (Neuropsychiatric Genetics), 141B,* 551–565.

Bodrova, E., & Leong, D. J. (2007). *Tools of the mind: The Vygotskian approach to early childhood education* (2nd ed.). Upper Saddle River, NJ: Merrill/Prentice Hall.

Body, J. J., Bergmann, P., Boonen, S., Boutsen, Y., Bruyere, O., Devogelaer, J. P., et al. (2011). Non-pharmacological management of osteoporosis: A consensus of the Belgian Bone Club. *Osteoporosis International, 22,* 2769–2788.

Bogaert, A. F. (2005). Age at puberty and father absence in a national probability sample. *Journal of Adolescence, 28,* 541–546.

Bogin, B. (2001). *The growth of humanity.* New York: Wiley-Liss.

Bohannon, J. N., & Bonvillian, J. D. (2009). Theoretical approaches to language acquisition. In J. B. Gleason & B. Ratner (Ed.), *The development of language* (7th ed., pp. 227–284). Boston: Allyn and Bacon.

Bohannon, J. N., III, & Stanowicz, L. (1988). The issue of negative evidence: Adult responses to children's language errors. *Developmental Psychology, 24,* 684–689.

Bohlmeijer, E. T., Roemer, M., Cuijpers, P., & Smit, F. (2007). The effects of life-review on psychological well-being in older adults: A meta-analysis. *Aging and Mental Health, 11,* 291–300.

Boldizar, J. P. (1991). Assessing sex typing and androgyny in children: The children's sex role inventory. *Developmental Psychology, 27,* 505–515.

Bolen, R. M. (2001). *Child sexual abuse.* New York: Kluwer Academic.

Bolkan, C., & Hooker, K. (2012). Self-regulation and social cognition in adulthood: The gyroscope of personality. In S. K. Whitbourne & M. J. Sliwinski (Eds.), *Wiley-Blackwell handbook of adulthood and aging* (pp. 357–380). Malden, MA: Wiley-Blackwell.

Bonilla, S., Kehl, S., Kwong, K. Y., Morphew, T., Kachru, R., & Jones, C. A. (2005). School absenteeism in children with asthma in a Los Angeles inner-city school. *Journal of Pediatrics, 116,* 802–806.

Bonnick, S. L. (2008). Osteoporosis in men and women. *Management of Osteoporosis, 8,* 28–36.

Bono, M. A., & Stifter, C. A. (2003). Maternal attention-directing strategies and infant focused attention during problem solving. *Infancy, 4,* 235–250.

Bookman, A., & Kimbrel, D. (2011). Families and elder care in the twenty-first century. *Future of Children, 21,* 117–140.

Boom, J., Wouters, H., & Keller, M. (2007). A cross-cultural validation of stage development: A Rasch re-analysis of longitudinal socio-moral reasoning data. *Cognitive Development, 22,* 213–229.

Booth, A., Scott, M. E., & King, V. (2010). Father residence and adolescent problem behavior: Are youth always better off in two-parent families? *Journal of Family Issues, 31,* 585–605.

Borduin, C. M. (2007). Multisystemic treatment of violent youth and their families. In T. A. Cavell & K. T. Malcolm (Eds.), *Anger, aggression and interventions for interpersonal violence* (pp. 239–265). Mahwah, NJ: Erlbaum.

Bornstein, M. H. (1989). Sensitive periods in development: Structural characteristics and causal interpretations. *Psychological Bulletin, 105,* 179–197.

Bornstein, M. H., & Arterberry, M. E. (1999). Perceptual development. In M. H. Bornstein & M. E. Lamb (Eds.), *Developmental psychology: An advanced textbook* (pp. 231–274). Mahwah, NJ: Erlbaum.

Bornstein, M. H., & Arterberry, M. E. (2003). Recognition, discrimination, and categorization of smiling by 5-month-old infants. *Developmental Science, 6,* 585–599.

Bornstein, M. H., Arterberry, M. E., & Mash, C. (2010). Infant object categorization transcends object-context relations. *Infant Behavior and Development, 33,* 7–15.

Bornstein, M. H., & Sawyer, J. (2006). Family systems. In K. McCartney & D. Phillips (Eds.), *Blackwell handbook of early childhood development* (pp. 381–398). Malden, MA: Blackwell.

Bornstein, M. H., Vibbert, M., Tal, J., & O'Donnell, K. (1992). Toddler language and play in the second year: Stability, covariation, and influences of parenting. *First Language, 12,* 323–338.

Boroughs, D. S. (2004). Female sexual abusers of children. *Children and Youth Services Review, 26,* 481–487.

Borst, C. G. (1995). *Catching babies: The professionalization of childbirth, 1870–1920.* Cambridge, MA: Harvard University Press.

Bortfeld, H., Leon, S., Bloom, J., Schober, M., & Brennan, S. (2001). Disfluency rates in conversation: Effects of age, relationship, topic, role, and gender. *Language and Speech, 44,* 123–147.

Bos, H. M. W., & Sandfort, T. G. M. (2010). Children's gender identity in lesbian and heterosexual two-parent families. *Sex Roles, 62,* 114–126.

Bos, H. M. W., van Balen, F., & van den Boom, D. C. (2007). Child adjustment and parenting in planned lesbian-parent families. *American Journal of Orthopsychiatry, 77,* 38–48.

Bosacki, S. L., & Moore, C. (2004). Preschoolers' understanding of simple and complex emotions: Links with gender and language. *Sex Roles, 50,* 659–675.

Bost, K. K., Shin, N., McBride, B. A., Brown, G. L., Vaughn, B. E., & Coppola, G. (2006). Maternal secure base scripts, children's attachment security, and mother–child narrative styles. *Attachment and Human Development, 8,* 241–260.

Boswell, G. H., Kahana, E., & Dilworth-Anderson, P. (2006). Spirituality and healthy lifestyle behaviors: Stress counter-balancing effects on the well-being of older adults. *Journal of Religion and Health, 45,* 587–602.

Botton, J., Heude, B., Maccario, J., Ducimetiére, P., & Charles, M. A. (2008). Postnatal weight and height growth velocities at different ages between birth and 5y and body composition in adolescent boys and girls. *American Journal of Clinical Nutrition, 87,* 1760–1768.

Bouchard, T. J. (2004). Genetic influence on human psychological traits: A survey. *Current Directions in Psychological Science, 13,* 148–151.

Bouchard, T. J., & Loehlin, J. C. (2001). Genes, evolution, and personality. *Behavior Genetics, 31,* 243–274.

Boucher, O., Bastien, C. H., Saint-Amour, D., Dewailly, E., Ayotte, P., Jacobson, J. L., Jacobson, et al. (2010). Prenatal exposure to methylmercury and PCBs affects distinct stages of information processing: An event-related potential study with Inuit children. *Neurotoxicology, 31,* 373–384.

Boucher, O., Muckle, G., & Bastien, C. H. (2009). Prenatal exposure to polychlorinated biphenyls: A neuropsychologic analysis. *Environmental Health Perspectives, 117,* 7–16.

Boukydis, C. F. Z., & Lester, B. M. (1998). Infant crying, risk status and social support in families of preterm and term infants. *Early Development and Parenting, 7,* 31–39.

Boulton, M. J. (1999). Concurrent and longitudinal relations between children's playground behavior and social preference, victimization, and bullying. *Child Development, 70,* 944–954.

Bowen, C. E., Noack, M. G., & Staudinger, U. M. (2011). Aging in the work context. In K. W. Schaie & S. L. Willis (Eds.), *Handbook of the psychology of aging* (7th ed., pp. 263–277). San Diego, CA: Academic Press.

Bowen, N. K., Bowen, G. L., & Ware, W. B. (2002). Neighborhood social disorganization, families, and the educational behavior of adolescents. *Journal of Adolescent Research, 17,* 468–490.

Bowlby, J. (1969). *Attachment and loss: Vol. 1. Attachment.* New York: Basic Books.

Bowlby, J. (1980). *Attachment and loss: Vol. 3. Loss: Sadness and depression.* New York: Basic Books.

Bowman, N. A. (2011a). College diversity experiences and cognitive development: A meta-analysis. *Review of Educational Research, 80,* 4–33.

Bowman, N. A. (2011b). Promoting participation in a diverse democracy: A meta-analysis of college diversity experiences and civic engagement. *Review of Educational Research, 81,* 29–68.

Bowman, S. A., Gortmaker, S. L., Ebbeling, C. B., Pereira, M. A., & Ludwig, D. S. (2004). Effects of fast-food consumption on energy intake and diet quality among children in a national household survey. *Pediatrics, 113,* 112–113.

Boyce, W., Doherty-Poirier, M., MacKinnon, D., Fortin, C., Saab, H., King, M., & Gallupe, O. (2006). Sexual health of Canadian youth: Findings from the Canadian Youth, Sexual Health and HIV/AIDS Study. *Canadian Journal of Human Sexuality, 15,* 59–68.

Boyle, P. A., Barnes, L. L., Buchman, A. S., & Bennett, D. A. (2009). Purpose in life is associated with mortality among community-dwelling older persons. *Psychosomatic Medicine, 71,* 574–579.

Boysson-Bardies, B. de, & Vihman, M. M. (1991). Adaptation to language: Evidence from babbling and first words in four languages. *Language, 67,* 297–319.

Bozionelos, N., Bozionelos, G., Kostopoulos, K., & Polychroniou, P. (2011). How providing mentoring relates to career success and organizational commitment: A study in the general managerial population. *Career Development International, 16,* 446–468.

Bracci, R., Perrone, S., & Buonocore, G. (2006). The timing of neonatal brain damage. *Biology of the Neonate, 90,* 145–155.

Bradbury, J. C. (2009). Peak athletic performance and ageing: Evidence from baseball. *Journal of Sports Sciences, 27,* 599–610.

Bradford, K., Barber, B. K., Olsen, J. A., Maughan, S. L., Erickson, L. D., Ward, D., & Stolz, H. E. (2003). A multi-national study of interparental conflict, parenting, and adolescent functioning: South Africa, Bangladesh, China, India, Bosnia, Germany, Palestine, Colombia, and the United States. *Marriage and Family Review, 35,* 107–137.

Bradley, R. H., & Caldwell, B. M. (1982). The consistency of the home environment and its relation to child development. *International Journal of Behavioral Development, 5,* 445–465.

Bradley, R. H., Whiteside, L., Mundfrom, D. J., Casey, P. H., Kelleher, K. J., & Pope, S. K. (1994). Early indications of resilience and their relation to experiences in the home environments of low birthweight, premature children living in poverty. *Child Development, 65,* 346–360.

Braine, L. G., Schauble, L., Kugelmass, S., & Winter, A. (1993). Representation of depth by children: Spatial strategies and lateral biases. *Developmental Psychology, 29,* 466–479.

Brame, B., Nagin, D. S., & Tremblay, R. E. (2001). Developmental trajectories of physical aggression from school entry to late adolescence. *Journal of Child Psychology and Psychiatry, 42,* 503–512.

Brand, S., Gerber, M., Beck, J., Hatzinger, M., Puhse, U., & Holsboer-Trachsler, E. (2010). High exercise levels are related to favorable sleep and psychological functioning in adolescence: A comparison of athletes and controls. *Journal of Adolescent Health, 46,* 133–141.

Braswell, G. S., & Callanan, M. A. (2003). Learning to draw recognizable graphic representations during mother–child interactions. *Merrill-Palmer Quarterly, 49,* 471–494.

Braungart-Rieker, J. M., Hill-Soderlund, A. L., & Karrass, J. (2010). Fear and anger reactivity trajectories from 4 to 16 months: The roles of temperament, regulation, and maternal sensitivity. *Developmental Psychology, 46,* 791–804.

Braveman, P., Cubbin, C., Egerter, S., Williams, D. R., & Pamuk, E. (2010). Socioeconomic disparities in health in the United States: What the patterns tell us. *American Journal of Public Health, 100,* S186–S196.

Bray, J. H. (1999). From marriage to remarriage and beyond: Findings from the Developmental Issues in Stepfamilies Research Project. In E. M. Hetherington (Ed.), *Coping with divorce, single parenting, and remarriage: A risk and resiliency perspective* (pp. 295–319). Mahwah, NJ: Erlbaum.

Bremner, J. G. (2010). Cognitive development: Knowledge of the physical world. In J. G. Bremner & T. D. Wachs (Eds.), *Wiley-Blackwell handbook of infant development: Vol. 1. Basic research* (2nd ed., pp. 204–242). Oxford, UK: Wiley.

Brendgen, M., Markiewicz, D., Doyle, A. B., & Bukowski, W. M. (2001). The relations between friendship quality, ranked-friendship preference, and adolescents' behavior with their friends. *Merrill-Palmer Quarterly, 47,* 395–415.

Brenner, E., & Salovey, P. (1997). Emotional regulation during childhood: Developmental, interpersonal, and individual considerations. In P. Salovey & D. Sluyter (Eds.), *Emotional literacy and emotional development* (pp. 168–192). New York: Basic Books.

Brenner, J. (2013). *Pew Internet: Social Networking.* Washington, DC: Pew Research Center.

Brent, R. L., Christian, M. S., & Diener, R. M. (2011). Evaluation of the reproductive and developmental risks of caffeine. *Developmental and Reproductive Toxicology, 92,* 152–187.

Bretherton, I., & Munholland, K. A. (2008). Internal working models in attachment relationships. In J. Cassidy & P. R. Shaver (Eds.), *Handbook of attachment: Theory, research, and clinical applications* (2nd ed., pp. 102–127). New York: Guilford.

Brewaeys, A., Ponjaert, I., Van Hall, E. V., & Golombok, S. (1997). Donor insemination: Child development and family functioning in lesbian mother families. *Human Reproduction, 12,* 1349–1359.

Bridge, J. A., Goldstein, T. R., & Brent, D. A. (2006). Adolescent suicide and suicidal behavior. *Journal of Child Psychology and Psychiatry, 47,* 372–394.

Bridgett, D. J., Gartstein, M. A., Putnam, S. P., McKay, T., Iddins, R., Robertson, C., et al. (2009). Maternal and contextual influences and the effect of temperament development during infancy on parenting in toddlerhood. *Infant Behavior and Development, 32,* 103–116.

Bright, G. M., Mendoza, J. R., & Rosenfeld, R. G. (2009). Recombinant human insulin-like growth factor-1 treatment: Ready for primetime. *Endocrinology and Metabolism Clinics of North America, 38,* 625–638.

Bright, J. E. H., Pryor, R. G. L., Wilkenfeld, S., & Earl, J. (2005). The role of social context and serendipitous events in career decision making. *International Journal for Educational and Vocational Guidance, 5,* 19–36.

Brim, O. G., Ryff, C. D., & Kessler, R. C. (2005). The MIDUS National Survey: An overview. In O. G. Brim, C. D. Ryff, & R. C. Kessler (Eds.), *How healthy are we? A national study of well-being at midlife* (pp. 1–34). Chicago: University of Chicago Press.

Brodaty, H., Seeher, K., & Gibson, L. (2012). Dementia time to death: A systematic literature review on survival time and years of life lost in people with dementia. *International Psychogeriatrics, 24,* 1034–1045.

Brody, G. H., & Flor, D. L. (1998). Maternal resources, parenting practices, and child competence in rural, single-parent African American families. *Child Development, 69,* 803–816.

Brody, G. H., & Murry, V. M. (2001). Sibling socialization of competence in rural, single-parent African American families. *Journal of Marriage and Family, 63,* 996–1008.

Brody, G. H., Stoneman, Z., & McCoy, J. K. (1994). Forecasting sibling relationships in early adolescence from child temperaments and family processes in middle childhood. *Child Development, 65,* 771–784.

Brody, L. (1999). *Gender, emotion, and the family.* Cambridge, MA: Harvard University Press.

Brody, L. R. (1997). Gender and emotion: Beyond stereotypes. *Journal of Social Issues, 53,* 369–393.

Brodzinsky, D. M. (2011). Children's understanding of adoption: Developmental and clinical implications. *Professional Psychology: Research and Practice, 42,* 200–207.

Broidy, L. M., Nagin, D. S., Tremblay, R. E., Bates, J. E., Brame, B., Dodge, K. A., et al. (2003). Developmental trajectories of childhood disruptive behaviors and adolescent delinquency: A six-site, cross-national study. *Developmental Psychology, 39,* 222–245.

Bronfenbrenner, U., & Morris, P. A. (2006). The bioecological model of human development. In R. M. Lerner (Ed.), *Handbook of child psychology: Vol. 1. Theoretical models of human development* (6th ed., pp. 297–342). Hoboken, NJ: Wiley.

Bronson, G. W. (1994). Infants' transitions toward adult-like scanning. *Child Development, 65,* 1243–1261.

Bronstein, P. (2006). The family environment: Where gender role socialization begins. In J. Worell & C. D. Goodheart (Eds.), *Handbook of girls' and women's psychological health: Gender and well-being across the lifespan* (pp. 262–271). New York: Oxford University Press.

Bronte-Tinkew, J., Moore, K. A., & Carrano, J. (2006). The father–child relationship, parenting styles, and adolescent risk behaviors in intact families. *Journal of Family Issues, 27,* 850–881.

Brooks, L., McCabe, P., & Schneiderman, N. (2011). Stress and cardiometabolic syndrome. In R. J. Contrada & A. Baum (Eds.), *Handbook of stress science: Biology, psychology, and health* (pp. 399–410). New York: Springer.

Brooks, P. J., Hanauere, J. B., Padowska, B., & Rosman, H. (2003). The role of selective attention in preschoolers' rule use in a novel dimensional card sort. *Cognitive Development, 18,* 195–215.

Brooks, R., & Meltzoff, A. N. (2008). Infant gaze following and pointing predict accelerated vocabulary growth through two years of age: A longitudinal, growth curve modeling study. *Journal of Child Language, 35,* 207–220.

Brooks-Gunn, J. (1988). Antecedents and consequences of variations in girls' maturational timing. *Journal of Adolescent Health Care, 9,* 365–373.

Brooks-Gunn, J. (2003). Do you believe in magic? What we can expect from early childhood intervention programs. *Social Policy Report of the Society for Research in Child Development, 17,* 3–14.

Brooks-Gunn, J. (2004). Intervention and policy as change agents for young children. In P. L. Chase-Lansdale, K. Kiernan, & R. J. Friedman (Eds.), *Human development across lives and generations: The potential for change* (pp. 293–340). New York: Cambridge University Press.

Brooks-Gunn, J., Han, W.-J., & Waldfogel, J. (2002). Maternal employment and child cognitive outcomes in the first three years of life: The NICHD study of early child care. *Child Development, 73,* 1052–1072.

Brooks-Gunn, J., Han, W.-J., & Waldfogel, J. (2010). First-year maternal employment and child development in the first 7 years. *Monographs of the Society for research in Child Development, 75*(No. 2, Serial No. 296), 59–69.

Brooks-Gunn, J., Klebanov, P. K., Smith, J., Duncan, G. J., & Lee, K. (2003). The black–white test score gap in young children. Contributions of test and family characteristics. *Applied Developmental Science, 7,* 239–252.

Brown, A. M., & Miracle, J. A. (2003). Early binocular vision in human infants: Limitations on the generality of the Superposition Hypothesis. *Vision Research, 43,* 1563–1574.

Brown, A. S. (2006). Prenatal infection as a risk factor for schizophrenia. *Schizophrenia Bulletin, 32,* 200–202.

Brown, B. B., & Dietz, E. L. (2009). Informal peer groups in middle childhood and adolescence. In K. H. Rubin, W. M. Bukowski, & B. Laursen (Eds.), *Handbook of peer interactions, relationships, and groups* (pp. 361–376). New York: Guilford Press.

Brown, B. B., Herman, M., Hamm, J. V., & Heck, D. (2008). Ethnicity and image: Correlates of minority adolescents' affiliation with individual-based versus ethnically defined peer crowds. *Child Development, 79,* 529–546.

Brown, C., & Lowis, M. J. (2003). Psychosocial development in the elderly: An investigation into Erikson's ninth stage. *Journal of Aging Studies, 17,* 415–426.

Brown, C. S., & Bigler, R. S. (2004). Children's perceptions of gender discrimination. *Developmental Psychology, 40,* 714–726.

Brown, G. L., Schoppe-Sullivan, S. J., Mangelsdorf, S. C., & Neff, C. (2010). Observed and reported supportive coparenting as predictors of infant–mother and infant–father attachment security. *Early Child Development and Care, 180,* 121–137.

Brown, J. D., & L'Engle, K. L. (2009). X-rated: Attitudes and behaviors associated with U.S. early adolescents' exposure to sexually explicit media. *Communication Research, 36,* 129–151.

Brown, L. H., & Rodin, P. A. (2004). Grandparent–grandchild relationships and the life course perspective. In J. Demick & C. Andreoletti (Eds.), *Handbook of adult development* (pp. 459–474). New York: Springer.

Brown, R. W. (1973). *A first language: The early stages.* Cambridge, MA: Harvard University Press.

Brown, S. A., & Ramo, D. E. (2005). Clinical course of youth following treatment for alcohol and drug problems. In H. A. Liddle & C. L. Rowe (Eds.), *Adolescent substance abuse: Research and clinical advances* (pp. 79–103). Cambridge, UK: Cambridge University Press.

Brown, S. L., & Kawamura, S. (2010). Relationships quality among cohabitors and marrieds in older adulthood. *Social Science Research, 39,* 777–786.

Brown, S. L., & Lin, I.-F. (2012). *Divorce in middle and later life: New estimates from the 2009 American Community Survey.* Bowling Green, OH: Center for Family and Demographic Research, Bowling Green University.

Brown, T. M., & Rodriguez, L. F. (2009). School and the co-construction of dropout. *International Journal of Qualitative Studies in Education, 22,* 221–242.

Browne, C. A., & Woolley, J. D. (2004). Preschoolers' magical explanations for violations of physical, social, and mental laws. *Journal of Cognition and Development, 5,* 239–260.

Brownell, C. A., Zerwas, S., & Ramani, G. B. (2007). "So big": The development of body self-awareness in toddlers. *Child Development, 78,* 1426–1440.

Brugman, G. M. (2006). Wisdom and aging. In J. E. Birren & K. W. Schaie (Eds.), *Handbook of the psychology of aging* (6th ed., pp. 445–476). Burlington, MA: Elsevier Academic Press.

Brussoni, M. J., and Boon, S. D. (1998). Grandparental impact in young adults' relationships with their closest grandparents: The role of relationship strength and emotional closeness. *International Journal of Aging and Human Development, 45,* 267–286.

Bruzzese, J.-M., & Fisher, C. B. (2003). Assessing and enhancing the research consent capacity of children and youth. *Applied Developmental Science, 7,* 13–26.

Bryan, A. E., & Dix, T. (2009). Mothers' emotions and behavioral support during interactions with toddlers: The role of child temperament. *Social Development, 18,* 647–670.

Bryant, B. K., Zvonkovic, A. M., & Reynolds, P. (2006). Parenting in relation to child and adolescent vocational development. *Journal of Vocational Behavior, 69,* 149–175.

Bryant, P., & Nunes, T. (2002). Children's understanding of mathematics. In U. Goswami (Ed.), *Blackwell handbook of childhood cognitive development* (pp. 412–439). Malden, MA: Blackwell.

Buchanan, C. M., Eccles, J. S., & Becker, J. B. (1992). Are adolescents the victims of raging hormones? Evidence for activational effects of hormones on moods and behavior at adolescence. *Psychological Bulletin, 111,* 62–107.

Buchanan, C. M., Maccoby, E. E., & Dornbusch, S. M. (1996). *Adolescents after divorce.* Cambridge, MA: Harvard University Press.

Buchanan-Barrow, E., & Barrett, M. (1998). Children's rule discrimination within the context of the school. *British Journal of Developmental Psychology, 16,* 539–551.

Buehler, C., & O'Brien, M. (2011). Mothers' part-time employment: Associations with mother and family well-being. *Journal of Family Psychology, 25,* 895–906.

Bugental, D. B., Ellerson, P. C., Lin, E. K., Rainey, B., & Kokotovic, A. (2002). A cognitive approach to child abuse prevention. *Journal of Family Psychology, 16,* 243–258.

Bugental, D. B., & Happaney, K. (2004). Predicting infant maltreatment in low-income families: The interactive effects of maternal attributions and child status at birth. *Developmental Psychology, 40,* 234–243.

Buhl, H. M., & Lanz, M. (2007). Emerging adulthood in Europe: Common traits and variability across five European countries. *Journal of Adolescent Research, 22,* 439–443.

Buhrmester, D. (1996). Need fulfillment, interpersonal competence, and the developmental contexts of early adolescent friendship. In W. M. Bukowski, A. F. Newcomb, & W. W. Hartup (Eds.), *The company they keep: Friendship during childhood and adolescence* (pp. 158–185). New York: Cambridge University Press.

Buhrmester, D., & Furman, W. (1990). Perceptions of sibling relationships during middle childhood and adolescence. *Child Development, 61,* 1387–1398.

Buhs, E. S., Ladd, G. W., & Herald-Brown, S. L. (2010). Victimization and exclusion: Links to peer rejection, classroom engagement, and achievement. In S. R. Jimerson, S. M. Swearer, & D. L. Espelage (Eds.), *Handbook of bullying in schools: An international perspective* (pp. 163–172). New York: Routledge.

Bukowski, W. M. (2001). Friendship and the worlds of childhood. In D. W. Nangle & C. A. Erdley (Eds.), *The role of friendship in psychological adjustment* (pp. 93–105). San Francisco: Jossey-Bass.

Bullo, M., Lamuela-Raventos, R., & Salas-Salvadó, J. (2011). Mediterranean diet and oxidation: Nuts and olive oil as important sources of fat and antioxidants. *Current Topics in Medicinal Chemistry, 11,* 1797–1810.

Bumpus, M. F., Crouter, A. C., & McHale, S. M. (2006). Linkages between negative work-to-family spillover and mothers' and fathers' knowledge of their young adolescents' daily lives. *Journal of Early Adolescence, 26,* 36–59.

Bunge, S. A., & Wright, S. B. (2007). Neurodevelopmental changes in working memory and cognitive control. *Current Opinion in Neurobiology, 17,* 243–250.

Bunting, L., & McAuley, C. (2004). Teenage pregnancy and parenthood: The role of fathers. *Child and Family Social Work, 9,* 295–303.

Burchinal, M., Vandergrift, N., & Pianta, R. (2010). Threshold analysis of association between child care quality and child outcomes for low-income children in prekindergarten programs. *Early Childhood Research Quarterly, 25,* 166–176.

Burden, M. J., Jacobson, S. W., & Jacobson, J. L. (2005). Relation of prenatal alcohol exposure to cognitive processing speed and efficiency in childhood. *Alcoholism: Clinical and Experimental Research, 29,* 1473–1483.

Burgess-Champoux, T. L., Larson, N., Neumark-Sztainer, D., Hannan, P. J., & Story, M. (2009). Are family meal patterns associated with overall diet quality during the transition from early to middle adolescence? *Journal of Nutrition Education and Behavior, 41,* 79–86.

Burke, D. M., & Shafto, M. A. (2004). Aging and language production. *Current Directions in Psychological Science, 13,* 21–24.

Burleson, B. R., & Kunkel, A. W. (2006). Revisiting the different cultures thesis: An assessment of sex differences and similarities in communication. In K. Dindia & D. J. Canary (Eds.), *Sex differences and similarities in communication* (2nd ed., pp. 137–159). Mahwah, NJ: Erlbaum.

Burts, D.C., Hart, C. H., Charlesworth, R., Fleege, P. O., Mosely, J., & Thomasson, R. H. (1992). Observed activities and stress behaviors of children in developmentally appropriate and inappropriate kindergarten classrooms. *Early Childhood Research Quarterly, 7,* 297–318.

Buscemi, L., & Turchi, C. (2011). An overview of the genetic susceptibility to alcoholism. *Medicine, Science, and the Law, 51,* S2–S6.

Bush, K. R., & Peterson, G. W. (2008). Family influences on child development. In T. P. Gullotta & G. M. Blau (Eds.), *Handbook of child behavioral issues: Evidence-based approaches to prevention and treatment* (pp. 43–67). New York: Routledge.

Bushman, B. J., & Huesmann, L. R. (2001). Effects of televised violence on aggression. In D. G. Singer & J. L. Singer (Eds.), *Handbook of children and the media* (pp. 223–254). Thousand Oaks, CA: Sage.

Bushnell, E. W., & Boudreau, J. P. (1993). Motor development and the mind: The potential role of motor abilities as a determinant of aspects of perceptual development. *Child Development, 64,* 1005–1021.

Buss, D. (2012). *Evolutionary psychology: The new science of the mind* (4th ed.). Upper Saddle River, NJ: Pearson.

Buss, D. M., Shackelford, T. K., Kirkpatrick, L. A., & Larsen, R. J. (2001). A half century of mate preferences: The cultural evolution of values. *Journal of Marriage and Family, 63,* 491–503.

Bussey, K. (1992). Lying and truthfulness: Children's definitions, standards, and evaluative reactions. *Child Development, 63,* 129–137.

Bussey, K. (1999). Children's categorization and evaluation of different types of lies and truths. *Child Development, 70,* 1338–1347.

Buswell, S. D., & Spatz, D. L. (2007). Parent–infant co-sleeping and its relationship to breastfeeding. *Journal of Pediatric Health Care, 21,* 22–28.

Butler, M., & Meaney, J. (Eds.). (2005). *Genetics of developmental disabilities.* Boca Raton, FL: Taylor & Francis.

Butler, R. N. (1968). The life review: An interpretation of reminiscence in the aged. In B. Neugarten (Ed.), *Middle age and aging* (pp. 486–496). Chicago: University of Chicago Press.

Buttelmann, D., Carpenter, M., & Tomasello, M. (2009). Eighteen-month-old infants show false belief understanding in an active helping paradigm. *Cognition, 112,* 337–342.

Buunk, B. P. (2002). Age and gender differences in mate selection criteria for various involvement levels. *Personal Relationships, 9,* 271–278.

Bybee, J. A., & Wells, Y. V. (2003). The development of possible selves during adulthood. In J. Demick & C. Andreoletti (Eds.), *Handbook of adult development* (pp. 257–270). New York: Springer.

Byrnes, J. P. (2003). Cognitive development during adolescence. In G. R. Adams & M. D. Berzonsky (Eds.), *Blackwell handbook of adolescence* (pp. 227–246). Malden, MA: Blackwell.

C

Cabrera, N. J., & Bradley, R. H. (2012). Latino fathers and their children. *Child Development Perspectives, 6,* 232–238.

Cabrera, N. J., & García-Coll, C. (2004). Latino fathers: Uncharted territory in need of much exploration. In M. E. Lamb (Ed.), *The role of the father in child development* (4th ed., pp. 98–120). Hoboken, NJ: Wiley.

Cahill, K. E., Giandrea, M. D., & Quinn, J. F. (2006). Retirement patterns from career employment. *Gerontologist, 46,* 514–523.

Cai, H., Cong, W., Ji, S., Rathman, S., Maudsley, S., & Martin, B. (2012). Metabolic dysfunction in Alzheimer's disease and related neurodegenerative disorders. *Current Alzheimer Research, 9,* 5–17.

Cain, K. M., & Dweck, C. S. (1995). The relation between motivational patterns and achievement cognitions through the elementary school years. *Merrill-Palmer Quarterly, 41,* 25–52.

Cairns, R. B., & Cairns, B. D. (2006). The making of developmental psychology. In R. M. Lerner (Ed.), *Handbook of child psychology: Vol. 1. Theoretical models of human development* (6th ed., pp. 89–165). Hoboken, NJ: Wiley.

Caldera, Y. M., & Lindsey, E. W. (2006). Coparenting, mother–infant interaction, and infant–parent attachment relationships in two-parent families. *Journal of Family Psychology, 20,* 275–283.

Caldwell, B. M., & Bradley, R. H. (1994). Environmental issues in developmental follow-up research. In S. L. Friedman & H. C. Haywood (Eds.), *Developmental follow-up* (pp. 235–256). San Diego: Academic Press.

Calhoun, L. G., Tedeschi, R. G., Cann, A., & Hanks, E. A. (2010). Positive outcomes following bereavement: Paths to posttraumatic growth. *Psychologica Belgica, 50,* 125–143.

Callanan, M. A., & Oakes, L. M. (1992). Preschoolers' questions and parents' explanations: Causal thinking in everyday activity. *Cognitive Development, 7,* 213–233.

Calvert, S. L., Rideout, V. J., Woolard, J. L., Barr, R. F., & Strouse, G. A. (2005). Age, ethnicity, and socioeconomic patterns in early computer use: A national survey. *American Behavioral Scientist, 48,* 590–607.

Cameron, C. A., & Lee, K. (1997). The development of children's telephone communication. *Journal of Applied Developmental Psychology, 18,* 55–70.

Cameron-Faulkner, T., Lieven, E., & Tomasello, M. (2003). A construction based analysis of child-directed speech. *Cognitive Science, 27,* 843–873.

Campbell, A., Shirley, L., & Candy, J. (2004). A longitudinal study of gender-related cognition and behaviour. *Developmental Science, 7,* 1–9.

Campbell, A. L., & Binstock, R. H. (2011). Politics and aging in the United States. In R. H. Binstock & L. K. George (Eds.), *Handbook of aging and the social sciences* (pp. 265–280). San Diego, CA: Academic Press.

Campbell, D. A., Lake, M. F., Falk, M., & Backstrand, J. R. (2006). A randomized control trial of continuous support in labor by a lay doula. *Journal of Obstetrics and Gynecology and Neonatal Nursing, 35,* 456–464.

Campbell, D. A., Scott, K. D., Klaus, M. H., & Falk, M. (2007). Female relatives or friends trained as labor doulas: Outcomes at 6 to 8 weeks postpartum. *Birth, 34,* 220–227.

Campbell, F. A., Pungello, E. P., Miller-Johnson, S., Burchinal, M., & Ramey, C. T. (2001). The development of cognitive and academic abilities: Growth curves from an early childhood educational experiment. *Developmental Psychology, 37,* 231–242.

Campbell, F. A., & Ramey, C. T. (2010). Carolina Abecedarian Project. In A. Reynolds, A. J. Rolick, M. M. Englund, & J. A. Temple (Eds.), *Childhood* programs and practices in the first decade of life: A human capital integration (pp. 76–98). New York: Cambridge University Press.

Campbell, F. A., Ramey, C. T., Pungello, E. P., Sparling, J., & Miller-Johnson, S. (2002). Early childhood education: Young adult outcomes from the Abecedarian Project. *Applied Developmental Science, 6,* 42–57.

Campbell, J., & Glass, N. (2009). Safety planning, danger, and lethality assessment. In C. Mitchell & D. Anglin (Eds.), *Intimate partner violence: A healthbased perspective* (pp. 319–334). New York: Oxford University Press.

Campbell, S. B., Brownell, C. A., Hungerford, A., Spieker, S. J., Mohan, R., & Blessing, J. S. (2004). The course of maternal depressive symptoms and maternal sensitivity as predictors of attachment security at 36 months. *Development and Psychopathology, 16,* 231–252.

Campos, J. J., Anderson, D. I., Barbu-Roth, M. A., Hubbard, E. M., Hertenstein, J. J., & Witherington, D. (2000). Travel broadens the mind. *Infancy, 1,* 149–219.

Campos, J. J., Witherington, D., Anderson, D. I., Frankel, C. I., Uchiyama, I., & Barbu-Roth, M. (2008). Rediscovering development in infancy. *Child Development, 79,* 1625–1632.

Camras, L. A., Oster, H., Campos, J. J., & Bakeman, R. (2003). Emotional facial expressions in European-American, Japanese, and Chinese infants. *Annals of the New York Academy of Sciences, 1000,* 1–17.

Camras, L. A., Oster, H., Campos, J., Campos, R., Ujie, T., Miyake, K., Wang, L., & Meng, Z. (1998). Production of emotional and facial expressions in European American, Japanese, and Chinese infants. *Developmental Psychology, 34,* 616–628.

Camras, L. A., Oster, H., Campos, J. J., Miyake, K., & Bradshaw, D. (1992). Japanese and American infants' responses to arm restraint. *Developmental Psychology, 28,* 578–583.

Canada Campaign 2000. (2009). *2009 Report Card on Child and Family Poverty in Canada: 1989–2009.* Retrieved from www.campaign2000.ca/reportcards.html

Candy, B., Holman, A., Leurent, S., & Jones, D. L. (2011). Hospice care delivered at home, in nursing homes and in dedicated hospice facilities: A systematic review of quantitative and qualitative evidence. *International Journal of Nursing Studies, 48,* 121–133.

Cannella, C., Savina, C., & Donini, L. M. (2009). Nutrition, longevity and behavior. *Archives of Gerontology and Geriatrics, 49*(Suppl. 1), 19–27.

Canobi, K. H. (2004). Individual differences in children's addition and subtraction knowledge. *Cognitive Development, 19,* 81–93.

Canobi, K. H., Reeve, R. A., & Pattison, P. E. (2003). The role of conceptual understanding in children's addition problem solving. *Developmental Psychology, 39,* 521–534.

Capaldi, D., DeGarmo, D., Patterson, G. R., & Forgatch, M. (2002). Contextual risk across the early life span and association with antisocial behavior. In J. B. Reid, G. R. Patterson, & J. Snyder (Eds.), *Antisocial behavior in children and adolescents* (pp. 123–145). Washington, DC: American Psychological Association.

Cappeliez, P., Rivard, V., & Guindon, S. (2007). Functions of reminiscence in later life: Proposition of a model and applications. *European Review of Applied Psychology, 57,* 151–156.

Cappeliez, P., & Robitaille, A. (2010). Coping mediates the relationships between reminiscence and psychological well-being among older adults. *Aging and Mental Health, 14,* 807–818.

Card, N. A., Stucky, B. D., Sawalani, G. M., & Little, T. D. (2008). Direct and indirect aggression during childhood and adolescence: A meta-analytic review of gender differences, intercorrelations, and relations to maladjustment. *Child Development, 79,* 1185–1229.

Carek, P. J., Laibstain, S. E., & Carek, S. M. (2011). Exercise for the treatment of depression and anxiety. *International Journal of Psychiatry in Medicine, 41,* 15–28.

Carey, S., & Markman, E. M. (1999). Cognitive development. In B. M. Bly & D. E. Rumelhart (Eds.), *Cognitive science* (pp. 201–254). San Diego: Academic Press.

Carlo, G., Koller, S. H., Eisenberg, N., Da Silva, M., & Frohlich, C. (1996). A cross-national study on the relations among prosocial moral reasoning, gender role orientations, and prosocial behaviors. *Developmental Psychology, 32,* 231–240.

Carlo, G., Mestre, M. V., Samper, P., Tur, A., & Armenta, B. E. (2011). The longitudinal relations among dimensions of parenting styles, sympathy, prosocial moral reasoning, and prosocial behaviors. *International Journal of Behavioral Development, 35,* 116–124.

Carlson, S. M., & Meltzoff, A. N. (2008). Bilingual experience and executive functioning in young children. *Developmental Science, 11,* 282–298.

Carlson, V. J., & Harwood, R. L. (2003). Attachment, culture, and the caregiving system: The cultural patterning of everyday experiences among Anglo and Puerto Rican mother–infant pairs. *Infant Mental Health Journal, 24,* 53–73.

Carnelley, K. B., Wortman, C. B., Bolger, N., & Burke, C. T. (2006). The time course of grief reactions to spousal loss: Evidence from a national probability sample. *Journal of Personality and Social Psychology, 91,* 476–492.

Carnes, B. A., Olshansky, S. J., & Hayflick, L. (2013). Can human biology allow most of us to become centenarians? *Journal of Gerontology, 68A,* 136–142.

Carpenter, M., Akhtar, N., & Tomasello, M. (1998). Fourteen- through eighteen-month-old infants differentially imitate intentional and accidental actions. *Infant Behavior and Development, 21,* 315–330.

Carr, D. (2003). A "good death" for whom? Quality of spouse's death and psychological distress among older widowed persons. *Journal of Health and Social Behavior, 44,* 215–232.

Carr, D. (2004). Psychological well-being across three cohorts: A response to shifting work–family opportunities and expectations? In O. G. Brim, C. D. Ryff, & R. C. Kessler (Eds.), *How healthy are we? A national study of well-being at midlife* (pp. 452–484). Chicago: University of Chicago Press.

Carr, D., House, J. S., Wortman, C., Nesse, R., & Kessler, R. C. (2001). Psychological adjustment to sudden and anticipated spousal loss among older widowed persons. *Journal of Gerontology, 56B,* S237–S248.

Carroll, D., Phillips, A. C., Hunt, K., & Der, G. (2007). Symptoms of depression and cardiovascular reactions to acute psychological stress: Evidence from a population study. *Biological Psychology, 75,* 68–74.

Carroll, J. B. (2005). The three-stratum theory of cognitive abilities. In D. P. Flanagan & P. L. Harrison (Eds.), *Contemporary intellectual assessment: Theories, tests, and issues* (2nd ed., pp. 69–76). New York: Guilford.

Carroll, J. S., Badger S., Willoughby, B. J., Nelson, L. J., Madsen, S. D., & Barry, C. M. (2009). Ready or not?: Criteria for marriage readiness among emerging adults. *Journal of Adolescent Research, 24,* 349–375.

Carstensen, L. L. (2006). The influence of sense of time on human development. *Science, 312,* 1913–1915.

Carstensen, L. L., Fung, H. H., & Charles, S. T. (2003). Socioemotional selectivity theory and the regulation of emotion in the second half of life. *Motivation and Emotion, 27,* 103–123.

Carstensen, L. L., Turan, B., Scheibe, S., Ram, N., Ersner-Hershfield, H., Samanez-Larkin, G. R., et al. (2011). Emotional experience improves with age: Evidence based on over 10 years of experience sampling. *Psychology and Aging, 26,* 21–33.

Carter, C. S., Hofer, T., Seo, A. Y., & Leeuwenburgh, C. (2007). Molecular mechanisms of life- and health-span extension: Role of calorie restriction and exercise intervention. *Applied Physiology, Nutrition, and Metabolism, 32,* 954–966.

Carver, C. S. (2011). Coping. In R. J. Contrada & A. Baum (Eds.), *Handbook of stress science: Biology, psychology, and health* (pp. 221–245). New York: Springer.

Carver, K., Joyner, K., & Udry, J. R. (2003). National estimates of adolescent romantic relationships. In P. Florsheim (Ed.), *Adolescent romantic relations and sexual behavior: Theory, research, and practical implications* (pp. 23–56). Mahwah, NJ: Erlbaum.

Carver, P. R., Egan, S. K., & Perry, D. G. (2004). Children who question their heterosexuality. *Developmental Psychology, 40,* 43–53.

Casalis, S., & Cole, P. (2009). On the relationship between morphological and phonological awareness: Effects of training in kindergarten and in first-grade reading. *First Language, 29,* 113–142.

Casas, J. F., Weigel, S. M., Crick, N. R., Ostrov, J. M., Woods, K. E., Yeh, E. A. J., & Huddleston-Casas, C. A. (2006). Early parenting and children's relational and physical aggression in the preschool and home contexts. *Applied Developmental Psychology, 27,* 209–227.

Casasola, M., Cohen, L. B., & Chiarello, E. (2003). Six-month-old infants' categorization of containment spatial relations. *Child Development, 74,* 679–693.

Casavant, M. J., Blake, K., Griffith, J., Yates, A., & Copley, L. M. (2007). Consequences of use of anabolic androgenic steroids. *Pediatric Clinics of North America, 54,* 677–690.

Case, R. (1996). Introduction: Reconceptualizing the nature of children's conceptual structures and their development in middle childhood. In R. Case & Y. Okamoto (Eds.), The role of central conceptual structures in the development of children's thought. *Monographs of the Society for Research in Child Development, 246*(61, Serial No. 246), pp. 1–26.

Case, R. (1998). The development of central conceptual structures. In D. Kuhn & R. Siegler (Eds.), *Handbook of child psychology: Vol. 2. Cognition, perception, and language* (5th ed., pp. 745–800). New York: Wiley.

Case, R., & Okamoto, Y. (Eds.). (1996). The role of central conceptual structures in the development of children's thought. *Monographs of the Society for Research in Child Development, 61*(1–2, Serial No. 246).

Caserta, M., Lund, D., Utz, R., & de Vries, B. (2009). Stress-related growth among the recently bereaved. *Aging and Mental Health, 13,* 463–476.

Caserta, M. S., Lund, D. A., & Obray, S. J. (2004). Promoting self-care and daily living skills among older widows and widowers: Evidence from the Pathfinders Demonstration Project. *Omega, 49,* 217–236.

Casper, L. M., & Smith, K. E. (2002). Dispelling the myths: Self-care, class, and race. *Journal of Family Issues, 23,* 716–727.

Caspi, A., Elder, G. H., Jr., & Bem, D. J. (1987). Moving against the world: Life-course patterns of explosive children. *Developmental Psychology, 23,* 308–313.

Caspi, A., Elder, G. H., Jr., & Bem, D. J. (1988). Moving away from the world: Life-course patterns of shy children. *Developmental Psychology, 24,* 824–831.

Caspi, A., Harrington, H., Milne, B., Amell, J. W., Theodore, R. F., & Moffitt, T. E. (2003). Children's behavioral styles at age 3 are linked to their adult personality traits at age 26. *Journal of Personality, 71,* 495–513.

Caspi, A., Lynam, D., Moffitt, T. E., & Silva, P. A. (1993). Unraveling girls' delinquency: Biological, dispositional, and contextual contributions to adolescent misbehavior. *Developmental Psychology, 29,* 19–30.

Caspi, A., McClay, J., Moffitt, T. E., Mill, J., Martin, J., & Craig, I. W. (2002). Role of genotype in the cycle of violence in maltreated children. *Science, 297,* 851–854.

Caspi, A., Moffitt, T. E., Morgan, J., Rutter, M., Taylor, A., Kim-Cohen, J., & Polo-Tomas, M. (2004). Maternal expressed emotion predicts children's antisocial behavior problems: Using monozygotic-twin differences to identify environmental effects on behavioral development. *Developmental Psychology, 40,* 149–161.

Caspi, A., & Roberts, B. W. (2001). Personality development across the life course: The argument for change and continuity. *Psychological Inquiry, 12,* 49–66.

Caspi, A., & Shiner, R. L. (2006). Personality development. In N. Eisenberg (Ed.), *Handbook of child psychology: Vol. 3. Social, emotional, and personality development* (6th ed., pp. 300–365). Hoboken, NJ: Wiley.

Cassia, V. M., Turati, C., & Simion, F. (2004). Can a nonspecific bias toward top-heavy patterns explain newborns' face preference? *Psychological Science, 15,* 379–383.

Cassidy, J. (2001). Adult romantic attachments: A developmental perspective on individual differences. *Review of General Psychology, 4,* 111–131.

Cassidy, J., & Berlin, L. J. (1994). The insecure/ ambivalent pattern of attachment: Theory and research. *Child Development, 65,* 971–991.

Castel, A. D., McGillivray, S., & Friedman, M. C. (2011). Metamemory and memory efficiency in older adults: Learning about the benefits of priority processing and value-directed remembering. In M. Naveh-Benjamin & N. Ohta (Eds.), *Memory and aging: Current issues and future directions* (pp. 245–270). New York: Psychology Press.

Castillo, E. M., & Comstock, R. D. (2007). Prevalence of use of performance-enhancing substances among United States adolescents. *Pediatric Clinics of North America, 54,* 663–675.

Caton, D., Corry, M. P., Frigoletto, F. D., Hokins, D. P., Liberman, E., & Mayberry, L. (2002). The nature and management of labor pain: Executive summary. *American Journal of Obstetrics and Gynecology, 186,* S1–S15.

Cauley, J. A. (2011). Defining ethnic and racial differences in osteoporosis and fragility fractures. *Clinical Orthopedics and Related Research, 469,* 1891–1899.

Ceci, S. J. (1991). How much does schooling influence general intelligence and its cognitive components? A reassessment of the evidence. *Developmental Psychology, 27,* 703–722.

Ceci, S. J. (1999). Schooling and intelligence. In S. J. Ceci & W. M. Williams (Eds.), *The nature–nurture debate: The essential readings* (pp. 168–175). Oxford, UK: Blackwell.

Ceci, S. J., Rosenblum, T. B., & Kumpf, M. (1998). The shrinking gap between high- and low-scoring groups: Current trends and possible causes. In U. Neisser (Ed.), *The rising curve* (pp. 287–302). Washington, DC: American Psychological Association.

Ceci, S. J., & Williams, W. M. (1997). Schooling, intelligence, and income. *American Psychologist, 52,* 1051–1058.

Ceci, S. J., & Williams, W. M. (2010). *The mathematics of sex: How biology and society conspire to limit talented women and girls.* New York: Oxford University Press.

Cecil, J. E., Watt, P., Murrie, I. S. L., Wrieden, W., Wallis, D. J., Hetherington, M. M., Bolton-Smith, C., & Palmer, C. N. A. (2005). Childhood obesity and socioeconomic status: A novel role for height

growth limitation. *International Journal of Obesity, 29,* 1199–1203.

Center for Communication and Social Policy. (Ed.). (1998). *National Television Violence Study* (Vol. 2). Newbury Park, CA: Sage.

Center for Hearing and Communication. (2012). *Facts about hearing loss.* Retrieved from www.chchearing .org/about-hearing-loss/facts-about-hearing-loss

Center to Advance Palliative Care. (2012). *Growth of palliative care in U.S. hospitals: 2012 snapshot.* Retrieved from www.capc.org/capc-growthanalysis-snapshot-2011.pdf

Centers for Disease Control and Prevention. (2007). *School Health Policies and Programs Study.* Atlanta, GA: Author.

Centers for Disease Control and Prevention. (2010). *Hip fractures in older adults.* Retrieved from www.cdc.gov/homeandrecreationalsafety/falls/ adulthipfx.html

Centers for Disease Control and Prevention. (2011a). *Breastfeeding report card—United States 2011.* Retrieved from www.cdc.gov/breastfeeding/ pdf/2011BreastfeedingReportCard.pdf

Centers for Disease Control and Prevention. (2011b). *HIV Surveillance Report: Diagnoses of HIV infection and AIDS in the United States and dependent areas, 2009.* Atlanta, GA: U.S. Department of Health and Human Services.

Centers for Disease Control and Prevention. (2011c). *Sexually transmitted disease surveillance 2010.* Atlanta, GA: U.S. Department of Health and Human Services.

Centers for Disease Control and Prevention. (2011d). *2009 assisted reproductive technology success rates: National summary and fertility clinic reports.* Atlanta, GA: Author.

Centers for Disease Control and Prevention. (2012a). *CDC vital signs: Child injury.* Retrieved from www.cdc.gov/vitalsigns/ChildInjury

Centers for Disease Control and Prevention. (2012b). Vital signs: Current cigarette smoking among adults aged ≥18 years—United States, 2005–2010. *Morbidity and Mortality Weekly Report, 60,* 1207–1212.

Centers for Disease Control and Prevention. (2013). *Multiple cause of death, 1999–2010.* Retrieved from wonder.cdc.gov/wonder/help/mcd.html

Centers for Medicare and Medicaid Services. (2012a). *National health expenditure projections.* Retrieved from www.cms.gov/Research-Statistics-Data-and-Systems/Statistics-Trends-and-Reports/ NationalHealthExpendData/ NationalHealthAccountsProjected.html

Centers for Medicare and Medicaid Services. (2012b). *Nursing home data compendium: 2012 edition.* Retrieved from www.cms.gov/Medicare/ Provider-Enrollment-and-Certification/ CertificationandComplianc/downloads/ nursinghomedatacompendium_508.pdf

Cerella, J. (1990). Aging and information processing rate. In J. E. Birren & K. W. Schaie (Eds.), *Handbook of the psychology of aging* (3rd ed.), (pp. 201–221). San Diego: Academic Press.

Cernoch, J. M., & Porter, R. H. (1985). Recognition of maternal axillary odors by infants. *Child Development 56,* 1593–1598.

Cevenini, E., Invidia, L., Lescai, F., Salvioli, S., Tieri, P., Castellani, G., & Franceschi, G. (2008). Human models of aging and longevity. *Expert Opinion on Biological Therapy, 8,* 1393–1405.

CFAH (Center for Advancement of Health). (2003). *Report on Phase 1 of the Grief Research Gaps, Needs and Actions Project.* Washington, DC: Author.

Chakravarty, E. F., Hubert, H. B., Krishnan, E., Bruce, B. B., Lingala, V. B., & Fries, J. F. (2012). Lifestyle risk factors predict disability and death in healthy aging adults. *American Journal of Medicine, 125,* 190–197.

Chalabaev, A., Sarrazin, P., & Fontayne, P. (2009). Stereotype endorsement and perceived ability as mediators of the girls' gender orientation–soccer performance relationship. *Psychology of Sport and Exercise, 10,* 297–299.

Chamberlain, P. (2003). Antisocial behavior and delinquency in girls. In P. Chamberlain (Ed.), *Treating chronic juvenile offenders* (pp. 109–127). Washington, DC: American Psychological Association.

Champion, T. B. (2003a). "A matter of vocabulary": Performances of low-income African-American Head Start children on the Peabody Picture Vocabulary Test. *Communication Disorders Quarterly, 24,* 121–127.

Champion, T. B. (2003b). *Understanding storytelling among African-American children: A journey from Africa to America.* Mahwah, NJ: Erlbaum.

Chan, A., Meints, K., Lieven, E., & Tomasello, M. (2010). Young children's comprehension of English SVO word order revisited: Testing the same children in act-out and intermodal preferential looking tasks. *Cognitive Development, 25,* 30–45.

Chan, L. K. S., & Moore, P. J. (2006). Development of attributional beliefs and strategic knowledge in years 5–9: A longitudinal analysis. *Educational Psychology, 26,* 161–185.

Chan, R. W., Raboy, B., & Patterson, C. J. (1998). Psychosocial adjustment among children conceived via donor insemination by lesbian and heterosexual mothers. *Child Development, 69,* 443–457.

Chan, S. M. (2010). Aggressive behaviour in early elementary school children: Relations to authoritarian parenting, children's negative emotionality and coping strategies. *Early Child Development and Care, 180,* 1253–1269.

Chandola, T., & Marmot, M. G. (2011). Socioeconomic status and stress. In R. J. Contrada & A. Baum (Eds.), *Handbook of stress science: Biology, psychology, and health* (pp. 185–193). New York: Springer.

Chandra, A., Martino, S. C., Collins, R. L., Elliott, M. N., Berry, S. H., Kanouse, D. E., & Miu, A. (2008). Does watching sex on television predict teen pregnancy? Findings from a national longitudinal survey of youth. *Pediatrics, 122,* 1047–1054.

Chang, E., Wilber, K. H., & Silverstein, M. (2010). The effects of childlessness on the care and psychological well-being of older adults with disabilities. *Aging and Mental Health, 14,* 712–719.

Chang, L., Schwartz, D., Dodge, D. A., & McBride-Chang, C. (2003). Harsh parenting in relation to child emotion regulation and aggression. *Journal of Family Psychology, 17,* 598–606.

Chao, R. K. (1994). Beyond parental control and authoritarian parenting style: Understanding Chinese parenting through the cultural notion of training. *Child Development, 65,* 1111–1119.

Chao, R. K., & Good, G. E. (2004). Nontraditional students' perspectives on college education: A qualitative study. *Journal of College Counseling, 7,* 5–12.

Chao, R. K., & Tseng, V. (2002). Parenting of Asians. In M. H. Bornstein (Ed.), *Handbook of parenting: Vol. 4* (2nd ed., pp. 59–94). Mahwah, NJ: Erlbaum.

Charles, S. T. (2010). Strength and vulnerability integration: A model of emotional well-being across adulthood. *Psychological Bulletin, 136,* 1068–1091.

Charles, S. T. (2011). Emotional experience and regulation in later life. In K. W. Schaie & S. L. Willis (Eds.), *Handbook of the psychology of aging* (7th ed., pp. 295–310). San Diego, CA: Academic Press.

Charles, S. T., & Carstensen, L. L. (2009). Socio-emotional selectivity theory. In H. Reis & S. Sprecher (Eds.), *Encyclopedia of human relationships* (pp. 1578–1581). Thousand Oaks, CA: Sage.

Charles, S. T., & Carstensen, L. L. (2010). Social and emotional aging. *Annual Review of Psychology, 61,* 383–409.

Charman, T., Baron-Cohen, S., Swettenham, J., Baird, G., Cox, A., & Drew, A. (2001). Testing joint attention, imitation, and play as infancy precursors to language and theory of mind. *Cognitive Development, 15,* 481–49.

Charman, W. N. (2008). The eye in focus: Accommodation and presbyopia. *Optometry, 91,* 207–225.

Charpak, N., Ruiz-Peláez, J. G., & Figueroa, Z. (2005). Influence of feeding patterns and other factors on early somatic growth of healthy, preterm infants in home-based kangaroo mother care: A cohort study. *Journal of Pediatric Gastroenterology and Nutrition, 41,* 430–437.

Chase-Lansdale, P. L., Gordon, R., Brooks-Gunn, J., & Klebanov, P. K. (1997). Neighborhood and family influences on the intellectual and behavioral competence of preschool and early school-age children. In J. Brooks-Gunn, G. Duncan, & J. L. Aber (Eds.), *Neighborhood poverty: Context and consequences for development* (pp. 79–118). New York: Russell Sage Foundation.

Chauhan, G. S., Shastri, J., & Mohite, P. (2005). Development of gender constancy in preschoolers. *Psychological Studies, 50,* 62–71.

Chavajay, P., & Rogoff, B. (1999). Cultural variation in management of attention by children and their caregivers. *Developmental Psychology, 35,* 1079–1090.

Chavajay, P., & Rogoff, B. (2002). Schooling and traditional collaborative social organization of problem solving by Mayan mothers and children. *Developmental Psychology, 38,* 55–66.

Chawarska, K., & Shic, F. (2009). Looking but not seeing: Atypical visual scanning and recognition of faces in 2- and 4-year-old children with autism spectrum disorder. *Journal of Autism and Developmental Disorders, 39,* 1663–1672.

Cheadle, J. E., & Amato, P. R. (2011). A quantitative assessment of Lareau's qualitative conclusions about class, race, and parenting. *Journal of Family Issues, 32,* 679–706.

Cheah, C. S. L., Leung, C. Y. Y., Tahseen, M., & Schultz, D. (2009). Authoritative parenting among immigrant Chinese mothers of preschoolers. *Journal of Family Psychology, 23,* 311–320.

Checkley, W., Epstein, L. D., Gilman, R. H., Cabrera, L., & Black, R. E. (2003). Effects of acute diarrhea on linear growth in Peruvian children. *American Journal of Epidemiology, 157,* 166–175.

Chen, E. S. L., & Rao, N. (2011). Gender socialization in Chinese kindergartens: Teachers' contributions. *Sex Roles, 64,* 103–116.

Chen, J. J. (2005). Relation of academic support from parents, teachers, and peers to Hong Kong adolescents' academic achievement: The mediating role of academic engagement. *Genetic, Social, and General Psychology Monographs, 131,* 77–127.

Chen, J. J., Howard, K. S., & Brooks-Gunn, J. (2011). How do neighborhoods matter across the life span? In K. L. Fingerman, C. A. Berg, J. Smith, & T. C. Antonucci (Eds.), *Handbook of life-span development* (pp. 805–836). New York: Springer.

Chen, R. (2012). Institutional characteristics and college student dropout risks: A multilevel event history analysis. *Research in Higher Education, 53,* 487–505.

Chen, X., & French, D. C. (2008). Children's social competence in cultural context. *Annual Review of Psychology, 59,* 591–616.

Chen, X., Wang, L., & DeSouza, A. (2006). Temperament, socioemotional functioning, and peer relationships in Chinese and North American children. In X. Chen, D. C. French, & B. H. Schneider (Eds.), *Peer relationships in cultural context* (pp. 123–147). New York: Cambridge University Press.

Chen, X., Wu, H., Chen, H., Wang, L., & Cen, G. (2001). Parenting practices and aggressive behavior in Chinese children. *Parenting: Science and Practice, 1,* 159–184.

Chen, Y.-C., Yu, M.-L., Rogan, W., Gladen, B., & Hsu, C.-C. (1994). A 6-year follow-up of behavior and activity disorders in the Taiwan Yu-cheng children. *American Journal of Public Health, 84,* 415–421.

Chen, Y.-J., & Hsu, C.-C. (1994). Effects of prenatal exposure to PCBs on the neurological function of children: A neuropsychological and neurophysiological study. *Developmental Medicine and Child Neurology, 36,* 312–320.

Cherlin, A. J. (2009). *The marriage-go-round.* New York: Knopf.

Cherlin, E. J., Barry, C. L., Prigerson, H. G., Schulman-Green, D., Johnson-Hurzeler, R., Kasl, S. V., & Bradley, E. H. (2007). Bereavement services for family caregivers: How often used, why, and why not. *Journal of Palliative Medicine, 10,* 148–158.

Chess, S., & Thomas, A. (1984). *Origins and evolution of behavior disorders.* New York: Brunner/Mazel.

Cheung, F. M., & Halpern, D. F. (2010). Women at the top: Powerful leaders define success as work + family in a culture of gender. *American Psychologist, 65,* 182–193.

Chhin, C. S., Bleeker, M. M., & Jacobs, J. E. (2008). Gender-typed occupational choices: The long-term impact of parents' beliefs and expectations. In H. M. G. Watt & J. S. Eccles (Eds.), *Gender and occupational outcomes: Longitudinal assessments of individual, social, and cultural influences* (pp. 215–234). Washington, DC: American Psychological Association.

Chi, M. T. H. (2006). Laboratory methods for assessing experts' and novices' knowledge. In K. A. Ericsson, N. Charness, P. J. Feltovich, & R. R. Hoffman (Eds.), *The Cambridge handbook of expertise and expert performance* (pp. 167–184). New York: Cambridge University Press.

Chi, M. T. H., Glaser, R., & Farr, M. J. (Eds.). (1988). *The nature of expertise.* Hillsdale, NJ: Erlbaum.

Child Trends. (2007). *Late or no prenatal care.* Retrieved from www.childtrendsdatabank.org/indicators/25PrenatalCare.cfm

Child Trends. (2011). *Teen births.* Retrieved from www.childtrendsdatabank.org/?q=node/52

Child Trends. (2012). *Late or no prenatal care.* Retrieved from www.childtrendsdatabank.org/sites/default/files/25_Prenatal_Care.pdf

Chin, T., & Phillips, M. (2004). Social reproduction and child-rearing practices: Social class, children's agency, and the summer activity gap. *Sociology of Education, 77*(3), 185–210.

Chinn, C. A., & Malhotra, B. A. (2002). Children's responses to anomalous scientific data: How is conceptual change impeded? *Journal of Educational Psychology, 94,* 327–343.

Choi, J., Fauce, S. R., & Effros, R. B. (2008). Reduced telomerase activity in human T lymphocytes exposed to cortisol. *Brain, Behavior, and Immunity, 22,* 600–605.

Choi, N., & Kim, J. (2011). The effect of time volunteering and charitable donations in later life on psychological well-being. *Ageing and Society, 31,* 590–611.

Chomsky, C. (1969). *The acquisition of syntax in children from five to ten.* Cambridge, MA: MIT Press.

Chomsky, N. (1957). *Syntactic structures.* The Hague: Mouton.

Chomtho, S., Wells, J. C., Williams, J. E., Davies, P. S., Lucas, A., & Fewtrell, M. S. (2008). Infant growth and later body composition: Evidence from the 4-component model. *American Journal of Clinical Nutrition, 87,* 1776–1784.

Chouinard, M. M. (2007). Children's questions: A mechanism for cognitive development. *Monographs of the Society for Research in Child Development, 72*(1, Serial No. 286).

Chouinard, M. M., & Clark, E. V. (2003). Adult reformulations of child errors as negative evidence. *Journal of Child Language, 30,* 637–669.

Christ, G. H., Siegel, K., & Christ, A. E. (2002). "It never really hit me . . . until it actually happened." *Journal of the American Medical Association, 288,* 1269–1278.

Christakis, D. A., Zimmerman, F. J., DiGiuseppe, D. L., & McCarty, C. A. (2004). Early television exposure and subsequent attentional problems in children. *Pediatrics, 113,* 708–713.

Christensen, A.-D., & Larsen, J. E. (2008). Gender, class, and family: Men and gender equality in a Danish context. *Social Politics: International Studies in Gender, State and Society, 15,* 53–78.

Christenson, S. L., & Thurlow, M. L. (2004). School dropouts: Prevention considerations, interventions, and challenges. *Current Directions in Psychological Science, 13,* 36–39.

Christiansen, M. H., & Chater, N. (2008). Language as shaped by the brain. *Behavioral and Brain Sciences, 31,* 489–558.

Chu, J., Zhou, C. C., Lu, N., Zhang, X., & Dong, F. T. (2008). Genetic variants in three genes and smoking show strong associations with susceptibility to exudative age-related macular degeneration in a Chinese population. *Chinese Medical Journal, 121,* 2525–2533.

Chudley, A. E., Conry, J., Cook, J. L., Loock, C., Rosales, T., & LeBlanc, N. (2005). Fetal alcohol spectrum disorder: Canadian guidelines for diagnosis. *Canadian Medical Association Journal, 172,* S1–S21.

Chumlea, W. C., Schubert, C. M., Roche, A. F., Kulin, H. E., Lee, P. A., Himes, J. H., & Sun, S. S. (2003). Age at menarche and racial comparisons in U.S. girls. *Pediatrics, 111,* 110–113.

Chung, H. L., Mulvey, E. P., & Steinberg, L. (2011). Understanding the school outcomes of juvenile offenders: An exploration of neighborhood influences and motivational resources. *Journal of Youth and Adolescence, 40,* 1025–1038.

Church, E. (2004). *Understanding stepmothers: Women share their struggles, successes, and insights.* Toronto: HarperCollins.

CIA (Central Intelligence Agency). (2012). *World fact book.* Retrieved from www.cia.gov/library/publications/download/download-2012/index.html

Cicchetti, D. (2007). Intervention and policy implications of research on neurobiological functioning in maltreated children. In J. L. Aber, S. J. Bishop-Josef, S. M. Jones, K. T. McLearn, & D. A. Phillips (Eds.), *Child development and social policy* (pp. 167–184). Washington, DC: American Psychological Association.

Cicirelli, V. G. (1995). *Sibling relationships across the life span.* New York: Plenum.

Cicirelli, V. G. (2001). Personal meanings of death in older adults and young adults in relation to their fears of death. *Death Studies, 25,* 663–683.

Cicirelli, V. G. (2002). *Older adults' views on death.* New York: Springer.

Cillessen, A. H. N., & Bellmore, A. D. (2004). Social skills and interpersonal perception in early and middle childhood. In P. K. Smith & C. H. Hart (Eds.), *Blackwell handbook of childhood social development* (pp. 355–374). Malden, MA: Blackwell.

Cipriano, E. A., & Stifter, C. A. (2010). Predicting preschool effortful control from toddler temperament and parenting behavior. *Journal of Applied Developmental Psychology, 31,* 221–230.

Clark, C. A., Woodward, L. J., Horwood, L. J., & Moor, S. (2008). Development of emotional and behavioral regulation in children born extremely preterm and very preterm: Biological and social influences. *Child Development, 79,* 1444–1462.

Clark, K. E., & Ladd, G. W. (2000). Connectedness and autonomy support in parent–child relationships: Links to children's socio-emotional orientation and peer relationships. *Developmental Psychology, 36,* 485–498.

Clarke, B. L., & Khosla, S. (2010). Physiology of bone loss. *Radiologic Clinics of North America, 48,* 483–495.

Clarke, L. H. (2005). Remarriage in later life: Older women's negotiations of power, resources and domestic labor. *Journal of Women and Aging, 17,* 21–41.

Clarke, P., & Smith, J. (2011). Aging in a cultural context: Cross-national differences in disability and the moderating role of personal control among older adults in the United States and England. *Journal of Gerontology, 66B,* 457–467.

Clarkson, T. W., Magos, L., & Myers, G. J. (2003). The toxicology of mercury—current exposures and clinical manifestations. *New England Journal of Medicine, 349,* 1731–1737.

Clarke-Stewart, K. A., & Brentano, C. (2006). *Divorce: Causes and consequences.* New Haven: Yale University Press.

Clarke-Stewart, K. A., & Hayward, C. (1996). Advantages of father custody and contact for the psychological well-being of school-age children. *Journal of Applied Developmental Psychology, 17,* 239–270.

Claxton, A., O'Rourke, N., Smith, J. Z., & DeLongis, A. (2011). Personality traits and marital satisfaction within enduring relationships: An intra-couple discrepancy approach. *Journal of Social and Personal Relationships, 29,* 375–396.

Clay, R. A. (2009). Mini-multitaskers. *Monitor on Psychology, 40*(2), 38–40.

Clearfield, M. W., & Nelson, N. M. (2006). Sex differences in mothers' speech and play behavior with 6-, 9-, and 14-month-old infants. *Sex Roles, 54,* 127–137.

Clearfield, M. W., Obsborn, C. N., & Mullen, M. (2008). Learning by looking: Infants' social looking behavior across the transition from crawling to walking. *Journal of Experimental Child Psychology, 100,* 297–307.

Clegg, L. X., Reichman, M. E., Miller, B. A., Hankey, B. F., Singh, G. K., Lin, Y. D., et al. (2009). Impact of socioeconomic status on cancer incidence and stage at diagnosis: Selected findings from the surveillance, epidemiology, and end results: National Longitudinal Mortality Study. *Cancer Causes and Control, 20,* 417–435.

Clements, D. H., & Sarama, J. (2003). Young children and technology: What does the research say? *Young Children, 58*(6), 34–40.

Cleveland, E. S., & Reese, E. (2005). Maternal structure and autonomy support in conversations about the past: Contributions to children's autobiographical memory. *Developmental Psychology, 41,* 376–388.

Clinchy, B. M. (2002). Revisiting women's ways of knowing. In B. K. Hofer & P. R. Pintrich (Eds.), *Personal epistemology: The psychological beliefs about knowledge and knowing* (pp. 63–87). Mahwah, NJ: Erlbaum.

Clingempeel, W. G., & Henggeler, S. W. (2003). Aggressive juvenile offenders transitioning into emerging adulthood: Factors discriminating persistors and desistors. *American Journal of Orthopsychiatry, 73,* 310–323.

Coatsworth, J. D., Sharp, E. H., Palen, L., Darling, N., Cumsille, P., & Marta, M. (2005). Exploring adolescent self-defining leisure activities and identity experiences across three countries. *International Journal of Behavioral Development, 29,* 361–370.

Cohen, L. B. (2003). Commentary on Part I: Unresolved issues in infant categorization. In D. H. Rakison & L. M. Oakes (Eds.), *Early category and concept development: Making sense of the blooming, buzzing confusion* (pp. 193–209). New York: Oxford University Press.

Cohen, L. B. (2010). A bottom-up approach to infant perception and cognition: A summary of evidence and discussion of issues. In S. P. Johnson (Ed.), *Neoconstructivism: The new science of cognitive development* (pp. 335–346). New York: Oxford University Press.

Cohen, L. B., & Brunt, J. (2009). Early word learning and categorization: Methodological issues and recent empirical evidence. In J. Colombo, P. McCardle, & L. Freund (Eds.), *Infant pathways to language: Methods, models, and research disorders* (pp. 245–266). New York: Psychology Press.

Cohen, L. B., & Cashon, C. H. (2006). Infant cognition. In D. Kuhn & R. Siegler (Eds.), *Handbook of child psychology: Vol. 2. Cognition, perception, and language* (6th ed., pp. 214–251). Hoboken, NJ: Wiley.

Cohen-Bendahan, C. C. C., van de Beek, C., & Berenbaum, S. A. (2005). Prenatal sex hormones effects on child and adult sex-typed behavior: Methods and findings. *Neuroscience and Biobehavioral Reviews, 29,* 353–384.

Cohen-Shalev, A. (1986). Artistic creativity across the adult life span: An alternative approach. *Interchange, 17*(4), 1–16.

Cohler, B. J., & Hostetler, A. J. (2007). Gay lives in the Third Age: Possibilities and paradoxes. In J. B. James & P. Wink (Eds.), *Annual review of gerontology and geriatrics* (Vol. 26, pp. 193–209). New York: Springer.

Coie, J. D., Dodge, K. A., & Coppotelli, H. (1982). Dimensions and types of social status: A cross-age perspective. *Developmental Psychology, 18,* 557–570.

Coke, M. M. (1992). Correlates of life satisfaction among elderly African Americans. *Journal of Gerontology, 47,* P316–P320.

Coker, A. D. (2003). African American female adult learners: Motivations, challenges, and coping strategies. *Journal of Black Studies, 33,* 654–674.

Colby, A., Kohlberg, L., Gibbs, J., & Lieberman, M. (1983). A longitudinal study of moral judgment. *Monographs of the Society for Research in Child Development, 48*(1–2, Serial No. 200).

Colcombe, S. J., Erickson, K. I., Scalf, P. E., Kim, J. S., Prakash, R., & McAuley, E. (2006). Aerobic exercise training increases brain volume in aging humans. *Journal of Gerontology, 61A,* 1166–1170.

Colcombe, S. J., Kramer, A. F., Erickson, K. I., Scalf, P., McAuley, E., & Cohen, N. J. (2004). Cardiovascular fitness, cortical plasticity, and aging. *Proceedings of the National Academy of Sciences, 101,* 3316–3321.

Cole, D. A., Martin, J. M., Peeke, L. A., Seroczynski, A. D., & Fier, J. (1999). Children's over- and underestimation of academic competence: A longitudinal study of gender differences, depression, and anxiety. *Child Development, 70,* 459–473.

Cole, E. R., & Stewart, A. J. (1996). Meanings of political participation among black and white women: Political identity and social responsibility. *Journal of Personality and Social Psychology, 71,* 130–140.

Cole, M. (1990). Cognitive development and formal schooling: The evidence from cross-cultural research. In L. C. Moll (Ed.), *Vygotsky and education* (pp. 89–110). New York: Cambridge University Press.

Cole, P. M., Armstrong, L. M., & Pemberton, C. K. (2010). The role of language in the development of emotion regulation. In S. D. Calkins & M. A. Bell (Eds.), *Child development at the intersection of emotion and cognition* (pp. 59–77). Washington, DC: American Psychological Association.

Coleman, M., Ganong, L., & Leon, K. (2006). Divorce and postdivorce relationships. In A. L. Vangelisti & D. Perlman (Eds.), *The Cambridge handbook of personal relationships* (pp. 157–173). New York: Cambridge University Press.

Coleman, P. G., Ivani-Chalian, C., & Robinson, M. (2004). Religious attitudes among British older people: Stability and change in a 20-year longitudinal study. *Ageing and Society, 24,* 167–188.

Coles, C. D., Goldstein, F. C., Lynch, M. E., Chen, X., Kable, J. A., Johnson, K. C., et al. (2011). Memory and brain volume in adults prenatally exposed to alcohol. *Brain and Cognition, 75,* 67–77.

Coles, L. (2004). Demography of human supercentenarians. *Journal of Gerontology, 59A,* 579–586.

Coley, R. L., Morris, J. E., & Hernandez, D. (2004). Out-of-school care and problem behavior trajectories among low-income adolescents: Individual, family, and neighborhood characteristics as added risks. *Child Development, 75,* 948–965.

Coley, R. L., Votruba-Drzal, E., & Schindler, H. S. (2009). Fathers' and mothers' parenting predicting and responding to adolescent sexual risk behaviors. *Child Development, 80,* 808–827.

Collings, P. (2001). "If you got everything, it's good enough": Perspectives on successful aging in a Canadian Inuit community. *Journal of Cross-Cultural Gerontology, 16,* 127–155.

Collins, N. L., Guichard, A. C., Ford, M. B., & Feeney, B. C. (2006). Responding to need in intimate relationships: Normative processes and individual differences. In M. Mikulincer & G. S. Goodman (Eds.), *Dynamics of romantic love* (pp. 149–189). New York: Guilford.

Collins, W. A., & Laursen, B. (2004). Parent–adolescent relationships and influences. In R. M. Lerner & L. Steinberg (Eds.), *Handbook of adolescent psychology* (2nd ed., pp. 331–361). New York: Wiley.

Collins, W. A., & Madsen, S. D. (2006). Personal relationships in adolescence and early adulthood. In A. L. Vangelisti & D. Perlman (Eds.), *The Cambridge handbook of personal relationships* (pp. 191–209). New York: Cambridge University Press.

Collins, W. A., Madsen, S. D., & Susman-Stillman, A. (2002). Parenting during middle childhood. In M. H. Bornstein (Ed.), *Handbook of parenting: Vol. 1* (2nd ed., pp. 73–101). Mahwah, NJ: Erlbaum.

Collins, W. A., & van Dulmen, M. (2006a). "The course of true love(s) . . .": Origins and pathways in the development of romantic relationships. In A. Booth & A. Crouter (Eds.), *Romance and sex in adolescence and emerging adulthood: Risks and opportunities* (pp. 63–86). Mahwah, NJ: Erlbaum.

Collins, W. A., & van Dulmen, M. (2006b). Friendships and romantic relationships in emerging adulthood: Continuities and discontinuities. In J. J. Arnett & J. Tanner (Eds.), *Emerging adults in America: Coming of age in the 21st century* (pp. 219–234). Washington, DC: American Psychological Association.

Collins, W. A., Welsh, D. P., & Furman, W. (2009). Adolescent romantic relationships. *Annual Review of Psychology, 60,* 631–652.

Collins, W. K., & Steinberg, L. (2006). Adolescent development in interpersonal context. In N. Eisenberg (Ed.), *Handbook of child psychology: Vol. 3. Social, emotional, and personality development* (6th ed., pp. 1003–1067). Hoboken, NJ: Wiley.

Colman, R. A., Hardy, S. A., Albert, M., Raffaelli, M., & Crockett, L. (2006). Early predictors of self-regulation in middle childhood. *Infant and Child Development, 15,* 421–437.

Colom, R., Escorial, S., Shih, P. C., & Privado, J. (2007). Fluid intelligence, memory span, and temperament difficulties predict academic performance of young adolescents. *Personality and Individual Differences, 42,* 1503–1514.

Colombo, J. (2002). Infant attention grows up: The emergence of a developmental cognitive neuroscience perspective. *Current Directions in Psychological Science, 11,* 196–199.

Colombo, J., Shaddy, D. J., Richman, W. A., Maikranz, J. M., & Blaga, O. M. (2004). The developmental course of habituation in infancy and preschool outcome. *Infancy, 5,* 1–38.

Commission on Adolescent Suicide Prevention. (2005). Targeted youth suicide prevention programs. In D. L. Evans, E. B. Foa, R. E. Gur, H. Hending, & C. P. O'Brien (Eds.), *Treating and preventing adolescent mental health disorders: What we know and what we don't know* (pp. 463–469). New York: Oxford University Press.

Commission on Children at Risk. (2008). Hardwired to connect: The new scientific case for authoritative communities. In K. K. Kline (Ed.), *Authoritative communities: The scientific case for nurturing the whole child* (pp. 3–68). New York: Springer.

Compton, J. I., Cox, E., & Laanan, F. S. (2006). Adult learners in transition. In F. S. Lanaan (Eds.), *New directions for student services* (Vol. 114, pp. 73–800). San Francisco: Jossey-Bass.

Comunian, A. L., & Gielen, U. P. (2000). Sociomoral reflection and prosocial and antisocial behavior: Two Italian studies. *Psychological Reports, 87,* 161–175.

Comunian, A. L., & Gielen, U. P. (2006). Promotion of moral judgment maturity through stimulation of social role-taking and social reflection: An Italian intervention study. *Journal of Moral Education, 35,* 51–69.

Conboy, B. T., & Thal, D. J. (2006). Ties between the lexicon and grammar: Cross-sectional and longitudinal studies of bilingual toddlers. *Child Development, 77,* 712–735.

Conchas, G. Q. (2006). *The color of success: Race and high-achieving urban youth.* New York: Teachers College Press.

Conde-Agudelo, A., Belizan, J. M., and Diaz-Rossello, J. (2011). Kangaroo mother care to reduce morbidity and mortality in low birthweight infants. *Cochrane Database of Systematic Reviews, 3,* CD002771.

Conger, K. J., Stocker, C., & McGuire, S. (2009). Sibling socialization: The effects of stressful life events and experiences. In L. Kramer & K. J. Conger (Eds.), *Siblings as agents of socialization: New directions for child and adolescent development* (No. 126, pp. 44–60). San Francisco: Jossey-Bass.

Conger, R. D., & Donnellan, M. B. (2007). An interactionist perspective on the socioeconomic context of human development. *Annual Review of Psychology, 58,* 175–199.

Connell, M. W., Sheridan, K., & Gardner, H. (2003). On abilities and domains. In R. J. Sternberg & E. Grigorenko (Eds.), *Perspectives on the psychology of abilities, competencies, and expertise* (pp. 126–155). New York: Cambridge University Press.

Conner, D. B., & Cross, D. R. (2003). Longitudinal analysis of the presence, efficacy, and stability of maternal scaffolding during informal problem-solving interactions. *British Journal of Developmental Psychology, 21,* 315–334.

Connidis, I. A. (2010). *Family ties and aging* (2nd ed.). Thousand Oaks, CA: Pine Forge Press.

Connolly, J., Craig, W., Goldberg, A., & Pepler, D. (2004). Mixed-gender groups, dating, and romantic relationships in early adolescence. *Journal of Research on Adolescence, 14,* 185–207.

Connolly, J., & Goldberg, A. (1999). Romantic relationships in adolescence: The role of friends and peers in their emergence and development. In W. Furman, B. B. Brown, & C. Feiring (Eds.), *The development of romantic relationships in adolescence* (pp. 266–290). New York: Cambridge University Press.

Connolly, J. A., & Doyle, A. B. (1984). Relations of social fantasy play to social competence in preschoolers. *Developmental Psychology, 20,* 797–806.

Connor, L. T., Spiro, A., Obler, L. K., & Albert, M. L. (2004). Change in object naming ability during adulthood. *Journal of Gerontology, 59B,* P203–P209.

Conway, C. C., Rancourt, D., Adelman, C. B., Burk, W. J., & Prinstein, M. J. (2011). Depression

socialization within friendship groups at the transition to adolescence: The roles of gender and group centrality as moderators of peer influence. *Journal of Abnormal Psychology, 120,* 857–867.

Conway, L. (2007, April 5). Drop the Barbie: Ken Zucker's reparatist treatment of gender-variant children. *Trans News Updates.* Retrieved from ai.eecs.umich.edu/people/conway/TS/News/Drop%20the%20Barbie.htm

Conway, M. A., Wang, Q., Hanyu, K., & Haque, S. (2005). A cross-cultural investigation of autobiographical memory. On the universality and cultural variation of the reminiscence bump. *Journal of Cross-Cultural Psychology, 36,* 739–749.

Conwell, Y., Duberstein, P. R., Hirsch, J., & Conner, K. R. (2010). Health status and suicide in the second half of life. *Geriatric Psychiatry, 25,* 371–379.

Conwell, Y., Van Orden, K., & Caine, E. D. (2011). Suicide in older adults. *Psychiatric Clinics of North America, 34,* 451–468.

Cook, C. R., Williams, K. R., Guerra, N. G., & Kim, T. E. (2010). Variability in the prevalence of bullying and victimization: A cross-national and methodological analysis. In S. R. Jimerson, S. M. Swearer, & D. L. Espelage (Eds.), *Handbook of bullying in schools: An international perspective* (pp. 347–362). New York: Routledge.

Cooke, L. P. (2010). The politics of housework. In J. Treas & S. Drobnic (Eds.), *Dividing the Domestic: Men, women, and household work in cross-national perspective* (pp. 59–78). Stanford, CA: Stanford University Press.

Cooney, T. M., & Mortimer, J. T. (1999). Family structure differences in the timing of leaving home: Exploring mediating factors. *Journal of Research on Adolescence, 9,* 367–393.

Cooper, C., Harvey, N., Cole, Z., Hanson, M., & Dennison, E. (2009). Developmental origins of osteoporosis: The role of maternal nutrition. In B. Koletzko, T. Decsi, D. Molnár, & A. de la Hunty (Eds.), *Early nutrition programming and health outcomes in later life: Obesity and beyond* (pp. 31–39). New York: Springer Science + Business Media.

Cooper, C., Sayer, A., & Dennison, E. M. (2006). The developmental environment: Clinical perspectives on effects on the musculoskeletal system. In P. Gluckman & M. Hanson (Eds.), *Developmental origins of health and disease* (pp. 392–405). Cambridge, UK: Cambridge University Press.

Cooper, R., & Huh, C. R. (2008). Improving academic possibilities of students of color during the middle school to high school transition: Conceptual and strategic considerations in a U.S. context. In J. K. Asamen, M. L. Ellis, & G. L. Berry (Eds.), *Sage handbook of child development, multiculturalism, and media* (pp. 143–162). Thousand Oaks, CA: Sage.

Copen, C. E., Chandra A., & Martinez G. (2012). *Prevalence and timing of oral sex with opposite-sex partners among females and males aged 15–24 years: United States, 2007–2010.* National Health Statistics Reports, No. 56. Hyattsville, MD: U.S. Department of Health and Human Services.

Coplan, R. J., & Arbeau, K. A. (2008). The stresses of a "brave new world": Shyness and school adjustment in kindergarten. *Journal of Research in Childhood Education, 22,* 377–389.

Coplan, R. J., Arbeau, K. A., & Armer, M. (2008). "Don't fret, be supportive!" Maternal characteristics linking child shyness to psychosocial and school adjustment in kindergarten. *Journal of Abnormal Child Psychology, 36,* 359–371.

Coplan, R. J., & Armer, M. (2007). A "multitude" of solitude: A closer look at social withdrawal and nonsocial play in early childhood. *Child Development Perspectives, 1,* 26–32.

Coplan, R. J., Gavinsky-Molina, M. H., Lagace-Seguin, D., & Wichmann, C. (2001). When girls versus boys

play alone: Gender differences in the associates of nonsocial play in kindergarten. *Developmental Psychology, 37,* 464–474.

Coplan, R. J., Prakash, K., O'Neil, K., & Armer, M. (2004). Do you "want" to play? Distinguishing between conflicted shyness and social disinterest in early childhood. *Developmental Psychology, 40,* 244–258.

Copple, C., & Bredekamp, S. (2009). *Developmentally appropriate practice in early childhood programs* (3rd ed.). Washington, DC: National Association for the Education of Young Children.

Corenblum, B. (2003). What children remember about ingroup and outgroup peers: Effects of stereotypes on children's processing of information about group members. *Journal of Experimental Child Psychology, 86,* 32–66.

Cornish, A. M., McMahon, C. A., Ungerer, J. A., Barnett, B., Kowalenko, N., & Tennant, C. (2005). Postnatal depression and infant cognitive and motor development in the second postnatal year: The impact of depression chronicity and infant gender. *Infant Behavior and Development, 28,* 407–417.

Cornwell, A. C., & Feigenbaum, P. (2006). Sleep biological rhythms in normal infants and those at high risk for SIDS. *Chronobiology International, 23,* 935–961.

Corr, C. A., & Corr, D. M. (2007). Historical and contemporary perspectives on loss, grief, and mourning. In C. A. Corr & D. M. Corr (Eds.), *Handbook of thanatology* (pp. 131–142). New York: Routledge.

Corr, C. A., & Corr, D. M. (2013). *Death and dying, life and living* (2nd ed.). Belmont, CA: Cengage.

Correa-Chávez, M., Rogoff, B., & Mejía-Arauz, R. (2005). Cultural patterns in attending to two events at once. *Child Development, 76,* 664–678.

Costello, J. (2006). Dying well: Nurses' experiences of "good and bad" deaths in hospital. *Journal of Advanced Nursing, 54,* 594–601.

Côté, J. E. (2006). Emerging adulthood as an institutionalized moratorium: Risks and benefits to identity formation. In J. J. Arnett (Ed.), *Emerging adults in America: Coming of age in the 21st century* (pp. 85–116). Washington, DC: American Psychological Association.

Côté, J. E. (2009). Identity formation and self-development in adolescence. In R. M. Lerner & L. Steinberg (Eds.), *Handbook of adolescent psychology: Vol. 1. Individual bases of adolescent development* (3rd ed., pp. 266–304). Hoboken, NJ: Wiley.

Côté, J. E., & Bynner, J. M. (2008). Changes in the transition to adulthood in the UK and Canada: The role of structure and agency in emerging adulthood. *Journal of Youth Studies, 11,* 251–268.

Côté, S. M., Vaillancourt, T., Barker, E. D., Nagin, D., & Tremblay, R. E. (2007). The joint development of physical and indirect aggression: Predictors of continuity and change during childhood. *Development and Psychopathology, 19,* 37–55.

Coudin, G., & Alexopoulos, T. (2010). "Help me! I'm old": How negative aging stereotypes create dependency among older adults. *Aging and Mental Health, 14,* 516–523.

Coulton, C. J., Crampton, D. S., Irwin, M., Spilsbury, J. C., & Korbin, J. E. (2007). How neighborhoods influence child maltreatment: A review of the literature and alternative pathways. *Child Abuse and Neglect, 31,* 1117–1142.

Courage, M. L., & Howe, M. L. (1998). The ebb and flow of infant attentional preferences: Evidence for longterm recognition memory in 3-month-olds. *Journal of Experimental Child Psychology, 18,* 98–106.

Courage, M. L., & Howe, M. L. (2002). From infant to child: The dynamics of cognitive change in the second year of life. *Psychological Bulletin, 128,* 250–277.

Courchesne, E., Carper, R., & Akshoomoff, N. (2003). Evidence of brain overgrowth in the first year of life in autism. *Journal of the American Medical Association, 290,* 337–344.

Couturier, J. L., & Lock, J. (2006). Denial and minimization in adolescents with anorexia nervosa. *International Journal of Eating Disorders, 39,* 212–216.

Cowan, C. P., & Cowan, P. A. (2000). *When partners become parents: The big life change for couples.* Mahwah, NJ: Erlbaum.

Cowan, N., & Alloway, T. (2009). Development of working memory in childhood. In M. L. Courage & N. Cowan (Eds.), *Development of memory in infancy and childhood* (pp. 303–342). Hove, UK: Psychology Press.

Cowan, P. A., & Cowan, C. P. (2002). Interventions as tests of family systems theories: Marital and family relationships in children's development and psychopathology. *Development and Psychopathology, 14,* 731–759.

Cowan, P. A., & Cowan, C. P. (2004). From family relationships to peer rejection to antisocial behavior in middle childhood. In J. B. Kupersmidt & K. A. Dodge (Eds.), *Children's peer relations: From development to intervention* (pp. 159–177). Washington, DC: American Psychological Association.

Cox, G. (2002). The Native American patient. In R. B. Gilbert (Ed.), *Health care and spirituality: Listening, assessing, caring* (pp. 107–127). Amityville, NY: Baywood.

Coyl, D. D., Newland, L. A., & Freeman, H. (2010). Predicting preschoolers' attachment security from parenting behaviours, parents' attachment relationships and their use of social support. *Early Child Development and Care, 180,* 499–512.

Coyne, S. M., Robinson, S. L., & Nelson, D. A. (2010). Does reality backbite? Verbal and relational aggression in reality television programs. *Journal of Broadcasting and Electronic Media, 54,* 282–298.

Craft, S., Baker, L. D., Montine, T. J., Minoshima, S., Watson, G. S., Arbuckle, M., et al. (2012). Intranasal insulin therapy for Alzheimer disease and amnestic mild cognitive impairment: A pilot clinical trial. *Archives of Neurology, 69,* 29–38.

Crago, M. B., Annahatak, B., & Ningiuruvik, L. (1993). Changing patterns of language socialization in Inuit homes. *Anthropology and Education Quarterly, 24,* 205–223.

Craig, C. M., & Lee, D. N. (1999). Neonatal control of sucking pressure: Evidence for an intrinsic tau guide. *Experimental Brain Research, 124,* 371–382.

Crain, W. (2005). *Theories of development* (5th ed.). Upper Saddle River, NJ: Prentice-Hall.

Crair, M. C., Gillespie, D. C., & Stryker, M. P. (1998). The role of visual experience in the development of columns in cat visual cortex. *Science, 279,* 566–570.

Cramer, R. E., Schaefer, J. T., & Reid, S. (2003). Identifying the ideal mate: More evidence for male–female convergence. In N. J. Pallone (Ed.), *Love, romance, sexual interaction: Research perspectives from current psychology* (pp. 61–73). New Brunswick, NJ: Transaction Publishers.

Cratty, B. J. (1986). *Perceptual and motor development in infants and children* (3rd ed.), Englewood Cliffs, NJ: Prentice-Hall.

Crawford, N. (2003, September). Understanding children's atypical gender behavior. *APA Monitor,* p. 40.

Crawley, L., Payne, R., Bolden, J., Payne, T., Washington, P., & Williams, S. (2000). Palliative and end-of-life care in the African American community. *Journal of the American Medical Association, 284,* 2518–2521.

Creasey, G., & Jarvis, P. (2009). Attachment and marriage. In M. C. Smith & N. DeFrates-Densch

(Eds.), *Handbook of research on adult learning and development* (pp. 269–304). New York: Routledge/Taylor & Francis Group.

Creasey, G. L., Jarvis, P. A., & Berk, L. E. (1998). Play and social competence. In O. N. Saracho & B. Spodek (Eds.), *Multiple perspectives on play in early childhood education* (pp. 116–143). Albany: State University of New York Press.

Crick, N. R., & Nelson, D. A. (2002). Relational and physical victimization within friendships: Nobody told me there'd be friends like these. *Journal of Abnormal Child Psychology, 30,* 599–607.

Crick, N. R., Ostrov, J. M., Appleyard, K., Jansen, E., & Casas, J. F. (2004). Relational aggression in early childhood: You can't come to my birthday party unless. . . . In M. Putallaz & K. Bierman (Eds.), *Aggression, antisocial behavior, and violence among girls: A developmental perspective* (pp. 71–89). New York: Guilford.

Crick, N. R., Ostrov, J. M., Burr, J. E., Cullerton-Sen, C., Jansen-Yeh, E., & Ralston, P. (2006). A longitudinal study of relational and physical aggression in preschool. *Journal of Applied Developmental Psychology, 27,* 254–268.

Crick, N. R., Ostrov, J. M., & Werner, N. E. (2006). A longitudinal study of relational aggression, physical aggression, and social-psychological adjustment. *Journal of Abnormal Child Psychology, 34,* 131–142.

Crimmins, E. M., Kim, J. K., & Solé-Auró, A. (2011). Gender differences in health: Results from SHARE, ELSA and HRS. *European Journal of Public Health, 21,* 81–91.

Criss, M. M., & Shaw, D. S. (2005). Sibling relationships as contexts for delinquency training in low income families. *Journal of Family Psychology, 19,* 592–600.

Crockenberg, S., & Leerkes, E. (2003). Infant negative emotionality, caregiving, and family relationships. In A. C. Crouter & A. Booth (Eds.), *Children's influence on family dynamics* (pp. 57–78). Mahwah, NJ: Erlbaum.

Crockenberg, S., & Leerkes, E. (2004). Infant and maternal behaviors regulate infant reactivity to novelty at 6 months. *Developmental Psychology, 40,* 1123–1132.

Crockett, L. J., Raffaelli, M., & Shen, Y.-L. (2006). Linking self-regulation and risk proneness to risky sexual behavior: Pathways through peer pressure and early substance use. *Journal of Research on Adolescence, 16,* 503–525.

Croker, R. (2007). *The boomer century: 1946–2046: How America's most influential generation changed everything.* New York: Springboard Press.

Cross, S., & Markus, H. (1991). Possible selves across the life span. *Human Development, 34,* 230–255.

Crouch, J. L., Skowronski, J. J., Milner, J. S., & Harris, B. (2008). Parental responses to infant crying: The influence of child physical abuse risk and hostile priming. *Child Abuse and Neglect, 32,* 702–710.

Crouter, A. C., & Bumpus, M. F. (2001). Linking parents' work stress to children's and adolescents' psychological adjustment. *Current Directions in Psychological Science, 10,* 156–159.

Crouter, A. C., & Head, M. R. (2002). Parental monitoring and knowledge of children. In M. H. Bornstein (Ed.), *Handbook of parenting: Vol. 3. Being and becoming a parent* (2nd ed., pp. 461–483). Mahwah, NJ: Erlbaum.

Crouter, A. C., Whiteman, S. D., McHale, S. M., & Osgood, D. W. (2007). Development of gender attitude traditionality across middle childhood and adolescence. *Child Development, 78,* 911–926.

Crowley, K. (2011). Sleep and sleep disorders in older adults. *Neuropsychological Review, 21,* 41–53.

Crystal, D. S., Killen, M., & Ruck, M. D. (2008). It is who you know that counts: Intergroup contact and judgments about race-based exclusion. *British Journal of Developmental Psychology, 26,* 51–70.

Crystal, D. S., Killen, M., & Ruck, M. D. (2010). Fair treatment by authorities is related to children's and adolescents' evaluations of interracial exclusion. *Applied Developmental Science, 14,* 125–136.

Csikszentmihalyi, M., & Nakamura, J. (2005). The role of emotions in the development of wisdom. In R. J. Sternberg & J. Jordan (Eds.), *A handbook of wisdom: Psychological perspectives* (pp. 220–242). New York: Cambridge University Press.

Csikszentmihalyi, M., & Rathunde, K. (1990). The psychology of wisdom: An evolutionary interpretation. In R. J. Sternberg (Ed.), *Wisdom: Its nature, origins, and development* (pp. 25–51). New York: Cambridge University Press.

Culbertson, F. M. (1997). Depression and gender: An international review. *American Psychologist, 52,* 25–51.

Cumming, E., & Henry, W. E. (1961). *Growing old: The process of disengagement.* New York: Basic Books.

Cummings, E. M., Goeke-Morey, M. C., & Papp, L. M. (2004). Everyday marital conflict and child aggression. *Journal of Abnormal Child Psychology, 32,* 91–202.

Cummings, E. M., & Merrilees, C. E. (2010). Identifying the dynamic processes underlying links between marital conflict and child adjustment. In M. S. Schulz, M. K. Pruett, P. K. Kerig, & R. D. Parke (Eds.), *Strengthening couple relationships for optimal child development* (pp. 27–40). Washington, DC: American Psychological Association.

Curby, T. W., LoCasale-Crouch, J., Konold, T. R., Pianta, R. C., Howes, C., Burchinal, M., et al. (2009). The relations of observed pre-K classroom quality profiles to children's achievement and social competence. *Early Education and Development, 20,* 346–372.

Curlin, F. A., Nwodim, C., Vance, J. L., Chin, M. H., & Lantos, J. D. (2008). To die, to sleep: U.S. physicians' religious and other objections to physician-assisted suicide, terminal sedation, and withdrawal of life support. *American Journal of Hospice and Palliative Medicine, 25,* 112–120.

Curtiss, K., Hayslip, B., Jr., & Dolan, D. C. (2007). Motivational style, length of residence, voluntariness, and gender as influences on adjustment to long term care: A pilot study. *Journal of Human Behavior in the Social Environment, 15,* 13–34.

Cutchin, M. P. (2013). The complex process of becoming at-home in assisted living. In G. D. Rowles & M. Bernard (Eds.), *Environmental gerontology: Making meaningful places in old age* (pp. 105–124). New York: Springer.

Cutler, L. J. (2007). Physical environments of assisted living: Research needs and challenges. *Gerontologist, 47*(Special Issue III), 68–82.

Cutler, R. G., & Mattson, M. P. (2006). Introduction: The adversities of aging. *Ageing Research Reviews, 5,* 221–238.

Cutler, S. J., Hendricks, J., & O'Neill, G. (2011). Civic engagement and aging. In R. H. Binstock & L. K. George (Eds.), *Handbook of aging and the social sciences* (7th ed., pp. 221–233). San Diego, CA: Academic Press.

Cutrona, C. E., Hessling, R. M., Bacon, P. L., & Russell, D. W. (1998). Predictors and correlates of continuing involvement with the baby's father among adolescent mothers. *Journal of Family Psychology, 12,* 369–387.

Cutter, W. J., Daly, E. M., Robertson, D. M. W., Chitnis, X. A., van Amelsvoort, T. A. M. J., & Simmons, A. (2006). Influence of X chromosome and hormones on human brain development: A magnetic resonance imaging and proton magnetic resonance spectroscopy study of Turner syndrome. *Biological Psychiatry, 59,* 273–283.

Cvencek, D., Meltzoff, A. N., & Greenwald, A. G. (2011). Math–gender stereotypes in elementary school children. *Child Development, 82,* 766–779.

Cyr, M., McDuff, P., & Wright, J. (2006). Prevalence and predictors of dating violence among adolescent female victims of child sexual abuse. *Journal of Interpersonal Violence, 21*, 1000–1017.

D

Dabrowska, E. (2000). From formula to schema: The acquisition of English questions. *Cognitive Linguistics, 11*, 1–20.

Daher, M. (2012). Cultural beliefs and values in cancer patients. *Annals of Oncology, 23*(Suppl. 3), 66–69.

Dahl, R. E., & Lewin, D. S. (2002). Pathways to adolescent healthy sleep regulation and behavior. *Journal of Adolescent Health, 31*, 175–184.

Dahlberg, L. L., & Simon, T. R. (2006). Predicting and preventing youth violence: Developmental pathways and risk. In L. L. Dahlberg & T. R. Simon (Eds.), *Preventing violence: Research and evidence-based intervention strategies* (pp. 97–124). Washington, DC: American Psychological Association.

Dal Santo, J. A., Goodman, R. M., Glik, D., & Jackson, K. (2004). Childhood unintentional injuries: Factors predicting injury risk among preschoolers. *Journal of Pediatric Psychology, 29*, 273–283.

Damjanovic, A. M., Yang, Y., Glaser, R., Kiecolt-Glaser, J. K., & Nguyen, H. (2007). Accelerated telomere erosion is associated with a declining immune function of caregivers of Alzheimer's disease patients. *Journal of Immunology, 179*, 4249–4254.

Damon, W. (1988a). *The moral child.* New York: Free Press.

Damon, W. (1988b). *Self-understanding in childhood and adolescence.* New York: Cambridge University Press.

Damon, W. (1990). Self-concept, adolescent. In R. M. Lerner, A. C. Petersen, & J. Brooks-Gunn (Eds.), *The encyclopedia of adolescence* (Vol. 2, pp. 87–91). New York: Garland.

Damon, W. (2004). *The moral advantage: How to succeed in business by doing the right thing.* San Francisco: Berrett-Koehler.

Damon, W., & Hart, D. (1988). *Self-understanding in childhood and adolescence.* New York: Cambridge University Press.

Dane, E., Baer, M., Pratt, M. G., & Oldham, G. R. (2011). Rational versus intuitive problem solving: How thinking "off the beaten path" can stimulate creativity. *Psychology of Aesthetics, Creativity, and the Arts, 5*, 3–12.

Daniels, E., & Leaper, C. (2006). A longitudinal investigation of sport participation, peer acceptance, and self-esteem among adolescent girls and boys. *Sex Roles, 55*, 875–880.

Daniels, P., Noe, G. F., & Mayberry, R. (2006). Barriers to prenatal care among black women of low socioeconomic status. *American Journal of Health Behavior, 30*, 188–198.

Dannemiller, J. L., & Stephens, B. R. (1988). A critical test of infant pattern preference models. *Child Development, 59*, 210–216.

Darling-Hammond, L. (2010). *The flat world and education: How America's commitment to equity will determine our future.* New York: Teachers College Press.

Darroch, J. E., Frost, J. J., & Singh, S. (2001). *Teenage sexual and reproductive behavior in developed countries: Can more progress be made?* New York: Alan Guttmacher Institute.

Darwin, C. (1936). *On the origin of species by means of natural selection.* New York: Modern Library. (Original work published 1859)

Daubenmier, J., Lin, J., Blackburn, E., Hecht, F. M., Kristeller, J., Maninger, N., et al. (2012). Changes in stress, eating, and metabolic factors are related to changes in telomerase activity in a randomized mindfulness intervention pilot study. *Psychoneuroendocrinology, 37*, 917–928.

D'Augelli, A. R. (2002). Mental health problems among lesbian, gay, and bisexual youths ages 14 to 21. *Clinical Child Psychology and Psychiatry, 7*, 433–456.

D'Augelli, A. R. (2006). Developmental and contextual factors and mental health among lesbian, gay, and bisexual youths. In A. M. Omoto & H. S. Howard (Eds.), *Sexual orientation and mental health: Examining identity and development in lesbian, gay, and bisexual people* (pp. 37–53). Washington, DC: American Psychological Association.

D'Augelli, A. R., Grossman, A. H., Salter, N. P., Vasey, J. J., Starks, M. T., & Sinclair, K. O. (2005). Predicting the suicide attempts of lesbian, gay, and bisexual youth. *Suicide and Life-Threatening Behavior, 35*, 646–660.

D'Augelli, A. R., Grossman, A. H., & Starks, M. T. (2008). Families of gay, lesbian, and bisexual youth: What do parents and siblings know and how do they react? *Journal of GBLT Family Studies, 4*, 95–115.

Davey, A., & Takagi, E. (2013). Adulthood and aging in families. In G. W. Peterson & K. R. Bush (Eds.), *Handbook of marriage and family* (pp. 377–399). New York: Springer.

Davidov, M., & Grusec, J. E. (2006). Untangling the links of parental responsiveness to distress and warmth to child outcomes. *Child Development, 77*, 44–58.

Davies, J. (2008). Differential teacher positive and negative interactions with male and female pupils in the primary school setting. *Educational and Child Psychology, 25*, 17–26.

Davis, K. F., Parker, K. P., & Montgomery, G. L. (2004). Sleep in infants and young children. Part 1: Normal sleep. *Journal of Pediatric Health Care, 18*, 65–71.

Dawley, K., Loch, J., & Bindrich, I. (2007). The Nurse–Family Partnership. *American Journal of Nursing, 107*, 60–67.

Dawson, G., Ashman, S. B., Panagiotides, H., Hessl, D., Self, J., Yamada, E., & Embry, L. (2003). Preschool outcomes of children of depressed mothers: Role of maternal behavior, contextual risk, and children's brain activity. *Child Development, 74*, 1158–1175.

Dawson, T. L. (2002). New tools, new insights: Kohlberg's moral judgment stages revisited. *International Journal of Behavioral Development, 26*, 154–166.

Ddungu, H. (2011). Palliative care: What approaches are suitable in developing countries? *British Journal of Haematology, 154*, 728–735.

Deák, G. O., Ray, S. D., & Brenneman, K. (2003). Children's perseverative appearance–reality errors are related to emerging language skills. *Child Development, 74*, 944–964.

DeAngelo, L., Hurtado, S., & Pryor, J. H. (2010). *Your first college year: National norms for the 2008 YFCY survey.* Los Angeles: Higher Education Research Institute, UCLA.

Dearing, E., Wimer, C., Simpkins, S. D., Lund, T., Bouffard, S. M., Caronongan, P., & Kreider, H. (2009). Do neighborhood and home contexts help explain why low-income children miss opportunities to participate in activities outside of school? *Developmental Psychology, 45*, 1545–1562.

Deary, I. J. (2001). *g* and cognitive elements of information progressing: An agnostic view. In R. J. Sternberg & E. L. Grigorenko (Eds.), *The general factor of intelligence: How general is it?* (pp. 447–479). Mahwah, NJ: Erlbaum.

Deary, I. J., Strand, S., Smith, P., & Fernandes, C. (2007). Intelligence and educational achievement. *Intelligence, 35*, 13–21.

Deary, I. J., Yang, J., Davies, G., Harris, S. E., Tenesa, A., Liewald, D., et al. (2012). Genetic contributions to stability and change in intelligence from childhood to old age. *Nature, 481*, 212–215.

Deater-Deckard, K., Lansford, J. E., Dodge, K. A., Pettit, G. S., & Bates, J. E. (2003). The development of attitudes about physical punishment: An 8-year longitudinal study. *Journal of Family Psychology, 17*, 351–360.

Deater-Deckard, K., Pike, A., Petrill, S. A., Cutting, A. L., Hughes, C., & O'Connor, T. G. (2001). Nonshared environmental processes in socialemotional development: An observational study of identical twin differences in the preschool period. *Developmental Science, 4*, F1–F6.

Debes, F., Budtz-Jorgensen, E., Weihe, P., White, R. F., & Grandjean, P. (2006). Impact of prenatal methylmercury exposure on neurobehavioral function at age 4 years. *Neurotoxicology and Teratology, 28*, 536–547.

DeBoer, T., Scott, L. S., & Nelson, C. A. (2007). Methods for acquiring and analyzing infant eventrelated potentials. In M. de Haan (Ed.), *Infant EEG and event-related potentials* (pp. 5–37). New York: Psychology Press.

de Bruyn, E. H. (2005). Role strain, engagement and academic achievement in early adolescence. *Educational Studies, 31*, 15–27.

de Bruyn, E. H., & Cillessen, A. H. N. (2006). Popularity in early adolescence: Prosocial and antisocial subtypes. *Journal of Adolescent Research, 21*, 607–627.

de Calignon, A., Polydoro, M., Suárez-Calvet, M., William, C., Adamowicz, D. H., Kopeikina, K. J., et al. (2012). Propagation of tau pathology in a model of early Alzheimer's disease. *Neuron, 73*, 685–697.

Dechanet, C., Anahory, T., Mathieu, T., Mathieu, D. J. C., Quantin, X., Ryftmann, L., et al. (2011). Effects of cigarette smoking on reproduction. *Human Reproduction Update, 17*, 76–95.

Deci, E. L., La Guardia, J. G., Moller, A. C., Scheiner, M. J., & Ryan, R. M. (2006). On the benefits of giving as well as receiving autonomy support: Mutuality in close friendships. *Personality and Social Psychology Bulletin, 32*, 313–327.

Degner, J., & Wentura, D. (2010). Automatic prejudice in childhood and early adolescence. *Journal of Personality and Social Psychology, 98*, 356–374.

De Goede, I. H. A., Branje, S. J. T., & Meeus, W. H. J. (2009). Developmental changes and gender differences in adolescents' perceptions of friendships. *Journal of Adolescence, 32*, 1105–1123.

de Haan, M., & Johnson, M. H. (2003). Mechanisms and theories of brain development. In M. de Haan & M. H. Johnson (Eds.), *The cognitive neuroscience of development* (pp. 1–18). Hove, UK: Psychology Press.

Deissinger, T. (2007). "Making schools practical": Practice firms and their function in the full-time vocational school system in Germany. *Education + Training, 49*, 364–378.

deJong, A., & Franklin, B. A. (2004). Prescribing exercise for the elderly: Current research and recommendations. *Current Sports Medicine Reports, 3*, 337–343.

Dekker, M. C., Ferdinand, R. F., van Lang, D. J., Bongers, I. L., van der Ende, J., & Verhulst, F. C. (2007). Developmental trajectories of depressive symptoms from early childhood to late adolescence: Gender differences and adult outcome. *Journal of Child Psychology and Psychiatry, 48*, 657–666.

DeKosky, S. T., Williamson, J. D., Fitzpatrick, A. L., Kronmal, R. A., Ives, D. G., & Saxton, J. A. (2008). Ginkgo biloba for prevention of dementia: A randomized controlled trial. *Journal of the American Medical Association, 300*, 2253–2262.

Dekovi?, M., & Buist, K. L. (2005). Multiple perspectives within the family: Family relationship patterns. *Journal of Family Issues, 26*, 467–490.

DeLamater, J. (2012). Sexual expression in later life: A review and synthesis. *Journal of Sex Research, 49*, 125–141.

DeLamater, J., & Moorman, S. M. (2007). Sexual behavior in later life. *Journal of Aging and Health, 19*, 921–945.

DeLoache, J. S. (1987). Rapid change in symbolic functioning of very young children. *Science, 238,* 1556–1557.

DeLoache, J. S. (2002). The symbol-mindedness of young children. In W. Hartup & R. A. Weinberg (Eds.), *Minnesota Symposia on Child Psychology* (Vol. 32, pp. 73–101). Mahwah, NJ: Erlbaum.

DeLoache, J. S., Uttal, D. H., & Rosengren, K. S. (2004). Scale errors offer evidence for a perception–action dissociation early in life. *Science, 304,* 1027–1029.

Delobel-Ayoub, M., Arnaud, C., White-Koning, M., Casper, C., Pierrat, V., Garel, M., et al. (2009). Behavioral problems and cognitive performance at 5 years of age after very preterm birth: The EPIPAGE Study. *Pediatrics, 123,* 485–1492.

De Marco, A. C., & Berzin, S. C. (2008). The influence of family economic status on home-leaving patterns during emerging adulthood. *Families in Society, 89,* 208–218.

DeMarie, D., Miller, P. H., Ferron, J., & Cunningham, W. R. (2004). Path analysis tests of theoretical models of children's memory performance. *Journal of Cognition and Development, 5,* 461–492.

Demetriou, A., Christou, C., Spanoudis, G., & Platsidou, M. (2002). The development of mental processing: Efficiency, working memory, and thinking. *Monographs of the Society for Research in Child Development, 67*(1, Serial No. 268).

Demiray, B., Gülgöz, S., & Bluck, S. (2009). Examining the life story account of the reminiscence bump: Why we remember more from young adulthood. *Memory, 17,* 708–723.

DeNavas-Walt, C., Proctor, B. D., & Smith, J. C. (2011). Income, poverty, and health insurance coverage in the United States: 2010. *U.S. Census Bureau, Current Population Reports,* P60–P239. Washington, DC: U.S. Government Printing Office.

Denissen, J. J. A., Zarrett, N. R., & Eccles, J. S. (2007). I like to do it, I'm able, and I know I am: Longitudinal couplings between domain-specific achievement, self-concept, and interest. *Child Development, 78,* 430–447.

Denmark, F. L., & Klara, M. D. (2007). Empowerment: A prime time for women over 50. In V. Mulhbauer & J. C. Chrisler (Eds.), *Women over 50* (pp. 182–203). New York: Springer.

Dennerstein, L., & Lehert, P. (2004). Modeling midaged women's sexual functioning: A prospective, population-based study. *Journal of Sex and Marriage Therapy, 30,* 173–183.

Denney, N. W. (1990). Adult age differences in traditional and practical problem solving. *Advances in Psychology, 72,* 329–349.

Denney, N. W., & Pearce, K. A. (1989). A developmental study of practical problem solving in adults. *Psychology and Aging, 4,* 438–442.

Dennis, T., Bendersky, M., Ramsay, D., & Lewis, M. (2006). Reactivity and regulation in children prenatally exposed to cocaine. *Developmental Psychology, 42,* 688–697.

Dent, A., & Stewart, A. (2004). *Sudden death in childhood: Support for the bereaved family.* London: Butterworth-Heinemann.

Deocampo, J. A. (2003, April). *Tools on TV: A new paradigm for testing dual representational understanding.* Poster presented at the biennial meeting of the Society for Research in Child Development, Tampa, FL.

DePaulo, B. M., & Morris, W. L. (2005). Singles in society and in science. *Psychological Inquiry, 16,* 142–149.

Deprest, J. A., Devlieger, R., Srisupundit, K., Beck, V., Sandaite, I., Rusconi, S., et al. (2010). Fetal surgery is a clinical reality. *Seminars in Fetal and Neonatal Medicine, 15,* 58–67.

Der, G., Batty, G. D., & Deary, I. J. (2006). Effect of breastfeeding on intelligence in children: Prospective study, sibling pairs analysis, and meta-analysis. *British Medical Journal, 333,* 945.

Der, G., & Deary, I. J. (2006). Age and sex differences in reaction time in adulthood: Results from the United Kingdom Health and Lifestyle Survey. *Psychology and Aging, 21,* 62–73.

deRegnier, R.-A. (2005). Neurophysiologic evaluation of early cognitive development in high-risk infants and toddlers. *Mental Retardation and Developmental Disabilities, 11,* 317–324.

deRegnier, R.-A., Long, J. D., Geogieff, M. K., & Nelson, C. A. (2007). Using event-related potentials and brain development in infants of diabetic mothers. *Developmental Neuropsychology, 31,* 379–396.

DeRoche, K., & Welsh, M. (2008). Twenty-five years of research on neurocognitive outcomes in early-treated phenylketonuria: Intelligence and executive function. *Developmental Neuropsychology, 33,* 474–504.

DeRose, L. M., & Brooks-Gunn, J. (2006). Transition into adolescence: The role of pubertal processes. In L. Balter & C. S. Tamis-LeMonda (Eds.), *Child psychology: A handbook of contemporary issues* (2nd ed., pp. 385–414). New York: Psychology Press.

DeRosier, M. E. (2007). Peer-rejected and bullied children: A safe schools initiative for elementary school students. In J. E. Zins, M. J. Elias, & C. A. Maher (Eds.), *Bullying, victimization, and peer harassment* (pp. 257–276). New York: Haworth.

DeRosier, M. E., & Thomas, J. M. (2003). Strengthening sociometric prediction: Scientific advances in the assessment of children's peer relations. *Child Development, 75,* 1379–1392.

de Rosnay, M., Copper, P. J., Tsigaras, N., & Murray, L. (2006). Transmission of social anxiety from mother to infant: An experimental study using a social referencing paradigm. *Behavior Research and Therapy, 44,* 1165–1175.

de Rosnay, M., & Hughes, C. (2006). Conversation and theory of mind: Do children talk their way to socio-cognitive understanding? *British Journal of Developmental Psychology, 24,* 7–37.

Derwinger, A., Neely, A. S., & Bäckman, L. (2005). Design your own memory strategies! Self-generated strategy training versus mnemonic training in old age: An 8-month follow-up. *Neuropsychological Rehabilitation, 15,* 37–54.

De Souza, E., Alberman, E., & Morris, J. K. (2009). Down syndrome and paternal age, a new analysis of case-control data collected in the 1960s. *American Journal of Medical Genetics, 149A,* 1205–1208.

Dessel, A. (2010). Prejudice in schools: Promotion of an inclusive culture and climate. *Education and Urban Society, 42,* 407–429.

Deutsch, N. L., & Schmertz, B. (2011). Starting from Ground Zero: Constraints and experiences of adult women returning to college. *Review of Higher Education, 34,* 477–504.

Deveson, A. (1994). *Coming of age: Twenty-one interviews about growing older.* Newham, Australia: Scribe.

Devi, N. P. G., Shenbagvalli, R., Ramesh, K., & Rathinam, S. N. (2009). Rapid progression of HIV infection in infancy. *Indian Pediatrics, 46,* 53–56.

de Villiers, J. G., & de Villiers, P. A. (1973). A cross-sectional study of the acquisition of grammatical morphemes in child speech. *Journal of Psycholinguistic Research, 2,* 267–278.

DeVries, R. (2001). Constructivist education in preschool and elementary school: The sociomoral atmosphere as the first educational goal. In S. L. Golbeck (Ed.), *Psychological perspectives on early childhood education* (pp. 153–180). Mahwah, NJ: Erlbaum.

De Weerd, A. W., & van den Bossche, A. S. (2003). The development of sleep during the first months of life. *Sleep Medicine Reviews, 7,* 179–191.

de Weerth, C., & Buitelaar, J. K. (2005). Physiological stress reactivity in human pregnancy—a review. *Neuroscience and Biobehavioral Reviews, 29,* 295–312.

De Wolff, M. S., & van IJzendoorn, M. H. (1997). Sensitivity and attachment: A meta-analysis on parental antecedents of infant attachment. *Child Development, 68,* 571–591.

Dey, J. G., & Hill, C. A. (2007). *Behind the pay gap.* Washington, DC: American Association of University Women.

Diamond, A. (2009). The interplay of biology and the environment broadly defined. *Developmental Psychology, 45,* 1–8.

Diamond, L. M. (1998). Development of sexual orientation among adolescent and young adult women. *Developmental Psychology, 34,* 1085–1095.

Diamond, L. M. (2003). Love matters: Romantic relationships among sexual-minority adolescents. In P. Florsheim (Ed.), *Adolescent romantic relations and sexual behavior* (pp. 85–108). Mahwah, NJ: Erlbaum.

Diamond, L. M. (2006). The intimate same-sex relationships of sexual minorities. In A. L. Vangelisti & D. Perlman (Eds.), *The Cambridge handbook of personal relationships* (pp. 293–312). New York: Cambridge University Press.

Diamond, L. M. (2008). Female bisexuality from adolescence to adulthood: Results from a 10-year longitudinal study. *Developmental Psychology, 44,* 5–14.

Diamond, L. M., Fagundes, C. P., & Butterworth, M. R. (2010). Intimate relationships across the lifespan. In M. E. Lamb, A. M. Freund, & R. M. Lerner, (Eds.), *The handbook of life-span development, Vol. 2: Social and emotional development* (pp. 379–433). Hoboken, NJ: Wiley.

Diamond, L. M., & Lucas, S. (2004). Sexual-minority and heterosexual youths' peer relationships: Experiences, expectations, and implications for well-being. *Journal of Research on Adolescence, 14,* 313–340.

Dias, M. G., & Harris, P. L. (1988). The effect of makebelieve play on deductive reasoning. *British Journal of Developmental Psychology, 6,* 207–221.

Dias, M. G., & Harris, P. L. (1990). The influence of the imagination on reasoning by young children. *British Journal of Developmental Psychology, 8,* 305–318.

Dick, D. M., Prescott, C., & McGue, M. (2008). The genetics of substance use and substance use disorders. In Y.-K. Kim (Ed.), *Handbook of behavior genetics* (pp. 433–453). New York: Springer.

Dick, D. M., Rose, R. J., Viken, R. J., & Kaprio, J. (2000). Pubertal timing and substance use: Associations between and within families across late adolescence. *Developmental Psychology, 36,* 180–189.

Dickinson, D. K., Golinkoff, R. M., & Hirsh-Pasek, K. (2010). Speaking out for language: Why language is central to reading development. *Educational Researcher, 39,* 305–310.

Dickinson, D. K., & McCabe, A. (2001). Bringing it all together: The multiple origins, skills, and environmental supports of early literacy. *Learning Disabilities Research and Practice, 16,* 186–202.

Dick-Read, G. (1959). *Childbirth without fear.* New York: Harper & Row.

Dickson, R. A., Pillemer, D. B., & Bruehl, E. C. (2011). The reminiscence bump for salient personal memories: Is a cultural life script required? *Memory and Cognition, 39,* 977–991.

Dickstein, M. (1992). After utopia: The 1960s today. In B. L. Tischler (Ed.), *Sights on the sixties* (pp. 13–24). New Brunswick, NJ: Rutgers University Press.

DiDonato, M. D., & Berenbaum, S. A. (2011). The benefits and drawbacks of gender typing: How different dimensions are related to psychological adjustment. *Archives of Sexual Behavior, 40,* 457–463.

Diehl, M., & Berg, K. M. (2007). Personality and involvement in leisure activities during the Third Age: Findings from the Ohio Longitudinal Study. In J. B. James & P. Wink (Eds.), *Annual review of gerontology and geriatrics* (Vol. 26, pp. 211–226). New York: Springer.

Diehl, M., Coyle, N., & Labouvie-Vief, G. (1996). Age and sex differences in strategies of coping and defense across the life span. *Psychology and Aging, 11*, 127–139.

Diehl, M., Youngblade, L. M., Hay, E. L., & Chui, H. (2011). The development of self-representations across the life span. In K. L. Fingerman, C. A. Berg, J. Smith, & H. Chui (Eds.), *Handbook of lifespan development* (pp. 611–646). New York: Springer.

Diener, E., Gohm, C. L., Suh, E., & Oishi, S. (2000). Similarity of the relations between marital status and subjective well-being across cultures. *Journal of Cross-Cultural Psychology, 31*, 419–436.

Dildy, G. A., Jackson, G. M., Fowers, G. K., Oshiro, B. T., Varner, M. W., & Clark, S. L. (1996). Very advanced maternal age. Pregnancy after age 45. *American Journal of Obstetrics and Gynecology, 175*, 668–674.

Dillon, M., & Wink, P. (2004). American religion, generativity, and the therapeutic culture. In E. de St. Aubin & D. P. McAdams (Eds.), *The generative society: Caring for future generations* (pp. 15–31). Washington, DC: American Psychological Association.

Dillon, M., & Wink, P. (2007). *In the course of a lifetime: Tracing religious belief, practice, and change.* Berkeley: University of California Press.

Dilworth-Anderson, P., Goodwin, P. Y., & Williams, S. W. (2004). Can culture help explain the physical health effects of caregiving over time among African American caregivers? *Journal of Gerontology, 59B*, S138–S145.

DiPietro, J. A., Bornstein, M. H., Costigan, K. A., Pressman, E. K., Hahn, C.-S., & Painter, K. (2002). What does fetal movement predict about behavior during the first two years of life? *Developmental Psychobiology, 40*, 358–371.

DiPietro, J. A., Hodgson, D. M., Costigan, K. A., & Hilton, S. C. (1996). Fetal neurobehavioral development. *Child Development, 67*, 2553–2567.

Dirix, C. E. H., Nijhuis, J. G., Jongsma, H. W., & Hornstra, G. (2009). Aspects of fetal learning and memory. *Child Development, 80*, 1251–1258.

Dirks, J. (1982). The effect of a commercial game on children's Block Design scores on the WISC-R test. *Intelligence, 6*, 109–123.

Dishion, T. J., Shaw, D., Connell, A., Gardner, F., Weaver, C., & Wilson, M. (2008). The Family Check-Up with high-risk indigent families: Preventing problem behavior by increasing parents' positive behavior support in early childhood. *Child Development, 79*, 1395–1414.

Dix, T., Stewart, A. D., Gershoff, E. T., & Day, W. H. (2007). Autonomy and children's reactions to being controlled: Evidence that both compliance and defiance may be positive markers in early development. *Child Development, 78*, 1204–1221.

Djahanbakhch, O., Ezzati, M., & Zosmer, A. (2007). Reproductive ageing in women. *Journal of Pathology, 211*, 219–231.

Dodd, V. L. (2005). Implications of kangaroo care for growth and development in preterm infants. *JOGNN, 34*, 218–232.

Dodge, K. A., Coie, J. D., & Lynam, D. (2006). Aggression and antisocial behavior in youth. In N. Eisenberg (Ed.), *Handbook of child psychology: Vol. 3. Social, emotional, and personality development* (6th ed., pp. 719–788). New York: Wiley.

Dodge, K. A., McLoyd, V. C., & Lansford, J. E. (2006). The cultural context of physically disciplining children. In V. C. McLoyd, N. E. Hill, & K. A. Dodge (Eds.), *African-American family life: Ecological and cultural diversity* (pp. 245–263). New York: Guilford.

Dodson, T. A., & Borders, L. D. (2006). Men in traditional and nontraditional careers: Gender role attitudes, gender role conflict, and job satisfaction. *Career Development Quarterly, 54*, 283–296.

Dohnt, H., & Tiggemann, M. (2006). The contribution of peer and media influences to the development of body satisfaction and self-esteem in young girls: A prospective study. *Developmental Psychology, 42*, 929–936.

Doka, K. J. (2008). Disenfranchised grief in historical and cultural perspective. In M. S. Stroebe, R. O. Hansson, H. Schut, & W. Stroebe (Eds.), *Handbook of bereavement research and practice* (pp. 223–240). Washington, DC: American Psychological Association.

Doka, K. J., & Martin, T. L. (2010). *Grieving beyond gender: Understanding the ways men and women mourn* (rev. ed.). New York: Routledge.

Dolbin-MacNab, M. L. (2006). Just like raising your own? Grandmothers' perceptions of parenting a second time around. *Family Relations, 55*, 564–575.

Dombrowski, S. C., Noonan, K., & Martin, R. P. (2007). Low birth weight and cognitive outcomes: Evidence for a gradient relationship in an urban, poor, African American birth cohort. *School Psychology Quarterly, 22*, 26–43.

Donatelle, R. J. (2012). *Health: The basics* (10th ed.). San Francisco: Benjamin Cummings.

Dondi, M., Simion, F., & Caltran, G. (1999). Can newborns discriminate between their own cry and the cry of another newborn infant? *Developmental Psychology, 35*, 418–426.

Done, D. J., & Thomas, J. A. (2001). Training in communication skills for informal carers of people suffering from dementia: A cluster randomized clinic trial comparing a therapist led workshop and booklet. *International Journal of Geriatric Psychiatry, 16*, 816–821.

Donnellan, M. B., Larsen-Rife, D., & Conger, R. D. (2005). Personality, family history, and competence in early adult romantic relationships. *Journal of Personality and Social Psychology, 88*, 562–576.

Donnellan, M. B., & Lucas, R. E. (2008). Age differences in the big five across the life span: Evidence from two national samples. *Psychology and Aging, 23*, 558–566.

D'Onofrio, B. M., Turkheimer, E., Emery, R. E., Slutske, W. S., Heath, A. C., Madden, P. A., & Martin, N. G. (2006). A genetically informed study of the processes underlying the association between parental marital instability and offspring adjustment. *Developmental Psychology, 42*, 486–499.

Dorris, M. (1989). *The broken cord*. New York: Harper & Row.

Doss, B. D., Rhoades, G. K., Stanley, S. M., & Markman, H. J. (2009). The effect of the transition to parenthood on relationship quality: An 8-year prospective study. *Journal of Personality and Social Psychology, 96*, 601–619.

Double, E. B., Mabuchi, K., Cullings, H. M., Preston, D. L., Kodama, K., Shimizu, Y., et al. (2011). Long-term radiation-related health effects in a unique human population: Lessons learned from the atomic bomb survivors of Hiroshima and Nagasaki. *Disaster Medicine and Public Health Preparedness, 5*(Suppl. 1), S122–S133.

Dowd, M. D. (2013). Prevention and treatment of traumatic stress in children: Few answers, many questions. *Pediatrics, 31*, 591–592.

Dowling, E. M., Gestsdottir, S., Anderson, P. M., von Eye, A., Almerigi, J., & Lerner, R. M. (2004). Structural relations among spirituality, religiosity, and thriving in adolescence. *Applied Developmental Psychology, 8*, 7–16.

Downing, J. E. (2010). *Academic instruction for students with moderate and severe intellectual disabilities.* Thousand Oaks, CA: Corwin.

Drayton, S., Turley-Ames, K. J., & Guajardo, N. R. (2011). Counterfactual thinking and false belief: The role of executive function. *Journal of Experimental Child Psychology, 108*, 532–548.

Drewnowski, A., & Shultz, J. M. (2001). Impact of aging on eating behaviors, food choices, nutrition, and health status. *Journal of Nutrition, Health, and Aging, 5*, 75–79.

Driscoll, M. C. (2007). Sickle cell disease. *Pediatrics in Review, 28*, 259–268.

Driver, J., Tabares, A., Shapiro, A. F., & Gottman, J. M. (2012). Couple interaction in happy and unhappy marriages: Gottman Laboratory studies. In F. Walsh (Ed.), *Normal family processes: Growing diversity and complexity* (pp. 57–77). New York: Guilford.

Drotar, D., Witherspoon, D. O., Zebracki, K., & Peterson, C. C. (2006). *Psychological interventions in childhood chronic illness.* Washington, DC: American Psychological Association.

Dubé, E. M., Savin-Williams, R. C., & Diamond, L. M. (2001). Intimacy development, gender, and ethnicity among sexual-minority youths. In A. R. D'Augelli & C. J. Patterson (Eds.), *Lesbian, gay, and bisexual identities and youth* (pp. 129–152). New York: Oxford University Press.

DuBois, D. L., Burk-Braxton, C., Swenson, L. P., Tevendale, H. D., Lockerd, E. M., & Moran, B. L. (2002). Getting by with a little help from self and others: Self-esteem and social support as resources during early adolescence. *Developmental Psychology, 38*, 822–939.

DuBois, D. L., Felner, R. D., Brand, S., & George, G. R. (1999). Profiles of self-esteem in early adolescence: Identification and investigation of adaptive correlates. *American Journal of Community Psychology, 27*, 899–932.

Dubois, M-F., Bravo, C., Graham, J., Wildeman, S., Cohen, C., Painter, K., et al. (2011). Comfort with proxy consent to research involving decisionally impaired older adults: Do type of proxy and risk–benefit profile matter? *International Psychogeriatrics, 23*, 1479–1488.

Duckworth, A. L., & Seligman, M. E. P. (2005). Self-discipline outdoes IQ in predicting academic performance of adolescents. *Psychological Science, 12*, 939–944.

Dudani, A., Macpherson, A., & Tamim, H. (2010). Childhood behavior problems and unintentional injury: A longitudinal, population-based study. *Journal of Developmental and Behavioral Pediatrics, 31*, 276–285.

Duggan, A., McFarlane, E., Fuddy, L., Burrell, L., Higman, S. M., Windham, A., & Sia, C. (2004). Randomized trial of a statewide home visiting program: Impact in preventing child abuse and neglect. *Child Abuse and Neglect, 28*, 597–622.

Dumas, J. A., & Hartman, M. (2003). Age differences in temporal and item memory. *Psychology and Aging, 18*, 573–586.

Duncan, G. J., Dowsett, C. J., Claessens, A., Magnuson, K., Huston, A. C., Klebanov, P., et al. (2007). School readiness and later achievement. *Developmental Psychology, 43*, 1428–1446.

Duncan, G. J., & Magnuson, K. A. (2003). Off with Hollingshead: Socioeconomic resources, parenting, and child development. In M. H. Bornstein & R. H. Bradley (Eds.), *Socioeconomic status, parenting, and child development* (pp. 83–106). Mahwah, NJ: Erlbaum.

Duncan, S. R., Paterson, D. S., Hoffman, J. M., Mokler, D. J., Borenstein, M. S., Belliveau, R. A., et al. (2010). Brainstem serotonergic deficiency in sudden infant death syndrome. *Journal of the American Medical Association, 303*, 430–437.

Dunham, Y., Baron, A. S., & Banaji, M. R. (2006). From American city to Japanese village: A cross-cultural investigation of implicit race attitudes. *Child Development, 77,* 1129–1520.

Dunham, Y., Baron, A. S., & Carey, S. (2011). Consequences of "minimal" group affiliations in children. *Child Development, 82,* 793–811.

Dunlosky, J., & Hertzog, C. (2001). Measuring strategy production during associative learning: The relative utility of concurrent versus retrospective reports. *Memory and Cognition, 29,* 247–253.

Dunn, J. (1989). Siblings and the development of social understanding in early childhood. In P. G. Zukow (Ed.), *Sibling interaction across cultures* (pp. 106–116). New York: Springer-Verlag.

Dunn, J. (1994). Temperament, siblings, and the development of relationships. In W. B. Carey & S. C. McDevitt (Eds.), *Prevention and early intervention* (pp. 50–58). New York: Brunner/Mazel.

Dunn, J. (2002). The adjustment of children in stepfamilies: Lessons from community studies. *Child and Adolescent Mental Health, 7,* 154–161.

Dunn, J. (2004). Sibling relationships. In P. K. Smith & C. H. Hart (Eds.), *Handbook of childhood social development* (pp. 223–237). Malden, MA: Blackwell.

Dunn, J. (2005). Moral development in early childhood and social interaction in the family. In M. Killen & J. G. Smetana (Eds.), *Handbook of moral development* (pp. 331–350). Mahwah, NJ: Erlbaum.

Dunn, J., Brown, J. R., & Maguire, M. (1995). The development of children's moral sensibility: Individual differences and emotion understanding. *Developmental Psychology, 31,* 649–659.

Dunn, J., Cheng, H., O'Connor, T. G., & Bridges, L. (2004). Children's perspectives on their relationships with their nonresident fathers: Influences, outcomes and implications. *Journal of Child Psychology and Psychiatry, 45,* 553–566.

Dunn, J. R., Schaefer-McDaniel, N. J., & Ramsay, J. T. (2010). Neighborhood chaos and children's development: Questions and contradictions. In G. W. Evans & T. D. Wachs (Eds.), *Chaos and its influence on children's development: An ecological perspective* (pp. 173–189). Washington, DC: American Psychological Association.

Dunne, E. J., & Dunne-Maxim, K. (2004). Working with families in the aftermath of suicide. In F. Walsh & M. McGoldrick (Eds.), *Living beyond loss: Death in the family* (2nd ed., pp. 272–284). New York: Norton.

Durbin, D. L., Darling, N., Steinberg, L., & Brown, B. B. (1993). Parenting style and peer group membership among European-American adolescents. *Journal of Research on Adolescence, 3,* 87–100.

Durlak, J. A., & Weissberg, R. P. (2007). *The impact of after-school programs that promote personal and social skills.* Chicago: Collaborative for Academic, Social, and Emotional Learning.

Durston, S., & Casey, B. J. (2006). What have we learned about cognitive development from neuroimaging? *Neuropsychologia, 44,* 2149–2157.

Durston, S., & Conrad, K. (2007). Integrating genetic, psychopharmacological and neuroimaging studies: A converging methods approach to understanding the neurobiology of ADHD. *Developmental Review, 27,* 374–395.

Dusek, J. B. (1987). Sex roles and adjustment. In D. B. Carter (Ed.), *Current conceptions of sex roles and sex typing* (pp. 211–222). New York: Praeger.

Duszak, R. S. (2009). Congenital rubella syndrome—major review. *Optometry, 80,* 36–43.

Dutta, A., Henley, W., Lang, I., Llewellyn, D., Guralnik, J., Wallace, R. B., et al. (2011). Predictors of extraordinary survival in the Iowa Established Populations for Epidemiological Study of the Elderly: Cohort follow-up to "extinction." *Journal of the American Geriatrics Society, 59,* 963–971.

Dutton, D. G. (2007). *The abusive personality: Violence and control in intimate relationships* (2nd ed.). New York: Guilford.

Dutton, D. G. (2012). The case against the role of gender in intimate partner violence. *Aggression and Violent Behavior, 17,* 99–104.

Dutton, D. G., Nicholls, T. L., & Spidel, A. (2005). Female perpetrators of intimate abuse. In F. P. Buttell & M. M. Carney (Eds.), *Women who perpetrate relationship violence: Moving beyond political correctness* (pp. 1–31). New York: Haworth Press.

Dweck, C. S. (2002). Messages that motivate: How praise molds students' beliefs, motivation, and performance (in surprising ways). In J. Aronson (Ed.), *Improving academic achievement: Impact of psychological factors on education* (pp. 37–60). San Diego, CA: Academic Press.

Dweck, C. S. (2009). Prejudice: How it develops and how it can be undone. *Human Development, 52,* 371–376.

Dykiert, D., Der, G., Starr, J. M., & Deary, I. J. (2012). Sex differences in reaction time mean and intraindividual variability across the life span. *Developmental Psychology, 48,* 1262–1276.

Dykstra, P. A. (2009). Older adult loneliness: Myths and realities. *European Journal of Ageing, 6,* 91–100.

E

Eagly, A. H., & Carli, L. L. (2007). *Through the labyrinth: The truth about how women become leaders.* Boston, MA: Harvard Business School Press.

Eagly, A. H., & Wood, W. (2012). Social role theory. In P. A. M. Van Lange, A. W. Kruglanski, & E. T. Higgins (Eds.), *Handbook of theories of social psychology* (Vol. 2, pp. 458–476). Thousand Oaks, CA: Sage.

Eaker, E. D., Sullivan. L. M., Kelly-Hayes, M., D'Agostino, R. B., & Benjamin, E. J. (2004). Anger and hostility predict the development of atrial fibrillation in men in the Framingham Offspring Study. *Circulation, 109,* 1267–1271.

Eaker, E. D., Sullivan, L. M., Kelly-Hayes, M., D'Agostino, R. B., & Benjamin, E. J. (2007). Marital status, marital strain, and risk of coronary heart disease or total mortality: The Framingham Offspring Study. *Psychosomatic Medicine, 69,* 509–513.

Early Head Start National Resource Center. (2013). *Early Head Start program facts for Fiscal Year 2012.* Retrieved from eclkc.ohs.acf.hhs.gov/hslc/tta-system/ehsnrc/Early Head Start/about.html

Eaton, D. K., Davis, K. S., Barrios, L., Brener, N. D., & Noonan, R. K. (2007). Associations of dating violence victimization with lifetime participation, cooccurrence, and early initiation of risk behaviors among U.S. high school students. *Journal of Interpersonal Violence, 22,* 585–602.

Eaves, L., Silberg, J., Foley, D., Bulik, C., Maes, H., & Erkanli, A. (2004). Genetic and environmental influences on the relative timing of pubertal change. *Twin Research, 7,* 471–481.

Ebner, N. C., Freund, A. M., & Baltes, P. B. (2006). Developmental changes in personal goal orientation from young to late adulthood: From striving for gains to maintenance and prevention of losses. *Psychology and Aging, 21,* 664–678.

Eccles, J. S. (2004). Schools, academic motivation, and stage–environment fit. In R. M. Lerner & L. Steinberg (Eds.), *Handbook of Adolescent Psychology* (2nd ed., pp. 125–154). Hoboken, N. J.: Wiley.

Eccles, J. S., & Gootman, J. (Eds.). (2002). *Community programs to promote youth development.* Washington, DC: National Academy Press.

Eccles, J. S., Jacobs, J. E., & Harold, R. D. (1990). Gender-role stereotypes, expectancy effects, and parents' role in the socialization of gender differences in self-perceptions and skill acquisition. *Journal of Social Issues, 46,* 183–201.

Eccles, J. S., & Roeser, R. W. (2009). Schools, academic motivation, and stage–environment fit. In R. M. Lerner & L. Steinberg (Eds.), *Handbook of adolescent psychology* (Vol. 1, pp. 404–434). Hoboken, NJ: Wiley.

Eccles, J. S., Templeton, J., Barber, B., & Stone, M. (2003). Adolescence and emerging adulthood: The critical passageways to adulthood. In M. H. Bornstein, L. Davidson, C. L. M., Keyes, K. A. Moore, & the Center for Child Well-Being (Eds.), *Well-being: Positive development across the life course* (pp. 383–406). Mahwah, NJ: Erlbaum.

Eder, R. A., & Mangelsdorf, S. C. (1997). The emotional basis of early personality development: Implications for the emergent self-concept. In R. Hogan, J. Johnson, & S. Briggs (Eds.), *Handbook of personality psychology* (pp. 209–240). San Diego, CA: Academic Press.

Edwards, B. A., O'Driscoll, D. M., Ali A., Jordan, A. S., Trinder, J., & Malhotra, A. (2010). Aging and sleep: Physiology and pathophysiology. *Seminars in Respiratory Critical Care Medicine, 31,* 618–633.

Edwards, O. W., & Oakland, T. D. (2006). Factorial invariance of Woodcock-Johnson III scores for African Americans and Caucasian Americans. *Journal of Psychoeducational Assessment, 24,* 358–366.

Egan, S. K., & Perry, D. G. (2001). Gender identity: A multidimensional analysis with implications for psychosocial adjustment. *Developmental Psychology, 37,* 451–463.

Eggebeen, D. J., Dew, J., & Knoester, C. (2010). Fatherhood and men's lives at middle age. *Journal of Family Issues, 31,* 113–130.

Eggebeen, D. J., & Sturgeon, S. (2006). Demography of the baby boomers. In S. K. Whitbourne & S. L. Willis (Eds.), *The baby boomers grow up: Contemporary perspectives on midlife* (pp. 3–21). Mahwah, NJ: Erlbaum.

Ehrensaft, M. K. (2009). Family and relationship predictors of psychological and physical aggression. In D. K. O'Leary & E. M. Woodin (Eds.), *Psychological and physical aggression in couples: Causes and interventions* (pp. 99–118). Washington, DC: American Psychological Association.

Ehrensaft, M. K., Moffitt, T. E., & Caspi, A. (2004). Clinically abusive relationships in an unselected birth cohort: Men's and women's participation and developmental antecedents. *Journal of Abnormal Psychology, 113,* 258–270.

Ehri, L. C., & Roberts, T. (2006). The roots of learning to read and write: Acquisition of letters and phonemic awareness. In D. K. Dikinson & S. B. Neuman (Eds.), *Handbook of early literacy research* (Vol. 2, pp. 113–131). New York: Guildford.

Einstein, G. O., McDaniel, M. A., & Scullin, M. K. (2012). Prospective memory and aging: Understanding the variability. In M. Naveh-Benjamin & N. Ohta (Eds.), *Memory and aging: Current issues and future directions* (pp. 153–179). New York: Psychology Press.

Eisenberg, N. (2003). Prosocial behavior, empathy, and sympathy. In M. H. Bornstein & L. Davidson (Eds.), *Well-being: Positive development across the life course* (pp. 253–265). Mahwah, NJ: Erlbaum.

Eisenberg, N. (2010). Empathy-related responding: Links with self-regulation, moral judgment, and moral behavior. In M. Mikulincer & P. R. Shaver (Eds.), *Prosocial motives, emotions, and behavior: The better angels of our nature* (pp. 129–148). Washington, DC: American Psychological Association.

Eisenberg, N., Eggum, N. D., & Edwards, A. (2010). Empathy-related responding and moral development. In W. F. Arsenio & E. A. Lemerise (Eds.), *Emotions, aggression, and morality in children* (pp. 115–135). Washington, DC: American Psychological Association.

Eisenberg, N., Fabes, R. A., Shepard, S. A., Murphy, B. C., Jones, S., & Guthrie, I. K. (1998). Contemporaneous and longitudinal prediction of children's sympathy from dispositional regulation and emotionality. *Developmental Psychology, 34*, 910–924.

Eisenberg, N., Sadovsky, A., Spinrad, T. L., Fabes, R. A., Losoya, S., & Valiente, C. (2005a). The relations of problem behavior status to children's negative emotionality, effortful control, and impulsivity: Concurrent relations and prediction of change. *Developmental Psychology, 41*, 193–211.

Eisenberg, N., & Silver, R. C. (2011). Growing up in the shadow of terrorism. *American Psychologist, 66*, 468–481.

Eisenberg, N., Smith, C. L., Sadovsky, A., & Spinrad, T. L. (2004). Effortful control: Relations with emotion regulation, adjustment, and socialization in childhood. In R. Baumeister & K. D. Vohs (Eds.), *Handbook of self-regulation: Research, theory, and applications* (pp. 259–282). New York: Guilford.

Eisenberg, N., Zhou, Q., Spinrad, T. L., Valiente, C., Fabes, R. A., & Liew, J. (2005b). Relations among positive parenting, children's effortful control, and externalizing problems: A three-wave longitudinal study. *Child Development, 76*, 1055–1071.

Elavsky, S., & McAuley, E. (2007). Physical activity and mental health outcomes during menopause: A randomized controlled trial. *Annals of Behavioral Medicine, 33*, 132–142.

Elder, G. H., Jr., & Conger, R. (2000). *Children of the land: Adversity and success in rural America.* Chicago: University of Chicago Press.

Elder, G. H., Jr., Nguyen, T. V., & Caspi, A. (1985). Linking family hardship to children's lives. *Child Development, 56*, 361–375.

Elfenbein, D. S., & Felice, M. E. (2003). Adolescent pregnancy. *Pediatric Clinics of North America, 50*, 781–800.

Elias, C. L., & Berk, L. E. (2002). Self-regulation in young children: Is there a role for sociodramatic play? *Early Childhood Research Quarterly, 17*, 1–17.

Elkind, D. (1994). *A sympathetic understanding of the child: Birth to sixteen* (3rd ed.). Boston: Allyn and Bacon.

Elkind, D., & Bowen, R. (1979). Imaginary audience behavior in children and adolescents. *Developmental Psychology, 15*, 33–44.

Elliott, D. B., & Simmons, T. (2011, August). *Marital events of Americans: 2009. American Community Survey Reports, ACS-13.* Washington, DC: U.S. Census Bureau. Retrieved from www.census.gov/prod/2011pubs/acs-13.pdf

Elliott, J. G. (1999). School refusal: Issues of conceptualization, assessment, and treatment. *Journal of Child Psychology and Psychiatry and Allied Disciplines, 40*, 1001–1012.

Ellis, A. E., & Oakes, L. M. (2006). Infants flexibly use different dimensions to categorize objects. *Developmental Psychology, 42*, 1000–1011.

Ellis, B. J. (2004). Timing of pubertal maturation in girls: An integrated life history approach. *Psychological Bulletin, 130*, 920–958.

Ellis, B. J., & Essex, M. J. (2007). Family environments, adrenarche, and sexual maturation: A longitudinal test of a life history model. *Child Development, 78*, 1799–1817.

Ellis, L., & Bonin, S. L. (2003). Genetics and occupation-related preferences: Evidence from adoptive and non-adoptive families. *Personality and Individual Differences, 35*, 929–937.

Ellis, W. E., & Zarbatany, L. (2007). Explaining friendship formation and friendship stability: The role of children's and friends' aggression and victimization. *Merrill-Palmer Quarterly, 53*, 79–104.

Else-Quest, N. M., Hyde, J. S., Goldsmith, H. H., & Van Hulle, C. A. (2006). Gender differences in temperament: A meta-analysis. *Psychological Bulletin, 132*, 33–72.

El-Sheikh, M., Cummings, E. M., & Reiter, S. (1996). Preschoolers' responses to ongoing interadult conflict: The role of prior exposure to resolved versus unresolved arguments. *Journal of Abnormal Child Psychology, 24*, 665–679.

Eltzschig, H. K., Lieberman, E. S., & Camann, W. R. (2003). Regional anesthesia and analgesia for labor and delivery. *New England Journal of Medicine, 384*, 319–332.

Eluvathingal, T. J., Chugani, H. T., Behen, M. E., Juhasz, C., Muzik, O., Maqbook, M., et al. (2006). Abnormal brain connectivity in children after early severe socioemotional deprivation: A diffusion tensor imaging study. *Pediatrics, 117*, 2093–2100.

Elwert, F., & Christakis, N. A. (2006). Widowhood and race. *American Sociological Review, 71*, 16–41.

Emery, R. E., Sbarra, D., & Grover, T. (2005). Divorce mediation: Research and reflections. *Family Court Review, 43*, 22–37.

Englund, M. E., Egeland, B., & Collins, W. A. (2008). Exceptions to high school dropout predictions in a low-income sample: Do adults make a difference? *Journal of Social Issues, 64*, 77–93.

Ennemoser, M., & Schneider, W. (2007). Relations of television viewing and reading: Findings from a 4-year longitudinal study. *Journal of Educational Psychology, 99*, 349–368.

Entringer, S., Kumsta, R., Hellhammer, D. H., Wadhwa, P. D., & Wüst, S. (2009). Prenatal exposure to maternal psychosocial stress and HPA axis regulation in young adults. *Hormones and Behavior, 55*, 292–298.

Entwisle, D. R., Alexander, K. L., & Olson, L. S. (2005). First grade and educational attainment by age 22: A new story. *American Journal of Sociology, 110*, 1458–1502.

Epel, E. S., Linn, J., Wilhelm, F., Mendes, W., Adler, N., & Dolbier, C. (2006). Cell aging in relation to stress arousal and cardiovascular disease risk factors. *Psychoneuroendocrinology, 31*, 277–287.

Epel, E. S., Merkin, S. S., Cawthon, R., Blackburn, E. H., Adler, N. E., Pletcher, M. J., & Seeman, T. S. (2009). The rate of leukocyte telomere shortening predicts mortality from cardiovascular disease in elderly men: A novel demonstration. *Aging, 1*, 81–88.

Epstein, L. H., Roemmich, J. N., & Raynor, H. A. (2001). Behavioral therapy in the treatment of pediatric obesity. *Pediatric Clinics of North America, 48*, 981–983.

Erath, S. A., Bierman, K. L., & the Conduct Problems Prevention Research Group. (2006). Aggressive marital conflict, maternal harsh punishment, and child aggressive-disruptive behavior: Evidence for direct and mediate relations. *Journal of Family Psychology, 20*, 217–226.

Erickson, K. I., Colcombe, S. J., Wadhwa, R., Bherer, L., Peterson, M. S., & Scalf, P. E. (2007). Training-induced plasticity in older adults: Effects of training on hemispheric asymmetry. *Neurobiology of Aging, 28*, 272–283.

Erickson, K. I., Raji, C. A., Lopez, O. L., Becker, J. T., Rosano, C., Newman, A. B., et al. (2010). Physical activity predicts gray matter volume in late adulthood: The Cardiovascular Health Study. *Neurology, 75*, 1415–1422.

Erikson, E. H. (1950). *Childhood and society.* New York: Norton.

Erikson, E. H. (1968). *Identity, youth, and crisis.* New York: Norton.

Erikson, E. H. (1998). *The life cycle completed. Extended version with new chapters on the ninth stage by Joan M. Erikson.* New York: Norton.

Ernst, M., Moolchan, E. T., & Robinson, M. L. (2001). Behavioral and neural consequences of prenatal exposure to nicotine. *Journal of the American Academy of Child and Adolescent Psychiatry, 40*, 630–641.

Ernst, M., & Spear, L. (2009). Reward systems. In M. de Haan & M. Gunnar (Eds.), *Handbook of developmental social neuroscience* (pp. 324–341). New York: Guilford.

Erol, R. Y., & Orth, U. (2011). Self-esteem development from age 14 to 30 years: A longitudinal study. *Journal of Personality and Social Psychology, 101*, 607–619.

Ertekin-Tanner, N. (2007). Genetics of Alzheimer's disease: A centennial review. *Neurologic Clinics, 25*, 611–667.

Espy, K. A., Fang, H., Johnson, C., Stopp, C., & Wiebe, S. A. (2011). Prenatal tobacco exposure: Developmental outcomes in the neonatal period. *Developmental Psychology, 47*, 153–156.

Espy, K. A., Molfese, V. J., & DiLalla, L. F. (2001). Effects of environmental measures on intelligence in young children: Growth curve modeling of longitudinal data. *Merrill-Palmer Quarterly, 47*, 42–73.

Estourgie-van Burk, G. F., Bartels, M., van Beijsterveldt, T. C., Delemarre-van de Waal, H. A., & Boomsma, D. I. (2006). Body size in five-year-old twins: Heritability and comparison to singleton standards. *Twin Research and Human Genetics, 9*, 646–655.

Ethier, K. A., Kershaw, T., Niccolai, L., Lewis, J. B., & Ickovics, J. R. (2003). Adolescent women underestimate their susceptibility to sexually transmitted infections. *Sexually Transmitted Infections, 79*, 408–411.

Etnier, J. L., & Labban, J. D. (2012). Physical activity and cognitive function: Theoretical bases, mechanisms, and moderators. In E. O. Acebedo (Ed.), *Oxford Handbook of exercise psychology* (pp. 76–96). New York: Oxford University Press.

Evans, A. M. (2008). Growing pains: Contemporary knowledge and recommended practice. *Journal of Foot and Ankle Research, 1*, 4.

Evans, E., Hawton, K., & Rodham, K. (2004). Factors associated with suicidal phenomena in adolescents: A systematic review of population-based studies. *Clinical Psychology Review, 24*, 957–979.

Evans, G. W., & Schamberg, M A. (2009). Childhood poverty, chronic stress, and adult working memory. *Proceedings of the National Academy of Sciences, 106*, 6545–6549.

Evans, N., & Levinson, S. C. (2009). The myth of language universals: Language diversity and its importance for cognitive science. *Behavioral and Brain Sciences, 32*, 429–492.

F

Fabes, R. A., Eisenberg, N., Hanish, L. D., & Spinrad, T. L. (2001). Preschoolers' spontaneous emotion vocabulary: Relations to likeability. *Early Education and Development, 12*, 11–27.

Fabes, R. A., Eisenberg, N., McCormick, S. E., & Wilson, M. S. (1988). Preschoolers' attributions of the situational determinants of others' naturally occurring emotions. *Developmental Psychology, 24*, 376–385.

Fabes, R. A., Martin, C. L., & Hanish, L. D. (2003). Young children's play qualities in same-, other-, and mixed-sex peer groups. *Child Development, 74*, 921–932.

Fabiani, M. (2012). It was the best of times, it was the worst of times: A psychophysiologist's view of cognitive aging. *Psychophysiology, 49*, 283–304.

Fagan, J. F., Holland, C. R., & Wheeler, K. (2007). The prediction, from infancy, of adult IQ and achievement. *Intelligence, 35*, 225–231.

Fagard, J., Spelke, E., & von Hofsten, C. (2009). Reaching and grasping a moving object in 6-, 8-, and 10-month-old infants: Laterality and performance. *Infant Behavior and Development, 32*, 137–146.

Fagot, B. I. (1985). Changes in thinking about early sex role development. *Developmental Review, 5*, 83–98.

Fagot, B. I., & Hagan, R. I. (1991). Observations of parent reactions to sex-stereotyped behaviors: Age and sex effects. *Child Development, 62,* 617–628.

Fagot, B. I., & Leinbach, M. D. (1989). The young child's gender schema: Environmental input, internal organization. *Child Development, 60,* 663–672.

Fagundes, C. P., Bennett, J. M., Derry, H. M., & Kiecolt-Glaser, J. K. (2011). Relationships and inflammation across the lifespan: Social developmental pathways to disease. *Social and Personality Psychology Compass, 5,* 891–903.

Fahrmeier, E. D. (1978). The development of concrete operations among the Hausa. *Journal of Cross-Cultural Psychology, 9,* 23–44.

Fairburn, C. G., & Harrison, P. J. (2003). Eating disorders. *Lancet, 361,* 407–416.

Faircloth, B. S., & Hamm, J. V. (2005). Sense of belonging among high school students representing four ethnic groups. *Journal of Youth and Adolescence, 34,* 293–309.

Falagas, M. E., & Zarkadoulia, E. (2008). Factors associated with suboptimal compliance to vaccinations in children in developed countries: A systematic review. *Current Medical Research and Opinion, 24,* 1719–1741.

Falbo, T. (1992). Social norms and the one-child family: Clinical and policy implications. In F. Boer & J. Dunn (Eds.), *Children's sibling relationships* (pp. 71–82). Hillsdale, NJ: Erlbaum.

Falbo, T., & Poston, D. L., Jr. (1993). The academic, personality, and physical outcomes of only children in China. *Child Development, 64,* 18–35.

Falbo, T., Poston, D. L., Jr., Triscari, R. S., & Zhang, X. (1997). Self-enhancing illusions among Chinese schoolchildren. *Journal of Cross-Cultural Psychology, 28,* 172–191.

Falk, D. (2005). Brain lateralization in primates and its evolution in hominids. *American Journal of Physical Anthropology, 30,* 107–125.

Family Caregiver Alliance. (2009). *Fact sheet: Selected caregiver statistics.* Retrieved from www.caregiver .org/caregiver/jsp/content_node.jsp?nodeid=439

Fanslow, C. A. (1981). Death: A natural facet of the life continuum. In D. Krieger (Ed.), *Foundations for holistic health nursing practices: The renaissance nurse* (pp. 249–272). Philadelphia: Lippincott.

Fantz, R. L. (1961, May). The origin of form perception. *Scientific American, 204*(5), 66–72.

Farah, M. J., Shera, D. M., Savage, J. H., Betancourt, L., Giannetta, J. M., Brodsky, N. L., et al. (2006). Childhood poverty: Specific associations with neurocognitive development. *Brain Research, 110,* 166–174.

Faraone, S. V., & Mick, E. (2010). Molecular genetics of attention deficit hyperactivity disorder. *Psychiatric Clinics of North America, 33,* 159–180.

Farmer, T. W., Irvin, M. J., Leung, M.-C., Hall, C. M., Hutchins, B. C., & McDonough, E. (2010). Social preference, social prominence, and group membership in late elementary school: Homophilic concentration and peer affiliation configurations. *Social Psychology of Education, 13,* 271–293.

Farr, R. J., Forssell, S. L., & Patterson, C. J. (2010). Parenting and child development in adoptive families: Does parental sexual orientation matter? *Applied Developmental Science, 14,* 164–178.

Farrant, K., & Reese, E. (2000). Maternal style and children's participation in reminiscing: Stepping stones in children's autobiological memory development. *Journal of Cognition and Development, 1,* 193–225.

Farrington, D. P. (2009). Conduct disorder, aggression and delinquency. In R. M. Lerner & L. Steinberg (Eds.), *Handbook of adolescent psychology: Vol. 1. Individual bases of adolescent development* (3rd ed., pp. 683–722). Hoboken, NJ: Wiley.

Farroni, T., Massaccesi, S., Menon, E., & Johnson, M. H. (2007). Direct gaze modulates face recognition in young infants. *Cognition, 102,* 396–404.

Farver, J. M., & Branstetter, W. H. (1994). Preschoolers' prosocial responses to their peers' distress. *Developmental Psychology, 30,* 334–341.

Farver, J. M., Kim, Y. K., & Lee, Y. (1995). Cultural differences in Korean- and Anglo-American preschoolers' social interaction and play behaviors. *Child Development, 66,* 1088–1099.

Fattibene, P., Mazzei, F., Nuccetelli, C., & Risica, S. (1999). Prenatal exposure to ionizing radiation: Sources, effects, and regulatory aspects. *Acta Paediatrica, 88,* 693–702.

Fearon, R. P., Bakermans-Kranenburg, M. J., Lapsley, A., & Roisman, G. I. (2010). The significance of insecure attachment and disorganization in the development of children's externalizing behavior: A meta-analytic study. *Child Development, 81,* 435–456.

Federal Interagency Forum on Aging Related Statistics. (2012). *Older Americans: Key indicators of well-being.* Washington, DC: U.S. Government Printing Office.

Federal Interagency Forum on Child and Family Statistics. (2011). *America's children: Key national indicators of well-being, 2011.* Retrieved from www.childstats.gov

Federico, M. J., & Liu, A. H. (2003). Overcoming childhood asthma disparities of the inner-city poor. *Pediatric Clinics of North America, 50,* 655–675.

Feeney, J. A. (1999). Adult romantic attachment and couple relationships. In J. Cassidy & P. R. Shaver (Eds.), *Handbook of attachment* (pp. 355–377). New York: Guilford.

Feeney, J. A., Hohaus, L., Noller, P., & Alexander, R. P. (2001). *Becoming parents: Exploring the bonds between mothers, fathers, and their infants.* New York: Cambridge University Press.

Fehr, B. (1994). Prototype based assessment of laypeoples' views of love. *Personal Relationships, 1,* 309–331.

Feigelman, W., & Gorman, B. S. (2008). Assessing the effects of peer suicide on youth suicide. *Suicide and Life-Threatening Behavior, 38,* 181–194.

Feinberg, M. E., McHale, S. M., Crouter, A. C., & Cumsille, P. (2003). Sibling differentiation: Sibling and parent relationship trajectories in adolescence. *Child Development, 74,* 1261–1274.

Feldman, A. F., & Matjasko, J. L. (2007). Profiles and portfolios of adolescent school-based extracurricular activity participation. *Journal of Adolescence, 30,* 313–332.

Feldman, D. C., & Beehr, T. A. (2011). A three-phase model of retirement decision making. *American Psychologist, 66,* 193–203.

Feldman, D. C., & Vogel, R. M. (2009). The aging process and person–environment fit. In S. G. Baugh & S. E. Sullivan (Eds.), *Research in careers* (pp. 1–25). Charlotte, NC: Information Age Press.

Feldman, P. J., & Steptoe, A. (2004). How neighborhoods and physical functioning are related: The roles of neighborhood socioeconomic status, perceived neighborhood strain, and individual health risk factors. *Annals of Behavioral Medicine, 27,* 91–99.

Feldman, R. (2003). Infant–mother and infant–father synchrony: The coregulation of positive arousal. *Infant Mental Health Journal, 24,* 1–23.

Feldman, R. (2006). From biological rhythms to social rhythms: Physiological precursors of mother–infant synchrony. *Developmental Psychology, 42,* 175–188.

Feldman, R. (2007). Maternal versus child risk and the development of parent–child and family relationships in five high-risk populations. *Development and Psychopathology, 19,* 293–312.

Feldman, R., Eidelman, A. I., & Rotenberg, N. (2004). Parenting stress, infant emotion regulation, maternal sensitivity, and the cognitive development

of triplets: A model for parent and child influences in a unique ecology. *Child Development, 75,* 1774–1791.

Feldman, R., Gordon, I., Schneiderman, I., Weisman, O., & Zagoory-Sharon, O. (2010). Natural variations in maternal and paternal care are associated with systematic changes in oxytocin following parent–infant contact. *Psychoneuroendocrinology, 35,* 1133–1141.

Feldman, R., Granat, A., Pariente, C., Kanety, H., Kuint, J., & Gilboa-Schechtman, E. (2009). Maternal depression and anxiety across the postpartum year and infant social engagement, fear regulation, and stress reactivity. *Journal of the American Academy of Child and Adolescent Psychiatry, 48,* 919–927.

Feldman, R., Greenbaum, C. W., & Yirmiya, N. (1999). Mother–infant affect synchrony as an antecedent of the emergence of self-control. *Developmental Psychology, 35,* 223–231.

Feldman, R., & Klein, P. S. (2003). Toddlers' self-regulated compliance to mothers, caregivers, and fathers: Implications for theories of socialization. *Developmental Psychology, 39,* 680–692.

Feldman, R., Sussman, A. L., & Zigler, E. (2004). Parental leave and work adaptation at the transition to parenthood: Individual, marital, and social correlates. *Applied Developmental Psychology, 25,* 459–479.

Felner, R. D., Favazza, A., Shim, M., Brand, S., Gu, K., & Noonan, N. (2002). Whole school improvement and restructuring as prevention and promotion: Lessons from STEP and the Project on High Performance Learning Communities. *Journal of School Psychology, 39,* 177–202.

Felsman, D. E., & Blustein, D. L. (1999). The role of peer relatedness in late adolescent career development. *Journal of Vocational Behavior, 54,* 279–295.

Feret, A., Steinweg, S., Griffin, H. C., & Glover, S. (2007). Macular degeneration: Types, causes, and possible interventions. *Geriatric Nursing, 28,* 387–392.

Ferguson, L. R. (2010). Meat and cancer. *Meat Science, 84,* 308–313.

Fergusson, D. M., & Woodward, L. J. (1999). Breastfeeding and later psychosocial adjustment. *Paediatric and Perinatal Epidemiology, 13,* 144–157.

Fernald, A., Perfors, A., & Marchman, V. A. (2006). Picking up speed in understanding: Speech processing efficiency and vocabulary growth across the 2nd year. *Developmental Psychology, 42,* 98–116.

Fernald, A., Taeschner, T., Dunn, J., Papousek, M., Boyssen-Bardies, B., & Fukui, I. (1989). A cross-language study of prosodic modifications in mothers' and fathers' speech to preverbal infants. *Journal of Child Language, 16,* 477–502.

Fernald, L. C., & Grantham-McGregor, S. M. (1998). Stress response in school-age children who have been growth-retarded since early childhood. *American Journal of Clinical Nutrition, 68,* 691–698.

Ferrari, P. F., & Coudé, G. (2011). Mirror neurons and imitation from a developmental and evolutionary perspective. In A. Vilain, C. Abry, J.-L. Schwartz, & J. Vauclair (Eds.), *Primate communication and human language* (pp. 121–138). Amsterdam, Netherlands: John Benjamins.

Ferrari, P. F., Visalberghi E., Paukner A., Fogassi L., Ruggiero A., Suomi, S. (2006). Neonatal imitation in rhesus macaques. *PLoS Biology, 4,* e302.

Ferry, A. L., Hespos, S. J., & Waxman, S. R. (2010). Categorization in 3- and 4-month-old infants: An advantage of words over tones. *Child Development, 81,* 472–479.

Ficca, G., Fagioli, I., Giganti, F., & Salzarulo, P. (1999). Spontaneous awakenings from sleep in the first year of life. *Early Human Development, 55,* 219–228.

Field, D. (1997). "Looking back, what period of your life brought you the most satisfaction?" *International Journal of Aging and Human Development, 45,* 169–194.

Field, D. (1999). Stability of older women's friendships: A commentary on Roberto. *International Journal of Aging and Human Development, 48,* 81–83.

Field, D., & Millsap, R. E. (1991). Personality in advanced old age: Continuity or change? *Journal of Gerontology, 46,* 299–308.

Field, T. (2001). Massage therapy facilitates weight gain in preterm infants. *Current Directions in Psychological Science, 10,* 51–54.

Field, T. (2011). Prenatal depression effects on early development: A review. *Infant Behavior and Development, 34,* 1–14.

Field, T., Hernandez-Reif, M., Feijo, L., & Freedman, J. (2006). Prenatal, perinatal and neonatal stimulation: A survey of neonatal nurseries. *Infant Behavior and Development, 29,* 24–31.

Field, T., Hernandez-Reif, M., & Freedman, J. (2004). Stimulation programs for preterm infants. *Social Policy Report of the Society for Research in Child Development, 18*(1).

Fiese, B. H., & Schwartz, M. (2008). Reclaiming the family table: Mealtimes and child health and well-being. *Social Policy Report of the Society for Research in Child Development, 22*(4), 3–18.

Fifer, W. P., Byrd, D. L., Kaku, M., Eigsti, I. M., Isler, J. R., Grose-Fifer, J., et al. (2010). Newborn infants learn during sleep. *Proceedings of the National Academy of Sciences, 107,* 10320–10323.

Figner, B., Mackinlay, R. J., Wilkening, F., & Weber, E. U. (2009). Affective and deliberative processes in risky choice: Age differences in risk taking in the Columbia Card Task. *Journal of Experimental Psychology: Learning, Memory, and Cognition, 35,* 709–770.

Fincham, F. D., & Bradbury, T. N. (2004). Marital satisfaction, depression, and attributions: A longitudinal analysis. In R. M. Kowalski & M. R. Leary (Eds.), *The interface of social and clinical psychology: Key readings* (pp. 129–146). New York: Psychology Press.

Finchum, T., & Weber, J. A. (2000). Applying continuity theory to elder adult friendships. *Journal of Aging and Identity, 5,* 159–168.

Findlay, L. C., & Coplan, R. J. (2008). Come out and play: Shyness in childhood and the benefits of organized sports participation. *Canadian Journal of Behavioural Science, 40,* 153–161.

Fine, M. A., Ganong, L. H., & Demo, D. H. (2010). Divorce: A risk and resilience perspective. In S. J. Price, C. A. Price, & P. C. McKenry (Eds.), *Families and change: Coping with stressful events and transitions* (pp. 211–234). Thousand Oaks, CA: Sage.

Fingerman, K. L. (2004). The role of offspring and in-laws in grandparents' ties to their grandchildren. *Journal of Family Issues, 25,* 1026–1049.

Fingerman, K. L., & Birditt, K. S. (2003). Do we get better at picking our battles? Age group differences in descriptions of behavioral reactions to interpersonal tensions. *Journal of Gerontology, 60B,* P121–P128.

Fingerman, K. L., & Birditt, K. S. (2011). Relationships between adults and their aging parents. In K. W. Schaie & S. L. Willis (Eds.), *Handbook of the psychology of aging* (pp. 219–232). San Diego, CA: Academic Press.

Fingerman, K. L., Cheng, Y.-P., Birditt, K., & Zarit, S. (2012a). Only as happy as the least happy child: Multiple grown children's problems and successes and middle-aged parents' well-being. *Journal of Gerontology, 67B,* 184–193.

Fingerman, K. L., Cheng, Y-P., Tighe, L., Birditt, K. S., & Zarit, S. (2012b). Relationships between young adults and their parents. In A. Booth, S. L. Brown, N. S. Landale, W. D. Manning, & S. M. McHale (Eds.), *Early adulthood in a family context* (pp. 59–85). New York: Springer.

Fingerman, K. L., Cheng, Y-P., Wesselmann, D., Zarit, S., Furstenberg, F., & Birditt, K. S. (2012c).

Helicopter parents and landing pad kids: Intense parental support of grown children. *Journal of Marriage and Family, 74,* 880–896.

Fingerman, K. L., Hay, E. L., Dush, C. M. K., Cichy, K. E., & Hosterman, S. J. (2007). Parents' and offspring's perceptions of change and continuity when parents experience the transition to old age. *Advances in Life Course Research, 12,* 275–305.

Fingerman, K. L., Pitzer, L. M., Chan, W., Birditt, K., Franks, M. M., & Zarit, S. (2011a). Who gets what and why? Help middle-aged adults provide to parents and grown children. *Journal of Gerontology, 66B,* 87–98.

Fingerman, K. L., Pitzer, L., Lefkowitz, E. S., Birditt, K. S., & Mroczek, D. (2008). Ambivalent relationship qualities between adults and their parents: Implications for both parties' well-being. *Journal of Gerontology, 63B,* P362–P371.

Fingerman, K. L., VanderDrift, L. E., Dotterer, A. M., Birditt, K. S., & Zarit, S. H. (2011b). Support to aging parents and grown children in black and white families. *Gerontologist, 51,* 441–452.

Finkel, D., Reynolds, C. A., McArdle, J. J., & Pedersen, N. L. (2007). Age changes in processing speed as a leading indicator of cognitive aging. *Psychology and Aging, 22,* 558–568.

Finkel, E. J., Eastwick, P. W., Karney, B. R., Reis, H. T., & Sprecher, S. (2012). Online dating: A critical analysis from the perspective of psychological science. *Psychological Science in the Public Interest, 13,* 3–66.

Finkelhor, D. (2009). The prevention of childhood sexual abuse. *Future of Children, 19,* 169–194.

Finucane, M. L., Mertz, C. K., Slovic, P., & Schmidt, E. S. (2005). Task complexity and older adults' decision-making competence. *Psychology and Aging, 20,* 71–84.

Fiori, K. L., Antonucci, T., & Cortina, K. S. (2006). Social network typologies and mental health among older adults. *Journal of Gerontology, 61B,* 25–32.

Fiori, K. L., Smith, J., & Antonucci, T. C. (2007). Social network types among older adults: A multidimensional approach. *Journal of Gerontology, 62B,* P322–P330.

Fischer, K. W., & Bidell, T. R. (2006). Dynamic development of action and thought. In R. M. Lerner (Ed.), *Handbook of child psychology: Vol. 1. Theoretical models of human development* (6th ed., pp. 313–399). Hoboken, NJ: Wiley.

Fischman, M. G., Moore, J. B., & Steele, K. H. (1992). Children's one-hand catching as a function of age, gender, and ball location. *Research Quarterly for Exercise and Sport, 63,* 349–355.

Fish, M. (2004). Attachment in infancy and preschool in low socioeconomic status rural Appalachian children: Stability and change and relations to preschool and kindergarten competence. *Development and Psychopathology, 16,* 293–312.

Fisher, C. B. (1993, Winter). Integrating science and ethics in research with high-risk children and youth. *Social Policy Report of the Society for Research in Child Development, 7*(4), 1–27.

Fisher, S. E., Francks, C., McCracken, J. T., McGough, J. J., Marlow, A. J., & MacPhie, I. L. (2002). A genomewide scan for loci involved in attention-deficit/hyperactivity disorder. *American Journal of Human Genetics, 70,* 1183–1196.

Fisher, S. K., Easterly, S., & Lazear, K. J. (2008). Lesbian, gay, bisexual and transgender families and their children. In T. P. Gullotta & G. M. Blau (Eds.), *Family influences on child behavior and development: Evidence-based prevention and treatment approaches* (pp. 187–208). New York: Routledge.

Fitzpatrick, J., & Sollie, D. L. (1999). Influence of individual and interpersonal factors on satisfaction and stability in romantic relationships. *Personal Relationships, 6,* 337–350.

Fivush, R., & Haden, C. A. (2005). Parent–child reminiscing and the construction of a subjective self. In B. D. Homer & C. S. Tamis-LeMonda (Eds.), *The development of social cognition and communication* (pp. 315–336). Mahwah, NJ: Erlbaum.

Flanagan, C. A., Stout, M., & Gallay, L. S. (2008). It's my body and none of your business: Developmental changes in adolescents' perceptions of rights concerning health. *Journal of Social Issues, 64,* 815–834.

Flannery, D. J., Hussey, D. L., Biebelhausen, L., & Wester, K. L. (2003). Crime, delinquency, and youth gangs. In G. R. Adams & M. D. Berzonsky (Eds.), *Blackwell handbook of adolescence* (pp. 502–522). Malden, MA: Blackwell.

Flannery, K. A., & Liederman, J. (1995). Is there really a syndrome involving the co-occurrence of neurodevelopmental disorder, talent, non–right handedness and immune disorder among children? *Cortex, 31,* 503–515.

Flavell, J. H., Flavell, E. R., & Green, F. L. (2001). Development of children's understanding of connections between thinking and feeling. *Psychological Science, 12,* 430–432.

Flavell, J. H., Green, F. L., & Flavell, E. R. (1987). Development of knowledge about the appearance-reality distinction. *Monographs of the Society for Research in Child Development, 51*(1, Serial No. 212).

Flavell, J. H., Green, F. L., & Flavell, E. R. (1995). Young children's knowledge about thinking. *Monographs of the Society for Research in Child Development, 60*(1, Serial No. 243).

Flegal, K. M., Carroll, M. D., Kit, B. K., & Ogden, C. L. (2012). Prevalence of obesity and trends in the distribution of body mass index among U.S. adults, 1999–2010. *Journal of the American Medical Association, 307,* 491–497.

Fleischman, D. A., Wilson, R. S., Gabrieli, J. D. E., Bienias, J. L., & Bennett, D. A. (2004). A longitudinal study of implicit and explicit memory in old persons. *Psychology and Aging, 19,* 617–625.

Fletcher, A. C., Nickerson, P., & Wright, K. L. (2003). Structured leisure activities in middle childhood: Links to well-being. *Journal of Community Psychology, 31,* 641–659.

Flom, R., & Bahrick, L. E. (2010). The effects of intersensory redundancy on attention and memory: Infants' long-term memory for orientation in audiovisual events. *Developmental Psychology, 46,* 428–436.

Flom, R., & Pick, A. D. (2003). Verbal encouragement and joint attention in 18-month-old infants. *Infant Behavior and Development, 26,* 121–134.

Flood, D. G., & Coleman, P. D. (1988). Cell type heterogeneity of changes in dendritic extent in the hippocampal region of the human brain in normal aging and in Alzheimer's disease. In T. L. Petit & G. O. Ivy (Ed.), *Neural plasticity: A lifespan approach* (pp. 265–281). New York: Alan R. Liss.

Florian, V., & Mikulincer, M. (1998). Symbolic immortality and the management of the terror of death: The moderating role of attachment style. *Journal of Personality and Social Psychology, 74,* 725–734.

Florsheim, P., & Smith, A. (2005). Expectant adolescent couples' relations and subsequent parenting behavior. *Infant Mental Health Journal, 26,* 533–548.

Flynn, E. (2006). A microgenetic investigation of stability and continuity in theory of mind development. *British Journal of Developmental Psychology, 24,* 631–654.

Flynn, J. R. (2007). *What is intelligence? Beyond the Flynn effect.* New York: Cambridge University Press.

Flynn, J. R. (2011). Secular changes in intelligence. In R. J. Sternberg & S. B. Kaufman (Eds.), *Cambridge handbook of intelligence* (pp. 647–665). New York: Cambridge University Press.

Foehr, U. G. (2006). *Media multitasking among American youth: Prevalence, predictors, and pairings.* Menlo Park. CA: Kaiser Family Foundation.

Foerde, K., Knowlton, B. J., & Poldrack, R. A. (2006). Modulation of competing memory systems by distraction. *Proceedings of the National Academy of Sciences, 103,* 11778–11783.

Fogel, A. (1993). *Developing through relationships: Origins of communication, self and culture.* New York: Harvester Wheatsheaf.

Fomon, S. J., & Nelson, S. E. (2002). Body composition of the male and female reference infants. *Annual Review of Nutrition, 22,* 1–17.

Fonda, S. J., Clipp, E. C., & Maddox, G. L. (2002). Patterns in functioning among residents of an affordable assisted living housing facility. *Gerontologist, 42,* 178–187.

Fong, T. G., Tulebaev, S. R., & Inouye, S. K. (2009). Delirium in elderly adults: Diagnosis, prevention and treatment. *Nature Reviews Neurology, 5,* 210–220.

Fontana, L. (2008). Calorie restriction and cardiometabolic health. *European Journal of Cardiovascular Prevention and Rehabilitation, 15,* 3–9.

Fontana, L. (2009). The scientific basis of caloric restriction leading to longer life. *Current Opinion in Gastroenterology, 25,* 144–150.

Fontana, L., Klein, S., & Holloszy, J. O. (2010). Effects of long-term calorie restriction and endurance exercise on glucose tolerance, insulin action, and adipokine production. *Age, 32,* 97–108.

Fontana, L., Meyer, T. E., Klein, S., & Holloszy, J. O. (2004). Long-term calorie restriction is highly effective in reducing the risk for atherosclerosis in humans. *Proceedings of the National Academy of Sciences, 101,* 6659–6663.

Forman, D. R., Aksan, N., & Kochanska, G. (2004). Toddlers' responsive imitation predicts preschoolage conscience. *Psychological Science, 15,* 699–704.

Forman, D. R., O'Hara, M. W., Stuart, S., Gorman, L. L., Larsen, K. E., & Coy, K. C. (2007). Effective treatment for postpartum depression is not sufficient to improve the developing mother–child relationship. *Development and Psychopathology, 19,* 585–602.

Forry, N. D., Leslie, L. A., & Letiecq, B. L. (2007). Marital quality in interracial relationships: The role of sex role ideology and perceived fairness. *Journal of Family Issues, 28,* 1538–1552.

Forste, R., & Heaton, T. B. (2004). The divorce generation: Well-being, family attitudes, and socioeconomic consequences of marital disruption. *Journal of Divorce and Remarriage, 42,* 95–114.

Fortenberry, J. D. (2010). Fate, desire, and the centrality of the relationship to adolescent condom use. *Journal of Adolescent Health, 47,* 219–220.

Foster, M. A., Lambert, R., Abbott-Shim, M., McCarty, F., & Franze, S. (2005). A model of home learning environment and social risk factors in relation to children's emergent literacy and social outcomes. *Early Childhood Research Quarterly, 20,* 13–36.

Fowler, J. W., & Dell, M. L. (2006). Stages of faith from infancy through adolescence: Reflections on three decades of faith development theory. In E. C. Roehlkepartain, P. E. King, L. Wagener, & P. L. Benson (Eds.), *Handbook of spiritual development in childhood and adolescence* (pp. 34–45). Thousand Oaks, CA: Sage.

Fox, C. L., & Boulton, M. J. (2006). Friendship as a moderator of the relationship between social skills problems and peer victimization. *Aggressive Behavior, 32,* 110–121.

Fox, N. A. (1991). If it's not left, it's right: Electroencephalograph asymmetry and the development of emotion. *American Psychologist, 46,* 863–872.

Fox, N. A., & Calkins, S. D. (2003). The development of self-control of emotion: Intrinsic and extrinsic influences. *Motivation and Emotion, 27,* 7–26.

Fox, N. A., & Davidson, R. J. (1986). Taste-elicited changes in facial signs of emotion and the asymmetry of brain electrical activity in newborn infants. *Neuropsychologia, 24,* 417–422.

Fox, N. A., Henderson, H. A., Pérez-Edgar, K., & White, L. K. (2008). The biology of temperament: An integrative approach. In C. A. Nelson & M. Luciana (Eds.), *Handbook of developmental cognitive neuroscience* (2nd ed., pp. 839–853). Cambridge, MA: MIT Press.

Franchak, J. M., & Adolph, K. E. (2012). What infants know and what they do: Perceiving possibilities for walking through openings. *Developmental Psychology, 48,* 1254–1261.

Frankenburg, E., & Orfield, G. (2007). *Lessons in integration: Realizing the promise of racial diversity in American schools.* Charlottesville: University of Virginia Press.

Franklin, V. P. (2012). "The teachers' unions strike back?" No need to wait for "Superman": Magnet schools have brought success to urban public school students for over 30 years. In D. T. Slaughter-Defoe, H. C. Stevenson, E. G. Arrington, & D. J. Johnson (Eds.), *Black educational choice: Assessing the private and public alternatives to traditional K–12 public schools* (pp. 217–220). Santa Barbara, CA: Praeger.

Frazier, L., Barreto, M., & Newman, F. (2012). Self-regulation and eudaimonic well-being across adulthood. *Experimental Aging Research, 38,* 394–410.

Frazier, L. D. (2002). Perceptions of control over health: Implications for sense of self in healthy and ill older adults. In S. P. Shohov (Ed.), *Advances in psychology research* (Vol. 10, pp. 145–163). Huntington, NY: Nova Science Publishers.

Frazier, L. D., & Hooker, K. (2006). Possible selves in adult development: Linking theory and research. In C. Dunkel & J. Kerpelman (Eds.), *Possible selves: Theory, research and applications* (pp. 41–59). Hauppauge, NY: Nova Science.

Frederickson, B. L., & Carstensen, L. L. (1990). Relationship classification using grade of membership analysis: A typology of sibling relationships in later life. *Journal of Gerontology, 45,* S43–S51.

Fredricks, J. A. (2012). Extracurricular participation and academic outcomes: Testing the overscheduling hypothesis. *Journal of Youth and Adolescence, 41,* 295–306.

Fredricks, J. A., & Eccles, J. S. (2002). Children's competence and value beliefs from childhood through adolescence: Growth trajectories in two male-sex-typed domains. *Developmental Psychology, 38,* 519–533.

Fredricks, J. A., & Eccles, J. S. (2006). Is extracurricular participation associated with beneficial outcomes? Concurrent and longitudinal relations. *Developmental Psychology, 42,* 698–713.

Freedman, M. (1999). *Prime time: How baby boomers will revolutionize retirement and transform America.* New York: Public Affairs.

Freeman, D. (1983). *Margaret Mead and Samoa: The making and unmaking of an anthropological myth.* Cambridge, MA: Harvard University Press.

Freeman, H., & Newland, L. A. (2010). New directions in father attachment. *Early Child Development and Care, 180,* 1–8.

Freeman, L., Caserta, M., Lund, D., Rossa, S., Dowdy, A., & Partenheimer, A. (2006). Music thanatology: Prescriptive harp music as palliative care for the dying patient. *American Journal of Hospice and Palliative Care, 23,* 100–104.

Freitag, C. M., Rohde, L. A., Lempp, T., & Romanos, M. (2010). Phenotypic and measurement influences on heritability estimates in childhood ADHD. *European Child and Adolescent Psychiatry, 19,* 311–323.

Freud, A. (1969). Adolescence as a developmental disturbance. In G. Caplan & S. Lebovici (Eds.), *Adolescence* (pp. 5–10). New York: Basic Books.

Freud, S. (1973). *An outline of psychoanalysis.* London: Hogarth. (Original work published 1938)

Freud, S. (1974). *The ego and the id.* London: Hogarth. (Original work published 1923)

Freund, A. M., & Baltes, P. B. (1998). Selection, optimization, and compensation as strategies of life management: Correlations with subjective indicators of successful aging. *Psychology and Aging, 13,* 531–543.

Freund, A. M., & Smith, J. (1999). Content and function of the self-definition in old and very old age. *Journal of Gerontology, 54B,* P55–P67.

Frey, A., Ruchkin, V., Martin, A., & Schwab-Stone, M. (2009). Adolescents in transition: School and family characteristics in the development of violent behaviors entering high school. *Child Psychiatry and Human Development, 40,* 1–13.

Fried, L. P., Xue, Q.-L., Cappola, A. R., Ferrucci, L., Chaves, P., Varadhan, R., et al. (2009). Nonlinear multisystem physiological dysregulation associated with frailty in older women: Implications for etiology and treatment. *Journal of Gerontology, 64A,* 1049–1052.

Friedman, C., McGwin, G., Jr., Ball, K. K., & Owsley, C. (2013). Association between higher-order visual processing abilities and a history of motor vehicle collision involvement by drivers age 70 and over. *Investigative Ophthalmology and Visual Science, 54,* 778–782.

Friedman, E. M., & Lawrence, D. A. (2002). Environmental stress mediates changes in neuroimmunological interactions. *Toxicological Sciences, 67,* 4–10.

Fries, J. F., Bruce, B., & Chakravarty, E. (2011). Compression of morbidity 1980–2011: A focused review of paradigms and progress. *Journal of Aging Research,* Article ID 261702. Retrieved from www.hindawi.com/journals/jar/2011/261702

Frith, U. (2003). *Autism: Explaining the enigma* (2nd ed.). Malden, MA: Blackwell.

Fry, C. L. (1985). Culture, behavior, and aging in the comparative perspective. In J. E. Birren & K. W. Schaie (Eds.), *Handbook of the psychology of aging* (2nd ed., pp. 216–244). New York: Van Nostrand Reinhold.

Fry, P. S. (2001). Predictors of health-related quality of life perspectives, self-esteem, and life satisfactions of older adults following spousal loss: An 18-month follow-up study of widows and widowers. *Gerontologist, 41,* 787–798.

Fry, P. S. (2003). Perceived self-efficacy domains as predictors of fear of the unknown and fear of dying among older adults. *Psychology and Aging, 18,* 474–486.

Fry, P. S., & Debats, D. L. (2006). Sources of life strengths as predictors of late-life mortality and survivorship. *International Journal of Aging and Human Development, 62,* 303–334.

Fryer, S. L., Crocker, N. A., & Mattson, S. N. (2008). Exposure to teratogenic agents as a risk factor for psychopathology. In T. P. Beauchaine & S. P. Hinshaw (Eds.), *Child and adolescent psychopathology* (pp. 180–207). Hoboken, NJ: Wiley.

Fryling, T., Summers, R., & Hoffman, A. (2006). Elder abuse: Definition and scope of the problem. In R. W. Summers & A. M. Hoffman (Eds.), *Elder abuse: A public health perspective* (pp. 5–18). Washington, DC: American Public Health Association.

Fuchs, D., Fuchs, L. S., Mathes, P. G., & Martinez, E. A. (2002a). Preliminary evidence on the standing of students with learning disabilities in PALS and no-PALS classrooms. *Learning Disabilities Research and Practice, 17,* 205–215.

Fuchs, L. S., Fuchs, D., Yazkian, L., & Powell, S. R. (2002b). Enhancing first-grade children's mathematical development with peer-assisted learning strategies. *School Psychology Review, 31,* 569–583.

Fukunaga, A., Uematsu, H., & Sugimoto, K. (2005). Influences of aging on taste perception and oral somatic sensation. *Journal of Gerontology, 60A,* 109–113.

Fuligni, A. J. (1998). The adjustment of children from immigrant families. *Current Directions in Psychological Science, 7,* 99–103.

Fuligni, A. J. (2004). The adaptation and acculturation of children from immigrant families. In U. P. Gielen & J. Roopnarine (Eds.), *Childhood and adolescence: Cross-cultural perspectives* (pp. 297–318). Westport, CT: Praeger.

Fuligni, A. J., Yip. T., & Tseng, V. (2002). The impact of family obligation on the daily activities and psychological well-being of Chinese-American adolescents. *Child Development, 73,* 302–314.

Fuller, C., Keller, L., Olson, J., Plymale, A., & Gottesman, M. (2005). Helping preschoolers become healthy eaters. *Journal of Pediatric Health Care, 19,* 178–182.

Fuller-Iglesias, H. (2010, November). Coping across borders: Transnational families in Mexico. In M. Mulso, *Families Coping across Borders.* Paper symposium presented at the National Council on Family Relations Annual Conference, Minneapolis, MN.

Fuller-Thomson, E., & Minkler, M. (2000). The mental and physical health of grandmothers who are raising their grandchildren. *Journal of Mental Health and Aging, 6,* 311–323.

Fuller-Thomson, E., & Minkler, M. (2005). Native American grandparents raising grandchildren: Findings from the Census 2000 Supplementary Survey and implications for social work practice. *Social Work, 50,* 131–139.

Fuller-Thomson, E., & Minkler, M. (2007). Mexican American grandparents raising grandchildren: Findings from the Census 2000 American Community Survey. *Families in Society, 88,* 567–574.

Fullerton, J. T., Navarro, A. M., & Young, S. H. (2007). Outcomes of planned home birth: An integrative review. *Journal of Midwifery and Women's Health, 52,* 323–333.

Fulmer, T. (2008). Screening for mistreatment of older adults. *American Journal of Nursing, 108,* 52–56.

Fülöp, T., Larbi, A., Kotb, R., de Angelis, F., & Pawelec, G. (2011). Aging, immunity, and cancer. *Discovery Medicine, 11,* 537–550.

Fung, H. H., Carstensen, L. L., & Lang, F. R. (2001). Age-related patterns in social networks among European Americans and African Americans: Implications for socioemotional selectivity across the life span. *International Journal of Aging and Human Development, 52,* 185–206.

Furchtgott-Roth, D. (2009). *Testimony on the gender pay gap* (testimony before the Joint Economic Committee, U.S. House of Representatives). Washington, DC: Hudson Institute.

Furnham, A. (2009). Sex differences in mate selection preferences. *Personality and Individual Differences, 47,* 262–267.

Furstenberg, F. F. (2010). On a new schedule: Transitions to adulthood and family change. *Future of Children, 20,* 67–87.

Furstenberg, F. F., Jr., & Harris, K. M. (1993). When and why fathers matter: Impact of father involvement on children of adolescent mothers. In R. I. Lerman & T. J. Ooms (Eds.), *Young unwed fathers* (pp. 117–138). Philadelphia: Temple University Press.

Fuson, K. C. (2009). Avoiding misinterpretations of Piaget and Vygotsky: Mathematical teaching without learning, learning without teaching, or

helpful learning-path teaching? *Cognitive Development, 24,* 343–361.

Fuson, K. C., & Burghard, B. H. (2003). Multidigit addition and subtraction methods invented in small groups and teacher support of problem solving and reflection. In J. J. Baroody & A. Dowker (Eds.), *The development of arithmetic concepts and skills* (pp. 267–304). Mahwah, NJ: Erlbaum.

Fussell, E., & Furstenberg, F. F., Jr. (2005). The transition to adulthood during the twentieth century. In R. A. Settersten, Jr., F. F. Furstenberg, Jr., & R. G. Rumbaut (Eds.), *On the frontier of adulthood* (pp. 29–75). Chicago: University of Chicago Press.

Fussell, E., & Gauthier, A. H. (2005). American women's transition to adulthood in comparative perspective. In R. A. Settersten, Jr., F. F. Furstenberg, Jr., & R. G. Rumbaut (Eds.), *On the frontier of adulthood: Theory, research, and public policy* (pp. 76–109). Chicago: University of Chicago Press.

Fuster, J. J., & Andres, V. (2006). Telomere biology and cardiovascular disease. *Circulation Research, 99,* 1167–1180.

Fyfe, M. (2006, April). Music and love help defy the doctors. Retrieved from www.theage.com.au/news/national/music-and-love-help-dying-defythedoctors/2006/03/31/1143441339517.html

G

Gabbay, S. G., & Wahler, J. J. (2002). Lesbian aging: Review of a growing literature. *Journal of Gay and Lesbian Social Services, 14,* 1–21.

Gabriel, Z., & Bowling, A. (2004). Quality of life from the perspectives of older people. *Ageing and Society, 24,* 675–691.

Gailliot, M. T., Schmeichel, B. J., & Baumeister, R. F. (2006). Self-regulatory processes defend against the threat of death: Effects of self-control depletion and trait self-control on thoughts and fears of dying. *Journal of Personality and Social Psychology, 91,* 49–62.

Galambos, N. L., Almeida, D. M., & Petersen, A. C. (1990). Masculinity, femininity, and sex role attitudes in early adolescence: Exploring gender intensification. *Child Development, 61,* 1905–1914.

Galambos, N. L., & Maggs, J. L. (1991). Children in self-care: Figures, facts, and fiction. In J. V. Lerner & N. L. Galambos (Eds.), *Employed mothers and their children* (pp. 131–157). New York: Garland.

Galambos, N. L., & Martinez, M. L. (2007). Poised for emerging adulthood in Latin America: A pleasure for the privileged. *Child Development Perspectives, 1,* 109–114.

Galinsky, E., Aumann, K., & Bond, J. T. (2009). *Times are changing: Gender and generation at work and at home.* New York: Families and Work Institute.

Galler, J. R., Ramsey, C. F., Morley, D. S., Archer, E., & Salt, P. (1990). The long-term effects of early kwashiorkor compared with marasmus. IV. Performance on the National High School Entrance Examination. *Pediatric Research, 28,* 235–239.

Galloway, J., & Thelen, E. (2004). Feet first: Object exploration in young infants. *Infant Behavior and Development, 27,* 107–112.

Gallup News Service. (2006). *Religion most important to blacks, women, and older Americans.* Retrieved from www.gallup.com/poll/25585/Religion-Most-Important-Blacks-Women-Older-Americans.aspx?version=print

Gallup News Service. (2012). *Seven in 10 Americans are very or moderately religious.* Retrieved from www.gallup.com/poll/159050/sevenamericansmoderatelyreligious.aspx

Ganea, P. A., Allen, M. L., Butler, L., Carey, S., & DeLoache, J. S. (2009). Toddlers' referential understanding of pictures. *Journal of Experimental Child Psychology, 104,* 283–295.

Ganea, P. A., Pickard, M. B., & DeLoache, J. S. (2008). Transfer between picture books and the real world

by very young children. *Journal of Cognition and Development, 9,* 46-66.

Ganea, P. A., Shutts, K., Spelke, E., & DeLoache, J. S. (2007). Thinking of things unseen: Infants' use of language to update object representations. *Psychological Science, 8,* 734–739.

Ganger, J., & Brent, M. R. (2004). Reexamining the vocabulary spurt. *Developmental Psychology, 40,* 621–632.

Ganong, L., Coleman, M., Fine, M., & Martin, P. (1999). Step-parents' affinity-seeking and affinity-maintaining strategies with stepchildren. *Journal of Family Issues, 20,* 299–327.

Ganong, L. H., & Coleman, M. (1994). *Remarried family relationships.* Thousand Oaks, CA: Sage.

Ganong, L. H., & Coleman, M. (2004). *Stepfamily relationships: Development, dynamics, and interventions.* New York: Kluwer/Plenum.

Ganong, L. H., Coleman, M., & Jamison, Y. (2011). Patterns of stepchild–stepparent relationship development. *Journal of Marriage and Family, 73,* 396–413.

Gans, D., & Silverstein, M. (2006). Norms of filial responsibility for aging parents across time and generations. *Journal of Marriage and Family, 68,* 961–976.

Garces, E., Thomas, D., & Currie, J. (2002). Longer-term effects of Head Start. *American Economic Review, 92,* 999–1012.

Garcia, M. M., Shaw, D. S., Winslow, E. B., & Yaggi, K. E. (2000). Destructive sibling conflict and the development of conduct problems in young boys. *Developmental Psychology, 36,* 44–53.

Garcia-Bournissen, F., Tsur, L., Goldstein, L. H., Staroselsky, A., Avner, M., & Asrar, F. (2008). Fetal exposure to isotretinoin—an international problem. *Reproductive Toxicology, 25,* 124–128.

García Coll, C., & Magnuson, K. (1997). The psychological experience of immigration: A developmental perspective. In A. Booth, A. C. Crouter, & N. Landale (Eds.), *Immigration and the family* (pp. 91–131). Mahwah, NJ: Erlbaum.

Gardner, H. (1982). *Artful Scribbles.* New York: Basic Books.

Gardner, H. (1983). *Frames of mind: The theory of multiple intelligences.* New York: Basic Books.

Gardner, H. (1993). *Multiple intelligences: The theory in practice.* New York: Basic Books.

Gardner, H. E. (1998). Are there additional intelligences? The case of the naturalist, spiritual, and existential intelligences. In J. Kane (Ed.), *Educational information and transformation.* Upper Saddle River, NJ: Prentice-Hall.

Gardner, H. E. (2000). *Intelligence reframed: Multiple intelligences for the twenty-first century.* New York: Basic Books.

Gardner, J. P., Li, S., Srinivasan, S. R., Chen, W., Kimura, M., & Lu, X. (2005). Rise in insulin resistance is associated with escalated telomere attrition. *Circulation, 111,* 2171–2177.

Garner, P. W. (2003). Child and family correlates of toddlers' emotional and behavioral responses to a mishap. *Infant Mental Health Journal, 24,* 580–596.

Garner, P. W., & Estep, K. (2001). Emotional competence, emotion socialization, and young children's peer-related social competence. *Early Education and Development, 12,* 29–48.

Gartstein, M. A., & Rothbart, M. K. (2003). Studying infant temperament via the revised infant behavior questionnaire. *Infant Behavior and Development, 26,* 64–86.

Gartstein, M. A., Slobodskaya, H. R., Zylics, P. O., Gosztyla, D., & Nakagawa, A. (2010). A crosscultural evaluation of temperament: Japan, USA, Poland and Russia. *International Journal of Psychology and Psychological Therapy, 10,* 55–75.

Gasden, V. (1999). Black families in intergenerational and cultural perspective. In M. E. Lamb (Ed.),

Parenting and child development in "nontraditional" families (pp. 221–246). Mahwah, NJ: Erlbaum.

Gaskill, R. L., & Perry, B. D. (2012). Child sexual abuse, traumatic experiences, and their impact on the developing brain. In P. Goodyear-Brown (Ed.), *Handbook of child sexual abuse: Identification, assessment, and treatment* (pp. 29–47). Hoboken, NJ: Wiley.

Gaskins, S. (1999). Children's daily lives in a Mayan village: A case study of culturally constructed roles and activities. In R. Göncü (Ed.), *Children's engagement in the world: Sociocultural perspectives* (pp. 25–61). Cambridge, UK: Cambridge University Press.

Gaskins, S. (2000). Children's daily activities in a Mayan village: A culturally grounded description. *Cross-Cultural Research, 34,* 375–389.

Gaskins, S., Haight, W., & Lancy, D. F. (2007). The cultural construction of play. In A. Göncü & S. Gaskins (Eds.), *Play and development: Evolutionary, sociocultural, and functional perspectives* (pp. 179–202). Mahwah, NJ: Erlbaum.

Gates, G. J. (2011). *How many people are lesbian, gay, bisexual, and transgender?* Berkeley: The Williams Institute, University of California School of Law.

Gates, G. J., Badgett, M. V. L., Macomber, J. E., & Chambers, K. (2007). *Adoption and foster care by gay and lesbian parents in the United States.* Los Angeles, CA: Williams Institute of the UCLA School of Law.

Gathercole, S. E., Adams, A.-M., & Hitch, G. (1994). Do young children rehearse? An individual-differences analysis. *Memory and Cognition, 22,* 201–207.

Gathercole, S. E., & Alloway, T. P. (2008). Working memory and classroom learning. In S. K. Thurman & C. A. Fiorello (Eds.), *Applied cognitive research in K-3 classrooms* (pp. 17–40). New York: Routledge/Taylor & Francis Group.

Gathercole, S. E., Lamont, E., & Alloway, T. P. (2006). Working memory in the classroom. In S. Pickering (Ed.), *Working memory and education* (pp. 219–240). San Diego: Elsevier.

Gathercole, S. E., Tiffany, C., Briscoe, J., Thorn, A., & ALSPAC Team. (2005). Developmental consequences of poor phonological short-term memory function in childhood: A longitudinal study. *Journal of Child Psychology and Psychiatry, 46,* 598–611.

Gathercole, V., Sebastián, E., & Soto, P. (1999). The early acquisition of Spanish verb morphology: Across-the-board or piecemeal knowledge? *International Journal of Bilingualism, 3,* 133–182.

Gauvain, M. (2004). Bringing culture into relief: Cultural contributions to the development of children's planning skills. In R. V. Kail (Ed.), *Advances in child development and behavior* (pp. 39–71). San Diego, CA: Elsevier.

Gauvain, M., de la Ossa, J. L., & Hurtado-Ortiz, M. T. (2001). Parental guidance as children learn to use cultural tools: The case of pictorial plans. *Cognitive Development, 16,* 551–575.

Gavrilova, N. S., & Gavrilov, L. A. (2012). Comments on dietary restriction, Okinawa diet and longevity. *Gerontology, 58,* 221–223.

Gazzaley, A., Cooney, J. W., Rissman, J., & D'Esposito, M. (2005). Top-down suppression deficit underlies working memory impairment in normal aging. *Nature Neuroscience, 8,* 1298–1300.

Ge, X., Brody, G. H., Conger, R. D., Simons, R. L., & Murry, V. (2002). Contextual amplification of the effects of pubertal transition on African American children's deviant peer affiliation and externalized behavioral problems. *Developmental Psychology, 38,* 42–54.

Ge, X., Conger, R. D., & Elder, G. H., Jr. (1996). Coming of age too early: Pubertal influences on girls' vulnerability to psychological distress. *Child Development, 67,* 3386–3400.

Ge, X., Conger, R. D., & Elder, G. H., Jr. (2001). The relation between puberty and psychological distress in adolescent boys. *Journal of Research on Adolescence, 11,* 49–70.

Ge, X., Jin, R., Natsuaki, M. N., Frederick, X., Brody, G. H., Cutrona, C. E., & Simons, R. L. (2006). Pubertal maturation and early substance use risks among African American children. *Psychology of Addictive Behaviors, 20,* 404–414.

Ge, X., Natsuaki, M. N., Jin, R., & Biehl, M. C. (2011). A contextual amplification hypothesis: Pubertal timing and girls' emotional and behavior problems. In M. Kerr, H. Stattin, R. C. M. E. Engels, G. Overbeek, & A.-K. Andershed (Eds.), *Understanding girls' problem behavior* (pp. 11–28). Chichester, UK: Wiley-Blackwell.

Geangu, E., Benga, O., Stahl, D., & Striano, T. (2010). Contagious crying beyond the first days of life. *Infant Behavior and Development, 33,* 279–288.

Geary, D. C. (2006a). Development of mathematical understanding. In D. Kuhn & R. Siegler (Eds.), *Handbook of child psychology: Vol. 2. Cognition, perception, and language* (pp. 777–810). Hoboken, NJ: Wiley.

Geary, D. C. (2006b). Evolutionary developmental psychology: Current status and future directions. *Developmental Review, 26,* 113–119.

Gee, C. B., & Rhodes, J. E. (2003). Adolescent mothers' relationship with their children's biological fathers: Social support, social strain, and relationship continuity. *Journal of Family Psychology, 17,* 370–383.

Geerts, C. C., Bots, M. L., van der Ent, C. K., Grobbee, D. E., & Uiterwaal, C. S. (2012). Parental smoking and vascular damage in their 5-year-old children. *Pediatrics, 129,* 45–54.

Geist, C. (2010). Men's and women's reports about housework. In J. Treas & S. Drobnic (Eds.), *Dividing the Domestic: Men, women, and household work in cross-national perspective* (pp. 217–240). Stanford, CA: Stanford University Press.

Gelman, R. (1972). Logical capacity of very young children: Number invariance rules. *Child Development, 43,* 75–90.

Gelman, S. A. (2003). *The essential child.* New York: Oxford University Press.

Gelman, S. A., & Kalish, C. W. (2006). Conceptual development. In D. Kuhn & R. Siegler (Eds.), *Handbook of child psychology: Vol. 2. Cognition, perception, and language* (6th ed., pp. 687–733). Hoboken, NJ: Wiley.

Gelman, S. A., Taylor, M. G., & Nguyen, S. P. (2004). Mother–child conversations about gender. *Monographs of the Society for Research in Child Development, 69*(1, Serial No. 275), pp. 1–127.

Genesee, F., & Nicoladis, E. (2007). Bilingual first language acquisition. In E. Hoff & M. Shatz (Eds.), *Blackwell handbook of language development* (pp. 324–342). Malden, MA: Blackwell.

Gentile, B., Twenge, J. M., & Campbell, W. K. (2010). Birth cohort differences in self-esteem, 1988–2008: A cross-temporal meta-analysis. *Review of General Psychology, 14,* 261–268.

George, S. A. (2002). The menopause experience: A woman's perspective. *Journal of Obstetric, Gynecologic, and Neonatal Nursing, 31,* 71–85.

Gere, J., Schimmack, U., Pinkus, R. T., & Lockwood, P. (2011). The effects of romantic partners' goal congruence on affective well-being. *Journal of Research in Personality, 45,* 549–559.

Gergely, G., & Watson, J. (1999). Early socioemotional development: Contingency perception and the social-biofeedback model. In P. Rochat (Ed.), *Early social cognition: Understanding others in the first months of life* (pp. 101–136). Mahwah, NJ: Erlbaum.

Gergen, M., & Gergen, K. J. (2003). Positive aging. In J. F. Gubrim & J. A. Holstein (Eds.), *Ways of aging* (pp. 203–224). Malden: Blackwell Publishers Ltd.

Gershoff, E. T. (2002a). Corporal punishment by parents and associated child behaviors and experiences: A meta-analytic and theoretical review. *Psychological Bulletin, 128,* 539–579.

Gershoff, E. T., Grogan-Kaylor, A., Lansford, J. E., Chang, L., Zelli, A., Deater-Deckard, K., et al. (2010). Parent discipline practices in an international sample: Associations with child behaviors and moderation by perceived normativeness. *Child Development, 81,* 487–502.

Gershoff, E. T., Lansford, J. E., Sexton, H. R., Davis-Kean, P., & Sameroff, A. J. (2012). Longitudinal links between spanking and children's externalizing behaviors in a national sample of white, black, Hispanic, and Asian American families. *Child Development, 83,* 838–843.

Gerstorf, D., Ram, N., Estabrook, R., Schupp, J., Wagner, G. G., & Lindenberger, U. (2008). Life satisfaction shows terminal decline in old age: Longitudinal evidence from the German socioeconomic panel study. *Developmental Psychology, 44,* 1148–1159.

Gervai, J. (2009). Environmental and genetic influences on early attachment. *Child and Adolescent Psychiatry and Mental Health, 3,* 25. Retrieved from www.capmh.com/content/3/1/25

Gesell, A. (1933). Maturation and patterning of behavior. In C. Murchison (Ed.), *A handbook of child psychology.* Worcester, MA: Clark University Press.

Gest, S. D., Domitrovich, C. E., & Welsh, J. A. (2005). Peer academic reputation in elementary school: Associations with changes in self-concept and academic skills. *Journal of Educational Psychology, 97,* 337–346.

Geuze, R. H., Schaafsma, S. M., Lust, J. M., Bouma, A., Schiefenhovel, W., Groothuis, T. G. G., et al. (2012). Plasticity of lateralization: Schooling predicts hand preference but not hand skill asymmetry in a nonindustrial society. *Neuropsychologia, 50,* 612–620.

Gewirtz, A., Forgatch, M. S., & Wieling, E. (2008). Parenting practices as potential mechanisms for child adjustment following mass trauma. *Journal of Marital and Family Therapy, 34,* 177–192.

Ghavami, N., Fingerhut, A., Peplau, L. A., Grant, S. K., & Wittig, M. A. (2011). Testing a model of minority identity achievement, identity affirmation, and psychological well-being among ethnic minority and sexual minority individuals. *Cultural Diversity and Ethnic Minority Psychology, 17,* 79–88.

Gibbs, J. C. (2006). Should Kohlberg's cognitive developmental approach to morality be replaced with a more pragmatic approach? Comment on Krebs and Denton (2005). *Psychological Review, 113,* 666–671.

Gibbs, J. C. (2013). *Moral development & reality: Beyond the theories of Kohlberg, Hoffman, and Haidt* (3rd ed.) New York: Oxford University Press.

Gibbs, J. C., Basinger, K. S., Grime, R. L., & Snarey, J. R. (2007). Moral judgment development across cultures: Revisiting Kohlberg's universality claims. *Developmental Review, 24,* 443–500.

Gibbs, J. C., Moshman, D., Berkowitz, M. W., Basinger, K. S., & Grime, R. L. (2009). Taking development seriously: Critique of the 2008 *JME* special issue on moral functioning. *Journal of Moral Education, 38,* 271–282.

Gibson, E. J. (1970). The development of perception as an adaptive process. *American Scientist, 58,* 98–107.

Gibson, E. J. (2000). Perceptual learning in development: Some basic concepts. *Ecological Psychology, 12,* 295–302.

Gibson, E. J. (2003). The world is so full of a number of things: On specification and perceptual learning. *Ecological Psychology, 15,* 283–287.

Gibson, E. J., & Walk, R. D. (1960). The "visual cliff." *Scientific American, 202,* 64–71.

Gibson, J. J. (1979). *The ecological approach to visual perception.* Boston: Houghton Mifflin.

Gibson, P. A. (2005). Intergenerational parenting from the perspective of American grandmothers. *Family Relations, 54,* 280–297.

Giles, J. W., & Heyman, G. D. (2005). Young children's beliefs about the relationship between gender and aggressive behavior. *Child Development, 76,* 107–121.

Gill, M., Daly, G., Heron, S., Hawi, Z., & Fitzgerald, M. (1997). Confirmation of association between attention deficit hyperactivity disorder and a dopamine transporter polymorphism. *Molecular Psychiatry, 2,* 311–313.

Gillet, J.-P., Macadangdang, B., Rathke, R. L., Gottesman, M. M., & Kimchi-Sarfaty, C. (2009). The development of gene therapy: From monogenic recessive disorders to complex diseases such as cancer. *Methods in Molecular Biology, 542,* 5–54.

Gillies, R. M. (2000). The maintenance of cooperative and helping behaviours in cooperative groups. *British Journal of Educational Psychology, 70,* 97–111.

Gillies, R. M. (2003). The behaviors, interactions, and perceptions of junior high school students during small-group learning. *Journal of Educational Psychology, 95,* 137–147.

Gilligan, C. F. (1982). *In a different voice.* Cambridge, MA: Harvard University Press.

Gilliom, M., Shaw, D. S., Beck, J. E., Schonberg, M. A., & Lukon, J. L. (2002). Anger regulation in disadvantaged preschool boys: Strategies, antecedents, and the development of self-control. *Developmental Psychology, 38,* 222–235.

Gillum, R. F., Dana, E. K., Thomas, O. O., & Harold, G. K. (2008). Frequency of attendance at religious services and mortality in a U.S. national cohort. *Annals of Epidemiology, 18,* 124–129.

Ginsburg, H. P., Lee, J. S., & Boyd, J. S. (2008). Mathematics education for young children: What it is and how to promote it. *Social Policy Report of the Society for Research in Child Development, 12*(1).

Ginsburg, K. R. (2007). The importance of play in promoting healthy child development and maintaining strong parent–child bonds. *Pediatrics, 119,* 182–191.

Ginsburg-Block, M. D., Rohrbeck, C. A., & Fantuzzo, J. W. (2006). A meta-analytic review of social, self-concept, and behavioral outcomes of peer-assisted learning. *Journal of Educational Psychology, 98,* 732–749.

Gitlin, L. N., Belle, S. H., Burgio, L. D., Szaja, S. J., Mahoney, D., & Gallagher-Thompson, D. (2003). Effect of multicomponent interventions on caregiver burden and depression: The REACH multisite initiative at 6-month follow-up. *Psychology and Aging, 18,* 361–374.

Gladstone, I. M., & Katz, V. L. (2004). The morbidity of the 34- to 35-week gestation: Should we reexamine the paradigm? *American Journal of Perinatology, 21,* 9–13.

Glasgow, K. L., Dornbusch, S. M., Troyer, L., Steinberg, L., & Ritter, P. L. (1997). Parenting styles, adolescents' attributions, and educational outcomes in nine heterogeneous high schools. *Child Development, 68,* 507–523.

Gleitman, L. R., Cassidy, K., Nappa, R., Papfragou, A., & Trueswell, J. C. (2005). Hard words. *Language Learning and Development, 1,* 23–64.

Glover, V., Bergman, K., & O'Connor, T. G. (2008). The effects of maternal stress, anxiety, and depression during pregnancy on the neurodevelopment of the child. In S. D. Stone & A. E. Menken (Eds.), *Perinatal and postpartum mood disorders: Perspectives and treatment guide for the health care practitioner* (pp. 3–5). New York: Springer.

Glowinski, A. L., Madden, P. A. F., Bucholz, K. K., Lynskey, M. T., & Heath, A. C. (2003). Genetic epidemiology of self-reported lifetime DSM-IV major depressive disorder in a population-based twin sample of female adolescents. *Journal of Child Psychology and Psychiatry and Allied Disciplines, 44,* 988–996.

Glück, J., & Bluck, S. (2007). Looking back across the lifespan: A life story account of the reminiscence bump. *Memory and Cognition, 35,* 1928–1939.

Gluckman, P. D., Sizonenko, S. V., & Bassett, N. S. (1999). The transition from fetus to neonate—an endocrine perspective. *Acta Paediatrica Supplement, 88*(428), 7–11.

Go, A. S., Mozaffarian, V. L., Roger, E. J., Benjmin, J. D., Berry, J. D., Borden, W. B, et al. (2013). Heart disease and stroke statistics—2013 update. A report from the American Heart Association. *Circulation, 127,* e1–e241.

Goering, J. (Ed.). (2003). *Choosing a better life? How public housing tenants selected a HUD experiment to improve their lives and those of their children: The Moving to Opportunity Demonstration Program.* Washington, DC: Urban Institute Press.

Gögele, M., Pattaro, C., Fuchsberger, C., Minelli, C., Pramstaller, P. P., & Wjst, M. (2011). Heritability analysis of life span in a semi-isolated population followed across four centuries reveals the presence of pleiotropy between life span and reproduction. *Journal of Gerontology, 66A,* 26–37.

Goldberg, A. E. (2010). *Lesbian and gay parents and their children: Research on the family life cycle.* Washington, DC: American Psychological Association.

Goldberg, A. P., Dengel, D. R., & Hagberg, J. M. (1996). Exercise physiology and aging. In E. L. Schneider & J. W. Rowe (Eds.), *Handbook of the biology of aging* (pp. 331–354). San Diego: Academic Press.

Goldenberg, C., Gallimore, R., Reese, L., & Garnier, H. (2001). Cause or effect? Immigrant Latino parents' aspirations and expectations, and their children's school performance. *American Educational Research Journal, 38,* 547–582.

Goldschmidt, L., Richardson, G. A., Cornelius, M. D., & Day, N. L. (2004). Prenatal marijuana and alcohol exposure and academic achievement at age 10. *Neurotoxicology and Teratology, 26,* 521–532.

Goldsmith, H. H., Pollak, S. D., & Davidson, R. J. (2008). Developmental neuroscience perspectives on emotion regulation. *Child Development Perspectives, 2,* 132–140.

Goldsmith, L. T. (2000). Tracking trajectories of talent: Child prodigies growing up. In R. C. Friedman & B. M. Shore (Eds.), *Talents unfolding: Cognition and development* (pp. 89–122). Washington, DC: American Psychological Association.

Goldsteen, M., Houtepen, R., Proot, I. M., Abu-Saad, H. H., Spreeuwenberg, C., & Widdershoven, G. (2006). What is a good death? Terminally ill patients dealing with normative expectations around death and dying. *Patient Education and Counseling, 64,* 378–386.

Goldstein, M. H., & Schwade, J. A. (2008). Social feedback to infants' babbling facilitates rapid phonological learning. *Psychological Science, 19,* 515–523.

Goldstein, S. (2011). Attention-deficit/hyperactivity disorder. In S. Goldstein & C. R. Reynolds (Eds.), *Handbook of neurodevelopmental and genetic disorders in children* (2nd ed., pp. 131–150). New York: Guilford.

Goldston, D. B., Molock, S. D., Whitbeck, L. B., Murakami, J. L., Zayas, L. H., & Hall, G. C. N. (2008). Cultural considerations in adolescent suicide prevention and psychosocial treatment. *American Psychologist, 63,* 14–31.

Golinkoff, R. M., & Hirsh-Pasek, K. (2008). How toddlers begin to learn verbs. *Trends in Cognitive Sciences, 12,* 397–403.

Golomb, C. (2004). *The child's creation of a pictorial world* (2nd ed.). Mahwah, NJ: Erlbaum.

Golombok, S., Lycett, E., MacCallum, F., Jadva, V., Murray, C., Rust, J., Abdalla, H., Jenkins, J., & Margar, R. (2004). Parenting of infants conceived by gamete donation. *Journal of Family Psychology, 18,* 443–452.

Golombok, S., Perry, B., Burston, A., Murray, C., Mooney-Somers, J., Stevens, M., & Golding, J. (2003). Children with lesbian parents: A community study. *Developmental Psychology, 39,* 20–33.

Göncü, A., Patt, M. B., & Kouba E. (2004). Understanding young children's pretend play in context. In P. K. Smith & C. H. Hart (Eds.), *Blackwell handbook of childhood social development* (pp. 418–437). Malden, MA: Blackwell.

Gonzalez, A.-L., & Wolters, C. A. (2006). The relation between perceived parenting practices and achievement motivation in mathematics. *Journal of Research in Childhood Education, 21,* 203–217.

Good, T. L., & Brophy, J. (2003). *Looking in classrooms* (9th ed.). Boston: Allyn and Bacon.

Goode, V., & Goode, J. D. (2007). De facto zero tolerance: An exploratory study of race and safe school violations. In J. L. Kincheloe & K. Hayes (Eds.), *Teaching city kids: Understanding and appreciating them* (pp. 85–96). New York: Peter Lang.

Goodman, A. Schorge, J., & Greene, M. F. (2011). The long-term effects of in utero exposures—the DES story. *New England Journal of Medicine, 364,* 2083–2084.

Goodman, C. C. (2012). Caregiving grandmothers and their grandchildren: Well-being nine years later. *Children and Youth Services Review, 34,* 648–654.

Goodman, J., Dale, P., & Li, P. (2008). Does frequency count? Parental input and the acquisition of vocabulary. *Journal of Child Language, 35,* 515–531.

Goodnow, J. J. (2010). Culture. In M. H. Bornstein (Ed.), *Handbook of cultural developmental science* (pp. 3–20). New York: Psychology Press.

Goodvin, R., Meyer, S., Thompson, R. A., & Hayes, R. (2008). Self-understanding in early childhood: Associations with child attachment security and maternal negative affect. *Attachment and Human Development, 10,* 433–450.

Goodwin, R., & Pillay, U. (2006). Relationships, culture, and social change. In A. L. Vangelisti & D. Perlman (Eds.), *The Cambridge handbook of personal relationships* (pp. 760–779). New York: Cambridge University Press.

Goodyear-Brown, P., Fath, A., & Myers, L. (2012). Child sexual abuse: The scope of the problem. In P. Goodyear-Brown (Ed.), *Handbook of child sexual abuse: Identification, assessment, and treatment* (pp. 3–28). Hoboken, NJ: Wiley.

Gooren, E. M. J. C., Pol, A. C., Stegge, H., Terwogt, M. M., & Koot, H. M. (2011). The development of conduct problems and depressive symptoms in early elementary school children: The role of peer rejection. *Journal of Clinical Child and Adolescent Psychology, 40,* 245–253.

Gopnik, A., & Nazzi, T. (2003). Words, kinds, and causal powers: A theory theory perspective on early naming and categorization. In D. H. Rakison & L. M. Oakes (Eds.), *Early category and concept development* (p. 303–329). New York: Oxford University Press.

Gopnik, A., & Tenenbaum, J. B. (2007). Bayesian networks, Bayesian learning and cognitive development. *Developmental Science, 10,* 281–287.

Gorelick, P. B., Scuteri A., Black S. E., DeCarli, C., Greenberg, S. M., Constantino, I., et al. (2011). Vascular contributions to cognitive impairment and dementia: A statement for healthcare professionals from the American Heart Association/American Stroke Association. *Stroke, 42,* 2672–2713.

Gormally, S., Barr, R. G., Wertheim, L., Alkawaf, R., Calinoiu, N., & Young, S. N. (2001). Contact and nutrient caregiving effects on newborn infant pain responses. *Developmental Medicine and Child Neurology, 43,* 28–38.

Goronzy, J. J., Shao, L., & Weyand, C. M. (2010). Immune aging and rheumatoid arthritis. *Rheumatoid Disease Clinics of North America, 36,* 297–310.

Gosselin, P. A., & Gagne, J.-P. (2011). Older adults expend more listening effort than young adults recognizing audiovisual speech in noise. *International Journal of Audiology, 50,* 786–792.

Goswami, U. (1996). Analogical reasoning and cognitive development. In H. Reese (Ed.), *Advances in child development and behavior* (Vol. 26, pp. 91–138). New York: Academic Press.

Gothe, N., Mullen, S. P., Wójcicki, T. R., Mailey, E. L., White, S. M., Olson, E. A. (2011). Trajectories of change in self-esteem in older adults: Exercise intervention effects. *Journal of Behavioral Medicine, 34,* 298–306.

Gott, M., & Hinchliff, S. (2003). How important is sex in later life? The views of older people. *Social Science and Medicine, 56,* 1617–1628.

Gott, M., Seymour, J., Bellamy, G., Clark, D., & Ahmedzai, S. (2004). Older people's views about home as a place of care at the end of life. *Palliative Medicine, 18,* 460–467.

Gottfredson, G. D., & Duffy, R. D. (2008). Using a theory of vocational personalities and work environments to explore subjective well-being. *Journal of Career Assessment, 16,* 44–59.

Gottfredson, L. S. (2005). Applying Gottfredson's theory of circumscription and compromise in career guidance and counseling. In S. D. Brown & R. W. Lent (Eds.), *Career development and counseling* (pp. 71–100). Hoboken, NJ: Wiley.

Gottfried, A. E., Gottfried, A. W., & Bathurst, K. (2002). Maternal and dual-earner employment status and parenting. In M. H. Bornstein (Ed.), *Handbook of parenting. Vol. 2: Biology and ecology of parenting* (2nd ed., pp. 207–229). Mahwah, NJ: Erlbaum.

Gottlieb, G. (2007). Probabilistic epigenesis. *Developmental Science, 10,* 1–11.

Gottlieb, G., Wahlsten, D., & Lickliter, R. (2006). The significance of biology for human development: A developmental psychobiological systems view. In R. M. Lerner (Ed.), *Handbook of child psychology: Vol. 1. Theoretical models of human development* (6th ed., pp. 210–257). Hoboken, NJ: Wiley.

Gottman, J. M. (2011). *The science of trust: Emotional attunement for couples.* New York: Norton.

Gottman, J. M., & Levenson, R. W. (2000). The timing of divorce: Predicting when a couple will divorce over a 14-year period. *Journal of Marriage and Family, 62,* 737–745.

Gould, E. (2007). How widespread is adult neurogenesis in mammals? *Nature Reviews: Neuroscience, 8,* 481–488.

Gould, F., Clarke, J., Heim, C., Harvey, P. D., Majer, M., & Nemeroff, C. B. (2010). The effects of child abuse and neglect on cognitive functioning in adulthood. *Journal of Psychiatric Research, 46,* 500–506.

Gould, J. L., & Keeton, W. T. (1996). *Biological science* (6th ed.). New York: Norton.

Graber, J. A. (2003). Puberty in context. In C. Hayward (Ed.), *Gender differences at puberty* (pp. 307–325). New York: Cambridge University Press.

Graber, J. A. (2004). Internalizing problems during adolescence. In R. M. Lerner & L. Steinberg (Eds.), *Handbook of adolescent psychology* (2nd ed., pp. 587–626). Hoboken, NJ: Wiley.

Graber, J. A., Brooks-Gunn, J., & Warren, M. P. (2006). Pubertal effects on adjustment in girls: Moving from demonstrating effects to identifying pathways. *Journal of Youth and Adolescence, 35,* 413–423.

Graber, J. A., Nichols, T., Lynne, S. D., Brooks-Gunn, J., & Botwin, G. J. (2006). A longitudinal examination of family, friend, and media influences on competent

versus problem behaviors among urban minority youth. *Applied Developmental Science, 10,* 75–85.

Graber, J. A., Seeley, J. R., Brooks-Gunn, J., & Lewinsohn, P. M. (2004). Is pubertal timing associated with psychopathology in young adulthood? *Journal of the American Academy of Child and Adolescent Psychiatry, 43,* 718–726.

Graber, J. A., & Sontag, L. M. (2009). Internalizing problems during adolescence. In R. M. Lerner & L. Steinberg (Eds.), *Handbook of adolescent psychology: Vol. 1. Individual bases of adolescent development* (3rd ed., pp. 642–682). Hoboken, NJ: Wiley.

Grabowski, D. C., Aschbrenner, K. A., Rome, V. F., & Bartels, S. J. (2010). Quality of mental health care for nursing home residents: A literature review. *Medical Care Research and Review, 67,* 627–656.

Graham-Bermann, S. A., & Howell, K. H. (2011). Child maltreatment in the context of intimate partner violence. In J. E. B. Myers (Ed.), *Child maltreatment* (3rd ed., pp. 167–180). Thousand Oaks, CA: Sage.

Gralinski, J. H., & Kopp, C. B. (1993). Everyday rules for behavior: Mothers' requests to young children. *Developmental Psychology, 29,* 573–584.

Grall, T. S. (2011, December). *Custodial mothers and fathers and their child support: 2007. Current Population Reports,* P60–240. Washington, DC: U.S. Department of Commerce.

Granger, R. C. (2008). After-school programs and academics: Implications for policy, practice, and research. *Social Policy Report of the Society for Research in Child Development, 22*(2), 3–11.

Granier-Deferre, C., Bassereau, S., Ribeiro, A., Jacquet, A.-Y., & Lecanuet, J.-P. (2003). *Cardiac "orienting" response in fetuses and babies following in utero melody-learning.* Paper presented at the 11th European Conference on Developmental Psychology, Milan, Italy.

Granillo, T., Jones-Rodriguez, G., & Carvajal, S. C. (2005). Prevalence of eating disorders in Latina adolescents: Associations with substance use and other correlates. *Journal of Adolescent Health, 36,* 214–220.

Granot, T. (2005). *Without you: Children and young people growing up with loss and its effects.* London: Jessica Kingsley.

Grantham-McGregor, S., Powell, C., Walker, S., Chang, S., & Fletcher, P. (1994). The long-term follow-up of severely malnourished children who participated in an intervention program. *Child Development, 65,* 428–439.

Grantham-McGregor, S., Schofield, W., & Powell, C. (1987). Development of severely malnourished children who received psychosocial stimulation: Six-year follow-up. *Pediatrics, 79,* 247–254.

Grantham-McGregor, S., Walker, S. P., & Chang, S. (2000). Nutritional deficiencies and later behavioral development. *Proceedings of the Nutrition Society, 59,* 47–54.

Graves, L. M., Ohlott, P. J., & Ruderman, M. N. (2007). Commitment to family roles: Effects on managers' attitudes and performance. *Journal of Applied Psychology, 92,* 44–56.

Gray, K. A., Day, N. L., Leech, S., & Richardson, G. A. (2005). Prenatal marijuana exposure: Effect on child depressive symptoms at ten years of age. *Neurotoxicology and Teratology, 27,* 439–448.

Gray, M. R., & Steinberg, L. (1999). Unpacking authoritative parenting: Reassessing a multidimensional construct. *Journal of Marriage and the Family, 61,* 574–587.

Gray-Little, B., & Carels, R. (1997). The effects of racial and socioeconomic consonance on self-esteem and achievement in elementary, junior high, and high school students. *Journal of Research on Adolescence, 7,* 109–131.

Gray-Little, B., & Hafdahl, A. R. (2000). Factors influencing racial comparisons of self-esteem:

A quantitative review. *Psychological Bulletin, 126,* 26–54.

Green, G. E., Irwin, J. R., & Gustafson, G. E. (2000). Acoustic cry analysis, neonatal status and longterm developmental outcomes. In R. G. Barr, B. Hopkins, & J. A. Green (Eds.), *Crying as a sign, a symptom, and a signal* (pp. 137–156). Cambridge, UK: Cambridge University Press.

Greenberger, E., O'Neil, R., & Nagel, S. K. (1994). Linking workplace and homeplace: Relations between the nature of adults' work and their parenting behavior. *Developmental Psychology, 30,* 990–1002.

Greendorfer, S. L., Lewko, J. H., & Rosengren, K. S. (1996). Family and gender-based socialization of children and adolescents. In F. L. Smoll & R. E. Smith (Eds.), *Children and youth in sport: A biopsychological perspective* (pp. 89–111). Dubuque, IA: Brown & Benchmark.

Greene, M. L., Way, N., & Pahl, K. (2006). Trajectories of perceived adult and peer discrimination among black, Latino, and Asian American adolescents: Patterns and psychological correlates. *Developmental Psychology, 42,* 218–238.

Greene, S. M., Anderson, E., Hetherington, E. M., Forgath, M. S., & DeGarmo, D. S. (2003). Risk and resilience after divorce. In R. Walsh (Ed.), *Normal family processes* (pp. 96–120). New York: Guilford.

Greenfield, P. (1992, June). *Notes and references for developmental psychology.* Conference on Making Basic Texts in Psychology More Culture-Inclusive and Culture-Sensitive, Western Washington University, Bellingham, WA.

Greenfield, P. M. (2004). *Weaving generations together: Evolving creativity in the Maya of Chiapas.* Santa Fe, NM: School of American Research.

Greenfield, P. M., Suzuki, L. K., & Rothstein-Fish, C. (2006). Cultural pathways through human development. In K. A. Renninger & I. E. Sigel (Eds.), *Handbook of child psychology: Vol. 4. Child psychology in practice* (6th ed., pp. 655–699). Hoboken, NJ: Wiley.

Greenhill, L. L., Halperin, J. M., & Abikoff, H. (1999). Stimulant medications. *Journal of the American Academy of Child and Adolescent Psychiatry, 38,* 503–512.

Greenough, W. T., & Black, J. E. (1992). Induction of brain structure by experience: Substrates for cognitive development. In M. R. Gunnar & C. A. Nelson (Eds.), *Minnesota Symposia on Child Psychology* (pp. 155–200). Hillsdale, NJ: Erlbaum.

Gregg, V., Gibbs, J. C., & Fuller, D. (1994). Patterns of developmental delay in moral judgment by male and female delinquents. *Merrill-Palmer Quarterly, 40,* 538–553.

Gregory, A., & Weinstein, R. S. (2004). Connection and regulation at home and in school: Predicting growth in achievement for adolescents. *Journal of Adolescent Research, 19,* 405–427.

Greve, W., & Bjorklund, D. F. (2009). The Nestor effect: Extending evolutionary developmental psychology to a lifespan perspective. *Developmental Review, 29,* 163–179.

Griffin, Z. M., & Spieler, D. H. (2006). Observing the what and when of language production for different age groups by monitoring speakers' eye movements. *Brain and Language, 99,* 272–288.

Grob, A., Krings, F., & Bangerter, A. (2001). Life markers in biographical narratives of people from three cohorts: A life span perspective in its historical context. *Human Development, 44,* 171–190.

Grolnick, W. S., Kurowski, C. O., Dunlap, K. G., & Hevey, C. (2000). Parental resources and the transition to junior high. *Journal of Research on Adolescence, 10,* 466–488.

Grossbaum, M. F., & Bates, G. W. (2002). Correlates of psychological well-being at midlife: The role of generativity, agency and communion, and narrative themes. *International Journal of Behavioral Development, 26,* 120–127.

Grossman, A. H. (2006). Physical and mental health of older lesbian, gay, and bisexual adults. In D. Kimmel, T. Rose, & S. David (Eds.), *Lesbian, gay, bisexual, and transgender aging* (pp. 53–69). New York: Columbia University Press.

Grossmann, K., Grossmann, K. E., Spangler, G., Suess, G., & Unzner, L. (1985). Maternal sensitivity and newborns' orientation responses as related to quality of attachment in Northern Germany. In I. Bretherton & E. Waters (Eds.), Growing points of attachment theory and research. *Monographs of the Society for Research in Child Development, 50*(1–2, Serial No. 209).

Gruendel J., & Aber, J. L. (2007). Bridging the gap between research and child policy change: The role of strategic communications in policy advocacy. In J. L. Aber, S. J. Bishop-Josef, S. M. Jones, K. T. McLearn, & D. Phillips (Eds.), *Child development and social policy: Knowledge for action* (pp. 43–58). Washington, DC: American Psychological Association.

Gruenewald, D. A., & White, E. J. (2006). The illness experience of older adults near the end of life: A systematic review. *Anesthesiology Clinics of North America, 24,* 163–180.

Grundy, E. (2005). Reciprocity in relationships: Socio-economic and health influences on intergenerational exchanges between Third Age parents and their adult children in Great Britain. *British Journal of Sociology, 56,* 233–255.

Grundy, E., & Henretta, J. C. (2006). Between elderly parents and adult children: A new look at the "sandwich generation." *Aging and Society, 26,* 707–722.

Grusec, J. E. (1988). *Social development: History, theory, and research.* New York: Springer.

Grusec, J. E. (2006). The development of moral behavior and conscience from a socialization perspective. In M. Killen & J. Smetana (Eds.), *Handbook of moral development* (pp. 243–265). Philadelphia: Erlbaum.

Guedes, G., Tsai, J. C., & Loewen, N. A. (2011). Glaucoma and aging. *Current Aging Science, 4,* 110–117.

Guerra, N. G., Graham, S., & Tolan, P. H. (2011). Raising healthy children: Translating child development research into practice. *Child Development, 82,* 7–16.

Guglielmi, R. S. (2008). Native language proficiency, English literacy, academic achievement, and occupational attainment in limited-English-proficient students: A latent growth modeling perspective. *Journal of Educational Psychology, 100,* 322–342.

Guignard, J.-H., & Lubart, T. I. (2007). A comparative study of convergent and divergent thinking in intellectually gifted children. *Gifted and Talented International, 22*(1), 9–15.

Guildner, S. H., Loeb, S., Morris, D., Penrod, J., Bramlett, M., Johnston, L., & Schlotzhauer, P. (2001). A comparison of life satisfaction and mood in nursing home residents and community-dwelling elders. *Archives of Psychiatric Nursing, 15,* 232–240.

Guilford, J. P. (1985). The structure-of-intellect model. In B. B. Wolman (Ed.), *Handbook of intelligence* (pp. 225–266). New York: Wiley.

Gullone, E. (2000). The development of normal fear: A century of research. *Clinical Psychology Review, 20,* 429–451.

Gulotta, T. P. (2008). How theory influences treatment and prevention practice within the family. In T. P. Gulotta (Ed.), *Family influences on child behavior and development: Evidence-based prevention and treatment approaches* (pp. 1–20). New York: Routledge.

Gunnar, M. R., & Cheatham, C. L. (2003). Brain and behavior interfaces: Stress and the developing brain. *Infant Mental Health Journal, 24,* 195–211.

Gunnar, M. R., Morison, S. J., Chisholm, K., & Schuder, M. (2001). Salivary cortisol levels in children adopted from Romanian orphanages. *Development and Psychopathology, 13,* 611–628.

Gunnarsdottir, I., Schack-Nielsen, L., Michaelson, K. F., Sørensen, T. I., & Thorsdottir, I. (2010). Infant weight gain, duration of exclusive breast-feeding, and childhood BMI—two similar follow-up cohorts. *Public Health Nutrition, 13,* 201–207.

Gunnoe, M. L., & Mariner, C. L. (1997). Toward a developmental-contextual model of the effects of parental spanking on children's aggression. *Archives of Pediatrics and Adolescent Medicine, 151,* 768–775.

Gunstad, J., Spitznagel, M. B., Luyster, F., Cohen, R. A., & Paul, R. H. (2007). Handedness and cognition across the healthy lifespan. *International Journal of Neuroscience, 117,* 477–485.

Gure, A., Ucanok, Z., & Sayil, M. (2006). The associations among perceived pubertal timing, parental relations and self-perception in Turkish adolescents. *Journal of Youth and Adolescence, 35,* 541–550.

Gureje, O., Ogunniyi, A., Baiyewu, O., Price, B., Unverzagt, F. W., & Evans, R. M. (2006). APOE epsilon-4 is not associated with Alzheimer's disease in elderly Nigerians. *Annals of Neurology, 59,* 182–185.

Gustafson, G. E., Wood, R. M., & Green, J. A. (2000). Can we hear the causes of infants' crying? In R. G. Barr & B. Hopkins (Eds.), *Crying as a sign, a symptom, and a signal: Clinical, emotional, and developmental aspects of infant and toddler crying* (pp. 8–22). New York: Cambridge University Press.

Guterman, N. B., Lee, S. J., Taylor, C. A., & Rathouz, P. J. (2009). Parental perceptions of neighborhood processes, stress, personal control, and risk for physical child abuse and neglect. *Child Abuse and Neglect, 33,* 897–906.

Gutman, L. M. (2006). How student and parent goal orientations and classroom goal structures influence the math achievement of African Americans during the high school transition. *Contemporary Educational Psychology, 31,* 44–63.

Gutman, L. M., & Midgley, C. (2000). The role of protective factors in supporting the academic achievement of poor African-American students during the middle school transition. *Journal of Youth and Adolescence, 29,* 223–248.

Gutmann, D. (1977). The cross-cultural perspective: Notes toward a comparative psychology of aging. In J. E. Birren & K. W. Schaie (Eds.), *Handbook of the psychology of aging* (pp. 302–326). New York: Van Nostrand Reinhold.

Gutmann, D. L., & Huyck, M. H. (1994). Development and pathology in post-parental men: A community study. In E. Thompson, Jr. (Ed.), *Older men's lives* (pp. 65–84). Thousand Oaks, CA: Sage.

Gutteling, B. M., de Weerth, C., Zandbelt, N., Mulder, E. J. H., Visser, G. H. A., & Buitelaar, J. K. (2006). Does maternal prenatal stress adversely affect the child's learning and memory at age six? *Journal of Abnormal Child Psychology, 34,* 789–798.

Guttuso, T., Jr. (2012). Effective and clinically meaningful non-hormonal hot flash therapies. *Maturitas, 72,* 6–12.

Gwiazda, J., & Birch, E. E. (2001). Perceptual development: Vision. In E. B. Goldstein (Ed.), *Blackwell handbook of perception* (pp. 636–668). Oxford, UK: Blackwell.

H

Haentjens, P., Magaziner, J., Colón-Emeric, C. S., Vanderschueren, D., Milisen, K., Velkeniers, B., et al. (2010). Meta-analysis: Excess mortality after hip fracture among older women and men. *Annals of Internal Medicine, 16,* 380–390.

Hagberg, B., & Samuelsson, G. (2008). Survival after 100 years of age: A multivariate model of exceptional survival in Swedish centenarians. *Journal of Gerontology, 63A,* 1219–1226.

Hagerman, R. J., Berry-Kravis, E., Kaufmann, W. E., Ono, M. Y., Tartaglia, N., & Lachiewicz, A. (2009). Advances in the treatment of fragile X syndrome. *Pediatrics, 123,* 378–390.

Hahn, S., & Chitty, L. S. (2008). Noninvasive prenatal diagnosis: Current practice and future perspectives. *Current Opinion in Obstetrics and Gynecology, 20,* 146–151.

Haidt, J. (2001). The emotional dog and its rational tail: A social intuitionist approach to moral judgment. *Psychological Review, 108,* 814–834.

Haidt, J., & Kesebir, S. (2010). Morality. In S. T. Fiske & D. Gilbert (Eds.), *Handbook of social psychology* (5th ed., pp. 797–832). Hoboken, NJ: Wiley.

Haight, W. L., & Miller, P. J. (1993). *Pretending at home: Early development in a sociocultural context.* Albany: State University of New York Press.

Hainline, L. (1998). The development of basic visual abilities. In A. Slater (Ed.), *Perceptual development: Visual, auditory, and speech perception in infancy* (pp. 37–44). Hove, UK: Psychology Press.

Hakman, M., & Sullivan, M. (2009). The effect of task and maternal verbosity on compliance in toddlers. *Infant and Child Development, 18,* 195–205.

Hakuta, K., Bialystok, E., & Wiley, E. (2003). Critical evidence: A test of the critical-period hypothesis for second-language acquisitions. *Psychological Science, 14,* 31–38.

Hale, C. M., & Tager-Flusberg, H. (2003). The influence of language on theory of mind: A training study. *Developmental Science, 6,* 346–359.

Hale, S., Rose, N. S., Myerson, J., Strube, M. J., Sommers, M., Tye-Murray, N., et al. (2011). The structure of working memory abilities across the adult life span. *Psychology and Aging, 26,* 92–110.

Hales, C. N., & Ozanne, S. E. (2003). The dangerous road of catch-up growth. *Journal of Physiology, 547,* 5–10.

Haley, W. E. (2013). Family caregiving at end-of-life: Current status and future directions. In R. C. Talley & R. J. V. Montgomery (Eds.), *Caregiving across the lifespan: Research, practice, and policy* (pp. 157–175). New York: Springer.

Halfon, N., & McLearn, K. T. (2002). Families with children under 3: What we know and implications for results and policy. In N. Halfon & K. T. McLearn (Eds.), *Child rearing in America: Challenges facing parents with young children* (pp. 367–412). New York: Cambridge University Press.

Halford, G. S., & Andrews, G. (2006). Reasoning and problem solving. In D. Kuhn & R. Siegler (Eds.), *Handbook of child psychology: Vol. 2. Cognition, perception, and language* (6th ed., pp. 557–608). Hoboken, NJ: Wiley.

Halgunseth, L. C., Ispa, J. M., & Rudy, D. (2006). Parental control in Latino families: An integrated review of the literature. *Child Development, 77,* 1282–1297.

Hall, C. B., Derby, C., LeValley, A., Katz, M. J., Verghese, J., & Lipton, R. B. (2007). Education delays accelerated decline on a memory test in persons who develop dementia. *Neurology, 69,* 1657–1664.

Hall, C. B., Lipton, R. B., Sliwinski, M., Katz, M. J., Derby, C. A., & Verghese, J. (2009). Cognitive activities delay onset of memory decline in persons who develop dementia. *Neurology, 73,* 356–361.

Hall, G. S. (1904). *Adolescence.* New York: Appleton.

Hall, J. G. (2003). Twinning. *Lancet, 362,* 735–743.

Hall, K., Murrell, J., Ogunniyi, A., Deeg, M., Baiyewu, O., & Gao, S. (2006). Cholesterol, APOE genotype, and Alzheimer disease: An epidemiologic study of Nigerian Yoruba. *Neurology, 66,* 223–227.

Halle, T. G. (2003). Emotional development and wellbeing. In M. H. Bornstein, L. Davidson,

C. L. M. Keyes, K. A. Moore, & the Center for Child Well-Being (Eds.), *Well-being: Positive development across the life course* (pp. 125–138). Mahwah, NJ: Erlbaum.

Haller, J. (2005). Vitamins and brain function. In H. R. Lieberman, R. B. Kanarek, & C. Prasad (2005). *Nutritional neuroscience* (pp. 207–233). Philadelphia: Taylor & Francis.

Hallinan, M. T., & Kubitschek, W. N. (1999). Curriculum differentiation and high school achievement. *Social Psychology of Education, 3,* 41–62.

Halpern, C. T., Udry, J. R., & Suchindran, C. (1997). Testosterone predicts initiation of coitus in adolescent females. *Psychosomatic Medicine, 59,* 161–171.

Halpern, D. F. (2004). A cognitive-process taxonomy for sex differences in cognitive abilities. *Current Directions in Psychological Science, 13,* 135–139.

Halpern, D. F. (2005a). How time-flexible work policies can reduce stress, improve health, and save money. *Stress and Health, 21,* 157–168.

Halpern, D. F. (2005b). Psychology at the intersection of work and family: Recommendations for employers, working families, and policymakers. *American Psychologist, 60,* 397–409.

Halpern, D. F., Wai, J., & Saw, A. (2005). A psychobiological model: Why females are sometimes greater than and sometimes less than males in math achievement. In D. F. Halpern, J. Wai, & A. Saw (Eds.), *Gender differences in mathematics: An integrative psychological approach* (pp. 48–72). New York: Cambridge University Press.

Halpern-Felsher, B. L., Biehl, M., Kropp, R. Y., & Rubinstein, M. L. (2004). Perceived risks and benefits of smoking: Differences among adolescents with different smoking experiences and intentions. *Preventive Medicine, 39,* 559–567.

Haltzman, S., Holstein, N., & Moss, S. B. (2007). Men, marriage, and divorce. In J. E. Grant & M. N. Potenza (Eds.), *Textbook of men's mental health* (pp. 283–305). Washington, DC: American Psychiatric Publishing.

Hamberger, L. K., Lohr, J. M., Parker, L. M., & Witte, T. (2009). Treatment approaches for men who batter their partners. In C. Mitchell & D. Anglin (Eds.), *Intimate partner violence: A health-based perspective* (pp. 459–471). New York: Oxford University Press.

Hamer, D. H., Hu, S., Magnuson, V. L., Hu, N., & Pattatucci, A. M. L. (1993). A linkage between DNA markers on the X chromosome and male sexual orientation. *Science, 261,* 321–327.

Hammes, B., & Laitman, C. J. (2003). Diethylstilbestrol (DES) update: Recommendations for the identification and management of DES-exposed individuals. *Journal of Midwifery and Women's Health, 48,* 19–29.

Hampton, K. N., Goulet, L. S., Rainie, L., & Purcell, K. (2011). *Social networking sites and our lives.* Washington, DC: Pew Research Center Internet & American Life Project. Retrieved from www.pewinternet.org/Reports/2011/Technology-and-social-networks.aspx

Hane, A. A., Cheah, C., Rubin, K. H., & Fox, N. A. (2008). The role of maternal behavior in the relation between shyness and social reticence in early childhood and social withdrawal in middle childhood. *Social Development, 17,* 795–811.

Hanioka, T., Ojima, M., Tanaka, K., & Yamamoto, M. (2011). Does secondhand smoke affect the development of dental caries in children? A systematic review. *International Journal of Environmental Research and Public Health, 8,* 1503–1509.

Hankin, B. L., & Abela, J. R. Z. (2005). Depression from childhood through adolescence and adulthood: A developmental vulnerability and stress perspective. In B. L. Hankin & J. R. Z. Abela (Eds.), *Development*

of psychopathology: A vulnerability-stress perspective (pp. 245–288). Thousand Oaks, CA: Sage.

Hankin, B. L., Stone, L., & Wright, P. A. (2010). Corumination, interpersonal stress generation, and internalizing symptoms: Accumulating effects and transactional influences in a multiwave study of adolescents. *Development and Psychopathology, 22,* 217–235.

Hannon, E. E., & Johnson, S. P. (2004). Infants use meter to categorize rhythms and melodies: Implications for musical structure learning. *Cognitive Psychology, 50,* 354–377.

Hannon, E. E., & Trehub, S. E. (2005a). Metrical categories in infancy and adulthood. *Psychological Science, 16,* 48–55.

Hannon, E. E., & Trehub, S. E. (2005b). Tuning in to musical rhythms: Infants learn more readily than adults. *Proceedings of the National Academy of Sciences, 102,* 12639–12643.

Hannon, T. S., Rao, G., & Arslanian, S. A. (2005). Childhood obesity and type 2 diabetes mellitus. *Pediatrics, 116,* 473–480.

Hansell, N. K., Wright, M. J., Geffen, G. M., Geffen, L. B., Smith, G. A., & Martin, N. G. (2001). Genetic influence on ERP slow wave measures of working memory. *Behavioral Genetics, 31,* 603–614.

Hansen, M., Janssen, I., Schiff, A., Zee, P. C., & Dubocovich, M. L. (2005). The impact of school daily schedule on adolescent sleep. *Pediatrics, 115,* 1555–1561.

Hansen, M. B., & Markman, E. M. (2009). Children's use of mutual exclusivity to learn labels for parts of objects. *Developmental Psychology, 45,* 592–596.

Hansson, R. O., & Stroebe, M. S. (2007). The dual process model of coping with bereavement and development of an integrative risk factor framework. In R. O. Hansson & M. S. Stroebe (Eds.), *Bereavement in late life: Coping, adaptation, and developmental influences* (pp. 41–60). Washington, DC: American Psychological Association.

Hao, L., & Woo, H. S. (2012). Distinct trajectories in the transition to adulthood: Are children of immigrants advantaged? *Child Development, 83,* 1623–1639.

Harachi, T. W., Fleming, C. B., White, H. R., Ensminger, M. E., Abbott, R. D., Catalano, R. F., & Haggerty, K. P. (2006). Aggressive behavior among girls and boys during middle childhood: Predictors and sequelae of trajectory group membership. *Aggressive Behavior, 32,* 279–293.

Harden, K. Paige, & Tucker-Drob, E. M. (2011). Individual differences in the development of sensation seeking and impulsivity during adolescence: Further evidence for a dual systems model. *Developmental Psychology, 47,* 739–746.

Hardy, S. A., & Carlo, G. (2005). Religiosity and prosocial behaviours in adolescence: The mediating role of prosocial values. *Journal of Moral Education, 34,* 231–249.

Hardy, S. A., & Carlo, G. (2011). Moral identity: What is it, how does it develop, and is it linked to moral action? *Child Development Perspectives, 5,* 212–218.

Hardy, S. A., Pratt, M. W., Pancer, S. M., Olsen, J. A., & Lawford, H. L. (2011). Community and religious involvement as contexts of identity change across late adolescence and emerging adulthood. *International Journal of Behavioral Development, 35,* 125–135.

Harley, B., & Jean, G. (1999). Vocabulary skills of French immersion students in their second language. *Zeitschrift für Interkulturellen Fremdsprachenunterricht, 4*(2). Retrieved from www.ualberta.ca

Harley, K., & Reese, E. (1999). Origins of autobiographical memory. *Developmental Psychology, 35,* 1338–1348.

Harlow, H. F., & Zimmerman, R. (1959). Affectional responses in the infant monkey. *Science, 130,* 421–432.

Harris, R. C., Robinson, J. B., Chang, F., & Burns, B. M. (2007). Characterizing preschool children's attention regulation in parent–child interactions: The roles of effortful control and motivation. *Journal of Applied Developmental Psychology, 28,* 25–39.

Harris, Y. R., & Graham, J. A. (2007). *The African American child: Development and challenges.* New York: Springer.

Harris Interactive. (2011). *Large majorities support doctor-assisted suicide for terminally ill patients in great pain.* Retrieved from www.harrisinteractive.com/NewsRoom/HarrisPolls/tabid/447/mid/1508/articleId/677/ctl/ReadCustom%20Default/Default.aspx

Hart, B., & Risley, T. R. (1995). *Meaningful differences in the everyday experience of young American children.* Baltimore: Paul H. Brookes.

Hart, C. H., Burts, D. C., Durland, M. A., Charlesworth, R., DeWolf, M., & Fleege, P. O. (1998). Stress behaviors and activity type participation of preschoolers in more and less developmentally appropriate classrooms: SES and sex differences. *Journal of Research in Childhood Education, 13,* 176–196.

Hart, C. H., Newell, L. D., & Olsen, S. F. (2003). Parenting skills and social–communicative competence in childhood. In J. O. Greene & B. R. Burleson (Eds.), *Handbook of communication and social interaction skills* (pp. 753–797). Mahwah, NJ: Erlbaum.

Hart, C. H., Yang, C., Nelson, L. J., Robinson, C. C., Olsen, J. A., Nelson, D. A., Porter, C. L., Jin, S., Olsen, S. F., & Wu, P. (2000). Peer acceptance in early childhood and subtypes of socially withdrawn behavior in China, Russia, and the United States. *International Journal of Behavioral Development, 24,* 73–81.

Hart, D., & Fegley, S. (1995). Prosocial behavior and caring in adolescence: Relations to self-understanding and social judgment. *Child Development, 66,* 1346–1359.

Hart, H., & Rubia, K. (2012). Neuroimaging of child abuse: A review. *Frontiers in Human Neuroscience, 6,* 52.

Hart, H. M., McAdams, D. P., Hirsch, B. J., & Bauer, J. J. (2001). Generativity and social involvement among African Americans and white adults. *Journal of Research in Personality, 35,* 208–230.

Harter, S. (1999). *The construction of self: A developmental perspective.* New York: Guilford.

Harter, S. (2003). The development of self-representations during childhood and adolescence. In M. R. Leary & J. P. Tangney (Eds.), *Handbook of self and identity* (pp. 610–642). New York: Guilford.

Harter, S. (2006). The self. In N. Eisenberg (Ed.), *Handbook of child psychology: Vol. 3. Social, emotional, and personality development* (6th ed., pp. 505–570). Hoboken, NJ: Wiley.

Harter, S., & Whitesell, N. (1989). Developmental changes in children's understanding of simple, multiple, and blended emotion concepts. In C. Saarni & P. Harris (Eds.), *Children's understanding of emotion* (pp. 81–116). Cambridge, UK: Cambridge University Press.

Hartley, A. (2006). Changing role of the speed of processing construct. In J. E. Birren & K. W. Schaie (Eds.), *Handbook of the psychology of aging* (6th ed., pp. 183–207). Burlington, MA: Academic Press.

Hartman, J., & Warren, L. H. (2005). Explaining age differences in temporal working memory. *Psychology and Aging, 20,* 645–656.

Hartshorn, K., Rovee-Collier, C., Gerhardstein, P., Bhatt, R. S., Wondoloski, T. L., Klein, P., Gilch, J., Wurtzel, N., & Campos-de-Carvalho, M. (1998). The ontogeny of long-term memory over the first year-and-a-half of life. *Developmental Psychobiology, 32,* 69–89.

Hartup, W. W. (2006). Relationships in early and middle childhood. In A. L. Vangelisti & D. Perlman (Eds.), *Cambridge handbook of personal relationships* (pp. 177–190). New York: Cambridge University Press.

Hartup, W. W., & Abecassis, M. (2004). Friends and enemies. In P. K. Smith & C. H. Hart (Eds.), *Blackwell handbook of childhood social development* (pp. 285–306). Malden, MA: Blackwell.

Hartup, W. W., & Stevens, N. (1999). Friendships and adaptation across the life span. *Current Directions in Psychological Science, 8,* 76–79.

Harvey, M. W. (2001). Vocational-technical education: A logical approach to dropout prevention for secondary special education. *Preventing School Failure, 45,* 108–113.

Harwood, M. D., & Farrar, M. J. (2006). Conflicting emotions: The connection between affective perspective taking and theory of mind. *British Journal of Developmental Psychology, 24,* 401–418.

Harwood, R., Leyendecker, B., Carlson, V., Asencio, M., & Miller, A. (2002). Parenting among Latino families in the U.S. In M. H. Bornstein (Ed.), *Handbook of parenting: Vol. 4. Social conditions and applied parenting* (4th ed., pp. 21–46). Mahwah, NJ: Erlbaum.

Hasebe, Y., Nucci, L., & Nucci, M. S. (2004). Parental control of the personal domain and adolescent symptoms of psychopathology: A cross-national study in the United States and Japan. *Child Development, 75,* 815–828.

Hasher, L., Lustig, C., & Zacks, R. T. (2007). Inhibitory mechanisms and the control of attention. In A. R. A. Conway, C. Jarrold, M. Kane, A. Miyake, & J. N. Towse (Eds.), *Variation in working memory* (pp. 227–249). New York: Oxford University Press.

Hastrup, B. (2007). Healthy aging in Denmark? In M. Robinson, W. Novelli, C. Pearson, & L. Norris (Eds.), *Global health and global aging* (pp. 71–84). San Francisco: Jossey-Bass.

Hatch, L. R., & Bulcroft, K. (2004). Does long-term marriage bring less frequent disagreements? *Journal of Family Issues, 25,* 465–495.

Hatfield, E., Rapson, R. L, & Martel, L. D. (2007). Passionate love and sexual desire. In S. Kitayama & D. Cohen (Eds.), *Handbook of cultural psychology* (pp. 760–779). New York: Guilford.

Hatfield, E., & Sprecher, S. (1995). Men's and women's mate preferences in the United States, Russia, and Japan. *Journal of Cross-Cultural Psychology, 26,* 728–750.

Hau, K.-T., & Ho, I. T. (2010). Chinese students' motivation and achievement. In M. H. Bond (Ed.), *Oxford handbook of Chinese psychology* (pp. 187–204). New York: Oxford University Press.

Hauf, P., Aschersleben, G., & Prinz, W. (2007). Baby do–baby see! How action production influences action perception in infants. *Cognitive Development, 22,* 16–32.

Haukkala, A., Konttinen, H., Laatikainen, T., Kawachi, I., & Uutela, A. (2010). Hostility, anger control, and anger expression as predictors of cardiovascular disease. *Psychosomatic Medicine, 72,* 556–562.

Hausfather, A., Toharia, A., LaRoche, C., & Engelsmann, F. (1997). Effects of age of entry, day-care quality, and family characteristics on preschool behavior. *Journal of Child Psychology and Psychiatry, 38,* 441–448.

Hawkins, J. N. (1994). Issues of motivation in Asian education. In H. F. O'Neil, Jr., & M. Drillings (Eds.), *Motivation: Theory and research* (pp. 101–115). Hillsdale, NJ: Erlbaum.

Hawkley, L. C., & Cacioppo, J. T. (2004). Stress and the aging immune system. *Brain, Behavior and Immunity, 18,* 114–119.

Haworth, C. M. A., Wright, M. J., Luciano, M., Martin, N. G., de Geus, E. J. C., van Beijsterveldt, C. E. M., et al. (2010). The heritability of general cognitive ability increases linearly from childhood to young adulthood. *Molecular Psychiatry, 15,* 1112–1120.

Haws, R. A., Yakoob, M. Y., Soomro, T., Menezes, E. V., Darmstadt, G. L., & Bhutta, Z. A. (2009). Reducing stillbirths: Screening and monitoring during pregnancy and labour. *BMC Pregnancy and Childbirth, 9*(Suppl. S1).

Hawton, A., Green, C., Dickens, A. P., Richards, S. H., Taylor, R. S., & Edwards, R. (2011). The impact of social isolation on the health status and healthrelated quality of life of older people. *Quality of Life Research, 20,* 57–67.

Hay, D. F., Pawlby, S., Waters, C. S., Perra, O., & Sharp, D. (2010). Mothers' antenatal depression and their children's antisocial outcomes. *Child Development, 81,* 149–165.

Hay, E. L., & Diehl, M. (2010). Reactivity to daily stressors in adulthood: The importance of stressor type in characterizing risk factors. *Psychology and Aging, 25,* 118–131.

Hay, P., & Bacaltchuk, J. (2004). Bulimia nervosa. *Clinical Evidence, 12,* 1326–1347.

Haycock, P. C. (2009). Fetal alcohol spectrum disorders: The epigenetic perspective. *Biology of Reproduction, 81,* 607–617.

Hayflick, L. (1994). *How and why we age.* New York: Ballantine.

Hayflick, L. (1998). How and why we age. *Experimental Gerontology, 33,* 639–653.

Hayne, H., Herbert, J., & Simcock, G. (2003). Imitation from television by 24- and 30-month-olds. *Developmental Science, 6,* 254–261.

Hayne, H., Rovee-Collier, C., & Perris, E. E. (1987). Categorization and memory retrieval by three-month-olds. *Child Development, 58,* 750–767.

Hayslip, B., Jr., & Kaminski, P. L. (2005). Grandparents raising their grandchildren. *Marriage and Family Review, 37,* 147–169.

Haywood, H. C., & Lidz, C. S. (2007). *Dynamic assessment in practice.* New York: Cambridge University Press.

Haywood, K. M., & Getchell, N. (2005). *Life span motor development* (4th ed.). Champaign, IL: Human Kinetics.

Haywood, K. M., & Getchell, N. (2009). *Life span motor development* (5th ed.). Champaign, IL: Human Kinetics.

Hazen, N. L., McFarland, L., Jacobvitz, D., & Boyd-Soisson, E. (2010). Fathers' frightening behaviours and sensitivity with infants: Relations with fathers' attachment representations, father–infant attachment, and children's later outcomes. *Early Child Development and Care, 180,* 51–69.

Head Start Bureau. (2010). *Head Start Program fact sheet.* Retrieved from eclkc.ohs.acf.hhs.gov/hslc/mr/factsheets/fHeadStartProgr.htm

Healthy Families America. (2011). *Healthy Families America FAQ.* Retrieved from www.healthyfamiliesamerica.org/about_us/faq.shtml

Heath, S. B. (1990). The children of Trackton's children: Spoken and written in social change. In J. Stigler, G. Herdt, & R. A. Shweder (Eds.), *Cultural psychology: Essays on comparative human development* (pp. 496–519). New York: Cambridge University Press.

Hebblethwaite, S., & Norris, J. (2011). Expressions of generativity through family leisure: Experiences of grandparents and adult grandchildren. *Family Relations, 60,* 121–133.

Heckhausen, J., Wrosch, C., & Schultz, R. (2010). A motivational theory of life-span development. *Psychological Review, 117,* 32–60.

Heckman, J. J., Seong, H. M., Pinto, R., Savelyev, P., & Yavitz, A. (2010). A new cost–benefit and rate of return for the Perry Preschool Program: A summary. In A. J. Reynolds, A. J. Rolnick, M. M. Englund, & J. Temple (Eds.), *Childhood programs and practices in the first decade of life: A human capital integration* (pp. 199–213). New York: Cambridge University Press.

Hedberg, K., Hopkins, D., Leman, R., & Kohn, M. (2009). The 10-year experience of Oregon's Death with Dignity Act: 1998–2007. *Journal of Clinical Ethics, 20,* 124–132.

Hedge, J. W., Borman, W. C., & Lammlein, S. E. (2006). *The aging workforce: Realities, myths, and implications for organizations.* Washington, DC: American Psychological Association.

Hediger, M. L., Overpeck, M. D., Ruan, W. J., & Troendle, J. F. (2002). Birthweight and gestational age effects on motor and social development. *Paediatric and Perinatal Epidemiology, 16,* 33–46.

Heino, R., Ellison, N., & Gibbs, J. (2010). Relationshopping: Investigating the market metaphor in online dating. *Journal of Social and Personal Relationships, 27,* 427–447.

Hellemans, K. G., Sliwowska, J. H., Verma, P., & Weinberg, J. (2010). Prenatal alcohol exposure: Fetal programming and later life vulnerability to stress, expression and anxiety disorders. *Neuroscience and Biobehavioral Reviews, 34,* 791–807.

Helm, H. M., Hays, J. C., Flint, E. P., Koenig, H. G., & Blazer, D. G. (2000). Does private religious activity prolong survival? A six-year follow-up study of 3,851 older adults. *Journal of Gerontology, 55A,* M400–M405.

Helson, R. (1992). Women's difficult times and the rewriting of the life story. *Psychology of Women Quarterly, 16,* 331–347.

Helson, R., Jones, C. J., & Kwan, V. S. Y. (2002). Personality change over 40 years of adulthood: Hierarchical linear modeling analyses of two longitudinal samples. *Journal of Personality and Social Psychology, 83,* 752–766.

Helson, R., & Picano, J. (1990). Is the traditional role bad for women? *Journal of Personality and Social Psychology, 59,* 311–320.

Helson, R., Soto, C. J., & Cate, R. A. (2006). From young adulthood through the middle ages. In D. K. Mroczek & T. D. Little (Eds.), *Handbook of personality development* (pp. 337–352). Mahwah, NJ: Erlbaum.

Heltzner, E. P., Cauley, J. A., Pratt, S. R., Wisniewski, S. R., Zmuda, J. M., & Talbott, E. O. (2005). Race and sex differences in age-related hearing loss: The health, aging and body composition study. *Journal of the American Geriatrics Society, 53,* 2119–2127.

Helwig, C. C. (2006). Rights, civil liberties, and democracy across cultures. In M. Killen & J. G. Smetana (Eds.), *Handbook of moral development* (pp. 185–210). Philadelphia: Erlbaum.

Helwig, C. C., & Jasiobedzka, U. (2001). The relation between law and morality: Children's reasoning about socially beneficial and unjust laws. *Child Development, 72,* 1382–1393.

Helwig, C. C., & Prencipe, A. (1999). Children's judgments of flags and flag-burning. *Child Development, 70,* 132–143.

Helwig, C. C., Zelazo, P. D., & Wilson, M. (2001). Children's judgments of psychological harm in normal and canonical situations. *Child Development, 72,* 66–81.

Henggeler, S. W., Schoenwald, S. K., Bourduin, C. M., Rowland, M. D., & Cunningham, P. B. (2009). *Multisystemic therapy for antisocial behavior in children and adolescents* (2nd ed.). New York: Guilford.

Hendrick, S. S., & Hendrick, C. (2002). Love. In C. R. Snyder & S. J. Lopez (Eds.), *Handbook of positive psychology* (pp. 472–484). New York: Oxford University Press.

Hendricks, J., & Cutler, S. J. (2004). Volunteerism and socioemotional selectivity in later life. *Journal of Gerontology, 59B,* S251–S257.

Hendrie, H. H. (2001). Exploration of environmental and genetic risk factors for Alzheimer's disease: The value of cross-cultural studies. *Current Directions in Psychological Science, 10,* 98–101.

Hendry, L. B., & Kloep, M. (2007). Conceptualizing emerging adulthood: Inspecting the emperor's new clothes? *Child Development Perspectives, 1,* 74–79.

Hendry, L. B., & Kloep, M. (2010). How universal is emerging adulthood? An empirical example. *Journal of Youth Studies, 13,* 169–179.

Hendry, M., Paserfield, D., Lewis, R., Carter, B., Hodgson, D., & Wilinson, C. (2012). Why do we want the right to die? A systematic review of the international literature on the views of patients, carers and the public on assisted dying. *Palliative Medicine, 27,* 13–26.

Henig, R. M., & Henig, S. (2012). *Twenty something: Why do young adults seem stuck?* New York: Hudson Street Press.

Henning, K., Jones, A. R., & Holdford, R. (2005). Attributions of blame among male and female domestic violence offenders. *Journal of Family Violence, 20,* 131–139.

Henrich, C. C., Brookmeyer, K. A., Shrier, L. A., & Shahar, G. (2006). Supportive relationships and sexual risk behavior in adolescence: An ecological–transactional approach. *Journal of Pediatric Psychology, 31,* 286–297.

Henrich, C. C., Kuperminc, G. P., Sack, A., Blatt, S. J., & Leadbeater, B. J. (2000). Characteristics and homogeneity of early adolescent friendship groups: A comparison of male and female clique and nonclique members. *Applied Developmental Science, 4,* 15–26.

Henricsson, L., & Rydell, A.-M. (2004). Elementary school children with behavior problems: Teacher–child relations and self-perception. A prospective study. *Merrill-Palmer Quarterly, 50,* 111–138.

Henry, J. D., MacLeod, M. S., Phillips, L. H., & Crawford, J. R. (2004). A meta-analytic review of prospective memory and aging. *Psychology and Aging, 19,* 27–39.

Herbenick, D., Reece, M., Schick, V., Sanders, S. A., Dodge, B., & Fortenberry, J. D. (2010). Sexual behavior in the United States: Results from a national probability sample of men and women ages 14–94. *Journal of Sexual Medicine, 7*(Suppl. 5), 255–265.

Herbst, J. H., McCrae, R. R., Costa, P. T., Jr., Feaganes, J. R., & Siegler, I. C. (2000). Self-perceptions of stability and change in personality at midlife: The UNC Alumni Heart Study. *Assessment, 7,* 379–388.

Herd, P., Robert, S. A., & House, J. S. (2011). Health disparities among older adults: Life course influences and policy solutions. *Handbook of aging and the social sciences* (7th ed., pp. 121–134). San Diego: Academic Press.

Herman, M. (2004). Forced to choose: Some determinants of racial identification in multiracial adolescents. *Child Development, 75,* 730–748.

Herman-Giddens, M. E. (2006). Recent data on pubertal milestones in United States children: The secular trend toward earlier development. *International Journal of Andrology, 29,* 241–246.

Herman-Giddens, M. E., Steffes, J., Harris, D., Slora, E., Hussey, M., Dowshen, S. A., et al. (2012). Secondary sexual characteristics in boys: Data from the Pediatric Research in Office Settings Network. *Pediatrics, 130,* e1058–e1068.

Hernandez, D. J., Denton, N. A., & Macartney, S. E. (2008). Children in immigrant families: Looking to America's future. *Social Policy Report of the Society for Research in Child Development, 12*(11).

Hernandez, M., & Newcomer, R. (2007). Assisted living and special populations: What do we know about differences in use and potential access barriers? *Gerontologist, 47*(Special Issue III), 110–117.

Herrnstein, R. J., & Murray, C. (1994). *The bell curve.* New York: Free Press.

Hershey, D. A., Jacobs-Lawson, J. M., McArdle, J. J., & Hamagami, F. (2007). Psychological foundations of financial planning for retirement. *Journal of Adult Development, 14,* 26–36.

Hertzog, C., & Dunlosky, J. (2011). Metacognition in later adulthood: Spared monitoring can benefit older adults' self-regulation. *Current Directions in Psychological Science, 20,* 167–173.

Hertzog, C., Kramer, A. F., Wilson, R. S., & Lindenberger, U. (2009). Enrichment effects on adult cognitive development. *Psychological Science in the Public Interest, 9*(1), 1–65.

Herzog, D. B., Eddy, K. T., & Beresin, E. V. (2006). Anorexia and bulimia nervosa. In M. K. Dulcan & J. M. Wiener (Eds.), *Essentials of child and adolescent psychiatry* (pp. 527–560). Washington, DC: American Psychiatric Publishing.

Hespos, S. J., & Baillargeon, R. (2008). Young infants' actions reveal their developing knowledge of support variables: Converging evidence for violation-ofexpectation findings. *Cognition, 107,* 304–316.

Hespos, S. J., Ferry, A. L., Cannistraci, C. J., Gore, J., & Park, S. (2010). Using optical imaging to investigate functional cortical activity in human infants. In A. W. Roe (Ed.), *Imaging the brain with optical methods* (pp. 159–176). New York: Springer Science + Business Media.

Hess, T. M., & Hinson, J. T. (2006). Age-related variation in the influences of aging stereotypes on memory in adulthood. *Psychology and Aging, 21,* 621–625.

Hess, T. M., Hinson, J. T., & Statham, J. A. (2004). Explicit and implicit stereotype activation effects on memory: Do age and awareness moderate the impact of priming? *Psychology and Aging, 19,* 495–505.

Hetherington, E. M. (1999). Should we stay together for the sake of the children? In E. M. Hetherington (Ed.), *Coping with divorce, single-parenting, and remarriage: A risk and resiliency perspective* (pp. 93–116). Hillsdale, NJ: Erlbaum.

Hetherington, E. M., Henderson, S. H., & Reiss, D. (1999). Adolescent siblings in stepfamilies: Family functioning and adolescent adjustment. *Monographs of the Society for Research in Child Development, 64*(4, Serial No. 259).

Hetherington, E. M., & Kelly, J. (2002). *For better or for worse: Divorce reconsidered.* New York: Norton.

Hetherington, E. M., & Stanley-Hagan, M. (2000). Diversity among stepfamilies. In D. H. Demo, K. R. Allen, & M. A. Fine (Eds.), *Handbook of family diversity* (pp. 173–196). New York: Oxford University Press.

Hewlett, B. S. (2004). Fathers in forager, farmer, and pastoral cultures. In M. E. Lamb (Ed.), *The role of the father in child development* (4th ed., pp. 182–195). Hoboken, NJ: Wiley.

Hewlett, S. (2003). *Creating a life.* New York: Miramax.

Heyman, G. D., & Dweck, C. S. (1998). Children's thinking about traits: Implications for judgments of the self and others. *Child Development, 69,* 391–403.

Heyman, G. D., & Legare, C. H. (2004). Children's beliefs about gender differences in the academic and social domains. *Sex Roles, 50,* 227–239.

Hickling, A. K., & Wellman, H. M. (2001). The emergence of children's causal explanations and theories: Evidence from everyday conversation. *Developmental Psychology, 37,* 668–683.

Hietanen, A., Era, P., Sorri, M., & Heikkinen, E. (2004). Changes in hearing in 80-year-old people: A 10-year follow-up study. *International Journal of Audiology, 43,* 126–135.

Higginbottom, G. M. A. (2006). "Pressure of life": Ethnicity as a mediating factor in mid-life and older peoples' experience of high blood pressure. *Sociology of Health and Illness, 28,* 583–610.

Higgins, C. A., Duxbury, L. E., & Lyons, S. T. (2010). Coping with overload and stress: Men and women in dual-earner families. *Journal of Marriage and Family 72,* 847–859.

High, P. C., LaGasse, L., Becker, S., Ahlgren, I., & Gardner, A. (2000). Literacy promotion in primary care pediatrics: Can we make a difference? *Pediatrics, 105,* 927–934.

Hildreth, K., & Rovee-Collier, C. (2002). Forgetting functions of reactivated memories over the first year of life. *Developmental Psychobiology, 41,* 277–288.

Hildreth, K., Sweeney, B., & Rovee-Collier, C. (2003). Differential memory-preserving effects of reminders at 6 months. *Journal of Experimental Child Psychology, 84,* 41–62.

Hilgers, K. K., Akridge, M., Scheetz, J. P., & Kinance, D. E. (2006). Childhood obesity and dental development. *Pediatric Dentistry, 28,* 18–22.

Hill, J. L., Brooks-Gunn, J., & Waldfogel, J. (2003). Sustained effects of high participation in an early intervention for low-birth-weight premature infants. *Developmental Psychology, 39,* 730–744.

Hill, N. E., & Taylor, L. C. (2004). Parental school involvement and children's academic achievement: Pragmatics and issues. *Current Directions in Psychological Science, 13,* 161–164.

Hill, N. M., & Schneider, W. (2006). Brain changes in the development of expertise: Neuroanatomical and neurophysiological evidence about skill-based adaptations. In K. A. Ericsson, N. Charness, P. J. Feltovich, & R. R. Hoffman (Eds.), *The Cambridge handbook of expertise and expert performance* (pp. 653–682). New York: Cambridge University Press.

Hillis, S. D., Anda, R. F., Dube, S. R., Felitti, V. J., Marchbanks, P. A., & Marks, J. S. (2004). The association between adverse childhood experiences and adolescent pregnancy, long-term psychosocial consequences, and fetal death. *Pediatrics, 113,* 320–327.

Hilt, L. M. (2004). Attribution retaining for therapeutic change: Theory, practice, and future directions. *Imagination, Cognition, and Personality, 23,* 289–307.

Hinojosa, T., Sheu, C.-F., & Michael, G. F. (2003). Infant hand-use preference for grasping objects contributes to the development of a hand-use preference for manipulating objects. *Developmental Psychobiology, 43,* 328–334.

Hirasawa, R., & Feil, R. (2010). Genomic imprinting and human disease. *Essays in Biochemistry, 48,* 187–200.

Hirsch, C. (1996). Understanding the influence of gender role identity on the assumption of family caregiving roles by men. *International Journal of Aging and Human Development, 42,* 103–121.

Hirsh-Pasek, K., & Golinkoff, R. M. (2003). *Einstein never used flash cards.* New York: Rodale.

Hirsh-Pasek, K., Golinkoff, R. M., Berk, L. E., & Singer, D. G. (2009). *A mandate for playful learning in preschool: Presenting the evidence.* New York: Oxford University Press.

Hoch-Espada, A., Ryan, E., & Deblinger, E. (2006). Child sexual abuse. In J. E. Fisher & W. T. O'Donohue (Eds.), *Practitioner's guide to evidence-based psychotherapy* (pp. 177–188). New York: Springer.

Hodges, R. M., & French, L. A. (1988). The effect of class and collection labels on cardinality, class inclusion, and number conservation tasks. *Child Development, 59,* 1387–1396.

Hodnett, E. D., Gates, S., Hofmeyr, G. J., & Sakala, C. (2003). Continuous support for women during childbirth. *Cochrane Database of Systematic Reviews, 3,* CD003766.

Hoenig, H., Taylor, D. H., Jr., & Sloan, F. A. (2003). Does assistive technology substitute for personal assistance among the disabled elderly? *American Journal of Public Health, 93,* 330–337.

Hoerr, T. (2004). How MI informs teaching at New City School. *Teachers College Record, 106*, 40–48.

Hoff, B. (2001). *Full report of the prevalence, incidence, and consequences of violence against women.* Washington, DC: U.S. Department of Justice.

Hoff, E. (2003). The specificity of environmental influence: Socioeconomic status affects early vocabulary development via maternal speech. *Child Development, 74*, 1368–1378.

Hoff, E. (2006). How social contexts support and shape language development. *Developmental Review, 26*, 55–88.

Hoff, E. (2013). Interpreting the early language trajectories of children from low-SES and language minority homes: Implications for closing achievement gaps. *Developmental Psychology, 49*, 4–14.

Hoff, E., Laursen, B., & Tardif, T. (2002). Socioeconomic status and parenting. In M. H. Bornstein (Ed.), *Handbook of parenting* (pp. 231–252). Mahwah, NJ: Erlbaum.

Hofferth, S. L. (2010). Home media and children's achievement and behavior. *Child Development, 81*, 1598–1619.

Hoffman, L. W. (2000). Maternal employment: Effects of social context. In R. D. Taylor & M. C. Wang (Eds.), *Resilience across contexts: Family, work, culture, and community* (pp. 147–176). Mahwah, NJ: Erlbaum.

Hoffman, M. L. (2000). *Empathy and moral development.* New York: Cambridge University Press.

Hogan, B. E., & Linden, W. (2004). Anger response styles and blood pressure: At least don't ruminate about it! *Annals of Behavioral Medicine, 27*, 38–49.

Hogan, M. J., & Strasburger, V. C. (2008). Body image, eating disorders, and the media. *Adolescent Medicine, 19*, 521–546.

Holditch-Davis, D., Belyea, M., & Edwards, L. J. (2005). Prediction of 3-year developmental outcomes from sleep development over the preterm period. *Infant Behavior and Development, 79*, 49–58.

Holdren, J. P., & Lander, E. (2012). *Engage to excel: Producing one million additional college graduates with degrees in science, technology, engineering, and mathematics.* Washington, DC: President's Council of Advisors on Science and Technology.

Holland, J. L. (1985). *Making vocational choices: A theory of vocational personalities and work environments.* Englewood Cliffs, NJ: Prentice-Hall.

Holland, J. L. (1997). *Making vocational choices: A theory of vocational personalities and work environments* (3rd ed.). Odessa, FL: Psychological Assessment Resources.

Hollich, G. J., Hirsh-Pasek, K., & Golinkoff, R. M. (2000). Breaking the language barrier: An emergentist coalition model for the origins of word learning. *Monographs of the Society for Research in Child Development, 65*(3, Serial No. 262).

Holobow, N., Genesee, F., & Lambert, W. (1991). The effectiveness of a foreign language immersion program for children from different ethnic and social class backgrounds: Report 2. *Applied Psycholinguistics, 12*, 179–198.

Honein, M. A., Paulozzi, L. J., & Erickson, J. D. (2001). Continued occurrence of Accutane exposed pregnancies. *Teratology, 64*, 142–147.

Hong, Z.-R., Veach, P. M., & Lawrenz, F. (2003). An investigation of the gender stereotyped thinking of Taiwanese secondary school boys and girls. *Sex Roles, 48*, 495–504.

Hoobler, J. M., Lemmon, G., & Wayne, S. J. (2011). Women's underrepresentation in upper management: New insights on a persistent problem. *Organizational Dynamics, 40*, 151–156.

Hooper, L., Summerbell, C. D., Thompson, R., Sills, F., Roberts, F. G., Moore, H. J., et al. (2012). Reduced or modified dietary fat for preventing cardiovascular disease. *Cochrane Database of Systematic Reviews* [Online], 5: CD002137.

Hooyman, N. R., & Kiyak, H. A. (2011). *Social gerontology: A multidisciplinary perspective* (9th ed.). Boston, MA: Pearson.

Hopkins, B., & Westra, T. (1988). Maternal handling and motor development: An intracultural study. *Genetic, Social and General Psychology Monographs, 14*, 377–420.

Hoppmann, C. A., Gerstorf, D., Smith, J., & Klumb, P. L. (2007). Linking possible selves and behavior: Do domain-specific hopes and fears translate into daily activities in very old age? *Journal of Gerontology, 62B*, P104–P111.

Horn, J. L., Donaldson, G., & Engstrom, R. (1981). Apprehension, memory, and fluid intelligence decline through the "vital years" of adulthood. *Research on Aging, 3*, 33–84.

Horn, J. L., & Noll, J. (1997). Human cognitive capabilities: Gf-Gc theory. In D. P. Flanagan, J. L., Genshaft, & P. L. Harrison (Eds.), *Beyond traditional intellectual assessment* (pp. 53–91). New York: Guilford.

Horner, T. M. (1980). Two methods of studying stranger reactivity in infants: A review. *Journal of Child Psychology and Psychiatry, 21*, 203–219.

Hornor, G. (2010). Child sexual abuse: Consequences and implications. *Journal of Pediatric Health Care, 24*, 358–364.

Hospice Foundation of America. (2005). *The dying process: A guide for caregivers.* Washington, DC: Author.

Hospice Foundation of America. (2013). *Hospice services and expenses.* Retrieved from www.hospicefoundation.org/servicesandexpenses

Hostetler, A. J., & Sweet, S., & Moen, P. (2007). Gendered career paths: A life course perspective on returning to school. *Sex Roles, 56*, 85–103.

Houlihan, J., Kropp. T., Wiles, R., Gray, S., & Campbell, C. (2005). *Body burden: The pollution in newborns.* Washington, DC: Environmental Working Group.

House, J. S., Lantz, P. M., & Herd, P. (2005). Continuity and change in the social stratification of aging and health over the life course: Evidence from a nationally representative longitudinal study from 1986 to 2001/2002 (Americans' Changing Lives Study). *Journal of Gerontology, 60B*(Special Issue II), 15–26.

Houts, R. M., Barnett-Walker, K. C., Paley, B., & Cox, M. J. (2008). Patterns of couple interaction during the transition to parenthood. *Personal Relationships, 15*, 103–122.

Howard, A. L., Galambos, N. L., & Krahn, H. J. (2010). Paths to success in young adulthood from mental health and life transitions in emerging adulthood. *International Journal of Behavioral Development, 34*, 538–546.

Howard, B. V., Manson, J. E., Stefanick, M. L., Beresford, S. A., Frank, G., & Jones, B. (2006). Low-fat dietary pattern and weight change over 7 years: The Women's Health Initiative Dietary Modification Trial. *Journal of the American Medical Association, 295*, 39–49.

Howard, K., & Walsh, M. E. (2010). Conceptions of career choice and attainment: Developmental levels in how children think about careers. *Journal of Vocational Behavior, 76*, 143–152.

Howe, M. L., Courage, M. L., & Rooksby, M. (2009). The genesis and development of autobiographical memory. In M. L. Courage & N. Cowan (Eds.), *The development of memory in infancy and childhood* (pp. 177–196). Hove, UK: Psychology Press.

Howe, N., Aquan-Assee, J., & Bukowski, W. M. (2001). Predicting sibling relations over time: Synchrony between maternal management styles and sibling relationship quality. *Merrill-Palmer Quarterly, 47*, 121–141.

Howell, K. K., Coles, C. D., & Kable, J. A. (2008). The medical and developmental consequences of prenatal drug exposure. In J. Brick (Ed.), *Handbook of the medical consequences of alcohol and drug abuse* (2nd ed., pp. 219–249). New York: Haworth Press.

Howell, K. K., Lynch, M. E., Platzman, K. A., Smith, G. H., & Coles, C. D. (2006). Prenatal alcohol exposure and ability, academic achievement, and school functioning in adolescence: A longitudinal follow-up. *Journal of Pediatric Psychology, 31*, 116–126.

Howell, L. C., & Beth, A. (2002). Midlife myths and realities: Women reflect on their experiences. *Journal of Women and Aging, 14*, 189–204.

Hoyer, W. J., & Verhaeghen, P. (2006). Memory aging. In J. E. Birren & K. W. Schaie (Eds.), *Handbook of the psychology of aging* (6th ed., pp. 209–232). Burlington, MA: Elsevier Academic Press.

Hoza, B., Gerdes, A. C., Hinshaw, S. P., Bukowski, W. M., Gold, J. A., Kraemer, H. C., Pelham, W. E., Jr., Wigal, T., & Arnold, L. E. (2005). What aspects of peer relationships are impaired in children with attention-deficit/hyperactivity disorder? *Journal of Consulting and Clinical Psychology, 73*, 411–423.

HSBC & Oxford Institute of Ageing. (2007). *The future of retirement.* London: HSBC Insurance.

HSBC & Oxford Institute of Ageing. (2011). *The future of retirement: The power of planning.* London: HSBC Insurance.

Huang, A. Subak, L., Thom, D., Van Den Eeden, S., Ragins, A., Kuppermann, M., et al. (2009). Sexual function and aging in racially and ethnically diverse women. *Journal of the American Geriatrics Society, 57*, 1362–1368.

Huang, C. Y., & Stormshak, E. A. (2011). A longitudinal examination of early adolescence ethnic identity trajectories. *Cultural Diversity and Ethnic Minority Psychology, 17*, 261–270.

Huang, Q., & Sverke, M. (2007). Women's occupational career patterns over 27 years: Relations to family of origin, life careers, and wellness. *Journal of Vocational Behavior, 70*, 369–397.

Hubbs-Tait, L., Nation, J. R., Krebs, N. F., & Bellinger, D. C. (2005). Neurotoxicants, micronurtrients, and social environments: Individual and combined effects on children's development. *Psychological Science in the Public Interest, 6*, 57–121.

Huddleston, J., & Ge, X. (2003). Boys at puberty: Psychosocial implications. In C. Hayward (Ed.), *Gender differences at puberty* (pp. 113–134). New York: Cambridge University Press.

Hudson, J. A., Fivush, R., & Kuebli, J. (1992). Scripts and episodes: The development of event memory. *Applied Cognitive Psychology, 6*, 483–505.

Hudson, J. A., & Mayhew, E. M. Y. (2009). The development of memory for recurring events. In M. L. Courage & N. Cowan (Eds.), *The development of memory in infancy and childhood* (pp. 69–91). Hove, UK: Psychology Press.

Hudson, J. M. (2008). Automatic memory processes in normal ageing and Alzheimer's disease. *Cortex, 44*, 345–349.

Hudziak, J. J., & Rettew, D. C. (2009). Genetics of ADHD. In T. E. Brown (Ed.), *ADHD comorbidties: Handbook for ADHD complications in children and adults* (pp. 23–36). Arlington, VA: American Psychiatric Publishing.

Huebner, C. E., & Payne, K. (2010). Home support for emergent literacy: Follow-up of a community-based implementation of dialogic reading. *Journal of Applied Developmental Psychology, 31*, 195–201.

Huesmann, L. R. (1986). Psychological processes promoting the relation between exposure to media violence and aggressive behavior by the viewer. *Journal of Social Issues, 42*, 125–139.

Huesmann, L. R., Moise-Titus, J., Podolski, C. & Eron, L. D. (2003). Longitudinal relations between children's exposure to TV violence and their aggressive and violent behavior in young adulthood: 1977–1992. *Developmental Psychology, 39,* 201–221.

Huffman, M. L. (2012). Introduction: Gender, race, and management. *Annals of the American Academy of Political and Social Science, 639,* 6–12.

Hughes, C. (2010). Conduct disorder and antisocial behavior in the under-5s. In C. L. Cooper, J. Field, U. Goswami, R. Jenkins, & B. J. Sahakian (Eds.), *Mental capital and well-being* (pp. 821–827). Malden, MA: Wiley-Blackwell.

Hughes, C., & Dunn, J. (1998). Understanding mind and emotion: Longitudinal associations with mental-state talk between young friends. *Developmental Psychology, 34,* 1026–1037.

Hughes, C., & Ensor, R. (2007). Executive function and theory of mind: Predictive relations from ages 2 to 4. *Developmental Psychology, 43,* 1447–1459.

Hughes, C., & Ensor, R. (2010). Do early social cognition and executive function predict individual differences in preschoolers' prosocial and antisocial behavior? In B. W. Sokol, U. Müller, J. I. M. Carpendale, A. R. Young, & G. Iarocci (Eds.), *Social interaction and the development of social understanding and executive functions* (pp. 418–441). New York: Oxford University Press.

Hughes, C., Ensor, R., & Marks, A. (2010). Individual differences in false belief understanding are stable from 3 to 6 years of age and predict children's mental state talk with school friends. *Journal of Experimental Child Psychology, 108,* 96–112.

Hughes, D., Rodriguez, J., Smith, E. P., Johnson, D. J., Stevenson, H. C., & Spicer, P. (2006). Parents' ethnic-racial socialization practices: A review of research and directions for future study. *Developmental Psychology, 42,* 747–770.

Hughes, J. N., Cavell, T. A., & Grossman, P. B. (1997). A positive view of self: Risk or protection for aggressive children? *Development and Psychopathology, 9,* 75–94.

Hughes, J. N., & Kwok, O. (2006). Classroom engagement mediates the effect of teacher–student support on elementary students' peer acceptance. *Journal of School Psychology, 43,* 465–480.

Hughes, J. N., & Kwok, O. (2007). Influence of student–teacher and parent–teacher relationships on lower achieving readers' engagement and achievement in the primary grades. *Journal of Educational Psychology, 99,* 39–51.

Huizenga, H., Crone, E. A., & Jansen, B. (2007). Decision making in healthy children, adolescents and adults explained by the use of increasingly complex proportional reasoning rules. *Developmental Science, 10,* 814–825.

Huizink, A. C., Bartels, M., Rose, R. J., Pulkkinen, L., Eriksson, C. J., & Kaprio, J. (2008). Chernobyl exposure as a stressor during pregnancy and hormone levels in adolescent offspring. *Journal of Epidemiology and Community Health, 62,* e5.

Huizink, A. C., & Mulder, E. J. (2006). Maternal smoking, drinking or cannabis use during pregnancy and neurobehavioral and cognitive functioning in human offspring. *Neuroscience and Biobehavioral Reviews, 30,* 24–41.

Hultsch, D. F., Hertzog, C., Dixon, R. A., & Small, B. J. (1998). *Memory change in the aged.* New York: Cambridge University Press.

Hultsch, D. F., MacDonald, S. W. S., & Dixon, R. A. (2002). Variability in reaction time performance of younger and older adults. *Journal of Gerontology, 57B,* P101–P115.

Human Genome Project. (2008). *How many genes are in the human genome?* Retrieved from www.ornl .gov/sci/techresources/Human_Genome/faq/ genenumber.shtml

Human Rights Campaign. (2008). *Surrogacy laws: State by state.* Retrieved from http://66.151.111.225/ issues/parenting/surrogacy/surrogacy_laws.asp

Humes, L. E., Dubno, J. R., Gordon-Salant, S., Lister, J. J., Cacace, A. T., Cruickshanks, K. J., et al. (2012). Central presbycusis: A review and evaluation of the evidence. *Journal of the American Academy of Audiology, 23,* 635–666.

Humphrey, T. (1978). Function of the nervous system during prenatal life. In U. Stave (Ed.), *Perinatal physiology* (pp. 651–683). New York: Plenum.

Hunnius, S., & Geuze, R. H. (2004a). Developmental changes in visual scanning of dynamic faces and abstract stimuli in infants: A longitudinal study. *Infancy, 6,* 231–255.

Hunnius, S., & Geuze, R. H. (2004b). Gaze shifting in infancy: A longitudinal study using dynamic faces and abstract stimuli. *Infant Behavior and Development, 27,* 397–416.

Hunt, C. E., & Hauck, F. R. (2006). Sudden infant death syndrome. *Canadian Medical Association Journal, 174,* 1861–1869.

Huotilainen, M., Kujala, A., Hotakainen, M., Parkkonen, L., Taulu, S., & Simola, J. (2005). Short-term memory functions of the human fetus recorded with magneto-encephalography. *NeuroReport, 16,* 81–84.

Hursti, U. K. (1999). Factors influencing children's food choice. *Annals of Medicine, 31,* 26–32.

Hurt, H., Betancourt, L. M., Malmud, E. K., Shera, D. M., Giannetta, J. M., Brodsky, N. L., et al. (2009). Children with and without gestational cocaine exposure: A neurocognitive systems analysis. *Neurotoxicology and Teratology, 31,* 334–341.

Hurtig, W. A., & Stewin, L. (2006). The effect of death education and eperience on nursing students' attitude toward death. *Journal of Advanced Nursing, 15,* 29–34.

Huston, A. C., & Alvarez, M. M. (1990). The socialization context of gender role development in early adolescence. In R. Montemayor, G. R. Adams, & T. P. Gullotta (Eds.), *From childhood to adolescence: A transitional period?* (pp. 156–179). Newbury Park, CA: Sage.

Huttenlocher, P. R. (2002). *Neural plasticity: The effects of environment on the development of the cerebral cortex.* Cambridge, MA: Harvard University Press.

Huyck, M. H. (1990). Gender differences in aging. In J. E. Birren & K. W. Schaie (Eds.), *Handbook of the psychology of aging* (3rd ed., pp. 124–134). New York: Academic Press.

Huyck, M. H. (1996). Continuities and discontinuities in gender identity in midlife. In V. L. Bengtson (Ed.), *Adulthood and aging* (pp. 98–121). New York: Springer-Verlag.

Huyck, M. H. (1998). Gender roles and gender identity in midlife. In S. L. Willis & J. D. Reid (Eds.), *Life in the middle* (pp. 209–232). San Diego: Academic Press.

Hyde, J. S., Essex, M. J., Clark, R., & Klein, M. H. (2001). Maternity leave, women's employment, and marital incompatibility. *Journal of Family Psychology, 15,* 476–491.

Hyde, J. S., Mezulis, A. H., & Abramson, L. Y. (2008). The ABCs of depression: Integrating affective, biological, and cognitive models to explain the emergence of the gender difference in depression. *Psychological Review, 115,* 291–313.

Hyman, B. T., Phelps, C. H., Beach, T. G., Bigio, E. H., Cairns, N. J., Carrillo, M. C., et al. (2012). National Institute on Aging–Alzheimer's Association guidelines for the neuropathologic assessment of Alzheimer's disease. *Alzheimer's and Dementia, 8,* 1–13.

Hymel, S., Vaillancourt, T., McDougall, P., & Renshaw, P. D. (2004). Peer acceptance and rejection in childhood. In P. K. Smith & C. H. Hart (Eds.), *Blackwell handbook of childhood social development* (pp. 265–284). Malden, MA: Blackwell.

I

Iacoboni, M. (2009). Imitation, empathy, and mirror neurons. *Annual Review of Psychology, 60,* 653–670.

Ickes, M. J. (2011). Stigmatization of overweight and obese individuals: Implications for mental health promotion. *International Journal of Mental Health Promotion, 13,* 37–45.

Ida, M. (2010). [The concept of death in the revised Organ Transplant Law in Japan.] *Nihon Rinsho [Japanese Journal of Clinical Medicine], 68,* 2223–2228.

Iglowstein, I., Jenni, O. G., Molinari, L., & Largo, R. H. (2003). Sleep duration from infancy to adolescence: Reference values and generational trends. *Pediatrics, 111,* 302–307.

Imai, M., & Haryu, E. (2004). The nature of wordlearning biases and their roles for lexical development: From a cross-linguistic perspective. In D. G. Hall & S. R. Waxman (Eds.), *Weaving a lexicon* (pp. 411–444). Cambridge, MA: MIT Press.

Impett, E. A., Sorsoli, L., Schooler, D., Henson, J. M., & Tolman, D. L. (2008). Girls' relationship authenticity and self-esteem across adolescence. *Developmental Psychology, 44,* 722–733.

Inhelder, B., & Piaget, J. (1958). *The growth of logical thinking from childhood to adolescence: An essay on the construction of formal operational structures.* New York: Basic Books. (Original work published 1955)

Irvine, A. B., Ary, D. V., & Bourgeois, M. S. (2003). An interactive multimedia program to train professional caregivers. *Journal of Applied Gerontology, 22,* 269–288.

Isabella, R. (1993). Origins of attachment: Maternal interactive behavior across the first year. *Child Development, 64,* 605–621.

Isabella, R., & Belsky, J. (1991). Interactional synchrony and the origins of infant–mother attachment: A replication study. *Child Development, 62,* 373–384.

Ishihara, K., Warita, K., Tanida, T., Sugawara, T., Kitagawa, H., & Hoshi, N. (2007). Does paternal exposure to 2, 3, 7, 8-tetrachlorodibenzo-p-dioxin (TCDD) affect the sex ratio of offspring? *Journal of Veterinary Medical Science, 69,* 347–352.

Israel, M., Johnson, C., & Brooks, P. J. (2000). From states to events: The acquisition of English passive participles. *Cognitive Linguistics, 11,* 103–129.

Itti, E., Gaw, G. I. T., Pawlikowska-Haddal, A., Boone, K. B., Mlikotic, A., & Itti, L. (2006). The structural brain correlates of cognitive deficits in adults with Klinefelter's syndrome. *Journal of Clinical Endocrinology and Metabolism, 91,* 1423–1427.

Ivorra, J. L., Sanjuan, J., Jover, M., Carot, J. M., de Frutos, R., & Molto, M. D. (2010). Gene-environment interaction of child temperament. *Journal of Developmental and Behavioral Pediatrics, 31,* 545–554.

Izard, C. E., & Ackerman, B. P. (2000). Motivational, organizational, and regulatory functions of discrete emotions. In M. Lewis & J. M. Haviland-Jones (Eds.), *Handbook of emotions* (2nd ed., pp. 253–264). New York: Guilford.

J

Jaccard, J., Dodge, T., & Dittus, P. (2002). Parent–adolescent communication about sex and birth control: A conceptual framework. In S. S. Feldman & D. A. Rosenthal (Eds.), *Talking sexuality: Parent–adolescent communication* (pp. 9–41). San Francisco: Jossey-Bass.

Jaccard, J., Dodge, T., & Dittus, P. (2003). Maternal discussions about pregnancy and adolescents' attitudes toward pregnancy. *Journal of Adolescent Health, 33,* 84–87.

Jackson, G. R., & Owsley, C. (2000). Scotopic sensitivity during adulthood. *Vision Research, 40,* 2467–2473.

Jackson, J. J., Hill, P. L., Payne, B. R., Roberts, B. W., & Steine-Morrow, E. A. L. (2012). Can an old dog learn (and want to experience) new tricks? Cognitive training increases openness to experience in older adults. *Psychology and Aging, 27*, 286–292.

Jackson, V. A., Sullivan, A. M., Gadmer, N. M., Seltzer, D., Mitchell, A. M., & Lakoma, M. D. (2005). "It was haunting . . . ": Physicians' descriptions of emotionally powerful patient deaths. *Academic Medicine, 80*, 648–656.

Jacobs, J. A., & King, R. B. (2002). Age and college completion: A life-history analysis of women aged 15–44. *Sociology of Education, 75*, 211–230.

Jacobs, J. E., & Klaczynski, P. A. (2002). The development of judgment and decision making during childhood and adolescence. *Current Directions in Psychological Science, 11*, 145–149.

Jacobs, J. E., Lanza, S., Osgood, D. W., Eccles, J. S., & Wigfield, A. (2002). Changes in children's self-competence and values: Gender and domain differences across grades one through twelve. *Child Development, 73*, 509–527.

Jacobs, J. N., & Kelley, M. L. (2006). Predictors of paternal involvement in childcare in dual-earner families with young children. *Fathering, 4*, 23–47.

Jacobson, J. L., & Jacobson, S. W. (2003). Prenatal exposure to polychlorinated biphenyls and attention at school age. *Journal of Pediatrics, 143*, 780–788.

Jacobson, K. C., & Crockett, L. J. (2000). Parental monitoring and adolescent adjustment: An ecological perspective. *Journal of Research on Adolescence, 10*, 65–97.

Jacobson, S. W., Jacobson, J. L., Sokol, R. J., Chiodo, L. M., & Corobana, R. (2004). Maternal age, alcohol abuse history, and quality of parenting as moderators of the effects of prenatal alcohol exposure on 7.5-year intellectual function. *Alcoholism: Clinical and Experimental Research, 28*, 1732–1745.

Jadack, R. A., Hyde, J. S., Moore, C. F., & Keller, M. L. (1995). Moral reasoning about sexually transmitted diseases. *Child Development, 66*, 167–177.

Jaffee, S. R., & Hyde, J. S. (2000). Gender differences in moral orientation: A meta-analysis. *Psychological Bulletin, 126*, 703–706.

James, J., Ellis, B. J., Schlomer, G. L., & Garber, J. (2012). Sex-specific pathways to early puberty, sexual debut, and sexual risk taking: Tests of an integrated evolutionary–developmental model. *Developmental Psychology, 48*, 687–702.

James, J. B., Lewkowicz, C., Libhaber, J., & Lachman, M. (1995). Rethinking the gender identity crossover hypothesis: A test of a new model. *Sex Roles, 32*, 185–207.

James, J. B., & Wink, P. (2007). The Third Age: A rationale for research. In J. B. James & P. Wink (Eds.), *Annual review of gerontology and geriatrics* (Vol. 26, pp. xix–xxxii). New York: Springer.

James, J. B., & Zarrett, N. (2007). Ego integrity in the lives of older women. *Journal of Adult Development, 13*, 61–75.

Jang, Y., Bergman, E., Schonfeld, L., & Molinari, V. (2007). The mediating role of health perceptions in the relation between physical and mental health: A study of older residents in assisted living facilities. *Journal of Aging and Health, 19*, 439–452.

Janosz, M., Le Blanc, M., Boulerice, B., & Tremblay, R. E. (2000). Predicting different types of school dropouts: A typological approach with two longitudinal samples. *Journal of Educational Psychology, 92*, 171–190.

Jansen, A., Theunissen, N., Slechten, K., Nederkoorn, C., Boon, B., Mulkens, S., & Roefs, A. (2003). Overweight children overeat after exposure to food cues. *Eating Behaviors, 4*, 197–209.

Jansen, J., de Weerth, C., & Riksen-Walraven, J. M. (2008). Breastfeeding and the mother–infant relationship. *Developmental Review, 28*, 503–521.

Janssen, S. M., Rubin, D. C., & St. Jacques, P. L. (2011). The temporal distribution of autobiographical memory: Changes in reliving and vividness over

the life span do not explain the reminiscence bump. *Memory and Cognition, 39*, 1–11.

Janssens, J. M. A. M., & Dekovi?, M. (1997). Child rearing, prosocial moral reasoning, and prosocial behaviour. *International Journal of Behavioral Development, 20*, 509–527.

Jarvis, J. F., & van Heerden, H. G. (1967). The acuity of hearing in the Kalahari Bushman: A pilot study. *Journal of Laryngology and Otology, 81*, 63–68.

Jaudes, P. K., & Mackey-Bilaver, L. (2008). Do chronic conditions increase young children's risk of being maltreated? *Child Abuse and Neglect, 32*, 671–681.

Jayakody, R., & Kalil, A. (2002). Social fathering in low-income, African-American families with preschool children. *Journal of Marriage and Family, 64*, 504–516.

Jedrychowski, W., Perera, F. P., Jankowski, J., Mrozek-Budzyn, D., Mroz, E., Flak, E., et al. (2009). Very low prenatal exposure to lead and mental development of children in infancy and early childhood. *Neuroepidemiology, 32*, 270–278.

Jellinger, K. A. (2004). Head injury and dementia. *Current Opinion in Neurology, 17*, 719–723.

Jellinger, K. A. (2008). Morphologic diagnosis of "vascular dementia"—a critical update. *Journal of the Neurological Sciences, 270*, 1–12.

Jenkins, C., Lapelle, N., Zapka, J. G., & Kurent, J. E. (2005). End-of-life care and African Americans: Voices from the community. *Journal of Palliative Medicine, 8*, 585–592.

Jenkins, J. M., Rasbash, J., & O'Connor, T. G. (2003). The role of the shared family context in differential parenting. *Developmental Psychology, 39*, 99–113.

Jenkins, K. R., Pienta, A. M., & Horgas, A. L. (2002). Activity and health-related quality of life in continuing care retirement communities. *Research on Aging, 24*, 124–149.

Jenni, O. G., Achermann, P., & Carskadon, M. A. (2005). Homeostatic sleep regulation in adolescents. *Sleep, 28*, 1446–1454.

Jennings, B. J., Ozanne, S. E., Dorling, M. W., & Hales, C. N. (1999). Early growth determines longevity in male rats and may be related to telomere shortening in the kidney. *FEBS Letters, 448*, 4–8.

Jensen, A. R. (1969). How much can we boost IQ and scholastic achievement? *Harvard Educational Review, 39*, 1–123.

Jensen, A. R. (1998). *The g factor: The science of mental ability.* New York: Praeger.

Jensen, A. R. (2001). Spearman's hypothesis. In J. M. Collis & S. Messick (Eds.), *Intelligence and personality: Bridging the gap in theory and measurement* (pp. 3–24). Mahwah, NJ: Erlbaum.

Jeon, Y.-H., Brodaty, H., & Chesterson, J. (2005). Respite care for caregivers and people with severe mental illness: Literature review. *Journal of Advanced Nursing, 49*, 297–306.

Jeong, S.-H., & Fishbein, M. (2007). Predictors of multitasking with media: Media factors and audience factors. *Media Psychology, 10*, 364–384.

Jerome, E. M., Hamre, B. K., & Pianta, R. C. (2009). Teacher–child relationships from kindergarten to sixth grade: Early childhood predictors of teacher-perceived conflict and closeness. *Social Development, 18*, 915–945.

Jeynes, W. (2012). A meta-analysis of the efficacy of different types of parental involvement programs for urban students. *Urban Education, 47*, 706–742.

Jeynes, W. H. (2007). The impact of parental remarriage on children: A meta-analysis. *Marriage and Family Review, 40*, 75–102.

Jiao, S., Ji, G., & Jing, Q. (1996). Cognitive development of Chinese urban only children and children with siblings. *Child Development, 67*, 387–395.

Jipson, J. L., & Gelman, S. A. (2007). Robots and rodents: Children's inferences about living and nonliving kinds. *Child Development, 78*, 1675–1688.

Joh, A. S., & Adolph, K. E. (2006). Learning from falling. *Child Development, 77*, 89–102.

Johansson, A. K., & Grimby, A. (2013). Anticipatory grief among close relatives of patients in hospice and palliative wards. *American Journal of Hospice and Palliative Medicine, 29*, 134–138.

Johnson, C. L., & Troll, L. E. (1994). Constraints and facilitators to friendships in late life. *Gerontologist, 34*, 79–87.

Johnson, E. K., & Seidl, A. (2008). Clause segmentation by 6-month-old infants: A crosslinguistic perspective. *Infancy, 13*, 440–455.

Johnson, J. G., Cohen, P., Smailes, E. M., Kasen, S., & Brook, J. S. (2002). Television viewing and aggressive behavior during adolescence and adulthood. *Science, 295*, 2468–2471.

Johnson, K. S., Elbert-Avila, K. I., & Tulsky, J. A. (2005). The influence of spiritual beliefs and practices on the treatment preferences of African Americans: A review of the literature. *Journal of the American Geriatrics Society, 53*, 711–719.

Johnson, K. S., Juchibhtla, M., Tanis, D., & Tulsky, J. A. (2008). Racial differences in hospice revocation to pursue aggressive care. *Archives of Internal Medicine, 168*, 218–224.

Johnson, M. D., Cohan, C. L., Davilla, J., Lawrence, E., Rogge, R. D., Karney, B. R., Sullivan, K. T., & Bradbury, T. N. (2005). Problem-solving skills and affective expressions as predictors of change in marital satisfaction. *Journal of Consulting and Clinical Psychology, 73*, 15–27.

Johnson, M. H. (1999). Ontogenetic constraints on neural and behavioral plasticity: Evidence from imprinting and face processing. *Canadian Journal of Experimental Psychology, 55*, 77–90.

Johnson, M. H. (2011). Developmental neuroscience, psychophysiology, and genetics. In M H. Bornstein & M. E. Lamb (Eds.), *Developmental science: An advanced textbook* (6th ed., pp. 187–222). Mahwah, NJ: Erlbaum.

Johnson, M. H., & Mareschal, D. (2001). Cognitive and perceptual development during infancy. *Current Opinion in Neurobiology, 11*, 213–218.

Johnson, R. W., & Mommaerts, C. (2010). *Will health care costs bankrupt aging boomers?* Washington, DC: Urban Institute.

Johnson, S. P., Slemmer, J. A., & Amso, D. (2004). Where infants look determines how they see: Eye movements and object perception performance in 3-month-olds. *Infancy, 6*, 185–201.

Johnston, L. D., O'Malley, P. M., Bachman, J. G., & Schulenberg, J. E. (2011). *Monitoring the future: National results on adolescent drug use. Overview of key findings, 2010.* Bethesda, MD: National Institute on Drug Abuse.

Johnston, L. D., O'Malley, P. M., Bachman, J. G., & Schulenberg, J. E. (2012). *Monitoring the Future: National results on adolescent drug use: Overview of key findings, 2011.* Ann Arbor: Institute for Social Research, University of Michigan.

Jokhi, R. P., & Whitby, E. H. (2011). Magnetic resonance imaging of the fetus. *Developmental Medicine and Child Neurology, 53*, 18–28.

Jome, L. M., Surething, N. A., & Taylor, K. K. (2005). Relationally oriented masculinity, gender nontraditional interests, and occupational traditionality of employed men. *Journal of Career Development, 32*, 183–197.

Jones, F. (2003). *Religious commitment in Canada, 1997 and 2000. Religious Commitment Monograph No. 3.* Ottawa: Christian Commitment Research Institute.

Jones, J., Lopez, A., & Wilson, M. (2003). Congenital toxoplasmosis. *American Family Physician, 67*, 2131–2137.

Jones, J. M. (2012). *Expected retirement age in U.S.: Up to 67.* Princeton, NJ: Gallup. Retrieved from www.gallup.com/poll/154178/expected-retirement-age.aspx

Jones, K. M., Whitbourne, S. K., & Skultety, K. M. (2006). Identity processes and the transition to midlife among the baby boomers. In S. K. Whitbourne & S. L. Willis (Eds.), *The baby boomers grow up: Contemporary perspectives on midlife* (pp. 149–164). Mahwah, NJ: Erlbaum.

Jones, M. C., & Mussen, P. H. (1958). Self-conceptions, motivations, and interpersonal attitudes of early- and late-maturing girls. *Child Development, 29,* 491–501.

Jones, S. (2009). The development of imitation in infancy. *Philosophical Transactions of the Royal Society B, 364,* 2325–2335.

Jopp, D., & Rott, C. (2006). Adaptation in very old age: Exploring the role of resources, beliefs, and attitudes for centenarians' happiness. *Psychology and Aging, 21,* 266–280.

Jordan, B. (1993). *Birth in four cultures.* Prospect Heights, IL: Waveland.

Jordon, J., & Neimeyer, R. (2003). Does grief counseling work? *Death Studies, 27,* 765–786.

Jose, A., O'Leary, D., & Moyer, A. (2010). Does premarital cohabitation predict subsequent marital stability and martial quality? A meta-analysis. *Journal of Marriage and Family, 72,* 105–116.

Joseph, R. M., & Tager-Flusberg, H. (2004). The relationship of theory of mind and executive functions to symptom type and severity in children with autism. *Development and Psychopathology, 16,* 137–155.

Juby, H., Billette, J.-M., Laplante, B., & Le Bourdais, C. (2007). Nonresident fathers and children: Parents' new unions and frequency of contact. *Journal of Family Issues, 28,* 1220–1245.

Julkunen, J., & Ahlström, R. (2006). Hostility, anger, and sense of coherence as predictors of health-related quality of life. Results of an ASCOT substudy. *Journal of Psychosomatic Research, 61,* 33–39.

Jürgensen, M., Hiort, O., Holterhus, P.-M., & Thyen, U. (2007). Gender role behavior in children with XY karyotype and disorders of sex development. *Hormones and Behavior, 51,* 443–453.

Jusczyk, P. W. (2002). Some critical developments in acquiring native language sound organization. *Annals of Otology, Rhinology and Laryngology, 189,* 11–15.

Jusczyk, P. W., & Hohne, E. A. (1997). Infants' memory for spoken words. *Science, 277,* 1984–1986.

Jutras-Aswad, D., DiNieri, J. A., Harkany, T., & Hurd, Y. L. (2009). Neurobiological consequences of maternal cannabis on human fetal development and its neuropsychiatric outcome. *European Archives of Psychiatry and Clinical Neuroscience, 259,* 395–412.

K

Kaczmarczyk, M. M., Miller, M. J., & Freund, G. G. (2012). The health benefits of dietary fiber: Beyond the usual suspects of type 2 diabetes mellitus, cardiovascular disease and colon cancer. *Metabolism: Clinical and Experimental, 61,* 1058–1066.

Kagan, J. (2003). Behavioral inhibition as a temperamental category. In R. J. Davidson, K. R. Scherer, & H. H. Goldsmith (Eds.), *Handbook of affective science* (pp. 320–331). New York: Oxford University Press.

Kagan, J. (2008a). Behavioral inhibition as a risk factor for psychopathology. In T. P. Beauchaine & S. P. Hinshaw (Eds.), *Child and adolescent psychopathology* (pp. 157–179). Hoboken, NJ: Wiley.

Kagan, J. (2008b). In defense of qualitative changes in development. *Child Development, 79,* 1606–1624.

Kagan, J. (2010). Emotions and temperament. In M. H. Bornstein (Ed.), *Handbook of cultural developmental science* (pp. 175–194). New York: Psychology Press.

Kagan, J., Arcus, D., Snidman, N., Feng, W. Y. Hendler, J., & Greene, S. (1994). Reactivity in infants: A cross-national comparison. *Developmental Psychology, 30,* 342–345.

Kagan, J., & Fox, N. A. (2006). Biology, culture, and temperamental biases. In N. Eisenberg (Ed.), *Handbook of child psychology: Vol. 3. Social, emotional, and personality development* (6th ed., pp. 167–225). Hoboken, NJ: Wiley.

Kagan, J., & Saudino, K. J. (2001). Behavioral inhibition and related temperaments. In R. N. Emde & J. K. Hewitt (Eds.), *Infancy to early childhood: Genetic and environmental influences on developmental change* (pp. 111–119). New York: Oxford University Press.

Kagan, J., Snidman, N., Kahn, V., & Towsley, S. (2007). The preservation of two infant temperaments into adolescence. *Monographs of the Society for Research in Child Development, 72*(2, Serial No. 287).

Kagan, J., Snidman, N., Zentner, M., & Peterson, E. (1999). Infant temperament and anxious symptoms in school-age children. *Development and Psychopathology, 11,* 209–224.

Kahana, E., King, C., Kahana, B., Menne, H., Webster, N. J., & Dan, A. (2005). Successful aging in the face of chronic disease. In M. L. Wykle, P. J. Whitehouse, & D. L. Morris (Eds.), *Successful aging through the life span* (pp. 101–126). New York: Springer.

Kahn, R. S., Khoury, J., Nichols, W. C., & Lanphear, B. M. (2003). Role of dopamine transporter genotype and maternal prenatal smoking in childhood hyperactive-impulsive, inattentive, and oppositional behaviors. *Journal of Pediatrics, 143,* 104–110.

Kail, R. (1993). The role of a global mechanism in developmental change in speed of processing. In M. L. Howe & R. Pasnak (Eds.), *Emerging themes in cognitive development: Vol. 1. Foundations.* New York: Springer-Verlag.

Kail, R. (1997). Processing time, imagery, and spatial memory. *Journal of Experimental Child Psychology, 64,* 67–78.

Kail, R. V. (2003). Information processing and memory. In M. H. Bornstein, L. Davidson, C. L. M. Keyes, K. A. Moore, and the Center for Child Well-Being (Eds.), *Well-being: Positive development across the life course* (pp. 269–280). Mahwah, NJ: Erlbaum.

Kaisa, A., Stattin, H., & Nurmi, J. (2000). Parenting styles and adolescents' achievement strategies. *Journal of Adolescence, 23,* 205–222.

Kakihara, F., Tilton-Weaver, L., Kerr, M., & Stattin, H. (2010). The relationship of parental control to youth adjustment: Do youths' feelings about their parents play a role? *Journal of Youth and Adolescence, 39,* 1442–1456.

Kalil, A., Levine, J. A., & Ziol-Guest, K. M. (2005). Following in their parents' footsteps: How characteristics of parental work predict adolescents' interest in parents' working jobs. In B. Schneider & L. J. Waite (Eds.), *Being together, working apart: Dual-career families and the work–life balance* (pp. 422–442). New York: Cambridge University Press.

Kalisch, T., Kattenstroth, J.-C., Kowalewski, R., Tegenthoff, M., & Dinse, H. R. (2012). *PLoS ONE, 7*(1), e30420.

Kalpouzos, G., & Nyberg, L. (2012). *Multimodal neuroimaging in normal aging: Structure–function interactions* (pp. 273–304). New York: Psychology Press.

Kaminski, J. W., Puddy, R. W., Hall, D. M., Cashman, S. Y., Crosby, A. E., & Ortega, L. G. (2010). The relative influence of different domains of social connectedness on self-directed violence in adolescence. *Journal of Youth and Adolescence, 39,* 460–473.

Kamo, Y. (1998). Asian grandparents. In M. E. Szinovacz (Ed.), *Handbook on grandparenthood* (pp. 97–112). Westport, CT: Greenwood Press.

Kane, P., & Garber, J. (2004). The relations among depression in fathers, children's psychopathology, and father–child conflict: A meta-analysis. *Clinical Psychology Review, 24,* 339–360.

Kane, R. A., Lum, T. Y., Cutler, L. J., Degenholtz, H. B., & Yu, T.-C. (2007). Resident outcomes in small-house nursing homes: A longitudinal evaluation of the initial Green House program. *Journal of the American Geriatrics Society, 55,* 836–839.

Kang, N. H., & Hong, M. (2008). Achieving excellence in teacher workforce and equity in learning opportunities in South Korea. *Educational Researcher, 37,* 200–207.

Kaplow, J. B., & Widom, C. S. (2007). Age of onset of child maltreatment predicts long-term mental health outcomes. *Journal of Abnormal Psychology, 116,* 176–187.

Kaplowitz, P. (2006). Pubertal development in girls: Secular trends. *Current Opinion in Obstetrics and Gynecology, 18,* 487–491.

Kaplowitz, P. B. (2007). Link between body fat and the timing of puberty. *Pediatrics, 121,* S208–S217.

Karafantis, D. M., & Levy, S. R. (2004). The role of children's lay theories about the malleability of human attributes in beliefs about and volunteering for disadvantaged groups. *Child Development, 75,* 236–250.

Karasawa, M., Curhan, K. B., Markus, H. R., Kitayama, S. S., Love, G. D., Radler, B. T., et al. (2011). Cultural perspectives on aging and well-being: A comparison of Japan and the U.S. *International Journal of Aging and Human Development, 73,* 73–98.

Karasik, L. B., Tamis-LeMonda, C. S., & Adolph, K. E. (2011). Transition from crawling to walking affects infants' social actions with objects. *Child Development, 82,* 1199–1209.

Karasik, L. B., Tamis-LeMonda, C. S., Adolph, K. E., & Dimitroupoulou, K. A. (2008). How mothers encourage and discourage infants' motor actions. *Infancy, 13,* 366–392.

Karel, M. J., Gatz, M., & Smyer, M. A. (2012). Aging and mental health in the decade ahead: What psychologists need to know. *American Psychologist, 67,* 184–198.

Karevold, E., Ystrom, E., Coplan, R. J., Sanson, A. V., & Mathiesen, K. S. (2012). A prospective longitudinal study of shyness from infancy to adolescence: Stability, age-related changes, and prediction of socio-emotional functioning. *Journal of Abnormal Child Psychology, 40,* 1167–1177.

Karger, H. J., & Stoesz, D. (2010). *American social welfare policy* (6th ed.). Upper Saddle River, NJ: Pearson Education.

Karlsson, C., & Berggren, I. (2011). Dignified end-of-life care in the patients' own homes. *Nursing Ethics, 18,* 374–385.

Kassel, J. D., Weinstein, S., Skitch, S. A., Veilleux, J., & Mermelstein, R. (2005). The development of substance abuse in adolescence: Correlates, causes, and consequences. In J. D. Kassel, S. Weinstein, S. A. Skitch, J. Veilleux, & R. Mermelstein (Eds.), *Development of psychopathology: A vulnerability-stress perspective* (pp. 355–384). Thousand Oaks, CA: Sage.

Kastenbaum, R. (2008). Grieving in contemporary society. In M. S. Stroebe, R. O. Hansson, H. Schut, & W. Stroebe (Eds.), *Handbook of bereavement research and practice* (pp. 67–85). Washington, DC: American Psychological Association.

Kastenbaum, R. J. (2012). *Death, society, and human experience* (11th ed.). Upper Saddle River, NJ: Pearson.

Kato, I., Franco, P., Groswasser, J., Scaillet, S., Kelmanson, I., Togari, H., & Kahn, A. (2003). Incomplete arousal processes in infants who were victims of sudden death. *American Journal of Respiratory and Critical Care, 168,* 1298–1303.

Katzman, D. K. (2005). Medical complications in adolescents with anorexia nervosa: A review of the literature. *International Journal of Eating Disorders, 37,* S52–S59.

Katz-Wise, S. L., Priess, H. A., & Hyde, J. S. (2010). Gender-role attitudes and behavior across the transition to parenthood. *Developmental Psychology, 46*, 18–28.

Kaufman, A. S. (2001). WAIS-III IQs, Horn's theory, and generational changes from young adulthood to old age. *Intelligence, 29*, 131–167.

Kaufman, A. S., & Horn, J. L. (1996). Age changes on tests of fluid and crystallized intelligence in females and males on the Kaufman Adolescent and Adult Intelligence Test (KAIT) at ages 17 to 94 years. *Archives of Clinical Neuropsychology, 11*, 97–121.

Kaufman, J. C., & Sternberg, R. J. (2007, July/August). Resource review: Creativity. *Change, 39*, 55–58.

Kavanaugh, R. D. (2006). Pretend play. In B. Spodek & O. N. Saracho (Eds.), *Handbook of research on the education of young children* (2nd ed., pp. 269–278). Mahwah, NJ: Erlbaum.

Kavšek, M. (2004). Predicting later IQ from infant visual habituation and dishabituation: A metaanalysis. *Journal of Applied Developmental Psychology, 25*, 369–393.

Kavšek, M., Yonas, A., & Granrud, C. E. (2012). Infants' sensitivity to pictorial depth cues: A review and meta-analysis. *Infant Behavior and Development, 35*, 109–128.

Kaya, Y., & Cook, K. J. (2010). A cross-national analysis of physical intimate partner violence against women. *International Journal of Comparative Sociology, 51*, 423–444.

Kaye, W. (2008). Neurobiology of anorexia and bulimia nervosa. *Physiology and Behavior, 94*, 121–135.

Keegan, L., & Drick, C. A. (2011). *End of life: Nursing solutions for death with dignity.* New York: Springer.

Keil, F. C. (1986). Conceptual domains and the acquisition of metaphor. *Cognitive Development, 1*, 73–96.

Keil, F. C., & Lockhart, K. L. (1999). Explanatory understanding in conceptual development. In E. K. Scholnick, K. Nelson, S. A. Gelman & P. H. Miller (Eds.), *Conceptual development: Piaget's legacy* (pp. 103–130). Mahwah, NJ: Erlbaum.

Keith, P. M., & Schafer, R. B. (1991). *Relationships and well-being over the life stages.* New York: Praeger.

Keith, T. Z., Keith, P. B., Quirk, K. J., Sperduto, J., Santillo, S., & Killings, S. (1998). Longitudinal effects of parent involvement on high school grades: Similarities and differences across gender and ethnic groups. *Journal of School Psychology, 36*, 335–363.

Keller, H., Borke, Y. J., Kärtner, J., Jensen, H., & Papaligoura, Z. (2004). Developmental consequences of early parenting experiences: Self-recognition and self-regulation in three cultural communities. *Child Development, 75*, 1745–1760.

Keller, H., Kärtner, J., Borke, J., Yovsi, R., & Kleis, A. (2005). Parenting styles and the development of the categorical self: A longitudinal study on mirror self-recognition in Cameroonian Nso and German families. *International Journal of Behavioral Development, 29*, 496–504.

Keller, P. A., & Lusardi, A. (2012). Employee retirement savings: What we know and are discovering for helping people prepare for life after work. In G. D. Mick, S. Pettigrew, C. Pechmann, & J. L. Ozanne (Eds.), *Transformative consumer research for personal and collective well-being* (pp. 445–464). New York: Routledge.

Kelley, S. A., Brownell, C. A., & Campbell, S. B. (2000). Mastery motivation and self-evaluative affect in toddlers: Longitudinal relations with maternal behavior. *Child Development, 71*, 1061–1071.

Kellman, P. J., & Arterberry, M. E. (2006). Infant visual perception. In D. Kuhn & R. Siegler (Eds.), *Handbook of child psychology: Vol. 2. Cognition, perception, and language* (6th ed., pp. 109–160). Hoboken, NJ: Wiley.

Kelly, D. J., Liu, S., Ge, L., Quinn, P. C., Slater, A. M., Lee, K., Liu, Q., & Pascalis, O. (2007). Cross-race preferences for same-race faces extend beyond the African versus Caucasian contrast in 3-month-old infants. *Infancy, 11*, 87–95.

Kelly, D. J., Quinn, P. C., Slater, A. M., Lee, K., Ge, L., & Pascalis, O. (2009). Development of the other-race effect during infancy: Evidence toward universality? *Journal of Experimental Child Psychology, 104*, 105–114.

Kelly, N., & Norwich, B. (2004). Pupils' perceptions of self and of labels: Moderate learning difficulties in mainstream and special schools. *British Journal of Educational Psychology, 74*, 411–435.

Kemkes-Grottenhaler, A. (2003). Postponing or rejecting parenthood? Results of a survey among female academic professionals. *Journal of Biosocial Science, 35*, 213–226.

Kempen, G., Ranchor, A. V., van Sonderen, E., van Jaarsveld, C. H. M., & Sanderman, R. (2006). Risk and protective factors of different functional trajectories in older persons: Are these the same? *Journal of Gerontology, 61B*, P95–P101.

Kemper, S. (2012). The interaction of linguistic constraints, working memory, and aging on language production and comprehension. In M. Naveh-Benjamin & N. Ohta (Eds.), *Memory and aging: Current issues and future directions* (pp. 31–47). New York: Psychology Press.

Kendig, H., Dykstra, P. A., van Gaalen, R. I., & Melkas, T. (2007). Health of aging parents and childless individuals. *Journal of Family Issues, 28*, 1457–1486.

Kendler, K. S., Thornton, L. M., Gilman, S. E., & Kessler, R. C. (2000). Sexual orientation in a U.S. national sample of twin and non-twin sibling pairs. *American Journal of Psychiatry, 157*, 1843–1846.

Kendrick, D., Barlow, J., Hampshire, A., Stewart-Brown, S., & Polnay, L. (2008). Parenting interventions and the prevention of unintentional injuries in childhood: Systematic review and meta-analysis. *Child: Care, Health and Development, 34*, 682–695.

Kennedy, G. E., & Kennedy, C. E. (1993). Grandparents: A special resource for children in stepfamilies. *Journal of Divorce and Remarriage, 19*, 45–68.

Kenney, G. M., Lynch, V., Cook, A., & Phong, S. (2010). Who and where are the children yet to enroll in Medicaid and the Children's Health Insurance Program? *Health Affairs, 29*, 1920–1929.

Kerckhoff, A. C. (2002). The transition from school to work. In J. T. Mortimer & R. Larson (Eds.), *The changing adolescent experience* (pp. 52–87). New York: Cambridge University Press.

Keren, M., Feldman, R., Namdari-Weinbaum, I., Spitzer, S., & Tyano, S. (2005). Relations between parents' interactive style in dyadic and triadic play and toddlers' symbolic capacity. *American Journal of Orthopsychiatry, 75*, 599–607.

Kerestes, M., & Youniss, J. E. (2003). Rediscovering the importance of religion in adolescent development. In R. M. Lerner, F. Jacobs, & D. Wertlieb (Eds.), *Handbook of applied developmental science* (Vol. 1, pp. 165–184). Thousand Oaks, CA: Sage.

Kerestes, M., Youniss, J., & Metz, E. (2004). Longitudinal patterns of religious perspective and civic integration. *Applied Developmental Science, 8*, 39–46.

Kernis, M. H. (2002). Self-esteem as a multifaceted construct. In T. M. Brinthaupt & R. P. Lipka (Eds.), *Understanding early adolescent self and identity* (pp. 57–88). Albany: State University of New York Press.

Kernohan, W. G., Hasson, F., Hutchison, P., & Cochrane, B. (2006). Patient satisfaction with hospice day care. *Supportive Care in Cancer, 14*, 462–468.

Kerr, D. C. R., Lopez, N. L., Olson, S. L., & Sameroff, A. J. (2004). Parental discipline and externalizing behavior problems in early childhood: The roles of moral regulation and child gender. *Journal of Abnormal Child Psychology, 32*, 369–383.

Kesler, S. R. (2007). Turner syndrome. *Child and Adolescent Psychiatric Clinics of North America, 16*, 709–722.

Kettl, P. (1998). Alaska Native suicide: Lessons for elder suicide. *International Psychogeriatrics, 10*, 205–211.

Key, J. D., Gebregziabher, M. G., Marsh, L. D., & O'Rourke, K. M. (2008). Effectiveness of an intensive, school-based intervention for teen mothers. *Journal of Adolescent Health, 42*, 394–400.

Keyes, C. L. M., Shmotkin, D., & Ryff, C. D. (2002). Optimizing well-being: The empirical encounter of two traditions. *Journal of Personality and Social Psychology, 82*, 1007–1022.

Keyes, C. L. M., & Westerhof, G. J. (2012). Chronological and subjective age differences in flourishing mental health and major depressive episode. *Aging and Mental Health, 16*, 67–74.

Khashan, A. S., Baker, P. N., & Kenny, L. C. (2010). Preterm birth and reduced birthweight in first and second teenage pregnancies: A register-based cohort study. *BMC Pregnancy and Childbirth, 10*, 36.

Khavkin, J., & Ellis, D. A. (2011). Aging skin: Histology, physiology, and pathology. *Facial Plastic Surgery Clinics of North America, 19*, 229–234.

Kidd, A. R., III, & Bao, J. (2012). Recent advances in the study of age-related hearing loss: A mini-review. *Gerontology, 58*, 490–496.

Kieffer, M. J. (2008). Catching up or falling behind? Initial English proficiency, concentrated poverty and the reading growth of language minority learners in the United States. *Journal of Educational Psychology, 100*, 851–868.

Killen, M., Crystal, D., & Watanabe, H. (2002). The individual and the group: Japanese and American children's evaluations of peer exclusion, tolerance of difference, and prescriptions for conformity. *Child Development, 73*, 1788–1802.

Killen, M., Henning, A., Kelly, M. C., Crystal, D., & Ruck, M. (2007). Evaluations of interracial peer encounters by majority and minority U.S. children and adolescents. *International Journal of Behavioral Development, 31*, 491–500.

Killen, M., Kelly, M. C., Richardson, C., Crystal, D., & Ruck, M. (2010). European American children's and adolescents' evaluations of interracial exclusion. *Group Processes and Intergroup Relations, 13*, 283–300.

Killen, M., Lee-Kim, J., McGlothlin, H., & Stangor, C. (2002). How children and adolescents evaluate gender and racial exclusion. *Monographs of the Society for Research in Child Development, 67*(4, Serial No. 271).

Killen, M., Margie, N. G., & Sinno, S. (2006). Morality in the context of intergroup relationships. In M. Killen & J. G. Smetana (Eds.), *Handbook of moral development* (pp. 155–183). Mahwah, NJ: Erlbaum.

Killen, M., & Nucci, L. P. (1995). Morality, autonomy, and social conflict. In M. Killen & D. Hart (Eds.), *Morality in everyday life: Developmental perspectives* (pp. 52–86). Cambridge, UK: Cambridge University Press.

Killoren, S. E., Thayer, S. M., & Updegraff, K. A. (2008). Conflict resolution between Mexican origin adolescent siblings. *Journal of Marriage and Family, 70*, 1200–1212.

Kilpatrick, S. W., & Sanders, D. M. (1978). Body image stereotypes: A developmental comparison. *Journal of Genetic Psychology, 132*, 87–95.

Kim, J. E., & Moen, P. (2002a). Is retirement good or bad for subjective well-being? *Current Directions in Psychological Science, 10*, 83–86.

Kim, J. E., & Moen, P. (2002b). Moving into retirement: Preparation and transitions in late midlife. In M. E. Lachman (Ed.), *Handbook of midlife development* (pp. 487–527). New York: Wiley.

Kim, J. M. (1998). Korean children's concepts of adult and peer authority and moral reasoning. *Developmental Psychology, 34*, 947–955.

Kim, J. M., & Turiel, E. (1996). Korean children's concepts of adult and peer authority. *Social Development, 5*, 310–329.

Kim, J.-Y., McHale, S. M., Crouter, A. C., & Osgood, D. W. (2007). Longitudinal linkages between sibling relationships and adjustment from middle childhood through adolescence. *Developmental Psychology, 43*, 960–973.

Kim, J.-Y., McHale, S. M., Osgood, D. W., & Crouter, A. C. (2006). Longitudinal course and family correlates of sibling relationships from childhood through adolescence. *Child Development, 77*, 1746–1761.

Kim, M., McGregor, K. K., & Thompson, C. K. (2000). Early lexical development in English- and Korean-speaking children: Language-general and language-specific patterns. *Journal of Child Language, 27*, 225–254.

Kim, S., & Hasher, L. (2005). The attraction effect in decision making: Superior performance by older adults. *Quarterly Journal of Experimental Psychology, 58A*, 120–133.

Kimbro, R. T. (2006). On-the-job moms: Work and breastfeeding initiation and duration for a sample of low-income women. *Maternal and Child Health Journal, 10*, 19–26.

King, A. C. (2001). Interventions to promote physical activity by older adults. *Journal of Gerontology, 56A*, 36A–46A.

King, A. C., & Bjorklund, D. F. (2010). Evolutionary developmental psychology. *Psicothema, 22*, 22–27.

King, A. C., Kiernan, M., Oman, R. F., Kraemer, H., Hull, M., & Ahn, D. (1997). Can we identify who will adhere to long-term physical activity? Signal detection methodology as a potential aid to clinical decision making. *Health Psychology, 16*, 380–389.

King, L. A., & Hicks, J. A. (2007). Whatever happened to "What might have been"? *American Psychologist, 62*, 625–636.

King, P. E., & Furrow, J. L. (2004). Religion as a resource for positive youth development: Religion, social capital, and moral outcomes. *Developmental Psychology, 40*, 703–713.

King, P. M., & Kitchener, K. S. (1994). *Developing reflective judgment: Understanding and promoting intellectual growth and critical thinking in adolescents and adults.* San Francisco: Jossey-Bass.

King, P. M., & Kitchener, K. S. (2002). The reflective judgment model: Twenty years of research on epistemic cognition. In B. K. Hofer & P. R. Pintrich (Eds.), *Personal epistemology: The psychological beliefs about knowledge and knowing* (pp. 37–61). Mahwah, NJ: Erlbaum.

King, V. (2007). When children have two mothers: Relationships with nonresident mothers, stepmothers, and fathers. *Journal of Marriage and Family, 69*, 1178–1193.

King, V. (2009). Stepfamily formation: Implications for adolescent ties to mothers, nonresident fathers, and stepfathers. *Journal of Marriage and Family, 71*, 954–968.

Kingsberg, S. A. (2002). The impact of aging on sexual function in women and their partners. *Archives of Sexual Behavior, 31*, 431–437.

Kinney, D. (1999). From "headbangers" to "hippies": Delineating adolescents' active attempts to form an alternative peer culture. In J. A. McLellan & M. J. V. Pugh (Eds.), *The role of peer groups in adolescent social identity: Exploring the importance of stability and change* (pp. 21–35). San Francisco: Jossey-Bass.

Kinney, H. C. (2009). Brainstem mechanisms underlying the sudden infant death syndrome: Evidence from human pathologic studies. *Developmental Psychobiology, 51*, 223–233.

Kinnunen, M.-L., Pietilainen, K., & Rissanen, A. (2006). Body size and overweight from birth to adulthood. In L. Pulkkinen & J. Kaprio (Eds.), *Socioemotional development and health from adolescence to adulthood* (pp. 95–107). New York: Cambridge University Press.

Kinsella, M. T., & Monk, C. (2009). Impact of maternal stress, depression and anxiety on fetal neurobehavioral development. *Clinical Obstetrics and Gynecology, 52*, 425–440.

Kinser, K., & Deitchman, J. (2007). Tenacious persisters: Returning adult students in higher education. *Journal of College Student Retention, 9*, 75–94.

Kirby, D. (2002a). Antecedents of adolescent initiation of sex, contraceptive use, and pregnancy. *American Journal of Health Behavior, 26*, 473–485.

Kirby, D. (2002b). Effective approaches to reducing adolescent unprotected sex, pregnancy, and childbearing. *Journal of Sex Research, 39*, 51–57.

Kirby, D., & Laris, B. A. (2009). Effective curriculumbased sex and STD/HIV education programs for adolescents. *Child Development Perspectives, 3*, 21–29.

Kirchner, G. (2000). *Children's games from around the world.* Boston: Allyn and Bacon.

Kiriakidis, S. P., & Kavoura, A. (2010). Cyberbullying: A review of the literature on harassment through the Internet and other electronic means. *Family and Community Health, 33*, 82–93.

Kirk, K. M., Bailey, J. M., Dunne, M. P., & Martin, N. G. (2000). Measurement models for sexual orientation in a community twin sample. *Behavior Genetics, 30*, 345–356.

Kirkham, N. Z., Cruess, L., & Diamond, A. (2003). Helping children apply their knowledge to their behavior on a dimension-switching task. *Developmental Science, 6*, 449–476.

Kirkham, N. Z., Slemmer, J. A., & Johnson, S. P. (2002). Visual statistical learning in infancy: Evidence for a domain general learning mechanism. *Cognition, 83*, B35–B42.

Kirkwood, T. (2010, November). Why women live longer. *Scientific American, 303*, 34–35.

Kirshenbaum, A. P., Olsen, D. M., & Bickel, W. K. (2009). A quantitative review of the ubiquitous relapse curve. *Journal of Substance Abuse Treatment, 36*, 8–17.

Kisilevsky, B. S., Hains, S. M. J., Brown, C. A., Lee, C. T., Cowperthwaite, B., & Stutzman, S. S. (2009). Fetal sensitivity to properties of maternal speech and language. *Infant Behavior and Development, 32*, 59–71.

Kisilevsky, B. S., Hains, S. M. J., Lee, K., Xie, X., Huang, H., Ye, H. H., Zhang, K., & Wang, Z. (2003). Effects of experience on fetal voice recognition. *Psychological Science, 14*, 220–224.

Kisilevsky, B. S., & Low, J. A. (1998). Human fetal behvior: 100 years of study. *Developmental Review, 18*, 1–29.

Kite, M. E., Stockdale, G. D., Whitley, B. E., Jr., & Johnson, B. T. (2005). Attitudes toward younger and older adults: An updated meta-analytic review. *Journal of Social Issues, 61*, 241–266.

Kito, M. (2005). Self-disclosure in romantic relationships and friendships among American and Japanese college students. *Journal of Social Psychology, 145*, 127–145.

Kitzman, H. J., Olds, D. L., Cole, R. E., Hanks, C. A., Anson, E. A., Arcoleo, K. J., et al. (2010). Enduring effects of prenatal and infancy home visiting by nurses on children: Follow-up of a randomized trial among children at age 12 years. *Archives of Pediatric and Adolescent Medicine, 164*, 412–418.

Kitzmann, K. M., Cohen, R., & Lockwood, R. L. (2002). Are only children missing out? Comparison of the peer-related social competence of only children and siblings. *Journal of Social and Personal Relationships, 19*, 299–316.

Kiuru, N., Aunola, K., Vuori, J., & Nurmi, J.-E. (2009). The role of peer groups in adolescents' educational expectation and adjustment. *Journal of Youth and Adolescence, 36*, 995–1009.

Kivipelto, M., Rovio, S., Ngandu, T., Karenhold, I., Eskelinen, M., & Winblad, B. (2008). Apolipoprotein E epsilon4 magnifies lifestyle risks for dementia: A population-based study. *Journal of Cellular and Molecular Medicine, 12*, 2762–2771.

Kjønniksen, L., Anderssen, N., & Wold, B. (2009). Organized youth sport as a predictor of physical activity in adulthood. *Scandinavian Journal of Medicine and Science in Sports, 19*, 646–654.

Kjønniksen, L., Torsheim, T., & Wold, B. (2008). Tracking of leisure-time physical activity during adolescence and young adulthood: A 10-year longitudinal study. *International Journal of Behavioral Nutrition and Physical Activity, 5*, 69.

Klaczynski, P. A. (2001). Framing effects on adolescent task representations, analytic and heuristic processing, and decision making: Implications for the normative/descriptive gap. *Applied Developmental Psychology, 22*, 289–309.

Klaczynski, P. A., & Narasimham, G. (1998). Development of scientific reasoning biases: Cognitive versus ego-protective explanations. *Developmental Psychology, 34*, 175–187.

Klaczynski, P. A., Schuneman, M. J., & Daniel, D. B. (2004). Theories of conditional reasoning: A developmental examination of competing hypotheses. *Developmental Psychology, 40*, 559–571.

Klareskog, L., Padyukov, L., Rönnelid, J., & Alfredsson, L. (2006). Genes, environment and immunity in the development of rheumatoid arthritis. *Current Opinion in Immunology, 18*, 650–655.

Klass, D. (2004). The inner representation of the dead child in the psychic and social narratives of bereaved parents. In R. A. Neimeyer (Ed.), *Meaning reconstruction and the experience of loss* (pp. 77–94). Washington, DC: American Psychological Association.

Klaw, E. L., Rhodes, J. E., & Fitzgerald, L. F. (2003). Natural mentors in the lives of African-American adolescent mothers: Tracking relationships over time. *Journal of Youth and Adolescence, 32*, 223–232.

Klebanov, P. K., Brooks-Gunn, J., McCarton, C., & McCormick, M. C. (1998). The contribution of neighborhood and family income to developmental test scores over the first three years of life. *Child Development, 69*, 1420–1436.

Kleespies, P. M. (2004). Concluding thoughts on suffering, dying and choice. In P. M. Kleespies (Ed.), *Life and death decisions: Psychological and ethical considerations in end-of-life care* (pp. 163–167). Washington, DC: American Psychological Association.

Klein, P. J., & Meltzoff, A. N. (1999). Long-term memory, forgetting, and deferred imitation in 12-month-old infants. *Developmental Science, 2*, 102–113.

Kleinspehn-Ammerlahn, A., Kotter-Grühn, D., & Smith, J. (2008). Self-perceptions of aging: Do subjective age and satisfaction with aging change during old age? *The Journals of Gerontology Series B: Psychological Sciences and Social Sciences, 63*, 377–385.

Klesges, L. M., Johnson, K. C., Ward, K. D., & Barnard, M. (2001). Smoking cessation in pregnant women. *Obstetrics and Gynecology Clinics of North America, 28*, 269–282.

Kliegel, M., Jäger, T., & Phillips, L. H. (2008). Adult age differences in event-based prospective memory: A meta-analysis on the role of focal versus nonfocal cues. *Psychology and Aging, 23*, 203–208.

Kliewer, W., Fearnow, M. D., & Miller, P. A. (1996). Coping socialization in middle childhood: Tests of maternal and paternal influences. *Child Development, 67*, 2339–2357.

Klimstra, T. A., Hale, W. W., III, Raaijmakers, Q. A. W., Branje, S. J. T., & Meeus, W. H. J. (2010). Identity formation in adolescence: Change or stability? *Journal of Youth and Adolescence, 39,* 150–162.

Kline, G. H., Stanley, S. M., Markman, H. J., Olmos-Gallo, P. A., St. Peters, M., Whitton, S. W., & Prado, L. M. (2004). Timing is everything: Preengagement cohabitation and increased risk for poor marital outcomes. *Journal of Family Psychology, 18,* 311–318.

Klingman, A. (2006). Children and war trauma. In K. A. Renninger & I. E. Sigel (Eds.), *Handbook of child psychology: Vol. 4. Child psychology in practice* (6th ed., pp. 619–652). Hoboken, NJ: Wiley.

Kloep, M., & Hendry, L. B. (2007). Retirement: A new beginning? *The Psychologist, 20,* 742–745.

Klomsten, A. T., Skaalvik, E. M., & Espnes, G. A. (2004). Physical self-concept and sports: Do gender differences exist? *Sex Roles, 50,* 119–127.

Klump, K. L., Kaye, W. H., & Strober, M. (2001). The evolving foundations of eating disorders. *Psychiatric Clinics of North America, 24,* 215–225.

Kluwer, E. S., & Johnson, M. D. (2007). Conflict frequency and relationship quality across the transition to parenthood. *Journal of Marriage and Family, 69,* 1089–1106.

Knafo, A., Zahn-Waxler, C., Davidov, M., Hulle, C. V., Robinson, J. L., & Rhee, S. H. (2009). Empathy in early childhood: Genetic, environmental, and affective contributions. In O. Vilarroya, S. Altran, A. Navarro, K. Ochsner, & A. Tobena (Eds.), *Values, empathy, and fairness across social barriers* (pp. 103–114). New York: New York Academy of Sciences.

Knickmeyer, R. C., Gouttard, S., Kang, C., Evans, D., Wilber, K., Smith, J. K., et al. (2008). A structural MRI study of human brain development from birth to 2 years. *Journal of Neuroscience, 28,* 12176–12182.

Knight, B. J., & Sayegh, P. (2010). Cultural values and caregiving: The updated sociocultural stress and coping model. *Journal of Gerontology, 65B,* 5–13.

Knopf, M., Kraus, U., & Kressley-Mba, R. A. (2006). Relational information processing of novel unrelated actions by infants. *Infant Behavior and Development, 29,* 44–53.

Knox, D., Langehough, S. O., & Walters, C. (1998). Religiosity and spirituality among college students. *College Student Journal, 32,* 430–432.

Ko, K. J., Berg, C. A., Butner, J., Uchino, B. N., & Smith, T. W. (2007). Profiles of successful aging in middle-age and older adult married couples. *Psychology and Aging, 22,* 705–718.

Kobayashi, T., Hiraki, K., & Hasegawa, T. (2005). Auditory-visual intermodal matching of small numerosities in 6-month-old infants. *Developmental Science, 8,* 409–419.

Kobayashi, T., Kazuo, H., Ryoko, M., & Hasegawa, T. (2004). Baby arithmetic: One object plus one tone. *Cognition, 91,* B23–B34.

Kobayashi, Y. (1994). Conceptual acquisition and change through social interaction. *Human Development, 37,* 233–241.

Kochanska, G. (1991). Socialization and temperament in the development of guilt and conscience. *Child Development, 62,* 1379–1392.

Kochanska, G., & Aksan, N. (2006). Children's conscience and self-regulation. *Journal of Personality, 74,* 1587–1617.

Kochanska, G., Aksan, N., & Joy, M. E. (2007). Children's fearfulness as a moderator of parenting in early socialization: Two longitudinal studies. *Developmental Psychology, 43,* 222–237.

Kochanska, G., Aksan, N., & Nichols, K. E. (2003). Maternal power assertion in discipline and moral discourse contexts: Commonalities, differences, and implications for children's moral conduct and cognition. *Developmental Psychology, 39,* 949–963.

Kochanska, G., Aksan, N., Prisco, T. R., & Adams, E. E. (2008). Mother-child and father-child mutually responsive orientation in the first 2 years and children's outcomes at preschool age: Mechanisms of influence. *Child Development, 79,* 30–44.

Kochanska, G., Casey, R. J., & Fukumoto, A. (1995). Toddlers' sensitivity to standard violations. *Child Development, 66,* 643–656.

Kochanska, G., Forman, D. R., Aksan, N., & Dunbar, S. B. (2005). Pathways to conscience: Early mother–child mutually responsive orientation and children's moral emotion, conduct, and cognition. *Journal of Child Psychology and Psychiatry, 46,* 19–34.

Kochanska, G., Gross, J. N., Lin, M.-H., & Nichols, K. E. (2002). Guilt in young children: Development, determinants, and relations with broader system standards. *Child Development, 73,* 461–482.

Kochanska, G., & Knaack, A. (2003). Effortful control as a personality characteristic of young children: Antecedents, correlates, and consequences. *Journal of Personality, 71,* 1087–1112.

Kochanska, G., Murray, K. T., & Harlan, E. T. (2000). Effortful control in early childhood: Continuity and change, antecedents, and implications for social development. *Developmental Psychology, 36,* 220–232.

Kochanska, G., Philibert, R. A., & Barry, R. A. (2009). Interplay of genes and early other–child relationship in the development of self-regulation from toddler to preschool age. *Journal of Child Psychology and Psychiatry, 50,* 1331–1338.

Koestner, R., Franz, C., & Weinberger, J. (1990). The family origins of empathic concern: A 26-year longitudinal study. *Journal of Personality and Social Psychology, 58,* 709–717.

Kohen, D. E., Leventhal, T., Dahinten, V. S., & McIntosh, C. N. (2008). Neighborhood disadvantage: Pathways of effects for young children. *Child Development, 79,* 156–169.

Kohlberg, L. (1969). Stage and sequence: The cognitivedevelopmental approach to socialization. In D. A. Goslin (Ed.), *Handbook of socialization theory and research* (pp. 347–480). Chicago: Rand McNally.

Kohlberg, L., Levine, C., & Hewer, A. (1983). *Moral stages: A current formulation and a response to critics.* Basel, Switzerland: Karger. Kohn, M. L. (2006). *Change and stability: A cross-national analysis of social structure and personality.* Greenbrae, CA: Paradigm Press.

Komp, D. M. (1996). The changing face of death in children. In H. M. Spiro, M. G. M. Curnen, & L. P. Wandel (Eds.), *Facing death: Where culture, religion, and medicine meet* (pp. 66–76). New Haven: Yale University Press.

Konner, M. (2010). *The evolution of childhood: Relationships, emotion, mind.* Cambridge, MA: Harvard University Press.

Konold, T. R., & Pianta, R. C. (2005). Empirically derived, person-oriented patterns of school readiness in typically developing children: Description and prediction to first-grade achievement. *Applied Developmental Science, 9,* 174–187.

Kopp, C. B., & Neufeld, S. J. (2003). Emotional development during infancy. In R. Davidson, K. R. Scherer, & H. H. Goldsmith (Eds.), *Handbook of affective sciences* (pp. 347–374). Oxford, UK: Oxford University Press.

Kooijman, V., Hagoort, P., & Cutler, A. (2009). Prosodic structure in early word segmentation: ERP evidence from Dutch ten-month-olds. *Infancy, 14,* 591–612.

Kopeikina, K. J., Carlson, G. A., Pitstick, R., Ludvigson, A. E., Peters, A., et al. (2011). Tau accumulation causes mitochondrial distribution deficits in neurons in a mouse model of tauopathy and in human Alzheimer's disease brain. *American Journal of Pathology 179,* 2071–2082.

Kornhaber, M. L. (2004). Using multiple intelligences to overcome cultural barriers to identification for gifted education. In D. Boothe & J. C. Stanley (Eds.), *In the eyes of the beholder: Critical issues for diversity in gifted education* (pp. 215–225). Waco, TX: Prufrock Press.

Kotkin, J. (2012, July 16). Are Millennials the screwed generation? *Newsweek.* Retrieved from www .thedailybeast.com/newsweek/2012/07/15/ aremillennials-the-screwed-generation.html

Kotre, J. (1999). *Make it count: How to generate a legacy that gives meaning to your life.* New York: Free Press.

Kozer, E., Costei, A. M., Boskovic, R., Nulman, I., Nikfar, S., & Koren, G. (2003). Effects of aspirin consumption during pregnancy on pregnancy outcomes: Meta-analysis. *Birth Defects Research, Part B, Developmental and Reproductive Toxicology, 68,* 70–84.

Kozol, J. (2005). *The shame of the nation: The restoration of apartheid schooling in America.* New York: Three Rivers Press.

Kragstrup, T. W., Kjaer, M., & Mackey, A. L. (2011). Structural, biochemical, cellular, and functional changes in skeletal muscle extracellular matrix with aging. *Scandinavian Journal of Medicine and Science in Sports, 21,* 749–757.

Kral, T. V. E., & Faith, M. S. (2009). Influences on child eating and weight development from a behavioral genetics perspective. *Journal of Pediatric Psychology, 34,* 596–605.

Kramer, A. F., Fabiani, M., & Colcombe, S. J. (2006). Contributions of cognitive neuroscience to the understanding of behavior and aging. In J. E. Birren & K. W. Schaie (Eds.), *Handbook of the psychology of aging* (6th ed., pp. 57–83). Burlington, MA: Elsevier Academic Press.

Kramer, A. F., Hahn, S., & Gopher, D. (1998). Task coordination and aging: Explorations of executive control processes in the task switching paradigm. *Acta Psychologica, 101,* 339–378.

Kramer, A. F., & Kray, J. (2006). Aging and attention. In E. Bialystok & F. I. M. Fergus (Eds.), *Lifespan cognition: Mechanisms of change* (pp. 57–69). New York: Oxford University Press.

Kramer, A. F., & Madden, D. J. (2008). Attention. In F. I. M. Craik & T. A. Salthouse (Eds.), *Handbook of aging and cognition* (pp. 189–249). New York: Psychology Press.

Kramer, D. A. (2003). The ontogeny of wisdom in its variations. In J. Demick & C. Andreoletti (Eds.), *Handbook of adult development* (pp. 131–151). New York: Springer.

Kramer, S. E., Kapteyn, T. S., Kuik, D. J., & Deeg, D. J. (2002). The association of hearing impairment and chronic diseases with psychosocial health status in older age. *Journal of Aging and Health, 14,* 122–137.

Krampe, R. T., & Charness, N. (2007). Aging and expertise. In K. A. Ericsson, N. Charness, P. J. Feltovich, & R. R. Hoffman (Eds.), *Cambridge handbook of expertise and expert performance* (pp. 723–742). New York: Cambridge University Press.

Krause, N. (2001). Social support. In R. H. Binstock & L. K. George (Eds.), *Handbook of aging and the social sciences* (5th ed., pp. 272–294). San Diego, CA: Academic Press.

Krause, N. (2012). Religious involvement, humility, and change in self-rated health over time. *Journal of Psychology and Theology, 40,* 199–210.

Krcmar, M., Grela, B., & Linn, K. (2007). Can toddlers learn vocabulary from television? An experimental approach. *Media Psychology, 10,* 41–63.

Krebs, D., & Denton, K. (2005). Toward a more pragmatic approach to morality: A critical evaluation of Kohlberg's model. *Psychological Review, 112,* 629–649.

Kreppner, J. M., Kumsta, R., Rutter, M., Beckett, C., Castle, J., Stevens, S., et al. (2010). Developmental course of deprivation specific psychological patterns: Early manifestations, persistence to age 15, and clinical features. *Monographs of the Society for Research in Child Development, 75*(1, Serial No. 295), 79–101.

Kreppner, J. M., Rutter, M., Beckett, C., Castle, J., Colvert, E., Groothues, C., Hawkins, A., & O'Connor, T. G. (2007). Normality and impairment following profound early institutional deprivation: A longitudinal follow-up into early adolescence. *Developmental Psychology, 43*, 931–946.

Krettenauer, T. (2005). The role of epistemic cognition in adolescent identity formation: Further evidence. *Journal of Youth and Adolescence, 34*, 185–198.

Krevans, J., & Gibbs, J. C. (1996). Parents' use of inductive discipline: Relations to children's empathy and prosocial behavior. *Child Development, 67*, 3263–3277.

Krishnamoorthy, J. S., Hart, C., & Jelalian, E. (2006). The epidemic of childhood obesity: Review of research and implications for public policy. *Social Policy Report of the Society for Research in Child Development, 9*(2).

Kroger, J. (2007). *Identity development: Adolescence through adulthood* (2nd ed.). Thousand Oaks, CA: Sage.

Kroger, J., Martinussen, M., & Marcia, J. E. (2010). Identity status change during adolescence and young adulthood: A meta-analysis. *Journal of Adolescence, 33*, 683–698.

Kropf, N. P., & Pugh, K. L. (1995). Beyond life expectancy: Social work with centenarians. *Journal of Gerontological Social Work, 23*, 121–137.

Krumhansl, C. L., & Jusczyk, P. W. (1990). Infants' perception of phrase structure in music. *Psychological Science, 1*, 70–73.

Kubicek, B., Korunka, C., Raymo, J. M., & Hoonakker, P. (2011). Psychological well-being in retirement: The effects of personal and gendered contextual resources. *Journal of Occupational Health Psychology, 16*, 230–246.

Kubik, M. Y., Lytle, L. A., Hannan, P. J., Perry, C. L., & Story, M. (2003). The association of the school food environment with dietary behaviors of young adolescents. *American Journal of Public Health, 93*, 1168–1173.

Kübler-Ross, E. (1969). *On death and dying*. New York: Macmillan.

Kubotera, T. (2004). Japanese religion in changing society: The spirits of the dead. In J. D. Morgan & P. Laungani (Eds.), *Death and bereavement around the world: Vol. 4. Asia, Australia, and New Zealand* (pp. 95–99). Amityville, NY: Baywood Publishing Company.

Kuchner, J. (1989, April). *Chinese-American and European-American mothers and infants: Cultural influences in the first three months of life*. Paper presented at the biennial meeting of the Society for Research in Child Development, Kansas City, MO.

Kuczynski, L. (1984). Socialization goals and mother–child interaction: Strategies for long-term and short-term compliance. *Developmental Psychology, 20*, 1061–1073.

Kuczynski, L., & Lollis, S. (2002). Four foundations for a dynamic model of parenting. In J. R. M. Gerris (Ed.), *Dynamics of parenting*. Hillsdale, NJ: Erlbaum.

Kudo, N., Nonaka, Y., Noriko, M., Katsumi, M., & Okanoya, K. (2011). On-line statistical segmentation of a non-speech auditory stream in neonates as demonstrated by event-related brain potentials. *Developmental Science, 14*, 1100–1106.

Kuebli, J., Butler, S., & Fivush, R. (1995). Mother–child talk about past emotions: Relations of maternal language and child gender over time. *Cognition and Emotion, 9*, 265–283.

Kugelmass, J., & Ainscow, M. (2004). Leadership for inclusion: A comparison of international practices. *Journal of Research in Special Educational Needs, 4*, 133–141.

Kuhl, P. K., Tsao, F.-M., & Liu, H.-M. (2003). Foreign language experience in infancy: Effects of short-term exposure and social interaction on phonetic learning. *Proceedings of the National Academy of Sciences, 100*, 9096–9101.

Kuhn, D. (2000). Theory of mind, metacognition, and reasoning: A life-span perspective. In P. Mitchell & K. J. Riggs (Eds.), *Children's reasoning and the mind* (pp. 301–326). Hove, UK: Psychology Press.

Kuhn, D. (2002). What is scientific thinking, and how does it develop? In U. Goswami (Ed.), *Blackwell handbook of childhood cognitive development* (pp. 371–393). Malden, MA: Blackwell.

Kuhn, D. (2009). Adolescent thinking. In R. M. Lerner & L. Steinberg (Eds.), *Handbook of adolescent psychology, Vol. 1: Individual bases of adolescent development* (3rd ed., pp. 152–186). Hoboken, NJ: Wiley.

Kuhn, D., Amsel, E., & O'Loughlin, M. (1988). *The development of scientific thinking skills*. Orlando, FL: Academic Press.

Kuhn, D., & Dean, D. (2004). Connecting scientific reasoning and causal inference. *Journal of Cognition and Development, 5*, 261–288.

Kuhn, D., & Franklin, S. (2006). The second decade: What develops (and how)? In D. Kuhn & R. S. Siegler (Eds.), *Handbook of child psychology: Vol. 2. Cognition, perception, and language* (6th ed.). Hoboken, NJ: Wiley.

Kuhn, D., Iordanou, K., Pease, M., & Wirkala, C. (2008). Beyond control of variables: What needs to develop to achieve skilled scientific thinking? *Cognitive Development, 23*, 435–451.

Kuhn, D., & Pease, M. (2006). Do children and adults learn differently? *Journal of Cognition and Development, 7*, 279–293.

Kuklinski, M. R., & Weinstein, R. S. (2001). Classroom and developmental differences in a path model of teacher expectancy effects. *Child Development, 72*, 1554–1578.

Kulik, K. (2001). Marital relationships in late adulthood: Synchronous versus asynchronous couples. *International Journal of Aging and Human Development, 52*, 323–339.

Kumar, S., & O'Brien, A. (2004). Recent developments in fetal medicine. *British Medical Journal, 328*, 1002–1006.

Kunemund, H., Motel-Klingebiel, A., & Kohli, M. (2005). Do intergenerational transfers from elderly parents increase social inequality among their middle-aged children? Evidence from the German Aging Survey. *Journal of Gerontology, 60B*, S30–S36.

Kunnen, E. S., & Bosma, H. A. (2003). Fischer's skill theory applied to identity development: A response to Kroger. *Identity, 3*, 247–270.

Kunnen, E. S., Sappa, V., van Gert, P. L. C., & Bonica, L. (2008). The shapes of commitment development in emerging adulthood. *Journal of Adult Development, 15*, 113–131.

Kuppens, S., Grietens, H., Onghena, P., & Michiels, D. (2009). Associations between parental control and children's overt and relational aggression. *British Journal of Developmental Psychology, 27*, 607–623.

Kurdek, L. A. (2005). Gender and marital satisfaction early in marriage: A growth curve approach. *Journal of Marriage and Family, 67*, 68–84.

Kurdek, L. A. (2006). Differences between partners from heterosexual, gay, and lesbian cohabiting couples. *Journal of Marriage and Family, 68*, 509–528.

Kurdek, L. A., & Fine, M. A. (1994). Family acceptance and family control as predictors of adjustment in young adolescents: Linear, curvilinear, or interactive effects? *Child Development, 65*, 1137–1146.

Kurtz-Costes, B., Rowley, S. J., Harris-Britt, A., & Woods, T. A. (2008). Gender stereotypes about mathematics and science and self-perceptions of ability in late childhood and early adolescence. *Merrill-Palmer Quarterly, 54*, 386–409.

Kwon, Y. H., Fingert, J. H., Kuehn, M. H., & Alward, W. L. (2009). Primary open-angle glaucoma. *New England Journal of Medicine, 360*, 1113–1124.

L

Labouvie-Vief, G. (1980). Beyond formal operations: Uses and limits of pure logic in life-span development. *Human Development, 23*, 141–160.

Labouvie-Vief, G. (1985). Logic and self-regulation from youth to maturity: A model. In M. Commons, F. Richards, & C. Armon (Eds.), *Beyond formal operations: Late adolescent and adult cognitive development* (pp. 158–180). New York: Praeger.

Labouvie-Vief, G. (2003). Dynamic integration: Affect, cognition, and the self in adulthood. *Current Directions in Psychological Science, 12*, 201–206.

Labouvie-Vief, G. (2005). Self-with-other representations and the organization of the self. *Journal of Research in Personality, 39*, 185–205.

Labouvie-Vief, G. (2006). Emerging structures of adult thought. In J. J. Arnett & J. L. Tanner (Eds.), *Emerging adults in America: Coming of age in the 21st century* (pp. 59–84). Washington, DC: American Psychological Association.

Labouvie-Vief, G. (2008). When differentiation and negative affect lead to integration and growth. *American Psychologist, 63*, 564–565.

Labouvie-Vief, G., Chiodo, L. M., Goguen, L. A., Diehl, M., & Orwoll, L. (1995). Representations of self across the life span. *Psychology and Aging, 10*, 404–415.

Labouvie-Vief, G., & Diehl, M. (1999). Self and personality development. In J. C. Kavanaugh & S. K. Whitbourne (Eds.), *Gerontology: An interdisciplinary perspective* (pp. 238–268). New York: Oxford University Press.

Labouvie-Vief, G., & Diehl, M. (2000). Cognitive complexity and cognitive-affective integration: Related or separate domains of adult development? *Psychology and Aging, 15*, 490–504.

Labouvie-Vief, G., Diehl, M., Jain, E., & Zhang, F. (2007). Six-year change in affect optimization and affect complexity across the adult life span: A further examination. *Psychology and Aging, 22*, 738–751.

Labouvie-Vief, G., Grühn, S., & Studer, J. (2010). Dynamic integration of emotion and cognition: Equilibrium regulation in development and aging. In W. Overton & R. M. Lerner (Eds.), *Handbook of life-span development: Vol. 2. Social and emotional development* (pp. 79–115). Hoboken, NJ: Wiley.

Lachance-Grzela, M., & Bouchard, G. (2010). Why do women do the lion's share of housework? A decade of research. *Sex Roles, 63*, 767–780.

Lachman, M. E. (2004). Development in midlife. *Annual Review of Psychology, 55*, 305–331.

Lachman, M. E., Neupert, S. D., & Agrigoroaei, S. (2011). The relevance of control beliefs for health and aging. In K. W. Schaie & S. L. Willis (Eds.), *Handbook of the psychology of aging* (7th ed., pp. 175–190). San Diego, CA: Elsevier.

Lacourse, E., Nagin, D., Tremblay, R. E., Vitaro, F., & Claes, M. (2003). Developmental trajectories of boys' delinquent group membership and facilitation of violent behaviors during adolescence. *Development and Psychopathology, 15*, 183–197.

Ladd, G. W. (2005). *Children's peer relationships and social competence: A century of progress*. New Haven, CT: Yale University Press.

Ladd, G. W., Birch, S. H., & Buhs, E. S. (1999). Children's social and scholastic lives in kindergarten: Related spheres of influence? *Child Development, 70*, 1373–1400.

Ladd, G. W., Buhs, E. S., & Seid, M. (2000). Children's initial sentiments about kindergarten: Is school liking an antecedent of early classroom participation and achievement? *Merrill-Palmer Quarterly, 46*, 255–279.

Ladd, G. W., & Burgess, K. B. (1999). Charting the relationship trajectories of aggressive, withdrawn, and aggressive/withdrawn children during early grade school. *Child Development, 70,* 910–929.

Ladd, G. W., Herald, S. L., & Kochel, K. P. (2006). School readiness: Are there social prerequisites? *Early Education and Development, 17,* 115–150.

Ladd, G. W., Kochenderfer-Ladd, B., Eggum, N. D., Kochel, K. P., & McConnell, E. M. (2011). Characterizing and comparing the friendships of anxious-solitary and unsociable preadolescents. *Child Development, 82,* 1434–1453.

Ladd, G. W., LeSieur, K., & Profilet, S. M. (1993). Direct parental influences on young children's peer relations. In S. Duck (Ed.), *Learning about relationships* (Vol. 2, pp. 152–183). London: Sage.

Ladd, G. W., & Pettit, G. S. (2002). Parenting and the development of children's peer relationships. In M. Bornstein (Ed.), *Handbook of parenting* (2nd ed.). Mahwah, NJ: Erlbaum.

Ladd, G. W., & Price, J. M. (1987). Predicting children's social and school adjustment following the transition from preschool to kindergarten. *Child Development, 58,* 1168–1189.

LaFraniere, S. (2011, April 6). As China ages, birthrate policy may prove difficult to reverse. *New York Times.* Retrieved from www.nytimes.com/2011/04/07/world/asia/07population.html?pagewanted=all

Lagattuta, K. H., Wellman, H. M., & Flavell, J. H. (1997). Preschoolers' understanding of the link between thinking and feeling: Cognitive cuing and emotional change. *Child Development, 68,* 1081–1104.

Lagnado, L. (2001, November 2). Kids confront Trade Center trauma. *Wall Street Journal,* pp. B1, B6.

Laible, D. (2004). Mother–child discourse in two contexts: Links with child temperament, attachment security, and socioemotional competence. *Developmental Psychology, 40,* 979–992.

Laible, D. (2007). Attachment with parents and peers in late adolescence: Links with emotional competence and social behavior. *Personality and Individual Differences, 43,* 1185–1197.

Laible, D., & Song, J. (2006). Constructing emotional and relational understanding: The role of affect and mother–child discourse. *Merrill-Palmer Quarterly, 52,* 44–69.

Laird, R. D., Jordan, K. Y., Dodge, K. A., Pettit, G. S., & Bates, J. E. (2001). Peer rejection in childhood, involvement with antisocial peers in early adolescence, and the development of external-izing behavior problems. *Development and Psychopathology, 13,* 337–354.

Laird, R. D., Pettit, G. S., Dodge, K. A., & Bates, J. E. (2005). Peer relationship antecedents of delinquent behavior in late adolescence: Is there evidence of demographic group differences in developmental processes? *Development and Psychopathology, 17,* 127–144.

Lamarche, V., Brendgen, M., Boivin, M., Vitaro, F., Perusse, D., & Dionne, G. (2006). Do friendships and sibling relationships provide protection against peer victimization in a similar way? *Social Development, 15,* 373–393.

Lamaze, F. (1958). *Painless childbirth.* London: Burke.

Lamb, M. E., & Ahnert, L. (2006). Nonparental child care: Context, concepts, correlates, and consequences. In K. A. Renninger & I. E. Sigel (Eds.), *Handbook of child psychology: Vol. 4. Child psychology in practice* (6th ed., pp. 700–778). Hoboken, NJ: Wiley.

Lamb, M. E., & Lewis, C. (2004). The development and significance of father–child relationships in twoparent families. In M. E. Lamb (Ed.), *The role of the father in child development* (4th ed., pp. 272–306). Hoboken, NJ: Wiley.

Lamb, M. E., Thompson, R. A., Gardner, W., Charnov, E. L., & Connell, J. P. (1985). Infant–mother attachment: The origins and developmental significance of individual differences in the Strange Situation: Its study and biological interpretation. *Behavioral and Brain Sciences, 7,* 127–147.

Lamberg, L. (2007). Menopause not always to blame for sleep problems in midlife women. *Journal of the American Medical Association, 297,* 1865–1866.

Lambert, S. M., Masson, P., & Fisch, H. (2006). The male biological clock. *World Journal of Urology, 24,* 611–617.

Lang, F. R., & Baltes, M. M. (1997). Being with people and being alone in later life: Costs and benefits for everyday functioning. *International Journal of Behavioral Development, 21,* 729–749.

Lang, F. R., Rohr, M. K., & Williger, B. (2010). Modeling success in life-span psychology: The principles of selection, optimization, and compensation. In L. Fingerman, C. A. Berg, J. Smith, & T. C. Antonucci (Eds.), *Handbook of life-span development* (pp. 57–85). New York: Springer.

Lang, F. R., Staudinger, U. M., & Carstensen, L. L. (1998). Perspectives on socioemotional selectivity in late life: How personality and social context do (and do not) make a difference. *Journal of Gerontology, 53B,* P21–P30.

Lang, I. A., Llewellyn, D. J., Langa, K. M., Wallace, R. B., Huppert, F. A., & Melzer, D. (2008). Neighborhood deprivation, individual socioeconomic status, and cognitive function in older people: Analyses from the English Longitudinal Study of Ageing. *Journal of the American Geriatric Society, 56,* 191–198.

Lang, M. (2010). Can mentoring assist in the school-to-work transition? *Education + Training, 52,* 359–367.

Langer, G. (2004). *ABC New Prime Time Live Poll: The American Sex Survey.* Retrieved from abcnews.go.com/Primetime/News/story?id=174461&page=1

Langer, J., Gillette, P., & Arriaga, R. I. (2003). Toddlers' cognition of adding and subtracting objects in action and in perception. *Cognitive Development, 18,* 233–246.

Langhinrichsen-Rohling, J., Friend, J., & Powell, A. (2009). Adolescent suicide, gender, and culture: A rate and risk factor analysis. *Aggression and Violent Behavior, 14,* 402–414.

Langosch, D. (2012). Grandparents parenting again: Challenges, strengths, and implications for practice. *Psychoanalytic Inquiry, 32,* 163–170.

Langsetmo, L., Hitchcock, C., Kingwell, E. J., Davison, K. S., Berger, C., Forsmo, S., et al. (2012). Physical activity, body mass index and bone mineral density-associations in a prospective population-based cohort of women and men: The Canadian Multicentre Osteoporosis Study. *Bone, 50,* 401–408.

Lansford, J. E. (2009). Parental divorce and children's adjustment. *Perspectives on Psychological Science, 4,* 140–152.

Lansford, J. E., Antonucci, T. C., Akiyama, H., & Takahashi, K. (2005). A quantitative and qualitative approach to social relationships and well-being in the United States and Japan. *Journal of Comparative Family Studies, 36,* 1–22.

Lansford, J. E., Criss, M. M., Dodge, K. A., Shaw, D. S., Pettit, G. S., & Bates, J. E. (2009). Trajectories of physical discipline: Early childhood antecedents and developmental outcomes. *Child Development, 80,* 1385–1402.

Lansford, J. E., Criss, M. M., Laird, R. D., Shaw, D. S., Pettit, G. S., Bates, J. E., et al. (2011). Reciprocal relations between parents' physical discipline and children's externalizing behavior during middle childhood and adolescence. *Development and Psychopathology, 23,* 225–238.

Lansford, J. E., Criss, M. M., Pettit, G. S., Dodge, K. A., & Bates, J. E. (2003). Friendship quality, peer group affiliation, and peer antisocial behavior as moderators of the link between negative parenting and adolescent externalizing behavior. *Journal of Research on Adolescence, 13,* 161–184.

Lansford, J. E., Deater-Deckard, K., Dodge, K. A., Bates, J. E., & Pettit, G. S. (2004). Ethnic differences in the link between physical discipline and later adolescent externalizing behaviors. *Journal of Child Psychology and Psychiatry, 45,* 801–812.

Lansford, J. E., Malone, P. S., Castellino, D. R., Dodge, K. A., Pettit, G., & Bates, J. E. (2006). Trajectories of internalizing, externalizing, and grades for children who have and have not experienced their parents' divorce or separation. *Journal of Family Psychology, 20,* 292–301.

Lapierr, S., Erlangsen, A., Waern, M., De Leo, D., Oyama, H., Scocco, P., et al. (2011). A systematic review of elderly suicide prevention programs. *Crisis, 32,* 88–98.

Larbi, A., Fülöp, T., & Pawelec, G. (2008). Immune receptor signaling, aging and autoimmunity. In A. B. Sigalov (Ed.), *Multichain immune recognition receptor signaling: From spatiotemporal organization to human disease* (pp. 312–324). New York: Springer.

Largo, R. H., Caflisch, J. A., Hug, F., Muggli, K., Molnar, A. A., & Molinari, L. (2001). Neuromotor development from 5 to 18 years. Part 1: Timed performance. *Developmental Medicine and Child Neurology, 43,* 436–443.

Larsen, J. A., & Nippold, M. A. (2007). Morphological analysis in school-age children: Dynamic assessment of a word learning strategy. *Language, Speech, and Hearing Services in Schools, 38,* 201–212.

Larsen, J. T., To, Y. M., & Fireman, G. (2007). Childen's understanding and experience of mixed emotions. *Psychological Science, 18,* 186–191.

Larsen, P. (2009, January). A review of cardiovascular changes in the older adult. *Gerontology Update, December 2008/January 2009, 3,* 9.

Larson, D. G., & Hoyt, W. T. (2007). What has become of grief counseling? An evaluation of the empirical foundations of the new pessimism. *Professional Psychology: Research and Practice, 38,* 347–355.

Larson, R. W. (2001). How U.S. children and adolescents spend time: What it does (and doesn't) tell us about their development. *Current Directions in Psychological Science, 10,* 160–164.

Larson, R. W., & Lampman-Petraitis, C. (1989). Daily emotional states as reported by children and adolescents. *Child Development, 60,* 1250–1260.

Larson, R. W., Mannell, R., & Zuzanek, J. (1986). Daily well-being of older adults with friends and family. *Psychology and Aging, 1,* 117–126.

Larson, R. W., Moneta, G., Richards, M. H., & Wilson, S. (2002). Continuity, stability, and change in daily emotional experience across adolescence. *Child Development, 73,* 1151–1165.

Larson, R. W., & Richards, M. (1998). Waiting for the weekend: Friday and Saturday night as the emotional climax of the week. In A. C. Crouter & R. Larson (Eds.), *Temporal rhythms in adolescence: Clocks, calendars, and the coordination of daily life* (pp. 37–51). San Francisco: Jossey-Bass.

Larsson, M., Öberg, C., & Bäckman, L. (2005). Odor identification in old age: Demographic, sensory and cognitive correlates. *Aging, Neuropsychology, and Cognition, 12,* 231–244.

Larzelere, R. E., Schneider, W. N., Larson, D. B., & Pike, P. L. (1996). The effects of discipline responses in delaying toddler misbehavior recurrences. *Child and Family Behavior Therapy, 18,* 35–57.

Lashley, F. R. (2007). Essentials of clinical genetics in nursing practice. New York: Springer.

Lattanzi-Licht, M., & Doka, K. J. (Eds.). (2003). *Living with grief: Coping with public tragedy.* New York: Brunner-Routledge.

Latz, S., Wolf, A. W., & Lozoff, B. (1999). Sleep practices and problems in young children in Japan and the United States. *Archives of Pediatric and Adolescent Medicine, 153,* 339–346.

Lau, C. Q. (2012). The stability of same-sex cohabitation, different-sex cohabitation, and marriage. *Journal of Marriage and Family, 74*, 973–988.

Lauer, P. A., Akiba, M., Wilkerson, S. B., Apthorp, H. S., Snow, D., & Martin-Glenn, M. (2006). Out-of-school time programs: A meta-analysis of effects for at-risk students. *Review of Educational Research, 76*, 275–313.

Laumann, E. O., Gagnon, J. H., Michael, R. T., & Michaels, S. (1994). *The social organization of sexuality.* Chicago: University of Chicago Press.

Laumann, E. O., Paik, A., & Rosen, R. C. (1999). Sexual dysfunction in the United States: Prevalence and predictors. *Journal of the American Medical Association, 281*, 537–544.

Laureys, S., & Boly, M. (2007). What is it like to be vegetative or minimally conscious? *Current Opinion in Neurology, 20*, 609–613.

Laursen, B., & Collins, W. A. (2009). Parent–child relationships during adolescence. In R. M. Lerner (Ed.), *Handbook of adolescent psychology: Vol. 2. Contextual influences on adolescent development* (3rd ed., pp. 3–42). Hoboken, NJ: Wiley.

Lavelli, M., & Fogel, A. (2005). Developmental changes in the relationship between the infant's attention and emotion during early face-to-face communication: The 2-month transition. *Developmental Psychology, 41*, 265–280.

Lavner, J. A., & Bradbury, T. N. (2012). Why do even satisfied newlyweds eventually go on to divorce? *Journal of Family Psychology, 26*, 1–10.

Law, K. L., Stroud, L. R., Niaura, R., LaGasse, L. L., Giu, J., & Lester, B. M. (2003). Smoking during pregnancy and newborn neurobehavior. *Pediatrics, 111*, 1318–1323.

Lawn, J. E., Mwanza-Kambafwile J., Horta, B. L., Barros, F. C., & Cousens, S. (2010). Kangaroo mother care to prevent neonatal deaths due to preterm birth complications. *International Journal of Epidemiology, 39*(Supplement 1), i144–i154.

Lawrence, A. R., & Schigelone, A. R. S. (2002). Reciprocity beyond dyadic relationships: Aging-related communal coping. *Research on Aging, 24*, 684–704.

Lawrence, E., Rothman, A., Cobb, R. J., & Bradbury, T. N. (2010). Marital satisfaction across the transition to parenthood. In M. S. Schulz, M. K. Pruett, P. K. Kerig, & R. D. Parke (Eds.), *Strengthening couple relationships for optimal child development* (pp. 97–114). Washington, DC: American Psychological Association.

Lawson, K. R., & Ruff, H. A. (2004). Early attention and negative emotionality predict later cognitive and behavioral function. *International Journal of Behavioral Development, 28*, 157–165.

Lawton, J. S. (2011). Sex and gender differences in coronary artery disease. *Seminars in Thoracic Surgery, 23*, 126–130.

Lazar, I., & Darlington, R. (1982). Lasting effects of early education: A report from the Consortium for Longitudinal Studies. *Monographs of the Society for Research in Child Development, 47*(2–3, Serial No. 195).

Lazarus, R. S., & Lazarus, B. N. (1994). *Passion and reason.* New York: Oxford University Press.

Lazinski, M. J., Shea, A. K., & Steiner, M. (2008). Effects of maternal prenatal stress on offspring development: A commentary. *Archives of Women's Mental Health, 11*, 363–375.

Le, T. N. (2011). Life satisfaction, openness value, selftranscendence, and wisdom. *Journal of Happiness Studies, 12*, 171–182.

Leaper, C. (1994). Exploring the correlates and consequences of gender segregation: Social relationships in childhood, adolescence, and adulthood. In C. Leaper (Ed.), *New directions for child development* (No. 65, pp. 67–86). San Francisco: Jossey-Bass.

Leaper, C., Anderson, K. J., & Sanders, P. (1998). Moderators of gender effects on parents' talk to their children: A meta-analysis. *Developmental Psychology, 34*, 3–27.

Leaper, C., & Friedman, C. K. (2007). The socialization of gender. In J. E. Grusec & P. D. Hastings (Eds.), *Handbook of socialization: Theory and research* (pp. 561–587). New York: Guilford.

Leaper, C., Tenenbaum, H. R., & Shaffer, T. G. (1999). Communication patterns of African-American girls and boys from low-income, urban backgrounds. *Child Development, 70*, 1489–1503.

LeBlanc, L. A., Goldsmith, T., & Patel, D. R. (2003). Behavioral aspects of chronic illness in children and adolescents. *Pediatric Clinics of North America, 50*, 859–878.

Lecanuet, J.-P., Granier-Deferre, C., Jacquet, A.-Y., Capponi, I., & Ledru, L. (1993). Prenatal discrimination of a male and female voice uttering the same sentence. *Early Development and Parenting, 2*, 217–228.

Lecuyer, E., & Houck, G. M. (2006). Maternal limitsetting in toddlerhood: Socialization strategies for the development of self-regulation. *Infant Mental Health Journal, 27*, 344–370.

Lee, C.-Y. S., & Doherty, W. J. (2007). Marital satisfaction and father involvement during the transition to parenthood. *Fathering, 5*, 75–96.

Lee, E. E., & Farran, C. J. (2004). Depression among Korean, Korean American, and Caucasian American family caregivers. *Journal of Transcultural Nursing, 15*, 18–25.

Lee, E. O., & Sharpe, T. (2007). Understanding religious/spiritual coping and support resources among African American older adults: A mixed method approach. *Journal of Religion, Spirituality and Aging, 19*, 55–75.

Lee, J. C., Hasnain-Wynia, R., & Lau, D. T. (2011). Delay in seeing a doctor due to cost: Disparity between older adults with and without disabilities in the United States. *Health Services Research, 47*, 698–720.

Lee, J. M., Appugliese, D., Kaciroti, N., Corwyn, R. F., Bradley, R. H., & Lumeng, J. C. (2007). Weight status in young girls and the onset of puberty. *Pediatrics, 119*, e624–e630.

Lee, S. J., Ralston, H. J., Partridge, J. C., & Rosen, M. A. (2005). Fetal pain: A systematic multidisciplinary review of the evidence. *Journal of the American Medical Association, 294*, 947–954.

Lee, V. E., & Burkam, D. T. (2002). *Inequality at the starting gate.* Washington, DC: Economic Policy Institute.

Leerkes, E. M. (2010). Predictors of maternal sensitivity to infant distress. *Parenting: Science and Practice, 10*, 219–239.

Legacy Project. (2012). *Fast facts on grandparenting and intergenerational mentoring.* Retrieved from www.legacyproject.org/specialreports/fastfacts.html

Lehman, D. R., & Nisbett, R. E. (1990). A longitudinal study of the effects of undergraduate training on reasoning. *Developmental Psychology, 26*, 952–960.

Lehman, M., & Hasselhorn, M. (2007). Variable memory strategy use in children's adaptive intratask learning behavior: Developmental changes and working memory influences in free recall. *Child Development, 78*, 1068–1082.

Lehman, M., & Hasselhorn, M. (2010). The dynamics of free recall and their relation to rehearsal between 8 and 10 years of age. *Child Development, 81*, 1006–1020.

Lehr, V. T., Zeskind, P. S., Ofenstein, J. P., Cepeda, E., Warrier, I., & Aranda, J. V. (2007). Neonatal facial coding system scores and spectral characteristics of infant crying during newborn circumcision. *Clinical Journal of Pain, 23*, 417–424.

Lehrer, E. L., & Chen, Y. (2011). *Women's age at first marriage and marital instability: Evidence from the 2006–2008 National Survey of Family Growth.*

Discussion Paper No. 5954. Chicago: University of Illinois at Chicago.

Lehrer, J. A., Pantell, R., Tebb, K., & Shafer, M. A. (2007). Forgone health care among U.S. adolescents: Associations between risk characteristics and confidentiality. *Journal of Adolescent Health, 40*, 218–226.

Leiter, M. P., Gascón, S., & Martínez-Jarreta, B. (2010). Making sense of work life: A structural model of burnout. *Journal of Applied Social Psychology, 40*, 57–75.

Lemaitre, H., Goldman, A. L., Sambataro, F., Verchinski, B. A., Meyer-Lindenberg, A., & Mattay, V. S. (2012). Normal age-related brain morphometric changes: Nonuniformity across cortical thickness, surface area and gray matter volume? *Neurobiology of Aging, 33*, 617.

Leman, P. J. (2005). Authority and moral reasons: Parenting style and children's perceptions of adult rule justifications. *International Journal of Behavioral Development, 29*, 265–270.

Lempert, H. (1990). Acquisition of passives: The role of patient animacy, salience, and lexical accessibility. *Journal of Child Language, 17*, 677–696.

Lengua, L. J., Wolchik, S., Sandler, I. N., & West, S. G. (2000). The additive and interactive effects of parenting and temperament in predicting problems of children of divorce. *Journal of Clinical Psychology, 29*, 232–244.

Lenhart, A., Ling, R., Campbell, S., & Purcell, K. (2010). *Teens and mobile phones.* Washington, DC: Pew Internet & American Life Project.

Lenroot, R. K., & Giedd, J. N. (2006). Brain development in children and adolescents: Insights from anatomical magnetic resonance imaging. *Neuroscience and Biobehavioral Reviews, 30*, 718–729.

Leon, K. (2003). Risk and protective factors in young children's adjustment to parental divorce: A review of the research. *Family Relations, 52*, 258–270.

Leonesio, M. V., Bridges, B., Gesumaria, R., & Del Bene, L. (2012). The increasing labor force participation of older workers and its effect on the income of the aged. *Social Security Bulletin, 72*(1). Retrieved from www.ssa.gov/policy/docs/ssb/v72n1/v72n1p59.html

Lepage, J.-F., & Théoret, H. (2007). The mirror neuron system: Grasping others' actions from birth? *Developmental Science, 10*, 513–523.

Lerman, R. I. (2010). Capabilities and contributions of unwed fathers. *Future of Children, 20*, 63–85.

Lerner, R. M. (2006). Developmental science, developmental systems, and contemporary theories of human development. In R. M. Lerner (Ed.), *Handbook of child psychology: Vol. 1. Theoretical models of human development* (6th ed., pp. 1–17). Hoboken, NJ: Wiley.

Lerner, R. M., Leonard, K., Fay, K., & Issac, S. S. (2011). Continuity and discontinuity in development across the life span: A developmental systems perspective. In K. L. Fingerman, C. A. Berg, J. Smith, & T. C. Antonucci (Eds.), *Handbook of life-span development* (pp. 141–160). New York: Springer.

Lerner, R. M., & Overton, W. F. (2008). Exemplifying the integrations of the relational developmental system. *Journal of Adolescent Research, 23*, 245–255.

Leslie, A. M. (2004). Who's for learning? *Developmental Science, 7*, 417–419.

Lester, B. M., & Lagasse, L. L. (2010). Children of addicted women. *Journal of Addictive Diseases, 29*, 259–276.

Letherby, G. (2002). Childless and bereft? Stereotypes and realities in relation to "voluntary" and "involuntary" childlessness and womanhood. *Sociological Inquiry, 72*, 7–20.

Leuner, B., Glasper, E. R., & Gould, E. (2010). Parenting and plasticity. *Trends in Neurosciencess, 33*, 465–473.

Leung, M. C. M., Zhang, J., & Zhang, J. (2004). An economic analysis of life expectancy by gender with application to the United States. *Journal of Health Economics, 23,* 737–759.

LeVay, S. (1993). *The sexual brain.* Cambridge, MA: MIT Press.

Levendosky, A. A., Bogat, G. A., Huth-Bocks, A. C., Rosenblum, K., & von Eye, A. (2011). The effects of domestic violence on the stability of attachment from infancy to preschool. *Journal of Clinical Child and Adolescent Psychology, 40,* 398–410.

Leventhal, T., & Brooks-Gunn, J. (2003). Children and youth in neighborhood contexts. *Current Directions in Psychological Science, 12,* 27–31.

Leventhal, T., Dupere, V., & Brooks-Gunn, J. (2009). Neighborhood influences on adolescent development. In R. M. Lerner & L. Steinberg (Eds.), *Handbook of adolescent psychology: Vol. 2* (3rd ed., pp. 411–443). Hoboken, NJ: Wiley.

Levi, J., Vinter, S., Richardson, L., St. Laurent, R., & Segal, L. M. (2009). *F as in fat: How obesity policies are failing in America.* Washington, DC: Trust for America's Health.

Levine, L. J. (1995). Young children's understanding of the causes of anger and sadness. *Child Development, 66,* 697–709.

LeVine, R. A., Dixon, S., LeVine, S., Richman, A., Leiderman, P. H., Keefer, C. H., & Brazelton, T. B. (1994). *Child care and culture: Lessons from Africa.* New York: Cambridge University Press.

Levinson, D. J. (1978). *The seasons of a man's life.* New York: Knopf.

Levinson, D. J. (1996). *The seasons of a woman's life.* New York: Knopf.

Levitt, M. J., & Cici-Gokaltun, A. (2011). Close relationships across the lifespan. In K. Fingerman, C. A. Berg, J. Smith, & T. C. Antonucci (Eds.), *Handbook of life-span development* (pp. 457–486). New York: Springer.

Levy, B. R., & Leifheit-Limson, E. (2009). The stereotype-matching effect: Greater influence on functioning when age stereotypes correspond to outcomes. *Psychology and Aging, 24,* 230–233.

Levy, B. R., Slade, M. D., Kunkel, S. R., & Kasl, S. V. (2002). Longevity increased by positive self-perceptions of aging. *Journal of Personality and Social Psychology, 83,* 261–270.

Levy, S. R., & Dweck, C. S. (1999). The impact of children's static vs. dynamic conceptions of people on stereotype formation. *Child Development, 70,* 1163–1180.

Lewis, M. (1992). *Shame: The exposed self.* New York: Free Press.

Lewis, M. (1995). Embarrassment: The emotion of self-exposure and evaluation. In J. P. Tangney & K. W. Fischer (Eds.), *Self-conscious emotions* (pp. 198–218). New York: Guilford.

Lewis, M. (1998). Emotional competence and development. In D. Pushkar, W. M. Bukowski, A. E. Schwartzman, E. M. Stack, & D. R. White (Eds.), *Improving competence across the lifespan* (pp. 27–36). New York: Plenum.

Lewis, M., & Brooks-Gunn, J. (1979). *Social cognition and the acquisition of self.* New York: Plenum.

Lewis, M., Ramsay, D. S., & Kawakami, K. (1993). Differences between Japanese infants and Caucasian American infants in behavioral and cortisol response to inoculation. *Child Development, 64,* 1722–1731.

Lewis, M., Sullivan, M. W., Stanger, C., & Weiss, M. (1989). Self development and self-conscious emotions. *Child Development, 60,* 146–156.

Leyk, D., Rüther, T., Wunderlich, M., Sievert, A., Ebfeld, D., Witzki, A., et al. (2010). Physical performance in middle age and old age. *Deutsches Ärzteblatt International, 107,* 809–816.

Li, D.-K., Willinger, M., Petitti, D. B., Odouli, R., Liu, L., & Hoffman, H. J. (2006). Use of a dummy (pacifier) during sleep and risk of sudden infant death syndrome (SIDS): Population based casecontrol study. *British Medical Journal, 332,* 18–21.

Li, S.-C., Lindenberger, U., Hommel, B., Aschersleben, G., Prinz, W., & Baltes, P. B. (2004). Transformation in the couplings among intellectual abilities and constituent cognitive processes across the life span. *Psychological Science, 15,* 155–163.

Liang, J., Krause, N. M., & Bennett, J. M. (2001). Social exchange and well-being: Is giving better than receiving? *Psychology and Aging, 16,* 511–523.

Liben, L. S. (2006). Education for spatial thinking. In K. A. Renninger & I. E. Sigel (Eds.), *Handbook of child psychology: Vol. 4. Child psychology in practice* (6th ed., pp. 197–247). Hoboken, NJ: Wiley.

Liben, L. S. (2009). The road to understanding maps. *Current Directions in Psychological Science, 18,* 310–315.

Liben, L. S., & Bigler, R. S. (2002). The developmental course of gender differentiation: Conceptualizing, measuring, and evaluating constructs and pathways. *Monographs of the Society for Research in Child Development, 6*(4, Serial No. 271).

Liben, L. S., Bigler, R. S., & Krogh, H. R. (2001). Pink and blue collar jobs: Children's judgments of job status and job aspirations in relation to sex of worker. *Journal of Experimental Child Psychology, 79,* 346–363.

Liben, L. S., & Downs, R. M. (1993). Understanding person–space–map relations: Cartographic and developmental perspectives. *Developmental Psychology, 29,* 739–752.

Lidstone, J. S. M., Meins, E., & Fernyhough, C. (2010). The roles of private speech and inner speech in planning during middle childhood: Evidence from a dual task paradigm. *Journal of Experimental Child Psychology, 107,* 438–451.

Lidz, J. (2007). The abstract nature of syntactic representations. In E. Hoff & M. Shatz (Eds.), *Blackwell handbook of language development* (pp. 277–303). Malden, MA: Blackwell.

Lieven, E., Pine, J., & Baldwin, G. (1997). Lexically based learning and early grammatical development. *Journal of Child Language, 24,* 187–220.

Li-Grining, C. P. (2007). Effortful control among low-income preschoolers in three cities: Stability, change, and individual differences. *Developmental Psychology, 43,* 208–221.

Lillard, A. (2003). Pretend play and cognitive development. In U. Goswami (Ed.), *Blackwell handbook of childhood cognitive development* (pp. 189–205). Malden, MA: Blackwell.

Lillard, A. (2007). *Montessori: The science behind the genius.* New York: Oxford University Press.

Lillard, A., & Else-Quest, N. (2006). Evaluating Montessori education. *Science, 313,* 1893–1894.

Lin, F. R., Ferrucci, L., Metter, E. J., An, Y., Zonderman, A. B., & Resnick, S. M. (2011). Hearing loss and cognition in the Baltimore Longitudinal Study of Aging. *Neuropsychology, 25,* 763–770.

Linares, T. J., Singer, L. T., Kirchner, H., Lester, H., Short, E. J., & Min, M. O. (2006). Mental health outcomes of cocaine-exposed children at 6 years of age. *Journal of Pediatric Psychology, 31,* 85–97.

Lindblad, F., & Hjern, A. (2010). ADHD after fetal exposure to maternal smoking. *Nicotine and Tobacco Research, 12,* 408–415.

Lindau, S. T., Schumm, L. P., Laumann, E. O., Levinson, W., O'Muircheartaigh, C. A., & Waite, L. J. (2007). A study of sexuality and health among older adults in the United States. *New England Journal of Medicine, 357,* 762–774.

Lindauer, M. S., Orwoll, L., & Kelley, M. C. (1997). Aging artists on the creativity of their old age. *Creativity Research Journal, 10,* 133–152.

Lindsay-Hartz, J., de Rivera, J., & Mascolo, M. F. (1995). Differentiating guilt and shame and their effects on motivation. In J. P. Tangney & K. W. Fischer (Eds.), *Self-conscious emotions* (pp. 274–300). New York: Guilford.

Lindsey, E. W., Colwell, M. J., Frabutt, J. M., Chambers, J. C., & MacKinnon-Lewis, C. (2008). Mother–child dyadic synchrony in European-American families during early adolescence: Relations with self-esteem and prosocial behavior. *Merrill-Palmer Quarterly, 54,* 289–315.

Lindsey, E. W., & Mize, J. (2000). Parent–child physical and pretense play: Links to children's social competence. *Merrill-Palmer Quarterly, 46,* 565–591.

Linebarger, D. L., Kosanic, A. Z., Greenwood, C. R., & Doku, N. S. (2004). Effects of viewing the television program *Between the Lions* on the emergent literacy skills of young children. *Journal of Educational Psychology, 96,* 297–308.

Linebarger, D. L., & Piotrowski, J. T. (2010). Structure and strategies in children's educational television: The roles of program type and learning strategies in children's learning. *Child Development, 81,* 1582–1597.

Linley, P. A. (2003). Positive adaptation to trauma: Wisdom as both process and outcome. *Journal of Traumatic Stress, 16,* 601–610.

Linn, R. L., & Welner, K. G. (2007). *Race-conscious policies for assigning students to schools: Social science research and the Supreme Court cases.* Washington, DC: National Academy Press.

Linver, M. R., Martin, A., & Brooks-Gunn, J. (2004). Measuring infants' home environment: The ITHOME for infants between birth and 12 months in four national data sets. *Parenting: Science and Practice, 4,* 115–137.

Lippe, T. van der (2010). Women's employment and housework. In J. Treas & S. Drobnic (Eds.), *Dividing the Domestic: Men, women, and household work in cross-national perspective* (pp. 41–58). Stanford, CA: Stanford University Press.

Lips, H. M. (2013). The gender pay gap: Challenging the rationalizations. Perceived equity, discrimination, and the limits of human capital models. *Sex Roles, 68,* 169–185.

Lipsitt, L. P. (2003). Crib death: A biobehavioral phenomenon? *Psychological Science, 12,* 164–170.

Lipton, J., & Spelke, E. (2004). Discrimination of large and small numerosities by human infants. *Infancy, 5,* 271–290.

Liu, C-C., Kanekiyo, T., Xu, H., & Bu, G. (2013). Apolipoprotein E and Alzheimer disease: Risk, mechanisms and therapy. *Nature Reviews Neurology, 9,* 106–118.

Liu, J., Raine, A., Venables, P. H., Dalais, C., & Mednick, S. A. (2003). Malnutrition at age 3 years and lower cognitive ability at age 11 years. *Archives of Paediatric and Adolescent Medicine, 157,* 593–600.

Liu, K., Daviglus, M. L., Loria, C. M., Colangelo, L. A., Spring, B., Moller, A. C., et al. (2012). Healthy lifestyle through young adulthood and the presence of low cardiovascular disease risk profile in middle age: The Coronary Artery Risk Development in (Young) Adults (CARDIA) study. *Circulation, 125,* 996–1004.

Liu, L., Drouet, V., Wu, J. W., Witter, M. P., Small, S. A., Clelland C., et al. (2012). Trans-synaptic spread of tau pathology in vivo. *PLoS One, 7,* e31302.

Livingston, G., & Cohn, D. (2010). *Childlessness up among all women; down among women with advanced degrees.* Washington, DC: Pew Research Center. Retrieved from pewresearch.org/pubs/1642/more-women-without-children

Lloyd, M. E., Doydum, A. O., & Newcombe, N. S. (2009). Memory binding in early childhood: Evidence for a retrieval deficit. *Child Development, 80,* 1321–1328.

Lochman, J. E., & Dodge, K. A. (1998). Distorted perceptions in dyadic interactions of aggressive and nonaggressive boys: Effects of prior expectations, context, and boys' age. *Development and Psychopathology, 10,* 495–512.

Lock, J., & Kirz, N. (2008). Eating disorders: Anorexia nervosa. In W. E. Graighead, D. J. Miklowitz, & L. W. Craighead (Eds.), *Psychopathology: History, diagnosis, and empirical foundations* (pp. 467–494). Hoboken, NJ: Wiley.

Loehlin, J. C., Horn, J. M., & Willerman, L. (1997). Heredity, environment, and IQ in the Texas Adoption Project. In R. J. Sternberg & E. L. Grigorenko (Eds.), *Intelligence, heredity, and environment* (pp. 105–125). New York: Cambridge University Press.

Loehlin, J. C., Jonsson, E. G., Gustavsson, J. P., Stallings, M. C., Gillespie, N. A., Wright, M. J., & Martin, N. G. (2005). Psychological masculinity–femininity via the gender diagnosticity approach: Heritability and consistency across ages and populations. *Journal of Personality, 73,* 1295–1319.

Loehlin, J. C., & Martin, N. G. (2001). Age changes in personality traits and their heritabilities during the adult years: Evidence from Australian twin registry samples. *Personality and Individual Differences, 30,* 1147–1160.

Loganovskaja, T. K., & Loganovsky, K. N. (1999). EEG, cognitive and psychopathological abnormalities in children irradiated in utero. *International Journal of Psychophysiology, 34,* 211–224.

Loganovsky, K. N., Loganovskaja, T. K., Nechayev, S. Y., Antipchuk, Y. Y., & Bomko, M. A. (2008). Disrupted devlopment of the dominant hemisphere following prenatal irradiation. *Journal of Neuropsychiatry and Clinical Neurosciences, 20,* 274–291.

Lohman, D. F. (2000). Measures of intelligence: Cognitive theories. In A. E. Kazdin (Ed.), *Encyclopedia of psychology: Vol. 5* (pp. 147–150). Washington, DC: American Psychological Association.

Lohrmann, S., & Bambara, L. M. (2006). Elementary education teachers' beliefs about essential supports needed to successfully include students with developmental disabilities who engage in challenging behaviors. *Research and Practice for Persons with Severe Disabilities, 31,* 157–173.

Loman, M. M., & Gunnar, M. R. (2010). Early experience and the development of stress reactivity and regulation in children. *Neuroscience and Biobehavioral Reviews, 34,* 867–876.

Long, D. D. (1985). A cross-cultural examination of fears of death among Saudi Arabians. *Omega, 16,* 43–50.

Loock, C., Conry, J., Cook, J. L., Chudley, A. E., & Rosales, T. (2005). Identifying fetal alcohol spectrum disorder in primary care. *Canadian Medical Association Journal, 172,* 628–630.

Loomans, E. M. Van der Stelt, O., van Eijsden, M., Gemke, R. J., Vrijkotte, T., & den Bergh, B. R. (2011). Antenatal maternal anxiety is associated with problem behaviour at age five. *Early Human Development, 87,* 565–570.

Lopez, C. M., Driscoll, K. A., & Kistner, J. A. (2009). Sex differences and response styles: Subtypes of rumination and associations with depressive symptoms. *Journal of Clinical Child and Adolescent Psychology, 38,* 27–35.

Lorenz, K. (1952). *King Solomon's ring.* New York: Crowell.

Lou, E., Lalonde, R. N., & Giguère, B. (2012). Making the decision to move out: Bicultural young adults and the negotiation of cultural demands and family relationships. *Journal of Cross-Cultural Psychology, 43,* 663–670.

Louie, V. (2001). Parents' aspirations and investment: The role of social class in the educational experiences of 1.5- and second-generation Chinese Americans. *Harvard Educational Review, 71,* 438–474.

Louis, J., Cannard, C., Bastuji, H., & Challemel, M. J. (1997). Sleep ontogenesis revisited: A longitudinal 24-hour home polygraphic study on 15 normal infants during the first two years of life. *Sleep, 20,* 323–333.

Lourenco, O. (2003). Making sense of Turiel's dispute with Kohlberg: The case of the child's moral competence. *New Ideas in Psychology, 21,* 43–68.

Lövdén, M., Bergman, L., Adolfsson, R., Lindenberger, U., & Nilsson, L.-G. (2005). Studying individual aging in an interindividual context: Typical paths of age-related, dementia-related, and mortality-related cognitive development in old age. *Psychology and Aging, 20,* 303–316.

Lövdén, M., Schmiedek, F., Kennedy, K. M., Rodrigue, K. M., Lindenberger, U., & Raz, N. (2012). Does variability in cognitive performance correlated with frontal brain volume? *NeuroImage, 64,* 209–215.

Love, J. M., Chazan-Cohen, R., & Raikes, H. (2007). Forty years of research knowledge and use: From Head Start to Early Head Start and beyond. In J. L. Aber, S. J. Bishop-Josef, S. M. Jones, K. T. McLearn, & D. Phillips (Eds.), *Child development and social policy: Knowledge for action* (pp. 79–95). Washington, DC: American Psychological Association.

Love, J. M., Harrison, L., Sagi-Schwartz, A., van IJzendoorn, M. H., Ross, C., & Ungerer, J. A. (2003). Child care quality matters: How conclusions may vary with context. *Child Development, 74,* 1021–1033.

Love, J. M., Kisker, E. E., Ross, C., Raikes, H., Constantine, J., Boller, K., & Brooks-Gunn, J. (2005). The effectiveness of Early Head Start for 3-year-old children and their parents: Lessons for policy and programs. *Developmental Psychology, 41,* 885–901.

Love, J. M., Tarullo, L. B., Raikes, H., & Chazan-Cohen, R. (2006). Head Start: What do we know about its effectiveness? What do we need to know? In K. McCartney & D. Phillips (Eds.), *Blackwell handbook of early childhood development* (pp. 550–575). Malden, MA: Blackwell.

Low, S. M., & Stocker, C. (2012). Family functioning and children's adjustment: Associations among parents' depressed mood, marital hostility, parent–child hostility, and children's adjustment. *Journal of Family Psychology, 19,* 394–403.

Lowenstein, A., Katz, R., & Gur-Yaish, N. (2007). Reciprocity in parent–child exchange and life satisfaction among the elderly: A cross-national perspective. *Journal of Social Issues, 63,* 865–883.

Lown, A. E., Nayak, M. B., Korcha, R. A., & Greenfield, T. K. (2011). Child physical and sexual abuse: A comprehensive look at alcohol consumption patterns, consequences, and dependence from the National Alcohol Survey. *Alcoholism: Clinical and Experimental Research, 35,* 317–325.

Lubart, T. I. (2003). In search of creative intelligence. In R. J. Sternberg, J. Lautrey, & T. I. Lubart (Eds.), *Models of intelligence: International perspectives* (pp. 279–292). Washington, DC: American Psychological Association.

Lubart, T. I., Georgsdottir, A., & Besançon, M. (2009). The nature of creative giftedness and talent. In T. Balchin, B. Hymer, & D. J. Matthews (Eds.), *The Routledge international companion to gifted education* (pp. 42–49). New York: Routledge.

Lubart, T. I., & Sternberg, R. J. (1998). Life span creativity: An investment theory approach. In C. E. Adams-Price (Ed.), *Creativity and successful aging.* New York: Springer.

Luby, J., Belden, A., Sullivan, J., Hayen, R., McCadney, A., & Spitznagel, E. (2009). Shame and guilt in preschool depression: Evidence for elevations in self-conscious emotions in depression as early as age 3. *Journal of Child Psychology and Psychiatry, 50,* 1156–1166.

Lucas, R. E., Clark, A. E., Georgellis, Y., & Diener, E. (2003). Reexamining adaptation and the set point model of happiness: Reactions to changes in marital status. *Journal of Personality and Social Psychology, 84,* 803–805.

Lucas, S. R., & Behrends, M. (2002). Sociodemographic diversity, correlated achievement, and de facto tracking. *Sociology of Education, 75,* 328–348.

Lucas-Thompson, R., & Clarke-Stewart, K. A. (2007). Forecasting friendship: How marital quality, maternal mood, and attachment security are linked to children's peer relationships. *Journal of Applied Developmental Psychology, 28,* 499–514.

Luciana, M. (2003). The neural and functional development of the human prefrontal cortex. In M. de Haan & M. H. Johnson (Eds.), *The cognitive neuroscience of development* (pp. 157–180). New York: Psychology Press.

Luciana, M. (2007). Special issue: Developmental cognitive neuroscience. *Developmental Review, 27,* 277–282.

Ludemann, P. M. (1991). Generalized discrimination of positive facial expressions by seven-and ten-month-old infants. *Child Development, 62,* 55–67.

Luecken, L. J. (2008). Long-term consequences of parental death in childhood: Psychological and physiological manifestations. In M. S. Stroebe, R. O. Hansson, H. Schut, & W. Stroebe (Eds.), *Handbook of bereavement research and practice* (pp. 397–416). Washington, DC: American Psychological Association.

Lukas, C., & Seiden, H. M. (2007). *Silent grief: Living in the wake of suicide* (rev. ed.). London, U.K.: Jessica Kingsley.

Luke, A., Cooper, R. S., Prewitt, T. E., Adeyemo, A. A., & Forrester, T. E. (2001). Nutritional consequences of the African diaspora. *Annual Review of Nutrition, 21,* 47–71.

Lukowski, A. F., Koss, M., Burden, M. J., Jonides, J., Nelson, C. A., Kaciroti, N., et al. (2010). Iron deficiency in infancy and neurocognitive functioning at 19 years: Evidence of long-term deficits in executive function and recognition memory. *Nutritional Neuroscience, 13,* 54–70.

Luna, B., Garver, K. E., Urban, T. A., Lazar, N. A., & Sweeney, J. A. (2004). Maturation of cognitive processes from late childhood to adulthood. *Child Development, 75,* 1357–1372.

Luna, B., Thulborn, K. R., Monoz, D. P., Merriam, E. P., Garver, K. E., Minshew, N. J., Keshavan, M. S., Genovese, C. R., Eddy, W. F., & Sweeney, J. A. (2001). Maturation of widely distributed brain function subserves cognitive development. *Neuroimage, 13,* 786–793.

Lund, D., Caserta, M., Utz, R., & de Vries, B. (2010). Experiences and early coping of bereaved spouses/partners in an intervention based on the dual process model (DPM). *Omega, 61,* 291–313.

Lund, D. A. (1996). Bereavement and loss. In J. E. Birren (Ed.), *Encyclopedia of gerontology* (pp. 173–183). San Diego: Academic Press.

Lund, D. A. (1998). Statements and perspectives from leaders in the field of aging in Utah. In *Utah sourcebook on aging.* Salt Lake City: Empire Publishing.

Lund, D. A. (2005). *My journey* [Sue's letter]. Unpublished document. Salt Lake City, UT: University of Utah.

Lund, D. A., & Caserta, M. S. (2001). When the unexpected happens: Husbands coping with the deaths of their wives. In D. Lund (Ed.), *Men coping with grief* (pp. 147–166). Amityville, NY: Baywood.

Lund, D. A., & Caserta, M. S. (2004a). Facing life alone: Loss of a significant other in later life. In D. Doda (Ed), *Living with grief: Loss in later life* (pp. 207–223). Washington, DC: Hospice Foundation of America.

Lund, D. A., & Caserta, M. S. (2004b). Older men coping with widowhood. *Geriatrics and Aging, 7*(6), 29–33.

Lund, D. A., Caserta, M. S., de Vries, B., & Wright, S. (2004). Restoration after bereavement. *Generations Review, 14,* 9–15.

Lund, D. A., Caserta, M. S., & Dimond, M. F. (1993). The course of spousal bereavement in later life. In M. S. Stroebe, W. Stroebe, & R. O. Hansson (Eds.), *Handbook of bereavement* (pp. 240–245). New York: Cambridge University Press.

Lund, D. A., Utz, R., Caserta, M., & de Vries, B. (2008–2009). Humor, laughter, and happiness in the daily lives of recently bereaved spouses. *Omega, 58,* 87–105.

Lund, D. A., Utz, R., Caserta, M. S., & Wright, S. D. (2009). Examining what caregivers do during respite time to make respite more effective. *Journal of Applied Gerontology, 28,* 109–131.

Lund, D. A., Wright, S. D., Caserta, M. S., Utz, R. L., Lindfelt, C., Bright, O., et al. (2010). *Respite services: Enhancing the quality of daily life for caregivers and care receivers.* San Bernardino, CA: California State University at San Bernardino.

Lund, N., Pedersen, L. H., & Henriksen, T. B. (2009). Selective serotonin reuptake inhibitor exposure in utero and pregnancy outcomes. *Archives of Pediatrics and Adolescent Medicine, 163,* 949–954.

Lundy, B. L. (2003). Father- and mother-infant face-to-face interactions: Differences in mind-related comments and infant attachment? *Infant Behavior and Development, 26,* 200–212.

Luo, L., & Craik, F. I. M. (2008). Aging and memory: A cognitive approach. *Canadian Journal of Psychiatry, 53,* 346–353.

Luo, Y., & Baillargeon, R. (2005). When the ordinary seems unexpected: Evidence for incremental physical knowledge in young infants. *Cognition, 95,* 297–328.

Luong, G., Charles, S. T., & Fingerman, K. L. (2011). Better with age: Social relationships across adulthood. *Journal of Social and Personal Relationships, 28,* 9–23.

Luster, T., & Haddow, J. L. (2005). Adolescent mothers and their children: An ecological perspective. In T. Luster & J. L. Haddow (Eds.), *Parenting: An ecological perspective* (2nd ed., pp. 73–101). Mahwah, NJ: Erlbaum.

Luthar, S. S., & Becker, B. E. (2002). Privileged but pressured: A study of affluent youth. *Child Development, 73,* 1593–1610.

Luthar, S. S., & Goldstein, A. S. (2008). Substance use and related behaviors among suburban late adolescents: The importance of perceived parent containment. *Development and Psychopathology, 20,* 591–614.

Luthar, S. S., & Latendresse, S. J. (2005). Children of the affluent: Challenges to well-being. *Current Directions in Psychological Science, 14,* 49–53.

Luxembourg Income Study. (2011). LIS key figures. Retrieved from www.lisdatacenter.org/data-access/key-figures/download-key-figures

Luyckx, K., Goossens, L., & Soenens, B. (2006). A developmental contextual perspective on identity construction in emerging adulthood: Change dynamics in commitment formation and commitment evaluation. *Developmental Psychology, 42,* 366–380.

Luyckx, K., Goossens, L., Soenens, B., & Beyers, W. (2006). Unpacking commitment and exploration: Preliminary validation of an integrative model of late adolescent identity formation. *Journal of Adolescence, 29,* 361–378.

Luyckx, K., Soenens, B., Vansteenkiste, M., Goossens, L., & Berzonsky, M. D. (2007). Parental psychological control and dimensions of identity formation in emerging adulthood. *Journal of Family Psychology, 21,* 546–550.

Lynch, S. K., Turkheimer, E., D'Onofrio, B. M., Mendle, J., Emery, R. E., Slutske, W. S., & Martin, N. G. (2006). A genetically informed study of the association between harsh punishment and offspring behavioral problems. *Journal of Family Psychology, 20,* 190–198.

Lyness, K. S., & Heilman, M. E. (2006). When fit is fundamental: Performance evaluations and promotions of upper-level female and male managers. *Journal of Applied Psychology, 90,* 777–785.

Lyon, T. D., & Flavell, J. H. (1994). Young children's understanding of "remember" and "forget." *Child Development, 65,* 1357–1371.

Lytton, H., & Gallagher, L. (2002). Parenting twins and the genetics of parenting. In M. H. Bornstein (Ed.), *Handbook of parenting* (Vol. 1, pp. 227–253). Mahwah, NJ: Erlbaum.

M

Ma, F., Xu, F., Heyman, G. D., & Lee, K. (2011). Chinese children's evaluations of white lies: Weighing the consequences for recipients. *Journal of Experimental Child Psychology, 108,* 308–321.

Maas, F. K. (2008). Children's understanding of promising, lying, and false belief. *Journal of General Psychology, 13,* 301–321.

Maas, F. K., & Abbeduto, L. J. (2001). Children's judgments about intentionally and unintentionally broken promises. *Journal of Child Language, 28,* 517–529.

Macaluso, A., & De Vito, G. (2004). Muscle strength, power and adaptations to resistance training in older people. *European Journal of Applied Physiology, 91,* 450–472.

Maccoby, E. E. (1984). Socialization and developmental change. *Child Development, 55,* 317–328.

Maccoby, E. E. (1998). *The two sexes: Growing up apart, coming together.* Cambridge, MA: Belknap.

Maccoby, E. E. (2002). Gender and group process: A developmental perspective. *Current Directions in Psychological Science, 11,* 54–58.

MacDonald, S. W. S., Hultsch, D. F., & Dixon, R. A. (2011). Aging and the shape of cognitive change before death: Terminal decline or terminal drop? *Journal of Gerontology, 66,* 292–301.

MacDonald, S. W. S., Li, S-C., & Bäckman, L. (2009). Neural underpinnings of within-person variability in cognitive functioning. *Psychology and Aging, 24,* 792–808.

MacDonald, W. L., & DeMaris, A. (1996). The effects of stepparent's gender and new biological children. *Journal of Family Issues, 17,* 5–25.

Macek, P., Bejĉek, J., & Vaníĉková, J. (2007). Contemporary Czech emerging adults: Generation growing up in the period of social changes. *Journal of Adolescent Research, 22,* 444–475.

Machin, G. A. (2005). Multiple birth. In H. W. Taeusch, R. A. Ballard, & C. A. Gleason (Eds.), *Avery's diseases of the newborn* (8th ed., pp. 57–62). Philadelphia: Saunders.

Mackey, K., Arnold, M. L., & Pratt, M. W. (2001). Adolescents' stories of decision making in more and less authoritative families: Representing the voices of parents in narrative. *Journal of Adolescent Research, 16,* 243–268.

Mackie, S., Show, P., Lenroot, R., Pierson, R., Greenstein, D. K., & Nugent, T. F., III. (2007). Cerebellar development and clinical outcome in attention deficit hyperactivity disorder. *American Journal of Psychiatry, 164,* 647–655.

Mackinnon, S. P., Nosko, A., Pratt, M. W., & Norris, J. E. (2011). Intimacy in young adults' narratives of romance and friendship predicts Eriksonian generativity: A mixed mother analysis. *Journal of Personality, 79,* 587–617.

MacLean, P. S., Bergouignan, A., Cornier, M-A., & Jackman, M. R. (2011). Biology's response to dieting: The impetus for weight gain. *American Journal of Physiology—Regular, Integrated, and Comparative Physiology, 301,* R581–R600.

MacWhinney, B. (2005). Language development. In M. H. Bornstein & M. E. Lamb (Eds.), *Developmental science: An advanced textbook* (5th ed., pp. 359–387). Mahwah, NJ: Erlbaum.

Maddi, S. R. (2005). On hardiness and other pathways to resilience. *American Psychologist, 60,* 261–262.

Maddi, S. R. (2006). Hardiness: The courage to be resilient. In J. C. Thomas, D. L. Segal, & M. Hersen (Eds.), *Comprehensive handbook of personality and psychopathology: Vol. 1. Personality and everyday functioning* (pp. 306–321). Hoboken, NJ: Wiley.

Maddi, S. R. (2007). The story of hardiness: Twenty years of theorizing, research, and practice. In A. Monat, R. S. Lazarus, & G. Reevy (Eds.), *Praeger handbook on stress and coping* (Vol. 2, pp. 327–340). Wastport, CT: Praeger.

Maddi, S. R. (2011). Personality hardiness as a pathway to resilience under educational stresses. In G. M. Reevy & E. Frydenberg (Eds.), *Personality, stress, and coping: Implications for education* (pp. 293–313). Charlotte, NC: Information Age Publishing.

Maddox, G. L. (1963). Activity and morale: A longitudinal study of selected elderly subjects. *Social Forces, 42,* 195–204.

Madey, S. F., & Rodgers, L. (2009). The effect of attachment and Sternberg's triangular theory of love on relationship satisfaction. *Individual Differences Research, 7,* 76–84.

Madigan, S., Bakermans-Kranenburg, M. J., van IJzendoorn, M. H., Moran, G., Pederson, D. R., & Benoit, D. (2006). Unresolved states of mind, anomalous parental behavior, and disorganized attachment: A review and meta-analysis of a transmission gap. *Attachment and Human Development, 8,* 89–111.

Madnawat, A. V. S., & Kachhawa, P. S. (2007). Age, gender, and living circumstances: Discriminating older adults on death anxiety. *Death Studies, 31,* 763–769.

Madon, S., Jussim, L., & Eccles, J. (1997). In search of the powerful self-fulfilling prophecy. *Journal of Personality and Social Psychology, 72,* 791–809.

Madsen, S. A., & Juhl, T. (2007). Paternal depression in the postnatal period assessed with traditional and male depression scales. *Journal of Men's Health and Gender, 4,* 26–31.

Maglio, C. J., & Robinson, S. E. (1994). The effects of death education on death anxiety: A meta-analysis. *Omega, 29,* 319–335.

Magnuson, K., & Shager H. (2010). Early education: Progress and promise for children from low-income families. *Children and Youth Services Review, 32,* 1186–1198.

Magolda, M. B., Abes, E., & Torres, V. (2009). Epistemological, intrapersonal, and interpersonal development in the college years and young adulthood. In M. C. Smith & N. DeFrates-Densch (Eds.), *Handbook of research on adult learning and development* (pp. 183–219). New York: Routledge.

Mahanran, L. G., Bauman, P. A., Kalman, D., Skolnik, H., & Pele, S. M. (1999). Master athletes: Factors affecting performance. *Sports Medicine, 28,* 273–285.

Main, M., & Goldwyn, R. (1998). *Adult attachment classification system.* London: University College.

Main, M., & Solomon, J. (1990). Procedures for identifying infants as disorganized/disoriented during the Ainsworth Strange Situation. In M. Greenberg, D. Cicchetti, & M. Cummings (Eds.), *Attachment in the preschool years: Theory, research, and intervention* (pp. 121–160). Chicago: University of Chicago Press.

Majdandžić, M., & van den Boom, D. C. (2007). Multimethod longitudinal assessment of temperament in early childhood. *Journal of Personality, 75,* 12.

Makishita, H., & Matsunaga, K. (2008). Differences of drivers' reaction times according to age and mental workload. *Accident Analysis Prevention, 40,* 567–575.

Makrantonaki, E., & Xouboulis, C. C. (2007). Molecular mechanisms of skin aging: State of the art. *Annals of the New York Academy of Sciences, 1119,* 40–50.

Malatesta, C. Z., Grigoryev, P., Lamb, C., Albin, M., & Culver, C. (1986). Emotion socialization and expressive development in preterm and full-term infants. *Child Development, 57,* 316–330.

Malina, R. M., & Bouchard, C. (1991). *Growth, maturation, and physical activity.* Champaign, IL: Human Kinetics.

Malone, M. M. (1982). Consciousness of dying and projective fantasy of young children with malignant disease. *Developmental and Behavioral Pediatrics, 3,* 55–60.

Mandara, J., Varner, F., Greene, N., & Richman, S. (2009). Intergenerational family predictors of the black–white achievement gap. *Journal of Educational Psychology, 101,* 867–878.

Mandler, J. M. (2004). Thought before language. *Trends in Cognitive Sciences, 8,* 508–513.

Mandler, J. M., & McDonough, L. (1998). On developing a knowledge base in infancy. *Developmental Psychology, 34,* 1274–1288.

Mangelsdorf, S. C., Schoppe, S. J., & Buur, H. (2000). The meaning of parental reports: A contextual approach to the study of temperament and behavior problems. In V. J. Molfese & D. L. Molfese (Eds.), *Temperament and personality across the life span* (pp. 121–140). Mahwah, NJ: Erlbaum.

Mani, T. M., Bedwell, J. S., & Miller, L. S. (2005). Age-related decrements in performance on a brief continuous performance task. *Archives of Clinical Neuropsychology, 20,* 575–586.

Manole, M. D., & Hickey, R. W. (2006). Preterminal gasping and effects on the cardiac function. *Critical Care Medicine, 34*(Suppl.), S438–S441.

Maquestiaux, F., Laguë-Beauvais, M., Ruthruff, E., Hartley, A., & Bherer, L. (2010). Learning to bypass the central bottleneck: Declining automaticity with advancing age. *Psychology and Aging, 25,* 177–192.

Maratsos, M. (2000). More overregularizations after all: New data and discussion on Marcus, Pinker, Ullman, Hollander, Rosen, & Xu. *Journal of Child Language, 27,* 183–212.

Marcon, R. A. (1999a). Differential impact of preschool models on development and early learning of inner-city children: A three-cohort study. *Developmental Psychology, 35,* 358–375.

Marcon, R. A. (1999b). Positive relationships between parent–school involvement and public school inner-city preschoolers' development and academic performance. *School Psychology Review, 28,* 395–412.

Marcus, G. F. (1995). Children's overregularization of English plurals: A quantitative analysis. *Journal of Child Language, 22,* 447–459.

Marcus-Newhall, A., Thompson, S., & Thomas, C. (2001). Examining a gender stereotype: Menopausal women. *Journal of Applied Social Psychology, 31,* 698–719.

Margrett, J. A., Daugherty, K., Martin, P., MacDonald, M., Davey, A., Woodard, J. L., et al. (2011). Affect and loneliness among centenarians and the oldest old: The role of individual and social resources. *Aging and Mental Health, 15,* 385–396.

Marian, V., Neisser, U., & Rochat, P. (1996). *Can 2-month-old infants distinguish live from videotaped interactions with their mothers?* (Emory Cognition Project, Report #33). Atlanta, GA: Emory University.

Mariano, K. A., & Harton, H. C. (2005). Similarities in aggression, inattention/hyperactivity, depression, and anxiety in middle childhood friendships. *Journal of Social and Clinical Psychology, 24,* 471–496.

Marjoribanks, J., Farquhar, C., Roberts, H., & Lethaby, A. (2012). Long term hormone therapy for perimenopausal and postmenopausal women. *Cochrane Database of Systematic Reviews, Issue 7,* Art. No.: CD004143.

Markey, P. M., & Markey, C. N. (2007). Romantic ideas, romantic obtainment, and relationship experiences: The complementarity of interpersonal traits among romantic partners. *Journal of Social and Personal Relationships, 24,* 517–533.

Markman, E. M. (1992). Constraints on word learning: Speculations about their nature, origins, and domain specificity. In M. R. Gunnar & M. P.

Markova, G., & Legerstee, M. (2006). Contingency, imitation, and affect sharing: Foundations of infants' social awareness. *Developmental Psychology, 42,* 132–141.

Markovits, H., Benenson, J., & Dolensky, E. (2001). Evidence that children and adolescents have internal models of peer interactions that are gender differentiated. *Child Development, 72,* 879–886.

Markovits, H., & Vachon, R. (1990). Conditional reasoning, representation, and level of abstraction. *Developmental Psychology, 26,* 942–951.

Marks, G. N., Cresswell, J., & Ainley, J. (2006). Explaining socioeconomic inequalities in student achievement: The role of home and school factors. *Educational Research and Evaluation, 12,* 105–128.

Marks, N. F. (1996). Caregiving across the lifespan: National prevalence and predictors. *Family Relations, 45,* 27–36.

Marks, N. F., Bumpass, L. L., & Jun, H. (2004). Family roles and well-being during the middle life course. In O. G. Brim, C. D. Ryff, & R.C. Kessler (Eds.), *How healthy are we? A national study of well-being at midlife* (pp. 514–549). Chicago: University of Chicago Press.

Marks, N. F., & Greenfield, E. A. (2009). The influence of family relationships on adult psychological well-being and generativity. In M. C. Smith & N. DeFrates-Densch (Eds.), *Handbook of research on adult learning and development* (pp. 306–349). New York: Routledge.

Marks, N. F., & Lambert, J. D. (1998). Marital status continuity and change among young and midlife adults. *Journal of Family Issues, 19,* 652–686.

Marks, R. (2010). Hip fracture epidemiological trends, outcomes, and risk factors, 1970–2009. *International Journal of General Medicine, 3,* 1–17.

Markstrom, C. A., & Kalmanir, H. M. (2001). Linkages between the psychosocial stages of identity and intimacy and the ego strengths of fidelity and love. *Identity, 1,* 179–196.

Markstrom, C. A., Sabino, V., Turner, B., & Berman, R. (1997). The Psychosocial Inventory of Ego Strengths: Development and validation of a new Eriksonian measure. *Journal of Youth and Adolescence, 26,* 705–732.

Markus, H. R., & Herzog, A. R. (1992). The role of self-concept in aging. In K. W. Schaie & M. P. Lawton (Eds.), *Annual review of gerontology and geriatrics* (pp. 110–143). New York: Springer.

Marlier, L., & Schaal, B. (2005). Human newborns prefer human milk: Conspecific milk odor is attractive without postnatal exposure. *Child Development, 76,* 155–168.

Marra, R., & Palmer, B. (2004). Encouraging intellectual growth: Senior college student profiles. *Journal of Adult Development, 11,* 111–122.

Marsee, M. A., & Frick, P. J. (2010). Callous-unemotional traits and aggression in youth. In W. F. Arsenio & E. A. Lemerise (Eds.), *Emotions, aggression, and morality in children: Bridging development and psychopathology* (pp. 137–156). Washington, DC: American Psychological Association.

Marsh, H. W. (1990). The structure of academic self-concept: The Marsh/Shavelson model. *Journal of Educational Psychology, 82,* 623–636.

Marsh, H. W., & Ayotte, V. (2003). Do multiple dimensions of self-concept become more differentiated with age? The differential distinctiveness hypothesis. *Journal of Educational Psychology, 95,* 687–706.

Marsh, H. W., Craven, R., & Debus, R. (1998). Structure, stability, and development of young children's self-concepts: A multicohort–multioccasion study. *Child Development, 69,* 1030–1053.

Marsh, H. W., Ellis, L. A., & Craven, R. G. (2002). How do preschool children feel about themselves? Unraveling measurement and multidimensional self-concept structure. *Developmental Psychology, 38,* 376–393.

Marsh, H. W., Gerlach, E., Trautwein, U., Lüdtke, O., & Brettschneider, W.-D. (2007). Longitudinal study of predadolescent sport self-concept and performance: Reciprocal effects and causal ordering. *Child Development, 78,* 1640–1656.

Marsh, H. W., Trautwein, U., Lüdtke, O., Koller, O., & Baumert, J. (2005). Academic self-concept, interest, grades, and standardized test scores: Reciprocal effects models of causal ordering. *Child Development, 76,* 397–416.

Marshall, B. J., & Davies, B. (2011). Bereavement in children and adults following the death of a sibling. In R. Neimeyer, D. Harris, H. Winokuer, G. Thornton (Eds.), *Grief and bereavement in contemporary society: Bridging research and practice* (pp. 107–116). New York: Routledge.

Marshall-Baker, A., Lickliter, R., & Cooper, R. P. (1998). Prolonged exposure to a visual pattern may promote behavioral organization in preterm infants. *Journal of Perinatal and Neonatal Nursing, 12,* 50–62.

Martin, C. L., & Fabes, R. A. (2001). The stability and consequences of young children's same-sex peer interactions. *Developmental Psychology, 37,* 431–446.

Martin, C. L., & Halverson, C. F. (1987). The role of cognition in sex role acquisition. In D. B. Carter (Ed.), *Current conceptions of sex roles and sex typing: Theory and research* (pp. 123–137). New York: Praeger.

Martin, C. L., & Ruble, D. (2004). Children's search for gender cues: Cognitive perspectives on gender development. *Current Directions in Psychological Science, 13,* 67–70.

Martin, C. L., Ruble, D. N., & Szkrybalo, J. (2002). Cognitive theories of early gender development. *Psychological Bulletin, 128,* 903–933.

Martin, G. L., & Pear, J. (2011). *Behavior modification: What it is and how to do it* (9th ed.). Upper Saddle River, NJ: Pearson.

Martin, K. A. (1996). *Puberty, sexuality and the self: Girls and boys at adolescence.* New York: Routledge.

Martin, P., Long, M. V., & Poon, L. W. (2002). Age changes and differences in personality traits and states of the old and very old. *Journal of Gerontology, 57B,* P144–P152.

Martin, R. (2008). Meiotic errors in human oogenesis and spermatogenesis. *Reproductive Biomedicine Online, 16,* 523–531.

Martinez-Frias, M. L., Bermejo, E., Rodríguez-Pinilla, E., & Frías, J. L. (2004). Risk for congenital anomalies associated with different sporadic and daily doses of alcohol consumption during pregnancy: A case-control study. *Birth Defects Research, Part A, Clinical and Molecular Teratology, 70,* 194–200.

Martinot, D., & Désert, M. (2007). Awareness of a gender stereotype, personal beliefs, and self-perceptions regarding math ability: When boys do not surpass girls. *Social Psychology of Education, 10,* 455–471.

Maruta, T., Colligan, R. C., Malinchoc, M., & Offord, K. P. (2002). Optimism–pessimism assessed in the 1960s and self-reported health status 30 years later. *Mayo Clinic Proceedings, 77,* 748–753.

Marzolf, D. P., & DeLoache, J. S. (1994). Transfer in young children's understanding of spatial representations. *Child Development, 65,* 1–15.

Masataka, N. (1996). Perception of motherese in a signed language by 6-month-old deaf infants. *Developmental Psychology, 32,* 874–879.

Mascolo, M. F., & Fischer, K. W. (2007). The codevelopment of self and sociomoral emotions during the toddler years. In C. A. Brownell & C. B. Kopp (Eds.), *Socioemotional development in the toddler years: Transitions and transformations* (pp. 66–99). New York: Guilford.

Mashburn, A. J. (2008). Quality of social and physical environments in preschools and children's development of academic, language, and literacy skills. *Applied Developmental Science, 12,* 113–127.

Mashburn, A. J., Pianta, R. C., Mamre, B. K., Downer, J. T., Barbarin, O. A., Bryant, D., et al. (2008). Measures of classroom quality in prekindergarten and children's development of academic, language, and social skills. *Child Development, 79,* 732–749.

Maslach, C., Schaufeli, W. B., & Leiter, M. P. (2001). Job burnout. *Annual Review of Psychology, 52,* 397–422.

Mason, M. G., & Gibbs, J. C. (1993a). Role-taking opportunities and the transition to advanced moral judgment. *Moral Education Forum, 18,* 1–12.

Mason, M. G., & Gibbs, J. C. (1993b). Social perspective taking and moral judgment among college students. *Journal of Adolescent Research, 8,* 109–123.

Masoro, E. J. (2011). Terminal weight loss, frailty, and mortality. In E. J. Masoro & S. N. Austad (Eds.), *Handbook of the biology of aging* (7th ed., pp. 321–331). San Diego, CA: Academic Press.

Massachusetts Expert Panel on End-of-Life Care. (2010, October). *Patient-centered care and human mortality: The urgency of health system reforms to ensure respect for patients' wishes and accountability for excellence in care.* Retrieved from www.mass .gov/hqcc/docs/expert-panel/final-expert-panel-report.pdf

Masten, A. S. (2001). Ordinary magic: Resilience processes in development. *American Psychologist, 56,* 227–238.

Masten, A. S., Burt, K. B., Roisman, G. I., Obradovic, J., Long, J. D., & Tellegen, A. (2004). Resources and resilience in the transition to adulthood: Continuity and change. *Development and Psychopathology, 16,* 1071–1094.

Masten, A. S., & Gewirtz, A. H. (2006). Vulnerability and resilience in early child development. In K. McCartney & D. Phillips (Eds.), *Blackwell handbook of early childhood development* (pp. 22–43). Malden, MA: Blackwell.

Masten, A. S., & Powell, J. L. (2003). A resilience framework for research, policy, and practice. In S. S. Luthar (Ed.), *Resilience and vulnerability* (pp. 1–25). New York: Cambridge University Press.

Masten, A. S., & Reed, M. J. (2002). Resilience in development. In C. R. Snyder & S. J. Lopez (Eds.), *Handbook of positive psychology* (pp. 74–88). New York: Oxford University Press.

Masten, A. S., & Shaffer, A. (2006). How families matter in child development: Reflections from research on risk and resilience. In A. S. Masten & A. Shaffer (Eds.), *Families count: Effects on child and adolescent development* (pp. 5–25). New York: Cambridge University Press.

Masters, R. K. (2012). Uncrossing the U.S. black–white mortality crossover: The role of cohort forces in life course mortality risk. *Demography, 49,* 773–796.

Mastropieri, D., & Turkewitz, G. (1999). Prenatal experience and neonatal responsiveness to vocal expression of emotion. *Developmental Psychobiology, 35,* 204–214.

Mather, M. (2010, May). *U.S. children in single-mother families* (PRB Data Brief). Washington, DC: Population Reference Bureau.

Mather, M., & Carstensen, L. L. (2005). Aging and motivated cognition: The positivity effect in attention and memory. *Trends in Cognitive Sciences, 9,* 496–502.

Mathews, T. J., & MacDorman, M. F. (2008). Infant mortality statistics from the 2005 period linked birth/infant death data set. *National Vital Statistics Reports, 57*(2), 1–32.

Matthews, K. A., Gump, B. B., Harris, K. F., Haney, T. L., & Barefoot, J. C. (2004). Hostile behaviors predict cardiovascular mortality among men enrolled in the Multiple Risk Factor Intervention Trial. *Circulation, 109,* 66–70.

Mattison, J. A., Roth, G. S., Beasley, T. M., Tilmont, E. M., Handy, A. M., Herbert, R. L., et al. (2012). Impact of caloric restriction on health and survival in rhesus monkeys from the NIA study. *Nature, 489,* 318–321.

Mattson, S. N., Calarco, K. E., & Lang, A. R. (2006). Focused and shifting attention in children with heavy prenatal alcohol exposure. *Neuropsychology, 20,* 361–369.

Maume, D. J., Jr. (2004). Is the glass ceiling a unique form of inequality? *Work and Occupations, 31,* 250–274.

Maurer, T. J. (2001). Career-relevant learning and development, worker age, and beliefs about self-efficacy for development. *Journal of Management, 27,* 123–140.

Maurer, T. J., Wrenn, K. A., & Weiss, E. M. (2003). Toward understanding and managing stereotypical beliefs about older workers' ability and desire for learning and development. In J. J. Martocchio & G. R. Ferris (Eds.), *Research in personnel and human resources management* (Vol. 22, pp. 253–285). Stamford, CT: JAI Press.

Mayberry, R. I. (2010). Early language acquisition and adult language ability: What sign language reveals about the critical period for language. In M. Marshark & P. E. Spencer (Eds.), *Oxford handbook of deaf studies, language, and education* (Vol. 2, pp. 281–291). New York: Oxford University Press.

Mayeux, L., & Cillessen, A. H. N. (2003). Development of social problem solving in early childhood: Stability, change, and associations with social competence. *Journal of Genetic Psychology, 164,* 153–173.

Maynard, A. E. (2002). Cultural teaching: The development of teaching skills in Maya sibling interactions. *Child Development, 73,* 969–982.

Maynard, A. E., & Greenfield, P. M. (2003). Implicit cognitive development in cultural tools and children: Lessons from Maya Mexico. *Cognitive Development, 18,* 489–510.

Maynard, A. E., Subrahmanyam, K., & Greenfield, P. M. (2005). Technology and the development of intelligence: From the loom to the computer. In R. J. Sternberg & D. D. Preiss (Eds.), *Intelligence and technology: The impact of tools in the nature and development of human abilities* (pp. 29–53). Mahwah, NJ: Erlbaum.

Mazerolle, M., Régner, I., Morisset, P., Rigalleau, F., & Huguet, P. (2012). Stereotype threat strengthens automatic recall and undermines controlled processes in older adults. *Psychological Science, 23,* 723–727.

McAdams, D. P., & Cox, K. S. (2010). Self and identity across the life span. In M. Lamb & A. Freund (Eds.), *Handbook of life-span development: Vol. 2. Social and emotional development* (pp. 158–207). Hoboken, NJ: Wiley.

McAdams, D. P., & de St. Aubin, E. (1992). A theory of generativity and its assessment through self-report, behavioral acts, and narrative themes in autobiography. *Journal of Personality and Social Psychology, 62,* 1003–1015.

McAdams, D. P., Hart, H. M., & Maruna, S. (1998). The anatomy of generativity. In D. P. McAdams & E. de St. Aubin (Eds.), *Generativity and adult development* (pp. 7–43). Washington, DC: American Psychological Association.

McAdams, D. P., & Logan, R. L. (2004). What is generativity? In E. de St. Aubin & D. P. McAdams (Eds.), *The generative society: Caring for future generations* (pp. 15–31). Washington, DC: American Psychological Association.

McAlister, A., & Peterson, C. C. (2006). Mental playmates: Siblings, executive functioning and theory of mind. *British Journal of Developmental Psychology, 24,* 733–751.

McAlister, A., & Peterson, C. C. (2007). A longitudinal study of child siblings and theory of mind development. *Cognitive Development, 22,* 258–270.

McAuley, E., & Elavsky, S. (2008). Self-efficacy, physical activity, and cognitive function. In W. W. Spirduso, L. W. Poon, & W. Chodzko-Zajko (Eds.), *Exercise and its mediating effects on cognition* (pp. 69–84). Champaign, IL: Human Kinetics.

McBee, M. T. (2006). A descriptive analysis of referral sources for gifted identification screening by race and socioeconomic status. *Journal of Secondary Gifted Education, 17,* 103–111.

McBride-Chang, C., & Kail, R. V. (2002). Cross-cultural similarities in the predictors of reading acquisition. *Child Development, 73,* 1392–1407.

McCabe, A. (1997). Developmental and cross-cultural aspects of children's narration. In M. Bamberg (Ed.), *Narrative development: Six approaches* (pp. 137–174). Mahwah, NJ: Erlbaum.

McCall, R. B., & Carriger, M. S. (1993). A meta-analysis of infant habituation and recognition memory performance as predictors of later IQ. *Child Development, 64,* 57–79.

McCartney, K., Dearing, E., Taylor, B., & Bub, K. (2007). Quality child care supports the achievement of low-income children: Direct and indirect pathways through caregiving and the home environment. *Journal of Applied Developmental Psychology, 28,* 411–426.

McCartney, K., Harris, M. J., & Bernieri, F. (1990). Growing up and growing apart: A developmental meta-analysis of twin studies. *Psychological Bulletin, 107,* 226–237.

McCartney, K., Owen, M., Booth, C., Clarke-Stewart, A., & Vandell, D. (2004). Testing a maternal attachment model of behavior problems in early childhood. *Journal of Child Psychology and Psychiatry, 45,* 765–778.

McCarton, C. (1998). Behavioral outcomes in low birth weight infants. *Pediatrics, 102,* 1293–1297.

McCarty, M. E., & Ashmead, D. H. (1999). Visual control of reaching and grasping in infants. *Developmental Psychology, 35,* 620–631.

McCarty, M. E., & Keen, R. (2005). Facilitating problem-solving performance among 9- and 12-month-old infants. *Journal of Cognition and Development, 6,* 209–228.

McClain, C. S., Rosenfeld, B., & Breitbart, W. (2003). Effect of spiritual well-being on end-of-life despair in terminally ill cancer patients. *Lancet, 361,* 1603–1607.

McClain-Jacobson, C., Rosenfeld, B., Kosinski, A., Pessin, H., Cimino, J. E., & Breitbart, W. (2004). Belief in an afterlife, spiritual well-being and end-of-life despair in patients with advanced cancer. *General Hospital Psychiatry, 26,* 484–486.

McClure, S., Laibson, D., Loewenstein, G., & Cohen, J. (2004). Separate neural systems value immediate and delayed monetary rewards. *Science, 306,* 503–507.

McColgan, K. L., & McCormack, T. (2008). Searching and planning: Young children's reasoning about past and future event sequences. *Child Development, 79,* 1477–1479.

McCrae, R. R., & Costa, P. T., Jr. (2006). Cross-cultural perspectives on adult personality trait development. In D. K. Mroczek & T. D. Little (Eds.), *Handbook of personality development* (pp. 129–146). Mahwah, NJ: Erlbaum.

McCrae, R. R. (2011). Personality theories for the 21st century. *Teaching of Psychology, 38,* 209–214.

McCune, L. (1993). The development of play as the development of consciousness. In M. H. Bornstein & A. O'Reilly (Eds.), *New directions for child development* (No. 59, pp. 67–79). San Francisco: Jossey-Bass.

McCurry, S. M., Logsdon, R. G., Teri, L., & Vitello, M. V. (2007). Evidence-based psychological treatments for insomnia in older adults. *Psychology and Aging, 22*, 18–27.

McDaniel, M. A., Einstein, G. O., & Rendell, P. G. (2007). The puzzle of inconsistent age-related declines in prospective memory: A multiprocess explanation. In M. Kliegel, M. A. McDaniel, & G. O. Einstein (Eds.), *Prospective memory: Cognitive, neuroscience, developmental, and applied perspectives* (pp. 141–160). Mahwah, NJ: Erlbaum.

McDill, T., Hall, S. K., & Turell, S. C. (2006). Aging and creating families: Never-married heterosexual women over forty. *Journal of Women and Aging, 18*, 37–50.

McDonagh, M. S., Osterweil, P., & Guise, J. M. (2005). The benefits and risks of inducing labour in patients with prior cesarean delivery: A systematic review. *BJOG, 112*, 1007–1015.

McDonald, L., & Robb, A. L. (2004). The economic legacy of divorce and separation for women in old age. *Canadian Journal on Aging, 23*(Suppl. 1), S83–S97.

McDonough, L. (1999). Early declarative memory for location. *British Journal of Developmental Psychology, 17*, 381–402.

McElhaney, K. B., Allen, J. P., Stephenson, J. C., & Hare, A. L. (2009). Attachment and autonomy during adolescence. In R. M. Lerner & L. Steiberg (Eds.), *Handbook of adolescent psychology: Vol. 1. Individual bases of adolescent development* (3rd ed., pp. 358–403). Hoboken, NJ: Wiley.

McElwain, N. L., & Booth-LaForce, C. (2006). Maternal sensitivity to infant distress and nondistress as predictors of infant–mother attachment security. *Journal of Family Psychology, 20*, 247–255.

McEwen, B. S. (2007). Physiology and neurobiology of stress an adaptation: Central role of the brain. *Physiological Reviews, 87*, 873–904.

McFarlane, J., Malecha, A., Watson, K., Gist, J., Batten, E., Hall, I., & Smith, S. (2005). Intimate partner assault against women: Frequency, health consequences, and treatment outcomes. *Obstetrics and Gynecology, 105*, 99–108.

McGee, L. M., & Richgels, D. J. (2012). *Literacy's beginnings: Supporting young readers and writers* (6th ed.). Boston: Allyn and Bacon.

McGoldrick, M. (2004). Echoes from the past: Helping families deal with their ghosts. In F. Walsh & M. McGoldrick (Eds.), *Living beyond loss* (pp. 99–118). New York: Norton.

McGoldrick, M., Schlesinger, J. M., Lee, E., Hines, P. M., Chan, J., & Almeida, R. (2004). Mourning in different cultures. In F. Walsh & M. McGoldrick (Eds.), *Living beyond loss* (pp. 1119–160). New York: Norton.

McGoldrick, M., & Shibusawa, T. (2012). The family life cycle. In F. Walsh (Ed.), *Normal family processes: Growing diversity and complexity* (pp. 375–398). New York: Guilford.

McGrath, S. K., & Kennell, J. H. (2008). A randomized controlled trial of continuous labor support for middle-class couples: Effect on cesarean delivery rates. *Birth: Issues in Perinatal Care, 35*, 9–97.

McGue, M., Elkins, I., Walden, B., & Iacono, W. G. (2005). Perceptions of the parent–adolescent relationship: A longitudinal investigation. *Developmental Psychology, 41*, 971–984.

McHale, J. P., Khazan, I., Erera, P., Rotman, T., DeCourcey, W., & McConnell, M. (2002a). Coparenting in diverse family systems. In M. H. Bornstein (Ed.), *Handbook of parenting: Vol. 3* (2nd ed., pp. 75–107). Mahwah, NJ: Erlbaum.

McHale, J. P., Kuersten-Hogan, R., & Rao, N. (2004). Growing points for coparenting theory and research. *Journal of Adult Development, 11*, 221–234.

McHale, J. P., Lauretti, A., Talbot, J., & Pouquette, C. (2002b). Retrospect and prospect in the psychological study of coparenting and family group process. In J. P. McHale & W. S. Grolnick (Eds.), *Retrospect and prospect in the psychological study of families* (pp. 127–165). Mahwah, NJ: Erlbaum.

McHale, J. P., & Rotman, T. (2007). Is seeing believing? Expectant parents' outlooks on coparenting and later coparenting solidarity. *Infant Behavior and Development, 30*, 63–81.

McHale, S. M., Crouter, A. C., Kim, J.-Y., Burton, L. M., Davis, K. D., Dotterer, A. M., & Swanson, D. P. (2006). Mothers' and fathers' racial socialization in African-American families: Implications for youth. *Child Development, 77*, 1387–1402.

McIntosh, H., Metz, E., & Youniss, J. (2005). Community service and identity formation in adolescents. In J. S. Mahoney, R. W. Larson, & J. S. Eccles (Eds.), *Organized activities as contexts of development: Extracurricular activities, after-school and community programs* (pp. 331–351). Mahwah, NJ: Erlbaum.

McIntosh, W. D., Locker, L., Briley, K., Ryan, R., & Scott, A. J. (2011). What do older adults seek in their potential romantic partners? Evidence from online personal ads. *International Journal of Aging and Human Development, 72*, 67–82.

McKenna, J. J. (2001). Why we never ask "Is it safe for infants to sleep alone?" *Academy of Breast Feeding Medicine News and Views, 7*(4), 32, 38.

McKenna, J. J. (2002, September/October). Breastfeeding and bedsharing still useful (and important) after all these years. *Mothering, 114.* Retrieved from www.mothering.com/articles/new_baby/sleep/mckenna.html

McKenna, J. J., & McDade, T. (2005). Why babies should never sleep alone: A review of the co-sleeping controversy in relation to SIDS, bedsharing, and breastfeeding. *Paediatric Respiratory Reviews, 6*, 134–152.

McKenna, J. J., & Volpe, L. E. (2007). Sleeping with baby: An Internet-based sampling of parental experiences, choices, perceptions, and interpretations in a Western industrialized context. *Infant and Child Development, 16*, 359–385.

McKeown, M. G., & Beck, I. L. (2009). The role of metacognition in understanding and supporting reading comprehension. In D. J. Hacker, J. Dunlosky, & A. C. Graesser (Eds.), *Handbook of metacognition in education* (pp. 7–25). New York: Routledge.

McKim, W. A., & Hancock, S. (2013). *Drugs and behavior* (7th ed.). Upper Saddle River, NJ: Pearson.

McKinney, C., Donnelly, R., & Renk, K. (2008). Perceived parenting, positive and negative perceptions of parents, and late adolescent emotional adjustment. *Child and Adolescent Mental health, 13*, 66–73.

McKown, C., & Strambler, M. J. (2009). Developmental antecedents and social and academic consequences of stereotype-consciousness in middle childhood. *Child Development, 80*, 1643–1659.

McKown, C., & Weinstein, R. S. (2003). The development and consequences of stereotype consciousness in middle childhood. *Child Development, 74*, 498–515.

McKown, C., & Weinstein, R. S. (2008). Teacher expectations, classroom context, and the achievement gap. *Journal of School Psychology, 46*, 235–261.

McKusick, V. A. (2011). *Online Mendelian inheritance in man.* Retrieved from www.nslij-genetics.org/search_omim.html

McLanahan, S. (1999). Father absence and the welfare of children. In E. M. Hetherington (Ed.), *Coping with divorce, single parenting, and remarriage: A risk and resiliency perspective* (pp. 117–145). Mahwah, NJ: Erlbaum.

McLaughlin, K. A., Fox, N. A., Zeanah, C. H., & Nelson, C. A. (2011). Adverse rearing environments and neural development in children: The development of frontal electroencephalogram asymmetry. *Biological Psychiatry, 70*, 1008–1015.

McLean, K. C. (2008). Stories of the young and the old: Personal continuity and narrative identity. *Developmental Psychology, 44*, 254–264.

McLoyd, V. C., Aikens, N. L., & Burton, L. M. (2006). Child poverty, policy, and practice. In K. A. Renninger & I. E. Sigel (Eds.), *Handbook of child psychology: Vol. 4. Child psychology in practice* (6th ed., pp. 700–778). Hoboken, NJ: Wiley.

McLoyd, V. C., Kaplan, R., Hardaway, C. R., & Wood, D. (2007). Does endorsement of physical discipline matter? Assessing moderating influences on the maternal and child psychological correlates of physical discipline in African-American families. *Journal of Family Psychology, 21*, 165–175.

McLoyd, V. C., & Smith, J. (2002). Physical discipline and behavior problems in African-American, European-American, and Hispanic children: Emotional support as a moderator. *Journal of Marriage and Family, 64*, 40–53.

McMahon, C. A., Barnett, B., Kowalenko, N. M., & Tennant, C. C. (2006). Maternal attachment state of mind moderates the impact of postnatal depression on infant attachment. *Journal of Child Psychology and Psychiatry, 47*, 660–669.

Mead, M. (1928). *Coming of age in Samoa.* Ann Arbor, MI: Morrow.

Meade, C. S., Kershaw, T. S., & Ickovics, J. R. (2008). The intergenerational cycle of teenage motherhood: An ecological approach. *Health Psychology, 27*, 419–429.

Meadus, R. J., & Twomey, J. C. (2011). Men student nurses: The nursing education experience. *Nursing Forum, 46*, 269–279.

Meegan, S. P., & Berg, C. A. (2002). Contexts, functions, forms, and processes of collaborative everyday problem solving in older adulthood. *International Journal of Behavioral Development, 26*, 6–15.

Meeus, W., Oosterwegel, A., & Vollebergh, W. (2002). Parental and peer attachment and identity development in adolescence. *Journal of Adolescence, 25*, 93–106.

Meeus, W., van de Schoot, R., Keijsers, L., & Branje, S. (2012). Identity statuses as developmental trajectories: A five-wave longitudinal study in early-to-middle and middle-to-late adolescents. *Journal of Youth and Adolescence, 41*, 1008–1021.

Meeus, W. H. J., Branje, S. J. T., van der Valk, I., & de Wied, M. (2007). Relationships with intimate partner, best friend, and parents in adolescence and early adulthood: A study of the saliency of the intimate partnership. *International Journal of Behavioral Development, 31*, 569–580.

Mehlmadrona, L., & Madrona, M. M. (1997). Physician- and midwife-attended home births—effects of breech, twin, and post-dates outcome data on mortality rates. *Journal of Nurse-Midwifery, 42*, 91–98.

Mehlson, M., Platz, M., & Fromholt, P. (2003). Life satisfaction across the life course: Evaluations of the most and least satisfying decades of life. *International Journal of Aging and Human Development, 57*, 217–236.

Meier, A., & Allen, G. (2009). Romantic relationships from adolescence to young adulthood: Evidence from the National Longitudinal Study of Adolescent Health. *Sociological Quarterly, 50*, 308–335.

Meins, E., Fernyhough, C., Russell, J., & Clark-Carter, D. (1998). Security of attachment as a predictor of symbolic and mentalizing abilities: A longitudinal study. *Social Development, 7*, 1–24.

Meins, E., Fernyhough, C., Wainwright, R., Clark-Carter, D., Gupta, M. D., Fradley, E., & Tucker, M. (2003). Pathways to understanding mind: Construct validity and predictive validity of maternal mind-mindedness. *Child Development, 74,* 1194–1211.

Melby, M. K., Lock, M., & Kaufert, P. (2005). Culture and symptom reporting at menopause. *Human Reproduction Update, 11,* 495–512.

Melby-Lervag, M., & Hulme, C. (2010). Serial and free recall in children can be improved by training: Evidence for the importance of phonological and semantic representations in immediate memory tasks. *Psychological Science, 21,* 1694–1700.

Melenhorst, A. S., Fisk, A. D., Mynatt, E. D., & Rogers, W. A. (2004). Potential intrusiveness of aware home technology: Perceptions of older adults. In *Proceedings of the Human Factors and Ergonomics Society 48th annual meeting* (pp. 266–270). Santa Monica, CA: Human Factors and Ergonomics Society.

Meltzoff, A. N. (2007). "Like me": A foundation for social cognition. *Developmental Science, 10,* 126–134.

Meltzoff, A. N., & Kuhl, P. K. (1994). Faces and speech: Intermodal processing of biologically relevant signals in infants and adults. In D. J. Lewkowicz & R. Lickliter (Eds.), *The development of intersensory perception* (pp. 335–369). Hillsdale, NJ: Erlbaum.

Meltzoff, A. N., & Moore, M. K. (1977). Imitation of facial and manual gestures by human neonates. *Science, 198,* 75–78.

Meltzoff, A. N., & Moore, M. K. (1994). Imitation, memory, and the representation of persons. *Infant Behavior and Development, 17,* 83–99.

Meltzoff, A. N., & Moore, M. K. (1999). Persons and representations: Why infant imitation is important for theories of human development. In J. Nadel & G. Butterworth (Eds.), *Imitation in infancy* (pp. 9–35). Cambridge, UK: Cambridge University Press.

Meltzoff, A. N., & Williamson, R. A. (2010). The importance of imitation for theories of social-cognitive development. In J. G. Bremner & T. D. Wachs (Eds.), *Wiley-Blackwell handbook of infant development* (2nd ed., pp. 345–364). Oxford, UK: Wiley.

Melzi, G., & Ely, R. (2009). Language development in the school years. In J. B. Gleason & N. B. Ratner (Eds.), *The development of language* (7th ed., pp. 391–435). Boston: Allyn and Bacon.

Mendle, J., Turkheimer, E., & Emery, R. E. (2007). Detrimental psychological outcomes associated with early pubertal timing in adolescent girls. *Developmental Review, 27,* 151–171.

Meneilly, G. S. (2006). Diabetes in the elderly. *Medical Clinics of North America, 90,* 909–923.

Mennella, J. A., & Beauchamp, G. K. (1998). Early flavor experiences: Research update. *Nutrition Reviews, 56,* 205–211.

Menon, U. (2001). Middle adulthood in cultural perspective: The imagined and the experienced in three cultures. In M. E. Lachman (Ed.), *Handbook of midlife development* (pp. 40–74). New York: Wiley.

Ment, L. R., Vohr, B., Allan, W., Katz, K. H., Schneider, K. C., Westerveld, M., Cuncan, C. C., & Makuch, R. W. (2003). Change in cognitive function over time in very low-birth-weight infants. *Journal of the American Medical Association, 289,* 705–711.

Merikangas, K. R., He, J.-P. Burstein, M., Swanson, S. A. Avenevoli, S., Cui, L., Benjet, C., et al. (2010). Lifetime prevalence of mental disorders in U.S. adolescents: Results from the National Comorbidity Survey Replication—Adolescent Supplement (NCS-A). *Journal of the American Academy of Child and Adolescent Psychiatry, 49,* 980–989.

Messman, S. J., Canary, D. J., & Hause, K. S. (2000). Motives to remain platonic, equity, and the use of maintenance strategies in opposite-sex friendships. *Journal of Social and Personal Relationships, 17,* 67–94.

Methven, L., Allen, V. J., Withers, C. A., & Gosney, M. A. (2012). Aging and taste. *Proceedings of the Nutrition Society, 71,* 556–565.

MetLife. (2011). *MetLife study of caregiving costs to working caregivers: Double jeopardy for baby boomers caring for their parents.* Westport, CT: National Alliance for Caregiving and MetLife Mature Market Institute.

Meyer, B. J. F., Russo, C., & Talbot, A. (1995). Discourse comprehension and problem solving: Decisions about the treatment of breast cancer by women across the lifespan. *Psychology and Aging, 10,* 84–103.

Meyer, B. J. F., Talbot, A. P., & Ranalli, C. (2007). Why older adults make more immediate treatment decisions about cancer than younger adults. *Psychology and Aging, 22,* 505–524.

Meyer, I. H. (2003). Prejudice, social stress, and mental health in lesbian, gay, and bisexual populations: Conceptual issues and research evidence. *Psychological Bulletin, 129,* 674–697.

Meyer, J. (2012). *Centenarians: 2010.* Washington, DC: U.S. Government Printing Office.

Meyer, R. (2009). Infant feeding in the first year. 1: Feeding practices in the first six months of life. *Journal of Family Health Care, 19,* 13–16.

Meyer-Bahlburg, H. F. L., Ehrhardt, A. A., Rosen, L. R., Gruen, R. S., Veridiano, N. P., Vann, F. H., & Neuwalder, H. F. (1995). Prenatal estrogens and the development of homosexual orientation. *Developmental Psychology, 31,* 12–21.

Meyers, A. B., & Berk, L. E. (2014). In L. Brooker, S. Edwards, & M. Blaise (Eds.), *Sage Handbook of play and learning in early childhood.* London: Sage.

Mezei, L., & Murinson, B. B. (2011). Pain education in North American medical schools. *Journal of Pain, 12,* 1199–1208.

Mezulis, A. H., Hyde, J. S., & Clark, R. (2004). Father involvement moderates the effect of maternal depression during a child's infancy on child behavior problems in kindergarten. *Journal of Family Psychology, 18,* 575–588.

Michael, R. T., Gagnon, J. H., Laumann, E. O., & Kolata, G. (1994). *Sex in America.* Boston: Little, Brown.

Michalik, N. M., Eisenberg, N., Spinrad, T. L., Ladd, B., Thompson, M., & Valiente, C. (2007). Longitudinal relations among parental emotional expressivity and sympathy and prosocial behavior in adolescence. *Social Development, 16,* 286–309.

Michels, K. B., Willett, W. C., Graubard, B. I., Vaidya, R. L., Cantwell, M. M., Sansbury, L. B., & Forman, M. R. (2007). A longitudinal study of infant feeding and obesity throughout the life course. *International Journal of Obesity, 31,* 1078–1085.

Mienaltowski, A. (2011). Everyday problem solving across the adult life span. *Annals of the New York Academy of Sciences, 1235,* 75–85.

Mikami, A. Y., Lerner, M. D., & Lun, J. (2010). Social context influences on children's rejection by their peers. *Child Development Perspectives, 4,* 123–130.

Mikulincer, M., Florian, V., & Hirschberger, G. (2003). The existential function of close relationships: Introducing death into the science of love. *Personality and Social Psychology Review, 7,* 20–40.

Mikulincer, M., & Shaver, P. R. (2008). An attachment perspective on bereavement. In M. S. Stroebe, R. O. Hansson, H. Schut, & W. Stroebe (Eds.), *Handbook of bereavement research and practice* (pp. 87–112). Washington, DC: American Psychological Association.

Milevsky, A., Schlechter, M., Netter, S., & Keehn, D. (2007). Maternal and paternal parenting styles in adolescents: Associations with self-esteem, depression, and life satisfaction. *Journal of Child and Family Studies, 16,* 39–47.

Milkie, M. A., Bierman, A., & Schieman, S. (2008). How adult children influence older parents' mental health: Integrating stress-process and life-course perspectives. *Social Psychology Quarterly, 71,* 86–105.

Miller, D. I., Taler, V., Davidson, P. S. R., & Messier, C. (2012). Measuring the impact of exercise on

cognitive aging: Methodological issues. *Neurobiology of Aging, 33,* 622.e29–622.e43.

Miller, D. N. (2011). *Child and adolescent suicidal behavior: School-based prevention, assessment, and intervention.* New York: Guilford.

Miller, J. G. (2006). Insights into moral development from cultural psychology. In M. Killen & J. Smetana (Eds.), *Handbook of moral development* (pp. 375–398). Philadelphia: Erlbaum.

Miller, J. G., & Bersoff, D. M. (1995). Development in the context of everyday family relationships: Culture, interpersonal morality, and adaptation. In M. Killen & D. Hart (Eds.), *Morality in everyday life: Developmental perspectives* (pp. 259–282). Cambridge, UK: Cambridge University Press.

Miller, L. T., & Vernon, P. A. (1992). The general factor in short-term memory, intelligence, and reaction time. *Intelligence, 16,* 5–29.

Miller, P. H. (2009). *Theories of developmental psychology* (5th ed.). New York: Worth.

Miller, P. J., Fung, H., Lin, S., Chen, E. C., & Boldt, B. R. (2012). How socialization happens on the ground: Narrative practices as alternate socializing pathways in Taiwanese and European-American families. *Monographs of the Society for Research in Child Development, 77*(1, Serial No. 302).

Miller, P. J., Hengst, J. A., & Wang, S. (2003). Ethnographic methods: Applications from developmental cultural psychology. In P. M. Carnic & J. E. Rhodes (Eds.), *Qualitative research in psychology* (pp. 219–242). Washington, DC: American Psychological Association.

Miller, P. J., Wang, S., Sandel, T., & Cho, G. E. (2002). Self-esteem as folk theory: A comparison of European American and Taiwanese mothers' beliefs. *Parenting: Science and Practice, 2,* 209–239.

Miller, P. J., Wiley, A. R., Fung, H., & Liang, C. H. (1997). Personal storytelling as a medium of socialization in Chinese and American families. *Child Development, 68,* 557–568.

Miller, S., Lansford, J. E., Costanzo, P., Malone, P. S., Golonka, M., & Killeya-Jones, L. A. (2009). Early adolescent romantic partner status, peer standing, and problem behavior. *Journal of Early Adolescence, 29,* 839–861.

Miller, S. A., Hardin, C. A., & Montgomery, D. E. (2003). Young children's understanding of the conditions for knowledge acquisition. *Journal of Cognition and Development, 4,* 325–356.

Milligan, K., Astington, J. W., & Dack, L. A. (2007). Language and theory of mind: Meta-analysis of the relation between language ability and false-belief understanding. *Child Development, 78,* 622–646.

Mills, D., Plunkett, K., Prat, C., & Schafer, G. (2005). Watching the infant brain learn words: Effects of language and experience. *Cognitive Development, 20,* 19–31.

Mills, R., & Grusec, J. (1989). Cognitive, affective, and behavioral consequences of praising altruism. *Merrill-Palmer Quarterly, 35,* 299–326.

Mills, R. S. L. (2005). Taking stock of the developmental literature on shame. *Developmental Review, 25,* 26–63.

Mills, T. L., Gomez-Smith, Z., & De Leon, J. M. (2005). Skipped generation families: Sources of psychological distress among grandmothers of grandchildren who live in homes where neither parent is present. *Marriage and Family Review, 37,* 191–212.

Miner-Rubino, K., Winter, D. G., & Stewart, A. J. (2004). Gender, social class, and the subjective experience of aging: Self-perceived personality change from early adulthood to late midlife. *Personality and Social Psychology Bulletin, 30,* 1599–1610.

Minkler, M., & Fuller-Thomson, E. (2005). African American grandparents raising grandchildren: A national study using the Census 2000 American Community Survey. *Journal of Gerontology, 60B,* S82–S92.

Misailidi, P. (2006). Young children's display rule knowledge: Understanding the distinction between apparent and real emotions and the motives underlying the use of display rules. *Social Behavior and Personality, 34,* 1285–1296.

Mishra, G., & Kuh, D. (2006). Perceived change in quality of life during the menopause. *Social Science and Medicine, 62,* 93–102.

Mistry, R. S., Biesanz, J. C., Chien, N., Howes, C., & Benner, A. D. (2008). Socioeconomic status, parental investments, and the cognitive and behavioral outcomes of low-income children from immigrant and native households. *Early Childhood Research Quarterly, 23,* 193–212.

Mitchell, A., & Boss, B. J. (2002). Adverse effects of pain on the nervous systems of newborns and young children: A review of the literature. *Journal of Neuroscience Nursing, 34,* 228–235.

Mitchell, B. A., & Lovegreen, L. D. (2009). The empty nest syndrome in midlife families: A multimethod exploration of parental gender differences and cultural dynamics. *Journal of Family Issues, 30,* 1651–1670.

Mitchell, B. D., Hsueh, W. C., King, T. M., Pollin, T. I., Sorkin, J., Agarwala, R., Schäffer, A. A., & Shuldiner, A. R. (2001). Heritability of life span in the Old Order Amish. *American Journal of Medical Genetics, 102,* 346–352.

Mitchell, P., Teucher, U., Kikuno, H., & Bennett, M. (2010). Cultural variations in developing a sense of knowing your own mind: A comparison between British and Japanese children. *International Journal of Behavioral Development, 34,* 248–258.

Miura, I. T., & Okamoto, Y. (2003). Language supports for mathematics understanding and performance. In A. J. Baroody & A. Dowker (Eds.), *The development of arithmetic concepts and skills* (pp. 229–242). Mahwah, NJ: Erlbaum.

Mize, J., & Pettit, G. S. (2010). The mother–child playgroup as socialisation context: A short-term longitudinal study of mother–child–peer relationship dynamics. *Early Child Development and Care, 180,* 1271–1284.

Moen, P., & Altobelli, J. (2007). Strategic selection as a retirement project: Will Americans develop hybrid arrangements? In J. B. James & P. Wink (Eds.), *Annual review of gerontology and geriatrics* (Vol. 26, pp. 61–82). New York: Springer.

Moen, P., & Roehling, P. V. (2005). *The career mystique.* Boulder, CO: Rowman & Littlefield.

Moens, E., Braet, C., & Soetens, B. (2007). Observation of family functioning at mealtime: A comparison between families of children with and without overweight. *Journal of Pediatric Psychology, 32,* 52–63.

Moffitt, T. E. (2007). Life-course-persistent vs. adolescence-limited antisocial behavior. In D. Cicchetti & D. J. Cohen (Eds.), *Developmental psychopathology* (2nd ed., pp. 570–598). Hoboken, NJ; Wiley.

Mohr, J. J., & Daly, C. A. (2008). Sexual minority stress and changes in relationship quality in same-sex couples. *Journal of Social and Personal Relationships, 25,* 989–1007.

Mohr, J. J., & Fassinger, R. E. (2006). Sexual orientation identity and romantic relationship quality in same-sex couples. *Personality and Social Psychology Bulletin, 32,* 1085–1099.

Mok, M. M. C., Kennedy, K. J., & Moore, P. J. (2011). Academic attribution of secondary students: Gender, year level and achievement level. *Educational Psychology, 31,* 87–104.

Moll, H., & Meltzoff, A. N. (2011). How does it look? Level 2 perspective-taking at 36 months of age. *Child Development, 82,* 661–673.

Moll, H., & Tomasello, M. (2006). Level I perspective-taking at 24 months of age. *British Journal of Developmental Psychology, 24,* 603–613.

Mollenkopf, H., Hieber, A., & Wahl, H-W. (2011). Continuity and change in older adults' perceptions of out-of-home mobility over ten years: A qualitative–quantitative approach. *Ageing and Society, 31,* 782–802.

Moller, K., Hwang, C. P., & Wickberg, B. (2008). Couple relationship and transition to parenthood: Does workload at home matter? *Journal of Reproductive and Infant Psychology, 26,* 57–68.

Mondloch, C. J., Lewis, T., Budreau, D. R., Maurer, D., Dannemiller, J. L., Stephens, B. R., & Kleiner-Gathercoal, K. A. (1999). Face perception during early infancy. *Psychological Science, 10,* 419–422.

Monin, J. K., & Schulz, R. (2009). Interpersonal effects of suffering in older adult caregiving relationships. *Psychology and Aging, 24,* 681–695.

Monk, C., Sloan, R., Myers, M. M., Ellman, L., Werner, E., Jeon, J., et al. (2010). Neural circuitry of emotional face processing in autism spectrum disorders. *Journal of Psychiatry and Neuroscience, 35,* 105–114.

Monsour, M. (2002). *Women and men as friends.* Mahwah, NJ: Erlbaum.

Montemayor, R., & Eisen, M. (1977). The development of self-conceptions from childhood to adolescence. *Developmental Psychology, 37,* 826–838.

Montepare, J. M. (2006). Body consciousness across the adult years: Variations with actual and subjective age. *Journal of Adult Development, 13,* 102–107.

Montgomery, M. J. (2005). Psychosocial intimacy and identity: From early adolescence to emerging adulthood. *Journal of Adolescent Research, 20,* 346–374.

Montgomery, M. J., & Côté, J. E. (2003). College as a transition to adulthood. In G. R. Adams & M. D. Berzonsky (Eds.), *Blackwell handbook of adolescence* (pp. 149–172). Malden, MA: Blackwell.

Montgomery-Goodnough, A., & Gallagher, S. J. (2007). Review of research on spiritual and religious formation in higher education. In S. M. Nielsen & M. S. Plakhotnik (Eds.), *Proceedings of the sixth annual College of Education Research Conference: Urban and international education section* (pp. 60–65). Miami, FL: International University.

Montorsi, F. (2005). Assessment, diagnosis, and investigation of erectile dysfunction. *Clinical Cornerstone, 7,* 29–35.

Montoya, A. G., Sorrentino, R., Lukas, S. E., & Price, B. H. (2002). Long-term neuropsychiatric consequences of "ecstasy" (MDMA): A review. *Harvard Review of Psychiatry, 10,* 212–220.

Moon, C., Cooper, R. P., & Fifer, W. P. (1993). Two-day-old infants prefer their native language. *Infant Behavior and Development, 16,* 495–500.

Moon, R. Y., Horne, R. S. C., & Hauck, F. R. (2007). Sudden infant death syndrome. *Lancet, 370,* 1578–1587.

Moore, A., & Stratton, D. C. (2002). *Resilient widowers.* New York: Springer.

Moore, D. R., & Florsheim, P. (2001). Interpersonal processes and psychopathology among expectant and nonexpectant adolescent couples. *Journal of Consulting and Clinical Psychology, 69,* 101–113.

Moore, E. G. J. (1986). Family socialization and the IQ test performance of traditionally and transracially adopted black children. *Developmental Psychology, 22,* 317–326.

Moore, K. L., & Persaud, T. V. N. (2008). *Before we are born* (7th ed.). Philadelphia: Saunders.

Moore, K. L., Persaud, T. V. N., & Torchia, M. G. (2013). *Before we are born: Essentials of embryology and birth defects* (8th ed.). Philadelphia, PA: Saunders.

Moore, M. K., & Meltzoff, A. N. (2004). Object permanence after a 24-hr delay and leaving the locale of disappearance: The role of memory, space, and identity. *Developmental Psychology, 40,* 606–620.

Moore, M. K., & Meltzoff, A. N. (2008). Factors affecting infants' manual search for occluded objects and the genesis of object permanence. *Infant Behavior and Development, 31,* 168–180.

Moore, M. R., & Brooks-Gunn, J. (2002). Adolescent parenthood. In M. H. Bornstein (Ed.), *Handbook of parenting: Vol. 3* (2nd ed., pp. 173–214). Mahwah, NJ: Erlbaum.

Moore, W. S. (2002). Understanding learning in a postmodern world: Reconsidering the Perry scheme of ethical and intellectual development. In B. K. Hofer & P. R. Pintrich (Eds.), *Personal epistemology* (pp. 17–36). Mahwah, NJ: Erlbaum.

Moran, G., Forbes, L., Evans, E., Tarabulsy, G. M., & Madigan, S. (2008). Both maternal sensitivity and atypical maternal behavior independently predict attachment security and disorganization in adolescent mother–infant relationships. *Infant Behavior and Development, 31,* 321–325.

Moran, S., & Gardner, H. (2006). Extraordinary achievements: A developmental and systems analysis. In D. Kuhn & R. Siegler (Eds.), *Handbook of child psychology: Vol. 2. Cognition, perception, and language* (6th ed., pp. 905–949). Hoboken, NJ: Wiley.

Morawska, A., & Sanders, M. (2011). Parental use of time out revisited: A useful or harmful parenting strategy? *Journal of Child and Family Studies, 20,* 1–8.

Morelli, G., Rogoff, B., Oppenheim, D., & Goldsmith, D. (1992). Cultural variation in infants' sleeping arrangements: Questions of independence. *Developmental Psychology, 28,* 604–613.

Morelli, G. A., Rogoff, B., & Angelillo, C. (2003). Cultural variation in young children's access to work or involvement in specialized child-focused activities. *International Journal of Behavioral Development, 27,* 264–274.

Moreno, A. J., Klute, M. M., & Robinson, J. L. (2008). Relational and individual resources as predictors of empathy in early childhood. *Social Development, 17,* 613–637.

Morgan, J. D., Laungani, P., & Palmer, S. (2009). General introduction to series. In J. D. Morgan, P. Laungani, & S. Palmer (Eds.), *Death and bereavement around the world: Vol. 5. Reflective essays* (pp. 1–4). Amityville, NY: Baywood.

Morgan, P. L., Farkas, G., Hillemeier, M. M., & Maczuga, S. (2009). Risk factors for learning-related behavior problems at 24 months of age: Population-based estimates. *Journal of Abnormal Child Psychology, 37,* 401–413.

Moro-García, M. A., Alonso-Arias, R., López-Vázquez, A., Suárez-García, F. M., Solano-Jaurrieta, J. J., Baltar, J., et al. (2012). Relationship between functional ability in older people, immune system status, and intensity of response to CMV. *Age, 34,* 479–495.

Morrill, M. I., Hines, D. A., Mahmood, S., & Córdova, J. V. (2010). Pathways between marriage and parenting for wives and husbands: The role of coparenting. *Family Process, 49,* 59–73.

Morris, A. S., Silk, J. S., Morris, M. D. S., & Steinberg, L. (2011). The influence of mother–child emotion regulation strategies on children's expression of anger and sadness. *Developmental Psychology, 47,* 213–225.

Morris, W. L., DePaulo, B. M., Hertel, J., & Taylor, L. C. (2008). Singlism—another problem that has no name: Prejudice, stereotypes, and discrimination against singles. In M. A. Morrison & T. G. Morrison (Eds.), *The psychology of modern prejudice* (pp. 165–194). Hauppauge, NY: Nova Science Publishers.

Morrison, V. (2008). Ageing and physical health. In B. Woods & L. Clare (Eds.), *Handbook of the clinical psychology of ageing* (2nd ed., pp. 57–74). Chichester, UK: Wiley.

Morrongiello, B. A., Fenwick, K. D., & Chance, G. (1998). Crossmodal learning in newborn infants:

Inferences about properties of auditory-visual events. *Infant Behavior and Development, 21,* 543–554.

Morrongiello, B. A., Midgett, C., & Shields, R. (2001). Don't run with scissors: Young children's knowledge of home safety rules. *Journal of Pediatric Psychology, 26,* 105–115.

Morrongiello, B. A., Ondejko, L., & Littlejohn, A. (2004). Understanding toddlers' in-home injuries: I. Context, correlates, and determinants. *Journal of Pediatric Psychology, 29,* 415–431.

Morrow, D. F. (2006). Gay, lesbian, and transgender adolescents. In D. F. Morrow & L. Messinger (Eds.), *Sexual orientation and gender expression in social work practice* (pp. 177–195). New York: Columbia University Press.

Morse, S. B., Zheng, H., Tang, Y., & Roth, J. (2009). Early school-age outcomes of late preterm infants. *Pediatrics, 123,* e622–e629.

Mosby, L., Rawls, A. W., Meehan, A. J., Mays, E., & Pettinari, C. J. (1999). Troubles in interracial talk about discipline: An examination of African American child rearing narratives. *Journal of Comparative Family Studies, 30,* 489–521.

Mosca, L., Barrett-Connor, E., & Wenger, N. K. (2012). Sex/gender differences in cardiovascular disease prevention: What a difference a decade makes. *Circulation, 124,* 2145–2154.

Moses, L. J., Baldwin, D. A., Rosicky, J. G., & Tidball, G. (2001). Evidence for referential understanding in the emotions domain at twelve and eighteen months. *Child Development, 72,* 718–735.

Mosher, W. D., Chandra, A., & Jones, J. (2005). *Sexual behavior and selected health measures: Men and women 15–44 years of age, United States 2002,* Vol. 362. Atlanta: Centers for Disease Control and Prevention.

Moshman, D. (1998). Identity as a theory of oneself. *Genetic Epistemologist, 26*(3), 1–9.

Moshman, D. (2003). Developmental change in adulthood. In J. Demick & C. Andreoletti (Eds.), *Handbook of adult development* (pp. 43–61). New York: Plenum.

Moshman, D. (2005). *Adolescent psychological development: Rationality, morality, and identity* (2nd ed.). Mahwah, NJ: Erlbaum.

Moshman, D. (2011). *Adolescent rationality and development: Cognition, morality, and identity* (3rd ed.). New York: Psychology Press.

Moshman, D., & Franks, B. A. (1986). Development of the concept of inferential validity. *Child Development, 57,* 153–165.

Moshman, D., & Geil, M. (1998). Collaborative reasoning: Evidence for collective rationality. *Thinking and Reasoning, 4,* 231–248.

Moss, E., Cyr, C., Bureau, J.-F., Tarabulsy, G. M., & Dubois-Comtois, K. (2005). Stability of attachment during the preschool period. *Developmental Psychology, 41,* 773–783.

Mossey, P. A., Little, J., Munger, R. G., Dixon, M. J., & Shaw, W. C. (2009). Cleft lip and palate. *Lancet, 374,* 1773–1785.

Moss-Racusin, C. A., Dovidio, J. F., Brescoll, V. L., Graham, M. J., & Handelsman, J. (2012). Science faculty's subtle gender biases favor male students. *Proceedings of the National Academy of Sciences, 109,* 16474–16479.

Mottus, R., Indus, K., & Allik, J. (2008). Accuracy of only children stereotype. *Journal of Research in Personality, 42,* 1047–1052.

Mounts, N. S., Valentiner, D. P., Anderson, K. L., & Boswell, M. K. (2006). Shyness, sociability, and parental support for the college transition: Relation to adolescents' adjustment. *Journal of Youth and Adolescence, 35,* 71–80.

Moxley, D. P., Najor-Durack, A., & Dumbrigue, C. (2001). *Keeping students in higher education.* London: Kogan Page.

Mroczek, D. K., & Spiro, A., III. (2007). Personality change influences mortality in older men. *Psychological Science, 18,* 371–376.

Mroczek, D. K., Spiro, A., & Turiano, N. A. (2009). Do health behaviors explain the effect of neuroticism on mortality? *Journal of Research in Personality, 43,* 653–659.

Mrug, S., Hoza, B., & Gerdes, A. C. (2001). Children with attention-deficit/hyperactivity disorder: Peer relationships and peer-oriented interventions. In D. W. Nangle & C. A. Erdley (Eds.), *The role of friendship in psychological adjustment* (pp. 51–77). San Francisco: Jossey-Bass.

Mueller, C. M., & Dweck, C. S. (1998). Intelligence praise can undermine motivation and performance. *Journal of Personality and Social Psychology, 75,* 33–52.

Muenchow, S., & Marsland, K. W. (2007). Beyond baby steps: Promoting the growth and development of U.S. child-care policy. In J. L. Aber, S. J. Bishop-Josef, S. M. Jones, K. T. McLearn, & D. Phillips (Eds.), *Child development and social policy: Knowledge for action* (pp. 97–112). Washington, DC: American Psychological Association.

Müller, O., & Krawinkel, M. (2005). Malnutrition and health in developing countries. *Canadian Medical Association Journal, 173,* 279–286.

Müller, U., Liebermann-Finestone, D. P., Carpendale, J. I. M., Hammond, S. I., & Bibok, M. B. (2012). Knowing minds, controlling actions: The developmental relations between theory of mind and executive function from 2 to 4 years of age. *Journal of Experimental Child Psychology, 111,* 331–348.

Müller, U., Overton, W. F., & Reese, K. (2001). Development of conditional reasoning: A longitudinal study. *Journal of Cognition and Development, 2,* 27–49.

Mulvaney, M. K., McCartney, K., Bub, K. L., & Marshall, N. L. (2006). Determinants of dyadic scaffolding and cognitive outcomes in first graders. *Parenting: Science and Practice, 6,* 297–310.

Mumme, D. L., Bushnell, E. W., DiCorcia, J. A., & Lariviere, L. A. (2007). Infants' use of gaze cues to interpret others' actions and emotional reactions. In R. Flom, K. Lee, & D. Muir (Eds.), *Gaze-following: Its development and significance* (pp. 143–170). Mahwah, NJ: Erlbaum.

Munakata, Y. (2001). Task-dependency in infant behavior: Toward an understanding of the processes underlying cognitive development. In F. Lacerda, C. von Hofsten, & M. Heimann (Eds.), *Emerging cognitive abilities in early infancy* (pp. 29–52). Mahwah, NJ: Erlbaum.

Munakata, Y. (2006). Information processing approaches to development. In D. Kuhn & R. S. Siegler (Eds.), *Handbook of child psychology: Vol. 3. Cognition, perception, and language* (6th ed., pp. 426–463). Hoboken, NJ: Wiley.

Mundy, P., & Stella, J. (2000). Joint attention, social orienting, and nonverbal communication in autism. In A. M. Wetherby & B. M. Prizant (Eds.), *Autism spectrum disorders* (Vol. 9, pp. 55–77). Baltimore, MD: Paul H. Brookes.

Munnell, A. H., Webb, A., Delorme, L., & Golub-Sass, F. (2012). *National retirement risk index: How much longer do we need to work?* Chestnut Hill, MA: Center for Retirement Research at Boston College. Retrieved from crr.bc.edu/briefs/national-retirement-risk-index-how-much-longer-do-we-need-to-work

Munroe, R. L., & Romney, A. K. (2006). Gender and age differences in same-sex aggregation and social behavior. *Journal of Cross-Cultural Psychology, 37,* 3–19.

Muris, P., Merckelbach, H., Ollendick, T. H., King, N. J., & Bogie, N. (2001). Children's nighttime fears: Parent–child ratings of frequency, content, origins,

coping behaviors, and severity. *Behaviour Research and Therapy, 39,* 13–28.

Murphy, S. A. (2008). The loss of a child: Sudden death and extended illness perspectives. In M. S. Stroebe, R. O. Hansson, H. Schut, & W. Stroebe (Eds.), *Handbook of bereavement research and practice* (pp. 375–396). Washington, DC: American Psychological Association.

Murray, S. L. (2008). Risk regulation in relationships: Self-esteem and the if–then contingencies of interdependent life. In J. V. Wood, A. Tesser, & J. G. Holmes (Eds.), *The self and social relationships* (pp. 3–25). New York: Psychology Press.

Mussen, P., & Eisenberg-Berg, N. (1977). *Roots of caring, sharing, and helping.* San Francisco: Freeman.

Mustanski, B. S., Viken, R. J., Kaprio, J., Pulkkinen, L., & Rose, R. J. (2004). Genetic and environmental influences on pubertal development: Longitudinal data from Finnish twins at ages 11 and 14. *Developmental Psychology, 40,* 1188–1198.

Mutchler, J. E., Burr, J. A., & Caro, F. G. (2003). From paid worker to volunteer: Leaving the paid workforce and volunteering in later life. *Social Forces, 81,* 1267–1293.

Mutran, E. J., Danis, M., Bratton, K. A., Sudha, S., & Hanson, L. (1997). Attitudes of the critically ill toward prolonging life: The role of social support. *Gerontologist, 37,* 192–199.

Myers, D. G. (2000). The funds, friends, and faith of happy people. *American Psychologist, 55,* 56–67.

Myers, M. G., Brown, S. A., Tate, S., Abrantes, A., & Tomlinson, K. (2001). *Adolescents, alcohol, and substance abuse* (pp. 275–296). New York: Guilford.

Myerson, J., Hale, S., Wagstaff, D., Poon, L. W., & Smith, G. A. (1990). The information-loss model: A mathematical theory of age-related cognitive slowing. *Psychological Review, 97,* 475–487.

Myowa-Yamakoshi, M., Tomonaga, M., Tanaka, M., & Matsuzawa, T. (2004). Imitation in neonatal chimpanzees *(Pan troglodytes). Developmental Science, 7,* 437–442.

N

Nadel, J., Prepin, K., & Okanda, M. (2005). Experiencing contingency and agency: First step toward self-understanding in making a mind? *Interaction Studies, 6,* 447–462.

Nader, P. R., Bradley, R. H., Houts, R. M., McRitchie, S. L., & O'Brien, M. (2008). Moderate-to-vigorous physical activity from ages 9 to 15 years. *Journal of the American Medical Association, 16,* 295–305.

Nagy, E., Compagne, H., Orvos, H., Pal, A., Molnar, P., & Janszky, I. (2005). Index finger movement imitation by human neonates: Motivation, learning, and left-hand preference. *Pediatric Research, 58,* 749–753.

Nagy, W. E., & Scott, J. A. (2000). Vocabulary processes. In M. L. Kamil & P. B. Mosenthal (Eds.), *Handbook of reading research* (Vol. 3, pp. 269–284). Mahwah, NJ: Erlbaum.

Naigles, L. R., & Swenson, L. D. (2007). Syntactic supports for word learning. In E. Hoff & M. Shatz (Eds.), *Blackwell handbook of language development* (pp. 212–231). Malden, MA: Blackwell.

Naito, M., & Seki, Y. (2009). The relationship between second-order false belief and display rules reasoning: Integration of cognitive and affective social understanding. *Developmental Science, 12,* 150–164.

Nakamura, J., & Csikszentmihalyi, M. (2009). Flow theory and research. In C. R. Snyder & S. J. Lopez (Eds.), *Oxford handbook of positive psychology* (2nd ed., pp. 195–206). New York: Oxford University Press.

Nánez, J., Sr., & Yonas, A. (1994). Effects of luminance and texture motion on infant defensive reactions to optical collision. *Infant Behavior and Development, 17,* 165–174.

Narayan, C. (2008). Is there a double standard of aging? Older men and women and ageism. *Educational Gerontology, 34,* 782–787.

Narr, K. L., Woods, R. P., Lin J., Kim, J., Phillips, O. R., Del'Homme, M., et al. (2009). Widespread cortical thinning is a robust anatomical marker for attention-deficit/hyperactivity disorder. *Journal of the American Academy of Child and Adolescent Psychiatry, 48,* 1014–1022.

Nastasi, B. K., & Clements, D. H. (1994). Effectance motivation, perceived scholastic competence, and higher-order thinking in two cooperative computer environments. *Journal of Educational Computing Research, 10,* 249–275.

Natale, R., & Dodman, N. (2003). Birth can be a hazardous journey: Electronic fetal monitoring does not help. *JOGC, 25,* 1007–1009.

National Academies Committee on National Statistics. (2010, January). *Meeting on research issues in elder mistreatment and abuse and financial fraud: Meeting report.* Washington, DC: National Institute on Aging.

National Association for Sport and Physical Education. (2010). *2010 Shape of the nation report: Status of physical education in the USA.* Reston, VA: Author.

National Center on Elder Abuse, U.S. Administration on Aging. (2013). *Frequently asked questions.* Retrieved from www.ncea.aoa.gov/faq/index.aspx

National Council of Youth Sports. (2008). *Report on trends and participation in organized youth sports.* Stuart, FL: Author.

National Institute on Aging. (2012). *2011–2012 Alzheimer's disease progress report: Intensifying the research effort.* Retrieved from www.nia.nih.gov/alzheimers/publication/2011-2012-alzheimers-disease-progress-report

National Institute on Drug Abuse. (2012). *Drug facts: MDMA (Ecstasy).* Retrieved from www.drugabuse.gov/publications/drugfacts/mdma-ecstasy

National Institutes of Health. (2011). *Dental caries (tooth decay) in children (age 2 to 11).* Retrieved from www.nidcr.nih.gov/DataStatistics/FindDataByTopic/DentalCaries/DentalCariesChildren2to11

National Institutes of Health. (2012). *Genes and disease.* Retrieved from www.ncbi.nlm.nih.gov/books/NBK22183

National Research Council. (2007). *Race conscious policies for assigning students to schools: Social science research and the Supreme Court cases.* Washington, DC: National Academy Press.

National Women's Law Center. (2007). *When girls don't graduate we all fail.* Washington, DC: Author.

Natsuaki, M. N., Biehl, M. C., & Ge, X. (2009). Trajectories of depressed mood from early adolescence to young adulthood: The effects of pubertal timing and adolescent dating. *Journal of Research on Adolescence, 19,* 47–74.

Naveh-Benjamin, M. (2000). Adult age differences in memory performance: Tests of an associative deficit hypothesis. *Journal of Experimental Psychology: Learning, Memory, and Cognition, 26,* 1170–1187.

Naveh-Benjamin, M. (2012). Age-related differences in explicit associative memory: Contributions of effortful-strategic and automatic processes. In M. Naveh-Benjamin & N. Ohta (Eds.), *Memory and aging: Current issues and future directions* (pp. 71–95). New York: Psychology Press.

Naveh-Benjamin, M., Brav, T. K., & Levy, D. (2007). The associative memory deficit of older adults: The role of strategy utilization. *Psychology and Aging, 22,* 202–208.

Naveh-Benjamin, M., Hussain, Z., Guez, J., & Bar-On, M. (2003). Adult age differences in episodic memory: Further support for an associative-deficit hypothesis. *Journal of Experimental Psychology: Learning, Memory, and Cognition, 29,* 826–837.

Neal, M. B., & Hammer, L. B. (2007). *Working couples caring for children and aging parents.* Mahwah, NJ: Erlbaum.

Needham, B. L., & Austin, E. L. (2010). Sexual orientation, parental support, and health during the transition to young adulthood. *Journal of Youth and Adolescence, 39,* 1189–1198.

Neff, K. D., & Helwig, C. C. (2002). A constructivist approach to understanding the development of reasoning about rights and authority within cultural contexts. *Cognitive Development, 17,* 1429–1450.

Neff, L. A., & Karney, B. R. (2008). Compassionate love in early marriage. In B. Fehr, S. Sprecher, & L. G. Underwood, (Eds.), *The science of compassionate love: Theory, research, and applications* (pp. 201–221). Malden, MA: Wiley-Blackwell.

Neimeyer, R., Currier, J. M., Coleman, R., Tomer, A., & Samuel, E. (2011). Confronting suffering and death at the end of life: The impact of religiosity, psychosocial factors, and life regret among hospice patients. *Death Studies, 35,* 777–800.

Neimeyer, R. A. (Ed.). (1994). *Death anxiety handbook.* Washington, DC: Taylor & Francis.

Neimeyer, R. A., Burke, L. A., Mackay, M. M., & Stringer, J G. van D. (2010). Grief therapy and the reconstruction of meaning: From principles to practice. *Journal of Contemporary Psychotherapy, 40,* 73–83.

Neimeyer, R. A., & Van Brunt, D. (1995). Death anxiety. In H. Waas & R. A. Neimeyer (Eds.), *Dying: Facing the facts* (3rd ed., pp. 49–88). Washington, DC: Taylor & Francis.

Neitzel, C., & Stright, A. D. (2003). Mothers' scaffolding of children's problem solving: Establishing a foundation of academic self-regulatory competence. *Journal of Family Psychology, 17,* 147–159.

Nelson, C. A. (1995). The ontogeny of human memory: A cognitive neuroscience perspective. *Developmental Psychology, 31,* 723–738.

Nelson, C. A. (2001). The development and neural bases of face recognition. *Infant and Child Development, 10,* 3–18.

Nelson, C. A. (2002). Neural development and lifelong plasticity. In R. M. Lerner, F. Jacobs, & D. Wertlieb (Eds.), *Handbook of applied developmental science* (Vol. 1, pp. 31–60). Thousand Oaks, CA: Sage.

Nelson, C. A. (2007b). A neurobiological perspective on early human deprivation. *Child Development Perspectives, 1,* 13–18.

Nelson, C. A. (2011). Neural development and lifelong plasticity. In D. P. Keating (Ed.), *Nature and nurture in early child development* (pp. 45–69). New York: Cambridge University Press.

Nelson, C. A., & Bosquet, M. (2000). Neurobiology of fetal and infant development: Implications for infant mental health. In C. H. Zeanah, Jr. (Ed.), *Handbook of infant mental health* (2nd ed., pp. 37–59). New York: Guilford.

Nelson, C. A., Thomas, K. M., & de Haan, M. (2006). Neural bases of cognitive development. In D. Kuhn & R. Siegler (Eds.), *Handbook of child psychology: Vol. 2. Cognition, perception, and language* (6th ed., pp. 3–57). Hoboken, NJ: Wiley.

Nelson, C. A., Zeanah, C. H., Fox, N. A., Marshall, P. J., Smyke, A. T., & Guthrie, D. (2007). Cognitive recovery in socially deprived young children: The Bucharest Early Intervention Project. *Science, 318,* 1937–1940.

Nelson, D. A., Hart, C. H., Yang, C., Olsen, J. A., & Jin, S. (2006a). Aversive parenting in China: Associations with child physical and relational aggression. *Child Development, 77,* 554–572.

Nelson, D. A., Nelson, L. J., Hart, C. H., Yang, C., & Jin, S. (2006b). Parenting and peer-group behavior in cultural context. In X. Chen, D. French, & B. Schneider (Eds.), *Peer relations in cultural context* (pp. 213–246). New York: Cambridge University Press.

Nelson, D. A., Robinson, C. C., & Hart, C. H. (2005). Relational and physical aggression of preschool-age children: Peer status linkages across informants. *Early Education and Development, 16,* 115–139.

Nelson, H. D. (2008). Menopause. *Lancet, 371,* 760–770.

Nelson, K. (2003). Narrative and the emergence of a consciousness of self. In G. D. Fireman & T. E. McVay, Jr. (Eds.). *Narrative and consciousness: Literature, psychology, and the brain* (pp. 17–36). London: Oxford University Press.

Nelson, L. J. (2009). An examination of emerging adulthood in Romanian college students. *International Journal of Behavioral Development, 33,* 402–411.

Nelson, L. J., & Chen, X. (2007). Emerging adulthood in China: The role of social and cultural factors. *Child Development Perspectives, 1,* 86–91.

Nelson, L. J., Padilla-Walker, L. M., Carroll, J. S., Madsen, S. D., Barry, C. M., & Badger, S. (2007). "If you want me to treat you like an adult, start acting like one!" Comparing the criteria that emerging adults and their parents have for adulthood. *Journal of Family Psychology, 21,* 665–674.

Nelson, L. J., Padilla-Walker, L. M., Christensen, K. J., Evans, C. A., & Carroll, J. S. (2011). Parenting in emerging adulthood: An examination of parenting clusters and correlates. *Journal of Youth and Adolescence, 40,* 730–743.

Nemet, D., Barkan, S., Epstein, Y., Friedland, O., Kowen, G., & Eliakim, A. (2005). Short- and long-term beneficial effects of a combined dietary–behavioral–physical activity intervention for the treatment of childhood obesity. *Pediatrics, 115,* e443–e449.

Nepomnyaschy, L., & Waldfogel, J. (2007). Paternity leave and fathers' involvement with their young children. *Community, Work and Family, 10,* 427–453.

Nerenberg, L. (2010). Elder abuse prevention: A review of the field. In J. C. Cavanaugh & C. K. Cavanaugh (Eds.), *Aging in America. Vol. 3: Societal issues* (pp. 53–80). Santa Barbara, CA: Praeger.

Neri, Q., Takeuchi, T., & Palermo, G. D. (2008). An update of assisted reproductive technologies in the United States. *Annals of the New York Academy of Sciences, 1127,* 41–48.

Nesdale, D., Durkin, K., Maas, A., & Griffiths, J. (2004). Group status, outgroup ethnicity, and children's ethnic attitudes. *Applied Developmental Psychology, 25,* 237–251.

Nesdale, D., Durkin, K., Maas, A., & Griffiths, J. (2005). Threat, group identification, and children's ethnic prejudice. *Social Development, 14,* 189–205.

Nettelbeck, T., & Burns, N. R. (2010). Processing speed, working memory and reasoning ability from childhood to old age. *Personality and Individual Differences, 48,* 379–384.

Netz, Y., Wu, M.-J., Becker, B. J., & Tenenbaum, G. (2005). Physical activity and psychological well-being in advanced age: A meta-analysis of intervention studies. *Psychology and Aging, 20,* 272–284.

Neugarten, B. L. (1968a). Adult personality: Toward a psychology of the life cycle. In B. Neugarten (Ed.), *Middle age and aging* (pp. 137–147). Chicago: University of Chicago Press.

Neugarten, B. L. (1968b). The awareness of middle aging. In B. L. Neugarten (Ed.), *Middle age and aging* (pp. 93–98). Chicago: University of Chicago Press.

Neugarten, B. L. (1979). Time, age, and the life cycle. *American Journal of Psychiatry, 136,* 887–894.

Neuhouser, M. L., Wasserthel-Smoller, S., Thomson, C., Aragaki, A., Anderson, G. L., & Manson, J. E. (2009). Multivitamin use and risk of cancer and cardiovascular disease in the Women's Health Initiative cohorts. *Archives of Internal Medicine, 169,* 294–304.

Neuman, S. B. (2003). From rhetoric to reality: The case for high-quality compensatory prekindergarten programs. *Phi Delta Kappan, 85*(4), pp. 286–291.

Neville, H. J., & Bavelier, D. (2002). Human brain plasticity: Evidence from sensory deprivation and altered language experience. In M. A. Hofman, G. J. Boer, A. J. G. D. Holtmaat, E. J. W. van Someren, J. Berhaagen, & D. F. Swaab (Eds.), *Plasticity in the adult brain: From genes to neurotherapy* (pp. 177–188). Amsterdam: Elsevier Science.

Newbury, J. (2011). The drama of end of life care at home. *Nursing Times, 107*(11), 20–23.

Newcomb, A. F., Bukowski, W. M., & Pattee, L. (1993). Children's peer relations: A meta-analytic review of popular, rejected, neglected, controversial, and average sociometric status. *Psychological Bulletin, 113*, 99–128.

Newcomb, M. D., Abbott, R. D., Catalano, R. F., Hawkins, J. D., Battin-Pearson, S., & Hill, K. (2002). Mediational and deviance theories of late high school failure: Process roles of structural strains, academic competence, and general versus specific problem behavior. *Journal of Counseling Psychology, 49*, 172–186.

Newland, L. A., Coyl, D. D., & Freeman, H. (2008). Predicting preschoolers' attachment security from fathers' involvement, internal working models, and use of social support. *Early Child Development and Care, 178*, 785–801.

Newnham, C. A., Milgrom, J., & Skouteris, H. (2009). Effectiveness of a modified mother–infant transaction program on outcomes for preterm infants from 3 to 24 months of age. *Infant Behavior and Development, 32*, 17–26.

Newport, E. L. (1991). Contrasting conceptions of the critical period for language. In S. Cary & R. Gelman (Eds.), *The epigenesis of mind: Essays on biology and cognition* (pp. 111–130). Hillsdale, NJ: Erlbaum.

Newsom, J. T. (1999). Another side to caregiving: Negative reactions to being helped. *Current Directions in Psychological Science, 8*, 183–187.

Newsom, J. T., & Schulz, R. (1998). Caregiving from the recipient's perspective: Negative reactions to being helped. *Health Psychology, 17*, 172–181.

Newton, N. J., & Stewart, A. J. (2010). The middle ages: Change in women's personalities and social roles. *Psychology of Women Quarterly, 34*, 75–84.

Ng, F. F., Pomerantz, E. M., & Lam, S. (2007). European American and Chinese parents' responses to children's success and failure: Implications for children's responses. *Developmental Psychology, 43*, 1239–1255.

Ngata, P. (2004). Death, dying, and grief: A Maori perspective. In J. D. Morgan & P. Laungani (Eds.), *Death and bereavement around the world: Vol. 4. Asia, Australia, and New Zealand* (pp. 95–99). Amityville, NY: Baywood.

Nguyen, U.-S. D. T., Rothman, K. J., Demissie, S., Jackson, D. J., Lang, J. M., & Ecker, J. L. (2010). Epidural analgesia and risks of cesarean and operative vaginal deliveries in nulliparous and multiparous women. *Maternal and Child Health Journal, 14*, 705–712.

NHPCO (National Hospice and Palliative Care Organization). (2005). 83% of *Americans want to die at home.* Retrieved from www.nhpco.org/templates/1/homepage.cfm

NHPCO (National Hospice and Palliative Care Organization). (2012). *Hospice care in America.* Retrieved from www.nhpco.org/sites/default/files/public/Statistics_Research/2012_Facts_Figures.pdf

Ni, Y. (1998). Cognitive structure, content knowledge, and classificatory reasoning. *Journal of Genetic Psychology, 159*, 280–296.

NICHD (National Institute of Child Health and Human Development) Early Child Care Research Network. (1997). The effects of infant child care on infant–

mother attachment security: Results of the NICHD Study of Early Child Care. *Child Development, 68*, 860–879.

NICHD (National Institute of Child Health and Human Development) Early Child Care Research Network. (1998). Relations between family predictors and child outcomes: Are they weaker for children in child care? *Developmental Psychology, 34*, 1119–1128.

NICHD (National Institute of Child Health and Human Development) Early Child Care Research Network. (1999). Child care and mother–child interaction in the first 3 years of life. *Developmental Psychology, 35*, 1399–1413.

NICHD (National Institute of Child Health and Human Development) Early Child Care Research Network. (2000a). Characteristics and quality of child care for toddlers and preschoolers. *Applied Developmental Science, 4*, 116–135.

NICHD (National Institute of Child Health and Human Development) Early Child Care Research Network. (2000b). The relation of child care to cognitive and language development. *Child Development, 71*, 960–980.

NICHD (National Institute of Child Health and Human Development) Early Child Care Research Network. (2001). Before Head Start: Income and ethnicity, family characteristics, child care experiences, and child development. *Early Education and Development, 12*, 545–575.

NICHD (National Institute of Child Health and Human Development) Early Child Care Research Network. (2003a). Does amount of time spent in child care predict socioemotional adjustment during the transition to kindergarten? *Child Development, 74*, 976–1005.

NICHD (National Institute of Child Health and Human Development) Early Child Care Research Network. (2003b). Does quality of child care affect child outcomes at age 4½? *Developmental Psychology, 39*, 451–469.

NICHD (National Institute of Child Health and Human Development) Early Child Care Research Network. (2004). Trajectories of physical aggression from toddlerhood to middle childhood. *Monographs of the Society for Research in Child Development, 69*(4, Serial No. 278).

NICHD (National Institute of Child Health and Human Development) Early Child Care Research Network. (2006). Child-care effect sizes for the NICHD Study of Early Child Care and Youth Development. *American Psychologist, 61*, 99–116.

Nichols, W. C., & Pace-Nichols, M. A. (2000). Childless married couples. In W. C. Nichols, M. A. Pace-Nichols, D. S. Becvar, & A. Y. Napier (Eds.), *Handbook of family development and intervention* (pp. 171–188). New York: Wiley.

Nicholson, J. M., Sanders, M. R., Halford, W. K., Phillips, M., & Whitton, S. W. (2008). The prevention and treatment of children's adjustment problems in stepfamilies. In J. Pryor (Ed.), *International handbook of stepfamilies: Policy and practice in legal, research, and clinical environments* (pp. 485–521). Hoboken, NJ: Wiley.

Nickman, S. L., Rosenfeld, A. A., Fine, P., MacIntyre, J. C., Pilowsky, D. J., & Howe, R. A. (2005). Children in adoptive families: Overview and update. *Journal of the American Academy of Child and Adolescent Psychiatry, 44*, 987–995.

Niehaus, M. D., Moore, S. R., Patrick, P. D., Derr, L. L., Lorntz, B., Lima, A. A., & Gurerrant, R. L. (2002). Early childhood diarrhea is associated with diminished cognitive function 4 to 7 years later in children in a northeast Brazilian shanty-town. *American Journal of Tropical Medicine and Hygiene, 66*, 590–593.

Nielsen, L. S., Danielsen, K. V., & Sørensen, T. I. (2011). Short sleep duration as a possible cause of obesity:

Critical analysis of the epidemiological evidence. *Obesity Reviews, 12*, 78–92.

Nielsen, N. M., Hansen, A. V., Simonsen, J., & Hviid, A. (2011). Prenatal stress and risk of infectious diseases in offspring. *American Journal of Epidemiology, 173*, 990–997.

Nippold, M. A., Taylor, C. L., & Baker, J. M. (1996). Idiom understanding in Australian youth: A cross-cultural comparison. *Journal of Speech and Hearing Research, 39*, 442–447.

Nisbett, R. E. (2009). *Intelligence and how to get it.* New York: Norton.

Nishitani, S., Miyamura, T., Tagawa, M., Sumi, M., Takase, R., Doi, H., et al. (2009). The calming effect of a maternal breast milk odor on the human newborn infant. *Neuroscience Research, 63*, 66–71.

Noble, K. G., Fifer, W. P., Rauh, V. A., Nomura, Y., & Andrews, H. F. (2012). Academic achievement varies with gestational age among children born at term. *Pediatrics, 130*, e257–e264.

Noble, K. G., McCandliss, B. D., & Farah, M. J. (2007). Socioeconomic gradients predict individual differences in neurocognitive abilities. *Developmental Science, 10*, 464–480.

Noice, H., & Noice, T. (2006). What studies of actors and acting can tell us about memory and cognitive functioning. *Current Directions in Psychological Science, 15*, 14–18.

Noice, H., Noice, T., & Staines, G. (2004). A short-term intervention to enhance cognitive and affective functioning in older adults. *Journal of Aging and Health, 16*, 562–585.

Nolen-Hoeksema, S. (2006). The etiology of gender differences in depression. In C. M. Mazure & G. Puryear (Eds.), *Understanding depression in women: Applying empirical research to practice and policy* (pp. 9–43). Washington, DC: American Psychological Association.

Nolen-Hoeksema, S., & Aldao, A. (2011). Gender and age differences in emotion regulation and their relationship to depressive symptoms. *Personality and Individual Differences, 51*, 704–708.

Noller, P., Feeney, J. A., Sheehan, G., Darlington, Y., & Rogers, C. (2008). Conflict in divorcing and continuously married families: A study of marital, parent–child and sibling relationships. *Journal of Divorce and Remarriage, 49*, 1–24.

Nomaguchi, K. M., & Brown, S. L. (2011). Parental strains and rewards among mothers: The role of education. *Journal of Marriage and Family, 73*, 621–636.

Nomaguchi, K. M., & Milkie, M. A. (2003). Costs and rewards of children: The effects of becoming a parent on adults' lives. *Journal of Marriage and Family, 65*, 356–374.

Nordhus, I. H. (2008). Manifestations of depression and anxiety in older adults. In B. Woods & L. Clare (Eds.), *Handbook of the clinical psychology of ageing* (pp. 97–110). Hoboken, NJ: Wiley-Interscience.

Nosarti, C., Walshe, M., Rushe, T. M., Rifkin, L., Wyatt, J., Murray, R. M.; et al. (2011). Neonatal ultrasound results following very preterm birth predict adolescent behavioral and cognitive outcome. *Developmental Neuropsychology, 36*, 118–135.

Noterdaeme, M., Mildenberger, K., Minow, F., & Amorosa, H. (2002). Evaluation of neuromotor deficits in children with autism and children with a specific speech and language disorder. *European Child and Adolescent Psychiatry, 11*, 219–225.

Nucci, L. (2008). *Nice is not enough: Facilitating moral development.* Upper Saddle River, NJ: Prentice Hall.

Nucci, L. P. (1996). Morality and the personal sphere of action. In E. Reed, E. Turiel, & T. Brown (Eds.), *Values and knowledge* (pp. 41–60). Hillsdale, NJ: Erlbaum.

Nucci, L. P. (2001). *Education in the moral domain.* New York: Cambridge University Press.

Nucci, L. P. (2002). The development of moral reasoning. In U. Goswami (Ed.), *Blackwell handbook of childhood cognitive development* (pp. 303–325). Malden, MA: Blackwell.

Nucci, L. P. (2005). Culture, context, and the psychological sources of human rights concepts. In W. Edelstein & G. Nunner-Winkler (Eds.), *Morality in context* (pp. 365–394). Amsterdam, Netherlands: Elsevier.

Nuland, S. B. (1993). *How we die.* New York: Random House.

Numan, M., & Insel, T. (2003). *Neurobiology of parental behavior.* New York: Springer-Verlag.

Nunez-Smith, M., Wolf, E., Huang, H. M., Chen, P. G., Lee, L., Emanuel, E. J., et al. (2008). *The impact of media on child and adolescent health.* Retrieved from www.commonsensemedia.org/sites/default/files/media_child_health_exec_summary_0.pdf

O

Oakes, L. M., Coppage, D. J., & Dingel, A. (1997). By land or by sea: The role of perceptual similarity in infants' categorization of animals. *Developmental Psychology, 33,* 396–407.

Oakes, L. M., Horst, J. S., Kovack-Lesh, K. A., & Perone, S. (2009). How infants learn categories. In A. Woodward & A. Needham (Eds.), *Learning and the infant mind* (pp. 144–171). New York: Oxford University Press.

Oberecker, R., & Friederici, A. D. (2006). Syntactic event-related potential components in 24-month-olds' sentence comprehension. *NeuroReport, 17,* 1017–1021.

Oberecker, R., Friedrich, M., & Friederici, A. D. (2005). Neural correlates of syntactic processing in two-year-olds. *Journal of Cognitive Neuroscience, 17,* 1667–1678.

Obermeyer, C. M. (2000). Menopause across cultures: A review of the evidence. *Menopause, 7,* 184–192.

Obradović, J., Long, J. D., Cutuli, J. J., Chan, C. K., Hinz, E., Heistad, D., & Masten, A. S. (2009). Academic achievement of homeless and highly mobile children in an urban school district: Longitudinal evidence on risk, growth, and resilience. *Development and Psychopathology, 21,* 493–518.

O'Brien, M. A., Hsing, C., & Konrath, S. (2010, May). *Empathy is declining in American college students.* Poster presented at the annual meeting of the Association for Psychological Science, Boston.

O'Connor, E., & McCartney, K. (2007). Examining teacher–child relationships and achievement as part of an ecological model of development. *American Educational Research Journal, 44,* 340–369.

O'Connor, P. (2003). Dying in the hospital. In I. Corless, B. B. Germino, & M. A. Pitman (Eds.), *Dying, death, and bereavement: A challenge for the living* (2nd ed., pp. 87–103). New York: Springer.

O'Connor, P. G. (2012). Alcohol abuse and dependence. In L. Goldman & D. A. Ausiello (Eds.), *Cecil Medicine* (23rd ed.), Philadelphia, PA: Elsevier.

O'Connor, T. G., Rutter, M., Beckett, C., Keaveney, L., Dreppner, J. M., & the English and Romanian Adoptees Study Team. (2000). The effects of global severe privation on cognitive competence: Extension and longitudinal follow-up. *Child Development, 71,* 376–390.

OECD (Organisation for Economic Cooperation and Development). (2006). *Starting strong II: Early childhood education and care.* Paris: OECD Publishing. Retrieved from www.sourceoecd.org/education/9264035451

OECD (Organisation for Economic Cooperation and Development). (2010a). *Education at a glance 2010: OECD indicators.* Paris: Author. Retrieved from www.oecd.org/document/52/0,3746,en_2649_39263238_45897844_1_1_1,00.html

OECD (Organisation for Economic Cooperation and Development). (2010b). *OECD Health data: 2010.* Retrieved from www.oecd.org/document/44/0,3746,en_2649_37407_2085228_1_1_1_37407,00.html

OECD (Organisation for Economic Cooperation and Development). (2011). *OECD health data 2011.* Retrieved from stats.oecd.org/index.aspx?DataSetCode=HEALTH_STAT

OECD (Organisation for Economic Cooperation and Development). (2012a). *Education at a glance 2012: OECD indicators.* Paris: Author.

OECD (Organisation for Economic Cooperation and Development). (2012b). *Health data: 2012.* Retrieved from www.oecd.org/health/healthpoliciesanddata/oecdhealthdata2012.htm

Ogan, A., & Berk, L. E. (2009, April). *Effects of two approaches to make-believe play training on self-regulation in Head Start children.* Paper presented at the biennial meeting of the Society for Research in Child Development, Denver, CO.

Ogawa, J. R., Sroufe, L. A., Weinfield, N. S., Carlson, E. A., & Egeland, B. (1997). Development and the fragmented self: Longitudinal study of dissociative symptomatology in a nonclinical sample. *Development and Psychopathology, 9,* 855–879.

Ogden, C. L., Carroll, M. D., Curtin, L. R., Lamb, M. M., & Flegal, K. M. (2010). Prevalence of high body mass index in U.S. children and adolescents, 2007–2008. *Journal of the American Medical Association, 303,* 242–249.

O'Halloran, C. M., & Altmaier, E. M. (1996). Awareness of death among children: Does a life-threatening illness alter the process of discovery? *Journal of Counseling and Development, 74,* 259–262.

Ohannessian, C. M., & Hesselbrock, V. M. (2008). Paternal alcoholism and youth substance abuse: The indirect effects of negative affect, conduct problems, and risk taking. *Journal of Adolescent Health, 42,* 198–200.

Okagaki, L., & Sternberg, R. J. (1993). Parental beliefs and children's school performance. *Child Development, 64,* 36–56.

Okami, P., Weisner, T., & Olmstead, R. (2002). Outcome correlates of parent–child bedsharing: An eighteen-year longitudinal study. *Developmental and Behavioral Pediatrics, 23,* 244–253.

O'Keefe, M. J., O'Callaghan, M., Williams, G. M., Najman, J. M., & Bor, W. (2003). Learning, cognitive, and attentional problems in adolescents born small for gestational age. *Pediatrics, 112,* 301–307.

O'Laughlin, E. M., & Anderson, V. N. (2001). Perceptions of parenthood among young adults: Implications for career and family planning. *American Journal of Family Therapy, 29,* 95–108.

Old, S. R., & Naveh-Benjamin, M. (2008). Age-related changes in memory: Experimental approaches. In S. M. Hofer & D. F. Alwin (Eds.), *Handbook of cognitive aging: Interdisciplinary perspectives* (pp. 151–167). Thousand Oaks, CA: Sage.

Olds, D. L., Kitzman, H., Cole, R., Robinson, J., Sidora, K., Luckey, D. W., et al. (2004). Effects of nurse home-visiting on maternal life course and child development: Age 6 follow-up results of a randomized trial. *Pediatrics, 114,* 1550–1559.

Olds, D. L., Kitzman, H., Hanks, C., Cole, R., Anson, E., Sidora-Arcoleo, K., et al. (2007). Effects of nurse home visiting on maternal and child functioning: Age-9 follow-up of a randomized trial. *Pediatrics, 120,* e832–e845.

Olfman, S., & Robbins, B. D. (Eds.). (2012). *Drugging our children.* New York: Praeger.

Olineck, K. M., & Poulin-Dubois, D. (2007). Imitation of intentional actions and internal state language in infancy predict preschool theory of mind skills. *European Journal of Developmental Psychology, 4,* 14–30.

Olineck, K. M., & Poulin-Dubois, D. (2009). Infants' understanding of intention from 10 to 14 months: Interrelations among violation of expectancy and imitation tasks. *Infant Behavior and Development, 32,* 404–415.

Oliveira, F. L., Patin, R. V., & Escrivao, M. A. (2010). Atherosclerosis prevention and treatment in children and adolescents. *Expert Review of Cardiovascular Therapy, 8,* 513–528.

Ollendick, T. H., King, N. J., & Muris, P. (2002). Fears and phobias in children: Phenomenology, epidemiology, and aetiology. *Child and Adolescent Mental Health, 7,* 98–106.

Olshansky, S. J., Hayflick, L., & Perls, T. T. (2004). Antiaging medicine: The hype and the reality—Part II. *Journal of Gerontology, 59A,* 649–651.

Omar, H., McElderry, D., & Zakharia, R. (2003). Educating adolescents about puberty: What are we missing? *International Journal of Adolescent Medicine and Health, 15,* 79–83.

Ondrusek, N., Abramovitch, R., Pencharz, P., & Koren, G. (1998). Empirical examination of the ability of children to consent to clinical research. *Journal of Medical Ethics, 24,* 158–165.

O'Neill, M., Bard, K. A., Kinnell, M., & Fluck, M. (2005). Maternal gestures with 20-month-old infants in two contexts. *Developmental Science, 8,* 352–359.

Ong, A. D., Bergeman, C. S., & Bisconti, T. L. (2004). The role of daily positive emotions during conjugal bereavement. *Journal of Gerontology, 59B,* 168–176.

Ong, A. D., Mroczek, D. K., & Riffin, C. (2011). The health significance of positive emotions in adulthood and later life. *Social and Personality Psychology Compass, 5/8,* 538–551.

Ontai, L. L., & Thompson, R. A. (2008). Attachment, parent–child discourse and theory-of-mind development. *Social Development, 17,* 47–60.

Ophir, E., Nass, C., & Wagner, A. D. (2009). Cognitive control in media multitaskers. *Proceedings of the National Academy of Sciences, 106,* 15583–15587.

Oosterwegel, A., & Oppenheimer, L. (1993). *The self-system: Developmental changes between and within self-concepts.* Hillsdale, NJ: Erlbaum.

Orbio de Castro, B., Veerman, J. W., Koops, W., Bosch, J. D., & Monshouwer, H. J. (2002). Hostile attribution of intent and aggressive behavior: A meta-analysis. *Child Development, 73,* 916–934.

Oregon Public Health Division. (2013). *Oregon's Death with Dignity Act—2012.* Retrieved from public.health.oregon.gov/ProviderPartnerResources/EvaluationResearch/DeathwithDignityAct/Documents/year15.pdf

O'Rourke, N., Cappeliez, P., & Claxton, A. (2011). Functions of reminiscence and the psychological well-being of young-old and older adults over time. *Aging and Mental Health, 15,* 272–281.

Orth, U., Robins, R. W., & Widaman, K. F. (2012). Lifespan development of self-esteem and its effects on important life outcomes. *Personality Processes and Individual Differences, 102,* 1271–1288.

Orth, U., Trzesniewski, K. H., & Robins, R. W. (2010). Self-esteem development from young adulthood to old age: A cohort-sequential longitudinal study. *Journal of Personality and Social Psychology, 98,* 645–658.

Osherson, D. N., & Markman, E. M. (1975). Language and the ability to evaluate contradictions and tautologies. *Cognition, 2,* 213–226.

Ostrov, J. M., Crick, N. R., & Stauffacher, K. (2006). Relational aggression in sibling and peer relationships during early childhood. *Applied Developmental Psychology, 27,* 241–253.

Ostrov, J. M., Gentile, D. A., & Crick, N. R. (2006). Media exposure, aggression, and prosocial behavior during early childhood: A longitudinal study. *Social Development, 15,* 612–627.

Oswald, F., Jopp, D., Rott, C., & Wahl, H.-W. (2010). Is aging in place a resource for or risk to life satisfaction? *Gerontologist, 51*, 238–250.

Oswald, F., & Wahl, H.-W. (2013). Creating and sustaining homelike places in residential living. In G. D. Rowles & M. Bernard (Eds.), *Environmental gerontology: Making meaningful places in old age* (pp. 53–78). New York: Springer.

Otis, N., Grouzet, F. M. E., & Pelletier, L. G. (2005). Latent motivational change in an academic setting: A three-year longitudinal study. *Journal of Educational Psychology, 97*, 170–183.

Otto, M. W., Henin, A., Hirshfeld-Becker, D. R., Pollack, M. H., Biederman, J., & Rosenbaum, J. (2007). Posttraumatic stress disorder symptoms following media exposure to tragic events: Impact of 9/11 on children at risk for anxiety disorders. *Journal of Anxiety Disorders, 21*, 888–902.

Oude, L. H., Baur, L., Jansen, H., Shrewsbury, V. A., O'Malley, C., Stolk, R. P., & Summerbell, C. D. (2009). Interventions for treating obesity in children. *Cochrane Database of Systematic Reviews, Issue 4*. Chichester, UK: Wiley.

Ouko, L. A., Shantikumar, K., Knezovich, J., Haycock, P., Schnugh, D. J., & Ramsay, M. (2009). Effect of alcohol consumption on CpG methylation in the differentially methylated regions of H19 and IGDMR in male gametes: Implications for fetal alcohol spectrum disorders. *Alcoholism, Clinical and Experimental Research, 33*, 1615–1627.

Ovando, C. J., & Collier, V. P. (1998). *Bilingual and ESL classrooms: Teaching in multicultural contexts.* Boston: McGraw-Hill.

Overton, W. F. (2010). Life-span development: Concepts and issues. In W. F. Overton (Ed.), *Handbook of lifespan development: Cognition, biology, and methods* (pp. 1–29). Hoboken, NJ: Wiley.

Owen, C. G., Whincup, P. H., Kaye, S. J., Martin, R. M., Smith, G. D., Cook, D. G., et al. (2008). Does initial breastfeeding lead to lower blood cholesterol in adult life? A quantitative review of the evidence. *American Journal of Clinical Nutrition, 88*, 305–314.

Owsley, C. (2011). Aging and vision. *Vision Research, 51*, 1610–1622.

Oyserman, D., Bybee, D., Mowbray, C., & Hart-Johnson, T. (2005). When mothers have serious mental health problems: Parenting as a proximal mediator. *Journal of Adolescence, 28*, 443–463.

Özçaliskan, S. (2005). On learning to draw the distinction between physical and metaphorical motion: Is metaphor an early emerging cognitive and linguistic capacity? *Journal of Child Language, 32*, 291–318.

Özçaliskan, S., & Goldin-Meadow, S. (2005). Gesture is at the cutting edge of early language development. *Cognition, 96*, B101–B113.

Ozer, E. M., & Irwin, C. E., Jr. (2009). Adolescent and young adult health: From basic health status to clinical interventions. In R. M. Lerner & L. Steinberg (Eds.), *Handbook of adolescent psychology: Vol. 1. Individual bases of adolescent development* (pp. 618–641). Hoboken, NJ: Wiley.

P

Padilla-Walker, L. M., & Nelson, L. J. (2012). Black Hawk down?: Establishing helicopter parenting as a distinct construct from other forms of parental control during emerging adulthood. *Journal of Adolescence, 35*, 1177–1190.

Pagani, L. S., Japel, C., Vitaro, F., Tremblay, R. E., Larose, S., & McDuff, P. (2008). When predictions fail: The case of unexpected pathways toward high school dropout. *Journal of Social Issues, 64*, 175–193.

Pager, D., & Shepherd, H. (2008). The sociology of discrimination: Racial discrimination in employment, housing, credit, and consumer markets. *Annual Review of Sociology, 34*, 181–209.

Pager, D., Western, B., & Bonkowski, B. (2009). Discrimination in a low-wage labor market: A field experiment. *American Sociological Review, 74*, 777–799.

Paik, A. (2010). "Hookups," dating, and relationship quality: Does the type of sexual involvement matter? *Social Science Research, 39*, 739–753.

Painter, J. A., Allison, L., Dhingra, P., Daughtery, J., Cogdill, K., & Trujillo, L. G. (2012). Fear of falling and its relationship with anxiety, depression, and activity engagement among community-dwelling older adults. *American Journal of Occupational Therapy, 66*, 169–176.

Palincsar, A. S. (2003). Advancing a theoretical model of learning and instruction. In B. J. Zimmerman (Ed.), *Educational psychology: A century of contributions* (pp. 459–475). Mahwah, NJ: Erlbaum.

Palop, J. J., Chin, J., Roberson, E. D., Wang, J., Thwin, M. T., & Bien-Ly, N. (2007). Aberrant excitatory neuronal activity and compensatory remodeling of inhibitory hippocampal circuits in mouse models of Alzheimer's disease. *Neuron, 55*, 697–711.

Pan, B. A., & Snow, C. E. (1999). The development of conversation and discourse skills. In M. Barrett (Ed.), *The development of language* (pp. 229–249). Hove, UK: Psychology Press.

Pan, H. W. (1994). Children's play in Taiwan. In J. L. Roopnarine, J. E. Johnson, & F. H. Hooper (Eds.), *Children's play in diverse cultures* (pp. 31–50). Albany, NY: SUNY Press.

Panish, J. B., & Stricker, G. (2002). Perceptions of childhood and adult sibling relationships. *NYS Psychologist, 14*, 33–36.

Papadakis, A. A., Prince, R. P., Jones, N. P., & Strauman, T. J. (2006). Self-regulation, rumination, and vulnerability to depression in adolescent girls. *Development and Psychopathology, 18*, 815–829.

Paquette, D. (2004). Theorizing the father–child relationship: Mechanisms and developmental outcomes. *Human Development, 47*, 193–219.

Paradis, J. (2007). Second language acquisition in childhood. In E. Hoff & M. Shatz (Eds.), *Blackwell handbook of language development* (pp. 387–405). Malden, MA: Blackwell.

Paradise, R., & Rogoff, B. (2009). Side by side: Learning by observing and pitching in. *Ethos, 27*, 102–138.

Paramei, G. V. (2012). Color discrimination across four life decades assessed by the Cambridge Color Test. *Journal of the Optical Society of America, 29*, A290–A297.

Pardini, D. A., Fite, P. J., & Burke, J. D. (2008). Bidirectional associations between parenting practices and conduct problems in boys from childhood to adolescence: The moderating effect of age and African-American ethnicity. *Journal of Abnormal Child Psychology, 36*, 647–662.

Parent, A., Teilmann, G., Juul, A., Skakkebaek, N. E., Toppari, J., & Bourguignon, J. (2003). The timing of normal puberty and the age limits of sexual precocity: Variations around the world, secular trends, and changes after migration. *Endocrine Reviews, 24*, 668–693.

Paris, S. G., & Paris, A. H. (2006). Assessments of early reading. In K. A. Renninger & I. E. Sigel (Eds.), *Handbook of child psychology: Vol. 4. Child psychology in practice* (6th ed., pp. 48–74). Hoboken, NJ: Wiley.

Park, D. C. (2002). Judging meaning improves function in the aging brain. *Trends in Cognitive Sciences, 6*, 227–229.

Park, D. C., Lautenschlager, G., Hedden, T., Davidson, N. S., Smith, A. D., & Smith, P. K. (2002). Models of visuospatial and verbal memory across the adult life span. *Psychology and Aging, 17*, 299–320.

Park, W. (2009). Acculturative stress and mental health among Korean adolescents in the United States. *Journal of Human Behavior in the Social Environment, 19*, 626–634.

Parke, R. D., & Buriel, R. (2006). Socialization in the family: Ethnic and ecological perspectives. In N. Eisenberg (Ed.), *Handbook of child psychology: Vol. 3. Social, emotional, and personality development* (6th ed., pp. 429–504). Hoboken, NJ: Wiley.

Parke, R. D., Simpkins, S. D., McDowell, D. J., Kim, M., Killian, C., Dennis, J., Flyr, M. L., Wild, M., & Rah, Y. (2004). Relative contributions of families and peers to children's social development. In P. K. Smith & C. H. Hart (Eds.), *Blackwell handbook of childhood social development* (pp. 156–177). Malden, MA: Blackwell.

Parker, F. L., Boak, A. Y., Griffin, K. W., Ripple, C., & Peay, L. (1999). Parent–child relationship, home learning environment, and school readiness. *School Psychology Review, 28*, 413–425.

Parker, J. G., Low, C. M., Walker, A. R., & Gamm, B. K. (2005). Friendship jealousy in young adolescents: Individual differences and links to sex, self-esteem, aggression, and social adjustment. *Developmental Psychology, 41*, 235–250.

Parker, P. D., Schoon, I., Tsai, Y.-M., Nagy, G., Trautwein, U., & Eccles, J. (2012). Achievement, agency, gender, and socioeconomic background as predictors of postschool choices: A multicontext study. *Developmental Psychology, 48*, 1629–1642.

Parten, M. (1932). Social participation among preschool children. *Journal of Abnormal and Social Psychology, 27*, 243–269.

Pascalis, O., de Haan, M., & Nelson, C. A. (2002). Is face processing species-specific during the first year of life? *Science, 296*, 1321–1323.

Pascarella, E. T., & Terenzini, P. T. (1991). *How college affects students.* San Francisco: Jossey-Bass.

Pascarella, E. T., & Terenzini, P. T. (2005). *How college affects students: Vol. 2. A third decade of research.* San Francisco: Jossey-Bass.

Pasterski, V. L., Geffner, M. E., Brain, C., Hindmarsh, P., & Brook, C. (2005). Prenatal hormones and postnatal socialization by parents as determinants of male-typical toy play in girls with congenital adrenal hyperplasia. *Child Development, 76*, 264–278.

Patock-Peckam, J. A., & Morgan-Lopez, A. A. (2009). Mediational links among parenting styles, perceptions of parental confidence, self-esteem, and depression on alcohol-related problems in emerging adulthood. *Journal of Studies on Alcohol and Drugs, 70*, 215–226.

Patrick, R. B., & Gibbs, J. C. (2011). Inductive discipline, parental expression of disappointed expectations, and moral identity in adolescence. *Journal of Youth and Adolescence, 41*, 973–983.

Pattenden, S., Antova, T., Neuberger, M., Nikiforov, B., De Sario, M., Grize, L., & Heinrich, J. (2006). Parental smoking and children's respiratory health: Independent effects of prenatal and postnatal exposure. *Tobacco Control, 15*, 294–301.

Patterson, C. J., & Riskind, R. G. (2010). To be a parent: Issues in family formation among gay and lesbian adults. *Journal of GLBT Family Studies, 6*, 326–340.

Patterson, G. R., & Fisher, P. A. (2002). Recent developments in our understanding of parenting: Bidirectional effects, causal models, and the search for parsimony. In M. H. Bornstein (Ed.), *Handbook of parenting* (Vol. 5, pp. 59–88). Mahwah, NJ: Erlbaum.

Patterson, G. R., & Yoerger, K. (2002). A developmental model for early- and late-onset delinquency. In J. B. Reid & G. R. Patterson (Eds.), *Antisocial behavior in children and adolescents* (pp. 147–172). Washington, DC: American Psychological Association.

Paukner, A., Ferrari, P. F., & Suomi, S. J. (2011). Delayed imitation of lipsmacking gestures by infant rhesus macaques (*Macaca mulatta*). *PLoS ONE 6*(12), e28848.

Paul, J. J., & Cillessen, A. H. N. (2003). Dynamics of peer victimization in early adolescence: Results from a four-year longitudinal study. *Journal of Applied School Psychology, 19,* 25–43.

Pauli, S. A., Berga, S. L., Shang, W., & Session, D. R. (2009). Current status of the approach to assisted reproduction. *Pediatric Clinics of North America, 56,* 467–488.

Paulussen-Hoogeboom, M. C., Stams, G. J. J. M., Hermanns, J. M. A., & Peetsma, T. T. D. (2007). Child negative emotionality and parenting from infancy to preschool: A meta-analytic review. *Developmental Psychology, 43,* 438–453.

Payne, B. R., Gao, X., Noh, S. R., Anderson, C. J., & Stine-Morrow, E. A. L. (2012). The effects of print exposure on sentence processing and memory in older adults: Evidence for efficiency and reserve. *Aging, Neuropsychology, and Cognition, 19,* 122–149.

Pea, R., Nass, C., Meheula, L., Rance, M., Kumar, A., Bamford, H., et al. (2012). Media use, face-to-face communication, media multitasking, and social well-being among 8- to 12-year-old girls. *Developmental Psychology, 48,* 327–336.

Peake, A., & Harris, K. L. (2002). Young adults' attitudes toward multiple role planning: The influence of gender, career traditionality, and marriage plans. *Journal of Vocational Behavior, 60,* 405–421.

Pearlman, D. N., Zierler, S., Meersman, S., Kim, H. K., Viner-Brown, S. I., & Caron, C. (2006). Race disparities in childhood asthma: Does where you live matter? *Journal of the National Medical Association, 98,* 239–247.

Peck, R. C. (1968). Psychological developments in the second half of life. In B. L. Neugarten (Ed.), *Middle age and aging* (pp. 88–92). Chicago: University of Chicago Press.

Pederson, D. R., & Moran, G. (1996). Expressions of the attachment relationship outside of the Strange Situation. *Child Development, 67,* 915–927.

Peets, K., Hodges, E. V. E., Kikas, E., & Salmivalli, C. (2007). Hostile attributions and behavioral strategies in children: Does relationship type matter? *Developmental Psychology, 43,* 889–900.

Peirano, P., Algarin, C., & Uauy, R. (2003). Sleep–wake states and their regulatory mechanisms throughout early human development. *Journal of Pediatrics, 43,* S70–S79.

Peiró, J., Tordera, N., & Potocnik, K. (2012). Retirement practices in different countries. In M. Wang (Ed.), *Oxford handbook of retirement* (pp. 509–540). New York: Oxford University Press.

Pellegrini, A. D. (1992). Kindergarten children's social cognitive status as a predictor of first grade success. *Early Childhood Research Quarterly, 7,* 565–577.

Pellegrini, A. D. (2003). Perceptions and functions of play and real fighting in early adolescence. *Child Development, 74,* 1522–1533.

Pellegrini, A. D. (2004). Rough-and-tumble play from childhood through adolescence: Development and possible functions. In P. K. Smith & C. H. Hart (Eds.), *Blackwell handbook of childhood social development* (pp. 438–453). Malden, MA: Blackwell.

Pellegrini, A. D., & Holmes, R. M. (2006). The role of recess in primary school. In D. G. Singer, R. M. Golinkoff & K. Hirsh-Pasek (Eds.), *Play = learning* (pp. 36–53). New York: Oxford University Press.

Pellegrini, A. D., Huberty, P. D., & Jones, I. (1995). The effects of recess timing on children's playground and classroom behaviors. *American Educational Research Journal, 32,* 845–864.

Pellegrini, A. D., Kato, K., Blatchford, P., & Baines, E. (2002). A short-term longitudinal study of children's playground games across the first year of school: Implications for social competence and adjustment to school. *American Educational Research Journal, 39,* 991–1015.

Pellegrini, A. D., & Smith, P. K. (1998). Physical activity play: The nature and function of a neglected aspect of play. *Child Development, 69,* 577–598.

Pendlebury, S. T., Rothwell, P. M. (2009). Prevalence, incidence, and factors associated with pre-stroke and post-stroke dementia: A systematic review and meta-analysis. *Lancet Neurology, 8,* 1006–1018.

Pennington, B. F., Snyder, K. A., & Roberts, R. J., Jr. (2007). Developmental cognitive neuroscience: Origins, issues, and prospects. *Developmental Review, 27,* 428–441.

Penny, H., & Haddock, G. (2007). Anti-fat prejudice among children: The "mere proximity" effect in 5–10 year olds. *Journal of Experimental Social Psychology, 43,* 678–683.

Pepler, D. J., Craig, W. M., Connolly, J. A., Yuile, A., McMaster, L., & Jiang, D. (2006). A developmental perspective on bullying. *Aggressive Behavior, 32,* 376–384.

Peralta de Mendoza, O. A., & Salsa, A. M. (2003). Instruction in early comprehension and use of a symbol–referent relation. *Cognitive Development, 18,* 269–284.

Perelli-Harris, B., & Gassen, N. S. (2012). How similar are cohabitation and marriage? Legal approaches to cohabitation across Western Europe. *Population and Development Review, 38,* 435–467.

Perkins, H. W. (1991). Religious commitment, yuppie values, and well-being in post-collegiate life. *Review of Religious Research, 32,* 244–251.

Perlmutter, M. (1984). Continuities and discontinuities in early human memory: Paradigms, processes, and performances. In R. V. Kail, Jr., & N. R. Spear (Eds.), *Comparative perspectives on the development of memory* (pp. 253–287). Hillsdale, NJ: Erlbaum.

Perlmutter, M., Kaplan, M., & Nyquist, L. (1990). Development of adaptive competence in adulthood. *Human Development, 33,* 185–197.

Perls, T., Levenson, R., Regan, M., & Puca, A. (2002). What does it take to live to 100? *Mechanisms of Ageing and Development, 123,* 231–242.

Perls, T., & Terry, D. (2003). Understanding the determinants of exceptional longevity. *Annals of Internal Medicine, 139,* 445–449.

Perone, S., Madole, K. L., Ross-Sheehy, S., Carey, M., & Oakes, L. M. (2008). The relation between infants' activity with objects and attention to object appearance. *Developmental Psychology, 44,* 1242–1248.

Perry, W. G., Jr. (1981). Cognitive and ethical growth. In A. Chickering (Ed.), *The modern American college* (pp. 76–116). San Francisco: Jossey-Bass.

Perry, W. G., Jr. (1998). *Forms of intellectual and ethical development in the college years: A scheme.* San Francisco: Jossey-Bass. (Originally published 1970)

Perry-Jenkins, M., Repetti, R. L., & Crouter, A. C. (2000). Work and family in the 1990s. *Journal of Marriage and the Family, 62,* 981–998.

Peshkin, A. (1997). *Places of memory: Whiteman's schools and Native American communities.* Mahwah, NJ: Erlbaum.

Pesonen, A.-K., Räikkönen, K., Heinonen, K., & Komsi, N. (2008). A transactional model of temperamental development: Evidence of a relationship between child temperament and maternal stress over five years. *Social Development, 17,* 326–340.

Peters, R. D. (2005). A community-based approach to promoting resilience in young children, their families, and their neighborhoods. In R. D. Peters, B. Leadbeater, & R. J. McMahon (Eds.), *Resilience in children, families, and communities: Linking context to practice and policy* (pp. 157–176). New York: Kluwer Academic.

Peters, R. D., Petrunka, K., & Arnold, R. (2003). The Better Beginnings, Better Futures Project: A universal, comprehensive, community-based prevention approach for primary school children and their families. *Journal of Clinical Child and Adolescent Psychology, 32,* 215–227.

Peterson, B. E. (2002). Longitudinal analysis of midlife generativity, intergenerational roles, and caregiving. *Psychology and Aging, 17,* 161–168.

Peterson, B. E. (2006). Generativity and successful parenting: An analysis of young adult outcomes. *Journal of Personality, 74,* 847–869.

Peterson, B. E., & Duncan, L. E. (2007). Midlife women's generativity and authoritarianism: Marriage, motherhood, and 10 years of aging. *Psychology and Aging, 22,* 411–419.

Peterson, B. E., Smirles, K. A., & Wentworth, P. A. (1997). Generativity and authoritarianism: Implications for personality, political involvement, and parenting. *Journal of Personality and Social Psychology, 72,* 1202–1216.

Peterson, C., Warren, K. L., & Short, M. M. (2011). Infantile amnesia across the years: A 2-year follow-up of children's earliest memories. *Child Development, 82,* 1092–1105.

Peter-Wight, M., & Martin, M. (2011). Older spouses' individual and dyadic problem solving. *European Psychologist, 16,* 288–294.

Petitto, L. A., Holowka, S., Sergio, L. E., Levy, B., & Ostry, D. J. (2004). Baby hands that move to the rhythm of language: Hearing babies acquiring sign languages babble silently on the hands. *Cognition, 93,* 43–73.

Petitto, L. A., Holowka, S., Sergio, L. E., & Ostry, D. (2001, September 6). Language rhythms in babies' hand movements. *Nature, 413,* 35–36.

Petitto, L. A., & Marentette, P. F. (1991). Babbling in the manual mode: Evidence for the ontogeny of language. *Science, 251,* 1493–1496.

Petrofsky, J., Berk, L., & Al-Nakhli, H. (2012). The influence of autonomic dysfunction associated with aging and type 2 diabetes on daily life activities. *Experimental Diabetes Research,* Article ID 657103.

Pettigrew, T. F., & Tropp, L. R. (2006). A meta-analytic test of intergroup contact theory. *Journal of Personality and Social Psychology, 90,* 751–783.

Pettit, G. S., Keiley, M. K., Laird, R. D., Bates, J. E., & Dodge, K. A. (2007). Predicting the developmental course of mother-reported monitoring across childhood and adolescence from early proactive parenting, child temperament, and parents' worries. *Journal of Family Psychology, 21,* 206–217.

Pew Forum on Religion and Public Life. (2010). *Religion among the Millennials.* Washington, DC: Pew Research Center.

Pew Research Center. (2006). *Strong public support for right to die.* Retrieved from www.people-press.org/2006/01/05/strong-public-support-for-right-to-die

Pew Research Center. (2010a). *The decline of marriage and rise of new families.* Washington, DC: Author.

Pew Research Center. (2010b). *Religion among the millennials.* Washington, DC: Pew Form on Religion and Public Life.

Pew Research Center. (2013). *Growing support for gay marriage: Changed minds and changing demographics.* Washington, DC: Author. Retrieved from www.people-press.org/files/legacy-pdf/3-20-13%20Gay%20Marriage%20Release%20UPDATE.pdf

Pharo, H., Sim, C., Graham, M., Gross, J., & Hayne, H. (2011). Risky business: Executive function, personality, and reckless behavior during adolescence and emerging adulthood. *Behavioral Neuroscience, 125,* 970–978.

Phinney, J. S. (2007). Ethnic identity exploration in emerging adulthood. In J. J. Arnett & J. L. Tanner (Eds.), *Emerging adults in America: Coming of age in the 21st century* (pp. 117–134). Washington, DC: American Psychological Association.

Phinney, J. S., & Chavira, V. (1995). Parental ethnic socialization and adolescent outcomes in ethnic minority families. *Journal of Research on Adolescence, 5,* 31–53.

Phinney, J. S., Horenczyk, G., Liebkind, K., & Vedder, P. (2001). Ethnic identity, immigration, and well-being: An interactional perspective. *Journal of Social Issues, 57,* 493–510.

Phinney, J. S., Ong, A., & Madden, T. (2000). Cultural values and intergenerational value discrepancies in immigrant and non-immigrant families. *Child Development, 71,* 528–539.

Phuong, D. D., Frank, R., & Finch, B. R. (2012). Does SES explain more of the black/white health gap than we thought? Revisiting our approach toward understanding racial disparities in health. *Social Science and Medicine, 74,* 1385–1393.

Piaget, J. (1926). *The language and thought of the child.* New York: Harcourt, Brace & World. (Original work published 1923)

Piaget, J. (1930). *The child's conception of the world.* New York: Harcourt, Brace, & World. (Original work published 1926)

Piaget, J. (1951). *Play, dreams, and imitation in childhood.* New York: Norton. (Original work published 1945)

Piaget, J. (1952). *The origins of intelligence in children.* New York: International Universities Press. (Original work published 1936)

Piaget, J. (1967). *Six psychological studies.* New York: Vintage.

Piaget, J. (1971). *Biology and knowledge.* Chicago: University of Chicago Press.

Pianta, R., Egeland, B., & Erickson, M. F. (1989). The antecedents of maltreatment: Results of the Mother–Child Interaction Research Project. In D. Cicchetti & V. Carlson (Eds.), *Child maltreatment* (pp. 203–253). New York: Cambridge University Press.

Pierroutsakos, S. L., & Troseth, G. L. (2003). Video verité: Infants' manual investigation of objects on video. *Infant Behavior and Development, 26,* 183–199.

Pietz, J., Peter, J., Graf, R., Rauterberg, R. I., Rupp, A., & Sontheimer, D. (2004). Physical growth and neurodevelopmental outcome of nonhandicapped low-risk children born preterm. *Early Human Development, 79,* 131–143.

Piirto, J. (2007). *Talented children and adults* (3rd ed.). Waco, TX: Prufrock Press.

Pillow, B. (2002). Children's and adults' evaluation of the certainty of deductive inferences, inductive inferences, and guesses. *Child Development, 73,* 779–792.

Pinquart, M. (2003). Loneliness in married, widowed, divorced, and never-married older adults. *Journal of Social and Personal Relationships, 20,* 31–53.

Pinquart, M., & Schindler, I. (2009). Change of leisure satisfaction in the transition to retirement: A latent-class analysis. *Leisure Sciences, 31,* 311–329.

Pinquart, M., & Sörensen, S. (2001). Gender differences in self-concept and psychological well-being in old age: A meta-analysis. *Journal of Gerontology, 56B,* P195–P213.

Pinquart, M., & Sörensen, S. (2006). Gender differences in caregiver stressor, social resources, and health: An updated meta-analysis. *Journal of Gerontology, 61B,* P33–P45.

Pirie, K., Peto, R., Reeves, G. K., Green, J., Beral, V., & the Million Women Study Collaborators. (2012). The 21st century hazards of smoking and benefits of stopping: A prospective study of one million women in the UK. *Lancet, 308,* 133–141.

Pitkin, J. (2010). Cultural issues and the menopause. *Menopause International, 16,* 156–161.

Pizarro, D. A., & Bloom, P. (2003). The intelligence of the moral intuitions: Comment on Haidt (2001). *Psychological Review, 110,* 193–196.

Plante, I., Théoret, M., & Favreau, O. E. (2009). Student gender stereotypes: Contrasting the perceived maleness and femaleness of mathematics and language. *Educational Psychology, 29,* 385–405.

Pleck, J. H., & Masciadrelli, B. P. (2004). Paternal involvement by U.S. residential fathers: Levels, sources, and consequences. In M. E. Lamb (Ed.), *The role of the father in child development* (4th ed., pp. 222–271). Hoboken, NJ: Wiley.

Plomin, R. (1994). *Genetics and experience: The interplay between nature and nurture.* Thousand Oaks, CA: Sage.

Plomin, R. (2009). The nature of nurture. In K. McCartney & R. A. Weinberg (Eds.), *Experience and development: A festschrift in honor of Sandra Wood Scarr* (pp. 61–80). New York: Psychology Press.

Plomin, R., & Davis, O. S. P. (2009). The future of genetics in psychology and psychiatry: Microarrays, genome-wide association, and non-coding RNA. *Journal of Child Psychology and Psychiatry, 50,* 63–71.

Plomin, R., & Spinath, F. M. (2004). Intelligence: Genetics, genes, and genomics. *Journal of Personality and Social Psychology, 86,* 112–129.

Plucker, J. A., & Makel, M. C. (2010). Assessment of creativity. In J. C. Kaufman & R. J. Sternberg (Eds.), *Cambridge handbook of creativity* (pp. 48–73). New York: Cambridge University Press.

Pluess, M., & Belsky, J. (2011). Prenatal programming of postnatal plasticity? *Development and Psychopathology, 23,* 29–38.

Poehlmann, J., Schwichtenberg, A. J. M., Shlafer, R. J., Hahn, E., Bianchi, J.-P., & Warner, R. (2011). Emerging self-regulation in toddlers born preterm or low birth weight: Differential susceptibility to parenting. *Developmental and Psychopathology, 23,* 177–193.

Pogarsky, G., Thornberry, T. P., & Lizotte, A. J. (2006). Developmental outcomes for children of young mothers. *Journal of Marriage and Family, 68,* 332–344.

Polderman, T. J. C., de Geus, J. C., Hoekstra, R. A., Bartels, M., van Leeuwen, M., Verhulst, F. C., et al. (2009). Attention problems, inhibitory control, and intelligence index overlapping genetic factors: A study in 9-, 12-, and 18-year-old twins. *Neuropsychology, 23,* 381–391.

Polka, L., & Werker, J. F. (1994). Developmental changes in perception of non-native vowel contrasts. *Journal of Experimental Psychology: Human Perception and Performance, 20,* 421–435.

Pomerantz, E. M., & Dong, W. (2006). Effects of mothers' perceptions of children's competence: The moderating role of mothers' theories of competence. *Developmental Psychology, 42,* 950–961.

Pomerantz, E. M., & Eaton, M. M. (2000). Developmental differences in children's conceptions of parental control: "They love me, but they make me feel incompetent." *Merrill-Palmer Quarterly, 46,* 140–167.

Pomerantz, E. M., Ng, F. F., & Wang, Q. (2008). Culture, parenting, and motivation: The case of East Asia and the United States. In M. L. Maehr, S. A., Karabenick, & T. C. Urdan (Eds.), *Advances in motivation and achievement: Social psychological perspectives* (Vol. 15, pp. 209–240). Bingley, UK: Emerald Group.

Pomerantz, E. M., & Ruble, D. N. (1998). The multidimensional nature of control: Implications for the development of sex differences in self-evaluation. In J. Heckhausen & C. S. Dweck (Eds.), *Motivation and self-regulation across the lifespan* (pp. 159–184). New York: Cambridge University Press.

Pomerantz, E. M., & Saxon, J. L. (2001). Conceptions of ability as stable and self-evaluative processes: A longitudinal examination. *Child Development, 72,* 152–173.

Pomerleau, A., Scuccimarri, C., & Malcuit, G. (2003). Mother–infant behavioral interactions in teenage and adult mothers during the first six months

postpartum: Relations with infant development. *Infant Mental Health Journal, 24,* 495–509.

Pong, S., Johnston, J., & Chen, V. (2010). Authoritarian parenting and Asian adolescent school performance. *International Journal of Behavioral Development, 34,* 62–72.

Pong, S., & Landale, N. S. (2012). Academic achievement of legal immigrants' children: The roles of parents' pre- and postmigration characteristics in origin-group differences. *Child Development, 83,* 1543–1559.

Ponnappan, S., & Ponnappan, U. (2011). Aging and immune function: Molecular mechanisms to interventions. *Antioxidants & Redox Signaling, 14,* 1551–1585.

Pons, F., Lawson, J., Harris, P. L., & de Rosnay, M. (2003). Individual differences in children's emotion understanding: Effects of age and language. *Scandinavian Journal of Psychology, 44,* 347–353.

Poobalan, A. S., Aucott, L. S., Precious, E., Crombie, I. K., & Smith, W. C. S. (2010). Weight loss interventions in young people (18 to 25 year olds): A systematic review. *Obesity Reviews, 11,* 580–592.

Poon, L. W., Goodman, S. G., Bugiardini, R., Bierman, A. S., Eagle, K. A., Johnston, N., et al. (2012). Bridging the gender gap: Insights from a contemporary analysis of sex-related differences in the treatment and outcomes of patients with acute coronary syndromes. *American Heart Journal, 163,* 66–73.

Portes, A., & Rumbaut, R. G. (2005). Introduction: The second generation and the Children of Immigrants Longitudinal Study. *Ethnic and Racial Studies, 28,* 983–999.

Posner, M. I., & Rothbart, M. K. (2007). Temperament and learning. In M. I. Posner & M. K. Rothbart (Eds.), *Educating the human brain* (pp. 121–146). Washington, DC: American Psychological Association.

Posthuma, R. A., & Campion, M. A. (2009). Age stereotypes in the workplace: Common stereotypes, moderators, and future research directions. *Journal of Management, 35,* 158–188.

Poti, J. M., & Popkin, B. M. (2011). Trends in energy intake among U.S. children by eating location and food source, 1977–2006. *Journal of the American Dietetic Association, 111,* 1156–1164.

Poulin-Dubois, D., Serbin, L. A., Eichstedt, J. A., Sen, M. G., & Beissel, C. F. (2002). Men don't put on make-up: Toddlers' knowledge of the gender stereotyping of household activities. *Social Development, 11,* 166–181.

Powdthavee, N. (2008). Putting a price tag on friends, relatives, and neighbors: Using surveys of life satisfaction to value social relationships. *Journal of Socio-economics, 37,* 1459–1480.

Powlishta, K. K., Serbin, L. A., & Moller, L. C. (1993). The stability of individual differences in gender typing: Implications for understanding gender segregation. *Sex Roles, 29,* 723–737.

Prager, K. J., & Bailey, J. M. (1985). Androgyny, ego development, and psychological crisis resolution. *Sex Roles, 13,* 525–535.

Pratt, M. W., Norris, J. E., Hebblethwaite, S., & Arnold, M. L. (2008). Intergenerational transmission of values: Family generativity and adolescents' narratives of parent and grandparent value teaching. *Journal of Personality, 76,* 171–198.

Pratt, M. W., Skoe, E. E., & Arnold, M. L. (2004). Care reasoning development and family socialization patterns in later adolescence: A longitudinal analysis. *International Journal of Behavioral Development, 28,* 139–147.

Preece, J., & Findsen, B. (2007). Keeping people active: Continuing education programs that work. In M. Robinson, W. Novelli, C. Pearson, & L. Norris (Eds.), *Global health and global aging* (pp. 313–322). San Francisco: Jossey-Bass.

Pressley, M., & Hilden, D. (2006). Cognitive strategies. In D. Kuhn & R. Siegler (Eds.), *Handbook of child psychology: Vol. 2. Cognition, perception, and language* (6th ed., pp. 511–556). Hoboken, NJ: Wiley.

Pressley, M., Wharton-McDonald, R., Raphael, L. M., Bogner, K., & Roehrig, A. (2002). Exemplary first-grade teaching. In B. M. Taylor & P. D. Pearson (Eds.), *Teaching reading: Effective schools, accomplished teachers* (pp. 73–88). Mahwah, NJ: Erlbaum.

Prevatt, F. (2003). Dropping out of school: A review of intervention programs. *Journal of School Psychology, 41,* 377–399.

Previc, F. H. (1991). A general theory concerning the prenatal origins of cerebral lateralization. *Psychological Review, 98,* 299–334.

Price, J., Jordan, J., Prior, L., & Parkes, J. (2011). Living through the death of a child: A qualitative study of bereaved parents' experiences. *International Journal of Nursing Studies, 48,* 1384–1392.

Priess, H. A., Lindberg, S. M., & Hyde, J. S. (2009). Adolescent gender-role identity and mental health: Gender intensification revisited. *Child Development, 80,* 1531–1544.

Prince, M., Bryce, R., Albanese, E., Wimo, A., Ribeiro, W., & Ferri, C. P. (2013). The global prevalence of dementia: A systematic review and meta-analysis. *Alzheimer's and Dementia, 9,* 63–75.

Prinstein, M. J., Boergers, J., & Vernberg, E. M. (2001). Overt and relational aggression in adolescents: Social–psychological adjustment of aggressors and victims. *Journal of Clinical Child Psychology, 30,* 479–491.

Prinstein, M. J., & Cillessen, A. H. N. (2003). Forms and functions of adolescent peer aggression associated with high levels of peer status. *Merrill-Palmer Quarterly, 49,* 310–342.

Prinstein, M. J., & La Greca, A. M. (2002). Peer crowd affiliation and internalizing distress in childhood and adolescence: A longitudinal follow-back study. *Journal of Research on Adolescence, 12,* 325–351.

Proctor, M. H., Moore, L. L., Gao, D., Cupples, L. A., Bradlee, M. L., Hood, M. Y., & Ellison, R. C. (2003). Television viewing and change in body fat from preschool to early adolescence: The Framingham Children's Study. *International Journal of Obesity, 27,* 827–833.

Programme for International Student Assessment. (2009). *PISA profiles by country/economy.* Retrieved from stats.oecd.org/PISA2009Profiles

Proulx, K., & Jacelon, C. (2004). Dying with dignity: The good patient versus the good death. *American Journal of Hospice and Palliative Care, 21,* 116–120.

Pruden, S. M., Hirsh-Pasek, K., Golinkoff, R. M., & Hennon, E. A. (2006). The birth of words: Ten-month-olds learn words through perceptual salience. *Child Development, 77,* 266–280.

Pryor, J. H., Hurtado, S., DeAngelo, L., Blake, L. P., & Tran, S. (2009). *The American freshman: National norms for fall 2009.* Los Angeles: Higher Education Research Institute, UCLA.

Prysak, M., Lorenz, R. P., & Kisly, A. (1995). Pregnancy outcome in nulliparous women 35 years and older. *Obstetrics and Gynecology, 85,* 65–70.

Puhl, R. M., & Heuer, C. A. (2010). Obesity stigma: Important considerations for public health. *American Journal of Public Health, 100,* 1019–1028.

Puhl, R. M., Heuer, C. A., & Brownell, D. K. (2010). Stigma and social consequences of obesity. In P. G. Kopelman, I. D. Caterson, & W. H. Dietz (Eds.), *Clinical obesity in adults and children* (3rd ed., pp. 25–40). Hoboken, NJ: Wiley.

Puhl, R. M., & Latner, J. D. (2007). Stigma, obesity, and the health of the nation's children. *Psychological Bulletin, 133,* 557–580.

Pujol, J., Soriano-Mas, C., Ortiz, H., Sebastián-Gallés, N., Losilla, J. M., & Deus, J. (2006). Myelination of language-related areas in the developing brain. *Neurology, 66,* 339–343.

Punamaki, R. L. (2006). Ante- and perinatal factors and child characteristics predicting parenting experience among formerly infertile couples during the child's first year: A controlled study. *Journal of Family Psychology, 20,* 670–679.

Putallaz, M., Grimes, C. L., Foster, K. J., Kupersmidt, J. B., Coie, J. D., & Dearing, K. (2007). Overt and relational aggression and victimization: Multiple perspectives within the school setting. *Journal of School Psychology, 45,* 523–547.

Putnam, S. P., Samson, A. V., & Rothbart, M. K. (2000). Child temperament and parenting. In V. J. Molfese & D. L. Molfese (Eds.), *Temperament and personality across the life span* (pp. 255–277). Mahwah, NJ: Erlbaum.

Pyka, G., Lindenberger, E., Charette, S., & Marcus, R. (1994). Muscle strength and fiber adaptations to a year-long resistance training program in elderly men and women. *Journal of Gerontology, 49,* M22–27.

Pyszczynski, T., Greenberg, J., Solomon, S., Arndt, J., & Schimel, J. (2004). Why do people need self-esteem? A theoretical and empirical view. *Psychological Bulletin, 130,* 435–468.

Q

Qian, Z., & Lichter, D. T. (2011). Changing patterns of interracial marriage in a multiracial society. *Journal of Marriage and Family, 73,* 1065–1084.

Quill, T. E. (1991). Death and dignity: A case of individualized decision making. *New England Journal of Medicine, 324,* 691–694.

Quine, S., Wells, Y., de Vaus, D., & Kendig, H. (2007). When choice in retirement decisions is missing: Qualitative and quantitative findings of impact on well-being. *Australasian Journal on Ageing, 26,* 173–179.

Quinn, P. C. (2008). In defense of core competencies, quantitative change, and continuity. *Child Development, 79,* 1633–1638.

Quinn, P. C., Kelly, D. J., Lee, K., Pascalis, O., & Slater, A. (2008). Preference for attractive faces extends beyond conspecifics. *Developmental Science, 11,* 76–83.

Quinn, P. C., Yahr, J., Kuhn, A., Slater, A. M., & Pascalis, O. (2002). Representation of the gender of human faces by infants: A preference for female. *Perception, 31,* 1109–1121.

R

Raaijmakers, Q. A. W., Engels, R. C. M. E., & van Hoof, A. (2005). Delinquency and moral reasoning in adolescence and young adulthood. *International Journal of Behavioral Development, 29,* 247–258.

Rabbitt, P., Lunn, M., & Wong, D. (2008). Death, dropout, and longitudinal measurements of cognitive change in old age. *Journal of Gerontology, 63B,* P271–P278.

Rabig, J., Thomas, W., Kane, R., Cutler, L. J., & McAlilly, S. (2006). Radical redesign of nursing homes: Applying the Green House concept in Tupelo, Mississippi. *Gerontologist, 46,* 533–539.

Radler, B. T., & Ryff, C. D. (2010). Who participates? Accounting for longitudinal retention in the MIDUS national study of health and well-being. *Journal of Aging and Health, 22,* 307–331.

Ragow-O'Brien, D., Hayslip, B., Jr., & Guarnaccia, C. A. (2000). The impact of hospice on attitudes toward funerals and subsequent bereavement adjustment. *Omega, 41,* 291–305.

Rahman, Q., & Wilson, G. D. (2003). Born gay? The psychobiology of human sexual orientation. *Personality and Individual Differences, 34,* 1337–1382.

Raikes, H. A., Robinson, J. L., Bradley, R. H., Raikes, H. H., & Ayoub, C. C. (2007). Developmental trends in self-regulation among low-income toddlers. *Social Development, 16,* 128–149.

Raikes, H. A., & Thompson, R. A. (2006). Family emotional climate, attachment security, and young children's emotion knowledge in a high-risk sample. *British Journal of Developmental Psychology, 24,* 89–104.

Raikes, H. H., Chazan-Cohen, R., Love, J. M., & Brooks-Gunn, J. (2010). Early Head Start impacts at age 3 and a description of the age 5 follow-up study. In A. J. Reynolds, A. J. Rolnick, M. M. Englund, & J. Temple (Eds.), *Childhood programs and practices in the first decade of life: A human capital integration* (pp. 99–118). New York: Cambridge University Press.

Räikkönen, K., Matthews, K. A., Flory, J. D., Owens, J. F., & Gump, B. B. (1999). Effects of optimism, pessimism, and trait anxiety on ambulatory blood pressure and mood during everyday life. *Journal of Personality and Social Psychology, 76,* 104–113.

Rait, G., Walters, K., Bottomley, C., Petersen, I., Iliffe, S., & Nazareth, I. (2010). Survival of people with clinical diagnosis of dementia in primary care: Cohort study. *British Medical Journal, 341,* c3584.

Rakison, D. H. (2005). Developing knowledge of objects' motion properties in infancy. *Cognition, 96,* 183–214.

Rakison, D. H. (2006). Make the first move: How infants learn about self-propelled objects. *Developmental Psychology, 42,* 900–912.

Rakison, D. H. (2010). Perceptual categorization and concepts. In J. G. Bremner & T. D. Wachs (Eds.), *Wiley-Blackwell handbook of infant development* (2nd ed., pp. 243–270). Oxford, UK: Wiley.

Rakison, D. H., & Lupyan, G. (2008). Developing object concepts in infancy: An associative learning perspective. *Monographs of the Society for Research in Child Development, 73*(1, Serial No. 289).

Rakoczy, H., Tomasello, M., & Striano, T. (2004). Young children know that trying is not pretending: A test of the "behaving-as-if" construal of children's early concept of pretense. *Developmental Psychology, 40,* 388–399.

Rakoczy, H., Tomasello, M., & Striano, T. (2005). How children turn objects into symbols: A cultural learning account. In L. Namy (Ed.), *Symbol use and symbol representation* (pp. 67–97). New York: Erlbaum.

Ralston, S. H., & Uitterlinden, A. G. (2010). Genetics of osteoporosis. *Endocrine Reviews, 31,* 629–662.

Ramaswami, A., & Dreher, G. F. (2007). The benefits associated with workplace mentoring relationships. In T. D. Allen & L. T. Eby (Eds.), *Blackwell handbook of mentoring: A multiple perspectives approach* (pp. 211–231). Malden, MA: Blackwell.

Ramaswami, A., Dreher, G. F., Bretz, R., & Wiethoff, C. (2010). Gender, mentoring, and career success: The importance of organizational context. *Personnel Psychology, 63,* 385–405.

Ramchandani, P. G., Stein, A., O'Connor, T. G., Heron, J., Murray, L., & Evans, J. (2008). Depression in men in the postnatal period and later child psychopathology: A population cohort study. *Journal of the American Academy of Child and Adolescent Psychiatry, 47,* 390–398.

Ramey, C. T., Ramey, S. L., & Lanzi, R. G. (2006). Children's health and education. In K. A. Renninger & I. E. Sigel (Eds.), *Handbook of child psychology: Vol. 4. Child psychology in practice* (6th ed., pp. 864–892). Hoboken, NJ: Wiley.

Ramirez, A., & Zhang, S. (2007). When online meets offline: The effect of modality switching on relational communication. *Communication Monographs, 74,* 287–310.

Ramos, E., Frontera, W. R., Llorpart, A., & Feliciano, D. (1998). Muscle strength and hormonal levels in adolescents: Gender related differences. *International Journal of Sports Medicine, 19*, 526–531.

Ramos, M. C., Guerin, D. W., Gottfried, A. W., Bathurst, K., & Oliver, P. H. (2005). Family conflict and children's behavior problems: The moderating role of child temperament. *Structural Equation Modeling, 12*, 278–298.

Rampell, C. (2010, March 9). The gender wage gap, around the world. *New York Times online.* Retrieved from economix.blogs.nytimes.com/2010/03/09/the-gender-wage-gap-around-the-world

Ramsey-Rennels, J. L., & Langlois, J. H. (2006). Differential processing of female and male faces. *Current Directions in Psychological Science, 15*, 59–62.

Ramus, F. (2002). Language discrimination by newborns: Teasing apart phonotactic, rhythmic, and intonational cues. *Annual Review of Language Acquisition, 2*, 85–115.

Rando, T. A. (1995). Grief and mourning: Accommodating to loss. In H. Wass & R. A. Neimeyer (Eds.), *Dying: Facing the facts* (3rd ed., pp. 211–241). Washington, DC: Taylor & Francis.

Raqib, R., Alam, D. S., Sarker, P., Ahmad, S. M., Ara, G., & Yunus, M. (2007). Low birth weight is associated with altered immune function in rural Bangladeshi children: A birth cohort study. *American Journal of Clinical Nutrition, 85*, 845–852.

Rasmussen, C., Ho, E., & Bisanz, J. (2003). Use of the mathematical principle of inversion in young children. *Journal of Experimental Child Psychology, 85*, 89–102.

Rasmussen, E. R., Neuman, R. J., Heath, A. C., Levy, F., Hay, D. A., & Todd, R. D. (2004). Familial clustering of latent class and DSM-IV defined attention-deficit hyperactivity disorder (ADHD) subtypes. *Journal of Child Psychology and Psychiatry, 45*, 589–598.

Rathunde, K., & Csikszentmihalyi, M. (2005). The social context of middle school: Teachers, friends, and activities in Montessori and traditional school environments. *Elementary School Journal, 106*, 59–79.

Rauber, M. (2006, May 18). Parents aren't sitting still as recess disappears. *Parents in Action.* Retrieved from healthyschoolscampaign.org/news/media/food/2006-05_recess_disappears.php

Ravid, D., & Tolchinsky, L. (2002). Developing linguistic literacy: A comprehensive model. *Journal of Child Language, 29*, 417–447.

Ravitch, D. (2010). *The death and life of the great American school system: How testing and choice are undermining education.* New York: Basic Books.

Rawlins, W. K. (2004). Friendships in later life. In J. F. Nussbaum & J. Coupland (Eds.), *Handbook of communication and aging research* (2nd ed., pp. 273–299). Mahwah, NJ: Erlbaum.

Rayner, K., Pollatsek, A., & Starr, M. S. (2003). Reading. In A. F. Healy & R. W. Proctor (Eds.), *Handbook of psychology: Experimental psychology* (Vol. 4, pp. 549–574). New York: Wiley.

Raz, N., Ghisletta, P., Rodrigue, K. M., Kennedy, K. M., & Lindenberger, U. (2010). Trajectories of brain aging in middle-aged and older adults: Regional and individual differences. *NeuroImage, 51*, 501–511.

Reay, A. C., & Browne, K. D. (2008). Elder abuse and neglect. In B. Woods & L. Clare (Eds.), *Handbook of the clinical psychology of ageing* (pp. 311–322). Chichester, UK: Wiley.

Reddin, J. (1997). High-achieving women: Career development patterns. In H. S. Farmer (Ed.), *Diversity and women's career development* (pp. 95–126). Thousand Oaks, CA: Sage.

Redman, L. M., Martin, C. K., Williamson, D. A., & Ravussin, E. (2008). Effect of caloric restriction in non-obese humans on physiological, psychological and behavioral outcomes. *Physiology and Behavior, 94*, 643–648.

Redman, L. M., & Ravussin, E. (2011). Caloric restriction in humans: Impact on physiological, psychological, and behavioral outcomes. *Antioxidants & Redox Signaling, 14*, 275–287.

Reich, S. M., Subrahmanyam, K., & Espinoza, G. (2012). Friending, IMing, and hanging out face-to-face: Overlap in adolescents' online and offline social networks. *Developmental Psychology, 48*, 356–368.

Reid, H. M., & Fine, A. (1992). Self-disclosure in men's friendships: Variations associated with intimate relations. In P. M. Nardi (Ed.), *Men's friendships* (pp. 153–171). Newbury Park, CA: Sage.

Reid, K. F., & Fielding, R. A. (2012). Skeletal muscle power: A critical determinant of physical functioning in older adults. *Exercise and Sports Sciences Reviews, 40*, 4–12.

Reis, O., & Youniss, J. (2004). Patterns in identity change and development in relationships with mothers and friends. *Journal of Adolescent Research, 19*, 31–44.

Reis, S. M. (2004). We can't change what we don't recognize: Understanding the special needs of gifted females. In S. Baum (Ed.), *Twice-exceptional and special populations of gifted students* (pp. 67–80). Thousand Oaks, CA: Corwin Press.

Reiss, D. (2003). Child effects on family systems: Behavioral genetic strategies. In A. C. Crouter & A. Booth (Eds.), *Children's influence on family dynamics: The neglected side of family relationships* (pp. 3–36). Mahwah, NJ: Erlbaum.

Reiss, N. S., & Tishler, C. L. (2008). Suicidality in nursing home residents: Part II. Prevalence, risk factors, methods, assessment, and management. *Professional Psychology: Research and Practice, 39*, 271–275.

Reitzes, D. C., & Mutran, E. J. (2002). Self-concept as the organization of roles: Importance, centrality, and balance. *Sociological Quarterly, 43*, 647–667.

Reitzes, D. C., & Mutran, E. J. (2004). Grandparenthood: Factors influencing frequency of grandparent–grandchildren contact and grandparent role satisfaction. *Journal of Gerontology, 59*, S9–S16.

Repacholi, B. M., & Gopnik, A. (1997). Early reasoning about desires: Evidence from 14- and 18-month-olds. *Developmental Psychology, 33*, 12–21.

Reppucci, N. D., Meyer, J. R., & Kostelnik, J. O. (2011). Tales of terror from juvenile justice and education. In M. S. Aber, K. I. Maton, & E. Seidman (Eds.), *Empowering settings and voices for social change* (pp. 155–172). New York: Oxford University Press.

Resnick, M., & Silverman, B. (2005). *Some reflections on designing construction kits for kids.* Proceedings of the Conference on Interaction Design and Children, Boulder, CO.

Rest, J. R. (1979). *Development in judging moral issues.* Minneapolis: University of Minnesota Press.

Reuter-Lorenz, P. A., & Cappell, K. A. (2008). Neurocognitive aging and the compensation hypothesis. *Current Directions in Psychological Science, 17*, 177–182.

Reyes-Ortiz, C. A., Kuo, Y.-F., DiNuzzo, A. R., Ray, L. A., Raji, M. A., & Markides, K. S. (2005). Near vision impairment predicts cognitive decline: Data from the Hispanic established populations for epidemiologic studies of the elderly. *Journal of the American Geriatric Society, 53*, 681–686.

Reyna, V. F., & Farley, F. (2006). Risk and rationality in adolescent decision making: Implications for theory, practice, and public policy. *Psychological Science in the Public Interest, 7*, 1–44.

Rhoades, B. L., Greenberg, M. T., & Domitrovich, C. E. (2009). The contribution of inhibitory control to preschoolers' social-emotional competence. *Journal of Applied Developmental Psychology, 30*, 310–320.

Rhoades, G. K., Stanley, S. M., & Markman, H. J. (2006). Pre-engagement cohabitation and gender

asymmetry in marital commitment. *Journal of Family Psychology, 20*, 553–560.

Rhone, M., & Basu, A. (2008). Phytochemicals and age-related eye diseases. *Nutrition Reviews, 66*, 465–472.

Richardson, H. L., Walker, A. M., & Horne, R. S. C. (2008). Sleep position alters arousal processes maximally at the high-risk age for sudden infant death syndrome. *Journal of Sleep Research, 17*, 450–457.

Richardson, H. L., Walker, A. M., & Horne, R. S. C. (2009). Maternal smoking impairs arousal patterns in sleeping infants. *Pediatric Sleep, 32*, 515–521.

Richardson, V. E. (2007). A dual process model of grief counseling: Findings from the changing lives of older couples (CLOC) study. *Journal of Gerontological Social Work, 48*, 311–329.

Richie, B. S., Fassinger, R. E., Linn, S. G., Johnson, J., Prosser, J., & Robinson, S. (1997). Persistence, connection, and passion: A qualitative study of the career development of highly achieving African American–black and white women. *Journal of Counseling Psychology, 44*, 133–148.

Richler, J., Luyster, R., Risi, S., Hsu, W.-L., Dawson, G., & Bernier, R. (2006). Is there a "regressive phenotype" of autism spectrum disorder associated with the measles-mumps-rubella vaccine? A CPEA study. *Journal of Autism and Developmental Disorders, 36*, 299–316.

Richmond, J., Colombo, M., & Hayne, H. (2007). Interpreting visual preferences in the visual paired-comparison task. *Journal of Experimental Psychology: Learning, Memory, and Cognition, 33*, 823–831.

Rideout, V., & Hamel, E. (2006). *The media family: Electronic media in the lives of infants, toddlers, preschoolers and their parents.* Menlo Park, CA: Henry J. Kaiser Family Foundation.

Rideout, V. J., Foehr, U. G., & Roberts, D. F. (2010). *Generation M2: Media in the lives of 8- to 18-year-olds.* Menlo Park. CA: Henry J. Kaiser Family Foundation.

Riediger, M., Li, S.-C., & Lindenberger, U. (2006). Selection, optimization, and compensation as developmental mechanisms of adaptive resource allocation: Review and preview. In J. E. Birren & K. W., Schaire (Eds.), *Handbook of the psychology of aging* (6th ed.) (pp. 289–313). Burlington, MA: Academic Press.

Riley, J. R., & Masten, A. S. (2004). Resilience in context. In R. D. Peters, B. Leadbeater, & R. McMahon (Eds.), *Resilience in children, families, and communities: Linking context to practice and policy* (pp. 13–25). New York: Kluwer Academic.

Riley, L. D., & Bowen, C. P. (2005). The sandwich generation: Challenges and coping strategies of multigenerational families. *Counseling and Therapy for Couples and Families, 13*, 52–58.

Rinaldo, L. A., & Ferraro, K. F. (2012). Inequality, health. In G. Ritzer (Ed.), *Wiley-Blackwell encyclopedia of globalization.* Hoboken, NJ: Wiley-Blackwell.

Ripple, C. H., & Zigler, E. (2003). Research, policy, and the federal role in prevention initiatives for children. *American Psychologist, 58*, 482–490.

Ritchie, L. D., Spector, P., Stevens, M. J., Schmidt, M. M., Schreiber, G. B., Striegel-Moore, R. H., et al. (2007). Dietary patterns in adolescence are related to adiposity in young adulthood in black and white females. *Journal of Nutrition, 137*, 399–406.

Riva, D., & Giorgi, C. (2000). The cerebellum contributes to higher functions during development: Evidence from a series of children surgically treated for posterior fossa tumours. *Brain, 123*, 1051–1061.

Rivlin, R. S. (2007). Keeping the young-elderly healthy: Is it too late to improve our health through nutrition? *American Journal of Clinical Nutrition, 86*(Suppl.), 1572S–1576S.

Rizvi, S. I., & Jha, R. (2011). Strategies for the discovery of anti-aging compounds. *Expert Opinion on Drug Discovery, 6,* 89–102.

Rizzolatti, G., & Craighero, L. (2004). The mirror-neuron system. *Annual Review of Neuroscience, 27,* 169–192.

Roberts, B. W., & DelVecchio, W. E. (2000). The rank-order consistency of personality traits from childhood to old age: A quantitative review of longitudinal studies. *Psychological Bulletin, 126,* 3–25.

Roberts, B. W., Kuncel, N., Shiner, R., Caspi, A., & Goldberg, L. R. (2007). The power of personality: A comparative analysis of the predictive validity of personality traits, SES, and IQ. *Perspectives on Psychological Science, 2,* 313–345.

Roberts, B. W., & Mroczek, D. (2008). Personality and trait change in adulthood. *Current Directions in Psychological Science, 17,* 31–35.

Roberts, B. W., Walton, K. E., & Viechtbauer, W. (2006). Patterns of mean-level change in personality traits across the life course: A meta-analysis of longitudinal studies. *Psychological Bulletin, 132,* 3–25.

Roberts, D. F., Henriksen, L., & Foehr, U. G. (2004). Adolescents and media. In R. M. Lerner & L. Steinberg (Eds.), *Handbook of adolescent psychology* (2nd ed., pp. 627–664). Hoboken, NJ: Wiley.

Roberts, D. F., Henriksen, L., & Foehr, U. G. (2009). Adolescence, adolescents, and media. In R. M. Lerner & L. Steinberg (Eds.), *Handbook of adolescent psychology: Vol. 2. Contextual influences on adolescent development* (3rd ed., pp. 314–344). Hoboken, NJ: Wiley.

Roberts, J. E., Burchinal, M. R., & Durham, M. (1999). Parents' report of vocabulary and grammatical development of American preschoolers: Child and environment associations. *Child Development, 70,* 92–106.

Roberts, P. (2006). From my space to our space: The functions of Web memorials in bereavement. *The Forum, 32,* 1–4.

Robertson, J. (2008). Stepfathers in families. In J. Pryor (Ed.), *International handbook of stepfamilies: Policy and practice in legal, research, and clinical environments* (pp. 125–150). Hoboken, NJ: Wiley.

Robertson, K. F., Smeets, S., Lubinski, D., & Benbow, C. P. (2010). Beyond the threshold hypothesis: Even among the gifted and top math/science graduate students, cognitive abilities, vocational interests, and lifestyle preferences matter for career choice, performance, and persistence. *Current Directions in Psychological Science, 19,* 346–351.

Robin, A. L., & Le Grange, D. (2010). Family therapy for adolescents with anorexia nervosa. In J. R. Weisz & A. E. Kazdin (Eds.), *Evidence-based psychotherapies for children and adolescents* (2nd ed., pp. 359–374). New York: Guilford.

Robinson, C. C., Anderson, G. T., Porter, C. L., Hart, C. H., & Wouden-Miller, M. (2003). Sequential transition patterns of preschoolers' social interactions during child-initiated play: Is parallel-aware play a bi-directional bridge to other play states? *Early Childhood Research Quarterly, 18,* 3–21.

Robinson, K. M. (2010). Policy issues in mental health among the elderly. *Nursing Clinics of North America, 45,* 627–634.

Robinson, S., Goddard, L., Dritschel, B., Wisley, M., & Howlin, P. (2009). Executive functions in children with autism spectrum disorders. *Brain and Cognition, 71,* 362–368.

Robles, T. F., & Carroll, J. E. (2011). Restorative biological processes and health. *Social and Personality Psychology Compass, 5,* 518–537.

Roca, A. Carcia-Esteve, L., Imaz, M. L., Torres, A., Hernández, S., & Botet, F. (2011). Obstetrical and neonatal outcomes after prenatal exposure to selective serotonin reuptake inhibitors: The relevance of dose. *Journal of Affective Disorders, 135,* 208–215.

Rochat, P. (1989). Object manipulation and exploration in 2- to 5-month-old infants. *Developmental Psychology, 25,* 871–884.

Rochat, P. (2003). Five levels of self-awareness as they unfold early in life. *Consciousness and Cognition, 12,* 717–731.

Rochat, P., & Goubet, N. (1995). Development of sitting and reaching in 5- to 6-month-old infants. *Infant Behavior and Development, 18,* 53–68.

Rochat, P., & Hespos, S. J. (1997). Differential rooting responses by neonates: Evidence for an early sense of self. *Early Development and Parenting, 6,* 105–112.

Rochat, P., & Striano, T. (2002). Who's in the mirror? Self-other discrimination in specular images by four- and nine-month-old infants. *Infant and Child Development, 11,* 289–303.

Rochat, P., Striano, T., & Blatt, L. (2002). Differential effects of happy, neutral, and sad still-faces on 2-, 4-, and 6-month-old infants. *Infant and Child Development, 11,* 289–303.

Rodkin, P. C., Farmer, T. W., Pearl, R., & Van Acker, R. (2000). Heterogeneity of popular boys: Antisocial and prosocial configurations. *Developmental Psychology, 36,* 14–24.

Rodrigue, K. M., & Kennedy, K. M. (2011). The cognitive consequences of structural changes to the aging brain. In K. W. Schaie & S. L. Willis (Eds.), *Handbook of the psychology of aging* (7th ed., pp. 73–91). San Diego, CA: Academic Press.

Rodríguez, B., & López, M. J. R. (2011). El "nido repleto": La resolución de conflictos familiares cuando los hijos mayores se quedan en el hogar. [The "full nest": The resolution of family conflicts when older children remain in the home.] *Cultura y Educación, 23,* 89–104.

Roelfsema, N. M., Hop, W. C., Boito, S. M., & Wladimiroff, J. W. (2004). Three-dimensional sonographic measurement of normal fetal brain volume during the second half of pregnancy. *American Journal of Obstetrics and Gynecology, 190,* 275–280.

Roeser, R. W., Eccles, J. S., & Freedman-Doan, C. (1999). Academic functioning and mental health in adolescence: Patterns, progressions, and routes from childhood. *Journal of Adolescent Research, 14,* 135–174.

Rogers, W. A., & Fisk, A. D. (2005). Aware home technology: Potential benefits for older adults. *Public Policy and Aging Report, 15*(4), 28–30.

Rogoff, B. (1998). Cognition as a collaborative process. In D. Kuhn & R. S. Siegler (Eds.), *Handbook of child psychology: Vol. 2. Cognition, perception, and language* (5th ed., pp. 679–744). New York: Wiley.

Rogoff, B. (2003). *The cultural nature of human development.* New York: Oxford University Press.

Rogoff, B., & Chavajay, P. (1995). What's become of research on the cultural basis of cognitive development? *American Psychologist, 50,* 859–877.

Rogoff, B., Malkin, C., & Gibride, K. (1984). Interaction with babies as guidance in development. In B. Rogoff & J. V. Wertsch (Eds.), *Children's learning in the "zone of proximal development" (New directions for child development,* No. 23, pp. 31–44). San Francisco: Jossey-Bass.

Rogoff, B., Paradise, R., Arauz, R. M., Correa-Chávez, M., & Angelillo, C. (2003). Firsthand learning through intent participation. *Annual Review of Psychology, 54,* 175–203.

Rogoff, B., & Waddell, K. J. (1982). Memory for information organized in a scene by children from two cultures. *Child Development, 53,* 1224–1228.

Rogol, A. D., Roemmich, J. N., & Clark, P. A. (2002). Growth at puberty. *Journal of Adolescent Health, 31,* 192–200.

Rohner, R. P., & Veneziano, R. A. (2001). The importance of father love: History and contemporary evidence. *Review of General Psychology, 5,* 382–405.

Roid, G. (2003). *The Stanford-Binet Intelligence Scales, Fifth Edition, interpretive manual.* Itasca, IL: Riverside Publishing.

Roisman, G. I., Madsen, S. D., Hennighausen, K. H., Sroufe, L. A., & Collins, W. A. (2001). The coherence of dyadic behavior across parent–child and romantic relationships as mediated by the internalized representation of experience. *Attachment and Human Development, 3,* 156–172.

Roisman, G. I., Padron, E., Sroufe, L. A., & Egeland, B. (2002). Earned-secure attachment status in retrospect and prospect. *Child Development, 73,* 1204–1219.

Rokach, A. (2001). Perceived causes of loneliness in adulthood. *Journal of Social Behavior and Personality, 15,* 67–84.

Rokach, A. (2003). Strategies of coping with loneliness throughout the lifespan. In N. J. Pallone (Ed.), *Love, romance, sexual interaction: Research perspectives from current psychology* (pp. 225–344). New Brunswick, NJ: Transaction.

Rokach, R., Cohen, O., & Dreman, S. (2004). Who pulls the trigger? Who initiates divorce among over 45-year-olds. *Journal of Divorce and Remarriage, 42,* 61–83.

Romano, E., Babchishin, L., Pagani, L. S., & Kohen, D. (2010). School readiness and later achievement: Replication and exgtension using a nationwide Canadian survey. *Developmental Psychology, 46,* 995–1007.

Rome-Flanders, T., & Cronk, C. (1995). A longitudinal study of infant vocalizations during mother–infant games. *Journal of Child Language, 22,* 259–274.

Romero, A. J., & Roberts, R. E. (2003). The impact of multiple dimensions of ethnic identity on discrimination and adolescents' self-esteem. *Journal of Applied Social Psychology, 33,* 2288–2305.

Rönnqvist, L., & Domellöf, E. (2006). Quantitative assessment of right and left reaching movements in infants: A longitudinal study from 6 to 36 months. *Developmental Psychobiology, 48,* 444–459.

Roopnarine, J. L., & Evans, M. E. (2007). Family structural organization, mother–child and father–child relationships and psychological outcomes in English-speaking African Caribbean and Indo Caribbean families. In M. Sutherland (Ed.), *Psychological of development in the Caribbean.* Kingston, Jamaica: Ian Randle.

Roopnarine, J. L., Hossain, Z., Gill, P., & Brophy, H. (1994). Play in the East Indian context. In J. L. Roopnarine, J. E. Johnson, & F. H. Hooper (Eds.), *Children's play in diverse cultures* (pp. 9–30). Albany: State University of New York Press.

Roopnarine, J. L., Krishnakumar, A., Metindogan, A., & Evans, M. (2006). Links between parenting styles, parent–child academic interaction, parent–school interaction, and early academic skills and social behaviors in young children of English-speaking Caribbean immigrants. *Early Childhood Research Quarterly, 21,* 238–252.

Roopnarine, J. L., Talukder, E., Jain, D., Joshi, P., & Srivastav, P. (1990). Characteristics of holding, patterns of play, and social behaviors between parents and infants in New Delhi, India. *Developmental Psychology, 26,* 667–673.

Rosander, K., & von Hofsten, C. (2004). Infants' emerging ability to represent occluded object motion. *Cognition, 91,* 1–22.

Rose, A. J., Carlson, W., & Waller, E. M. (2007). Prospective associations of co-rumination with friendship and emotional adjustment: Considering the socioemotional trade-offs of corumination. *Developmental Psychology, 43,* 1019–1031.

Rose, A. J., Swenson, L. P., & Waller, E. M. (2004). Overt and relational aggression and perceived popularity:

Developmental differences in concurrent and prospective relations. *Developmental Psychology, 40,* 378–387.

Rose, S. A., Feldman, J. F., & Jankowski, J. J. (2001). Attention and recognition memory in the 1st year of life: A longitudinal study of preterm and full-term infants. *Developmental Psychology, 37,* 135–151.

Rose, S. A., Jankowski, J. J., & Senior, G. J. (1997). Infants' recognition of contour-deleted figures. *Journal of Experimental Psychology: Human Perception and Performance, 23,* 1206–1216.

Rosen, A. B., & Rozin, P. (1993). Now you see it, now you don't: The preschool child's conception of invisible particles in the context of dissolving. *Developmental Psychology, 29,* 300–311.

Rosen, C. S., & Cohen, M. (2010). Subgroups of New York City children at high risk of PTSD after the September 11 attacks: A signal detection analysis. *Psychiatric Services, 61,* 64–69.

Rosen, D. (2003). Eating disorders in children and young adolescents: Etiology, classification, clinical features, and treatment. *Adolescent Medicine: State of the Art Reviews, 14,* 49–59.

Rosen, S., Bergman, M., & Plester, D. (1962). Presbycusis study of a relatively noise-free population in the Sudan. *Transactions of the American Otological Society, 50,* 135–152.

Rosenbaum, J. E. (2009). Patient teenagers? A comparison of the sexual behavior of virginity pledgers and matched nonpledgers. *Pediatrics, 123,* e110–e120.

Rosenblatt, P. C. (2008). Grief across cultures: A review and research agenda. In M. S. Stroebe, R. O. Hansson, H. Schut, & W. Stroebe (Eds.), *Handbook of bereavement research and practice* (pp. 207–222). Washington, DC: American Psychological Association.

Rosenman, R. H., Brand, R. J., Jenkins, C. D., Friedman, M., Strauss, R., & Wurm, M. (1975). Coronary heart disease in the Western Collaborative Group Study: Final follow-up experience of 8½ years. *Journal of the American Medical Association, 223,* 872–877.

Rosenstein, D. L. (2011). Depression and end-of-life care for patients with cancer. *Dialogues in Clinical Neuroscience, 13,* 101–108.

Roseth, C. J., Pellegrini, A. D., Bohn, C. M., van Ryzin, M., & Vance, N. (2007). Preschoolers' aggression, affiliation, and social dominance relationships: An observational, longitudinal study. *Journal of School Psychology, 45,* 479–497.

Rosetta, L., & Baldi, A. (2008). On the role of breastfeeding in health promotion and the prevention of allergic diseases. *Advances in Experimental Medicine and Biology, 606,* 467–483.

Ross, C. E., & Sastry, J. (1999). The sense of personal control: Social-structural causes and emotional consequences. In C. S. Aneshensel & J. C. Phelan (Eds.), *Handbook of the sociology of mental health* (pp. 369–394). New York: Springer.

Rossen, E. K., Knafl, K. A., & Flood, M. (2008). Older women's perceptions of successful aging. *Activities, Adaptation and Aging, 32,* 73–88.

Rossi, A. S. (2005). The menopausal transition and aging processes. In O. G. Brim, C. D. Ryff, & R. C. Kessler (Eds.), *How healthy are we? A national study of well-being at midlife* (pp. 153–201). Chicago: University of Chicago Press.

Rothbart, M. K. (2003). Temperament and the pursuit of an integrated developmental psychology. *Merrill-Palmer Quarterly, 50,* 492–505.

Rothbart, M. K., Ahadi, S. A., & Evans, D. E. (2000). Temperament and personality: Origins and outcome. *Journal of Personality and Social Psychology, 78,* 122–135.

Rothbart, M. K., & Bates, J. E. (2006). Temperament. In N. Eisenberg (Ed.), *Handbook of child psychology: Vol. 3. Social, emotional, and personality development* (6th ed., pp. 99–166). Hoboken, NJ: Wiley.

Rothbart, M. K., Posner, M. I., & Kieras, J. (2006). Temperament, attention, and the development of self-regulation. In K. McCartney & D. Phillips (Eds.), *Blackwell handbook of early childhood development* (pp. 338–357). Malden, MA: Blackwell.

Rothbaum, F., Kakinuma, M., Nagaoka, R., & Azuma, H. (2007). Attachment and amae: Parent–child closeness in the United States and Japan. *Journal of Cross-Cultural Psychology, 38,* 465–486.

Rothbaum, F., Pott, M., Azuma, H., Miyake, K., & Weisz, J. (2000a). The development of close relationships in Japan and the United States: Paths of symbiotic harmony and generative tension. *Child Development, 71,* 1121–1142.

Rothblum, E. D., Balsam, K. F., & Solomon, S. E. (2011). The longest "legal" U.S. same-sex couples reflect on their relationships. *Journal of Social Issues, 67,* 302–315.

Rothman, S. M., & Mattson, M. P. (2012). Sleep disturbances in Alzheimer's and Parkinson's diseases. *Neuromolecular Medicine, 14,* 194–204.

Routledge, C., & Juhl, J. (2010). When death thoughts lead to death fears: Mortality salience increases death anxiety for individuals who lack meaning in life. *Cognition and Emotion, 24,* 848–854.

Rovee-Collier, C. K. (1999). The development of infant memory. *Current Directions in Psychological Science, 8,* 80–85.

Rovee-Collier, C. K., & Bhatt, R. S. (1993). Evidence of long-term memory in infancy. *Annals of Child Development, 9,* 1–45.

Rovee-Collier, C. K., & Cuevas, K. (2009). Multiple memory systems are unnecessary to account for infant memory development: An ecological model. *Developmental Psychology, 45,* 160–174.

Rowe, M. L. (2008). Child-directed speech: Relation to socioeconomic status, knowledge of child development and child vocabulary skill. *Journal of Child Language, 35,* 185–205.

Rowe, M. L., & Goldin-Meadow, S. (2009). Early gesture selectively predicts later language learning. *Developmental Science, 12,* 182–187.

Rowland, C. F. (2007). Explaining errors in children's questions. *Cognition, 104,* 106–134.

Rowland, C. F., & Pine, J. M. (2000). Subject-auxiliary inversion errors and wh-question acquisition: "What children do know?" *Journal of Child Language, 27,* 157–181.

Rowley, S. J., Kurtz-Costes, B., Mistry, R., & Feagans, L. (2007). Social status as a predictor of race and gender stereotypes in late childhood and early adolescence. *Social Development, 16,* 150–168.

Roy, K. M., & Lucas, K. (2006). Generativity as second chance: Low-income fathers and transformation of the difficult past. *Research in Human Development, 3,* 139–159.

Rubenstein, L. Z., Stevens, J. A., & Scott, V. (2008). Interventions to prevent falls among older adults. In L. S. Doll, S. E. Bonzo, D. A. Sleet, J. A. Mercy, & E. N. Haas (Eds.), *Handbook of injury and violence prevention* (pp. 37–53). New York: Springer.

Rubin, C., Maisonet, M., Kieszak, S., Monteilh, C., Holmes, A., Flanders, D., et al. (2009). Timing of maturation and predictors of menarche in girls enrolled in a contemporary British cohort. *Paediatric and Perinatal Epidemiology, 23,* 492–504.

Rubin, D., Downes, K., O'Reilly, A., Mekonnen, R., Luan, X., & Localio, R. (2008). Impact of kinship care on behavioral well-being for children in out of home care. *Archives of Pediatrics and Adolescent Medicine, 162,* 550–556.

Rubin, D. C. (2002). Autobiographical memory across the lifespan. In P. Graf & N. Ohta (Eds.), *Lifespan development of human memory* (pp. 159–184). Cambridge, MA: MIT Press.

Rubin, D. C., Rahhal, T. A., & Poon, L. W. (1998). Things learned in early adulthood are remembered best. *Memory and Cognition, 26,* 3–19.

Rubin, D. M., O'Reilly, A. L., Luan, X., Dai, D., Localio, A. R., et al. (2011). Variation in pregnancy outcomes following statewide implementation of a prenatal home visitation program. *Archives of Pediatrics and Adolescent Medicine, 165,* 198–204.

Rubin, K. H., Bowker, J., & Gazelle, H. (2010). Social withdrawal in childhood and adolescence: Peer relationships and social competence. In K. H. Rubin & R. J. Coplan (Eds.), *The development of shyness and social withdrawal* (pp. 131–156). New York: Guilford.

Rubin, K. H., Bukowski, W. M., & Parker, J. G. (2006). Peer interactions, relationships, and groups. In N. Eisenberg (Ed.), *Handbook of child psychology: Vol. 3. Social, emotional, and personality development* (6th ed., pp. 571–645). Hoboken, NJ: Wiley.

Rubin, K. H., & Burgess, K. B. (2002). Parents of aggressive and withdrawn children. In M. Bornstein (Ed.), *Handbook of parenting* (2nd ed., pp. 383–418). Hillsdale, NJ: Erlbaum.

Rubin, K. H., Coplan, J., Chen, X., Buskirk, A. A., & Wojslawowicz, J. C. (2005). Peer relationships in childhood. In M. H. Bornstein & M. E. Lamb (Eds.), *Developmental science: An advanced textbook* (pp. 469–512). Mahwah, NJ: Erlbaum.

Rubin, K. H., Fein, G. G., & Vandenberg, B. (1983). Play. In E. M. Hetherington (Ed.), *Handbook of child psychology: Vol. 4. Socialization, personality, and social development* (4th ed., pp. 693–744). New York: Wiley.

Rubin, K. H., Watson, K. S., & Jambor, T. W. (1978). Free-play behaviors in preschool and kindergarten children. *Child Development, 49,* 539–536.

Ruble, D. N., Alvarez, J., Bachman, M., Cameron, J., Fuligni, A., García Coll, C., & Rhee, E. (2004). The development of a sense of "we": The emergence and implications of children's collective identity. In M. Bennett & F. Sani (Eds.), *The development of the social self* (pp. 29–76). Hove, UK: Psychology Press.

Ruble, D. N., Martin, C. L., & Berenbaum, S. A. (2006). Gender development. In N. Eisenberg (Ed.), *Handbook of child psychology: Vol. 3. Social, emotional, and personality development* (6th ed., pp. 226–299). Hoboken, NJ: Wiley.

Ruble, D. N., Taylor, L. J., Cyphers, L., Greulich, F. K., Lurye, L. E., & Shrout, P. E. (2007). The role of gender constancy in early gender development. *Child Development, 78,* 1121–1136.

Rudolph, K. D., Lambert, S. F., Clark, A. G., & Kurlakowsky, K. D. (2001). Negotiating the transition to middle school: The role of self-regulatory processes. *Child Development, 72,* 929–946.

Ruff, H. A., & Capozzoli, M. C. (2003). Development of attention and distractibility in the first 4 years of life. *Developmental Psychology, 39,* 877–890.

Ruffman, T., & Langman, L. (2002). Infants' reaching in a multi-well A not B task. *Infant Behavior and Development, 25,* 237–246.

Ruffman, T., Perner, J., Olson, D. R., & Doherty, M. (1993). Reflecting on scientific thinking: Children's understanding of the hypothesis–evidence relation. *Child Development, 64,* 1617–1636.

Ruffman, T., Slade, L., Devitt, K., & Crowe, E. (2006). What mothers say and what they do: The relation between parenting, theory of mind, language, and conflict/cooperation. *British Journal of Developmental Psychology, 24,* 105–124.

Ruitenberg, A., Ott, A., van Swieten, J. C., Hofman, A., & Breteler, M. M. B. (2001). Incidence of dementia: Does gender make a difference? *Neurobiology of Aging, 22,* 575–580.

Runco, M. A. (1992). Children's divergent thinking and creative ideation. *Developmental Review, 12,* 233–264.

Runco, M. A., Cramond, B., & Pagnani, A. R. (2010). Gender and creativity. In J. C. Chrisler & D. R. McCreary (Eds.), *Handbook of gender research in psychology* (Vol. 1, pp. 343–357). New York: Springer.

Rurup, M. L., Muller, M. T., Onwuteaka-Philipsen, B. D., van der Heide, A., van der Wal, G., & van der Maas, P. J. (2005). Requests for euthanasia or physician-assisted suicide from older persons who do not have a severe disease: An interview study. *Psychological Medicine, 35,* 665–671.

Rusconi, A. (2004). Different pathways out of the parental home: A comparison of West Germany and Italy. *Journal of Comparative Family Studies, 35,* 627–649.

Rushton, J. L., Forcier, M., & Schectman, R. M. (2002). Epidemiology of depressive symptoms in the National Longitudinal Study of Adolescent Health. *Journal of the American Academy of Child and Adolescent Psychiatry, 41,* 199–205.

Rushton, J. P., & Bons, T. A. (2005). Mate choice and friendship in twins. *Psychological Science, 16,* 555–559.

Rushton, J. P., & Jensen, A. R. (2005). Thirty years of research on race differences in cognitive ability. *Psychology, Public Policy, and Law, 11,* 235–294.

Rushton, J. P., & Jensen, A. R. (2006). The totality of available evidence shows the race IQ gap still remains. *Psychological Science, 17,* 921–924.

Rushton, J. P., & Jensen, A. R. (2010). The rise and fall of the Flynn effect as a reason to expect a narrowing of the black–white IQ gap. *Intelligence, 38,* 213–219.

Russac, R. J., Gatliff, C., Reece, M., & Spottswood, D. (2007). Death anxiety across the adult years: An examination of age and gender effects. *Death Studies, 31,* 549–561.

Russell, A., Mize, J., & Bissaker, K. (2004). Parent–child relationships. In P. K. Smith & C. H. Hart (Eds.), *Blackwell handbook of childhood social development* (pp. 204–222). Malden, MA: Blackwell.

Russell, J. A. (1990). The preschooler's understanding of the causes and consequences of emotion. *Child Development, 61,* 1872–1881.

Russell, J. A., Douglas, A. J., & Ingram, C. D. (2001). Brain preparations for maternity—adaptive changes in behavioral and neuroendocrine systems during pregnancy and lactation. *Progress in Brain Research, 133,* 1–38.

Russell, R. B., Petrini, J. R., Damus, K., Mattison, D. R., & Schwarz, R. H. (2003). The changing epidemiology of multiple births in the United States. *Obstetrics and Gynecology, 101,* 129–135.

Rutland, A., Killen, M., & Abrams, D. (2010). A new social-cognitive developmental perspective on prejudice: The interplay between morality and group identity. *Perspectives on Psychological Science, 5,* 279–291.

Rutter, M. (2007). Gene-environment interdependence. *Developmental Science, 10,* 12–18.

Rutter, M. (2011). Biological and experiential influences on psychological development. In D. P. Keating (Ed.), *Nature and nurture in early child development* (pp. 7–44). New York: Cambridge University Press.

Rutter, M., Colvert, E., Kreppner, J., Beckett, C., Castle, J., & Groothues, C. (2007). Early adolescent outcomes for institutionally deprived and nondeprived adoptees. I: Disinhibited attachment. *Journal of Child Psychology and Psychiatry, 48,* 17–30.

Rutter, M., & the English and Romanian Adoptees Study Team. (1998). Developmental catch-up, and deficit, following adoption after severe global early privation. *Journal of Child Psychology and Psychiatry, 39,* 465–476.

Rutter, M., O'Connor, T. G., & English and Romanian Adoptees (ERA) Study Team. (2004). Are there biological programming effects for psychological development? Findings from a study of Romanian adoptees. *Developmental Psychology, 40,* 81–94.

Rutter, M., Pickles, A., Murray, R., & Eaves, L. (2001). Testing hypotheses on specific environmental causal effects on behavior. *Psychological Bulletin, 127,* 291–324.

Rutter, M., Sonuga-Barke, E. J, Beckett, C., Castle, J., Kreppner, J., Kumsta, R., et al. (2010). Deprivation-specific psychological patterns: Effects of institutional deprivation. *Monographs of the Society for Research in Child Development, 75*(1, Serial No. 295), 48–78.

Ryan, E. B., Jin, Y., Anas, A. P., & Luh, J. J. (2004). Communication beliefs about youth and old age in Asia and Canada. *Journal of Cross-Cultural Gerontology, 19,* 343–360.

Rybash, J. M., & Hrubi-Bopp, K. L. (2000). Isolating the neural mechanisms of age-related changes in human working memory. *Nature Neuroscience, 3,* 509–515.

Ryff, C. D. (1991). Possible selves in adulthood and old age: A tale of shifting horizons. *Psychology and Aging, 6,* 286–295.

Ryff, C. D., Friedman, E., Fuller-Rowell, T., Love, G., Miyamoto, Y., Morozink, J., et al. (2012). Varieties of resilience in MIDUS. *Social and Personality Psychology Compass, 6,* 792–806.

Ryff, C. D., & Keyes, C. L. M. (1995). The structure of psychological well-being revisited. *Journal of Personality and Social Psychology, 69,* 719–727.

Ryff, C. D., Singer, B. H., & Seltzer, M. M. (2002). Pathways through challenge: Implications for well-being and health. In L. Pulkkinen & A. Caspi (Eds.), *Paths to successful development* (pp. 302–328). Cambridge, UK: Cambridge University Press.

Rynearson, E. K., & Salloum, A. (2011). Restorative retelling: Revising the narrative of violent death. In R. A. Neimeyer, D. L. Harris, H. R. Winokuer, & G. F. Thornton (Eds.), *Grief and bereavement in contemporary society: Bridging research and practice* (pp. 177–188). New York: Routledge.

S

Saarni, C. (2000). Emotional competence: A developmental perspective. In R. Bar-On & J. D. A. Parker (Eds.), *Handbook of emotional intelligence* (pp. 68–91). San Francisco: Jossey-Bass.

Saarni, C., Campos, J. J., Camras, L. A., & Witherington, D. (2006). Emotional development: Action, communication, and understanding. In N. Eisenberg (Ed.), *Handbook of child psychology: Vol. 3. Social, emotional, and personality development* (6th ed., pp. 226–299). Hoboken, NJ: Wiley.

Sabo, D., & Veliz, P. (2011). *Progress without equity: The provision of high school athletic opportunity in the United States, by gender 1993–94 through 2005–06.* East Meadow, NY: Women's Sports Foundation.

Sacca, S. C., Bolognesi, C., Battistella, A., Bagnis, A., & Izzotti, A. (2009). Gene-environment interactions in ocular diseases. *Mutation Research, 667,* 98–117.

Sacks, P. (2005). "No child left": What are schools for in a democratic society? In S. Olfman (Ed.), *Childhood lost: How American culture is failing our kids* (pp. 185–202). Westport, CT: Praeger.

Sadeh, A. (1997). Sleep and melatonin in infants: A preliminary study. *Sleep, 20,* 185–191.

Sadeh, A., Flint-Ofir, E., Tirosh, T., & Tikotzky, L. (2007). Infant sleep and parental sleep-related cognitions. *Journal of Family Psychology, 21,* 74–87.

Sadler, P., Ethier, N., & Woody, E. (2011). Interpersonal complementarity. In L. M. Horowitz & S. Strack (Eds.), *Handbook of interpersonal psychology* (pp. 123–156). Hoboken, NJ: Wiley.

Sadler, T. W. (2010). *Langman's medical embryology* (11th ed.). Baltimore, MD: Lippincott Williams & Wilkins.

Safe Kids USA. (2008). *Report to the nation: Trends in unintentional childhood injury mortality and parental views on child safety.* Retrieved from www.safekids.org/assets/docs/ourwork/research/research-report-safe-kids-week-2008.pdf

Safe Kids USA. (2011a). *A look inside American family vehicles: National study of 79,000 car seats, 2009–2010.* Retrieved from www.safekids.org/assets/docs/safety-basics/safety-tips-by-risk-area/sk-car-seat-report-2011.pdf

Safe Kids USA. (2011b). *Injury trends fact sheet.* Retrieved from www.safekids.org/our-work/research/fact-sheets/injury-trends-fact-sheet.html

Saffran, J. R. (2009). Acquiring grammatical patterns: Constraints on learning. In J. Colombo, P. McCardle, & L. Freund (Eds.), *Infant pathways to language: Methods, models, and research disorders* (pp. 31–47). New York: Psychology Press.

Saffran, J. R., Aslin, R. N., & Newport, E. L. (1996). Statistical learning by 8-month-old infants. *Science, 27,* 1926–1928.

Saffran, J. R., & Thiessen, E. D. (2003). Pattern induction by infant language learners. *Developmental Psychology, 39,* 484–494.

Saffran, J. R., Werker, J. F., & Werner, L. A. (2006). The infant's auditory world: Hearing, speech, and the beginnings of language. In D. Kuhn & R. Siegler (Eds.), *Handbook of child psychology: Vol. 2. Cognition, perception, and language* (6th ed., pp. 58–108). Hoboken, NJ: Wiley.

Safren, S. A., & Pantalone, D. W. (2006). Social anxiety and barriers to resilience among lesbian, gay, and bisexual adolescents. In A. M. Omoto & H. S. Kurtzman (Eds.), *Sexual orientation and mental health: Examining identity and development in lesbian, gay, and bisexual young people* (pp. 55–71). Washington, DC: American Psychological Association.

Saginak, K. A., & Saginak, M. A. (2005). Balancing work and family: Equity, gender, and marital satisfaction. *Counseling and Therapy for Couples and Families, 13,* 162–166.

Sahathevan, R., Brodtmann, A., & Donnan, G. (2011). Dementia, stroke, and vascular risk factors: A review. *International Journal of Stroke, 7,* 61–73.

Sahlberg, P. (2010). Educational change in Finland. In A. Hargreaves, M. Fullan, A. Lieberman, & D. Hopkins (Eds.), *Second international handbook of educational change.* New York: Springer.

Saito, Y., Auestad, R. A., & Waerness, K. (2010). *Meeting the challenges of elder care: Japan and Norway.* Kyoto, Japan: Kyoto University Press.

Salari, S. (2011). Elder mistreatment. In R. A. Settersten, Jr., & J. L. Angel (Eds.), *Handbook of sociology of aging* (pp. 415–430). New York: Springer.

Sale, A., Berardi, N., & Maffei, L. (2009). Enrich the environment to empower the brain. *Trends in Neurosciences, 32,* 233–239.

Salerno, M., Micillo, M., Di Maio, S., Capalbo, D., Ferri, P., & Lettiero, T. (2001). Longitudinal growth, sexual maturation and final height in patients with congenital hypothyroidism detected by neonatal screening. *European Journal of Endocrinology, 145,* 377–383.

Salihu, H. M., Shumpert, M. N., Slay, M., Kirby, R. S., & Alexander, G. R. (2003). Childbearing beyond maternal age 50 and fetal outcomes in the United States. *Obstetrics and Gynecology, 102,* 1006–1014.

Salley, B. J., & Dixon, W. E., Jr. (2007). Temperamental and joint attentional predictors of language development. *Merrill-Palmer Quarterly, 53,* 131–154.

Salmivalli, C., & Voeten, M. (2004). Connections between attitudes, group norms, and behaviour in bullying situations. *International Journal of Behavioral Development, 28,* 246–258.

Salomon, J. A., Wang, H., Freeman, M. K., Vos, T., Flaxman, A. D., Lopez, A. D., et al. (2012). Healthy life expectancy for 187 countries, 1990–2010: A systematic analysis for the Global Burden Disease Study 2010. *Lancet, 380,* 2144–2162.

Salter, D., McMillan, D., Richards, M., Talbot, T., Hodges, J., Bentovim, A., & Hastings, R. (2003). Development of sexually abusive behavior in sexually victimized males: A longitudinal study. *Lancet, 361,* 471–476.

Salthouse, T. A. (1996). Constraints on theories of cognitive aging. *Psychonomic Bulletin and Review, 3,* 287–299.

Salthouse, T. A. (2006). Aging of thought. In E. Bialystok & F. I. M. Craik (Eds.), *Lifespan cognition: Mechanisms of change* (pp. 274–284). New York: Oxford University Press.

Salthouse, T. A. (2011). Neuroanatomical substrates of age-related cognitive decline. *Psychological Bulletin, 137,* 753–784.

Salthouse, T. A., & Caja, S. J. (2000). Structural constraints on process explanations in cognitive aging. *Psychology and Aging, 15,* 44–55.

Salvioli, S., Capri, M., Santoro, A., Raule, N., Sevini, F., & Lukas, S. (2008). The impact ofd mitochondrial DNA on human lifespan: A view from studies on centenarians. *Biotechnology Journal, 3,* 740–749.

Samarel, N. (1995). The dying process. In H. Wass & R. A. Neimeyer (Eds.), *Dying: Facing the facts* (3rd ed., pp. 89–116). Washington, DC: Taylor & Francis.

Samek, D. R., & Rueter, M. A. (2011). Considerations of elder sibling closeness in predicting younger sibling substance use: Social learning versus social bonding explanations. *Journal of Family Psychology, 25,* 931–941.

Sameroff, A. (2006). Identifying risk and protective factors for healthy child development. In A. Clarke-Stewart & J. Dunn (Eds.), *Families count: Effects on child and adolescent development* (pp. 53–76). New York: Cambridge University Press.

Sampselle, C. M., Harris, V., Harlow, S. D., & Sowers, M. (2002). Midlife development and menopause in African-American and Caucasian women. *Health Care for Women International, 23,* 351–363.

Sanchez, M. M., & Pollak, S. D. (2009). Socioemotional development following early abuse and neglect: Challenges and insight from translational research. In M. de Haan & M. R. Gunnar (Eds.), *Handbook of developmental social neuroscience* (pp. 497–520). New York: Guilford.

Sanders, O. (2006). *Evaluating the Keeping Ourselves Safe Programme.* Wellington, NZ: Youth Education Service, New Zealand Police. Retrieved from www.nzfvc.org.nz/accan/papers-presentations /abstract11v.shtml

Sanderson, J. A., & Siegal, M. (1988). Conceptions of moral and social rules in rejected and nonrejected preschoolers. *Journal of Clinical Child Psychology, 17,* 66–72.

Sangrigoli, S., Pallier, C., Argenti, A. M., Ventureyra, V. A. G., & de Schonen, S. (2005). Reversibility of the other-race effect in face recognition during childhood. *Psychological Science, 16,* 440–444.

San Juan, V., & Astington, J. W. (2012). Bridging the gap between implicit and explicit understanding: How language development promotes the processing and representation of false belief. *British Journal of Developmental Psychology, 30,* 105–122.

Sann, C., & Streri, A. (2007). Perception of object shape and texture in human newborns: Evidence from cross-modal transfer tasks. *Developmental Science, 10,* 399–410.

Sann, C., & Streri, A. (2008). The limits of newborn's grasping to detect texture in a cross-modal transfer task. *Infant Behavior and Development, 31,* 523–531.

Sansavini, A., Bertoncini, J., & Giovanelli, G. (1997). Newborns discriminate the rhythm of multisyllabic stressed words. *Developmental Psychology, 33,* 3–11.

Santtila, P., Wager, I., Witting, K., Harlaar, N., Jern, P., Johansson, A., Varjonen, M., & Sandnabba, K. (2008). Discrepancies between sexual desire and sexual activity: Gender differences and associations with relationship satisfaction. *Journal of Sex and Marital Therapy, 34,* 31–44.

Sanz, A., Pamplona, R., & Barja, G. (2006). Is the mitochondrial free radical theory of aging intact? *Antioxidants and Redox Signaling, 8,* 582–599.

Sarnecka, B. W., & Gelman, S. A. (2004). Six does not just mean a lot: Preschoolers see number words as specific. *Cognition, 92,* 329–352.

Satin, J. R., Linden, W., Phillips, M. J. (2009). Depression as a predictor of disease progression and mortality in cancer patients. *Cancer, 115,* 5349–5361.

Sato, T., Matsumoto, T., Kawano, H., Watanabe, T., Uematsu, Y., & Semine, K. (2004). Brain masculinization requires androgen receptor function. *Proceedings of the National Academy of Sciences, 101,* 1673–1678.

Saucier, J. F., Sylvestre, R., Doucet, H., Lambert, J., Frappier, J. Y., Charbonneau, L., & Malus, M. (2002). Cultural identity and adaptation to adolescence in Montreal. In F. J. C. Azima & N. Grizenko (Eds.), *Immigrant and refugee children and their families: Clinical, research, and training issues* (pp. 133–154). Madison, WI: International Universities Press.

Saudino, K. J. (2003). Parent ratings of infant temperament: Lessons from twin studies. *Infant Behavior and Development, 26,* 100–107.

Saunders, B. E. (2012). Determining best practice for treating sexually victimized children. In P. Goodyear-Brown (Ed.), *Handbook of child sexual abuse: Identification, assessment, and treatment* (pp. 173–198). Hoboken, NJ: Wiley.

Sautter, J. M., Thomas, P. A., Dupre, M., & George, L. K. (2012). Socioeconomic status and the black–white mortality crossover. *American Journal of Public Health, 102,* 1566–1571.

Savin-Williams, R. C. (2001). A critique of research on sexual minority youths. *Journal of Adolescence, 24,* 5–13.

Savin-Williams, R. C., & Diamond, L. M. (2004). Sex. In R. M. Lerner & L. Steinberg (Eds.), *Handbook of adolescent development* (2nd ed., pp. 189–231). Hoboken, NJ: Wiley.

Savin-Williams, R. C., & Ream, G. L. (2003). Sex variations in the disclosure to parents of same-sex attractions. *Journal of Family Psychology, 17,* 429–438.

Sawyer, A. M., & Borduin, C. M. (2011). Effects of multisystemic therapy through midlife: A 21.9-year follow-up to a randomized clinical trial with serious and violent juvenile offenders. *Journal of Consulting and Clinical Psychology, 79,* 643–652.

Sayer, L. C. (2010). Trends in housework. In J. Treas & S. Drobnic (Eds.), *Dividing the domestic: Men, women, and household work in cross-national perspective* (pp. 19–38). Stanford, CA: Stanford University Press.

Saygin, A. P., Leech, R., & Dick, F. (2010). Nonverbal auditory agnosia with lesion to Wernicke's area. *Neuropsychologia, 48,* 107–113.

Saylor, M. M. (2004). Twelve- and 16-month-old infants recognize properties of mentioned absent things. *Developmental Science, 7,* 599–611.

Saylor, M. M., Baldwin, D. A., & Sabbagh, M. A. (2005). Word learning: A complex product. In G. Hall & S. Waxman (Eds.), *Weaving a lexicon.* Cambridge, MA: MIT Press.

Saylor, M. M., & Troseth, G. L. (2006). Preschoolers use information about speakers' desires to learn new words. *Cognitive Development, 21,* 214–231.

Scarlett, W. G., & Warren, A. E. A. (2010). Religious and spiritual development across the life span: A behavioral and social science perspective. In M. Lamb & A. Freund (Eds.), *Handbook of lifespan development: Vol. 2. Social and emotional development* (pp. 631–682). Hoboken, NJ: Wiley.

Scarmeas, N., Luchsinger, J. A., Mayeux, R., & Stern, Y. (2007). Mediterranean diet and Alzheimer disease mortality. *Neurology, 69,* 1084–1093.

Scarr, S., & McCartney, K. (1983). How people make their own environments: A theory of genotype environment effects. *Child Development, 54,* 424–435.

Scarr, S., & Weinberg, R. A. (1983). The Minnesota Adoption Studies: Genetic differences and malleability. *Child Development, 54,* 260–267.

Schaal, B., Marlier, L., & Soussignan, R. (2000). Human fetuses learn odours from their pregnant mother's diet. *Chemical Senses, 25,* 729–737.

Schacht, P. M., Cummings, E. M., & Davies, P. T. (2009). Fathering in family context and child adjustment: A longitudinal analysis. *Journal of Family Psychology, 23,* 790–797.

Schäfer, S., Huxhold, O., & Lindenberger, U. (2006). Healthy mind in healthy body? A review of sensorimotor–cognitive interdependencies in old age. *European Review of Aging and Physical Activity, 3,* 45–54.

Schaie, K. W. (1994). The course of adult intellectual development. *American Psychologist, 49,* 304–313.

Schaie, K. W. (1996). *Intellectual development in adulthood: The Seattle Longitudinal Study.* New York: Cambridge University Press.

Schaie, K. W. (1998). The Seattle Longitudinal Studies of Adult Intelligence. In M. P. Lawton & T. A. Salthouse (Eds.), *Essential papers on the psychology of aging* (pp. 263–271). New York: New York University Press.

Schaie, K. W. (2005). *Developmental influences on adult intelligence: The Seattle Longitudinal Study.* New York: Oxford University Press.

Schaie, K. W. (2011). Historical influences on aging and behavior. In K. W. Schaie & S. L. Willis (Eds.), *Handbook of the psychology of aging* (7th ed., pp. 41–55). San Diego, CA: Academic Press.

Schalet, A. (2007). Adolescent sexuality viewed through two different cultural lenses. In M. S. Tepper & A. F. Owens (Eds.), *Sexual health: Vol. 3. Moral and cultural foundations* (pp. 365–387). Westport, CT: Praeger.

Scheibe, S., Freund, A. M., & Baltes, P. B. (2007). Toward a developmental psychology of Sehnsucht (life longings): The optimal (utopian) life. *Developmental Psychology, 43,* 778–795.

Schewe, P. A. (2007). Interventions to prevent sexual violence. In L. S. Doll, S. E. Bonzo, D. A. Sleet, & J. A. Mercy (Eds.), *Handbook of injury and violence prevention* (pp. 223–240). New York: Springer Science + Business Media.

Schiamberg, L. B., Barboza, G. G., Oehmke, J., Zhang, Z., Griffore, R. J., Weatherhill, R. P., et al. (2011). Elder abuse in nursing homes: An ecological perspective. *Journal of Elder Abuse and Neglect, 23,* 190–211.

Schieman, S., & Plickert, G. (2007). Functional limitations and changes in levels of depression among older adults: A multiple-hierarchy stratification perspective. *Journal of Gerontology, 62B,* S36–S42.

Schindler, H. S. (2010). The importance of parenting and financial contributions in promoting fathers' psychological health. *Journal of Marriage and Family, 72,* 318–332.

Schlaggar, B. L., & McCandliss, B. D. (2007). Development of neural systems for reading. *Annual Review of Neuroscience, 30,* 475–503.

Schlegel, A., & Barry, H., III. (1991). *Adolescence: An anthropological inquiry.* New York: Free Press.

Schlossberg, N. (2004). *Retire smart, retire happy: Finding your true path in life.* Washington, DC: American Psychological Association.

Schmidt, K.-H., Neubach, B., & Heuer, H. (2007). Self-control demands, cognitive control deficits, and burnout. *Work and Stress, 21,* 142–154.

Schmidt, L. A., Fox, N. A., Rubin, K. H., Sternberg, E. M., Gold, P. W., & Smith, C. C. (1997). Behavioral and neuroendocrine responses in shy children. *Developmental Psychobiology, 35,* 119–135.

Schmidt, L. A., Fox, N. A., Schulkin, J., & Gold, P. W. (1999). Behavioral and psychophysiological correlates of self-presentation in temperamentally shy children. *Developmental Psychobiology, 30,* 127–140.

Schmidt, L. A., Santesso, D. L., Schulkin, J., & Segalowitz, S. J. (2007). Shyness is a necessary but not sufficient condition for high salivary cortisol in typically developing 10-year-old children. *Personality and Individual Differences, 43,* 1541–1551.

Schmitt, D. P., Allik, J., McCrae, R. R., & Benet-Martínez, V. (2007). The geographic distribution of the Big Five personality traits: Patterns and profiles of human self-description across 56 countries. *Journal of Cross-Cultural Psychology, 38,* 173–212.

Schmitz, S., Fulker, D. W., Plomin, R., Zahn-Waxler, C., Emde, R. N., & DeFries, J. C. (1999). Temperament and problem behaviour during early childhood. *International Journal of Behavioural Development, 23,* 333–355.

Schneewind, K. A., & Gerhard, A. (2002). Relationship personality, conflict resolution, and marital satisfaction in the first 5 years of marriage. *Family Relations, 51,* 63–71.

Schneider, B. H., Atkinson, L., & Tardif, C. (2001). Child–parent attachment and children's peer relations: A quantitative review. *Developmental Psychology, 37,* 87–100.

Schneider, W. (2002). Memory development in childhood. In U. Goswami (Ed.), *Blackwell handbook of childhood cognitive development* (pp. 236–256). Malden, MA: Blackwell.

Schneider, W., & Bjorklund, D. F. (1992). Expertise, aptitude, and strategic remembering. *Child Development, 63,* 461–473.

Schneider, W., & Bjorklund, D. F. (1998). Memory. In D. Kuhn & R. S. Siegler (Eds.), *Handbook of child psychology: Vol. 2. Cognition, perception, and language* (5th ed., pp. 467–521). New York: Wiley.

Schneider, W., & Pressley, M. (1997). *Memory development between two and twenty* (2nd ed.). Mahwah, NJ: Erlbaum.

Schneiders, J., Nicolson, N. A., Berkhof, J., Feron, F. J., van Os, J., & deVries, M. W. (2006). Mood reactivity to daily negative events in early adolescence: Relationship to risk for psychopathology. *Developmental Psychology, 42,* 543–554.

Schneller, D. P., & Arditti, J.A. (2004). After the breakup: Interpreting divorce and rethinking intimacy. *Journal of Divorce and Remarriage, 42,* 1–37.

Schnohr, P., Nyboe, J., Lange, P., & Jensen, G. (1998). Longevity and gray hair, baldness, facial wrinkles, and arcus senilis in 13,000 men and women: The Copenhagen City Heart Study. *Journal of Gerontology, 53,* M347–350.

Scholl, B. J., & Leslie, A. M. (2000). Minds, modules, and meta-analysis. *Child Development, 72,* 696–701.

Scholnick, E. K. (1995, Fall). Knowing and constructing plans. *SRCD Newsletter,* pp. 1–2, 17.

Schonberg, R. L., & Tifft, C. J. (2007). Birth defects and prenatal diagnosis. In M. L. Batshaw, L. Pellegrino, & N. J. Roizen (Eds.), *Children with disabilities* (6th ed., pp. 83–96). Baltimore: Paul H. Brookes.

Schooler, C., Mulatu, M. S., & Oates, G. (1999). The continuing effects of substantively complex work on the intellectual functioning of older workers. *Psychology and Aging, 14,* 483–506.

Schoon, L., & Parsons, S. (2002). Teenage aspirations for future careers and occupational outcomes. *Journal of Vocational Behavior, 60,* 262–288.

Schoppe-Sullivan, S. J., Brown, G. L., Cannon, E. A., Mangelsdorf, S. C., & Sokolowski, M. S. (2008). Maternal gatekeeping, coparenting quality, and

fathering behavior in families with infants. *Journal of Family Psychology, 22,* 389–398.

Schoppe-Sullivan, S. J., Mangelsdorf, S. C., Frosch, C. A., & McHale, J. (2004). Associations between coparenting and marital behavior from infancy to the preschool years. *Journal of Family Psychology, 18,* 194–207.

Schott, J. M., & Rossor, M. N. (2003). The grasp and other primitive reflexes. *Journal of Neurological and Neurosurgical Psychiatry, 74,* 558–560.

Schroeder, R. D., Bulanda, R. E., Giordano, P. C., & Cernkovich, S. A. (2010). Parenting and adult criminality: An examination of direct and indirect effects by race. *Journal of Adolescent Research, 25,* 64–98.

Schroots, J. J. F., van Dijkum, C., & Assink, M. H. J. (2004). Autobiographical memory from a life span perspective. *International Journal of Aging and Human Development, 58,* 69–85.

Schuckit, M. A. (2009). Alcohol-use disorders. *Lancet, 373,* 492–501.

Schuetze, P., & Eiden, R. D. (2006). The association between maternal cocaine use during pregnancy and physiological regulation in 4- to 8-week-old infants: An examination of possible mediators and moderators. *Journal of Pediatric Psychology, 31,* 15–26.

Schull, W. J. (2003). The children of atomic bomb survivors: A synopsis. *Journal of Radiological Protection, 23,* 369–394.

Schulte-Ruther, M., Markowitsch, H. J., Fink, G. R., & Piefke, M. (2007). Mirror neuron and theory of mind mechanisms involved in face-to-face interactions: A functional magnetic resonance imaging approach to empathy. *Journal of Cognitive Neuroscience, 19,* 1354–1372.

Schultz, R., Burgio, L., Burns, R., Eisdorfer, C., Gallagher-Thompson, D., Gitlin, L. N., & Mahoney, D. F. (2003). Resources for enhancing Alzheimer's caregiver health (REACH): Overview, site-specific outcomes, and future directions. *Gerontologist, 43,* 514–520.

Schulz, R., & Curnow, C. (1988). Peak performance and age among superathletes: Track and field, swimming, baseball, tennis, and golf. *Journal of Gerontology, 43,* P113–P120.

Schumann, C. M., & Amaral, D. G. (2010). The human amygdala in autism. In P. J. Whalen & E. A. Phelps (Eds.), *The human amygdala* (pp. 362–381). New York: Guilford.

Schumann, C. M., Barnes, C. C., Lord, C., & Courchesne, E. (2009). Amygdala enlargement in toddlers and autism related to severity of social and communication impairments. *Biological Psychiatry, 66,* 942–949.

Schwanenflugel, P. J., Henderson, R. L., & Fabricius, W. V. (1998). Developing organization of mental verbs and theory of mind in middle childhood: Evidence from extensions. *Developmental Psychology, 34,* 512–524.

Schwartz, B. L., & Frazier, L. D. (2005). Tip-of-the-tongue states and aging: Contrasting psycholinguistic and metacognitive perspectives. *Journal of General Psychology, 132,* 377–391.

Schwartz, J. P., & Waldo, M. (2004). Group work with men who have committed partner abuse. In J. L. DeLucia-Waack, D. A. Gerrity, C. R. Kalodner, & M. T. Riva (Eds.), *Handbook of group counseling and psychotherapy* (pp. 576–592). Thousand Oaks, CA: Sage.

Schwartz, S. J., Beyers, W., Luyckx, K., Soenens, B. Zamboanga, B. L., Forthun, L. F., et al. (2011). Examining the light and dark sides of emerging adults' identity: A study of identity status differences in positive and negative psychosocial functioning. *Journal of Youth and Adolescence, 40,* 839–859.

Schwartz, S. J., Côté, J. E., & Arnett, J. J. (2005). Identity and agency in emerging adulthood: Two

developmental routes in the individualization process. *Youth and Society, 37,* 201–229.

Schwartz, S. J., Pantin, H., Prado, G., Sullivan, S., & Szapocznik, J. (2005). Family functioning, identity, and problem behavior: Immigrant early adolescents. *Journal of Early Adolescence, 25,* 392–420.

Schwebel, D. C., & Brezausek, C. M. (2007). Father transitions in the household and young children's injury risk. *Psychology of Men and Masculinity, 8,* 173–184.

Schweiger, W. K., & O'Brien, M. (2005). Special needs adoption: An ecological systems approach. *Family Relations, 54,* 512–522.

Schweinhart, L. J. (2010). The challenge of the High/Scope Perry Preschool study. In A. J. Reynolds, A. J. Rolnick, M. M. Englund, & J. Temple (Eds.), *Childhood programs and practices in the first decade of life: A human capital integration* (pp. 199–213). New York: Cambridge University Press.

Schweinhart, L. J., Montie, J., Xiang, Z., Barnett, W. S., Belfield, C. R., & Nores, M. (2005). *Lifetime effects: The High/Scope Perry Preschool Study through age 40.* Ypsilanti, MI: High/Scope Press.

Schweizer, K., Moosbrugger, H., & Goldhammer, F. (2006). The structure of the relationship between attention and intelligence. *Intelligence, 33,* 589–611.

Schwenck, C., Bjorklund, D. F., & Schneider, W. (2007). Factors influencing the incidence of utilization deficiencies and other patterns of recall/strategy-use relations in a strategic memory task. *Child Development, 22,* 197–212.

Schwier, C., van Maanen, C., Carpenter, M., & Tomasello, M. (2006). Rational imitation in 12-month-old infants. *Infancy, 10,* 303–311.

Scott, L. D. (2003). The relation of racial identity and racial socialization to coping with discrimination among African Americans. *Journal of Black Studies, 20,* 520–538.

Scott, L. S., & Monesson, A. (2009). The origin of biases in face perception. *Psychological Science, 20,* 676–680.

Scullin, M. K., Bugg, J. M., McDaniel, M. A., & Einstein, G. O. (2011). Prospective memory and aging: Preserved spontaneous retrieval, but impaired deactivation, in older adults. *Memory and Cognition, 39,* 1232–1240.

Seale, C. (2009). Legalisation of euthanasia or physician-assisted suicide: Survey of doctors' attitudes. *Palliative Medicine, 23,* 205–212.

Seaton, E. K., Scottham, K. M., & Sellers, R. M. (2006). The status model of racial identity development in African American adolescents: Evidence of structure, trajectories, and well-being. *Child Development, 77,* 1416–1426.

Seeman, E. (2008). Structural basis of growth-related gain and age-related loss of bone strength. *Rheumatology, 47,* iv2–iv8.

Seeman, T. E., Huang, M.-H., Bretsky, P., Crimmins, E., Launer, L., & Guralnik, J. M. (2005). Education and APOE-e4 in longitudinal cognitive decline: MacArthur Studies of Successful Aging. *Journal of Gerontology, 60B,* P74–P83.

Seiberling, K. A., & Conley, D. B. (2004). Aging and olfactory and taste function. *Otolaryngologic Clinics of North America, 37,* 1209–1228.

Seibert, A. C., & Kerns, K. A. (2009). Attachment figures in middle childhood. *International Journal of Behavioral Development, 33,* 347–355.

Seidman, E., Aber, J. L., & French, S. E. (2004). Assessing the transitions to middle and high school. *Journal of Adolescent Research, 19,* 3–30.

Seidman, E., Lambert, L. E., Allen, L., & Aber, J. L. (2003). Urban adolescents' transition to junior high school and protective family transactions. *Journal of Early Adolescence, 23,* 166–193.

Seitz, V., & Apfel, N. H. (2005). Creating effective school-based interventions for pregnant teenagers. In R. DeV. Peters, B. Leadbeater, & R. J. McMahon

(Eds.), *Resilience in children, families, and communities: Linking context to practice and policy* (pp. 65–82). New York: Kluwer Academic.

Sekita, A., Ninomiya, T., Tanizaki, Y., Doi, Y., Hata, J., Yonemoto, K., et al. (2010). Trends in prevalence of Alzheimer's disease and vascular dementia in a Japanese community: The Hisayama Study. *Acta Psychiatrica Scandivavica, 122,* 319–325.

Selfhout, M. H. W., Branje, S. J. T., & Meeus, W. H. J. (2008). The development of delinquency and perceived friendship quality in adolescent best friendship dyads. *Journal of Abnormal Child Psychology, 36,* 471–485.

Selwood, A., & Cooper, C. (2009). Abuse of people with dementia. *Reviews in Clinical Gerontology, 19,* 35–43.

Selwood, A., Johnston, K., Katona, C., Lyketsos, C., & Livingston, G. (2007). Systematic review of the effect of psychological interventions on family caregivers of people with dementia. *Journal of Affective Disorders, 101,* 75–89.

Selwyn, P. A. (1996). Before their time: A clinician's reflections on death and AIDS. In H. M. Spiro, M. G. M. Curnen, & L. P. Wandel (Eds.), *Facing death: Where culture, religion, and medicine meet* (pp. 33–37). New Haven, CT: Yale University Press.

Semanik, P. A., Chang, R. W., & Dunlop, D. D. (2012). Aerobic activity in prevention and symptom control of osteoarthritis. *PM&R, 4,* S37–S44.

Senju, A., Csibra, G., & Johnson, M. H. (2008). Understanding the referential nature of looking: Infants' preference for object-directed gaze. *Cognition, 108,* 303–319.

Senju, A., Southgate, V., Snape, C., Leonard, M., & Csibra, G. (2011). Do 18-month-olds really attribute mental states to others? A critical test. *Psychological Science, 22,* 878–880.

Serafini, T. E., & Adams, G. R. (2002). Functions of identity: Scale construction and validation. *Identity: An International Journal of Theory and Research, 2,* 361–389.

Serbin, L. A., Powlishta, K. K., & Gulko, J. (1993). The development of sex typing in middle childhood. *Monographs of the Society for Research in Child Development, 58*(2, Serial No. 232).

Sergeant, J. F., Ekerdt, D. J., & Chapin, R. (2008). Measurement of late-life residential relocation: Why are rates for such a manifest event so varied? *Journal of Gerontology, 63B,* S92–S98.

Serra, L., Perri, R., Cercignani, M., Spano, B., Fadda, L., Marra, C. et al. (2010). Are behavioral symptoms of Alzheimer's disease directly associated with neurodegeneration? *Journal of Alzheimer's Disease, 21,* 627–639.

Service Canada. (2009). *Guide to Canada Pension Plan disability benefits.* Retrieved from www .servicecanada.gc.ca/eng/isp/pub/cpp/disability/guide/sectionb.shtml

Sesame Workshop. (2009). *Sesame Workshop Annual Report 2009.* Retrieved from www.sesameworkshop .org/assets/290/src/Annual%20Report%202009.pdf

Settersten, R. A. (2003). Age structuring and the rhythm of the life course. In J. T. Mortimer & M. J. Shanahan (Eds.), *Handbook of the life course* (pp. 81–98). New York: Kluwer Academic.

Settersten, R. A. (2007). The new landscape of adult life: Road maps, signposts, and speed lines. *Research in Human Development, 4,* 239–252.

Settles, I. H., Cortina, L. M., Malley, J., & Stewart, A. J. (2006). The climate for women in academic science: The good, the bad, and the changeable. *Psychology of Women Quarterly, 30,* 47–58.

Sevigny, P. R., & Loutzenhiser, L. (2010). Predictors of parenting self-efficacy in mothers and fathers of toddlers. Child Care, *Health and Development, 36,* 179–189.

Seymour, S. C. (1999). *Women, family, and child care in India.* Cambridge, UK: Cambridge University Press.

Shaeer, O., & Shaeer, K. (2012). The Global Online Sexual Survey (GOSS): The United States of America in 2011. Chapter I: Erectile dysfunction among English-speakers. *Journal of Sexual Medicine, 9,* 3018–3027.

Shah, T., Sullivan, K., & Carter, J. (2006). Sudden infant death syndrome and reported maternal smoking during pregnancy. *American Journal of Public Health, 96,* 1757–1759.

Shalev, I. (2012). Early life stress and telomere length: Investigating the connection and possible mechanisms. *BioEssays, 34,* 943–952.

Shanahan, L., McHale, S. M., Crouter, A. C., & Osgood, D. W. (2007). Warmth with mothers and fathers from middle childhood to late adolescence: Within- and between-families comparisions. *Developmental Psychology, 43,* 551–563.

Shapka, J. D., & Keating, D. P. (2005). Structure and change in self-concept during adolescence. *Canadian Journal of Behavioural Science, 37,* 83–96.

Sharp, E. A., & Ganong, L. (2011). "I'm a loser, I'm not married, let's just all look at me": Ever-single women's perceptions of their social environment. *Journal of Family Issues, 32,* 956–980.

Shatz, M. (2007). On the development of the field. In E. Hoff & M. Shatz (Eds.), *Blackwell handbook of language development* (pp. 1–20). Malden, MA: Blackwell.

Shaver, P., Furman, W., & Buhrmester, D. (1985). Transition to college: Network changes, social skills, and loneliness. In S. Duck & D. Perlman (Eds.), *Understanding personal relationships: An interdisciplinary approach* (pp. 193–219). London: Sage.

Shaw, B. A. (2005). Anticipated support from neighbors and physical functioning during later life. *Research on Aging, 27,* 503–525.

Shaw, D. S., Gilliom, M., Ingoldsby, E. M., & Nagin, D. S. (2003). Trajectories leading to school-age conduct problems. *Developmental Psychology, 39,* 189–200.

Shaw, P., Eckstrand, K., Sharp, W., Blumenthal, J., Lerch, J. P., & Greenstein, D. (2007, November 16). Attention-deficit/hyperactivity disorder is characterized by a delay in cortical maturation. *Proceedings of the National Academy of Sciences Online.* Retrieved from www.pnas.org/cgi/content/abstract/0707741104v1

Shay, J. W., & Wright, W. E. (2011). Role of telomeres and telomerase in cancer. *Seminars in Cancer Biology, 21,* 349–353.

Shea, J. L. (2006). Cross-cultural comparison of women's midlife symptom-reporting: A China study. *Culture, Medicine, and Psychiatry, 30,* 331–362.

Shedler, J., & Block, J. (1990). Adolescent drug use and psychological health: A longitudinal inquiry. *American Psychologist, 45,* 612–630.

Sherman, A. M., de Vries, B., & Lansford, J. E. (2000). Friendship in childhood and adulthood: Lessons across the life span. *International Journal of Aging and Human Development, 51,* 31–51.

Sherman, A. M., Lansford, J. E., & Volling, B. L. (2006). Sibling relationships and best friendships in young adulthood: Warmth, conflict, and well-being. *Personal Relationships, 13,* 151–165.

Sherman, C. W., Rosenblatt, D. E., & Antonucci, T. C. (2008). Elder abuse and mistreatment: A life span and cultural context. *Indian Journal of Gerontology, 22.*

Sherman, S. L., Freeman, S. B., Allen, E. G., & Lamb, N. E. (2005). Risk factors for nondisjunction of trisomy 21. *Cytogenetic Genome Research, 111,* 273–280.

Sherrod, L. R., & Spiewak, G. S. (2008). Possible interrelationships between civic engagement, positive youth development, and spirituality/religiosity. In R. M. Lerner, R. W. Roeser, & E. Phelps (Eds.), *Positive youth development and spirituality: From theory to research* (pp. 322–338). West Conshohocken, PA: Templeton Foundation Press.

Sherry, B., McDivitt, J., Brich, L. L., Cook, F. H., Sanders, S., Prish, J. L., et al. (2004). Attitudes, practices, and concerns about child feeding and child weight status among socioeconomically diverse white, Hispanic, and African-American mothers. *Journal of the American Dietetic Association, 104,* 215–221.

Shield, R. R., Wetle, T., Teno, J., Miller, S. C., & Welch, L. C. (2010). Vigilant at the end of life: Family advocacy in the nursing home. *Journal of Palliative Medicine, 13,* 573–579.

Shields, G., King, W., Fulks, S., & Fallon, L. F. (2002). Determinants of perceived safety among the elderly: An exploratory study. *Journal of Gerontological Social Work, 38,* 73–83.

Shierholz, H., Sabadish, N., & Wething, H. (2012, May 3). *The class of 2012: Labor market for young graduates remains grim.* EPI Briefing Paper #340. Washington, DC: Economic Policy Institute.

Shifren, J. L., Monz, B. U., Russo, P. A., Segreti, A., & Johannes, C. B. (2008). Sexual problems and distress in United States women. *Obstetrics and Gynecology, 112,* 970–978.

Shimizu, H. (2001). Japanese adolescent boys' senses of empathy (omoiyari) and Carol Gilligan's perspectives on the morality of care: A phenomenological approach. *Culture and Psychology, 7,* 453–475.

Shin, J. S., Hong, A., Solomon, M. J., & Lee, C. S. (2006). The role of telomeres and telomerase in the pathology of human cancer and aging. *Pathology, 38,* 103–113.

Shonkoff, J. P., & Bales, S. N. (2011). Science does not speak for itself: Translating child development research for the public and its policymakers. *Child Development, 82,* 17–32.

Shonkoff, J. P., & Phillips, D. (Eds.). (2001). *Neurons to neighborhoods: The science of early childhood development.* Washington, DC: National Academy Press.

Shor, E., Roelfs, D. J., Curreli, M., Clemow, L., Burg, M. M., & Schwartz, J. E. (2012). Widowhood and mortality: A meta-analysis and meta-regression. *Demography, 49,* 575–606.

Shuey, K., & Hardy, M. A. (2003). Assistance to aging parents and parents-in-law: Does lineage affect family allocation decisions? *Journal of Marriage and Family, 65,* 418–431.

Shultz, K. S., & Wang, M. (2007). The influence of specific physical health conditions on retirement decisions. *International Journal of Aging and Human Development, 65,* 149–161.

Shure, M. B., & Aberson, B. (2005). Enhancing the process of resilience through effective thinking. In S. Goldstein & R. B. Brooks (Eds.), *Handbook of resilience in children* (pp. 373–394). New York: Kluwer Academic.

Shuwairi, S. M., Albert, M. K., & Johnson, S. P. (2007). Discrimination of possible and impossible objects in infancy. *Psychological Science, 18,* 303–307.

Shwalb, D. W., Nakawaza, J., Yamamoto, T., & Hyun, J.-H. (2004). Fathering in Japanese, Chinese, and Korean cultures: A review of the research literature. In M. E. Lamb (Ed.), *The role of the father in child development* (4th ed., pp. 146–181). Hoboken, NJ: Wiley.

Shweder, R. A., Goodnow, J. J., Hatano, G., LeVine, R. A., Markus, H. R., & Miller, P. J. (2006). The cultural psychology of development: One mind, many mentalities. In R. M. Lerner (Ed.), *Handbook of child psychology: Vol. 1. Theoretical models of human development* (6th ed., pp. 716–792). Hoboken, NJ: Wiley.

Sibley, C. G., & Overall, N. C. (2010). Modeling the hierarchical structure of personality–attachment associations: Domain diffusion versus domain differentiation. *Journal of Social and Personal Relationships, 27,* 47–70.

Sidebotham, P., Heron, J., & the ALSPAC Study Team. (2003). Child maltreatment in the "children of the nineties": The role of the child. *Child Abuse and Neglect, 27,* 337–352.

Siebenbruner, J., Zimmer-Gembeck, M. J., & Egeland, B. (2007). Sexual partners and contraceptive use: A 16-year prospective study predicting abstinence and risk behavior. *Journal of Research on Adolescence, 17,* 179–206.

Siegal, M., Iozzi, L., & Surian, L. (2009). Bilingualism and conversational understanding in young children. *Cognition, 110,* 115–122.

Siega-Riz, A. M., Deming, D. M., Reidy, K. C., Fox, M. K., Condon, E., & Briefel, R. R. (2010). Food consumption patterns of infants and toddlers: Where are we now? *Journal of the American Dietetic Association, 110,* S38–S51.

Siegel, R., Naishadham, D., & Jemal, A. (2012). Cancer statistics, 2012. *CA: A Cancer Journal for Clinicians, 62,* 10–29.

Sieger, K., & Renk, K. (2007). Pregnant and parenting adolescents: A study of ethnic identity, emotional and behavioral functioning, child characteristics, and social support. *Journal of Youth and Adolescence, 36,* 567–581.

Siegler, R. S. (1996). *Emerging minds: The process of change in children's thinking.* New York: Oxford University Press.

Siegler, R. S. (2007). Cognitive variability. *Developmental Science, 10,* 104–109.

Siegler, R. S. (2009). Improving preschoolers' number sense using information-processing theory. In O. A. Barbarin & B. H. Wasik (Eds.), *Handbook of child development and early education* (pp. 429–454). New York: Guilford.

Siegler, R. S., & Mu, Y. (2008). Chinese children excel on novel mathematics problems even before elementary school. *Psychological Science, 19,* 759–763.

Siegler, R. S., & Svetina, M. (2006). What leads children to adopt new strategies? A microgenetic/cross-sectional study of class inclusion. *Child Development, 77,* 997–1015.

Siervogel, R. M., Maynard, L. M., Wisemandle, W. A., Roche, A. F., Guo, S. S., Chumlea, W. C., & Towne, B. (2000). Annual changes in total body fat and fat-free mass in children from 8 to 18 years in relation to changes in body mass index: The Fels Longitudinal Study. *Annals of the New York Academy of Sciences, 904,* 420–423.

Silk, J. S., Morris, A. S., Kanaya, T., & Steinberg, L. (2003). Psychological control and autonomy granting: Opposite ends of a continuum or distinct constructs? *Journal of Research on Adolescence, 13,* 113–128.

Silvén, M. (2001). Attention in very young infants predicts learning of first words. *Infant Behavior and Development, 24,* 229–237.

Silver, M. H., & Perls, T. T. (2000). Is dementia the price of a long life? An optimistic report from centenarians. *Journal of Geriatric Psychiatry, 33,* 71–79.

Silverman, P. R. (2004). Dying and bereavement in historical perspective. In J. Berzoff & P. R. Silverman (Eds.), *Living with dying: A handbook for end-of-life healthcare practitioners* (pp. 128–149). New York: Columbia University Press.

Silverman, P. R., & Nickman, S. L. (1996). Children's construction of their dead parents. In D. Klass, P. R. Silverman, & S. L. Nickman (Eds.), *Continuing bonds: New understandings of grief* (pp. 73–86). Washington, DC: Taylor & Francis.

Silverman, W. K., & Pina, A. A. (2008). Psychosocial treatments for phobic and anxiety disorders in youth. In R. G. Steele, T. D. Elkin, & M. Roberts (Eds.), *Handbook of evidence-based therapies for*

children and adolescents: Bridging science and practice* (pp. 65–82). New York: Springer.

Silverstein, M., Conroy, S., Wang, H., Giarrusso, R., & Bengtson, V. L. (2002). Reciprocity in parent–child relations over the adult life course. *Journal of Gerontology, 57B,* S3–S13.

Silverstein, M., & Giarrusso, R. (2010). Aging and family life: A decade review. *Journal of Marriage and Family, 72,* 1039–1058.

Silverstein, M., & Marenco, A. (2001). How Americans enact the grandparent role across the family life course. *Journal of Family Issues, 22,* 493–522.

Simcock, G., & DeLoache, J. (2006). Get the picture? The effects of iconicity on toddlers' reenactment from picture books. *Developmental Psychology, 42,* 1352–1357.

Simcock, G., & Hayne, H. (2002). Breaking the barrier? Children fail to translate their preverbal memories into language. *Psychological Science, 13,* 225–231.

Simcock, G., & Hayne, H. (2003). Age-related changes in verbal and nonverbal memory during early childhood. *Developmental Psychology, 39,* 805–814.

Simon, N. M., Smoller, J. W., McNamara, K. L., Maser, R. S., Zlata, A. K., & Pollack, M. H. (2006). Telomere shortening and mood disorders: Preliminary support for a chronic stress model of accelerated aging. *Biological Psychiatry, 60,* 432–435.

Simoneau, M., & Markovits, H. (2003). Reasoning with premises that are not empirically true: Evidence for the role of inhibition and retrieval. *Developmental Psychology, 39,* 964–975.

Simons, J. S., Dodson, C. S., Bell, D., & Schachter, D. L. (2004). Specific-and partial-source memory: Effects of aging. *Psychology and Aging, 19,* 689–694.

Simonton, D. K. (2000). Creativity: Cognitive, personal, developmental, and social aspects. *American Psychologist, 55,* 151–158.

Simonton, D. K. (2006). Historiometric methods. In K. A. Ericsson, N. Charness, P. J. Feltovich, & R. R. Hoffman (Eds.), *The Cambridge handbook of expertise and expert performance* (pp. 319–335). New York: Cambridge University Press.

Simonton, D. K. (2012). Creative productivity and aging. In S. K. Whitbourne & M. J. Sliwinski (Eds.), *Wiley-Blackwell handbook of adulthood and aging* (pp. 477–496). Malden, MA: Blackwell Publishing.

Simpson, E. A., Varga, A., Frick, J. E., & Fragaszy, D. (2011). Infants experience perceptual narrowing for nonprimate faces. *Infancy, 16,* 318–328.

Simpson, J. A., & Harris, B. A. (1994). Interpersonal attraction. In A. L. Weber & J. H. Harvey (Eds.), *Perspectives on close relationships* (pp. 45–66). Boston: Allyn and Bacon.

Simpson, J. A., Rholes, W. S., Campbell, L., Tran, S., & Wilson, C. L. (2003). Adult attachment, the transition to parenthood, and depressive symptoms. *Journal of Personality and Social Psychology, 84,* 1172–1187.

Simpson, R. (2004). Masculinity at work: The experiences of men in female dominated occupations. *Work, Employment and Society, 18,* 349–368.

Simpson, R. (2005). Men in non-traditional occupations: Career entry, career orientation and experience of role strain. *Gender, Work and Organization, 12,* 363–380.

Singer, D. G., & Singer, J. L. (2005). *Imagination and play in the electronic age.* Cambridge, MA: Harvard University Press.

Singer, Y., Bachner, Y. G., Shvartzman, P., & Carmel, S. (2005). Home death—the caregivers' experiences. *Journal of Pain and Symptom Management, 30,* 70–74.

Singleton, J. L., & Newport, E. L. (2004). When learners surpass their models: The acquisition of American Sign Language from inconsistent input. *Cognitive Psychology, 49,* 370–407.

Sinkkonen, J., Anttila, R., & Siimes, M. A. (1998). Pubertal maturation and changes in self-image in early adolescent Finnish boys. *Journal of Youth and Adolescence, 27,* 209–218.

Sirsch, U., Erher, E., Mayr, E., & Willinger, U. (2009). What does it take to be an adult in Austria? *Journal of Adolescent Research, 24,* 275–292.

Skully, R., & Saleh, A. S. (2011). Aging and the effects of vitamins and supplements. *Clinical Geriatric Medicine, 27,* 591–607.

Slack, K. S., & Yoo, J. (2005). Food hardship and child behavior problems among low-income children. *Social Service Review, 79,* 511–536.

Slater, A., Brown, E., Mattock, A., & Bornstein, M. H. (1996). Continuity and change in habituation in the first 4 months from birth. *Journal of Reproductive and Infant Psychology, 14,* 187–194.

Slater, A., Quinn, P. C., Kelly, D. J., Lee, K., Longmore, C. A., McDonald, P. R., & Pascalis, O. (2011). The shaping of the face space in early infancy: Becoming a native face processor. *Child Development Perspectives, 4,* 205–211.

Slater, A., Riddell, P., Quinn, P. C., Pascalis, O., Lee, K., & Kelly, D. J. (2010). Visual perception. In J. G. Bremner & T. D. Wachs (Eds.), *Wiley-Blackwell handbook of infant development: Vol. 1. Basic research* (2nd ed., pp. 40–80). Chichester, UK: Wiley-Blackwell.

Sloter, E., Schmid, T. E., Marchetti, F., Eskenazi, B., & Nath, J. (2006). Quantitative effects of male age on sperm motion. *Human Reproduction, 21,* 2868–2875.

Slutske, W. S., Hunt-Carter, E. E., Nabors-Oberg, R. E., Sher, K. J., Bucholz, K. K., & Madden, P. A. F. (2004). Do college students drink more than their non-college-attending peers? Evidence from a population-based longitudinal female twin study. *Journal of Abnormal Psychology, 113,* 530–540.

Smahel, D., Brown, B. B., & Blinka, L. (2012). Associations between online friendship and Internet addiction among adolescents and emerging adults. *Developmental Psychology, 48,* 381–388.

Small, B. J., Rawson, K. S., Eisel, S., & McEvoy, C. L. (2012). Memory and aging. In S. K. Whitbourne & M. J. Sliwinski (Eds.), *Wiley-Blackwell handbook of adulthood and aging* (pp. 174–189). Malden, MA: Wiley-Blackwell.

Smart, J., & Hiscock, H. (2007). Early infant crying and sleeping problems: A pilot study of impact on parental well-being and parent-endorsed strategies for management. *Journal of Paediatrics and Child Health, 43,* 284–290.

Smetana, J. G. (2002). Culture, autonomy, and personal jurisdiction in adolescent–parent relationships. In R. V. Kail & H. W. Reese (Eds.), *Advances in child development and behavior* (Vol. 29, pp. 51–87). San Diego, CA: Academic Press.

Smetana, J. G. (2006). Social-cognitive domain theory: Consistencies and variations in children's moral and social judgments. In M. Killen & J. G. Smetana (Eds.), *Handbook of moral development* (pp. 119–154). Mahwah, NJ: Erlbaum.

Smetana, J. G., Metzger, A., & Campione-Barr, N. (2004). African-American late adolescents' relationships with parents: Developmental transitions and longitudinal patterns. *Child Development, 75,* 932–947.

Smith, A. N., Brief, A. P., & Colella, A. (2010). Bias in organizations. In J. F. Dovidio, M. Hewstone, P. Glick, & V. M. Esses (Eds.), *Treatment of childhood disorders* (3rd ed., pp. 65–136). New York: Guilford.

Smith, B. H., Barkley, R. A., & Shapiro, C. J. (2006). Attention-deficit/hyperactivity disorder. In E. J. Mash & R. A. Barkley (Eds.), *Treatment of childhood disorders* (3rd ed., pp. 65–136). New York: Guilford.

Smith, C., Perou, R., & Lesesne, C. (2002). Parent education. M. H. Bornstein (Ed.), *Handbook of parenting* (Vol. 4, pp. 389–410). Mahwah, NJ: Erlbaum.

Smith, C., & Snell, P. (2009). *Souls in transition: The religious & spiritual lives of emerging adults.* New York: Oxford University Press.

Smith, C. D., Chebrolu, H., Wekstein, D. R., Schmitt, F. A., & Markesbery, W. R. (2007). Age and gender effects on human brain anatomy: A voxel-based morphometric study in healthy elderly. *Neurobiology of Aging, 28,* 1075–1087.

Smith, C. L., Calkins, S. D., Keane, S. P., Anastopoulos, A. D., & Shelton, T. L. (2004). Predicting stability and change in toddler behavior problems: Contributions of maternal behavior and child gender. *Developmental Psychology, 40,* 29–42.

Smith, C. M., & Cotter, V. T. (2008). Age-related changes in health. In E. Capezuti, D. Zwicker, M. Mezey, T. T. Fulmer, & D. Gray-Miceli (Eds.), *Evidence-based geriatric nursing protocols for best practice* (3rd ed., pp. 431–458). New York: Springer.

Smith, D. G., Xiao, L., & Bechara, A. (2012). Decision making in children and adolescents: Impaired Iowa gambling task performance in early adolescence. *Developmental Psychology, 48,* 1180–1187.

Smith, G. C., Rodriguez, J. M., & Palmieri, P. A. (2010). Patterns and predictors of support group use by custodial grandmothers and grandchildren. *Families in Society, 91,* 385–393.

Smith, J., & Freund, A. M. (2002). The dynamics of possible selves in old age. *Journal of Gerontology, 57B,* P492–P500.

Smith, J., & Infurna, F. J. (2011). Early precursors of later health. In K. L. Fingerman, C. A. Berg, J. Smith, & T. C. Antonucci (Eds.), *Handbook of life-span development* (pp. 213–238). New York: Springer.

Smith, J. C., Nielson, K. A., Woodard, J. L., Seidenberg, M., & Rao, S. M. (2013). Physical activity and brain function in older adults at increased risk for Alzheimer's disease. *Brain Science, 3,* 54–83.

Smith, L. B., Jones, S. S., Gershkoff-Stowe, L., & Samuelson, L. (2002). Object name learning provides on-the-job training for attention. *Psychological Science, 13,* 13–19.

Smith, N., Young, A., & Lee, C. (2004). Optimism, health-related hardiness and well-being among older Australian women. *Journal of Health Psychology, 9,* 741–752.

Smith, T. W. (2011a). *Cross-national differences in attitudes toward homosexuality.* Chicago: National Opinion Research Center/University of Chicago.

Smith, T. W. (2011b). *Public attitudes toward homosexuality.* Chicago: National Opinion Research Center/University of Chicago.

Smith, T. W., & Cundiff, J. M. (2011). An interpersonal perspective on risk for coronary heart disease. In L. Horowitz & S. Strack (Eds.), *Handbook of interpersonal psychology: Theory, research, assessment, and therapeutic interventions* (pp. 471–489). Hoboken, NJ: Wiley.

Smith, T. W., Glazer, K., Ruiz, J. M., & Gallo, L. C. (2004). Hostility, anger, aggressiveness, and coronary heart disease: An interpersonal perspective on personality, emotion, and health. *Journal of Personality, 72,* 1217–1270.

Smith, T. W., Uchino, B. N., Berg, C. A., & Florsheim, P. (2012). Marital discord and coronary artery disease: A comparison of behaviorally defined discrete groups. *Journal of Consulting and Clinical Psychology, 80,* 87–92.

Smyke, A. T., Zeanah, C. H., Fox, N. A., & Nelson, C. A. (2009). A new model of foster care for young children: The Bucharest Early Intervention Project. *Child and Adolescent Psychiatric Clinics of North America, 18,* 721–734.

Smyke, A. T., Zeanah, C. H., Fox, N. A., Nelson, C. A., & Guthrie, D. (2010). Placement in foster care enhances quality of attachment among young institutionalized children. *Child Development, 81,* 212–223.

Snarey, J., Son, L., Kuehne, V. S., Hauser, S., & Vaillant, G. (1987). The role of parenting in men's psychosocial development: A longitudinal study of early adulthood infertility and midlife generativity. *Developmental Psychology, 23,* 593–603.

Sneed, J. R., Whitbourne, S. K., & Culang, M. E. (2006). Trust, identity, and ego integrity: Modeling Erikson's core stages over 34 years. *Journal of Adult Development, 13,* 148–157.

Sneed, J. R., Whitbourne, S. K., Schwartz, S. J., & Huang, S. (2012). The relationship between identity, intimacy, and midlife well-being: Findings from the Rochester Adult Longitudinal Study. *Psychology and Aging, 27,* 318–323.

Snidman, N., Kagan, J., Riordan, L., & Shannon, D. C. (1995). Cardiac function and behavioral reactivity. *Psychophysiology, 32,* 199–207.

Snow, C. E., & Beals, D. E. (2006). Mealtime talk that supports literacy development. In R. W. Larson, A. R. Wiley, & K. R. Branscomb (Eds.), *Family mealtime as a context of development and socialization* (pp. 51–66). San Francisco: Jossey-Bass.

Snow, C. E., & Kang, J. Y. (2006). Becoming bilingual, biliterate, and bicultural. In K. A. Renninger & I. E. Sigel (Eds.), *Handbook of child psychology: Vol. 4. Child psychology in practice* (6th ed., pp. 75–102). Hoboken, NJ: Wiley.

Snyder, J., Brooker, M., Patrick, M. R., Snyder, A., Schrepferman, L., & Stoolmiller, M. (2003). Observed peer victimization during early elementary school: Continuity, growth, and relation to risk for child antisocial and depressive behavior. *Child Development, 74,* 1881–1898.

Snyder, J. S., & Cameron, H. A. (2012). Could adult hippocampal neurogenesis be relevant for human behavior? *Behavioural Brain Research, 227,* 384–390.

Soares, C. N. (2007). Menopausal transition and depression: Who is at risk and how to treat it? *Expert Review of Neurotherapeutics, 7,* 1285–1293.

Sobel, D. M. (2006). How fantasy benefits young children's understanding of pretense. *Developmental Science, 9,* 63–75.

Society for Research in Child Development. (2007). *SRCD ethical standards for research with children.* Retrieved from www.srcd.org/about-us/ethical-standards-research

Soderstrom, M., Dolbier, C., Leiferman, J., & Steinhardt, M. (2000). The relationship of hardiness, coping strategies, and perceived stress to symptoms of illness. *Journal of Behavioral Medicine, 23,* 311–328.

Soderstrom, M., Seidl, A., Nelson, D. G. K., & Jusczyk, P. W. (2003). The prosodic bootstrapping of phrases: Evidence from prelinguistic infants. *Journal of Memory and Language, 49,* 249–267.

Sofi, F., Cesari, F., Abbate, R., Gensini, G, F., & Casini, A. (2008). Adherence to Mediterranean diet and health status: Meta-analysis. *British Medical Journal, 337,* a1344.

Soli, A. R., McHale, S. M., & Feinberg, M. E. (2009). Risk and protective effects of sibling relationships among African American adolescents. *Family Relations, 58,* 578–592.

Solomon, J. C., & Marx, J. (1995). "To grandmother's house we go": Health and school adjustment of children raised solely by grandparents. *Gerontologist, 35,* 386–394.

Son, J., & Wilson, J. (2011). Generativity and volunteering. *Sociological Forum, 26,* 644–667.

Sondergaard, C., Henriksen, T. B., Obel, C., & Wisborg, K. (2002). Smoking during pregnancy and infantile colic. *Journal of the American Academy of Child and Adolescent Psychiatry, 41,* 147.

Sörensen, S., & Pinquart, M. (2005). Racial and ethnic differences in the relationship of caregiving stressors, resources, and sociodemographic variables to caregiver depression and perceived physical health. *Aging and Mental Health, 9,* 482–495.

Soska, K. C., Adolph, K. E., & Johnson, S. P. (2010). Systems in development: Motor skill acquisition facilitates three-dimensional object completion. *Developmental Psychology, 46,* 129–138.

Soto, C. J., John, O. P., Gosling, S. D., & Potter, J. (2011). Age differences in personality traits from 10 to 65: Big five domains and facets in a large cross-sectional sample. *Journal of Personality and Social Psychology, 100,* 330–348.

South African Department of Health. (2009). *2008 National Antenatal Sentinel HIV and Syphilis Prevalence Survey.* Retrieved from www.info.gov.za/view/DownloadFileAction?id=109007

Sowell, E. R., Thompson, P. M., Welcome, S. E., Henkenius, A. L., Toga, A. W., & Peterson, B. S. (2003). Cortical abnormalities in children and adolescents with attention-deficit hyperactivity disorder. *Lancet, 362,* 1699–1707.

Sowell, E. R., Trauner, D. A., Gamst, A., & Jernigan, T. (2002). Development of cortical and subcortical brain structures in childhood and adolescence: A structural MRI study. *Developmental Medicine and Child Neurology, 44,* 4–16.

Sowers, M. F., Zheng, H., Tomey, K., Karvonen-Gutierrez, M. J., Li, X., Matheos, Y., & Symons, J. (2007). Changes in body composition in women over six years at midlife: Ovarian and chronological aging. *Journal of Clinical Endocrinology and Metabolism, 92,* 895–901.

Speakman, J. R., & Selman, C. (2011). The free-radical damage theory: Accumulating evidence against a simple link of oxidative stress to ageing and lifespan. *Bioessays, 33,* 255–259.

Speece, D. L., Ritchey, K. D., Cooper, D. H., Roth, F. P., & Schatschneider, C. (2004). Growth in early reading skills from kindergarten to third grade. *Contemporary Educational Psychology, 29,* 312–332.

Spelke, E. S. (2000). Core knowledge. *American Psychologist, 55,* 1233–1242.

Spelke, E. S. (2004). Core knowledge. In N. Kanwisher & J. Duncan (Eds.), *Attention and performance* (Vol. 20, pp. 29–56). Oxford, UK: Oxford University Press.

Spelke, E. S., & Kinzler, K. D. (2007). Core knowledge. *Developmental Science, 10,* 89–96.

Spence, M. J., & DeCasper, A. J. (1987). Prenatal experience with low-frequency maternal voice sounds influences neonatal perception of maternal voice samples. *Infant Behavior and Development, 10,* 133–142.

Spencer, J. P., & Perone, S. (2008). Defending qualitative change: The view from dynamical systems theory. *Child Development, 79,* 1639–1647.

Spencer, J. P., Verejiken, B., Diedrich, F. J., & Thelen, E. (2000). Posture and the emergence of manual skills. *Developmental Science, 3,* 216–233.

Spera, C. (2005). A review of the relationship among parenting practices, parenting styles, and adolescent school achievement. *Educational Psychology Review, 17,* 125–146.

Spere, K. A., Schmidt, L. A., Theall-Honey, L. A., & Martin-Chang, S. (2004). Expressive and receptive language skills of temperamentally shy preschoolers. *Infant and Child Development, 13,* 123–133.

Spielmann, G., McFarlin, B. K., O'Connor, D. P., Smith, P. J., Pircher, H., & Simpson, R. J. (2011). Aerobic fitness is associated with lower proportions of senescent blood T-cells in man. *Brain, Behavior, and Immunity, 25,* 1521–1529.

Spinrad, T. L., & Eisenberg, N. (2009). Empathy, prosocial behavior, and positive development in schools. In R. Gilman, E. S. Huebner, & M. J. Furlong (Eds.), *Handbook of positive psychology in schools* (pp. 119–129). New York: Routledge

Spitze, G., & Gallant, M. P. (2004). "The bitter with the sweet": Older adults' strategies for handling ambivalence in relations with their adult children. *Research on Aging, 26,* 387–412.

Spock, B., & Needlman, R. (2012). *Dr. Spock's baby and child care* (9th ed.). New York: Gallery Books.

Spokane, A. R., & Cruza-Guet, M. C. (2005). Holland's theory of vocational personalities in work environments. In S. D. Brown & R. W. Lent (Eds.), *Career development and counseling* (pp. 24–41). Hoboken, NJ: Wiley.

Sprecher, S. (1999). "I love you more today than yesterday": Romantic partners' perceptions of changes in love and related affect over time. *Journal of Personality and Social Psychology, 76,* 46–53.

Sprecher, S., & Fehr, B. (2011). Dispositional attachment and relationship-specific attachment as predictors of compassionate love for partner. *Journal of Social and Personal Relationships, 28,* 558–574.

Srivastava, S., John, O. P., Gosling, S. D., & Potter, J. (2003). Development of personality in early and middle adulthood: Set like plaster or persistent change? *Journal of Personality and Social Psychology, 84,* 1041–1053.

Sroufe, L. A., Coffino, B., & Carlson, E. A. (2010). Conceptualizing the role of early experience: Lessons from the Minnesota Longitudinal Study. *Developmental Review, 30,* 36–51.

Sroufe, L. A., Egeland, B., Carlson, E., & Collins, W. (2005). *Minnesota Study of Risk and Adaptation from birth to maturity: The development of the person.* New York: Guilford.

Sroufe, L. A., & Waters, E. (1976). The ontogenesis of smiling and laughter: A perspective on the organization of development in infancy. *Psychological Review, 83,* 173–189.

Sroufe, L. A., & Wunsch, J. P. (1972). The development of laughter in the first year of life. *Child Development, 43,* 1324–1344.

Stackert, R. A., & Bursik, K. (2003). Why am I unsatisfied? Adult attachment style, gendered irrational relationship beliefs, and young adult romantic relationship satisfaction. *Personality and Individual Differences, 34,* 1419–1429.

Stahl, S. A., & Miller, P. D. (2006). Whole language and language experience approaches for beginning reading: A quantitative research synthesis. In K. A. Dougherty Stahl & M. C. McKenna (Eds.), *Reading research at work: Foundations of effective practice* (pp. 9–35). New York: Guilford.

Stams, G. J. M., Brugman, D., Deković, M., van Rosmalen, L., van der Laan, P., & Gibbs, J. C. (2006). The moral judgment of juvenile delinquents: A meta-analysis. *Journal of Abnormal Child Psychology, 34,* 697–713.

Stams, G. J. M., Juffer, F., & van IJzendoorn, M. H. (2002). Maternal sensitivity, infant attachment, and temperament in early childhood predict adjustment in middle childhood: The case of adopted children and their biologically unrelated parents. *Developmental Psychology, 38,* 806–821.

Stanovich, K. E. (2013). *How to think straight about psychology* (10th ed.). Upper Saddle River, NJ: Pearson.

Starr, R. J. (1999). Music therapy in hospice care. *American Journal of Hospice and Palliative Care, 16,* 739–742.

Stattin, H., & Magnusson, D. (1990). *Pubertal maturation in female development.* Hillsdale, NJ: Erlbaum.

Staudinger, U. M. (1996). Wisdom and the social-interactive foundation of the mind. In P. B. Baltes & U. M. Staudinger (Eds.), *Interactive minds: Life-span perspectives on the social foundation of cognition* (pp. 276–315). New York: Cambridge University Press.

Staudinger, U. M. (2008). A psychology of wisdom: History and recent developments. *Research in Human Development, 5,* 107–120.

Staudinger, U. M., & Bowen, C. E. (2010). Life-span perspectives on positive personality development in adulthood and old age. In M. E. Lamb, A. M. Freund, & R. M. Lerner (Eds.), *Handbook of lifespan*

development: Vol. 2. Social and emotional development* (pp. 254–297). Hoboken, NJ: Wiley.

Staudinger, U. M., Dörner, J., & Mickler, C. (2005). Wisdom and personality. In R. J. Sternberg & J. Jordan (Eds.), *A handbook of wisdom: Psychological perspectives* (pp 191–219). New York: Cambridge University Press.

Staudinger, U. M., & Lindenberger, U. (2003). Understanding human development takes a metatheory and multiple disciplines. In U. M. Staudinger & U. Lindenberger (Eds.), *Understanding human development: Dialogues with life span psychology* (pp. 1–13). Norwell, MA: Kluwer.

Staudinger, U. M., Smith, J., & Baltes, P. B. (1992). Wisdom-related knowledge in a life-review task: Age differences and the role of professional specialization. *Psychology and Aging, 7,* 271–281.

Steele, C. M. (1997). A threat in the air: How stereotypes shape intellectual identity and performance. *American Psychologist, 52,* 613–629.

Steele, H., Steele, M., & Fonagy, P. (1996). Associations among attachment classifications of mothers, fathers, and their infants. *Child Development, 67,* 541–555.

Steele, S., Joseph, R. M., & Tager-Flusberg, H. (2003). Developmental change in theory of mind abilities in children with autism. *Journal of Autism and Developmental Disorders, 33,* 461–467.

Stein, C. H. (2009). "I owe it to them": Understanding felt obligation toward parents in adulthood. In K. Shifren (Ed.), *How caregiving affects development* (pp. 119–145). Washington, DC: American Psychological Association.

Stein, J. H., & Reiser, L. W. (1994). A study of white middle-class adolescent boys' responses to "semenarche" (the first ejaculation). *Journal of Youth and Adolescence, 23,* 373–384.

Stein, N., & Levine, L. J. (1999). The early emergence of emotional understanding and appraisal: Implications for theories of development. In T. Dalgleish & M. J. Power (Eds.), *Handbook of cognition and emotion* (pp. 383–408). Chichester, UK: Wiley.

Steinberg, L. (2008). A social neuroscience perspective on adolescent risk-taking. *Developmental Review, 28,* 78–106.

Steinberg, L., Albert, D., Cauffman, E., Banich, M., & Graham, S. (2008). Age differences in sensation seeking and impulsivity as indexed by behavior and self-report: Evidence for a dual systems model. *Developmental Psychology, 44,* 1764–1778.

Steinberg, L., Blatt-Eisengart, I., & Cauffman, E. (2006). Patterns of competence and adjustment among adolescents from authoritative, authoritarian, indulgent, and neglectful homes: A replication in a sample of serious juvenile offenders. *Journal of Research on Adolescence, 16,* 47–58.

Steinberg, L., Graham, S., O'Brien, L., Woolard, J., Cauffman, E., & Banich, M. (2009). Age differences in future orientation and delay discounting. *Child Development, 80,* 28–44.

Steinberg, L., & Monahan, K. C. (2011). Adolescents' exposure to sexy media does not hasten the initiation of sexual intercourse. *Developmental Psychology, 47,* 562–576.

Steinberg, L. D., Darling, N. E., & Fletcher, A. C. (1995). Authoritative parenting and adolescent development: An ecological journey. In P. Moen, G. H. Elder, Jr., & K. Luscher (Eds.), *Examining lives in context* (pp. 423–466). Washington, DC: American Psychological Association.

Steinberg, L. D., & Silk, J. S. (2002). Parenting adolescents. In M. H. Bornstein (Ed.), *Handbook of parenting* (Vol. 1, pp. 103–134). Mahwah, NJ: Erlbaum.

Steiner, J. E. (1979). Human facial expression in response to taste and smell stimulation. In H. W. Reese & L. P. Lipsitt (Eds.), *Advances in child development and behavior* (Vol. 13, pp. 257–295). New York: Academic Press.

Steiner, J. E., Glaser, D., Hawilo, M. E., & Berridge, D. C. (2001). Comparative expression of hedonic impact: Affective reactions to taste by human infants and other primates. *Neuroscience and Biobehavioral Review, 25,* 53–74.

Steinhausen, C. (2006). Eating disorders: Anorexia nervosa and bulimia nervosa. In C. Gillberg, R. Harrington, & H. Steinhausen (Eds.), *A clinician's handbook of child and adolescent psychiatry* (pp. 272–303). New York: Cambridge University Press.

Stenberg, C. (2003). Effects of maternal inattentiveness on infant social referencing. *Infant and Child Development, 12,* 399–419.

Stenberg, C., & Campos, J. J. (1990). The development of anger expressions in infancy. In N. Stein, B. Leventhal, & T. Trabasso (Eds.), *Psychological and biological approaches to emotion* (pp. 247–282). Hillsdale, NJ: Erlbaum.

Stephens, B. E., & Vohr, B. R. (2009). Neurodevelopmental outcome of the premature infant. *Pediatric Clinics of North America, 56,* 631–646.

Stephens, M. A. P., Franks, M. M., Martire, L. M., Norton, T. R., & Atienza, A. A. (2009). Women at midlife: Stress and rewards of balancing parent care with employment and family roles. In K. Shifren (Ed.), *How caregiving affects development* (pp. 147–167). Washington, DC: American Psychological Association.

Stephens, P. C., Sloboda, Z., Stephens, R. C., Teasdale, B., Grey, S. F., Hawthorne, R. D., & Williams, J. (2009). Universal school-based substance abuse prevention programs: Modeling targeted mediators and outcomes for adolescent cigarette, alcohol, and marijuana use. *Drug and Alcohol Dependence, 102,* 19–29.

Stern, D. (1985). *The interpersonal world of the infant.* New York: Basic Books.

Stern, Y. (2009). Cognitive reserve. *Neuropsychologia, 47,* 2015–2028.

Sternberg, R. J. (1988). Triangulating love. In R. J. Sternberg & M. L. Barnes (Eds.), *The psychology of love* (pp. 119–138). New Haven, CT: Yale University Press.

Sternberg, R. J. (2000). *Cupid's arrow: The course of love through time.* Cambridge, UK: Cambridge University Press.

Sternberg, R. J. (2001). Why schools should teach for wisdom: The balance theory of wisdom in educational settings. *Educational Psychologist, 36,* 227–245.

Sternberg, R. J. (2003). The development of creativity as a decision-making process. In R. K. Sawyer, V. John-Steiner, S. Moran, R. J. Sternberg, D. H. Feldman, J. Nakamura, & M. Csikszentmihalyi (Eds.), *Creativity and development* (pp. 91–138). New York: Oxford University Press.

Sternberg, R. J. (2005). The triarchic theory of successful intelligence. In D. P. Flanagan & P. L. Harrison (Eds.), *Contemporary intellectual assessment: Theories, tests, and issues* (pp. 103–119). New York: Guilford.

Sternberg, R. J. (2006). A duplex theory of love. In R. J. Sternberg & K. Weis (Eds.), *The new psychology of love* (pp. 184–199). New Haven, CT: Yale University Press.

Sternberg, R. J. (2008). The triarchic theory of successful intelligence. In N. Salkind (Ed.), *Encyclopedia of educational psychology* (Vol. 2, pp. 988–994). Thousand Oaks, CA: Sage.

Sternberg, R. J., Forsythe, G. B., Hedlund, J., Horvath, J. A., Wagner, R. K., Williams, W. M., Snook, S. A., & Grigorenko, E. L. (2000). *Practical intelligence in everyday life.* Cambridge, UK: Cambridge University Press.

Sternberg, R. J., & Grigorenko, E. L. (2002). *Dynamic testing.* New York: Cambridge University Press.

Sternberg, R. J., & Lubart, T. I. (2001). Wisdom and creativity. In J. E. Birren & K. W. Schaie (Eds.),

Handbook of the psychology of aging (pp. 500–522). San Diego: Academic Press.

Stevens, J., Katz, E. G., & Huxley, R. R. (2010). Associations between gender, age and waist circumference. *European Journal of Clinical Nutrition, 64,* 6–15.

Stevens, J. C., & Cruz, L. A. (1996). Spatial acuity of touch: Ubiquitous decline with aging revealed by repeated threshold testing. *Somatosensory and Motor Research, 13,* 1–10.

Stevenson, H. W., Lee, S., & Mu, X. (2000). Successful achievement in mathematics: China and the United States. In C. F. M. van Lieshout & P. G. Heymans (Eds.), *Developing talent across the life span* (pp. 167–183). Philadelphia: Psychology Press.

Stewart, A. J., & Malley, J. E. (2004). Women of the greatest generation. In C. Daiute & C. Lightfoot (Eds.), *Narrative analysis: Studying the development of individuals in society* (pp. 223–244). Thousand Oaks, CA: Sage.

Stewart, A. J., Ostrove, J. M., & Helson, R. (2001). Middle aging in women: Patterns of personality change from the 30s to the 50s. *Journal of Adult Development, 8,* 23–37.

Stewart, A. J., & Vandewater, E. A. (1999). "If I had to do over again . . .": Midlife review, midcourse corrections, and women's well-being in midlife. *Journal of Personality and Social Psychology, 76,* 270–283.

Stewart, A. L., Verboncoeur, C. J., McLellan, B. Y., Gillis, D. E., Rush, S., & Mills, K. M. (2001). Physical activity outcomes of CHAMPS II: A physical activity promotion program for older adults. *Journal of Gerontology, 56A,* M465–M470.

Stewart, P. W., Lonky, E., Reihman, J., Pagano, J., Gump, B. B., & Darvill, T. (2008). The relationship between prenatal PCB exposure and intelligence (IQ). *Environmental Health Perspectives, 116,* 1416–1422.

Stewart, R. B., Jr. (1990). *The second child: Family transition and adjustment.* Newbury Park, CA: Sage.

Stewart, S., Stinnett, H., & Rosenfeld, L. B. (2000). Sex differences in desired characteristics of short-term and long-term relationship partners. *Journal of Social and Personal Relationships, 17,* 843–853.

Stice, E. (2003). Puberty and body image. In C. Hayward (Ed.), *Gender differences at puberty* (pp. 61–76). New York: Cambridge University Press.

Stice, E., Presnell, K., & Bearman, S. K. (2001). Relation of early menarche to depression, eating disorders, substance abuse, and comorbid psychopathology among adolescent girls. *Developmental Psychology, 37,* 608–619.

Stiles, J. (2008). *Fundamentals of brain development.* Cambridge, MA: Harvard University Press.

Stiles, J. (2012). The effects of injury to dynamic neural networks in the mature and developing brain. *Developmental Psychobiology, 54,* 343–349.

Stiles, J., Reilly, J., Paul, B., & Moses, P. (2005). Cognitive development following early brain injury: Evidence for neural adaptation. *Trends in Cognitive Sciences, 9,* 136–143.

Stiles, J., Stern, C., Appelbaum, M., & Nass, R. (2008). Effects of early focal brain injury on memory for visuospatial patterns: Selective deficits of global-local processing. *Neuropsychology, 22,* 61–73.

Stilson, S. R., & Harding, C. G. (1997). Early social context as it relates to symbolic play: A longitudinal investigation. *Merrill-Palmer Quarterly, 43,* 682–693.

Stinchcomb, J. B., Bazemore, G., & Riestenberg, N. (2006). Beyond zero tolerance: Restoring justice in secondary schools. *Youth Violence and Juvenile Justice, 4,* 123–147.

Stine-Morrow, E. A. L., & Basak, C. (2011). Cognitive interventions. In K. W. Schaie & S. L. Willis (Eds.), *Handbook of the psychology of aging* (7th ed.,pp. 153–171). New York: Elsevier.

Stine-Morrow, E. A. L., & Miller, L. M. S. (2009). Aging, self-regulation, and learning from text. *Psychology of Learning and Motivation, 51,* 255–285.

Stipek, D. J., Feiler, R., Daniels, D., & Milburn, S. (1995). Effects of different instructional approaches on young children's achievement and motivation. *Child Development, 66,* 209–223.

Stipek, D. J., Gralinski, J. H., & Kopp, C. B. (1990). Self-concept development in the toddler years. *Developmental Psychology, 26,* 972–977.

St James-Roberts, I. (2007). Helping parents to manage infant crying and sleeping: A review of the evidence and its implications for services. *Child Abuse Review, 16,* 47–69.

St James-Roberts, I., Alvarez, M., Csipke, E., Abramsky, T., Goodwin, J., & Sorgenfrei, E. (2006). Infant crying and sleeping in London, Copenhagen and when parents adopt a "proximal" form of care. *Pediatrics, 117,* e1146–e1155.

St James-Roberts, I., Goodwin, J., Peter, B., Adams, D., & Hunt, S. (2003). Individual differences in responsivity to a neurobehavioural examination predict crying patterns of 1-week-old infants at home. *Developmental Medicine and Child Neurology, 45,* 400–407.

St. Louis, G. R., & Liem, J. H. (2005). Ego identity, ethnic identity, and the psychosocial well-being of ethnic minority and majority college students. *Identity, 5,* 227–246.

Stoch, M. B., Smythe, P. M., Moodie, A. D., & Bradshaw, D. (1982). Psychosocial outcome and CT findings after growth undernourishment during infancy: A 20-year developmental study. *Developmental Medicine and Child Neurology, 24,* 419–436.

Stocker, C. M., Burwell, R. A., & Briggs, M. L. (2002). Sibling conflict in middle childhood predicts children's adjustment in early adolescence. *Journal of Family Psychology, 16,* 50–57.

Stohs, S. J. (2011). The role of free radicals in toxicity and disease. *Journal of Basic and Clinical Physiology and Pharmacology, 6,* 205–228.

Stone, A. A., Schwartz, J. E., Broderick, J. E., & Deaton, A. (2010). A snapshot of the age distribution of psychological well-being in the United States. *Proceedings of the National Academy of Sciences, 107,* 9985–9990.

Stone, M. R., & Brown, B. B. (1999). Identity claims and projections: Descriptions of self and crowds in secondary school. In J. A. McLellan & M. J. V. Pugh (Eds.), *The role of peer groups in adolescent social identity: Exploring the importance of stability and change* (pp. 7–20). San Francisco: Jossey-Bass.

Stone, R. I., & Reinhard, S. C. (2007). The place of assisted living in long-term care and related service systems. *Gerontologist, 47,* 23–32.

Stoppa, T. M., & Lefkowitz, E. S. (2010). Longitudinal changes in religiosity among emerging adult college students. *Journal of Research on Adolescence, 20,* 23–38.

Stormshak, E. A., Bierman, K. L., McMahon, R. J., Lengua, L. J., & the Conduct Problems Prevention Research Group. (2000). Parenting practices and child disruptive behavior problems in early elementary school. *Journal of Clinical Child Psychology, 29,* 17–29.

Story, R. (2007). Asthma and obesity in children. *Current Opinion in Pediatrics, 19,* 680–684.

Stouthamer-Loeber, M., Wei, E., Loeber, R., & Masten, A. S. (2004). Desistance from persistent serious delinquency in the transition to adulthood. *Development and Psychopathology, 16,* 897–918.

Strapp, C. M., & Federico, A. (2000). Imitations and repetitions: What do children say following recasts? *First Language, 20,* 273–290.

Straus, M. A., & Stewart, J. H. (1999). Corporal punishment by American parents: National data on prevalence, chronicity, severity, and duration, in

relation to child and family characteristics. *Clinical Child and Family Psychology Review, 2,* 55–70.

Strawbridge, W. J., Shema, S. J., Cohen, R. D., & Kaplan, G. A. (2001). Religious attendance increases survival by improving and maintaining good health behaviors. *Annals of Behavioral Medicine, 23,* 68–74.

Strazdins, L., Clements, M. S., Korda, R. J., Broom, D. H., & D'Souza, R. M. (2006). Unsociable work? Nonstandard work schedules, family relationships, and children's well-being. *Journal of Marriage and the Family, 68,* 394–410.

Street, A. E., Bell, M., & Ready, C. B. (2011). Sexual assault. In D. Benedek & G. Wynn (Eds.), *Clinical manual for the management of PTSD* (pp. 325–348). Arlington, VA: American Psychiatric Press.

Streissguth, A. P., Bookstein, F. L., Barr, H. M., Sampson, P. D., O'Malley, K., & Young, J. K. (2004). Risk factors for adverse life outcomes in fetal alcohol syndrome and fetal alcohol effects. *Journal of Developmental and Behavioral Pediatrics, 25,* 228–238.

Streissguth, A. P., Treder, R., Barr, H. M., Shepard, T., Bleyer, W. A., Sampson, P. D., & Martin, D. (1987). Aspirin and acetaminophen use by pregnant women and subsequent child IQ and attention decrements. *Teratology, 35,* 211–219.

Striano, T., & Rochat, P. (2000). Emergence of selective social referencing in infancy. *Infancy, 1,* 253–264.

Striegel-Moore, R. H., & Franko, D. L. (2006). Adolescent eating disorders. In R. H. Striegel-Moore & D. L. Franko (Eds.), *Child and adolescent psychopathology: Theoretical and clinical implications* (pp. 160–183). New York: Routledge.

Stright, A. D., Herr, M. Y., & Neitzel, C. (2009). Maternal scaffolding of children's problem solving and children's adjustment in kindergarten: Hmong families in the United States. *Journal of Educational Psychology, 101,* 207–218.

Stright, A. D., Neitzel, C., Sears, K. G., & Hoke-Sinex, L. (2002). Instruction begins in the home: Relations between parental instruction and children's self-regulation in the classroom. *Journal of Educational Psychology, 93,* 456–466.

Stringer, K., Kerpelman, J., & Skorikov, V. (2011). Career preparation: A longitudinal, process-oriented examination. *Journal of Vocational Behavior, 79,* 158–169.

Stringer, K. J., & Kerpelman, J. L. (2010). Career identity development in college students: Decision making, parental support, and work experience. *Identity, 10,* 181–200.

Stroebe, M., & Schut, H. (2010). The dual process model of coping with bereavement: A decade on. *Omega, 61,* 273–289.

Stroebe, M. S., & Schut, H. (1999). The dual process model of coping with bereavement: Rationale and description. *Death Studies, 23,* 197–224.

Stroebe, M. S., van der Houwen, K., & Schut, H. (2008). Bereavement support, intervention, and research on the Internet: A critical review. In M. S. Stroebe, R. O. Hansson, H. Schut, & W. Stroebe (Eds.), *Handbook of bereavement research and practice* (pp. 551–574). Washington, DC: American Psychological Association.

Strohschein, L. (2005). Parental divorce and child mental health trajectories. *Journal of Marriage and Family, 67,* 1286–1300.

Strough, J., Hicks, P. J., Swenson, L. M., Cheng, S., & Barnes, K. A. (2003). Collaborative everyday problem solving: Interpersonal relationships and problem dimensions. *International Journal of Aging and Human Development, 56,* 43–66.

Strough, J., Leszczynski, J. P., Neely, T. L., Flinn, J. A., & Margrett, J. (2007). From adolescence to later adulthood: Femininity, masculinity, and androgyny in six age groups. *Sex Roles, 57,* 385–396.

Strough, J., McFall, J. P., Flinn, J. A., & Schuller, K. L. (2008). Collaborative everyday problem solving among same-gender friends in early and later adulthood. *Psychology and Aging, 23*, 517–530.

Strouse, D. L. (1999). Adolescent crowd orientations: A social and temporal analysis. In J. A. McLellan & M. J. V. Pugh (Eds.), *The role of peer groups in adolescent social identity: Exploring the importance of stability and change* (pp. 37–54). San Francisco: Jossey-Bass.

Stuart, M., & Weinrich, M. (2001). Home- and community-based long-term care: Lessons from Denmark. *Gerontologist, 41*, 474–480.

Sturaro, C., van Lier, P. A. C., Cuijpers, P., & Koot, H. M. (2011). The role of peer relationships in the development of early school-age externalizing problems. *Child Development, 82*, 758–765.

Sturge-Apple, M. L., Davies, P. T., Winter, M. A., Cummings, E. M., & Schermerhorn, A. (2008). Interparental conflict and children's school adjustment: The explanatory role of children's internal representations of interparental and parent–child relationships. *Developmental Psychology, 44*, 1678–1690.

Styne, D. M. (2003). The regulation of pubertal growth. *Hormone Research, 60*(Suppl. 1), 22–26.

Su, T. F., & Costigan, C. L. (2008). The development of children's ethnic identity in immigrant Chinese families in Canada: The role of parenting practices and children's perceptions of parental family obligation expectations. *Journal of Early Adolescence, 29*, 638–663.

Suarez-Morales, L., & Lopez, B. (2009). The impact of acculturative stress and daily hassles on preadolescent psychological adjustment: Examining anxiety symptoms. *Journal of Primary Prevention, 30*, 335–349.

Suárez-Orozco, C., Todorova, I., & Qin, D. B. (2006). The well-being of immigrant adolescents: A longitudinal perspective on risk and protective factors. In F. A. Villarruel & T. Luster (Eds.), *The crisis in youth mental health: Critical issues and effective programs: Vol. 2. Disorders in adolescence* (pp. 53–83). Westport, CT: Praeger.

Subbotsky, E. (2004). Magical thinking in judgments of causation: Can anomalous phenomena affect ontological causal beliefs in children and adults? *British Journal of Developmental Psychology, 22*, 123–152.

Subrahmanyam, K., Gelman, R., & Lafosse, A. (2002). Animate and other separably moveable things. In G. Humphreys (Ed.), *Category-specificity in brain and mind* (pp. 341–371). London: Psychology Press.

Subrahmanyam, K., & Greenfield, P. M. (2008). Online communication and adolescent relationships. *Future of Children, 18*, 119–146.

Subrahmanyam, K., Smahel, D., & Greenfield, P. (2006). Connecting developmental constructions to the Internet: Identity presentation and sexual exploration in online teen chat rooms. *Developmental Psychology, 42*, 395–406.

Substance Abuse and Mental Health Services Administration. (2011). *Results from the 2010 National Survey on Drug Use and Health: Vol. 1. Summary of national findings*. Rockville, MD: Author.

Sullivan, M. C., McGrath, M. M. Hawes, K., & Lester, B. M. (2008). Growth trajectories of preterm infants: Birth to 12 years. *Journal of Pediatric Health Care, 22*, 83–93.

Sullivan, M. W., & Lewis, M. (2003). Contextual determinants of anger and other negative expressions in young infants. *Developmental Psychology, 39*, 693–705.

Summers, R. W., & Hoffman, A. M. (Eds.). (2006). *Elder abuse: A public health perspective*. Washington, DC: American Public Health Association.

Super, C. M. (1981). Behavioral development in infancy. In R. H. Monroe, R. L. Monroe, & B. B. Whiting (Eds.), *Handbook of cross-cultural human development* (pp. 181–270). New York: Garland.

Super, C. M., & Harkness, S. (2002). Culture structures the environment for development. *Human Development 45*, 270–274.

Super, C. M., & Harkness, S. (2010). Culture and infancy. In J. G. Bremner & T. D. Wachs (Eds.), *Wiley-Blackwell handbook of infant development: Vol. 1. Basic research* (2nd ed., pp. 623–649). Chichester, UK: Wiley-Blackwell.

Super, D. E. (1990). A life span, life space approach to career development. In D. Brown & L. Brooks (Eds.), *Career choice and development* (2nd ed., pp. 197–261). San Francisco: Jossey-Bass.

Super, D. E. (1994). A life span, life space perspective on convergence. In M. L. Savikas & R. W. Lent (Eds.), *Convergence in career development theories* (pp. 62–71). Palo Alto, CA: Consulting Psychologists Press.

Supple, A. J., Ghazarian, S. R., Peterson, G. W., & Bush, K. R. (2009). Assessing the cross-cultural validity of a parental autonomy granting measure: Comparing adolescents in the United States, China, Mexico, and India. *Journal of Cross-Cultural Psychology, 40*, 816–833.

Supple, A. J., & Small, S. A. (2006). The influence of parental support, knowledge, and authoritative parenting on Hmong and European American adolescent development. *Journal of Family Issues, 27*, 1214–1232.

Susman, E. J., & Dorn, L. D. (2009). Puberty: Its role in development. In R. M. Lerner & L. Steinberg (Eds.), *Handbook of adolescent psychology: Vol. 1. Individual bases of adolescent development* (3rd ed., pp. 116–151). Hoboken, NJ: Wiley.

Sussman, S., Skara, S., & Ames, S. L. (2008). Substance abuse among adolescents. *Substance Use and Misuse, 43*, 1802–1828.

Sutton, M. J., Brown, J. D., Wilson, K. M., & Klein, J. D. (2002). Shaking the tree of forbidden fruit: Where adolescents learn about sexuality and contraception. In J. D. Brown, J. R. Steele, & K. Walsh-Childers (Eds.), *Sexual teens, sexual media* (pp. 25–55). Mahwah, NJ: Erlbaum.

Swartz, T. T. (2009). Intergenerational family relations in adulthood: Patterns, variations, and implictions in the contemporary United States. *Annual Review of Sociology, 25*, 191–212.

Sweet, S., & Moen, P. (2007). Integrating educational careers in work and family. *Community, Work and Family, 10*, 231–250.

Swinson, J., & Harrop, A. (2009). Teacher talk directed to boys and girls and its relationship to their behaviour. *Educational Studies, 35*, 515–524.

Symons, D. K. (2001). A dyad-oriented approach to distress and mother–child relationship outcomes in the first 24 months. *Parenting: Science and Practice, 1*, 101–122.

Szaflarski, J. P., Rajogopal, A., Altaye, M., Byars, A. W., Jacola, L., Schmithorst, V. J., et al. (2012). Lefthandedness and language lateralization in children. *Brain Research, 1433*, 85–97.

Szlemko, W. J., Wood, J. W., & Thurman, P. J. (2006). Native Americans and alcohol: Past, present, and future. *Journal of General Psychology, 133*, 435–451.

T

Tabibi, Z., & Pfeffer, K. (2007). Finding a safe place to cross the road: The effect of distractors and the role of attention in children's identification of safe and dangerous road-crossing sites. *Infant and Child Development, 16*, 193–206.

Taga, G., Asakawa, K., Maki, A., Konishi, Y., & Koizumi, H. (2003). Brain imaging in awake infants by near-infrared optical topography. *Proceedings of the National Academy of Sciences, 100*, 10722–10727.

Tager-Flusberg, H., & Zukowski, A. (2009). Putting words together: Morphology and syntax in the preschool years. In J. B. Gleason & B. Ratner (Ed.), *The development of language* (7th ed., pp. 139–191). Boston: Allyn and Bacon.

Tahir, L., & Gruber, H. E. (2003). Developmental trajectories and creative work in late life. In J. Demick & C. Andreoletti (Eds.), *Handbook of adult development* (pp. 239–255). New York: Springer.

Takagi, E., Silverstein, M., & Crimmins, E. (2007). Intergenerational coresidence of older adults in Japan: Conditions for cultural plasticity. *Journal of Gerontology, 62B*, S330–S339.

Takahashi, K. (1990). Are the key assumptions of the "Strange Situation" procedure universal? A view from Japanese research. *Human Development, 33*, 23–30.

Takamura, J., & Williams, B. (2002). *Informal caregiving: Compassion in action*. Arlington, TX: Arc of the United States.

Talbot, L. S., McGlinchey, E. L., Kaplan, K. A., & Dahl, R. E. (2010). Sleep deprivation in adolescents and adults: Changes in affect. *Emotion, 10*, 831–841.

Tamis-LeMonda, C. S., & Bornstein, M. H. (1989). Habituation and maternal encouragement of attention in infancy as predictors of toddler language, play, and representational competence. *Child Development, 60*, 738–751.

Tamis-LeMonda, C. S., Shannon, J. D., Cabrera, N. J., & Lamb, M. E. (2004). Fathers and mothers at play with their 2- and 3-year-olds: Contributions to language and cognitive development. *Child Development, 75*, 1806–1820.

Tamis-LeMonda, C. S., Way, N., Hughes, D., Yoshikawa, H., Kalman, R. K., & Niwa, E. Y. (2008). Parents' goals for children: The dynamic coexistence of individualism and collectivism in cultures and individuals. *Social Development, 17*, 183–209.

Tammelin, T., Näyhä, S., Hills, A. P., & Järvelin, M. (2003). Adolescent participation in sports and adult physical activity. *American Journal of Preventive Medicine, 24*, 22–28.

Tamrouti-Makkink, I. D., Dubas, J. S., Gerris, J. R. M., & van Aken, A. G. (2004). The relation between the absolute level of parenting and differential parental treatment with adolescent siblings' adjustment. *Journal of Child Psychology and Psychiatry, 45*, 1397–1406.

Tanaka, H., & Seals, D. R. (2003). Dynamic exercise performance in master athletes: Insight into the effects of primary human aging on physiological functional capacity. *Journal of Applied Physiology, 95*, 2152–2162.

Tangney, J. P., Stuewig, J., & Mashek, D. J. (2007). Moral emotions and moral behavior. *Annual Review of Psychology, 58*, 345–372.

Tanimura, M., Takahashi, K., Kataoka, N., Tomita, K., Tanabe, I., Yasuda, M., et al. (2004). Proposal: Heavy television and video viewing poses a risk for infants and young children. *Nippon Shonika Gakkai Zasshi, 108*, 709–712 (in Japanese).

Tanner, J. M., Healy, M., & Cameron, N. (2001). *Assessment of skeletal maturity and prediction of adult height (TW3 method)* (3rd ed.). Philadelphia: Saunders.

Tanner, J. L., & Arnett, J. J. (2011). Presenting "emerging adulthood": What makes it developmentally distinctive? In J. J. Arnett, M. Kloep, L. B. Hendry, & J. L. Tanner (Eds.), *Debating emerging adulthood: Stage or process?* (pp. 13–30). New York: Oxford University Press.

Tanner, J. L., Arnett, J. J., & Leis, J. A. (2009). Emerging adulthood: Learning and development during the first stage of adulthood. In M. C. Smith & N. DeFrates-Densch (Eds.), *Handbook of research on adult learning and development* (pp. 34–67). New York: Routledge.

Tardif, T. (2006). But are they really verbs? Chinese words for action. In K. Hirsh-Pasek & R. M. Golinkoff (Eds.), *Action meets word: How children learn verbs* (pp. 477–498). New York: Oxford University Press.

Tardif, T., Fletcher, P., Liang, W., & Kaciroti, N. (2009). Early vocabulary development in Mandarin (Putonghua) and Cantonese. *Journal of Child Language, 36,* 1115–1144.

Tardif, T., Fletcher, P., Liang, W., Zhang, Z., Kaciroti, N., & Marchman, V. A. (2008). Baby's first 10 words. *Developmental Psychology, 44,* 929–938.

Tardif, T., Wellman, H. M., & Cheung, K. M. (2004). False belief understanding in Cantonese-speaking children. *Journal of Child Language, 31,* 779–800.

Tarry-Adkins, J. L., Martin-Gronert, M. S., Chen, J. H., Cripps, R. L., & Ozanne, S. E. (2008). Maternal diet influences DNA damage, aortic telomere length, oxidative stress, and antioxidant defense capacity in rats. *FASEB Journal, 22,* 2037–2044.

Tarter, R. E., Vanyukov, M., & Kirisci, L. (2008). Etiology of substance use disorder: Developmental perspective. In Y. Kaminer & O. G. Bukstein (Eds.), *Adolescent substance abuse: Psychiatric comorbidity and high-risk behaviors* (pp. 5–27). New York: Routledge.

Tasker, F. (2005). Lesbian mothers, gay fathers, and their children: A review. *Developmental and Behavioral Pediatrics, 26,* 224–240.

Taylor, C. A., Manganello, J. A., Lee, S. J., & Rice, J. C. (2010). Mother's spanking of 3-year-old children and subsequent risk of children's aggressive behavior. *Pediatrics, 125,* e1057–e1065.

Taylor, J. L. (2009). Midlife impacts of adolescent parenthood. *Journal of Family Issues, 30,* 484–510.

Taylor, M. C., & Hall, J. A. (1982). Psychological androgyny: Theories, methods, and conclusions. *Psychological Bulletin, 92,* 347–366.

Taylor, M. G., Rhodes, M., & Gelman, S. A. (2009). Boys will be boys; cows will be cows: Children's essentialist reasoning about gender categories and animal species. *Child Development, 80,* 461–481.

Taylor, P., Wang, W., Parker, K., Passel, J. S., Patten, E., & Motel, S. (2012). *The rise of intermarriage.* Washington, DC: Pew Research Center.

Taylor, R. D. (2010). Risk and resilience in low-income African American families: Moderating effects of kinship social support. *Cultural Diversity and Ethnic Minority Psychology, 16,* 344–351.

Taylor, R. J., Lincoln, K. D., & Chatters, L. M. (2005). Supportive relationships with church members among African Americans. *Family Relations, 54,* 501–511.

Taylor, W. C., Sallis, J. F., Lees, E., Hepworth, J. T., Feliz, K., Volding, D. C., Cassels, A., & Tobin, J. N. (2007). Changing social and built environments to promote physical activity: Recommendations from low-income, urban women. *Journal of Physical Activity and Health, 4,* 54–65.

Teasdale, B., & Bradley-Engen, M. S. (2010). Adolescent same-sex attraction and mental health: The role of stress and support. *Journal of Homosexuality, 57,* 287–309.

Teinonen, T., Fellman, V., Näätänen, R., Alku, P., & Huotilainen, M. (2009). Statistical language learning in neonates revealed by event-related brain potentials. *BMC Neuroscience, 10,* 21.

Temkin-Greener, H., Bajorska, A., Peterson, D. R., Kunitz, S. J., Gross, D., & Williams, T. F. (2004). Social support and risk-adjusted mortality in a frail older population. *Medical Care, 42,* 779–788.

Temple, J. L., Giacomelli, A. M., Roemmich, J. N., & Epstein, L. H. (2007). Overweight children habituate slower than nonoverweight children to food. *Physiology and Behavior, 9,* 250–254.

ten Brummelhuis, L. L., ter Hoeven, C. L., De Jong, M. D. T., & Peper, B. (2012). Exploring the linkage between the home domain and absence from work: Health, motivation, or both? *Journal of Organizational Behavior, 33.* Accessed online at http://onlinelibrary.wiley.com/doi/10.1002/job.1789/abstract

Tenenbaum, H. R., Hill, D., Joseph, N., & Roche, E. (2010). "It's a boy because he's painting a picture": Age differences in children's conventional and unconventional gender schemas. *British Journal of Psychology, 101,* 137–154.

Tenenbaum, H. R., & Leaper, C. (2002). Are parents' gender schemas related to their children's gender-related cognitions? A meta-analysis. *Developmental Psychology, 38,* 615–630.

Tenenbaum, H. R., & Leaper, C. (2003). Parent–child conversations about science: The socialization of gender inequities? *Developmental Psychology, 39,* 34–47.

Tenenbaum, H. R., Snow, C. E., Roach, K. A., & Kurland, B. (2005). Talking and reading science: Longitudinal data on sex differences in mother–child conversations in low-income families. *Journal of Applied Developmental Psychology, 26,* 1–19.

ten Tusscher, G. W., & Koppe, J. G. (2004). Perinatal dioxin exposure and later effects—a review. *Chemosphere, 54,* 1329–1336.

Terwel, J., Gillies, R. M., van den Eeden, P., & Hoek, D. (2001). Cooperative learning processes of students: A longitudinal multilevel perspective. *British Journal of Educational Psychology, 71,* 619–645.

Teti, D. M., Saken, J. W., Kucera, E., & Corns, K. M. (1996). And baby makes four: Predictors of attachment security among preschool-age firstborns during the transition to siblinghood. *Child Development, 67,* 579–596.

Teyber, E. (2001). *Helping children cope with divorce* (rev. ed.). San Francisco: Jossey-Bass.

Thacker, H. L. (2011). Assessing risks and benefits of nonhormonal treatments for vasomotor symptoms in perimenopausal and postmenopausal women. *Journal of Women's Health, 20,* 1007–1016.

Thacker, S. B., & Stroup, D. F. (2003). Revisiting the use of the electronic fetal monitor. *Lancet, 361,* 445–446.

Thatcher, R. W., Walker, R. A., & Giudice, S. (1987). Human cerebral hemispheres develop at different rates and ages. *Science, 236,* 1110–1113.

Thelen, E., Schöner, G., Scheier, C., & Smith, L. B. (2001). The dynamics of embodiment: A field theory of infant perseverative reaching. *Behavioral and Brain Sciences, 24,* 1–34.

Thelen, E., & Smith, L. B. (1998). Dynamic systems theories. In R. M. Lerner (Ed.), *Handbook of child psychology: Vol. 1. Theoretical models of human development* (5th ed., pp. 563–634). New York: Wiley.

Thelen, E., & Smith, L. B. (2006). Dynamic systems theories. In R. M. Lerner (Ed.), *Handbook of child psychology: Vol. 1. Theoretical models of human development* (6th ed., pp. 258–312). Hoboken, NJ: Wiley.

Thiessen, E. D., & Saffran, J. R. (2007). Learning to learn: Infants' acquisition of stress-based strategies for work segmentation. *Language Learning and Development, 3,* 73–100.

Thoermer, C., Sodian, B., Vuori, M., Perst, H., & Kristen, S. (2012). Continuity from an implicit to an explicit understanding of false belief from infancy to preschool age. *British Journal of Developmental Psychology, 30,* 172–187.

Thomaes, S., Stegge, H., Bushman, B. J., & Olthof, T. (2008). Trumping shame by blasts of noise: Narcissism, self-esteem, shame, and aggression in young adolescents. *Child Development, 79,* 1792–1801.

Thomas, A., & Chess, S. (1977). *Temperament and development.* New York: Brunner/Mazel.

Thomas, A., Chess, S., & Birch, H. G. (1968). *Temperament and behavior disorders in children.* New York: New York University Press.

Thomas, C. L., & Dimitrov, D. M. (2007). Effects of a teen pregnancy prevention program on teens'

attitudes toward sexuality: A latent trait modeling approach. *Developmental Psychology, 43,* 173–185.

Thomas, K. A., & Tessler, R. C. (2007). Bicultural socialization among adoptive families: Where there is a will, there is a way. *Journal of Family Issues, 28,* 1189–1219.

Thomas, R. M. (2005). *Comparing theories of child development* (6th ed.). Belmont, CA: Wadsworth.

Thombs, B. D., Roseman, M., & Arthurs, E. (2010). Prenatal and postpartum depression in fathers and mothers. *Journal of the American Medical Association, 304,* 961.

Thompson, A., Hollis, C., & Richards, D. (2003). Authoritarian parenting attitudes as a risk for conduct problems: Results of a British national cohort study. *European Child and Adolescent Psychiatry, 12,* 84–91.

Thompson, P. M., Giedd, J. N., Woods, R. P., MacDonald, D., Evans, A. C., & Toga, A. W. (2000). Growth patterns in the developing brain detected by using continuum mechanical tensor maps. *Nature, 404,* 190–192.

Thompson, R. A. (2000). The legacy of early attachments. *Child Development, 71,* 145–152.

Thompson, R. A. (2006). The development of the person: Social understanding, relationships, conscience, self. In N. Eisenberg (Ed.), *Handbook of child psychology: Vol. 3. Social, emotional, and personality development* (6th ed., pp. 24–98). Hoboken, NJ: Wiley.

Thompson, R. A. (2008). Early attachment and later development. In J. Cassidy & P. R. Shaver (Eds.), *Handbook of attachment: Theory, research, and clinical applications* (2nd ed., pp. 348–365). New York: Guilford.

Thompson, R. A., & Goodman, M. (2010). Development of emotion regulation: More than meets the eye. In A. M. Kring & D. M. Sloan (Eds.), *Emotion regulation and psychopathology: A transdiagnostic approach to etiology and treatment* (pp. 38–58). New York: Guilford.

Thompson, R. A., & Goodvin, R. (2007). Taming the tempest in the teapot. In C. A. Brownell & C. B. Kopp (Eds.), *Socioemotional development in the toddler years: Transitions and transformations* (pp. 320–341). New York: Guilford.

Thompson, R. A., & Meyer, S. (2007). Socialization of emotion regulation in the family. In J. J. Gross (Ed.), *Handbook of emotion regulation* (pp. 249–268). New York: Guilford.

Thompson, R. A., Meyer, S., & McGinley, M. (2006). Understanding values in relationships: The development of conscience. In M. Killen & J. G. Smetana (Eds.), *Handbook of moral development* (pp. 267–298). Mahwah, NJ: Erlbaum.

Thompson, R. A., & Raikes, H. A. (2007). The social and emotional foundations of school readiness. In D. F. Perry, R. K. Kaufmann, & J. Knitzer (Eds.), *Social and emotional health in early childhood: Building bridges between services and systems* (pp. 13–35). Baltimore, MD: Paul H. Brookes.

Thompson, W. W., Price, C., Goodson, B., Shay, D. K., Benson, P., Hinrichsen, V. L., et al. (2007). Early thimerosal exposure and neuropsychological outcomes at 7 to 10 years. *New England Journal of Medicine, 357,* 1281–1292.

Thorne, B. (1993). *Gender play: Girls and boys in school.* New Brunswick, NJ: Rutgers University Press.

Thornton, J., Edwards, R., Mitchell, P., Harrison, R. A., Buchan, I., & Kelly, S. P. (2005). Smoking and age-related macular degeneration: A review of association. *Eye, 19,* 935–944.

Thornton, S. (1999). Creating conditions for cognitive change: The interaction between task structures and specific strategies. *Child Development, 70,* 588–603.

Tienari, P., Wahlberg, K. E., & Wynne, L. C. (2006). Finnish adoption study of schizophrenia: Implications for family interventions. *Families, Systems, and Health, 24,* 442–451.

Tiet, Q. Q., Huizinga, D., & Byrnes, H. F. (2010). Predictors of resilience among inner city youths. *Journal of Child and Family Studies, 19,* 360–378.

Tiggemann, M., & Anesbury, T. (2000). Negative stereotyping of obesity in children: The role of controllability beliefs. *Journal of Applied Social Psychology, 30,* 1977–1993.

Tofler, I. R., Knapp, P. K., & Drell, M. J. (1998). The achievement by proxy spectrum in youth sports: Historical perspective and clinical approach to pressured and high-achieving children and adolescents. *Child and Adolescent Psychiatric Clinics of North America, 7,* 803–820.

Tokunaga, R. S. (2010). Following you home from school: A critical review and synthesis of research on cyberbullying victimization. *Computers in Human behavior, 26,* 277–287.

Tomasello, M. (1999). Having intentions, understanding intentions, and understanding communicative intentions. In P. D. Zelazo, J. W. Astington, & J. Wilde (Eds.), *Developing theories of intention: Social understanding and self-control* (pp. 63–75). Mahwah, NJ: Erlbaum.

Tomasello, M. (2003). *Constructing a language: A usage-based theory of language acquisition.* Cambridge, MA: Harvard University Press.

Tomasello, M. (2006). Acquiring linguistic constructions. In D. Kuhn & R. Siegler (Eds.), *Handbook of child psychology: Vol. 2: Cognition, perception, and language* (6th ed., pp. 255–298). Hoboken, NJ: Wiley.

Tomasello, M. (2011). Language development. In U. Goswami (Ed.), *Wiley-Blackwell handbook of childhood cognitive development* (2nd ed., pp. 239–257). Malden, MA: Wiley-Blackwell.

Tomasello, M., & Akhtar, N. (1995). Two-year-olds use pragmatic cues to differentiate reference to objects and actions. *Cognitive Development, 10,* 201–224.

Tomasello, M., & Brandt, S. (2009). Flexibility in the semantics and syntax of children's early verb use. *Monographs of the Society for Research in Child Development, 72*(2, Serial No. 293), 113–126.

Tomasello, M., Carpenter, M., & Liszkowski, U. (2007). A new look at infant pointing. *Child Development, 78,* 705–722.

Tomer, A., Eliason, G., & Smith, J. (2000). Beliefs about the self, life, and death: Testing aspects of a comprehensive model of death anxiety and death attitudes. *Death attitudes and the older adult: Theories, concepts, and applications* (pp. 109–122). Philadelphia: Taylor & Francis.

Tong, V. T., Jones, J. R., Dietz, P. M., D'Angelo, D., & Bombard, J. M. (2009, May 29). Trends in smoking before, during, and after pregnancy—Pregnancy Risk Assessment Monitoring System (PRAMS), United States, 31 Sites, 2000–2005. *Morbidity and Mortality Weekly Report, 58* (No. SS-4).

Torges, C. M., Stewart, A. J., & Miner-Rubino, K. (2005). Personality after the prime of life: Men and women coming to terms with regrets. *Journal of Research in Personality, 39,* 148–165.

Tornstam, L. (2000). Transcendence in later life. *Generations, 23*(10), 10–14.

Tornstam, L. (2011). Maturing into gerotranscendence. *Journal of TransPersonal Psychology, 43,* 166–180.

Toro-Morn, M., & Sprecher, S. (2003). A cross-cultural comparison of mate preferences among university students: The United States vs. the People's Republic of China (PRC). *Journal of Comparative Family Studies, 34,* 151–170.

Torrance, E. P. (1988). The nature of creativity as manifest in its testing. In R. J. Sternberg (Ed.), *The nature of creativity: Contemporary psychological perspectives* (pp. 43–75). New York: Cambridge University Press.

Tottenham, N., Hare, T. A., Millner, A., Gilhooly, T., Zevin, J. D., & Casey, B. J. (2011). Elevated amygdala response to faces following early deprivation. *Developmental Science, 14,* 190–204.

Touwslager, R. N., Gielen, M., Derom, C., Mulder, A. L., Gerver, W. J., Zimmermann, L. J., et al. (2011). Determinants of infant growth in four age windows: A twin study. *Journal of Pediatrics, 158,* 566–572.

Tracy, J. L., Robins, R. W., & Lagattuta, K. H. (2005). Can children recognize pride? *Emotion, 5,* 251–257.

Trafford, A. (2004). *My time: Making the most of the rest of your life.* New York: Basic Books.

Trappe, S. (2007). Marathon runners: How do they age? *Sports Medicine, 37,* 302–305.

Trautner, H. M., Gervai, J., & Nemeth, R. (2003). Appearance–reality distinction and development of gender constancy understanding in children. *International Journal of Behavioral Development, 27,* 275–283.

Trautner, H. M., Ruble, D. N., Cyphers, L., Kirsten, B., Behrendt, R., & Hartmann, P. (2005). Rigidity and flexibility of gender stereotypes in childhood: Developmental or differential? *Infant and Child Development, 14,* 365–381.

Treasure, J., & Schmidt, U. (2005). Anorexia nervosa. *Clinical Evidence, 13,* 1148–1157.

Trehub, S. E. (2001). Musical predispositions in infancy. *Annals of the New York Academy of Sciences, 930,* 1–16.

Tremblay, L., & Frigon, J.-Y. (2005). Precocious puberty in adolescent girls: A biomarker of later psychosocial adjustment problems. *Child Psychiatry and Human Development, 36,* 73–94.

Tremblay, R. E. (2000). The development of aggressive behaviour during childhood: What have we learned in the past century? *International Journal of Behavioral Development, 24,* 129–141.

Tremblay, R. E., Japel, C., Perusse, D., Voivin, M., Zoccolillo, M., Montplaisir, J., & McDuff, P. (1999). The search for the age of "onset" of physical aggression: Rousseau and Bandura revisited. *Criminal Behavior and Mental Health, 9,* 8–23.

Trentacosta, C. J., & Shaw, D. S. (2009). Emotional self-regulation, peer rejection, and antisocial behavior: Developmental associations from early childhood to early adolescence. *Journal of Applied Developmental Psychology, 30,* 356–365.

Triandis, H. C. (1995). *Individualism and collectivism.* Boulder, CO: Westview Press.

Triandis, H. C. (2005). Issues in individualism and collectivism research. In R. M. Sorrentino, D. Cohen, J. M. Olson, & M. P. Zanna (Eds.), *Culture and social behavior: The Ontario Symposium* (Vol. 10, pp. 207–225). Mahwah, NJ: Erlbaum.

Triandis, H. C. (2007). Culture and psychology: A history of the study of their relationship. In S. Kitayama & D. Cohen (Eds.), *Handbook of cultural psychology* (pp. 59–76). New York: Guilford.

Trocmé, N., & Wolfe, D. (2002). *Child maltreatment in Canada: The Canadian Incidence Study of Reported Child Abuse and Neglect.* Retrieved from www.hc-sc.gc.ca/pphb-dgspsp/cm-vee

Tronick, E., Morelli, G., & Ivey, P. (1992). The Efe forager infant and toddler's pattern of social relationships: Multiple and simultaneous. *Developmental Psychology, 28,* 568–577.

Tronick, E. Z., Thomas, R. B., & Daltabuit, M. (1994). The Quechua manta pouch: A caretaking practice for buffering the Peruvian infant against the multiple stressors of high altitude. *Child Development, 65,* 1005–1013.

Troop-Gordon, W., & Asher, S. R. (2005). Modifications in children's goals when encountering obstacles to conflict resolution. *Child Development, 76,* 568–582.

Troseth, G. L., Saylor, M. M., & Archer, A. H. (2006). Young children's use of video as a source of socially relevant information. *Child Development, 77,* 786–799.

Troyer, A. K., Häfliger, A., Cadieux, M. J., & Craik, F. I. M. (2006). Name and face learning in older adults: Effects of level of processing, self-generation, and intention to learn. *Journal of Gerontology, 61B,* P67–P74.

Trudel, G., Villeneuve, V., Anderson, A., & Pilon, G. (2008). Sexual and marital aspects of old age: An update. *Sexual and Relationship Therapy, 23,* 161–169.

True, M. M., Pisani, L., & Oumar, F. (2001). Infant–mother attachment among the Dogon of Mali. *Child Development, 72,* 1451–1466.

Trusty, J. (1999). Effects of eighth-grade parental involvement on late adolescents' educational expectations. *Journal of Research and Development in Education, 32,* 224–233.

Trzesniewski, K. H., & Donnellan, M. B. (2009). Reevaluating the evidence for increasingly positive self-views among high school students: More evidence for consistency across generations. *Psychological Science, 20,* 920–922.

Trzeniewski, K. H., & Donnellan, M. B. (2010). Rethinking "generation me": A study of cohort effects from 1976–2006. *Perspectives on Psychological Science, 5,* 58–75.

Trzesniewski, K. H., Donnellan, M. B., & Robins, R. W. (2003). Stability of self-esteem across the life span. *Journal of Personality and Social Psychology, 84,* 205–220.

Tsang, P. S., & Shaner, T. L. (1998). Age, attention, expertise, and time-sharing performance. *Psychology and Aging, 13,* 323–347.

Tsujimoto, S. (2008). The prefrontal cortex: Functional neural development during early childhood. *Neuroscientist, 14,* 345–358.

Tucker, C. J., McHale, S. M., & Crouter, A. C. (2001). Conditions of sibling support in adolescence. *Journal of Family Psychology, 15,* 254–271.

Tucker, C. J., McHale, S. M., & Crouter, A. C. (2003). Dimensions of mothers' and fathers' differential treatment of siblings: Links with adolescents' sex-typed personal qualities. *Family Relations, 52,* 82–89.

Turati, C. (2004). Why faces are not special to newborns: An account of the face preference. *Current Directions in Psychological Science, 13,* 5–8.

Turesson, C., & Matteson, E. L. (2006). Genetics of rheumatoid arthritis. *Mayo Clinic Proceedings, 81,* 94–101.

Turiel, E. (2006). The development of morality. In N. Eisenberg (Ed.), *Handbook of child psychology: Vol. 3. Social, emotional, and personality development* (6th ed., pp. 789–857). Hoboken, NJ: Wiley.

Turiel, E., & Killen, M. (2010). Taking emotions seriously: The role of emotions in moral development. In W. F. Arsenio & E. A. Lemerise (Eds.), *Emotions, aggression, and morality in children: Bridging development and psychopathology* (pp. 33–52). Washington, DC: American Psychological Association.

Turnbull, K. P., Anthony, A. B., Justice, L., & Bowles, R. (2009). Preschoolers' exposure to language stimulation in classrooms serving at-risk children: The contribution of group size and activity context. *Early Education and Development, 20,* 53–79.

Turnbull, M., Hart, D., & Lapkin, S. (2003). Grade 6 French immersion students' performance on large-scale reading, writing, and mathematics tests: Building explanations. *Alberta Journal of Educational Research, 49,* 6–23.

Turner, B. F. (1982). Sex-related differences in aging. In B. B. Wolman (Ed.), *Handbook of developmental psychology* (pp. 912–936). Englewood Cliffs, NJ: Prentice-Hall.

Turner, L. B. (2011). A meta-analysis of fat intake, reproduction, and breast cancer risk: An evolutionary perspective. *American Journal of Human Biology, 23,* 601–608.

Turner, P. J., & Gervai, J. (1995). A multidimensional study of gender typing in preschool children and their parents: Personality, attitudes, preferences, behavior, and cultural differences. *British Journal of Developmental Psychology, 11*, 323–342.

Turner, R. N., Hewstone, M., & Voci, A. (2007). Reducing explicit and implicit outgroup prejudice via direct and extended contact: The mediating role of self-disclosure and intergroup anxiety. *Journal of Personality and Social Psychology, 93*, 369–388.

Tuyen, J. M., & Bisgard, K. (2003). *Community setting: Pertussis outbreak.* Atlanta, GA: Centers for Disease Control and Prevention. Retrieved from www.cdc .gov/pertussis/outbreaks/guide/downloads/ chapter-10.pdf

Twenge, J. M. (1997). Changes in masculine and feminine traits over time: A meta-analysis. *Sex Roles, 36*, 305–325.

Twenge, J. M. (2001). Changes in women's assertiveness in response to status and roles: A cross-temporal meta-analysis, 1931–1993. *Journal of Personality and Social Psychology, 81*, 133–145.

Twenge, J. M., & Campbell, W. K. (2001). Age and birth cohort differences in self-esteem: A crosstemporal meta-analysis. *Personality and Social Psychology Review, 5*, 321–344.

Twenge, J. M., Campbell, W. K., & Freeman, E. C. (2012). Generational differences in young adults' life goals, concern for others, and civic orientation, 1966–2009. *Journal of Personality and Social Psychology, 102*, 1045–1062.

Twenge, J. M., & Crocker, J. (2002). Race and self-esteem: Meta-analyses comparing whites, blacks, Hispanics, Asians, and America Indians and comment on Gray-Little and Hafdahl (2000). *Psychological Bulletin, 128*, 371–408.

Tzuriel, D., & Kaufman, R. (1999). Mediated learning and cognitive modifiability: Dynamic assessment of young Ethiopian immigrant children to Israel. *Journal of Cross-Cultural Psychology, 30*, 359–380.

U

Uauy, R., Kain, J., Mericq, V., Rojas, J., & Corvalán, C. (2008). Nutrition, child growth, and chronic disease prevention. *Annals of Medicine, 40*, 11–20.

Uchino, B. N. (2009). Understanding the links between social support and physical health. *Perspectives on Psychological Science, 4*, 236–255.

Udechuku, A., Nguyen, T., Hill, R., & Szego, K. (2010). Antidepressants in pregnancy: A systematic review. *Australian and New Zealand Journal of Psychiatry, 44*, 978–996.

Uhlenberg, P., & Hammill, B. G. (1998). Frequency of grandparent contact with grandchild sets: Six factors that make a difference. *Gerontologist, 38*, 276–285.

Ukrainetz, T. A., Justice, L. M., Kaderavek, J. N., Eisenberg, S. L., Gillam, R., & Harm, H. M. (2005). The development of expressive elaboration in fictional narratives. *Journal of Speech, Language, and Hearing Research, 48*, 1363–1377.

Umana-Taylor, A. J., & Alfaro, E. C. (2006). Ethnic identity among U.S. Latino adolescents: Measurement and implications for well-being. In F. A. Villarruel & T. Luster (Eds.), *The crisis in youth mental health: Critical issues and effective programs: Vol. 2. Disorders in adolescence* (pp. 195–211). Westport, CT: Praeger.

Umana-Taylor, A. J., & Updegraff, K. A. (2007). Latino adolescents' mental health: Exploring the interrelations among discrimination, ethnic identity, cultural orientation, self-esteem, and depressive symptoms. *Journal of Adolescence, 30*, 549–567.

Underhill, K., Montgomery, P., & Operario, D. (2007). Sexual abstinence only programmes to prevent HIV infection in high-income countries: Systematic review. *British Medical Journal, 335*, 248.

Underwood, M. K. (2003). *Social aggression among girls.* New York: Guilford.

UNICEF (United Nations Children's Fund). (2007). *An overview of child well-being in rich countries, Innocenti Report Card 7.* Florence, Italy: UNICEF Innocenti Research Centre.

UNICEF (United Nations Children's Fund). (2009). *Infant and young child feeding 2000–2007.* Retrieved from www.childinfo.org/breastfeeding_countrydata .php

UNICEF (United Nations Children's Fund). (2010a). *Children and AIDS: Fifth stocktaking report.* New York: United Nations.

UNICEF (United Nations Children's Fund). (2010b). *Young champions for education: A progress review.* Retrieved from www.ungei.org/resources/files/ Young_Champions_Evaluation_7_Jan.pdf

UNICEF (United Nations Children's Fund). (2011). *Children in conflict and emergencies.* Retrieved from www.unicef.org/protection/armedconflict.html

United Nations. (2011). *World population prospects: The 2011 revision. Population database.* Retrieved from esa.un.org/wpp/unpp/panel_population.htm

Uotinen, V., Rantanen, T., Suutama, T., & Ruoppila, I. (2006). Change in subjective age among older people over an eight-year follow-up: "Getting older and feeling younger"? *Experimental Aging Research, 32*, 381–393.

U.S. Census Bureau. (2012a). International database. Retrieved from sasweb.ssd.census.gov/idb/ranks .html

U.S. Census Bureau. (2012b). *Statistical abstract of the United States* (131st ed.). Washington, DC: U.S. Government Printing Office.

U.S. Census Bureau. (2013). *Statistical abstract of the United States* (132nd ed.). Washington, DC: U.S. Government Printing Office.

U.S. Department of Agriculture. (2011a). *Food security in the United States: Key statistics and graphics.* Retrieved from www.ers.usda.gov/Briefing/ FoodSecurity/stats_graphs.htm

U.S. Department of Agriculture. (2011b). *WIC: The Special Supplemental Nutrition Program for Women, Infants, and Children.* Nutrition Program Facts. Retrieved from www.fns.usda.gov/wic/wic-fact-sheet.pdf

U.S. Department of Agriculture. (2012). *Expenditures on children by families, 2011.* Retrieved from www .cnpp.usda.gov/Publications/CRC/crc2011.pdf

U.S. Department of Education. (2007). *The Nation's Report Card: Mathematics 2007.* Retrieved from nces.ed.gov/pubsearch/pubsinfo.asp?pubid=2007494

U.S. Department of Education. (2009). *The Nation's Report Card: Mathematics 2009.* Retrieved from nces.ed.gov/nationsreportcard/pdf/main2009/ 2010451.pdf

U.S. Department of Education. (2010). *The nation's report card: Reading 2009.* Retrieved from nces.ed .gov/pubsearch/pubsinfo.asp?pubid=2010458

U.S. Department of Education. (2012a). *The condition of education 2012.* Retrieved from nces.ed.gov/ pubsearch/pubsinfo.asp?pubid=2012045

U.S. Department of Education. (2012b). *Digest of education statistics: 2011.* Washington, DC: U.S. Government Printing Office.

U.S. Department of Health and Human Services. (2010a). Births: Final data for 2008. *National Vital Statistics Reports, 59*(1).

U.S. Department of Health and Human Services. (2010b). *Breastfeeding.* Retrieved from www .womenshealth.gov/breastfeeding/index.cfm

U.S. Department of Health and Human Services. (2010c). *Drugs, brains, and behavior: The science of addiction.* Bethesda, MD: National Institute of Drug Abuse.

U.S. Department of Health and Human Services. (2010d). *Head Start Impact Study: Final report.* Washington, DC: U.S. Government Printing Office.

U.S. Department of Health and Human Services. (2010e). National, state, and local vaccination coverage among children aged 19–35 months— United States, 2009. *Morbidity and Mortality Weekly Report, 59*, 1171–1177.

U.S. Department of Health and Human Services. (2011a). *Births: Preliminary data for 2010.* Retrieved from www.cdc.gov/nchs/data/nvsr/ nvsr60/nvsr60_02.pdf

U.S. Department of Health and Human Services. (2011b). *Child maltreatment 2010.* Retrieved from www.acf.hhs.gov/programs/cb/resource/child-maltreatment-2010

U.S. Department of Health and Human Services. (2011c). *Health, United States 2010: With special feature on death and dying.* Washington, DC: U.S. Government Printing Office.

U.S. Department of Health and Human Services. (2011d). *Results from the 2010 National Survey on Drug Use and Health: Summary of national findings.* Rockville, MD: Substance Abuse and Mental Health Services Administration.

U.S. Department of Health and Human Services. (2011e). *The Surgeon General's call to action to prevent and decrease overweight and obesity: Overweight children and adolescents.* Retrieved from www.surgeongeneral.gov/library/calls/obesity/ fact_adolescents.html

U.S. Department of Health and Human Services. (2012a). *Facts about Down syndrome.* Retrieved from www.education.com/reference/article/ Ref_Facts_About_Down

U.S. Department of Health and Human Services. (2012b). *Key statistics from the National Survey of Family Growth: Impaired fecundity.* Retrieved from www.cdc.gov/nchs/nsfg/abc_list_i.htm#impaired

U.S. Department of Health and Human Services. (2012c). *Morbidity and mortality: 2012 chart book on cardiovascular, lung and blood diseases.* Bethesda, MD: Author.

U.S. Department of Health and Human Services. (2012d). *Older persons' health: Health care utilization.* Retrieved from www.cdc.gov/nchs/ fastats/older_americans.htm

U.S. Department of Health and Human Services. (2012e). *A profile of older Americans 2012: Key indicators of well-being.* Washington, DC: U.S. Government Printing Office.

U.S. Department of Health and Human Services. (2012f). Youth Risk Behavior Surveillance—United States, 2011. *Morbidity and Mortality Weekly Report, 61*(No. 4). Retrieved from www.cdc.gov/mmwr/ pdf/ss/ss6104.pdf

U.S. Department of Justice. (2010). *Crime in the United States, 2009.* Retrieved from www2.fbi.gov/ucr/ cius2009

U.S. Department of Transportation. (2012). *Traffic safety facts: Research note. 2011 motor vehicle crashes: Overview.* Retrieved from www-nrd.nhtsa .dot.gov/Pubs/811701.pdf

U.S. Living Will Registry. (2005). *Advance directive forms.* Retrieved from uslwr.com/formslist.shtm

Usher-Seriki, K. K., Bynum, M. S., & Callands, T. A. (2008). Mother–daughter communication about sex and sexual intercourse among middle- to upper-class African American girls. *Journal of Family Issues, 29*, 901–917.

Usta, I. M., & Nassar, A. H. (2008). Advanced maternal age. Part I: Obstetric complications. *American Journal of Perinatology, 25*, 521–534.

Utz, R. L., Carr, D., Nesse, R., & Wortman, C. B. (2002). The effect of widowhood on older adults' social participation: An evaluation of activity, disengagement, and continuity theories. *Gerontologist, 42*, 522–533.

V

Vacha-Haase, T., Hill, R. D., & Bermingham, D. W. (2012). Aging theory and research. In N. A. Fouad, J. A. Carter, & L. M. Subich (Eds.), *APA handbook of counseling psychology: Vol. 1. Theories, research, and methods* (pp. 491–505). Washington, DC: American Psychological Association.

Vaillancourt, T., Brittain, H., Bennett, L., Arnocky, S., McDougall, P., Hymel, S., et al. (2010a). Places to avoid: Population-based study of student reports of unsafe and high bullying areas at school. *Canadian Journal of School Psychology, 25*, 40–54.

Vaillancourt, T., Clinton, J., McDougall, P., Schmidt, L. A., & Hymel, S. (2010b). The neurobiology of peer victimization and rejection. In S. Jimerson, S. M. Swearer, & D. L. Espelage (Eds.), *Handbook of bullying in schools: An international perspective* (pp. 293–304). New York: Routledge.

Vaillancourt, T., & Hymel, S. (2006). Aggression and social status: The moderating roles of sex and peer-valued characteristics. *Aggressive Behavior, 32*, 396–408.

Vaillancourt, T., McDougall, P., Hymel, S., & Sunderani, S. (2010c). Respect or fear? The relationship between power and bullying behavior. In S. R. Jimerson, S. M. Swearer, & D. L. Espelage (Eds.), *Handbook of bullying in schools: An international perspective* (pp. 211–222). New York: Routledge.

Vaillant, G. E. (1977). *Adaptation to life*. Boston: Little, Brown.

Vaillant, G. E. (2002). *Aging well*. Boston: Little, Brown.

Vaillant, G. E., & Koury, S. H. (1994). Late midlife development. In G. H. Pollock & S. I. Greenspan (Eds.), *The course of life* (pp. 1–22). Madison, CT: International Universities Press.

Vaillant, G. E., & Mukamal, K. (2001). Successful aging. *American Journal of Psychiatry, 158*, 839–847.

Vaillant, G. E., & Vaillant, C. O. (1990). Determinants and consequences of creativity in a cohort of gifted women. *Psychology of Women Quarterly, 14*, 607–616.

Vakil, E., Blachstein, H., Sheinman, M., & Greenstein, Y. (2009). Developmental changes in attention tests norms: Implications for the structure of attention. *Child Neuropsychology, 15*, 21–39.

Valdés, G. (1998). The world outside and inside schools: Language and immigrant children. *Educational Researcher, 27*(6), 4–18.

Valentine, J. C., DuBois, D. L., & Cooper, H. (2004). The relation between self-beliefs and academic achievement: A meta-analytic review. *Educational Psychologist, 39*, 111–133.

Valian, V. (1999). Input and language acquisition. In W. C. Ritchie & T. K. Bhatia (Eds.), *Handbook of child language acquisition* (pp. 497–530). San Diego: Academic Press.

Valiente, C., Eisenberg, N., Fabes, R. A., Shepard, S. A., Cumberland, A., & Losoya, S. H. (2004). Prediction of children's empathy-related responding from their effortful control and parents' expressivity. *Developmental Psychology, 40*, 911–926.

Valiente, C., Lemery-Chalfant, K., Swanson, J., & Reiser, M. (2008). Prediction of children's academic competence from their effortful control, relationships, and classroom participation. *Journal of Educational Psychology, 100*, 67–77.

Valkenburg, P. M., & Peter, J. (2007a). Internet communication and its relation to well-being: Identifying some underlying mechanisms. *Media Psychology, 9*, 43–58.

Valkenburg, P. M., & Peter, J. (2007b). Preadolescents' and adolescents' online communication and their closeness to friends. *Developmental Psychology, 43*, 267–277.

Valkenburg, P. M., & Peter, J. (2009). Social consequences of the Internet for adolescents: A decade of research. *Current Directions in Psychological Science, 18*, 1–5.

Valkenburg, P. M., & Peter, J. (2011). Online communication among adolescents: An integrated model of its attraction, opportunities, and risks. *Journal of Adolescent Health, 48*, 121–127.

van Aken, C., Junger, M., Verhoeven, M., van Aken, M. A. G., & Dekovi?, M. (2007). The interactive effects of temperament and maternal parenting on toddlers' externalizing behaviours. *Infant and Child Development, 16*, 553–572.

van Asselt, D. (2006). Advance directives: Prerequisites and usefulness. *Zeitschrift für Gerontologie und Geriatrie, 39*, 371–375.

van Baarsen, B. (2002). Theories on coping with loss: The impact of social support and self-esteem on adjustment to emotional and social loneliness following a partner's death in later life. *Journal of Gerontology, 57B*, S33–S42.

Van Cleave, J., Gortmaker, S. L., & Perrin, J. M. (2010). Dynamics of obesity and chronic health conditions among children and youth. *Journal of the American Medical Association, 303*, 623–630.

Vandell, D. L., Belsky, J., Burchinal, M., Steinberg, L., Vandergrift, N., & NICHD Early Child Care Research Network. (2010). Do effects of early child care extend to age 15 years? Results from the NICHD Study of Early Child Care and Youth Development. *Child Development, 81*, 737–756.

Vandell, D. L., & Posner, J. K. (1999). Conceptualization and measurement of children's after-school environments. In S. L. Friedman & T. D. Wachs (Eds.), *Measuring environment across the life span* (pp. 167–196). Washington, DC: American Psychological Association.

Vandell, D. L., Reisner, E. R., & Pierce, K. M. (2007). *Outcomes linked to high-quality after-school programs: Longitudinal findings from the Study of Promising After-School Programs*. Retrieved from www.gse.uci .edu/childcare/pdf/afterschool/PP%20Longitudinal %20Findings%20Final%20Report.pdf

Vandell, D. L., Reisner, E. R., Pierce, K. M., Brown, B. B., Lee, D., Bolt, D., & Pechman, E. M. (2006). *The study of promising after-school programs: Examination of longer term outcomes after two years of program experiences*. Madison, WI: University of Wisconsin. Retrieved from www.wcer.wisc.edu/ childcare/statements.html

van den Akker, A. L. Deković, M., Prinzie, P., & Asscher, J. J. (2010). Toddlers' temperament profiles: Stability and relations to negative and positive parenting. *Journal of Abnormal Child Psychology, 38*, 485–495.

Van den Bergh, B. R. H., & De Rycke, L. (2003). Measuring the multidimensional self-concept and global self-worth of 6- to 8-year-olds. *Journal of Genetic Psychology, 164*, 201–225.

Van den Bergh, B. R. H., Van Calster, B., Smits, T., Van Huffel, S., & Lagae, L. (2008). Antenatal maternal anxiety is related to HPA-axis dysregulation and self-reported depressive symptoms in adolescence: A prospective study on the fetal origins of depressed mood. *Neuropsychopharmacology, 33*, 536–545.

van den Dries, L., Juffer, F., van IJzendoorn, M. H., & Bakermans-Kranenburg, M. J. (2009). Fostering security? A meta-analysis of attachment in adopted children. *Children and Youth Services Review, 31*, 410–421.

Vanderbilt-Adriance, E., & Shaw, D. S. (2008). Protective factors and the development of resilience in the context of neighborhood disadvantage. *Journal of Abnormal Child Psychology, 36*, 887–901.

van der Wal, M. F., van Eijsden, M., & Bonsel, G. J. (2007). Stress and emotional problems during pregnancy and excessive infant crying. *Developmental and Behavioral Pediatrics, 28*, 431–437.

Van de Vijver, P. J. R., Hofer, J., & Chasiotis, A. (2010). Methodology. In M. H. Bornstein (Ed.), *Handbook of cultural developmental science* (pp. 21–37). New York: Psychology Press.

Vandewater, E. A., & Stewart, A. J. (1997). Women's career commitment patterns and personality development. In M. E. Lachman & J. B. James (Eds.), *Multiple paths of midlife development* (pp. 375–410). Chicago: University of Chicago Press.

Van Eyk, J., & Dunn, M. J. (Eds.). (2008). *Clinical proteomics*. Weinheim, Germany: Wiley-VCH.

Van Eyken, E., Van Camp, G., & Van Laer, L. (2007). The complexity of age-related hearing impairment: Contributing environmental and genetic factors. *Audiology and Neurotology, 12*, 345–358.

Van Hiel, A., & Vansteenkiste, M. (2009). Ambitions fulfilled? The effects of intrinsic and extrinsic goal attainment on older adults' ego integrity and death attitudes. *International Journal of Aging and Human Development, 68*, 27–51.

Van Hulle, C. A., Goldsmith, H. H., & Lemery, K. S. (2004). Genetic, environmental, and gender effects on individual differences in toddler expressive language. *Journal of Speech, Language, and Hearing Research, 47*, 904–912.

van IJzendoorn, M. H. (1995). Adult attachment representations, parental responsiveness, and infant attachment: A meta-analysis on the predictive validity of the Adult Attachment Interview. *Psychological Bulletin, 117*, 387–403.

van IJzendoorn, M. H., & Bakermans-Kranenburg, M. J. (2006). DRD4 7-repeat polymorphism moderates the association between maternal unresolved loss or trauma and infant disorganization. *Attachment and Human Development, 8*, 291–307.

van IJzendoorn, M. H., Juffer, F., & Poelhuis, C. W. K. (2005). Adoption and cognitive development: A meta-analytic comparison of adopted and nonadopted children's IQ and school performance. *Psychological Bulletin, 131*, 301–316.

van IJzendoorn, M. H., & Kroonenberg, P. M. (1988). Cross-cultural patterns of attachment: A meta-analysis of the Strange Situation. *Child Development, 59*, 147–156.

van IJzendoorn, M. H., & Sagi-Schwartz, A. (2008). Cross-cultural patterns of attachment: Universal and contextual dimensions. In J. Cassidy & P. R. Shaver (Eds.), *Handbook of attachment* (2nd ed., pp. 880–905). New York: Guilford.

van IJzendoorn, M. H., Schuengel, C., & Bakermans-Kranenburg, M. J. (1999). Disorganized attachment in early childhood: Meta-analysis of precursors, concomitants, and sequelae. *Development and Psychopathology, 11*, 225–249.

van IJzendoorn, M. H., Vereijken, C. M. J. L., Bakermans-Kranenburg, M. J., & Riksen-Walraven, J. M. (2004). Assessing attachment security with the Attachment Q Sort: Meta-analytic evidence for the validity of the Observer AQS. *Child Development, 75*, 1188–1213.

van Solinge, H., & Henkens, K. (2008). Adjustment to and satisfaction with retirement: Two of a kind? *Psychology and Aging, 23*, 422–434.

van Tol, D., Rietjens, J., & van der Heide, A. (2010). Judgment of unbearable suffering and willingness to grant a euthanasia request by Dutch general practitioners. *Health Policy, 97*, 166–172.

Van Volkom, M. (2006). Sibling relationships in middle and older adulthood: A review of the literature. *Marriage and Family Review, 40*, 151–170.

Varendi, H., & Porter, R. H. (2001). Breast odour as the only maternal stimulus elicits crawling toward the odour source. *Acta Paediatrica, 90*, 372–375.

Varnhagen, C. (2007). Children and the Web. In J. Gackenbach (Ed.), *Psychology and the Internet* (2nd ed., pp, 37–54). Amsterdam: Elsevier.

Vartanian, L. R., & Powlishta, K. K. (1996). A longitudinal examination of the social-cognitive foundations of adolescent egocentrism. *Journal of Early Adolescence, 16*, 157–178.

Vaughn, B. E., Bost, K. K., & van IJzendoorn, M. H. (2008). Attachment and temperament. In J. Cassidy & P. R. Shaver (Eds.), *Handbook of attachment: Theory, research, and clinical applications* (2nd ed., pp. 192–216). New York: Guilford.

Vaughn, B. E., Kopp, C. B., & Krakow, J. B. (1984). The emergence and consolidation of self-control from eighteen to thirty months of age: Normative trends and individual differences. *Child Development, 55,* 990–1004.

Vazsonyi, A. T., Hibbert, J. R., & Snider, J. B. (2003). Exotic enterprise no more? Adolescent reports of family and parenting processes from youth in four countries. *Journal of Research on Adolescence, 13,* 129–160.

Veenstra, R., Lindenberg, S., Munniksma, A., & Dijkstra, J. K. (2010). The complex relation between bullying, victimization, acceptance, and rejection: Giving special attention to status, affection, and sex differences. *Child Development, 81,* 480–486.

Velderman, M. K., Bakermans-Kranenburg, M. J., Juffer, F., & van IJzendoorn, M. H. (2006). Effects of attachment-based interventions on maternal sensitivity and infant attachment: Differential susceptibility of highly reactive infants. *Journal of Family Psychology, 20,* 266–274.

Velleman, R. D. B., Templeton, L. J., & Copello, A. G. (2005). The role of the family in preventing and intervening with substance use and misuse: A comprehensive review of family interventions, with a focus on young people. *Drug and Alcohol Review, 24,* 93–109.

Venet, M., & Markovits, H. (2001). Understanding uncertainty with abstract conditional premises. *Merrill-Palmer Quarterly, 47,* 74–99.

Venezia, M., Messinger, D. S., Thorp, D., & Mundy, P. (2004). The development of anticipatory smiling. *Infancy, 6,* 397–406.

Veneziano, R. A. (2003). The importance of paternal warmth. *Cross-Cultural Research, 37,* 265–281.

Ventura, S. J., Curtin, S. C., & Abma, J. C. (2012). Estimated pregnancy rates and rates of pregnancy outcomes for the United States, 1990–2008. *National Vital Statistics Reports, 60*(7). Retrieved from www.cdc.gov/nchs/data/nvsr/nvsr60/nvsr60_07.pdf

Verhaeghen, P. (2012). Age-related differences in working-memory functioning and cognitive control. In M. Naveh-Benjamin & N. Ohta (Eds.), *Memory and aging: Current issues and future directions* (pp. 3–30). New York: Psychology Press.

Verhaeghen, P., & Cerella, J. (2008). Everything we know about aging and response times: A meta-analytic integration. In S. M. Hofer & D. F. Alwin (Eds.), *Handbook of cognitive aging: Interdisciplinary perspectives* (pp. 134–150). Thousand Oaks, CA: Sage.

Verhulst, F. C. (2008). International adoption and mental health: Long-term behavioral outcome. In M. E. Garralda & J.-P. Raynaud (Eds.), *Culture and conflict and adolescent mental health* (pp. 83–105). Lanham, MD: Jason Aronson.

Veríssimo, M., & Salvaterra, F. (2006). Maternal secure-base scripts and children's attachment security in an adopted sample. *Attachment and Human Development, 8,* 261–273.

Vernon-Feagans, L., Pancsofar, N., Willoughby, M., Odom, E., Quade, A., & Cox, M. (2008). Predictors of maternal language to infants during a picture book task in the home: Family SES, child characteristics and the parenting environment. *Journal of Applied Developmental Psychology, 29,* 213–226.

Vesco, K. K., Haney, E. M., Humphrey, L., Fu, R., & Nelson, H. D. (2007). Influence of menopause on mood: A systematic review of cohort studies. *Climacteric, 10,* 448–465.

Vidaeff, A. C., Carroll, M. A., & Ramin, S. M. (2005). Acute hypertensive emergencies in pregnancy. *Critical Care Medicine, 33,* S307–S312.

Vinden, P. G. (1996). Junín Quechua children's understanding of mind. *Child Development, 67,* 1707–1716.

Vinden, P. G. (2002). Understanding minds and evidence for belief: A study of Mofu children in Cameroon.

International Journal of Behavioral Development, 26, 445–452.

Visher, E. B., Visher, J. S., & Pasley, K. (2003). Remarriage, families and stepparenting. In F. Walsh (Ed.), *Normal family processes* (pp. 153–175). New York: Guilford.

Vitali, P., Migliaccio, R., Agosta, F., Rosen, H. J., & Geschwind, M. D. (2008). Neuroimaging in dementia. *Seminars in Neurology, 28,* 467–483.

Vitrup, B., & Holden, G. W. (2010). Children's assessments of corporal punishment and other disciplinary practices: The role of age, race, SES, and exposure to spanking. *Journal of Applied Developmental Psychology, 31,* 211–220.

Vivanti, G., Nadig, A., Ozonoff, S., & Rogers, S. J. (2008). What do children with autism attend to during imitation tasks? *Journal of Experimental Psychology, 101,* 186–205.

Vogels, N., Diepvens, K., & Westerterp-Plantenga, M. S. (2005). Predictors of long-term weight maintenance. *Obesity Research, 13,* 2162–2168.

Volling, B. L. (2001). Early attachment relationships as predictors of preschool children's emotion regulation with a distressed sibling. *Early Education and Development, 12,* 185–207.

Volling, B. L., & Belsky, J. (1992). Contribution of mother–child and father–child relationships to the quality of sibling interaction: A longitudinal study. *Child Development, 63,* 1209–1222.

Volling, B. L., McElwain, N. L., & Miller, A. L. (2002). Emotion regulation in context: The jealousy complex between young siblings and its relations with child and family characteristics. *Child Development, 73,* 581–600.

Volling, B. L., McElwain, N. L., Notaro, P. C., & Herrera, C. (2002). Parents' emotional availability and infant emotional competence: Predictors of parent–infant attachment and emerging self-regulation. *Journal of Family Psychology, 16,* 447–465.

Vondra, J. I., Shaw, D. S., Searingen, L., Cohen, M., & Owens, E. B. (2001). Attachment stability and emotional and behavioral regulation from infancy to preschool age. *Development and Psychopathology, 13,* 13–33.

von Hofsten, C. (2004). An action perspective on motor development. *Trends in Cognitive Sciences, 8,* 266–272.

Vouloumanos, A., & Werker, J. F. (2004). Tuned to the signal: The privileged status of speech for young infants. *Developmental Science, 7,* 270–276.

Vuoksimaa, E., Koskenvuo, M., Rose, R. J., & Kaprio, J. (2009). Origins of handedness: A nationwide study of 30,1671 adults. *Neuropsychologia, 47,* 1294–301.

Vygotsky, L. S. (1978). *Mind in society: The development of higher mental processes.* Cambridge, MA: Harvard University Press. (Original works published 1930, 1933, and 1935)

Vygotsky, L. S. (1987). Thinking and speech. In R. W. Rieber, & A. S. Carton (Eds.), & N. Minick (Trans.), *The collected works of L. S. Vygotsky: Vol. 1. Problems of general psychology* (pp. 37–285). New York: Plenum. (Original work published 1934)

W

Waber, D. P. (2010). *Rethinking learning disabilities.* New York: Guilford.

Wachs, T. D., & Bates, J. E. (2001). Temperament. In G. Bremner & A. Fogel (Eds.), *Blackwell handbook of infant development* (pp. 465–501). Oxford, UK: Blackwell.

Wadsworth, M. E., & Santiago, C. D. (2008). Risk and resiliency processes in ethnically diverse families in poverty. *Journal of Family Psychology, 22,* 399–410.

Wagenaar, K., van Wessenbruch, M. M., van Leeuwen, F. E., Cohen-Kettenis, P. T., Delemarre-van de Waal, H. A., Schats, R., et al. (2011). Self-reported behavioral and socioemotional functioning of

11- to 18-year-old adolescents conceived by in vitro fertilization. *Fertility and Sterility, 95,* 611–616.

Wainryb, C. (1997). The mismeasure of diversity: Reflections on the study of cross-cultural differences. In H. D. Saltzstein (Ed.), *New directions for child development* (No. 76, pp. 51–65). San Francisco: Jossey-Bass.

Waite, L., & Das, A. (2013). Families, social life, and well-being at older ages. *Demography, 47,* S87–S109.

Waite, L. J., Laumann, E. O., Das, A., & Schumm, L. P. (2009). Sexuality: Measures of partnerships, practices, attitudes, and problems in the National Social Life, Health, and Aging Study. *Journal of Gerontology, 64B,* i56–i66.

Wakeley, A., Rivera, S., & Langer, J. (2000). Can young infants add and subtract? *Child Development, 71,* 1477–1720.

Walberg, H. J. (1986). Synthesis of research on teaching. In M. C. Wittrock (Ed.), *Handbook of research on teaching* (3rd ed., pp. 214–229). New York: Macmillan.

Waldfogel, J. (2001). International policies toward parental leave and child care. *Future of Children 11,* 52–61.

Waldfogel, J., Craigie, T. A., & Brooks-Gunn, J. (2010). Fragile families and child well-being. *Future of Children, 20,* 87–112.

Waldman, I. D., Rowe, D. C., Abramowitz, A., Kozel, S. T., Mohr, J. H., & Sherman, S. L. (1998). Association and linkage of the dopamine transporter gene and attention-deficit hyperactivity disorder in children: Heterogeneity owing to diagnostic subtype and severity. *American Journal of Human Genetics, 63,* 1767–1776.

Waldrip, A. M. (2008). With a little help from your friends: The importance of high-quality friendships on early adolescent adjustment. *Social Development, 17,* 832–852.

Walenski, M., Tager-Flusberg, H., & Ullman, M. T. (2006). Language in autism. In S. O. Moldin & J. L. R. Rubenstein (Eds.), *Understanding autism: From basic neuroscience to treatment* (pp. 175–203). Boca Raton, FL: CRC Press.

Walker, L. J. (1995). Sexism in Kohlberg's moral psychology? In W. M. Kurtines & J. L. Gewirtz (Eds.), *Moral development: An introduction* (pp. 83–107). Boston: Allyn and Bacon.

Walker, L. J. (2004). Progress and prospects in the psychology of moral development. *Merrill-Palmer Quarterly, 50,* 546–557.

Walker, L. J. (2006). Gender and morality. In M. Killen & J. G. Smetana (Eds.), *Handbook of moral development* (pp. 93–118). Philadelphia: Erlbaum.

Walker, L. J., & Taylor, J. H. (1991a). Family interactions and the development of moral reasoning. *Child Development, 62,* 264–283.

Walker, L. J., & Taylor, J. H. (1991b). Stage transitions in moral reasoning: A longitudinal study of developmental processes. *Developmental Psychology, 27,* 330–337.

Wall, M., & Côté, J. (2007). Developmental activities that lead to dropout and investment in sport. *Physical Education and Sport Pedagogy, 12,* 77–87.

Walsh, C. A., Ploeg, J., Lohfeld, L., Horne, J., MacMillan, H., & Lai, D. (2007). Violence across the lifespan: Interconnections among forms of abuse as described by marginalized Canadian elders and their caregivers. *British Journal of Social Work, 37,* 491–514.

Walsh, F., & McGoldrick, M. (2004). Loss and the family: A systemic perspective. In F. Walsh & M. McGoldrick (Eds.), *Living beyond loss: Death in the family* (2nd ed., pp. 3–26). New York: Norton.

Walsh, K. E., & Berman, J. R. (2004). Sexual dysfunction in the older woman: An overview of the current understanding and management. *Therapy in Practice, 21,* 655–675.

Walston, J., Hadley, E. C., Ferrucci, L., Guralnik, J. M., Newman, A. B., Studenski, S. A., et al. (2006). Research agenda for frailty in older adults: Toward a better understanding of physiology and etiology: Summary from the American Geriatrics Society/National Institute on Aging Research Conference on Frailty in Older Adults. *Journal of the American Geriatrics Society, 54,* 991–1001.

Wang, H., & Amato, P. R. (2000). Predictors of divorce adjustment: Stressors, resources, and definitions. *Journal of Marriage and Family, 62,* 655–668.

Wang, H., & Wellman, B. (2010). Social connectivity in America: Changes in adult friendship network size from 2002 to 2007. *American Behavioral Scientist, 53,* 1148–1169.

Wang, M. (2011). Retirement: An adult development perspective. In S. K. Whitbourne & M. J. Sliwinski (Eds.), *Wiley-Blackwell handbook of adulthood and aging* (pp. 416–429). Malden, MA: Wiley-Blackwell.

Wang, M., Adams, G. A., Beehr, T. A., & Shultz, K. S. (2009). Career issues at the end of one's career: Bridge employment and retirement. In S. G. Baugh & S. E. Sullivan (Eds.), *Maintaining focus, energy, and options over the life span* (pp. 135–162). Charlotte, NC: Information Age Publishing.

Wang, M., & Shultz, K. (2010). Employee retirement: A review and recommendations for future investigation. *Journal of Management, 36,* 172–206.

Wang, Q. (2006). Relations of maternal style and child self-concept to autobiographical memories in Chinese, Chinese immigrant, and European American 3-year-olds. *Child Development, 77,* 1794–1809.

Wang, Q., Pomerantz, E. M., & Chen, H. (2007). The role of parents' control in early adolescents' psychological functioning: A longitudinal investigation in the United States and China. *Child Development, 78,* 1592–1610.

Wang, Q., Shao, Y., & Li, Y. J. (2010). "My way or mom's way?" The bilingual and bicultural self in Hong Kong Chinese children and adolescents. *Child Development, 81,* 555–567.

Wang, S., Baillargeon, R., & Paterson, S. (2005). Detecting continuity violations in infancy: A new account and new evidence from covering and tube events. *Cognition, 95,* 129–173.

Wang, Z., & Deater-Deckard, K. (2013). Resilience in gene–environment transactions. In S. Goldstein & R. Brooks (Eds.), *Handbook of resilience in children* (2nd ed., pp. 57–72). New York: Springer Science + Business Media.

Wark, G. R., & Krebs, D. L. (1996). Gender and dilemma differences in real-life moral judgment. *Developmental Psychology, 32,* 220–230.

Warner, L. A., Valdez, A., Vega, W. A., de la Rosa, M., Turner, R. J., & Canino, G. (2006). Hispanic drug abuse in an evolving cultural context: An agenda for research. *Drug and Alcohol Dependence, 84*(Suppl. 1), S8–S16.

Warner, L. M., Ziegelmann, J. P., Schüz, B., Wurm, S., Tesch-Römer, C., & Schwarzer, R. (2011). Maintaining autonomy despite multimorbidity: Self-efficacy and the two faces of social support. *European Journal of Ageing, 8,* 3–12.

Warnock, F., & Sandrin, D. (2004). Comprehensive description of newborn distress behavior in response to acute pain (newborn male circumcision). *Pain, 107,* 242–255.

Warr, P. (2001). Age and work behavior: Physical attributes, cognitive abilities, knowledge, personality traits, and motives. *International Review of Industrial and Organizational Psychology, 16,* 1–36.

Warren, A. R., & Tate, C. S. (1992). Egocentrism in children's telephone conversations. In R. M. Diaz & L. E. Berk (Eds.), *Private speech: From social interaction to self-regulation* (pp. 245–264). Hillsdale, NJ: Erlbaum.

Warshaw, C., Brashler, P., & Gil, J. (2009). Mental health consequences of intimate partner violence. In C. Mitchell & D. Anglin (Eds.), *Intimate partner violence: A health-based perspective* (pp. 147–171). New York: Oxford University Press.

Wass, H. (2004). A perspective on the current state of death education. *Death Studies, 28,* 289–308.

Wasserman, E. A., & Rovee-Collier, C. (2001). Pick the flowers and mind your As and 2s! Categorization by pigeons and infants. In M. E. Carroll & J. B. Overmier (Eds.), *Animal research and human health: Advancing human welfare through behavioral science* (pp. 263–279). Washington, DC: American Psychological Association.

Watamura, S. E., Phillips, D., Morrissey, T. W., McCartney, K., & Bub, K. (2011). Double jeopardy: Poorer social-emotional outcomes for children in the NICHD SECCYD experiencing home and childcare environments that confer risk. *Child Development, 82,* 48–65.

Waterman, A. S., & Whitbourne, S. K. (1982). Androgyny and psychosocial development among college students and adults. *Journal of Personality, 50,* 121–133.

Waters, E., & Cummings, E. M. (2000). A secure base from which to explore close relationships. *Child Development, 71,* 164–172.

Waters, E., Merrick, S., Treboux, D., Crowell, J., & Albersheim, L. (2000). Attachment security in infancy and early adulthood: A twenty-year longitudinal study. *Child Development, 71,* 684–689.

Waters, E., Vaughn, B. E., Posada, G., & Kondo-Ikemura, K. (Eds.). (1995). Caregiving, cultural, and cognitive perspectives on secure-base behavior and working models: New growing points of attachment theory and research. *Monographs of the Society for Research in Child Development, 60*(2–3, Serial No. 244).

Watson, J. B., & Raynor, R. (1920). Conditioned emotional reactions. *Journal of Experimental Psychology, 3,* 1–14.

Watson, M. (1990). Aspects of self-development as reflected in children's role playing. In D. Cicchetti & M. Beeghly (Eds.), *The self in transition: Infancy to childhood* (pp. 281–307). Chicago: University of Chicago Press.

Wax, J. R., Pinette, M. G., & Cartin, A. (2010). Home versus hospital birth—process and outcome. *Obstetric and Gynecological Survey, 65,* 132–140.

Waxman, S. R., & Senghas, A. (1992). Relations among word meanings in early lexical development. *Developmental Psychology, 28,* 862–873.

Webb, N. M., Franke, M. L., Ing, M., Chan, A., De, T., Freund, D., & Battey, D. (2008). The role of teacher instructional practices in student collaboration. *Contemporary Educational Psychology, 35,* 360–381.

Weber, C., Hahne, A., Friedrich, M., & Friederici, A. (2004). Discrimination of word stress in early infant perception: Electrophysiological evidence. *Cognitive Brain Research, 18,* 149–161.

Webster-Stratton, C., & Reid, M. J. (2010a). The Incredible Years Parents, Teachers, and Children Training Series: A multifaceted treatment approach for young children with conduct disorders. In J. R. Weisz & A. E. Kazdin (Eds.), *Evidence-based psychotherapies for children and adolescents* (2nd ed., pp. 194–210). New York: Guilford.

Webster-Stratton, C., & Reid, M. J. (2010b). The Incredible Years program for children from infancy to pre-adolescence: Prevention and treatment of behavior problems. In R. C. Murrihy, A. D. Kidman, & T. H. Ollendick (Eds.), *Clinical handbook of assessing and treating conduct problems in youth* (pp. 117–138). New York: Springer Science + Business Media.

Webster-Stratton, C., Rinaldi, J., & Reid, J. M. (2011). Long-term outcomes of Incredible Years parenting

program: Predictors of adolescent adjustment. *Child and Adolescent Mental Health, 16,* 38–46.

Wechsler, D. (2002). *WPPSI-III: Wechsler Preschool and Primary Scale of Intelligence* (3rd ed.). San Antonio, TX: Psychological Corporation.

Wechsler, D. (2003). *WISC-IV: Wechsler Intelligence Scale for Children* (4th ed.). San Antonio, TX: Psychological Corporation.

Weems, C. F., & Costa, N. M. (2005). Developmental differences in the expression of childhood anxiety symptoms and fears. *Journal of the American Academy of Child and Adolescent Psychiatry, 44,* 656–663.

Wegesin, D. J., Jacobs, D. M., Zubin, N. R., & Ventura, P. R. (2000). Source memory and encoding strategy in normal aging. *Journal of Clinical and Experimental Neuropsychology, 22,* 455–464.

Wehren, A., De Lisi, R., & Arnold, M. (1981). The development of noun definition. *Journal of Child Language, 8,* 165–175.

Weikum, W. M., Vouloumanos, A., Navarra, J., Soto-Faraco, S., Sebastián-Gallés, N., & Werker, J. F. (2007). Visual language discrimination in infancy. *Science, 316,* 1159.

Weinberg, M. K., & Tronick, E. Z. (1994). Beyond the face: An empirical study of infant affective configurations of facial, vocal, gestural, and regulatory behaviors. *Child Development, 65,* 1503–1515.

Weinberger, M. I., & Whitbourne, S. K. (2010). Depressive symptoms, self-reported physical functioning, and identity in community-dwelling older adults. *Aging International, 35,* 276–285.

Weindruch, R., Keenan, K. P., Carney, J. M., Fernandes, G., Feuers, R. J., & Floyd, R. A. (2001). Caloric restriction mimetics: Metabolic interventions. *Journal of Gerontology, 56A,* 20–33.

Weiner, J., & Tardif, C. (2004). Social and emotional functioning of children with learning disabilities: Does special education placement make a difference? *Learning Disabilities Research and Practice, 19,* 20–32.

Weinfield, N. S., Sroufe, L. A., & Egeland, B. (2000). Attachment from infancy to early adulthood in a high-risk sample: Continuity, discontinuity, and their correlates. *Child Development, 71,* 695–702.

Weinfield, N. S., Whaley, G. J. L., & Egeland, B. (2004). Continuity, discontinuity, and coherence in attachment from infancy to late adolescence: Sequelae of organization and disorganization. *Attachment and Human Development, 6,* 73–97.

Weinstein, R. S. (2002). *Reaching higher: The power of expectations in schooling.* Cambridge, MA: Harvard University Press.

Weinstein, S. M., Mermelstein, R. J., Hedeker, D., Hankin, B. L., & Flay, B. R. (2006). The time-varying influences of peer and family support on adolescent daily positive and negative affect. *Journal of Clinical Child and Adolescent Psychology, 35,* 420–430.

Weinstock, M. (2008). The long-term behavioural consequences of prenatal stress. *Neuroscience and Biobehavioral Reviews, 32,* 1073–1086.

Weisfield, G. E. (1997). Puberty rites as clues to the nature of human adolescence. *Cross-Cultural Research, 31,* 27–54.

Weisgram, E. S., Bigler, R. S., & Liben, L. S. (2010). Gender, values, and occupational interests among children, adolescents, and adults. *Child Development, 81,* 778–796.

Weissberg, R. W. (2006). Modes of expertise in creative thinking: Evidence from case studies. In K. A. Ericsson, N. Charness, P. J. Feltovich, & R. R. Hoffman (Eds.), *The Cambridge handbook of expertise and expert performance* (pp. 761–787). New York: Cambridge University Press.

Weisz, A. N., & Black, B. M. (2002). Gender and moral reasoning: African American youths respond to dating dilemmas. *Journal of Human Behavior in the Social Environment, 6,* 17–34.

Weizman, Z. O., & Snow, C. E. (2001). Lexical output as related to children's vocabulary acquisition: Effects of sophisticated exposure and support for meaning. *Developmental Psychology, 37,* 265–279.

Wekerle, C., & Avgoustis, E. (2003). Child maltreatment, adolescent dating, and adolescent dating violence. In P. Florsheim (Ed.), *Adolescent romantic relations and sexual behavior: Theory, research, and practical implications* (pp. 213–242). Mahwah, NJ: Erlbaum.

Wekerle, C., Wall, A.-M., Leung, E., & Trocmé, N. (2007). Cumulative stress and substantiated maltreatment: The importance of caregiver vulnerability and adult partner violence. *Child Abuse and Neglect, 31,* 427–443.

Wellman, H. M. (2002). Understanding the psychological world: Developing a theory of mind. In U. Goswami (Ed.), *Blackwell handbook of child cognitive development* (pp. 167–187). Malden, MA: Blackwell.

Wellman, H. M. (2011). Developing a theory of mind. In U. Goswami (Ed.), *Wiley-Blackwell handbook of childhood cognitive development* (2nd ed., pp. 258–284). Malden, MA: Wiley-Blackwell.

Wellman, H. M., & Hickling, A. K. (1994). The mind's "I": Children's conception of the mind as an active agent. *Child Development, 65,* 1564–1580.

Welsh, M. C. (2002). Developmental and clinical variations in executive functions. In J. Kirk & D. Molfese (Eds.), *Developmental variations in language and learning* (pp. 139–185). Mahwah, NJ: Erlbaum.

Welsh, M. C., Friedman, S. L., & Spieker, S. J. (2008). Executive functions in developing children: Current conceptualizations and questions for the future. In K. McCartney & D. Phillips (Eds.), *Blackwell handbook of early childhood development* (pp. 167–187). Malden, MA: Blackwell Publishing.

Wenger, G. C. (2009). Childlessness at the end of life: Evidence from rural Wales. *Ageing and Society, 29,* 1243–1259.

Wenger, G. C., & Burholdt, V. (2001). Differences over time in older people's relationships with children, grandchildren, nieces and nephews in rural North Wales. *Ageing and Society, 21,* 567–590.

Wentworth, N., Benson, J. B., & Haith, M. M. (2000). The development of infants' reaches for stationary and moving targets. *Child Development, 71,* 576–601.

Wentzel, K. R., Barry, C. M., & Caldwell, K. A. (2004). Friendships in middle school: Influences on motivation and school adjustment. *Journal of Educational Psychology, 96,* 195–203.

Werner, E. E. (1991). Grandparent–grandchild relationships amongst U.S. ethnic groups. In P. K. Smith (Ed.), *The psychology of grandparenthood: An international perspective* (pp. 68–82). London: Routledge.

Werner, E. E. (2013). What can we learn about resilience from large-scale longitudinal studies? In S. Goldstein & R. Brooks (Eds.), *Handbook of resilience in children* (2nd ed., pp. 87–102). New York: Springer Science + Business Media.

Werner, N. E., & Crick, N. R. (2004). Maladaptive peer relationships and the development of relational and physical aggression during middle childhood. *Social Development, 13,* 495–514.

Westerhof, G. J. (2008). Age identity. In D. Carr (Ed.), *Encyclopedia of the life course and human development* (pp. 10–14). Farmington Hills, MI: Macmillan.

Westerhof, G. J., & Barrett, A. E. (2005). Age identity and subjective well-being: A comparison of the United States and Germany. *Journal of Gerontology, 60S,* 129–136.

Westerhof, G. J., Bohlmeijer, E., & Webster, J. D. (2010). Reminiscence and mental health: A review of recent

progress in theory, research and interventions. *Ageing and Society, 30,* 697–721.

Westerhof, G. J., Whitbourne, S. K., & Freeman, G. P. (2012). The aging self in a cultural context: The relation of conceptions of aging to identity processes and self-esteem in the United States and the Netherlands. *Journal of Gerontology, 67B,* 52–60.

Westermann, G., Mareschal, D., Johnson, M. H., Sirois, S., Spratling, M. W., & Thomas, M. S. C. (2007). Neuroconstructivism. *Developmental Science, 10,* 75–83.

Westermann, G., Sirois, S., Shultz, T. R., & Mareschal, D. (2006). Modeling developmental cognitive neuroscience. *Trends in Cognitive Sciences, 10,* 227–232.

Westermeyer, J. F. (2004). Predictors and characteristics of Erikson's life cycle model among men: A 32-year longitudinal study. *International Journal of Aging and Human Development, 58,* 29–48.

Wethington, E. (2000). Expecting stress: Americans and the "midlife crisis." *Motivation and Emotion, 24,* 85–103.

Wethington, E., Kessler, R. C., & Pixley, J. E. (2004). Turning points in adulthood. In O. G. Brim, C. D. Ryff, & R. C. Kessler (Eds.), *How healthy are we? A national study of well-being at midlife* (pp. 586–613). Chicago: University of Chicago Press.

Wetle, T., Shield, R., Teno, J., Miller, S. C., & Welch, L. (2005). Family perspectives on end-of-life care experiences in nursing homes. *Gerontologist, 45,* 642–650.

Wetmore, C. M., & Mokdad, A. H. (2012). In denial: Misperceptions of weight change among adults in the United States. *Preventive Medicine, 55,* 93–100.

Whincup, P. H., Kaye, S. J., Owen, C. G., Huxley, R., Cook, D. G., Anazawa, S., et al. (2008). Birth weight and risk of type 2 diabetes: A systematic review. *Journal of the American Medical Association, 24,* 2886–2897.

Whipple, E. E. (2006). Child abuse and neglect: Consequences of physical, sexual, and emotional abuse of children. In H. E. Fitzgerald, B. M. Lester, & B. Zuckerman (Eds.), *The crisis in youth mental health: Critical issues and effective programs: Vol. 1. Childhood disorders* (pp. 205–229). Westport, CT: Praeger.

Whipple, N., Bernier, A., & Mageau, G. A. (2011). Broadening the study of infant security of attachment: Maternal autonomy-support in the context of infant exploration. *Social Development, 20,* 17–32.

Whisman, M. A., Uebelacker, L. A., Tolejko, N., Chatav, Y., & McKelvie, M. (2006). Marital discord and well-being in older adults: Is the association confounded by personality? *Psychology and Aging, 21,* 626–631.

Whitaker, D. J., Baker, C. K., & Arias, I. (2007). Interventions to prevent intimate partner violence. In L. S. Doll, S. E., Bonzo, D. A. Sleet, & J. A. Mercy (Eds.), *Handbook of injury and violence prevention* (pp. 203–221). New York: Springer Science + Business Media.

Whitbourne, S. K. (1996). *The aging individual: Physical and psychological perspectives.* New York: Springer.

Whitbourne, S. K. (2002). *The aging individual: Physical and psychological perspectives.* New York: Springer.

Whitbourne, S. K., & Meeks, S. (2011). Psychopathology, bereavement, and aging. In K. W. Schaie & S. L. Willis (Eds.), *Handbook of the psychology of aging* (7th ed., pp. 311–323). San Diego, CA: Elsevier.

Whitbourne, S. K., & Willis, S. L. (2006). Preface. In S. K. Whitbourne & S. L. Willis (Eds.), *The baby boomers grow up* (pp. vii–ix). Mahwah, NJ: Erlbaum.

Whitbourne, S. K., Zuschlag, M. K., Elliot, L. B., & Waterman, A. S. (1992). Psychosocial development in adulthood: A 22-year sequential study. *Journal of Personality and Social Psychology, 63,* 260–271.

White, H. R., McMorris, B. J., Catalano, R. F., Fleming, C. B., Haggerty, K. P., & Abbott, R. D. (2006). Increases in alcohol and marijuana use during the transition out of high school into emerging adulthood: The effects of leaving home, going to college, and high school protective factors. *Journal of Studies on Alcohol, 67,* 810–822.

White, L. (2001). Sibling relationships over the life course: A panel analysis. *Journal of Marriage and Family, 63,* 555–568.

White, Y. A., Woods, D. C., Takai, Y., Ishihara, O., Seki, H., & Tilly, J. L. (2012). Oocyte formation by mitotically active germ cells purified from ovaries of reproductive-age women. *Nature Medicine, 18,* 413–421.

Whiteman, S. D., & Loken, E. (2006). Comparing analytic techniques to classify dyadic relationships: An example using siblings. *Journal of Marriage and Family, 68,* 1370–1382.

Whiteman, S. D., McHale, S. M., & Crouter, A. C. (2010). Family relationships from adolescence to early adulthood: Changes in the family system following firstborns' leaving home. *Journal of Research on Adolescence, 21,* 461–474.

Whitesell, N. R., Mitchell, C. M., Spicer, P., and the Voices of Indian Teens Project Team. (2009). A longitudinal study of self-esteem, cultural identity, and academic success among American Indian adolescents. *Cultural Diversity and Ethnic Minority Psychology, 15,* 38–50.

Whiteside-Mansell, L., Bradley, R. H., Owen, M. T., Randolph, S. M., & Cauce, A. M. (2003). Parenting and children's behavior at 36 months: Equivalence between African-American and European-American mother–child dyads. *Parenting: Science and Practice, 3,* 197–234.

Whitfield, K. E., Thorpe, R., & Szanton, S. (2011). Health disparities, social class, and aging. In K. Warner Schaie & S. L. Willis (Eds.), *Handbook of the psychology of aging* (7th ed., pp. 207–218). San Diego, CA: Academic Press.

Whitlock, J. L., Powers, J. L., & Eckenrode, J. (2006). The virtual cutting edge: The Internet and adolescent self-injury. *Developmental Psychology, 42,* 407–417.

Whitmer, R. A., Gustafson, D. R., Barrett-Connor, E., Haan, M. N., Gunderson, E. P., & Yaffe, K. (2008). Central obesity and increased risk of dementia more than three decades later. *Neurology, 71,* 1057–1064.

Wichmann, C., Coplan, R. J., & Daniels, T. (2004). The social cognitions of socially withdrawn children. *Social Development, 13,* 377–392.

Wichstrøm, L. (2006). Sexual orientation as a risk factor for bulimic symptoms. *International Journal of Eating Disorders, 39,* 448–453.

Wickens, A. P. (2001). Aging and the free radical theory. *Respiration Physiology, 128,* 379–391.

Wigfield, A., Battle, A., Keller, L. B., & Eccles, J. S. (2002). Sex differences in motivation, self-concept, career aspiration, and career choice: Implications for cognitive development. In A. McGillicudy-De Lisi & R. De Lisi (Eds.), *Biology, society, and behavior: The development of sex differences in cognition* (pp. 93–124). Westport, CT: Ablex.

Wigfield, A., & Eccles, J. S. (1994). Children's competence beliefs, achievement values, and general self-esteem change across elementary and middle school. *Journal of Early Adolescence, 14,* 107–138.

Wigfield, A., Eccles, J. S., Schiefele, U., Roeser, R. W., & Davis-Kean, P. (2006). Development of achievement motivation. In N. Eisenberg (Ed.), *Handbook of child psychology: Vol. 3. Social, emotional, and personality development* (6th ed., pp. 933–1002). Hoboken, NJ: Wiley.

Wigfield, A., Eccles, J. S., Yoon, K. S., Harold, R. D., Arbreton, A. J., Freedman-Doan, C., & Blumenfeld, P. C. (1997). Changes in children's competence beliefs and subjective task values across the elementary school years: A three-year study. *Journal of Educational Psychology, 89,* 451–469.

Wikby, A., Maxson, P., Olsson, J., Johansson, B., & Ferguson, F. G. (1998). Changes in CD8 and CD4 lymphocyte subsets, T cell proliferation responses and non-survival in the very old: The Swedish longitudinal OCTO-immune study. *Mechanisms of Ageing and Development, 102,* 187–198.

Wilbur, J., Chandler, P. J., Dancy, B., & Lee, H. (2003). Correlates of physical activity in urban Midwestern African-American women. *American Journal of Preventive Medicine, 25,* 45–52.

Wilbur, J., Vassalo, A., Chandler, P., McDevitt, J., & Miller, A. M. (2005). Midlife women's adherence to home-based walking during maintenance. *Nursing Research, 54,* 33–40.

Wilcox, A. J., Weinberg, C. R., & Baird, D. D. (1995). Timing of sexual intercourse in relation to ovulation: Effects on the probability of conception, survival of the pregnancy, and sex of the baby. *New England Journal of Medicine, 333,* 1517–1519.

Wilkie, S. S., Guenette, J. A., Dominelli, P. B., & Sheel, A. W. (2012). Effects of an aging pulmonary system on expiratory flow limitation and dyspnoea during exercise in healthy women. *European Journal of Applied Physiology, 112,* 2195–2204.

Wilkinson, R. B. (2004). The role of parental and peer attachment in the psychological health and self-esteem of adolescents. *Journal of Youth and Adolescence, 33,* 479–493.

Wilkinson, R. G., & Pickett, K. E. (2006). Income inequality and population health: A review and explanation of the evidence. *Social Science and Medicine, 62,* 1768–1784.

Willatts, P. (1999). Development of means–end behavior in young infants: Pulling a support to retrieve a distant object. *Developmental Psychology, 35,* 651–667.

Williams, J. M., & Currie, C. (2000). Self-esteem and physical development in early adolescence: Pubertal timing and body image. *Journal of Early Adolescence, 20,* 129–149.

Williams, K., & Dunne-Bryant, A. (2006). Divorce and adult psychological well-being: Clarifying the role of gender and age. *Journal of Marriage and Family, 68,* 1178–1196.

Williams, N., & Torrez, D. J. (1998). Grandparenthood among Hispanics. In M. E. Szinovacz (Ed.), *Handbook on grandparenthood* (pp. 87–96). Westport, CT: Greenwood Press.

Williams, P. E., Weis, L. G., & Rolfhus, E. (2003). *WISC-IV: Theoretical model and test blueprint.* San Antonio, TX: Psychological Corporation.

Williams, R., McNeilly, A., & Sutherland, C. (2012). Insulin resistance in the brain: An old-age or new-age problem? *Biochemical Pharmacology, 84,* 737–745.

Williams, S., & Dale, J. (2006). The effectiveness of treatment for depression/depressive symptoms in adults with cancer: A systematic review. *British Journal of Cancer, 94,* 372–390.

Williams, T. S., Connolly, J., Pepler, D., Craig, W., & Loporte, L. (2008). Risk models of dating aggression across different adolescent relationships: A developmental psychopathology approach. *Journal of Consulting and Clinical Psychology, 76,* 622–632.

Williamson, J., Softas-Nall, B., & Miller, J. (2003). Grandmothers raising grandchildren: An exploration of their experiences and emotions. *Counseling and Therapy for Couples with Families, 11,* 13–32.

Willinger, M., Ko, C.-W., Hoffman, H. J., Kessler, R. C., & Corwin, M. J. (2003). Trends in infant bed sharing in the United States. *Archives of Pediatrics and Adolescent Medicine, 157,* 43–49.

Willis, S. L., & Schaie, K. W. (1999). Intellectual functioning in midlife. In S. L. Willis & J. D. Reid

(Eds.), *Life in the middle* (pp. 105–146). San Diego: Academic Press.

Wilson, D. J., Mitchell, J. M., Kemp, B. J., Adkins, R. H., & Mann, W. (2009). Effects of assistive technology on functional decline in people aging with a disability. *Assistive Technology, 21,* 208–217.

Wilson, E. K., Dalberth, B. T., Koo, H. P., & Gard, J. C. (2010). Parents' perspectives on talking to preteenage children about sex. *Perspectives on Sexual and Reproductive Health, 42,* 56–63.

Wilson, R. S., Beckett, L. A., Evans, D. A., & Bennett, D. A. (2003). Terminal decline in cognitive function. *Neurology, 60,* 1782–1787.

Windsor, T. D., Anstey, K. J., & Rodgers, B. (2008). Volunteering and psychological well-being among young–old adults: How much is too much? *Gerontologist, 48,* 59–70.

Wink, P. (2006). Who is afraid of death? Religiousness, spirituality, and death anxiety in late adulthood. *Journal of Religion, Spirituality and Aging, 18,* 93–110.

Wink, P. (2007). Everyday life in the Third Age. In J. B. James & P. Wink (Eds.), *Annual review of gerontology and geriatrics* (Vol. 26, pp. 243–261). New York: Springer.

Wink, P., & Dillon, M. (2002). Spiritual development across the adult life course: Findings from a longitudinal study. *Journal of Adult Development, 9,* 79–94.

Wink, P., & Dillon, M. (2008). Religiousness, spirituality, and psychosocial functioning in late adulthood: Findings from a longitudinal study. *Psychology of Religion and Spirituality 5,* 102–115.

Wink, P., & Helson, R. (1993). Personality change in women and their partners. *Journal of Personality and Social Psychology, 65,* 597–605.

Wink, P., & Schiff, B. (2002). To review or not to review? The role of personality and life events in life review and adaptation to older age. In J. D. Webster & B. K. Haight (Eds.), *Critical advances in reminiscence work* (pp. 44–75). New York: Springer.

Wink, P., & Scott, J. (2005). Does religiousness buffer against the fear of death and dying in late adulthood? Findings from a longitudinal study. *Journal of Gerontology, 60B,* P207–P214.

Winkler, I., Háden, G. P., Ladinig, O., Sziller, I., & Honing, H. (2009). Newborn infants detect the beat in music. *Proceedings of the National Academy of Sciences, 106,* 2468–2471.

Winner, E. (1986, August). Where pelicans kiss seals. *Psychology Today, 20*(8), 25–35.

Winner, E. (1988). *The point of words: Children's understanding of metaphor and irony.* Cambridge, MA: Harvard University Press.

Winner, E. (2000). The origins and ends of giftedness. *American Psychologist, 55,* 159–169.

Winner, E. (2003). Creativity and talent. In M. H. Bornstein, L. Davidson, C. L. M. Keyes, K. A. Moore, & the Center for Child Well-Being (Eds.), *Well-being: Positive development across the life course* (pp. 371–380). Mahwah, NJ: Erlbaum.

Winsler, A. (2009). Still talking to ourselves after all these years: A review of current research on private speech. In A. Winsler, C. Fernyhough, & I. Montero (Eds.), *Private speech executive functioning, and the development of self-regulation.* New York: Cambridge University Press.

Winsler, A., Fernyhough, C., & Montero, I. (Eds.). (2009). *Private speech, executive functioning, and the development of verbal self-regulation.* New York: Cambridge University Press.

Winsler, A., Naglieri, J., & Manfra, L. (2006). Children's search strategies and accompanying verbal and motor strategic behavior: Developmental trends and relations with task performance among children age 5 to 17. *Cognitive Development, 21,* 232–248.

Winslow, R. D., Mehta, D., & Fuster, V. (2005). Sudden cardiac death: Mechanisms, therapies and challenges. *Cardiovascular Medicine, 2,* 352–360.

Wiseman, F. K., Alford, K. A., Tybulewicz, V. L. J., & Fisher, E. M. C. (2009). Down syndrome—recent progress and future prospects. *Human Molecular Genetics, 8,* R75–R83.

Wissink, I. B., Deković, M., & Meijer, A. M. (2006). Parenting behavior, quality of the parent–adolescent relationship, and adolescent functioning in four ethnic groups. *Journal of Early Adolescence, 26,* 133–159.

Witherington, D. C. (2005). The development of prospective grasping control between 5 and 7 months: A longitudinal study. *Infancy, 7,* 143–161.

Wolak, J., Finkelhor, D., Mitchell, K. J., & Ybarra, M. L. (2008). Online "predators" and their victims: Myths, realities, and implications for prevention and treatment. *American Psychologist, 63,* 111–128.

Wolak, J., Mitchell, K. J., & Finkelhor, D. (2003). Escaping or connecting? Characteristics of youth who form close online relationships. *Journal of Adolescence, 26,* 105–119.

Wolak, J., Mitchell, K., & Finkelhor, D. (2007). Unwanted and wanted exposure to online pornography in a national sample of youth Internet users. *Pediatrics, 119,* 247–257.

Wolchik, S. A., Wilcox, K. L., Tein, J.-Y. & Sandler, I. N. (2000). Maternal acceptance and consistency of discipline as buffers of divorce stressors on children's psychological adjustment problems. *Journal of Abnormal Child Psychology, 28,* 87–102.

Wolfe, V. V. (2006). Child sexual abuse. In E. J. Mash & R. A. Barkley (Eds.), *Treatment of childhood disorders* (3rd ed., pp. 647–727). New York: Guilford.

Wolff, P. H. (1966). The causes, controls and organization of behavior in the neonate. *Psychological Issues, 5*(1, Serial No. 17).

Wolff, P. H., & Fesseha, G. (1999). The orphans of Eritrea: A five-year follow-up study. *Journal of Child Psychology and Psychiatry and Allied Disciplines, 40,* 1231–1237.

Wolfinger, N. H. (2005). *Understanding the divorce cycle.* New York: Cambridge University Press.

Wolinsky, F. D., Unverzagt, F. W., Smith, D. M., Jones, R., Stoddard, A., & Tennstedt, S. L. (2006). The ACTIVE cognitive training trail and health-related quality of life: Protection that lasts for 5 years. *Journal of Gerontology, 61A,* 1324–1329.

Wong, C. A., Eccles, J. S., & Sameroff, A. (2003). The influence of ethnic discrimination and ethnic identification on African American adolescents' school and socioemotional adjustment. *Journal of Personality, 71,* 1197–1232.

Wood, E., Desmarais, S., & Gugula, S. (2002). The impact of parenting experience on gender stereotyped toy play of children. *Sex Roles, 47,* 39–49.

Wood, J. J., Emmerson, N. A., & Cowan, P. A. (2004). Is early attachment security carried forward into relationships with preschool peers? *British Journal of Developmental Psychology, 22,* 245–253.

Wood, J. T. (2009). Communication, gender differences in. In H. T. Reis & S. K. Sprecher (Eds.), *Encyclopedia of human relationships* (Vol. 1, pp. 252–256). Thousand Oaks, CA: Sage.

Wood, R. M. (2009). Changes in cry acoustics and distress ratings while the infant is crying. *Infant and Child Development, 18,* 163–177.

Woods, N. F., Smith-DiJulio, K., Percival, D. B., Tao, E. Y., Mariella, A., & Mitchell, E. S. (2008). Depressed mood during the menopausal transition and early postmenopause: Observations from the Seattle Midlife Women's Health Study. *Menopause, 15,* 223–232.

Woolley, J. D., & Cox, V. (2007). Development of beliefs about storybook reality. *Developmental Science, 10,* 681–693.

Woolley, M. E., Kol, K. L., & Bowen, G. L. (2009). The social context of school success for Latino middle school students: Direct and indirect influences of teachers, family, and friends. *Journal of Early Adolescence 29*, 43–70.

Worden, J. W. (2000). Toward an appropriate death. In T. A. Rando (Ed.), *Clinical dimensions of anticipatory mourning* (pp. 267–277). Champaign, IL: Research Press.

Worden, J. W. (2009). *Grief counseling and grief therapy* (4th ed.). New York: Springer.

World Cancer Research Fund/American Institute for Cancer Research. (2007). *Food, nutrition, physical activity, and the prevention of cancer: A global perspective.* Washington, DC: American Institute for Cancer Research.

World Federation of Right to Die Societies. (2006). *Public opinion.* Retrieved from www.worldrtd.net

World Health Organization. (2008). *World report on child injury prevention.* Geneva, Switzerland: Author.

World Health Organization. (2010). *World health statistics 2010.* Geneva, Switzerland: Author.

World Health Organization. (2011). *The world's women 2010: Trends and statistics.* Retrieved from unstats.un.org/unsd/demographic/products/Worldswomen/Executive%20summary.htm

World Health Organization. (2012a). *Countdown to 2015: Building a future for women and children.* Geneva, Switzerland: Author.

World Health Organization. (2012b). *The World Health Organization's infant feeding recommendation.* Retrieved from www.who.int/nutrition/topics/infantfeeding_recommendation/en/index.html

World Health Organization. (2012c). *World health statistics 2012.* Geneva: Author.

World Health Organization. (2013a). *Obesity and overweight.* Retrieved from www.who.int/mediacentre/factsheets/fs311/en

World Health Organization. (2013b). *Suicide prevention (SUPRE).* Retrieved from www.who.int/mental_health/prevention/suicide/suicideprevent/en

Worrell, F. C., & Gardner-Kitt, D. L. (2006). The relationship between racial and ethnic identity in black adolescents: The cross-racial identity scale and the multigroup ethnic identity measure. *Identity, 6,* 293–315.

Worthy, J., Hungerford-Kresser, H., & Hampton, A. (2009). Tracking and ability grouping. In L. Christenbury, R. Bomer, & P. Smargorinsky (Eds.), *Handbook of adolescent literacy research* (pp. 220–235). New York: Guilford.

Wright, B. C. (2006). On the emergence of the discriminative mode for transitive inference. *European Journal of Cognitive Psychology, 18,* 776–800.

Wright, J. C., Huston, A. C., Murphy, K. C., St. Peters, M., Pinon, M., Scantlin, R., & Kotler, J. (2001). The relations of early television viewing to school readiness and vocabulary of children from low-income families: The Early Window Project. *Child Development, 72,* 1347–1366.

Wright, K. (2003). Relationships with death: The terminally ill talk about dying. *Journal of Marital and Family Therapy, 29,* 439–454.

Wright, M. J., Gillespie, N. A., Luciano, M., Zhu, G., & Martin, N. G. (2008). Genetics of personality and cognition in adolescents. In J. J. Hudziak (Ed.), *Developmental psychology and wellness: Genetic and environmental influences* (pp. 85–107). Washington, DC: American Psychiatric Publishing.

Wright, M. O., & Masten, A. S. (2005). Resilience processes in development. In S. Goldstein & R. B. Brooks (Eds.), *Handbook of resilience in children* (pp. 17–37). New York: Springer.

Wrotniak, B. H., Epstein, L. H., Raluch, R. A., & Roemmich, J. N. (2004). Parent weight change as a predictor of child weight change in family-based

behavioral obesity treatment. *Archives of Pediatric and Adolescent Medicine, 158,* 342–347.

Wu, A. M. S., Tang, C. S. K., & Kwok, T. C. Y. (2002). Death anxiety among Chinese elderly people in Hong Kong. *Journal of Aging and Health, 14,* 42–56.

Wu, L. L., Bumpass, L. L., & Musick, K. (2001). Historical and life course trajectories of nonmarital childbearing. In L. L. Wu & B. Wolfe (Eds.), *Out of wedlock: Causes and consequences of nonmarital fertility* (pp. 3–48). New York: Russell Sage Foundation.

Wu, P., Robinson, C. C., Yang, C., Hart, C. H., Olsen, S. F., Porter, C. L., Jin, S., Wo, J., & Wu, X. (2002). Similarities and differences in mothers' parenting of preschoolers in China and the United States. *International Journal of Behavioral Development, 26,* 481–491.

Wu, T., Mendola, P., & Buck, G. M. (2002). Ethnic differences in the presence of secondary sex characteristics and menarche among U.S. girls: The Third National Health and Nutrition Examination Survey, 1988–1994. *Pediatrics, 110,* 752–757.

Wu, W., Brickman, A. M., Luchsinger, J., Ferrazzano, P., Pichiule, P., Yoshita, M., & Brown, T. (2008). The brain in the age of old: The hippocampal formation is targeted differentially by diseases of late life. *Annals of Neurology, 64,* 698–706.

Wu, Z., & Schimmele, C. M. (2007). Uncoupling in late life. *Generations, 31,* 41–46.

Wulczyn, F. (2009). Epidemiological perspectives on maltreatment prevention. *Future of Children, 19,* 39–66.

Wyatt, J. M., & Carlo, G. (2002). What will my parents think? Relations among adolescents' expected parental reactions, prosocial moral reasoning, and prosocial and antisocial behaviors. *Journal of Adolescent Research, 16,* 646–666.

Wyman, E., Rakoczy, H., & Tomasello, M. (2009). Normativity and context in young children's pretend play. *Cognitive Development, 24,* 146–155.

Wynn, K., Bloom, P., & Chiang, W.-C. (2002). Enumeration of collective entities by 5-month-old infants. *Cognition, 83,* B55–B62.

Wynne-Edwards, K. E. (2001). Hormonal changes in mammalian fathers. *Hormones and Behavior, 40,* 139–145.

Wysong, A., Lee, P. P., & Sloan, F. A. (2009). Longitudinal incidence of adverse outcomes of age-related macular degeneration. *Archives of Ophthalmology, 127,* 320–327.

X

Xu, F., Spelke, E. S., & Goddard, S. (2005). Number sense in human infants. *Developmental Science, 8,* 88–101.

Xu, X., & Lai, S.-C. (2004). Gender ideologies, marital roles, and marital quality in Taiwan. *Journal of Family Issues, 25,* 318–355.

Xue, Y., & Meisels, S. J. (2004). Early literacy instruction and learning in kindergarten: Evidence from the early childhood longitudinal study—kindergarten classes of 1998–1999. *American Educational Research Journal, 41,* 191–229.

Y

Yaari, R., & Corey-Bloom, J. (2007). Alzheimer's disease. *Seminars in Neurology, 27,* 32–41.

Yaffe, K., Fox, P., Newcomer, R., Sands, L., Lindquist, K., Dane, K., & Covinsky, K. E. (2002). Patient and caregiver characteristics and nursing home placement in patients with dementia. *Journal of the American Medical Association, 287,* 2090–2097.

Yaffe, K., Lindquist K., Schwartz, A. V., Vitartas C., Vittinghoff, E., Satterfield, S., et al. (2011). Advanced glycation end product level, diabetes, and accelerated cognitive aging. *Neurology, 77,* 1351–1356.

Yale, M. E., Messinger, D. S., Cobo-Lewis, A. B., Oller, D. K., & Eilers, R. E. (1999). An event-based analysis of the coordination of early infant vocalizations and facial actions. *Developmental Psychology, 35,* 505–513.

Yamamoto, K. (2004). The care of the dying and the grieving in Japan. In J. D. Morgan & P. Laungani (Eds.), *Death and bereavement around the world: Vol. 4. Death and bereavement in Asia, Australia, and New Zealand* (pp. 101–107). Amityville, NY: Baywood Publishing Company.

Yang, B., Ollendick, T. H., Dong, Q., Xia, Y., & Lin, L. (1995). Only children and children with siblings in the People's Republic of China: Levels of fear, anxiety, and depression. *Child Development, 66,* 1301–1311.

Yang, C. (2008, April). *The influence of one-child policy on child rearing, family, and society in post-Mao China.* Invited address, Illinois State University.

Yang, C.-K., & Hahn, H.-M. (2002). Cosleeping in young Korean children. *Developmental and Behavioral Pediatrics, 23,* 151–157.

Yang, F.-Y., & Tsai, C.-C. (2010). Reasoning about science-related uncertain issues and epistemological perspectives among children. *Instructional Science, 38,* 325–354.

Yao, L., & Robert, S. A. (2008). The contributions of race, individual socioeconomic status, and neighborhood socioeconomic context to the self-rated health trajectories and mortality of older adults. *Research on Aging, 30,* 251–273.

Yap, M. B. H., Allen, N. B., & Ladouceur, C. D. (2008). Maternal socialization of positive affect: The impact of invalidation on adolescent emotion regulation and depressive symptomatology. *Child Development, 79,* 1415–1431.

Yates, L. B., Djouseé, L., Kurth, T., Buring, J. E., & Gaziano, J. M. (2008). Exceptional longevity in men: Modifiable factors associated with survival and function to age 90 years. *Archives of Internal Medicine, 168,* 284–290.

Yau, J. P., Tasopoulos-Chan, M., & Smetana, J. G. (2009). Disclosure to parents about everyday activities among American adolescents from Mexican, Chinese, and European backgrounds. *Child Development, 80,* 1481–1498.

Yeh, C. J., Kim, A. B., Pituc, S. T., & Atkins, M. (2008). Poverty, loss, and resilience: The story of Chinese immigrant youth. *Journal of Counseling Psychology, 55,* 34–48.

Yeh, S. S. (2010). Understanding and addressing the achievement gap through individualized instruction and formative assessment. *Assessment in Education: Principles, Policy and Practice, 17,* 169–182.

Yeung, W. (1996). Buddhism, death, and dying. In J. K. Parry & A. S. Ryan (Eds.), *A cross-cultural look at death, dying, and religion* (pp. 74–83). Chicago: Nelson-Hall.

Yirmiya, N., Erel, O., Shaked, M., & Solomonica-Levi, D. (1998). Meta-analyses comparing theory of mind abilities of individuals with autism, individuals with mental retardation, and normally developing individuals. *Psychological Bulletin, 124,* 283–307.

Yoshida, H., & Smith, L. B. (2003). Known and novel noun extensions: Attention at two levels of abstraction. *Child Development, 74,* 564–577.

Yoshikawa, H., Weisner, T. S., Kalil, A., & Way, N. (2008). Mixing qualitative and quantitative research in developmental science: Uses and methodological choices. *Developmental Psychology, 44,* 344–354.

Youn, G., Knight, B. G., Jeon, H., & Benton, D. (1999). Differences in familism values and caregiving outcomes among Korean, Korean American, and White American dementia caregivers. *Psychology and Aging, 14,* 355–364.

Young, J. F., & Mroczek, D. K. (2003). Predicting intraindividual self-concept trajectories during adolescence. *Journal of Adolescence, 26,* 589–603.

Young, S. E., Friedman, N. P., Miyake, A., Willcutt, E. G., Corley, R. P., Haberstick, B. C., et al. (2009). Behavioral disinhibition: Liability for externalizing spectrum disorders and its genetic and environmental relation to response inhibition across adolescence. *Journal of Abnormal Psychology, 118,* 117–130.

Young, T., Rabago, D., Zgierska, A., Austin, D., & Finn, L. (2002). Objective and subjective sleep quality in premenopausal, perimenopausal, and postmenopausal women in the Wisconsin Sleep Cohort Study. *Epidemiology, 26,* 667–672.

Youngblade, L. M., & Dunn, J. (1995). Individual differences in young children's pretend play with mother and sibling: Links to relationships and understanding of other people's feelings and beliefs. *Child Development, 66,* 1472–1492.

Young-Hyman, D., Tanofsky-Kraff, M., Yanovski, S. Z., Keil, M., Cohen, M. L., & Peyrot, M. (2006). Psychological status and weight-related distress in overweight or at-risk-for-overweight children. *Obesity, 14,* 2249–2258.

Yu, B. P. (2006). Why calorie restriction would work for human longevity. *Biogerontology, 7,* 179–182.

Yuan, A. S. V., & Hamilton, H. A. (2006). Stepfather involvement and adolescent well-being: Do mothers and nonresidential fathers matter? *Journal of Family Issues, 27,* 1191–1213.

Yunger, J. L., Carver, P. R., & Perry, D. G. (2004). Does gender identity influence children's psychological well-being? *Developmental Psychology, 40,* 572–582.

Z

Zacks, R. T., & Hasher, L. (2006). Aging and long-term memory: Deficits are not inevitable. In E. Bialystok & F. I. M. Craik (Eds.), *Lifespan cognition: Mechanisms of change* (pp. 162–177). New York: Oxford University Press.

Zahn-Waxler, C., Radke-Yarrow, M., & King, R. M. (1979). Child-rearing and children's prosocial initiations toward victims of distress. *Child Development, 50,* 319–330.

Zakowski, S. G., Hall, M. H., Klein, L. C., & Baum, A. (2001). Appraised control, coping, and stress in a community sample: A test of the goodness-of-fit hypothesis. *Annals of Behavioral Medicine, 23,* 158–165.

Zane, N., & Yeh, M. (2002). The use of culturally based variables in assessment: Studies on loss of face. In K. Kurasaki, S. Okazaki, & S. Sue (Eds.), *Asian American mental health: Assessment theories and methods* (pp. 123–138). Dordrecht, Netherlands: Kluwer Academic.

Zaretsky, M. D. (2003). Communication between identical twins: Health behavior and social factors are associated with longevity that is greater among identical than fraternal U.S. World War II veteran twins. *Journal of Gerontology, 58,* 566–572.

Zaslow, M. J., Weinfield, N. S., Gallagher, M., Hair, E. C., Ogawa, J. R., Egeland, B., Tabors, P. O., & De Temple, J. M. (2006). Longitudinal prediction of child outcomes from differing measures of parenting in a low-income sample. *Developmental Psychology, 42,* 27–37.

Zeanah, C. H. (2000). Disturbances of attachment in young children adopted from institutions. *Journal of Developmental and Behavioral Pediatrics, 21,* 230–236.

Zeifman, D. M. (2003). Predicting adult responses to infant distress: Adult characteristics associated with perceptions, emotional reactions, and timing of intervention. *Infant Mental Health Journal, 24,* 597–612.

Zelazo, N. A., Zelazo, P. R., Cohen, K. M., & Zelazo, P. D. (1993). Specificity of practice effects on elementary neuromotor patterns. *Developmental Psychology, 29,* 686–691.

Zelazo, P. D., Carlson, S. M., & Kesek, A. (2008). The development of executive function in childhood. In C. A. Nelson & M. Luciana (Eds.), *Handbook of cognitive developmental neuroscience* (2nd ed., pp. 553–574). Cambridge, MA: MIT Press.

Zelazo, P. D., & Lee, W. S. C. (2010). Brain development: An overview. In W. Overton & R. M. Lerner (Eds.), *Handbook of life-span development: Vol. 1. Cognition biology, and methods* (pp. 89–114). Hoboken, NJ: Wiley.

Zelinski, E., & Kennison, R. F. (2007). Not your parents' test scores: Cohort reduces psychometric aging effects. *Psychology and Aging, 22,* 546–557.

Zeman, J., Shipman, K., & Suveg, C. (2002). Anger and sadness regulation: Predictions to internalizing and externalizing symptoms in children. *Journal of Clinical Child and Adolescent Psychology, 31,* 393–398.

Zeskind, P. S., & Barr, R. G. (1997). Acoustic characteristics of naturally occurring cries of infants with "colic." *Child Development, 68,* 394–403.

Zhan, H. J., & Montgomery, R. J. V. (2003). Gender and elder care in China: The influence of filial piety and structural constraints. *Gender and Society, 17,* 209–229.

Zhang, L., & Sternberg, R. J. (2011). Revisiting the investment theory of creativity. *Creativity Research Journal, 23,* 229–238.

Zhang, Q. F. (2004). Economic transition and new patterns of parent–adult child coresidence in urban China. *Journal of Marriage and Family, 66,* 1231–1245.

Zhang, T.-Y., & Meaney, M. J. (2010). Epigenetics and the environmental regulation of the genome and its function. *Annual Review of Psychology, 61,* 439–466.

Zhang, Y., & Jordan, J. M. (2010). Epidemiology of osteoarthritis. *Clinics of Geriatric Medicine, 26,* 355–369.

Zhao, J., Settles, B. H., & Sheng, X. (2011). Family-to-work conflict: Gender, equity and workplace policies. *Journal of Comparative Family Studies, 42,* 723–738.

Zheng, N. T., Mukamel, D. B., Caprio, T. V., & Temkin-Greener, H. (2012). Hospice utilization in nursing homes: Association with facility end-of-life care practices. *Gerontologist, 52.* Retrieved from gerontologist.oxfordjournals.org.libproxy.lib.ilstu .edu/search?fulltext=Zheng&submit=yes&x=13&y=9

Zhou, M., & Bankston, C. L. (1998). *Growing up American: How Vietnamese children adapt to life in the United States.* New York: Russell Sage Foundation.

Zhou, Q., Lengua, L. J., & Wang, Y. (2009). The relations of temperament reactivity and effortful control to children's adjustment problems in China and the United States. *Developmental Psychology, 45,* 724–739.

Zhou, X., Huang, J., Wang, Z., Wang, B., Zhao, Z., Yang, L., & Zheng-zheng, Y. (2006). Parent–child interaction and children's number learning. *Early Child Development and Care, 176,* 763–775.

Zhu, W. X., & Hesketh, T. (2009). China's excess males, sex selective abortion, and one child policy: Analysis of data from 2005 national intercensus survey. *British Medical Journal, 338,* b1211.

Zickuhr, K., & Madden, M. (2012). *Pew Internet: Older adults and Internet use.* Washington, DC: Pew Research Center.

Zimmer-Gembeck, M., & Helfand, M. J. (2008). Ten years of longitudinal research on U.S. adolescent sexual behavior: Developmental correlates of sexual intercourse, and the importance of age, gender and ethnic background. *Developmental Review, 28,* 153–224.

Zimmerman, B. J., & Cleary, T. J. (2009). Motives to self-regulate learning: A social cognitive account. In K. R. Wenzel & A. Wigfield (Eds.), *Handbook of motivation at school* (pp. 247–264). New York: Routledge.

Zimmerman, B. J., & Moylan, A. R. (2009). Self-regulation: Where metacognition and motivation intersect. In D. J. Hacker, J. Dunlosky, & A. C. Graesser (Eds.), *Handbook of metacognition in education* (pp. 299–315). New York: Routledge.

Zimmerman, C. (2007). The development of scientific thinking skills in elementary and middle school. *Developmental Review, 27,* 172–223.

Zimmerman, C. (2012). Acceptance of dying: A discourse analysis of palliative care literature. *Social Science and Medicine, 78,* 217–224.

Zimmerman, F. J., & Christakis, D. A. (2005). Children's television viewing and cognitive outcomes. *Archives of Pediatrics and Adolescent Medicine, 159,* 619–625.

Zimmerman, F. J., Christakis, D. A., & Meltzoff, A. N. (2007). Television and DVD/video viewing in children younger than 2 years. *Archives of Pediatrics and Adolescent Medicine, 161,* 473–479.

Zimmerman, F. J., Gilkerson, J., Richards, J. A., Christakis, D. A., Xu, D., Gray, S., & Yapanel, U. (2009). Teaching by listening: The importance of adult–child conversations to language development. *Pediatrics, 124,* 342–348.

Zimmerman, L. K., & Stansbury, K. (2004). The influence of emotion regulation, level of shyness, and habituation on the neuroendocrine response of three-year-old children. *Psychoneuroendocrinology, 29,* 973–982.

Zimmerman, P., & Becker-Stoll, F. (2002). Stability of attachment representations during adolescence: The influence of ego-identity status. *Journal of Adolescence, 25,* 107–124.

Zolotor, A. J., & Puzia, M. E. (2010). Bans against corporal punishment: A systematic review of the laws, changes in attitudes and behaviours. *Child Abuse Review, 19,* 229–247.

Zosuls, K. M., Ruble, D. N., Bornstein, M. H., & Greulich, F. K. (2009). The acquisition of gender labels in infancy: Implications for gender-typed play. *Developmental Psychology, 45,* 688–701.

Zucker, A. N., Ostrove, J. M., & Stewart, A. J. (2002). College-educated women's personality development in adulthood: Perceptions and age differences. *Psychology and Aging, 17,* 236–244.

Zukow-Goldring, P. (2002). Sibling caregiving. In M. H. Bornstein (Ed.), *Handbook of parenting: Vol. 3* (2nd ed., pp. 253–286). Hillsdale, NJ: Erlbaum.

Name Index

Italic n *following page number indicates page with an illustration or table.*

A

Aalsma, M., 308
Aarnoudse-Moens, C. S., 78
AARP, 433
Abakoumkin, G., 524
Abbeduto, L. J., 210
Abbey, A., 355
Abecassis, M., 268
Abela, J. R. Z., 334
Abele, A. E., 386
Abelson, H., 332
Aber, J. L., 48, 50, 309, 310
Aberson, B., 213
Abes, E., 358, 359
Abikoff, H., 239
Abma, J. C., 300, 301
Aboud, F. E., 266
Abrams, D., 267, 325
Abrams, K. Y., 156
Abramson, L. Y., 335
Achenbach, T. M., 80
Achermann, P., 292
Acierno, R., 497
Acker, M. M., 209, 377
Ackerman, B. P., 145
Ackerman, P. L., 416
Ackerman, S., 424
ACT, 362
Adachi-Mejia, A. M., 229
Adams, A.-M., 185
Adams, G. A., 442
Adams, G. R., 320
Adams, K. B., 490, 491
Adams, R. G., 294
Adamson, D., 42
Addington-Hall, J., 516
Adhikari, B., 352
Adolph, K. E., 82, 106, 107, 111, 112, 114, 160
Afifi, T. O., 208
Afterschool Alliance, 278
Aggarwal, R., 171
Agrigoroaei, S., 429, 455, 484
Agronick, G., 280
Agüero-Torres, H., 466
Aguiar, A., 121
Ahadi, S. A., 149
Ahlskog, J. E., 464
Ahlström, R., 409
Ahnert, L., 51, 134, 192
Ahrens, C. J. C., 429
Ahuja, J., 441
Ai, A. L., 483
Aikens, J. W., 154, 310
Aikens, N. L., 135, 191
Ainley, J., 313
Ainscow, M., 252
Ainsworth, M. D. S., 154, 154n, 156
Aisen, P. S., 457
Ajrouch, K. J., 485, 492, 497
Akhtar, N., 122, 194
Akimoto, S. A., 147
Akinbami, L. J., 230
Akiyama, H., 431, 438, 439, 487, 492
Aksan, N., 144, 149, 161, 207, 208
Akshoomoff, N. A., 96, 188

Alberman, E., 41
Albers, C. A., 133
Albert, M. K., 111
Aldao, A., 356
Aldwin, C. M., 411, 502
Alessandri, S. M., 145
Alexander, J. M., 240
Alexander, K. L., 313
Alexopoulos, T., 455
Alfaro, E. C., 322
Algarin, C., 83
Alink, L. R. A., 211
Alkema, G. E., 467
Allemand, M., 483
Allen, G., 333, 334
Allen, J. P., 302
Allen, M., 392
Allen, N. B., 334
Allen, P. A., 415
Allen, S. E. M., 248
Allen, T. D., 393
Allik, J., 273
Allison, B. N., 294
Alloway, T. P., 126, 237
Almeida, D. M., 328, 356, 428
Almeida, J., 299
Almkvist, O., 455
Al-Nakhli, H., 460
Al-Namlah, A. S., 182
Alonso-Férnandez, P., 346
Alsaker, F. D., 295
Alterovitz, S. S. R., 493, 493n
Althaus, J., 78
Altmaier, E. M., 512
Altobelli, J., 385
Alvarez, M. M., 328
Alzheimer's Association, 437, 461, 462, 464, 465
Amaral, D. G., 188
Amato, P. R., 47, 218, 274, 275, 276, 277, 384, 390, 391
Amba, J. C., 390
American Academy of Orthopaedic Surgeons, 408, 409
American Academy of Pediatrics, 71, 99, 101n, 124
American Cancer Society, 407, 408
American College of Sports Medicine, 352
American Heart Association, 346, 509
American Hospice Foundation, 511
American Psychiatric Association, 239, 253
American Psychological Association, 31, 31n
Ames, S. L., 303
Amsel, E., 307, 307n
Amso, D., 111
Amsterlaw, J., 186
An, J. S., 424
Anand, S. S., 229
Andel, R., 467
Anderson, C. A., 212
Anderson, D. M., 193

Anderson, E., 195
Anderson, J. L., 109
Anderson, K. J., 139, 271
Anderson, P. B., 355, 357n
Anderson, V. N., 386
Anderssen, N., 232
Andreoletti, C., 456
Andres, V., 345
Andrews, G., 181, 235, 236
Anesbury, T., 229
Aneshensel, C. S., 48
Anetzberger, G. J., 498
Angelillo, C., 184
Anisfeld, M., 105
Annahatak, B., 246
Annett, M., 169
Anstey, K. J., 501
Anttila, R., 295
Anzuini, F., 351
Apfel, N. H., 302
Apgar, V., 76, 76n
Aquan-Assee, J., 159
Aquilino, W. S., 373
Arbeau, K. A., 150, 204
Archer, A. H., 124
Archer, J., 374
Archibald, A. B., 288, 290
Arcus, D., 45
Ardelt, M., 472, 483, 511
Arditti, J. A., 432
Arias, L., 385
Arking, R., 343, 344, 346, 347n
Armer, M., 150, 204
Armstrong, L. M., 148, 202
Armstrong, T. D., 483
Arnett, J. J., 318, 354, 369, 370, 371, 372, 374
Arnold, M., 248
Arnold, M. L., 218, 326
Arnold, R., 49
Arnon, S., 80
Arriaga, R. I., 125
Arslanian, S. A., 229
Arterberry, M. E., 87, 111, 113, 128, 174
Arthurs, E., 145
Artman, L., 236, 306
Ary, D. V., 465
Asakawa, K., 95n
Aschersleben, G., 109
Asher, S. R., 270, 271
Ashmead, D. H., 108
Aslin, R. N., 109, 136, 139
Assink, M. H. J., 470
Astington, J. W., 186, 187, 240
Atchley, R. C., 488, 490, 501
Atkins, R., 327
Atkinson, L., 159
Au, T. K., 179
Auestad, R. A., 437
Aumann, K., 157, 158, 158n, 273
Aunola, K., 218, 219, 311
Austin, E. L., 299
Auth, E. A., 490, 491

Averhart, C. J., 266
Aveyard, P., 352
Avgoustis, E., 334
Avis, N. E., 403
Avni-Babad, D., 306
Avolio, B. J., 440
Axelin, A., 86
Axia, G., 248
Ayala, G. X., 229
Ayotte, V., 261, 262

B

Bacallao, M. L., 26
Bacaltchuk, J., 297
Bäckman, L., 416, 452, 473
Bagwell, C. L., 269
Bahrick, L. E., 104, 113, 114, 125, 128
Bailey, J. M., 300, 430
Baillargeon, R., 121, 121n, 125, 186
Baillargeon, R. H., 211
Bair, D., 493
Baird, B. M., 53
Baird, D. D., 62
Baker, C. K., 385
Baker, J. M., 248
Baker, P. N., 301
Bakermans-Kranenburg, M. J., 156
Balasch, J., 348
Baldi, A., 101n
Baldi, R., 356
Baldwin, D. A., 194
Baldwin, G., 195
Bale, J. F., 70
Bales, S. N., 52
Balis, T., 335
Ball, K., 473
Ball, M. M., 491
Balsam, K. F., 389
Baltes, M. M., 484
Baltes, P. B., 5, 6, 54, 468, 471, 472, 473, 502
Bambara, L. M., 253
Banaji, M. R., 266
Bancroft, J., 354
Bandstra, E. S., 68
Bandura, A., 14, 207
Banish, M. T., 96
Banks, M. S., 87
Bankston, C. L., 26
Bao, J., 452
Barber, B. K., 219, 309, 329
Barber, B. L., 218, 321
Bard, K. A., 160
Barelds, D. P. H., 384
Barenbaum, J., 280
Bar-Haim, Y., 113
Barja, G., 344
Barker, D. J., 71
Barkley, R. A., 239
Barnes, G. M., 336
Barnes, J., 48
Barnes-Farrell, J., 440
Barnett, D., 154
Barnett, W. S., 191
Baron, A. S., 266

Baron, I. S., 78
Baron-Cohen, S., 188
Baroni, R., 248
Barr, H. M., 67, 69
Barr, R., 122, 124
Barr, R. G., 85
Barreto, M., 401, 440
Barrett, A. E., 425
Barrett, K. C., 147
Barrett, M., 265
Barrett, T. M., 108
Barrett-Conner, E., 408
Barros, R. M., 233
Barry, C. M., 332, 370, 380
Barry, H., III, 294
Barry, R. A., 152, 219
Bartlik, B., 407
Bartocci, M., 86
Bartrip, J., 113
Bartsch, K., 186
Basak, C., 6, 416, 473
Basow, S. A., 328
Bass, S., 482
Bassett, N. S., 75
Bassuk, S. S., 351
Bastien, C. H., 70
Basu, A., 451
Bates, E. A., 136
Bates, G. W., 424
Bates, J. E., 53, 148, 149, 150
Bathurst, K., 20, 278
Battistella, A., 351
Batty, G. D., 101
Bauer, C. R., 68
Bauer, P. J., 122, 129, 185
Baum, N., 432
Baumeister, R. F., 207, 267, 512
Baumgartner, M. S., 440
Baumrind, D., 217, 219
Bauserman, R., 276
Bavelier, D., 96
Baydar, N., 159
Bayer, A., 32
Bayley, N., 106n, 108n, 132
Bazemore, G., 338
Beals, D. E., 249
Bean, R. A., 329
Bearman, P. S., 335
Bearman, S. K., 295
Beauchamp, G. K., 86
Beautrais, A. L., 335
Bechara, A., 291
Beck, I. L., 241
Becker, B. E., 48
Becker, G., 50
Becker, J. B., 293
Becker, K., 57
Beckerman, M. B., 418
Becker-Stoll, F., 321
Beckett, C., 97
Bedford, O. A., 203
Bedwell, J. S., 415
Beehr, T. A., 500
Behnke, M., 68
Behrends, M., 312
Behrens, K. Y., 157
Beier, M. E., 416
Bejček, J., 369
Bekkouche, N. S., 356

Subject Index

Figures and tables are indicated by f and t following page numbers.

A

A-not-B search error in sensorimotor
stage, 120, 122
AARP, 52
Abortion
in adolescent pregnancy, 301
spontaneous. *See* Miscarriage
Abstinence from sexual activity,
301–302
Abstract thinking, 304
consequences of changes in, 307
and expertise, 360
in formal operational stage, 304, 305,
306
and moral development, 324
and self-concept, 318
Abuse
of child. *See* Child maltreatment
in dating relationships, 333–334
of elderly, 497–499
of substances. *See* Substance abuse
Academic achievement
in adolescence, 310–313
child-rearing styles affecting,
218–219, 311
cultural influences on, 311
divorce of parents affecting, 275
early intervention programs affecting,
191–192
family beliefs on, 26
gender stereotypes on, 215, 263, 271
of immigrant youths, 26
intelligence quotient as predictor of,
190, 242
international comparisons of, 255t,
255–256
mathematical abilities affecting, 189
parent–school partnerships affecting,
311
reading skills affecting, 189
recess time affecting, 233
school characteristics affecting,
311–313
school transitions affecting, 309–310
and self-esteem, 261
and social skills, 205
in teenage pregnancy, 301
Academic learning, 250–256, 309–314.
See also Education
Academic programs in preschool and
kindergarten, 190
Acceptance
of change in late adulthood, 483, 502
in child rearing, 217, 218, 218t, 219
in coping with dying, 480, 513
in peer relations. *See* Peer acceptance
of self. *See* Self-acceptance
Accidental injuries. *See* Injuries,
unintentional
Accommodation in cognitive
development, 118, 119, 177
Accommodation of eyes, 402
Acculturative stress, 322, 329
Accutane (isotretinoin), 66–67
Acetylcholine
in Alzheimer's disease, 463
drug therapy affecting, 466
Achievement
ability and effort in, 263, 264
academic. *See* Academic achievement
attributions related to, 263–264
gender stereotypes on, 215, 263, 271

and identity, 319, 320t
and learned helplessness, 263
and self-esteem, 263–264
Acquired immune deficiency syndrome.
See AIDS
ACTIVE (Advanced Cognitive Training
for Independent and Vital Elderly)
study, 473
Active correlation, 55
Activities of daily living in late
adulthood, 449
cognitive interventions affecting, 473
control versus dependency in, 484,
485
problem solving in, 471
Activity level and temperament, 148,
149, 149t
Activity theory of aging, 487
Actors, memory strategies of, 417
Adaptation
of baby to labor and delivery, 75
coping strategies in. *See* Coping
strategies
Darwin on, 11
to dying, contextual influences on,
514–516
in early adulthood, 375
ethology of, 17
evolutionary developmental
psychology on, 18
to family changes, 46–47, 87–88
and habituation, 46
of immigrant youths, 26
in late adulthood, 454–456, 471,
494–495
in middle adulthood, 409–412, 426
Piaget on, 15, 118–119
and practical intelligence, 244
and resilience, 8
Vaillant on, 375, 426
in widowhood, 494–495
Adaptation to Life (Vaillant), 374
Addiction, 303, 352
to alcohol, 353
of infants, 68
Adjustment
in adolescence, 287, 309–310, 332
affluence affecting, 48
child-care facilities affecting, 157
child maltreatment affecting, 221
child-rearing styles affecting, 218, 219
divorce of parents affecting, 275, 276
early intervention programs affecting,
191
and friendships, 332
of immigrant youths, 26
and infant sleeping arrangements, 99
to parenthood, 87–88
peer acceptance affecting, 269, 271
to retirement, 500–501
Adolescence (11 to 18 years old), 6t,
286–339
academic achievement in, 310–313
in adoption, 45
aggression in, 233
arousal states in, 292
autonomy in, 296, 329–330, 387
bereavement interventions in, 528
biological perspective of, 287
in blended families, 277
body composition in, 289
body proportions in, 288

body size in, 288, 289f
brain development in, 291–292, 303,
308, 309
cognitive–affective complexity in,
359, 359f
cognitive development in, 290–291,
304–314
conflicts in, 294, 329–330, 331
cultural influences on, 287, 288, 293,
294, 297–298, 329
dating in, 333–334
death concept in, 512
death of parent or sibling during, 525
decision making in, 308–309
delinquency in, 336–338
depression in, 334–335
divorce of parents during, 275
dropping out of school during,
313–314
eating disorders in, 296–297
emotional and social development in,
317–339
employment in, 364
family in, 329–330, 387
fetal alcohol exposure affecting, 69
formal operational stage in, 304–306
free time in, 330
friendships in, 330–332
gender typing in, 328
health issues in, 295–303
hormone changes in, 288, 293
hypothetico-deductive reasoning in,
304–305
idealism and criticism in, 308
identity development in, 318,
319–321
identity versus role confusion in,
13t, 318
of immigrant youths, 26
impulsivity and sensation seeking in,
292, 292f
information processing in, 306–307
initiation ceremonies in, 293
language development in, 304
learning in school during, 309–314
media multitasking in, 311, 312
memory of events in late adulthood,
470
milestones of development in,
340–341
moodiness in, 293
moral development in, 321–328
motor development in, 289–290
nutrition in, 290, 295–297
obesity in, 228, 229
parent relationships in, 294, 329–330.
See also Parent–adolescent
relationships
peer relations in, 294, 295, 330–334
physical attractiveness in, 294–295
physical development in, 287–303
play in, 233
pregnancy in, 72, 300–302. *See also*
Teenage pregnancy and parenthood
propositional thought in, 305
psychosexual and psychosocial
development in, 13t
puberty in, 288–295. *See also* Puberty
school transitions in, 309–310
scientific reasoning in, 306–307
self-consciousness and self-focusing
in, 308

self-understanding in, 318–321
sex differences in, 288–289, 290, 291t,
292–293, 330–331
sexual abuse in, 279, 280
sexuality in, 297–302
sexually transmitted diseases in, 300
sexual maturation in, 290
shyness in, 150
sibling relationships in, 330
sleep schedule in, 292
social perspective of, 287
substance use and abuse in, 289, 294,
300, 302–303, 333
suicide in, 335–336
time spent with family in, 330
vocational choice in, 362
Adoption, 44–45
attachment security in, 155
deprivation prior to, 97–98
and environmental influences on gene
expression, 56
by gay and lesbian couples, 392
intelligence and IQ research in,
245–246
schizophrenia research in, 56
in surrogate motherhood, 42–43
Adrenal androgens, 288
Adult Development and Enrichment
Project (ADEPT), 473
Adulthood
brain plasticity in, 96
death concept in, 511–512
death of intimate partner in, 525
diversity of lifestyles in, 388–393
early, 6t, 342–397. *See also* Early
adulthood
late, 6t, 446–505. *See also* Late
adulthood
middle, 6t, 400–443. *See also* Middle
adulthood
Advanced Cognitive Training for
Independent and Vital Elderly
(ACTIVE) study, 473
Advance medical directives, 520–521
Affect optimization in late adulthood,
480
Affluence, 48
Afghanistan, life expectancy in, 448
Africa. *See also specific countries*
breastfeeding and bottle-feeding in,
100
menopause in, 405, 405f
African Americans
academic achievement of, 311, 312
adolescent, 298
as adult learners, 419
aging parents of, 436, 490
Alzheimer's disease of, 463
anorexia nervosa of, 296
asthma of, 230
body image of, 295
body size of, 92
cardiovascular diseases of, 346, 351,
408
child-rearing practices of, 209,
219–220
communication style of, 246, 249
cosleeping of parents and infants, 99
death beliefs of, 516, 527
dementia of, 461, 463
departure from parental home, 381
diabetes mellitus of, 460